Contents

Using the Guide

Many of the countries in this guide are divided into regions, within which the site locations are listed in alphabetical order. Those not divided into regions are in alphabetical order of location. Regions and locations are shown on the country maps at the back of the book, and are listed in the index.

Sample entry

LOCATION **REGION**

Name of Campsite

Address of campsite
☎ telephone number 🖷 fax number
e-mail: email@campsite.com
web: www.campsite.fr

Description of campsite, which may mention its setting, such as mountains, forest etc, how far it is from the beach, and other general details of the site.

dir: *General directions from nearest main road or large town.*

GPS: 03.1958, -3.1875

Open: Apr-Sep **Site:** 2HEC **For hire:** **Prices:** 15.50-20 Mobile home hire 160-370 **Facilities:** Wi-fi Play Area **Services:** **Leisure:** P **Off-site:** S Symbols are explained at the bottom of the page, throughout the body of the guide.

Campsite entries

In order to update our information we send a questionnaire each year to every campsite. Inevitably a number of the questionnaires are not returned in time for publication, in which case the campsite name is printed in italics, and prices are omitted. Most of the sites accept both tents and caravans unless otherwise stated.

Websites

Campsite web addresses are included where available. The AA cannot be held responsible for the content of any of these websites.

Opening times

Dates shown are inclusive. All information was correct at the time of going to press, but we recommend you check with the site before arriving. Sometimes only restricted facilities are available between October and April.

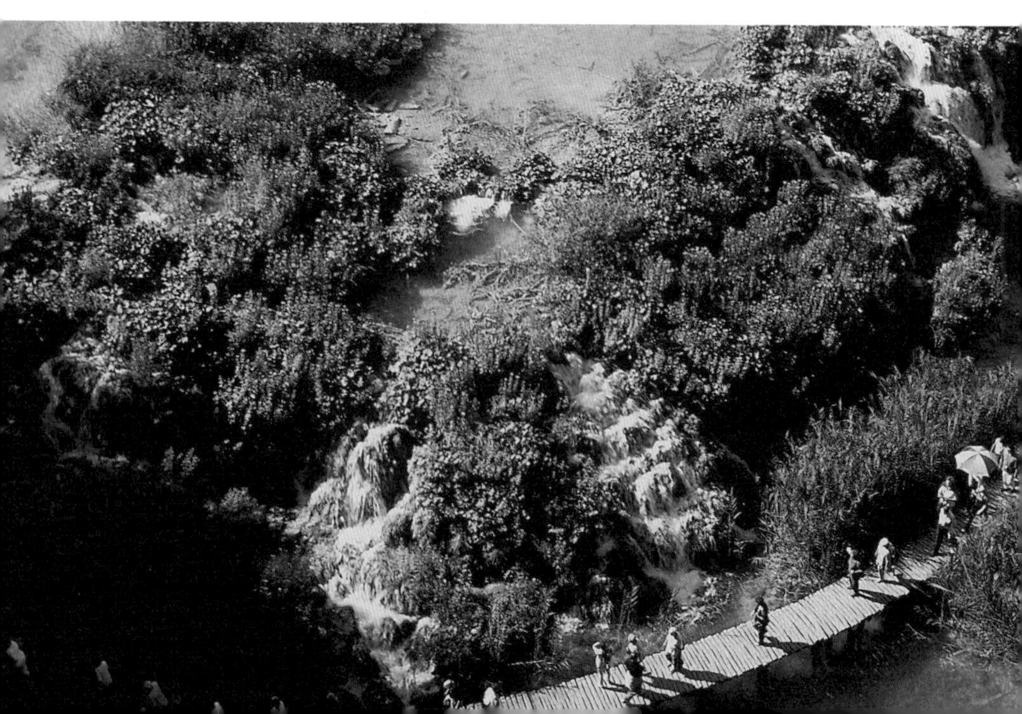

Prices

Prices are given per night, and include two adults, a car, and caravan or tent. We also quote prices for weekly hire of static caravans/mobile homes. Prices are given in euros except for Switzerland (Francs), Czech Republic (Koruna), Hungary (Forint), and Poland (New Złotych).

Booking

It is best to book well in advance for peak holiday seasons, or for your first and last stop close to a ferry crossing port. However, we do find that some sites do not accept reservations. Specimen booking letters in English, French, German, Italian and Spanish are on page 8.
Please note: Although it is not common practice, some campsites may regard your deposit as a booking fee which is not deductible from the final account.

Complaints

If you have any complaint about a site, discuss the problem with the site proprietor immediately so that the matter can be dealt with promptly. We regret that the AA cannot act as intermediary in any dispute, or attempt to gain refunds or compensation. Your comments, however, help us to update new editions. Please contact us at lifestyleguides@theAA.com

Disabled travellers

We have asked each campsite if it is fully accessible for wheelchair users. Where a site has answered "yes" to this question we have included a wheelchair symbol (♿) in their entry. If you require further information on the site's suitability for wheelchair use, or any other disability, please contact the site directly.

Symbols

Abbreviations and symbols are explained at the foot of the gazetteer pages. Please note also:

CM camping municipal, parque municipal de campismo, or parque de la camara municipal (local authority site)

Route Planning / Sat Nav / GPS

For route planning you should use a road atlas, such as AA Road Atlas Europe. AA road atlases are also available for France, Germany, Italy, Spain and Portugal. The AA Route Planner Europe on theAA.com covers many of the countries in the guide. (Please be cautious when using route-planning services. Ensure that they are suitable for your type of vehicle or combination.)
Each site was asked to supply GPS positioning data for use in Sat Nav programming. Where this data could be verified by us, we have printed it. These coordinates can be entered into navigation devices to provide routes to the campsite location. For more details regarding how to enter coordinates please refer to your device manual.

Camping and Caravanning Club

For the 2012 edition of the Guide, the Camping and Caravanning Club has inspected over a hundred of the sites in the guide. These are highlighted by a tinted background and feature the Camping and Caravanning Club logo.

Online Information

This selection of websites contains useful travel information.

Camping

Official site of Calor Gas
www.calor.co.uk

Official site of LP Gas, suppliers of liquid petroleum gas
www.uklpg.org

Britain's major caravan clubs
www.campingand
caravanningclub.co.uk
www.caravanclub.co.uk

Caravan news/info
www.practicalcaravan.com
www.outandaboutlive.co.uk
www.caravantimes.co.uk

Suppliers of camping & outdoor gear
www.tentastic.co.uk
www.outdoorgear.co.uk
www.campmania.co.uk
www.outdoorworlddirect.co.uk
www.outdoorworld.co.uk
www.gear-zone.co.uk
www.gooutdoors.co.uk
www.blacks.co.uk

European Federation of Campingsite Organisations and Holiday Park Associations
www.campingeurope.com

UK Government

The Foreign & Commonwealth Office travel information
www.fco.gov.uk/travel

HM Revenue & Customs
www.hmrc.gov.uk

Home Office Identity & Passport Office
www.direct.gov.uk/en/
TravelAndTransport/Passports

Pet travel information and quarantine regulations
www.defra.gov.uk/wildlife-pets/pets/
travel/

EU, Euro, Currency

The European Union
europa.eu
www.ecb.int

Tourism

Andorra
www.andorra.ad

Austria
www.austria.info

Belgium
www.belgiumtheplaceto.be
www.visitbelgium.com
www.visitflanders.co.uk

Bulgaria
www.bulgariatravel.org
www.bulgarian-tourism.com

Czech Republic
www.czechtourism.com

Croatia
www.croatia.hr
www.croatiatouristcenter.com

France
uk.franceguide.com
www.francetourism.com

Germany
www.germany.travel

Greece
www.visitgreece.gr
www.greek-tourism.gr

Holland
www.holland.com

Hungary
www.hungary.com
www.gotohungary.com

Italy
www.italia.it
www.enit.it

Luxembourg
www.luxembourg.co.uk
www.visitluxembourg.com

Poland
www.poland.travel

Portugal
www.visitportugal.com
www.travel-in-portugal.com

Romania
www.romaniatourism.com
www.bestromania.com

Slovenia
www.slovenia.info
www.slovenia.si

Spain
www.spain.info
www.tourspain.org/

Switzerland
www.myswitzerland.com

Turkey
www.turkeytourism.com
www.gototurkey.co.uk

Low Emission Zones (LEZs) in Europe

www.lowemissionzones.eu

Disabled Parking Info

www.fiadisabledtravellers.com

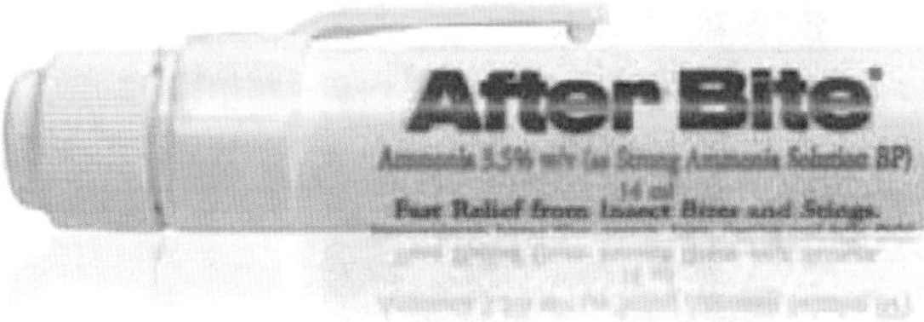

Booking Letters

Please use capitals and enclose an International Reply Coupon, obtainable from a Post Office. Be sure to include your name, address, post code, email address and country.

English

Dear Sir

I intend to stay at your site for ... days, arriving on ... (date and month) and departing on ... (date and month).

We are a party of ... people, including ... adults and ... children (aged ...) and would like a pitch for... tent(s) and/or parking space for our car/caravan/caravan trailer.

We would like to hire a tent/caravan/bungalow. Please quote full charges when replying and advise on the deposit required, which will be forwarded without delay.

French

Monsieur

Je me propose de séjourner à votre terrain de camping pour ... jours, depuis le ... jusqu'au ...

Nous sommes ... personnes en tout, y compris ... adultes et ... enfants (âgés de ...) et nous aurons besoin d'un emplacement pour ... tente(s), et/ou un parking pour notre voiture/caravane/remorque.

Nous voudrions louer une tente/caravane/bungalow.

Veuillez me donner dans votre réponse une idée de vos prix, m'indiquant en même temps le montant qu'il faut payer en avance, ce qui vous sera envoyé sans délai.

German

Sehr geehrter Herr!

Ich beabsichtige, mich auf Ihrem Campingplatz ... Tage aufzuhalten, und zwar vom ... bis zum ...

Wir sind im ganzen ... Personen, ... Erwachsene und ... Kinder (in Alter von ...), und benötigen Platz für Zelt(e) und/oder unseren Wagen/Wohnwagen/Wohnwagenanhänger.

Wir möchten ein Zelt/Wohnwagen/Bungalow mieten.

Bitte, geben Sie mir in Ihrem Antwortschreiben die vollen Preise bekannt, und ebenso die Höhe der von mir zu leistenden Anzahlung, die Ihnen alsdann unverzüglich überwiesen wird.

Italian

Egregio Signore

Ho intenzione di remanere presso di voi per ... giorni. Arriverò il ... e partirò il ...

Siamo un gruppo di ... persone in totale, compreso ... adulti e ... bambini (de età ...) e vorrremo un posto per ... tenda(tende) e/o spazio per parcheggiare la nostra vetture/carovana/roulette.

Desideriamo affittare una tenda/carovana/bungalow.

Vi preghiamo di quotare i prezzi completi quando ci risponderete, e darci informazioni sul deposito richiesto, che vi sarà rimesso senza ritardo.

Spanish

Muy señor mio

Desearia me reservara espacio por ... dias, a partir del ... hasta el ...

Nuestro grupo comprende .....personas todo comprendido, ... adultos y ... niños (... de años de edad). Necesitarimos un espacio por ... tienda(s) y/o espacio para apacar nuestro choche/caravana/remolque.

Deseariamos alquilar una tienda de campana/caravan/bungalow.

Le ruego nos comunique los precios y nos informe sobre el depósito que debemos remitirle.

Visiting Europe

Planning your journey before leaving

General advice for driving in Europe is available at www.theaa.com/motoring_advice/overseas/index.html. You can also buy AA European Breakdown Cover online at the website or call 0800 072 3279.

Before departure, it may be worth having your car checked by AA Vehicle Inspections.

For more information and charges visit www.theaa.com/vehicle-inspections or call 0800 056 8040.

AA UK travel news

When heading for your UK port of departure, check the traffic on the AA's information line 0906 88 84322 (land line) or 84322 ('theaa') from your mobile (calls cost up to 60p per minute). Or click on to Travel or Traffic at theAA.com.

BBC World Service

The international radio arm of the BBC broadcasts in English and a large number of other languages. World news is on the hour every hour and there are regular bulletins of British news. If you want to listen to the World Service when you are abroad, go to www.bbc.co.uk/worldservice or write for information to:

BBC World Service, Bush House, Strand
London WC2B 4PH

Camping Card International (CCI)

A CCI is recognised at most campsites in Europe. At some campsites a reduction to the advertised charge may be allowed on presentation of the card. The CCI, which is valid for 12 months, provides third-party insurance cover for up to 11 people camping away from home, staying in rented accommodation or at a hotel.

For more information, visit:
www.campingcardinternational.com

AA personal members may purchase a CCI from the Camping & Caravanning Club, or the Caravan Club. If you require further information please call:

Camping & Caravanning Club on 0845 130 7701
or Caravan Club on 01342 327410 (Mon-Fri 9.15-5.15).

In either case, be prepared to quote your AA membership number.

Caravans & trailers

Take a list of contents, especially if any valuable or unusual equipment is being carried, as this may be required at some frontiers.

In some countries, a towed vehicle - boat trailer, caravan or trailer - must have a unique chassis number. The identification plate should be in an accessible position and show the name of the maker of the vehicle and the production or serial number.

If the towed vehicle does not have a unique chassis number, you can obtain a trailer plate from the AA.

Direction indicators

Most standard car-flasher units will be overloaded by the extra lamps of a caravan or trailer, and a special heavy duty unit or relay device should be fitted.

Visiting Europe

Disabled travellers

The AA Disability Helpline provides information on a range of disability related subjects, such as motoring in the UK and overseas. AA members can call this service free on 0800 26 20 50.

A standard blue parking badge for disabled people has been introduced throughout the EU. All EU member states with reciprocal arrangements in place operate the Blue Badge parking scheme. Badge holders across the participating EU states can enjoy the same parking concessions provided in the host country by displaying the badge issued under their own national scheme. (Badge holders should check local notices to ensure that they are parking within the law.) These arrangements apply only to badge holders themselves and are not for the benefit of non-disabled companions. Wrongful display of the badge may incur a fine.

For details of the Blue Badge parking scheme or for planning a trip abroad contact:

Department for Transport,
Great Minster House,
33 Horseferry Road
London SW1P 4DR
Tel 020 7944 9643
www.dft.gov.uk/transportforyou/access/
www.direct.gov.uk/DisabledPeople

Information on the Blue Badge scheme in 29 European countries is also available from the AA's website:
www.theAA.com/motoring_advice/overseas/blue-badge-users.html

The FIA Guide for the Disabled Traveller is at
www.fiadisabledtravellers.com

Documents & insurance

Always carry your national driving licence (and International Driving Permit if necessary), the original vehicle registration document and your passport. Remember, if the registration document is not in your name, ask the registered keeper to provide you with a letter of authority. If the vehicle is hired or leased ask the company concerned to supply you with a Vehicle on Hire Certificate. (VC103b)

The IDP, for which a statutory charge is made, is issued by the AA to applicants who hold a valid full British driving licence and who are aged 18 and over.

Go to www.theAA.com/getaway/idp/index.html or call 0870 600 0371.

When driving abroad you must carry your certificate of motor insurance with you at all times. Third-party is the minimum legal requirement in most countries. Before taking a vehicle, caravan or trailer abroad, contact your insurer or broker to notify them of your intentions and ask their advice. Check that you are covered against damage in transit (e.g. on the ferry) when the vehicle is not being driven. Motorists can obtain all types of insurance at www.theAA.com or call 0800 316 2456.

Electrical

The electricity supply in Europe is usually 220 volts (50 cycles) AC (alternating current), but can be as low as 110 volts.

In some isolated areas, low voltage DC (direct current) is provided. Continental circular two-pin plugs and screw-type bulbs are usually the rule. Check for correct polarity when using a mains hook-up on a touring caravan.

Electrical adaptors (not voltage transformers), which can be used in Continental power sockets, shaver points and light bulb sockets, are available in the UK from electrical retailers or from on-board ferry shops.

Euro

The currency of the majority of countries in this guide is the euro. For further information visit the European Central Bank at www.ecb.int.

Notes have denominations of 5, 10, 20, 50, 100, 200 and 500 euros; the coins 1 and 2 euros, and 1, 2, 5, 10, 20 and 50 cents. There is no limit to the amount of sterling notes you may take abroad. Some countries have currency import or export restrictions and you should check this with your bank or currency supplier.

Credit and debit cards can be used abroad. Their use is subject to the conditions set out by the issuing bank.

Establishments display the symbols of cards that they accept. However, it is recommended that you don't rely exclusively on any one payment method. A combination of traveller's cheques, a payment card and a small amount of local currency is suggested. Traveller's cheques can often be used like cash. Your bank will be able to recommend currency traveller's cheques for the countries you are visiting.

The AA has a pre-loaded Travel Currency Card, which can be used at 32 million locations worldwide:
www.theaa.com/currency-card/

Countries in this guide that do not have the Euro as their national currency are: Switzerland (Francs), Bulgaria (Leva), Croatia (Kuna), Czech Republic (Koruna), Hungary (Forint), Poland (Złotych), Romania (New Lei), and Turkey (New Lira). Campsites in Bulgaria, Croatia, Romania and Turkey have given their prices in Euros.

Visiting Europe

Fire extinguisher/first aid kit

In some countries it is compulsory to equip your vehicle with these items (see country introductions).

Foodstuffs

Most countries have regulations governing the types and quantities of foodstuffs that may be imported. Although they are usually not strictly applied, visitors should know that they exist and only take reasonable quantities of food with them.

Lights

When driving on the Continent, you must adjust the headlamp beam pattern to suit driving on the right so that the dipped beam doesn't dazzle oncoming drivers. Never go without adjusting the headlamp pattern, as it is an offence to dazzle oncoming traffic.

Headlamp beam converter kits are widely available, but don't leave adjustment to the last minute, as it may need to be made by your dealer.

Some models feature an internal 'shutter' that can be moved into place by a screw or lever adjustment at the back of the headlamp unit. Some designs are less convenient so the dealer will need to do it.

Some modern halogen-type headlamps, HID headlights and Xenon headlamps are of very complex design. The fitting of the masks for these may take practice due to the lack of markings on the headlamp glass. Check with your dealer or car handbook for advice.

Remember to remove your converters as soon as you return to the UK.

AA Headlamp Beam Converters and/or AA Bulb Kits, or an AA Eurotravel Kit, which includes a highviz vest, first aid kit, GB magnetic plate, headlamp beam converters and warning triangle, can be purchased from the AA's Dover shop (Eastern Docks Terminal), the AA's Folkestone shop (Eurotunnel Passenger Terminal)
or online at www.theAA.com/shop

Medical treatment

EU/EEA nationals temporarily visiting another country in the European Economic Area (EEA) or Switzerland are entitled to receive state-provided medical care in the case of illness or an accident. A European Health Insurance Card entitles you to reduced-cost or free public medical treatment for an illness or accident while you're in a European Economic Area (EEA) country or Switzerland. The EHIC can be obtained online via www.ehic.org.uk, or call 0845 606 2030, or pick up a EHIC form from the Post Office.

Nationality plate

Vehicles must display a nationality sticker of the approved design on a vertical surface at the rear (and caravan or trailer). Fines are imposed for failing to display the correct distinguishing sign.

UK registration plates displaying the GB Euro-symbol (Euro-Plates) must comply with British Standard AU 145d. These plates make the display of a conventional sticker unnecessary when circulating within the EU. The Euro-Plate is only legally recognised in the EU; it is still a requirement to display a GB sticker when travelling outside the EU.

A GB sign can be purchased from the AA's Dover shop (Eastern Docks Terminal), the AA's Folkestone shop (Eurotunnel Passenger Terminal) or online at
www.theAA.com/shop

Passports

Each person must hold a valid passport. Always carry your passport and a separate note of the number, date and place of issue.

All passports issued to children under the age of 16 years are for 5 years only. After 5 years a new application must be made. To obtain a passport application call 0300 222 0000 or visit the UK Passport Service at
www.passport.gov.uk.

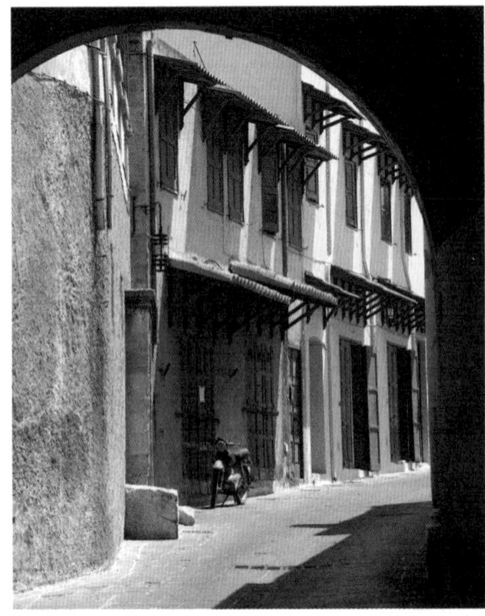

Pet Travel Scheme

For information on how to bring pet cats and dogs back into the UK from certain countries without quarantine contact the Pets Helpline on 0870 241 1710 or visit the Department for Environment, Food & Rural Affairs (DEFRA) website
www.defra.gov.uk/wildlife-pets/pets/travel/quarantine/

Vehicle licence

When taking a vehicle out of the UK for a temporary visit, the vehicle licence (tax disc) must be valid throughout your journey and on your return.

Agreement within the EU provides for the temporary use of foreign-registered vehicles within the member states. A vehicle which is properly registered and taxed in its home country should not be subject to the domestic taxation and registration laws of the host country during a temporary stay.

Visas

EU citizens travelling within the EU do not require visas. A visa is not normally required by United Kingdom and Republic of Ireland passport holders when visiting non-EU countries within western Europe for periods of three months or less. However, if you hold a passport of any other nationality, a UK passport not issued in this country, or if you are in any doubt at all, check with the embassies or consulates of the countries you intend to visit.

Warning triangle & reflective jacket

The use of a warning triangle is compulsory in most European countries in the event of accident or breakdown. In certain circumstances two triangles are required. Additionally, reflective jackets/waistcoats are now compulsory in several European countries.

Warning triangles and reflective jackets or waistcoats can be purchased from the AA's Dover shop (Eastern Docks Terminal), the AA's Folkestone shop (Eurotunnel Passenger Terminal) or online at
www.theAA.com/shop

Weather

For weather information on the Continent visit
www.metoffice.gov.uk
or call the Met Office on 0870 900 0100, from outside the UK on +44 (0)1392 885680.

During your journey

Accidents

If you are in an accident you must stop. A warning triangle should be placed on the road at the appropriate distance; the use of hazard warning lights does not affect the regulations governing the use of warning triangles. The accident must be reported to the police if the accident has caused death or bodily injury; or if an unoccupied vehicle or property has been damaged. The emergency telephone number is 112. If the accident necessitates calling the police, leave the vehicle in position. If it obstructs other traffic, mark the position of the vehicle on the road and get the details confirmed by independent witnesses before moving it. Notify your insurance company (by letter) within 24 hours, making sure all the essential particulars are noted (see the conditions of your policy).

If a third party is injured, contact your insurers for advice or, if you have a Green Card, notify the company or bureau given on the back of your Green Card; this company or bureau will deal with any compensation claim from the injured party.

It is useful to take photographs of the scene. Include the other vehicles involved, their registration plates and any background that could help later enquiries or when completing the insurance company's accident form.

Emergency numbers

All the countries in this guide use 112 as the principal emergency telephone number that can be dialled free of charge from any telephone or any mobile phone in order to reach emergency services (ambulances, fire-fighters and the police). Turkey only uses 112 for medical services. Other Turkish numbers are listed in Turkey's opening section.

Visiting Europe

Breakdown

Try to move the car to the side of the road so that it does not obstruct traffic flow. Place a warning triangle to the rear of the vehicle at the appropriate distance. Find the nearest telephone to call for assistance. On motorways emergency telephones are generally located every 2km and automatically connect you to the official motorway breakdown service.

Motorists are advised to take out *AA European Breakdown Cover* and travel insurance from the AA. They are available at www.theaa.com/breakdown-cover/european-breakdown-cover.jsp or call 0800 072 3279.

Beaches

Pollution of seawater at certain Continental coastal resorts can represent a health hazard. Countries of the European Union publish detailed information on the quality of their bathing beaches, including maps, which are available from national authorities and the European Union.

In many (though not all) popular resorts where the water quality may present risk, signs (generally small) forbid bathing:

France	
No bathing	Défense de se baigner
Bathing prohibited	Il est défendu de se baigner
Italy	
No bathing	Vietato bagnarsi
Bathing prohibited	Evietato bagnarsi
Spain	
No bathing	Prohibido bañarse
Bathing prohibited	Se prohibe bañarse
Germany	
Bathing prohibited	Baden verboten

British Embassies/Consulates

Many Continental countries have at least one British consulate in addition to the British embassy. British consulates (and consular sections in embassies) can help British travellers in distress overseas but there are limitations to what they can do. For example, they cannot pay your hotel, medical or any other bills, nor will they do the work of a travel agent, information bureau or the police.

Report any loss or theft of property to the local police in the first instance, not to the consular offices. If you need to obtain an emergency passport or guidance on how to transfer funds from the UK, contact the nearest British embassy or consulate. Note that the hours and functions of honorary consuls are more restricted than full consular posts.

For up-to-date advice on travelling abroad,
visit www.fco.gov.uk/knowbeforeyougo
or call 0845 850 2829.

Cycle carriers

If you are taking bicycles on a rear-mounted cycle rack, make sure that they do not obstruct rear lights and/or number plate, or you risk an on-the-spot fine.

N.B. Rear-mounted cycle racks are illegal in Portugal. When travelling in Spain or Italy a reflectorised sign has to be placed on the back of a rear-mounted carrier. For further information please see www.theaa.com/motoring_advice/overseas/countrybycountry.html

Crash helmets

The wearing of crash or safety helmets by motorcyclists and their passengers is compulsory in all countries.

Customs regulations

People travelling within the EU are free to take not only personal belongings but a motor vehicle, boat, caravan or trailer across the internal frontiers without being subject to customs formalities. The EU countries are Austria, Belgium, Bulgaria, Cyprus, Czech Republic, Denmark, Estonia, Finland, France, Germany, Greece, Hungary, Republic of Ireland, Italy, Latvia, Lithuania, Luxembourg, Malta, the Netherlands, Poland, Portugal, Romania, Slovakia, Slovenia, Spain (but not the Canaries), Sweden and the UK (but not the Channel Islands). Gibraltar is part of the EU, but customs allowances for outside the EU apply.

When you return to the UK, use the blue exit reserved for EU travellers. You do not have to pay any tax or duty in the UK on goods you have bought in other EU countries for your own use. The law sets out guidelines for the amount of alcohol and tobacco you can bring into the UK. If you bring in more, you must be able to satisfy the customs officer that the goods are for your own use. If you cannot, the goods may be taken from you, and your vehicle may also be seized.
The guidelines are:
800 cigarettes, 400 cigarillos, 200 cigars, 1kg smoking tobacco, 10 litres spirits, 20 litres fortified wine, 90 litres wine, 110 litres beer. (Bulgaria and Romania have a limit of 200 cigarettes, but there are no limits on other tobacco products as long as they are for your own use).
People under 17 are not allowed to bring in alcohol or tobacco.
When you enter the UK from a non-EU country, or from an EU country having travelled through a non-EU country, you must pass through customs. If you have any goods over the allowance, or if you are not sure what to declare you must use the red exit. If you do not declare items on which you should pay duty you are breaking the law.
Customs allowances for travellers from outside the EU are:
200 cigarettes or 100 cigarillos or 50 cigars or 250g tobacco; 4 litres still table wine; 16 litres of beer; 1 litre of spirits or strong liqueurs over 22% volume or 2 litres fortified wine, sparkling wine or other liqueurs; £390 worth of all other goods including perfume, gifts and souvenirs.
For more information, see the HM Revenue & Customs website www.hmrc.gov.uk/customs/arriving/index.htm or call 0845 010 9000.

Fines

Some countries impose on-the-spot fines for minor traffic offences. Fines are paid in the currency of the country concerned to the police or local post office against a ticket issued. A receipt should be obtained as proof of payment. If you drink, don't drive - the laws are strict and the penalties severe.

Horn

In built-up areas, the general rule is that you should not use it unless safety demands it. In many large towns and resorts, and in areas indicated by the international sign (a horn inside a red circle, crossed through) use of the horn is banned.

Hot weather

In hot weather and at high altitude, excessive heat can cause engine problems. If towing a caravan, consult the manufacturers of your vehicle about the limitations of the cooling system, and the operating temperature of the gearbox fluid for automatics.

Journey times

As there are many factors to consider when travelling abroad it is extremely difficult to estimate how long a journey will take. Volume of traffic, road and weather conditions will all affect calculations. On motorways the average speed will be about 60mph (96km/ph), on all-purpose roads out of town the average can be about 45mph (72km/ph), and in urban areas it may be as low as 15-20mph (24-32km/ph). Remember to allow for refreshments, petrol and toilet stops, and if making for a port or airport to add extra time for checking in and unforeseen delays. At peak travel periods delays may occur on some main routes and at frontier crossing points. Mountain passes and alpine roads may be closed during the winter months.

Mobile phones

The use of hand-held mobile phones while driving is prohibited in most countries. In Spain the use of an earpiece or headphones while driving is banned. Only fully hands-free phone systems are permitted.

Off-site camping

Off-site camping may contravene local regulations. You are strongly advised never to camp by the roadside or in isolated areas.

Parking

Heavy fines are imposed for parking offences and unaccompanied offending cars can be towed away. Make sure you understand all parking related signs. Always park on the right-hand side of the road or at an authorised place. If possible, park off the main carriageway.

Petrol & diesel

You will find familiar brands and comparable grades of petrol along the main routes in most countries. However, leaded petrol is no longer generally available in northern European countries. Diesel fuel is generally known as diesel or gas-oil. While you may wish to carry a reserve can of fuel, remember that all ferry and some rail operators will either forbid the carriage of fuel in spare cans or insist that spare cans must be empty. In Luxembourg motorists are forbidden to carry petrol in cans in the vehicle.

Road signs

Most road signs throughout Europe conform to international standards and most will be familiar. Watch for road markings - do not cross a solid white or yellow line marked on the road centre. In Belgium there are three official languages, and signs will be in Dutch, French or German. In the Basque and Catalonian areas of Spain local and national place names appear on signposts.

Road signs also indicate priority or loss of priority, and tourists must be sure that they understand such signs. Particular care should be exercised when circulating
anti-clockwise on a roundabout. It is advisable to keep to the outside lane if possible, to make your exit easier.

Rules of the road

In all countries in this guide, drive on the right and overtake on the left.

When overtaking on roads with two lanes or more in each direction, signal in good time, and also signal your return to the inside lane. Do not remain in any other lane. Failure to comply with this regulation, particularly in France, will incur an on-the-spot fine (immediate deposit in France).

Do not overtake at level crossings, intersections, the crest of a hill or pedestrian crossings. When being overtaken, keep to the right and reduce speed if necessary.

Seat belts

All countries in this guide require seat belts to be worn. Regulations relating to children and seat belts are generally strict and should be checked in advance of travel. See country openers.

Signposting

Signposting between major towns and along main roads is generally efficient, but on some secondary roads and in open country advance direction signs may be less frequent. Signs are often of the pointer type and placed on walls or railings on the far side of the turn; they tend to point across the road they indicate which can be confusing at first. Difficulties may arise with spellings when crossing frontiers, and place names may not be so easily recognised when written in a different language. Extra difficulties may arise in countries with two or more official languages or dialects, although some towns may have both spellings, eg San Sebastian - Donostia in Spain, Antwerpen - Anvers in Belgium, Basel - Bâle in Switzerland.

Speed limits

Speed limits for individual countries are listed in the country openers. They are listed in km per hour only to avoid confusion. Lower limits may apply to motorcycles and new drivers in some countries and also generally when towing a trailer unless indicated otherwise. It can be an offence to travel so slowly as to obstruct traffic flow without good reason or due to poor weather conditions.

Tolls

Tolls are payable on most motorways in Croatia, France, Greece, Italy, Portugal, Spain and on sections in Austria and Poland. Over long distances, charges can be considerable. Always have some local currency ready to pay the tolls, as traveller's cheques are not accepted at toll booths. Credit cards are accepted at toll booths in France and Spain. In Austria, Czech Republic, Hungary, Slovakia and Switzerland, authorities levy a tax for using motorway networks. See country openers. In some countries a "vignette" (tax sticker) may be required for the use of motorways, major roads or for entering environmental zones. In Portugal, on some sections of motorway, an electronic device is required. This must be pre-loaded with currency. Further info at www.theaa.com/allaboutcars/overseas/european_tolls_select.jsp

Trams

Trams take priority over other vehicles. Always give way to passengers boarding and alighting. Never position a vehicle so that it impedes the free passage of a tram. Trams must be overtaken on the right, except in one-way streets.

Channel Crossings

Brittany Ferries

Tel: 0871 244 0744
www.brittany-ferries.com
Cork to Roscoff
Plymouth to Roscoff
Plymouth to Santander
Portsmouth to Caen
Poole to Cherbourg
Portsmouth to Bilbao
Portsmouth to Cherbourg
Portsmouth to St Malo
Portsmouth to Santander

Condor Ferries

Tel: 0845 609 1024
www.condorferries.co.uk
Poole to St Malo
(via Channel Islands)
Weymouth to St Malo
(via Channel Islands)
Portsmouth to Cherbourg
(seasonal)
Portsmouth to St Malo
(via Channel Islands)

Eurotunnel

Tel: 08443 35 35 35
www.eurotunnel.com
Folkestone to Calais

Irish Ferries

Tel: 0818 300 400 (from ROI)
08717 300 400 (from GB)
www.irishferries.com
Rosslare to Cherbourg
Rosslare to Roscoff

Stena Line

Tel: 08447 70 70 70
www.stenaline.co.uk
Harwich to Hook of Holland

LD Lines/ Transmanche Ferries

Tel: 0844 576 8836
www.ldlines.co.uk
Portsmouth to Le Havre
Newhaven to Dieppe
Nantes St-Nazaire to Gijón

Norfolkline Ferries

Tel: 0871 574 7235
www.norfolkline.com
Dover to Dunkerque
Rosyth to Zeebrugge
Newcastle to Amsterdam

P&O Ferries

Tel: 08716 64 21 21
www.poferries.com
Portsmouth to Bilbao
Dover to Calais
Hull to Zeebrugge
Hull to Rotterdam

The Camping and Caravanning Club

The Camping and Caravanning Club is the world's oldest and largest club for people who enjoy camping, however they choose to camp.

If you love the great outdoors, you'll love The Camping and Caravanning Club. Whether you like striking out on your own, or you want the reassurance of a great place to stay, The Club can provide you with as much or as little of your camping needs as you want.

Early Days

The Camping and Caravanning Club was founded in 1901 by six young men camping at Wantage, then in Berkshire. Little did those founder members realise how big their club would grow –The Club's membership grew to a new high of 280,000 households during 2011.

Famous Names

A number of notable people have been associated with the history of The Club. Captain Robert Falcon Scott – Scott of the Antarctic – was an early President. Legend has it that he took his Club pennon (pennant) on his tragic journey to the South Pole. Another President was Lord Baden-Powell, the father of Scouting. His grandson, the third Lord Baden-Powell, was also President of The Club for a decade. The current President, Professor David Bellamy OBE, is highly respected and known throughout the world for his environmental campaigning.

The Outdoor Life

Proud of its history as an innovator and pioneer of camping trends, The Club constantly looks at what campers need to make the most of their outdoor lifestyle adventures. As it's a Club owned and run by its members – people who love the outdoors as much as you do – it's a not for profit organisation which means that any money made, is ploughed back into providing better site facilities, locations and services for members.

There's nothing quite like getting out in the open: fresh air; freedom; new destinations; old and new friends. The Camping and Caravanning Club exists to help you and your family get even more out of the great outdoors. Whether taking the kids on a weekend's camping just half an hour from where you live, or going it alone to explore Europe, the USA or even Australia and New Zealand, The Club can help to make it a real adventure.

Member benefits

In addition to providing members with a foreign travel service which can offer individually tailored holidays, The Club also offers members over 100 award-winning UK Club Sites - all with a reputation for cleanliness and friendliness. There is also a choice of 1,400 smaller and often more rural sites which are exclusive to members. Thanks to a partnership with The Forestry Commission, 'Camping in the Forest' offers over 20 Camping and Caravanning Sites, and 'Forest Holidays' offer seven cabin sites in some of the UK's most beautiful and secluded woodland locations.

Club members can also benefit from publications which help you make the most out of your camping adventures plus products and services including

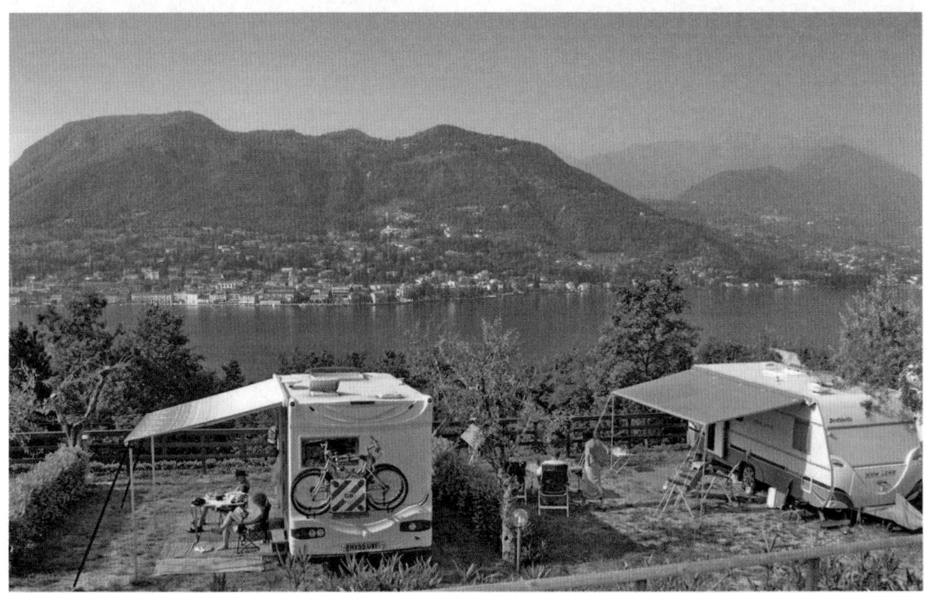

tent, caravan and motorhome insurance – designed by campers, for campers.

Family membership of The Camping and Caravanning Club costs just £39.00 per year. And with special site rates you soon recoup your membership fee with just a few nights' stay at UK Club Sites

Once you become a member of The Camping and Caravanning Club, we're always here to help. If you have a query, a technical problem or simply need some reliable advice, you can call us on 0845 130 7632, Monday to Friday between 8:00am and 8:00pm (from 10am to 7pm on Wednesdays). For a more detailed reply, you're also more than welcome to email us from the Club's website.

To see what other benefits are available to members or to join or find out more about The Club click on: www.thefriendlyclub.co.uk or speak to an advisor on: 0845 130 7632

The Club in Europe

Carefree, the overseas travel service from The Camping and Caravanning Club are experts in providing holidays for people who enjoy spending their time camping throughout Europe. Carefree now sends over 75,000 people abroad each year. Regardless of whether you're a first time camper or an expert overseas explorer, it provides a one-stop-shop travel service.

Peace of mind is assured. Carefree holiday packages are ABTA protected (or ATOL protected if you're taking a fly-drive motorhome holiday outside of Europe). Also, each European campsite suggested for your trip is personally inspected by Carefree's dedicated team against standards agreed with The Royal Society for the Prevention of Accidents (RoSPA). All of this means that you can be assured that your holiday will be one to remember – for all the right reasons.

Abroad for the first time

However you choose to camp, going overseas for the first time is made simpler and safer with The Club. The Carefree brochures have pages of helpful ideas and tips for those travelling abroad with a tent, motorhome or caravan. You will find help on a multitude of subjects - from whether or not to take a universal travel sink plug, to how to take your pet with you, both safely and legally. The AA and Carefree's helpful European Driver's Handbook, along with this AA Caravan & Camping Europe guide, are the perfect partnership to help you find your way around Europe.

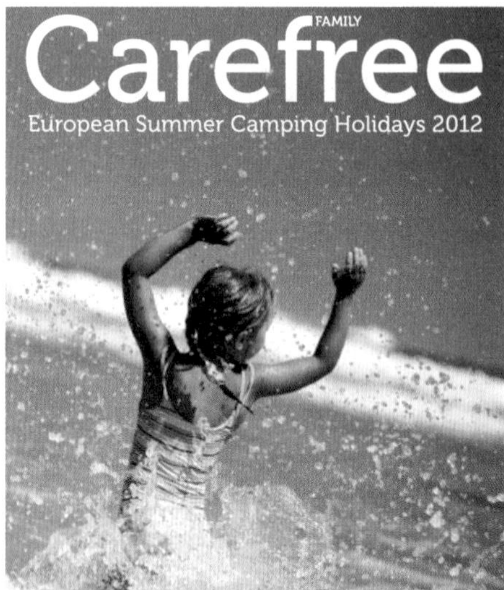

One excellent way to take advantage of other Club members' experience of travelling outside the UK is to visit a Carefree Holiday Rally. Here, campers can meet up with other Club members on site, secure in the knowledge that there will be an experienced Holiday Steward on hand to help if there are any problems. Please click on www.thefriendlyclub.co.uk/travelabroad/rallies for an up-to-date list.

Carefree staff are experienced and incredibly knowledgeable about Carefree destinations. They are able to give campers travelling abroad for the first time the most up-to-date information at their fingertips and you can talk to team members who have visited the sites themselves. You can speak to a European Travel Specialist on 0845 130 7701.

Summer holidays

The summer months are a great time to see much of Europe. From fabulous regional variations in France to fascinating Eastern Europe, there is an ever-increasing array of campsites for you to choose from. European campsites can be simple or include a vast array of facilities, restaurants and activities. Swimming pools offer a cooling break from the summer heat or from trekking, shopping or other pastimes. Many sites allow you to hire bikes or boats etc depending on how you want to go out and enjoy the area.

The sites featuring a **C&CC Report** in this guide guarantee a good standard of facilities and are inspected regularly by C&CC staff. Look for the sites with **C&CC Report** and you'll be guaranteed quality.

In Tune with the Seasons

Be aware too of the differences between high season and low season. High season across Europe is geared to family holidays, family activities and on many coastal sites in particular this includes lively night-times. Each country's high season tends to tie in with the school holiday dates for that country. Children stay up late on many Spanish, Italian and lively French sites – be prepared, be local and go with the flow! The Club produces a family edition of its European Summer Camping brochure so families can easily select the best sites for them.

Low season is the ideal time for couples looking to explore abroad and the European Summer Camping brochure is full of sites and ideas for making the most

The Camping and Caravanning Club

of Europe. Facilities on many sites in low season run at an absolute minimum – there are often simply not enough people on site to justify opening facilities. If a particular facility is important to you it is always recommended you establish whether or not this is available before you book a site.

Winter sun holidays

When the weather gets colder, there is a camping opportunity to travel to sunnier climes. A large number of sites operate during the winter months across European destinations such as France, Spain and Portugal, each helping you to create new memories and providing a base for exploration. Many northern Europeans – British, Dutch, German and Scandinavian in particular – have been wintering here for years and have got the art of 'snowbirding' down to a fine art.

European campsites – what to expect

Most British campers are amazed at the quality of continental sites when they travel abroad. You can definitely leave behind any notions of the 1950s and 'holes in the ground'! The vast majority of continental campsites have swimming pools for their campers. These can range from small traditional swimming pools, to Californian-style pools with waterslides and 'magic rivers', right through to amazing complexes with indoor and outdoor pools, jacuzzis and steam rooms. Sites with pools nearly always have a paddling pool for babies and toddlers. Further sports facilities can include tennis courts, fitness rooms, cycle hire, crazy-golf, multisports courts and of course, in France, the almost obligatory boules pitch.

Carefree
European Camping Holidays 2012
Enjoy the freedom of 'go-as-you-please' year round camping holidays and Rallies to some of Europe's most popular beach, rural, alpine and city destinations
VALUE
YOU CAN
TRUST IN

Similarly, forget any worries about dated wash block facilities. Continental wash blocks are contemporary and well equipped, with modern toilets, efficient showers and nearly always washbasins in cubicles. The further south you go, the more open the wash blocks become, benefitting from the gentler climate. You might like to visit Camping la Paz at Vidiago in northern Spain where you can enjoy a view of the Picos de Europa mountain range from the showers. Travel to

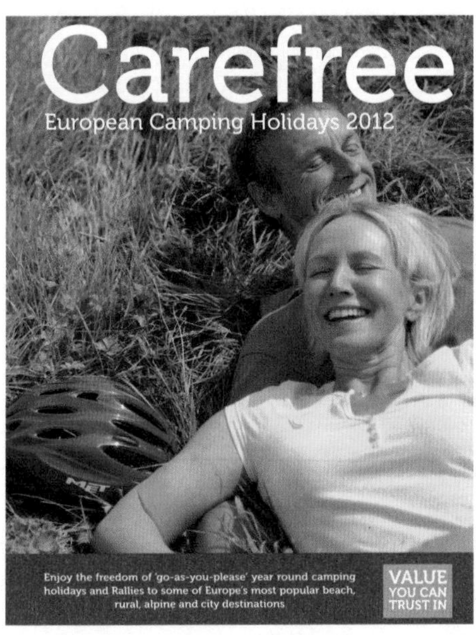

Germany and Austria and you will see some wash blocks worthy of a 5-star hotel, with superb quality bathroom fittings and ceramic tiling. Some sites even offer family bathrooms that you can rent for your exclusive use during your stay on site. Many sites also have great children's facilities, with baby baths and mini-showers, mini-loos and mini-basins, all at children's height.

On many sites you won't need to go far for an evening meal. Lots of sites have take-aways or snack bars, and most of the highest rated sites have very nice restaurants too. You can also usually sample the local specialities just a short stroll away from your pitch. Bars are found on most sites too, ranging from either just a small set of optics and a few bottles behind reception to fabulous terraces overlooking beaches, lakes or the surrounding countryside.

High Season

In high season, many of Europe's bigger and most popular sites offer fabulous activity and entertainment programmes. You can join in with as much or as little as you like, and often it's completely free of charge. Activities might range from Children's Clubs, with sports and craft activities, to walks and bike rides in the local area, to coach excursions to places of interest, to musical evenings and dances. When the French, Spanish and Italians go on holiday, expect them to let their hair down and watch the whole family party until late at night (or early in the morning). If you go to Germany, Holland or any other northern European country, expect the night times to be rather more like campsites at home.

Continental Pitches

In terms of pitches, campers and caravanners travelling abroad for the first time will find one significant difference to many British campsites.

Pitches on the continent are usually quite clearly marked out by either hedges, shrubs or trees. They can range in size from as small as 60m^2 to as spacious as 200m^2. So for the most part you will find that you are pitched much closer to your neighbour than you would generally be in the UK. Electric hook-up supplies are generally good, with a typical choice of a 6, 10 or sometimes 16 amp supply.

There are an increasing number of sites now that offer 'premium' pitches too, aimed specifically at the British tourer with a large caravan or motorhome. The style of these pitches vary from site to site but always offer the largest available pitches, with electricity, water and drainage. There is also usually a variety of added extras such as garden furniture, barbecue, washbasin, fridge and free Wi-fi access.

Simple Pitches

However, should you wish to leave all the facilities and sophisticated camping behind, throughout Europe you will find some of the simplest and most delightful little sites you could wish to experience. Surrounded by countryside, adjacent to small villages, or heading up to the mountains, Europe's sheer range of campsites is quite superb. There is bound to be something out there for you. With the help of this guide you are guaranteed fun in exploring and finding it.

Country Regions

Most of the countries in this guide are divided into regions. See the country maps at the end of the guide. The lists below of country regions show the corresponding national departments, districts or administrative areas.

Austria

TIROL — Tirol
CARINTHIA — Kärnten
STYRIA — Steiermark
LOWER AUSTRIA — Niederösterreich, Burgenland
UPPER AUSTRIA — Oberösterreich, Salzburg
VORARLBERG — Vorarlberg
VIENNA — Wien

Belgium

SOUTH WEST/COAST — Hainaut, West-Vlaanderen
NORTH/CENTRAL — Brabant, Oost-Vlaanderen
NORTH EAST — Antwerpen, Limburg
SOUTH EAST — Liège, Luxembourg, Namur

France

ALPS/EAST — Ain, Doubs, Hautes-Alpes, Haute-Saône, Haute-Savoie, Jura, Isère, Savoie, Territoire-de-Belfort
ALSACE/LORRAINE — Bas-Rhin, Haut-Rhin, Meurthe-et-Moselle, Meuse, Moselle, Vosges
BURGUNDY/CHAMPAGNE — Aube, Ardennes, Côte-d'Or, Haute-Marne, Marne, Nièvre, Saône-et-Loire, Yonne
SOUTH WEST/ PYRENEES — Ariège, Dordogne, Gers, Gironde, Haute-Garonne, Hautes-Pyrénées, Landes, Lot, Lot-et-Garonne, Pyrénées-Atlantiques, Tarn, Tarn-et-Garonne
LOIRE/CENTRAL — Charente, Charente-Maritime, Cher, Corrèze, Creuse, Deux-Sèvres, Eure-et-Loir, Haute-Vienne, Indre, Indre-et-Loire, Loire-Atlantique, Loiret, Loir-et-Cher, Maine-et-Loire, Mayenne, Sarthe, Vendée, Vienne
BRITTANY/NORMANDY — Calvados, Côtes-d'Armor, Eure, Finistère, Ille-et-Vilaine, Manche, Morbihan, Orne, Seine-Maritime
PARIS/NORTH — Aisne, Essonne, Nord, Oise, Paris, Pas-de-Calais, Seine-et-Marne, Somme, Val d'Oise, Yvelines
AUVERGNE — Allier, Aveyron, Cantal, Haute-Loire, Loire, Lozère, Puy-de-Dôme, Rhône
SOUTH COAST/RIVIERA — Alpes-Maritimes, Alpes-de-Haute-Provence, Ardèche, Aude, Bouches-du-Rhône, Drôme, Gard, Hérault, Pyrénées-Orientales, Var, Vaucluse
CORSICA — Corse-du-Sud, Haute-Corse

Germany

SOUTH EAST — Bayern
SOUTH WEST — Baden-Württemberg
BERLIN AND EASTERN PROVINCES — Brandenburg, Mecklenburg-Vorpommern, Sachsen, Thüringen
CENTRAL — Hessen, Nordrhein-Westfalen, Rheinland-Pfalz, Saarland
NORTH — Bremen, Niedersachsen, Schleswig-Holstein

Italy

NORTH WEST/ALPS & LAKES — Aosta, Bolzano, Brescia, Como, Cuneo, Novara, Sondrio, Trento, Torino, Varese
VENICE/NORTH — Belluno, Gorizia, Padova, Rovigo, Trieste, Udine, Venezia, Verona, Vicenza
NORTH WEST/MED COAST — Arezzo, Firenze, Genova, Grosseto, Imperia, Livorno, Lucca, Massa Carrara, Pisa, Pistoia, Savona, Siena, La Spezia
NORTH EAST/ADRIATIC — Ancona, L'Aquila, Ascoli Piceno, Bologna, Campobasso, Chieti, Fermo, Ferrara, Forli, Modena, Parma, Perugia, Pescara, Pesaro & Urbino, Ravenna, Teramo, Terni
ROME — Latina, Roma, Viterbo
SOUTH — Brindisi, Caserta, Catanzaro, Cosenza, Foggia, Lecce, Napoli, Salerno, Taranto
SARDINIA — Cagliari, Nuoro, Sassari
SICILY — Agrigento, Catania, Messina, Palermo, Ragusa, Siracusa, Trapani

Netherlands

NORTH — Drenthe, Friesland, Groningen
CENTRAL — Flevoland, Gelderland, Noord-Holland, Overijssel, Utrecht
SOUTH — Limburg, Noord-Brabant, Zeeland, Zuid-Holland

Portugal

SOUTH — Algarve, Baixo Alentejo
NORTH — Douro Litoral, Minho, Trás os Montes
CENTRAL — Alto Alentejo, Beira Alta, Beira Baixa, Beira Litoral, Estremadura

Spain

NORTH EAST COAST — Barcelona, Girona
CENTRAL — Badajoz, Cáceres, Cuenca, Madrid, Salamanca, Segovia, Teruel, Toledo
SOUTH EAST COAST — Alicante, Castellón, Tarragona, Valencia
NORTH COAST — Asturias, Cantabria, Guipúzcoa, La Coruña, Lugo
NORTH EAST — Burgos, Huesca, Lleida, La Rioja, Navarra, Zaragoza
NORTH WEST — Léon, Pontevedra, Valladolid
SOUTH — Almeria, Cádiz, Cordoba, Granada, Huelva, Jaén, Málaga, Murcia

Switzerland

NORTH — Aargau, Basel, Solothurn
NORTH EAST — Appenzell, St-Gallen, Schaffhausen, Thurgau, Zürich
NORTH WEST/CENTRAL — Bern, Luzern, Neuchâtel, Nidwalden, Obwalden, Schwyz, Uri, Zug
EAST — Graubünden
SOUTH — Ticino
SOUTH WEST — Fribourg, Genève, Valais, Vaud

Drinking and driving

The maximum permitted level of alcohol in the bloodstream is 0.049%. If the level of alcohol in the bloodstream is between 0.05% and 0.079% a fine will be imposed, 0.08% or more, a severe fine and/or driving ban for Austria are imposed. A lower limit of 0.01% is applicable to new drivers who have held their licence under 2 years.

Driving licence

Minimum age at which a UK licence holder may use a temporarily imported car 18, motorcycle (up to 50cc) with a maximum design speed of 45km/h 16, and motorcycle (over 50cc) 18. NOTE UK driving licences that do not incorporate a photograph are only valid when accompanied by photographic proof of identity, e.g. passport.

Fines

On-the-spot. The officer collecting the fine should issue an official receipt. For higher fines the driver will be asked to pay a deposit and remainder of the fine within two weeks. Parked vehicles that obstruct traffic may be towed away.

Fuel

Unleaded petrol (95 and 98 octane) and diesel available. No leaded petrol (lead substitute additive available) and limited LPG available. Petrol in a can permitted, maximum 10 litres. Credit cards are accepted by larger filling stations; check with your card issuer for usage in Austria before travel.

Lights

Passing lights (dipped headlights) on cars must be used when visibility is poor due to bad weather conditions.

Motorcycles

Wearing of crash helmets compulsory for both the driver and passenger. It is prohibited to drive with side lights (position lights only). The use of dipped headlights during the day is compulsory.

Motor insurance

Third-party compulsory, including trailers.

Passengers/children in cars

Children under 14 and less than 1.50 metres in height cannot travel as a front or rear seat passenger unless using suitable restraint system for their height/weight. Vehicles without such protection e.g. two-seater sports cars or vans/lorries may not be used at all to transport children under 14 years of age. Children under 14 years but over 1.50 metres in height must use the adult seat belt. Children 14 or over and over 1.35 metres in height are allowed to use a 'Dreipunktgurt' (three point seat belt) without a special child seat, if the belt does not cover the throat/neck of the child.

Seat belts

Compulsory for front and rear seat occupants to wear seat belts, if fitted. Fine for non-compliance 35.

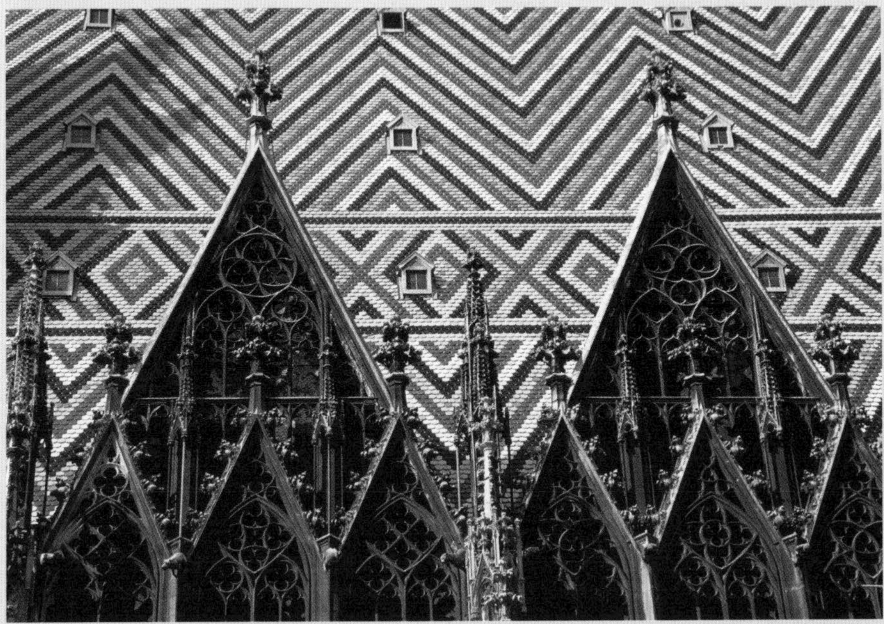

Pictured: St Stephen's Cathedral (Stephansdom), Vienna

Speed limits

Standard legal limits, which may be varied by signs

Private vehicles without trailers	
In built-up areas	50km/h
Outside built- up areas	100km/h
Motorways	130km/h
Vehicle towing a trailer not exceeding 750kg	
Motorways	100km/h
Other roads	100km/h
Vehicle with trailer of a maximum weight exceeding 750kg [when the weight of the trailer does not exceed that of the vehicle and the maximum weight of both vehicles does not exceed 3,500kg]	
Motorways	100km/h
Other roads	80km/h
Vehicle with trailer of a maximum weight exceeding 750kg [when the total weight exceeds 3,500 kg]	
Motorways	70km/h
Other roads	60km/h

Vehicles not capable of sustaining a minimum speed of 60km/h are not permitted on motorways. Mopeds must not exceed 45km/h. The maximum recommended speed limit for vehicles with snow chains is 50km/h. Vehicles equipped with spiked tyres must not exceed 100km/h on motorways and 80km/h on other roads. A number of towns have a general speed limit of 30km/h.

Compulsory equipment in Austria

Warning triangle – Must conform to EC regulation 27 (for vehicles with more than two wheels).

First-aid kit - Must be in a strong dirt proof box.

Reflective jacket - Every car driver has to carry a reflectorised jacket/waistcoat (compliant with European regulation EN471) which has to be used in the case of a breakdown or accident and even when setting up a warning triangle on the road. This regulation does not apply to mopeds/motorcycles, however it is recommended.

Winter equipment – All motorists have the legal obligation to adapt their vehicle to winter weather conditions (see information below).

Between the 1st November and the 15th April vehicles must be fitted with winter tyres (which must be marked M&S on the side walls and have a minimum tread depth of 4mm) or all-season tyres which must be marked M&S (mud and snow) and if roads have a covering of snow, slush or ice outside these dates.

Theoretically snow chains on summer tyres can be used as an alternative to winter tyres where the road is heavily covered with snow and no damage to the road surface is caused by the snow chains. In practice, because road conditions and the weather can not be predicted, use of winter tyres is effectively compulsory.

Note: It is the driver's legal responsibility to carry the required winter equipment; therefore, it is essential to check that it is included in any hire car.

Other rules/requirements

All vehicles using Austrian motorways and expressways must display motorway tax sticker (vignette). The stickers, which are valid for one calendar year, two months or 10 days, may be purchased at some petrol stations located close to the border in neighbouring countries and in Austria: at the frontier, at petrol stations, post offices or in ÖAMTC offices.

A special vignette the 'Korridor Vignette' is required for vehicles travelling from Hohenehms to Horbranz on the German Border if a standard vignette has not been purchased. Fines for driving without a vignette can be severe, minimum 120.

Tolls are also payable when passing through certain motorway tunnels. The use of the horn is generally prohibited in Vienna and in the vicinity of hospitals.

When a school bus has stopped to let children on and off, indicated by a yellow flashing light, drivers travelling in the same direction are not permitted to overtake.

Spiked tyres may be used from the 1st October until the 31st May, special local regulations may extend this period.

It is prohibited to use radar detectors.

If a voucher is required for parking they can be obtained from most tobacconists, banks and some petrol stations.

Tolls Vignette Currency Euro (€)	Car	Car Towing Caravan/Trailer
10 day vignette	€7.90	€7.90
2 month vignette	€23.00	€23.00
Annual vignette	€76.50	€76.50
A10 Tauern Autobahn	€10.00	€10.00
A13 Innsbruck-Brenner Pass	€8.00	€8.00
A16 (S16) Arlberg Expressway (Arlberg tunnel)	€8.50	
Gross Glockner Alpine Road	€28.00	
Bridges and Tunnels		
On A9 Bosruck Tunnel	€4.50	€4.50
On A9 Gleinalm Tunnel	€7.50	€7.50
On A11 Karawanken Tunnel	€6.50	€6.50

TIROL

ASCHAU IM ZILLERTAL TIROL

Erlebnis Comfort Camping Aufenfeld

Aufenfeldweg 10, 6274
☎ 05282 2916 📠 05282 291611
e-mail: info@camping-zillertal.at
web: www.camping-zillertal.at

A well-equipped family site on level meadowland backed by thickly wooded slopes.

dir: *Signed from Aschau road.*

GPS: 47.2631, 11.8997

Open: 4 Dec-4 Nov **Site:** 12HEC **For hire:** **Prices:** 21.60-35.90 **Facilities:** Wi-fi (charged) Kids' Club Play Area **Services:** **Leisure:** L P **Off-site:**

EHRWALD TIROL

Dr Lauth

Zugspitzstr 34, 6632
☎ 05673 2666 📠 05673 26664
e-mail: info@campingehrwald.at
web: www.campingehrwald.at

On undulating grassland, surrounded by high conifers, below the Wetterstein mountain range. Cars may park by tents in winter.

dir: *To right of access road to Zugspitz funicular.*

Open: All Year. **Site:** 1HEC **For hire:** **Facilities:** **Services:** **Off-site:** P

Tiroler Zugspitze

Obermoos 1, 6632
☎ 05673 2309 📠 05673 230951
e-mail: camping@zugspitze-resort.at
web: www.zugspitze-resort.at

A well-equipped site on several grassy terraces surrounded by woodland. Modern sanitary installations with bathrooms.

dir: *Near Zugspitz funicular station.*

Open: All Year. **Site:** 5HEC **Prices:** 37-44 **Facilities:** Wi-fi (charged) Kids' Club Play Area **Services:** **Leisure:** P

FIEBERBRUNN TIROL

Tirol-Camp

6391
☎ 05354 56666 📠 05354 52516
e-mail: office@tirol-camp.at
web: www.tirol-camp.at

A summer and winter site in pleasant Alpine surroundings.

Open: 6 Dec-Apr & 20 May-6 Nov **Site:** 7HEC **Facilities:** Kids' Club Play Area **Services:** **Leisure:** L P

FÜGEN TIROL

Zillertal Camping

Gageringerstr 1, 6263
☎ 05288 62203 📠 05288 622034
e-mail: info@zillertal-camping.at
web: www.zillertal-camping.at

Meadow setting around a farm with fine views of the surrounding mountains.

dir: *1km N of Fügen on B169.*

GPS: 47.3592, 11.8517

Open: All Year. **Site:** 4HEC **For hire:** **Prices:** 30.50-36.50 **Facilities:** Wi-fi (charged) Kids' Club Play Area **Services:** **Leisure:** P **Off-site:** L

HAIMING TIROL

Center Oberland

Bundestr 9, 6425
☎ 05266 88294 📠 05266 882949
e-mail: camping-oberland@qmx.at
web: www.camping-oberland.at

On a sloping meadow in a picturesque mountain setting. A variety of leisure facilities are available, including table tennis and a bouncy castle. 2km from Area 47 theme park.

dir: *Off B171 at Km485.*

Open: May-Oct **Site:** 4HEC **For hire:** **Prices:** 21.60-25 **Facilities:** Wi-fi (charged) Play Area **Services:** **Off-site:** L P R

HALL IN TIROL — TIROL

Camping Schwimmbad Hall

Scheidensteinstr, 6060

☎ 0699 81655268

e-mail: h.niedrist@hall.ag

web: www.camping-hall.at

400 metres from the historic town, this tidy site has leisure facilities including mini-golf, beach volleyball and tennis.

dir: *1.5km from motorway exit Hall Mitte.*

GPS: 47.2839, 11.5003

Open: May-Sep **Site:** 1.2HEC **Prices:** 20-23 **Facilities:** Wi-fi (charged) Play Area **Services:** **Leisure:** P **Off-site:**

HEITERWANG — TIROL

Heiterwangersee

Hotel Fischer am See, 6611

☎ 05674 5116 📠 05674 5260

e-mail: hotel@fischeramsee.at

web: www.fischeramsee.at

A quiet meadow location beside a lake behind the hotel.

dir: *By Hotel Fischer am See.*

Open: All Year. **Site:** 1HEC **Prices:** 26 **Facilities:** Wi-fi Play Area **Services:** **Leisure:** L

HUBEN — TIROL

Ötztaler Naturcamping

6444

☎ 05253 5855 📠 05253 5538

e-mail: info@oetztalernaturcamping.com

web: www.oetztalernaturcamping.com

A well-kept site in a beautiful wooded location beside a mountain stream.

dir: *S of town, signed from Km27 on B186.*

Open: All Year. **Site:** 0.5HEC **Prices:** 22.20-23.60 **Facilities:** Wi-fi (charged) **Services:** **Off-site:** L P

IMST — TIROL

Campingpark Imst-West

Langgasse 62, 6460

☎ 05412 66293 📠 05412 6629319

e-mail: fink.franz@aon.at

web: www.imst-west.com

On open meadowland in the Langgasse area.

dir: *Off bypass near turning for the Pitztal.*

GPS: 47.2286, 10.7433

Open: All Year. **Site:** 1HEC **Prices:** 15-19 **Facilities:** Wi-fi (charged) Play Area **Services:** **Off-site:** L P R

INNSBRUCK — TIROL

Camping Kranebitterhof

Kranebitter Allee 216, 6020

☎ 0512 279558 📠 0512 279558140

e-mail: info@camping-kranebitterhof.at

web: www.camping-kranebitterhof.at

A comfortable and functional site located ten minutes from Innsbruck's historical city centre, between the River Inn and the massive mountain ranges of Tirol. There is a bus connection to the city centre.

Open: All Year. **Site:** 1.5HEC **Prices:** 20-30 **Facilities:** Wi-fi Play Area **Services:** **Off-site:** L R

ITTER — TIROL

Schlossberg

Brixentalerstr 11, 6305

☎ 05335 2181 📠 05335 2182

e-mail: info@camping-itter.at

web: www.camping-itter.at

A family site on terraced meadowland below Schloss Itter on the Brixental Ache. Good leisure facilities.

dir: *2km W on B170.*

Open: Dec-15 Nov **Site:** 4HEC **Prices:** 19-28 **Facilities:** Wi-fi (charged) Kids' Club Play Area **Services:** **Leisure:** P R **Off-site:** L

KITZBÜHEL TIROL

Schwarzsee Camp

6370

☎ 05356 62806 05356 6447930

e-mail: office@bruggerhof-camping.at

web: www.bruggerhof-camping.at

Meadowland site on the edge of a wood behind a large restaurant. There are a sauna, steam room, jacuzzi and gym available.

dir: *B170 from town towards Wörgl, 2km turn right, 400m after Schwarzsee railway station.*

Open: All Year. **Site:** 6HEC **Prices:** 28-42 **Facilities:** Wi-fi Play Area **Services:** **Leisure:** L P

KÖSSEN TIROL

Wilder Kaiser

Kranebittau 18, 6345

☎ 05375 6444 05375 2113

e-mail: info@eurocamp-koessen.com

web: www.eurocamp-koessen.com

Situated in a lovely position below Unterberg. The level site is adjoined on three sides by woodland. Kids' club in July and August.

dir: *Road to Unterberg lift & turn right for 200m.*

GPS: 47.6539, 12.415

Open: 8 Dec-4 Nov **Site:** 5HEC **For hire:** **Prices:** 20.40-24.40 **Facilities:** Wi-fi (charged) Kids' Club Play Area **Services:** **Leisure:** P **Off-site:** L

KRAMSACH TIROL

Camping Seeblick Toni

The Camping and Caravanning Club
The Friendly Club

Moosen 46, 6233

☎ 05337 63544 05337 63544305

e-mail: info@camping-seeblick.at

web: www.camping-seeblick.at

Rural site near the Brantlhof above Lake Reintaler. A kids' club is available during high season.

C&CC Report *A simply beautiful base for some Tyrolean relaxation, for hiking and for day trips to Innsbruck, Kitzbühel and Italy. With both summer and winter activities, a lakeside location, great places to visit and excellent washblocks, Seeblick Toni is top-notch at any time of year. The panoramic traditional restaurant offers superb local cuisine.*

dir: *A12 (Kufstein-Innsbruck) exit Kramsach.*

GPS: 47.4611, 11.9067

Open: All Year. **Site:** 4.5HEC **For hire:** **Prices:** 29.50-40.50 **Facilities:** Wi-fi (charged) Kids' Club Play Area **Services:** **Leisure:** L **Off-site:** P

Stadlerhof

6233

☎ 05337 63371 05337 65311

e-mail: camping.stadlerhof@chello.at

web: www.camping-stadlerhof.at

A pleasant, year-round site on the Reintaler See with well-defined pitches and good leisure facilities.

dir: *Via A12.*

Open: All Year. **Site:** 3HEC **For hire:** **Facilities:** Wi-fi (charged) Play Area **Services:** **Leisure:** L P **Off-site:** R

KUFSTEIN TIROL

Parkcamping Hager

Kufsteinerstrasse 38, 6336

☎ 05372 64170 05332 7296635

e-mail: office@hager-stb.at

Site situated on level meadowland.

Open: All Year. **Site:** 0.5HEC **Facilities:** Play Area **Services:** **Off-site:** L R

LANDECK TIROL

Riffler

Bruggfeldstr, 6500

☎ 05442 64898 05442 648984

e-mail: lorenz.schimpfoessl@aon.at

web: www.camping-riffler.at

Site on meadowland between residential housing and the banks of the Sanna.

Open: Jun-Apr **Site:** 0.2HEC **Prices:** 22.60-25.10 **Facilities:** **Services:** **Leisure:** R **Off-site:** P

LÄNGENFELD TIROL

Camping Ötztal

6444

☎ 05253 5348 05253 53484

e-mail: info@camping-oetztal.com

web: www.camping-oetztal.com

Meadowland with some tall trees on the edge of woodland.

dir: *Turn right off E186 at fire station.*

GPS: 47.0723, 10.9640

Open: All Year. **Site:** 2.6HEC **For hire:** **Facilities:** Wi-fi (charged) Play Area **Services:** **Off-site:** P

AUSTRIA

LERMOOS TIROL

Happy Camp Hofherr

Garmischer Str 21, 6631
☎ 05673 2980 🖷 05673 29805
e-mail: info@camping-lermoos.com
web: www.camping-lermoos.com

Well-equipped site in a wooded location with fine views of the surrounding mountains.

dir: *0.5km from town, off B187 towards Ehrwald.*

Open: 16 Dec-Oct **Site:** 0.8HEC **Facilities:** **Services:** **Off-site:** P R

LEUTASCH TIROL

Holiday-Camping

6105
☎ 05214 65700 🖷 05214 657030
e-mail: info@holiday-camping.at
web: www.holiday-camping.at

A modern site on level grassland screened by trees on the Leutascher Ache.

dir: *Off B313 Mittenwald-Scharnitz towards Leutasch.*

GPS: 47.3984, 11.1797

Open: 7 Dec-5 Nov **Site:** 2.6HEC **Prices:** 21-32 **Facilities:** Wi-fi Play Area **Services:** **Leisure:** P R

LIENZ TIROL

Falken

Falkenweg 7, 9900
☎ 04852 64022 🖷 04852 640226
e-mail: camping.falken@tirol.com
web: www.camping-falken.com

On open ground on the outskirts of the town with modern sanitary facilities.

dir: *S of Lienz, signed from B100.*

GPS: 46.8224, 12.7715

Open: 15 Dec-20 Oct **Site:** 2.5HEC **Facilities:** Wi-fi (charged) Play Area **Services:** **Off-site:** L P R

MAURACH TIROL

Karwendel - Camping

6212
☎ 05243 6116 🖷 05243 20036
e-mail: info@karwendel-camping.at
web: www.karwendel-camping.at

On a level meadow with fine views of the surrounding mountains.

dir: *Off B181 in town onto Pertisau road.*

Open: All Year. **Site:** 1.8HEC **For hire:** **Prices:** 21-23 **Facilities:** Wi-fi (charged) Play Area **Services:** **Off-site:** L P

MAYRHOFEN TIROL

Mayrhofen

Laubichl 125, 6290
☎ 05285 6258051 🖷 05285 6258060
e-mail: camping@alpenparadies.com
web: www.alpenparadies.com

A modern site with good facilities, a short walk from the village.

dir: *Near farm at N entrance to village.*

Open: 21 Dec-Oct **Site:** 2HEC **Facilities:** Wi-fi (charged) Play Area **Services:** **Leisure:** P **Off-site:** R

NATTERS TIROL

Natterer See

Natterer See 1, 6161
☎ 0512 546732 🖷 0512 54673216
e-mail: info@natterersee.com
web: www.natterersee.com

A terraced site beautifully situated among woodland and mountains. Extensive entertainment programme. Dogs not accepted in July and August.

dir: *Brenner motorway exit Innsbruck Süd, via Natters, onto B182 & signed.*

GPS: 47.2383, 11.3389

Open: All Year. **Site:** 9HEC **For hire:** **Prices:** 19.90-36 Mobile home hire 351.50-638.50 **Facilities:** Wi-fi (charged) Kids' Club Play Area **Services:** **Leisure:** L **Off-site:** P

NAUDERS TIROL

Alpencamping Nauders

6543

05473 87217 05473 8721750

e-mail: alpencamping@tirol.com

web: www.camping-nauders.at

A year-round family site in a delightful Alpine location with good recreational facilities.

dir: *Via B315.*

Open: 17 Dec-Oct **Site:** 3HEC **Facilities:** **Services:** **Off-site:** L

PETTNEU AM ARLBERG TIROL

Arlberg

6574

05448 22266 05448 2226630

e-mail: info@camping-arlberg.at

web: www.camping-arlberg.at

Site in the Tyrolean mountains suitable for hiking and mountaineering in summer and close to winter sports resorts.

dir: *S16 exit for Pettneu.*

Open: All Year. **Site:** 4.8HEC **For hire:** **Facilities:** **Services:** **Leisure:** P R

PILL TIROL

Plankenhof

6136

05242 641950 05242 72344

e-mail: hotel@plankenhof.com

Site in meadow behind a hotel near the Womperbach river.

dir: *On B171 near Gasthof Plankenhof.*

Open: May-1 Oct **Site:** 0.6HEC **Prices:** 24-27 **Facilities:** **Services:** **Off-site:** L P R

PRUTZ TIROL

Aktiv-Camping Prutz

Pontlatzstrasse 22, 6522

05472 2648 05472 26484

e-mail: info@aktiv-camping.at

web: www.aktiv-camping.at

A pleasant site in a beautiful mountain setting, close to the Inn River and Kaunertal Glacier, with modern facilities.

dir: *From E60 onto B180, via Reschen Pass.*

GPS: 47.0803, 10.6594

Open: All Year. **Site:** 1.5HEC **For hire:** **Prices:** 18.80-30.80 **Facilities:** Wi-fi (charged) Play Area **Services:** **Leisure:** R **Off-site:** L P

REUTTE TIROL

Seespitze

6600

05672 78121 05672 63372

e-mail: agrar.breitenwang@aon.at

web: www.camping-plansee.at

A quiet location on the shore of Plansee lake.

dir: *On road from Reutte to Oberammergau.*

GPS: 47.4739, 10.7869

Open: May-15 Oct **Site:** 2HEC **Prices:** 20-23 **Facilities:** Play Area **Services:** **Leisure:** L **Off-site:** P

Sennalpe

6600

05672 78115 05672 63372

e-mail: agrar.breitenwang@aon.at

web: www.camping-plansee.at

A quiet location next to Lake Plansee.

dir: *On Reutte-Oberammergau road, 200m from Hotel Forelle.*

Open: 15 Dec-15 Oct **Site:** 4HEC **Prices:** 20-23 **Facilities:** Play Area **Services:** **Leisure:** L **Off-site:**

RIED BEI LANDECK TIROL

Dreiländereck

6531

05472 6025 05472 60254

e-mail: camping-dreilandereck@tirol.com

web: www.tirolcamping.at

Level site in centre of village beside a lake, with spectacular views.

Open: All Year. **Site:** 1HEC **For hire:** **Prices:** 19.40-27.50 **Facilities:** Wi-fi (charged) Play Area **Services:** **Off-site:** L P R

RINN TIROL

Camping Judenstein

Judenstein 40, 6074

05223 78098 05223 7887715

e-mail: camping@kbrinn.at

web: www.kbrinn.at/camping

A wooded location with fine views.

dir: *From motorway exit Hall.*

Open: 15 Apr-15 Oct **Site:** 0.6HEC **Prices:** 13.50-15.50 **Facilities:** **Services:** **Off-site:** L P

Facilities shower electric points for razors electric points for caravans motorvan service point parking by tents permitted compulsory separate car park shop **Services** café/restaurant bar Camping Gaz International gas other than Camping Gaz first aid facilities laundry **Leisure** swimming L-Lake P-Pool R-River S-Sea **Off-site** All facilities within 5km

ST JOHANN — TIROL

Michelnhof

Weiberndorf 6, 6380
05352 62584 05352 625844
e-mail: camping@michelnhof.at
web: www.camping-michelnhof.at
Family-owned site with clean, well-equipped facilities. A small animal zoo is run by the same family.

dir: *1.5km S via B161 St-Johann-Kitzbühel.*

Open: All Year. **Site:** 3HEC **Facilities:** **Services:** **Off-site:** P R

SEEFELD — TIROL

Camp-Alpin

Leutascher Str 810, 6100
05212 4848 05212 484810
e-mail: info@camp-alpin.at
web: www.camp-alpin.at
Terraced site on an alpine plateau with fine mountain views, ideal for summer activities and winter sports.

Open: All Year. **Site:** 3HEC **For hire:** **Prices:** 21.40-39.10 **Facilities:** Wi-fi Kids' Club Play Area **Services:** **Off-site:** L P

SÖLDEN — TIROL

Sölden

Wohlfahrtstr 22, 6450
05254 26270 05254 26275
e-mail: info@camping-soelden.com
web: www.camping-soelden.com
Situated on meadowland on the Ötztaler tributary. Beautiful views of the surrounding mountains.

dir: *B186 exit K.*

GPS: 46.9578, 11.0119

Open: Jan-mid Apr, mid Jun-mid Sep, mid Oct-Dec **Site:** 1.3HEC **Prices:** 25.40 **Facilities:** Wi-fi Play Area **Services:** **Off-site:** L P

THIERSEE — TIROL

Rueppenhof

Seebauern 8, 6335
05376 5694
e-mail: rueppenhof@gmail.com
web: www.rueppenhof.com
Site made up of several meadows surrounding a farm on the banks of a lake.

dir: *A12 exit Kufstein-Nord, signed Thiersee.*

Open: 15 Apr-15 Oct **Site:** 1.5HEC **For hire:** **Prices:** 17.60-19.10 **Facilities:** Wi-fi (charged) Play Area **Services:** **Leisure:** L **Off-site:** P

UMHAUSEN — TIROL

Ötztal Arena

6441
05255 5390 05255 5390
e-mail: info@oetztal-camping.at
web: www.oetztal-camping.at
At an altitude of 1050 metres, site on meadowland.

dir: *Signed from B186.*

Open: All Year. **Site:** 1HEC **For hire:** **Prices:** 20-22 **Facilities:** **Services:** **Leisure:** L R

WAIDRING — TIROL

Steinplatte

Unterwasser 43, 6384
05353 5345 05353 5406
e-mail: camping-steinplatte@aon.at
web: www.camping-steinplatte.at
On a level meadow with fine panoramic views of the surrounding mountains.

Open: All Year. **Site:** 4HEC **For hire:** **Facilities:** **Services:** **Leisure:** L **Off-site:** P R

WALCHSEE — TIROL

Seespitz

Seespitz 1, 6344
05374 5359 05374 5845
e-mail: info@camping-seespitz.at
web: www.camping-seespitz.at
Pleasant surroundings beside the Walchsee with good recreational facilities.

dir: *Between B172 & lake.* **GPS:** 47.6492, 12.3143

Open: All Year. **Site:** 4HEC **Prices:** 24.50-30 **Facilities:** Play Area **Services:** **Leisure:** L **Off-site:** P

Terrassencamping Süd-See

Seestr 76, 6344
☎ 05374 5339 🖹 05374 5529
e-mail: campingwalchsee@aon.at
web: www.camp-sud-see.com

A lakeside site in wooded surroundings with extensive terracing and fine mountain views.

dir: *0.5km W on B172 onto no through road, continue 1.5km.*

Open: All Year. **Site:** 11HEC **Facilities:** **Services:** **Leisure:** L **Off-site:** P

WEER TIROL

Alpencamping Mark

Bundesstrasse 12, 6114
☎ 05224 68146 🖹 05244 681466
e-mail: alpcamp.mark@aon.at
web: www.alpencampingmark.com

Situated on meadowland by a farm on the edge of a forest.

dir: *Off B171.*

GPS: 47.3061, 11.6494

Open: Apr-Oct **Site:** 2HEC **For hire:** **Prices:** 16-21 **Facilities:** Wi-fi (charged) Kids' Club Play Area **Services:** **Leisure:** P **Off-site:** L

WESTENDORF TIROL

Panorama

Mühltal 70, 6363
☎ 05334 6166 🖹 05334 6843
e-mail: info@panoramacamping.at
web: www.panoramacamping.at

A beautiful Alpine setting with modern facilities.

dir: *B170 W towards Wörgl.*

Open: 14 Dec-Oct **Site:** 2.2HEC **Facilities:** **Services:** **Off-site:** P

ZELL AM ZILLER TIROL

Hofer

Gerlosstr 33, 6280
☎ 05282 2248 🖹 05282 22488
e-mail: info@campingdorf.at
web: www.campingdorf.at

Meadowland site with some fruit trees. Free ski bus service every 15 minutes in winter.

dir: *Site at end of Zillertal off road to Gerlos Pass.*

Open: All Year. **Site:** 1.5HEC **For hire:** **Prices:** 19.30-29.60 **Facilities:** Wi-fi (charged) Play Area **Services:** **Leisure:** P

CARINTHIA

DELLACH KÄRNTEN

Neubauer

9872
☎ 04766 2532 🖹 04766 25324
e-mail: info@camping-neubauer.at
web: www.camping-neubauer.at

A terraced site with direct access to the Millstättersee.

dir: *Off B100 Leinz-Spittal, signed in village.*

Open: May-15 Oct **Site:** 1.5HEC **Facilities:** **Services:** **Leisure:** L **Off-site:**

DELLACH IM DRAUTAL KÄRNTEN

Waldbad

9772
☎ 04714 288 🖹 04714 2343
e-mail: info@camping-waldbad.at
web: www.camping-waldbad.at

A small site, suitable for families, in a delightful wooded setting with two large swimming pools, adventure playground and sports facilities.

dir: *Off A10 at Spittal onto B100.*

Open: May-Sep **Site:** 3HEC **For hire:** **Prices:** 17-26.50 **Facilities:** Wi-fi (charged) Play Area **Services:** **Leisure:** P **Off-site:** R

DÖBRIACH KÄRNTEN

Brunner am See

Glanzerstr 108, 9873
☎ 04246 7189 🖹 04246 718914
e-mail: office@camping-brunner.at
web: www.camping-brunner.at

A tidily arranged site with award-winning facilities. Situated on the banks of Lake Millstatt with a private bathing area. Shop open June to September and kids' club available in July and August. Cycling, walking and hiking nearby.

dir: *Off A10, at E end of Lake Millstatt.*

GPS: 46.7676, 13.6485

Open: All Year. **Site:** 3.5HEC **For hire:** **Prices:** 19.56-39.76 **Facilities:** Wi-fi (charged) Kids' Club Play Area **Services:** **Leisure:** L **Off-site:** P

AUSTRIA

Burgstaller

Seefeldstr 16, 9873
☎ 04246 7774 04246 77744
e-mail: info@burgstaller.co.at
web: www.burgstaller.co.at
A quiet site 100 metres from the lake, with modern facilities.
dir: *From B98 towards SE end of Lake Millstatt for 1km.*
GPS: 46.7697, 13.6481
Open: 30 Mar-4 Nov **Site:** 12HEC **For hire:** **Prices:** 21.60-45.26 **Facilities:** Wi-fi (charged) Kids' Club Play Area **Services:** **Leisure:** L P

DÖLLACH KÄRNTEN

Zirknitzer

9843
☎ 04825 451 04825 451
e-mail: camping.zirknitzer@utanet.at
web: web.utanet.at/zirknitp
Beside the River Möll.
dir: *Between Km8 & Km9 on B107 Glocknerstr.*
Open: All Year. **Site:** 0.6HEC **For hire:** **Prices:** 15.60-17.60 **Facilities:** Play Area **Services:** **Leisure:** R **Off-site:** P

FAAK AM SEE KÄRNTEN

Strandcamping Arneitz

Seeuferlandesstrasse 53, 9583
☎ 04254 2137 04254 3044
e-mail: camping@arneitz.at
web: www.arneitz.at
On a wooded peninsula jutting into the Faakersee with good sports facilities.
Open: 28 Apr-Sep **Site:** 6HEC **Facilities:** Wi-fi (charged) Play Area **Services:** **Leisure:** L

Strandcamping Sandbank

Badeweg 3, 9583
☎ 04254 2261 04254 3943
e-mail: info@camping-sandbank.at
web: www.camping-sandbank.at
A partially shaded site between the lakeside and the road.
dir: *From road by Hotel Fürst.*
Open: May-25 Sep **Site:** 5HEC **For hire:** **Facilities:** **Services:** **Leisure:** L **Off-site:**

FELDKIRCHEN KÄRNTEN

Seewirt-Spiess

Maltschach am See 2, 9560
☎ 04277 2637 04277 26374
e-mail: office@seewirt-spiess.com
web: www.seewirt-spiess.com
A pleasant wooded location on the shore of the Maltschacher See.
dir: *Off B95 towards Klagenfurt.*
Open: May-Sep **Site:** 1.2HEC **For hire:** **Facilities:** **Services:** **Leisure:** L **Off-site:** P

HEILIGENBLUT KÄRNTEN

Nationalpark-Camping Grossglockner

9844
☎ 04824 2048 04824 24622
e-mail: nationalpark-camping@heiligenblut.at
web: www.heiligenblut.at/nationalpark-camping
Meadowland site surrounded by woodland within a national park.
Open: May-Oct & Dec-Apr **Site:** 2.5HEC **Prices:** 20.50-22 **Facilities:** Wi-fi (charged) Play Area **Services:** **Leisure:** R **Off-site:** P

HERMAGOR KÄRNTEN

Naturpark Schluga Seecamping

9620
☎ 04282 2760 04282 288120
e-mail: camping@schluga.com
web: www.schluga.com
A well-equipped family site 200 metres north of a lake in meadowland with some terraces and fine views.
dir: *6km E of Hermagor.*
Open: 10 May-20 Sep **Site:** 8.8HEC **For hire:** **Prices:** 16-36 **Facilities:** Wi-fi (charged) Kids' Club Play Area **Services:** **Leisure:** L **Off-site:** P R

Schluga Camping Hermagor

Vellach 15, 9620
☎ 04282 2051 04282 288120
e-mail: camping@schluga.com
web: www.schluga.com
Well-equipped family site in a rural setting, 4km from lake Presseger See.
Open: All Year. **Site:** 5.5HEC **For hire:** **Prices:** 16-36 **Facilities:** Wi-fi (charged) Kids' Club Play Area **Services:** **Leisure:** L P **Off-site:** R

AUSTRIA

KEUTSCHACH — KÄRNTEN

Camping Reichmann

Reauz 5, 9074

☎ 0664 1430437

e-mail: info@camping-reichmann.at

web: www.camping-reichmann.at

On the east bank of Rauschelesee Lake, with a pebble beach. Sporting facilities include football, swimming and fishing.

Open: May-Sep **Site:** 4.8HEC **For hire:** **Prices:** 25.70 Mobile home hire 415 **Facilities:** Wi-fi (charged) Play Area **Services:** **Leisure:** L

Strandcamping Süd

Dobeinitz 30, 9074

☎ 04273 2773 04273 2773-4

e-mail: info@strandcampingbruecklersued.at

web: www.keutschachsued.at

A pleasant setting among shrubs and trees on south side of the Keutschachersee.

dir: *Motorway exit Valden, towards Keutschacher-Seental.*

Open: May-Sep **Site:** 2HEC **Prices:** 22.80-27.60 **Facilities:** Kids' Club Play Area **Services:** **Leisure:** L

KLAGENFURT — KÄRNTEN

Camping Klagenfurt Wörthersee

Metnitz Strand 5, 9020

☎ 0463 287810 0463 2878103

e-mail: info@campingfreund.at

web: www.camping-klagenfurt.at

Large site divided into sections by trees and bushes.

dir: *B83 from town centre towards Velden, left just outside town towards bathing area.*

GPS: 46.6175, 14.2578

Open: 15 Apr-Sep **Site:** 4HEC **For hire:** **Prices:** 22.90-29.90 **Facilities:** Wi-fi (charged) Kids' Club Play Area **Services:** **Leisure:** L **Off-site:** P R

KÖTSCHACH-MAUTHEN — KÄRNTEN

Alpencamp Kärnten

9640

☎ 04715 429 04715 429

e-mail: info@alpencamp.at

web: www.alpencamp.at

On level meadowland beside River Gail with good facilities for water sports.

dir: *S of village, off B110, 0.8km towards Lesachtal.*

GPS: 46.6697, 12.9911

Open: 15 Dec-Oct **Site:** 1.8HEC **For hire:** **Prices:** 17.70-26.20 Mobile home hire 390-590 **Facilities:** Wi-fi (charged) Play Area **Services:** **Off-site:** P R

MALTA — KÄRNTEN

Maltatal

9854

☎ 04733 2340 04733 23416

e-mail: info@maltacamp.at

web: www.maltacamp.at

On a gently rising alpine meadow with breathtaking views of the surrounding mountains and close to the Hohe Tauern National Park.

dir: *A10 exit Gmünd.*

GPS: 46.9497, 13.5094

Open: 31 Mar-Oct **Site:** 3.5HEC **For hire:** **Prices:** 22.70-31.50 Mobile home hire 366-940 **Facilities:** Wi-fi (charged) Play Area **Services:** **Leisure:** P R

OBERVELLACH — KÄRNTEN

Activ Sport Erlebnis Camp

9821

☎ 04782 2727 04782 27274

e-mail: info@sporterlebnis.at

web: www.sporterlebnis.at

Family campsite specialising in leisure activities such as rafting, kayaking etc.

dir: *A10 at Spittal exit onto B100 signed Lienz-Mallnitz then B106 signed Obervellach.*

Open: May-Sep **Site:** 10HEC **For hire:** **Prices:** 17-19 **Facilities:** Wi-fi Play Area **Services:** **Leisure:** R **Off-site:** P

OSSIACH KÄRNTEN

Ossiach

9570
☎ 04243 436 📠 04243 8171
e-mail: martinz@camping.at
web: www.terrassen.camping.at

Divided into pitches with generally well-placed terraces.

dir: *Off B94 on E bank of Kale Ossiacher.*

Open: May-Sep **Site:** 10HEC **For hire:** **Facilities:** **Services:** **Leisure:** L

Parth

Ostriach 10, 9570
☎ 04243 2744 📠 04243 274415
e-mail: camping@parth.at
web: www.parth.at

On the south shore of Lake Ossiacher, pitches are on hilly ground but with some terraces. Kids' club available in July and August. Camping Card International (CCI) compulsory 8 July to 25 August.

dir: *From Salzburg A10 (direction Villach) exit Ossiacher See-Sud.*

GPS: 46.6636, 13.9747

Open: Apr-Oct & 26 Dec-10 Jan **Site:** 1.8HEC **For hire:** **Prices:** 16-29.50 **Facilities:** Wi-fi (charged) Kids' Club Play Area **Services:** **Leisure:** L

Seecamping Berghof

Ossiachersee-Süduferstr 241, 9523
☎ 04242 41133 📠 04242 4113330
e-mail: office@seecamping-berghof.at
web: www.seecamping-berghof.at

Attractive, terraced meadowland site with a 0.8km-long promenade and bathing areas.

dir: *E shore of Lake Ossiacher.*

Open: Apr-17 Oct **Site:** 10HEC **For hire:** **Prices:** 22.80-33.90 **Facilities:** Wi-fi (charged) Kids' Club Play Area **Services:** **Leisure:** L

SACHSENBURG KÄRNTEN

Drau Camping

Ringmauergasse 8, 9751
☎ 04769 3131 📠 04769 292520
e-mail: info@draucamping.at
web: www.draucamping.at

A modern family site with good facilities in a delightful mountain setting.

dir: *A10 between Spittal & Lienz.*

GPS: 46.8283, 13.3483

Open: May-Sep **Site:** 1.3HEC **Prices:** 19-27 **Facilities:** Wi-fi (charged) Play Area **Off-site:** P

ST PRIMUS KÄRNTEN

Strandcamping Turnersee Breznik

9123
☎ 04239 2350 📠 04239 235032
e-mail: info@breznik.at
web: www.breznik.at

A quiet site in a picturesque mountain setting with a variety of recreational facilities. Kids' club available in high season.

dir: *B70 Klagenfurt-Graz towards Klopeinersee.*

GPS: 46.5857, 14.5660

Open: 14 Apr-Sep **Site:** 7.5HEC **For hire:** **Prices:** 17.10-28.20 Mobile home hire 280-686 **Facilities:** Wi-fi (charged) Kids' Club Play Area **Services:** **Leisure:** L **Off-site:**

SEEBODEN KÄRNTEN

Strandcamping Winkler

Seepromenade 33, 9871
☎ 04762 81822 (winter) 📠 04762 81822
web: www.campsite.at/strandcamping-winkler

Located next to Lake Millstatt, with pitches accessed by asphalt paths. Ideal for exploring the surrounding mountainous countryside.

dir: *A10 exit at Millstätter See onto B98.*

GPS: 46.8152, 13.5204

Open: May-1 Oct **Site:** 0.7HEC **Prices:** 25.40-32.40 **Facilities:** Play Area **Services:** **Leisure:** L **Off-site:**

SPITTAL AN DER DRAU KÄRNTEN

Draufluss

Schwaig 10, 9800
☎ 04762 2466 📠 04762 2466
e-mail: drauwirt@aon.at
web: www.drauwirt.com

A long, narrow riverside site, partly surrounded by a hedge.

dir: *From town centre to river towards Goldeckbahn.*

Open: May-Sep **Site:** 0.7HEC **Facilities:** **Services:** **Leisure:** R **Off-site:** P

STOCKENBOI KÄRNTEN

Ronacher

Möse 6, 9714

☎ 04761 256 🖷 04761 2564

e-mail: info@campingronacher.at

web: www.campingronacher.at

Situated on meadow between forest slopes, gently sloping to the shore of Weissensee.

dir: *Approach for caravans via Weissensee.*

Open: May-10 Oct **Site:** 1.7HEC **Facilities:** Wi-fi (charged) Play Area **Services:** **Leisure:** L

VILLACH KÄRNTEN

Camping Gerli

St Georgenerstr 140, 9500

☎ 04242 57402 🖷 04242 582909

e-mail: gerli.meidl@utanet.at

web: www.campgerli.com

Level, isolated site with a heated swimming pool.

dir: *Off B100, turn right just before Villach & continue 2km.*

Open: All Year. **Site:** 2.3HEC **For hire:** **Prices:** 15.20-18.90 **Facilities:** Wi-fi Play Area **Services:** **Leisure:** P **Off-site:**

Seecamping Berghof

Ossiacher See Süduferstr 241, 9523

☎ 04242 41133 🖷 04242 4113330

e-mail: office@seecamping-berghof.at

web: www.seecamping-berghof.at

On the southern shore of Lake Ossiach, pitches overlook the lake or have wonderful mountain views. Wide range of leisure facilities including a sailing and surfing school and live evening entertainment. Dogs allowed except July and August.

GPS: 46.6533, 13.9333

Open: 15 Apr-16 Oct **Site:** 10HEC **For hire:** **Facilities:** Wi-fi (charged) Kids' Club Play Area **Services:** **Leisure:** L

WERTSCHACH KÄRNTEN

Alpenfreude

9612

☎ 04256 2708 🖷 04256 27084

e-mail: camping.alpenfreude@aon.at

web: www.alpenfreude.at

With wonderful views of the surrounding mountains, well-established family site with large swimming pool area.

Open: May-Sep **Site:** 5HEC **For hire:** **Prices:** 14-19.40 **Facilities:** Wi-fi Kids' Club Play Area **Services:** **Leisure:** P **Off-site:** R

STYRIA

AUSSEE, BAD STEIERMARK

Camping An Der Traun

Grundlseer Str 21, 8990

☎ 03622 54565 🖷 03622 52427

e-mail: office@staudnwirt.at

web: www.staudnwirt.at

Pleasant wooded surroundings attached to hotel.

dir: *2.5km from Bad Aussee towards Grundlsee.*

Open: All Year. **Site:** 0.4HEC **Prices:** 19.90 **Facilities:** Wi-fi Play Area **Services:** **Leisure:** R **Off-site:** L

GROSSLOBMING STEIERMARK

Camping Murinsel

Teichweg 1, 8734

☎ 0664 3045045 🖷 03512 600884

e-mail: office@camping-murinsel.at

web: www.camping-murinsel.at

Located next to a lake, a peaceful and secure site.

dir: *4km from S36.*

GPS: 47.1933, 14.8067

Open: 1wk before Etr-Oct **Site:** 5HEC **For hire:** **Prices:** 15-25 **Facilities:** Wi-fi Play Area **Services:** **Leisure:** L R **Off-site:** P

HIRSCHEGG STEIERMARK

Hirschegg

8584

☎ 03141 2201

e-mail: info@camping-hirschegg.at

web: www.camping-hirschegg.at

Delightful Alpine setting.

dir: *A2 towards Klagenfurt, exit Modriach.*

Open: All Year. **Site:** 2HEC **For hire:** **Facilities:** **Services:** **Off-site:** L R

AUSTRIA

AUSTRIA

LANGENWANG-MÜRTZAL STEIERMARK

Europa Camping

Siglstr 5, 8665

☎ 03854 2950

e-mail: europa.camping.stmk@aon.at

web: www.campsite.at/europa.camping.langenwang

On level meadow with some trees, surrounded by hedges. The site occupies an attractive alpine setting.

dir: *S6 bypasses town. Exit 6km S of Mürzzuschlag.*

Open: All Year. **Site:** 0.55HEC **Prices:** 14.55-16.40 **Facilities:** Play Area **Services:** **Off-site:** L R

LEIBNITZ STEIERMARK

Leibnitz

R-H-Bartsch-Gasse 33, 8430

☎ 03452 82463 03452 71491

e-mail: camping@leibnitz.at

web: www.camping-steiermark.at

A well-equipped site in pleasant wooded surroundings with plenty of leisure facilities.

dir: *Signed W of town.*

GPS: 46.7788, 15.5290

Open: May-15 Oct **Site:** 0.7HEC **Prices:** 20.10 **Facilities:** Wi-fi (charged) Play Area **Services:** **Leisure:** P R **Off-site:** L

MARIA LANKOWITZ STEIERMARK

Piberstein

Am See 1, 8591

☎ 03144 7095910 03144 7095974

e-mail: office@piberstein.at

web: www.piberstein.at

Large well-equipped site surrounding a series of lakes. Plenty of sports facilities.

dir: *S of Maria Lankowitz towards Pack.*

Open: May-15 Oct **Site:** 5.6HEC **For hire:** **Facilities:** **Services:** **Leisure:** L **Off-site:**

MITTERNDORF, BAD STEIERMARK

Camping & Pension Grimmingsicht

8983

☎ 03623 2985 03623 2985

e-mail: camping@grimmingsicht.at

web: www.grimmingsicht.at

Small, friendly campsite, quietly situated near a village with beautiful views of the surrounding mountains.

dir: *Off B145.*

GPS: 47.5551, 13.9224

Open: All Year. **Site:** 0.6HEC **For hire:** **Prices:** 16-22 **Facilities:** Play Area **Services:** **Leisure:** R **Off-site:** P

MÜHLEN STEIERMARK

Camping am Badesee

Hitzmannsdorf 2, 8822

☎ 03586 2418 03586 2204

e-mail: office@camping-am-badesee.at

web: www.camping-am-badesee.at

A small, family site with direct access to the lake. Ideally located for fishing and hiking.

dir: *N via B92, signed.*

GPS: 47.0369, 14.4875

Open: 30 Apr-Sep **Site:** 1.5HEC **For hire:** **Prices:** 14-19.40 **Facilities:** Wi-fi Kids' Club Play Area **Services:** **Leisure:** L **Off-site:** P

OBERWÖLZ STEIERMARK

Rothenfels

Bromach 1, 8832

☎ 0664 1412514

e-mail: camping@rothenfels.at

web: www.camping-rothenfels.at

Set in the grounds of a castle in picturesque Alpine surroundings. Good recreational facilities.

dir: *On SE outskirts.*

Open: All Year. **Site:** 8HEC **For hire:** **Prices:** 17-18.50 **Facilities:** Play Area **Services:** **Leisure:** L **Off-site:** P R

ST GEORGEN STEIERMARK

Olachgut

8861
☎ 03532 2162 🖷 03532 21624
e-mail: office@olachgut.at
web: www.olachgut.at

On a level meadow, surrounded by beautiful mountain scenery. The site owns a farm with a riding school.

dir: *W of Murau, off B97.*

Open: All Year. **Site:** 10HEC **For hire:** **Facilities:** Wi-fi (charged) Play Area **Services:** **Leisure:** L **Off-site:** P R

ST SEBASTIAN STEIERMARK

Erlaufsee

Erlaufseestr 3, 8630
☎ 03882 4937 🖷 03882 214822
e-mail: gemeinde@st-sebastian.at
web: www.st-sebastian.at

A picturesque Alpine setting in woodland, 100 metres from the lake.

Open: May-15 Sep **Site:** 1HEC **Prices:** 16.50 **Facilities:** **Off-site:** L P R

SCHLADMING STEIERMARK

Camping-Hotel Zirngast

Linke Ennsau 633, 8970
☎ 03687 23195 🖷 03687 231954
e-mail: camping@zirngast.at
web: www.zirngast.at

Meadowland site on the River Enns next to the railway.

dir: *Off B308 towards town, site by fuel station.*

Open: All Year. **Site:** 1.5HEC **Prices:** 23.50-35 **Facilities:** Wi-fi (charged) **Services:** **Leisure:** R **Off-site:** P

UNGERSDORF BEI FROHNLEITEN STEIERMARK

Lanzmaierhof

Ungersdorf 16, 8130
☎ 03126 2360 🖷 03126 4174
e-mail: lanzmaierhof@tele2.at
web: www.camping-steiermark.at

A quiet site and an ideal base for walking and climbing.

dir: *Signed 2km S of Frohnleiten on Graz road.*

GPS: 47.1512, 15.1907

Open: Apr-15 Oct **Site:** 0.5HEC **For hire:** **Prices:** 18.30-21.40 **Facilities:** Play Area **Services:** **Off-site:** P

WEISSKIRCHEN STEIERMARK

50Plus Campingpark Fisching

Fisching 9, 8741
☎ 03577 82284 🖷 03577 822846
e-mail: campingpark@fisching.at
web: www.camping50plus.at

A modern site with fine sanitary and sports facilities, catering for over-50s. 8km from the Formula 1 circuit (Red Bull Ring) in Zeltweg.

dir: *S36 exit Zeltweg-Ost for Obdach & signs for B78, signed from centre of Fisching.*

Open: Apr-15 Oct **Site:** 1.5HEC **For hire:** **Prices:** 26 **Facilities:** Wi-fi (charged) **Services:** **Leisure:** P **Off-site:**

WILDALPEN STEIERMARK

Wildalpen

8924
☎ 03636 342 & 341 🖷 03636 313
e-mail: camping@wildalpen.at
web: www.wildalpen.at

Located in a nature reserve beside the River Salza with good canoeing facilities.

Open: Apr-Oct **Site:** 0.8HEC **Facilities:** Wi-fi (charged) **Services:** **Leisure:** R **Off-site:** P

LOWER AUSTRIA

GMÜND NIEDERÖSTERREICH

Sole-Felsen-Bad

Albrechtser Str 10, 3950
02852 202030 02852 202033
e-mail: info@sole-felsen-bad.at
web: www.sole-felsen-bad.at
A pleasant location with a variety of recreational facilities.
dir: *Signed off B41.*
Open: Apr-Oct **Site:** 0.5HEC **Facilities:** **Services:** **Off-site:** L P

JENNERSDORF BURGENLAND

Jennersdorf

Freizeitzentrum 3, 8380
03329 46133 03329 4626121
e-mail: post@jennersdorf.bgld.gv.at
web: www.jennersdorf.eu
A pleasant site in wooded surroundings.
dir: *A2 exit Fürstenfeld.*
Open: 16 Mar-Oct **Site:** 1HEC **Facilities:** **Services:** **Leisure:** P **Off-site:** R

KAUMBERG NIEDERÖSTERREICH

Paradise Garden Camping

Hoefnerbraben 2, 2572
0676 4741966 02765 3883
e-mail: grandl@camping-noe.at
web: www.camping-noe.at
Not far from Vienna, in a picturesque valley setting surrounded by meadows where sheep graze and the proprietor grows 120 varieties of fruit. Quiet site with nearby cycle paths and walking trails for exploring the countryside.
Open: Apr-14 Sep **Site:** 5HEC **For hire:** **Prices:** 16-21 **Facilities:** Wi-fi (charged) Play Area **Services:** **Leisure:** R **Off-site:** L P

MARBACH NIEDERÖSTERREICH

Marbacher

3671
07413 20733 07413 20733
e-mail: info@marbach-freizeit.at
web: www.marbach-freizeit.at
A pleasant location beside the River Danube.
dir: *A1 exit Pöchlarn.*
Open: Apr-Oct **Site:** 0.35HEC **For hire:** **Facilities:** Wi-fi **Services:** **Leisure:** R **Off-site:** P

MARKT ST MARTIN BURGENLAND

Markt St Martin

Mühlweg 2, 7341
02618 2239 02618 22394
e-mail: post@markt-st-martin.bgld.gv.at
web: www.marktstmartin.at
On a level meadow with plenty of trees and bushes.
dir: *S31 exit Weppersdorf/St Martin.*
Open: May-Sep **Site:** 0.5HEC **For hire:** **Facilities:** Play Area **Services:** **Leisure:** L R **Off-site:** P

RECHNITZ BURGENLAND

GC

Hauptpl 10, 7471
03363 79202 03363 7920222
e-mail: post@rechnitz.bgld.gv.at
web: www.rechnitz.at
On an artificial lake in the heart of the beautiful Faludi Valley.
Open: Jun-Aug **Site:** 1HEC **Facilities:** **Services:** **Leisure:** L **Off-site:**

SCHÖNBÜHEL NIEDERÖSTERREICH

Stumpfer

3392
02752 8510 02752 851017
e-mail: office@stumpfer.com
web: www.stumpfer.com
A small site in a wooded location attached to a guesthouse close to the River Donau.
dir: *SW of town.*
Open: Apr-Oct **Site:** 1.5HEC **For hire:** **Prices:** 19.90-25.50 **Facilities:** Wi-fi (charged) **Services:** **Leisure:** R

TRAISEN NIEDERÖSTERREICH

Terrassen-Camping Traisen

Kulmhof 1, 3160
☎ 02762 62900 🖷 02762 629004
e-mail: info@camping-traisen.at
web: www.camping-traisen.at

Set out in a circular formation around the main buildings with plenty of trees around the pitches. There is a wonderful view.

dir: *0.6km W via B20.*

GPS: 48.0424, 15.6029

Open: 15 Feb-15 Nov **Site:** 2.1HEC **For hire:** **Prices:** 19-22 **Facilities:** Wi-fi Play Area **Services:** **Leisure:** P **Off-site:** R

TULLN NIEDERÖSTERREICH

Donaupark-Camping Tulln

Donaulände 76, 3430
☎ 02272 65200 🖷 02272 65201
e-mail: camptulln@oeamtc.at
web: www.campingtulln.at

A modern site in a peaceful location with good facilities, close to the River Danube. Summer bus service to Vienna and guided cycling tours.

dir: *20km from the A1. Exit 41 St Christopher.*

GPS: 48.3325, 16.0719

Open: 30 Mar-15 Oct **Site:** 10HEC **For hire:** **Facilities:** Wi-fi (charged) **Services:** **Leisure:** L **Off-site:** P R

WAIDHOFEN AN DER THAYA NIEDERÖSTERREICH

Thayapark

Badgasse 9, 3830
☎ 0664 5904433 🖷 02842 50399
web: www.waidhofen-thaya.at

A family site in wooded surroundings close to the River Thaya.

dir: *Signed from village.*

Open: May-Sep **Site:** 10HEC **For hire:** **Facilities:** **Services:** **Leisure:** R **Off-site:** P

UPPER AUSTRIA/SALZBURG

ABERSEE SALZBURG

Seecamping Wolfgangblick

Seestrasse 115, 5342
☎ 06227 3475 🖷 06227 3664
e-mail: camping@wolfgangblick.at
web: www.wolfgangblick.at

A pleasant position on the Wolfgangsee.

dir: *Signed from village. 6km from St Gilgen via B1598.*

GPS: 47.7367, 13.4328

Open: 20 Apr-Sep **Site:** 2HEC **Prices:** 16.60-20.70 **Facilities:** Play Area **Services:** **Leisure:** L R **Off-site:**

ABTENAU SALZBURG

Oberwötzlhof

Erlfeld 37, 5441
☎ 06243 2698 🖷 06243 269855
e-mail: oberwoetzlhof@sbg.at
web: www.oberwoetzlhof-camp.at

A summer and winter site on a level meadow with panoramic views of the surrounding mountains.

dir: *NW of Abtenau.*

Open: All Year. **Site:** 2HEC **For hire:** **Facilities:** **Services:** **Leisure:** P **Off-site:** R

BRUCK AN DER GROSSGLOCKNERSTRASSE SALZBURG

Sportcamp Woferlgut

The Camping and Caravanning Club The Friendly Club

Kroessenbach 40, 5671
☎ 06545 73030 🖷 06545 73033
e-mail: info@sportcamp.at
web: www.sportcamp.at

Set in a beautiful valley beside a lake with extensive recreational facilities included in the camping price. There is a new mini-golf course suitable for all the family.

C&CC Report *An exceptional family site in outstanding scenery, justly renowned for its range of high quality facilities. All but fishing, solarium, mini-golf, canoe lessons and massages are free, while the private bathrooms are pure camping luxury. With the Hohe Tauern National Park on the doorstep, the great outdoors is just waiting to be enjoyed.*

dir: *Via Bruck-Süd or Grossglockner on B311.*

GPS: 47.2836, 12.8167

Open: All Year. **Site:** 18HEC **For hire:** **Prices:** 23-32.80 Mobile home hire 441-819 **Facilities:** Wi-fi (charged) Kids' Club Play Area **Services:** **Leisure:** L P **Off-site:** R

GLEINKERAU OBERÖSTERREICH

Pyhrn Priel

4582
07562 7066
e-mail: pyhrn-priel@aon.at
web: www.pyhrn-priel.at

A year-round site with a variety of facilities.

dir: *A9 exit 52 signed Gleinkerau.*

Open: All Year. **Site:** 1HEC **Prices:** 20.30-24.80 **Facilities:** Play Area **Services:** **Off-site:** L P R

KAPRUN SALZBURG

Mühle

N-Gassner Str 66, 5710
06547 8254 06547 825489
e-mail: muehle@kaprun.at
web: www.muehle-kaprun.at

A pleasant family site on long stretch of meadow by the Kapruner Ache.

dir: *S end of village towards cable lift.*

Open: All Year. **Site:** 1.5HEC **Prices:** 24.50-28.50 **Facilities:** **Services:** **Leisure:** P

MAISHOFEN SALZBURG

Kammerlander

Oberreit 18, 5751
06542 68755 06542 687555
e-mail: landhaus-christa@sbg.at
web: www.sbg.at/landhaus-christa

Quiet, family friendly site, ideal for hiking or cycling in the surrounding countryside.

dir: *On B168.*

Open: May-15 Sep **Site:** **Prices:** 12-15 **Facilities:** Play Area **Off-site:** L

MAUTERNDORF SALZBURG

Camping Mauterndorf

5570
06472 72023 06472 7202320
e-mail: info@camping-mauterndorf.at
web: www.camping-mauterndorf.at

Located in an area ideal for hiking and skiing, a family friendly site with health spa. Swimming pool available in summer. Charge for dogs.

dir: *On B99.*

Open: All Year. **Site:** 2.5HEC **Facilities:** Wi-fi (charged) Kids' Club Play Area **Services:** **Leisure:** P R

MONDSEE OBERÖSTERREICH

Mond-See-Land

Punzau 21, 5310
06232 2600 06232 27218
e-mail: austria@campmondsee.at
web: www.campmondsee.at

A picturesque and peaceful site between the lakes Mondsee and Irrsee, with good facilities.

dir: *A1 exit Mondsee, B154 towards Strasswalden for 1.5km, onto Haider-Mühle road for 2km.*

GPS: 47.8664, 13.3064

Open: Apr-Oct **Site:** 3HEC **For hire:** **Prices:** 21.80 **Facilities:** Wi-fi (charged) Play Area **Services:** **Leisure:** P

NUSSDORF OBERÖSTERREICH

Seecamping Gruber

Dorfstr 63, 4865
07666 80450 07666 80456
e-mail: office@camping-gruber.at
web: www.camping-gruber.at

On fairly long meadow parallel to the promenade.

dir: *S of village. Off B151 at Km19.7 towards Attersee.*

Open: 15 Apr-15 Oct **Site:** 2.6HEC **Prices:** 22.40-28.40 **Facilities:** Wi-fi Kids' Club Play Area **Services:** **Leisure:** L P **Off-site:**

PERWANG AM GRABENSEE OBERÖSTERREICH

Perwang

5166
06217 8288 06217 824715
e-mail: gemeinde@perwang.ooe.gv.at
web: www.perwang.at

Family site beside lake.

Open: Apr-Oct **Site:** 1.5HEC **Prices:** 12.10-18.60 **Facilities:** Play Area **Services:** **Leisure:** L **Off-site:**

RADSTADT SALZBURG

Forellencamp

Gaismairallee 51, 5550
06452 7861
e-mail: info@forellencamp.com
web: www.forellencamp.com

Flat meadowland near town.

dir: *SW via B99.*

Open: All Year. **Site:** 1HEC **Prices:** 21.70-23 **Facilities:** Play Area **Services:** **Off-site:** P R

ST JOHANN IM PONGAU — SALZBURG

Wieshof

Wieshofgasse 8, 5600
☎ 06412 8519 📠 06412 85191
e-mail: info@camping-wieshof.at
web: www.camping-wieshof.at

Terraced, spacious pitches with views of surrounding mountains and countryside. Modern sanitation facilities.

dir: *Off B311 towards Zell am Zee.*

Open: All Year. **Site:** 1.6HEC **Prices:** 19.50 **Facilities:** Wi-fi Play Area **Services:** **Off-site:** L P

ST MARTIN BEI LOFER — SALZBURG

Park Grubhof

5092
☎ 06588 8237 📠 06588 82377
e-mail: home@grubhof.com
web: www.grubhof.com

Situated in meadowland on the banks of the River Saalach. Separate sections for dog owners, families, teenagers and groups. Extra large pitches available with mountain views. Sauna and spa available.

dir: *B311 S of Lofer, 1.5km turn left.*

Open: All Year. **Site:** 10HEC **For hire:** **Prices:** 18-27.50 **Facilities:** Wi-fi (charged) Play Area **Services:** **Leisure:** R **Off-site:** P

ST WOLFGANG — OBERÖSTERREICH

Appesbach

Au 99, 5360
☎ 06138 2206 📠 06138 220633
e-mail: camping@appesbach.at
web: www.appesbach.at

On sloping meadow facing lake with no shade at upper end.

dir: *0.8km E of St Wolfgang between lake & Strobl road.*

Open: Mar-Oct **Site:** 2.2HEC **For hire:** **Facilities:** **Services:** **Leisure:** L **Off-site:**

Berau

Schwarzenbach 16, 5360
☎ 06138 2543 📠 06138 25435
e-mail: camping@berau.at
web: www.berau.at

A family-run site in a picturesque setting on the edge of the Wolfgangsee. Spacious, level pitches and modern facilities. There is a kids' club during July and August.

dir: *A1 exit Talgau, N158 signed Hof/Bad Ischl, through Strobl towards St Wolfgang & signed.*

Open: All Year. **Site:** 2HEC **For hire:** **Prices:** 17.40-27 **Facilities:** Wi-fi (charged) Kids' Club Play Area **Services:** **Leisure:** L

SALZBURG — SALZBURG

Camping Nord Sam

Samstr 22A, 5023
☎ 0662 660494 📠 0662 660494
e-mail: office@camping-nord-sam.com
web: www.camping-nord-sam.com

Pitches divided by trees and shrubs with cycle route directly from site to city centre. Cycle rental available.

dir: *Salzburg Nord autobahn exit, site 400m.*

GPS: 47.8269, 13.0631

Open: 15 Apr-2 Nov, 7-11 Dec, 27 Dec-8 Jan **Site:** 1.4HEC **Prices:** 23-31 **Facilities:** Wi-fi (charged) Play Area **Services:** **Leisure:** P **Off-site:**

Panorama Camping Stadtblick

Rauchenbichlerstr 21, 5020
☎ 0662 450652 📠 0662 458018
e-mail: info@ panorama-camping.at
web: www.panorama-camping.at

A terraced site affording spectacular views of the surrounding mountains.

dir: *Motorway exit Salzburg-Nord & signed.*

Open: 20 Mar-5 Nov, 5-15 Dec & 27 Dec-6 Jan **Site:** 0.8HEC **Prices:** 24-28 **Facilities:** Wi-fi (charged) Play Area **Services:** **Off-site:** L

Schloss Aigen

5026

0662 622079 0662 622079

e-mail: camping.aigen@elsnet.at

web: www.campingaigen.com

Site divided into pitches in partial clearing on mountain slope.

dir: *Motorway exit Salzburg-Süd, Anif & Glasenbach.*

GPS: 47.7806, 13.0899

Open: May-Sep **Site:** 25HEC **Prices:** 15-16 **Facilities:** Play Area **Services:** **Off-site:** P R

SCHLÖGEN OBERÖSTERREICH

Freizeitanlage Schlögen

4083

07279 8241 07279 824122

e-mail: info@freizeitanlage-schloegen.at

web: www.freizeitanlage-schloegen.at

On level ground beside the River Donau, backed by woods and mountains.

Open: Apr-20 Oct **Site:** 2.8HEC **Prices:** 21 **Facilities:** Play Area **Services:** **Leisure:** P R

SEEKIRCHEN SALZBURG

See-camping Zell am Wallersee

Bayerham 40, 5201

06212 4080 06212 4080

e-mail: info@see-camping.at

web: www.see-camping.at

Level meadowland separated from the lake by the lido.

dir: *A1 exit Wallersee, via Seekirchen to Zell.*

Open: Apr-Oct **Site:** 3HEC **Facilities:** Wi-fi (charged) Play Area **Services:** **Leisure:** L **Off-site:** P

Strandcamping Seekirchen

Seestr 2, 5201

06212 4088 06212 4088

e-mail: info@camping-seekirchen.at

web: www.camping-seekirchen.at

Beside the Wallersee in a beautiful meadow.

Open: 15 Apr-15 Oct **Site:** 2HEC **Facilities:** Wi-fi Play Area **Services:** **Leisure:** L P R **Off-site:**

UNTERACH AM ATTERSEE OBERÖSTERREICH

Insel Camping

4866

07665 8311 07665 83115

e-mail: camping@inselcamp.at

web: www.inselcamp.at

Quiet family site on the shore of Lake Attersee, divided into two by the River Seeache. Fishing available.

dir: *Entrance below B152 towards Steinbach at Km24.5, 300m from B151 junct.*

Open: May-15 Sep **Site:** 1.8HEC **Prices:** 15.60-19.80 **Facilities:** **Services:** **Leisure:** L R **Off-site:**

WALD SALZBURG

S.N.P

Lahn 65, 5742

06565 84460 06565 84464

e-mail: info@snp-camping.at

web: www.snp-camping.at

A small family site in a beautiful Alpine setting.

dir: *W of town.*

Open: All Year. **Site:** 0.7HEC **Facilities:** **Services:** **Off-site:** L P

ZELL AM SEE SALZBURG

Panorama Camp Zell am See

Seeuferstr 196, 5700

06542 56228 06542 562284

e-mail: info@panoramacamp.at

web: www.panoramacamp.at

A family site on level ground in a picturesque spot on the southern bank of the Zeller See. Ideal starting point for hiking and bike tours in the summer, as well as cross-country skiing and alpine skiing in the winter.

dir: *S via B311 exit for Thumersbach before tunnel entrance, after 500m, turn left. Follow road to S of lake, site on right.*

GPS: 47.3012, 12.8163

Open: All Year. **Site:** 1HEC **For hire:** **Prices:** 19.20-27.40 **Facilities:** Wi-fi (charged) Play Area **Services:** **Off-site:** L P R

Seecamp Zell am See

Thumersbacherstr 34, 5700
06542 72115 06542 7211515
e-mail: zell@seecamp.at
web: www.seecamp.at

Pleasant wooded location beside the lake with excellent site and recreational facilities.

dir: *B311 N of lake towards Thumersbach, signed.*

Open: All Year. **Site:** 3.2HEC **Facilities:** Wi-fi (charged) **Services:** **Leisure:** L **Off-site:** P

VORARLBERG

BEZAU **VORARLBERG**

Bezau

Ach 206, 6870
05514 2964
e-mail: campingplatz.bezau@aon.at
web: www.campingfuehrer.at

Small family-owned site with modern sanitary facilities. Free Bregenzerwald Card, if staying for more than 3 nights, allowing use of cable cars, public transport and swimming pools.

dir: *S via B200 Dornbirn-Warth.*

GPS: 47.3808, 9.8889

Open: All Year. **Site:** 0.5HEC **Prices:** 18.60-20.10 **Facilities:** **Off-site:** P R

BRAZ **VORALBERG**

Traube

Klostertalerstr 12, 6751
05552 28103 05552 2810340
e-mail: office@traubebraz.at
web: www.campingtraube.at

On sloping grassland in the picturesque Klostertal Valley with modern facilities.

dir: *7km SE of Bludenz. Off S16 near railway, signed.*

Open: All Year. **Site:** 2HEC **Facilities:** Wi-fi Play Area **Services:** **Leisure:** P **Off-site:** R

DALAAS **VORARLBERG**

Erne

Klostertalerstr 64, 6752
05585 7223 05585 20049
e-mail: info@etpc.at
web: www.etpc.at

Site in the town, attached to a guesthouse and next to the swimming pool.

dir: *S16 exit Dalass.*

Open: All Year. **Site:** 0.6HEC **Facilities:** Wi-fi (charged) **Services:** **Leisure:** R **Off-site:** P

DORNBIRN **VORARLBERG**

In der Enz

6850
05572 29119
e-mail: camping@camping-enz.at
web: www.camping-enz.at

A municipal site beside a public park, in a wooded area 100 metres beyond the Karren cable lift.

dir: *Autobahn exit Dornbirn-Süd.*

Open: Apr-Sep **Site:** 10HEC **Facilities:** **Services:** **Off-site:** P R

LINGENAU **VORARLBERG**

Feurstein

Haidach 185, 6951
05513 6114 05513 61144

A small site located in a meadow adjacent to farm buildings with sufficient facilities for a pleasant stay.

dir: *B200 for Müselbach, then B205.*

Open: All Year. **Site:** 1HEC **Prices:** 18.60-19.60 **Facilities:** Wi-fi **Services:** **Off-site:**

NENZING **VORARLBERG**

Alpencamping Nenzing

6710
05525 62491 05525 624916
e-mail: office@alpencamping.at
web: www.alpencamping.at

A well-appointed site in magnificent Alpine scenery. Recreational facilities include indoor and outdoor swimming pools, climbing wall, sun terrace and sauna. Also modern sanitary blocks with 20 private bathrooms.

dir: *Signed from B190 from Nenzing, 2km towards Gurtis.*

Open: All Year. **Site:** 3HEC **For hire:** **Prices:** 19-29 **Facilities:** Wi-fi (charged) Kids' Club Play Area **Services:** **Leisure:** P **Off-site:** S

AUSTRIA

NÜZIDERS VORALBERG

Terrassencamping Sonnenberg

Hinteroferst 12, 6714
☎ 05552 64035 📠 05552 33900
e-mail: sonnencamp@aon.at
web: www.camping-sonnenberg.com

Clean site with modern facilities, terraces and splendid mountain scenery. Kids' club in high season.

dir: *E60 (A14), exit 57 via Bludenz-Nüziders, follow road into Nüziders, site signed.*

GPS: 47.1702, 9.8077

Open: May-3 Oct **Site:** 1.9HEC **For hire:** **Prices:** 20.50-30 **Facilities:** Wi-fi (charged) Kids' Club Play Area **Services:** **Off-site:** P R

RAGGAL-PLAZERA VORARLBERG

Grosswalsertal

6741
☎ 05553 209 📠 05553 2094
e-mail: info@camping-grosswalsertal.at
web: www.camping-grosswalsertal.at

A family site in a quiet location on gently sloping terrain, with pleasant views. Leisure facilities include beach volleyball.

dir: *On NE outskirts.*

Open: May-Sep **Site:** 0.8HEC **Prices:** 17-20 **Facilities:** Wi-fi (charged) Play Area **Services:** **Leisure:** P **Off-site:**

TSCHAGGUNS VORARLBERG

Zelfen

6774
☎ 0664 2002326
e-mail: kunsttischlerei.tschofen@utanet.at
web: www.camping-zelfen.at

Partly uneven, grassy site in a wooded location beside River Ill. Good recreational facilities.

dir: *A14 to Bludenz, then B188 to Tschagguns.*

Open: All Year. **Site:** 2HEC **Prices:** 21-22 **Facilities:** Kids' Club Play Area **Services:** **Leisure:** P R

VIENNA (WIEN)

WIEN (VIENNA) WIEN

Camping Wien Süd

Breitenfurter Str 269, 1230
☎ 01 8673649 📠 01 8675843
e-mail: sued@campingwien.at
web: www.campingwien.at/ws

8km SW of the city centre, located in a former Palace Park, surrounded by old trees. Shaded tent pitches.

Open: Jun-Aug **Site:** 2HEC **Prices:** 25.10-28.60 **Facilities:** Wi-fi Play Area **Services:**

Donaupark Camping Klosterneuburg

In der Au, 3400
☎ 02243 25877 📠 02243 25878
e-mail: campklosterneuburg@oeamtc.at
web: www.campingklosterneuburg.at

A modern site in delightful wooded surroundings with fine recreational facilities and within easy reach of the city centre.

dir: *A1 onto B19 to Tulln then B14 to Klosterneuburg.*

GPS: 48.3106, 16.3272

Open: Apr-Oct **Site:** 2.25HEC **For hire:** **Prices:** 21.50-26.50 **Facilities:** Wi-fi (charged) **Services:** **Off-site:** P R

Neue Donau

Am Kleehäufel, 1220
☎ 01 2024010 📠 01 2024020
e-mail: neuedonau@campingwien.at
web: www.campingwien.at

Situated in a meadow surrounded by trees beside the Danube within a leisure park.

dir: *On E bank of river via A4 & A22.*

Open: Etr-Sep **Site:** 3.3HEC **For hire:** **Facilities:** **Services:** **Off-site:** L P R

Wien West

Hüttelbergstr 80, 1140
☎ 01 9142314 📠 01 9113594
e-mail: west@campingwien.at
web: www.campingwien.at

30 minutes from the city centre by bus or underground, with facilities including satellite TV and bicycle rental.

dir: *End of A1 Linz-Wien to Bräuhausbrücke, turn left & across road to Linz for 1.8km.*

Open: Jan & Mar-Dec **Site:** 2.5HEC **For hire:** **Facilities:** Wi-fi Play Area **Services:**

Belgium

Drinking and driving

Maximum permitted level of alcohol in the bloodstream is 0.049%. If the level of alcohol in the bloodstream is between 0.05 and 0.08% you will be banned from driving for three hours and issued an on-the-spot fine of 137.50. If you refuse to pay the fine, the public prosecutor will prosecute and impose a fine up to 2,750. 0.08% or more, an on-the-spot fine of up to 550 and a ban from driving for at least six hours; if more than 0.15%, a fine up to 11,000 and a licence suspension up to five years. However, if you have held your licence for less than two years an on-the-spot fine will not be imposed, you will automatically be prosecuted.

Driving licence

Minimum age at which a UK driving licence holder may drive temporarily imported car and/or motorcycle 18.

Fines

On-the-spot. The officer collecting the fine must issue an official receipt showing the amount of the fine. Motorists can refuse to pay an on-the-spot fine. A foreign motorist refusing to do so may be invited to make a consignation (deposit) and if he does not pay a deposit his vehicle will be impounded, by the police and permanently confiscated if the deposit is not paid within 96 hours. The amount of the deposit is the same as the on-the-spot fine. Fines can be paid for in cash euros or debit/credit card.

Fuel

Unleaded petrol (95 and 98 octane), diesel and LPG available. No leaded petrol (anti-wear additive available). Petrol in a can is permitted, but forbidden aboard ferries. Credit cards are accepted at filling stations; check with your card issuer for usage in Belgium before travel.

Lights

Dipped headlights on cars should be used in poor daytime visibility.

Motorcycles

Use of dipped headlights during the day compulsory. The wearing of crash helmets is compulsory for both driver and passenger.

Motor insurance

Third-party compulsory. The police can impound an uninsured vehicle.

Passengers/children in cars

Children under 18 and less than 1.35m must use a suitable child-restraint system whether seated in the front or rear seat of a vehicle. Exception: When two child restraint systems are being used on the rear seats and there isn't adequate room to place a third child restraint system, then the third child may travel on the back seat protected by the adult seat belt. A child under 3 can not be transported in a vehicle without a child seat/restraint. It is prohibited to use a rear facing child seat on a front seat with a frontal airbag unless it is deactivated.

Pictured: Brabo Fountain, Guildhouses, Antwerp's Grote Markt

Belgium

Seat belts

Compulsory for front and rear seat occupants to wear seat belts, if fitted.

Speed limits

Standard legal limits, which may be varied by signs

Private vehicles with or without trailers	
Built-up areas	50km/h
Outside built-up areas	90km/h
Motorways and dual carriageways separated by a central reservation	120km/h
Minimum speed on motorways	70km/h
Vehicles with spiked tyres	
Normal roads	60km/h
Motorways/dual carriageways	90km/h

A limit of 30km/h may be indicated at the entrance to a built up area.

Compulsory equipment in Belgium

Reflective jacket - Drivers stranded on a Belgian motorway or on a major road (usually four-lane roads, called 'route pour automobiles' - sign E17), stopping on places where parking is not allowed, must wear a reflective safety jacket as soon as they leave their vehicle. Fine for non-compliance 50 is applicable, but the amount can be much higher (55 - 1,375) if the driver refuses to pay or in a circumstance where the driver has to go to court (for example in the event of an accident).

Warning triangle - Compulsory for vehicles with more than two wheels.

Other rules/requirements

First-aid kit and fire extinguisher recommended as their carriage is compulsory for Belgian-registered vehicles.

The majority of roundabouts have signs showing that traffic on the roundabout has priority. If there is no sign present, (very few roundabouts) traffic joining from the right has priority.

A road sign has been introduced banning the use of cruise control on congested motorways and can also appear during motorway road works.

A white disc bordered in red, bearing the word 'Peage' in black indicates that drivers must stop. The Dutch word 'Tol' sometimes replaces 'Peage'.

Any vehicle standing must have its engine switched off, unless absolutely necessary.

A car navigation system with maps indicating the location of fixed speed cameras is permitted but equipment which actively searches for speed cameras or interferes with police equipment is prohibited.

The police can impound a vehicle with an unsafe load.

Spiked tyres are permitted from the 1st November until the 31st March on vehicles weighing up to a maximum of 3.5t. Snow chains are only permitted on snow or ice covered roads. Winter tyres are permitted from the 1st October until the 30th April, a lower speed limit needs to be adhered to and the maximum designed speed for the tyres displayed on a sticker on the dashboard.

Vehicles with spiked tyres must display at the rear a white disc with a red reflectorised border showing the figure "60", when the spiked tyres are applied.

The majority of level crossings in Belgium are equipped with cameras. Crossing a level crossing when not permitted to do so i.e. when the lights are red carries a fine of up to 2,250

Tolls Vignette Currency Euro (€)	Car	Car Towing Caravan/Trailer
Tunnels		
On R2 Llefkenshoek Tunnel	€5.50	€18

SOUTH WEST/COAST

BLANKENBERGE WEST-VLAANDEREN

Bonanza 1

Zeebruggelaan 137, 8370
050 416658 050 427349
e-mail: info@bonanza1.be
web: www.bonanza1.be

A family site in wooded surroundings 1km from both the village and the sea.

Open: 15 Mar-15 Sep **Site:** 4.5HEC **Facilities:** **Services:** **Off-site:** L P S

Dallas

A.Ruzettelaan 191, 8370
050 418157 050 429479
e-mail: campingdallas@skynet.be
web: www.campingdallas.com

Well-equipped family site near a large department store 50 metres from the beach.

Open: 15 Mar-1 Oct **Site:** 2.65HEC **Facilities:** Wi-fi (charged) Play Area **Services:** **Off-site:** L P S

BREDENE WEST-VLAANDEREN

Asterix

Duinenstr 200, 8450
059 331000 059 324202
web: www.camping-asterix.be

A family site in wooded surroundings, 0.5km from the sea.

dir: *N34 from Oostende towards Knokke-Heist, 7km right for Bredene-Dorp.*

Open: All Year. **Site:** 3HEC **Prices:** 20-24 **Facilities:** **Services:** **Off-site:** L P S

Camping Astrid

Koningin Astridlaan 1, 8450
059 321247
e-mail: info@camping-astrid.be
web: www.camping-astrid.be

Family camp site 100 metres from the beach and dunes. Spacious pitches and cycle routes available.

Open: All Year. **Site:** 4.7HEC **For hire:** **Facilities:** Wi-fi (charged) Play Area **Services:** **Leisure:** S **Off-site:** P

JABBEKE WEST-VLAANDEREN

Recreatiepark Klein Strand

Varsenareweg 29, 8490
050 811440 050 814289
e-mail: info@kleinstrand.be
web: www.kleinstrand.be

A lakeside site with modern facilities and a variety of leisure activities.

dir: *Off Oostende-Brugge road.*

Open: All Year. **Site:** 28HEC **For hire:** **Facilities:** Wi-fi (charged) Kids' Club Play Area **Services:** **Leisure:** L P **Off-site:** R

KNOKKE-HEIST WEST-VLAANDEREN

De Vuurtoren

Heistlaan 168, 8301
059 333342
e-mail: info@campingdevuurtoren.be
web: www.campingdevuurtoren.be

On level meadow with tarmacked roads. 700 metres from the sea, and 500 metres from the city centre.

dir: *From Knokke to Oostende for 4km, turn S & signed.*

GPS: 51.3319, 3.2362

Open: 15 Mar-15 Oct **Site:** 6.6HEC **For hire:** **Prices:** 19.50-28.50 Mobile home hire 294-812 **Facilities:** Wi-fi (charged) Play Area **Services:** **Off-site:** S

Zilvermeeuw

Heistlaan 166, 8301
050 512726 050 512703
e-mail: info.campingzilvermeeuw@skynet.be
web: www.camping-zilvermeeuw.be

Level site in wooded surroundings. 700 metres from the beach, and 8km from the Dutch/Belgian border.

dir: *SW via N300.*

Open: Mar-1 Nov **Site:** 7HEC **Facilities:** Wi-fi Kids' Club Play Area **Services:** **Off-site:** L P S

BELGIUM

KOKSIJDE — WEST-VLAANDEREN

Blekker & Blekkerdal

Jachtwakerstr 12, 8670
058 511633 058 511307
e-mail: camping.deblekker@belgacom.net
web: www.deblekker.be

A peaceful location surrounded by trees. Good modern facilities.

dir: *Between Dunkerque & Oostende, 5km from Belgian frontier. Motorway exit towards Veurne.*

Open: Apr-30 Oct **Site:** 3HEC **Facilities:** **Services:** **Off-site:** P S

LOMBARDSIJDE — WEST-VLAANDEREN

Lombarde

Elisabethlaan 4, 8434
058 236839 058 239908
e-mail: info@delombarde.be
web: www.delombarde.be

A well-equipped family site 400 metres from the sea and close to the centre of the village. 1 dog permitted per pitch.

dir: *E40 exit Nieuwpoort. At Nieuwpoort take N34 towards Oostende, site signed on right.*

GPS: 51.1564, 2.7537

Open: All Year. **Site:** 8.5HEC **For hire:** **Prices:** 18-32.50 **Facilities:** Wi-fi Play Area **Services:** **Off-site:** P S

Zomerzon

Elisabethlaan 1, 8434
058 237396 058 232817
web: www.zomerzon.be

A quiet location with good facilities, 0.8km from the dunes and beach.

Open: Mar-Oct **Site:** 10HEC **For hire:** **Facilities:** Wi-fi (charged) Play Area **Services:** **Off-site:** P S

MIDDELKERKE — WEST-VLAANDEREN

Mijn Plezier

Duinenweg 489, 8430
059 303020 059 314503
e-mail: camping@mijnplezier.be
web: www.mijnplezier.be

Wooded surroundings close to the castle. Only 150 metres from the beach.

GPS: 51.175, 2.7922

Open: Apr-Sep **Site:** 3HEC **Prices:** 21.50 **Facilities:** Wi-fi (charged) Play Area **Services:** **Off-site:** S

MONS — HAINAUT

Waux-Hall

av St-Pierre 17, 7000
065 337923 065 363848
e-mail: info.tourisme@ville.mons.be
web: www.monsregion.be

A secluded position 1km from the town centre, with direct access to the Parc du Waux-Hall.

dir: *From town ring road exit for Beaumont/Binche, Charleroi, right at lights & sharp right.*

Open: All Year. **Site:** 1.44HEC **Prices:** 13.50 **Facilities:** Play Area **Services:** **Off-site:** L P

NIEUWPOORT — WEST-VLAANDEREN

Kompas Camping

Brugsesteenweg 49, 8620
058 236037 058 232682
e-mail: nieuwpoort@kompascamping.be
web: www.kompascamping.be

A family site in pleasant wooded surroundings. Plenty of recreational facilities, including water sports and a kids' club is available in high season.

dir: *E40 exit 4 for Diksmuide & Nieuwpoort, signed from St Joris.*

Open: 23 Mar-12 Nov **Site:** 24HEC **For hire:** **Prices:** 26.30-39.30 Mobile home hire 340.90-844.90 **Facilities:** Wi-fi (charged) Kids' Club Play Area **Services:** **Leisure:** P **Off-site:** L R S

TOURNAI — HAINAUT

Orient

rue JB Moens, 7500
069 222635 069 890229
e-mail: campingorient@tournai.be
web: www.tournai.be

A pleasant site in an area of woodland with good recreational facilities.

dir: *Motorway exit Tournai Est for town centre, left at 1st x-rds & signed.*

Open: All Year. **Site:** 20HEC **Facilities:** **Services:** **Leisure:** L P

Site 6HEC (site size) 🌱 grass 🏖 sand 🪨 stone ♣ little shade ♣ partly shaded 🌳 mainly shaded ⌷ motorvans accepted 🏠 bungalows for hire 🚰 mobile homes for hire 🅰 tents for hire ⊗ no dogs 🦽 site fully accessible for wheelchairs **Prices** amount quoted is per night, for 2 adults and car, plus tent or caravan

WAREGEM — WEST-VLAANDEREN

Gemeentelijk

Zuiderlaan 13, 8790
☎ 056 609532 Fax 056 621290
e-mail: toerisme@waregem.be
web: www.waregem.be
Set in a sports and leisure centre south-east of the town centre.
dir: *Via E17 Kortrijk-Gent.*
Open: Apr-Sep **Site:** 1HEC **Facilities:** shower, electric points for razors, electric points for caravans, parking by tents permitted **Services:** first aid facilities **Off-site:** swimming P shop café/restaurant bar Camping Gaz International gas other than Camping Gaz

NORTH/CENTRAL

BACHTE-MARIA-LEERNE — OOST-VLAANDEREN

Groeneveld

Groeneveldreef 14, 9800
☎ 09 3801014 Fax 09 3801014
e-mail: info@campinggroeneveld.be
web: www.campinggroeneveld.be
Well-equipped, quiet site beside a fishing lake. One dog per pitch.
dir: *Approach via E17 or E40.*
Open: Apr-Sep **Site:** 1.7HEC **For hire:** **Facilities:** shower, electric points for razors, electric points for caravans, Wi-fi, parking by tents permitted **Services:** café/restaurant, bar, first aid facilities, laundry **Off-site:** swimming P R shop café/restaurant Camping Gaz International gas other than Camping Gaz

BEGYNENDYK — BRABANT

Roygaerden

Betekomsesteenweg 75, 3130
☎ 016 531087 Fax 016 531087
e-mail: deroygaerden@skynet.be
web: www.camping-deroygaerden.be
Pitches are in wooded surroundings beside a lake.
dir: *A2 exit 22/N10 for Begijnendijk.*
Open: All Year. **Site:** 5HEC **For hire:** **Prices:** 12-17 **Facilities:** shower, electric points for razors, electric points for caravans, parking by tents permitted **Services:** café/restaurant, bar, Camping Gaz International, gas other than Camping Gaz, first aid facilities, laundry **Off-site:** swimming L P shop

GENT (GAND) — OOST-VLAANDEREN

Blaarmeersen

The Camping and Caravanning Club — The Friendly Club

Zuiderlaan 12, 9000
☎ 09 2668160 Fax 09 2668166
e-mail: camping.blaarmeersen@gent.be
web: www.blaarmeersen.be
Pleasant wooded surroundings. Part of a spa and leisure centre.
C&CC Report *Apart from being a very well located en-route site, this is great for families of all ages and anyone wanting to visit some of Belgium's most popular places, many of which are less than an hour's drive away. Historic Gent is a short bus ride from the site and there is loads to do in and around the adjacent leisure centre and lake.*
dir: *E17/E40/R4.*
Open: Mar-15 Oct **Site:** 10HEC **For hire:** **Prices:** 16-21 **Facilities:** shop, shower, electric points for razors, electric points for caravans, motorvan service point, Wi-fi (charged), parking by tents permitted, disabled facilities **Services:** café/restaurant, bar, Camping Gaz International, first aid facilities, laundry **Leisure:** swimming L **Off-site:** swimming P gas other than Camping Gaz

GRIMBERGEN — BRABANT

Grimbergen

Veldkanstr 64, 1850
☎ 0479 760378 Fax 02 2701215
e-mail: camping.grimbergen@telenet.be
A charming and neat site with good public transport links to Brussels.
dir: *Bruxelles ring road exit 7.*
Open: Apr-Oct **Site:** 1.5HEC **Prices:** 18-21 **Facilities:** shower, electric points for razors, electric points for caravans, motorvan service point, compulsory separate car park, disabled facilities **Services:** first aid facilities, laundry **Off-site:** swimming P shop café/restaurant bar

TOURINNES-LA-GROSSE — BRABANT

Au Val Tourinnes

rue du Grand Brou 16A, 1320
☎ 010 866642
e-mail: info@campingauvaltourinnes.com
web: www.campingauvaltourinnes.com
Scenic natural location with two lakes near to Brussels and Leuven.
dir: *Autoroute E40 exit 23 towards Wavre, Hamme-Mille. Autoroute E19 exit 19 towards Wavre, Leuven & Hamme-Mille.*
Open: 15 Jan-15 Dec **Site:** 5HEC **For hire:** **Prices:** 18 Mobile home hire 385 **Facilities:** shop, shower, electric points for razors, electric points for caravans, motorvan service point, Wi-fi, Play Area, parking by tents permitted, disabled facilities **Services:** café/restaurant, bar, Camping Gaz International, gas other than Camping Gaz, first aid facilities, laundry

WACHTEBEKE **OOST-VLAANDEREN**

Puyenbroeck

Puyenbrug 1A, 9185
09 3424231 09 3424258
web: www.puyenbroeck.be

A large camping area with leisure facilities including bike rental, mini-golf and a boating lake.

Open: Apr-Sep **Site:** 9HEC **Facilities:** **Services:** **Off-site:** P

ZELE **OOST-VLAANDEREN**

Camping Groenpark

Gentsesteenweg 337, 9240
09 3679071
e-mail: groenpark@scarlet.be
web: www.campinggroenpark.be

Quiet, peaceful site close to the biggest lake in Belgium. Leisure facilities are close by.

dir: *E17 exit 11/12 follow signs for Donkmeer and Overmere then Zele.*

Open: Mar-Nov **Site:** 5HEC **For hire:** **Prices:** 15-23 **Facilities:** Wi-fi **Services:** **Off-site:** L P

NORTH EAST

EKSEL **LIMBURG**

Lage Kempen

Kiefhoek Str 19, 3941
011 402243 011 348812
e-mail: info@lagekempen.be
web: www.lagekempen.be

Situated in the middle of a forest with a variety of recreational facilities. Kids' club available in July and August.

dir: *Route 67 from Hasselt & signed left Lage Kampen.*

Open: 6 Apr-1 Nov **Site:** 3.75HEC **For hire:** **Prices:** 16-24 **Facilities:** Wi-fi (charged) Kids' Club Play Area **Services:** **Leisure:** P **Off-site:**

GIERLE **ANTWERPEN**

De Lilse Bergen

The Camping and Caravanning Club The Friendly Club

Strandweg 6, 2275
014 557901 014 554454
e-mail: info@lilsebergen.be
web: www.lilsebergen.be

Well-equipped family site surrounding a private lake.

C&CC Report *A very well-organised site with superb award-winning adventure park. Located in parkland, with many marked-out walks and cycle paths accessible from the site, De Lilse Bergen is a great holiday base both for exploring some beautiful Belgian cities – particularly Antwerp and Leuven – and for keeping the most active of children amused for days.*

dir: *E39 exit 22, campsite signed.*

Open: All Year. **Site:** 60HEC **For hire:** **Prices:** 20-26 Mobile home hire 355-540 **Facilities:** Wi-fi Play Area **Services:** **Leisure:** L

LANAKEN **LIMBURG**

Jocomo Parc

3620
089 722884 089 733087
e-mail: info@jocomo.be
web: www.jocomo.be

On the edge of Hoge Kempen National Park, there are both seasonal and touring pitches. Facilities include a boating and fishing pond and tennis court.

Open: Apr-Oct **Site:** 31HEC **For hire:** **Prices:** 19-22 Mobile home hire 325-425 **Facilities:** Wi-fi (charged) **Services:** **Leisure:** P **Off-site:**

MOL **ANTWERPEN**

Provinciaal Recreatie Domein Zilvermeer

Zilvermeerlaan 2, 2400
014 829500 014 829501
e-mail: info@zilvermeer.provant.be
web: www.zilvermeer.be

A pleasant lakeside site with good recreational facilities.

Site: 45HEC **For hire:** **Facilities:** **Services:** **Leisure:** L **Off-site:** P

Site 6HEC (site size) grass sand stone little shade partly shaded mainly shaded motorvans accepted bungalows for hire mobile homes for hire tents for hire no dogs site fully accessible for wheelchairs
Prices amount quoted is per night, for 2 adults and car, plus tent or caravan Mobile home hire is a weekly rate.

OPGLABBEEK — LIMBURG

Wilhelm Tell

Hoeverweg 87, 3660

089 854444 089 810010

e-mail: receptie@wilhelmtell.com

web: www.wilhelmtell.com

A family site set in a vast nature reserve with heathland, woodland and marshland. The large variety of water attractions on site include a water chute and a swimming pool with a wave machine. Also an indoor family pool and jacuzzi.

dir: *E313 exit 32 As to Opglabbeek.*

GPS: 51.0283, 5.5978

Open: All Year. **Site:** 4HEC **For hire:** **Prices:** 22.40-32 Mobile home hire 370-730 **Facilities:** Wi-fi Kids' Club Play Area **Services:** **Leisure:** P

OPOETEREN — LIMBURG

Camping Zavelbos

Kattebeekstr 1, 3680

089 758146 089 758148

e-mail: receptie@zavelbos.com

web: www.zavelbos.com

Peaceful and child friendly site with table tennis and fishing available.

dir: *A2 exit Maaseik to Opoeteren, site on right towards Opglabbeek.*

GPS: 51.0581, 5.6292

Open: All Year. **Site:** 6HEC **For hire:** **Prices:** 21-30 Mobile home hire 370-730 **Facilities:** Wi-fi Play Area **Services:** **Off-site:** P

RETIE — ANTWERPEN

Berkenstrand

Brand 78, 2470

014 377590 014 375139

e-mail: info@berkenstrand.be

web: www.berkenstrand.be

Wooded surroundings beside a lake.

dir: *3km NE on road to Postel.*

Open: Apr-Sep **Site:** 10HEC **For hire:** **Prices:** 15-18 **Facilities:** Wi-fi Kids' Club **Services:** **Leisure:** L

TURNHOUT — ANTWERPEN

Baalse Hei

Roodhuisstr 10, 2300

014 448470 014 448474

e-mail: info@baalsehei.be

web: www.baalsehei.be

An eco-friendly, family site in pleasant wooded surroundings with plenty of recreational facilities.

dir: *E34 exit 24 or take Tilburg/Baarle-Nassau/Turnhout road.*

GPS: 51.3575, 4.9589

Open: 16 Jan-15 Dec **Site:** 30HEC **For hire:** **Prices:** 18-25 Mobile home hire 370-545 **Facilities:** Wi-fi Play Area **Services:** **Leisure:** L

VORST-LAAKDAL — ANTWERPEN

Kasteel Meerlaer

Verboekt 115, 2430

013 661420 013 667512

e-mail: camp.meerlaer@skynet.be

web: www.camping.be/campings

On the site of an historic castle, well-kept pitches and sporting leisure facilities.

dir: *E313 exit 24 for Hasselt. Or exit 24 for Antwerp.*

Open: All Year. **Site:** 6HEC **Facilities:** **Services:** **Off-site:**

ZONHOVEN — LIMBURG

Holsteenbron

Hengelhoelseweg 9, 3520

011 817140 011 441789

e-mail: camping.holsteenbron@skynet.be

web: www.holsteenbron.be

A rural family site in a wooded location.

dir: *E314 exit 29 for Zonhoven.*

Open: Apr-11 Nov **Site:** 4HEC **For hire:** **Facilities:** **Services:**

BELGIUM

BELGIUM

SOUTH EAST

AISCHE-EN-REFAIL — NAMUR

Manoir de Là-Bas

rte de Gembloux 180, 5310
☎ 081 655353
e-mail: europa-camping.sa@skynet.be
web: www.camping-manoirdelabas.be

A beautiful location within the wooded grounds of a former manor house. Dogs accepted, please contact for details.

dir: *5km W of Eghezée, off E411.*

Open: Apr-Oct **Site:** 21HEC **Prices:** 15 **Facilities:** Wi-fi (charged) Play Area **Services:** **Leisure:** P **Off-site:**

AMBERLOUP — LUXEMBOURG

Camping Tonny

Tonny 35-36, 6680
☎ 061 688285 061 688285
e-mail: camping.tonny@skynet.be
web: www.campingtonny.be

Set in a pleasant valley beside the River Ourthe with fine sports facilities. Good location for hiking, fishing and cycling.

dir: *E25 or A4 to Bastogne, then N826.*

GPS: 50.0264, 5.5131

Open: 15 Mar-15 Nov **Site:** 2.48HEC **For hire:** **Facilities:** Wi-fi (charged) Play Area **Services:** **Leisure:** R **Off-site:**

BERTRIX — LUXEMBOURG

Ardennen Camping Bertrix

rte de Mortehan, 6880
☎ 061 412281 061 412588
e-mail: info@campingbertrix.be
web: www.campingbertrix.be

Well-equipped family site in a pleasant wooded setting.

dir: *Via E411 exit 25 onto N89.*

Open: 14 Mar-3 Nov **Site:** 14HEC **For hire:** **Facilities:** **Services:** **Leisure:** P

BURE — LUXEMBOURG

Parc la Clusure

30 chemin de la Clusure, 6927
☎ 084 360050 084 366777
e-mail: info@parclaclusure.be
web: www.parclaclusure.be

Pleasant site with good facilities in the centre of the Ardennes.

dir: *E411 & N846 from Tellin.*

Open: All Year. **Site:** 12HEC **For hire:** **Facilities:** Wi-fi Kids' Club Play Area **Services:** **Leisure:** P R

BÜTGENBACH — LIÈGE

Worriken

Worriken 9, 4750
☎ 080 446961 080 444247
e-mail: info@worriken.be
web: www.worriken.be

Situated on the shores of a lake. Kids' club available in high season.

Open: All Year. **Site:** 8HEC **For hire:** **Prices:** 18-29 **Facilities:** Wi-fi (charged) Kids' Club **Services:** **Leisure:** L P **Off-site:** R

CHEVETOGNE — NAMUR

Domaine Provincial

5590
☎ 083 687211 083 688677
e-mail: info.chevetogne@province.namur.be
web: www.domainedechevetogne.be

Located in the grounds of a castle and surrounded by fine ornamental gardens. There is a variety of leisure activities.

Open: All Year. **Site:** 0.5HEC **For hire:** **Facilities:** Play Area **Services:** **Off-site:** P

COO-STAVELOT — LIÈGE

Cascade

chemin des Faravennes 5, 4970
☎ 080 684312 080 684312
e-mail: info@camping-coo.be
web: www.camping-coo.be

A small touring and holiday site beside the River Amblève.

dir: *Motorway exit 10 or 11, site 3km from Trois-Ponts.*

Open: Apr-30 Oct **Site:** 0.75HEC **Facilities:** **Services:** **Leisure:** R **Off-site:**

Site 6HEC (site size) ♨ grass ⚌ sand ♨ stone ♣ little shade ♣ partly shaded ♨ mainly shaded ⛆ motorvans accepted ⚏ bungalows for hire ⛱ mobile homes for hire ⛰ tents for hire ⊗ no dogs ⛱ site fully accessible for wheelchairs **Prices** amount quoted is per night, for 2 adults and car, plus tent or caravan Mobile home hire is a weekly rate.

DOCHAMPS — LUXEMBOURG

Panorama Camping Petite Suisse

Al Bounire 27, 6960
☎ 084 444030 🖷 084 444455
e-mail: info@petitesuisse.be
web: www.petitesuisse.be

On a southern slope, terraced pitches with views over the surrounding area. Facilities include outdoor sports and mountain bike hire.

dir: *E25/A40.*

Open: All Year. **Site:** 7.5HEC **For hire:** **Prices:** 15-33 Mobile home hire 280-819 **Facilities:** Wi-fi (charged) Kids' Club Play Area **Services:** **Leisure:** P

FLORENVILLE — LUXEMBOURG

Rosière

Rive Gauche de la Semois, 6820
☎ 061 311937 🖷 061 314873
e-mail: larosiere@scarlet.be
web: www.larosiere.be

Wooded surroundings close to the town centre.

dir: *E411 exit 26 for Verlaine/Neufchâteau.*

Open: Apr-Oct **Site:** 10HEC **For hire:** **Facilities:** **Services:** **Leisure:** P

FORRIÈRES — LUXEMBOURG

Pré du Blason

rue de la Ramée 30, 6953
☎ 084 212867 🖷 084 223650
e-mail: info@camping-predublason.be
web: www.camping-predublason.be

This well-kept site lies on a meadow surrounded by wooded hills and is completely divided into pitches and crossed by rough, gravel drives.

dir: *Off N49 Masbourg road.*

Open: Apr-Oct **Site:** 3HEC **For hire:** **Prices:** 11-19.50 **Facilities:** Wi-fi (charged) Play Area **Services:** **Leisure:** R

GEMMENICH — LIÈGE

Kon Tiki

Terstraeten 141, 4851
☎ 087 785973
e-mail: info@campingkontiki.be
web: www.campingkontiki.be

Close to the borders with Holland and Germany, a relaxing site with leisure facilities including a games room and swimming pool area.

Open: All Year. **Site:** 12HEC **Facilities:** **Services:** **Leisure:** P R

GOUVY — LUXEMBOURG

Lac de Cherapont

Cherapont 2, 6670
☎ 080 517082 🖷 080 517093
e-mail: cherapont@skynet.be
web: www.cherapont.be

On an extensive lakeside tourist complex with a variety of recreational facilities.

dir: *E25 exit 51. Or E42 exit 15.*

Open: Apr-Oct **Site:** 10HEC **For hire:** **Prices:** 12-20 **Facilities:** Wi-fi Play Area **Services:** **Leisure:** L R **Off-site:**

GRAND-HALLEUX — LUXEMBOURG

Neuf Prés

av de la Résistance, 6698
☎ 080 216882
web: www.vielsalm.be

A family site in pleasant wooded surroundings beside a river.

dir: *Via E42.*

Open: Apr-Sep **Site:** 4HEC **Facilities:** **Services:** **Leisure:** P R **Off-site:**

HOGNE — NAMUR

Relais

16 rue de Serinchamps, 5377
☎ 0475 423049
e-mail: info@campinglerelais.com
web: www.campinglerelais.com

A pleasant site in a wooded park beside a lake.

dir: *N4 from Courrière to Hogne via Marche.*

Open: Mar-4 Jan **Site:** 12HEC **For hire:** **Facilities:** **Services:** **Leisure:** L R

HOUFFALIZE — LUXEMBOURG

Chasse et Pêche

rue de la Roche 63, 6660
061 288314 061 289660
e-mail: info@cpbuitensport.com
web: www.cpbuitensport.com

A pleasant site attached to a café-restaurant with good recreational facilities.

dir: *3km NW off E25.*

Open: All Year. **Site:** 2HEC **For hire:** **Prices:** 14.50-19.50 **Facilities:** **Services:** **Leisure:** R

Moulin de Rensiwez

Moulin de Rensiwez 1, 6663
061 289027 061 289027

A good stopover site on a series of terraces beside the River Ourthe, close to an old water-mill.

Open: All Year. **Site:** 5HEC **For hire:** **Prices:** 21-23 **Facilities:** **Services:** **Leisure:** R

LOUVEIGNÉ — LIÈGE

Moulin du Rouge-Thier

Rouge-Thier 8, 4141
041 608341 041 608341

A well-equipped site in a pleasant wooded location.

dir: *S of town towards Deigné.*

Open: Apr-30 Oct **Site:** 8HEC **For hire:** **Facilities:** **Services:**

MALONNE — NAMUR

Trieux

Les Tris 99, 5020
081 445583 081 445583
e-mail: camping.les.trieux@skynet.be
web: www.campinglestrieux.be

A quiet, peaceful site situated 3km from Namur which is easily accessible either on foot or by bike.

Open: Apr-30 Oct **Site:** 2.2HEC **For hire:** **Facilities:** **Services:** **Off-site:** P R

MARCHE-EN-FAMENNE — LUXEMBOURG

Euro Camping Paola

rue du Panorama 10, 6900
084 311704 084 314722
e-mail: camping.paola@skynet.be
web: www.campingpaola.be

A long site on a hill with beautiful views. The only noise comes from a railway line that passes the site.

dir: *Towards Hotton, right after cemetery for 1km.*

Open: All Year. **Site:** 13HEC **For hire:** **Facilities:** **Services:** **Off-site:** P

NEUFCHÂTEAU — LUXEMBOURG

Spineuse

rue de Malome 7, rte de Florenville, 6840
061 277320 061 277104
e-mail: info@camping-spineuse.be
web: www.camping-spineuse.be

Positioned on a river and with a fishing lake, site leisure facilities also include tennis courts and volleyball.

dir: *2km from Florenville towards Neufchâteau.*

Open: All Year. **Site:** 2.5HEC **For hire:** **Prices:** 19.30-21.30 Mobile home hire 245-450 **Facilities:** **Services:** **Leisure:** L P R

OLLOY-SUR-VIROIN — NAMUR

Try des Baudets

rue de la Champagne, 5670
060 390108 060 390108
e-mail: info@trydesbaudets.be
web: www.trydesbaudets.be

A peaceful site surrounded by forest. Plenty of facilities for children including a big playground and water-park on site. Entertainment in high season. Bike hire available.

dir: *N5 onto N99.*

GPS: 50.0688, 4.5964

Open: All Year. **Site:** 12HEC **For hire:** **Prices:** 12.50-20.50 Mobile home hire 262.45-587.45 **Facilities:** Wi-fi Kids' Club Play Area **Services:** **Leisure:** P **Off-site:** R

OTEPPE LIÈGE

Hirondelle

rue de la Burdinale 76A, 4210
085 711131 085 711021
e-mail: info@lhirondelle.be
web: www.lhirondelle.be
Ideal family site with modern facilities in the picturesque Burdinale Valley.
dir: *Signed N of town between E40 & E42.*
Open: Apr-Sep **Site:** 45HEC **For hire:** **Prices:** 13.75-21 Mobile home hire 305-639 **Facilities:** Wi-fi Play Area **Services:** **Leisure:** P **Off-site:**

RENDEUX LUXEMBOURG

Camping "Le Festival-Floreal"

rte de la Roche 89, 6987
084 477371 084 477364
e-mail: camping.festival@florealclub.be
Unspoiled surroundings beside the River Ourthe.
GPS: 50.2256, 5.5261
Open: Jan-Sep **Site:** 11HEC **For hire:** **Facilities:** Wi-fi (charged) Kids' Club **Services:** **Leisure:** R

ROBERTVILLE LIÈGE

Plage

33 rte des Bains, 4950
080 446658 080 446178
e-mail: info@campinglaplage.be
web: www.campinglaplage.be
Terraced pitches, 400 metres from the town centre. Ideal for hiking or cycling (rental available) in the surrounding forest. Other leisure facilities include an outdoor heated swimming pool and fishing.
Open: All Year. **Site:** 1.8HEC **For hire:** **Facilities:** **Services:** **Leisure:** L P R

ROCHE-EN-ARDENNE, LA LUXEMBOURG

Lohan

20a rte de Houffalize, 6980
084 411545 084 411545
Set in a park surrounded by woodland, on the north bank of the River Ourthe.
dir: *3km E of La Roche towards Maboge & Houffalize.*
Open: Apr-1 Nov **Site:** 4HEC **Prices:** 13-15.50 **Facilities:** Play Area **Services:** **Leisure:** R

Ourthe

6980
084 411459
e-mail: info@campingdelourthe.be
web: www.campingdelourthe.be
Well-kept site beside the River Ourthe.
dir: *On SW bank of Ourthe below N34.*
Open: 15 Mar-15 Oct **Site:** 2HEC **For hire:** **Facilities:** **Services:** **Leisure:** R **Off-site:** P

SART-LEZ-SPA LIÈGE

Touring Club

Stockay 17, 4845
087 474400 087 475277
e-mail: info@campingspador.be
web: www.campingspador.be
Located on the banks of the river Wayai, with good leisure facilities. Kids' club available in July and August. 8km from the Spa Francorchamps circuit, where the Belgian Formula One Grand Prix is held.
dir: *Signed E of Spa.*
Open: Apr-Oct **Site:** 6HEC **For hire:** **Prices:** 15.50-26.50 **Facilities:** Wi-fi (charged) Kids' Club Play Area **Services:** **Leisure:** P **Off-site:** L

SIPPENAEKEN LIÈGE

Vieux Moulin

114 Tebruggen, 4851
087 784255 087 883497
web: www.camping-vieuxmoulin.be
A family site with good recreational facilities, set in a pleasant wooded location close to a nature reserve.
dir: *E40 exit Battile for Aubel-Hombourg-Sippenaeken.*
Open: Apr-Sep **Site:** 6HEC **For hire:** **Facilities:** **Services:** **Leisure:** P R

SPA LIÈGE

Parc des Sources

rue de la Sauvenière 141, 4900
087 772311 087 475965
e-mail: info@parcdessources.be
web: www.parcdessources.be
On the outskirts of the town close to a forest.
dir: *S of town centre on N32 towards Malmédy.*
Open: Apr-Oct **Site:** 2.5HEC **Prices:** 17-19 **Facilities:** Wi-fi Play Area **Services:** **Leisure:** P **Off-site:**

STAVELOT — LIÈGE

Domaine de l'Eau Rouge

Cheneux 25, 4970

☎ 080 863075 📠 080 863075

web: www.eaurouge.eu

A pleasant riverside site with good sports facilities. 3km from the Formula One circuit at Spa.

dir: *Via E42 to Francorchamps or Malmédy.*

Open: All Year. **Site:** 4HEC **For hire:** **Prices:** 17 Mobile home hire 455 **Facilities:** Wi-fi Play Area **Services:** **Leisure:** R **Off-site:** P

TENNEVILLE — LUXEMBOURG

Pont de Berguème

rue Berguème 9, 6970

☎ 084 455443 📠 084 456231

e-mail: info@pontbergueme.be

web: www.pontbergueme.be

A peaceful wooded setting in the beautiful Ardennes area, with modern facilities.

dir: *Off N4 towards Berguème, then turn right.*

GPS: 50.0756, 5.5558

Open: All Year. **Site:** 3HEC **For hire:** **Prices:** 16 **Facilities:** Wi-fi (charged) Play Area **Services:** **Leisure:** R **Off-site:**

THOMMEN-REULAND — LIÈGE

Hohenbusch

Grüfflingen 44, 4791

☎ 080 227523 📠 080 420807

e-mail: info@hohenbusch.be

web: www.hohenbusch.be

A well-appointed family site on a wooded meadow with plenty of recreational facilities. There are apartments available to hire.

dir: *E42 exit 15, take N62 to the right.*

GPS: 50.2417, 6.0931

Open: Apr-Oct **Site:** 5HEC **For hire:** **Prices:** 15-22 **Facilities:** Play Area **Services:** **Leisure:** P

VIELSALM — LUXEMBOURG

Salm

chemin de la Vallée, 6690

☎ 080 216241 📠 080 217266

web: www.vielsalm.be

A hilly site with some shaded pitches and direct access to a pond.

Open: All Year. **Site:** 2.5HEC **Facilities:** **Services:** **Leisure:** R **Off-site:** L P

VIRTON — LUXEMBOURG

Colline de Rabais

clos des Horles 1, 6760

☎ 063 571195 📠 063 583342

e-mail: info@collinederabais.be

web: www.collinederabais.be

A secluded family site in the heart of the Gaume region close to a lake, with good recreational facilities.

dir: *NE of Virton between N87 & N82.*

Open: All Year. **Site:** 8HEC **For hire:** **Facilities:** **Services:** **Leisure:** P **Off-site:** L

WAIMES — LIÈGE

Anderegg

Bruyères 4, 4950

☎ 080 679393

e-mail: campinganderegg@skynet.be

web: www.campinganderegg.be

A peaceful location beside the Lac de Robertville, the site has modern sanitary facilities.

GPS: 50.4392, 6.1181

Open: All Year. **Site:** 1.5HEC **Prices:** 16.50 **Facilities:** Wi-fi (charged) Play Area **Services:** **Off-site:** L

Drinking and driving
Strictly forbidden for all drivers less than 24 years of age - 0% of alcohol allowed in driver's blood. Legal limit for drivers 24 years and over; alcohol in drivers blood is 0.05%, exceptions to this rule apply to professional drivers. Tests for narcotics may be performed, if tests prove positive severe consequences include confiscation of vehicle, severe fine and removal of driving licence. It is prohibited to drive after taking any medicine whose side effects may affect the ability to drive a motor vehicle.

Driving licence
Minimum age at which a UK licence holder may drive temporarily imported car and/or motorcycle (exceeding 125cc) 18.

Fines
The police officer will impose a fine on-the-spot; the fine must be paid within 8 days at a post office or bank. The police may hold your passport until evidence of payment is produced. The driving licence of a foreign motorist can be suspended for up to 8 days for driving with excess alcohol, driving without prescribed medical aids e.g. glasses, driving in a state of exhaustion or whilst ill. The licence must be collected within 3 days of the end of suspension. Illegally parked cars can be wheel clamped.

Fuel
Unleaded petrol (95 and 98 octane), diesel (dizel) available and LPG available at most filling stations located on motorways. It is forbidden to carry petrol in a can. Credit cards accepted at filling stations; check with your card issuer for usage in Croatia before travel.

Lights
Dipped headlights are compulsory for all vehicles in reduced visibility, fine imposed for non-compliance. Dipped headlights are compulsory in the daytime from the last Sunday in October to the last Sunday in March (out of the daylight saving time period), fine for non-compliance.

Motorcycles
Use of dipped headlights during the day compulsory. The wearing of crash helmets is compulsory for both the driver and passenger. Children under 12 cannot travel as a passenger. A fine will be imposed if the passenger on a motorcycle is found to be under the influence of alcohol or narcotics.

Motor insurance
Third-party compulsory. It is recommended that all visitors obtain a green card prior to travel to facilitate insurance formalities in case of an accident. The green card must cover Croatia (HR) as well as Bosnia Herzegovina if travelling on a 20km section of coastline at Neum, along the Dalmatian coastal highway.

Passengers/children in cars
Children under the age of 12 cannot travel as a front seat passenger, with the exception of a child under 2 years seated in a suitable child seat. The seat must be fitted facing in the opposite direction of travel with the passenger airbags turned off. Children from the age of 2 up to 5 years of age must be seated in a suitable child seat; other children must be seated using a suitable child restraint, using a booster seat where necessary.

Seat belts
Compulsory for front/rear-seat occupants to wear seat belts, if fitted.

Speed limits
Standard legal limits, which may be varied by signs

Private vehicles without trailers	
Built-up areas	50km/h
Outside built-up areas	90km/h
Expressways	110km/h
Motorways (unless otherwise indicated)	130km/h
If towing a trailer/caravan or over 3.5t	
Motoways	90km/h
Expressways/ordinary roads	80km/h
Motorists under 24 years of age	
Outside built-up areas	80km/h
Expressways	100km/h
Motorways	120km/h
Minimum speed on motorways	60km/h

Compulsory equipment
Spare bulbs - This does not apply if the vehicle is fitted with xenon, neon, LED or similar lights.

First-aid kit (excludes motorcycles)

Warning triangle - two triangles required if towing a trailer (excludes motorcycles).

Snow chains - During winter months, in the Gorski Kotar and Lika regions, chains are compulsory regardless of the type of tyre*

Reflective jacket - All drivers of motor vehicles (except motorcycles with sidecars and mopeds under 50cc) must have a reflective safety jacket (EN- 71) in the vehicle and wear it whenever they have to get out of the vehicle at the roadside, in an emergency. Be aware however that car hire companies may not supply them to persons hiring vehicles.

Other rules/requirements in Croatia

The use of spiked tyres is prohibited.

*It is generally necessary to have winter equipment ready between November and the end of April. This may consist of winter tyres marked M+S on the side walls or snow chains for the driving wheels. Vehicles not adapted to winter conditions may be prohibited from driving and can also encounter a fine. Snow tyres must have a minimum tread depth of 4 millimeters.

The authorities at the frontier must certify any visible damage to a vehicle entering Croatia and a certificate obtained; this must be produced when leaving the country.

Radar detectors are forbidden.

Tolls Currency: Kunas (HRK)	Car	Car Towing Caravan/Trailer
A1 (E65) Zagreb - Split - Dubrovnik	171HRK	265HRK
A6 (E65) Zagreb - Rijeka	60HRK	108HRK
A3+A5 (E70) Zagreb - Lipovac	105HRK	160HRK
A4 (E71) Zagreb - Gorican	36HRK	54HRK
A7 Rupa - Rijeka	5HRK	7HRK
Zagreb- Macelj (Zapresic Tollgate) A2 (E59)	42HRK	62HRK
Bridges and Tunnels		
Krk Bridge	30HRK	40HRK
A8 Ucka Tunnel (Kanfanar-Matuiji)	28HRK	40HRK
A9 Mirna Bridge (Kastel-Pula)	12HRK	21HRK

Please note: Although the official currency of Croatia is the Croatian kuna, the campsites featured in this guide have quoted their prices in Euros.

BIOGRAD NA MORU **ZADAR**

Camping Park Soline

Put Solina 17, 23210

☎ 023 383351 🖹 023 384823

e-mail: info@campsoline.com

web: www.campsoline.com

Set among pine trees with access to the sea and a pebble beach (with a sandy beach close by).

Open: 15 Apr-Sep **Site:** 20HEC **For hire:** **Facilities:** Wi-fi (charged) Kids' Club Play Area ♿ **Services:** **Leisure:** S **Off-site:** P

KOLAN (ISLAND OF PAG) **ZADAR**

Camping Village Šimuni

Šimuni bb, 23251

☎ 023 697441 🖹 023 657442

e-mail: info@camping-simuni.hr

web: www.camping-simuni.hr

Attractive site situated in oak and pine woods near a small fishing village on the Island of Pag, one of the largest Adriatic islands. The beach extends for 4km.

dir: *A1 motorway Karlovac-Split, before Zadar exit at Posedarje to Pag. 11km towards Novalia, site signed.*

GPS: 44.4619, 14.9702

Open: All Year. **Site:** 35HEC **For hire:** **Prices:** 35-50 Mobile home hire 260-400 **Facilities:** Wi-fi Kids' Club Play Area **Services:** **Leisure:** S

LOPAR (RAB) — GORSKI KOTAR

San Marino

Lopar bb, 51280
☎ 051 775133 📠 051 775290
e-mail: ac-sanmarino@imperial.hr
web: www.rab-camping.com

Situated in shady pinewoods next to the sandy Paradise Beach on the Island of Rab. Easy access to the sea.

dir: *Paradise Beach is 3km S of ferry landing at Crnika Bay.*

Open: Apr-Sep **Site:** 9HEC **For hire:** **Facilities:** **Services:** **Leisure:** S

OKRUG GORNJI (ISLAND OF ČIOVO) — DALMATIA

Camping Rožac

Šetalište Stjepana Radicá 56, 21220
☎ 021 806105 📠 021 882554
e-mail: booking@camp-rozac.hr
web: www.camp-rozac.hr

On the island of Čiovo, reached by bridge from Trogir. Surrounded by beach, the site is in a wooded setting.

dir: *From 8/E65 to Trogir, pass two bridges, turn right to island, follow road to site.*

GPS: 43.5058, 16.2583

Open: Apr-Oct **Site:** 2.5HEC **For hire:** **Prices:** 25.50-34 Mobile home hire 350-805 **Facilities:** Wi-fi (charged) Play Area **Services:** **Leisure:** S **Off-site:**

PAKOŠTANE — ZADAR

Camping Kozarica

Brune Bušica bb, 23211
☎ 023 381070 📠 023 381068
e-mail: kozarica@adria-more.hr
web: www.adria-more.hr

A family friendly site shaded by pines, with direct access to the beach where water sports are available.

Open: 2 Apr-Oct **Site:** 6HEC **For hire:** **Prices:** 16.60-32 Mobile home hire 252-882 **Facilities:** Wi-fi Kids' Club Play Area **Services:** **Leisure:** S **Off-site:** L

POREČ — ISTRIA

Lanterna

52440
☎ 52 404500
e-mail: lanterna@valamar.com
web: www.camping-adriatic.com

Large shady site on the beautiful Lanterna peninsula situated among pine and oak trees.

Open: Apr-5 Oct **Site:** 80HEC **For hire:** **Facilities:** Wi-fi Kids' Club **Services:** **Leisure:** P S **Off-site:**

PUNAT (ISLAND OF KRK) — GORSKI KOTAR

Pila

Šetalište Ivana Brusiča 2, 51521

☎ 051 854020 🖹 051 854020

e-mail: pila@hoteli-punat.hr

web: www.hoteli-punat.hr

Site set among pine woods in the south of the island of Krk which is connected to the mainland by a bridge. A tree-fringed promenade divides it from the sea and the beach.

dir: *From mainland take bridge to Krk, past Punat towards Stara Baaka, campsite 1st right.*

Open: Apr-14 Oct **Site:** 8.44HEC **For hire:** **Prices:** 20-40 **Facilities:** Play Area **Services:** **Leisure:** S **Off-site:**

ROVINJ — ISTRIA

Naturist Camping Valalta

Cesta za Valatu - Lim 7, 52210

☎ 052 804800 🖹 052 811463

e-mail: valalta@valalta.hr

web: www.valalta.hr

Large naturist site on the coast with sand and shingle beaches, located at the entrance to the Lim channel nature reserve. Modern facilities, salt water swimming pools, supermarket, sauna, beauty salon and entertainment.

dir: *7km NW from Rovinj, follow signs Valalta.*

GPS: 45.1228, 13.6311

Open: May-29 Sep **Site:** 90HEC **For hire:** **Prices:** 18.70-42 **Facilities:** Wi-fi (charged) Kids' Club Play Area **Services:** **Leisure:** P S

see advert on page 65

Polari

Polari bb, 52210

☎ 052 801501 🖹 052 811395

e-mail: polari@maistra.hr

web: www.campingrovinjvrsar.com

Located in a picturesque cove south of Rovinj. Extensive facilities with pitches shaded by evergreen trees. One part of the camp, Punta Eva, is reserved for naturists.

Open: 2 Apr-1 Oct **Site:** 60HEC **For hire:** **Facilities:** Wi-fi **Services:** **Leisure:** P S

SPLIT — DALMATIA

Camping Stobreč Split

Sv.Lovre 6, 21311

☎ 021 325426 🖹 021 325452

e-mail: camping.split@gmail.com

web: www.campingsplit.com

In the district of Stobreč, part of the city of Split, set in a forest. Surrounded on two sides by the sea and at the mouth of the Žrnovnica river, with both sandy and pebble beaches. Camping pitches are fenced and planted with seedlings.

dir: *A1 exit Dugopolje. Site just off D8.*

GPS: 43.5039, 16.5265

Open: All Year. **Site:** 5HEC **For hire:** **Prices:** 27.70-30.40 Mobile home hire 434-784 **Facilities:** Wi-fi (charged) Kids' Club Play Area **Services:** **Leisure:** R S **Off-site:** P

UMAG — ISTRIA

Campsite Finida

Krizine 55, 52470

☎ 052 700700 🖹 052 725969

e-mail: camp.finida@istraturist.hr

web: www.istracamping.com

Peaceful site located on the sea front in an area with secluded bays.

dir: *7km from centre of Umag towards Novigrad.*

Open: 23 Apr-25 Sep **Site:** 5HEC **Facilities:** **Services:** **Leisure:** S **Off-site:** P

Campsite Park Umag

Karigador bb, 52470

☎ 052 700700 🖹 052 725053

e-mail: camp.park.umag@istraturist.hr

web: www.istracamping.com

Large family campsite with many facilities for children, including swimming pools with waterfalls, castles and a pirate ship.

dir: *9km from town centre of Umag towards Novigrad.*

GPS: 45.3672, 13.5470

Open: 7 Apr-Sep **Site:** 101HEC **For hire:** **Prices:** 18-53 **Facilities:** Wi-fi (charged) Kids' Club Play Area **Services:** **Leisure:** P S **Off-site:**

Campsite Pineta

Istarska bb, 52475
052 709550 052 709559
e-mail: camp.pineta@istraturist.hr
web: www.istracamping.com
Quiet site among pine trees located near the beach close to a picturesque fishing village.

dir: *9km from town centre of Umag, at foot of lighthouse near village of Savudrija.*

GPS: 45.4867, 13.4925

Open: 7 Apr-Sep **Site:** 11.30HEC **For hire:** **Prices:** 14.60-29.40 **Facilities:** **Services:** **Leisure:** P S **Off-site:**

Campsite Stella Maris

Stella Maris 8, Monterol, 52470
052 700700 052 710909
e-mail: camp.stella.maris@istraturist.hr
web: www.istracamping.com
Meadowland site among pine trees and situated next to a picturesque lagoon with a fine beach.

dir: *2km from town centre of Umag.*

GPS: 45.4504, 13.5227

Open: 30 Mar-Sep **Site:** 5HEC **Prices:** 15-32.10 **Facilities:** Wi-fi (charged) Kids' Club Play Area **Services:** **Off-site:** P S

Naturist Kanegra FKK

Kanegra bb, 52470
052 700700 052 709499
e-mail: camping@istraturist.com
web: www.istracamping.com
A naturist site located on the seafront, with a pebble beach, 10km from Umag. Leisure facilities include a tennis school and bike rental.

dir: *10km from town centre.*

GPS: 45.4873, 13.5608

Open: 7 Apr-Sep **Site:** 4.8HEC **For hire:** **Prices:** 15.10-33 **Facilities:** Wi-fi Play Area **Services:** **Leisure:** S **Off-site:**

VRSAR ISTRIA

Porto Sole

Petalon, 52450
052 426500 052 426580
e-mail: portosole@maistra.hr
web: www.maistra.com
A small site by the shore in a sheltered bay set in sunny meadows and pinewoods. Extensive sports facilities.

Open: 26 Apr-3 Oct **Site:** **Facilities:** **Leisure:** P

CROATIA

Above: The walled city of Dubrovnik

Drinking and driving

Strictly forbidden. 0% of alcohol allowed in drivers' blood. Fine between 25,000 and 50,000 Czech crown (CZK) and withdrawal of the driving licence for up to two years. Frequent random testing takes place, police can also test for drugs by testing saliva. Driving under the influence of alcohol and drugs is considered a criminal offence.

Driving licence

Minimum age at which a UK licence holder may drive a temporarily imported car 18, motorcycle up to 125cc 17, over 125cc (max 25kW) 18 years. Photo card licences are accepted - licences that do not incorporate a photo must be accompanied by an International Driving Permit.

Fines

On-the-spot up to 5,000 CZK, maximum fine for traffic offence 100,000 CZK. An official receipt should be obtained. The police are empowered to retain the driving licence if a serious traffic offence has been committed. Illegally parked vehicles may be clamped or towed away.

Fuel

Unleaded petrol 'natural' (95 and 98 octane), diesel (nafta) and LPG (autoplyn or plyn) available. Up to 10 litres of petrol in a can permitted. Credit cards accepted at filling stations, check with your card issuer for usage in Czech Republic before travel.

Lights

Use of dipped headlights / daytime running lights during the day compulsory throughout the year. Fine for non-compliance: approximately 2,000 CZK. Any vehicle warning lights, other than those supplied with the vehicle as original equipment, must be made inoperative.

Motorcycles

Use of dipped headlights during the day compulsory throughout the year. The wearing of crash helmets is compulsory for driver and passenger of motorcycles. It is forbidden for motorcyclists to smoke while riding their machine.

Motor insurance

Third-party compulsory.

Passengers/children in cars

All passengers must use seat belts. Children with a weight under 36kg and under 150cm in height are not permitted to travel in a vehicle unless using a suitable restraint system, adapted to their size and weight. A child seated in the front seats of a vehicle using a suitable child restraint system where the airbag is activated must travel facing forward.

Seat belts

Compulsory for front and rear seat occupants to wear seat belts, if fitted.

Speed limits

Standard legal limits, which may be varied by signs

Private vehicles without trailers	
Built-up areas	50km/h
Outside built-up areas	90km/h
(with trailer or caravan)	80km/h
Motorways	130km/h
Expressways through built-up areas	80km/h
Maximum speed with snow chains	50km/h

At railway crossings drivers must not exceed 30km/h for 50m before the crossing. The arrival of a train is indicated by red flashing lights, or a red or yellow flag.

Vehicles that are constructed with a maximum speed of 80km/h or under are not permitted to travel on motorways.

Compulsory equipment in Czech Republic

First-aid kit
A set of replacement bulbs
A set of replacement fuses
Warning triangle - not required for two wheeled vehicles
Reflective Jacket – A reflective jacket is required on board all motor vehicles.

Winter equipment -Vehicles must be fitted with either winter tyres (which must be marked M&S) or carry snow chains between the 1st November and the 31st March. Dependant upon weather conditions (if roads are covered with snow) this period may be extended. As snow chains can only be used when roads are completely covered, we recommend that winter tyres are fitted. The minimum depth on winter tyres is 4 millimeters.

A road sign showing the picture of a car and a snowflake is used to designate these road sections; the same road sign with a line across indicates the end of this restriction. One of these sections is also on the motorway D1 from Prague to Brno.

Please note: From November 2011, it is highly likely that winter tyres will become compulsory on all roads during winter weather conditions.

Reflective jacket – EU standard EN471. The driver of a vehicle with 2 or more axles must carry a reflective waistcoat, it has to be worn in the event of a breakdown or emergency outside a built-up area, on all roads, expressways and motorways. It has to be worn when exiting the vehicle in such circumstances and therefore must be kept within the car (not in the boot). The waistcoat is recommended for car passengers and is compulsory for riders of mopeds and motorcycles.

Other rules/requirements

Motorway tax is payable for the use of motorways and express roads. A windscreen sticker must be displayed on all four-wheeled vehicles up to 3.5t as evidence of payment. Stickers can be purchased at the Czech frontier, UAMK branch offices, petrol stations or post offices for periods of one year, one month or ten consecutive days. Fines imposed for non-display.

The authorities at the frontier must certify any visible damage to a vehicle entering the Czech Republic. If any damage occurs inside the country a police report must be obtained at the scene of the accident. Damaged vehicles may only be taken out of the country on production of this evidence.

The use of an audible warning device is only permitted in built up areas to avoid imminent danger, they are prohibited between 2000hrs and 0600hrs, and in Prague.

The use of spiked tyres is prohibited.

A GPS based navigation system which has maps indicating the location of fixed speed cameras must have the 'fixed speed camera PoI (Points of Interest)' function deactivated. The use of radar detectors is prohibited.

Motorway Tax Sticker Currency: Czech Koruna (CZK)	Car	Car Towing Caravan/Trailer
1 week	250CZK	250CZK
1 month	350CZK	350CZK
1 year	1,200CZK	1,200CZK

BÍTOV **JIHOMORAVSKÝ**

Camp Bítov - Vranovská Přehrada

67110

☎ 605 842965 📠 515 296204

e-mail: info@camp-bitov.cz

web: www.camp-bitov.cz

Surrounded by deciduous forests, this site's leisure facilities include fishing, table tennis and concerts.

Open: May-15 Sep **Site:** **For hire:** **Facilities:** Wi-fi Play Area **Services:** **Leisure:** L

CERNÁ V POSUMAVÍ **BOHEMIA**

Camping Olsina

Ckyne 212, 38481

☎ 608 029982

e-mail: info@campingolsina.cz

web: www.campingolsina.cz

Partly forested campsite situated by Lake Lipno, near the village Cerná v Posumaví.

dir: *From Cerná v Posumaví towards Ceský Krumlov, after 1km turn left, campsite signed.*

Open: 20 Apr-20 Oct **Site:** 5.5HEC **For hire:** **Prices:** 340 **Facilities:** Wi-fi **Services:** **Leisure:** L **Off-site:**

Villa Bohemia

Lipno, 38223

☎ 380 744004

e-mail: camp@villabohemia.cz

web: www.villabohemia.cz

Situated on the shores of Lake Lipno with a kilometre long private beach. Fine views of the lake and the mountains beyond. Good facilities and high standard sanitary installations.

dir: *Ceský Krumlov-Cerná v Posumaví road. Directly after dam on Lipno lake follow sign for Jestrabi, site 1.5km.*

Open: May-Sep **Site:** 3.5HEC **For hire:** **Facilities:** **Services:** **Leisure:** L **Off-site:**

FRYMBURK — BOHEMIA

Frymburk

38279

☎ 380 735284 380 735283

e-mail: info@campingfrymburk.cz

web: www.campingfrymburk.cz

In an attractive location on Lake Lipno in southern Bohemia, Frymburk is ideal for swimming and water activities. Level pitches in terraces. A kids' club is available during high season.

dir: *On route 163, 1km S of Frymburk at Lipno Lake.*

Open: 27 Apr-1 Oct **Site:** 4.5HEC **For hire:** **Prices:** 484-734 Mobile home hire 700-18200 **Facilities:** Wi-fi Kids' Club **Services:** **Leisure:** L **Off-site:** P

HLUBOKÉ MAŠŮVKY — MORAVIA

Country

67152

☎ 515 255249 515 255249

e-mail: camping-country@cbox.cz

web: www.camp-country.com

Attractively landscaped site, close to the historical town of Znojmo. In a rural location close to a National Park and the Austrian border. Suitable for family camping with lots of activities for children.

dir: *7km N of Znojmo. Take E59 (Jihlava-Vienna), near Kravsko turn left, site 6km.*

GPS: 48.9217, 16.0281

Open: May-Oct **Site:** 2HEC **For hire:** **Prices:** 360-410 **Facilities:** Wi-fi Play Area **Services:** **Leisure:** P **Off-site:** R

HLUK — MORAVIA

Camping Babi Hora

68725

☎ 572 581180

e-mail: babihora@quick.cz

web: www.camping-babihora.com

Quiet meadowland site surrounded by woodland.

dir: *E50, take exit to Kunovice, then follow exit for Hluk & signs to campsite.*

Open: 15 May-15 Sep **Site:** 2.5HEC **For hire:** **Prices:** 300-400 **Facilities:** Wi-fi Play Area **Services:** **Leisure:** P

MARIANSKÉ LAZNĚ — ZÁPADOCESKY

Karolina

Brod nad Tichou, 34815

☎ 777 296990

e-mail: office@camp-k.cz

web: www.camp-k.cz

A quiet, comfortable, family-based camp site surrounded by forest and hills with a brook running through, on the edge of the West Bohemian spa region.

dir: *E50 motorway towards Plzen, exit 128 for Brod nad Tichou, 13km to campsite.*

GPS: 49.8339, 12.7411

Open: May-15 Oct **Site:** 2.8HEC **For hire:** **Facilities:** Play Area **Services:** **Leisure:** P R **Off-site:** L

NOVÉ STRAŠECÍ — BOHEMIA

Bucek

Trtice 170, 27101

☎ 313 564212

e-mail: info@campingbucek.cz

web: www.campingbucek.cz

Partly forested site beside a large lake with a sandy beach and suitable for all kinds of water sports. At peak times there is a small restaurant open in the grounds of the campsite. Modern sanitary facilities.

dir: *On E48/6 Prague-Karlovy Vary road, 4km past Nové Strašecí exit.*

Open: 25 Apr-15 Sep **Site:** 5HEC **For hire:** **Facilities:** Wi-fi Play Area **Services:** **Leisure:** L P

PASOHLÁVKY MORAVIA

Autocamp Merkur

69122

519 427751 519 427501

e-mail: camp@pasohlavky.cz

web: www.kemp-merkur.cz

Situated by the upper Novomlynskas reservoir, also called the Palava lakes, with views of surrounding hills. Ideal for swimming, fishing and water sports.

dir: *35km from Brno on right of E461 (Brno-Vienna).*

GPS: 48.9028, 16.5761

Open: Apr-Oct **Site:** 4.5HEC **For hire:** **Facilities:** Wi-fi Play Area **Services:** **Leisure:** L

PLZEŇ ZÁPADOCESKY

Autocamping Ostende

Malý Bolevec, 32300

377 520194 377 520194

e-mail: atc-ostende@cbox.cz

web: www.atc-ostende.cz

By the shore of the Grand Boulevec lake, surrounded by woods and forests. Good location for swimming and walking.

dir: *N of Plzeň, signposted on Plzeň-Most road.*

GPS: 49.7772, 13.39

Open: May-Sep **Site:** 3HEC **For hire:** **Prices:** 380-560 **Facilities:** Play Area **Services:** **Leisure:** L **Off-site:** P

PRAHA (PRAGUE) BOHEMIA

Family Camp Drusus

K Reporyjim 4, 15500

235 514391 235 514391

e-mail: drusus@drusus.com

web: www.drusus.com

Quiet site on outskirts of Prague within easy reach of the city.

dir: *From Pilsen/Slany D5 onto E50 direction Brno, take exit 19 (Reporyje/Orech).*

GPS: 50.0439, 14.2844

Open: Apr-5 Oct **Site:** 1.2HEC **For hire:** **Prices:** 420-580 **Facilities:** Wi-fi Play Area **Services:** **Off-site:** P

Prager

V Ladech 3, 14900

244 912854 244 912854

e-mail: petrgali@login.cz

web: www.pensioncampprague.com

Family run campsite in south-east Prague, within easy reach of the city centre.

dir: *E50 (Prague-Brno), exit 2/2A for Seberov.*

GPS: 50.0125, 14.5117

Open: Etr & May-Sep **Site:** 0.4HEC **For hire:** **Prices:** 400 **Facilities:** Wi-fi Play Area **Services:** **Leisure:** P **Off-site:** L

Triocamp Praha

Ústecká (Obsluzná 43), 18400

283 850793 283 850793

e-mail: triocamp.praha@telecom.cz

web: www.triocamp.cz

Located on the northern edge of Prague the site is convenient for visiting the city with good bus and tram links. The ground is slightly sloping but most pitches are level and in the shade of mature trees.

dir: *D8/E55 towards Teplice, exit Zdiby, route 608 to Dolni Cabry, site 3km on right.*

GPS: 50.1542, 14.4506

Open: All Year. **Site:** 1HEC **For hire:** **Prices:** 690-850 Mobile home hire 13300-17150 **Facilities:** Wi-fi (charged) Play Area **Services:** **Leisure:** P **Off-site:**

PROTIVÍN BOHEMIA

Blanice

Chelcického 889, 39811

721 589125

e-mail: info@campingblanice.nl

web: www.campingblanice.nl

Low-lying site in the pretty, flat valley of the Blanice river. Situated between two forks of the river, the site is accessed over a little bridge.

dir: *Take E49 from Ceske Budejovice-Pisek, site signed by exit for Protovín.*

Open: Apr-15 Sep **Site:** 1HEC **For hire:** **Facilities:** **Services:** **Off-site:** R

ROZNOV POD RADHOŠTĚM — MORAVIA

Roznov

Radhostska 940, 75661

☎ 571 648001/3 📠 571 620513

e-mail: info@camproznov.cz

web: www.camproznov.cz

Level site set amid a variety of fruit and other trees. Some pitches are small although the newer landscaped pitches are bigger. Situated by a main road although the surrounding trees help to reduce the traffic noise.

dir: *Between Dolni Becva & Roznov on E442, on right.*

Open: Apr-Oct **Site:** 3.9HEC **For hire:** **Prices:** 240-430 Mobile home hire 7000-8400 **Facilities:** Wi-fi Play Area **Services:** **Leisure:** P **Off-site:** R

SOBĚSLAV — BOHEMIA

ATC Karvánky

39201

☎ 381 521003

e-mail: karvanky@post.cz

web: www.karvanky.cz

Set in a wooded area where facilities include fishing.

dir: *E55.*

Open: May-Sep **Site:** 5HEC **For hire:** **Facilities:** Wi-fi (charged) Play Area **Services:** **Leisure:** L **Off-site:** R

STRÁZOV — SUMAVA

U Dvou Orechu

Splz 13, 34021

☎ 602 394496

e-mail: info@camping-tsjechie.nl

web: www.camping-tsjechie.nl

Partly terraced site in scenic forested surroundings with glacial lakes and fast flowing rivers.

dir: *Take route 191 (Nyrsko-Katovy), then route 171 to Strázov. In Strázov right towards Depoltice/Divisovice, site on left after 2km.*

GPS: 49.2814, 13.2400

Open: May-1 Oct **Site:** 1.5HEC **For hire:** **Prices:** 395 **Facilities:** Wi-fi **Services:** **Off-site:** P

TURNOV — LIBERECKÝ

Autocamp Sedmihorky

51101

☎ 481 389162 📠 481 389160

e-mail: camp@campsedmihorky.cz

web: www.campsedmihorky.cz

With good transport links, the site grounds are grassy and divided by asphalt paths. There is a pond where swimming is available, other facilities include cycle rental and grass courts for volleyball or badminton.

dir: *Off E442, SE of Turnov.*

GPS: 50.5580, 15.1867

Open: All Year. **Site:** 4.2HEC **For hire:** **Prices:** 155-340 Mobile home hire 5110-14210 **Facilities:** Wi-fi Kids' Club Play Area **Services:** **Leisure:** L **Off-site:** R

VRCHLABI — KRÁLOVÉHRADECKÝ

Holiday Park Lisci Farma

Dolní Branná 350, 54362

☎ 499 421473 📠 499 421656

e-mail: info@liscifarma.cz

web: www.liscifarma.cz

Pitches are fairly flat, although the terrain is slightly sloping and some pitches are terraced. There is shade and the site is well equipped for the whole family with many facilities. Close to a sandy lakeside beach.

dir: *Route 295 (Vrchlabi-Studenec), site on right.*

Open: All Year. **Site:** 8HEC **For hire:** **Facilities:** **Services:** **Leisure:** P **Off-site:** L R

CZECH REPUBLIC

Oase Praha

25241
☎ 241 932044
e-mail: info@campingoase.cz
web: www.campingoase.cz

The Camping and Caravanning Club The Friendly Club

A level, well-kept site, close to Prague. Leisure facilities include indoor and outdoor swimming pools. Wi-fi is chargeable in high season. Guided city tours can be arranged.

C&CC Report *This friendly, high quality, family-run site is on the edge of a village amid the gently rolling countryside of Bohemia, while access to the area from the Channel is by fast and cheap roads. For a small and cosy site, Oase Praha provides a surprisingly wide range of good quality facilities, and is particularly good for families who like relaxing and exploring. A mere ten miles (16 kilometres) from historic, romantic Prague, the bus stops at the site entrance. Other great attractions within reach are Konopiste and Karlstejn castles, old Kutna Hora and Prague zoo, with Aquapalace waterpark only 16km away.*

dir: *S of Prague follow R1 (Prague Ring Road), exit 82 Jesenice. In Jesenice turn left towards Zlatniky then left at rdbt, campsite 700m from village.*

GPS: 49.9514, 14.4747

Open: 28 Apr-15 Sep **Site:** 2.5HEC For hire: **Prices:** 300-500 Mobile home hire 9800-18200 **Facilities:** Wi-fi Kids' Club Play Area **Services:** **Leisure:** P **Off-site:** L

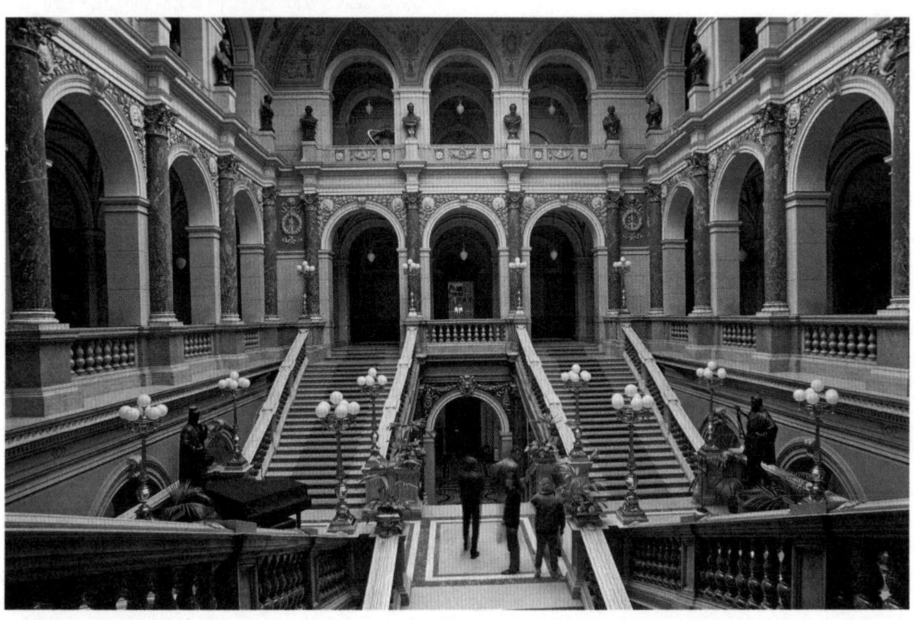

Above: National Museum, Prague

Drinking and driving

If the level of alcohol in the bloodstream is 0.05% or more (0.02% for bus/coach drivers), severe penalties include fine, imprisonment and/or confiscation of the driving licence. Saliva drug tests will be used to detect drivers under the influence of drugs – severe penalties as above.

Driving licence

Minimum age at which a UK licence holder may drive a temporarily imported car 18, motorcycle (up to 80cc) 16, motorcycle (over 80cc) 18.

Fines

On-the-spot fines or 'deposits' are severe. An official receipt should be issued. Vehicles parking contrary to regulations may be towed away and impounded.

Fuel

Unleaded petrol (95 and 98 octane), diesel (Gazole) and LPG available. No leaded petrol (lead replacement petrol "Super carburant" available or lead substitute additive). Petrol in a can is permitted but forbidden by ferry operators. Credit cards accepted at most filling stations; check with your card issuer for usage in France and Monaco before travel. There are many automatic petrol pumps operated by credit/debit card however, cards issued in the UK are not always accepted by these pumps.

A new type of fuel, the SP95-E10 (Sans Plomb 95 Octane, Ethanol 10% = Lead Free 95 Octane containing 10% of Ethanol) is now being sold throughout France. This fuel is not suitable for use in all cars and you should check compatibility with your vehicle manufacturer before using it. If in doubt use the standard SP95 or SP98, Octane unleaded fuel which continues to be available alongside the new fuel.

Lights

Dipped headlights must be used in poor daytime visibility. It is highly recommended by the French Government that vehicles with more than four wheels use dipped headlights day and night (already compulsory for motorcycles).

Motorcycles

Use of dipped headlights during the day compulsory. The wearing of crash helmets is compulsory for both driver and passenger of any two-wheel motorised vehicle.

Motor insurance

Third-party compulsory.

Passengers/children in cars

Children under the age of 10 are not permitted to travel on the front seats of vehicles, unless there are no rear seats or the rear seats are already occupied with children under 10, or there are no seat belts. In these circumstances a child must not be placed in the front seats with their back to the road if the vehicle is fitted with a passenger airbag, unless it is deactivated. They must travel in an approved child seat or restraint adapted to their size. A baby up to 13kg must be carried in a rear-facing baby seat. A child between 9 and 18kg must be seated in a child seat and a child from 15kg up to 10 years can use a booster seat with a seat belt or a harness. It is the driver's responsibility to ensure all passengers under 18 are appropriately restrained.

Seat belts

Compulsory for front/rear seat occupants to wear seat belts, if fitted.

Speed limits

Standard legal limits, which may be varied by signs

Private vehicles without trailers	
Built-up areas	50km/h
Outside built-up areas	90km/h
Urban motorways and dual carriageways separated by a central reservation	110km/h
Motorways	130km/h
In wet weather and for visiting motorists who have held a driving licence for less than two years	
Outside built-up areas	80km/h
Dual carriageways	100km/h
Motorways	110km/h
Vehicle towing a trailer or caravan [If less than 3.5t, speed limits are the same as those for private vehicles. If 3.5t to 12t, speed limits are the same as those for combinations of vehicles]	
Other roads	80km/h
Priority roads/Dual carriageways	90km/h
Motorways	90km/h
If the weight of the trailer exceeds that of the car	
if the excess is less than 30%	65km/h
if the excess is more than 30%	45km/h

In these cases, a disc showing maximum speed must be displayed on the rear of caravan/trailers. They may not be driven in the fast lane of a 3-lane motorway.

Minimum speed limit on motorways (all vehicles) 80km/h

Note: Holders of EU driving licences exceeding the speed limit by more than 40km/h will have their licences confiscated on the spot by the police.

Compulsory equipment in France and Monaco

Warning triangle - excludes motorcycles.

Snow chains - must be fitted to vehicles using snow-covered roads in compliance with the relevant road sign. Maximum speed limit 50km/h

Reflective jacket (EN471) - one reflective jacket in the vehicle. This does not apply to drivers of two-wheeled and three-wheeled vehicles.

Other rules/requirements

It is recommended that visitors equip their vehicle with a set of replacement bulbs.

Snow tyres marked M&S are recommended on roads covered with ice or snow. The minimum tread depth is 3.5mm.

In built-up areas give way to traffic coming from the right "priorité a droite".

At signed roundabouts bearing the words "Vous n'avez pas la priorité" or "Cédez le passage" traffic on the roundabout has priority; where no such sign exists traffic entering the roundabout has priority.

Overtaking stationary trams is prohibited when passengers are boarding/alighting.

Parking discs for 'blue zone' parking areas can be obtained from police stations, tourist offices and some shops.

In built-up areas the use of the horn is prohibited except in cases of immediate danger .

Apparatus with a screen which can distract a driver (such as television, video, DVD equipment) should be positioned in places where the driver is unable to see them. This excludes GPS systems. It is prohibited to touch or program the device unless parked in a safe place.

It is absolutely prohibited to carry, transport or use radar detectors. Failure to comply with this regulation involves a fine of up to 1500 Euros, and the vehicle and/or device may be confiscated. Road signs indicating the location of fixed speed cameras are being removed.

Pictured: Les Invalides as seen from the Eiffel Tower , Paris

Tolls Currency Euro (€)	Car	Car Towing Caravan/Trailer
A1 - Lille - Paris	€14.60	€21.50
A10 - Tours - Poitiers	€9.70	€16.00
A10 - Poitiers - Saintes	€10.60	€16.50
A10 - Paris - Tours	€22.80	€33.90
A10 - Tours - Bordeaux	€30.10	€47.40
A10/A71 - Paris - Clermont-Ferrand	€33.80	€54.30
A10/A837 - Bordeaux - La Rochelle	€12.60	€19.10
A11 - Angers - Nantes	€8.20	€12.40
A11 - Paris - Angers	€25.40	€39.00
A11/A81 - Paris - Rennes	€26.70	€40.80
A13 - Le Havre - St Saëns	€7.20	€10.80
A13/A131 - Le Havre - Paris	€24.30	€39.10
A13/A14 - Rouen - Paris	€13.40	€24.10
A13/A14 - Caen - Paris	€21.60	€36.40
A14 - Orgeval - Paris (La defense)	€7.80	€15.60
A16 - Calais - Paris	€20.40	€31.50
A2/A1 - Valenciennes - Paris	€13.00	€19.10
A2/A26 - Valenciennes - Reims	€11.90	€17.80
A26 - Reims - Troyes	€10.20	€15.20
A26 - Calais - Reims	€20.20	€30.20
A26/A1 - Calais - Paris	€18.90	€27.30
A26/A5 - Reims - Lyon	€37.30	€57.00
A26/A5/A39/A40 - Reims - Mont Blanc Tunnel (Tunnel du Mont Blanc)	€51.10	€78.30
A29 - Le Havre - St Saëns (A29)	€7.20	€10.80
A29/A16 - Neufchâtel en Bray - Amiens	€6.30	€9.80
A29/A26 - Amiens - Reims	€12.10	€18.30
A31 - Langres - Dijon	€2.10	€3.20
A31 - Dijon - Beaune	€2.70	€3.90
A31 - Nancy - Langres	€8.10	€12.70
A36 - Belfort - Mulhouse (German Frontier)	€2.80	€4.30
A36 - Beaune - Besançon	€7.00	€10.80
A36 - Besançon - Belfort	€7.10	€10.90
A39 - Dijon - Dole	€2.80	€4.20

Tolls Currency Euro (€)	Car	Car Towing Caravan/Trailer
A39 - Dole - Bourg-en-Bresse	€8.20	€13.00
A4 - Paris - Reims	€9.70	€14.70
A4 - Metz - Strasbourg	€12.00	€18.60
A4 - Paris - Metz	€22.90	€34.90
A4 - Paris - Strasbourg	€34.90	€53.50
A40 - Genève - Mont Blanc Tunnel (Tunnel Mont du Blanc)	€5.40	€9.90
A40 - Mâcon - Genève	€14.90	€24.10
A41 - Grenoble - Chambery	€5.50	€7.90
A41 - Chambery - Genève	€8.20	€12.40
A41/A40 - Chambery - Chamonix	€8.70	€14.20
A42/A40 - Lyon - Geneve	€14.40	€23.20
A43 - Lyon - Chambery	€10.30	€16.20
A43/A430 - Chambery - Albertville	€4.90	€7.60
A43/A48 - Lyon - Grenoble	€9.60	€15.50
A49 - Valence - Grenoble	€8.20	€12.90
A5/A31/A6 - Paris - Lyon (via Troyes)	€35.60	€55.10
A51 - Aix-en-Provence - La Saulce	€11.60	€17.60
A52/A50 - Aix-en-Provence - Toulon	€7.00	€10.70
A54/A7 - Montpellier - Aix-en-Provence	€10.10	€15.40
A57 - Toulon - Le Cannet de Maures	€3.80	€5.80
A6 - Paris - Beaune	€19.60	€30.40
A6 - Paris - Mâcon	€25.50	€39.80
A6 - Paris - Lyon	€30.90	€48.20
A61/A9 - Toulouse - Le Perthus (Spanish Frontier)	€17.90	€27.20
A61/A9 - Toulouse - Montpellier	€20.30	€30.70
A62 - Bordeaux - Toulouse	€16.70	€26.40
A63 - Bordeaux - Hendaye (Spanish Frontier)	€7.00	€10.70
A64 - Bayonne - Toulouse	€17.40	€27.80
A7/A8 - Lyon - Aix-en-Provence	€22.30	€35.30
A7/A9 - Lyon - Montpellier	€24.00	€37.50
A72 - Clermont-Ferrand - Lyon	€8.60	€13.30

Tolls	Car	Car Towing Caravan/Trailer
A8 - Nice - Menton (Italian frontier)	€2.10	€3.20
A8 - Cannes - Nice	€2.80	€4.30
A8 - Aix-en-Provence - Cannes	€13.20	€19.90
A83/A10 - Nantes - Bordeaux	€26.90	€40.90
A85 - Angers - Tours	€8.80	€12.40
A87 - Angers - Les Sables d'Olonne	€9.00	€14.60
A89 - Brive la Gaillarde - Clermont Ferrand	€9.60	€14.90
A89 - Bordeaux - Brive la Gaillarde	€16.10	€25.00
A9 - Orange - Montpellier	€1.10	€1.70
A9 - Montpellier - Le Perthus (Spanish frontier)	€12.60	€20.00
A9/A54 - Montpellier - Arles	€6.10	€9.40
E402 - Le Mans - Tours	€7.00	€11.00
E402 - Rouen - Le Mans	€19.60	€32.50
E604 - Tours - Bourges	€12.50	€20.00
E712 - Grenoble - Sisteron	€3.00	€4.70
E9 - Toulouse - Tunnel du Puymorens	€4.60	€6.90
E9 - Brive la Gaillarde - Toulouse	€14.40	€22.30

Bridges and Tunnels	Car	Car Towing Caravan/Trailer
Fréjus Tunnel (Tunnel du Fréjus) (French-Italian border)	€36.80	€48.70
D735 - La Rochelle - Ile de Ré (high season)	€16.50	€27.00
A75 - Millau Viaduct (July & August)	€8.20	€12.30
A75 - Millau Viaduct (rest of the year)	€6.40	€9.60
Mont Blanc Tunnel (French-Italian border)	€36.80	€48.70
Pont de Normandie (Le Havre)	€5.00	€5.80
Pont de Tancarville (Le Havre)	€2.30	€2.90
Tunnel Prado Carenage (cars only) (Marseille)	€2.60	
A159 nr Colmar - Tunnel de Sainte Marie aux Mines	€7.50	€16.00
Tunnel du Puymorens (Andorra-Spanish border)	€5.40	€10.90

ALPS/EAST

ABRETS, LES — ISÈRE

Coin Tranquille

The Camping and Caravanning Club The Friendly Club

6 chemin des Vignes, 38490
☎ 476321348 📠 476374067
e-mail: contact@coin-tranquille.com
web: www.coin-tranquille.com

Completely divided into pitches with attractive flower beds in rural surroundings. Kids' club available in July and August.

C&CC Report *This very pretty site is centrally located within easy reach of many favoured Alpine destinations. The nearby lakes, the Chartreuse (renowned as one of the finest walking areas of France) and the Vercors Regional Parks are favourites.*

dir: *2km E of village, 0.5km off N6.*

GPS: 45.5410, 5.6086

Open: Apr-1 Nov **Site:** 5HEC **For hire:**
Prices: 15-29 **Facilities:** Kids' Club Play Area
Services: **Leisure:** P **Off-site:** R

ALBENS — SAVOIE

Beauséjour

rte de la Rippe, 73410
☎ 479541520
web: www.campingbeausejour-albens.com

A peaceful wooded setting between Aix-les-Bains and Annecy.

dir: *SW via rte de la Chambotte, signed.*

Open: 15 Jun-20 Sep **Site:** 2HEC **For hire:**
Prices: 9.60-13.40 Mobile home hire 300-380 **Facilities:** Play Area **Services:** **Off-site:** R

ALLEVARD — ISÈRE

Clair Matin

20 rte de Pommiers, 38580
☎ 476975519 📠 476458715
e-mail: contact@camping-clair-matin.com
web: www.camping-clair-matin.com

Tranquil and shaded, gently sloping terraced site divided into pitches. Good recreational facilities, including bike hire. Hiking trails and paragliding nearby.

dir: *S of village, 300m off D525.*

GPS: 45.3885, 6.0644

Open: May-16 Oct **Site:** 5.5HEC **For hire:**
Prices: 14.40-20 Mobile home hire 195-434 **Facilities:** Wi-fi (charged) Kids' Club Play Area **Services:** **Leisure:** P **Off-site:** L R

ARBOIS — JURA

Vignes

av Gl-Leclerc, 39600
☎ 384661412 📠 384661412
e-mail: reservation@rsl39.com
web: www.jura-campings.com

Terraced site in an area famous for its wine and food.

dir: *E on D107 Mesnay road at stadium.*

Open: 16 Apr-2 Oct **Site:** 5HEC **For hire:**
Facilities: **Services:** **Off-site:** L P R

ARGENTIÈRE — HAUTE-SAVOIE

Glacier d'Argentière

161 chemin des Chosalets, 74400
☎ 450541736
e-mail: info@campingchamonix.com
web: www.campingchamonix.com

Set on terraced meadowland in a beautiful location at the foot of the Mont Blanc Massif. The site, which has been open since 1967, has views of Mont Blanc and the Chamonix Valley. Nearby are hiking and climbing.

dir: *1km S of Argentière. Off N506 towards Cableway Lognan/ Grandes Montets & 200m to site.*

GPS: 45.9745, 6.9231

Open: 15 May-Sep **Site:** 1.5HEC **For hire:**
Prices: 16.50 Mobile home hire 180 **Facilities:** **Services:** **Off-site:** P R

ARS-SUR-FORMANS — AIN

Bois de la Dame

chemin du Bois de la Dame, 01480
☎ 474007723

Separate car park for arrivals after 22.00hrs.

dir: *A6 exit Villefranche for Jassans-Riottier.*

Open: Apr-Sep **Site:** 1.5HEC **For hire:** **Facilities:** **Services:** **Leisure:** R **Off-site:**

FRANCE

AUTRANS ISÈRE

Joyeux Réveil

38880

476953344 476957298

e-mail: camping-au-joyeux-reveil@wanadoo.fr

web: www.camping-au-joyeux-reveil.fr

A beautiful location surrounded by woodland, with fine mountain views.

dir: *NE of town via rte de Montaud.*

Open: May-Sep **Site:** 1.5HEC **For hire:** **Prices:** 20-34 Mobile home hire 330-995 **Facilities:** Wi-fi Kids' Club Play Area **Services:** **Leisure:** P **Off-site:**

Le Vercors

Les Gaillards, 38880

476953188 476953682

e-mail: camping.le.vercors@wanadoo.fr

web: www.camping-du-vercors.fr

Ideal for summer or winter holidays, situated in the heart of the Vercors with easy access to skiing.

dir: *0.6km S via D106 towards Méaudre.*

Open: 20 May-20 Sep, Dec-Mar **Site:** 1HEC **For hire:** **Prices:** 14.50-18.20 Mobile home hire 300-640 **Facilities:** Wi-fi (charged) Play Area **Services:** **Leisure:** P **Off-site:** R

BARATIER HAUTES-ALPES

Verger

05200

492431587 492434981

web: www.campingleverger.fr

Terraced site in plantation of fruit trees with fine views of Alps. Divided into pitches.

dir: *From N94 drive 2.5km S of Embrun, 1.5km E on D40.*

Open: All Year. **Site:** 4HEC **For hire:** **Facilities:** **Services:** **Leisure:** P **Off-site:** L R

BELFORT TERRITOIRE-DE-BELFORT

Étang des Forges

The Camping and Caravanning Club The Friendly Club

rue du Général Béthouart, 90000

384225492 384227655

e-mail: contact@camping-belfort.com

web: www.camping-belfort.com

Situated on the banks of a pond in the regional nature reserve of Ballons des Vosges. Ideal terrain for hiking and not far from the historic city of Belfort.

C&CC Report *Sitting next to a pretty leisure lake and within walking distance of the city centre, this is a very convenient base for visiting historic Belfort and exploring the famous Ballons regional park. The Territoire de Belfort département is a land of contrasts between the Vosges and Jura mountain ranges, so L'Étang des Forges has much to offer, with day trips also into Switzerland or the wine areas of Southern Alsace and Germany. Also recommended is a boat trip through the spectacular Doubs Gorge, just over an hour's drive away on the Swiss border.*

dir: *A36 exit 13, follow centre ville, then Offemont, then camping.*

GPS: 47.6531, 6.8653

Open: 7 Apr-Sep **Site:** 3.5HEC **For hire:** **Prices:** 14.50-16.50 Mobile home hire 252-539 **Facilities:** Wi-fi (charged) Kids' Club Play Area **Services:** **Leisure:** P **Off-site:** L

BOURG-D'OISANS, LE ISÈRE

Camping-Caravaning le Vernis

38520

476800268

e-mail: levernis.camping@wanadoo.fr

web: www.oisans.com/levernis

Well-kept site at foot of mountain in summer skiing area. Walking, cycling and museums nearby.

dir: *2.5km of N91, rte de Briançon.*

Open: Jun-10 Sep **Site:** 1.5HEC **For hire:** **Prices:** 14-22 **Facilities:** Wi-fi Play Area **Services:** **Leisure:** P **Off-site:**

Cascade

rte de l'Alpe-d'Huez, 38520

476800242 476802263

e-mail: lacascade@wanadoo.fr

web: www.lacascadesarenne.com

Set at the foot of Alpe-d'Huez with a waterfall and modern, very well-kept sanitary arrangements. TV lounge, open fireplace and snacks/pizzas available. Booking recommended.

Open: 15 Dec-Sep **Site:** 2.5HEC **For hire:** **Facilities:** Wi-fi **Services:** **Leisure:** P R **Off-site:**

Facilities shower electric points for razors electric points for caravans motorvan service point parking by tents permitted compulsory separate car park shop **Services** café/restaurant bar Camping Gaz International gas other than Camping Gaz first aid facilities laundry **Leisure** swimming L-Lake P-Pool R-River S-Sea **Off-site** All facilities within 5km

Colporteur

le Mas du Plan, 38520
☎ 476791144 📠 476791149
e-mail: info@camping-colporteur.com
web: www.camping-colporteur.com

Situated 200m from the centre of Bourg-d'Oisans, in the centre of a plain surrounded by mountains. Activities for children.

Open: mid May-mid Sep **Site:** 4HEC **For hire:** **Facilities:** Wi-fi (charged) Play Area **Services:** **Leisure:** R **Off-site:** P

Rencontre du Soleil

The Camping and Caravanning Club The Friendly Club

rte de l'Alpe-d'Huez, 38520
☎ 476791222 📠 476802637
e-mail: rencontre.soleil@wanadoo.fr
web: www.alarencontredusoleil.com

Charming site in a lovely setting in the Dauphiné Alps at the foot of a mountain. Rustic common room with open fireplace. TV, playroom for children and a kids' club is available in July and August.

C&CC Report *A classic small family-run site – very friendly and in a spectacular alpine location. Bourg-d'Oisans is a thriving village on the main route to Briançon and Italy. This is a favourite haunt for the Tour de France and ideal base for exploring this outstanding region, with the Venosc and Ecrins National Parks close by. Rafting, canoeing, mountain biking, walking trips; visits to an alpine botanical garden, a hydro-electric station, a mountain railway and a mountain museum are all possible, locally.*

dir: *At foot of hairpin road to l'Alpe-d'Huez, off N91 in Le Bourg-d'Osians.*

Open: May-Sep **Site:** 1.6HEC **For hire:** **Facilities:** Wi-fi (charged) Kids' Club **Services:** **Leisure:** P **Off-site:** R

BOURG-EN-BRESSE — AIN

CM de Challes

5 allée du Centre Nautique, 01000
☎ 474453721 📠 474455995
e-mail: camping_municipal_bourgenbresse@wanadoo.fr

Set in a football ground near the swimming pool.

dir: *Signed from outskirts of town.*

Open: Apr-14 Oct **Site:** 2.7HEC **Prices:** 13.80-16.10 **Facilities:** Wi-fi Play Area **Services:** **Leisure:** P **Off-site:** L

BOURGET-DU-LAC, LE — SAVOIE

CM Ile aux Cygnes

73370
☎ 479250176 📠 479722825
e-mail: camping@lebourgetdulac.fr
web: www.lebourgetdulac.fr

A family site on the shore of the Lac du Bourget with plenty of recreational facilities and outdoor activities including sailing, cycling and hiking. First aid and kids' club available during July and August.

dir: *Via N514.*

Open: last wknd Apr-last wknd Sep **Site:** 4.5HEC **For hire:** **Prices:** 12.35-16.10 Mobile home hire 340-560 **Facilities:** Wi-fi Kids' Club Play Area **Services:** **Leisure:** L R **Off-site:**

BOURG-ST-MAURICE — SAVOIE

Versoyen

rte des Arcs, 73700
☎ 479070345 📠 479072541
e-mail: leversoyen@wanadoo.fr
web: www.leversoyen.com

Many secluded pitches in a wood with two communal sanitary blocks (one heated). Skiing facilities in winter.

dir: *Via RN90.*

Open: 28 May-2 Nov & 15 Dec-2 May **Site:** 4HEC **For hire:** **Facilities:** Wi-fi (charged) Play Area **Services:** **Off-site:** P R

BOUT-DU-LAC — HAUTE-SAVOIE

International du Lac Bleu

rte de la Plage, 74210
☎ 450443018 📠 450448435
e-mail: contact@camping-lac-bleu.com
web: www.camping-lac-bleu.com

Modern, well-kept site. Overflow area with own sanitary blocks.

dir: *On S shore of Lake Annecy via N508, opposite garage.*

Open: Apr-25 Sep **Site:** 4HEC **For hire:** **Facilities:** Wi-fi Kids' Club Play Area **Services:** **Leisure:** L P **Off-site:**

FRANCE

CHALEZEULE DOUBS

Plage

12 rte de Belfort, 25220
381880426 381505462
e-mail: contact@campingdebesancon.com
web: www.campingdebesancon.com
A modern site with good facilities near the main roads and close to the River Doubs. Swimming pool open from 20 June until end of August.
dir: *N83 towards Belfort.*
GPS: 47.2657, 6.0713
Open: Apr-Sep **Site:** 2.5HEC **For hire:** **Prices:** Mobile home hire 225-650 **Facilities:** Wi-fi Play Area **Services:** **Leisure:** P R **Off-site:**

CHAMONIX-MONT-BLANC HAUTE-SAVOIE

Cimes

28 rte des Tissieres, 74400
450535893
e-mail: infos@campinglescimesmontblanc.com
web: www.campinglescimesmontblanc.com
A wooded meadow at the foot of Mont Blanc Massif plus comfortable chalets to hire. Ideal for hiking and mountain tours.
GPS: 45.9022, 6.8367
Open: Jun-Sep **Site:** 0.8HEC **For hire:** **Prices:** 15.80 **Facilities:** Wi-fi **Services:** **Leisure:** R **Off-site:** L

Deux Glaciers

80 rte des Tissières, 74400
450531584 450559081
e-mail: glaciers@clubinternet.fr
web: www.les2glaciers.com
A glacial stream runs through the site. Pitches shaded by trees, very modern, well-kept sanitary installations. Rustic common room with open fires.
dir: *Off N506 towards road underpass, 250m to site.*
Open: All Year. **Site:** 16HEC **Facilities:** **Services:** **Off-site:**

Mer de Glace

200 chemin de la Bagna, 74400
450534403 450536083
e-mail: info@chamonix-camping.com
web: www.chamonix-camping.com
A forested setting with individual pitches separated by hedges or trees and with wonderful views of the Mont Blanc mountain range. Leisure facilities include walking, hiking, climbing, water sports and mountain biking trails.
dir: *2km NE to Les Praz. On approach to village (from Chamonix) turn right under railway bridge if less than 2.4m in height or continue to rdbt, right over railway line. After 500m right & right again, 200m on left.*
GPS: 45.9383, 6.89
Open: 27 Apr-Sep **Site:** 2.2HEC **Prices:** 20-24.10 **Facilities:** Wi-fi Play Area **Services:** **Off-site:** P

CHAMPAGNOLE JURA

CM Boyse

rue G-Vallery, 39300
384520032 384520116
e-mail: camping.boyse@wanadoo.fr
web: www.camping.champagnole.com
Clean and tidy site in the grounds of a municipal swimming pool with asphalt drives and divided into pitches.
dir: *Onto D5 before town & 1.3km to site.*
Open: Jun-15 Sep **Site:** 8HEC **For hire:** **Facilities:** **Services:** **Leisure:** P R

CHÂTEAUROUX-LES-ALPES HAUTES-ALPES

Cariamas

Fontmolines, 05380
492432263
e-mail: cariamas@hotmail.fr
web: les.cariamas.free.fr
On a meadow in an attractive mountain setting beside the River Durance and near to the Ecrin National Park.
dir: *1.5km SE.*
Open: Apr-Oct **Site:** 6HEC **For hire:** **Prices:** 16.75-20.75 Mobile home hire 390-630 **Facilities:** Wi-fi Play Area **Services:** **Leisure:** P **Off-site:** L R

FRANCE

CHÂTILLON JURA

Domaine de l'Epinette

15 rue de l'Epinette, 39130

☎ 384257144 📠 384257125

e-mail: contact@domaine-epinette.com

web: www.domaine-epinette.com

A small campsite situated beside the Ain river in an area of lakes and mountains. Kids' club available in July and August.

Open: 16 Jun-9 Sep **Site:** 7HEC **For hire:** **Prices:** 17-27 **Facilities:** Wi-fi Kids' Club Play Area **Services:** **Leisure:** P R

Grisière et Europe Vacances

39130

☎ 384258048 📠 384252234

e-mail: bailly@la-grisiere.com

web: www.la-grisiere.com

Fenced in meadowland with some trees, sloping down to the Grand Lac. The site is guarded during July and August.

dir: *From village centre off N78 onto D118 towards Châtel-de-Joux for 0.8km.*

Open: May-Sep **Site:** 11HEC **For hire:** **Facilities:** **Services:** **Leisure:** L

CHOISY HAUTE-SAVOIE

Chez Langin

74330

☎ 450774165 📠 450774101

e-mail: contact@chezlangin.com

web: www.chezlangin.com

Pleasant wooded surroundings. Nature trails, play areas, petting zoo.

dir: *1.3km NE via D3.*

Open: 14 Apr-Sep **Site:** 3HEC **For hire:** **Facilities:** **Services:** **Leisure:** P

CLUSAZ, LA HAUTE-SAVOIE

Plan du Fernuy

1800, rte des Confins, 74220

☎ 450024475 📠 450326702

e-mail: info@planduferuy.com

web:

Well placed for skiing or walking. Airing rooms. 30 ski-lifts nearby and several cable cars.

dir: *Off N50 E of La Clusaz towards Les Confins, 2km to site.*

Open: 17 Jun-2 Sep & 20 Dec-Apr **Site:** 1.31HEC **For hire:** **Facilities:** **Services:** **Leisure:** P **Off-site:**

CHORANCHE ISÈRE

Gouffre de la Croix

38680

☎ 476360713 📠 476360713

e-mail: camping.gouffre.croix@wanadoo.fr

web: www.camping-choranche.com

A quiet and charming location beside the River Bourne with fine views of the surrounding mountains and modern facilities.

dir: *A49 exit St-Marcellin or Hostun.*

Open: 30 Apr-15 Sep **Site:** 2.5HEC **For hire:** **Prices:** 14-22 Mobile home hire 325-450 **Facilities:** Play Area **Services:** **Leisure:** R

CORMORANCHE-SUR-SAÔNE AIN

Camping du Lac

365 rte du Lac, 01290

☎ 385239710 📠 385239711

e-mail: contact@lac-cormoranche.com

web: www.lac-cormoranche.com

8km South of Mâcon, the site is situated on a lake suitable for swimming, fishing and water sports. The beach is supervised and cleaned daily. Kids' club in July and August. Dogs accepted, restrictions apply.

dir: *A6 exit 29 Mâcon Sud then towards Cormoranche-sur-Saône.*

GPS: 46.2519, 4.8259

Open: May-Sep **Site:** 4.5HEC **For hire:** **Prices:** 15.10-17.60 Mobile home hire 220-485 **Facilities:** Wi-fi (charged) Kids' Club Play Area **Services:** **Leisure:** L **Off-site:**

CLAIRVAUX-LES-LACS JURA

Fayolan

39130

☎ 384258852 📠 384252620

e-mail: reservation@rsl39.com

web: www.jura-campings.com

Wooded location beside the lake. Lots of activities including aerobics, kayaking, and evening shows.

dir: *1.2km SE via D118.*

Open: 28 Apr-9 Sep **Site:** 17HEC **For hire:** **Prices:** 17-41 **Facilities:** Wi-fi Kids' Club Play Area **Services:** **Leisure:** L P **Off-site:**

FRANCE

DIVONNE-LES-BAINS AIN

Le Fleutron

Quartier Villard, 2465 Vie de l'Etraz, 01220
☎ 442204725 🖷 442950363
e-mail: info@homair.com
web: www.homair.co.uk

Set in wooded surroundings with large individual pitches.

dir: *35km from N5.*

Open: Apr-15 Oct **Site:** 8HEC **For hire:** **Prices:** 15-26 Mobile home hire 224-987 **Facilities:** Wi-fi (charged) Kids' Club Play Area **Services:** **Leisure:** P **Off-site:** L

DOLE JURA

Pasquier

18 chemin V et G Thévenot, 39100
☎ 384720261 🖷 384792344
e-mail: camping-pasquier@wanadoo.fr
web: www.camping-le-pasquier.com

Meadow site near River Doubs. Close to city centre.

dir: *0.9km SE of town centre.*

Open: 15 Mar-15 Oct **Site:** 2HEC **For hire:** **Facilities:** Wi-fi (charged) Play Area **Services:** **Leisure:** P R **Off-site:** L

DOUCIER JURA

Domaine de Chalain

39130
☎ 384257878 🖷 384257006
e-mail: chalain@chalain.com
web: www.chalain.com

A large site beside Lake Chalain with a variety of recreational facilities.

dir: *3km NE.*

GPS: 46.6642, 5.8139

Open: 27 Apr-18 Sep **Site:** 20HEC **For hire:** **Prices:** 21-39 Mobile home hire 240-658 **Facilities:** Wi-fi (charged) Kids' Club Play Area **Services:** **Leisure:** L P **Off-site:** R

DOUSSARD HAUTE-SAVOIE

Ferme de la Serraz

rue de la Poste, 74210
☎ 450443068
e-mail: info@campinglaserraz.com
web: www.campinglaserraz.com

Modern site divided into pitches with beautiful views of the surrounding mountains.

dir: *At E end of village, N508 onto D181 for 0.5km.*

Open: May-15 Sep **Site:** 4HEC **For hire:** **Prices:** 13.80-47.80 Mobile home hire 279-898 **Facilities:** Wi-fi (charged) Kids' Club Play Area **Services:** **Leisure:** P **Off-site:** L R

Ravoire

The Camping and Caravanning Club The Friendly Club

rte de la Ravoire, 74210
☎ 450443780 🖷 450329060
e-mail: info@camping-la-ravoire.fr
web: www.camping-la-ravoire.fr

A well-appointed, modern site on level ground 0.8km from Lake Annecy. Spectacular mountain views.

C&CC Report *Small, high quality, welcoming and relaxed, with facilities open all season, La Ravoire has been developed into a site that is much loved, both by couples and families who enjoy mountains and lakes, as well as the more adventurous who can join in with activities booked through reception. Picturesque Annecy is well worth a visit, as is a day trip to Chamonix and Mont Blanc.*

dir: *Autoroute exit Annecy Sud for Albertville, N508 to Duingt & signed.*

Open: 15 May-6 Sep **Site:** 2.3HEC **For hire:** **Prices:** 24.50-27.40 **Facilities:** Wi-fi Play Area **Services:** **Leisure:** P **Off-site:** L

ENTRE-DEUX-GUIERS ISÈRE

Arc en Ciel

37 chemin de Berges, 38380
☎ 476660697 🖷 476660697
e-mail: info@camping-arc-en-ciel.com
web: www.camping-arc-en-ciel.com

A wooded location by the river with well-shaded pitches.

dir: *On D520, 300m from N6.*

Open: 15 Apr-15 Oct **Site:** 1.2HEC **For hire:** **Prices:** 15-16.80 Mobile home hire 210-504 **Facilities:** Play Area **Services:** **Leisure:** P R **Off-site:**

FRANCE

FERRIÈRE-D'ALLEVARD — ISÈRE

CM Neige et Nature

chemin de Montarmand, 38580
476451984
e-mail: contact@neige-nature.fr
web: www.neige-nature.fr

A beautiful location with spectacular mountain views and modern facilities.

dir: *From Allevard D525A towards Le Pleynet.*

Open: 15 May-15 Sep **Site:** 1.2HEC **For hire:** **Prices:** 15-17.60 Mobile home hire 315-550 **Facilities:** Wi-fi **Services:** **Leisure:** P R **Off-site:**

GAP — HAUTES-ALPES

Alpes Dauphiné

rte Napoleon (RN85), 05000
492512995 492535892
e-mail: info@alpesdauphine.com
web: www.alpesdauphine.com

With panoramic views of the surrounding mountains, the site is in a natural meadowland setting with shaded pitches. Facilities include a weekly entertainment programme and a kids' club in July and August.

Open: 15 Apr-25 Oct **Site:** 6HEC **For hire:** **Facilities:** Wi-fi Kids' Club Play Area **Services:** **Leisure:** P

GRESSE-EN-VERCORS — ISÈRE

4 Saisons

38650
476343027
web: www.camping-les4saisons.com

A picturesque mountain setting with good facilities.

dir: *A51 Grenoble-Sisteron exit at Monestier de Clermont, follow signs Gresse-en-Vercors.*

GPS: 44.8966, 5.5556

Open: May-Sep & 20 Dec-15 Mar **Site:** 2.2HEC **For hire:** **Prices:** 15.90-17.50 Mobile home hire 330-660 **Facilities:** Wi-fi Play Area **Services:** **Leisure:** P **Off-site:** R

GUILLESTRE — HAUTES-ALPES

Camping la Rochette

rte des Campings, 05600
492450215
e-mail: guillestre@aol.com
web: www.campingguillestre.com

Located in the French Alps, quiet site with shaded pitches. A range of leisure facilities are available close by.

dir: *Access from RN91, RN85 or RN94.*

GPS: 44.6589, 6.6375

Open: 15 May-Sep **Site:** 4.5HEC **For hire:** **Prices:** 12.60-15.30 Mobile home hire 255-340 **Facilities:** Wi-fi (charged) Play Area **Services:** **Leisure:** P R **Off-site:**

Villard

Le Villard, 05600
492450654 492450052
e-mail: info@camping-levillard.com
web: www.camping-levillard.com

A magnificent location between the Ecrins and Queyras regional parks with good facilities.

dir: *2km W via D902A & N4 rte de Gap.*

Open: 15 Dec-1 Nov **Site:** 3HEC **For hire:** **Facilities:** Kids' Club Play Area **Services:** **Leisure:** P R **Off-site:** L

HUANNE-MONTMARTIN — DOUBS

Bois de Reveuge

25680
381843860 381844404
web: www.campingduboisdereveuge.com

A terraced site in a 20-hectare park surrounded by the Vosges and Jura mountains with good recreational facilities.

dir: *A36 exit Baumes-les-Dames.*

Open: 26 Apr-11 Sep **Site:** 24HEC **For hire:** **Facilities:** **Services:** **Leisure:** L P

ISLE-SUR-LE-DOUBS, L' — DOUBS

Camping les Lûmes

10 rue des Lûmes, 25250

381927305 381927305

e-mail: contact@les-lumes.com

web: les-lumes.com

The site lies close to the town. Common room with TV.

dir: *Off N83. Entrance near bridge over the River Doubs.*

Open: Apr-1 Oct **Site:** 1.5HEC **For hire:** **Prices:** 13-18 Mobile home hire 343-480 **Facilities:** Wi-fi Play Area **Services:** **Leisure:** R **Off-site:**

LANDRY — SAVOIE

Eden

73210

479076181 479076217

e-mail: info@camping-eden.net

web: www.camping-eden.net

A modern site with excellent sports and sanitary facilities, situated in the heart of the Savoie Olympic area.

Open: 18 Dec-8 May & Jun-15 Sep **Site:** 2.7HEC **For hire:** **Facilities:** **Services:** **Leisure:** P R **Off-site:**

LONS-LE-SAUNIER — JURA

Marjorie

640 bld de l'Europe, 39000

384242694 384240840

e-mail: info@camping-marjorie.com

web: www.camping-marjorie.com

Clean, tidy site with tent and caravan sections separated by a stream. Caravan pitches are gravelled and surrounded by hedges. Heated common room with TV, reading area and kitchen.

dir: *Near swimming stadium on outskirts of town.*

Open: Apr-15 Oct **Site:** 9HEC **For hire:** **Prices:** 15.95-21.90 Mobile home hire 240-630 **Facilities:** Kids' Club Play Area **Services:** **Off-site:** P

LUGRIN — HAUTE-SAVOIE

Myosotis

28 chemin du Grand Tronc, 74500

450760759

e-mail: campinglesmyosotis@wanadoo.fr

web: www.camping-les-myosotis.com

A terraced site with fine views over the lake and surrounding mountains.

dir: *Via D321.*

GPS: 46.3992, 6.6644

Open: 10 May-20 Sep **Site:** 0.9HEC **For hire:** **Prices:** 12.50-13.60 **Facilities:** **Services:** **Off-site:** L

Rys

rte le Rys, 74500

627491535 450760575

e-mail: jeanmichel.blanc@wanadoo.fr

Calm shady site with panoramic views of the lake and mountains. Ten minutes walk from the beach

dir: *Signed W of town.*

Open: 30 Apr-1 Oct **Site:** 2.3HEC **For hire:** **Prices:** 12-14 Mobile home hire 300-500 **Facilities:** **Services:** **Off-site:** L

Vieille Église

53 rte des Prés Parrau, 74500

450760195 450761312

e-mail: campingvieilleeglise@wanadoo.fr

web: www.camping-vieille-eglise.com

On rising meadowland between lake and mountains with good views. Close to lake Léman and its beaches.

dir: *D24 to Neuvecelle, onto D21, 1km on right after Maxilly.*

GPS: 46.4006, 6.6467

Open: 10 Apr-20 Oct **Site:** 1.5HEC **For hire:** **Prices:** 16.20-19.90 Mobile home hire 320-785 **Facilities:** Wi-fi (charged) Play Area **Services:** **Leisure:** P **Off-site:** L

MALBUISSON — DOUBS

Fuvettes

25160

381693150 381697046

e-mail: les-fuvettes@wanadoo.fr

web: www.camping-fuvettes.com

Mainly level site with some terraces at an altitude of 900 metres in the Jura mountains, gently sloping towards a lake.

dir: *0.5km S on D437.*

Open: Apr-Sep **Site:** 6HEC **For hire:** **Facilities:** Wi-fi (charged) Kids' Club Play Area **Services:** **Leisure:** L P

MARIGNY — JURA

Pergola

39130

384257003 384257596

e-mail: contact@lapergola.com

web: www.lapergola.com

Situated close to waterfalls and beautiful villages, a well-equipped, terraced family site with direct access to the lake.

dir: *S of Marigny off D27.*

GPS: 46.6769, 5.7814

Open: 29 Apr-9 Sep **Site:** 12HEC **For hire:** **Prices:** 19-38 Mobile home hire 297-980 **Facilities:** Wi-fi (charged) Kids' Club Play Area **Services:** **Leisure:** L P **Off-site:** R

MATAFELON-GRANGES — AIN

Gorges de l'Oignin

rue du Lac, 01580

474768097 474768097

e-mail: camping.lesgorgesdeloignin@wanadoo.fr

web: www.gorges-de-loignin.com

Rural site on the banks of a lake surrounded by low mountains. Kids' club available during July and August.

dir: *A404 exit 9, site signed after 1.6km.*

GPS: 46.2553, 5.5569

Open: 15 Apr-25 Sep **Site:** 2.6HEC **For hire:** **Prices:** 13.60-22.80 Mobile home hire 236-582 **Facilities:** Wi-fi Kids' Club Play Area **Services:** **Leisure:** L P **Off-site:** R

MÉAUDRE — ISÈRE

Buissonnets

38112

476952104

e-mail: camping-les-buissonnets@wanadoo.fr

web: www.camping-les-buissonnets.com

A quiet, friendly site in the heart of the Vercors regional park, with modern sanitary blocks and a range of summer and winter recreational facilities.

dir: *200m from village centre.*

Open: 15 Dec-1 Nov **Site:** 2.7HEC **For hire:** **Facilities:** **Services:** **Off-site:** P R

MESNOIS — JURA

Beauregard

The Camping and Caravanning Club — The Friendly Club

2 Grande Rue, 39130

384483251 384483251

e-mail: reception@juracampingbeuregard.com

web: www.juracampingbeauregard.com

Situated by the River Ain, spacious pitches divided by hedges. Both indoor and outdoor swimming pools are for guests' use.

C&CC Report *A real gem of a family-run site – friendly, attractive and very well-kept, with some excellent pitches and a very good wash block, all set in the beautiful Jura countryside, an area of lakes, waterfalls and hills. Lots of fresh air, open spaces and informality. For a day trip, Switzerland is just a short drive away.*

Open: Apr-Sep **Site:** 6HEC **For hire:** **Prices:** 18-25 Mobile home hire 300-650 **Facilities:** Wi-fi (charged) Play Area **Services:** **Leisure:** P R **Off-site:** L

MESSERY — HAUTE-SAVOIE

Relais du Léman

74140

450947111 450947766

e-mail: info@relaisduleman.com

web: www.relaisduleman.com

Well-equipped site in a wooded location on the shore of Lac Léman.

dir: *1.5km SW via D25.*

Open: Apr-Sep **Site:** 3.5HEC **For hire:** **Facilities:** Wi-fi Play Area **Services:** **Leisure:** P **Off-site:** L P

MEYRIEU-LES-ÉTANGS ISÈRE

Moulin

38440
474593034 474583612
e-mail: basedeloisirs.du.moulin@wanadoo.fr
web: www.camping-meyrieu.com
A quiet rural setting with good recreational facilities.
dir: *On D552 between Vienne & Bourgoin-Jallieu.*
Open: 15 Apr-Sep **Site:** 1.5HEC **For hire:** **Facilities:** **Services:** **Leisure:** L

MIRIBEL-LES-ÉCHELLES ISÈRE

Balcon de Chartreuse

950 chemin de la Foret, 38380
476552853 476552853
e-mail: info@camping-balcondechartreuse.com
web: www.camping-balcondechartreuse.com
A peaceful site in the heart of the Parc Régional de Chartreuse, with fine views of the surrounding mountains.
dir: *400m from village centre.*
Open: Apr-Oct **Site:** 2.5HEC **For hire:** **Prices:** 11.60-14.70 Mobile home hire 230-399 **Facilities:** **Services:** **Leisure:** P **Off-site:**

MONTMAUR HAUTES-ALPES

Mon Repos

05400
592580314
e-mail: campingmonrepos@gmail.com
Generally well-kept site on wooded terrain with shaded pitches.
dir: *1km E on D937 & D994.*
Open: May-Sep **Site:** 7HEC **For hire:** **Facilities:** **Services:** **Leisure:** L R

MONTREVEL-EN-BRESSE AIN

Plaine Tonique

Base de Plein Air, 01340
474308052 474308077
e-mail: plaine.tonique@wanadoo.fr
web: www.laplainetonique.com
A well-equipped site divided into a series of self contained sections beside the lake. Entrance closed between 22.00 and 07.00 hrs.
dir: *0.5km E on D28.*
Open: Apr-24 Sep **Site:** 17HEC **For hire:** **Facilities:** **Services:** **Leisure:** L P **Off-site:** R

MURS-ET-GELIGNIEUX AIN

Ile de la Comtesse

rte des Abrets, 01300
479872333 479872333
e-mail: camping.comtesse@wanadoo.fr
web: www.ile-de-la-comtesse.com
A stunning natural setting beneath the Alps next to Lake Cuchet (part of the Rhône), with direct access to the water.
dir: *A43 exit 10, D592 to La Bruyere, site off route to Belley.*
Open: 15 May-15 Sep **Site:** 3HEC **For hire:** **Facilities:** Wi-fi (charged) Kids' Club Play Area **Services:** **Leisure:** P R **Off-site:** L

NEYDENS HAUTE-SAVOIE

Colombière

74160
450351314 450351340
e-mail: la.colombiere@wanadoo.fr
web: www.camping-la-colombiere.com
A pleasant, friendly site with good recreational facilities.
dir: *Via A40.*
Open: Apr-Sep **Site:** 2.2HEC **For hire:** **Facilities:** **Services:** **Leisure:** P **Off-site:** R

ORNANS DOUBS

Chanet

9 chemin de Chanet, 25290
381622344 381621397
e-mail: contact@lechanet.com
web: www.lechanet.com
Comfortable site with good facilities, including an environmentally-friendly swimming pool, in the peaceful Loue Valley. Wi-fi is free for the first hour.
dir: *1.5km SW on D241, green signs.*
Open: Apr-Oct **Site:** 2.2HEC **For hire:** **Prices:** 15-22 Mobile home hire 250-640 **Facilities:** Wi-fi Kids' Club Play Area **Services:** **Leisure:** P **Off-site:** R

FRANCE

Facilities shower electric points for razors electric points for caravans motorvan service point parking by tents permitted compulsory separate car park shop **Services** café/restaurant bar Camping Gaz International gas other than Camping Gaz first aid facilities laundry **Leisure** swimming L-Lake P-Pool R-River S-Sea **Off-site** All facilities within 5km

ORPIERRE — HAUTES-ALPES

Princes d'Orange

05700

☎ 492662253 📠 492663108

e-mail: campingorpierre@wanadoo.fr

web: www.campingorpierre.com

The site lies on a meadow with terraces.

dir: *N75 exit Eyguians onto D30.*

GPS: 44.3108, 5.6965

Open: Apr-Oct **Site:** 20HEC **For hire:** **Prices:** 19.50-26.50 Mobile home hire 370-710 **Facilities:** Wi-fi Kids' Club Play Area **Services:** **Leisure:** P **Off-site:** L R

OUNANS — JURA

Plage Blanche

The Camping and Caravanning Club The Friendly Club

39380

☎ 384376963 📠 384376021

e-mail: reservation@la-plage-blanche.com

web: www.la-plage-blanche.com

Pleasant location with spacious pitches on the banks of the river Loue, with good recreational facilities. Outdoor activity centre, canoe and mountain bike hire nearby.

C&CC Report *Stretching along the banks of the river Loue, La Plage Blanche provides the perfect spot for outdoor pursuits. And it's not just this enviable location in the Jura which sets La Plage Blanche apart, but the carefully planned out and lovingly looked after grounds and facilities too. Children will be in their element with canoeing, treetop ropes and guided bike rides all on the doorstep. This spacious site caters for more peaceful moments too; take a quiet walk in the forest or fish in the private lake. Off-site you could visit the historic town of Dole, the nearby UNESCO world heritage Royal Saltworks site, or the Haut-Jura National Regional Park.*

dir: *A39 exit 7 (from S), exit 6 (from N) signed Pontarlier then Ounans.*

Open: Apr-Sep **Site:** 7HEC **For hire:** **Prices:** 13-22 Mobile home hire 350-690 **Facilities:** Wi-fi Kids' Club Play Area **Services:** **Leisure:** P R **Off-site:**

PARCEY — JURA

Bords de Loue

chemin du Val d'Amour, 39100

☎ 384710382 📠 384710342

e-mail: contact@jura-camping.fr

web: www.jura-camping.fr

A quiet site on the River Loue.

dir: *1.5km from village centre via N5, signed.*

Open: 20 Apr-10 Sep **Site:** 18HEC **For hire:** **Facilities:** **Services:** **Leisure:** P R **Off-site:**

PASSY — HAUTE-SAVOIE

Village Center Les Iles

245 rte des Lacs, 74190

☎ 499572121 📠 467516389

e-mail: contact@village-center.com

web: www.village-center.com/rhones-alpes/camping-montagne-iles.php

With unrestricted views of Mont Blanc, Les Iles is located on the edge of a lake, 3km from the centre of Passy.

dir: *A41 exit 21.*

GPS: 45.9236, 6.6506

Open: 16 Dec-11 Mar & 27 Apr-9 Sep **Site:** 4.5HEC **For hire:** **Prices:** 15-19 Mobile home hire 175-679 **Facilities:** Wi-fi (charged) Kids' Club Play Area **Services:** **Off-site:** L P

PATORNAY — JURA

Moulin

39130

☎ 384483121 📠 384447121

e-mail: contact@camping-moulin.com

web: www.camping-moulin.com

A modern site on a level meadow in a peaceful, wooded location on the banks of the River Ain.

dir: *NE via N78 rte de Clairvaux-les-Lacs.*

Open: 28 Apr-16 Sep **Site:** 5HEC **For hire:** **Prices:** 17.50-30 Mobile home hire 200-600 **Facilities:** Wi-fi (charged) Kids' Club Play Area **Services:** **Leisure:** P R **Off-site:** L

PLAGNE-MONTCHAVIN — SAVOIE

Montchavin les Coches

73210

☎ 479078323 📠 479078018

e-mail: campingmontchavin@wanadoo.fr

web: www.montchavin-lescoches.com

A summer and winter site overlooking the Tarentaise Valley with modern facilities.

dir: *RN90 then D225. In Bellentre follow direction Montchavin les Coches.*

GPS: 45.5566, 6.7365

Open: Nov-Sep **Site:** 1.33HEC **For hire:** **Prices:** 15 Mobile home hire 360-630 **Facilities:** Wi-fi (charged) Play Area **Services:** **Off-site:** P R

FRANCE

PONT-DE-VAUX — AIN

Ripettes

The Camping and Caravanning Club — The Friendly Club

St Benigne, Chavannes sur Reyssouze, 01190

385306658

e-mail: info@camping-les-ripettes.com

web: www.camping-les-ripettes.com

Small, friendly site with very large pitches, in peaceful countryside, but convenient for A6 motorway.

C&CC Report *A small, very well-kept and very pretty site, Les Ripettes' friendly atmosphere sets you right in the calm of the south Burgundy countryside. While the smallest pitches are big by any standards and the biggest are truly vast, the very experienced owners, Marc and Isabelle, are keen to maintain the cosy and convivial atmosphere. Great for bird spotters too.*

dir: *At Pont-de-Vaux take D2 signed Saint Triviers de Courtes. After 4km take next left after water tower & immediately left again.*

GPS: 46.4446, 4.9806

Open: Apr-Sep **Site:** 2.5HEC **For hire:** **Facilities:** Wi-fi Play Area **Services:** **Leisure:** P **Off-site:** R

Rives du Soleil

Port de Fleurville, 01190

385303365 385303123

e-mail: info@rivesdusoleil.com

web: www.rivesdusoleil.com

A family site beside the River Saône with good facilities. Kids' club available in July and August.

dir: *3km from Pont-de-Vaux via N6.*

GPS: 46.4453, 4.8985

Open: 20 Apr-15 Oct **Site:** 7HEC **For hire:** **Prices:** 23-26 **Facilities:** Wi-fi Kids' Club Play Area **Services:** **Leisure:** P R

PORT-SUR-SAÔNE — HAUTE-SAÔNE

CM Maladière

70170

384915132 384781809

A quiet, comfortable site with modern facilities, close to the River Saône.

dir: *S on D6, between River Saône & canal.*

Open: 15 May-15 Sep **Site:** 2HEC **Facilities:** **Services:** **Off-site:** P R

ROCHETTE, LA — SAVOIE

Lac St-Clair

73110

479257355 479257825

e-mail: campinglarochette@orange.fr

web: www.la-rochette.com

At the foot of the Belledonne mountains, 1km from a lake with good fishing.

dir: *Via D925B Grenoble-Albertville.*

Open: Jun-Sep **Site:** 3HEC **For hire:** **Facilities:** **Services:** **Leisure:** L **Off-site:** P

ROSIÈRE-DE-MONTVALEZAN, LA — SAVOIE

Camping "La Forêt"

73700

479068621 479401625

e-mail: contact@camping-larosiere.com

web: www.camping-larosiere.com

A peaceful site in pleasant wooded surroundings, with modern facilities. Snacks and regional specialities are available.

dir: *2km S via N90 towards Bourg-St-Maurice.*

GPS: 45.6234, 6.8555

Open: All Year. **Site:** 2.7HEC **For hire:** **Prices:** 14.90-19.40 Mobile home hire 395-745 **Facilities:** Wi-fi **Services:** **Leisure:** P **Off-site:** R

ROUGEMONT — DOUBS

Val de Bonnal

Bonnal, 25680

381869087 381860392

e-mail: val-de-bonnal@wanadoo.fr

web: www.camping-valdebonnal.fr

Quiet woodland site beside the River Ognon. Supervised swimming in lake with beach. Kids' club available in July and August.

dir: *RN19 exit at Vesoul onto D9 (Villersexel), exit at Esprels onto D87 towards Bonnal.*

GPS: 47.5052, 6.3519

Open: 6 May-7 Sep **Site:** 15HEC **For hire:** **Prices:** 25.50-45 Mobile home hire 450-990 **Facilities:** Wi-fi (charged) Kids' Club Play Area **Services:** **Leisure:** L P R

RUMILLY HAUTE-SAVOIE

Camping le Madrid

rte de Saint-Felix, 74150
450011257 450012949
e-mail: contact@camping-le-madrid.com
web: www.camping-le-madrid.com

Close to the Massif des Bauges Regional Park, a site with spacious pitches. Leisure facilities include a kids' club in July and August.

GPS: 45.8411, 5.9629

Open: All Year. **Site:** 3HEC **For hire:** **Prices:** 15-17 Mobile home hire 400-600 **Facilities:** Wi-fi (charged) Kids' Club Play Area **Services:** **Leisure:** P **Off-site:** L R

ST-CLAIR-DU-RHÔNE ISÈRE

Daxia

rte du Péage, D4 - av du Plateau des Frères, 38370
474563920 474564557
e-mail: info@campingledaxia.com
web: www.campingledaxia.com

A riverside site with good sanitary and recreational facilities.

dir: *Via N7/A7.*

Open: Apr-Sep **Site:** 7.5HEC **For hire:** **Facilities:** **Services:** **Leisure:** L P R

ST-CLAUDE JURA

Camping du Martinet

39200
384450040
e-mail: contact@camping-saint-claude.fr
web: www.camping-saint-claude.fr

A wooded location close to the Centre Nautique.

dir: *2km SE beside river.*

GPS: 46.3716, 5.8724

Open: May-Sep **Site:** 3HEC **Prices:** 10.30-12.80 **Facilities:** Wi-fi Play Area **Services:** **Leisure:** R **Off-site:** P

ST-GERVAIS-LES-BAINS HAUTE-SAVOIE

Dômes de Miage

197 rte des Contamines, 74170
450934596 450781075
e-mail: info@camping-mont-blanc.com
web: www.camping-mont-blanc.com

On a beautiful wooded plateau with fine views of the surrounding mountains.

dir: *2km S on D902.*

Open: May-12 Sep **Site:** 2.5HEC **For hire:** **Facilities:** Wi-fi Play Area **Services:** **Off-site:** P

ST-JEAN-DE-COUZ SAVOIE

International la Bruyère

73160
479657911
e-mail: camping-labruyere@orange.fr
web: www.campingsavoie.com

Wooded surroundings close to the Grande Chartreuse range with a variety of sports facilities.

dir: *15km S of Chambery, towards Les Echelles Valence.*

GPS: 45.4567, 5.8125

Open: 15 May-Sep **Site:** 1HEC **For hire:** **Prices:** 10.30 Mobile home hire 200-280 **Facilities:** Wi-fi Play Area **Services:** **Off-site:** P R

ST-JORIOZ HAUTE-SAVOIE

Europa

1444 rte d'Albertville, 74410
450685101 450685520
e-mail: info@camping-europa.com
web: www.camping-europa.com

Well-equipped site in picturesque surroundings close to Lake Annecy.

dir: *1.4km SE.*

Open: 25 Apr-19 Sep **Site:** 4.2HEC **For hire:** **Facilities:** **Services:** **Leisure:** P **Off-site:** L

International du Lac d'Annecy

1184 rte d'Albertville, 74410

450686793 450090122

e-mail: contact@camping-lac-annecy.com

web: www.camping-lac-annecy.com

Located 9km from Annecy and 400 metres from Lake Annecy with direct access to cycle paths. There are two swimming pools, leisure facilities and entertainment in high season.

dir: *N508 towards Albertville.*

GPS: 45.83, 6.182

Open: 8 May-15 Sep **Site:** 2.5HEC **For hire:** **Prices:** 15-28 Mobile home hire 300-740 **Facilities:** Wi-fi (charged) Kids' Club **Services:** **Leisure:** P **Off-site:** L

ST-LAURENT-EN-BEAUMONT — ISÈRE

Belvédère de l'Obiou

Lieu-dit les Egats, Rte Napoleon (RN 85), 38350

476304080 476304486

e-mail: info@camping-obiou.com

web: www.camping-obiou.com

Terraced meadow site in at the foot of mountains and in an area with several lakes. Basic supplies are available on-site.

dir: *1.6km from Ortsteil les Égâts on N85, signed.*

GPS: 44.8763, 5.8369

Open: 15 Apr-15 Oct **Site:** **For hire:** **Prices:** 13.50-18.50 Mobile home hire 294-616 **Facilities:** Wi-fi Play Area **Services:** **Leisure:** P **Off-site:** R

ST-MARTIN-SUR-LA-CHAMBRE — SAVOIE

Bois Joli

St Martin-sur-la-Chambre, 73130

479562128

e-mail: info@campingleboisjoli.com

web: www.campingleboisjoli.com

Well-kept site with pitches and individual washing cabins.

dir: *1km N of St-Avre, off N6-E70 via La Chambre.*

Open: 15 Apr-15 Oct **Site:** 4HEC **For hire:** **Facilities:** Wi-fi Play Area **Services:** **Leisure:** P **Off-site:** L

ST-PIERRE-DE-CHARTREUSE — ISÈRE

Martinière

rte du Col de Porte, 38380

476886036 476886910

e-mail: camping-de-martiniere@orange.fr

web: www.campingdemartiniere.com

Small family-run site set in the Chartreuse National Park with fine panoramic views. Restaurant open in July and August.

dir: *2km SW off D512.*

GPS: 45.3258, 5.7971

Open: 28 Apr-8 Sep **Site:** 2.5HEC **For hire:** **Prices:** 16-20.50 Mobile home hire 245-550 **Facilities:** Play Area **Services:** **Leisure:** P

SALLE-EN-BEAUMONT, LA — ISÈRE

Champ-Long

38350

476304181 476304721

e-mail: champlong38@orange.fr

web: www.camping-champlong.com

A beautiful Alpine setting at the entrance to the Ecrins park at an altitude of 700 metres.

dir: *1.5km NW off N85.*

GPS: 44.8556, 5.8451

Open: All Year. **Site:** 5.5HEC **For hire:** **Prices:** 14-16 Mobile home hire 390-560 **Facilities:** Wi-fi (charged) Play Area **Services:** **Leisure:** P **Off-site:** L R

SCIEZ — HAUTE-SAVOIE

Camping du Chatelet

658 chemin des Hutins Vieux, 74140

450725260 450723767

e-mail: info@camping-chatelet.com

web: www.camping-chatelet.com

Flat, grassy pitches, 500 metres from the shores of Lake Genève (Geneva).

GPS: 46.3409, 6.3970

Open: Apr-15 Oct **Site:** 3.2HEC **For hire:** **Prices:** 12.50-16.50 **Facilities:** Wi-fi (charged) Play Area **Services:** **Off-site:** L

FRANCE

SÉEZ — SAVOIE

Reclus

RN 90, 73700

479410105 479410105

e-mail: contact@campinglereclus.com

web: www.campinglereclus.com

Pleasant wooded location within easy reach of the ski slopes.

dir: *NW on N90.*

GPS: 45.6253, 6.7925

Open: All Year. **Site:** 2HEC **For hire:** **Prices:** 12.60-14.40 Mobile home hire 250-550 **Facilities:** Wi-fi Play Area **Services:** **Leisure:** R **Off-site:** L P

SERRES — HAUTES-ALPES

Barillons

05700

492671735

e-mail: camping.les.barillons@wanadoo.fr

Well-laid out with terraces.

dir: *1km SE on N75.*

Open: mid May-mid Sep **Site:** 3HEC **For hire:** **Prices:** 14.90-18.40 **Facilities:** Wi-fi (charged) Play Area **Services:** **Leisure:** P R **Off-site:** L

Domaine des 2 Soleils

05700

492670133 492670802

e-mail: dom.2.soleils@wanadoo.fr

web: www.domaine-2soleils.com

Well-kept terraced site in Buéch Valley.

dir: *S of town off N75, signed.*

Open: May-Sep **Site:** 12HEC **For hire:** **Facilities:** **Services:** **Leisure:** P **Off-site:** L R

SEVRIER — HAUTE-SAVOIE

Coeur du Lac

3233 RD1508, 74320

450524645 450190145

e-mail: info@aucoeurdulac.com

web: www.campingaucoeurdulac.com

Site adjacent to Lake Annecy with direct access to the lake, beach and cycle path and fine views of the Alps. Dogs permitted in low season.

dir: *Leave autoroute at Annecy in direction of Le Lac-Albertville.*

GPS: 45.8548, 6.1439

Open: Apr-Sep **Site:** 2.7HEC **For hire:** **Facilities:** Wi-fi (charged) Play Area **Services:** **Leisure:** L **Off-site:**

TALLOIRES — HAUTE-SAVOIE

Lanfonnet

948 rte d'Angon, 74290

450607212 450607212 & 450233882

e-mail: camping.le.lanfonnet@wanadoo.fr

web: www.camping-lanfonnet.com

A well-equipped site 100 metres from the lake.

dir: *1.5km SE.*

Open: May-Sep **Site:** 2.3HEC **For hire:** **Facilities:** Wi-fi **Services:** **Leisure:** L

THOISSEY — AIN

CM

01140

474040425

e-mail: campingthoissey@orange.fr

Situated between the rivers Saône and Chalaronne.

dir: *1km SW on D7.*

Open: Apr-Sep **Site:** 13HEC **For hire:** **Facilities:** Play Area **Services:** **Leisure:** P R **Off-site:**

TIGNES-LES-BRÉVIÈRES — SAVOIE

Camping Municipal des Brévières

rte des Ruines, 73320

684812250

e-mail: campingtignes@free.fr

A well-equipped site 1km from the centre of the village.

dir: *Signed from D902.*

Open: 15 Jun-15 Sep **Site:** 4.5HEC **Prices:** 13-15.40 **Facilities:** Play Area **Services:** **Off-site:** L P R

TREPT — ISÈRE

3 Lacs du Soleil

La Plaine, 38460

474929206 474929395

web: www.camping-les3lacsdusoleil.com

Situated at the gateway to the Alps, an undulating wooded area with small lakes.

dir: *2.5km W on D517.*

Open: May-10 Sep **Site:** 26HEC **For hire:** **Facilities:** **Services:** **Leisure:** L P

FRANCE

Site 6HEC (site size) grass sand stone little shade partly shaded mainly shaded motorvans accepted bungalows for hire mobile homes for hire tents for hire no dogs site fully accessible for wheelchairs
Prices amount quoted is per night, for 2 adults and car, plus tent or caravan Mobile home hire is a weekly rate.

VALLOUISE — HAUTES-ALPES

Camping Indigo Vallouise

05290

492233026

e-mail: vallouise@camping-indigo.com

web: www.camping-indigo.com

With views of the surrounding mountains, this site is in a natural setting bordered by two streams. Outdoor activities available locally are hiking and skiing. Kids' club available in July and August. Only 1 dog per pitch.

Open: 28 Jun-16 Sep **Site:** 6.5HEC **For hire:** **Prices:** 13.70-14.30 **Facilities:** Kids' Club Play Area **Services:** **Leisure:** P R **Off-site:**

VERNIOZ — ISÈRE

Kawan Resort Le Bontemps

5 Impasse du Bontemps, 38150

474578352 474578370

e-mail: info@camping-lebontemps.com

web: www.camping-lebontemps.com

A pleasantly landscaped site beside the River Varèze. Kids' club in high season.

dir: *N7 onto D131.*

Open: 31 Mar-Sep **Site:** 6HEC **For hire:** **Prices:** 19-26 Mobile home hire 420-714 **Facilities:** Wi-fi Kids' Club Play Area **Services:** **Leisure:** P R

VILLARD-DE-LANS — ISERE

L'Oursière

38250

476951477 476955811

e-mail: info@camping-oursiere.fr

web: www.camping-oursiere.fr

Peaceful site in the Vercors regional park. Summer and winter facilities.

dir: *N off D531 towards Grenoble.*

Open: 4 Dec-6 May & 22 May-Sep **Site:** 4.2HEC **For hire:** **Facilities:** Wi-fi Play Area **Services:** **Leisure:** R **Off-site:** P

VILLARS-LES-DOMBES — AIN

Camping Indigo Parc des Oiseaux

164 av des Nations, 01330

474980021 474980582

e-mail: parcdesoiseaux@camping-indigo.com

web: www.camping-indigo.com/fr/camping-nature-parc-des-oiseaux-dombes.html

Pleasant wooded site in the heart of the Dombes and 500 metres from Parc des Oiseaux, with spacious pitches and clean, modern facilities.

dir: *SW off N83.*

GPS: 45.9969, 5.0308

Open: 31 Mar-4 Nov **Site:** 4.5HEC **For hire:** **Prices:** 12.90-17.40 **Facilities:** Wi-fi Play Area **Services:** **Leisure:** P R **Off-site:**

ALSACE/LORRAINE

ANOULD — VOSGES

Acacias

88650

329571106

e-mail: contact@acaciascamp.com

web: www.acaciascamp.com

Pleasant surroundings with well-defined pitches in the heart of the Hautes-Vosges region.

dir: *NE of town centre towards ski slopes.*

Open: 5 Dec-5 Oct **Site:** 2.5HEC **For hire:** **Prices:** 11.20 Mobile home hire 450 **Facilities:** Wi-fi Play Area **Services:** **Leisure:** P **Off-site:** R

BAERENTHAL — MOSELLE

Ramstein Plage

Base de Baerenthal, Ramstein Plage, 57230

387065073 387065073

e-mail: camping.ramstein@wanadoo.fr

web: www.baerenthal.eu

The River Zinsel runs through this rural wooded site close to the border with Germany.

dir: *W via rue du Ramstein.*

Open: Apr-Sep **Site:** 14HEC **For hire:** **Facilities:** Wi-fi (charged) Play Area **Services:** **Leisure:** L P **Off-site:** R

FRANCE

BIESHEIM — HAUT-RHIN

Ile du Rhin

Zone Touristique, 68600
389725795 389721421
e-mail: camping@paysdebrisach.fr
web: www.campingiledurhin.com

On the Ile du Rhin, between the Canal d'Alsace and the River Rhine in pleasant wooded surroundings.

dir: *From Colmar N415 to Rhine bridge.*

Open: early Apr-early Oct **Site:** 3HEC **For hire:** **Facilities:** **Services:** **Off-site:** P R

BRESSE, LA — VOSGES

Belle Hutte

88250
329254975
e-mail: camping-belle-hutte@wanadoo.fr
web: www.camping-belle-hutte.com

Terraced site beside the River Moselotte.

dir: *D34 towards Col de la Schlucht.*

Open: Jan-15 Nov & 15-31 Dec **Site:** 5HEC **For hire:** **Prices:** 21.62-23.72 **Facilities:** Wi-fi (charged) Play Area **Services:** **Leisure:** P R **Off-site:** L

BUSSANG — VOSGES

Domaine de Champé

14 Les Champs Navés, 88540
329616151 329615690
e-mail: info@domaine-de-champe.com
web: www.domaine-de-champe.com

Pleasant surroundings beside the River Moselle.

dir: *On N57.*

Open: All Year. **Site:** 3.5HEC **For hire:** **Facilities:** **Services:** **Leisure:** P R **Off-site:** L

CERNAY — HAUT-RHIN

CM Acacias

16 rue Réne Guibert, 68700
389755697 389397229
e-mail: campoland.cernay@orange.fr
web: www.camping-les-acacias.com

Clean, quiet site on the River Thur.

dir: *Off N83 between Colmar & Belfort.*

Open: 15 Apr-15 Oct **Site:** 3HEC **For hire:** **Facilities:** **Services:** **Off-site:** P R

COLMAR — HAUT-RHIN

Intercommunal de l'Ill

1 allée du Camping, 68180
389411594 389411594
e-mail: camping@agglo-colmar.fr
web: www.campingdelill.com

On a meadow beside the river with modern facilities. Separate sections for campers in transit.

dir: *2km E on N415.*

Open: 21 Mar-6 Jan **Site:** 4.7HEC **Facilities:** **Services:** **Leisure:** R **Off-site:** P

CORCIEUX — VOSGES

Clos de la Chaume

The Camping and Caravanning Club — The Friendly Club

21 rue d'Alsace, 88430
329507676 329507676
e-mail: info@camping-closdelachaume.com
web: www.camping-closdelachaume.co.uk

Quiet level site located in the Ballons des Vosges Regional Park and 600 metres from the village. Run by a British and French family, there is a on site swimming pool.

C&CC Report *You can be assured of a warm and friendly welcome from Pascaline and Mike, the Franco-British owners of this charming little site on the outskirts of the typical Vosges village of Corcieux. The pride they take in the site is shown in the carefully tended plants and flowers on site and the spotless sanitation blocks. The site is well placed to discover the Alsace, with its villages full of flowers and its wine route, the Vosges, with its lakes, forests, waterfalls and legends, and the Lorraine, with its monuments, its history and its gastronomy.*

Open: 30 Apr-18 Sep **Site:** 4HEC **For hire:** **Prices:** 16-22.50 Mobile home hire 295-711 **Facilities:** Wi-fi (charged) Kids' Club Play Area **Services:** **Leisure:** P R **Off-site:** L

Domaine des Bans

rue J-Wiese, 88430
329516467 329516469
web: www.domaine-des-bans.fr

On meadowland, divided into pitches with a variety of recreational facilities.

dir: *E of village off D8.*

Open: 30 Apr-3 Sep **Site:** 35HEC **For hire:** **Facilities:** Wi-fi (charged) Kids' Club Play Area **Services:** **Leisure:** L P **Off-site:**

FRANCE

Site 6HEC (site size) grass sand stone little shade partly shaded mainly shaded motorvans accepted bungalows for hire mobile homes for hire tents for hire no dogs site fully accessible for wheelchairs
Prices amount quoted is per night, for 2 adults and car, plus tent or caravan Mobile home hire is a weekly rate.

DABO MOSELLE

Rocher

CD 45, 57850
387074751 387074751
e-mail: info@ot-dabo.fr
web: www.ot-dabo.fr
Beautiful position close to the historic town of Dabo in the Vosges mountains.
dir: *1.5km SW via D45.*
Open: 10 Apr-2 Nov **Site:** 0.5HEC **For hire:** **Facilities:** **Off-site:**

DAMBACH-LA-VILLE BAS-RHIN

L'Ours

rte d'Ebersheim, 67650
388924860
e-mail: camping-de-l-ours@orange.fr
web: www.pays-de-barr.com/dambach-la-ville
A wooded location close to the town centre.
dir: *1km E via D120.*
Open: 15 Mar-Dec **Site:** 1.8HEC **Facilities:** Play Area **Services:** **Off-site:**

EGUISHEIM HAUT-RHIN

Trois Châteaux

10 rue du Bassin, 68420
389231939
e-mail: camping.eguisheim@orange.fr
web: www.eguisheimcamping.fr
Peaceful location surrounded by vineyards at an altitude of 210 metres.
dir: *6km S of Colmar on N83.*
GPS: 48.0430, 7.3000
Open: Apr-25 Oct **Site:** 1.8HEC **For hire:** **Prices:** 11.50-13.50 Mobile home hire 322-630 **Facilities:** Wi-fi **Services:** **Off-site:**

FONTENOY-LE-CHÂTEAU VOSGES

Fontenoy

rue Colonel Gilbert, 88240
329363474
e-mail: marliesfontenoy@hotmail.com
web: www.campingfontenoy.com
Small family site set on a hill in peaceful, wooded surroundings.
dir: *2.2km S via D40.*
Open: 11 Apr-4 Oct **Site:** 1.2HEC **For hire:** **Facilities:** Wi-fi Play Area **Services:** **Leisure:** P **Off-site:** R

GEISHOUSE HAUT-RHIN

Au Relais du Grand Ballon

17 Grand Rue, 68690
389823047
e-mail: aurelaisgeishouse@wanadoo.fr
web: www.aurelaisdugrandballon.com
Situated at an altitude of 730 metres in a small village, a quiet site ideal for hiking in the surrounding countryside.
Open: All Year. **Site:** 0.3HEC **For hire:** **Prices:** 14.10-18.60 **Facilities:** Wi-fi (charged) Play Area **Services:** **Off-site:**

GEMAINGOUTTE VOSGES

CM Le Violu

88520
329577070 329517260
e-mail: mairie.gemaingoutte@wanadoo.fr
The site is near the river and has level grassy pitches.
dir: *W beside river via N59.*
Open: May-Sep **Site:** 0.9HEC **For hire:** **Facilities:** **Services:** **Leisure:** R **Off-site:**

GÉRARDMER VOSGES

Ramberchamp

21 chemin du Tour du Lac, 88400
329630382 329632609
e-mail: boespflug.helene@wanadoo.fr
web: www.camping-de-ramberchamp.com
On a level meadow on south side of Lac de Gérardmer.
dir: *2km from village centre via N417 or 486.*
Open: 13 Apr-18 Sep **Site:** 3.5HEC **For hire:** **Facilities:** **Services:** **Leisure:** L **Off-site:** P

GRANGES-SUR-VOLOGNE VOSGES

Château

2 Les Chappes, 88640
329575083
e-mail: camping-du-chateau@wanadoo.fr
A terraced site with good sports facilities 1km from the village, next to the forest.
GPS: 48.1542, 6.7947
Open: 15 Jun-15 Sep **Site:** 2HEC **For hire:** **Prices:** 12.50 Mobile home hire 250-320 **Facilities:** Wi-fi Play Area **Services:** **Leisure:** P **Off-site:** R

Gina-Park

88460

☎ 329514195

web: www.ginapark.com

A pleasant park at the foot of a wooded mountain. Streams cross the site and there is a lake and facilities for a variety of sports.

dir: *1km SE of town centre.*

Open: All Year. **Site:** 4.5HEC **For hire:** **Facilities:** **Services:** **Leisure:** P R **Off-site:**

HEIMSBRUNN — HAUT-RHIN

Chaumière

62 rue de la Galfingue, 68990

☎ 389819343 389819343

e-mail: reception@camping-lachaumiere.com

web: www.camping-lachaumiere.com

A pleasant wooded location with modern facilities.

dir: *Signed from village centre.*

Open: All Year. **Site:** 1HEC **For hire:** **Facilities:** Wi-fi **Services:** **Leisure:** P **Off-site:** R

HOHWALD, LE — BAS-RHIN

CM

67140

☎ 388083090 388083090

e-mail: lecamping.herrenhaus@orange.fr

A well-equipped terraced site in beautiful wooded surroundings.

dir: *W via D425.*

Open: All Year. **Site:** 2HEC **Prices:** 11.40 **Facilities:** Play Area **Services:** **Off-site:** R

ISSENHEIM — HAUT-RHIN

Florival

rte de Soultz, 68500

☎ 389742047 389811000

e-mail: contact@camping-leflorival.com

web: www.camping-leflorival.com

Level meadowland site, situated in a regional park and surrounded by a forest.

dir: *N83 Colmar-Mulhouse exit for Issenheim, site signed.*

Open: Apr-Oct **Site:** 3.5HEC **For hire:** **Prices:** 15.40 **Facilities:** Wi-fi Play Area **Services:** **Off-site:** P

KAYSERSBERG — HAUT-RHIN

CM

rue des Acacias, 68240

☎ 389471447 389471447

e-mail: camping@ville-kaysersberg.fr

Between a sports ground and the River Weiss. Subdivided by low hedges.

dir: *200m from N415, signed.*

Open: Apr-Sep **Site:** 1.5HEC **Facilities:** Wi-fi Play Area **Services:** **Leisure:** R **Off-site:** P

KRUTH — HAUT-RHIN

Schlossberg

rue du Bourbach, 68820

☎ 389822676 389822017

e-mail: contact@schlossberg.fr

web: www.schlossberg.fr

A quiet location in the heart of the Parc des Ballons with modern facilities.

dir: *2.3km NW via D13b.*

GPS: 47.9436, 6.9544

Open: Etr-1 Oct **Site:** 5.2HEC **For hire:** **Prices:** 13.50 **Facilities:** Wi-fi (charged) Play Area **Services:** **Leisure:** R **Off-site:** L

LAUTERBOURG — BAS-RHIN

CM des Mouettes

chemin des Mouettes, 67630

☎ 388546860 388546860

e-mail: camping-lauterbourg@wanadoo.fr

A level site on the shores of a lake.

dir: *D63 from Haguenau.*

Open: 19 Apr-Nov **Site:** 3HEC **For hire:** **Facilities:** **Services:** **Leisure:** L **Off-site:** R

LIÈPVRE — HAUT-RHIN

Camping du Haut Koenigsbourg

rte de la Vancelle, 68660

☎ 389584320 389589829

e-mail: camping.haut-koenigsbourg@orange.fr

web: www.liepvre.fr/camping

Tranquil and shady site, ideal for exploring the local wine-growing region.

GPS: 48.2731, 7.2906

Open: 15 Mar-15 Oct **Site:** 1HEC **For hire:** **Facilities:** Wi-fi Play Area **Services:** **Off-site:** R

LUTTENBACH HAUT-RHIN

Amis de la Nature

4 rue du Château, 68140

389773860 389772572

e-mail: camping.an@wanadoo.fr

web: www.camping-an.fr

Situated on a long strip of land, in the heart of Munster countryside. Divided into pitches.

dir: *D10 from Munster for 1km.*

Open: All Year. **Site:** 7HEC **Prices:** 9.90-11 **Facilities:** Wi-fi Play Area **Services:** **Leisure:** P R **Off-site:** P

MASEVAUX HAUT-RHIN

Masevaux

3 rue du Stade, 68290

389824229 389824229

e-mail: contact@camping-masevaux.com

web: www.camping-masevaux.com

Wooded surroundings beside the River Doller, 200 metres from small picturesque town.

Open: 15 Mar-Oct **Site:** 3.5HEC **Prices:** 13-17.30 **Facilities:** Wi-fi Play Area **Services:** **Off-site:** L P R

MITTLACH HAUT-RHIN

Camping Municipal

68380

389776377 389777436

e-mail: camping@mittlach.fr

web: www.mittlach.fr

Very quiet forested area by a small village.

dir: *From Munster signs for Metzeral then Mittlach D10.*

Open: May-Oct **Site:** 3HEC **Prices:** 10.65 **Facilities:** Play Area **Services:** **Leisure:** R **Off-site:**

MOOSCH HAUT-RHIN

Mine d'Argent

rue de la Mine d'Argent, 68690

389823066

A well-established site in a peaceful wooded setting.

dir: *1.5km SW off N66.*

GPS: 47.8506, 7.0306

Open: 15 Apr-15 Oct **Site:** 2.5HEC **For hire:** **Facilities:** Play Area **Services:** **Leisure:** R **Off-site:** L P R

MULHOUSE HAUT-RHIN

CM de L'Ill

av P-de-Coubertin, 68100

389062066 389611834

e-mail: campingdelill@wanadoo.fr

web: www.camping-de-lill.com

Set in the park between the canal and the River Ill, a short walk from the city centre.

dir: *From town centre signs for Fribourg & Allemagne, signed at Ile Napoléon.*

Open: Apr-15 Oct **Site:** 5.5HEC **For hire:** **Prices:** 16-19.45 Mobile home hire 320-550 **Facilities:** Wi-fi (charged) **Services:** **Leisure:** P **Off-site:** R

MUNSTER HAUT-RHIN

Village Center Le Parc de la Fecht

rte de Gunsbach, 68140

499572121 467516389

e-mail: contact@village-center.com

web: www.village-center.com/alsace/camping-montagne-parc-fecht.php

Quiet and friendly site close to the town centre.

dir: *On D417 via Colmar (direction of Epinal).*

GPS: 48.0396, 7.1425

Open: 27 Apr-9 Sep **Site:** 4.5HEC **For hire:** **Prices:** 15-17 Mobile home hire 175-699 **Facilities:** Wi-fi (charged) Play Area **Services:** **Leisure:** R **Off-site:** P

OBERBRONN BAS-RHIN

CM Oasis

3 rue du Frohret, 67110

388097196 388099787

e-mail: oasis.oberbronn@laregie.fr

web: oasis67110.jimdo.com

Site with 139 pitches, plus chalets with leisure facilities including a health spa.

dir: *Signed W from D28 Oberbronn-Zinswiller.*

Open: Apr-Sep **Site:** 9HEC **For hire:** **Facilities:** Wi-fi (charged) Play Area **Services:** **Leisure:** P **Off-site:**

FRANCE

OBERNAI — BAS-RHIN

CM

rue de Berlin, 67210
388953848 388483147
e-mail: camping@obernai.fr
web: www.obernai.fr

Partly terraced site in a park. Vaccination book required for dogs.

dir: *W on D426 towards Ottrott.*

GPS: 48.4645, 7.4678

Open: All Year. **Site:** 3HEC **Prices:** 18.50 **Facilities:** Wi-fi Play Area **Services:** **Off-site:** P R

REHAUPAL — VOSGES

Barba

45 le Village, 88640
329663557 329663557
e-mail: barba@campingdubarba.com
web: www.campingdubarba.com

Small, quiet, friendly site in beautiful hill country.

dir: *In Epinal D11 direction Gérardmer, before Tendon left (D30) direction Rehaupal.*

GPS: 48.1190, 6.7323

Open: May-Sep **Site:** 2HEC **For hire:** **Facilities:** Wi-fi **Services:** **Off-site:** L P

RIBEAUVILLE — HAUT-RHIN

Pierre de Coubertin

23 rue de Landau, 68150
389736671
e-mail: camping.ribeauville@wanadoo.fr
web: camping-alsace.com/-Camping-Pierre-de-Coubertin-Ribeauville-.html

Peaceful location, close to the town and leisure facilities.

dir: *Via D106.*

GPS: 48.1947, 7.3365

Open: 15 Mar-14 Nov **Site:** 3.5HEC **Prices:** 12-13 **Facilities:** Wi-fi Play Area **Services:** **Off-site:** P

RIQUEWIHR — HAUT-RHIN

Inter Communal

rte des Vins, 68340
389479008 389490563
e-mail: campingriquewihr@wanadoo.fr
web: www.camping-alsace.com/riquewihr/

Extensive site overlooking vineyards.

dir: *2km E on D16. Turn W off N83 at Ostheim.*

Open: Apr-Dec **Site:** 4HEC **Facilities:** **Services:** **Off-site:**

ST-MAURICE-SUR-MOSELLE — VOSGES

Deux Ballons

17 rue du Stade, 88560
329251714
e-mail: stan0268@orange.fr
web: www.camping-deux-ballons.fr

Well-maintained site beside a stream and surrounded by woodland and mountains.

dir: *1km W on N66 near fuel station.*

Open: 28 Apr-16 Sep **Site:** 4HEC **For hire:** **Prices:** 18-24.80 **Facilities:** Wi-fi (charged) Play Area **Services:** **Leisure:** P **Off-site:** R

ST-PIERRE — BAS-RHIN

Beau Séjour

rue de l'Église, 67140
388085224 388085224
e-mail: camping.saintpierre@laposte.net
web: www.pays-de-barr.com/beau-sejour/

Situated midway between Strasbourg and Colmar with modern facilities.

Open: 15 May-1 Oct **Site:** 0.6HEC **Facilities:** **Services:** **Leisure:** R **Off-site:**

STE-CROIX-EN-PLAINE — HAUT-RHIN

Clair Vacances

rte de Herrlisheim, 68127
389492728 389493137
e-mail: clairvacances@wanadoo.fr
web: www.clairvacances.com

A pleasant woodland setting with good facilities for a family holiday.

dir: *On D1 towards Herrlisheim.*

GPS: 48.0160, 7.3500

Open: Etr-17 Oct **Site:** 3.5HEC **For hire:** **Prices:** 16-21 **Facilities:** Wi-fi Play Area **Services:** **Leisure:** P **Off-site:**

Site 6HEC (site size) 🌱 grass 🏖 sand 🌱 stone ♣ little shade ♣ partly shaded ♣ mainly shaded 🚐 motorvans accepted
🏠 bungalows for hire 🚐 mobile homes for hire ⛺ tents for hire ⊗ no dogs ♿ site fully accessible for wheelchairs
Prices amount quoted is per night, for 2 adults and car, plus tent or caravan Mobile home hire is a weekly rate.

SÉLESTAT — BAS-RHIN

CM Cigognes

rue de la 1-er DFL, 67600

388920398

Rural setting at an altitude of 175 metres.

dir: *0.9km from town centre.*

Open: May-Sep **Site:** 0.7HEC **Facilities:** **Services:** **Off-site:** P

SEPPOIS-LE-BAS — HAUT-RHIN

Village Center Les Lupins

1 rue de la Gare, 68580

499572121 467516389

e-mail: contact@village-center.com

web: www.village-center.com/alsace/camping-campagne-lupins.php

Picturesque site close to the German and Swiss borders.

dir: *From Colmar/Mulhouse, through Altkirch in direction of Férette.*

GPS: 47.5377, 7.1825

Open: 24 Jun-4 Sep **Site:** 4HEC **For hire:** **Facilities:** Wi-fi Play Area **Services:** **Leisure:** P **Off-site:**

SIVRY-SUR-MEUSE — MEUSE

Brouzel

26 rue du Moulin, 55110

329748155

e-mail: lebrouzel@gmail.com

web: www.lebrouzel.com

Quiet site on the banks of a canal.

Open: Apr-1 Oct **Site:** 1.5HEC **For hire:** **Prices:** 10.80 Mobile home hire 250 **Facilities:** Play Area **Services:** **Leisure:** R **Off-site:** R

THOLY, LE — VOSGES

Noir Rupt

15 chemin de l'Étang de Noirrupt, 88530

329618127 329618305

e-mail: info@jpvacances.com

web: www.jpvacances.com

A peaceful site in a beautiful wooded location, 1km from Tholy. With plenty of facilities an ideal base whatever the season.

dir: *2km SE on D417.*

GPS: 48.0888, 6.7289

Open: May-15 Oct **Site:** 3HEC **For hire:** **Prices:** 14.91-21.30 **Facilities:** Wi-fi (charged) Play Area **Services:** **Leisure:** P **Off-site:** R

TURCKHEIM — HAUT-RHIN

Camping Municipal les Cigognes

68230

389270200

e-mail: municipc@calixo.net

web: www.turckheim-alsace.com

Relaxing site with recreational facilities on site or nearby. Folk events occasionally held.

dir: *N417 from Colmar to Wintzenheim then Turckheim, left before bridge, pass railway station & stadium.*

Open: 15 Mar-20 Dec **Site:** 2.5HEC **Prices:** 10.52 **Facilities:** Wi-fi Play Area **Services:** **Leisure:** R **Off-site:**

VAGNEY — VOSGES

Camping Champêtre du Mettey

rte du camping, 88120

623911608

e-mail: contact@campingdumettey.fr

web: www.campingdumettey.fr

Pleasant site, with good facilities, in a natural setting 15km from Gérardmer.

dir: *1.3km E on road to Gérardmer.*

Open: All Year. **Site:** 5HEC **For hire:** **Prices:** 13-17 **Facilities:** Wi-fi Kids' Club Play Area **Services:** **Leisure:** P **Off-site:** R

FRANCE

VERDUN — MEUSE

Breuils

allée des Breuils, 55100

☎ 329861531 🖹 329867576

e-mail: contact@camping-lesbreuils.com

web: www.camping-lesbreuils.com

A family site in peaceful surroundings. Pitches are divided by trees and bushes and the sanitary facilities are well-maintained.

dir: *SW via D34, signed.*

Open: Apr-Sep **Site:** 5.5HEC **For hire:** **Facilities:** **Services:** **Leisure:** P **Off-site:** L R

VILLERS-LÈS-NANCY — MEURTHE-ET-MOSELLE

Campéole le Brabois

The Camping and Caravanning Club — The Friendly Club

av Paul Muller, 54600

☎ 383271828 🖹 383400643

e-mail: campeoles.brabois@orange.fr

web: www.camping-brabois.com

Beautiful wooded surroundings with well-defined pitches and good recreational facilities.

C&CC Report *Good facilities, a British manager, a restaurant often featuring the site's own fresh produce, a location handy for Nancy's lovely historic centre – all these mean that this small and well-run site attracts both long and short stays. Nancy itself, the hub of the Art Nouveau movement, makes for a very rewarding visit. In Place Stanislas, a splendid UNESCO World Heritage Site, evenings from mid-June to mid-September present a spell-binding free sound and light show, with the region's history told by images projected onto the buildings.*

dir: *Motorway A33 junct 2b, follow signs. From centre of Nancy follow sign to Technopole de Brabois.*

Open: Apr-15 Oct **Site:** 6HEC **For hire:** **Facilities:** **Services:** **Off-site:** P

VITTEL — VOSGES

Vittel

270 rue Claude Bassot, 88800

☎ 329080271 🖹 386379583

e-mail: aquadis1@wanadoo.fr

web: www.aquadis-loisirs.com

Friendly site located in this spa town in the Vosges mountains.

dir: *NE via D68 rte de Domjulien.*

Open: Apr-Sep **Site:** 3HEC **For hire:** **Facilities:** **Services:** **Off-site:** P

WASSELONNE — BAS-RHIN

CM

Rue Des Sapins, 67310

☎ 388870008 🖹 388684890

e-mail: camping-wasselonne@wanadoo.fr

On a level meadow adjoining the local sports complex.

dir: *1km W on D224.*

Open: Apr-15 Oct **Site:** 2.5HEC **For hire:** **Facilities:** **Services:** **Leisure:** P **Off-site:**

WATTWILLER — HAUT-RHIN

Sources

rte des Crêtes, 68700

☎ 389754494 🖹 389757198

e-mail: camping.les.sources@wanadoo.fr

web: www.camping-les-sources.com

A family site on the edge of the Vosges forest close to the Route du Vin. Kids' club available in July and August.

dir: *N83 exit Cernay Nord.*

GPS: 47.8344, 7.1656

Open: 6 Apr-Sep **Site:** 15HEC **For hire:** **Prices:** 17.60-31.60 Mobile home hire 210-840 **Facilities:** Wi-fi Kids' Club Play Area **Services:** **Leisure:** P

WIHR-AU-VAL — HAUT-RHIN

Route Verte

13 rue de la Gare, 68230

☎ 389711010

e-mail: info@camping-routeverte.com

web: camping-routeverte.com

Near the centre of the village at an altitude of 320 metres.

dir: *Approach via D10.*

Open: end Apr-Sep **Site:** 1HEC **Facilities:** **Services:** **Off-site:** P R

XONRUPT/LONGEMER — VOSGES

Camping Les Jonquilles

rte du Lac, 88400

☎ 329633401 🖹 329600928

e-mail: info@camping-jonquilles.com

web: www.camping-jonquilles.com

A delightful wooded lakeside setting.

dir: *2km SE on D67A beside Lac de Longemer.*

Open: 21 Apr-7 Oct **Site:** 4HEC **Prices:** 13.50 **Facilities:** Wi-fi **Services:** **Leisure:** L **Off-site:**

Site 6HEC (site size) grass sand stone little shade partly shaded mainly shaded motorvans accepted bungalows for hire mobile homes for hire tents for hire no dogs site fully accessible for wheelchairs
Prices amount quoted is per night, for 2 adults and car, plus tent or caravan Mobile home hire is a weekly rate.

L'Eau-Vive

2799 rte de Colmar, 88400

329630737

e-mail: campingeauvive@wanadoo.fr

web: www.campingaleauvive.com

On a meadow surrounded by trees, close to the ski slopes.

dir: *2km SE on D67A next to Lac de Longemer.*

Open: All Year. **Site:** 1HEC **For hire:** **Facilities:** **Services:** **Leisure:** R **Off-site:** L

BURGUNDY/CHAMPAGNE

ACCOLAY YONNE

Moulin Jacquot

Rte de Bazarnes, 89460

386815687 386815687

e-mail: dominique-tilmant0971@orange.fr

A well-equipped site in a pleasant rural setting, close to the village.

dir: *W to Canal du Nivernais.*

Open: Apr-Sep **Site:** 0.8HEC **Prices:** 8.80-11.30 **Facilities:** Wi-fi Play Area **Services:** **Off-site:** R

ANCY-LE-FRANC YONNE

CM

rte de Cusy, 89160

386751321

A sheltered position just beyond the village.

dir: *Via Montbard road.*

Open: 15 Jun-15 Sep **Site:** 0.8HEC **Facilities:** **Services:** **Off-site:** R

ANDRYES YONNE

Au Bois Joli

89480

386817048 386817048

e-mail: info@campingauboisjoli.com

web: www.campingauboisjoli.com

Family friendly site, but suitable for all ages, set in pleasant Burgundian countryside.

dir: *0.6km SW via N151.*

Open: Apr-Oct **Site:** 5HEC **For hire:** **Prices:** 16.20-28 Mobile home hire 250-620 **Facilities:** Wi-fi **Services:** **Leisure:** P **Off-site:** L R

ARNAY-LE-DUC CÔTE-D'OR

Fouché

rue du 8 mai 1945, 21230

380900223 380901191

e-mail: info@campingfouche.com

web: www.campingfouche.com

A quiet location beside a lake with good recreational facilities, close to the medieval town of Arnay-le-Duc.

dir: *0.7km E on CD17.*

Open: Apr-15 Oct **Site:** 8HEC **For hire:** **Facilities:** Wi-fi Kids' Club Play Area **Services:** **Leisure:** L P

AUXERRE YONNE

CM

8 rte de Vaux, 89000

386521115 386511754

e-mail: camping.mairie@auxerre.com

Quiet, shady site with leisure facilities including table tennis and volleyball.

dir: *SE towards Vaux.*

Open: 15 Apr-15 Sep **Site:** 3HEC **Prices:** 9.60-11 **Facilities:** Play Area **Services:** **Off-site:** P R

AUXONNE CÔTE-D'OR

Arquebuse

rte d'Athée, 21130

380310689 380311302

e-mail: camping.arquebuse@wanadoo.fr

web: www.campingarquebuse.com

Clean, well-equipped site on the River Saône, near a bathing area.

dir: *N5 W from Auxonne for 3km, N onto D24 towards Athée & Pontailler-sur-Saône.*

Open: All Year. **Site:** 5HEC **For hire:** **Facilities:** **Services:** **Off-site:** P R

AVALLON YONNE

Sous-Roche

1 rue Sous-Roche, 89200

386341039 386341039

e-mail: campingsousroche@ville-avallon.fr

web: www.ville-avallon.fr

In a riverside setting within Morvan Regional Natural Park.

dir: *2km SE by D944 & D427.*

Open: Apr-15 Oct **Site:** 2HEC **Facilities:** **Services:** **Leisure:** R **Off-site:** P

FRANCE

BANNES HAUTE-MARNE

Hautoreille

52360

☎ 325848340 🖹 325848340

e-mail: campinghautoreille@orange.fr

web: www.campinghautoreille.com

Small grassy site with modern facilities, offering large pitches, many in shaded positions. Separate car park for late arrivals.

dir: *D74, S towards Langres.*

Open: All Year. **Site:** 3.5HEC **Facilities:** Wi-fi Play Area **Services:** **Off-site:** L R

BEAUNE CÔTE-D'OR

CM Cent Vignes

10 rue August Dubois, 21200

☎ 380220391 🖹 380201551

e-mail: campinglescentvignes@mairie-beaune.fr

On outskirts of town. Site divided into pitches, clean, well-looked after sanitary installations.

dir: *On N74 on Savigny-les-Beaune road.*

GPS: 47.0328, 4.8392

Open: 15 Mar-Oct **Site:** 2HEC **Prices:** 12.20-13.60 **Facilities:** Wi-fi **Services:** **Off-site:** L P

BOURBON-LANCY SAÔNE-ET-LOIRE

St-Prix

rue du St-Prix, 71140

☎ 385892098 🖹 386379583

e-mail: aquadis1@wanadoo.fr

web: www.aquadis-loisirs.com

A well-equipped family site close to an extensive water-sports centre.

dir: *By swimming pool off D979a.*

Open: Apr-Oct **Site:** 2.5HEC **For hire:** **Facilities:** **Services:** **Leisure:** P **Off-site:** L

BOURBONNE-LES-BAINS HAUTE-MARNE

Montmorency

rue du Stade, BP N7, 52400

☎ 325900864 🖹 325842374

e-mail: c.montmorency@wanadoo.fr

web: www.camping-montmorency.com

A well-equipped site in a pleasant natural setting.

Open: Apr-Oct **Site:** 2HEC **For hire:** **Facilities:** Play Area **Services:** **Off-site:** L P

BOURG HAUTE-MARNE

Croix d'Arles

rte de Dijon D974, 52200

☎ 325882402

e-mail: croix.arles@yahoo.fr

web: www.croixdarles.eu

A peaceful site in flat wooded surroundings close to Langres. Kids' club available in July and August.

dir: *A31 exit 6, D428 towards Langres, onto RN74 for Dijon, site 2km on right.*

GPS: 47.8128, 5.3205

Open: 15 Mar-1 Nov **Site:** 7HEC **For hire:** **Prices:** 13-16 Mobile home hire 238-595 **Facilities:** Wi-fi Kids' Club Play Area **Services:** **Leisure:** P **Off-site:**

BOURG-FIDÈLE ARDENNES

Camping de la Murée

35 rue Catherine de Clèves, 08230

☎ 324542445

e-mail: campingdelamuree@wanadoo.fr

web: www.campingdelamuree.com

A lakeside site in wooded surroundings.

dir: *1km N via D22.*

GPS: 49.8997, 4.3207

Open: 15 Jan-15 Dec **Site:** 1.3HEC **For hire:** **Prices:** 14.70 Mobile home hire 350 **Facilities:** **Services:** **Off-site:** L P

BUZANCY ARDENNES

Samaritaine

The Camping and Caravanning Club The Friendly Club

08240

☎ 324300888 🖹 324302939

e-mail: info@campinglasamaritaine.com

web: www.campinglasamaritaine.com

Site set in a peaceful location in a small village in the heart of the Ardennes. The forests in the area are well-suited for walking, horse-riding or cycling. Kids' club available in summer months.

C&CC Report *A very attractive site with large pitches separated by flowering shrubs, beautifully kept grounds and facilities, and a friendly atmosphere, in the lovely Ardennes countryside. Worth visiting are weekly farmers' markets, a beer museum, a zoo where day is turned into night, a historic iron furnace with a dazzling multimedia show, the Great War sites of the Maginot Line and Verdun, the Museum of War and Peace – and in Belgium, a brewery in a Trappist monastery.*

dir: *D12 onto D947 towards Buzancy for 17km.*

Open: May-20 Sep **Site:** 2.5HEC **For hire:** **Facilities:** Kids' Club Play Area **Services:** **Off-site:** L

CHAGNY SAÔNE-ET-LOIRE

Pâquier Fané

20 rue de Pâquier, 71150
☎ 385872142
e-mail: camping-chagny@orange.fr
web: www.camping-chagny.com
A clean site 0.6km west of the church, close to village.
dir: *D974 from village centre.*
Open: 15 Apr-Oct **Site:** 1.8HEC **Facilities:** Wi-fi **Services:** **Leisure:** R **Off-site:** P

CHÂLONS-EN-CHAMPAGNE MARNE

Camping de Châlons en Champagne

rue de Plaisance, 51000
☎ 326683800 386379583
e-mail: aquadis1@orange.fr
web: www.aquadis-loisirs.com
Pleasant wooded location with good recreational facilities.
dir: *N44 NE/N77 S.*
Open: Apr-Oct **Site:** 7.5HEC **Facilities:** Wi-fi Play Area **Services:** **Off-site:** P

CHAROLLES SAÔNE-ET-LOIRE

CM

rte de Viny, 71120
☎ 385240490
e-mail: camping@ville-charolles.fr
Pleasant wooded surroundings with modern sanitary facilities.
dir: *NE of town on D33 towards Viry, signed.*
Open: Apr-5 Oct **Site:** 0.6HEC **For hire:** **Prices:** 12.50 **Facilities:** Wi-fi **Services:** **Leisure:** P R **Off-site:**

CHÂTILLON-SUR-SEINE CÔTE-D'OR

CM Louis Rigoly

espl St-Vorles, 21400
☎ 380910305 380912146
e-mail: tourism-chatillon-sur-seine@wanadoo.fr
Hilly shaded site near the historic Renaissance church of St Vorles.
dir: *SE of town off D928 rte de Langres.*
Open: Apr-Sep **Site:** 0.8HEC **Facilities:** **Services:** **Off-site:** P

CHEVIGNY NIÈVRE

Hermitage de Chevigny

58230
☎ 386845097
A pleasant site with good facilities in wooded surroundings within the Morvan nature reserve. There is direct access to the lake and water sports are available.
dir: *On left bank of Lake Chevigny.*
Open: 15 Apr-Sep **Site:** 2.5HEC **Prices:** 16.50-20 **Facilities:** Play Area **Services:** **Leisure:** L R

CLAMECY NIÈVRE

Pont Picot

rte de Chenoches, 58500
☎ 386270597
A pleasant location between the River Yonne and the Canal du Nivernais.
Open: Apr-Sep **Site:** 1.2HEC **For hire:** **Facilities:** Wi-fi Play Area **Services:** **Leisure:** R **Off-site:** P

CLAYETTE, LA SAÔNE-ET-LOIRE

Bruyères

9 rte de Gibles, 71800
☎ 385280915 386379583
e-mail: aquadis1@wanadoo.fr
web: www.aquadis-loisirs.com
Peaceful, friendly site well located for visiting the Beaujolais region and 50km from Lyon.
dir: *A6 exit for Mâcon, take N88 to La Clayette.*
Open: Apr-Sep **Site:** 3HEC **For hire:** **Facilities:** **Services:** **Off-site:** P

CRÊCHES-SUR-SAÔNE SAÔNE-ET-LOIRE

CM Le Port d'Arciat

71680
☎ 385371183 385365791
e-mail: camping-creches.sur.saone@orange.fr
web: pagesperso-orange.fr/campingduportdarciat
Wooded location beside the River Saône.
dir: *1.5km E via D31.*
Open: 15 May-15 Sep **Site:** 6HEC **Prices:** 11-15 **Facilities:** Wi-fi Play Area **Services:** **Leisure:** L R **Off-site:**

FRANCE

DECIZE — NIÈVRE

Camping des Halles

allée Marcel Merle, 58300
386251405 386379583
e-mail: aquadis1@orange.fr
web: www.aquadis-loisirs.com
Located by the River Loire.
dir: *NW of town centre.*

Open: May-Sep **Site:** 4HEC **For hire:** **Facilities:** **Services:** **Off-site:** P R

DIGOIN — SAÔNE-ET-LOIRE

CM Chevrette

rue de la Chevrette, 71160
385531149 385885970
e-mail: lachevrette@wanadoo.fr
web: www.lachevrette.com
On the banks of the river Loire set in peaceful countryside.
dir: *W of village on N79 exit 23/24.*
GPS: 46.4794, 3.9672

Open: 15 Mar-15 Oct **Site:** 1.5HEC **For hire:** **Prices:** 13.50-19.50 **Facilities:** Wi-fi Play Area **Services:** **Leisure:** P R **Off-site:**

DIJON — CÔTE-D'OR

Lac Kir

3 bld Chanoine Kir, 21000
380435472 380455706
e-mail: campingdijon@wanadoo.fr
web: www.camping-dijon.com
A well-maintained site in natural surroundings, an ideal base for exploring the historic town of Dijon.
dir: *1.5km W on N5.*

Open: Apr-15 Oct **Site:** 2.5HEC **For hire:** **Facilities:** **Services:** **Off-site:** L P

DOMPIERRE-LES-ORMES — SAÔNE-ET-LOIRE

Village des Meuniers

71520
385503660
e-mail: contact@villagedesmeuniers.com
web: www.villagedesmeuniers.com
A well-equipped site in the heart of the southern Burgundy countryside. Kids' club available in July and August.
dir: *Via N79, signed.*
GPS: 46.3639, 4.4747

Open: 15 Mar-1 Nov **Site:** 4HEC **For hire:** **Prices:** 17.50-23 Mobile home hire 280-770 **Facilities:** Wi-fi Kids' Club Play Area **Services:** **Leisure:** P

ÉCLARON-BRAUCOURT — HAUTE-MARNE

Presqu'île de Champaubert

52290
325041320 325943351
e-mail: ilechampaubert@free.fr
web: www.lescampingsduder.com
Situated on a lake peninsula.

Open: Apr-Sep **Site:** 3.5HEC **Facilities:** **Services:** **Off-site:** L

EPINAC — SAÔNE-ET-LOIRE

Pont Vert

Rue de la Piscine, 71360
385820026 385821367
e-mail: info@campingdupontvert.com
web: www.campingdupontvert.com
Wooded location on the banks of the river. Modern facilities and motel within the site.
dir: *S via D43 beside River Drée.*

Open: Apr-Oct **Site:** 4HEC **For hire:** **Facilities:** **Services:** **Leisure:** R **Off-site:**

FRONCLES — HAUTE-MARNE

Deux Ponts

rue des Ponts, 52320
325023121 325020980
e-mail: mairie.froncles@wanadoo.fr
A peaceful location beside the River Marne.

Open: 15 Mar-15 Oct **Site:** 3HEC **Facilities:** **Off-site:** R

GIBLES SAÔNE-ET-LOIRE

Château de Montrouant

Montrouant, 71800

385845113

e-mail: campingdemontrouant@wanadoo.fr

web: www.chateau-de-montrouant.com

A small site in the Charollais hill region with access to extensive parkland.

dir: *1.6km NE beside lake.*

Open: Jun-9 Sep **Site:** 1HEC **For hire:** **Facilities:** **Services:** **Leisure:** L P R **Off-site:**

GIFFAUMONT MARNE

Plage

chemin de la Cachotte, Station Nautique, 51290

608513824

A well-maintained site at the Station Nautique.

dir: *2km from village.*

Open: May-10 Sep **Site:** 1.5HEC **Facilities:** **Services:** **Off-site:** L

GIGNY-SUR-SAÔNE SAÔNE-ET-LOIRE

Domaine du Château de l'Epervière

The Camping and Caravanning Club The Friendly Club

Château de l'Epervière, 71240

385941690 385941697

e-mail: info@domaine-eperviere.com

web: www.domaine-eperviere.com

Peaceful site in the park surrounding a 16th-century château. Close to the River Saône for fishing and sailing. Kids' club available in July and August.

C&CC Report *A beautiful site, with excellent services and a great location, in a lovely, fascinating region. Most services operate for most of the season, which makes l'Epervière an attractive base for exploring the beautiful Burgundian wine areas and countryside at any time. Popular and well-known by campers seeking both traditional France and a restful and high quality camp site.*

dir: *A6 exit 26 onto RN6 towards Mâcon/Tournus. Left onto D18, signed*

GPS: 46.6545, 4.9440

Open: Apr-Sep **Site:** 10HEC **For hire:**
Prices: 20.70-29.50 Mobile home hire 399-849 **Facilities:** Wi-fi Kids' Club Play Area **Services:** **Leisure:** P

GRANDPRÉ ARDENNES

CM

08250

324305071

A peaceful riverside site.

dir: *150m from village centre on D6.*

Open: Apr-Sep **Site:** 2HEC **Facilities:** **Services:** **Leisure:** R **Off-site:**

ISSY-L'ÉVÊQUE SAÔNE-ET-LOIRE

Flower Camping de l'Étang Neuf

71760

385249605

e-mail: info@issy-camping.com

web: www.issy-camping.com

A fine position beside the lake, with views of the château.

Open: 13 May-15 Sep **Site:** 4HEC **For hire:** **Facilities:** Wi-fi Play Area **Services:** **Leisure:** L P **Off-site:**

LAIVES SAÔNE-ET-LOIRE

Lacs La Heronnière

Rte de la Ferté, Les Bois de Laives, 71240

385449885 385449885

e-mail: contact@camping-laheronniere.com

web: camping-laheronniere.com

A family site, quiet and shady, in a pleasant environment surrounded by nature, very close to a leisure park. Between Chalon-sur-Saône and Mâcon, the campsite is surrounded by three lakes. Separate car park for arrivals after 22.00hrs.

dir: *Autoroute exit Chalon Sud towards Mâcon.*

GPS: 46.6719, 4.833

Open: 19 May-15 Sep **Site:** 2HEC **For hire:** **Facilities:** Play Area **Services:** **Leisure:** P **Off-site:** L R

FRANCE

MÂCON — SAÔNE-ET-LOIRE

Camping Municipal de Mâcon

rue des Grandes Varennes, 71000

☎ 385381622 🖷 385393918

Site divided into pitches with a water-sports centre and pool nearby.

dir: *A6 exit Mâcon Nord, follow signs for camp site.*

GPS: 46.3308, 4.8434

Open: 15 Mar-Oct **Site:** 5HEC **Prices:** 18.90-22.70 **Facilities:** Wi-fi **Services:** **Leisure:** P **Off-site:** R

MARCENAY — CÔTE-D'OR

Grebes du Lac de Marcenay

Lac de Marcenay, 21330

☎ 380816172 🖷 380816199

e-mail: info@campingmarcenaylac.com

web: www.campingmarcenaylac.com

A peaceful site in unspoiled contryside with separate hedged pitches. Direct access to lake.

Open: 30 Mar-Sep **Site:** 3HEC **For hire:** **Facilities:** **Services:** **Leisure:** L P **Off-site:** R

MATOUR — SAÔNE-ET-LOIRE

CM Le Paluet

Le Paluet, 71520

☎ 385597058 🖷 385597454

e-mail: lepaluet@matour.fr

web: www.matour.fr

Not far from the town centre in a pleasant countryside setting beside the river, pitches are shady and well-spaced. Family and large group gatherings can be facilitated.

Open: May-Sep **Site:** 2HEC **For hire:** **Facilities:** Wi-fi **Services:** **Leisure:** P R **Off-site:**

MESNIL-ST-PÈRE — AUBE

Kawan Resort Camping Le Lac d'Orient

rue du Lac, 10140

☎ 325406185 🖷 325709687

e-mail: info@camping-lacdorient.com

web: www.camping-lacdorient.com

Site with both indoor and outdoor swimming pools, set in wooded parkland leading down to a lake with a beach. The sheltered pitches have varying degrees of shade. During July and August an events programme, including a kids' club, takes place with occasional evening entertainment.

dir: *From N - A26 exit 23 towards Chaumont (N19). After 13.5km leave N19 towards Mesnil-St-Père.*

Open: 31 Mar-Sep **Site:** 10HEC **For hire:** **Prices:** 25-34 Mobile home hire 455-840 **Facilities:** Wi-fi Kids' Club Play Area **Services:** **Leisure:** P **Off-site:** L

see advert on this page

MEURSAULT — CÔTE-D'OR

Grappe d'Or

2 rte de Volnay, 21190

☎ 380212248 🖷 380216574

e-mail: info@camping-meursault.com

web: www.camping-meursault.com

Clean terraced site on an open meadow in Meursault, well-known for its wine. Mountain bikes are available for hire.

dir: *0.7km NE on D11b.*

GPS: 46.9856, 4.7683

Open: Apr-15 Oct **Site:** 5.5HEC **For hire:** **Prices:** 14-18 Mobile home hire 294-553 **Facilities:** Wi-fi (charged) **Services:** **Leisure:** P **Off-site:**

MONTAPAS — NIÈVRE

CM La Chênaie

La Chênaie, 58110

☎ 386583432 🖷 386582905

e-mail: mairiedemontapas@orange.fr

web: www.camping-nievre-montapas.net

Wooded location beside a lake with plenty of recreational facilities.

dir: *0.5km from town centre via D259, beside lake.*

Open: Apr-Oct **Site:** 1HEC **Facilities:** **Services:** **Leisure:** L **Off-site:**

MONTHERMÉ — ARDENNES

Camping d'Haulme

08800

☎ 324328161 🖹 324323766

e-mail: campinghaulme@cg08.fr

A pleasant wooded location.

dir: *0.8km NE beside the River Semoy.*

Open: Apr-Oct **Site:** 16HEC **Facilities:** **Services:** **Leisure:** R

MONTIGNY-LE-ROI — HAUTE-MARNE

Camping du Château

pl du Château, 52140

☎ 325873893 🖹 325873893

e-mail: campingmontigny52@wanadoo.fr

web: www.campingduchateau.com

On the site of a medieval château with panoramic views of the Meuse valley, a peaceful site with leisure facilities including tennis courts and petanque.

Open: 15 Apr-Sep **Site:** 6HEC **Prices:** 14-16 **Facilities:** Wi-fi Play Area **Services:** **Off-site:** R

MONTSAUCHE — NIÈVRE

Mesanges

Lac des Settons, Rive Gauche, 58230

☎ 386845577 🖹 386845577

e-mail: campinglesmesanges@orange.fr

web: www.campinglesmesanges.fr

On Lac des Settons.

dir: *D193 towards Lac des Settons, D520 to L'Huis Gaumont then left onto C4.*

Open: 15 May-15 Sep **Site:** 5HEC **Prices:** 16.50 **Facilities:** Wi-fi Play Area **Services:** **Off-site:** L P R

Plage du Midi

58230

☎ 386845197 🖹 386845731

e-mail: campplagedumidi@aol.com

web: www.settons-camping.com

Wooded setting on Lac des Settons with good facilities.

dir: *D193 from town centre to Les Settons & site.*

Open: Etr-15 Oct **Site:** 4HEC **For hire:** **Facilities:** **Services:** **Leisure:** L **Off-site:**

PARAY-LE-MONIAL — SÂONE-ET-LOIRE

Mambré

19 rue du Gué-Léger, 71600

☎ 385888920

e-mail: camping.plm@gmail.com

web: www.campingdemambre.com

Peaceful site on a level meadow with modern facilities.

dir: *N70, exit at Paray-le Monial-Sud. Site signposted along Canal-du-Centre on the D979 direction Moulins.*

GPS: 46.4573, 4.1050

Open: 3 May-Sep **Site:** 4.5HEC **For hire:** **Prices:** 16.90-19.50 Mobile home hire 340-450 **Facilities:** Play Area **Services:** **Leisure:** P **Off-site:** R

PEIGNEY — HAUTE-MARNE

Lac de la Liez

The Camping and Caravanning Club — The Friendly Club

rue des Voiliers, 52200

☎ 325902779 🖹 325906679

e-mail: campingliez@free.fr

There is a swimming pool with slides and a pony club. Kids' club available in July and August.

C&CC Report *In a convenient location, 18km from the A5 and 20km from the A31 motorway exits, in the recently designated Parc Naturel de la Haute Marne. An ideal site both for short stays en-route to and from sites further south, and for longer stays, with good fishing, cycling and walking routes nearby. Enjoy views over the lake from many pitches, be sure to eat in the excellent on-site restaurant and visit the fascinating ancient hilltop town of Langres, where an audio tour explains its history.*

dir: *A31 exit 7, then N19 S, then follow Vesoul & Lac de la Liez.*

GPS: 47.8714, 5.3806

Open: Apr-Sep **Site:** **For hire:** **Facilities:** Wi-fi (charged) Kids' Club Play Area **Services:** **Leisure:** P **Off-site:** L

PONT-SAINTE-MARIE — AUBE

CM de Troyes

7 rue Roger Salengro, 10150

☎ 325810264 🖹 325810264

e-mail: info@troyescamping.net

web: www.troyescamping.net

Wooded site a short walk from the town of Troyes, which has a large shopping centre. Ideally located for exploring the surrounding countryside.

dir: *Follow signs for 'Pont Saint Marie' and 'Municipal' through Troyes.*

Open: Apr-15 Oct **Site:** 3.8HEC **Facilities:** Wi-fi Play Area **Services:** **Leisure:** P **Off-site:**

FRANCE

POUGUES-LES-EAUX — NIÈVRE

CM Chanternes

av de Paris, 58320

☎ 386688618 386231697

Well equipped and cared for site.

dir: *7km N of Nevers on N7.*

Open: Jun-Sep **Site:** 1.4HEC **Prices:** 8.80 **Facilities:** **Services:** **Off-site:** P R

RADONVILLIERS — AUBE

Garillon

rue des Anciens Combattants, 10500

☎ 325922146

e-mail: camping-le-garillon@hotmail.fr

Beside the river, 250 metres from the lake.

Open: May-14 Nov **Site:** 1HEC **For hire:** **Facilities:** **Leisure:** P **Off-site:** L R

RIEL-LES-EAUX — CÔTE-D'OR

Riel-les-Eaux

21570

☎ 380937276

A lakeside site with fishing and boating facilities.

dir: *2.2km W via D13.*

Open: Apr-Oct **Site:** 0.2HEC **For hire:** **Facilities:** **Services:** **Leisure:** L **Off-site:**

ST-HILAIRE-SOUS-ROMILLY — AUBE

Domaine de La Noue des Rois

The Camping and Caravanning Club — The Friendly Club

chemin des Brayes, 10100

☎ 325244160 325243418

e-mail: contact@lanouedesrois.com

web: www.lanouedesrois.com

A quiet site between the A26 Calais-Troyes and A5 Paris-Troyes motorways.

C&CC Report *In a lakeside, woodland setting, with an on-site crêperie and the village and its services just 2.5km away.*

dir: *2km NE.*

Open: All Year. **Site:** 30HEC **For hire:** **Facilities:** **Services:** **Leisure:** L P

ST-HONORÉ — NIÈVRE

Bains

15 av J-Mermoz, 58360

☎ 386307344 386306188

e-mail: camping-les-bains@wanadoo.fr

web: www.campinglesbains.com

A family site with good facilities close to the Morvan national park.

dir: *Via A6 & D985.*

Open: Apr-Oct **Site:** 4.5HEC **For hire:** **Prices:** 11-16 Mobile home hire 150-490 **Facilities:** **Services:** **Leisure:** P **Off-site:**

ST MARCEL — SAÔNE-ET-LOIRE

Camping du Pont de Bourgogne

Rue Julien Leneveu, 71380

☎ 385482686 385485063

e-mail: campingchalon71@wanadoo.fr

web: www.camping-chalon.com

Situated on the banks of the river Saône, only a few minutes from the city centre of Chalon-sur-Saône, and within easy reach of the Autoroute. Restaurant open in high season and take-away meals available in low season.

dir: *A6 exit 26 (Chalon Sud), signed.*

GPS: 46.7843, 4.8723

Open: Apr-Sep **Site:** 3.3HEC **For hire:** **Prices:** 16-22.40 Mobile home hire 349-599 **Facilities:** Wi-fi **Services:**

ST-PÉREUSE — NIÈVRE

Manoir de Bezolle

58110

☎ 386844255 386844377

e-mail: info@camping-bezolle.com

web: www.camping-bezolle.com

A well-kept site divided by hedges in the grounds of a manor house, at the edge of a national park.

dir: *At x-rds of D11 & D978.*

Open: All Year. **Site:** 8HEC **For hire:** **Prices:** 20.44-32.44 Mobile home hire 260-550 **Facilities:** Wi-fi Play Area **Services:** **Leisure:** P

FRANCE

STE-MENEHOULD — MARNE

CM de la Grelette

51800

326608021

web: www.ste-menehould.fr

A well-equipped municipal site.

dir: *E of town towards Metz, beside River Aisne.*

GPS: 49.0894, 4.9097

Open: May-Sep **Site:** 1HEC **Facilities:** Play Area **Off-site:** P R

SAULIEU — CÔTE-D'OR

Camping le Perron

21210

380641619 386379583

e-mail: aquadis1@orange.fr

web: www.aquadis-loisirs.com

On level, open ground with good recreational facilities.

dir: *1km NW on N6.*

GPS: 47.2892, 4.2236

Open: All Year. **Site:** 3HEC **For hire:** **Facilities:** Wi-fi Play Area **Services:** **Leisure:** P **Off-site:** L

SEDAN — ARDENNES

CM de la Prairie

bld Fabert, 08200

324271305 324271305

A well-equipped municipal site on the banks of the River Meuse, close to the centre of the village.

Open: Apr-Sep **Site:** 1.5HEC **Facilities:** **Services:** **Leisure:** R **Off-site:** L P

SEURRE — CÔTE-D'OR

Piscine

21250

380204922 380203401

A well-equipped municipal site with direct access to the river.

dir: *N73 W from town centre for 0.6km towards Beaune.*

Open: 15 May-15 Sep **Site:** **Facilities:** **Services:** **Leisure:** P R **Off-site:**

SÉZANNE — MARNE

CM

rte de Launat, 51120

326805700

e-mail: campingdesezanne@wanadoo.fr

Close to the centre of town and surrounded by fields and trees, pitches offer a variety of shade.

dir: *1.5km W on D239.*

Open: Apr-1 Oct **Site:** 1HEC **Facilities:** **Services:** **Leisure:** P **Off-site:**

SIGNY-LE-PETIT — ARDENNES

Domaine de la Motte

Base de Loisirs, 08380

324535473 324535473

e-mail: campingprehugon@wanadoo.fr

web: www.domainedelamotte.eu

A pleasant site in wooded surroundings with a spa facility. Kids' club available in high season.

dir: *Via N43.*

Open: All Year. **Site:** 0.8HEC **For hire:** **Facilities:** Wi-fi Kids' Club Play Area **Services:** **Leisure:** P **Off-site:** L R

SOULAINES-DHUYS — AUBE

La Croix Badeau

10200

325270543

e-mail: steveheusghem@hotmail.com

web: www.croix-badeau.com

Close to local amenities, a small, quiet site. Leisure facilities include a tennis court and table tennis.

Open: Apr-Sep **Site:** 1.5HEC **For hire:** **Prices:** 10.90-12.40 **Facilities:** Wi-fi **Services:** **Off-site:** R

TAZILLY — NIÈVRE

Château de Chigy

58170

386301080 386300922

e-mail: reception@chateaudechigy.com.fr

web: www.chateaudechigy.com.fr

A beautiful location within the extensive grounds of a magnificent château. Good sports facilities and entertainment programme.

dir: *4km from Luzy on D973 Luzy-Moulins.*

Open: May-Sep **Site:** 7HEC **For hire:** **Facilities:** **Services:** **Leisure:** L P

FRANCE

THONNANCE-LES-MOULINS HAUTE-MARNE

Forge de Ste-Marie

The Camping and Caravanning Club — The Friendly Club

52230

☎ 325944200 🖷 325944143

e-mail: info@laforgedesaintemarie.com

web: www.laforgedesaintemarie.com

Partially terraced, on the site of an 18th-century forge containing a lake.

C&CC Report *This fabulous site, makes for a lovely restful setting. The welcome and helpfulness of Angela and Jacco and the beauty of the area make it impossible not to relax. Low season here is especially good, with a programme of walks, painting, cheese and wine tasting and other activities, plus the delicious restaurant meals.*

dir: *Via N67 & D427.*

GPS: 48.4065, 5.2711

Open: 21 Apr-7 Sep **Site:** 11HEC **For hire:** **Prices:** 20.60-32.60 Mobile home hire 230-620 **Facilities:** Wi-fi (charged) Kids' Club Play Area **Services:** **Leisure:** P R

TOULON-SUR-ARROUX SAÔNE-ET-LOIRE

CM du Val d'Arroux

rte d'Uxeau, 73120

☎ 385795122 🖷 385796217

e-mail: mairie.toulon@wanadoo.fr

On western outskirts beside the River Arroux.

dir: *D985 onto Uxeau road.*

Open: 18 Apr-18 Oct **Site:** 0.62HEC **Prices:** 9.60-12.80 **Facilities:** **Services:** **Leisure:** R **Off-site:**

TOURNUS SAÔNE-ET-LOIRE

Tournus

14 rue des Canes, 71700

☎ 385511658 🖷 385511658

e-mail: reception@camping-tournus.com

web: www.camping-tournus.com

Friendly campsite with large, grassy pitches which are easily accessible.

dir: *A6 autoroute, exit 27 for Tournus, follow RN6, campsite signposted.*

GPS: 46.5737, 4.9093

Open: Apr-Sep **Site:** 1.5HEC **Prices:** 16-20.60 **Facilities:** Wi-fi Play Area **Services:** **Off-site:** P

UCHIZY SAÔNE-ET-LOIRE

National 6

71700

☎ 385405390 🖷 385405390

e-mail: camping.uchizylen6@wanadoo.fr

web: www.camping-lenational6.com

Site surrounded by poplar trees on banks of river.

dir: *Off N6 towards Saône, 6km S of Tournus & continue 0.8km.*

Open: Apr-1 Oct **Site:** 6HEC **For hire:** **Facilities:** **Services:** **Leisure:** P R

VAL-DES-PRÉS MARNE

Gentianes

La Vachette, 05100

☎ 492212141 🖷 492212412

web: www.campinglesgentianes.com

A delightful wooded location bordered by a river and backed by imposing mountains.

dir: *On edge of village, 3km SE of Briançon.*

Open: All Year. **Site:** 2HEC **For hire:** **Facilities:** **Services:** **Leisure:** P R **Off-site:**

VANDENESSE-EN-AUXOIS CÔTE-D'OR

Lac de Panthier

21320

☎ 380492194 🖷 380492580

e-mail: info@lac-de-panthier.com

web: www.lac-de-panthier.com

A pleasant location beside a lake with plenty of facilities for families. Kids' club available in July and August.

dir: *A6 or A38 exit at Pouilly-en-Auxois towards Créancey.*

GPS: 47.2368, 4.6282

Open: 7 Apr-7 Oct **Site:** 7HEC **For hire:** **Prices:** 19-28 Mobile home hire 280-791 **Facilities:** Wi-fi (charged) Kids' Club Play Area **Services:** **Leisure:** L P

VENAREY-LES-LAUMES CÔTE-D'OR

Alésia

rue Dr-Roux, 21150

☎ 380960776 🖷 380960776

e-mail: camping.venarey@wanadoo.fr

web: www.alesia-tourisme.net

A peaceful site close to the lake and river.

GPS: 47.5446, 4.4508

Open: 15 Apr-15 Oct **Site:** 2HEC **For hire:** **Prices:** 11.70-15.70 **Facilities:** Play Area **Services:** **Off-site:** L R

FRANCE

VERMENTON YONNE

Coullemières

89270

☎ 386815302 🖷 386815302

e-mail: camping.vermenton@orange.fr

web: www.camping-vermenton.com

A peaceful meadowland site with good facilities.

dir: *On N6 S of Auxerre.*

Open: Apr-Sep **Site:** 1.5HEC **For hire:** **Facilities:** **Services:** **Leisure:** R **Off-site:**

VIGNOLES CÔTE-D'OR

Bouleaux

The Camping and Caravanning Club The Friendly Club

11 rue Jaune, 21200

☎ 380222688 🖷 380222688

Small, immaculately-kept site handy for A6 motorway.

C&CC Report *A small and pretty site suitable for short or long stays, in an excellent location. Always lovingly well-kept by the attentive and welcoming owners, Les Bouleaux is a good base for visits to any number of vineyards, or for ambling through the many wine villages in the lovely countryside of Burgundy. The unique old town of Beaune, with its ancient hospices, its decorated tiled roofs and its wine museums, whose names are so familiar from many a wine bottle label, is always worth a visit.*

dir: *From Beaune onto RD973 (towards Dole), turn left to Vignoles. 3km from Beaune centre.*

Open: All Year. **Site:** 1.4HEC **Prices:** 14.50 **Facilities:** **Services:** **Off-site:** L P

VILLENEUVE-LES-GENÊTS YONNE

Bois Guillaume

89350

☎ 386454541 🖷 386454920

e-mail: camping@bois-guillaume.com

web: www.bois-guillaume.com

Wooded surroundings with modern facilities. Heated swimming pool from mid June to mid September.

dir: *A77 exit Briare follow signs Blèneau on D22.*

GPS: 47.7576, 3.0992

Open: All Year. **Site:** 8HEC **For hire:** **Prices:** 15-20 Mobile home hire 320-530 **Facilities:** Wi-fi (charged) Play Area **Services:** **Leisure:** P **Off-site:** R

VINCELLES YONNE

Ceriselles

rte de Vincelottes, 89290

☎ 386425047 🖷 386423939

e-mail: camping@cc-payscoulangeois.fr

web: www.campingceriselles.com

Rural location beside the river Yonne, close to the local village.

dir: *D606 exit between Avallon & Auxerre, signed.*

Open: Apr-Oct **Site:** 2.5HEC **For hire:** **Facilities:** Wi-fi Play Area **Services:** **Leisure:** P **Off-site:** R

SOUTH WEST/PYRÉNÉES

AIGNAN GERS

Castex

32290

☎ 562092513 🖷 562092479

e-mail: info@domaine-castex.com

web: www.domaine-castex.com

Wooded site in peaceful surroundings.

dir: *0.8km from D48.*

GPS: 43.6927, 0.0748

Open: 15 Mar-15 Oct **Site:** 3HEC **For hire:** **Prices:** 15-18 **Facilities:** Wi-fi (charged) Play Area **Services:** **Leisure:** P **Off-site:** L R

AIRE-SUR-L'ADOUR LANDES

Ombrages de l'Adour

rue des Graviers, 40800

☎ 558717510 🖷 558713259

e-mail: hetapsarl@yahoo.fr

web: www.camping-adour-landes.com

A clean, tidy site next to a sports stadium beside the river. Clean sanitary installations.

Open: Apr-Oct **Site:** 2HEC **For hire:** **Facilities:** Wi-fi (charged) Play Area **Services:** **Leisure:** R **Off-site:** P

FRANCE

ALBI — TARN

Albirondack Park Camping Lodge & Spa

1 allée de la piscine, 81000
☎ 563603706
e-mail: ballario.andre.ballario@orange.fr
web: www.albirondack.fr

Shaded by 100 year old oak trees, the site's restaurant is based on an American Lodge with cathedral ceiling. Kids' club available in July and August. Dogs accepted but restrictions apply.

dir: *N99 from village towards Millau, left onto D100, left to site.*

GPS: 43.9337, 2.1663

Open: All Year. **Site:** 1.8HEC **For hire:** **Prices:** 15-28 Mobile home hire 300-800 **Facilities:** Wi-fi (charged) Kids' Club **Services:** **Leisure:** P **Off-site:**

ALLAS-LES-MINES — DORDOGNE

Domaine Le Cro Magnon

The Camping and Caravanning Club — The Friendly Club

24220
☎ 553291370 553291579
e-mail: contact@domaine-cro-magnon.com
web: www.domaine-cro-magnon.com

Spacious pitches in a generously wooded estate.

C&CC Report *The Léger family is rightly proud that this well-run, high quality and popular site is also noted by campers for its informal and friendly family atmosphere. The beautiful hilltop setting includes a viewpoint over the river, while its location makes the site a perfect base for visiting the very best of the wonderful villages and prehistoric sites for which the Dordogne is so famous. Large pitches, open and covered pools, a waterslide and excellent site facilities make this a great place for relaxation, too.*

dir: *D25 southwards exit Marnac Berbiguières.*

Open: 15 Jun-14 Sep **Site:** 22HEC **For hire:** **Prices:** 9.40-34.70 Mobile home hire 270-958 **Facilities:** Kids' Club Play Area **Services:** **Leisure:** P **Off-site:** R

ALLES-SUR-DORDOGNE — DORDOGNE

Port de Limeuil

24480
☎ 553632976 553630419
e-mail: didierbonvallet@aol.com
web: www.leportdelimeuil.com

Situated in a conservation area at the confluence of the Dordogne and Vézère rivers, with a 400 metre-long beach.

dir: *Signed off D51.*

GPS: 44.8837, 0.8895

Open: May-Sep **Site:** 7HEC **For hire:** **Prices:** 14-27.50 Mobile home hire 190 **Facilities:** Wi-fi Play Area **Services:** **Leisure:** P R

ANDERNOS-LES-BAINS — GIRONDE

Fontaine-Vieille

4 bld du Colonel Wurtz, 33510
☎ 556820167 556820981
e-mail: fontaine-vieille-sa@wanadoo.fr
web: www.fontaine-vieille.com

On level ground in sparse forest. Dogs allowed except in mobile homes. Shop, bar, café and restaurant open in July and August.

dir: *S of village centre.*

Open: Apr-Sep **Site:** 12.6HEC **For hire:** **Prices:** 26.18-30.18 Mobile home hire 608.26-983.26 **Facilities:** Wi-fi Kids' Club Play Area **Services:** **Leisure:** P S

ANGLARS-JUILLAC — LOT

Camping Base Nautique Floiras

46140
☎ 565362739
e-mail: campingfloiras@aol.com
web: www.campingfloiras.com

A quiet level site beside the River Lot, surrounded by vineyards in a hilly landscape dotted with villages, castles and caves. Facilities for boating.

dir: *SW via D8.*

GPS: 44.4765, 1.1991

Open: Apr-15 Oct **Site:** 1HEC **For hire:** **Prices:** 13.10-18.10 **Facilities:** Wi-fi **Services:** **Leisure:** R **Off-site:**

ANGLET — PYRÉNÉES-ATLANTIQUES

Parme

Quartier Brindos, 64600
☎ 559230300 559412955
e-mail: campingdeparme@wanadoo.fr
web: www.campingdeparme.com

Wooded area with good facilities on the outskirts of Biarritz.

dir: *3km SW off N10.*

Open: Apr-30 Oct **Site:** 3.5HEC **For hire:** **Prices:** 17.50-36 Mobile home hire 239-1035 **Facilities:** Wi-fi (charged) Kids' Club Play Area **Services:** **Leisure:** P **Off-site:** L R S

FRANCE

ARCACHON GIRONDE

Camping Club d'Arcachon

av de la Galaxie, Les Abatilles, 33120
556832415 557522851
e-mail: info@camping-arcachon.com
web: www.camping-arcachon.com
A delightful wooded position 1.8km from the town and beaches. Parking next to tents is permitted in certain areas only.
dir: *1.5km S.*
Open: 15 Dec-13 Nov **Site:** 6HEC **For hire:** **Prices:** 13-24 Mobile home hire 370-1100 **Facilities:** Wi-fi (charged) Kids' Club Play Area **Services:** **Leisure:** P **Off-site:** S

ARCIZANS-AVANT HAUTES-PYRÉNÉES

Lac

29 chemin d'Azun, 65400
562970188 562970188
e-mail: campinglac@campinglac65.fr
web: www.campinglac65.fr
Set in delightful Pyrenean surroundings on outskirts of village. Quiet and peaceful, with spacious and grassy pitches.
dir: *S on N21, onto D13 through St-Savin.*
Open: 20 May-20 Sep **Site:** 4HEC **For hire:** **Prices:** 16.90-24.50 **Facilities:** Wi-fi Play Area **Services:** **Leisure:** P **Off-site:** L R

ARÈS GIRONDE

Canadienne

rte de Lège, 82 r du Gl-de-Gaulle, 33740
556602491 557704085
e-mail: info@lacanadienne.com
web: www.lacanadienne.com
A family site surrounded by pine and oak trees with good facilities.
dir: *1km N off D106.*
Open: Feb-Nov **Site:** 2HEC **For hire:** **Facilities:** **Services:** **Leisure:** P **Off-site:** L

La Cigale

The Camping and Caravanning Club — The Friendly Club

53 rue du Génèral de Gaulle, 33740
556602259 557704166
e-mail: contact@camping-lacigale-ares.com
web: www.camping-lacigale-ares.com
Clean tidy site among pine trees. Grassy pitches and good recreational facilities.
C&CC Report *A small, immaculately kept site with a convivial family atmosphere, close to the magnificent Atlantic beaches and within walking distance of the town centre. The attention to detail shown by the friendly owners is apparent throughout the site. Nature lovers will want to visit the bird sanctuary at La Teste, while more energetic visitors may prefer the Dune du Pyla, the highest sand dune in Europe.*
dir: *0.5km N on D106, between sea & Arcachon Basin.*
GPS: 44.7728, -1.1414
Open: 23 Apr-Sep **Site:** 2.8HEC **For hire:** **Prices:** 20-38 **Facilities:** Wi-fi Play Area **Services:** **Leisure:** P **Off-site:** S

Goélands

av de la Libération, 33740
556825564 556820751
e-mail: camping-les-goelands@wanadoo.fr
Situated among oak trees 200 metres from the beach with good facilities.
dir: *1.7km SE.*
Open: Mar-Oct **Site:** 10HEC **For hire:** **Facilities:** Wi-fi Kids' Club **Services:** **Leisure:** P **Off-site:** L

Pasteur

1 rue du Pilote, 33704
556603333
web: www.atlantic-vacances.com
Comfortable family site with friendly atmosphere, near to the beach and 200 metres from village.
dir: *S of D3, 300m from the sea.*
Open: Apr-Sep **Site:** 1HEC **For hire:** **Prices:** 15-26 Mobile home hire 255-710 **Facilities:** Wi-fi **Services:** **Leisure:** P **Off-site:** S

FRANCE

ARREAU — HAUTES-PYRÉNÉES

Refuge International

RD 929, 65240

☎ 562986334 562986334

e-mail: camping.international.arreau@wanadoo.fr

web: www.camping-international-pyrenees.com

Enclosed terrace site on riverside close to village centre.

dir: *2km N on D929.*

Open: All Year. **Site:** 15HEC **For hire:** **Prices:** 13 Mobile home hire 350-400 **Facilities:** Play Area **Services:** **Leisure:** P R **Off-site:** L

ASCARAT — PYRÉNÉES-ATLANTIQUES

Europ' Camping

64220

☎ 559371278 559372982

e-mail: europcamping64@orange.fr

web: www.europ-camping.com

Rural surroundings of mountains and vineyards, 300 metres from the River Nive.

dir: *1km W of St-Jean-Pied-de-Port on D918.*

Open: Etr-Sep **Site:** 2HEC **For hire:** **Facilities:** Play Area **Services:** **Leisure:** P **Off-site:** R

ATUR — DORDOGNE

Grand Dague

24750

☎ 553042101 553042201

e-mail: info@legranddague.fr

web: www.legranddague.fr

Well-equipped family site in the heart of the Dordogne region, with pitches divided by bushes and hedges.

dir: *NE of Atur via D2.*

Open: 27 Apr-29 Sep **Site:** 22HEC **For hire:** **Prices:** 19-35 Mobile home hire 280-875 **Facilities:** Wi-fi (charged) Kids' Club Play Area **Services:** **Leisure:** P **Off-site:** R

AUREILHAN — LANDES

Village Center Aurilandes

1001 promenade de l'Étang, 40200

☎ 499572121 467516389

e-mail: contact@village-center.com

web: www.village-center.com/aquitaine/camping-mer-aurilandes.php

Quiet site on the banks of Lake Aureilhan.

dir: *D626, 2km before Mimizan, on right.*

GPS: 44.2230, -1.2036

Open: 27 Jun-9 Sep **Site:** 8HEC **For hire:** **Prices:** 15-25 Mobile home hire 154-889 **Facilities:** Wi-fi (charged) Kids' Club Play Area **Services:** **Leisure:** L P

Village Center Eurolac

Promenade de l'Étang, 40200

☎ 499572121 467516389

e-mail: contact@village-center.com

web: www.village-center.com/aquitaine/camping-eurolac.php

At the edge of Aureilhan Lake with exceptional views.

dir: *Off N10 at exit 16 to Mimizan onto D626 to Aureilhan.*

GPS: 44.2228, -1.2039

Open: 27 May-18 Sep **Site:** 7HEC **For hire:** **Facilities:** Wi-fi Kids' Club Play Area **Services:** **Leisure:** L P **Off-site:**

AZUR — LANDES

Camping Azu' Rivage

720 rte des Campings, Au bord du lac, 40140

☎ 558483072 558482556

e-mail: info@campingazurivage.com

web: www.campingazurivage.com

A family site in wooded surroundings close to Lac de Soustons and 8km from the coast. Kids' club available for 5-12 year olds.

dir: *2km S of Azur.*

Open: May-25 Sep **Site:** 7HEC **For hire:** **Prices:** 15-30 Mobile home hire 235-800 **Facilities:** Wi-fi Kids' Club **Services:** **Leisure:** L P R

FRANCE

BAGNÈRES-DE-BIGORRE HAUTES-PYRÉNÉES

Bigourdan

rte de Tarbes, 65200

562951357

web: www.camping-bigourdan.com

A level site recommended for caravans in a beautiful Pyrenean setting.

dir: *2.5km NW at Pouzac.*

Open: 31 Mar-21 Oct **Site:** 1HEC **For hire:** **Facilities:** **Services:** **Leisure:** P **Off-site:** R

Tilleuls

12 av Maréchal Alan Brooke, 65200

562952604

A well-equipped site at an altitude of 500 metres. There are good recreational facilities and a bakery operates during July and August.

Open: May-Sep **Site:** 2.6HEC **Facilities:** **Services:** **Off-site:** P

BASTIDE-DE-SEROU, LA ARIÈGE

Arize

rte de Nescus, 09240

561658151 561658334

e-mail: camparize@aol.com

web: www.camping-arize.com

A well-run site with a friendly atmosphere and offering a range of facilities in a peaceful wooded location at the foot of the Pyrénées. Available nearby, horse riding, trout fishing and hiking.

GPS: 43.0018, 1.4454

Open: 11 Mar-13 Nov **Site:** 3HEC **For hire:** **Facilities:** Wi-fi (charged) Kids' Club Play Area **Services:** **Leisure:** P R **Off-site:**

BEAUCENS-LES-BAINS HAUTES-PYRÉNÉES

Viscos

65400

562970545

e-mail: domaineviscos@orange.fr

web: www.domaineviscos.fr

A secluded location at the foot of the Pyrénées.

dir: *1km N on D13 rte de Lourdes. 4km from Argelès-Gazost (RN21).*

Open: May-15 Oct **Site:** 2HEC **For hire:** **Prices:** 11.70-16.20 Mobile home hire 250-480 **Facilities:** Play Area **Services:** **Leisure:** P **Off-site:** L R

BELVÈS DORDOGNE

Hauts de Ratebout

24170

553290210 553290828

e-mail: ratebout@franceloc.fr

web: www.camping-hauts-ratebout.fr

A well-equipped site on an old Périgord farm, set in extensive grounds on top of a hill.

dir: *D710 to Fumel, after Vaurez-de-Belvès onto D54 to Casals.*

Open: 28 Apr-12 Sep **Site:** 12HEC **For hire:** **Facilities:** **Services:** **Leisure:** P

Nauves

Bos Rouge, 24170

553291264

e-mail: campinglesnauves@hotmail.com

web: www.lesnauves.com

Located on a site with 40 different species of trees. A good base for touring the Perigord Noir.

dir: *4.5km SW via D53.*

GPS: 44.7544, 0.9822

Open: 11 Apr-14 Sep **Site:** 4.5HEC **For hire:** **Prices:** 11.20-22.20 Mobile home hire 130-756 **Facilities:** Wi-fi Kids' Club Play Area **Services:** **Leisure:** P **Off-site:** R

RCN Le Moulin de la Pique

24170

553290115 553282909

e-mail: moulin@rcn.fr

web: www.rcn-campings.fr

A quiet well-equipped site set out around an imposing villa and a small lake. There are fine entertainment facilities and modern sanitary installations.

dir: *0.5km S on D710.*

GPS: 44.7619, 1.0146

Open: 14 Apr-29 Sep **Site:** 12HEC **For hire:** **Prices:** 20.70-45.65 **Facilities:** Wi-fi (charged) Play Area **Services:** **Leisure:** L P R

BEYNAC-ET-CAZENAC DORDOGNE

Capeyrou

24220

553295495 553283627

e-mail: lecapeyrou@wanadoo.fr

web: www.campinglecapeyrou.com

Situated beside the River Dordogne close to the gates of the picturesque medieval town of Beynac. Great view of the castle.

dir: *Via D703.*

GPS: 44.8383, 1.1486

Open: 15 Apr-Sep **Site:** 5HEC **For hire:** **Prices:** 15-21.30 Mobile home hire 195-390 **Facilities:** Wi-fi Play Area **Services:** **Leisure:** P R **Off-site:**

BEZ, LE TARN

Plô

81260

563740082

e-mail: info@leplo.com

web: www.leplo.com

A pleasant small family site in wooded surroundings.

dir: *0.9km W via D30.*

GPS: 43.6081, 2.4713

Open: May-Sep **Site:** 4.2HEC **For hire:** **Facilities:** Wi-fi Play Area **Services:** **Leisure:** P **Off-site:** R

BIARRITZ PYRÉNÉES-ATLANTIQUES

Biarritz

28 rue d'Harcet, 64200

559230012 559437467

e-mail: biarritz.camping@wanadoo.fr

web: www.biarritz-camping.fr

A pleasant site with spacious pitches, 700 metres from the beach.

dir: *2km from town centre on N10, signed Espagne.*

Open: 9 Apr-2 Oct **Site:** 2.6HEC **For hire:** **Facilities:** Wi-fi (charged) Play Area **Services:** **Leisure:** P **Off-site:** S

BIAS LANDES

CM Le Tatiou

40710

558090476 558824430

e-mail: campingletatiou@wanadoo.fr

web: www.campingletatiou.com

Well-equipped family site in a forested setting, 4km from the sea.

dir: *2km W towards Lespecier.*

Open: Etr wknd-Sep **Site:** 10HEC **For hire:** **Prices:** 14.70 **Facilities:** Play Area **Services:** **Leisure:** P **Off-site:** L S

BIDART PYRÉNÉES-ATLANTIQUES

Ilbarritz

The Camping and Caravanning Club The Friendly Club

rte de Biarritz, 64210

559230029 559412459

e-mail: contact@camping-ilbarritz.com

web: www.camping-ilbarritz.com

Terraced site with numbered pitches, 0.8km from the sea.

C&CC Report *A great location for a site in the south west of France, with the beaches of Biarritz close at hand. The outdoor fun pool with waterslides is great for the family and with the covered pool too there is plenty of space for all. The Basque country is perfect for active members, with many walks and cycle paths in the area, whilst Biarritz is the surf capital of France.*

dir: *2km N on N106 Biarritz road.*

Open: 31 Mar-10 Nov **Site:** 7.7HEC **For hire:** **Facilities:** Wi-fi Kids' Club **Services:** **Leisure:** P **Off-site:** S

Oyam

Ferme Oyamburua, 64210

559549161 559547687

e-mail: accueil@camping-oyam.com

web: www.camping-oyam.com

Level meadow site near farm. Views of the Pyrénées. Simple but pleasant site. Shop, café and restaurant open July and August.

dir: *Turn off beyond church onto N10 towards Arbonne for 1km.*

Open: Jun-Sep **Site:** 7HEC **For hire:** **Prices:** 13-30 Mobile home hire 266-791 **Facilities:** Play Area **Services:** **Leisure:** P **Off-site:** S

FRANCE

Pavillon Royal

av Prince de Galles, 64210

559230054 559234447

e-mail: info@pavillon-royal.com

web: www.pavillon-royal.com

A beautiful, well-kept site beside a sandy beach, divided into pitches, most of which have a sea view.

dir: *A63 exit Biarritz.*

Open: 15 May-Sep **Site:** 4.5HEC **For hire:** **Prices:** 31-54 **Facilities:** Wi-fi (charged) Play Area **Services:** **Leisure:** P **Off-site:** S

Ruisseau

rte Burruntz, 64210

559419450 559419573

e-mail: francoise.dumont3@wanadoo.fr

web: www.camping-le-ruisseau.fr

A well-equipped family site in wooded surroundings set out around two lakes. There is a mini-farm for children and a kids' club in July and August. Leisure complex with two pools, one with slides.

dir: *2km E on D255.*

Open: 19 May-16 Sep **Site:** 18HEC **For hire:** **Prices:** 20-44 Mobile home hire 390-900 **Facilities:** Wi-fi (charged) Kids' Club Play Area **Services:** **Leisure:** P **Off-site:** S

Sunêlia Berrua

rue Berrua, 64210

559549666 559547830

e-mail: contact@berrua.com

web: www.berrua.com

A well-equipped family site 1km from the beach and 0.5km from the village. In a peaceful, shaded setting among trees, easy to get to and offering a view of the Pyrénées. The holiday park has a family atmosphere and lots of activities.

dir: *A63 exit Bayonne Nord for Pau.*

Open: 2 Apr-25 Sep **Site:** 5HEC **For hire:** **Facilities:** Wi-fi **Services:** **Leisure:** P **Off-site:** S

Ur-Onéa

rue de la Chapelle, 64210

559265361 559265394

e-mail: contact@uronea.com

web: www.uronea.com

A well-equipped site lying at the foot of the Pyrénées with good recreational facilities.

dir: *Off RN10.*

GPS: 43.4336, -1.5892

Open: 7 Apr-15 Sep **Site:** 5HEC **For hire:** **Prices:** 19-33 Mobile home hire 220-790 **Facilities:** Wi-fi (charged) Play Area **Services:** **Leisure:** P **Off-site:** R S

BIRON DORDOGNE

Moulinal

24540

553408460 553408149

e-mail: lemoulinal@franceloc.fr

web: www.lemoulinal.com

A pleasant location beside a lake close to the former mill of Château de Biron. The modern holiday village has a variety of recreational facilities.

dir: *2km S on the Lacapelle-Biron road.*

Open: 22 Mar-22 Sep **Site:** 18HEC **For hire:** **Facilities:** **Services:** **Leisure:** L P

BISCARROSSE LANDES

Camping les Petits Ecureuils

254 chemin Crastail, 40600

558780197 556884727

e-mail: bisca.petits.ecureuils@wanadoo.fr

web: www.les-petits-ecureuils.com

Family site, with facilities including a snack bar and ping-pong.

GPS: 44.4052, -1.1485

Open: 3 Apr-15 Oct **Site:** 1.7HEC **For hire:** **Prices:** 15-30 Mobile home hire 220-828 **Facilities:** Play Area **Services:** **Leisure:** P **Off-site:** L S

FRANCE

Ecureuils

Port Navarrosse, 40600

☎ 558098000 🖹 558098121

e-mail: camping.les.ecureuils@wanadoo.fr

web: www.ecureuils.fr

A pleasant wooded location 200 metres from the lake. Plenty of recreational facilities.

dir: *Via D652.*

GPS: 44.4294, -1.1669

Open: Apr-Sep **Site:** 7HEC **For hire:** **Facilities:** Wi-fi Kids' Club Play Area **Services:** **Leisure:** P **Off-site:** L

Rive

rte de Bordeaux, 40600

☎ 558781233 🖹 558781292

e-mail: info@larive.fr

web: www.larive.fr

Level site in tall pine forest on eastern side of lake. Private port and beach as well as restaurant and take away service.

dir: *N of town off D652 Sanguinet road.*

Open: 6 Apr-9 Sep **Site:** 15HEC **For hire:** **Prices:** 25.50-52 **Facilities:** Wi-fi (charged) Kids' Club Play Area **Services:** **Leisure:** L P

BOURNEL LOT-ET-GARONNE

Ferme de Bourgade

47210

☎ 553366715

e-mail: bourgade.gites@nordnet.fr

web: www.bourgade-holidays.co.uk

A small, tranquil site with good, clean facilities.

dir: *Signed from N21 between Castillonnès & Villeréal.*

Open: 15 Jun-15 Sep **Site:** 1HEC **Facilities:** **Services:** **Leisure:** L **Off-site:**

BRETENOUX LOT

Bourgnatelle

46130

☎ 565108904 🖹 565108918

e-mail: contact@dordogne-vacances.fr

web: www.dordogne-vacances.fr

A pleasant location beside the River Cére. Separate car park for arrivals after 22.30hrs.

dir: *D940 towards Rocamadour.*

Open: May-Sep **Site:** 3HEC **For hire:** **Facilities:** Wi-fi Play Area **Services:** **Leisure:** P R **Off-site:**

BRUGES GIRONDE

Le Village du Lac

bld Jacques Chaban, Delmas, 33520

☎ 557877060 🖹 557877061

e-mail: contact@camping-bordeaux.com

web: www.camping-bordeaux.com

Situated 8km from the centre of Bordeaux, with good bus and tram links to the city centre. There are spacious pitches and bike rental available. Shop on site open 15 June to 15 September.

GPS: 44.8974, -0.5827

Open: All Year. **Site:** 6HEC **For hire:** **Prices:** 18-31 Mobile home hire 210-1300 **Facilities:** Wi-fi (charged) Play Area **Services:** **Leisure:** P **Off-site:** L R

BUGUE, LE DORDOGNE

Brin d'Amour

Saint Cirq, 24260

☎ 553072373 🖹 553072373

e-mail: campingbrindamour@orange.fr

web: www.campings-dordogne.com/brindamour

A family site in a fine location overlooking the Vézère Valley with good facilities.

Open: Apr-Sep **Site:** 3.8HEC **For hire:** **Prices:** 10-19.50 Mobile home hire 180-640 **Facilities:** Wi-fi Play Area **Services:** **Leisure:** P **Off-site:** L R

Rocher de la Granelle

rte du Buisson, 24260

☎ 53072432

e-mail: info@lagranelle.com

web: www.lagranelle.com

Surrounded by woodland with pitches set out among trees and bushes on the banks of the Vézère with a variety of leisure facilities.

dir: *From Le Bugue centre over bridge & signed.*

Open: Apr-Sep **Site:** 8HEC **For hire:** **Facilities:** **Services:** **Leisure:** P R

St-Avit Loisirs

St-Avit-de-Vialard, 24260

553026400 553026439

e-mail: contact@saint-avit.loisirs.com

web: www.saint-avit-loisirs.com

A pleasant site in natural wooded surroundings with four swimming pools including an indoor heated pool. Leisure facilities include tennis and a golf driving range along with a kids' club available in July and August.

dir: *W of town via C201.*

Open: Apr-Sep **Site:** 7HEC **For hire:** **Prices:** 12.80-46.60 **Facilities:** Wi-fi (charged) Kids' Club Play Area **Services:** **Leisure:** P **Off-site:** R

CAHORS — LOT

Rivière de Cabessut

rue de la Rivière, 46000

565300630

e-mail: contact@cabessut.com

web: www.cabessut.com

1.5km from Cahors with quiet, shaded pitches.

dir: *N of town via Cabessut Bridge over River Lot.*

Open: Apr-Sep **Site:** 3HEC **For hire:** **Prices:** 17-19 Mobile home hire 210-540 **Facilities:** Wi-fi **Services:** **Leisure:** P R **Off-site:**

CALVIAC — LOT

Trois Sources

Le Peyratel, 46190

565330301 565330301

web: www.les-trois-sources.eu

Wooded location, family site with plenty of leisure facilities.

dir: *D653 onto D25 to Calviac.*

Open: 28 Apr-Sep **Site:** 7.5HEC **For hire:** **Facilities:** **Services:** **Leisure:** L P R

CAMPAGNE — DORDOGNE

Le Val de la Marquise

Le Moulin, 24260

553547410 553540070

e-mail: contact@levaldelamarquise.com

web: www.levaldelamarquise.com

Family-friendly site set in countryside, 3km from Le Bugue. Pitches are grassy, flat and divided by hedges. On-site fishing is available plus a swimming and paddling pool.

GPS: 44.9059, 0.9742

Open: Apr-Sep **Site:** 4HEC **For hire:** **Prices:** 11.10-19.60 Mobile home hire 182-651 **Facilities:** Wi-fi (charged) Kids' Club Play Area **Services:** **Leisure:** P **Off-site:**

CAP FERRET — GIRONDE

Truc Vert

rte Forestière, 33950

556608955 556609947

e-mail: camping.truc-vert@worldonline.fr

web: www.trucvert.com

A very pleasant location on a slope in a pine wood close to the beach.

dir: *On D106 towards Cap Ferret to Petit Piquey, turn right & signed.*

Open: May-Sep **Site:** 11HEC **Prices:** 16.50-21.50 **Facilities:** Wi-fi Play Area **Services:** **Off-site:** S

CARLUCET — LOT

Château de Lacomté

The Camping and Caravanning Club — The Friendly Club

46500

565387546 565331768

e-mail: chateaulacomte@wanadoo.fr

web: www.campingchateaulacomte.com

Set in wooded surroundings with good size, fully serviced pitches and a variety of recreational facilities. Site for adults only.

C&CC Report *Site for adults only. Popular with returning customers from all over Europe, this British-owned adults only site is a peaceful, rustic, rural retreat. A good base for trips to the Gouffre du Padirac, Rocamadour, Sarlat and Cahors, Lacomté has also delighted nature lovers with its swallowtail butterflies, rare orchids, three species of woodpecker and sightings of birds of prey, as well as the occasional visiting hare or deer. You can also take in the peaceful surroundings either while enjoying Sheila's cooking on the terrace or during a swim in the pool.*

dir: *Signed from D807/D32.*

Open: 15 May-Sep **Site:** 12HEC **For hire:** **Facilities:** Wi-fi **Services:** **Leisure:** P

FRANCE

CASTELJALOUX LOT-ET-GARONNE

CM de la Piscine

rte de Marmande, 47700

553935468 553934807

Close to the town centre and next to the olympic-size swimming pool.

dir: *NW on D933 Marmande road.*

Open: Apr-Nov **Site:** 1HEC **Facilities:** **Services:** **Off-site:** P R

Sarl Castel Chalets

rte de Mont-de-Marsan, 47700

553930745 553930745

e-mail: castel.chalets@orange.fr

web: www.castel-chalets.com

A large site with direct access to the 17-hectare Lac de Clarens and good recreational facilities.

dir: *A62 exit Marmande then towards Casteljaloux.*

Open: Apr-Nov **Site:** 2HEC **For hire:** **Prices:** 10 **Facilities:** Wi-fi Play Area **Services:** **Leisure:** L R **Off-site:** P

CASTELNAUD-LA-CHAPELLE DORDOGNE

Maisonneuve

24250

553295129 553302706

e-mail: contact@campingmaisonneuve.com

web: www.campingmaisonneuve.com

Picturesque surroundings 0.8km from the village, close to the River Céou in the Périgord Noir region.

dir: *10km S of Sarlat on D57.*

GPS: 44.8056, 1.1644

Open: 27 Mar-2 Nov **Site:** 6HEC **For hire:** **Prices:** 14.80-21.20 Mobile home hire 290-690 **Facilities:** Wi-fi Play Area **Services:** **Leisure:** P R **Off-site:**

CLAOUEY GIRONDE

Airotel les Viviers

rte du Cap Ferret, 33950

556607004 557703777

e-mail: reception@lesviviers.com

web: www.lesviviers.com

Extensive site in a beautiful forest divided by seawater channels.

dir: *On D106 1km S of the town.*

Open: 8 Apr-1 Oct **Site:** 33HEC **For hire:** **Facilities:** **Services:** **Leisure:** L P S

CONTIS-PLAGE LANDES

Lous Seurrots

606 av de l'Ocean, 40170

558428582 558424911

e-mail: info@lous-seurrots.com

web: www.lous-seurrots.com

Well-equipped site close to the beach in a pine forest on outskirts of village between a road and a stream. Kids' club July to August.

dir: *Via D41.*

GPS: 44.0886, -1.3166

Open: 4 Apr-16 Sep **Site:** 15HEC **For hire:** **Prices:** 17-45 **Facilities:** Wi-fi (charged) Kids' Club Play Area **Services:** **Leisure:** P R **Off-site:** S

CORDES TARN

Moulin de Julien

81170

563561110

A beautiful valley with good pitches for caravans and tents and plenty of modern facilities.

dir: *0.9km E on D600 & D922.*

Open: May-Sep **Site:** 6HEC **For hire:** **Facilities:** **Services:** **Leisure:** P **Off-site:** R

COUX-ET-BIGAROQUE DORDOGNE

Clou

Meynard, 24220

553316332 553316933

e-mail: info@camping-le-clou.com

web: www.camping-le-clou.com

Separate section for dog owners.

dir: *Via D703 Le Bugue-Delve road.*

Open: 18 Apr-4 Oct **Site:** 3.5HEC **For hire:** **Facilities:** **Services:** **Leisure:** P

FRANCE

Valades

Les Valades, 24220

☎ 553291427

e-mail: info@lesvalades.com

web: www.lesvalades.com

Wooded surroundings within a pleasant valley. Well-equipped pitches available. Every comfortable pitch has its own individual shower, toilet and sink. The site is also equipped with a sink for dishes, a refrigerator, a barbecue and wooden table.

dir: *5km N of town off N703.*

GPS: 44.8606, 0.9639

Open: Apr-Sep **Site:** 12HEC **For hire:** **Prices:** 26 Mobile home hire 240-700 **Facilities:** Wi-fi Play Area **Services:** **Leisure:** L P **Off-site:** R

CRÉON — GIRONDE

Bel Air

33670

☎ 556230190 556230838

web: www.camping-bel-air.com

A well-equipped, roomy site on a level meadow shaded by tall trees.

dir: *1.6km W of Créon on D671.*

Open: All Year. **Site:** 2HEC **For hire:** **Facilities:** **Services:** **Leisure:** P

DAGLAN — DORDOGNE

Moulin de Paulhiac

24250

☎ 553282088 553293345

e-mail: info@moulin-de-paulhiac.com

web: www.moulin-de-paulhiac.com

Picturesque wooded surroundings with wide, well-marked pitches and modern facilities.

dir: *4km N via D57 beside the Céou.*

Open: 15 May-15 Sep **Site:** 5HEC **For hire:** **Facilities:** **Services:** **Leisure:** P R

DAX — LANDES

Chênes

Au Bois-de-Boulogne, 40100

☎ 558900553 558904243

e-mail: camping-chenes@wanadoo.fr

web: www.camping-les-chenes.fr

A wooded park on the edge of the Bois-de-Boulogne with good facilities.

dir: *1.5km W of town beside River Adour.*

GPS: 43.7116, -1.0731

Open: 22 Mar-10 Nov **Site:** 5HEC **For hire:** **Prices:** 14.90-20.60 Mobile home hire 266-531 **Facilities:** Wi-fi (charged) **Services:** **Leisure:** P **Off-site:** R

DOMME — DORDOGNE

Perpetuum

La Rivière, 24250

☎ 553283518 553296364

e-mail: leperpetuum.domme@wanadoo.fr

web: www.campingleperpetuum.com

Situated on the edge of the Dordogne, a friendly, family site with flat, green pitches and leisure activities.

Open: May-10 Oct **Site:** 4.5HEC **For hire:** **Prices:** 12-20 Mobile home hire 220-700 **Facilities:** Wi-fi Kids' Club Play Area **Services:** **Leisure:** P R

DURAS — LOT-ET-GARONNE

Le Cabri

The Camping and Caravanning Club The Friendly Club

rte de Savignac, 47120

☎ 553838103 553830891

e-mail: holidays@lecabri.eu.com

web: www.lecabri.eu.com

Surrounded by vineyards in the countryside, yet only a ten minute walk to the historic village. Good facilities and spacious pitches.

C&CC Report *If you think that small is beautiful, you'll love le Cabri. With just a handful of pitches there's masses of space on site for your unit and your family, meaning total freedom for youngsters while mum and dad can relax and enjoy the restaurant and bar terrace. On this great little British-owned site a day out heading east brings you to the Dordogne, west to the Atlantic beaches, or south to the Midi-Pyrénées. Alternatively, just explore the unspoilt Lot-et-Garonne, enjoying its vineyards, châteaux, villages, festivals, walking and cycling routes, fishing, gardens and rivers.*

dir: *A89 exit 12, or A62 exit 5, then D708 to Duras.*

Open: All Year. **Site:** 6.5HEC **For hire:** **Prices:** 14-19 Mobile home hire 199-599 **Facilities:** Wi-fi (charged) Play Area **Services:** **Leisure:** P **Off-site:**

FRANCE

DURAVEL LOT

Club de Vacances

Port de Vire, 46700
☎ 565246506
e-mail: info@clubdevacances.eu
web: www.clubdevacances.eu
A pleasant site with good facilities beside the River Lot.
dir: *2.3km S via D58.*
Open: 25 Apr-Sep **Site:** 7HEC **For hire:** **Facilities:** **Services:** **Leisure:** P R

DURFORT ARIÈGE

Bourdieu

09130
☎ 561673017 561672900
e-mail: lebourdieu@wanadoo.fr
web: www.location-chalet-camping-ariege.com
Well-equipped site in a picturesque setting with fine views of the Pyrénées.
dir: *Off D14 Le Fossat-Saverdun.*
Open: All Year. **Site:** 20HEC **For hire:** **Facilities:** Wi-fi (charged) Play Area **Services:** **Leisure:** P **Off-site:**

ESQUIÈZE-SÈRE HAUTES-PYRÉNÉES

Camping Airotel Pyrénées

The Camping and Caravanning Club The Friendly Club

46 av du Barege, 65120
☎ 562928918 562929650
e-mail: airotel.pyrenees@wanadoo.fr
web: www.airotel-pyrenees.com
Family site with well equipped facilities and activities to suit all age groups.
C&CC Report *A superb setting, much enjoyed by campers of all ages. Whether you want to be active or just relax in the breathtaking scenery, this mountain location takes some beating – and it's only a short walk into the town, too. Visit mountains and passes made famous by the Tour de France, or try more adventurous activities such as white water rafting.*
dir: *Access directly off N927.*
Open: 27 Apr-Sep & Dec-13 Apr **Site:** 2.8HEC **For hire:** **Prices:** 14.50-27 Mobile home hire 199-795 **Facilities:** Wi-fi Play Area **Services:** **Leisure:** P **Off-site:**

ESTAING HAUTES-PYRÉNÉES

Pyrénées Natura

rte du Lac, 65400
☎ 562974544 562974581
e-mail: sarl.ruysschaert@wanadoo.fr
web: www.camping-pyrenees-natura.com
A well-run site at an altitude of 1000 metres, situated on the edge of the national park with views of the surrounding mountains.
dir: *8km from Argeles-Gazost turn left on D13 to Bun, cross the river then right on D103 to site.*
Open: May-20 Sep **Site:** 2.5HEC **For hire:** **Prices:** 17.40-25.90 Mobile home hire 280-640 **Facilities:** Wi-fi (charged) Play Area **Services:** **Leisure:** R **Off-site:** L P

ÉYZIES-DE-TAYAC, LES DORDOGNE

Pech Charmant

24620
☎ 553359708 553359709
e-mail: info@lepech.com
web: www.lepech.com
Located on the side of a wooded hill and contains a small farm with donkeys, goats, horses and chickens.
Open: 15 Apr-15 Sep **Site:** 17HEC **For hire:** **Facilities:** **Services:** **Leisure:** P **Off-site:** R

FIGEAC LOT

Les Rives du Célé - Camping le Domaine du Surgié

Domaine du Surgié, 46100
☎ 561648854 561648917
e-mail: contact@marc-montmija.com
web: www.lesrivesducele.com
A pleasant wooded location on the banks of the River Célé with plenty of leisure facilities. The site lies within a large recreation area. Separate car park for late arrivals. Mobile homes, gîtes and Ecolodges are available for rental.
dir: *Signed in town.*
GPS: 44.6118, 2.0494
Open: Apr-Sep **Site:** 2HEC **For hire:** **Facilities:** Kids' Club Play Area **Services:** **Leisure:** L P R **Off-site:**

FOIX — ARIÈGE

Camping du Lac

RN 20, 09000

561651158 561651998

e-mail: camping-du-lac@wanadoo.fr

web: www.campingdulac.com

On well-kept meadow beside the Lac de Labarre.

dir: *3km N on N20.*

Open: All Year. **Site:** 5HEC **For hire:** **Facilities:** Wi-fi Play Area **Services:** **Leisure:** L P **Off-site:**

FONTRAILLES — HAUTES-PYRÉNÉES

Fontrailles

65220

562356252

e-mail: detm.paddon@orange.fr

web: www.fontraillescamping.com

Set in a peaceful location, next to a shady oak wood and small fishing lake.

dir: *2km N of Trie-sur-Baise, left off D939 Tarbes-Mirande, signed.*

GPS: 43.345, 0.3697

Open: Jul-Sep **Site:** 1.5HEC **Prices:** 15 **Facilities:** Wi-fi Play Area **Services:** **Leisure:** P **Off-site:**

GAUGEAC — DORDOGNE

Village Center le Moulin de David

D2, 24540

499572121 467516389

e-mail: contact@village-center.com

web: www.village-center.com/aquitaine/camping-campagne-moulin-david.php

Situated in a wooded valley alongside a small stream, with well-defined pitches and good recreational facilities.

dir: *3km from town towards Villeréal.*

GPS: 44.6596, 0.8798

Open: 24 Jun-4 Sep **Site:** 16HEC **For hire:** **Facilities:** Wi-fi Kids' Club Play Area **Services:** **Leisure:** L P

GOURDON — LOT

Paradis

La Peyrugue, 46300

565416501 565416501

e-mail: contact@campingleparadis.com

web: www.campingleparadis.com

On a pleasant wooded meadow surrounded by hills.

dir: *1.6km SW off N673.*

Open: May-15 Sep **Site:** 2HEC **For hire:** **Prices:** 11-16 Mobile home hire 220-400 **Facilities:** Wi-fi Play Area **Services:** **Leisure:** P **Off-site:** L R

GOURETTE — PYRÉNÉES-ATLANTIQUES

Ley

64440

559051147 559051147

Terraced site with gravel and asphalt caravan pitches. TV, common room.

dir: *E from Laruns to Eaux-Bonnes & uphill to Gourette.*

Open: Dec-Apr & Jul-Aug **Site:** 2HEC **For hire:** **Prices:** 13.50 **Facilities:** **Services:** **Leisure:** R **Off-site:** L

GRADIGNAN — GIRONDE

Beausoleil

The Camping and Caravanning Club — The Friendly Club

371 cours Gén de Gaulle, 33170

556891766 556891766

e-mail: campingbeausoleil@wanadoo.fr

web: www.camping-gradignan.com

Quiet, shady site, close to cycle/foot paths from which to explore the surrounding countryside.

C&CC Report *Small friendly site in a good location not far from the Bordeaux ring-road, convenient transport links to Bordeaux and Gradignan and its services just 1.5km away.*

dir: *Off Bordeaux ring road, exit 16.*

Open: All Year. **Site:** 0.5HEC **For hire:** **Prices:** 17-20 Mobile home hire 75-425 **Facilities:** Wi-fi **Services:** **Off-site:**

FRANCE

cilities shower electric points for razors electric points for caravans motorvan service point parking by tents permitted
mpulsory separate car park shop **Services** café/restaurant bar Camping Gaz International gas other than Camping Gaz
first aid facilities laundry **Leisure** swimming L-Lake P-Pool R-River S-Sea **Off-site** All facilities within 5km

GRAULGES, LES — DORDOGNE

Crozes les Graulges

24340

553607473

e-mail: info@lesgraulges.com

web: www.lesgraulges.com

A picturesque setting in woodland beside a lake.

dir: *Off D939 between Angoulême & Périgueux.*

Open: Apr-Sep **Site:** 8HEC **For hire:** **Facilities:** **Services:** **Leisure:** L P R

GROLÉJAC — DORDOGNE

Granges

24250

553281115 553285713

e-mail: contact@lesgranges-fr.com

web: lesgranges-fr.com

Beautifully situated terraces on a hill with big pitches. The site has been constructed around a disused railway station, incorporating the old ticket office and the bridge into the modern design. Facilities for sports and entertainment. Kids' club available in high season.

dir: *Off D704 in village towards Domme.*

Open: 21 Apr-8 Sep **Site:** 6.5HEC **For hire:** **Prices:** 14.50-25 Mobile home hire 291-772 **Facilities:** Wi-fi Kids' Club Play Area **Services:** **Leisure:** P R **Off-site:** L

HASPARREN — PYRÉNÉES-ATLANTIQUES

Chapital

rte de Cambo, 64240

559296294

On level ground, surrounded by woodland. Good facilities for families.

dir: *0.5km W via D22. Or via A64 exit 3 for 10km.*

Open: May-Sep **Site:** 2.58HEC **For hire:** **Prices:** 15-21 Mobile home hire 200-540 **Facilities:** Play Area **Services:** **Off-site:** P

HAUTEFORT — DORDOGNE

Camping du Coucou

Le Bois du Coucou, 24390

553508697 553508697

e-mail: campingducoucou@orange.fr

web: www.campingducoucou.com

Located at the foot of the Château de Hautefort in rural countryside with modern amenities on site.

dir: *2km SW via D72 & D71, 100m from Coucou lake.*

GPS: 45.2477, 1.1379

Open: 23 Apr-15 Oct **Site:** 4HEC **For hire:** **Prices:** 11.70-15.10 Mobile home hire 190-430 **Facilities:** Wi-fi Play Area **Services:** **Leisure:** P **Off-site:** L R

HENDAYE — PYRÉNÉES-ATLANTIQUES

Acacias

64700

559207876 559207876

e-mail: info@les-acacias.com

web: www.les-acacias.com

A pleasant family site in parkland, 5 minutes from the beach.

dir: *1.8km E (rte de la Glacière).*

Open: Apr-Sep **Site:** 5HEC **For hire:** **Facilities:** **Services:** **Leisure:** L **Off-site:** S

HOURTIN — GIRONDE

Acacia

Ste-Hélène, 33990

556738080

e-mail: camping.lacacia@orange.fr

web: www.camping-lacacia.com

Pleasant, quiet site on the edge of a forest with good sanitary facilities. Compulsory car park for arrivals after 22.30hrs.

dir: *Off D3 towards lake.*

Open: Jun-Sep **Site:** 5HEC **For hire:** **Prices:** 13.90-15.90 Mobile home hire 250-350 **Facilities:** Play Area **Services:** **Off-site:** L

Ourmes

90 av du Lac, 33990
556091276 556092390
e-mail: info@lesourmes.com
web: www.lesourmes.com

A family campsite in wooded surroundings close to the beach and 0.5km from the largest freshwater lake in France.

dir: *D4 towards lake.*

GPS: 45.1819, -1.0756

Open: May-20 Sep **Site:** 7HEC **For hire:** **Prices:** 15.10-32.60 Mobile home hire 240-760 **Facilities:** Wi-fi Kids' Club Play Area **Services:** **Leisure:** P **Off-site:** L S

HOURTIN-PLAGE GIRONDE

Côte d'Argent

33990
556091025 556092496
e-mail: info@camping-cote-dargent.com
web: www.camping-cote-dargent.com

Set in a pine and oak forest with good facilities, 300 metres from the beach.

dir: *D101 from Hourtin.*

Open: 16 May-16 Sep **Site:** 20HEC **For hire:** **Prices:** 21-51 Mobile home hire 196-1134 **Facilities:** Wi-fi (charged) Kids' Club Play Area **Services:** **Leisure:** L P S

LABENNE LANDES

Pins Bleus

av de l'Océan, 40530
559454113 559454470
e-mail: camping@lespinsbleus.com
web: www.lespinsbleus.com

Tranquil, family site located close to the beach.

dir: *On RN10.*

Open: Apr-4 Nov **Site:** 6.5HEC **For hire:** **Facilities:** **Services:** **Leisure:** P **Off-site:** L R S

LABENNE-OCÉAN LANDES

Boudigau

40530
559454207 559457776
e-mail: info@boudigau.com
web: www.boudigau.com

Situated in a pine forest.

dir: *Turn right after bridge into site.*

Open: 15 May-15 Sep **Site:** 6HEC **For hire:** **Facilities:** **Services:** **Leisure:** P **Off-site:** S

Côte d'Argent

60 av de l'Océan, 40530
559454202 559457331
e-mail: info@camping-cotedargent.com
web: www.camping-cotedargent.com

Very well-managed modern site attached to holiday village. Bar, café and restaurant open June to September. Kids' club available in July and August.

dir: *D126 exit 8, RN10 direction Bayonne. At Labenne towards Labenne Ocean.*

GPS: 43.5953, -1.4565

Open: 30 Mar-Oct **Site:** 4HEC **For hire:** **Prices:** 10.70-28.90 Mobile home hire 285-820 **Facilities:** Wi-fi (charged) Kids' Club **Services:** **Leisure:** P **Off-site:** R S

Mer

38 rte de la Plage, 40530
559454209 559454307
e-mail: campinglamer@wanadoo.fr
web: www.campinglamer.com

Set in a pine forest 0.5km from the beach. A kids' club is available in July and August. Restrictions may apply to certain breeds of dog.

dir: *On D126 rte de la Plage.*

Open: 30 Mar-Sep **Site:** 11HEC **For hire:** **Prices:** 10.40-28.50 Mobile home hire 250-875 **Facilities:** Wi-fi (charged) Kids' Club Play Area **Services:** **Leisure:** P R **Off-site:** S

Yelloh Village Le Sylvamar

av de l'Océan, 40530

☎ 559457516 📠 559454639

e-mail: camping@sylvamar.fr

web: www.sylvamar.fr

Situated in a tranquil location in a pine forest, 900 metres from the sea. Paddling pool and heated spa area.

dir: *Access via D126.*

Open: 31 Mar-23 Sep **Site:** 21HEC **For hire:** **Prices:** 15-44 **Facilities:** Wi-fi (charged) Kids' Club Play Area **Services:** **Leisure:** P **Off-site:** L S

Yelloh Village Grands Pins

Plages Nord, 33680

☎ 556032077 📠 557700389

e-mail: reception@lesgrandspins.com

web: www.lesgrandspins.com

On very hilly terrain in woodland, 350 metres from the beach through dunes.

dir: *A10 exit 7, D6 to Lacanau.*

Open: 14 Apr-22 Sep **Site:** 12HEC **For hire:** **Prices:** 17-49 Mobile home hire 273-1673 **Facilities:** Wi-fi (charged) Kids' Club Play Area **Services:** **Leisure:** P **Off-site:** L S

LACANAU-OCÉAN GIRONDE

Airotel de l'Océan

24 Rue du Répos, 33680

☎ 556032445 📠 557700187

e-mail: web-airotel@wanadoo.fr

web: www.airotel-ocean.com

On rising ground in a pine forest, 0.8km from the beach.

Open: 8 Apr-24 Sep **Site:** 9.5HEC **For hire:** **Facilities:** **Services:** **Leisure:** P **Off-site:** S

Talaris

rte de l'Océan, 33680

☎ 556030415 📠 556262156

e-mail: talarisvacances@free.fr

web: www.talaris-vacances.fr

A family site in delightful wooded surroundings 1.2km from the lake. Separate car park for arrivals after 22.30hrs.

dir: *2km E on rte de Lacanau.*

Open: 7 Apr-15 Sep **Site:** 8.25HEC **For hire:** **Facilities:** **Services:** **Leisure:** P **Off-site:** L

Tedey

rte de Longarisse, 33680

☎ 556030015 📠 556030190

e-mail: camping@le-tedey.com

web: www.le-tedey.com

Quiet site in pine forest, on edge of Lake Lacanau. Dogs not accepted in July and August.

dir: *Off D6 onto narrow track through forest for 0.5km.*

GPS: 44.9869, -1.1364

Open: 22 Apr-15 Sep **Site:** 14HEC **For hire:** **Prices:** 17-30 Mobile home hire 330-735 **Facilities:** Wi-fi (charged) **Services:** **Leisure:** L **Off-site:** S

LACAPELLE-MARIVAL LOT

CM Bois de Sophie

rte d'Aynac, 46120

☎ 565408259

e-mail: lacapelle.mairie@wanadoo.fr

A pleasant wooded location with a variety of sports facilities.

dir: *1km NW via D940.*

Open: Mar-Oct **Site:** 2HEC **For hire:** **Prices:** 11.55 Mobile home hire 240-320 **Facilities:** Wi-fi Play Area **Services:** **Leisure:** P **Off-site:** L R

LANTON GIRONDE

Roumingue

33138

☎ 556829748 📠 556829609

web: www.roumingue.fr

Level terrain under a few deciduous trees partially in open meadow on the Bassin d'Arcachon. During July and August, shop, bar, café, restaurant, swimming pool bungalows/chalets are all available.

dir: *1km NW of village towards sea.*

GPS: 44.704, -1.048

Open: 15 Mar-15 Nov **Site:** 10HEC **For hire:** **Facilities:** Wi-fi Kids' Club Play Area **Services:** **Leisure:** P S **Off-site:**

FRANCE

LARNAGOL — LOT

Camping du Ruisseau de Treil

46160

565312339

e-mail: lotcamping@wanadoo.fr

web: www.lotcamping.com

A quiet site, with old stone walls, a stream and plenty of shrubs and trees. Located within a small valley on the southern edge of the Massif Central the site has large well-defined pitches and good leisure facilities.

dir: *0.6km E of Larnagol off D662 towards Cajarc.*

GPS: 44.4735, 1.7835

Open: 19 May-8 Sep **Site:** 3.2HEC **For hire:** **Facilities:** Wi-fi (charged) Play Area **Services:** **Leisure:** P **Off-site:** R

LARUNS — PYRÉNÉES-ATLANTIQUES

Gaves

64440

559053237 559054714

e-mail: campingdesgaves@wanadoo.fr

web: www.campingdesgaves.com

On the bank of the Gave d'Ossan amid beautiful Pyrenean scenery. Some pitches reserved for caravans.

dir: *1km S follow in the direction of Saragosse exit Gan to Laruns.*

GPS: 42.9823, -0.4173

Open: All Year. **Site:** 2.5HEC **For hire:** **Prices:** 14.30-19.90 Mobile home hire 252-630 **Facilities:** Wi-fi Play Area **Services:** **Leisure:** R **Off-site:** P

LECTOURE — GERS

Lac des Trois Vallées

32700

562688233 562688882

web: www.lacdes3vallees.fr

This rural site is part of a large park and lies next to a lake. It has spacious marked pitches.

dir: *3km SE on N21.*

Open: 20 May-10 Sep **Site:** 40HEC **For hire:** **Facilities:** **Services:** **Leisure:** L P

LÉON — LANDES

Airotel Lou Puntaou

av du Lac, 40550

558487430 558487042

e-mail: reception@loupuntaou.com

web: www.loupuntaou.com

Set in an oak wood with separate sections for caravans.

dir: *Off N652 in village onto D142 towards lake for 1.5km.*

Open: Apr-1 Oct **Site:** 8HEC **For hire:** **Facilities:** **Services:** **Leisure:** P **Off-site:** L R S

St-Antoine

St-Michel-Escalus, 40550

558487850

e-mail: campingstantoine@wanadoo.fr

A pleasant, well-equipped site beside a river in peaceful wooded surroundings.

dir: *N10 onto D142/N652 onto D142.*

GPS: 43.8778, -1.2381

Open: Apr-Sep **Site:** 6HEC **For hire:** **Prices:** 15 **Facilities:** **Services:** **Leisure:** R

LESCAR — PYRÉNÉES-ATLANTIQUES

Terrier

av du Vert Galant, 64230

559810182 559812683

e-mail: camping.terrier@wanadoo.fr

web: www.camping-terrier.com

Meadowland site divided in two with pitches surrounded by hedges in foreground.

dir: *From Pau N117 towards Bayonne for 6.5km, left onto D501 towards Monein to site towards bridge.*

Open: All Year. **Site:** 4HEC **For hire:** **Facilities:** Play Area **Services:** **Leisure:** P **Off-site:** L

LESPERON — LANDES

Parc de Couchoy

3000 rue de Linxe, 40260

558896015 558896015

e-mail: colinmrose@aol.com

web: parcdecouchoy.com

Situated in a pine forest, 3km from the village. Leisure activities include a swimming pool, paddling pool, table tennis and petanque.

Open: Jun-15 Sep **Site:** 1.5HEC **For hire:** **Prices:** 15-23 **Facilities:** Wi-fi Play Area **Services:** **Leisure:** P **Off-site:** R

FRANCE

LINXE — LANDES

CM Le Grandjean

rte de Mixe, 40260

558429000 558429467

A modern family site on the edge of a forest.

dir: *Off Castets road onto D42 towards Linxe.*

Open: 25 Jun-27 Aug **Site:** 2.7HEC **For hire:** **Facilities:** **Services:** **Off-site:**

LIT-ET-MIXE — LANDES

Village Center les Vignes

rte du Cap de l'Homy, 40170

558428560 558427436

e-mail: auvignes@village-center.fr

web: www.village-center.com/aquitaine/camping-mer-les-vignes.php

5km from the ocean, set in a pine forest with good sanitary and sports facilities.

dir: *N10 exit 13 onto D41.*

GPS: 44.0234, -1.2796

Open: 8 Apr-2 Oct **Site:** 15HEC **For hire:** **Prices:** Mobile home hire 1099 **Facilities:** Wi-fi (charged) Kids' Club Play Area **Services:** **Leisure:** P **Off-site:** S

LIVERS-CAZELLES — TARN

Rédon

81170

563561464 563561464

e-mail: info@campredon.com

web: www.campredon.com

A quiet site with modern facilities, and fine views over the surrounding area. Close to the medieval village of Cordes and the larger Albi, a UNESCO world heritage site. Kids' club in high season.

dir: *4km SE of Cordes on D600.*

GPS: 44.0418, 2.0162

Open: 31 Mar-14 Oct **Site:** 2HEC **For hire:** **Prices:** 15.80-22.80 Mobile home hire 375-695 **Facilities:** Wi-fi Kids' Club Play Area **Services:** **Leisure:** P **Off-site:**

LOUPIAC — LOT

Hirondelles

Al Pech, 46350

565376625

e-mail: contact@camping-leshirondelles.com

web: www.camping-leshirondelles.com

A natural setting in the heart of the Quercy region with a variety of recreational facilities. Kids' club in high season.

dir: *3km N via N20.*

Open: Apr-Sep **Site:** 2.5HEC **For hire:** **Prices:** 16.90-19.50 Mobile home hire 300-690 **Facilities:** Wi-fi Kids' Club Play Area **Services:** **Leisure:** P **Off-site:**

LOURDES — HAUTES-PYRÉNÉES

Arrouach

9 rue des Trois Archanges, Quartier Biscaye, 65100

562421143

e-mail: camping.arrouach@wanadoo.fr

web: www.camping-arrouach.com

Pleasant wooded surroundings on northern outskirts.

dir: *On D947 Soumoulou road.*

Open: 15 Mar-Oct **Site:** 13HEC **Prices:** 13.40 **Facilities:** Wi-fi **Services:** **Off-site:** L P R

Domec

rte de Julos, 65100

562940879 562940879

e-mail: campingdomec@free.fr

web: www.camping-domec-lourdes.com

In a quiet area near the city centre. Leisure facilities include a games room.

dir: *Off N21 Tarbes road N of town centre.*

Open: Etr-Oct **Site:** 2HEC **For hire:** **Facilities:** **Services:** **Off-site:** L P R

LUZ-ST-SAUVEUR — HAUTES-PYRÉNÉES

Le Bergons

rte de Barèges, 65120

562929077

e-mail: info@camping-bergons.com

web: www.camping-bergons.com

A beautiful setting on a level meadow surrounded by woodland close to the main Pyrenean ski resorts.

dir: *0.6km E on D618 Barèges road.*

Open: 3 Dec-22 Apr, 7 May-21 Oct **Site:** 1HEC **For hire:** **Prices:** 10.34-10.64 Mobile home hire 235-500 **Facilities:** Wi-fi (charged) Play Area **Services:** **Off-site:** P R

Camping International

rte de Lourdes, 65120

562928202 562929687

e-mail: camping.international.luz@wanadoo.fr

web: www.international-camping.fr

Set in a wooded valley at an altitude of 700 metres with panoramic views of the surrounding mountains.

dir: *1.3km NW on N21.*

Open: 15 Dec-20 Apr & Jun-Sep **Site:** 4HEC **For hire:** **Prices:** 13.60-23 Mobile home hire 200-660 **Facilities:** Wi-fi **Services:** **Leisure:** P **Off-site:** R

Pyrénévasion

rte de Luz-Ardiden, Sazos, 65120

562929154 562929834

e-mail: camping-pyrenevasion@wanadoo.fr

web: www.campingpyrenevasion.com

A quiet site in an idyllic mountain setting close to the ski-runs. The pitches are well-defined and all facilities are clean and modern.

dir: *2km from town on Luz-Ardiden road.*

Open: 20 Nov-20 Oct **Site:** 3HEC **For hire:** **Facilities:** Wi-fi Play Area **Services:** **Leisure:** P **Off-site:** R

MARCILLAC-ST-QUENTIN — DORDOGNE

Tailladis

24200

553591095 553294756

e-mail: tailladis@wanadoo.fr

web: www.tailladis.com

Well-maintained family site with good recreational facilities.

dir: *2km N near D48.*

GPS: 44.9742, 1.1872

Open: Mar-Nov **Site:** 4HEC **For hire:** **Prices:** 11-18.20 Mobile home hire 245-580 **Facilities:** Wi-fi (charged) Play Area **Services:** **Leisure:** L P

MARTRES-TOLOSANE — HAUTE-GARONNE

Le Moulin

31220

561988640 561986690

e-mail: info@campinglemoulin.com

web: www.campinglemoulin.com

A beautiful wooded location beside the River Garonne at the foot of the Pyrénées. Well maintained with a variety of recreational facilities. Kids' club available in July and August.

dir: *2km off A64 exit 21/22.*

GPS: 43.1906, 1.0179

Open: Apr-Sep **Site:** 12HEC **For hire:** **Prices:** 16-22.90 Mobile home hire 266-890 **Facilities:** Wi-fi Kids' Club Play Area **Services:** **Leisure:** P R **Off-site:** L

MAULÉON-LICHARRE — PYRÉNÉES-ATLANTIQUES

Camping Uhaitza Le Saison

rte de Libarrenx, 64130

559281879 559280623

e-mail: camping.uhaitza@wanadoo.fr

web: www.camping-uhaitza.com

Located near the town centre, this peaceful site is beside a river for swimming and fishing.

dir: *1.5km S on D918.*

GPS: 43.2079, -0.8967

Open: Apr-Sep **Site:** 1.13HEC **For hire:** **Prices:** 13-19.60 Mobile home hire 250-590 **Facilities:** Wi-fi Play Area **Services:** **Leisure:** R **Off-site:** P

MAZION — GIRONDE

Tilleuls

33390

557421813 557421301

e-mail: chateau_alberts@hotmail.com

web: www.chateau-les-alberts.com

In a shady setting amongst the vineyards of Château les Alberts.

dir: *5.5km NE on N937.*

Open: May-Oct **Site:** 0.5HEC **Prices:** 12.50-15.50 **Facilities:** **Services:** **Off-site:** P

FRANCE

MESSANGES — LANDES

Acacias

Quartier Delest, Route d'Azur, 40660
☎ 558480178 558482312
e-mail: lesacacias@lesacacias.com
web: www.lesacacias.com

The Camping and Caravanning Club — The Friendly Club

Quiet family site, close to sandy beaches, cycle paths and the forest of Landes. Kids' club available in high season.

C&CC Report *In an area with many large, busy sites, this is a small, friendly, more relaxed and traditional alternative which is generally very peaceful in low season. The welcoming owners, proximity to superb beaches, and well-sized pitches will make Camping Les Acacias a greatly-loved favourite, especially younger families and couples. The local cycle paths offer the chance to explore without taking the car, whilst the traditional surrounding Basque architecture, and towns of Bayonne and Dax, are a further delight.*

dir: *A63-RN10 direction Bordeaux-Bayonne exit 11 Magescq. Towards Azur/Messanges, then Vieux-Boucau. Left at rdbt by fire station, site 1km on left.*

GPS: 43.7983, -1.3758

Open: 25 Mar-25 Oct **Site:** 2.07HEC **For hire:** **Prices:** 10.80-17.50 Mobile home hire 240-650 **Facilities:** Wi-fi Kids' Club Play Area **Services:** **Off-site:** L P S

Airotel Le Vieux Port

Plage Sud, 40660
☎ 176767000 558480169
e-mail: contact@levieuxport.com
web: www.levieuxport.com

A family site in the heart of the Landes forest with direct access to the beach. Good recreational facilities, including a large pool area.

dir: *2.5km SW via D652.*

Open: 31 Mar-Sep **Site:** 30HEC **For hire:** **Prices:** 16-52 Mobile home hire 159-1393 **Facilities:** Wi-fi (charged) Kids' Club Play Area **Services:** **Leisure:** P S **Off-site:** L R

Albret Plage

rte Plagesud, 40660
☎ 558480367 558482191
e-mail: albretplage@wanadoo.fr
web: www.albretplage.fr

Family site with direct access to beach (300 metres). 1km from town of Vieux Boucau.

GPS: 43.7970, -1.4010

Open: Apr-Sep **Site:** 6HEC **For hire:** **Prices:** 12.40-19.02 Mobile home hire 215-535 **Facilities:** Wi-fi (charged) Play Area **Services:** **Leisure:** S **Off-site:** L P R

see advert on this page

Côte

BP 37, 40660
☎ 558489494 558489444
e-mail: info@campinglacote.com
web: www.campinglacote.com

A picturesque wooded area 1km from the beach.

dir: *2.3km S via D652.*

GPS: 43.8003, -1.3917

Open: Apr-Sep **Site:** 4HEC **For hire:** **Prices:** 11.20-22.50 Mobile home hire 240-720 **Facilities:** Wi-fi Play Area **Services:** **Leisure:** P **Off-site:** L S

Moïsan

rte de la Plage, 40660
☎ 558489206 558489206
e-mail: camping.moisan@orange.fr
web: www.camping-moisan.com

Family site set in a pine forest 0.8km from the sea with modern facilities.

GPS: 43.8161, -1.3908

Open: Apr-3 Oct **Site:** 7HEC **For hire:** **Facilities:** Wi-fi Play Area **Services:** **Off-site:** P S

MÉZOS LANDES

Sen Yan

40170

☎ 558426005 558426456

e-mail: reception@sen-yan.com

web: www.sen-yan.com

A pleasant site in exotic tropical gardens, surrounded by a pine wood. Dogs accepted but may be restricted on some pitches. Kids' club available for children aged 5 to10.

dir: *1km E between Mézos and Danglas.*

Open: May-12 Sep **Site:** 8HEC **For hire:** **Facilities:** Wi-fi (charged) Kids' Club Play Area **Services:** **Leisure:** P **Off-site:** R

MIERS LOT

Pigeonnier

46500

☎ 565337195 565337195

e-mail: camping-le-pigeonnier@orange.fr

web: www.campinglepigeonnier.com

Peaceful, shady site close to the River Dordogne amid spectacular scenery.

dir: *400m E via D91.*

Open: Apr-1 Oct **Site:** 1HEC **For hire:** **Facilities:** **Services:** **Leisure:** P **Off-site:** L

MIMIZAN LANDES

Camping de la Plage

bld de l'Atlantique, 40200

☎ 558090032 558094494

e-mail: contact@mimizan-camping.com

web: www.mimizan-camping.com

Well equipped secure site with thoughtfully divided areas and good facilities.

GPS: 44.2161, -1.2856

Open: 6 Apr-23 Sep **Site:** 16HEC **For hire:** **Prices:** 15-22.30 Mobile home hire 200-685 **Facilities:** Wi-fi (charged) Play Area **Services:** **Off-site:** S

Club Marina-Landes

rue Marina, 40200

☎ 558091266 558091640

e-mail: contact@clubmarina.com

web: www.marinalandes.com

Set in a pine wood 0.5km from the beach. Kids' club available in July and August.

dir: *D626 from Mimizan Plage.*

GPS: 44.2040, -1.2909

Open: 14 May-21 Sep **Site:** 9.5HEC **For hire:** **Facilities:** Wi-fi (charged) Kids' Club Play Area **Services:** **Leisure:** P **Off-site:** R S

MIRANDOL-BOURGNOUNAC TARN

Camping Les Clots

Les Clots, 81190

☎ 563769278

e-mail: campclots@wanadoo.fr

web: www.campinglesclots.info

A campsite for nature lovers situated in a wooded area within the Viaur Valley with good facilities.

dir: *5.5km N via D905, rte de Rieupeyroux.*

GPS: 44.1772, 2.1791

Open: Jun-mid Sep **Site:** 7HEC **For hire:** **Prices:** 25 **Facilities:** Wi-fi Play Area **Services:** **Leisure:** P R **Off-site:**

MOLIÈRES DORDOGNE

Lac du Malivert

Centre de Loisirs du Malivert, 82220

☎ 563677637 563676216

e-mail: molieres.82@wanadoo.fr

web: www.ville-molieres.fr

A pleasant lakeside setting.

dir: *To Molières from S, towards Centre de Loisirs & Lac Malivert.*

Open: May-Oct **Site:** 0.7HEC **For hire:** **Prices:** 9-11 Mobile home hire 430-480 **Facilities:** Wi-fi Play Area **Services:** **Leisure:** L **Off-site:**

FRANCE

MOLIETS-PLAGE — LANDES

Cigales

av de l'Océan, 40660

558485118 558483527

e-mail: reception@camping-les-cigales.fr

web: www.camping-les-cigales.fr

On undulating ground in pine trees.

dir: *300m from beach.*

Open: Apr-Sep **Site:** 23HEC **For hire:** **Facilities:** Wi-fi (charged) **Services:** **Off-site:** L R S

Le Saint Martin

av de l'Océan, 40660

558485230 558485073

e-mail: contact@camping-saint-martin.fr

web: www.camping-saint-martin.fr

Large site on the Atlantic coast with direct access to the largest sandy beach in the region. Wi-fi free out of season. Kids' club in July and August.

C&CC Report *A large, family-oriented site in a fantastic location, right on a huge beach and in the busy little village of Moliets-Plage, offering a quiet beach holiday in low season, with free indoor heated pool, or the full seaside experience in the busier times. If you want a change from the beach, take to the forest roads or cycle tracks or get special discounts for using the local golf club.*

dir: *Between village & beach.*

Open: 4 Apr-1 Nov **Site:** 18.5HEC **For hire:**
Prices: 18.80-54.40 Mobile home hire 220-1440
Facilities: Wi-fi (charged) Kids' Club Play Area
Services: **Leisure:** P S **Off-site:**

MONCRABEAU — LOT-ET-GARONNE

Mouliat

Le Mouliat, 47600

553654328 553654328

e-mail: campinglemouliat@gmail.com

A small family site in a wooded location on the banks of the River La Baïse. Several walking routes from the site.

dir: *On D219, 200m from D930.*

Open: Apr-Oct **Site:** 1.3HEC **For hire:**
Prices: 8.70-10.50 Mobile home hire 209-495 **Facilities:** Wi-fi **Services:** **Leisure:** P R

MONTCABRIER — LOT

Moulin de Laborde

46700

565246206

e-mail: moulindelaborde@wanadoo.fr

web: www.moulindelaborde.com

Well-equipped site, set by a 17th-century watermill, surrounded by woods and hills, in a picturesque valley on the River Thèze.

dir: *NW off D673.*

GPS: 44.5475, 1.0839

Open: 25 Apr-8 Sep **Site:** 12HEC
Prices: 18.96-23.70 **Facilities:** Wi-fi Play Area
Services: **Leisure:** L P R **Off-site:**

MONTIGNAC — DORDOGNE

Moulin du Bleufond

av Aristide Briand, 24290

553518395 553511992

e-mail: le.moulin.du.bleufond@wanadoo.fr

web: www.bleufond.com

Situated beside a river in the grounds of a 17th-century mill.

dir: *0.5km off D65 Montignac to Sergeac road.*

Open: Apr-12 Oct **Site:** 1.3HEC **For hire:** **Facilities:** **Services:** **Leisure:** P **Off-site:** R

NAGES — TARN

Village Center Rieumontagné

Lac du Laouzas, 81320

499572121 467516389

e-mail: contact@village-center.com

web: www.village-center.com/midi-pyrenees/camping-rieumontagne.php

Wooded location beside the Laouzas lake with good recreational facilities.

dir: *4.5km S via D62.*

GPS: 43.6487, 2.7781

Open: 24 Jun-4 Sep **Site:** 11HEC **For hire:**
Facilities: Wi-fi (charged) Kids' Club Play Area
Services: **Leisure:** P **Off-site:** L

FRANCE

OLORON-STE-MARIE PYRÉNÉES-ATLANTIQUES

Gite du Stade

chemin de Lagravette, 64400
559391126 559391126
e-mail: camping-du-stade@wanadoo.fr
web: www.camping-du-stade.com
Peaceful shady site in the Pyrénées with a sports complex nearby.
dir: *A64 exit for Pau, towards Oloron-Ste-Marie.*
GPS: 43.1788, -0.6233
Open: May-Sep **Site:** 3HEC **For hire:** **Prices:** 12-15 Mobile home hire 285-530 **Facilities:** Play Area **Services:** **Leisure:** R **Off-site:** P

ONESSE-ET-LAHARIE LANDES

Bienvenu

259 rte de Mimizan, 40110
558073049 558073049
e-mail: campingbienvenu.landes@orange.fr
A family site situated in a forest.
dir: *0.5km from village centre on D38.*
Open: 15 Mar-30 Oct **Site:** 1.2HEC **For hire:** **Facilities:** **Services:** **Leisure:** P **Off-site:** L R S

OUSSE PYRÉNÉES-ATLANTIQUES

Sapins

4 rte de Tarbes (D817), 64320
559817421
e-mail: lessapins64@orange.fr
web: www.camping-hotel-les-sapins.fr
Small, peaceful site with spacious pitches. Facilities include table tennis.
dir: *D817 exit Pau. Or A64 exit Soumoulou.*
GPS: 43.2887, -0.2697
Open: All Year. **Site:** 1HEC **For hire:** **Prices:** 10.50 Mobile home hire 320 **Facilities:** Wi-fi **Services:** **Off-site:**

PAUILLAC GIRONDE

CM Les Gabarreys

rte de la Rivière, 33250
556591003 556733068
e-mail: camping.les.gabarreys@wanadoo.fr
web: www.pauillac-medoc.com
A municipal site with good sports facilities plus a sauna and spa.
dir: *RN 215/D2.*
Open: 3 Apr-10 Oct **Site:** 2HEC **For hire:** **Prices:** 14.50-17 Mobile home hire 304.50-503 **Facilities:** Wi-fi (charged) Play Area **Services:** **Off-site:** P R

PAYRAC LOT

Flower Camping les Pins

46350
565379632 565379108
e-mail: info@les-pins-camping.com
web: www.les-pins-camping.com
A well-managed site, partly in forest, partly on meadowland. Sheltered from traffic noise.
dir: *S of village off D820.*
GPS: 44.7893, 1.4730
Open: 14 Apr-16 Sep **Site:** 3.5HEC **For hire:** **Prices:** 18-30.90 Mobile home hire 196-896 **Facilities:** Wi-fi Kids' Club Play Area **Services:** **Leisure:** P **Off-site:**

Panoramic

rte de Loupiac, 46350
565379845
e-mail: info@campingpanoramic.com
web: www.campingpanoramic.com
A peaceful family site 5km from the River Dordogne with good recreational facilities.
dir: *Off D820 N of Payrac.*
GPS: 44.8057, 1.4748
Open: All Year. **Site:** 1.85HEC **For hire:** **Prices:** 11-14 Mobile home hire 170-395 **Facilities:** Wi-fi Play Area **Services:** **Off-site:** P R

FRANCE

PÉRIGUEUX — DORDOGNE

Barnabé

80 rue des Bains, Boulazac, 24750
553534145 553541662
e-mail: contact@barnabe-perigord.com
web: www.barnabe-perigord.com

A well-appointed site in a wooded park-like location beside the river.

dir: *Signed from N89, 2km E of town centre.*

Open: Mar-Oct **Site:** 1.5HEC **Facilities:** **Services:** **Off-site:** P

PETIT-PALAIS — GIRONDE

Pressoir

Queyrai Petit-Palais, 33570
557697325 557697736
e-mail: contact@campinglepressoir.com
web: www.campinglepressoir.com

A renovated, former wine farm in the rolling countryside around St-Emilion.

dir: *N89 Bordeaux-Périgeux, exit St-Médard de Guizières & signed.*

Open: All Year. **Site:** 2.5HEC **For hire:** **Facilities:** Wi-fi Kids' Club Play Area **Services:** **Leisure:** P **Off-site:** R

PEZULS — DORDOGNE

Camping la Forêt

24510
553227169 553237779
e-mail: campinglaforet@dbmail.com
web: www.camping-la-foret.com

Set in extensive grounds on the edge of the forest with modern facilities.

dir: *3km from village centre, site 0.6km off D703.*

GPS: 44.9153, 0.8211

Open: Apr-Oct **Site:** 9HEC **For hire:** **Prices:** 10.80-12.20 Mobile home hire 192-440 **Facilities:** Wi-fi Play Area **Services:** **Leisure:** P

PONT-ST-MAMET — DORDOGNE

Lestaubière

Pont-St-Mamet, 24140
553829815 553829017
e-mail: lestaubiere@cs.com
web: www.lestaubiere.com

Secluded site in an attractive part of the Dordogne, occupying the former outbuildings and wooded grounds of the adjacent château. Fine views of the surrounding countryside.

dir: *Off N21. 0.5km N of Pont-St-Mamet.*

Open: 26 Apr-1 Oct **Site:** 22HEC **For hire:** **Facilities:** **Services:** **Leisure:** L P

PUYBRUN — LOT

Sole

46130
565385237 565109109
e-mail: camping.la.sole@wanadoo.fr
web: www.la-sole.com

A well-run site in pleasant wooded surroundings with good facilities.

dir: *D703 from village towards Bretenoux, 1st turning after garage.*

Open: Apr-Sep **Site:** 2.1HEC **For hire:** **Facilities:** **Services:** **Leisure:** P **Off-site:** L R

PYLA-SUR-MER — GIRONDE

Camping de la Dune

rte de Biscarrosse, 33115
556227217 556227401
e-mail: reception@campingdeladune.fr
web: www.campingdeladune.fr

A beautifully situated and quiet site located at the base of the highest sand dune in Europe.

dir: *Dune du Pyla following signs for camping - route de Biscarrosse.*

GPS: 44.5813, -1.2127

Open: Mar-Oct **Site:** 6HEC **For hire:** **Facilities:** Wi-fi (charged) Kids' Club Play Area **Services:** **Leisure:** P **Off-site:** L S

FRANCE

Pyla Camping

rte de Biscarrosse, 33115

556227456 556221031

e-mail: reception@pylacamping.fr

web: www.pyla-camping.com

Located at the southern end of the Dune du Pyla, a well-equipped family site with good recreational facilities and direct access to the sea. Kids' club in season.

GPS: 44.5779, -1.2135

Open: Apr-2 Oct **Site:** 10HEC **For hire:** **Prices:** 16-36 Mobile home hire 315-925 **Facilities:** Wi-fi (charged) Kids' Club Play Area **Services:** **Leisure:** P S

Sunêlia Petit Nice

rte de Biscarrosse, 33115

556227403 556221431

e-mail: info@petitnice.com

web: www.petitnice.com

Sandy terraced site, partly steep slopes in pine woodland, mainly suitable for tents. Paths and standings are strengthened with timber, and there are 220 steps down to the beach.

dir: *6km S on D218.*

Open: 4 Apr-Sep **Site:** 5.5HEC **For hire:** **Facilities:** **Services:** **Leisure:** P S

Village Center la Forêt

rte de Biscarrosse, 33115

499572121 467516389

e-mail: contact@village-center.com

web: www.village-center.com/aquitaine/camping-la-foret.php

Located in an ancient forest at the foot of the Dune du Pyla.

GPS: 44.5848, -1.2092

Open: 8 Apr-2 Oct **Site:** 12HEC **For hire:** **Facilities:** Wi-fi (charged) Kids' Club Play Area **Services:** **Leisure:** P S

Yelloh Village Panorama du Pyla

rte de Biscarrosse, 33115

556221044 556221012

e-mail: mail@camping-panorama.com

web: www.camping-panorama.com

Partially terraced site among dunes, on the edge of the 100 metres high Dune du Pyla. Views of the sea from some pitches.

dir: *Signed on D218.*

Open: 15 Apr-3 Oct **Site:** 15HEC **For hire:** **Facilities:** Wi-fi (charged) Kids' Club Play Area **Services:** **Leisure:** P S

RAUZAN — GIRONDE

Vieux Château

rte Départementale 123, 33420

557841538 557841834

e-mail: hoekstra.camping@wanadoo.fr

web: www.vieux-chateau.com

A family site in a peaceful valley surrounded by vineyards and overlooked by the ruined 12th-century Rauzan castle.

dir: *1.5km from D670.*

Open: Apr-Oct **Site:** 2.5HEC **For hire:** **Facilities:** **Services:** **Leisure:** P **Off-site:**

REYREVIGNES — LOT

Domaine de Vacances Papillon

46320

565401240 565401718

e-mail: info@domaine-papillon.com

web: www.domaine-papillon.com

A wooded park in the heart of the Haut-Quercy region with modern facilities.

dir: *Via N653.*

Open: May-Sep **Site:** 3HEC **For hire:** **Facilities:** **Services:** **Leisure:** P **Off-site:** L R

ROCAMADOUR — LOT

Relais du Campeur l'Hospitalet

46500

565336328 565106821

e-mail: lerelaisducampeur@orange.fr

web: www.lerelaisducampeur.com

Shady, level site with well-marked pitches and good facilities. Fine views of Rocamadour.

dir: *On D36.*

Open: 15 Feb-10 Nov **Site:** 1.7HEC **Facilities:** Wi-fi (charged) **Services:** **Leisure:** P **Off-site:**

Le Roc

Pech-Alis, 46500

565336850

e-mail: campingleroc@wanadoo.fr

web: www.camping-leroc.com

On the outskirts of Rocamadour this small site has spacious pitches.

GPS: 44.8194, 1.6544

Open: Apr-Oct **Site:** 2HEC **For hire:** **Prices:** 11.60-16.60 Mobile home hire 247-557 **Facilities:** Wi-fi (charged) Play Area **Services:** **Leisure:** P

FRANCE

ROCHE-CHALAIS, LA — DORDOGNE

Camping les Gerbes

rue de la Dronne, 24490
553914065 553903201
e-mail: campinggerbes@orange.fr
web: www.larochechalais.com
Well-appointed family site on banks of River Dronne.
dir: *Off D674 in village centre, signed.*
Open: 15 Apr-Sep **Site:** 3.5HEC **For hire:** **Prices:** 9.80-13.30 Mobile home hire 158-315 **Facilities:** Wi-fi Play Area **Services:** **Off-site:** P R

ROMIEU, LA — GERS

Camp de Florence

32480
562281558 562282004
e-mail: info@lecampdeflorence.com
web: www.lecampdeflorence.com
Well-equipped site in rural surroundings. Spaciously laid out with large pitches, many with views of the Gascony countryside.
dir: *D931 towards Agen-Condom, 3km before Condom left to La Romieu.*
GPS: 43.9830, 0.5018
Open: Apr-10 Oct **Site:** 10HEC **For hire:** **Prices:** 15.90-32.80 Mobile home hire 315-924 **Facilities:** Wi-fi (charged) Kids' Club Play Area **Services:** **Leisure:** P **Off-site:**

ROQUEFORT — LANDES

CM de Nauton

Cité Nauton, 40120
558455046 558455363
e-mail: mairie.roquefort@wanadoo.fr
A small municipal site with good facilities.
dir: *1.6km N on D932 towards Bordeaux.*
Open: Jun-Aug **Site:** 1.35HEC **Facilities:** **Services:** **Off-site:** L P R

ROQUELAURE — GERS

Talouch Yelloh Village

32810
562655243 562655368
e-mail: info@camping-talouch.com
web: www.camping-talouch.com
A family site in picturesque wooded surroundings in the heart of Gascony. There are good sports and entertainment facilities.
dir: *N21 onto D148.*
Open: 6 Apr-24 Sep **Site:** 9HEC **For hire:** **Prices:** 17-38 Mobile home hire 273-1113 **Facilities:** Play Area **Services:** **Leisure:** P

ST-ANTOINE-D'AUBEROCHE — DORDOGNE

Pélonie

La Pélonie, 24330
553075578 553037427
e-mail: lapelonie@aol.com
web: www.lapelonie.com
In a picturesque rural location in the heart of the Perigord.
dir: *Off N89 between St Pierre de Chignac & Fossmagne.*
GPS: 45.13, 0.93
Open: 20 Apr-10 Oct **Site:** 3HEC **For hire:** **Facilities:** Wi-fi Kids' Club Play Area **Services:** **Leisure:** P

ST-ANTOINE-DE-BREUILH — DORDOGNE

Rivière Fleurie

180 rue Théophile Cart, lieu dit St Aulaye de Breuilh, 24230
553248280 553248280
e-mail: info@la-riviere-fleurie.com
web: www.la-riviere-fleurie.com
Relaxing, friendly site with swimming pool and fishing available on the River Dordogne, 50 metres away.
dir: *Off D936 W of St-Antoine & 3km towards River Dordogne.*
GPS: 44.8289, 0.1225
Open: Apr-Sep **Site:** 2.4HEC **For hire:** **Prices:** 15.90-25.90 Mobile home hire 225-735 **Facilities:** Wi-fi Play Area **Services:** **Leisure:** P R **Off-site:**

ST-ANTONIN-NOBLE-VAL — TARN-ET-GARONNE

Trois Cantons

82140
563319857
e-mail: info@3cantons.fr
web: www.3cantons.fr
Divided into pitches, partly on sloping ground in an oak forest, near St Antonin Noble Val. Separate section for teenagers. Restaurant available mid May to September and kids' club available mid July to mid August.
dir: *8.5km NW near D926, signed.*
Open: 15 Apr-Sep **Site:** 15HEC **For hire:** **Prices:** 12-22 Mobile home hire 245-690 **Facilities:** Wi-fi Kids' Club Play Area **Services:** **Leisure:** P **Off-site:** R

ST-BERTRAND-DE-COMMINGES HAUTE-GARONNE

Es Pibous

chemin de St-Just, 31510
561883142 561956383
e-mail: es.pibous@wanadoo.fr
web: www.es-pibous.fr

A quiet, shaded site in an elevated position with good facilities.

dir: *A64 exit 17 onto RN125. Right towards Valcabrère on RD26.*

Open: Apr-Oct **Site:** 1.8HEC **For hire:** **Prices:** 15.72-16.82 Mobile home hire 380 **Facilities:** Play Area **Services:** **Leisure:** P **Off-site:** L R

ST-CÉRÉ LOT

CM le Soulhol

The Camping and Caravanning Club The Friendly Club

quai A-Salesse, 46400
565381237 565381237
e-mail: info@campinglesoulhol.com
web: www.campinglesoulhol.com

A family site bordered by two rivers with good recreational facilities. 500 metres from the town centre.

C&CC Report *Le Soulhol is a great site for exploring the lovely, unspoiled and fascinating Lot. There's a relaxing riverside setting, a friendly atmosphere, swimming pool, the town centre a short stroll away and more places to visit than can be fitted into one stay, including Figeac, Rocamadour, Cahors and Beaulieu-sur-Dordogne.*

dir: *Via A20, exit 52/54.*

GPS: 44.8581, 1.8977

Open: May-Sep **Site:** 4HEC **For hire:** **Prices:** 14.50-15.50 Mobile home hire 230-490 **Facilities:** Wi-fi (charged) Play Area **Services:** **Leisure:** P R **Off-site:**

ST-CIRQ-LAPOPIE LOT

Plage

46330
565302951
e-mail: camping-laplage@wanadoo.fr
web: www.campingplage.com

Family site beside the River Lot and close to one of the most beautiful villages in France. Boat and bicycle hire available.

dir: *Via D41 from N. Or D42 from S.*

Open: 15 Apr-15 Oct **Site:** 3HEC **For hire:** **Prices:** 15.80-18.80 Mobile home hire 280-640 **Facilities:** Wi-fi Kids' Club Play Area **Services:** **Leisure:** R **Off-site:**

ST-CRICQ GERS

Lac de Thoux Saint Cricq

32440
562657129 562657481
e-mail: contact@camping-lacdethoux.com
web: www.camping-lacdethoux.com

A family site with good facilities on the edge of the lake, 50 metres from the beach. Leisure facilities include a swimming pool with slide and a sailing club.

Open: Apr-15 Oct **Site:** 3HEC **For hire:** **Prices:** 16-26 Mobile home hire 228-889 **Facilities:** Wi-fi (charged) Kids' Club Play Area **Services:** **Leisure:** L P **Off-site:**

ST-CYPRIEN DORDOGNE

CM Garrit

24220
553292056 553292056
e-mail: pbecheau@aol.com
web: www.campingdugarritendordogneperigord.com

A peaceful location beside the River Dordogne with safe bathing.

dir: *1.5km S on D48.*

Open: May-Sep **Site:** 2HEC **For hire:** **Facilities:** **Services:** **Leisure:** P R **Off-site:** R

ST-ÉMILION GIRONDE

Yelloh Saint Emilion

Domaine de la Barbanne, 2 lieu dit les Combes, 33330
557247580 557246968
e-mail: info@camping-saint-emilion.com
web: www.camping-saint-emilion.com

A peaceful country setting among vineyards, close to a 5-hectare lake.

dir: *3km N via D122.*

GPS: 44.9170, -0.1417

Open: 14 Apr-22 Sep **Site:** 10HEC **For hire:** **Prices:** 17-38 Mobile home hire 273-1253 **Facilities:** Wi-fi (charged) Kids' Club Play Area **Services:** **Leisure:** P

FRANCE

BASQUE COAST
Le CAMPING ATLANTICA
SAINT-JEAN-DE-LUZ
www.campingatlantica.com
The ideal place for family holidays that combine the pleasures of both the sea and the mountain. You will find many kinds of entertainment, an aquatic park, quality services and catering.
F-64500 Saint-Jean-de-Luz / Phone: +33 (0)5 59 47 72 44

ST-GENIES DORDOGNE

Bouquerie

24590
☎ 553289822 🖹 553291975
e-mail: labouquerie@wanadoo.fr
web: www.labouquerie.com

A family site in wooded surroundings with a variety of facilities.

dir: *N of village on D704.*

Open: 19 Apr-19 Sep **Site:** 8HEC **For hire:** **Facilities:** **Services:** **Leisure:** L P

ST-GIRONS ARIÈGE

Pont du Nert

rte de Lacourt (D33), Encourtiech, 09200
☎ 561665848
e-mail: marie-anne.dreyfuss@wanadoo.fr

Grassy site between road and woodland.

dir: *3km SE at junct D33 & D3.*

Open: Jun-15 Sep **Site:** 1.5HEC **Prices:** 10-12 **Facilities:** **Off-site:** R

ST-JEAN-DE-LUZ PYRÉNÉES-ATLANTIQUES

Atlantica

Quartier Acotz, 64500
☎ 559477244 🖹 559547227
e-mail: info@campingatlantica.com
web: www.campingatlantica.com

A family site with good facilities at the foot of the Pyrénées close to the Spanish border, and 0.5km from the beach.

dir: *N10 exit St-Jean-de-Luz Nord for Biarritz, 1km on left.*

Open: Apr-Sep **Site:** 3.5HEC **For hire:** **Facilities:** **Services:** **Leisure:** P **Off-site:** S

see advert on this page

Camping International Erromardie

Plage Erromardie, 64500
☎ 559260774 🖹 251339404
e-mail: info@chadotel.com
web: www.chadotel.com

With direct access to the beach and 2km from the town centre, a family site, with pitches divided by hedges.

Open: 7 Apr-11 Nov **Site:** 5HEC **For hire:** **Facilities:** Wi-fi Play Area **Services:** **Leisure:** P S

Ferme d'Erromardie

64500
☎ 559263426 🖹 559512602
e-mail: contact@camping-erromardie.com
web: www.camping-erromardie.com

Site by the sea with several sections divided by roads and low hedges.

dir: *N to N10, over railway bridge & sharp right, signed.*

Open: 15 Mar-2 Oct **Site:** 2HEC **For hire:** **Prices:** 13.80-23 Mobile home hire 230-800 **Facilities:** Wi-fi Play Area **Services:** **Leisure:** R S **Off-site:**

Tamaris Plage

quartier d'Acotz, 64500
☎ 559265590 🖹 559477015
e-mail: tamaris1@wanadoo.fr
web: www.tamaris-plage.com

Level family site with good facilities divided into sections by drives and hedges. Kids' club available 10 July to 12 August.

dir: *Signed from N10 towards sea.*

Open: All Year. **Site:** 1.3HEC **For hire:** **Facilities:** Wi-fi Kids' Club Play Area **Services:** **Leisure:** S **Off-site:**

ST-JEAN-PIED-DE-PORT PYRÉNÉES-ATLANTIQUES

Narbaïtz

rte de Bayonne, Ascarat, 64220
☎ 559371013 🖹 559372142
e-mail: camping-narbaitz@wanadoo.fr
web: www.camping-narbaitz.com

A quiet, comfortable site beside the River Berroua with heated swimming pool.

dir: *2km NW towards Bayonne.*

GPS: 43.1775, -1.2594

Open: May-mid Sep **Site:** 2.5HEC **For hire:** **Prices:** 16-26 Mobile home hire 290 **Facilities:** Wi-fi Kids' Club Play Area **Services:** **Leisure:** P R **Off-site:**

ST-JULIEN-EN-BORN LANDES

Lette Fleurie

40170

558427409 558424151

e-mail: contact@camping-municipal-plage.com

web: www.camping-municipal-plage.com

On undulating ground in a pine wood with good facilities, 5 minutes from the beach.

Open: Apr-Sep **Site:** 18HEC **For hire:** **Prices:** 17.10-22.10 **Facilities:** Wi-fi Play Area **Services:** **Leisure:** P **Off-site:** R S

ST-JUSTIN LANDES

Camping le Pin

rte de Roquefort, 40240

558448891 558448891

e-mail: camping.lepin@wanadoo.fr

web: www.campinglepin.com

A quiet family site with a kids' club during July and August.

dir: *2.3km N on D626.*

Open: Mar-Oct **Site:** 3HEC **For hire:** **Facilities:** Wi-fi Kids' Club Play Area **Services:** **Leisure:** P **Off-site:**

ST-LÉON-SUR-VÉZÈRE DORDOGNE

Paradis

24290

553507264 553507590

e-mail: le-paradis@perigord.com

web: www.le-paradis.fr

Situated on the river bank in the picturesque Vézère Valley, ideal for walking and mountain biking.

dir: *S of village off D706 Les Eyzies road.*

GPS: 45.0018, 1.0710

Open: Apr-19 Oct **Site:** 7HEC **For hire:** **Prices:** 18.60-27.90 Mobile home hire 322-924 **Facilities:** Wi-fi (charged) Kids' Club Play Area **Services:** **Leisure:** P R

ST-MARTIN-DE-SEIGNANX LANDES

Lou P'tit Poun

The Camping and Caravanning Club — The Friendly Club

40390

559565579 559565371

e-mail: contact@louptitpoun.com

web: www.louptitpoun.com

A quiet site with well-defined pitches on terraces.

C&CC Report *One of the most friendly and lovingly kept sites around. A spacious, peaceful and relaxed site, with the Basque country's bustling resorts, lovely beaches, mountains and lively Bayonne all easily accessible. Many campers return here year after year to enjoy the distinctive culture of the region and Monsieur and Madame Sauvy's welcome.*

dir: *A63 exit Bayonne Nord for Pau.*

Open: Jun-11 Sep **Site:** 7HEC **For hire:** **Prices:** 17.90-29.20 **Facilities:** Play Area **Services:** **Leisure:** P

ST-NICOLAS-DE-LA-GRAVE TARN-ET-GARONNE

Plan d'Eau

Base de Plein Air, et de Loisirs, 82210

563955002 563955001

e-mail: basedeloisirs.stnicolas@cg82.fr

web: www.cg82.fr

Ideal site for water activity enthusiasts as fishing, windsurfing and sailing are available.

dir: *2.5km N via D15.*

Open: 15 Jun-15 Sep **Site:** 1.5HEC **Facilities:** **Services:** **Leisure:** L P R **Off-site:**

ST-PARDOUX-LA-RIVIÈRE DORDOGNE

Kawan Village Château le Verdoyer

24470

553569464 553563870

e-mail: chateau@verdoyer.fr

web: www.verdoyer.fr

A small, well-equipped site in the grounds of a restored castle.

dir: *3km N via D96.*

Open: 23 Apr-4 Oct **Site:** 25HEC **For hire:** **Facilities:** Wi-fi (charged) Kids' Club Play Area **Services:** **Leisure:** L P

FRANCE

ST-PAUL-LES-DAX LANDES

Pins du Soleil

RD459, 40990

☎ 558913791

web: www.pinsoleil.com

On a hotel complex with modern facilities.

dir: *SW via D954.*

GPS: 43.7205, -1.0936

Open: Apr-Oct **Site:** 6HEC **For hire:** **Facilities:** Wi-fi Kids' Club Play Area **Services:** **Leisure:** P **Off-site:** R

ST-PÉE-SUR-NIVELLE PYRÉNÉES-ATLANTIQUES

Goyetchea

64310

☎ 559541959

e-mail: info@camping-goyetchea.com

web: www.camping-goyetchea.com

Quiet, peaceful site in a wooded location at the foot of the Pyrénées. 10km from the beaches of Bidart.

dir: *2km from St Pée via D918.*

GPS: 43.3627, -1.5659

Open: 6 Jun-19 Sep **Site:** 4HEC **For hire:** **Prices:** 14-21 Mobile home hire 210-740 **Facilities:** Wi-fi (charged) Play Area **Services:** **Leisure:** P **Off-site:** L R

Ibarron

64310

☎ 559541043

e-mail: camping.dibarron@wanadoo.fr

web: www.camping-ibarron.com

A pleasant wooded location with level pitches and modern facilities.

dir: *2km W on D918.*

Open: May-Sep **Site:** 2.88HEC **For hire:** **Facilities:** Wi-fi Play Area **Services:** **Leisure:** P R **Off-site:** L

ST-PIERRE-LAFEUILLE LOT

Les Graves

46090

☎ 565368312 565368312

e-mail: infos@camping-lesgraves.com

web: www.camping-lesgraves.com

On a small hill on the northern outskirts of the village providing fine views over the surrounding countryside.

dir: *A20 exit 57, 10km N of Cahors.*

GPS: 44.5262, 1.4601

Open: 15 Apr-Sep **Site:** 1.5HEC **For hire:** **Prices:** 13.80-16.80 Mobile home hire 175-539 **Facilities:** Play Area **Services:** **Leisure:** P **Off-site:**

Quercy-Vacances

Le Mas de Lacombe, 46090

☎ 565368715

e-mail: quercyvacances@wanadoo.fr

web: www.quercy-vacances.com

A well-equipped site in pleasant wooded surroundings.

dir: *On N20. 12km N of Cahors.*

Open: Apr-Sep **Site:** 3HEC **For hire:** **Prices:** 15-18.80 Mobile home hire 230-650 **Facilities:** Wi-fi Play Area **Services:** **Leisure:** P **Off-site:** L R

STE-EULALIE-EN-BORN LANDES

Bruyères

chemin Laffont, 40200

☎ 558097336 558097558

e-mail: bonjour@camping-les-bruyeres.com

web: www.camping-les-bruyeres.com

Set in the middle of the Landes forest close to the lakes and the sea.

dir: *2.5km N via D652.*

Open: 14 May-29 Sep **Site:** 3HEC **For hire:** **Facilities:** Wi-fi (charged) **Services:** **Leisure:** P **Off-site:** L R

FRANCE

STE-NATHALÈNE DORDOGNE

Camping la Palombière

24200

☎ 553594234 🖹 553284540

e-mail: contact@lapalombiere.fr

web: www.lapalombiere.fr

Terraced pitches among pines and oaks. There is an aquatic complex, and during high season sports/spa activities are run during the day with entertainment in the evening. A kids' club is available.

dir: *8km NE of Sarlat.*

GPS: 44.9081, 1.2925

Open: 28 Apr-16 Sep **Site:** 11HEC **For hire:** **Prices:** 14.50-27.80 Mobile home hire 290-890 **Facilities:** Wi-fi Kids' Club Play Area **Services:** **Leisure:** P

Domaine des Mathevies

Les Mathevies, 24200

☎ 553592086

e-mail: mathevies@mac.com

web: www.mathevies.com

Suitable for couples and young families, the terraced pitches are generous in size and all have electricity, in addition there are wooden chalets, mobile homes and a traditional stone gîte. A shaded terrace offers stunning views over the valley and a beautiful Perigordine barn has been restored into a modern sanitary block and restaurant that offers local home cooked food.

dir: *7km NW of Sarlat-la-Caneda. A20, exit 55 (Souillac), follow signs to Routillac then signs to Carlux & continue to Ste-Nathalène.*

GPS: 44.9181, 1.2778

Open: Apr-Sep **Site:** 2.5HEC **For hire:** **Prices:** 16.50-35 Mobile home hire 245-840 **Facilities:** Wi-fi Play Area **Services:** **Leisure:** P **Off-site:** L R

SALIGNAC DORDOGNE

Peneyrals

Le Poujol, St-Crépin Carlucet, 24590

☎ 553288571 🖹 553288099

e-mail: camping.peneyrals@wanadoo.fr

web: www.peneyrals.com

Extensive leisure facilities are available, swimming pools with slides, tennis, mini-golf and so on. Entertainment from end of May to beginning of September with a kids' club available in July and August.

dir: *10km N of Sarlat on D60.*

GPS: 44.9577, 1.2729

Open: 12 May-15 Sep **Site:** 13HEC **For hire:** **Prices:** 16.90-30.10 **Facilities:** Wi-fi (charged) Kids' Club Play Area **Services:** **Leisure:** P

see advert on this page

SALLES LOT-ET-GARONNE

Bastides

47150

☎ 553408309 🖹 553408176

e-mail: info@campingdesbastides.com

web: www.campingdesbastides.com

Peaceful wooded surroundings overlooking the Lède Valley with good sports and entertainment facilities.

dir: *1km N via D150.*

GPS: 44.5524, 0.8813

Open: Etr-Sep **Site:** 6HEC **For hire:** **Facilities:** Wi-fi (charged) Kids' Club Play Area **Services:** **Leisure:** P

Camping Parc du Val de l'Eyre

8 rte de Minoy, 33770

☎ 556884703 🖹 556884727

e-mail: levaldeleyre2@wanadoo.fr

web: www.camping-parcduvaldeleyre.com

A well-equipped family site in a pleasant wooded location between the Landes forests and Bordeaux vineyards.

dir: *SW on D108 rte de Lugos.*

Open: Feb-22 Nov **Site:** 13HEC **For hire:** **Prices:** 7-16 Mobile home hire 253-790 **Facilities:** Wi-fi Kids' Club Play Area **Services:** **Leisure:** L P R **Off-site:**

FRANCE

SARLAT-LA-CANÉDA DORDOGNE

Maillac

Ste-Nathalène, 24200
553592212 553296017
e-mail: campingmaillac@wanadoo.fr
web: www.campingmaillac.fr

Wooded surroundings in the heart of the Périgord Noir region with good facilities for a family holiday. Separate car park for arrivals after 23.00hrs.

dir: *7km NE on D47.*

Open: 15 May-Oct **Site:** 6HEC **For hire:** **Facilities:** **Services:** **Leisure:** P **Off-site:** L R

Moulin du Roch

rte des Éyzies, Le Roch, 24200
553592027 553592095
e-mail: moulin.du.roch@wanadoo.fr
web: www.moulin-du-roch.com

A pleasant site with good facilities in a picturesque location between Sarlat and Les Eyzies. Kids' club available in July and August.

dir: *10km NW via D704, D6 & D47.*

GPS: 44.9081, 1.1155

Open: 28 Apr-16 Sep **Site:** 8HEC **For hire:** **Prices:** 15-32 Mobile home hire 270-980 **Facilities:** Wi-fi (charged) Kids' Club Play Area **Services:** **Leisure:** P

Les Périères

rue Jean Gabin, BP98, 24203
553590584 553285751
e-mail: les-perieres@wanadoo.fr
web: www.lesperieres.com

Very well-kept terraced site in parkland and woods in the heart of the Périgord Noir, with fine views over the Sarlat Valley. There are good recreational facilities.

dir: *1km NE of town on D47.*

GPS: 44.8939, 1.2275

Open: Apr-Sep **Site:** 11HEC **For hire:** **Prices:** 21-32 **Facilities:** Wi-fi Play Area **Services:** **Leisure:** P **Off-site:**

FRANCE

Rocher de la Cave

24200
553281426 553282710
e-mail: rocher.de.la-cave@wanadoo.fr
web: www.rocherdelacave.com

Pleasant family site on a level meadow beside the Dordogne, set in beautiful countryside.

dir: *Via D703 & D704.*

Open: May-Sep **Site:** 4HEC **For hire:** **Facilities:** Wi-fi Play Area **Services:** **Leisure:** P R

Val d'Ussel

La Fond d'Ussel, Proissans, 24200
553592873 553293825
e-mail: campinglevaldussel@orange.fr

A well-equipped site in woodland in the heart of the Périgord Noir region. Separate car park for late arrivals.

dir: *Off D704 or D56.*

Open: 25 Apr-19 Sep **Site:** 7HEC **For hire:** **Facilities:** Wi-fi (charged) Kids' Club Play Area **Services:** **Leisure:** P

Village Center Aqua Viva

rte de Sarlat-Souillac, Carsac-Aillac, 24200
499572121 467516389
e-mail: contact@village-center.com
web: www.village-center.com/aquitaine/camping-aqua-viva.php

6km from Sarlat on a sheltered site in beautiful wooded surroundings.

dir: *A20 exit 55.*

Open: 8 Apr-2 Oct **Site:** 13HEC **For hire:** **Facilities:** Wi-fi (charged) Kids' Club Play Area **Services:** **Leisure:** P

SAUVETERRE-LA-LEMANCE LOT-ET-GARONNE

Moulin du Périé

rte de Loubejac, 47500
553406726
web: camping-moulin-perie.com

In a wooded valley close to an 18th-century watermill with good, modern facilities.

dir: *3km E of town off D710. Follow signposts from the entrance to the village and keep to the valley road.*

Open: Apr-Sep **Site:** 5HEC **Facilities:** **Services:** **Leisure:** P R **Off-site:** L

SEIGNOSSE — LANDES

Chevreuils

2388 rte de Hossegor, à Vieux Boucau, 40510

☎ 558433280 558433280

e-mail: info@chevreuils.com

web: www.chevreuils.com

Set in a pine forest close to the sea with good recreational facilities. Compulsory separate car park for arrivals after midnight.

dir: *On CD79 rte de Hossegor.*

GPS: 43.7241, -1.4134

Open: May-27 Sep **Site:** 8HEC **For hire:** **Prices:** 18.40-28.20 Mobile home hire 231-987 **Facilities:** Kids' Club **Services:** **Leisure:** P **Off-site:** L S

Océliances

av des Tucs, 40510

☎ 558433030 558416421

e-mail: oceliances@wanadoo.fr

web: www.oceliances.com

Very clean and tidy site in a pine forest 0.6km from the sea.

dir: *200m from Seignosse town centre.*

Open: Apr-29 Sep **Site:** 13HEC **For hire:** **Facilities:** **Services:** **Leisure:** P **Off-site:** L S

Oyats

rte de la Plage des Casernes, 40510

☎ 558433794 558432329

e-mail: cployats@atciat.com

web: www.campeoles.fr

Level site, subdivided into fields and surrounded by woodland. Separate section for young people. Children's play area.

dir: *Off D79 in N outskirts towards Plage des Casernes.*

Open: 15 May-15 Sep **Site:** 17HEC **For hire:** **Facilities:** **Services:** **Leisure:** P **Off-site:** S

SEIX — ARIÈGE

Haut Salat

09140

☎ 561668178 561669417

e-mail: camping.le-haut-salat@wanadoo.fr

web: www.ariege.com/campinglehautsalat

Very clean, well-kept site beside stream. Big gravel pitches for caravans. Common room with TV.

dir: *0.8km NE on D3.*

Open: 2 Jan-14 Dec **Site:** 3HEC **For hire:** **Facilities:** **Services:** **Leisure:** P R

SÉRIGNAC-PÉBOUDOU — LOT-ET-GARONNE

Vallée de Gardeleau

47410

☎ 553369696 553369696

e-mail: valleegardeleau@wanadoo.fr

web: perso.wanadoo.fr/camping.valleegardeleau.fr

A shaded wooded position, offering peace and comfort in relaxing surroundings.

dir: *On RN21 between Lauzun & Castilonnès.*

Open: Mar-Oct **Site:** 2HEC **For hire:** **Facilities:** **Services:** **Leisure:** P

SOUILLAC — LOT

Domaine de la Paille Basse

The Camping and Caravanning Club — The Friendly Club

46200

☎ 565378548 565370958

e-mail: info@lapaillebasse.com

web: www.lapaillebasse.com

A family site in a picturesque wooded hilltop location in the grounds of an old farming hamlet.

C&CC Report *This classic Castels site, built on an old farmstead hamlet of great character and charm, offers modern facilities in an idyllic setting with open views. Busy, yet relaxed, the site has something for all nature-lovers – young children love the pet farm, while the active enjoy the group walks and cycling excursions. In low season this is a lovely haven and a convenient base for exploring the best parts of the Dordogne and Lot valleys, both within easy reach.*

dir: *6.5km NW off D15 Salignac-Eyvignes road.*

GPS: 44.9454, 1.4414

Open: 15 May-15 Sep **Site:** 12HEC **For hire:** **Facilities:** Wi-fi (charged) Kids' Club Play Area **Services:** **Leisure:** P

SOULAC-SUR-MER — GIRONDE

Amélie-Plage

L'Amélie-sur-Mer, 33780

☎ 556098727 556736426

e-mail: camping.amelie.plage@wanadoo.fr

web: www.camping-amelie-plage.com

Hilly wooded terrain. Lovely sandy beach.

dir: *3km S on Soulac road.*

Open: Mar-Dec **Site:** 12.5HEC **For hire:** **Facilities:** **Services:** **Leisure:** P S

FRANCE

Club de Soube

8 allée Michel Montaigne, 33780
☎ 556097763 📠 556099482
e-mail: contact@lelilhan.com
web: www.lelilhan.com
Located in an oak tree and pine forest, a short distance from the beach.
Open: Apr-Sep **Site:** 4HEC **For hire:** **Facilities:** **Services:** **Leisure:** P **Off-site:** S

Lacs

126 rte des Lacs, 33780
☎ 556097663 📠 556099802
e-mail: info@camping-les-lacs.com
web: www.camping-les-lacs.com
Site with marked pitches within easy reach of fine Atlantic beaches.
Open: Apr-5 Nov **Site:** 5.8HEC **For hire:** **Facilities:** **Services:** **Leisure:** P

Palace

65 bld Marsan de Montbrun, 33780
☎ 556098022 📠 556098423
e-mail: info@camping-palace.com
Well-kept site on sand dunes. Individual pitches, asphalt drives.
dir: *1km S from village centre. Access is via D1 and D101.*
Open: May-15 Sep **Site:** 16HEC **For hire:** **Facilities:** **Services:** **Leisure:** P **Off-site:** S

Pins

213 passe de Formose, Lilian, 33780
☎ 556098252 📠 5577365558
e-mail: contact@campingdespins.fr
web: www.campingdespins.fr
Situated in a beautiful pine forest close to the beach with plenty of sports facilities.
dir: *S on D101.*
Open: Apr-Oct **Site:** 3.2HEC **For hire:** **Facilities:** **Services:** **Leisure:** P **Off-site:** R S

Sables d'Argent

33 bld de l'Amélie, 33780
☎ 556098287 📠 556099482
e-mail: contact@sables-d-argent.com
web: www.sables-d-argent.com
Set in a pine forest bordered by dunes, with direct access to the beach.
dir: *1.5km SW of village.*
Open: Apr-Sep **Site:** 2.6HEC **For hire:** **Facilities:** Wi-fi (charged) Kids' Club **Services:** **Leisure:** S **Off-site:** P

SOUSTONS — LANDES

L'Airial

61 av Port d'Albret, 40140
☎ 558411248 📠 558415383
e-mail: contact@camping-airial.com
web: www.camping-airial.com
Situated in a shady park with plenty of recreational facilities and modern installations. Heated, covered swimming pool.
dir: *2km W on D652.*
GPS: 43.7545, -1.3517
Open: Apr-15 Oct **Site:** 12HEC **For hire:** **Facilities:** Wi-fi Kids' Club Play Area **Services:** **Leisure:** P **Off-site:** L S

TARASCON-SUR-ARIÈGE — ARIÈGE

Camping Village Le Pré Lombard

BP 90148, 09400
☎ 561056194 📠 561057893
e-mail: leprelombard@wanadoo.fr
web: www.prelombard.com
Beautiful wooded surroundings beside the River Ariège with modern facilities.
dir: *1.5km SE on D23.*
Open: 15 Mar-15 Oct **Site:** 3.5HEC **For hire:** **Facilities:** Wi-fi Kids' Club Play Area **Services:** **Leisure:** P R

TEILLET — TARN

Relais de l'Entre Deux Lacs

81120
☎ 563557445
e-mail: contact@campingdutarn.com
web: www.campingdutarn.com
Shady terraced site. Various activities arranged. Beautiful views.
dir: *Off D81 towards Lacaune.*
Open: 9 Apr-Sep **Site:** 4HEC **For hire:** **Facilities:** Wi-fi Play Area **Services:** **Leisure:** P **Off-site:** L R

THIVIERS — DORDOGNE

CM Le Repaire

24800

☎ 553526975

e-mail: camping.le.repaire@gmail.com

web: www.camping-thiviers-perigord.com

A well-appointed family site in a wooded valley in the Périgord Vert region of the Dordogne, a short walk from the ancient village of Thiviers.

dir: *On D707 1.5km towards Lanouaille.*

Open: All Year. **Site:** 11HEC **For hire:** **Prices:** 11.70-14.80 Mobile home hire 201-495 **Facilities:** Wi-fi Play Area **Services:** **Leisure:** P **Off-site:** L R

TOUZAC — LOT

Ch'Timi

46700

☎ 565365236 565365323

e-mail: info@campinglechtimi.com

web: www.campinglechtimi.com

A well-equipped site overlooking the River Lot. Entertainment available in summer.

dir: *0.8km from Touzac on D8.*

GPS: 44.4981, 1.0667

Open: Apr-Sep **Site:** 3.5HEC **For hire:** **Prices:** 14.40-20.20 Mobile home hire 305-580 **Facilities:** Wi-fi Kids' Club Play Area **Services:** **Leisure:** P R

Clos Bouyssac

46700

☎ 565365221 565246851

e-mail: camping.leclosbouyssac@wanadoo.fr

web: www.leclosbouyssac.eu

Friendly site, with English owners on the fringe of a wooded hillside by the sandy shore of the River Lot. Most pitches have direct river access. The area is ideal for exploring on foot, by car or even on horse back.

dir: *S of Touzac on D65.*

Open: Apr-Sep **Site:** 1.5HEC **For hire:** **Prices:** 14-17 Mobile home hire 449-599 **Facilities:** Wi-fi Play Area **Services:** **Leisure:** P R

TURSAC — DORDOGNE

Pigeonnier

24620

☎ 553069690 553069690

e-mail: campinglepigeonnier@wanadoo.fr

web: www.campinglepigeonnier.fr

A small, peaceful site in the heart of the Dordogne countryside.

dir: *Via D706 between Le Moustier & Les Éyzies.*

Open: Jun-Sep **Site:** 1.14HEC **Prices:** 15.94 **Facilities:** Play Area **Services:** **Leisure:** P **Off-site:** R

Vézère Périgord

The Camping and Caravanning Club — The Friendly Club

rte de Montignac, 24620

☎ 553069631 553067966

web: levezereperigord.com

A well-equipped site in wooded surroundings close to the river.

C&CC Report *The friendliness and traditional family camping style of this peaceful site draw campers back. Just 275 metres from the river Vézère with its fishing, canoeing and river beach, close by are also many of the unique prehistoric dwellings, paintings and sculptures for which the Dordogne is world renowned. The troglodyte dwellings just three miles away at La Roque-St-Christophe are fascinating, but perhaps it'll be the canoeing and the waterslides that your kids remember!*

dir: *0.8km NE on D706.*

Open: Etr-Oct **Site:** 6HEC **For hire:** **Facilities:** **Services:** **Leisure:** P **Off-site:** R

URRUGNE — PYRÉNÉES-ATLANTIQUES

Juantcho

rte de la Corniche, Socoa, 64122

☎ 559471197 559473179

e-mail: juantcho64@gmail.com

web: www.camping-juantcho.com

Situated on cliffs overlooking the Atlantic Ocean with terraced pitches divided by hedges and trees. The beach is a 10 minute walk on a footpath.

dir: *Exit A63 signed St Jean-de-Luz Sud, under RD810 onto D913. After 4km at rdbt towards Hendaye, 2nd rdbt towards Socoa.*

GPS: 43.3939, -1.6917

Open: May-Sep **Site:** 6HEC **For hire:** **Prices:** 14.10-23 Mobile home hire 290-610 **Facilities:** **Services:** **Off-site:** R S

Larrouleta

210 rte de Socoa, 64122
☎ 559473784 559474254
e-mail: info@larrouleta.com
web: www.larrouleta.com

Flat shaded site next to a lake, where there is a beach, fishing and pedaloes. 200 metres from a bus stop for exploring neighbouring towns.

C&CC Report *The Basque country is a fascinating area with its own identity separate from France, and this friendly site is well placed to explore both Spanish and French areas. With the Atlantic beaches just a short drive away you are spoilt for choice with the swimming pool (covered in low season) and lake swimming on site. Why not try one of the free pedaloes?*

dir: *Via RN10 or A63.*

Open: All Year. **Site:** 10HEC **Prices:** 15-20 **Facilities:** Wi-fi (charged) **Services:** **Leisure:** L P R **Off-site:** S

URT — PYRÉNÉES-ATLANTIQUES

Etche Zahar

allée de Mesplès, 64240
☎ 559562736
e-mail: info@etche-zahar.fr
web: www.etche-zahar.fr

A small, privately owned site in a wooded location and within easy reach of local tourist areas. Separate car parking for arrivals 22.00-08.00hrs. The owner speaks English and will help with any information needed. Special offers may be available. Wi-fi is free except in July and August. Dogs are permitted except 1-20 August.

dir: *A63 exit 8. Or A64 exit 4.*

GPS: 43.4917, -1.2966

Open: Mar-15 Nov **Site:** 2.5HEC **For hire:** **Prices:** 13-24 Mobile home hire 238-640 **Facilities:** Wi-fi Play Area **Services:** **Leisure:** P **Off-site:** R

VALEUIL — DORDOGNE

Bas Meygnaud

D393 Brantome, 24310
☎ 553055844
e-mail: camping-du-bas-meygnaud@wanadoo.fr
web: www.basmeygnaud.fr

A quiet, shady site in the Dronne Valley. English spoken.

dir: *Off D939 at Lasserre.*

Open: Apr-15 Oct **Site:** 1.7HEC **For hire:** **Prices:** 18.50-22 Mobile home hire 235-450 **Facilities:** Wi-fi Play Area **Services:** **Leisure:** P **Off-site:** R

VARILHES — ARIÈGE

Château

av du 8 Mai 45, 09120
☎ 561674284 561674284
e-mail: camping.du.chateau@orange.fr
web: www.campingdevarilhes.com

On the banks of the river and close to the town.

dir: *N on N20.*

GPS: 43.0468, 1.6324

Open: All Year. **Site:** 1.2HEC **For hire:** **Prices:** 12.10-16.55 Mobile home hire 330-460 **Facilities:** Wi-fi (charged) Play Area **Services:** **Leisure:** P R **Off-site:**

VAYRAC — LOT

Camping Les Chênes Clairs

Condat, 46110
☎ 565321632
e-mail: leschenesclairs@laposte.net
web: www.leschenesclairs.fr

With the Dordogne River a few kilometres to the south, this site has shaded pitches and a gîte for rent.

dir: *Off D20 between Condat & Vayrac.*

Open: May-Oct **Site:** 4HEC **For hire:** **Prices:** 11.40 **Facilities:** Wi-fi Play Area **Services:** **Leisure:** P **Off-site:** L R

VENDAYS-MONTALIVET — GIRONDE

Camping de Mayan

3 rte de Mayan, 33930
☎ 556417651
e-mail: campingmayan@sfr.fr
web: campingmayan.wifeo.com

A small site in a pine wood.

dir: *Via N215 & D102.*

Open: 15 Jun-15 Sep **Site:** 1HEC **Prices:** 9.55-12 **Facilities:** Wi-fi **Services:** **Off-site:** S

FRANCE

Chesnays

8 rte de Mayan, 33930

556417274 556417274

e-mail: lachesnays@camping-montalivet.com

web: www.camping-montalivet.com

Peaceful campsite, shaded by trees and situated between the sand beaches of the Atlantic shoreline and the Gironde Estuary.

dir: *Leave A10 at Saintes (junct 25) follow signs for Royan. Find Bac (ferry) to cross The Gironde. Follow N215 to Soulac, then D101 to campsite.*

GPS: 45.3758, -1.0822

Open: Apr-Sep **Site:** 2HEC **For hire:** **Prices:** 14.30-21 Mobile home hire 250-648 **Facilities:** Wi-fi Play Area **Services:** **Leisure:** P **Off-site:** R S

VERDON-SUR-MER, LE — GIRONDE

Royannais

88 rte de Soulac, 33123

556096112 556737067

e-mail: camping.le.royannais@wanadoo.fr

web: www.royannais.com

Level, sandy terrain under high pine and deciduous trees.

dir: *S of Le Verdon-sur-Mer in Le Royannais district on D1.*

Open: Apr-15 Oct **Site:** 3HEC **For hire:** **Facilities:** Kids' Club Play Area **Services:** **Leisure:** P **Off-site:** R S

VÉZAC — DORDOGNE

Deux Vallées

La Gare, 24220

553295355 553310981

e-mail: contact@campingles2vallees.com

web: www.campingles2vallees.com

A level site in a picturesque location in the Dordogne Valley with views of Beynac castle. Good facilities for families, with a kids' club available in July and August.

dir: *Via D57 from Sarlat. Or D703 from Bergerac.*

GPS: 44.8356, 1.1587

Open: 15 Feb-15 Nov **Site:** 3.8HEC **For hire:** **Prices:** 13.70-25 Mobile home hire 140-749 **Facilities:** Wi-fi Kids' Club Play Area **Services:** **Leisure:** P **Off-site:** R

Plage

La Roque Gageac, 24220

685232216

e-mail: campinglaplage24@orange.fr

web: www.camping-laplage.fr

Modest but attractive site in a pleasant riverside setting.

dir: *Via D703 beyond La Roque Gageac.*

Open: Apr-Sep **Site:** 3.5HEC **For hire:** **Facilities:** **Services:** **Leisure:** P R

VIELLE-ST-GIRONS — LANDES

Camping Campéole les Tourterelles

St-Girons-Plage, 40560

558479312 558479203

e-mail: tourterelles@campeole.com

web: www.camping-tourterelles.com

Large site situated close to the beach.

dir: *N10 exit Castets, Vielle-St-Girons.*

Open: 30 Apr-Sep **Site:** 19HEC **For hire:** **Facilities:** Wi-fi (charged) Kids' Club Play Area **Services:** **Leisure:** P **Off-site:** S

Eurosol

rte de la Plage, 40560

558479014 558477674

e-mail: contact@camping-eurosol.com

web: www.camping-eurosol.com

Well-maintained family site in a pine forest, 0.7km from one of the finest beaches in the country. Kids' club available in July and August and dogs not permitted in chalets or mobile homes.

dir: *A63 exit Castets.*

GPS: 43.9517, -1.3521

Open: 19 May-15 Sep **Site:** 18HEC **For hire:** **Prices:** 15-29 Mobile home hire 322-854 **Facilities:** Wi-fi (charged) Kids' Club Play Area **Services:** **Leisure:** P **Off-site:** S

Sunêlia Col Vert

1548 rte de l'Etang, 40560

890710001 558429188

e-mail: contact@colvert.com

web: www.colvert.com

Quiet site on lakeside in sparse pine woodland. Small natural harbour in the mouth of a stream.

dir: *Off D652 on N side of village, continue towards lake.*

GPS: 43.9026, -1.3104

Open: Apr-Sep **Site:** 30HEC **For hire:** **Prices:** 11.50-36.90 Mobile home hire 203-777 **Facilities:** Wi-fi (charged) Kids' Club Play Area **Services:** **Leisure:** L P

FRANCE

VIEUX-BOUCAU-LES-BAINS — LANDES

Camping Municipal les Sablères

bld du Marensin, 40480

558481229 558482070

e-mail: camping-lessableres@wanadoo.fr

web: www.camping-les-sableres.com

A family site with modern facilities and direct access to the beach.

dir: *Via N10 & D652.*

GPS: 43.7938, -1.4082

Open: Apr-15 Oct **Site:** 11HEC **For hire:** **Prices:** 13-23.40 Mobile home hire 226.80-625.80 **Facilities:** Wi-fi Play Area **Services:** **Off-site:** L S

VIGAN, LE — LOT

Rêve

Revers, 46300

565412520

e-mail: info@campinglereve.com

web: www.campinglereve.com

A modern family site in woodland setting.

dir: *D673 from Payrac towards Le Vigan & signed.*

GPS: 44.7714, 1.4432

Open: May-21 Sep **Site:** 10HEC **For hire:** **Prices:** 16.80-21 **Facilities:** Wi-fi (charged) Play Area **Services:** **Leisure:** P **Off-site:**

Val de l'Arre

Roudoulouse, rte du Point de la Croix, 30120

467810277 467817123

e-mail: valdelarre@wanadoo.fr

web: www.valdelarre.com

Wooded surroundings beside the River Arre. Separate car park for late arrivals.

dir: *2.5km E on D999.*

GPS: 43.9911, 3.6375

Open: Apr-Sep **Site:** 4HEC **For hire:** **Prices:** 13.90-18.40 Mobile home hire 189-651 **Facilities:** Wi-fi (charged) Play Area **Services:** **Leisure:** P R **Off-site:**

VILLEFRANCHE-DU-QUEYRAN — LOT-ET-GARONNE

Moulin de Campech

The Camping and Caravanning Club — The Friendly Club

47160

553887243 553880652

e-mail: camping@moulindecampech.co.uk

web: www.moulindecampech.co.uk

A beautiful site in a peaceful location beside a small lake stocked with trout.

C&CC Report *A little gem of a site, in the heart of the south-west, Moulin de Campech is an ideal base for exploring. Visit local markets, enjoy the many cycling and walking routes, or spend a day at the coast or south in the Pyrénées. When relaxing on this peaceful, welcoming British-owned site, you'll enjoy being on a tourers only site, where freshly picked, home-grown produce is used in the popular site restaurant. Nature lovers should keep an eye out for kingfishers, red squirrels, golden oriole, lizards and deer or even occasionally, wild boar.*

dir: *D11 towards Casteljaloux.*

GPS: 44.2747, 0.1964

Open: Apr-7 Oct **Site:** 4HEC **Prices:** 18-28 **Facilities:** Wi-fi (charged) **Services:** **Leisure:** P

VILLERÉAL — LOT-ET-GARONNE

Château de Fonrives

Rives, 47210

553366338 553360998

e-mail: chateau.de.fonrives@wanadoo.fr

web: www.campingchateaufonrives.com

A beautiful natural park in the grounds of a château with good facilities for all ages.

dir: *2.2km NW via D207.*

Open: 9 Apr-Sep **Site:** 20HEC **For hire:** **Facilities:** Wi-fi (charged) Kids' Club Play Area **Services:** **Leisure:** L P **Off-site:**

Fontaine du Roc

Dévillac, 47210

553360816 553616023

e-mail: fontaine.du.roc@wandadoo.fr

web: www.fontaineduroc.com

On a wooded hillside with views of Château Biron, spacious pitches vary in shade. Leisure facilities include swimming pool, plus children's pool and whirlpool. Cycles can be hired.

dir: *From Villeréal on D255 towards Dévillac or from Monflanquin on D272 towards Monpazier, follow green sign for Fontaine du Roc.*

Open: Apr-1 Oct **Site:** 3HEC **For hire:** **Prices:** 15-20 Mobile home hire 350-575 **Facilities:** Wi-fi Kids' Club Play Area **Services:** **Leisure:** P **Off-site:** L

FRANCE

Site 6HEC (site size) grass sand stone little shade partly shaded mainly shaded motorvans accepted bungalows for hire mobile homes for hire tents for hire no dogs site fully accessible for wheelchairs **Prices** amount quoted is per night, for 2 adults and car, plus tent or caravan Mobile home hire is a weekly rate.

VITRAC — DORDOGNE

Bouysse

Caudon, 24200

553283305 553303852

e-mail: info@labouysse.com

web: www.labouysse.com

Well-appointed site in a wooded valley beside the Dordogne.

dir: *2km E, near the River Dordogne.*

Open: Apr-Sep **Site:** 3HEC **For hire:** **Prices:** 17.70-25.60 Mobile home hire 250-710 **Facilities:** Wi-fi Kids' Club Play Area **Services:** **Leisure:** P R **Off-site:**

Domaine de Soleil Plage

The Camping and Caravanning Club The Friendly Club

Caudon par Montfort, 24200

553283333 553283024

e-mail: info@soleilplage.fr

web: www.soleilplage.fr

Set out around an old farmhouse bordering the Dordogne with excellent facilities. Kids' club available in July and August.

C&CC Report *A high quality, renowned site in an outstanding location, perfectly situated for visiting lovely Sarlat and all the western Dordogne. With excellent facilities open nearly all season, it's a great place to relax and watch the meandering river wind past the cliffs, either from the river bank or from one of the site's canoes. Pitches are in two separate areas, each with advantages – those with full facilities are by the river, others are closer to the site's main facilities.*

dir: *4km E on D703, turn by Camping Clos Bernard.*

Open: 15 Apr-29 Sep **Site:** 8HEC **For hire:** **Prices:** 21-33.50 Mobile home hire 290-830 **Facilities:** Wi-fi (charged) Kids' Club Play Area **Services:** **Leisure:** P R

LOIRE/CENTRAL

AIRVAULT — DEUX-SÈVRES

Camping de Courte Vallée

Courte Vallée, 79600

549647065 549647065

e-mail: info@caravanningfrance.com

web: www.caravanningfrance.com

Small, family-run site with large pitches and good facilities, situated in a river valley.

dir: *On NW outskirts of town, 0.5km towards Availles.*

Open: 24 Mar-27 Nov **Site:** 12HEC **Facilities:** Wi-fi (charged) Play Area **Services:** **Leisure:** P **Off-site:** P R

ALLONNES — MAINE-ET-LOIRE

Le Pô Doré

51 rte de Pô, 49650

241387880 241387880

e-mail: camping-lepodore@orange.fr

web: camping-lepodore.com

A family site in a pleasant rural setting in the heart of the Anjou region with good recreational facilities. Separate car park for arrivals after 22.00hrs. Wi-fi free for first three hours.

dir: *D35 from Tours. Or N147 from Angers.*

Open: 15 Mar-15 Nov **Site:** 2HEC **For hire:** **Prices:** 13.50-19 Mobile home hire 233-508 **Facilities:** Wi-fi (charged) **Services:** **Leisure:** P **Off-site:** L R

AMBRIÈRES-LES-VALLÉES — MAYENNE

Camping Le Parc de Vaux

35 rue des Colverts, 53300

243049025

e-mail: parcdevaux@camp-in-ouest.com

web: www.parcdevaux.com

Campsite with chalet, mobile homes, bungalows and tents. Kids' club in July and August.

GPS: 48.3919, -0.6171

Open: All Year. **Site:** 4HEC **For hire:** **Prices:** 11.40-14.40 Mobile home hire 165-685 **Facilities:** Wi-fi Kids' Club Play Area **Services:** **Off-site:**

ANCENIS — LOIRE-ATLANTIQUE

Ile Mouchet

Impasse de L'Ile Mouchet, 44150

240830843 240831619

e-mail: camping-ile-mouchet@orange.fr

web: www.camping-estivance.com

Peaceful, wooded site located on the banks of the Loire.

dir: *Off N23 Nantes-Ancenis.*

Open: Apr-8 Oct **Site:** 3HEC **For hire:** **Facilities:** **Services:** **Leisure:** P **Off-site:** R

FRANCE

ANGERS — MAINE-ET-LOIRE

Lac de Maine

av du Lac de Maine, 49000

☎ 241730503 📠 241730220

e-mail: camping@lacdemaine.fr

web: www.camping-angers.fr

Pleasant rural surroundings on the 100-hectare Lac de Maine. There are fine sports and entertainment facilities, and the historic town of Angers is within easy reach.

dir: *A11 exit Lac de Maine.*

Open: 25 Mar-10 Oct **Site:** 4HEC **For hire:** **Facilities:** **Services:** **Leisure:** P **Off-site:** L R

ANGLES — VENDÉE

Moncalm et Atlantique

85750

☎ 251975580 📠 251289109

e-mail: camping-apv@wanadoo.fr

web: www.camping-apv.com

Two distinct sites, but sharing the same recreational facilities in a wooded setting close to the beach.

Open: 31 Mar-22 Sep **Site:** 3HEC **For hire:** **Facilities:** **Services:** **Leisure:** P **Off-site:** R

ANGOULINS-SUR-MER — CHARENTE-MARITIME

Chirats

rte de la Platère, 17690

☎ 546569416 📠 546566595

web: www.campingleschirats.fr

Modern site with good facilities 100 metres from a small sandy beach and providing panoramic views over the Bay of Fouras. The more popular, larger beaches of the area are some 3km away.

dir: *7km S of La Rochelle.*

Open: Apr-Sep **Site:** 4.5HEC **For hire:** **Facilities:** **Services:** **Leisure:** P S

ARCES — CHARENTE-MARITIME

Chez Filleux

17120

☎ 546908433 📠 546908433

e-mail: laferme.chezfilleux@wanadoo.fr

web: www.camping-chezfilleux.com

A level meadow partly shaded by trees and bushes, with modern facilities, 10 minutes from the beaches.

Open: Jun-Sep **Site:** 3HEC **For hire:** **Facilities:** **Services:** **Leisure:** P

ARGENTAT — CORRÈZE

Gibanel

Le Gibanel, 19400

☎ 555281011 📠 555288685

e-mail: contact@camping-gibanel.com

web: www.camping-gibanel.com

Pleasant site in the grounds of a château next to a lake.

dir: *S from Tulle on N120.*

GPS: 45.1115, 1.9598

Open: Jun-1 Sep **Site:** 6.5HEC **For hire:** **Prices:** 17.50-23 Mobile home hire 380-900 **Facilities:** Wi-fi Play Area **Services:** **Leisure:** L P **Off-site:**

Saulou

Vergnolles, 19400

☎ 555281233 📠 555288067

e-mail: le.saulou@wanadoo.fr

web: www.saulou.net

A peaceful site in a wooded location beside the River Dordogne. Ideal for families.

dir: *6km S on D116.*

Open: Apr-Sep **Site:** 7.5HEC **For hire:** **Facilities:** **Services:** **Leisure:** P R

Vaurette

Monceaux-sur-Dordogne, 19400

☎ 555280967

e-mail: info@vaurette.com

web: www.vaurette.com

In a sheltered valley on the banks of the River Dordogne with sporting facilities including heated swimming pool and tennis court.

dir: *On D12 between Argentat & Beaulieu.*

GPS: 45.0458, 1.8839

Open: May-21 Sep **Site:** 4HEC **For hire:** **Prices:** 16.80-26.80 Mobile home hire 335-690 **Facilities:** Wi-fi (charged) Kids' Club Play Area **Services:** **Leisure:** P R

ARGENTON-LES-VALLÉES DEUX-SÈVRES

CM du Lac d'Hautibus

79150

549659508 549657084

e-mail: campinghautibus@orange.fr

Partly shaded, individually marked pitches on this site, close to the town.

dir: *0.4km S on D748.*

Open: Apr-Oct **Site:** 16.2HEC **For hire:**
Prices: 11.20 **Facilities:** Play Area
Services: **Off-site:** L P R

AUBAZINE CORRÈZE

Campéole le Coiroux

Centre Touristique du Coiroux, 19190

555272196 555271916

e-mail: coiroux@campeole.com

web: www.camping-coiroux.com

Peaceful, shady site with large pitches, 300 metres from a lakeside beach. Sporting facilities include volleyball and tennis courts. Shop, bar, café and restaurant available during July and August.

GPS: 45.1861, 1.7072

Open: Apr-Sep **Site:** 11HEC **For hire:**
Prices: 11-20.40 Mobile home hire 259-777 **Facilities:**
Wi-fi Kids' Club Play Area **Services:**
Leisure: L P **Off-site:** R

AUBETERRE SUR DRONNE CHARENTE

Camping Municipal d'Aubeterre

rte de Riberac, 16390

545986017

e-mail: camping.aubeterre-sur-dronne@orange.fr

web: www.camping-aubeterre.fr

200 metres from the village, grassy site bordered with hedges and trees. Kayak and canoe hire nearby.

GPS: 45.2705, 0.1731

Open: May-Sep **Site:** 4HEC **For hire:** **Facilities:**
Wi-fi **Services:** **Leisure:** R
Off-site:

AVRILLÉ VENDÉE

Domaine des Forges

The Camping and Caravanning Club
The Friendly Club

rue des Forges, 85440

251223885 251909870

e-mail: contact@campingdomainedesforges.com

web: www.campingdomainedesforges.com

A pleasant position beside a lake, 300 metres from the town centre. The site has a variety of leisure facilities.

C&CC Report *Approaching Domaine des Forges along a country lane, by the fishing lake, seeing the large pitches and pretty manor house courtyard, you realise this is not a typical Vendéen site. Set just outside the village of Avrillé, offering huge pitches in a parkland setting, this site provides a great base all year round for those who want the best of the Vendée or a few days' stopover en route south or north. A delightful inland site that combines easy access to the coast with the space and peace of the countryside, just half an hour from the A87 and 45 minutes from the A83.*

Open: All Year. **Site:** 14HEC **For hire:**
Facilities: Wi-fi Kids' Club Play Area
Services: **Leisure:** P **Off-site:**

Mancellières

rte de Longeville-sur-Mer, 85440

251903597 251903931

e-mail: camping.mancellieres@wanadoo.fr

web: www.lesmancellieres.com

A pleasant site in a wooded park 5km from the fine beaches of south Vendée. Separate car park for arrivals after 23.00hrs.

dir: *1.7km S on D105 towards Longeville.*

Open: May-15 Sep **Site:** 2.6HEC **For hire:**
Prices: 12.60-18 Mobile home hire 370-700 **Facilities:**
Services: **Leisure:** P

AZAY-LE-RIDEAU INDRE-ET-LOIRE

Parc du Sabot

rue du Stade, 37190

247454272 247454911

e-mail: camping.lesabot@wanadoo.fr

Site lies in a large meadow on the River Indre.

dir: *Near château in town centre.*

GPS: 47.2591, 0.4701

Open: Apr-Oct **Site:** 6HEC **Prices:** 11.90-12.90
Facilities: Wi-fi Play Area **Services:**
Leisure: R **Off-site:** P

FRANCE

BALLAN-MIRÉ — INDRE-ET-LOIRE

Mignardière

The Camping and Caravanning Club — The Friendly Club

22 av des Aubepines, 37510
247733100 247733101
e-mail: info@mignardiere.com
web: www.mignardiere.com

A well-maintained site with a variety of sports facilities.

C&CC Report *The facilities on site and across the quiet road make La Mignardière ideal for younger families. It's a great base for discovering the Loire châteaux and all of the central Loire valley. Buses to Tours centre stop 45 metres from the site entrance. The very welcoming and friendly owners provide tourist information and advice on the riverside cycle routes of the Loire and Cher valleys.*

dir: *2.5km NE of village.*

Open: 10 Apr-Sep **Site:** 3.5HEC **For hire:** **Facilities:** **Services:** **Leisure:** P **Off-site:**

BARROU — INDRE-ET-LOIRE

Camping Les Rioms

lieu dit Les Rioms, 37350
247945307
e-mail: campinglesrioms@orange.fr
web: www.lesrioms.com

Friendly site in a pleasant location on the banks of the River Creuse.

dir: *From Châtellerault towards Lesigny then Barrou. From Tours A10 exit 25 St Maure de Touraine then towards La Roche Posay.*

GPS: 46.8625, 0.7589

Open: Apr-Oct **Site:** 1.6HEC **For hire:** **Prices:** 9-10 Mobile home hire 195-510 **Facilities:** Wi-fi Play Area **Services:** **Leisure:** P R **Off-site:**

BATZ-SUR-MER — LOIRE-ATLANTIQUE

Govelle

10 rue de la Govelle, 44740
240239163

Direct access to the sea. Supervised beach and sea-fishing nearby.

dir: *On D45 between Le Pouliguen & Batz.*

Open: 20 Apr-Sep **Site:** 6.8HEC **For hire:** **Facilities:** **Services:** **Leisure:** S

BAULE, LA — LOIRE-ATLANTIQUE

Ajoncs d'Or

chemin du Rocher, 44500
240603329 240244437
e-mail: contact@ajoncs.com
web: www.ajoncs.com

A large wooded park with well-defined pitches, close to the beach.

dir: *Signed from entrance to town.*

Open: Apr-Sep **Site:** 6HEC **For hire:** **Facilities:** **Services:** **Leisure:** P **Off-site:** S

Bois d'Amour

10 allée de Diane, 44500
240601740
e-mail: accboisdamour@village-center.fr
web: www.village-center.fr

Site consists of two sections, one for caravans, one for tents, each with separate entrance. Bar available mid June to mid September and kids' club in July and August.

dir: *On NE outskirts near railway.*

Open: Apr-Oct **Site:** 4HEC **For hire:** **Prices:** 17-27 Mobile home hire 330-693 **Facilities:** Wi-fi (charged) Kids' Club Play Area **Services:** **Leisure:** P **Off-site:** S

Camping l'Eden

13/15 rte de Ker Rivaud, 44500
240600323 240119425
e-mail: eden-caravaning@wanadoo.fr
web: www.campingeden.com

Pleasant rural surroundings with good sports and sanitary facilities. Kids' club in July and August.

dir: *1km NW via N171 exit La Baule-Escoublac.*

GPS: 47.3028, -2.3738

Open: 26 Mar-6 Nov **Site:** 5HEC **For hire:** **Facilities:** Wi-fi (charged) Kids' Club Play Area **Services:** **Leisure:** P **Off-site:** S

Roseraie

20 av J-Sohier, 44500
240604666 240601184
e-mail: camping@laroseraie.com
web: www.laroseraie.com

A well-planned site in wooded surroundings with good recreational facilities.

dir: *E of N171 towards bay.*

Open: Apr-Sep **Site:** 5HEC **For hire:** **Facilities:** **Services:** **Leisure:** P **Off-site:** S

BEYNAT — CORRÈZE

Lac de Miel

19190

555855066 555855796

e-mail: info@camping-miel.com

web: www.camping-miel.com

A family site in a picturesque wooded setting close to the lake.

dir: *4km E on N121 Argentat road.*

Open: May-Sep **Site:** 42HEC **For hire:** **Facilities:** **Services:** **Leisure:** L P R

BOIS-DE-CENÉ — VENDÉE

Bois Joli

The Camping and Caravanning Club The Friendly Club

2 rue de Châteauneuf, 85710

251682005 251684640

e-mail: contact@camping-leboisjoli.com

web: www.camping-leboisjoli.com

Leisure facilities include a pool area, tennis and fishing. Storks return every year to the site to nest and breed.

C&CC Report *A traditional campers' and caravanners' site, with a warm welcome and good quality facilities. Tourers enjoy some very good-sized pitches and the recently rebuilt wash block is very good too. Le Bois Joli offers great value for money, and avoids the hustle and bustle of the coast, yet with the seaside not far away. Within easy reach too are Noirmoutier island, Challans and the beaches of St Jean-de-Monts.*

dir: *From Nantes take A83, exit for Machecoul/Challans.*

GPS: 46.9330, -1.8881

Open: Apr-Sep **Site:** 5HEC **For hire:** **Prices:** 13.50-18.50 Mobile home hire 240-650 **Facilities:** Wi-fi (charged) Play Area **Services:** **Leisure:** P **Off-site:**

BONNAC-LA-CÔTE — HAUTE-VIENNE

Château de Leychoisier

1 rte de Leychoisier, 87270

555399343 555399343

e-mail: contact@leychoisier.com

web: www.leychoisier.com

A well-managed site of roomy pitches sloping gently towards woods.

dir: *1km S off A20, exit 27.*

GPS: 45.9330, 1.2900

Open: 15 Apr-20 Sep **Site:** 4HEC **For hire:** **Facilities:** Wi-fi (charged) Play Area **Services:** **Leisure:** L P

BONNES — VIENNE

CM

rue de la Varenne, 86300

549564434 549564851

e-mail: camping_bonnes@hotmail.com

A quiet site with plenty of recreational facilities.

dir: *S beside River Vienne.*

Open: Jun-15 Sep **Site:** 1HEC **For hire:** **Facilities:** Wi-fi **Services:** **Leisure:** P R **Off-site:** L

BONNY-SUR-LOIRE — LOIRET

Camping du Val

chemin du Camping, 45420

238315771 238315771

e-mail: otsidebonny@wanadoo.fr

Woodland site beside the Loire, near the town centre.

dir: *A77 exit 21.*

Open: mid Apr-Sep **Site:** 0.8HEC **Prices:** 8 **Facilities:** **Leisure:** R **Off-site:**

BOURGES — CHER

CM Robinson

26 bld de l'Industrie, 18000

248201685 248503239

e-mail: camping@ville-bourges.fr

web: www.ville-bourges.fr/english/tourism/camping.php

In a wooded area, in the town not far from Lake Auron. Children's playground available.

dir: *Via A71, N144 or N76.*

Open: 15 Mar-15 Nov **Site:** 2.2HEC **Prices:** 13.40-14.60 **Facilities:** Wi-fi **Services:** **Off-site:** L P R

FRANCE

BOUSSAC-BOURG — CREUSE

Château de Poinsouze

The Camping and Caravanning Club — The Friendly Club

rte de La Châtre - BP 12, 23600
☎ 555650221 fax 555658649
e-mail: info@camping-de.poinsouze.com
web: www.camping-de-poinsouze.com

A picturesque location in the grounds of a château with modern facilities. Dogs permitted except mid July to mid August.

C&CC Report *It's all about space, quality and welcome at Château de Poinsouze – vast, spacious grounds, high-quality facilities in the beautifully restored château outbuildings, open green spaces, caring, attentive owners and very large pitches. The area is an unspoilt rural idyll, with many châteaux, forests and rivers to enjoy, ideal for anglers, walkers and cyclists, plus many quiet country lanes and footpaths. It's a lovely site for long and short stays alike.*

dir: *2km N via D917.*

GPS: 46.3706, 2.2072

Open: Jun-1 Sep **Site:** 22HEC grass, mainly shaded, motorvans accepted **For hire:** bungalows, mobile homes **Prices:** 19-35 Mobile home hire 240-450 **Facilities:** shop, shower, electric hook-up, launderette, chemical disposal point, Wi-fi (charged) Kids' Club Play Area parking, wheelchair accessible **Services:** café/restaurant, bar, gas, first aid, washing machine **Leisure:** swimming P **Off-site:** swimming R

BRACIEUX — LOIR-ET-CHER

Camping Indigo les Châteaux

11 rue Roger Brun, 41250
☎ 254464184 fax 254464121
e-mail: chateaux@camping-indigo.com
web: www.camping-indigo.com

A pleasant shady park close to the town centre and convenient for visiting the châteaux of Chambord, Cheverny and Villesavin. Kids' club July to August.

Open: 4 Apr-8 Nov **Site:** 8HEC grass, partly shaded **Facilities:** shower, electric hook-up, launderette, Kids' Club Play Area parking **Services:** first aid, washing machine **Leisure:** swimming P R **Off-site:** shop, café/restaurant, bar, gas, accommodation

BRAIN-SUR-L'AUTHION — MAINE-ET-LOIRE

CM Caroline

49800
☎ 241804218
e-mail: info@campingduportcaroline.fr
web: www.campingduportcaroline.fr

A modern site in a pleasant wooded setting close to the river.

Open: All Year. **Site:** 3.2HEC grass, mainly shaded **For hire:** bungalows, tents **Facilities:** shop, shower, electric hook-up, launderette, parking **Services:** first aid, washing machine **Leisure:** swimming P **Off-site:** swimming R, café/restaurant, bar, gas, accommodation

BREM-SUR-MER — VENDÉE

Chaponnet

The Camping and Caravanning Club — The Friendly Club

85470
☎ 251905556 fax 251909167
e-mail: campingchaponnet@wanadoo.fr
web: www.le-chaponnet.com

Situated 1.3km from the sea, a well-equipped site with good leisure facilities and swimming pool area.

C&CC Report *A super site all season round, with a great pool area and a popular high season activities programme to keep you well entertained. Here you can enjoy the best of all worlds; countryside and beach, peace and quiet, next to a busy little village. The local market is great, as is the local produce – try the wine from the vineyards surrounding Brem-sur-Mer. The cycle path network continues to grow in the Vendée, so why not cycle to Les Sables or St-Gilles-Croix-de-Vie and beat the traffic?*

Open: Apr-Sep **Site:** 6.7HEC grass, sand, little shade, partly shaded **For hire:** bungalows, mobile homes **Facilities:** shower, electric hook-up, launderette, Wi-fi (charged) Kids' Club Play Area parking **Services:** café/restaurant, bar, washing machine **Leisure:** swimming P **Off-site:** swimming R S, shop, gas, accommodation

BRESSUIRE — DEUX-SÈVRES

Puy Rond

Cornet, 79300
☎ 685603726
e-mail: puyrondcamping@gmail.com
web: www.puyrondcamping.com

Small family friendly site with many places to visit nearby, including Puy du Fou, Marais Poitevin and Futuroscope.

GPS: 46.8297, -0.5016

Open: Apr-Oct **Site:** 2.5HEC grass, partly shaded **For hire:** bungalows, mobile homes **Prices:** 12-16.50 Mobile home hire 270-470 **Facilities:** shower, electric hook-up, launderette, Play Area parking, wheelchair accessible **Services:** washing machine **Leisure:** swimming P **Off-site:** swimming L R, shop, café/restaurant, bar, gas, accommodation

BRÉTIGNOLLES-SUR-MER VENDÉE

Camping la Trévillière

The Camping and Caravanning Club The Friendly Club

rue de Bellevue, 85470
251900965 251339404
e-mail: info@chadotel.com
web: www.chadotel.com

Friendly, family site with many leisure activities and entertainment.

C&CC Report *This site offers the great combination of easy access to coast, countryside and village life. Tourers are well catered for and the upper part of the site has popular, sunny, good-sized pitches. High season life centres around the pool, slide and bar; the new covered pool is the perfect addition to the site. The bustling resort of Brétignolles, its shops, weekly market and services are all an easy stroll away. A bike ride or short drive takes you to the glorious beaches.*

dir: *0.9km from town centre. 2.5km from beach.*

GPS: 46.6363, -1.8584

Open: 7 Apr-22 Sep **Site:** 3HEC **For hire:** **Prices:** 15-30 **Facilities:** Wi-fi (charged) **Services:** **Leisure:** P **Off-site:** S

Dunes

Plage des Dunes, 85470
251905532 251905485
e-mail: infos@campinglesdunes.fr
web: www.campinglesdunes.com

Direct access to the beach. All plots surrounded by hedges. Kids' club available in July and August.

dir: *2km S turn right off D38, 1km across dunes, 150m from beach.*

Open: Apr-11 Nov **Site:** 12HEC **For hire:** **Facilities:** Kids' Club Play Area **Services:** **Leisure:** P **Off-site:** L S

Motine

4 rue des Morinières, 85470
251900442
e-mail: lamotine@free.fr
web: www.lamotine.com

Pleasant site 350 metres from the town centre and 400 metres from the beach, with good facilities.

Open: Apr-Sep **Site:** 1.8HEC **For hire:** **Prices:** 20-24 Mobile home hire 290-590 **Facilities:** **Services:** **Leisure:** P **Off-site:** L R S

Vagues

20 bld du Centre, 85470
251901948 240024988
e-mail: lesvagues@free.fr
web: www.campinglesvagues.fr

A family site in a delightful rural setting on the Côte de Lumière. Near shops and ocean.

dir: *N on D38 towards St-Gilles-Croix-de-Vie.*

Open: Apr-Sep **Site:** 5HEC **For hire:** **Prices:** 15-30 Mobile home hire 250-750 **Facilities:** Wi-fi Kids' Club Play Area **Services:** **Leisure:** P **Off-site:** L R S

BRISSAC-QUINCÉ MAINE-ET-LOIRE

L'Étang

The Camping and Caravanning Club The Friendly Club

rte de St Mathurin, 49320
241917061 241917265
e-mail: info@campingetang.com
web: www.campingetang.com

A lakeside site in the heart of the Anjou countryside with good recreational facilities. Free entry or special rates at the amusement park close to the site.

C&CC Report *A spacious and top quality site, in a peaceful setting to which the owning charity continue to add facilities. The luxury of its own vineyard, serving and selling its wines on site, and a fishing lake makes L'Etang an ideal place to unwind. Children are equally spoilt for choice owing to the two swimming pools on site and adjacent play park. The heritage and cuisine of the region are a delight to discover.*

dir: *D748 towards Poitiers.*

GPS: 47.3595, -0.4339

Open: 27 Apr-11 Sep **Site:** 6HEC **For hire:** **Prices:** 17-31 Mobile home hire 270-690 **Facilities:** Wi-fi (charged) Kids' Club Play Area **Services:** **Leisure:** P R **Off-site:** L

BRÛLON SARTHE

Camping le Septentrion

le Bord du Lac, 72350
243956896
e-mail: le.septentrion@orange.fr

A family friendly site located on Lake de Brûlon. Facilities include mini-golf.

Open: Apr-Oct **Site:** 3.5HEC **For hire:** **Prices:** 11.50-13.50 Mobile home hire 210-489 **Facilities:** Wi-fi Play Area **Services:** **Leisure:** L P R **Off-site:**

FRANCE

CANDÉ-SUR-BEUVRON LOIR-ET-CHER

Grande Tortue

3 rte de Pontlevoy, 41120
☎ 254441520 📠 254441945
e-mail: grandetortue@wanadoo.fr
web: www.la-grande-tortue.com

A family site in a peaceful wooded setting. There is a swimming pool with slides, jacuzzi and sauna. Kids' club available in July and August.

dir: *A10 exit 17, cross Loire river, turn right just after bridge. Cande on D751.*

GPS: 47.4900, 1.2583

Open: 7 Apr-22 Sep **Site:** 5.8HEC **For hire:** **Prices:** 19.30-32.80 Mobile home hire 239-798 **Facilities:** Wi-fi (charged) Kids' Club Play Area **Services:** **Leisure:** P **Off-site:** R

CHALARD, LE HAUTE-VIENNE

Vigères

Les Vigères, 87500
☎ 555093722
e-mail: lesvigeres@aol.com
web: www.lesvigeres.com

Generally level site in peaceful surroundings in an elevated position with fine views.

dir: *On D901 between Châlus & Le Chalard.*

GPS: 45.555, 1.1186

Open: All Year. **Site:** 20HEC **For hire:** **Prices:** 10.50-15.25 Mobile home hire 250-450 **Facilities:** Wi-fi Play Area **Services:** **Leisure:** L P **Off-site:** R

CHALONNES-SUR-LOIRE MAINE-ET-LOIRE

CM Candais

rte de Rochefort, 49290
☎ 241780227 📠 241741481
web: www.chalonnes-sur-loire.fr

On the banks of the River Loire at its confluence with the River Louet.

dir: *NE off D751 towards Rochefort.*

Open: 15 May-Sep **Site:** 3HEC **Facilities:** **Services:** **Off-site:** P

CHAPELLE HERMIER, LA VENDÉE

Pin Parasol

The Camping and Caravanning Club — The Friendly Club

Lac du Jaunay, Chateaulong, 85220
☎ 251346472 📠 251346462
e-mail: contact@campingpinparasol.fr
web: www.campingpinparasol.fr

Set in the heart of the Vendée on the shore of Lac du Jaunay with modern facilities.

C&CC Report *A truly excellent family-owned site, built and run to highest standards. Provides a superb location, away from coastal hassle, with the great indoor pool a real plus all season round. The relaxed atmosphere is perfect for couples, young families, anglers and canoeists alike.*

dir: *Between D6 & D12.*

Open: 20 Apr-25 Sep **Site:** 12HEC **For hire:** **Prices:** 14-31 Mobile home hire 225-885 **Facilities:** Wi-fi (charged) Kids' Club Play Area **Services:** **Leisure:** P **Off-site:** R S

CHARTRES EURE-ET-LOIR

CM des Bords de l'Eure

9 rue de Launay, 28000
☎ 237287943 📠 237282943
e-mail: camping-roussel-chartres@wanadoo.fr
web: www.auxbordsdeleure.com

Wooded surroundings beside the river.

dir: *Signed towards Orléans.*

Open: 10 Apr-10 Nov **Site:** 3.86HEC **For hire:** **Facilities:** **Services:** **Off-site:** P R

CHARTRE-SUR-LE-LOIR, LA SARTHE

Vieux Moulin

chemin des Bergivaux, 72340
☎ 243444118 📠 243442406
e-mail: camping@lachartre.com
web: www.le-vieux-moulin.fr

In a quiet, wooded situation on the River Loire. Leisure facilities include a heated swimming pool, fishing and petanque.

Open: Apr-Sep **Site:** 2.4HEC **For hire:** **Facilities:** **Services:** **Leisure:** P R **Off-site:** L P

FRANCE

CHARTRIER-FERRIÈRE — CORRÈZE

Magaudie

La Magaudie Ouest, 19600

555852606

e-mail: camping@lamagaudie.com

web: www.lamagaudie.com

A peaceful site covering 8 hectares, half of which is forested, 3km from Lac du Causse with beaches and water sports. The 18th-century buildings on the site have been converted to house sanitary facilities.

dir: *A20 exit 53, N20 for Cahors, at rdbt onto D19 for Chasteaux, D154 left for Chartrier & Nadaillac, 3rd right for La Magaudie, 1st right, site on left.*

GPS: 45.0698, 1.4307

Open: All Year. **Site:** 8HEC **For hire:** **Prices:** 15.40-18.90 **Facilities:** Play Area **Services:** **Leisure:** P

CHASSENEUIL-SUR-BONNIEURE — CHARENTE

CM Les Charmilles

rue des Écoles, 16260

545395536 545225245

e-mail: mairie.chasseneuil@wanadoo.fr

web: www.chasseneuil-sur-bonnieure.fr

Small site, close to local amenities.

dir: *W of town via D27, beside River Bonnieure.*

Open: Jun-Sep **Site:** 1.5HEC **Facilities:** **Services:** **Leisure:** R **Off-site:** P

CHÂTELAILLON-PLAGE — CHARENTE-MARITIME

2 Plages - le Village Corsaire

17340

546562753 546435118

e-mail: reception@2plages.com

web: www.2plages.com

Pleasant wooded surroundings 200 metres from the beach.

dir: *Bypass Marans.*

GPS: 46.0839, -1.0931

Open: May-Sep **Site:** 4.5HEC **For hire:** **Prices:** 21-30.90 Mobile home hire 358.40-921.40 **Facilities:** Wi-fi (charged) Play Area **Services:** **Leisure:** P **Off-site:** L S

CHÂTELLERAULT — VIENNE

Relais du Miel

rte d'Antran, 86100

549020627

e-mail: camping@lerelaisdumiel.com

web: www.lerelaisdumiel.com

Set in the grounds of Château de Valette, beside the River Vienne.

dir: *A10 exit 26 Châtellerault Nord.*

Open: 15 Jun-Aug **Site:** 7HEC **For hire:** **Facilities:** **Services:** **Leisure:** P R **Off-site:**

CHAUFFOUR-SUR-VELL — CORRÈZE

Feneyrolles

19500

0555 840958

e-mail: contact@camping-feneyrolles.com

web: www.camping-feneyrolles.com

A quiet wooded location with good facilities. Ideal for exploring the Dordogne Valley and surrounding area.

dir: *2.2km E.*

Open: 15 May-Sep **Site:** 3.5HEC **For hire:** **Prices:** 17.15-18.80 Mobile home hire 250-640 **Facilities:** Wi-fi Play Area **Services:** **Leisure:** P

CHEF-BOUTONNE — DEUX-SÈVRES

Camping le Moulin

The Camping and Caravanning Club — The Friendly Club

Treneuillet, 1 rte de Niort, 79110

549297346 549297346

e-mail: info@campingchef.com

web: www.campingchef.com

Small, secluded family site, child and dog friendly. Located in a rural setting but within walking distance of local town.

C&CC Report *If your ideal is a friendly welcome from a family of British owners, on an intimate site on the edge of a market town, in picturesque French countryside with lovely walks, then Camping le Moulin is for you. With its popular restaurant including the site's own year-round Chinese take-away meals, and the nearby shops in Chef-Boutonne, you will be well looked-after at any time of the year. Make sure you find time to visit the Château de Javarzay in Chef-Boutonne, and remember that Niort, lovely La Rochelle, the brandy cellars of Cognac, plus Poitiers and Futuroscope all offer rewarding visits.*

dir: *1km NE via D740.*

GPS: 46.1078, 0.0937

Open: All Year. **Site:** 2.5HEC **For hire:** **Prices:** 15.90-18.70 Mobile home hire 180-460 **Facilities:** Wi-fi Play Area **Services:** **Leisure:** P R **Off-site:** L

FRANCE

CHEMILLÉ-SUR-INDROIS INDRE-ET-LOIRE

Les Coteaux du Lac

Base de Loisirs, 37460
☎ 247927783
e-mail: lescoteauxdulac@wanadoo.fr
web: www.lescoteauxdulac.com

In peaceful countryside setting with leisure facilities including table-tennis and mountain bike rental.

Open: 26 Mar-15 Oct **Site:** **For hire:** **Facilities:** Wi-fi Kids' Club Play Area **Services:** **Leisure:** L P **Off-site:**

CHENONCEAUX INDRE-ET-LOIRE

Moulin Fort

37150
☎ 247238622 247238093
e-mail: lemoulinfort@wanadoo.fr
web: www.lemoulinfort.com

A peaceful site on the banks of the River Cher with well-maintained facilities. Booking recommended in high season.

dir: *2km SE between Francueil and Chisseaux.*

GPS: 47.3272, 1.0883

Open: Apr-Sep **Site:** 3HEC **Prices:** 15-23 **Facilities:** Wi-fi (charged) Play Area **Services:** **Leisure:** P R

CHÉVERNY LOIR-ET-CHER

Les Saules

rte de Contres, 41700
☎ 254799001 254792834
e-mail: contact@camping-cheverny.com
web: www.camping-cheverny.com

Set in the heart of the Val de Loire, bordered by a golf course and the Chéverny forest. Kids' club available July to 20 August.

C&CC Report *A very friendly, family-run site, excellent for adults and young families who want to visit the many châteaux and villages of the area. This is especially true for those who like to get around by bike; after the welcoming owners, Les Saules' biggest plus is its access to a huge network of cycle paths linking up some of the region's greatest châteaux, via some of its loveliest woodland.*

dir: *1.5km from town on D102 towards Contres.*

GPS: 47.4786, 1.4522

Open: Apr-23 Sep **Site:** 8HEC **For hire:** **Prices:** 16.50-27 **Facilities:** Wi-fi Kids' Club Play Area **Services:** **Leisure:** P

CLOYES-SUR-LE-LOIR EURE-ET-LOIR

Val Fleuri

rte de Montigny, 28220
☎ 237985053 237983384
e-mail: info@val-fleuri.fr
web: www.val-fleuri.fr

On the bank of the River Loir. Extensive leisure facilities. Separate section for teenagers.

dir: *N10 S from Châteaudun towards Cloyes, right onto Montigny-le-Gamelon road.*

Open: 15 Mar-15 Nov **Site:** 6HEC **For hire:** **Prices:** 15.50-21.90 Mobile home hire 295-707 **Facilities:** Wi-fi (charged) Play Area **Services:** **Leisure:** P R

COËX VENDÉE

Ferme du Latois

The Camping and Caravanning Club The Friendly Club

85220
☎ 251546730
e-mail: contact@camp-atlantique.com
web: www.rcn-campings.fr

Spacious pitches in sunny locations. Leisure facilities include table tennis, volleyball and cycle hire.

C&CC Report *A relaxing inland site with masses of space, from pitches to play areas to the surrounding countryside. A very popular site with Dutch campers, the area is ideal for those who prefer to avoid the overcrowding at the coast. Attractive facilities housed in the old farm buildings complement the lakes in the centre of the site, where campers enjoy fishing and boating. The nearest beaches are just under 16km away.*

dir: *2.5km S, access from D40 or D42.*

GPS: 46.6772, -1.7687

Open: 14 Apr-29 Sep **Facilities:** Wi-fi Play Area **Services:** **Leisure:** P

COGNAC CHARENTE

Camping de Cognac

rte de Ste-Sévère, bd de Châtenay, 16100
☎ 545321332 545321582
e-mail: infos@campingdecognac.com
web: www.campingdecognac.com

Wooded surroundings beside the River Charente with modern facilities.

dir: *2km N on D24.*

GPS: 45.709, -0.313

Open: May-Sep **Site:** 2HEC **For hire:** **Prices:** 13-20 Mobile home hire 275-490 **Facilities:** Wi-fi Play Area **Services:** **Leisure:** P R **Off-site:** P R

CONCOURSON-SUR-LAYON MAINE-ET-LOIRE

Vallée des Vignes

La Croix Patron, 49700
241598635 241590983
e-mail: info@campingvdv.com
web: www.campingvdv.com

Family-run site with leisure facilities including mini-golf, table tennis and boules.

C&CC Report *Vallée des Vignes is a superbly maintained and spacious site with a fine array of facilities that have been developed to complement its rural surroundings. An ideal base for Saumur, Angers and the local wine villages, as well as Doué's rose gardens and World Wildlife Fund recognised zoo. The Nicols organise friendly barbecue evenings, trips to local vineyards, wine appreciation lessons and provide cycle maps of the local lanes and tracks. Le Puy du Fou is not far away either.*

dir: *Located just outside Concourson on D960 direction Cholet. Signposted.*

Open: Apr-Sep **Site:** 3.5HEC **For hire:** **Prices:** 16.50-24 Mobile home hire 300-650 **Facilities:** **Services:** **Leisure:** P **Off-site:** R

CONDAT SUR GANAVEIX CORRÈZE

Moulin de la Geneste

19140
555989008 555989008
e-mail: la.geneste@lineone.net
web: www.lageneste.net

Undulating land with three small lakes and a small trout river. Part of the land and small wood have been left as a nature reserve with an abundance of wildlife.

dir: *From Limoges take A20 exit 44 Uzerche travelling S. Follow signs for Condat sur Ganaveix.*

Open: May-15 Sep **Site:** 4HEC **For hire:** **Facilities:** **Services:** **Off-site:**

CONTRES LOIR-ET-CHER

Charmoise

Sassay, 41700
254795515 254795515

On a level meadow with good facilities.

dir: *N956.*

Open: Apr-Oct **Site:** 1HEC **For hire:** **Facilities:** Play Area **Services:** **Off-site:** P R

CORRÈZE CORRÈZE

Au Bois de Calais

rue René Cassin, 19800
555262627 555213362
e-mail: auboisdecalais@orange.fr
web: www.auboisdecalais.com

Quiet, relaxing site in an attractive national park location close to a lake and river.

Open: Apr-Oct **Site:** 5HEC **For hire:** **Prices:** 12-20 Mobile home hire 300-400 **Facilities:** Wi-fi (charged) Play Area **Services:** **Leisure:** P **Off-site:** L R

COUHÉ-VERAC VIENNE

Peupliers

86700
549592116 549379209
e-mail: info@lespeupliers.fr
web: www.lespeupliers.fr

A family site in a forest beside the river.

dir: *N of village on N10 Poitiers road.*

GPS: 46.3118, 0.1800

Open: 2 May-Sep **Site:** 16HEC **For hire:** **Prices:** 16.80-28 Mobile home hire 180-1040 **Facilities:** Wi-fi (charged) Kids' Club Play Area **Services:** **Leisure:** P R **Off-site:**

COUTURES MAINE-ET-LOIRE

Parc de Montsabert

Montsabert, 49320
241579163 241579002
e-mail: camping@parcdemontsabert.com
web: www.parcdemontsabert.com

The site is situated in the old Castle Montsabert Park (adjacent to campground). Quiet with a natural setting, the pitches are spacious and well separated by hedges. Good facilities and amenities.

dir: *Off D751 along River Loire between Angers and Saumur.*

Open: 9 Apr-11 Sep **Site:** 10HEC **For hire:** **Facilities:** Wi-fi (charged) Kids' Club Play Area **Services:** **Leisure:** P **Off-site:**

FRANCE

CROISIC, LE — LOIRE-ATLANTIQUE

Océan

44490

240230769 240157063

e-mail: info@camping-ocean.com

web: www.camping-ocean.com

A quiet, well-appointed site 150 metres from the sea. In the heart of the peninsula of Le Croisic close to the town centre and harbour.

dir: *1.5km NW via D45.*

Open: 6 Apr-Sep **Site:** 7.5HEC **For hire:** **Prices:** 20-45 Mobile home hire 420-1330 **Facilities:** Wi-fi Kids' Club Play Area **Services:** **Leisure:** P **Off-site:** S

see advert on page 175

DISSAY — VIENNE

CM du Parc

rue du Parc, 86130

549628429 549625872

e-mail: accueil@dissay.fr

web: www.dissay.fr

Quiet, shady site at the foot of a 15th-century castle, close to Futuroscope, the lake of St-Cyr and the forest of Moulière.

GPS: 46.6983, 0.4258

Open: 14 Jun-Aug **Site:** 1.4HEC **Prices:** 12.50 **Facilities:** Play Area **Services:** **Off-site:** L P R

EYMOUTHIERS — CHARENTE

Gorges du Chambon

16220

545707170 545708002

e-mail: info@gorgesduchambon.fr

web: www.gorgesduchambon.fr

A beautiful location on a wooded hilltop. Kids' club available in high season.

dir: *3km N via D163.*

Open: 21 Apr-15 Sep **Site:** 7HEC **For hire:** **Prices:** 15.15-28.95 Mobile home hire 266-685 **Facilities:** Wi-fi (charged) Kids' Club Play Area **Services:** **Leisure:** P R

FRESNAY-SUR-SARTHE — SARTHE

CM Sans Souci

rue de Haut Ary, Allée André Chevalier, 72130

243973287 243337572

e-mail: camping-fresnay@wanadoo.fr

web: www.fresnaysursarthe.fr/camping

A family site with good facilities and direct access to the river.

dir: *1km SE on D310.*

Open: Apr-Sep **Site:** 2HEC **For hire:** **Facilities:** Play Area **Services:** **Leisure:** P R **Off-site:**

FRIAUDOUR — HAUTE-VIENNE

Freaudour

87250

555765722 555712393

A well-equipped site beside Lac de St-Pardoux.

dir: *A20 exit 25.*

Open: Jun-12 Sep **Site:** 3.5HEC **For hire:** **Facilities:** **Services:** **Leisure:** L P **Off-site:**

FROSSAY — LOIRE-ATLANTIQUE

Migron

Le Square de la Chaussée, 44320

240397272

A pleasant location beside the canal.

Open: Jul-Sep **Site:** 2.5HEC **Facilities:** **Services:** **Leisure:** R **Off-site:**

GENNES — MAINE-ET-LOIRE

Au Bord de Loire

av des Cadets de Saumur, 49350

241380467 241380712

e-mail: auborddeloire@free.fr

web: www.camping-auborddeloire.com

Peaceful location on the river.

dir: *Via D952-D751.*

GPS: 47.3425, -0.2317

Open: May-Sep **Site:** 3HEC **For hire:** **Prices:** 10 **Facilities:** Wi-fi Play Area **Services:** **Leisure:** R **Off-site:** L P

Site 6HEC (site size) grass sand stone little shade partly shaded mainly shaded motorvans accepted bungalows for hire mobile homes for hire tents for hire no dogs site fully accessible for wheelchairs **Prices** amount quoted is per night, for 2 adults and car, plus tent or caravan Mobile home hire is a weekly rate.

GIEN — LOIRET

Domaine Les Bois du Bardelet

rte de Bourges, Poilly, 45500
238674739 238382716
e-mail: contact@bardelet.com
web: www.bardelet.com

A family site with a variety of sports facilities.

C&CC Report *A picturesque setting, with lots to do both on and off site. There's plenty to occupy young families and the site's wide appeal also means it's popular with retired couples. In low season there's the benefit of heated indoor and outdoor pools, as well as the fitness room. An ideal base for exploring the countryside south of Paris and the eastern Loire region, but perfect for just relaxing on site too.*

dir: *D940 SW of Gien.*

GPS: 47.6415, 2.6152

Open: Apr-Sep **Site:** 18HEC **For hire:** **Prices:** 19.80-46 Mobile home hire 302-1036 **Facilities:** Wi-fi (charged) Kids' Club Play Area **Services:** **Leisure:** P

GUÉMENÉ-PENFAO — LOIRE-ATLANTIQUE

Hermitage

36 av du Paradis, 44290
240792348 240792348
e-mail: camping.hermitage@wanadoo.fr
web: www.campinglhermitage.com

A beautiful setting overlooking the Don valley with modern facilities.

dir: *1.5km E on rte de Châteaubriant.*

Open: Apr-Oct **Site:** 2.5HEC **For hire:** **Facilities:** Kids' Club **Services:** **Leisure:** P **Off-site:** R

GUÉRANDE — LOIRE-ATLANTIQUE

Domaine de Léveno

rte de l'Étang de Sandun, 44350
240247930 240620123
e-mail: domaine.leveno@wanadoo.fr
web: www.camping-leveno.com

Family site in a pleasant location with good facilities. Kids' club in July and August.

dir: *3km E via rte de Sandun.*

GPS: 47.3333, -2.3903

Open: 7 Apr-29 Sep **Site:** 12HEC **For hire:** **Prices:** 22-42 Mobile home hire 315-875 **Facilities:** Wi-fi Kids' Club Play Area **Services:** **Leisure:** P

see advert on page 175

HÉRIC — LOIRE-ATLANTIQUE

Camping la Pindière

La Denais, 44810
240576541
e-mail: contact@camping.la.pindiere.com
web: www.camping-la-pindiere.com

Located between Nantes and Rennes this relaxing family site on a level meadow has pitches divided by hedges and a wide range of facilities. Not far from sandy beaches and the Nantes to Brest canal.

dir: *1km from town on D16.*

Open: All Year. **Site:** 3HEC **For hire:** **Prices:** 11.70-14 Mobile home hire 225-540 **Facilities:** Wi-fi Play Area **Services:** **Leisure:** P **Off-site:** L R

HOUMEAU, L' — CHARENTE-MARITIME

Au Petit Port de l'Houmeau

17137
546509082 546500133
e-mail: info@aupetitport.com
web: www.aupetitport.com

Quiet site with grassed and shaded pitches. 800 metres to the sea.

dir: *NE via D106.*

GPS: 46.1958, -1.1875

Open: Apr-Sep **Site:** 2HEC **For hire:** **Prices:** 15.50-20 **Facilities:** Wi-fi Play Area **Services:** **Off-site:** S

ILE DE NOIRMOUTIER, BOIS DE LA CHAISE

Camping Indigo Noirmoutier

Bois de la Chaise, 23 Allée des Sableaux, 85330
251390624 251359763
e-mail: noirmoutier@camping-indigo.com
web: www.camping-indigo.com

In a unique location between pinewoods and beach, the campsite is well equipped.

dir: *From town centre towards Plage des Sableaux.*

GPS: 47.0055, -2.2563

Open: 5 Apr-7 Oct **Site:** 12HEC **For hire:** **Prices:** 14-21 **Facilities:** Play Area **Services:** **Leisure:** S **Off-site:** P

ILE DE NOIRMOUTIER, GUERINIERE, LA

Caravan'Ile

BP N4, 85680

☎ 251395029 📠 251358685

e-mail: contact@caravanile.com

web: www.caravanile.com

Located near fine sand beaches. Swimming pool with aquatic toboggan.

Open: 15 Mar-15 Nov **Site:** 9HEC **For hire:** **Prices:** 16-28 Mobile home hire 230-780 **Facilities:** Wi-fi (charged) Kids' Club Play Area **Services:** **Leisure:** P S

ILE D'OLÉRON, BOYARDVILLE

Camping Signol

17190

☎ 546470122 📠 546472346

e-mail: contact@signol.com

web: www.camp-atlantique.com

Attractive surroundings in a pine forest, close to the village centre and 0.8km from the beach. Spacious pitches and a wide range of leisure facilities.

dir: *D126 W from town by fuel station, signed for 0.6km.*

Open: 2 Apr-24 Sep **Site:** 8HEC **For hire:** **Facilities:** Kids' Club Play Area **Services:** **Leisure:** P **Off-site:** S

ILE D'OLÉRON, CHÂTEAU-D'OLÉRON, LE

Airotel d'Oléron

Domaine de Montreavail, 17480

☎ 546476182 📠 546477967

e-mail: info@camping-airotel-oleron.com

web: www.camping-airotel-oleron.com

A peaceful, park-like setting 1km from the beach and the town centre.

dir: *Signed from town centre.*

Open: Mar-1 Nov **Site:** 4HEC **For hire:** **Facilities:** **Services:** **Leisure:** L P S

Brande

rte des Huîtres, 17480

☎ 546476237 📠 546477170

e-mail: info@camping-labrande.com

web: www.camping-labrande.co.uk

A family site with good facilities in beautiful surroundings. Recreational facilities include a heated and covered pool.

dir: *2.5km NW, 250m from sea.*

Open: 30 Mar-11 Nov **Site:** 5.5HEC **For hire:** **Prices:** 16-38 Mobile home hire 270-1090 **Facilities:** Wi-fi Kids' Club Play Area **Services:** **Leisure:** P **Off-site:** S

ILE D'OLÉRON, DOLUS-D'OLÉRON

Ostréa

rte des Huitres, 17550

☎ 546476236 📠 546752001

e-mail: camping.ostrea@wanadoo.fr

web: www.camping-ostrea.com

A well-equipped site in wooded surroundings close to the beach.

dir: *3.5km NE.*

Open: Apr-Sep **Site:** 2HEC **For hire:** **Prices:** 17.15-24.50 Mobile home hire 285-635 **Facilities:** Wi-fi Kids' Club Play Area **Services:** **Leisure:** P S

ILE D'OLÉRON, ST-GEORGES-D'OLÉRON

Domaine d'Oléron

The Camping and Caravanning Club — The Friendly Club

La Jousselinière, 17190

☎ 546765497 📠 251339404

e-mail: info@chadotel.com

web: www.chadotel.com

Pitches shaded by oak trees, site located 2.5km from the beach.

C&CC Report *The toll-free bridge to the Ile d'Oléron allows you to try island life yet remain within easy reach of the mainland, while nearly 160km of cycle tracks help you explore the island's lovely beaches, quiet villages, salt marshes and oyster parks. Try a boat trip around famous Fort Boyard, a visit to the world famous Zoo de la Palmyre or relax on the island's beautiful beaches.*

dir: *2km from centre of St Pierre d'Oléron.*

GPS: 45.9675, -1.3193

Open: 7 Apr-22 Sep **Site:** 3HEC **For hire:** **Prices:** 15.50-31 **Facilities:** Wi-fi (charged) Play Area **Services:** **Leisure:** P **Off-site:** S

Les Gros Joncs

17190

☎ 546765229 📠 546766774

e-mail: info@les-gros-joncs.fr

web: www.camping-les-gros-joncs.com

Quiet location on undulating land in lovely pine woodland. Spa facilities are available all year.

dir: *After the Oléron bridge towards Grand-Village-La Cotinière. Site is 5km past La Cotinière.*

GPS: 45.9536, -1.3798

Open: Apr-Oct **Site:** 5.15HEC **For hire:** **Prices:** 16.10-44.40 **Facilities:** Wi-fi (charged) Kids' Club Play Area **Services:** **Leisure:** P S **Off-site:**

FRANCE

Signol

av de Albatros, Boyardville, 17190
546470122 546472346
e-mail: contact@signol.com
web: www.signol.com
Situated among pine and oak trees, 0.8km from a sandy beach.
Open: Apr-Sep **Site:** 8HEC **For hire:** **Facilities:** **Services:** **Leisure:** P **Off-site:** S

Suroît

rte Touristique Côte Ouest, l'Ileau, 17190
546470725 546750424
e-mail: info@camping-lesuroit.com
web: www.camping-lesuroit.com
Level ground sheltered by dunes with fine modern facilities.
dir: *5km SW of town.*
Open: Apr-Sep **Site:** 5HEC **For hire:** **Facilities:** **Services:** **Leisure:** P S **Off-site:**

ILE D'OLÉRON, ST-PIERRE-D'OLÉRON

Aqua Trois Masses

Le Marais Doux, 17310
546472396 546751554
e-mail: accueil@campingaqua3masses.com
web: www.campingaqua3masses.com
A well-equipped site in a picturesque location 2.5km from the beach.
Open: Apr-Sep **Site:** 3HEC **For hire:** **Facilities:** Wi-fi **Services:** **Leisure:** P **Off-site:** S

ILE DE RÉ, ARS-EN-RÉ

Cormoran

rte de Radia, 17590
546294604 546292936
e-mail: info@cormoran.com
web: www.cormoran.com
Situated on the edge of a forest 0.5km from village of Ars.
Open: 4 Apr-26 Sep **Site:** 3HEC **Facilities:** **Services:** **Leisure:** P **Off-site:** S

ILE DE RÉ, BOIS-PLAGE-EN-RÉ, LE

Sunêlia Interlude

8 rte de Gros Jonc, 17580
546091822 546092338
e-mail: infos@interlude.fr
web: www.interlude.fr
A pleasant wooded location 50 metres from the beach. A heated indoor swimming pool, with outdoor paddling pool and aquatic play for children is a recent addition. The site also has a fitness centre. Kids' club available during school holidays in April, July and August.
Open: 7 Apr-23 Sep **Site:** 7.5HEC **For hire:** **Prices:** 23-48 **Facilities:** Wi-fi (charged) Kids' Club Play Area **Services:** **Leisure:** P **Off-site:** S

ILE DE RÉ, COUARDE-SUR-MER, LA

Océan

50 rte d'Ars, 17670
546298770 546299213
e-mail: info@campingocean.com
web: www.campingocean.com
A fine position facing the sea, with modern facilities.
dir: *3km NW on N735.*
Open: 14 Apr-16 Sep **Site:** 9HEC **For hire:** **Prices:** 19.50-42.65 Mobile home hire 270-1530 **Facilities:** Wi-fi (charged) Kids' Club Play Area **Services:** **Leisure:** P **Off-site:** S

La Tour des Prises

rte d'Ars, BP 27, 17670
546298482 546298899
e-mail: camping@lesprises.com
web: www.lesprises.com
Located in the heart of the island, next to a wood, in a peaceful and quiet location. The trees dotted throughout the site offer many shady areas.
dir: *After bridge direction St Martin de Ré/la Couarde Sur Mer/ Ars-en-Ré.*
Open: 23 Mar-Sep **Site:** 2.5HEC **For hire:** **Prices:** 15-35 Mobile home hire 290-590 **Facilities:** Wi-fi Play Area **Services:** **Leisure:** P **Off-site:** S

FRANCE

ILE DE RÉ, FLOTTE, LA

Camping la Grainetière

rte de St-Martin-de-Ré, D735, 17630
546096886 546095313
e-mail: la-grainetiere@orange.fr
web: www.la-grainetiere.com

1.5km from village centre, a wooded, family friendly site with a wide range of leisure activites including a games room and cycle hire.

Open: 2 Apr-Sep **Site:** 2.7HEC **For hire:** **Facilities:** Wi-fi (charged) Play Area **Services:** **Leisure:** P **Off-site:** S

Camping Les Peupliers

17630
251331700 251331727
e-mail: contact@camp-atlantique.com
web: www.camp-atlantique.com

Situated in a large, wooded park 0.8km from the sea with good sports and entertainment facilities.

dir: *1.3km SE at the entrance of Ile de Ré.*

GPS: 46.1831, -1.3085

Open: 7 Apr-22 Sep **Site:** 4.4HEC **For hire:** **Prices:** 17-34 Mobile home hire 250-950 **Facilities:** Wi-fi (charged) Kids' Club Play Area **Services:** **Leisure:** P **Off-site:** S

ILE DE RÉ, LOIX

Ilates

Le Petit Boucheau, rte du Grouin, 17111
546290543 546290679
e-mail: ilates@wanadoo.fr
web: www.camping-loix.com

Pitches separated by hedges, and leisure facilities including outdoor swimming pool, tennis courts and table tennis.

dir: *E towards Pointe du Grouin, 0.5km from sea.*

Open: 21 Mar-4 Oct **Site:** 4.5HEC **For hire:** **Facilities:** **Services:** **Leisure:** P **Off-site:** S

ILE DE RÉ, ST-MARTIN-DE-RÉ

Camping Municipal

rue du Rempart, 17410
546092196 546099418
e-mail: camping.stmartindere@wanadoo.fr

Pleasant wooded surroundings at the foot of the 17th-century ramparts. Nearby are the port, shops and a family beach.

dir: *From Nantes take A83 then N137. From Bordeaux take A10, onto A837 then N137.*

Open: 15 Feb-15 Nov **Site:** 4HEC **For hire:** **Facilities:** Wi-fi Play Area **Services:** **Off-site:** S

ILE DE RÉ, STE MARIE-DE-RÉ

Camping les Grenettes

rte du Bois Plage, 17740
546302247 546302464
e-mail: contact@hotel-les-grenettes.com
web: www.campinglesgrenettes.com

Located 200 metres from the sea and set in pine woodland.

dir: *A10/RN11. After bridge onto RD201 (signed Intineraire Sud) towards Ste-Marie-de-Ré then le Bois-Plage-en-Ré.*

GPS: 46.1606, -1.3513

Open: All Year. **Site:** 7HEC **For hire:** **Prices:** 15-33 Mobile home hire 230-825 **Facilities:** Wi-fi **Services:** **Leisure:** P S

JARD-SUR-MER VENDÉE

Écureuils

rte des Goffineaux, 85520
251334274 251339114
e-mail: ecureuils@franceloc.fr
web: www.camping-ecureuils.com

Quiet woodland terrain 450 metres from the sea, with large pitches surrounded by hedges.

Open: Apr-Sep **Site:** 4.3HEC **For hire:** **Facilities:** **Services:** **Leisure:** P **Off-site:** S

Océano d'Or

58 rue G-Clemenceau, 85520
251336508 251339404
e-mail: info@chadotel.com
web: www.chadotel.com

A well-maintained site 1km from the beach and 0.5km from the town centre. An aqua park and entertainment caters for all ages.

dir: *Via D19, 400m from city centre.*

Open: 7 Apr-22 Sep **Site:** 8HEC **For hire:** **Prices:** 15.50-31 **Facilities:** Wi-fi (charged) Play Area **Services:** **Leisure:** P **Off-site:** S

JAUNAY CLAN — VIENNE

Croix du Sud

rte de Neuville, 86130

☎ 549625814

e-mail: camping@la-croix-du-sud.fr

web: www.la-croix-du-sud.fr

Within easy reach of Futuroscope, the European Park of the Moving Image.

dir: *Via A10 & D62.*

Open: 29 Mar-13 Sep **Site:** 4HEC **For hire:** **Facilities:** **Services:** **Leisure:** P **Off-site:**

LAGORD — CHARENTE-MARITIME

CM Parc

rue du Parc, 17140

☎ 546676154 546006201

e-mail: mairie.lagord@wanadoo.fr

Pleasant municipal site within easy reach of the coast.

dir: *Via N137/D735.*

Open: Jun-15 Sep **Site:** **For hire:** **Facilities:** **Services:** **Off-site:** P

LIMERAY — INDRE-ET-LOIRE

Jardin Botanique

9 rue de la Rivière, 37530

☎ 247301350 247301732

e-mail: info@camping-jardinbotanique.com

web: www.camping-jardinbotanique.com

Set in wooded shady parkland.

dir: *6km NE of Amboise on N152.*

Open: All Year. **Site:** 1.5HEC **For hire:** **Prices:** 13-17 Mobile home hire 180-450 **Facilities:** Wi-fi Play Area **Services:** **Leisure:** P **Off-site:** R

LINDOIS, LE — CHARENTE

Étang

16310

☎ 545650267 545650896

web: www.campingdeletang.com

Well-shaded site with a natural lake, ideal for swimming and fishing with a small beach.

dir: *From Rochefoucauld D13 towards Montemboeuf.*

Open: Apr-1 Nov **Site:** 10HEC **For hire:**
Prices: 16.50-20 **Facilities:** **Services:** **Leisure:** L **Off-site:**

LION D'ANGERS, LE — MAINE-ET-LOIRE

CM Frénes

49220

☎ 241953156

A municipal site on the banks of the River Oudon, 300 metres from the town centre.

dir: *NE on N162.*

Open: Jun-Aug **Site:** 2HEC **Facilities:** **Leisure:** R **Off-site:** P

LOCHES — INDRE-ET-LOIRE

Camping la Citadelle

1 av Aristide Briand, 37600

☎ 247590591 247590035

e-mail: camping@lacitadelle.com

web: www.lacitadelle.com

Family friendly site in a rural setting on the banks of the River Indre. A variety of pitches are available. In July and August children's activities take place including a kids' club. Dogs are permitted with a vaccination certificate. Bar and restaurant/grill open in July and August.

Open: 19 Mar-Sep **Site:** 4HEC **For hire:** **Prices:** 16-33.50 **Facilities:** Wi-fi (charged) Kids' Club Play Area **Services:** **Leisure:** P **Off-site:**

LONGEVILLE — VENDÉE

Brunelles

Le Bouil, 85560

☎ 251331700 251331727

e-mail: contact@camp-atlantique.com

web: www.camp-atlantique.com

A well-appointed site in a wooded location 0.7km from the beach. Indoor and outdoor pools, entertainment, spa and fitness, are available.

dir: *On coast between Longeville & Jard-sur-Mer.*

Open: 2 Apr-24 Sep **Site:** 13HEC **For hire:** **Prices:** 17-34 Mobile home hire 250-1200 **Facilities:** Wi-fi (charged) Kids' Club Play Area **Services:** **Leisure:** P **Off-site:** S

FRANCE

Camping Le Petit Rocher

The Camping and Caravanning Club The Friendly Club

85560

☎ 251331700

e-mail: ferme@rcn.fr

web: www.campinglepetitrocher.com

Close to the beach, with a swimming pool, slides and multi-sports area.

C&CC Report *A small site in a superb position, a short walk from one of the Vendée's glorious, long, sandy beaches. The site, the beach and the little village strip between them offer all you need on a day-to-day basis, while local services and the rest of the main Vendée attractions are just a short drive away. Further afield, Le Puy du Fou, canoeing in the marshes, museums and an Aquatic Park provide longer days out - if you can tear yourself away from the beach.*

dir: *Off D105 S of Longeville-sur-Mer.*

GPS: 46.4035, -1.5075

Open: 28 Apr-16 Sep **Facilities:** Wi-fi Play Area **Services:** **Leisure:** P

Clos des Pins

Les Conches, 85560

☎ 251903169 251903068

e-mail: info@campingclosdespins.com

web: www.campingclosdespins.com

A family-run site with good facilities, 250 metres from a sandy beach.

dir: *Between Longeville & La Tranche.*

Open: Apr-Sep **Site:** 1.6HEC **For hire:** **Facilities:** **Services:** **Leisure:** P **Off-site:** S

LUCHÉ-PRINGÉ — SARTHE

CM de la Chabotière

Place des Tilleuls, 72800

☎ 243451000 243451000

e-mail: contact@lachabotiere.com

web: www.lachabotiere.com

Site by a river just 100 metres from the village and a short drive from several Loire chateaux. Large marked sites on terraces above the river, and most cars are kept in a car park to ensure safe play areas for children. Kids' club available in July and August.

dir: *From Le Mans, RN23 then D13 at Clermont-Créans. In village, turn left before monument.*

GPS: 47.7022, 0.0734

Open: Apr-15 Oct **Site:** 2.5HEC **For hire:** **Prices:** 11.90-14.50 **Facilities:** Wi-fi Kids' Club Play Area **Services:** **Leisure:** P **Off-site:**

LUSIGNAN — VIENNE

Camping Municipal Vauchiron

chemin de la Plage, Vauchiron, 86600

☎ 549433008 549436119

e-mail: lusignan@cg86.fr

web: www.lusignan.fr

Close to a medieval city, a family friendly site in a quiet wooded location beside the River Vonne with good facilities. A bar is available on site in July and August. Dogs are permitted, on leads and with vaccination certificate.

dir: *0.5km NE on RD611.*

Open: 15 Apr-Sep **Site:** 4HEC **For hire:** **Prices:** 9.80 Mobile home hire 205-266 **Facilities:** Wi-fi **Services:** **Leisure:** R **Off-site:**

LUYNES — INDRE-ET-LOIRE

Granges

Les Granges, 37230

☎ 247557905 247409243

e-mail: reception@campinglesgranges.fr

web: www.campinglesgranges.fr

Quiet site close to the village. Ideal for visiting historical sites, fishing, and wine tasting

dir: *S via D49.*

Open: Apr-Sep **Site:** 1.82HEC **For hire:** **Prices:** 13.22-29.22 Mobile home hire 242.27-547.89 **Facilities:** Wi-fi Play Area **Services:** **Leisure:** P **Off-site:** R

MACHÉ — VENDÉE

Val de Vie

5 rue du Stade, 85190

☎ 251602102 251602102

e-mail: campingvaldevie@orange.fr

web: www.camping-val-de-vie.fr

Traditional, quiet, family-owned campsite.

dir: *Off D948 Aizenay-Challans, follow blue signs in 300m from village centre.*

GPS: 46.7531, -1.6860

Open: Apr-Sep **Site:** 2.2HEC **For hire:** **Prices:** 12.50-19.50 Mobile home hire 195-500 **Facilities:** **Services:** **Leisure:** P **Off-site:** L

Site 6HEC (site size) grass sand stone little shade partly shaded mainly shaded motorvans accepted bungalows for hire mobile homes for hire tents for hire no dogs site fully accessible for wheelchairs
Prices amount quoted is per night, for 2 adults and car, plus tent or caravan Mobile home hire is a weekly rate.

MAGNAC-BOURG HAUTE-VIENNE

Écureuils

rte de Limoges, 87380

555008028 555004909

e-mail: mairie.magnac-bourg@wanadoo.fr

A grassy site close to the historic village.

dir: *25km S on N20.*

Open: 15 May-15 Sep **Site:** 1.3HEC **Prices:** 13.30 **Facilities:** **Services:** **Off-site:**

MANSIGNÉ SARTHE

Plage

rte du Plessis, 72510

243461417

e-mail: camping-mansigne@orange.fr

web: www.atouvert.com

A holiday complex, with good recreational facilities, set in extensive parkland around a 24-hectare lake with a beach. Ideal for fishing and enjoying nature.

dir: *On D13, 4km from D307.*

Open: Apr-Oct **Site:** 3.4HEC **For hire:** **Prices:** 9-11.50 Mobile home hire 280-420 **Facilities:** Kids' Club Play Area **Services:** **Leisure:** L P **Off-site:**

MARANS CHARENTE-MARITIME

CM Le Bois Dinot

rte de Nantes, 17230

546011051 546660265

e-mail: campingboisdinot.marans@wanadoo.fr

web: www.ville-marans.fr

Separate car park for arrivals after 23.00hrs. Plenty of shade on site, and a children's playground.

dir: *Via N137.*

GPS: 46.3172, -0.9887

Open: Apr-Sep **Site:** 6HEC **For hire:** **Prices:** 12.94-21.54 **Facilities:** Wi-fi (charged) Play Area **Services:** **Leisure:** P **Off-site:** R

MARÇON SARTHE

Lac des Varennes

rte du Port Gauthier, 72340

243441372 243445431

e-mail: lacdesvarennes@camp-in-ouest.com

web: www.camp-in-ouest.com

An attractive site bordering the lake in the heart of the Loire Valley, with spacious pitches and new facilities. A kids' club is available in July and August.

GPS: 47.7125, 0.4997

Open: 4 Apr-30 Oct **Site:** 9HEC **For hire:** **Prices:** 11.90-15 Mobile home hire 240-670 **Facilities:** Wi-fi Kids' Club Play Area **Services:** **Leisure:** L R **Off-site:**

MATHES, LES CHARENTE-MARITIME

Estanquet

17570

546224732 546225146

e-mail: contact@campinglestanquet.com

web: www.campinglestanquet.com

Close to sandy beaches, site with shade provided by pine trees. Leisure activities include a swimming pool complex.

Open: Apr-Sep **Site:** 8HEC **For hire:** **Facilities:** Wi-fi Kids' Club Play Area **Services:** **Leisure:** P **Off-site:** S

Orée du Bois

225 rte de la Bouverie, La Fouasse, 17570

546224243 546225476

e-mail: info@camping-oree-du-bois.fr

web: www.camping-oree-du-bois.fr

A family site in a pine and oak forest, 5 minutes from the beach.

dir: *3.5km NW.*

Open: 28 Apr-15 Sep **Site:** 6HEC **For hire:** **Prices:** 19-42 Mobile home hire 220-780 **Facilities:** Wi-fi (charged) Kids' Club Play Area **Services:** **Leisure:** P **Off-site:** S

Pinède

2103 rte de la Fouasse, 17570

546224513 546225021

e-mail: contact@campinglapinede.com

web: www.campinglapinede.com

A modern family site in a wooded area around the large aquatic park. Excellent sports facilities. Entertainment available in July and August.

dir: *3km NW from D141 for approx 2km, site on left.*

Open: Apr-Sep **Site:** 7HEC **For hire:** **Facilities:** **Services:** **Leisure:** P

MAYENNE — MAYENNE

CM du Gue St Leonard

rue St-Léonard, 53100
243045714 243000199
e-mail: campingsaintleonard@orange.fr
web: www.paysdemayenne-tourisme.fr

Situated close to Mayenne town centre, on the banks of the river, the site offers attractive, shady grounds. Swimming pool available during July and August.

dir: *0.8km from town centre near N12.*

Open: 15 Mar-Sep **Site:** 1.8HEC **For hire:** **Prices:** 7.30-9.20 Mobile home hire 150-460 **Facilities:** Wi-fi Play Area **Services:** **Leisure:** P **Off-site:**

MEMBROLLE-SUR-CHOISILLE, LA — INDRE-ET-LOIRE

Camping Municipal de la Membrolle sur Choisille

rte de Fondettes, 37390
247412040
e-mail: mairie@ville-la-membrolle37.fr
web: www.la-membrolle-sur-choisille.fr

On level meadow in sports ground beside River Choisille.

dir: *N on N138 Le Mans road.*

Open: May-Sep **Site:** 1.5HEC **Facilities:** Play Area **Services:** **Leisure:** R **Off-site:** L

MERVENT — VENDÉE

Chêne Tord

34 chemin du Chêne Tord, 85200
251002063 251002063
e-mail: contact@camping-mervent.fr
web: www.camping-mervent.fr

A well-appointed site 200 metres from a large artificial lake in the heart of the Mervent forest.

dir: *Via D99 - autoroute.*

Open: Apr-Nov **Site:** 3HEC **For hire:** **Prices:** 11-13 Mobile home hire 292-423 **Facilities:** Wi-fi Play Area **Services:** **Off-site:** L R

MESLAND — LOIR-ET-CHER

Parc du Val de Loire

rte de Fleuray, 41150
254702718 254702171
e-mail: parcduvaldeloire@wanadoo.fr
web: www.parcduvaldeloire.com

A sheltered position among Touraine vineyards with good recreational facilities.

dir: *1.5km W between A10 & N152.*

Open: 8 Apr-11 Sep **Site:** 13.6HEC **For hire:** **Facilities:** Wi-fi Kids' Club Play Area **Services:** **Leisure:** P

MESQUER — LOIRE-ATLANTIQUE

Château du Petit Bois

44420
240426877 240426558
e-mail: info@campingdupetitbois.com
web: www.campingdupetitbois.com

Set in the extensive grounds of an 18th-century château with shaded, well-defined pitches.

Open: Apr-Sep **Site:** 10HEC **For hire:** **Facilities:** **Services:** **Leisure:** P **Off-site:** S

Praderoi

14 allée des Barges, Quimiac, 44420
240426672 240426672
e-mail: camping.praderoi@wanadoo.fr
web: www.camping-le-praderoi.com

On level ground 90 metres from Lanseria beach, 350 metres from shopping centre.

dir: *From Guérande on D774 onto D52.*

Open: 15 Jun-15 Sep **Site:** 0.5HEC **For hire:** **Prices:** 16-20.60 Mobile home hire 250-620 **Facilities:** Wi-fi Play Area **Services:** **Off-site:** S

Welcome

rue de Bel-Air, 44420
240425085 240425085
e-mail: contact@lewelcome.com
web: www.lewelcome.com

Pleasant wooded surroundings, 0.6km from the coast. Separate car park for arrivals after 22.30hrs.

dir: *1.8km NW via D352.*

Open: Apr-Oct **Site:** 2HEC **For hire:** **Facilities:** **Services:** **Leisure:** P **Off-site:** S

FRANCE

MESSÉ — DEUX-SÈVRES

Grande Vigne

79120
549293993
e-mail: grande.vigne@orange.fr
web: www.grande-vigne.com

Flat, orchard site bordered by fruit trees and set in rural countryside. No boundaries or marked pitches as only 5 pitches are let at any one time.

dir: *Off RN10 between Poitiers & Angoulême.*

GPS: 46.2561, 0.0886

Open: All Year. **Site:** 0.5HEC **For hire:** **Prices:** 15.50-18.50 **Facilities:** **Services:** **Leisure:** P

MISSILLAC — LOIRE-ATLANTIQUE

CM des Platanes

4-6 rue de la Fontaine St Jean, 44780
240883888

Level and sloping pitches with pond area and fishing available.

dir: *1km W via D2, 50m from the lake.*

Open: Jul-Aug **Site:** 2.04HEC **Prices:** 8.30 **Facilities:** Play Area **Services:** **Off-site:** L

MONTGIVRAY — INDRE

CM Solange Sand

2 rue du Pont, 36400
254061036 254061039
e-mail: mairie.montgivray@wanadoo.fr

A pleasant riverside site in the grounds of a château.

Open: 15 Mar-15 Oct **Site:** 1HEC **Facilities:** **Services:** **Leisure:** R **Off-site:** P

MONTLOUIS-SUR-LOIRE — INDRE-ET-LOIRE

Camping des Peupliers

RD 751, 37270
247508190 386379583
e-mail: aquadis1@orange.fr
web: www.aquadis-loisirs.com

On level meadow, near the town and close to the river.

dir: *1.5km W on N751, next to swimming pool near railway bridge.*

Open: Apr-17 Oct **Site:** 4HEC **For hire:** **Facilities:** Wi-fi Play Area **Services:** **Leisure:** P **Off-site:** R

MONTMORILLON — VIENNE

CM Allochon

av F-Tribot, 86500
549910233
e-mail: camping@ville-montmorillon.fr

A well-equipped municipal site close to the river and 1.5km from the town centre.

dir: *SE via D54.*

Open: Mar-Oct **Site:** 2HEC **Prices:** 5.04-8.29 **Facilities:** Wi-fi Play Area **Services:** **Off-site:** P R

MONTSOREAU — MAINE-ET-LOIRE

Isle Verte

av de la Loire, 49730
241517660 241510883
e-mail: isleverte@cvtloisirs.fr
web: www.campingisleverte.com

Situated in a pretty village, in wooded surroundings beside the River Loire. Kids' club available in high season.

dir: *On D947 between road & river.*

GPS: 47.2181, 0.0528

Open: Apr-Sep **Site:** 2HEC **For hire:** **Prices:** 16.90-22.90 Mobile home hire 280-840 **Facilities:** Wi-fi (charged) Kids' Club Play Area **Services:** **Leisure:** P R **Off-site:**

MORTEROLLES-SUR-SEMME — HAUTE-VIENNE

CM

87250
555766018 555766845
e-mail: ot.bessines@wanadoo.fr
web: www.tourisme-bessines87.fr

A small, quiet country campsite with spacious pitches.

dir: *A20 exit 24.*

GPS: 46.1483, 1.3656

Open: All Year. **Site:** 8HEC **Prices:** 7-10 **Facilities:** **Services:** **Off-site:** L R

FRANCE

MOUTIERS-EN-RETZ, LES — LOIRE-ATLANTIQUE

Domaine du Collet

44760

☎ 240214092 📠 240214512

e-mail: domaineducollet@orange.fr

web: www.domaine-du-collet.com

Site set in a large estate with leisure facilities including tennis courts and fishing.

Open: Apr-Oct **Site:** 12HEC **For hire:** **Prices:** 15-25 Mobile home hire 200-750 **Facilities:** Wi-fi (charged) Kids' Club Play Area **Services:** **Leisure:** L P R S

Village de la Mer

18 rue de Prigny, 44760

☎ 240646590

e-mail: vdmer@hotmail.com

web: www.village-mer.fr

Quiet site close to a village and the beach.

dir: *9km S of Pornic on D97.*

Open: 15 Jun-15 Sep **Site:** 7HEC **For hire:** **Prices:** 21.10-40.10 Mobile home hire 295-995 **Facilities:** Wi-fi (charged) **Services:** **Leisure:** P **Off-site:** S

MUIDES-SUR-LOIRE — LOIR-ET-CHER

Château des Marais

27 rue de Chambord, 41500

☎ 254870542 📠 254870543

e-mail: chateau.des.marais@wanadoo.fr

web: www.chateau-des-marais.com

A wooded site set in the spacious grounds of an old stone manor house. The site retains the atmosphere of a country estate and the water park features slides and spacious sun terraces. Recreational facilities include library, TV room, a pond for fishing and a kids' club in high season.

dir: *A10 exit 16 Mer-Chambord, at rdbt 2nd exit towards Blois-Mer, at next rdbt 1st exit towards Mer. In Mer left onto D112 and in Muides-sur-Loire right towards Chambord. Site on right after a series of bends in road.*

GPS: 47.6658, 1.5288

Open: 12 May-15 Sep **Site:** 12HEC **For hire:** **Prices:** 26-40 Mobile home hire 336-1180 **Facilities:** Wi-fi Kids' Club Play Area **Services:** **Leisure:** P **Off-site:** R

see advert on opposite page

NANTES — LOIRE-ATLANTIQUE

Petit Port

bld du Petit Port 21, 44300

☎ 240744794 📠 240742306

e-mail: camping-petit-port@nge-nantes.fr

web: www.nge-nantes.fr/camping

A modern, well-kept park by a river. A good base for exploring Nantes and the region's vineyards.

dir: *In N of town near Parc du Petit Port. N137 Rennes road from town centre & signed.*

Open: All Year. **Site:** 8.5HEC **For hire:** **Facilities:** **Services:** **Off-site:** P R

NÉRET — INDRE

Camping le Bonhomme

Mulles, 36400

☎ 254314611

e-mail: info@camping-lebonhomme.com

web: www.camping-lebonhomme.com

Small site on a sunny hillside, sheltered by hedges.

Open: 15 Apr-Sep **Site:** 1.5HEC **Facilities:** **Services:** **Leisure:** P

NEUVILLE-SUR-SARTHE — SARTHE

Vieux Moulin

72190

☎ 243253182 📠 243253811

web: www.lemanscamping.net

Close to the medieval town of Le Mans, a privately owned site of 4.8 hectares, close to the village. Beautifully landscaped mature parkland bordering the river Sarthe. Good sized pitches, outdoor swimming pool. Ideal as a stop-over, short holiday or for the 24 hour Le Mans motor race.

dir: *Via N138 & D197.*

Open: Jul-Aug **Site:** 4.8HEC **For hire:** **Facilities:** Play Area **Services:** **Leisure:** P **Off-site:** L R

FRANCE

NIBELLE — LOIRET

Nibelle

rte de Boiscommun, 45340
238322355 238320387
e-mail: info@camping-parcdenibelle.com
web: www.camping-parcdenibelle.com

Spacious, quiet, level site in the clearing of an oak woodland with a good range of leisure facilities.

dir: *Off D921 E to Nibelle, signed.*

Open: Mar-Nov **Site:** 10HEC **For hire:** **Prices:** 24-30 Mobile home hire 380-633 **Facilities:** Wi-fi Play Area **Services:** **Leisure:** P **Off-site:** L R

NOTRE-DAME-DE-MONTS — VENDÉE

Beauséjour

85690
251588388
e-mail: campingbeausejour85@orange.fr

1.5km from the beach, a relaxing, family-friendly site.

dir: *2km NW on D38.*

Open: Apr-Sep **Site:** 1.34HEC **For hire:** **Facilities:** Play Area **Services:** **Off-site:** P R S

Grand Jardin

50 rue de la Barre, 85690
228112175
e-mail: contact@legrandjardin.net
web: www.legrandjardin.net

A family site in a picturesque location facing the Ile d'Yeu. Modern sanitary installations and plenty of sports facilities. 1km from the beach.

dir: *0.6km N.*

Open: All Year. **Site:** 4HEC **For hire:** **Prices:** 22-25.80 Mobile home hire 260-690 **Facilities:** Wi-fi (charged) **Services:** **Leisure:** P R **Off-site:** S

NOTRE-DAME-DE-RIEZ — VENDÉE

Domaine des Renardières

85270
251551417
e-mail: caroline.raffin@free.fr

Pleasant countryside site with sandy beaches close by.

Open: May-2 Sep **Site:** 3.5HEC **For hire:** **Facilities:** **Services:** **Leisure:** P **Off-site:** S

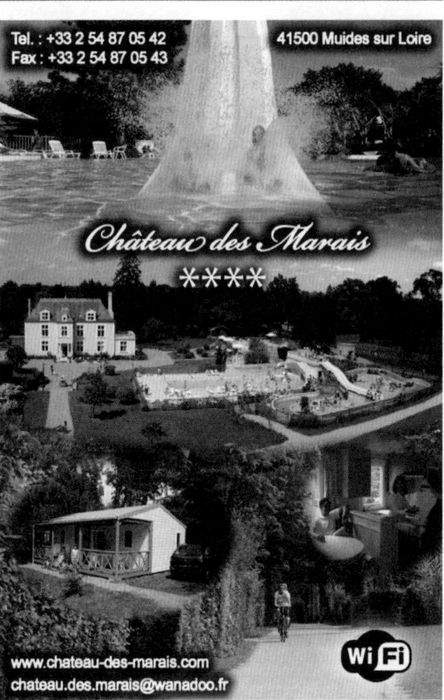

OLIVET — LOIRET

Camping Municipal Olivet

rue du Pont Bouchet, 45160
238635394 238635896
e-mail: campingolivet@wanadoo.fr
web: www.camping-olivet.org

Site lies partly on shaded peninsula, partly on open lawns beside river.

dir: *2km E, signed from village.*

GPS: 47.8561, 1.9254

Open: Apr-15 Oct **Site:** 1HEC **Prices:** 12.80-20.10 **Facilities:** Wi-fi Play Area **Services:** **Off-site:** L P R

FRANCE

OLONNE-SUR-MER VENDÉE

Domain de l'Oree

rte des Amis de la Nature, 85340
☎ 251331059 🖷 251331516
e-mail: loree@free.fr
web: www.l-oree.com

With direct access to a 1.5km long, sandy beach, pitches are divided by trees. The swimming pool complex includes both indoor and outdoor pools and waterslides. Organised activities for both children and adults.

dir: *3km N.*

Open: 16 Apr-18 Sep **Site:** 7HEC **For hire:** **Facilities:** Wi-fi Kids' Club Play Area **Services:** **Leisure:** P **Off-site:** S

Loubine

The Camping and Caravanning Club The Friendly Club

1 rte de la Mer, 85340
☎ 251331292 🖷 251331271
e-mail: camping.la.loubine@wanadoo.fr
web: www.la-loubine.fr

Situated on the edge of a forest near the coast.

C&CC Report *A lively site for older families and nightbirds, with many static units as well as tourers, and one of the best pool complexes in the area. Many people walk or cycle to the nearest sandy beach, plage de Sauveterre, and Les Sables d'Olonne, home of the world famous Vendée Globe yacht race, is just a short drive away. If you're an early riser, a trip to Les Sables' market hall is a great shopping experience.*

dir: *N via D87/D80.*

Open: 2 Apr-24 Sep **Site:** 8HEC **For hire:** **Facilities:** **Services:** **Leisure:** P **Off-site:** S

ONZAIN LOIR-ET-CHER

Domaine de Dugny

rte de Chambon-sur-Cisse, 41150
☎ 254207066 🖷 254337169
e-mail: ld.reception@siblu.fr
web: www.siblu.fr

On a small lake, surrounded by farmland with well-marked pitches shaded by poplars. Heated indoor pool and outdoor pool with slides. Activities include mini-golf, archery and tennis and there are pedaloes and kayaks to hire. Entertainment programme 21 March to 11 September. Dogs allowed on touring pitches.

dir: *CD45 from Onzain for Chambon-sur-Cisse.*

Open: 11 Feb-11 Nov **Site:** 10HEC **For hire:** **Prices:** 20-50 Mobile home hire 250-1000 **Facilities:** Wi-fi (charged) Kids' Club Play Area **Services:** **Leisure:** P **Off-site:**

PERRIER, LE VENDÉE

Maison Blanche

85300
☎ 251493923
e-mail: campingmaisonblanche@yahoo.fr
web: www.campingmaisonblanche.fr

A family site on level ground, with pitches divided by trees. 6km from the coast.

Open: May-Sep **Site:** 3.2HEC **For hire:** **Facilities:** **Services:** **Leisure:** P R **Off-site:** S

PIERREFITTE-SUR-SAULDRE LOIR-ET-CHER

Parc des Alicourts

Domaine des Alicourts, 41300
☎ 254886334 🖷 254885840
e-mail: info@lesalicourts.com
web: www.lesalicourts.com

In wooded surroundings at the heart of an extensive park, this family site is exceptionally well equipped and provides a wide variety of recreational facilities.

dir: *6km NE via D126 beside the lake.*

GPS: 47.5444, 2.1914

Open: 27 Apr-7 Sep **Site:** 25HEC **For hire:** **Prices:** 20-56 **Facilities:** Kids' Club Play Area **Services:** **Leisure:** L P **Off-site:** R

see advert on opposite page

PLAINE-SUR-MER, LA LOIRE-ATLANTIQUE

Tabardière

44770
☎ 240215883 🖷 240210268
e-mail: info@camping-la-tabardiere.com
web: www.camping-la-tabardiere.com

A wooded, terraced site 3km from the sea.

dir: *Off D13 between Pornic & La Plaine-sur-Mer.*

GPS: 47.1406, -2.1533

Open: 16 Apr-25 Sep **Site:** 6HEC **For hire:** **Facilities:** Wi-fi (charged) **Services:** **Leisure:** P **Off-site:** S

FRANCE

www.lesalicourts.com
My Holiday ?
My little prince discovered the baby pool and swims like Nemo. **My** eldest has made good friends with the ponies. Their dad has been improving his handicap on the 9 hole golf course!!! And me? I have learnt the meaning of total relaxation. You see when my **family** is happy I am too, so for once I can think about only **me**.
1,70
A lovely campsite located in the heart of Loire Valley for the whole family
My perfect world
Plenty of activities to share with your family : wellness centre, spa, gym, heated pools, wave pool, slides and water park, 9 hole golf, tennis court, football, volleyball, basketball, kayaking, archery, bike rental, fishing, kids club.
Les Alicourts
41 300 Pierrefitte-sur-Sauldre
Tél +33 (0) 2 54 88 63 34
Fax +33 (0) 2 54 88 58 40
infos@lesalicourts.com
Alan Rogers
LeadingCampings
les alicourts
resort by nature

lities shower electric points for razors electric points for caravans motorvan service point parking by tents permitted
pulsory separate car park shop **Services** café/restaurant bar Camping Gaz International gas other than Camping Gaz
first aid facilities laundry **Leisure** swimming L-Lake P-Pool R-River S-Sea **Off-site** All facilities within 5km

PONS — CHARENTE-MARITIME

Camping Chardon

13 rte des Bernards, 17800
☎ 546950125
e-mail: jacques.bier@cegetel.net
web: www.camping-chardon.fr

Quiet location on the edge of a small village, next to a farm.

dir: *D732 W from Pons towards Royan, site 2.5km on left. Or A10 exit 36, towards Pons, site 0.8km on right.*

Open: All Year. **Site:** 1.6HEC **For hire:** **Facilities:** **Services:** **Off-site:** R

PONT-L'ABBÉ-D'ARNOULT — CHARENTE-MARITIME

Parc de la Garenne

24 av Bernard Chambenoit, 17250
☎ 546970146
e-mail: info@lagarenne.net
web: www.lagarenne.net

Peaceful site in a parkland setting. Shady individual pitches.

dir: *Via A10, N137 & D18.*

Open: 15 May-Oct **Site:** 4.8HEC **For hire:** **Facilities:** Wi-fi Kids' Club Play Area **Services:** **Leisure:** P **Off-site:** R

PONTS-DE-CÉ, LES — MAINE-ET-LOIRE

Ile du Château

rte de Cholet, av de la Boire Salée, 49130
☎ 241446205 241446205
e-mail: ile-du-chateau@wanadoo.fr
web: www.camping-ileduchateau.com

Situated on a small island in the Loire close to the Château des Ponts-de-Cé. Separate car park for arrivals after 21.00hrs.

dir: *SW of Angers towards Cholet.*

Open: Apr-Sep **Site:** 2.3HEC **For hire:** **Facilities:** **Services:** **Leisure:** P R **Off-site:**

PORNIC — LOIRE-ATLANTIQUE

Boutinardière

23 rue de la Plage de la Boutinardière, 44210
☎ 240820568 240824901
e-mail: info@boutinardiere.com
web: www.camping-boutinardiere.com

A family campsite, 200 metres from the beach, has indoor and outdoor pools with 10 waterslides, as well as a sauna and steam-room. Kids' club available in July and August.

Open: Apr-Sep **Site:** 8HEC **For hire:** **Facilities:** Wi-fi Kids' Club Play Area **Services:** **Leisure:** P **Off-site:** S

see advert on opposite page

La Chênaie

The Camping and Caravanning Club The Friendly Club

42210
☎ 240820731
e-mail: accueil@campinglachenaie.com
web: www.campinglachenaie.com

Spacious pitches divided by hedges within easy reach of the coast.

C&CC Report *This friendly, well-kept and welcoming family site is set among trees and shrubs with plenty of open space. Its countryside setting belies its proximity to the beaches of the much loved resort of Pornic, while most services are open most of the season. The north Vendée and the island of Noirmoutier, south Brittany, Nantes, the Loire-Atlantique's beaches and salt marshes, and even a safari park and an ice cream factory, are all within an easy day trip.*

Open: 6 Apr-16 Sep **Site:** 6HEC **Facilities:** Play Area **Services:** **Leisure:** P

Patisseau

29 rue de Patisseau, 44210
☎ 240821039 240822281
e-mail: contact@lepatisseau.com
web: www.lepatisseau.com

Wooded surroundings close to the beach with good recreational facilities. There are two heated pools with slides. Shop open July and August. Bar and restaurant open weekends and during holidays.

dir: *3km E via D751.*

GPS: 47.1189, -2.0729

Open: 9 Apr-14 Sep **Site:** 4.3HEC **For hire:** **Prices:** 26-42 Mobile home hire 435-880 **Facilities:** Wi-fi (charged) Kids' Club Play Area **Services:** **Leisure:** P **Off-site:** L R S

PORNICHET LOIRE-ATLANTIQUE

Bel Air

av Bonne Source/av Chevissens, 44380

☎ 240611078

web: www.belairpornichet.fr

A pleasant wooded location 50 metres from the beach.

Open: Apr-Sep **Site:** 6HEC **For hire:** **Prices:** 22-40 Mobile home hire 350-1050 **Facilities:** Wi-fi Kids' Club Play Area **Services:** **Leisure:** P **Off-site:** S

Forges

98 rte de Villes Blais, 44380

☎ 240611884 240601184

e-mail: camping@campinglesforges.com

web: www.campinglesforges.com

Wooded surroundings with well-defined pitches and good recreational facilities.

dir: *Via N171.*

Open: Jul-Aug **Site:** 2HEC **For hire:** **Facilities:** **Services:** **Leisure:** P **Off-site:** L

PRAILLES DEUX-SÈVRES

Lambon

Plan d'eau du Lambon, 79370

☎ 549328511 549329492

e-mail: lambon.vacances@wanadoo.fr

web: www.lelambon.com

A peaceful rural site by a lake, with outdoor activities including archery, canoeing and climbing. There are organised activities for children three times a week.

dir: *A10 jnct 10 onto D948 from Niort towards Limoges, follow signs for Celles-sur-Belle then for base de loisirs de Lambon for 6km.*

Open: May-Sep **Site:** 1HEC **For hire:** **Prices:** 11.10 Mobile home hire 156-364 **Facilities:** Wi-fi Play Area **Services:** **Leisure:** L **Off-site:** R

PUILBOREAU CHARENTE-MARITIME

Beaulieu

3 rue du Treuil Gras, 17138

☎ 546680438 546358595

e-mail: contact@camping-la-rochelle.com

web: www.camping-la-rochelle.com

Shady pitches with hedges. Lots of activities for children and varied entertainment for all.

GPS: 46.1781, -1.1154

Open: All Year. **Site:** 5HEC ○ ○ ○ **For hire:** ○ ○ ○ **Prices:** 18-25 Mobile home hire 250-885 **Facilities:** ○ ○ ○ Wi-fi (charged) Kids' Club Play Area ○ **Services:** ○ ○ ○ ○ **Leisure:** ○ P **Off-site:** ○ S ○ ○ ○

RILLE INDRE-ET-LOIRE

Huttopia Rille

Lac de Rillé, 37340

☎ 247246297 247246361

e-mail: rille@huttopia.com

web: www.huttopia.com

Site located at the edge of a lake surrounded by forest in the châteaux area of the Loire. Home to some 190 species of birds. Spacious shady pitches. Kids' club available in July and August. 1 dog per pitch.

dir: *A85 exit 7, cross Langeais then D57 to Hommes, then Rille. Follow signs to lake.*

GPS: 47.4460, 0.3329

Open: 19 Apr-8 Nov **Site:** 4.5HEC ○ ○ **For hire:** ○ ○ ○ **Prices:** 15-26.70 Mobile home hire 404.25-805 **Facilities:** ○ ○ ○ ○ Kids' Club Play Area ○ ○ **Services:** ○ ○ ○ ○ **Leisure:** ○ L P

ROSIERS, LES MAINE-ET-LOIRE

Val de Loire

6 rue Ste-Baudruche, 49350

☎ 241519433 241518913

e-mail: contact@camping-valdeloire.com

web: www.camping-valdeloire.com

A comfortable site partly on the banks of the River Loire with good recreational facilities.

dir: *N via D59.*

Open: Apr-Sep **Site:** 3HEC ○ ○ **For hire:** ○ ○ **Facilities:** ○ ○ ○ ○ **Services:** ○ ○ ○ ○ ○ **Leisure:** ○ P **Off-site:** ○ R ○ ○

ROYAN CHARENTE-MARITIME

Clairefontaine

Rue du C Lachaud, Pontaillac, 17200

☎ 546390811 546381379

e-mail: clairefontaine@campeole.com

web: www.campeole.com

A well-equipped site in wooded surroundings 300 metres from the beach with a variety of recreational facilities.

Open: May-26 Sep **Site:** 5HEC ○ ○ **For hire:** ○ ○ **Facilities:** ○ ○ ○ ○ **Services:** ○ ○ ○ ○ ○ **Leisure:** ○ P **Off-site:** ○ S ○

SABLES-D'OLONNE, LES VENDÉE

Dune des Sables

rte de l'Aubraie - La Paracou, 85100

☎ 251323121 251339404

e-mail: info@chadotel.com

web: www.chadotel.com

A fine location facing the sea and with direct access to the beach. Various events take place during the summer season.

dir: *2km from town centre.*

GPS: 46.5123, -1.8146

Open: 7 Apr-22 Sep **Site:** 5.5HEC ○ ○ ○ **For hire:** ○ ○ **Prices:** 20-32.50 **Facilities:** ○ ○ ○ ○ Wi-fi (charged) Play Area ○ **Services:** ○ ○ ○ ○ ○ ○ **Leisure:** ○ P S **Off-site:** ○

Roses

1 rue des Roses, 85100

☎ 251951042 251339404

e-mail: info@chadotel.com

web: www.chadotel.com

A level site shaded by trees and bushes, 0.5km from the Remblai beach, set in the residential heart of les Sables-d'Olonne. Heated pool with waterslide and a programme of entertainment.

dir: *Close to town centre off D949, 0.5km from the beach.*

GPS: 46.4914, -1.7658

Open: 7 Apr-11 Nov **Site:** 3HEC ○ ○ **For hire:** ○ **Prices:** 20-32.50 **Facilities:** ○ ○ ○ ○ Wi-fi (charged) ○ **Services:** ○ ○ ○ ○ ○ **Leisure:** ○ P **Off-site:** ○ S ○

SABLÉ-SUR-SARTHE — SARTHE

Hippodrome

allée du Quebec, 72300
☎ 243954261 243927482
e-mail: camping@sablesursarthe.fr
web: www.tourisme.sablesursarthe.fr
A peaceful wooded setting with a great variety of recreational facilities.
dir: *450m from town.*
Open: Apr-Oct **Site:** 3HEC **For hire:** **Facilities:** Wi-fi Play Area **Services:** **Leisure:** P R **Off-site:**

ST-AIGNAN-SUR-CHER — LOIR-ET-CHER

Les Cochards

41110
☎ 254751559 254754472
e-mail: camping@lescochards.com
web: www.lescochards.com
On beautiful meadowland, completely surrounded by hedges. Activities for children in July and August.
dir: *1km from bridge on D17 towards Selles.*
Open: Apr-15 Oct **Site:** 4HEC **For hire:** **Prices:** 19-22 Mobile home hire 290-590 **Facilities:** Wi-fi (charged) Kids' Club **Services:** **Leisure:** P **Off-site:** R

ST-AMAND-MONTROND — CHER

CM Roche

chemin de la Roche, 18200
☎ 248960936 248960936
e-mail: camping-la-roche@wanadoo.fr
web: www.ville-saint-amand-montrond.fr
A lovely wooded location between the River Cher and the Berry Canal with modern facilities.
dir: *1.5km SW near river & canal.*
GPS: 46.7166, 2.4833
Open: Apr-Sep **Site:** 4HEC **For hire:** **Facilities:** Wi-fi Play Area **Services:** **Leisure:** R **Off-site:** P

ST-AVERTIN — INDRE-ET-LOIRE

CM Rives du Cher

61 rue de Rochepinard, 37550
☎ 247272760 247258289
e-mail: contact@camping-lesrivesducher.com
web: www.camping-lesrivesducher.com
Municipal site on the banks of the River Cher.
dir: *400m N of town centre. 4km from Tours.*
Open: Apr-15 Oct **Site:** 3HEC **For hire:** **Facilities:** **Services:** **Off-site:** L P R

ST-BRÉVIN-LES-PINS — LOIRE-ATLANTIQUE

CM Courance

100/110 av Ml-Foch, 44250
☎ 240272291 240272291
e-mail: info@campinglacourance.fr
web: www.campinglacourance.fr
Set in a pine forest with direct access to the beach.
dir: *S off D305.*
Open: All Year. **Site:** 4HEC **For hire:** **Facilities:** **Services:** **Leisure:** S **Off-site:** P

Fief

57 chemin du Fief, 44250
☎ 240272386 240644619
e-mail: camping@lefief.com
web: www.lefief.com
A family site adjacent to a long sandy beach. The pitches are surrounded by trees and bushes and there are modern facilities.
dir: *From town centre onto Route Bleue to Centre Leclerc & 2nd right to site.*
Open: 7 Apr-Sep **Site:** 7HEC **For hire:** **Prices:** 18-41 Mobile home hire 364-1575 **Facilities:** Wi-fi (charged) Kids' Club Play Area **Services:** **Leisure:** P **Off-site:** S

ST-BRÉVIN-L'OCÉAN — LOIRE-ATLANTIQUE

Pierres Couchées

L'Ermitage, 44250
☎ 240278564 240849703
e-mail: contact@pierres-couchees.com
web: www.pierres-couchees.com
Extensive, well-screened terrain made up of three sites.
dir: *300m from sea. 2km on D213 toward Pornic.*
Open: Apr-8 Oct **Site:** 14HEC **For hire:** **Facilities:** **Services:** **Leisure:** P **Off-site:** S

FRANCE

ST-CYR VIENNE

Camping du Lac de Saint-Cyr

The Camping and Caravanning Club The Friendly Club

86130
549625722 549522858
e-mail: contact@campinglacdesaintcyr.com
web: www.campinglacdesaintcyr.com

A delightful setting in a spacious park beside a lake. Futuroscope is within easy reach via the A10. Kids' club in July and August.

C&CC Report *A good modern site, convenient not only as a stopover between the ports and south-west France, but also for longer stays. It's great for both families and couples, with on-site leisure facilities as well as the nearby golf, fishing or watersports. It's also a good choice if all you want to do is relax or visit the local Vienne area, with Poitiers and the theme park of the moving image, Futuroscope, close by.*

dir: *1.5km NE via D4/D82.*

GPS: 46.7192, 0.4592

Open: Apr-Sep **Site:** 5HEC **For hire:** **Prices:** 13-26 Mobile home hire 310-749 **Facilities:** Wi-fi Kids' Club Play Area **Services:** **Leisure:** L P **Off-site:** R

SAINTES CHARENTE-MARITIME

Au Fil de l'Eau

6 rue de Courbiac, 17100
546930800
e-mail: campingaufildeleau@sfr.fr
web: www.camping-saintes-17.com

Site lies beside the River Charente, 0.9km from the town centre. Wi-fi free of charge for first hour.

dir: *A10 exit 35 towards town centre on D128.*

Open: May-Sep **Site:** 7HEC **For hire:** **Prices:** 17.52 Mobile home hire 300-500 **Facilities:** Wi-fi **Services:** **Leisure:** P R **Off-site:**

ST-FLORENT-LE-VIEIL MAINE-ET-LOIRE

Ile Batailleuse

44370
240834501
e-mail: serge.rabec@aliceadsl.fr
web: campingilebatailleuse.com.chez-alice.fr

On the banks of the Loire, relaxing site with shady pitches. Boat moorings available.

dir: *6km SE. N of Lac du Boudon.*

Open: 28 Apr-16 Nov **Site:** 2.7HEC **For hire:** **Prices:** 10.50-11.50 **Facilities:** Wi-fi Play Area **Services:** **Leisure:** R **Off-site:** P

ST-GEORGES-DE-DIDONNE CHARENTE-MARITIME

Bois Soleil

2 av de Suzac, 17110
546050594 546062743
e-mail: camping.bois.soleil@wanadoo.fr
web: www.bois-soleil.com

Pitches lie on different levels. Direct access to the beach.

dir: *2.5km S of town on D25 Meschers road.*

GPS: 45.5883, -0.9867

Open: 31 Mar-7 Oct **Site:** 10HEC **For hire:** **Prices:** 20-44 Mobile home hire 180-1190 **Facilities:** Wi-fi (charged) Kids' Club Play Area **Services:** **Leisure:** P S

Ideal Camping

16 av de Suzac, 17110
546052904 546063236
e-mail: info@ideal-camping.com
web: www.ideal-camping.com

A well-equipped, peaceful site in a pine forest 200 metres from Suzac beach.

dir: *W of St-Georges-de-Didonne via D25.*

GPS: 45.5852, -0.9855

Open: 5 May-9 Sep **Site:** 8HEC **For hire:** **Prices:** 16.50-28.80 Mobile home hire 260-770 **Facilities:** Wi-fi (charged) Play Area **Services:** **Leisure:** P **Off-site:** S

Village Center les Catalpas

45 chemin d'Enlias, 17110
499572121 467516389
e-mail: contact@village-center.com
web: www.village-center.com/poitou-charentes/camping-mer-catalpas.php

Close to the town centre and beach with clearly marked-out pitches. Leisure facilities available during the day and evening. Compulsory separate car park for arrivals 23.00-08.00hrs.

GPS: 45.6151, -0.9946

Open: 24 Jun-4 Sep **Site:** 2HEC **For hire:** **Prices:** Mobile home hire 497-833 **Facilities:** Wi-fi (charged) Kids' Club Play Area **Services:** **Leisure:** P **Off-site:** L S

FRANCE

ST-GEORGES-LÈS-BAILLARGEAUX VIENNE

Futuriste

86130
549524752 549372333
e-mail: camping-le-futuriste@wanadoo.fr
web: www.camping-le-futuriste.fr

An elevated position having fine views over the Clain Valley.

C&CC Report *Small, family run, very friendly site, less than a kilometre from the village centre and 4 km from Futuroscope.*

Open: All Year. **Site:** 4HEC **For hire:** **Prices:** 21-28.20 Mobile home hire 499-680 **Facilities:** Play Area **Services:** **Leisure:** L P **Off-site:** R

ST-GERMAIN-LES-BELLES HAUTE-VIENNE

Camping de Montréal

rue du Petit Moulin, 87380
555718620 555710083
e-mail: contact@campingdemontreal.com
web: www.campingdemontreal.com

With a lakeside setting, pitches separated by hedges with views of the surrounding hills.

dir: *A20 exit 42 towards St-Germain-les-Belles.*

GPS: 45.6114, 1.5011

Open: Apr-Oct **Site:** 2HEC **For hire:** **Prices:** 13.40-19.40 Mobile home hire 169-539 **Facilities:** Wi-fi (charged) Play Area **Services:** **Leisure:** L P **Off-site:**

ST-GILLES-CROIX-DE-VIE VENDÉE

Bahamas Beach

168 rte des Sables, 85800
251546916 251339404
e-mail: info@chadotel.com
web: www.chadotel.com

Site lies 1km from the beach. Sunny pitches, heated indoor and outdoor pools and varied entertainment.

C&CC Report *A modern, well-equipped site, very well situated on one of the most popular stretches of the Vendée coastline, just to the south of St-Gilles-Croix-de-Vie. There are many static units on site, yet touring pitches are still reasonably sized for such a good coastal location. A footpath direct from the site takes about 15 minutes to the beach while another path goes to St Gilles itself. There's a classic French holiday atmosphere on site, with English spoken at reception. Good pitches for sunseekers! Nearby St-Gilles-Croix-de-Vie is very popular for its shops and markets, including a high season evening market.*

dir: *2km from town centre.*

GPS: 46.6774, -1.9152

Open: 7 Apr-22 Sep **Site:** 4HEC **For hire:** **Prices:** 15.50-31 **Facilities:** Wi-fi (charged) Play Area **Services:** **Leisure:** P **Off-site:** R S

Domaine de Beaulieu

rue du Parc - Givrand, 85800
251555946 251339404
e-mail: info@chadotel.com
web: www.chadotel.com

A former farm, located 1km from the beach, this family site has facilities including a heated swimming pool and take away.

dir: *4km from town. 1km from beach.*

GPS: 46.6718, -1.9041

Open: 7 Apr-22 Sep **Site:** 7HEC **For hire:** **Prices:** 15-30 **Facilities:** Wi-fi (charged) Play Area **Services:** **Leisure:** P **Off-site:** R S

ST-HILAIRE-DE-RIEZ VENDÉE

Biches

rte de Notre-Dame-de-Riez, 85270
251543882 251543074
e-mail: info@camping-les-biches.com
web: www.camping-les-biches.com

A well-equipped site in a pine forest and close to the sea. Kids' club for 5 to 10 year olds - July to August.

dir: *2km N.*

Open: 15 May-15 Sep **Site:** 10HEC **For hire:** **Facilities:** **Services:** **Leisure:** P

FRANCE

Bois Tordu

84 av de la Pège, 85270
☎ 251543378 🖷 251540829
e-mail: info@leboistordu.com
web: www.leboistordu.com
Wooded location with good facilities.
dir: *5.3km NW.*

Open: 15 May-10 Sep **Site:** 2HEC **For hire:** **Facilities:** Play Area **Services:** **Leisure:** P **Off-site:** S

Chouans

108 av de la Faye, 85270
☎ 251540592
e-mail: info@camping-leschouans.com
web: www.camping-leschouans.com
Wooded location on the edge of a national forest.
dir: *2.5km NW.*

Open: May-Sep **Site:** 5HEC **For hire:** **Facilities:** Wi-fi (charged) Kids' Club Play Area **Services:** **Leisure:** P **Off-site:** S

Écureuils

100 av de la Pège, 85270
☎ 251543371 🖷 251556908
e-mail: info@camping-aux-ecureuils.com
web: www.camping-aux-ecureuils.com
Pleasant surroundings 250 metres from a fine sandy beach, with good recreational facilities. Kids' club available in July and August.
dir: *D178 & D753 from Nantes to St-Hilaire-de-Riez.*
GPS: 46.745, -2.0083

Open: 28 Apr-8 Sep **Site:** 4HEC **For hire:** **Prices:** 27.15-36.70 Mobile home hire 322-926 **Facilities:** Wi-fi (charged) Kids' Club Play Area **Services:** **Leisure:** P **Off-site:** S

Padrelle

1 rue Prévot, La Corniche de Sion/l'Océan, 85270
☎ 251553203
e-mail: contact@camping-la-padrelle.com
web: www.camping-la-padrelle.com
A rural setting 50 metres from the beach and 5 minutes from the town.
GPS: 46.7001, -1.9731

Open: May-15 Oct **Site:** 1.5HEC **For hire:** **Prices:** 12-20.44 Mobile home hire 281.54-656.16 **Facilities:** Play Area **Services:** **Off-site:** S

Parée Préneau

The Camping and Caravanning Club — The Friendly Club

23 av de la Parée Préneau, 85270
☎ 251543384 🖷 251552957
e-mail: contact@campinglapareepreneau.com
Less than 1km to the beach, site within landscaped grounds, pitches divided by plants. There are indoor and outdoor swimming pools.

C&CC Report *A long-established and well-located site, great for beaches and lively high season resorts. Ideal for campers who prefer smaller scale sites and who prefer entertainment and services nearby but not right on site – the popular resorts of St-Gilles-Croix-de-Vie and St Jean-de-Monts are both just a few kilometres away. Nearby too is 'Feeling Forest', a tree-based adventure park with aerial slides and walkways - great fun for all ages.*

dir: *From D38 St-Hilaire and St-Gilles C-de-Vie, then St-Hilaire centre ville, Sion-l'Océan and signed.*

Open: May-10 Sep **Site:** 1.5HEC **For hire:** **Facilities:** **Services:** **Leisure:** P **Off-site:** S

Plage

106 av de la Pège, 85270
☎ 251543393 🖷 251559702
e-mail: campinglaplage@campingscollinet.com
web: www.campingscollinet.com
On a meadow with trees. Access to beach via dunes.
dir: *5.7km NW.*

Open: Apr-Sep **Site:** 5.5HEC **For hire:** **Facilities:** **Services:** **Leisure:** P S **Off-site:**

Prairie

chemin des Roselières, 85270
☎ 251540856 🖷 251559702
e-mail: campinglaprairie@campingscollinet.com
web: www.campingscollinet.com
A family site with pitches shaded by trees. A big swimming pool complex and entertainment for adults and children, in July and August.
dir: *5.5km NW, 0.5km from beach.*

Open: 15 May-10 Sep **Site:** 4.7HEC **For hire:** **Facilities:** Wi-fi Kids' Club Play Area **Services:** **Leisure:** P **Off-site:** L S

Puerta del Sol

7 chemin des Hommeaux, 85270
251491010 251498484
e-mail: info@campinglapuertadelsol.com
web: www.campinglapuertadelsol.com

A peaceful site with well-defined pitches in a wooded location. Good facilities for family recreation.

dir: *4.5km N.*

Open: Apr-Sep **Site:** 4HEC **For hire:** **Facilities:** ⊙ **Services:** **Leisure:** P **Off-site:**

Sol-à-Gogo

61 av de la Pège, 85270
251542900 251548874
e-mail: info@solagogo.com
web: www.solagogo.com

A family site with good recreational facilities, including three aquaslides, with direct access to the beach.

dir: *4.8km NW of St-Hilaire, 6km S of St-Jean-de-Monts.*

Open: 15 May-13 Sep **Site:** 4HEC **For hire:** **Prices:** 28.80-36 Mobile home hire 350-860 **Facilities:** ⊙ Wi-fi Kids' Club Play Area **Services:** **Leisure:** P S **Off-site:**

ST-HILAIRE-LA-FORÊT VENDÉE

Batardières

85440
251333385

A pleasant site surrounded by mature trees and shrubs, with large pitches separated by hedges.

dir: *W on D70.*

Open: Jul-Aug **Site:** 1.6HEC **Prices:** 20-23.50 **Facilities:** ⊙ **Services:** **Off-site:** S

Grand' Métairie

8 rue de la Vineuse en Plaine, 85440
251333238 251332569
e-mail: info@camping-grandmetairie.com
web: www.la-grand-metairie.com

Site with flowers and trees with clearly marked pitches. Entertainment for children and teenagers. Free shuttle available to nearby sandy beach. Rental bikes, indoor and outdoor pool.

Open: Apr-Sep **Site:** 3.84HEC **For hire:** **Facilities:** ⊙ Wi-fi (charged) Kids' Club Play Area **Services:** **Leisure:** P **Off-site:** L S

ST-HILAIRE-PEYROUX CORRÈZE

Le Chazal

19560
555255248
e-mail: lechazal@neuf.fr
web: lechazal-19.perso.sfr.fr

A peaceful site on the edge of the Massif Central with fine views over the Couze Valley, good for walking holidays.

dir: *Off N89 at Malemort onto D141 at rdbt to Venarsal & 1.5m for St-Hilaire-Peyroux, left onto C13 for site.*

Open: Apr-1 Nov **Site:** 1.5HEC **For hire:** **Prices:** 12 **Facilities:** ⊙ Wi-fi **Services:** **Off-site:** R

ST-JEAN-D'ANGELY CHARENTE-MARITIME

Val de Boutonne

56 quai de Bernouet, 17400
546322616
e-mail: info@valba.net
web: www.valba.net

Wooded location near the river and 900 metres from the town centre.

dir: *A10 exit 34.*

GPS: 45.9486, -0.5364

Open: Apr-Sep **Site:** 3.5HEC **For hire:** **Prices:** 17 Mobile home hire 179-579 **Facilities:** ⊙ Wi-fi (charged) Play Area **Services:** **Off-site:** P

ST-JEAN-DE-MONTS VENDÉE

Amiaux

The Camping and Caravanning Club The Friendly Club

223 rte de Notre-Dame de Monts, 85169
251582222 251582609
e-mail: accueil@amiaux.fr
web: www.amiaux.fr

A well-equipped site on the edge of a forest, 0.7km from the beach.

C&CC Report *A great family site, with excellent pitches, where tourers are welcomed. The swimming pools and waterslides are superb, particularly the large indoor pool, and it's only 15 minutes walk along a woodland path to the nearest sandy beach. The cycle paths are first-rate too throughout the Vendée – cycle into St-Jean-de-Monts or to the Grand-Plage.*

dir: *3.5km NW of D38.*

GPS: 46.8075, -2.1049

Open: 3 May-Sep **Site:** 16HEC **For hire:** **Prices:** 19-34.50 Mobile home hire 290-810 **Facilities:** ⊙ Wi-fi (charged) Kids' Club Play Area **Services:** **Leisure:** P **Off-site:** S

ilities shower ⊙ electric points for razors electric points for caravans motorvan service point parking by tents permitted
npulsory separate car park shop **Services** café/restaurant bar Camping Gaz International gas other than Camping Gaz
first aid facilities laundry **Leisure** swimming L-Lake P-Pool R-River S-Sea **Off-site** All facilities within 5km

Bois Dormant

168 rue des Sables, 85160
251586262 251582997
e-mail: boisdormant@siblu.fr
web: www.siblu.fr/leboisdormant

Family-friendly site, close to beaches with swimming pool complex and organised activities.

Open: 24 Apr-5 Sep **Site:** 11.5HEC **For hire:** **Facilities:** **Services:** **Leisure:** P **Off-site:** S

Bois Joly

46 rue de Notre-Dame-de-Monts, BP 507, 85165
251591163 251591106
e-mail: campingboisjoly@wanadoo.fr
web: www.camping-leboisjoly.com

A pleasantly landscaped, terraced site set among pine trees. Close to the beach and town centre, heated covered pool with slides and entertainment in July and August. Dogs allowed except in chalets/mobile homes.

GPS: 46.7996, -2.0744

Open: 7 Apr-Sep **Site:** 7.5HEC **For hire:** **Prices:** 19-34 Mobile home hire 250-720 **Facilities:** Wi-fi (charged) Kids' Club Play Area **Services:** **Leisure:** P R **Off-site:** S

Bois Masson

149 rue des Sables, 85160
251586262 251582997
e-mail: boismasson@siblu.fr
web: www.siblu.com

A family site with a variety of facilities in a wooded setting near the beach. Aquatic complex includes covered and outdoor pools, water chutes, jacuzzi and sauna.

dir: *2km SE.*

Open: 27 Mar-18 Sep **Site:** 7.5HEC **For hire:** **Facilities:** **Services:** **Leisure:** P **Off-site:** S

Clarys Plage

av des Epines, 85160
251581024 251595196
e-mail: info@leclarys.com
web: www.leclarys.com

A family site with good facilities including an indoor swimming pool and an outdoor pool with a waterslide.

dir: *S of town 300m from beach.*

Open: 15 May-15 Sep **Site:** 8HEC **Prices:** 28.80-36 **Facilities:** Wi-fi Kids' Club Play Area **Services:** **Leisure:** P **Off-site:** S

FRANCE

Forêt

190 chemin de la Rive, 85160
251588463 251588463
e-mail: camping-la-foret@wanadoo.fr
web: www.hpa-laforet.com

A well-equipped family site in a pleasant rural setting, with direct access to the beach.

dir: *Off D38.*

Open: Apr-25 Sep **Site:** 1HEC **For hire:** **Prices:** 15-29 Mobile home hire 279-729 **Facilities:** Wi-fi (charged) Play Area **Services:** **Leisure:** P S **Off-site:**

Yole

chemin des Bosses, Orouet, 85160
251586717 251590535
e-mail: contact@la-yole.com
web: www.la-yole.com

Quiet site ideal for families with younger children. Set in rural surroundings, 1.5km from a fine sandy beach. Kids' club in July and August for 5 to 12 year olds.

dir: *Signed from D38 in Orouet.*

Open: 2 Apr-26 Sep **Site:** 9HEC **For hire:** **Prices:** 16-29.90 Mobile home hire 260-890 **Facilities:** Wi-fi (charged) Kids' Club Play Area **Services:** **Leisure:** P **Off-site:** S

Zagarella

Le Pey Blanc, Rte des Sables, 85160
251581982 251593528
e-mail: zagarella@zagarella.fr
web: www.zagarella.fr

In pine woods close to the sea.

GPS: 46.7811, -2.0169

Open: 7 Apr-12 Sep **Site:** 5HEC **For hire:** **Prices:** 24-33.50 Mobile home hire 230-900 **Facilities:** Wi-fi Kids' Club Play Area **Services:** **Leisure:** P **Off-site:** S

ST-JULIEN-DES-LANDES VENDÉE

Château de la Fôret

85150

☎ 251466211

e-mail: camping@domainelaforet.com

web: www.domainelaforet.com

A picturesque setting in the grounds of a château with well-defined pitches, modern facilities and a lake on site for fishing. 12km from the beach.

dir: *NE on D55, rte de Martinet.*

GPS: 46.6409, -1.7107

Open: 15 May-15 Sep **Site:** 50HEC **For hire:** **Prices:** 14.50-29 Mobile home hire 215-749 **Facilities:** Wi-fi (charged) Kids' Club Play Area **Services:** **Leisure:** P **Off-site:** R

Garangeoire

The Camping and Caravanning Club The Friendly Club

85150

☎ 251466539 251466985

e-mail: info@garangeoire.com

web: www.camping-la-garangeoire.com

Family site set in 200-hectare estate with a variety of recreational facilities. Pitches separated by hedges.

C&CC Report *An extremely popular site, with a well-deserved reputation for quality. La Garangeoire is particularly popular with British families, not least because of the very spacious pitches, friendly English-speaking staff and wide range of services operating virtually all season. Should you ever leave the site during your stay – many families don't! – you'll find the nearest beaches just quarter of an hour's drive away, while inland there are châteaux to visit at nearby Apremont and Avrillé.*

dir: *2km N of village.*

GPS: 46.6636, -1.7134

Open: 7 Apr-24 Sep **Site:** 19HEC **For hire:** **Prices:** 14.50-29.50 **Facilities:** Wi-fi (charged) Kids' Club Play Area **Services:** **Leisure:** P **Off-site:** L

Village de la Guyonnière

La Guyonnière, 85150

☎ 251466259 251466289

e-mail: info@laguyonniere.com

web: www.laguyonniere.com

A pleasant site with pitches divided by hedges with good sanitary and recreational facilities. Kids' club available in July and August.

dir: *7km from town centre towards La Mothe Achard.*

GPS: 46.6529, -1.7500

Open: 23 Apr-5 Sep **Site:** 30HEC **For hire:** **Prices:** 14.90-34.90 Mobile home hire 260-815 **Facilities:** Wi-fi Kids' Club Play Area **Services:** **Leisure:** L P

ST-JUST-LUZAC CHARENTE-MARITIME

Castel Camping Séquoia Parc

La Josephtrie, 17320

☎ 546855555 546855556

e-mail: info@sequoiaparc.com

web: www.sequoiaparc.com

Situated in a spacious park on the La Josephtrie estate, which contains an attractive château, 5km from the coast and beaches. There is a swimming pool complex with waterslides and a large paddling pool. Organised entertainment for children throughout the season and for adults in July and August. Dogs not permitted in rentals.

Open: 12 May-5 Sep **Site:** 45HEC **For hire:** **Prices:** 21-48 Mobile home hire 294-1050 **Facilities:** Wi-fi (charged) Kids' Club Play Area **Services:** **Leisure:** P **Off-site:** S

ST-LAURENT-NOUAN LOIR-ET-CHER

Camping Municipal de l'Amitié

rue du Camping, 41220

☎ 254870152

e-mail: camping@stlaurentnouan.eu

web: www.stlaurentnouan.fr/fr/information/34193/camping-amitie

On the shore of the River Loire between Blois and Orléans, 6km from the château of Chambord.

dir: *On D951.*

GPS: 47.6866, 1.5581

Open: All Year. **Site:** 2HEC **For hire:** **Facilities:** **Services:** **Off-site:** P

ST-LÉONARD-DE-NOBLAT HAUTE-VIENNE

Beaufort

87400

☎ 555560279 555560279

web: www.campingdebeaufort.fr

Set in pleasant wooded surroundings with good facilities.

dir: *Off D39.*

Open: 14 Apr-Sep **Site:** 2HEC **For hire:** **Facilities:** **Services:** **Leisure:** R **Off-site:**

FRANCE

ST-MALÔ-DU-BOIS VENDÉE

La Vallee de Poupet

85590

☎ 251923145 📠 251923865

e-mail: camping@valleedepoupet.com

web: www.valleedepoupet.com

A picturesque location beside the River Sèvre Nantaise, surrounded by woodland.

dir: *D72 from village, 1km left fork & signed.*

Open: 15 May-15 Sep **Site:** 3HEC **For hire:** **Prices:** 12.80-15.50 **Facilities:** Wi-fi Play Area **Services:** **Leisure:** P R **Off-site:**

ST-MARC-SUR-MER LOIRE-ATLANTIQUE

Yukadi Village L'Eve

rte du Fort de L'Eve, 44600

☎ 546223822 📠 240917659

e-mail: leve@yukadivillages.com

web: www.yukadivillages.com

Large, well-kept site divided into pitches and on a gentle slope. Access to sea through a private tunnel and a snack bar on-site. Dogs allowed except in mobile homes.

dir: *On D292.*

Open: 11 May-9 Sep **Site:** 6HEC **For hire:** **Prices:** 14.80-31.20 Mobile home hire 213-836.50 **Facilities:** Wi-fi Kids' Club Play Area **Services:** **Leisure:** P S

ST-PALAIS-SUR-MER CHARENTE-MARITIME

Côte de Beauté

The Camping and Caravanning Club The Friendly Club

157 av de la Grande Côte, 17420

☎ 546232059

e-mail: campingcotedebeaute@wanadoo.fr

web: www.camping-cote-de-beaute.com

Situated facing sea.

C&CC Report *This is a quiet little site in an excellent location just across the road from the Atlantic Ocean. With a fine sandy beach within 500 metres, it is a beach lover's dream and cyclists will enjoy the cycle path along the coast which is adjacent to the site. The friendly owners ensure that the sanitation is immaculately kept, and are always on hand to recommend one of the restaurants within walking distance.*

dir: *N of town on road to La Palmyre (D25).*

Open: May-Sep **Site:** 1HEC **For hire:** **Facilities:** **Off-site:** S

Ormeaux

44 av de Bernezac, 17420

☎ 546390207 📠 546385666

e-mail: campingormeaux@aliceadsl.fr

web: www.camping-ormeaux.com

Well-equipped site in wooded surroundings, 0.5km from the beach.

dir: *1km N.*

Open: Apr-Oct **Site:** 3.5HEC **For hire:** **Facilities:** **Services:** **Leisure:** P **Off-site:** L S

Yukadi Village Le Logis

22 rue des Palombes, 17420

☎ 546223822 📠 546231061

e-mail: reservations@ yukadivillages.com

web: www.yukadivillages.com

Situated on the edge Saint-Augustin forest and 800 metres from the sea. Facilities include a swimming pool with slides. Snacks and take-away meals are available.

dir: *2.5km NW on D25.*

Open: 27 Apr-9 Sep **Site:** 19HEC **For hire:** **Prices:** 15.50-37.50 Mobile home hire 225-917 **Facilities:** Wi-fi Kids' Club Play Area **Services:** **Leisure:** P **Off-site:** S

ST-PARDOUX-CORBIER CORRÈZE

Le Domaine Bleu

Plan d'eau, 19210

☎ 555735989

e-mail: ledomainebleu@orange.fr

web: www.ledomainebleu.eu

A quiet, peaceful campsite on a fishing lake between Limoges and Brive.

dir: *A20 exit 44 towards Lubersac. Follow signs for St-Pardoux-Corbier.*

GPS: 45.4297, 1.4547

Open: Jul-Aug **Site:** 1.5HEC **Prices:** 11.50 **Facilities:** Play Area **Leisure:** L **Off-site:** P R

FRANCE

ST-REVÉRÉND VENDÉE

Pont Rouge

av Georges Clémenceau, 85220
☎ 251546850 🖷 251546167
e-mail: camping.pontrouge@wanadoo.fr
web: www.camping-lepontrouge.com
Quiet site in the Vendée countryside within easy reach of the sea.
dir: *D6 E from St Gilles, turning to St-Revéŕend.*
Open: Apr-Oct **Site:** 1.6HEC **For hire:** **Facilities:** **Services:** **Leisure:** P **Off-site:** L R

ST-SATUR CHER

St-Satur

Quai de la Loire, 18300
☎ 248540467 🖷 386379583
e-mail: aquadis1@orange.fr
web: www.aquadis-loisirs.com
Quiet, shady site alongside the Loire at the foot of vineyard covered hills.
dir: *A71 exit for Sancerre.*
Open: May-Sep **Site:** 1.6HEC **Facilities:** **Services:** **Off-site:** P R

ST-SORNIN CHARENTE-MARITIME

Valerick

The Camping and Caravanning Club The Friendly Club

1 Domaine de La Mauvinière, 17600
☎ 546851595
e-mail: campingvalerick@orange.fr
web: www.camping-le-valerick.fr
Small, peaceful site in quiet surroundings.
C&CC Report *The most relaxing way to enjoy the delightful Charente-Maritime, away from the busy seaside resorts. Begin at St Sornin church for a rewarding start, then cross the sea bridge to the Ile d'Oléron on a weekday, or visit the Saturday market in Saintes. On site, all is picturesque and peaceful, with great warmth of welcome and personal attention from the resident site owners, Monsieur and Madame Vignaud. There is also plenty of wildlife around, such as the storks' nest visible from the site.*
Open: Apr-Sep **Site:** 1.5HEC **For hire:**
Prices: 15.40-19.20 **Facilities:** Play Area
Services: **Off-site:** R

ST-TROJAN-LES-BAINS CHARENTE-MARITIME

Indigo Oléron

11 av des Bris, 17370
☎ 546760239 🖷 546764295
e-mail: oleron@camping-indigo.com
web: www.camping-indigo.com
Recently renovated site nestled in a pine forest with spacious shady pitches. Snacks are available and there is a kids' club in July and August. One dog per pitch allowed.
dir: *From Paris/Nantes A10 exit 33 La Rochelle/Rochefort then follow signs to Surgeres/Rochefort/Ile d'Oleron.*
GPS: 45.8363, -1.2097
Open: 26 Apr-Sep **Site:** 5HEC **For hire:**
Prices: 14.20-21 **Facilities:** Kids' Club Play Area **Services:** **Leisure:** P **Off-site:** S

ST-USTRE VIENNE

Petit Trianon de St-Ustre

1 rue du Moulin, 86220
☎ 549026147 🖷 549026881
e-mail: chateau@petit-trianon.fr
web: www.petit-trianon.fr
Set in a beautiful park surrounding a small 18th-century château, the site has good entertainment and recreational facilities.
dir: *Off N10 at sign N of Ingrandes, site 1km.*
Open: 20 May-20 Sep **Site:** 7HEC **For hire:**
Facilities: **Services:** **Leisure:** P
Off-site:

ST-VINCENT-SUR-JARD VENDÉE

Bolée d'Air

rte du Bouil, 85520
☎ 251903605 🖷 251339404
e-mail: info@chadotel.com
web: www.chadotel.com
A family site on level ground with pitches divided by hedges. Good recreational facilities, including two pools, sauna, tennis and mini-golf, and 0.9km from Bouil beach.
dir: *2km E via D21. 900m from the beach.*
GPS: 46.4184, -1.5279
Open: 7 Apr-22 Sep **Site:** 6HEC **For hire:**
Prices: 15-30 **Facilities:** Wi-fi (charged) Play Area
Services: **Leisure:** P **Off-site:** S

FRANCE

STE-CATHERINE-DE-FIERBOIS INDRE-ET-LOIRE

Parc de Fierbois

37800

☎ 247654335 📠 247655375

e-mail: contact@fierbois.com

web: www.fierbois.com

Beside artificial lake, good bathing area. Kids' club available in July and August.

dir: *Off N10 onto D101, 1.5km SE.*

GPS: 47.1483, 0.6547

Open: 16 Apr-7 Sep **Site:** 40HEC **For hire:** **Prices:** 16-44 Mobile home hire 322-1246 **Facilities:** Wi-fi (charged) Kids' Club Play Area **Services:** **Leisure:** P

see advert below

STE-LUCE-SUR-LOIRE LOIRE-ATLANTIQUE

Belle Rivière

The Camping and Caravanning Club The Friendly Club

rte des Perrières, 44980

☎ 240258581 📠 240258581

e-mail: belleriviere@wanadoo.fr

web: www.belle-riviere.com

Located close to Nantes, on the banks of the Loire river. A peaceful site with landscaped grounds.

C&CC Report *Rural setting, close to the village of Ste Luce-sur-Loire, 8km from Nantes city centre, good for an overnight stay on the way South.*

dir: *Off Nantes eastern ring road.*

GPS: 47.2514, -1.4536

Open: All Year. **Site:** 4HEC **For hire:** **Facilities:** Wi-fi (charged) Play Area **Services:** **Leisure:** R **Off-site:** P

FRANCE

STE-REINE-DE-BRETAGNE LOIRE-ATLANTIQUE

Château du Deffay

BP 18, 44160
☎ 240880057 📠 240016655
e-mail: campingdudeffay@wanadoo.fr
web: www.camping-le-deffay.com
Set in the beautiful Parc de Brière providing fishing, walking and horse riding. Games and TV rooms.
dir: *4.5km W on D33 rte de Pontchâteau.*
GPS: 47.4410, -2.1598
Open: May-Sep **Site:** 13HEC **For hire:** **Prices:** 16.25-35.35 Mobile home hire 152-715 **Facilities:** Wi-fi (charged) Play Area **Services:** **Leisure:** P

SANTROP HAUTE-VIENNE

Camping de Santrop

87640
☎ 555710808 📠 386379583
e-mail: aquadis1@orange.fr
web: www.aquadis-loisirs.com
A well-equipped family site on the shore of Lac de St-Pardoux with good facilities for water sports.
dir: *A20 exit 25.*
Open: May-Oct **Site:** 4.5HEC **For hire:** **Facilities:** Play Area **Services:** **Leisure:** L **Off-site:** P

SAUMUR MAINE-ET-LOIRE

Chantepie

The Camping and Caravanning Club The Friendly Club

49400
☎ 241679534 📠 241679585
e-mail: info@campingchantepie.com
web: www.campingchantepie.com
A pleasant site with a fine view over the River Loire.
C&CC Report *A delightful family site perched in a prime position on the Loire. This high quality site provides a range of activities including wine-tasting, walks, canoeing and a children's club. The rustic charm of the site fits well with the local region where you can discover mushroom caves, châteaux and Saumur's vineyards.*
dir: *D751 towards Gennes.*
GPS: 47.2939, -0.1425
Open: 28 Apr-15 Sep **Site:** 10HEC **For hire:** **Prices:** 20-34 Mobile home hire 300-600 **Facilities:** Wi-fi (charged) Kids' Club Play Area **Services:** **Leisure:** P R S **Off-site:**

Ile d'Offard

bld de Verden, 49400
☎ 241403000 📠 241673781
On an island in the middle of the Loire near municipal stadium, facing the "Château of Saumur". Kids' club in high season.
Open: Mar-mid Nov **Site:** 5.5HEC **For hire:** **Facilities:** Wi-fi (charged) Kids' Club Play Area **Services:** **Leisure:** P R **Off-site:**

SELLE CRAONNAISE, LA MAYENNE

Rincerie

Base de Loisirs la Rincerie, 53800
☎ 243061752 📠 243075020
e-mail: contact@la-rincerie.com
web: www.la-rincerie.com
A modern site close to lake offering relaxation. An extensive selection of sports activities, plus facilities for fishing and wildlife observation. Children have their own activities during July and August. Separate car park for arrivals after 22.00hrs.
dir: *N of La Selle-Craonnaise towards Ballots.*
GPS: 47.8644, -1.0669
Open: Mar-Oct **Site:** 5HEC **For hire:** **Prices:** 6.60-13.50 **Facilities:** Wi-fi Play Area **Services:** **Off-site:**

SENONCHES EURE-ET-LOIRE

Huttopia Senonches

Etang de Badouleau, 28250
☎ 237378140 📠 237377893
e-mail: senonches@huttopia.com
web: www.huttopia.com
Located in the Perche region, this site has pitches within a wooded area. A natural swimming pool is on offer and campers can watch films on a large open-air screen. Guided nature walks at dusk. Kids' club in July and August, 1 dog per pitch.
dir: *N12 onto D928 towards Digny then Senonches, follow Huttopia signs.*
GPS: 48.5531, 1.0386
Open: 6 Apr-7 Nov **Site:** 10HEC **For hire:** **Prices:** 14.50-23.40 **Facilities:** Kids' Club Play Area **Services:** **Leisure:** L P **Off-site:**

FRANCE

SILLÉ-LE-GUILLAUME SARTHE

Camping Indigo Les Molières

Sillé Plage, 72140

☎ 243201612 ▤ 243245684

e-mail: molieres@camping-indigo.com

web: www.camping-indigo.com

Situated in the national forest of Sillé on the banks of a lake. Snacks are available. Kids' club in July and August. 1 dog per pitch.

dir: *A11 exit 7 Sillé-le-Guillaume, follow signs to Sillé then Sillé Plage.*

GPS: 48.2034, -0.1287

Open: 26 Apr-23 Sep **Site:** 8HEC **For hire:** **Prices:** 13-18 Mobile home hire 240.10-595 **Facilities:** Kids' Club Play Area **Services:** **Leisure:** L P **Off-site:**

SILLÉ-LE-PHILIPPE SARTHE

Castel Camping Château de Chanteloup

The Camping and Caravanning Club The Friendly Club

72460

☎ 243275107

e-mail: chanteloup.souffront@wanadoo.fr

web: www.chateau-de-chanteloup.com

Peaceful site set in wooded clearings and meadows within the grounds of a château. Kids' club available from 15 July to 18 August. Two hours of Wi-fi free of charge.

C&CC Report *The spacious grounds around the owning family's château provide pitches in a peaceful and beautiful setting, while there's both a relaxed, sociable atmosphere and lots of space, with woodland walks, fishing, cycle routes and fun outdoor family activities. An idyllic site, with friendly, attentive and caring owners, especially for younger families and those who genuinely want to take it easy. Great too for visiting Le Mans for the free nightime sound and light shows (July and August Tue-Sat only).*

dir: *16km NE of Le Mans on D301.*

GPS: 48.1058, 0.3410

Open: Jun-1 Sep **Site:** 22HEC **Prices:** 27.90-35 **Facilities:** Wi-fi (charged) Kids' Club Play Area **Services:** **Leisure:** P

SONZAY INDRE-ET-LOIRE

Camping l'Arada Parc

rue de la Baratière, 37360

☎ 247247269 ▤ 247247270

e-mail: info@laradaparc.com

web: www.laradaparc.com

Site with leisure facilities that include indoor and outdoor pools, plus spa and fitness room. Programme of events for both children and adults. Kids' club takes place in summer.

dir: *A28 exit 27, towards Neuillé Pont Pierre then Sonzay.*

GPS: 47.5262, 0.4509

Open: 31 Mar-18 Oct **Site:** 1.7HEC **For hire:** **Prices:** 15-24 Mobile home hire 259-714 **Facilities:** Wi-fi (charged) Kids' Club Play Area **Services:** **Leisure:** P

SUÈVRES LOIR-ET-CHER

Château de la Grenouillère

41500

☎ 254878037 ▤ 254878421

e-mail: la.grenouillere@wanadoo.fr

web: www.camping-loire.com

A family site in the Loire region, close to the château of Chambord. A large selection of pitches, all with electricity. Leisure facilities include swimming pools and entertainment is available.

dir: *A10 exit 16 Mer/Chambord, RN152 towards Blois. Site 2km after Mer on right.*

Open: 9 Apr-10 Sep **Site:** 12HEC **For hire:** **Facilities:** Wi-fi (charged) Kids' Club Play Area **Services:** **Leisure:** P

SULLY-SUR-LOIRE LOIRET

Hortus Jardin de Sully

rte de St Benoît - D60, 45600

☎ 238363594 ▤ 238363594

e-mail: info@camping-hortus.com

web: www.camping-hortus.com

On a level meadow beside the River Loire near to Sully and just 700 metres from the historic château.

dir: *W on D60 towards St-Benoît-sur-Loire.*

Open: Apr-20 Nov **Site:** 5HEC **For hire:** **Prices:** 15-20 **Facilities:** Wi-fi Play Area **Services:** **Leisure:** P R **Off-site:** L

TALMONT-ST-HILAIRE VENDÉE

Yelloh Village Le Littoral

Le Porteau, 85440
☎ 251220464 🖷 251220537
e-mail: info@campinglelittoral.com
web: www.campinglelittoral.com
Situated near Port Bourgenay, 80 metres from the sea. Good facilities, and entertainment available during the season. Bar, restaurant, grocery, bakery shop open from April to September.
dir: *In Talmont-St-Hilaire follow signs to aquarium, site close by.*
GPS: 46.4515, -1.7019
Open: 6 Apr-9 Sep **Site:** 8.5HEC **For hire:**
Prices: 17-43 Mobile home hire 273-1435 **Facilities:** Wi-fi (charged) Kids' Club Play Area **Services:** **Leisure:** P **Off-site:** S

TRANCHE-SUR-MER, LA VENDÉE

Baie d'Aunis

10 rue du Pertuis Breton, 85360
☎ 251274736 🖷 251274454
e-mail: info@camping-baiedaunis.com
web: www.camping-baiedaunis.com
On level land by the sea, 50 metres from the beach and 400 metres from the town centre with a variety of leisure activities. Dogs are not accepted in July and August.
dir: *300m E on D46.*
Open: 27 Apr-16 Sep **Site:** 2.4HEC **For hire:**
Prices: 25.70-34.20 Mobile home hire 320-820 **Facilities:** Wi-fi Play Area **Services:** **Leisure:** P S
Off-site:

Bel

The Camping and Caravanning Club The Friendly Club

rue du Bottereau, 85360
☎ 251304739 🖷 251277281
e-mail: campbel@wanadoo.fr
A quiet, family-run site 450 metres from a magnificent beach and a marine lake. Plenty of sports and entertainment facilities.
C&CC Report *Abandon your car at this small family run camp site, within easy walking distance of the popular resort of La Tranche-Sur-Mer. The friendly owners take pride in their facilities, and families with smaller children are particularly welcome. As well as the site pool there is also a water park in the resort with indoor pools and waterslides, but it'll be the great beaches in this area that keep the whole family happy.*
dir: *Follow town centre direction.*
Open: 26 May-4 Sep **Site:** 3.5HEC **Prices:** 30
Facilities: Wi-fi (charged) Play Area
Services: **Leisure:** P S **Off-site:**

Cottage Fleuri

La Grière-Plage, 85360
☎ 251303457 🖷 251277477
A level site with modern facilities.
dir: *2.5km E, 0.5km from beach.*
Open: Apr-Sep **Site:** 7.5HEC **For hire:**
Prices: 21-31 Mobile home hire 180-770 **Facilities:** Wi-fi (charged) Kids' Club Play Area **Services:**
Leisure: P **Off-site:** S

Jard

The Camping and Caravanning Club The Friendly Club

123 bld de Lattre-de-Tassigny, 85360
☎ 251274379 🖷 251274292
e-mail: info@campingdujard.fr
web: www.campingdujard.fr
A family site on level ground with clearly defined pitches, 0.7km from the beach, with plenty of recreational facilities.
C&CC Report *Great for all the family, this site is well placed to enjoy the sandy beaches of the sunny Southern Vendée. A short walk will take you to La Grière beach, one of the local favourites, if you can drag yourself away from the excellent pool complex and activity programme. Camping du Jard is a popular site with British campers and caravanners, many of whom return here year after year.*
dir: *Via D747.*
Open: May-15 Sep **Site:** 6HEC **For hire:**
Facilities: **Services:** **Leisure:**
P **Off-site:**

Village Center les Almadies

La Charrière des Bandes, 85360
☎ 499572121 🖷 467516389
e-mail: contact@village-center.com
web: www.village-center.com/pays-de-la-loire/camping-les-almadies.php
An 11 hectare park, 3km from beach.
dir: *A83 take exit for St Hermine, then onto D949 to Luçon, then D747 to La Tranche-sur-Mer.*
GPS: 46.3725, -1.4153
Open: 30 Mar-Sep **Site:** 11HEC **For hire:**
Prices: 15-27 Mobile home hire 182-799 **Facilities:** Wi-fi (charged) Kids' Club Play Area **Services:**
Leisure: P **Off-site:** S

FRANCE

TROCHE — CORRÈZE

Domaine Vert

Les Magnes, 19230

☎ 555735989

e-mail: ledomainevert@orange.fr

web: www.ledomainevert.nl

Peaceful farm site surrounded by grass and woodland where campers can select their own pitch. Well-kept facilities and the opportunity to try the organic produce from the farm.

dir: *A20 exit 45, to Vigeois, after Vigeois right onto D50 for Lubersac, site 5km.*

GPS: 45.4086, 1.4788

Open: Apr-1 Oct **Site:** 5HEC **For hire:** **Prices:** 18 **Facilities:** Wi-fi **Services:** **Off-site:** L R

TROGUES — INDRE-ET-LOIRE

Château de la Rolandière

37220

☎ 247585371

e-mail: contact@larolandiere.com

web: www.larolandiere.com

Situated in parkland surrounding a fine château. A good base for visiting the châteaux of the Loire.

dir: *A10 exit 25, road for Chinon for 6km.*

GPS: 47.1071, 0.5102

Open: 21 Apr-15 Sep **Site:** 4HEC **For hire:** **Prices:** 16.50-20.50 Mobile home hire 310-680 **Facilities:** Wi-fi (charged) Play Area **Services:** **Leisure:** P **Off-site:** R

Village Center le Parc des Allais

Les Allais, 37220

☎ 499572121 467516389

e-mail: contact@village-center.com

web: www.village-center.com/centre/camping-parc-des-allais.php

A natural environment site at the heart of the Loire châteaux. On the banks of the Vienne river and beside a fine lake.

dir: *A10 autoroute from Tours exit 25 Ste Maure de Touraine.*

GPS: 47.0974, 0.5020

Open: 8 Apr-2 Oct **Site:** 16HEC **For hire:** **Facilities:** Wi-fi Kids' Club Play Area **Services:** **Leisure:** P

TURBALLE, LA — LOIRE-ATLANTIQUE

Parc Ste-Brigitte

Chemin des Routes, 44420

☎ 240248891 240156572

e-mail: saintebrigitte@wanadoo.fr

web: www.campingsaintebrigitte.com

Parkland site in the grounds of a château, divided into pitches and surrounded by hedges.

dir: *E of village on D99 Guérande road.*

Open: Apr-Sep **Site:** 6HEC **For hire:** **Prices:** 20.06-23.60 Mobile home hire 380-695 **Facilities:** Wi-fi Play Area **Services:** **Leisure:** P **Off-site:** S

VARENNES-SUR-LOIRE — MAINE-ET-LOIRE

Domaine de la Brèche

L'Étang de la Brèche, 5 Impasse de la Brèche, 49730

☎ 241512292 241512724

e-mail: etang.breche@wanadoo.fr

web: www.etang-breche.com

Located close to Saumur, famous for its château, wine and architecture, this spacious site is ideal for couples and families. Extensive leisure facilities include heated swimming pools with slides, tennis courts, mini-golf and pony rides. Kids' club available in July and August.

dir: *A85 exit 3 Saumur then onto D952 towards Tours or A85 exit 4 Bourgueil then onto D952 towards Saumur.*

Open: 28 Apr-14 Sep **Site:** 25HEC **For hire:** **Prices:** 15-38 Mobile home hire 260-1168 **Facilities:** Wi-fi Kids' Club Play Area **Services:** **Leisure:** P **Off-site:** L

VAUX-SUR-MER — CHARENTE-MARITIME

Le Nauzan Plage

39 av de Nauzan Plage, 17640

☎ 546382913 546381843

e-mail: camping.le.nauzan@wanadoo.fr

web: www.campinglenauzanplage.com

450 metres from the beach with a wide range of leisure facilities including tennis and activities for children. In the evening, discos and casino nights take place.

GPS: 45.6427, -1.0723

Open: Apr-Sep **Site:** 5HEC **For hire:** **Prices:** 17-32 Mobile home hire 150-980 **Facilities:** Wi-fi (charged) Kids' Club Play Area **Services:** **Leisure:** P **Off-site:** L S

FRANCE

VELLES — INDRE

Grands Pins

Les Maisons Neuves, 36330
254366193
e-mail: contact@les-grands-pins.fr
web: www.les-grands-pins.fr

The site has individual pitches and has easy access to the countryside. Swimming pool only available July and August.

dir: *7km S of Châteauroux on D920 direction Les Maisons Neuves; between exits 14 & 15 of A20.*

Open: 10 Mar-15 Dec **Site:** 5HEC **Facilities:** Wi-fi **Services:** **Leisure:** P

VENDÔME — LOIR-ET-CHER

Au Coeur de Vendôme

rue G-Martel, 41100
254770027
web: www.aucoeurdevendome.com

Site lies on a meadow, next to a sports ground.

dir: *E of town on right bank of Loire.*

Open: 21 May-7 Sep **Site:** 3HEC **For hire:** **Facilities:** **Services:** **Leisure:** P R **Off-site:**

VILLIERS-LE-MORHIER — EURE-ET-LOIR

Ilots de St Val

28130
237827130 237827767
e-mail: lesilots@campinglesilotsdestval.com
web: www.campinglesilotsdestval.com

A peaceful rural setting between Maintenon and Nogent-le-Roi, nestling above the Eure river. A haven for wildlife.

dir: *On D983.*

Open: 15 Jan-15 Dec **Site:** 10HEC **For hire:** **Prices:** 16.20 Mobile home hire 260-380 **Facilities:** Play Area **Services:** **Off-site:** R

BRITTANY/NORMANDY

ALENÇON — ORNE

CM de Guéramé

65 rue de Guéramé, 61000
233263495 233263495
e-mail: campingguerame@ville-alencon.fr

Set in open country near a stream, 0.5km from town centre.

dir: *Via boulevard Périphérique in SW part of town.*

Open: Apr-Sep **Site:** 1.5HEC **Prices:** 10.50 **Facilities:** Wi-fi Play Area **Services:** **Leisure:** R **Off-site:** P

ALLINEUC — CÔTES-D'ARMOR

Lac de Bosméléac

Bosméléac, 22460
296288788 296288097
e-mail: bosmeleac@orange.fr
web: bosmeleac.monsite-orange.fr

Wooded site beside a lake with a beach.

dir: *RN12 Brest-Paris exit Loudéac.*

Open: 15 Jun-Sep **Site:** 1.15HEC **For hire:** **Prices:** 8-10.50 **Facilities:** Play Area **Services:** **Leisure:** L **Off-site:** P R

ARRADON — MORBIHAN

Penboch

9 chemin de Penboch, 56610
297447129 297447910
e-mail: camping.penboch@wanadoo.fr
web: www.camping-penboch.fr

An well-appointed site in a pleasant wooded location 200 metres from the beaches of the Gulf of Morbihan. The swimming pool has a large chute with 4 waterslides, plus an indoor pool and jacuzzi.

dir: *Signed from N165.*

Open: 6 Apr-29 Sep **Site:** 4HEC **For hire:** **Prices:** 15.90-47.90 **Facilities:** Wi-fi Play Area **Services:** **Leisure:** P S

FRANCE

ARZANO — FINISTÈRE

Camping le Ty Nadan

The Camping and Caravanning Club — The Friendly Club

Rte d'Arzano, 29310

☎ 298717547 🖹 298717731

e-mail: info@tynadan-vacances.fr

web: www.tynadan-vacances.fr

Located on the banks of the River Ellé and not far from the Devils Rock's, the site has extensive leisure facilities including indoor and outdoor pools with slides, and many other activities.

C&CC Report *An idyllic natural woodland river valley setting provides the backdrop to an activity lover's paradise for all ages, all season through, with a phenomenal range of activities. Though you won't need to go off-site, this area is very pretty indeed, so if you need a rest from all the on-site activities, Brittany's lovely beaches are close. Great for half-term and Easter breaks.*

dir: *N165 exit Quimperlé. D22 from Quimperlé to Arzano, site after 3km.*

GPS: 47.9047, -3.4750

Open: 31 Mar-2 Sep **Site:** **For hire:** **Prices:** 20.10-46 Mobile home hire 282-833 **Facilities:** Wi-fi (charged) Kids' Club Play Area **Services:** **Leisure:** P R

AUDIERNE — FINISTÈRE

Loquéran

BP 55, 29770

☎ 298749506 🖹 298749114

e-mail: campgite.loqueran@free.fr

web: campgite.loqueran.free.fr

A terraced woodland site in calm and peaceful surroundings, a short distance from the sea.

GPS: 48.0249, -4.5280

Open: May-Sep **Site:** 1HEC **Facilities:** Wi-fi **Services:** **Off-site:** S

BADEN — MORBIHAN

Mané Guernehué

The Camping and Caravanning Club — The Friendly Club

rue Mané er Groez, 56870

☎ 297570206 🖹 297571543

e-mail: info@camping-baden.com

web: www.camping-baden.com

A pleasant location at the head of the Gulf of Morbihan with good recreational facilities including a large pool complex with indoor and outdoor pools and waterslides, plus an equestrian centre.

C&CC Report *With one of the best camp site pool complexes in France, Mané-Guernehué is more than just a campsite, it's an activities paradise. Busy and lively, the many on-site activities include pony rides for tiny tots through to adults, archery, a treetop adventure park and a spa facility worthy of a top-class hotel. The pretty rural location is also perfect for visiting the Morbihan Gulf islands, the resorts of Carnac and La Trinité, as well as nearby Le Bono and Auray.*

dir: *1km SW via Mériadec road.*

GPS: 47.6139, -2.9252

Open: Apr-Oct **Site:** 10HEC **For hire:** **Prices:** 15-39 Mobile home hire 238-1300 **Facilities:** Wi-fi (charged) Kids' Club Play Area **Services:** **Leisure:** P **Off-site:** S

BARNEVILLE-CARTERET — MANCHE

Yelloh Village Les Vikings

St-Jean-de-la-Rivière, 50270

☎ 233538413

web: www.camping-lesvikings.com

A family site with level terrain, 400 metres from the sea and a fine sandy beach.

dir: *SE of Barneville-Carteret off D904.*

Open: 15 Mar-15 Nov **Site:** 6HEC **For hire:** **Facilities:** **Services:** **Leisure:** P

BAYEUX — CALVADOS

Camping des Bords de l'Aure

allée de Abattoirs, 14400

☎ 231920843 🖹 231920843

e-mail: campingmunicipal@mairiebayeux.fr

web: www.mairie-bayeux.fr

Very clean and tidy site with tarmac drive and hardstanding for caravans. Adjoins football field.

dir: *N side of town on Boulevard Circulaire.*

GPS: 49.2840, -0.6977

Open: Apr-Oct **Site:** 2.9HEC **For hire:** **Prices:** 12.60 Mobile home hire 450-700 **Facilities:** **Services:** **Off-site:** P R S

FRANCE

BEG-MEIL FINISTÈRE

Kervastard

chemin de Kervastard, 29170

298949152 298949983

e-mail: camping.le.kervastard@wanadoo.fr

web: www.campinglekervastard.com

A pleasant wooded site 250 metres from a fine sandy beach with plenty of leisure facilities, close to the village centre.

dir: *W of D45 leave this road just N of village.*

Open: May-Sep **Site:** 2HEC **For hire:**
Prices: 15.50-23.50 Mobile home hire 280-585 **Facilities:** Play Area **Services:** **Leisure:** P
Off-site: R S

Roche Percée

29170

298949415 298944805

e-mail: contact@camping-larochepercee.com

web: www.camping-larochepercee.com

Wooded family site 400 metres from the Roche Percée beach. The site has good facilities and a number of activities.

dir: *1km from Beg Meil towards Fouesnant.*

GPS: 47.8694, -3.9918

Open: 31 Mar-29 Sep **Site:** 2.35HEC **For hire:**
Facilities: Wi-fi (charged) Kids' Club Play Area
Services: **Leisure:** P **Off-site:** S

BÉNODET FINISTÈRE

L'Escale St-Gilles

Corniche de la Mer, 29950

298570537 298572752

e-mail: sunelia@stgilles.fr

web: www.stgilles.fr

Holiday site south of village, on fields by beach. Divided into sectors with individual pitches. Well-equipped sanitary blocks and a range of facilities, including a covered pool complex and spa.

dir: *D34 Quimper-Bénodet, signed in town. From N165 take exit for Concarneau, turn right following signs for Bénodet, site signed.*

GPS: 47.8604, -4.0901

Open: 6 Apr-23 Sep **Site:** 10HEC **For hire:**
Prices: 20-42 Mobile home hire 385-1225 **Facilities:**
Wi-fi (charged) Kids' Club Play Area **Services:**
Leisure: P S **Off-site:**

Letty

29950

298570469 298662256

e-mail: reception@campingduletty.com

web: www.campingduletty.com

Site bordering beach, divided into small paddocks. Good sanitary installations, ironing rooms and games room. Good beach for children. Use of car park compulsory after 23.00hrs.

C&CC Report *The best site in the popular resort of Bénodet has been further enhanced with a superb new indoor and outdoor pool complex. Extremely well-run, with no statics, this is a site where visitors always enjoy a warm welcome and a high quality range of facilities that suits campers and caravanners of all ages. A great site from which to experience Brittany, with many returning regularly.*

dir: *1km SE beside sea.*

GPS: 47.8672, -4.0908

Open: 12 Jun-6 Sep **Site:** 10HEC **For hire:**
Prices: 19-33.20 **Facilities:** Wi-fi Kids' Club
Play Area **Services:** **Leisure:** P S
Off-site:

BÉNOUVILLE CALVADOS

Hautes Coutures

av de la Côte de Nacre, 14970

231447308 231953080

e-mail: info@campinghautescoutures.com

web: www.campinghautescoutures.com

Pleasant site with good facilities near the Canal Maritime and within easy reach of the Caen-Portsmouth ferry. Restaurant and kids' club available in July and August.

C&CC Report *Primarily used as an overnight stop site, due to its proximity to the ferry port of Ouistreham, Les Hautes Coutures is well placed to visit the historic D-Day beaches. Pegasus Bridge, its superb museum and the Café Gondrée are a short stroll away, while Caen's Peace Memorial museum, the D-Day beaches and Bayeux, with its famous Norman tapestry, are all an easy drive away. The swimming pool complex will be popular with the children after being taken to see the historic sites of the region.*

dir: *From Caen towards Ouistreham on dual carriageway, exit Zone Activités Benouville, site after Pegasus Bridge exit.*

Open: Apr-Oct **Site:** 7HEC **For hire:**
Prices: 23-28.80 Mobile home hire 290-883 **Facilities:**
Wi-fi Kids' Club Play Area **Services:**
Leisure: P R **Off-site:** S

BINIC — CÔTES-D'ARMOR

Palmiers

Kerviarc'h, 22520

☎ 296737259 296737259

e-mail: campingpalmiers.chantal@laposte.net

web: www.campingpalmiers.com

A well-equipped site within the Parc Tropical de Bretagne, just over 1km from the town centre.

dir: *Via N12/D786.*

Open: Jun-Sep **Site:** 2HEC **For hire:** **Facilities:** **Services:** **Leisure:** P **Off-site:** R S

BLANGY-LE-CHÂTEAU — CALVADOS

Brévedent

The Camping and Caravanning Club – The Friendly Club

rte du Pin, Le Brévedent, 14130

☎ 231647288 231643341

e-mail: contact@campinglebrevedent.com

web: www.campinglebrevedent.com

Situated in the grounds of an 18th-century manor house with good facilities.

C&CC Report *Perfect for young families and couples, this top quality site offers an idyllic rural château setting, a splendid restaurant and charming site owners. The friendly little café by the château and the family bathrooms are welcome enhancements to the relaxed, family atmosphere. Visits to a local cider farm are organised by the site, or you may want to visit the cathedral city of Lisieux.*

dir: *3km SE on D510 (Lisieux to Pont-L'Eveque) beside lake.*

GPS: 49.2403, 0.2813

Open: May-Sep **Site:** 6HEC **For hire:** **Prices:** 22-32 Mobile home hire 250-630 **Facilities:** Wi-fi Kids' Club Play Area **Services:** **Leisure:** P

Domaine du Lac

rte du Mesnil, 14130

☎ 231652921 231650346

e-mail: info@domaine-du-lac.fr

web: www.domaine-du-lac.fr

In natural parkland close to lake and river, the site has good facilities and is close to the village.

Open: Apr-Oct **Site:** 7HEC **Prices:** 18.50 **Facilities:** Wi-fi Kids' Club Play Area **Services:** **Leisure:** L R **Off-site:**

BLANGY-SUR-BRESLE — SEINE-MARITIME

CM

rue des Étangs, 76340

☎ 235945565 235945565

In the middle of the local leisure park comprising 80 hectares of woodland, lakes and streams.

dir: *300m on N28.*

Open: Apr-Sep **Site:** 8HEC **Facilities:** **Services:** **Off-site:** R

BOURG-ACHARD — EURE

Clos Normand

235 rte de Pont-Audemer, 27310

☎ 232563484

web: www.leclosnormand.eu

A peaceful location within an apple orchard. Situated on the plateau of the Roumois, an ideal corner for those wanting to escape city life.

dir: *A13 exit Bourg-Achard, site 1km.*

Open: Apr-Sep **Site:** 1.5HEC **For hire:** **Facilities:** Play Area **Services:** **Leisure:** P **Off-site:**

CAHAGNOLLES — CALVADOS

Camping l'Escapade

rue de l'église, 14490

☎ 231216359 231920648

e-mail: escapadecamping@orange.fr

web: www.campinglescapade.net

Quiet site with wide pitches. Three ponds with fishing available. Only dogs below 10kg are accepted.

Open: Apr-Oct **Site:** 7HEC **For hire:** **Facilities:** Wi-fi (charged) Play Area **Services:** **Leisure:** P

CALLAC — CÔTES-D'ARMOR

CM Verte Vallée

BP58 Mairie de Callac, 22160

☎ 296455850

Between town and countryside, a few minutes' walk from the centre of Callac this quiet site borders a pretty lake. There are facilities for tennis or mini-golf.

dir: *W on D28 towards Morlaix.*

Open: 15 Jun-15 Sep **Site:** 1HEC **Prices:** 8.50-15 **Facilities:** **Off-site:**

FRANCE

Site 6HEC (site size) grass sand stone little shade partly shaded mainly shaded motorvans accepted bungalows for hire mobile homes for hire tents for hire no dogs site fully accessible for wheelchairs
Prices amount quoted is per night, for 2 adults and car, plus tent or caravan Mobile home hire is a weekly rate.

CAMARET-SUR-MER FINISTÈRE

Armorique

29570

298277733 298273838

e-mail: contact@campingarmorique.com

web: www.campingarmorique.com

Situated beside the sea on the edge of the Armorique regional park with a variety of recreational facilities.

dir: *3km NE on D355 rte de Roscanvel.*

Open: 29 Mar-Sep **Site:** 2.5HEC **For hire:** **Facilities:** **Services:** **Leisure:** P **Off-site:** S

Grand Large

Lambezen, 29570

298279141 298279372

e-mail: contact@campinglegrandlarge.com

web: www.campinglegrandlarge.com

Situated at the tip of the Armorique regional park, facing the sea.

dir: *Entering Camaret, at rdbt right onto D355, 2km turn right.*

Open: Apr-Sep **Site:** 2.8HEC **For hire:** **Facilities:** **Services:** **Leisure:** P **Off-site:** S

Plage de Trez Rouz

29570

298279396

e-mail: contact@trezrouz.com

web: www.trezrouz.com

On level ground 50 metres from the beach.

dir: *3km from Camaret-sur-Mer on D355 towards Pointe-des-Espagnols.*

Open: 15 Mar-15 Oct **Site:** 3.1HEC **For hire:** **Prices:** 12.70-16.50 Mobile home hire 230-690 **Facilities:** Wi-fi Play Area **Services:** **Leisure:** S

CANCALE ILLE-ET-VILAINE

Notre Dame du Verger

35260

299897284 299896011

web: www.camping-verger.com

Terraced site overlooking the sea with direct access to the beach.

dir: *2km from Pointe-du-Grouin on D201.*

Open: 29 Mar-28 Sep **Site:** 2.2HEC **Facilities:** **Services:** **Off-site:** S

CARANTEC FINISTÈRE

Mouettes

The Camping and Caravanning Club — The Friendly Club

50 rte de la Grande Grève, 29660

298670246 298783146

e-mail: camping@les-mouettes.com

web: www.les-mouettes.com

Level site divided by low shrubs and trees with extensive leisure facilities and activities for children. The swimming pool with slides is heated from 15 May.

C&CC Report *This very high quality, family-run, family-oriented and very busy site, is renowned for its range and quality of services, many being open all season. The superb water park, with an adults-only session at the start of each morning, comprises 1,000m2 of water, 180m of slides, sunbathing terraces and artificial river, with a bar terrace, shop and take-away adjacent. An entertainments room and second bar, a crêperie, plus a large stage and square add to the picture, while on-site sports facilities are good and there are watersports in Carantec. Close by, St Pol-de-Léon, Morlaix, the 'Pink Granite' coast and the inland moors are recommended visits.*

dir: *1.5km SW on rte de St-Pol-de-Léon towards sea.*

Open: 6 Apr-9 Sep **Site:** 14HEC **For hire:** **Prices:** 17-46 Mobile home hire 273-1519 **Facilities:** Wi-fi Kids' Club Play Area **Services:** **Leisure:** P **Off-site:** R S

CARENTAN MANCHE

CM le Haut Dick

30 chemin du Grand-Bas Pays, 50500

233421689

e-mail: lehautdick@aol.com

web: www.camping-municipal.com

A level site in wooded surroundings with well-defined pitches.

dir: *Village road off N13 towards Le Port.*

Open: 15 Jan-1 Nov **Site:** 2.5HEC **For hire:** **Facilities:** **Services:** **Off-site:** P R

CARNAC MORBIHAN

Bruyères

Kerogile, 56340

297523057 971704647

e-mail: contact@camping-lesbruyeres.com

web: www.camping-lesbruyeres.com

Partly wooded site with modern facilities close to the local beaches. Leisure facilities include a covered swimming pool.

dir: *N of Carnac on C4, 2km from Plouharnel.*

Open: Apr-Sep **Site:** 4.5HEC **For hire:** **Prices:** 14.70-18.40 Mobile home hire 246-670 **Facilities:** Wi-fi Kids' Club Play Area **Services:** **Leisure:** P S

FRANCE

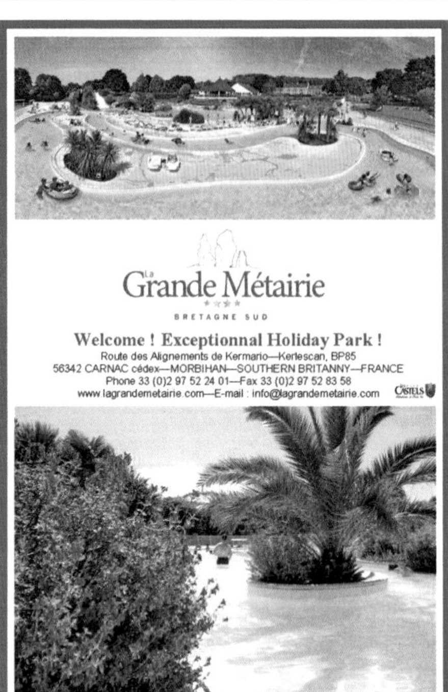

Druides

55 chemin de Beaumer, 56340

297520818 297529613

e-mail: contact@camping-les-druides.com

web: www.camping-les-druides.com

Family site with well-defined pitches, 400 metres from a fine sandy beach.

dir: *SE of town centre. Approach via D781 or D119.*

Open: May-13 Sep **Site:** 2.5HEC **For hire:** **Facilities:** **Services:** **Leisure:** P **Off-site:** S

Étang

67 rte de Kerlann, 56340

297521406

web: www.camping-etang.fr

A rural setting with pitches divided by hedges, 2.5km from the coast.

dir: *2km N at Kerlann on D119.*

Open: Apr-15 Oct **Site:** 2.5HEC **For hire:** **Prices:** 11.30-18.70 Mobile home hire 220-540 **Facilities:** Wi-fi (charged) Play Area **Services:** **Leisure:** P

Grande Métairie

rte des Alignements de Kermario, 56342

297522401 297528358

e-mail: info@lagrandemetairie.com

web: www.lagrandemetairie.com

Holiday site with modern amenities, completely divided into pitches. Kids' club available 19 May-8 Sep.

dir: *2.5km NE on D196.*

GPS: 47.5966, -3.0602

Open: 31 Mar-8 Sep **Site:** 15HEC **For hire:** **Prices:** 16-42 Mobile home hire 245-1160 **Facilities:** Wi-fi (charged) Kids' Club Play Area **Services:** **Leisure:** P S **Off-site:** L

see advert on this page

Men Dû

22 bis chemin de Beaumer, 56340

297520423

e-mail: mendu@wanadoo.fr

web: www.camping-mendu.com

Peaceful site in a wooded setting close to the beach.

dir: *1km from Carnac Plage via D781 & D186.*

GPS: 47.5789, -3.0535

Open: Apr-Oct **Site:** 1.5HEC **For hire:** **Prices:** 15-23 Mobile home hire 240-620 **Facilities:** Wi-fi (charged) **Services:** **Off-site:** R S

Menhirs

The Camping and Caravanning Club — The Friendly Club

allée St-Michel, 56343

297529467 297522538

e-mail: contact@lesmenhirs.com

web: www.lesmenhirs.com

A family site near the beach and shops with good recreational facilities and modern sanitary blocks, including toilets suitable for the disabled.

C&CC Report *Enjoying a superb location, just a short walk from the beach and shops, this bustling site has lots to do for active families – so forget about the car. Enjoy the pools, the waterslides, the bars and activity room complex. Carnac-Plage is a popular little resort, while the famous prehistoric standing stones, Quiberon peninsula and pretty Breton towns of Auray and Vannes should not be missed.*

Open: 14 Apr-22 Sep **Site:** 6HEC **For hire:** **Prices:** 24.15-47.20 Mobile home hire 290-980 **Facilities:** Wi-fi (charged) Kids' Club Play Area **Services:** **Leisure:** P **Off-site:** R S

see advert on opposite page

FRANCE

Site 6HEC (site size) grass sand stone little shade partly shaded mainly shaded motorvans accepted bungalows for hire mobile homes for hire tents for hire no dogs site fully accessible for wheelchairs
Prices amount quoted is per night, for 2 adults and car, plus tent or caravan Mobile home hire is a weekly rate.

Moulin de Kermaux

rte de Kerlescan, 56340
297521590 297528385
e-mail: moulin-de-kermaux@wanadoo.fr
web: www.camping-moulinkermaux.com

A quiet location surrounded by trees and bushes, with good facilities. Within easy reach of the coast and the local megaliths.

dir: *2.5km NE.*

Open: 7 Apr-15 Sep **Site:** 3HEC **For hire:** **Prices:** 20.40-32.40 Mobile home hire 240-880 **Facilities:** Wi-fi (charged) Kids' Club Play Area **Services:** **Leisure:** P **Off-site:** R S

Moustoir

The Camping and Caravanning Club The Friendly Club

71 rte du Moustoir, 56340
297521618 297528837
e-mail: info@lemoustoir.com
web: www.lemoustoir.com

Well-equipped site in a rural setting close to the sea. Kids' club in July and August.

C&CC Report *This site is in a great location, just a short drive away from Carnac resort, and enjoying a lovely countryside setting. The area is fascinating and remains popular with many campers who return each year to enjoy it out of the busy high season. A particularly good site, with much to see and do in the surrounding area. Carnac, La Trinité, Quiberon and the rugged Côte Sauvage peninsula are all close by, with Carnac's world-famous standing stone alignments literally just down the road.*

dir: *3km NE of Carnac.*

GPS: 47.6087, -3.0674

Open: Apr-Sep **Site:** 5HEC **For hire:** **Prices:** 15.40-29.40 Mobile home hire 240-780 **Facilities:** Wi-fi Kids' Club Play Area **Services:** **Leisure:** P **Off-site:** S

Ombrages

56430
297521652

Wooded location with shaded pitches divided by hedges.

dir: *Rte Carnac to Auray, left at fuel station.*

Open: 10 Jun-20 Sep **Site:** 1HEC **For hire:** **Prices:** 15.60 Mobile home hire 220-500 **Facilities:** Play Area **Services:** **Off-site:** L S

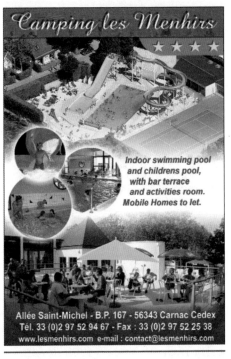

CAUREL CÔTES-D'ARMOR

Nautic International

The Camping and Caravanning Club The Friendly Club

rte de Beau Rivage, 22530
296285794 296260200
e-mail: contact@campingnautic.fr
web: www.campingnautic.fr

A terraced site in woodland on the edge of Lake Guerlédan with a variety of recreational facilities.

C&CC Report *A rare combination of relaxation, location and water activities is what makes this rustic site special. A short stroll to the pleasure cruisers, bars and eateries of the lakeside leaves the site an oasis of calm amid nearly 100 different species of tree and shrub. There are extensive cycle tracks in the area around the lake, and the children love the unique underwater arched windows of the site swimming pool. In the centre of Brittany, this is also a good base for day trips to almost anywhere in the region.*

dir: *N164 towards Beau Rivage.*

GPS: 48.2089, -3.0508

Open: 15 May-25 Sep **Site:** 3.6HEC **For hire:** **Prices:** 15.20-22.80 Mobile home hire 280-610 **Facilities:** **Services:** **Leisure:** L P **Off-site:**

FRANCE

CHAPELLE-AUX-FILZMÉENS, LA ILLE-ET-VILAINE

Domaine du Logis

35190

299452545 299453040

e-mail: domainedulogis@wanadoo.fr

web: www.domainedulogis.com

A quiet, pleasant site in the wooded grounds of an 18th-century château. Restaurant and kids' club available in July and August.

dir: *NE of town towards Combourg.*

GPS: 48.3811, -1.8327

Open: Apr-1 Nov **Site:** 6HEC **For hire:** **Prices:** 19.60-30.60 Mobile home hire 300-680 **Facilities:** Wi-fi Kids' Club **Services:** **Leisure:** P **Off-site:** R

CHÂTEAULIN FINISTÈRE

La Pointe

rte St-Coulitz, 29150

298865153

e-mail: lapointecamping@aol.com

web: www.lapointesuperbecamping.com

Set in a wooded valley close to the town, with modern facilities. Pitches divided by hedges.

dir: *D770 S from Châteaulin centre for Quimper, 1km left to St-Coulitz, site 100m on right.*

Open: 11 Mar-15 Oct **Site:** 2.5HEC **Facilities:** Wi-fi Play Area **Services:** **Leisure:** R **Off-site:** P

CHERRUEIX ILLE-ET-VILAINE

Camping le Tenzor de la Baie

10 bis rue Théophile Blin, 35120

299489813

e-mail: tenzor-de-la-baie@wanadoo.fr

web: www.tenzor-de-la-baie.com

Pretty, peaceful family site close to village amenities and 500 metres from Mont-St-Michel bay. Leisure activities include a heated swimming pool, mini-golf and horse-drawn carriage rides in season or by arrangement. Yurts can be hired.

Open: Apr-Sep **Site:** 2HEC **For hire:** **Prices:** 10.80-15.50 Mobile home hire 270-550 **Facilities:** Wi-fi (charged) Play Area **Services:** **Leisure:** P **Off-site:**

CLOÎTRE-ST-THEGONNEC, LE FINISTÈRE

Bruyères

29410

298797176

web: www.camping-bruyeres.com

A small, secluded site in a picturesque setting within the Amorique regional park, 30km from Roscoff.

dir: *12km S of Morlaix via D769.*

Open: Jul-Aug **Site:** 2.5HEC **Prices:** 16 **Facilities:** Play Area **Services:** **Off-site:**

COMBOURG ILLE-ET-VILAINE

Bois Coudrais

Cuguen, 35270

299732745

e-mail: info@vacancebretagne.com

web: www.vacancebretagne.com

A small family-run site with heated pool. Ideally located for exploring sites including Mont-St-Michel, St Malo, Rennes and Dinan.

dir: *Off D83.*

GPS: 48.4540, -1.6513

Open: May-Sep **Site:** 2.2HEC **For hire:** **Prices:** 10-20 **Facilities:** Wi-fi Play Area **Services:** **Leisure:** P **Off-site:**

CONCARNEAU FINISTÈRE

Camping les Sables Blancs

av du Dorlett, 29900

298971644 298971644

e-mail: contact@camping-lessablesblancs.com

web: www.camping-lessablesblancs.com

150 metres from the beach and a 15 minute walk to the town, the swimming pool overlooks the sea. Entertainment includes concerts and karaoke.

Open: 2 Apr-Oct **Site:** 3HEC **For hire:** **Facilities:** Wi-fi Kids' Club Play Area **Services:** **Leisure:** P S **Off-site:**

Les Prés Verts

Kernous Plage, BP612, 29900

298970974

e-mail: info@presverts.com

web: www.presverts.com

A landscaped site with good facilities overlooking Concarneau Bay.

dir: *1.2km NW.*

Open: May-Sep **Site:** 3HEC **For hire:** **Facilities:** Wi-fi (charged) **Services:** **Leisure:** P S **Off-site:**

Site 6HEC (site size) 👐 grass ⚓ sand 👐 stone ♨ little shade ♨ partly shaded 👐 mainly shaded 🚋 motorvans accepted
🚌 bungalows for hire 🚋 mobile homes for hire 🅰 tents for hire ⊗ no dogs ♿ site fully accessible for wheelchairs
Prices amount quoted is per night, for 2 adults and car, plus tent or caravan Mobile home hire is a weekly rate.

FRANCE

COURTILS MANCHE

Saint Michel

50220
☎ 233709690
e-mail: info@campingsaintmichel.com
web: www.campingsaintmichel.com

The Camping and Caravanning Club — The Friendly Club

Well kept site located in a peaceful, rural setting, 10km from Mont-St-Michel. Pitches are shaded by many trees and shrubs. On site is a small enclosure of farm animals kept to entertain visitors.

C&CC Report *A beautifully kept, very friendly site, both great for holidays and very convenient for all routes across northern France. The attractive bar, reception and shop all run together to create a welcoming feel as soon as you arrive. There are lots of quiet lanes for cycling and the staff are a mine of information. Though superbly located for visiting the Bay of Mont-St-Michel, including its shellfish centres, guided walks across the bay, and hugely improved visitor access to the mount for 2012, just a bit further afield are the medieval castle at Fougères, the picturesque copper-working centre of Villedieu-les-Poêles, and scenic coastal paths.*

dir: *From Caen A84, exit 34 in direction Mont-St-Michel through Courtils village. From Rennes take exit 33.*

Open: 5 Feb-13 Nov **Site:** 5.2HEC **For hire:** **Prices:** 21-25 Mobile home hire 511-770 **Facilities:** Wi-fi Kids' Club Play Area **Services:** **Leisure:** P **Off-site:** S

COUTERNE ORNE

Clos Normand

rte de Bagnoles-de l'Orne, 61410
☎ 233379243
e-mail: france.doffemont@voila.fr
web: www.camping-clos-normand.fr

A pleasant site in rural surroundings in a sheltered position close to the thermal spa of Bagnoles-de-l'Orne.

dir: *Approach D916.*

Open: Mar-Oct **Site:** 1.3HEC **For hire:** **Prices:** 9.80 Mobile home hire 285-415 **Facilities:** Wi-fi (charged) Play Area **Services:** **Off-site:** L P R

CRACH MORBIHAN

Fort Espagnol

rte de Fort Espagnol, 56950
☎ 297551488 Fax 297300104
e-mail: fort-espagnol@wanadoo.fr
web: www.fort-espagnol.com

A family site in a secluded, wooded location, with a variety of recreational facilities.

Open: Jun-10 Sep **Site:** 4.5HEC **For hire:** **Facilities:** **Services:** **Leisure:** P **Off-site:** R S

CRIEL-SUR-MER SEINE-MARITIME

Mouettes

rue de la Plage, 76910
☎ 235867073
e-mail: contact@camping-lesmouettes.fr
web: www.camping-lesmouettes.fr

Small grassy site overlooking the sea.

Open: Apr-2 Nov **Site:** 2HEC **For hire:** **Facilities:** **Services:** **Off-site:** R S

Parc Val d'Albion

1 rue de la Mer, Mesnil-Val-Plage, 76910
☎ 235862142 Fax 235867851

Terraced site in wooded parkland next to the sea.

dir: *3km S from Le Tréport on D126.*

GPS: 50.0433, 1.3311

Open: May-15 Sep **Site:** 3HEC **Prices:** 16.80 **Facilities:** **Services:** **Off-site:** S

CROZON FINISTÈRE

Pen ar Menez

bld de Pralognan, 29160
☎ 298271236
e-mail: pen.ar.menez@orange.fr
web: www.camping-pen-ar-menez.fr

On fringe of a pine wood. Water sports 5km away. 500 metres from the centre of Crozon.

Open: All Year. **Site:** 2.6HEC **For hire:** **Prices:** 13-14.40 **Facilities:** Wi-fi Play Area **Services:** **Off-site:** P S

FRANCE

Plage de Goulien

Kernaveno, 29160
☎ 608434932 🖹 298262316
e-mail: camping.delaplage.degoulien@presquile-crozon.com
web: www.camping-crozon-laplagedegoulien.com
Grassy site in wooded surroundings 150 metres from the sea.
dir: *5km W on D308.*
Open: 10 Jun-15 Sep **Site:** 3HEC **For hire:** **Prices:** 18.50 Mobile home hire 320-625 **Facilities:** Play Area **Services:** **Off-site:** S

DEAUVILLE — CALVADOS

Haras

chemin du Calvaire, Touques, 14800
☎ 231884484 🖹 231889708
e-mail: campingdesharas@orange.fr
A partially residential site in pleasant surroundings. Ideal for overnight stops.
dir: *N on D62, to Honfleur.*
Open: Feb-Nov **Site:** 4HEC **For hire:** **Facilities:** **Services:** **Off-site:** P

Vallée de Deauville

av de la Vallée, St Arnoult, 14800
☎ 231885817 🖹 231881157
e-mail: contact@campingdeauville.com
web: www.campingdeauville.com
A pleasant wooded setting with plenty of recreational facilities.
dir: *1km S via D27 & D275.*
Open: Apr-Oct **Site:** 19HEC **For hire:** **Facilities:** **Services:** **Leisure:** L P R **Off-site:** S

DIEPPE — SEINE-MARITIME

La Source

63 rue Tisserands, Petit Appeville, Hautot-sur-Mer, 76550
☎ 235842704 🖹 235822502
e-mail: reception@camping-la-source.fr
web: www.camping-la-source.fr
Quiet, green site with games room and fishing available.
Open: 15 Mar-15 Oct **Site:** 2.5HEC **For hire:** **Prices:** 23.70-25.80 Mobile home hire 350-535 **Facilities:** Wi-fi (charged) Play Area **Services:** **Leisure:** P R **Off-site:** S

DOL-DE-BRETAGNE — ILLE-ET-VILAINE

Domaine des Ormes

35120
☎ 299735300 🖹 299735355
e-mail: info@lesormes.com
web: www.lesormes.com
Site in grounds of a château, with a large indoor water park including a wave pool. 18 hole golf course and horse riding available.
dir: *7km S on N795 Rennes road.*
GPS: 48.49, -1.7267
Open: 28 May-23 Sep **Site:** 60HEC **For hire:** **Prices:** 27.50-57 Mobile home hire 385-1274 **Facilities:** Wi-fi Kids' Club Play Area **Services:** **Leisure:** P

Tendieres

rue des Tendieres, 35120
☎ 299481468 🖹 299481869
e-mail: campinglestendieres@orange.fr
web: www.camping-lestendieres.com
On level meadow.
dir: *SW from town centre on rte de Dinan 400m.*
Open: 15 May-15 Oct **Site:** 1.7HEC **For hire:** **Facilities:** **Services:** **Leisure:** R **Off-site:** P

Vieux Chêne

The Camping and Caravanning Club — The Friendly Club

Baguer-Pican, 35120
☎ 299480955
e-mail: vieux.chene@wanadoo.fr
web: www.camping-vieuxchene.fr
Spacious site in a pleasant lakeside location.
C&CC Report *Amid the beautiful countryside around the Bay of Mont-St-Michel, Vieux Chêne and its pretty fishing lake make a welcoming and comfortable base for children and adults alike. Spectacular Mont-St-Michel, a host of historic towns, picturesque coastline and the enchanting villages of Brittany are all within easy reach. Visitor access to Mont-St-Michel has recently been hugely improved.*
dir: *5km E of Dol-de-Bretagne on D576.*
Open: 12 May-25 Sep **Site:** 12HEC **For hire:** **Prices:** 16.50-25.50 Mobile home hire 255-755 **Facilities:** Wi-fi (charged) Kids' Club Play Area **Services:** **Leisure:** P

FRANCE

DOUARNENEZ FINISTÈRE

Camping de la Baie de Douarnenez

Poullan-Sur-Mer, 29100
☎ 298742639 298745597
e-mail: info@pil-koad.com
web: www.camping-douarnenez.com
A natural wooded setting with a variety of recreational facilities, including a covered swimming pool and jacuzzi.
dir: *E on D7 towards Douarnenez.*
Open: Apr-Sep **Site:** 5.5HEC **For hire:**
Prices: 17-32 **Facilities:** Wi-fi (charged) Kids' Club Play Area **Services:** **Leisure:** P
Off-site: S

Kerleyou

Tréboul, 29100
☎ 298741303 298740961
e-mail: campingdekerleyou@wanadoo.fr
web: www.camping-kerleyou.com
Family site in wooded surroundings near the beach. Separate car park for arrivals after 23.00hrs.
dir: *1km W on rue de Préfet-Collignon towards sea.*
Open: 10 Apr-19 Sep **Site:** 3HEC **For hire:**
Facilities: Wi-fi Play Area **Services:**
Leisure: P **Off-site:** S

ERDEVEN MORBIHAN

Ideal

rte de la plage, 56410
☎ 297556766
e-mail: info@camping-l-ideal.com
web: www.camping-l-ideal.com
Well-kept site located 800 metres from the beach. Leisure facilities include a covered swimming pool, trampoline, table tennis and fitness area. Nearby are walks, tennis, golf, squash and horse riding.
dir: *Via N781 to Plage de Kerhilio.*
GPS: 47.6214, -3.1629
Open: Apr-Sep **Site:** 0.5HEC **For hire:**
Prices: 18.40-33 Mobile home hire 240-780 **Facilities:**
Wi-fi (charged) Play Area **Services:** **Leisure:** P
Off-site: R S

Sept Saints

56410
☎ 297555265 297552267
e-mail: info@septsaints.com
web: www.septsaints.com
Wooded surroundings with good recreational facilities.
dir: *2km NW via D781 rte de Plouhinec.*
Open: 15 May-15 Sep **Site:** 5HEC **For hire:**
Facilities: **Services:** **Leisure:** P
Off-site: L R S

ERQUY CÔTES-D'ARMOR

Camping Bellevue

rte de la Libération, 22430
☎ 296723304
e-mail: campingbellevue@yahoo.fr
web: www.campingbellevue.fr
Situated 2km from a sandy beach and ideal for families. Pitches are separated by hedges, trees and plants. Dogs accepted, some restrictions apply.
GPS: 48.5943, -2.4848
Open: 6 Apr-20 Sep **Site:** 3HEC **For hire:**
Facilities: Wi-fi Kids' Club Play Area
Services: **Leisure:** P **Off-site:** S

Camping La Vallée

St Pabu, 22431
☎ 296720622
e-mail: campinglavalleeerquy@wanadoo.fr
web: campinglavallee.fr
0.5m from a sandy beach and with flat, well-drained pitches. Leisure activities include basketball, table tennis and cycle rental. There is a spa facility with sauna, hot tub and relaxation room.
Open: 30 Apr-15 Sep **Site:** 2HEC **For hire:**
Prices: 14-18.30 Mobile home hire 250-615 **Facilities:**
Wi-fi (charged) Play Area **Services:**
Off-site: S

Hautes Greés

123 rue St-Michel, 22430
☎ 296723478 296723015
e-mail: hautesgrees@wanadoo.fr
web: www.camping-hautes-grees.com
Good family site, 2km from the town centre and 400 metres from the beach.
dir: *2km before Erquy.*
Open: 7 Apr-Sep **Site:** 3HEC **For hire:**
Prices: 12.95-21.10 Mobile home hire 290-630 **Facilities:**
Wi-fi (charged) Kids' Club Play Area **Services:**
Leisure: P **Off-site:** S

FRANCE

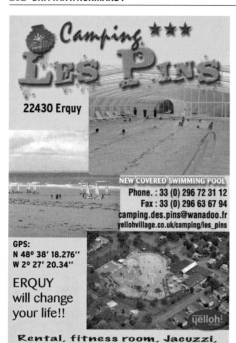

Pins

rte du Guen, 22430

☎ 296723112 🖷 296636794

e-mail: camping.des.pins@wanadoo.fr

A well equipped family site situated in a pine forest 800 metres from Erquy harbour and the Guen beach.

dir: *1km NE of village.*

Open: 12 Apr-15 Sep **Site:** 10HEC **For hire:** **Facilities:** **Services:** **Leisure:** P **Off-site:** S

see advert on this page

Roches

Caroual Village, 22430

☎ 296723290 🖷 296635784

e-mail: info@camping-les-roches.com

web: www.camping-les-roches.com

A quiet site in a rural setting with well-marked pitches, 0.8km from the beach.

dir: *3km SW off D786.*

Open: Apr-Sep **Site:** 3.1HEC **For hire:** **Prices:** 10-18.30 **Facilities:** Wi-fi Play Area **Services:** **Off-site:** S

St-Pabu

22430

☎ 296722465 🖷 296728717

e-mail: camping@saintpabu.com

web: www.saintpabu.com

On big open meadow with several terraces in beautiful, isolated location by sea. Divided into pitches.

dir: *W on D786, signed from la Coutre.*

Open: Apr-10 Oct **Site:** 5.5HEC **For hire:** **Prices:** 16-20.10 Mobile home hire 275-695 **Facilities:** Kids' Club Play Area **Services:** **Leisure:** S

Vieux Moulin

rue des Moulins, 22430

☎ 296723423 🖷 296723663

e-mail: camp.vieux.moulin@wanadoo.fr

web: www.camping-vieux-moulin.com

Clean tidy site divided into pitches and surrounded by a pine forest. Suitable for children.

dir: *On D783.*

Open: 9 Apr-11 Sep **Site:** 6.5HEC **For hire:** **Facilities:** Wi-fi (charged) Kids' Club Play Area **Services:** **Leisure:** P **Off-site:** S

ÉTABLES-SUR-MER CÔTES-D'ARMOR

Abri Côtier

The Camping and Caravanning Club — The Friendly Club

22680

☎ 296706157 🖷 296706523

e-mail: camping.abricotier@wanadoo.fr

web: www.camping-abricotier.fr

A pleasant family site in a wooded location close to the sea.

C&CC Report *This friendly, very well-kept and relaxing little site is much appreciated for its quiet, family atmosphere, attractive location and proximity to the superb beaches and coves of Brittany's lovely north coast. Add in the very helpful Anglo-French owners and it makes for an ideal site for any time of the season, both for first-timers and returners alike.*

dir: *1km N of town centre on D786.*

Open: 27 Apr-16 Sep **Site:** 6HEC **For hire:** **Prices:** 15.60-18.20 Mobile home hire 260-600 **Facilities:** Wi-fi (charged) **Services:** **Leisure:** P **Off-site:** S

FRANCE

ETRÉHAM — CALVADOS

Reine Mathilde

14400
231217655
e-mail: camping.reine-mathilde@wanadoo.fr
web: www.camping-normandie-rm.fr
A quiet rural setting 4km from the sea.
dir: *1km W via D123.*
Open: Apr-Sep **Site:** 6.5HEC **For hire:** **Facilities:** Wi-fi (charged) Play Area **Services:** **Leisure:** P **Off-site:**

FAOUËT, LE — MORBIHAN

Beg Er Roch

rte de Lorient, 56320
297231511 297231166
e-mail: camping.lefaouet@wanadoo.fr
Pleasant surroundings on the banks of a river. A popular site with modern sanitary facilities and opportunities for many sports.
Open: All Year. **Site:** 3.5HEC **For hire:**
Prices: 9.35-14.30 Mobile home hire 216-423 **Facilities:** Play Area **Services:** **Leisure:** R **Off-site:** P

FIQUEFLEUR-EQUAINVILLE — EURE

Domaine Catinière

rte d'Honfleur, 27210
232576351 232421257
e-mail: info@camping-catiniere.com
web: www.camping-catiniere.com
Picturesque site in a pretty valley.
dir: *From Le Havre E05/E44/D22.*
GPS: 49.4008, 0.3064
Open: 6 Apr-18 Sep **Site:** 5HEC **For hire:**
Prices: 20-28 Mobile home hire 260-760 **Facilities:** Wi-fi (charged) Play Area **Services:** **Leisure:** P R **Off-site:**

FORÊT-FOUESNANT, LA — FINISTÈRE

Camping Les Saules

rte de la Plage, 29440
298569857
e-mail: info@camping-les-saules.com
web: www.camping-les-saules.com
In a green shaded area with direct access to the beach. There is a swimming pool complex with waterslides.
GPS: 47.8987, -3.9612
Open: 3 Apr-2 Oct **Site:** 3.5HEC **For hire:** **Prices:** 15.82-27.92 Mobile home hire 205.44-937.76 **Facilities:** Wi-fi Kids' Club Play Area **Services:** **Leisure:** P S

see advert on page 204

Domaine du Saint Laurent

Kerleven, 29940
298569765 298569251
e-mail: saintlaurent@franceloc.fr
web: www.camping-du-saint-laurent.fr
On rocky coast. Divided into pitches.
dir: *3.5km SE of village.*
Open: Apr-Sep **Site:** 5.25HEC **For hire:** **Facilities:** **Services:** **Leisure:** P S **Off-site:**

Européen De La Plage

5 rte de Port la Forêt, 29940
678077228
e-mail: laplage.camp@wanadoo.fr
web: www.cedlp.com
Pitches divided by hedges, close to the sea.
dir: *2.5km SE on D783.*
Open: 15 Mar-15 Oct **Site:** 1HEC **Prices:** 16
Facilities: Wi-fi **Services:** **Leisure:** S
Off-site:

Kérantérec

29940
298569811 298568173
e-mail: info@camping-keranterec.com
web: www.camping-keranterec.com
Well-kept terraced site, divided into sections by hedges and extending to the sea.
dir: *3km SE.*
Open: 10 Apr-19 Sep **Site:** 6.5HEC **For hire:**
Facilities: **Services:** **Leisure:** P S **Off-site:**

FRANCE

CAMPING
LES SAULES
Holiday park in La Forêt-Fouesnant
Direct access to the beach • Heated aquatic park
Mobile home rental • Camping • Caravanning
Route de la plage Port-la-Forêt 29940 La Forêt Fouesnant
Tel. 02 98 56 98 57 www.camping-les-saules.com

Manoir de Penn Ar Ster

29940
☎ 298569775
e-mail: info@camping-pennarster.com
web: www.camping-pennarster.com

Well-tended site close to Port La Forêt, a major yachting arena.

dir: *NE off D44.*

Open: Feb-11 Nov **Site:** 3HEC **For hire:** **Facilities:** Wi-fi (charged) Play Area **Services:** **Off-site:** P S

FOUESNANT — FINISTÈRE

Domaine Le Grand Large

48 rte du Grand Large, Pointe de Mousterlin, 29170
☎ 298560406 298565826
e-mail: grand-large@franceloc.fr
web: www.campings-franceloc.fr

A family site in a wooded setting with direct access to the beach and plenty of modern facilities. A kids' club is available in July and August.

dir: *S of Fouesnant via D145.*

Open: 3 Apr-11 Sep **Site:** 6HEC **For hire:** **Prices:** 16-29 Mobile home hire 133-1001 **Facilities:** Wi-fi Kids' Club Play Area **Services:** **Leisure:** P S **Off-site:**

Piscine

51 Hent Kerleya, 29170
☎ 298565606 298565764
e-mail: contact@campingdelapiscine.com
web: www.campingdelapiscine.com

Family friendly site in a beautiful location, 1.5km from the beach. Recreational facilities include indoor and outdoor swimming pools with slides, a children's pool, and spa including sauna and jacuzzi. There is a charge for Wi-fi in July and August.

C&CC Report *The Caradecs lovingly run their very friendly, spacious site in pretty countryside close to the lovely Finistère coast. It's very well suited both to low season tourers and, with high season children's activities, to younger families. While the impressive pool complex now includes an indoor pool and a spa, popular day trips off-site include Océanopolis (the ocean discovery park in Brest), historic Quimper, many great beaches, and boat trips to the Glénan islands.*

dir: *4km NW towards Kerleya.*

GPS: 47.8667, -4.0158

Open: 11 May-16 Sep **Site:** 5HEC **For hire:** **Prices:** 18-31 Mobile home hire 240-720 **Facilities:** Wi-fi (charged) Kids' Club Play Area **Services:** **Leisure:** P **Off-site:** S

Sunêlia Atlantique

rte de Mousterlin, 29170
☎ 298561444 298561867
e-mail: sunelia@latlantique.fr
web: www.latlantique.fr

Modern site with plenty of amenities, 400 metres from the beach. Kids' club available in July and August.

C&CC Report *Popular and well known, lively l'Atlantique is a bustling site with lots going on and in a great location. A short walk through the woods brings you out over the dunes onto a long white sand beach – but there is plenty to keep you on site, from a great pool complex, to pony rides, a pet farm, good sports facilities and a relaxing spa centre. Nearby, Quimper and many great beaches make good trips out.*

dir: *4.5km S on road to Mousterlin.*

GPS: 47.8567, -4.0208

Open: 21 Apr-9 Sep **Site:** 10HEC **For hire:** **Prices:** 22-41 Mobile home hire 329-1225 **Facilities:** Wi-fi (charged) Kids' Club Play Area **Services:** **Leisure:** P **Off-site:** S

FOUGÈRES ILLE-ET-VILAINE

CM Paron

rte de la Chapelle Janson, 35300

299994081 299942794

e-mail: campingmunicipal35@orange.fr

A well-managed site suitable for overnight stays.

dir: *1.5km E via D17.*

Open: May-Sep **Site:** 2.5HEC **Prices:** 15-20 **Facilities:** Play Area **Services:** **Off-site:** L P R

GUILLIGOMARC'H FINISTÈRE

Bois des Ecureuils

29300

298717098 298717098

e-mail: bois-des-ecureuils@aliceadsl.fr

web: bois-des-ecureuils.com

Tranquil 1.6-hectare wooded site set among oak, chestnut and beech trees. An ideal base for walking, cycling, horse riding and fishing.

Open: Jun-1 Sep **Site:** 2.5HEC **Facilities:** **Services:**

GUILVINEC FINISTÈRE

Yelloh Village La Plage

rte de Penmarc'h, 29730

298586190 298588906

e-mail: info@yellohvillage-la-plage.com

web: www.villagelaplage.com

Site is on level meadow divided into pitches. Direct access to a flat beach suitable for children.

Open: Apr-15 Sep **Site:** 14HEC **For hire:** **Prices:** 17-43 Mobile home hire 245-1064 **Facilities:** Wi-fi Kids' Club Play Area **Services:** **Leisure:** P S

HAYE-DU-PUITS, LA MANCHE

Étang des Haizes

43 rue Cauticotte, 50250

233460116 233472380

e-mail: info@campingetangdeshaizes.com

web: www.campingetangdeshaizes.com

A well-equipped family site bordering a lake where fishing is available, shaded by apple trees. Activities are organised in summer including a kids' club in July and August.

dir: *D903 from Carentan.*

Open: Apr-15 Oct **Site:** 5HEC **For hire:** **Prices:** 16-37 Mobile home hire 360-784 **Facilities:** Wi-fi (charged) Kids' Club Play Area **Services:** **Leisure:** P **Off-site:**

HOULGATE CALVADOS

Vallée

88 rue de la Vallée, 14510

231244069 231244242

e-mail: camping.lavallee@wanadoo.fr

web: www.campinglavallee.com

Site with good recreational facilities, 0.9km from the beach.

dir: *1km S.*

Open: Apr-Sep **Site:** 11HEC **For hire:** **Prices:** 21-34 Mobile home hire 310-750 **Facilities:** Wi-fi (charged) Play Area **Services:** **Leisure:** P **Off-site:** S

ISIGNY SUR MER CALVADOS

Camping le Fanal

rue du Fanal, 14230

231213320 231221200

e-mail: info@camping-lefanal.com

web: www.camping-normandie-fanal.fr

Family friendly site with swimming pool complex. Entertainment includes concerts and plays. Kids' club available in July and August. Dogs allowed except July and August.

Open: Apr-Sep **Site:** 8HEC **For hire:** **Facilities:** Wi-fi (charged) Kids' Club Play Area **Services:** **Leisure:** L P **Off-site:** R

JULLOUVILLE MANCHE

Chaussée

1 av de la Libération, 50610

233618018 233614526

e-mail: jmb@camping-lachaussee.com

web: camping-lachaussee.com

On large meadow, completely divided into pitches. Separated from the beach and coast road by a row of houses.

Open: 10 Apr-20 Sep **Site:** 6HEC **For hire:** **Facilities:** **Services:** **Leisure:** P **Off-site:** S

FRANCE

cilities shower electric points for razors electric points for caravans motorvan service point parking by tents permitted npulsory separate car park shop **Services** café/restaurant bar Camping Gaz International gas other than Camping Gaz first aid facilities laundry **Leisure** swimming L-Lake P-Pool R-River S-Sea **Off-site** All facilities within 5km

JUMIÈGES **SEINE-MARITIME**

Forêt

rue Mainberthe, 76480
☎ 235379343 📠 235377648
e-mail: info@campinglaforet.com
web: www.campinglaforet.com

Located in the heart of the Brotonne regional park beside the Seine.

C&CC Report *Ideal for exploring a lovely part of France that is overlooked by many. The orchards, lush forests and tall white cliffs of the Seine valley are stunning, while old Norman farms and white stone villages pepper a lovely landscape that is topped off majestically by the region's medieval jewel, Rouen. Monet's inspiration for his famous water lily paintings, Giverny is within easy reach and the Route des Abbayes (Abbeys' Route) alone, could keep you going for days.*

dir: *A13 exit Bourg-Achard, site 10km.*

Open: 11 Apr-24 Oct **Site:** 2.5HEC **For hire:** **Facilities:** Wi-fi (charged) Play Area **Services:** **Leisure:** P **Off-site:** L R

KERLIN **FINISTÈRE**

Étangs de Trévignon

Pointe de Trévignon, Kerlin, 29910
☎ 298500041
e-mail: camp.etangdetrevignon@wanadoo.fr
web: www.camping-etangs.com

A family site with modern facilities including a covered pool and big waterslide. A path leads to the beach, 0.8km away.

GPS: 47.8103, -3.8486

Open: Jun-15 Sep **Site:** 3.5HEC **For hire:** **Prices:** 15-20.65 **Facilities:** Play Area **Services:** **Leisure:** P **Off-site:** S

LANDAUL **MORBIHAN**

Le Pied-à-Terre

Branzého, 56690
☎ 297245270
e-mail: jimrolland@wanadoo.fr
web: www.lepiedaterre.net

A pleasant, quiet location, 15 minutes from the sea.

dir: *1km from N165, signed from Landaul.*

Open: May-15 Sep **Site:** 2.6HEC **Prices:** 16 **Facilities:** Play Area **Services:** **Off-site:**

LANDÉDA **FINISTÈRE**

Camping des Abers

Dunes de Ste-Marguerite,
51 Toull Treaz, 29870
☎ 298049335 📠 298048435
e-mail: info@camping-des-abers.com
web: www.camping-des-abers.com

Very quiet beautiful site among dunes with off-shore islands accessible at low tide. Ideal for children.

C&CC Report *With a truly beautiful position and the owners' friendly, personal care for every camper, this traditional site's strong community sense is its trump card. Popular open stage evenings are a social highlight, with eclectic contributions from returning and new campers alike. The Abers country reinvigorates all season, with tidal watermills, Folgoët's basilica, an artists' colony and a seaweed-harvesting museum.*

dir: *2.5km NW on peninsula between bays Aber-Wrac'h & Aber Benoît.*

Open: May-Sep **Site:** 4.5HEC **For hire:** **Facilities:** Wi-fi Play Area **Services:** **Leisure:** S **Off-site:** R

LANLOUP **CÔTES D'ARMOR**

Camping le Neptune

Kerguistin 3, 22580
☎ 296223335
e-mail: contact@leneptune.com
web: www.leneptune.com

Two minutes from the sea and beaches, this site has grassy, spacious pitches separated by hedges. Entertainment includes concerts, sports and a mini-farm.

GPS: 48.7137, -2.9670

Open: Apr-17 Oct **Site:** 1.5HEC **For hire:** **Prices:** 15-21 Mobile home hire 229-729 **Facilities:** Wi-fi Play Area **Services:** **Leisure:** P **Off-site:** S

LESCONIL **FINISTÈRE**

Camping de la Grande Plage

71 rue P-Langevin, 29740
☎ 298878827 📠 298878827
e-mail: campinggrandeplage@hotmail.com
web: www.campinggrandeplage.com

Well-equipped level site, surrounded by woodland and 300 metres from the sea. Heated swimming pool with slides available.

Open: May-Sep **Site:** 2.5HEC **For hire:** **Facilities:** Wi-fi Play Area **Services:** **Leisure:** P **Off-site:** S

Site 6HEC (site size) grass sand stone little shade partly shaded mainly shaded motorvans accepted bungalows for hire mobile homes for hire tents for hire no dogs site fully accessible for wheelchairs
Prices amount quoted is per night, for 2 adults and car, plus tent or caravan Mobile home hire is a weekly rate.

Camping des Dunes

67 rue P-Langevin, 29740

298878178 298822705

e-mail: campingdesdunes@gmail.com

web: www.camping-lesdunes-29.com

A peaceful family site with spacious pitches surrounded by trees on slightly sloping landscaped ground. Located 0.8km from the town centre and harbour of Lesconil.

dir: *From Quimper towards Pont l'Abbé then Lesconil. Exit Lesconil towards the coast in direction of Treffiagat.*

Open: mid Apr-Sep **Site:** 2.8HEC **For hire:** **Prices:** 21.58 Mobile home hire 335-670 **Facilities:** Wi-fi Play Area **Services:** **Leisure:** S **Off-site:** P R

LITTEAU CALVADOS

Domaine de Litteau

14490

231222208 231218565

e-mail: hsm.dlt@siblu.fr

web: www.siblu.com/domainedelitteau

Peaceful site on the edge of the Cerisy forest. An ideal base for exploring the beaches of Normandy and the historic town of Bayeux. Recreational facilities include a pool with slide and two fishing ponds for campers, plus fishing rod hire. A kids' club is available in July and August.

Open: May-Sep **Site:** 19HEC **For hire:** **Prices:** 15-45 Mobile home hire 270-950 **Facilities:** Wi-fi (charged) Kids' Club Play Area **Services:** **Leisure:** P

LOUANNEC CÔTES-D'ARMOR

CM Ernest Renan

66 rte de Perros-Guirec, 22700

296231178 296490447

e-mail: mairie-louannec@orange.fr

Site next to the sea with heated swimming pool. Takeaway food, games room with other amenities close by.

dir: *1km W.*

GPS: 48.7966, -3.4266

Open: May-Sep **Site:** 4.5HEC **For hire:** **Prices:** 10.05-13.25 Mobile home hire 250-580 **Facilities:** Wi-fi (charged) Kids' Club Play Area **Services:** **Leisure:** L P R S **Off-site:**

LOUVIERS EURE

Bel Air

rte de la Haye Malherbe, 27400

232401077

e-mail: campinglebelair@aol.com

web: www.camping-lebelair.fr

Small site on the edge of a forest with landscaped pitches and good facilities.

dir: *3km from town centre via D81.*

GPS: 49.2152, 1.1332

Open: Mar-Oct **Site:** 2.5HEC **For hire:** **Facilities:** Wi-fi **Services:** **Leisure:** P

LUC-SUR-MER CALVADOS

Capricieuse

2 rue Brummel, 14530

231973443 231968278

e-mail: info@campinglacapricieuse.com

web: www.campinglacapricieuse.com

A large family site 100 metres from the beach.

dir: *On W outskirts. A13 exit Douvres.*

Open: Apr-Sep **Site:** 4.5HEC **For hire:** **Prices:** 20.10-22.75 Mobile home hire 305-699 **Facilities:** Wi-fi Play Area **Services:** **Off-site:** P S

MARCILLY-SUR-EURE EURE

Domaine de Marcilly

rte de St André, 27810

237484542 237485111

e-mail: domainedemarcilly@wanadoo.fr

Overlooking the Eure valley, spacious pitches in wooded surroundings separated by hedges and shrubs.

dir: *On D52.*

GPS: 48.83, 1.3321

Open: Apr-Oct **Site:** 15HEC **For hire:** **Facilities:** Wi-fi (charged) Play Area **Services:** **Leisure:** P **Off-site:**

FRANCE

MARTIGNY SEINE-MARITIME

2 Rivières

76880

☎ 235856082 235859516

e-mail: martigny.76@orange.fr

web: www.camping-2-RIVIERAes.com

On the shore of a lake in pleasant surroundings 8km from Dieppe.

dir: *Via D154.*

Open: 26 Mar-10 Oct **Site:** 6.8HEC **For hire:** **Facilities:** Play Area **Services:** **Off-site:** P

MARTRAGNY CALVADOS

Château de Martragny

14740

☎ 231802140 231081491

e-mail: chateau.martragny@wanadoo.fr

web: www.chateau-martragny.com

Peaceful family site in grounds of a château, which also offers accommodation.

C&CC Report *An exclusively touring site with a rural feel, in impressive, spacious grounds. Martragny is an ideal base for either short or long stays, especially for younger families and couples. The D-Day beaches, sites and museums and the Caen Peace Memorial are close by, as is Bayeux with its famous Norman tapestry. The D-Day Festival takes place throughout the area in the days around 6 June, but amid all the history don't ignore the simple pleasures of the beautiful Norman countryside, its lovely villages and the delicious regional produce.*

dir: *N13 exit Martragny, through St-Léger, site on right.*

Open: May-12 Sep **Site:** 12HEC **Prices:** 26.40-30.40 **Facilities:** Wi-fi Play Area **Services:** **Leisure:** P **Off-site:** R S

MAUPERTUS-SUR-MER MANCHE

Anse du Brick

50330

☎ 233543357 233544966

e-mail: welcome@anse-du-brick.com

web: www.anse-du-brick.com

Terraced site in a landscaped park between the sea and a forest.

dir: *10km E of Cherbourg ferry terminal.*

GPS: 49.6670, -1.4870

Open: Apr-Sep **Site:** 17HEC **For hire:** **Prices:** 20.30-39.60 Mobile home hire 385-870 **Facilities:** Wi-fi (charged) Kids' Club Play Area **Services:** **Leisure:** P S

MERVILLE-FRANCEVILLE CALVADOS

Camping Le Point du Jour

14810

☎ 231242334

e-mail: contact@camping-lepointdujour.com

web: www.camping-lepointdujour.com

Spacious pitches divided by hedges. Cycles are available to hire.

C&CC Report *Camping Point du Jour is very well located for Normandy beachside holidays, short breaks and stopovers before or after the Portsmouth-Caen ferry crossing. In the heart of the D-Day Normandy landing beaches, it's a fascinating area – history and modern day charm sit happily side by side. A kilometre walk will take you to the typical Normandy coastal village of Merville-Franceville where there is a choice of bars and restaurants.*

dir: *E of village on D514.*

GPS: 49.2832, -0.1913

Open: Apr-4 Sep **Site:** **Facilities:** Wi-fi Play Area **Services:** **Leisure:** P

Peupliers

allée des Pins, 14810

☎ 231240507 231240507

e-mail: contact@camping-peupliers.com

web: www.camping-peupliers.com

A rural setting 300 metres from the beach. The sanitary facilities include a bathroom for babies.

dir: *2km E from sign on D514.*

Open: Apr-Oct **Site:** 3.6HEC **For hire:** **Prices:** 23.80 Mobile home hire 720 **Facilities:** Wi-fi Kids' Club Play Area **Services:** **Leisure:** P **Off-site:** R S

MONTERBLANC MORBIHAN

Haras

Kersimon, Vannes-Meucon, 56250

☎ 297446606 297444941

e-mail: contact@campingvannes.com

web: www.campingvannes.com

Quiet well equipped family site with plenty of activities for children, close to Vannes and the Gulf of Morbihan.

dir: *4km from Vannes towards Vannes-Meucon.*

GPS: 47.7303, -2.7279

Open: All Year. **Site:** 14HEC **For hire:** **Prices:** 14-25 Mobile home hire 266-700 **Facilities:** Wi-fi Play Area **Services:** **Leisure:** P **Off-site:**

see advert on opposite page

FRANCE

MONT-ST-MICHEL, LE MANCHE

Gué de Beauvoir

5 rte du Mont-St-Michel, Beauvoir, 50170
☎ 233600923 ▤ 233582175
e-mail: nolleauyves@yahoo.fr
web: www.hotel-gue-de-beauvoir.fr
A level site in an orchard close to the River Couesnon.
dir: *4km S of Abbey on D776 Pontorson road.*
Open: Etr-Sep **Site:** 0.6HEC **For hire:** **Facilities:** Wi-fi **Services:** **Leisure:** R S **Off-site:**

MORGAT FINISTÈRE

Bruyères

Le Bouis, 29160
☎ 298261487 ▤ 298261487
e-mail: info@camping-bruyeres-crozon.com
web: www.camping-bruyeres-crozon.com
On a meadow surrounded by woodland with pitches divided by hedges on the edge of the Parc Naturel Régional d'Armorique.
dir: *From Morgat D255 towards Cap de la Chèvre, 1.5km right towards Bouis.*
Open: May-Sep **Site:** 3HEC **For hire:** **Facilities:** **Services:** **Off-site:**

MOYAUX CALVADOS

Le Colombier

14590
☎ 231636308 ▤ 231615017
e-mail: chateau@camping-lecolombier.com
web: www.camping-lecolombier.com
A charming, well-kept site in grounds of manor house.
dir: *3km NE on D143.*
Open: May-15 Sep **Site:** 10HEC **Prices:** 26-36 **Facilities:** Wi-fi (charged) Play Area **Services:** **Leisure:** P

NÉVEZ FINISTÈRE

Deux Fontaines

Feuntelin Vehan, 29920
☎ 298068191 ▤ 298067180
e-mail: info@les2fontaines.fr
web: www.les2fontaines.fr
Mainly level site, subdivided into several fields surrounded by woodland with good recreational facilities including an indoor swimming pool, waterslide, scuba diving, fitness area, archery lessons, 6 hole golf course and driving range. Pizzas and snacks are available.
dir: *0.7km from Ragunès beach.*
Open: 5 May-2 Sep **Site:** 7HEC **For hire:** **Prices:** 16-33.80 Mobile home hire 280-980 **Facilities:** Wi-fi Kids' Club Play Area **Services:** **Leisure:** P **Off-site:** R S

FRANCE

NOYAL-MUZILLAC MORBIHAN

Moulin de Cadillac

56190

☎ 297670347 297670002

e-mail: infos@moulin-cadillac.com

web: www.camping-moulin-cadillac.com

A well-equipped family site in a pleasant wooded location with good facilities including an indoor swimming pool.

dir: *Via N165, N through Muzillac.*

Open: May-Sep **Site:** 5HEC **For hire:** **Prices:** 16.80-27.80 Mobile home hire 260-610 **Facilities:** Wi-fi Play Area **Services:** **Leisure:** P

Yelloh Domaine d'Inly

rte de Couarne, BP24, 56760

☎ 299903509 299904093

e-mail: inly-info@wanadoo.fr

web: www.camping-inly.com

Set in the centre of a nature reserve close to the coast, with good recreational facilities.

dir: *2km SE via D201.*

GPS: 47.4715, -2.4670

Open: 6 Apr-22 Sep **Site:** 29HEC **For hire:** **Prices:** 17-44 Mobile home hire 273-1323 **Facilities:** Wi-fi Kids' Club Play Area **Services:** **Leisure:** L P **Off-site:** R S

PÉNESTIN-SUR-MER MORBIHAN

Camping des Iles

La Pointe du Bile - BP4, 56760

☎ 299903024 299904455

e-mail: contact@camping-des-iles.fr

web: www.camping-des-iles.fr

A family site with direct access to the beach and a separate residential section. The on-site shop is open all season. Leisure facilities include a heated swimming pool with slides and a kids' club is available in July and August.

dir: *3km S on D201.*

Open: 6 Apr-Sep **Site:** 4HEC **For hire:** **Prices:** 17-37 Mobile home hire 259-1022 **Facilities:** Wi-fi (charged) Kids' Club Play Area **Services:** **Leisure:** P S

Cénic

56760

☎ 299904565 299904505

e-mail: info@lecenic.com

web: www.lecenic.com

A forested area 2km from the sea. The spacious grassy pitches are ideal for families and there is a heated swimming pool with slides.

dir: *D34 from La Roche-Bernard.*

GPS: 47.4777, -2.4530

Open: Apr-Sep **Site:** 7HEC **For hire:** **Prices:** 15-28 Mobile home hire 285-700 **Facilities:** Kids' Club Play Area **Services:** **Leisure:** P **Off-site:** S

PENMARC'H FINISTÈRE

Camping les Genêts

rue Gouesnac'h Nevez, 29760

☎ 298586693

e-mail: campinglesgenets29@orange.fr

web: www.camping-lesgenets.com

1.5km from a sandy beach, this family site has large pitches and offers lots of activities.

Open: Apr-Sep **Site:** 3.5HEC **For hire:** **Facilities:** Wi-fi Kids' Club Play Area **Services:** **Leisure:** P **Off-site:** S

PENTREZ-PLAGE FINISTÈRE

Ker-Ys

29550

☎ 298265395 298265248

e-mail: camping-kerys@wanadoo.fr

web: www.ker-ys.com

Level site divided into pitches 20 metres from the beach.

dir: *Via D887.*

Open: Apr-14 Sep **Site:** 3HEC **For hire:** **Facilities:** **Services:** **Leisure:** P S **Off-site:**

FRANCE

PIEUX, LES — MANCHE

Grand Large

The Camping and Caravanning Club The Friendly Club

50340
☎ 233524075 🖹 233525820
e-mail: info@legrandlarge.com
web: www.legrandlarge.com

An unspoiled family site, with direct access to the sandy beach.

C&CC Report *Le Grand Large is a very well-run and well-established site in an outstanding location for great summer holidays. With direct access to the wonderful beach and its views over the Channel Islands, there are also many walking paths, a rugged coastline and historic towns, sites and battlegrounds of the Cotentin peninsula to explore. The site is also very handy for Cherbourg's ferry port and the amazing ocean attraction, Cité de la Mer.*

dir: *From Valognes, take D902. From Bricquebec towards Les Pieux, signed.*

GPS: 49.4936, -1.8425

Open: 7 Apr-23 Sep **Site:** 4HEC **For hire:** **Prices:** 17-32 Mobile home hire 250-890 **Facilities:** Wi-fi (charged) Play Area **Services:** **Leisure:** P S **Off-site:**

PLEUBIAN — CÔTES-D'ARMOR

Camping de Port la Chaîne

22610
☎ 296229238 🖹 296228792
e-mail: info@portlachaine.com
web: www.portlachaine.com

A peaceful and quiet terraced site on the Wild Peninsula, with direct access to the sea and plenty of tourist attractions nearby.

dir: *2km N via D20.*

Open: 9 Apr-22 Sep **Site:** 5HEC **For hire:** **Prices:** 14.40-23 Mobile home hire 252-672 **Facilities:** Wi-fi Play Area **Services:** **Leisure:** P S

PLOBANNALEC-LESCONIL — FINISTÈRE

Yelloh Village L'Océan Breton

The Camping and Caravanning Club The Friendly Club

29740
☎ 298822389 🖹 298822649
e-mail: info@yellohvillage-loceanbreton.com
web: www.oceanbreton.com

A peaceful site, with a large pool area, located in the grounds of a manor house, 2km from the beach.

C&CC Report *This busy, bustling site is a great family base for exploring stunning west Brittany. There is always something going on and families of all ages are particularly welcome, while cultural and children's entertainments keep everyone occupied. The new water park has added extra appeal to an already well-equipped site in the attractive grounds of a Breton manor house.*

Open: 28 Apr-9 Sep **Site:** 12HEC **For hire:** **Prices:** 17-42 Mobile home hire 245-1064 **Facilities:** Wi-fi Kids' Club Play Area **Services:** **Leisure:** P S

PLOËMEL — MORBIHAN

Kergo

The Camping and Caravanning Club The Friendly Club

56400
☎ 297568066 🖹 297568066
e-mail: camping.kergo@wanadoo.fr
web: campingkergo.com

Pleasant wooded surroundings close to the beaches. There is a jacuzzi and a sauna.

C&CC Report *This simple, peaceful alternative for visiting this ever-popular and busy area brings you a friendly welcome and beautiful natural surroundings. With attractive pitches and helpful owners, De Kergo is within easy reach of Carnac, La Trinité-sur-Mer, the Quiberon peninsula and the region's numerous prehistoric and other attractions.*

dir: *From N165 exit Carnac Quiberon, follow signs to Carnac Quiberon on D768 after 4km turn right, continue for 500m.*

Open: May-Sep **Site:** 2.5HEC **For hire:** **Prices:** 11.45-14.30 Mobile home hire 225-560 **Facilities:** Wi-fi (charged) Play Area **Services:** **Off-site:**

FRANCE

PLOEMEUR MORBIHAN

Ajoncs

Beg Minio, 56270
☎ 297863011 🖷 297863011
e-mail: contact@campingajoncs.fr
web: www.campingclub.asso.fr
A rural site set in an orchard.
dir: *From town centre towards Fort-Bloqué.*
Open: 18 Mar-Sep **Site:** 2HEC **Facilities:** **Services:** **Off-site:** L P S

PLOËRMEL MORBIHAN

Lac

Les Belles Rives, Taupont, 56800
☎ 297740122
e-mail: camping.du-lac@wanadoo.fr
web: www.camping-du-lac-ploermel.com
A lakeside family site with plenty of facilities for water sports.
dir: *2km from village centre beside lake.*
Open: Apr-Oct **Site:** 3HEC **For hire:** **Facilities:** **Services:** **Leisure:** L

Vallée du Ninian

Le Rocher, 56800
☎ 297935301 🖷 297935727
e-mail: infos@camping-ninian.fr
web: www.camping-ninian.fr
Peaceful family site beside the River Ninian in the heart of Brittany. The owners specialise in homemade cider.
dir: *W of Taupont towards river.*
Open: 5 Apr-Sep **Site:** 2.7HEC **For hire:** **Prices:** 11.60-15.20 Mobile home hire 230-600 **Facilities:** Wi-fi (charged) Play Area **Services:** **Leisure:** P R **Off-site:** L

PLOMEUR FINISTÈRE

Torche

Pointe de la Torche, 29120
☎ 298586282 🖷 298588969
e-mail: info@campingdelatorche.fr
web: www.campingdelatorche.fr
A family site with pitches surrounded by trees and bushes, 1.5km from the beach.
dir: *3.5km W.*
Open: 3 Apr-Sep **Site:** 4HEC **For hire:** **Facilities:** **Services:** **Leisure:** P **Off-site:** S

PLOMODIERN FINISTÈRE

Iroise

Plage de Pors-ar-Vag, 29550
☎ 298815272 🖷 298812610
e-mail: campingiroise@orange.fr
web: www.camping-iroise.fr
A family site with fine recreational facilities, providing magnificent views over the Bay of Douarnenez. Nearby are the Parc Naturel Marin d'Iroise and the Parc Naturel Régional d'Amorique.
dir: *5km SW, 150m from the beach.*
GPS: 48.1693, -4.2894
Open: 7 Apr-29 Sep **Site:** 2.5HEC **For hire:** **Prices:** 16.90-24.90 Mobile home hire 285-600 **Facilities:** Wi-fi (charged) Play Area **Services:** **Leisure:** P S **Off-site:**

PLONÉVEZ-PORZAY FINISTÈRE

Domaine de Kervel

29550
☎ 298925154 🖷 298925496
e-mail: camping.kervel@wanadoo.fr
web: www.kervel.com
One of the best sites in the region and 0.8km from the sea. Ideal for families.
dir: *SW of village on D107 Douarnenez road for 3km, turn at x-rds towards coast.*
Open: 30 Apr-10 Sep **Site:** 7HEC **For hire:** **Facilities:** **Services:** **Leisure:** P **Off-site:** S

Plage de Tréguer

Plage de Ste Anne la Palud, 29550
☎ 298925352 🖷 298925489
e-mail: camping-treguer-plage@wanadoo.fr
web: www.camping-treguer-plage.com
A level site with direct access to the beach.
dir: *1.3km N.*
Open: 7 Apr-29 Sep **Site:** 6HEC **For hire:** **Facilities:** **Services:** **Leisure:** P S **Off-site:**

FRANCE

PLOUESCAT FINISTÈRE

Village Center la Baie du Kernic

rue de Pen An Théven, 29430
499572121 467516389
e-mail: contact@village-center.com
web: www.village-center.com/bretagne/camping-mer-baie-kernic.php
In a countryside setting, 100 metres from the beach between Roscoff and Plouescat.
dir: *From Plouescat follow signs for Pors Guen-Porsmeur.*
GPS: 48.6600, -4.2162
Open: 13 Apr-9 Sep **Site:** 6HEC **For hire:** **Prices:** 15-23 Mobile home hire 175-699 **Facilities:** Wi-fi (charged) Kids' Club **Services:** **Leisure:** P **Off-site:** S

PLOUÉZEC CÔTES-D'ARMOR

Cap Horn

Port Lazo, 22470
296206428 296206388
e-mail: info@camping-capdesiles.com
web: www.lecaphorn.com
An elevated position overlooking the Ile de Bréhat with direct access to the beach.
dir: *2.3km NE via D77 at Port-Lazo.*
Open: Apr-Sep **Site:** 5HEC **For hire:** **Facilities:** **Services:** **Leisure:** P S **Off-site:**

PLOUEZOCH FINISTÈRE

Baie de Térénez

Moulin de Caneret, 29252
298672680
e-mail: campingbaiedeterenez@wanadoo.fr
web: www.campingbaiedeterenez.com
A well-equipped site in a pleasant rural setting, 1.5km from the beach.
dir: *3.5km NW via D76.*
GPS: 48.6597, -3.8483
Open: Apr-Sep **Site:** 3HEC **For hire:** **Prices:** 11-16 Mobile home hire 220-650 **Facilities:** Wi-fi Play Area **Services:** **Leisure:** P **Off-site:** R S

PLOUGASNOU FINISTÈRE

Le Domaine de Mesqueau

26930
298673745
e-mail: domaine-de-mesqueau@orange.fr
web: www.camping-bretagne-mer.com
Large site with good recreational facilities.
dir: *3.5km S via D46.*
Open: Apr-Sep **Site:** 7HEC **For hire:** **Facilities:** Wi-fi **Services:** **Leisure:** P R **Off-site:** S

Trégor

130 rte du Cosquerou, Kerjean, 29630
298673764
e-mail: bookings@campingdutregor.com
web: www.campingdutregor.com
A sheltered site with numbered, grassy pitches. Surrounded by hedges.
dir: *Off D46 towards Morlaix.*
GPS: 48.6849, -3.7852
Open: Etr-Oct **Site:** 1HEC **For hire:** **Prices:** 12-15.50 Mobile home hire 200-420 **Facilities:** Wi-fi (charged) **Services:** **Off-site:** S

PLOUGOULM FINISTÈRE

M du Bois de la Palud

The Camping and Caravanning Club The Friendly Club

29250
298298182 298299226
e-mail: mairie-de-plougoulm@wanadoo.fr
Well-defined pitches on a site with views over the sea and river valley, 15 minute walk to the beach.
C&CC Report *A super, simple little site, very close to Roscoff town and ferry port. Although an ideal site for an overnight stop, people who stay longer confirm that both the area and this tranquil little site offer real rest and relaxation, far from the madding crowd. Both the coast and the inland moors are great for walking and a boat trip to the island of Batz is also recommended. Plougoulm provides all the basic local services while St Pol-de-Léon is good for more extensive shopping.*
Open: 15 Jun-6 Sep **Site:** 2HEC **Facilities:** **Off-site:** S

FRANCE

PLOUHA — CÔTES-D'ARMOR

Domaine de Keravel

rte de Port Moguer, La Trinité, 22580

☎ 296224913

e-mail: keravel@wanadoo.fr

web: www.keravel.com

Forested family site built around an elegant country mansion with spacious pitches, good recreational facilities and entertainment. 1km from the sea.

Open: Jun-15 Sep **Site:** 5HEC **For hire:** **Prices:** 16.40-26.70 Mobile home hire 330-740 **Facilities:** Wi-fi Kids' Club Play Area **Services:** **Leisure:** P **Off-site:** S

PLOUHARNEL — MORBIHAN

Kersily

Ste-Barbe, 56340

☎ 297523965 297524476

e-mail: camping.kersily@wanadoo.fr

web: www.camping-kersily.com

1.8km from a sandy beach, family-friendly site with pitches divided by shrubs and trees. There is a swimming pool area and evening entertainment available.

Open: Apr-Oct **Site:** 4HEC **For hire:** **Facilities:** **Services:** **Leisure:** P **Off-site:** S

Lande

Kerzivienne, 56340

☎ 297523148

e-mail: contact@campingdelalande.com

web: www.campingdelalande.com

On partially shaded terrain, 0.6km from the beach.

Open: Jun-27 Sep **Site:** 1HEC **For hire:** **Prices:** 14.50 Mobile home hire 320-470 **Facilities:** Play Area **Services:** **Off-site:** S

Loperhet

56340

☎ 297523468 297523468

web: www.camping-loperhet.com

Close to a sandy beach with dunes, pitches of varying shade are available. Leisure facilities include a swimming pool area with a 42 metre flume, and a 9 hectare fishing lake.

dir: *Via D781.*

Open: Apr-Sep **Site:** 6HEC **For hire:** **Facilities:** **Services:** **Leisure:** P **Off-site:** S

PLOUHINEC — MORBIHAN

Moténo

rte du Magouer, 56680

☎ 297367663 297858184

e-mail: info@camping-moteno.com

web: www.camping-le-moteno.com

On slightly sloping ground, subdivided into several fields in a wooded area, 0.8km from the beach.

Open: 2 Apr-25 Sep **Site:** 4HEC **For hire:** **Facilities:** Wi-fi Kids' Club Play Area **Services:** **Leisure:** P **Off-site:** R S

PLOUMANACH — CÔTES-D'ARMOR

Claire Fontaine

Toul ar Lann, Perros-Guirec, 22700

☎ 296230355 296490619

web: www.camping-claire-fontaine.com

Spacious, level site in a rural setting.

dir: *1.2km SW of town centre, 0.8km from Trestraou beach.*

Open: Etr-Sep **Site:** 3HEC **For hire:** **Facilities:** **Services:** **Off-site:** S

Yelloh Village Ranolien

22700

☎ 296916565 296914190

e-mail: info@yellohvillage-ranolien.com

web: www.leranolien.fr

The site is divided into pitches by hedges, with separate sections for caravans.

dir: *0.5km from village.*

GPS: 48.8284, -3.4754

Open: 6 Apr-23 Sep **Site:** 15HEC **For hire:** **Prices:** 17-43 Mobile home hire 273-1389 **Facilities:** Wi-fi (charged) Kids' Club Play Area **Services:** **Leisure:** P **Off-site:** S

PLOZÉVET — FINISTÈRE

Corniche

The Camping and Caravanning Club The Friendly Club

rte de la Corniche, 29710
☎ 298913394
e-mail: infos@campinglacorniche.com
web: www.campinglacorniche.com
Peaceful rural site 1.5km from the sea.

C&CC Report *An absolutely immaculately kept site, with great coast both locally and within easy driving distance. The site is also very well situated for exploring some of lovely Finistère's best historic sites. An all-round favourite for those who like quiet relaxation on site, or getting out and about to lots of places of interest, all within under an hour's drive.*

Open: 3 Apr-2 Oct **Site:** 2HEC **For hire:** **Facilities:** **Services:** **Leisure:** P **Off-site:** L R S

PONTAUBAULT — MANCHE

Vallée de la Sélune

7 rue Mal Leclerc, 50220
☎ 233603900 233603900
e-mail: campselune@wanadoo.fr
web: www.campselune.com
This site is in a quiet village near the River Sélune. Ideal base for exploring the Normandy/Brittany area. 15km from Mont-St-Michel and 8km from Avranches.

dir: *Off N175 onto D43 towards Pontaubault. Site in village.*

GPS: 48.63, -1.3527

Open: Apr-20 Oct **Site:** 1.6HEC **For hire:** **Prices:** 14.40-16 Mobile home hire 150-380 **Facilities:** Wi-fi Play Area **Services:** **Off-site:** R

PONTORSON — MANCHE

Haliotis

chemin des Soupirs, 50170
☎ 233681159 233589536
e-mail: camping.haliotis@wanadoo.fr
web: www.camping-haliotis-mont-saint-michel.com
On the banks of a river, a short distance from Mont-St-Michel. Leisure facilities include a heated swimming pool, sauna and tennis. Cycle paths lead to Mont-St-Michel. Kids' club during July and August.

dir: *Off D976 towards Avranches.*

Open: 16 Mar-11 Nov **Site:** 6HEC **For hire:** **Prices:** 16.80-22.30 **Facilities:** Wi-fi Kids' Club Play Area **Services:** **Leisure:** P **Off-site:** R

PORDIC — CÔTES-D'ARMOR

Madières

rte le Vau Madec, 22590
☎ 296790248
e-mail: campinglesmadieres@wanadoo.fr
web: www.campinglesmadieres.com
A quiet coastal site in a well-shaded position.

dir: *1.5km from village on D786 towards St-Brieuc.*

Open: Apr-Oct **Site:** 2HEC **For hire:** **Prices:** 13-17.50 Mobile home hire 250-570 **Facilities:** Wi-fi Play Area **Services:** **Leisure:** P **Off-site:** S

PORT-EN-BESSIN — CALVADOS

Port'land

14520
☎ 231510706 231517649
e-mail: campingportland@wanadoo.fr
web: www.camping-portland.com
Situated in rural surroundings near Omaha Beach, with an indoor heated swimming pool on site. Kids' club available during July and August.

GPS: 49.3498, -0.7688

Open: Apr-4 Nov **Site:** 8.6HEC **For hire:** **Prices:** 25-40 Mobile home hire 371-1085 **Facilities:** Wi-fi Kids' Club Play Area **Services:** **Leisure:** P **Off-site:** S

PORT-MANECH — FINISTÈRE

St-Nicolas

29920
☎ 298068975 298067461
e-mail: info@campinglesaintnicolas.com
web: www.campinglesaintnicolas.com
Divided into hedge-lined pitches in beautiful surroundings close to the beach.

Open: May-Sep **Site:** 3.5HEC **For hire:** **Facilities:** Play Area **Services:** **Leisure:** P **Off-site:** S

FRANCE

POULDU, LE — FINISTÈRE

Camping Les Embruns

2 rue du Philosophe Alain, 29360
298399107 298399787
e-mail: camping-les-embruns@orange.fr
web: www.camping-les-embruns.com

A pleasant site with good facilities and easy access to the beach. Separate car park for arrivals after 22.00hrs.

GPS: 47.7687, -3.5451

Open: 6 Apr-22 Sep **Site:** 6HEC **For hire:** **Prices:** 10.50-31.50 Mobile home hire 250-820 **Facilities:** Wi-fi (charged) Kids' Club Play Area **Services:** **Leisure:** P **Off-site:** R S

QUETTEHOU — MANCHE

Rivage

75 rue Sainte Marie, 50630
233541376
e-mail: camping.lerivage@wanadoo.fr
web: www.camping-lerivage.fr

Quiet, sheltered site, 400 metres from the sea.

dir: *Via D14.*

GPS: 49.5911, -1.3020

Open: Apr-Sep **Site:** 2HEC **For hire:** **Prices:** 15.50-19.50 Mobile home hire 285-638 **Facilities:** Wi-fi (charged) Play Area **Services:** **Leisure:** P **Off-site:** S

QUIBERON — MORBIHAN

Le Bois d'Amour

87 rue St-Clement, 56170
442204725 442950363
e-mail: info@homair.com
web: www.homair.co.uk

A family site with plenty of recreational facilities close to the area's fine beaches.

Open: 24 Mar-3 Oct **Site:** 4.8HEC **For hire:** **Prices:** 15-40 Mobile home hire 224-994 **Facilities:** Wi-fi (charged) Kids' Club Play Area **Services:** **Leisure:** P **Off-site:** S

QUIMPER — FINISTÈRE

Orangerie de Lanniron

The Camping and Caravanning Club — The Friendly Club

Château de Lanniron,
Chemin de Lanniron, 29336
298906202 298521556
e-mail: camping@lanniron.com
web: www.lanniron.com

Set in the grounds of the former residence of the bishops of Quimper, beside the River Odet and surrounded by tropical vegetation.

C&CC Report *A top quality site in an exceptional setting. The heated aquapark, with its slides, fountains and spa, plus the wide variety of activities, will keep all ages entertained; or you might simply relax in the extensive château grounds, where the rhododendrons in May are absolutely glorious. Quimper, Finistère's pretty 'county town', is reachable by footpath from the site.*

dir: *2.5km from town centre via D34.*

Open: 15 May-15 Sep **Site:** 40HEC **For hire:** **Prices:** 19.80-35.80 Mobile home hire 420-1085 **Facilities:** Wi-fi (charged) Kids' Club Play Area **Services:** **Leisure:** P R

RAGUENÈS-PLAGE — FINISTÈRE

Airotel International Raguenès-Plage

The Camping and Caravanning Club — The Friendly Club

19 rue des Iles, Raguenez, 29920
298068069 298068905
e-mail: info@camping-le-raguenes-plage.com
web: www.camping-le-raguenes-plage.com

Site with asphalt drives, 300 metres from beaches.

C&CC Report *Le Raguenès-Plage is a superbly-located, much-loved, family-run, traditional site. All season round it's a great base for some wonderful places to visit, with its proximity to the beach a huge plus. Families love the pools and waterslides, but the site appeals to anyone seeking relaxation on the coast. The charming artists' town of Pont-Aven is only a short drive away, as is the fortified harbour of Concarneau, while much of west and south Brittany is also easily within a day trip.*

dir: *From Pont-Aven to Nevez, signs to Raguenès.*

Open: Apr-1 Oct **Site:** 7HEC **For hire:** **Prices:** 16.50-32.80 Mobile home hire 280-830 **Facilities:** Wi-fi (charged) Kids' Club Play Area **Services:** **Leisure:** P S

FRANCE

RAVENOVILLE-PLAGE — MANCHE

Le Cormoran

50480

☎ 233413394 🖹 233951608

e-mail: lecormoran@wanadoo.fr

web: www.lecormoran.com

A pleasant family site with well-defined pitches, 20 metres from the sea. Kids' club during July and August. Facilities include indoor and outdoor pools and a goats' enclosure.

dir: *300m from town towards Utah Beach.*

Open: 7 Apr-29 Sep **Site:** 8.5HEC **For hire:** **Prices:** 21-33 Mobile home hire 252-861 **Facilities:** Wi-fi (charged) Kids' Club Play Area **Services:** **Leisure:** P S **Off-site:**

ROCHE-BERNARD, LA — MORBIHAN

CM Patis

3 chemin du Patis, 56130

☎ 299906013 🖹 299908828

e-mail: camping.lrb@gmail.com

On banks of River Vilaine.

dir: *100m from village centre, on the port.*

Open: Apr-15 Oct **Site:** 1HEC **For hire:** **Facilities:** Wi-fi (charged) Play Area **Services:** **Leisure:** R **Off-site:** P

ROCHEFORT-EN-TERRE — MORBIHAN

Moulin Neuf

56220

☎ 297433752 🖹 297433545

A well-equipped site in wooded surroundings.

dir: *Signed from D744 in village.*

Open: May-Sep **Site:** 2.5HEC **Facilities:** **Services:** **Leisure:** P **Off-site:** L R

ROSTRENEN — CÔTES-D'ARMOR

Fleur de Bretagne

Kerandouaron, 22110

☎ 296291545 🖹 296291645

e-mail: contact@fleurdebretagne.com

web: www.fleurdebretagne.com

A spacious site in a picturesque, sheltered valley with modern facilities.

dir: *D764 from Rostrenen, 1.5km towards Pontivy.*

Open: All Year. **Site:** 6HEC **For hire:** **Prices:** 12-16 Mobile home hire 150-250 **Facilities:** Wi-fi Play Area **Services:** **Leisure:** L P **Off-site:**

ST-ALBAN — CÔTES-D'ARMOR

St-Vréguet

St-Vréguet, 22400

☎ 296329759

e-mail: vreguet@aliceadsl.fr

web: www.campingvreguet.fr

A peaceful site in a pleasant park with good sanitary and recreational facilities. Separate car park for arrivals after 23.00hrs.

Open: Jun-Sep **Site:** 1HEC **For hire:** **Prices:** 10-12 Mobile home hire 280 **Facilities:** Wi-fi Play Area **Services:** **Off-site:** P R S

ST-AUBIN-SUR-MER — CALVADOS

CM Mesnil

76740

☎ 235830283

A family site attached to a typical Norman farm.

dir: *2km W on D68.*

Open: Apr-Oct **Site:** 2.3HEC **For hire:** **Facilities:** Wi-fi Play Area **Services:** **Off-site:** S

Yelloh Village Côte de Nacre

17 rue du General Moulton, 14750

☎ 231971445 🖹 231972211

e-mail: camping-cote-de-nacre@wanadoo.fr

web: www.camping-cote-de-nacre.com

A pleasant site with good recreational facilities. Separate car park for arrivals after 22.00hrs.

Open: 30 Mar-23 Sep **Site:** 10HEC **For hire:** **Prices:** 25-44 Mobile home hire 273-1295 **Facilities:** Wi-fi Kids' Club Play Area **Services:** **Leisure:** P **Off-site:** S

ST-BRIEUC — CÔTES-D'ARMOR

Vallées

Parc de Brézillet, 22000

☎ 296940505

e-mail: campingdesvallees@wanadoo.fr

Situated on the edge of the town in a plateau crossed by wooded valleys. Restaurant only open July and August.

Open: All Year. **Site:** 4.8HEC **For hire:** **Facilities:** Play Area **Services:** **Leisure:** R **Off-site:** P S

FRANCE

ST-CAST-LE-GUILDO — CÔTES-D'ARMOR

Château de Galinée

The Camping and Caravanning Club — The Friendly Club

22380
☎ 296411056 🖹 296410372
e-mail: contact@chateaudegalinee.com
web: www.chateaudegalinee.com

A family site with swimming pool complex including waterslides and an indoor pool. Set in a wood incorporating the buildings of an old farm, 3km from the beaches.

C&CC Report *The large pitches and a spacious countryside setting appeal to seekers of peace and quiet, while younger families also love the leisure facilities, with the excellent indoor pool and the bar and terrace adding to everyone's enjoyment in both low and high season. Some of France's most beautiful and spectacular stretches of coastline are only a short drive away – if you don't yet know the stunning Côtes-d'Armor then a visit is long overdue.*

dir: *1km from CD786. Signed.*

Open: 12 May-5 Sep **Site:** 14HEC **For hire:** **Prices:** 16.50-33.10 Mobile home hire 280-735 **Facilities:** Wi-fi (charged) Kids' Club **Services:** **Leisure:** P **Off-site:** L S

ST-COULOMB — ILLE-ET-VILAINE

Camping des Chevrets

La Guimorais, 35350
☎ 299890190 🖹 299890116
e-mail: campingdeschevrets@wanadoo.fr
web: www.campingdeschevrets.fr

Tranquil site with direct access to a sandy beach, pitches are individually marked. Events take place throughout the season.

GPS: 48.6903, -1.9417

Open: 7 Apr-1 Nov **Site:** 21HEC **For hire:** **Prices:** 15-22 **Facilities:** Wi-fi (charged) Play Area **Services:** **Leisure:** S

ST-EFFLAM — CÔTES-D'ARMOR

CM

rue de Lan-Carré, 22310
☎ 296356215
e-mail: campingmunicipalplestin@wanadoo.fr
web: www.camping-municipal-bretagne.com

On a level meadow with well-defined pitches, 100 metres from a magnificent beach.

Open: Apr-Sep **Site:** 4HEC **For hire:** **Prices:** 9.99-11.75 Mobile home hire 194-439 **Facilities:** Wi-fi Kids' Club Play Area **Services:** **Leisure:** P **Off-site:** S

ST-GERMAIN-SUR-AY — MANCHE

Aux Grands Espaces

50430
☎ 233071014 🖹 233072259
web: www.auxgrandespaces.com

On slightly sloping ground among dunes, 0.5km from the sea. Children's play area.

dir: *Off D650 W of town onto D306 signed Plage.*

Open: May-15 Sep **Site:** 15HEC **For hire:** **Prices:** 22.40 Mobile home hire 300-690 **Facilities:** **Services:** **Leisure:** P **Off-site:** S

ST-GILDAS-DE-RHUYS — MORBIHAN

Menhir

rte de Port Crouesty, 56730
☎ 297452288
e-mail: campingmenhir@aol.com
web: www.camping-bretagnesud.com

A family site with good facilities, 1km from the beach.

dir: *3.5km N.*

Open: May-5 Sep **Site:** 3HEC **For hire:** **Facilities:** Wi-fi Play Area **Services:** **Leisure:** P **Off-site:** S

ST-JOUAN-DES-GUÉRÊTS — ILLE-ET-VILAINE

P'tit Bois

The Camping and Caravanning Club — The Friendly Club

La Chalandouze, 35430
☎ 299211430 🖹 299817414
e-mail: camping.ptitbois@wanadoo.fr
web: www.ptitbois.com

A pleasant family site in quiet wooded surroundings. Pitches are spacious and there are plenty of facilities and activities, including a kids' club in July and August. Located at the centre of the Gulf of St Malo and 5km from the sea and fine sandy beaches; nearby are the beaches of the Rance River.

C&CC Report *Plants and flowering shrubs border the pitches and roadways in immaculately kept grounds, while many facilities are open early in the season on this high quality, family-run site that boasts an excellent pool complex. Access to St Malo is easy and Dinan, Dinard and Rennes are great for days out, while the nearby coast and beaches delight all ages. Be sure to fit in lunch at Cancale too, and watch the oyster farmers in action.*

dir: *Via N137 exit St-Jouan-des-Guérêts, take D4.*

Open: 6 Apr-15 Sep **Site:** 6HEC **For hire:** **Prices:** 18.50-36.50 Mobile home hire 280-1008 **Facilities:** Wi-fi Kids' Club Play Area **Services:** **Leisure:** P **Off-site:** R

see advert on opposite page

ST-LÉGER-DU-BOURG-DENIS SEINE-MARITIME

Aubette

23 rue Vert Buisson, 76160

☎ 235084769 235084769

Set in a wooded valley, 3km East of Rouen.

Open: All Year. **Site:** 0.8HEC **Prices:** 9.10 **Facilities:** **Services:** **Off-site:** P R

ST-LUNAIRE ILLE-ET-VILAINE

Longchamp

bld de St-Cast, 35800

☎ 299463398 299460271

web: www.camping-longchamp.com

A beautiful wooded setting, 100 metres from the sea on the Emerald coast, with a good range of facilities.

dir: *Off D786 towards St-Briac at end of village, site on left.*

Open: Jun-10 Sep **Site:** 5HEC **Facilities:** Play Area **Services:** **Off-site:** S

Touesse

171 rue Ville Géhan, 35800

☎ 299466113 299160258

e-mail: camping.la.touesse@wanadoo.fr

web: www.campinglatouesse.com

A well-equipped family site, 300 metres from the beach.

dir: *2km E via D786.*

Open: Apr-Sep **Site:** 2.8HEC **For hire:** **Prices:** 15-22 Mobile home hire 196-686 **Facilities:** Wi-fi (charged) Play Area **Services:** **Off-site:** P S

ST-MALO ILLE-ET-VILAINE

CM le Nicet

av de la Varde Rotheneuf, 35400

☎ 299402632 299219262

e-mail: camping@ville-saint-malo.fr

Site 100 metres from the beach, access via stairs. Water sports and other activities available.

Open: Jul-Aug **Site:** 2.9HEC **Prices:** 14-20 **Facilities:** **Services:** **Leisure:** S **Off-site:**

Domaine de la Ville Huchet

rte de la Passagère, 35400

☎ 299811183 299815189

e-mail: info@lavillehuchet.com

web: www.lavillehuchet.com

A family campsite set around an old manor house. Leisure facilities include two heated swimming pools with slides, crazy golf and bike hire. Kids' club available in high season.

dir: *5km S via N137.*

GPS: 48.6153, -1.9864

Open: 6 Apr-23 Sep **Site:** 6.3HEC **For hire:** **Prices:** 22.40-35.10 Mobile home hire 238-630 **Facilities:** Wi-fi Kids' Club Play Area **Services:** **Leisure:** P **Off-site:** R S

FRANCE

ST-MARCAN ILLE-ET-VILAINE

Balcon de la Baie

35120

☎ 299802295

web: www.lebalcondelabaie.com

A quiet, family site set in a beautiful location overlooking the bay of Mont-St-Michel.

dir: *10km NW of Pontorson on D797.*

Open: Apr-Oct **Site:** 2.7HEC **For hire:** **Facilities:** Play Area **Services:** **Leisure:** P **Off-site:**

ST-MARTIN-DES-BESACES CALVADOS

Camping le Puits

14350

☎ 231678002

e-mail: enquiries@lepuits.com

web: www.lepuits.com

A small family-run site surrounded by a pleasant garden and lush fields.

dir: *A84 junct 41 for St Martin-des-Besaces.*

GPS: 49.0080, -0.86

Open: Mar-Oct **Site:** 3.6HEC **Prices:** 19 **Facilities:** Wi-fi (charged) Play Area **Services:** **Off-site:**

ST-MARTIN-EN-CAMPAGNE SEINE-MARITIME

Goélands

rue des Grèbes, Saint Martin Plage, 76370

☎ 235838290 235832179

e-mail: domainelesgoelands@orange.fr

web: www.lesdomaines.org

A pleasant, comfortable campsite ideal for those who love the sea. Kids' club available in July and August.

dir: *NE of Dieppe, 2km from D925.*

Open: Mar-mid Nov **Site:** 4.5HEC **For hire:** **Facilities:** Wi-fi (charged) Kids' Club Play Area **Services:** **Off-site:** P S

ST-PAIR-SUR-MER MANCHE

Camping la Mariennée

553 rte du Chesnay, 50380

☎ 233906005 233906005

e-mail: lamariennee@wanadoo.fr

web: www.camping-lamariennee.com

Set in the grounds of an old farm, 2km from the sea.

dir: *2km S of town on D21.*

Open: Apr-Sep **Site:** 1.2HEC **For hire:** **Prices:** 13.52 Mobile home hire 450 **Facilities:** **Services:** **Off-site:** P S

Ecutot

50380

☎ 233502629 233506494

e-mail: camping.ecutot@wanadoo.fr

web: www.ecutot.com

Set in an orchard, 1km from the sea.

dir: *On main road between Granville & Avranches.*

GPS: 48.8169, -1.5511

Open: Jun-15 Sep **Site:** 5HEC **For hire:** **Facilities:** **Services:** **Leisure:** P **Off-site:** S

Lez-Eaux

St-Aubin-des-Preaux, 50380

☎ 233516609 233519202

e-mail: bonjour@lez-eaux.com

web: www.lez-eaux.com

Quiet site situated in grounds of a château. Facilities include a bank, TV and reading room and swimming pools with waterslides. On-site fishing and a kids' club is available in July and August.

dir: *7km SE via D973 rte d'Avranches.*

Open: 30 Mar-17 Sep **Site:** 12HEC **For hire:** **Prices:** 21-49 Mobile home hire 462-886 **Facilities:** Wi-fi (charged) Kids' Club Play Area **Services:** **Leisure:** P **Off-site:** S

ST-PIERRE-DU-VAUVRAY EURE

St-Pierre

1 rue du Château, 27430

☎ 232610155

e-mail: eliane-darcissac@wanadoo.fr

web: www.lecampingdesaintpierre.com

Wooded surroundings with pitches divided by hedges, 50 metres from the River Seine.

dir: *Via A13/N15.*

Open: Mar-Oct **Site:** 3HEC **Prices:** 13.80-15 **Facilities:** **Services:** **Leisure:** P **Off-site:** R

FRANCE

ST-QUAY-PORTRIEUX CÔTES-D'ARMOR

Bellevue

68 bld du Littoral, 22410
296704184 269705546
e-mail: campingbellevue22@orange.fr
web: www.campingbellevue.net

A terraced site adjacent to the sea with numbered pitches.

dir: *0.8km from town centre off D786.*

Open: 28 Apr-16 Sep **Site:** 4HEC **For hire:**
Prices: 14.80-19.20 Mobile home hire 270-590 **Facilities:** Wi-fi Play Area **Services:** **Leisure:** P S **Off-site:**

ST-VAAST-LA-HOUGUE MANCHE

Gallouette

rue de la Gallouette, 50550
233542057 233541671
e-mail: contact@camping-lagallouette.fr
web: www.camping-lagallouette.fr

A well-equipped site, 300 metres from the town centre and with direct access to the beach.

dir: *N13 towards Cherbourg, exit Montebourg, towards Quettehou then St Vaast.*

GPS: 49.5844, -1.2681

Open: Apr-Sep **Site:** 3.5HEC **For hire:**
Prices: 16.20-23.50 **Facilities:** Wi-fi (charged) Kids' Club Play Area **Services:** **Leisure:** P **Off-site:** S

ST-YVI FINISTÈRE

Village Center le Bois de Pleuven

rte de St-Yvi, 29140
499572121 467516389
e-mail: contact@village-center.com
web: www.village-center.com/bretagne/camping-mer-bois-pleuven.php

A peaceful site set in a forest between Quimper and Concarneau.

dir: *D765 towards Rosporden, last site before St-Yvi.*

GPS: 47.9504, -3.9705

Open: 24 Jun-4 Sep **Site:** 17HEC **For hire:**
Facilities: Wi-fi (charged) Kids' Club Play Area
Services: **Leisure:** P **Off-site:** S

STE-MARIE-DU-MONT MANCHE

Utah Beach

La Madeleine, 50480
233715369 233710711
e-mail: utah.beach@wanadoo.fr
web: www.camping-utahbeach.com

On a level meadow 100 metres from the beach.

dir: *6km NE via D913 & D421.*

Open: Apr-Sep **Site:** 5.5HEC **For hire:**
Prices: 17.20-23.50 Mobile home hire 370-770 **Facilities:** Wi-fi Play Area **Services:** **Leisure:** P S

STE-MARINE FINISTÈRE

Hellès

55 rue du Petit Bourg, 29120
298563146
e-mail: contact@le-helles.com
web: www.le-helles.com

Family site close to the beach and village of Ste Marine.

dir: *400m from beach.*

Open: May-15 Sep **Site:** 3HEC **For hire:**
Prices: 15.80-21.50 Mobile home hire 225-566 **Facilities:** Wi-fi **Services:** **Leisure:** P **Off-site:** S

SARZEAU MORBIHAN

Bohat

The Camping and Caravanning Club The Friendly Club

56730
297417868 297417097
e-mail: contact@domainelebohat.com
web: www.camping-sarzeau.com

Spacious pitches built around an old farm with extensive leisure facilities including heated swimming pools, football and badminton.

C&CC Report *A very pretty site, ideal for families or couples who enjoy traditional sites. Loads of space for children to play safely, with great new play areas throughout the site. A lovely part of Brittany, with cycle routes and boat trips to take you around the Morbihan Gulf, plus a foot and cycle path route to Sarzeau village via a subway under the main by-pass.*

dir: *Bypass Sarzeau, keeping on D780, following signs to Arzon. Turn left (S) at site sign after 2km, site 300m on right.*

Open: Apr-Nov **Site:** **Facilities:** **Services:**
Leisure: P

FRANCE

Ferme de Lann Hoedic

rte du Roaliguen, rue Jean de la Fontaine, 56370
☎ 297480173
e-mail: contact@camping-lannhoedic.fr
web: www.camping-lannhoedic.fr

Quiet site 0.8km from a sheltered beach, accessible by foot or bike by a forest path. Pitches in sunny or shady locations, some surrounded by landscaped hedges.

dir: *From Vannes exit for Sarzeau, continue towards Arzon, left at 1st rdbt by Super U, 2km left for Lann Hoedic.*

GPS: 47.5075, -2.7611

Open: Apr-Oct **Site:** 3.6HEC **For hire:** **Prices:** 14.50-18 Mobile home hire 240-650 **Facilities:** Wi-fi Play Area **Services:** **Off-site:** P S

Trest

rte de la Plage du Roaliguen, 56370
☎ 297417960 297413621
web: www.an-trest.com

A family site with good facilities, 0.8km from Roaliguen beach.

dir: *2.5km S.*

Open: Jun-14 Sep **Site:** 5HEC **For hire:** **Facilities:** **Services:** **Leisure:** P **Off-site:** S

SUBLIGNY — MANCHE

Grand Chemin

50870
☎ 233513096

Small site in a rural setting with well-defined pitches within easy reach of the village.

dir: *N175 towards Avranches, onto D39 & signed.*

Open: All Year. **Site:** 2HEC **Facilities:** **Services:**

SURRAIN — CALVADOS

Camping la Roseraie d'Omaha

14170
☎ 231211771 231510220
e-mail: camping-laroseraie@orange.fr
web: www.camping-calvados-normandie.fr

Close to the Normandy landing beaches, relaxing site with indoor heated swimming pool and table tennis. Cycles can be hired.

Open: Apr-Sep **Site:** 2.6HEC **For hire:** **Prices:** 15.90-17.90 Mobile home hire 386-685 **Facilities:** Wi-fi (charged) Play Area **Services:** **Leisure:** P **Off-site:** S

TELGRUC-SUR-MER — FINISTÈRE

Panoramic

Le Penquer, 130 rte de la Plage, 29560
☎ 298277841 298273610
e-mail: info@camping-panoramic.com
web: www.camping-panoramic.com

Quiet terraced site, with views across a wide sandy beach and Douarnenez Bay, offering large, private pitches.

dir: *W on D887, S onto D208.*

Open: May-15 Sep **Site:** 4HEC **For hire:** **Prices:** 16-22 Mobile home hire 250-680 **Facilities:** Wi-fi Play Area **Services:** **Leisure:** P **Off-site:** S

THEIX — MORBIHAN

Rhuys

Le Poteau Rouge, rue Duguay Trouin, 56450
☎ 297541477
e-mail: campingderhuys@wanadoo.fr

Site directly on the sea with modern facilities.

dir: *3.5km NW via N165.*

Open: 10 Apr-15 Oct **Site:** 2HEC **For hire:** **Facilities:** Wi-fi Play Area **Services:** **Leisure:** P **Off-site:**

THURY-HARCOURT — CALVADOS

Vallée du Traspy

rue du Pont Benôit, 14220
☎ 231796180 231796180
web: www.campingtraspy.com

Level meadow site near a small reservoir, 250 metres from Centre Aquatique de la Suisse Normande.

Open: 15 Apr-Sep **Site:** 1.5HEC **For hire:** **Facilities:** **Services:** **Leisure:** L P R **Off-site:**

FRANCE

TINTÉNIAC — ILLE-ET-VILAINE

Peupliers

Manoir de la Besnelais, 35190
299454975
e-mail: camping.les.peupliers@wanadoo.fr
web: www.les-peupliers-camping.fr

A peaceful wooded site in the heart of Brittany with good facilities.

dir: *1km SE via N137.*

GPS: 48.3092, -1.8217

Open: Apr-Sep **Site:** 4.5HEC **For hire:** **Prices:** 18.20-22.70 Mobile home hire 245-590 **Facilities:** Wi-fi (charged) Play Area **Services:** **Leisure:** P **Off-site:**

TORIGNI-SUR-VIRE — MANCHE

Camping du Lac des Charmilles

rte de Vire, 50160
233569174 233559113
e-mail: contact@camping-lacdescharmilles.com
web: www.camping-lacdescharmilles.com

A family-friendly site on the banks of a lake. Facilities include a heated swimming pool, bike rental and a multi-sports area.

dir: *A84 exit 40.*

GPS: 49.0283, -0.9719

Open: Apr-Sep **Site:** 4HEC **For hire:** **Prices:** 14-20.90 Mobile home hire 384-609 **Facilities:** Wi-fi (charged) Play Area **Services:** **Leisure:** P **Off-site:**

TOURLAVILLE — MANCHE

Espace Loisirs de Collignon

50110
233201688 233448171
e-mail: camping-collignon@wanadoo.fr
web: www.mairie-tourlaville.fr

A pleasant site with good facilities, 1km from town centre.

Open: May-Sep **Site:** 2HEC **For hire:** **Facilities:** **Services:** **Leisure:** S **Off-site:** P

TOURNIÈRES — CALVADOS

Picard Holidays

14330
231228244
e-mail: paulpalmer@orange.fr
web: www.normandycampsite.com

A quiet site between Cherbourg and Caen, with pleasant sheltered pitches.

dir: *Via N13 & D15/D5.*

Open: All Year. **Site:** 2HEC **For hire:** **Prices:** 19.50 Mobile home hire 450-585 **Facilities:** Wi-fi Play Area **Services:** **Leisure:** L P **Off-site:** R

TRÉBEURDEN — CÔTES-D'ARMOR

Armor-Loisirs

rue de Kernévez-Pors-Mabo, 22560
296235231
e-mail: info@armorloisirs.com
web: www.armorloisirs.com

Modern site with individual pitches surrounded by hedges, including hard standings for caravans. Restaurant open in July and August.

dir: *0.5km S of Kernévez road.*

Open: Apr-Sep **Site:** 2.2HEC **For hire:** **Prices:** 12-22 Mobile home hire 220 **Facilities:** Wi-fi Play Area **Services:** **Leisure:** P **Off-site:** R S

TRÉDREZ-LOCQUÉMEAU — CÔTES-D'ARMOR

Capucines

Kervourdon, 22300
296357228 296357898
e-mail: les.capucines@wanadoo.fr
web: www.lescapucines.fr

A peaceful setting near the beach with a large variety of facilities, including a heated and covered swimming pool.

dir: *On D786 Lannion-Morlaix road.*

Open: 2 Apr-23 Sep **Site:** 4HEC **For hire:** **Prices:** 15.10-22.20 Mobile home hire 260-770 **Facilities:** Wi-fi Play Area **Services:** **Leisure:** P **Off-site:** S

FRANCE

TRÉGUNC — FINISTÈRE

Pommeraie

St-Philibert, 29910

☎ 298500273

e-mail: campinglapommeraie@orange.fr

web: www.campingdelapommeraie.com

A well-equipped site with good facilities for children, 1km from the beach.

dir: *S via D1.*

Open: Apr-15 Oct **Site:** 7HEC **For hire:** **Prices:** 19-27 Mobile home hire 150-885 **Facilities:** Wi-fi (charged) Kids' Club Play Area **Services:** **Leisure:** P **Off-site:** R S

TRÉLÉVERN — CÔTES-D'ARMOR

Port l'Epine

10 Venelle de Pors-Garo, 22660

☎ 296237194 296237783

e-mail: camping-de-port-lepine@wanadoo.fr

Well-shaded site directly by the sea.

Open: 8 May-25 Sep **Site:** 3HEC **For hire:** **Facilities:** **Services:** **Leisure:** P S

TRÉPORT, LE — SEINE-MARITIME

CM les Boucaniers

rue Mendes-France, 76470

☎ 235863547 235865582

e-mail: camping@ville-le-treport.fr

web: www.ville-le-treport.fr

Well-kept site on flat meadow on eastern edge of village. Sports and games nearby. Kids' club available in July and August.

Open: Apr-Sep **Site:** 5.5HEC **For hire:** **Facilities:** Wi-fi (charged) Kids' Club Play Area **Services:** **Off-site:** P R S

Parc International du Golf

102 rte de Dieppe, 76470

☎ 227280150 227280151

web: www.campings-treport.com

Set in a park on the cliffs in a wooded retreat. This comfortable and quiet area, is near the city centre, the port and the beach by the funicular.

dir: *1km W on D940.*

GPS: 50.0516, 1.3677

Open: Apr-20 Sep **Site:** 5HEC **Prices:** 15-16.40 **Facilities:** **Services:** **Off-site:** P S

TRÉVOU-TRÉGUIGNEC — CÔTES-D'ARMOR

Mât

38 rue de Trestel, 22660

☎ 296237152

web: www.campinglemat.com

A family site on level ground, 50 metres from the beach.

dir: *Via D38.*

Open: Apr-Sep **Site:** 1.6HEC **For hire:** **Facilities:** **Services:** **Leisure:** P **Off-site:** L S

TRINITÉ-SUR-MER, LA — MORBIHAN

Baie

Plage de Kervillen, 56470

☎ 297557342 276013337

e-mail: contact@campingdelabaie.com

web: www.campingdelabaie.com

Several strips of land divided by tall trees on the edge of a fine sandy beach. Kids' club available in July and August.

dir: *Signed towards Kerbihan & Plage de Kervillen.*

Open: 12 May-16 Sep **Site:** 2.4HEC **For hire:** **Prices:** 17.70-42.90 Mobile home hire 245-798 **Facilities:** Wi-fi (charged) Kids' Club Play Area **Services:** **Leisure:** P **Off-site:** S

Kervilor

rte du Latz, 56470

☎ 297557675 297558726

e-mail: camping.kevilor@wanadoo.fr

web: www.camping-kervilor.com

Large site with over 250 pitches in a pleasant wooded location 1.5km from the port. Plenty of recreational facilities including indoor and outdoor pools with slides, crazy golf, billiards and tennis.

dir: *1.6km N.*

Open: Apr-28 Sep **Site:** 5HEC **For hire:** **Prices:** 16-29.25 Mobile home hire 265-920 **Facilities:** Wi-fi Kids' Club Play Area **Services:** **Leisure:** P **Off-site:** S

FRANCE

Plage

Plage de Kervillen, 56470
297557328 276013305
e-mail: contact@camping-plage.com
web: www.camping-plage.com

A family site divided into pitches behind dunes, with direct access to the beach. Kids' club during July and August.

C&CC Report *You simply cannot beat the location of this classic beachside site just outside the fishing port of La Trinité-sur-Mer, one of France's premier yachting centres. Access to some of the pitches can be a bit tight, but this is more than compensated for by the direct access to the safe and sandy beach. A short walk along the beach takes you to the site shop, bar and restaurant where you can dine on the terrace and enjoy views over Quiberon bay.*

dir: *1km S towards Carnac-Plage.*

GPS: 47.5756, -3.0290

Open: 5 May-16 Sep **Site:** 3HEC **For hire:** **Prices:** 18-37.70 Mobile home hire 255-850 **Facilities:** Wi-fi (charged) Kids' Club Play Area **Services:** **Leisure:** P S **Off-site:**

VEULES-LES-ROSES SEINE-MARITIME

Camping Les Mouettes

76980
235976198
e-mail: camping-les-mouettes@wanadoo.fr
web: www.camping-lesmouettes-normandie.com

Located close to the beach and with leisure facilities and entertainment in high season.

C&CC Report *Camping Les Mouettes is a newly redeveloped site located in a very pretty part of Haute-Normandie, just over a kilometre away from the charming village of Veules-les-Roses, where you'll find the smallest river in France. Set on a hill, 300 metres from a pebble beach, this site is great for a stopover, short stay or longer holiday, with Normandy's coastal highlights all within easy reach and Dieppe just 25 kilometres drive away.*

dir: *Signed from D925 on outskirts of town.*

GPS: 49.8759, 0.8032

Open: Apr-4 Sep **Site:** 3.5HEC **Facilities:** Wi-fi Play Area **Services:** **Leisure:** P

VILLEDIEU-LES-POÊLES MANCHE

Camping des Chevaliers

2 impasse du Pré de la Rose, 50800
233610244 233494993
e-mail: contact@camping-deschevaliers.com
web: www.camping-deschevaliers.com

In an ideal location for exploring the surrounding tourist attractions, on-site leisure facilities include a heated swimming pool and cycle rental.

dir: *A84 exit 37/38.*

GPS: 48.8364, -1.2169

Open: Apr-Sep **Site:** 2HEC **For hire:** **Prices:** 14-21.90 Mobile home hire 384-609 **Facilities:** Wi-fi Play Area **Services:** **Leisure:** P **Off-site:**

PARIS/NORTH

ACY-EN-MULTIEN OISE

Ancien Moulin

60620
344872128 344872128
e-mail: ccdf_acy@cegetel.net
web: www.campingclub.asso.fr

Situated beside a river and a small lake with good sports facilities.

Open: All Year. **Site:** 5HEC **For hire:** **Facilities:** **Services:** **Leisure:** L R **Off-site:**

AMIENS SOMME

Parc des Cygnes

111 avenue des Cygnes, 80080
322432928 322435942
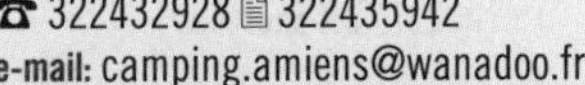
e-mail: camping.amiens@wanadoo.fr
web: www.parcdescygnes.com

A well maintained site on the outskirts of Amiens. Pitches are grassy and flat in varying sizes and some are specially designed for motor homes.

C&CC Report *A modern, good quality city site, convenient for the A16 motorway, the cathedral city of Amiens and exploring Picardy. A warm welcome is extended and there's plenty of information on hand about Amiens and its cathedral light show. Further afield, the First World War museums in Péronne and Albert and the moving Somme memorials are all highly recommended, while Paris is only one hour by train.*

dir: *A16 exit 20 Amiens Nord.*

Open: Apr-14 Oct **Site:** 3.2HEC **For hire:** **Facilities:** Wi-fi (charged) **Services:** **Off-site:** R

FRANCE

ARDRES — PAS-DE-CALAIS

St-Louis

223 rue Leulène, Autingues, 62610

☎ 321354683

e-mail: domirine@aol.com

web: www.campingstlouis.com

A well-equipped site in pleasant wooded surroundings.

dir: *Off N43 1km SE of Ardres onto D224 & signed.*

Open: Apr-Oct **Site:** 1.7HEC **Facilities:** Wi-fi Play Area **Services:** **Off-site:** L

BERCK-SUR-MER — PAS-DE-CALAIS

Orée du Bois

chemin Blanc 251, Rang-du-Fliers, 62180

☎ 321842851 321842856

e-mail: oree.du.bois@wanadoo.fr

web: www.loreedubois.com

A modern site in wooded surroundings with good sports facilities.

dir: *2km NE.*

Open: Apr-Oct **Site:** 18.5HEC **For hire:** **Facilities:** **Services:** **Off-site:**

BERNY-RIVIÈRE — AISNE

Croix du Vieux Pont

2290

☎ 323555002 323550513

e-mail: lacroixduvieuxpont@wanadoo.fr

web: www.la-croix-du-vieux-pont.com

Wooded surroundings beside the River Aisne with good facilities.

dir: *N of N31. Over River Aisne, site 0.5km E of Vic-sur-Aisne on D91.*

Open: All Year. **Site:** 34HEC **For hire:** **Facilities:** Wi-fi (charged) **Services:** **Leisure:** P **Off-site:**

BERTANGLES — SOMME

Camping du Château

rue du Château, 80260

☎ 360656836

e-mail: camping@chateaubertangles.com

web: www.chateaubertangles.com

Site in an old orchard of a château. ten kilometres north of Amiens and ideally located for visiting the battlefields of the Somme.

dir: *Signed off Amiens-Doullens road.*

GPS: 49.9736, 2.3033

Open: 20 Apr-10 Sep **Site:** 0.8HEC **Prices:** 14.80 **Facilities:** Play Area **Services:** **Off-site:**

BOIRY-NOTRE-DAME — PAS-DE-CALAIS

Paille Haute

145 rue de Sailly, 62156

☎ 321481540 321220724

e-mail: lapaillehaute@wanadoo.fr

web: www.la-paille-haute.com

On a level meadow with a variety of recreational facilities.

dir: *A1 exit 15 towards Cambrai, site on D34. Or A26 exit 8 towards Arras.*

Open: Apr-Oct **Site:** 4.9HEC **For hire:** **Prices:** 17-20 **Facilities:** Wi-fi Play Area **Services:** **Leisure:** P **Off-site:**

see advert on this page

BOUBERS-SUR-CANCHE — PAS-DE-CALAIS

Petit St Jean

27 rue de Frévent, 62270

☎ 321048520 321048520

e-mail: arielle.triart@wanadoo.fr

web: www.campingboubers.com

A peaceful rural setting within easy reach of the village.

dir: *E via D340 towards Frévent.*

Open: Apr-15 Oct **Site:** 1HEC **For hire:** **Facilities:** **Services:** **Off-site:** P R

BOULANCOURT — SEINE-ET-MARNE

Ile de Boulancourt

6 allée des Marronniers, 77760
164241338 164241043
e-mail: camping-ile-de-boulancourt@wanadoo.fr
web: www.camping-iledeboulancourt.com

A peaceful site shaded by mature trees in a convenient location in the Essonne Valley.

dir: *A6 exit 14 towards Malesherbes.*

GPS: 48.2558, 2.435

Open: All Year. **Site:** 5HEC **For hire:** **Prices:** 13-13.70 Mobile home hire 156-305 **Facilities:** Wi-fi (charged) Play Area **Services:** **Off-site:** P R

BRAY-DUNES — NORD

Perroquet-Plage

59123
328583737 328583701
e-mail: contact@campingleperroquet.com
web: www.campingleperroquet.com

Situated among dunes with direct access to the beach. A site with many activities and the opportunity to relax.

dir: *3km NE towards La Panne.*

Open: Apr-Sep **Site:** 28HEC **For hire:** **Prices:** 13.20-19.70 **Facilities:** Wi-fi Kids' Club Play Area **Services:** **Leisure:** S **Off-site:** P

CHARLY-SUR-MARNE — AISNE

Camping des Illettes

rte de Pavant, 02310
323821211 323821399
e-mail: mairie.charly@wanadoo.fr
web: www.charly-sur-marne.fr

Five minutes walk from the town centre, small site with some facilities for children.

GPS: 48.9735, 3.2820

Open: Apr-Sep **Site:** 1HEC **Prices:** 12-14.50 **Facilities:** Play Area **Services:** **Off-site:**

CONDETTE — PAS-DE-CALAIS

Caravaning du Château

21 rue Nouvelle, 62360
321875959 321875959
e-mail: campingduchateau@libertysurf.fr
web: camping-caravaning-du-chateau.com

Pleasant parkland bordered by a forest, 0.5km from the town centre. Separate car park for arrivals after 23.00hrs.

dir: *D940 towards Hardelot.*

GPS: 50.6464, 1.6253

Open: Apr-30 Oct **Site:** 1.2HEC **For hire:** **Prices:** 15.70-21.30 Mobile home hire 400-625 **Facilities:** Wi-fi (charged) Kids' Club Play Area **Services:** **Off-site:** L S

COUDEKERQUE — NORD

Bois des Forts

59280
328610441

Family site with good facilities close to village.

dir: *0.7km NW on D72.*

Open: All Year. **Site:** 4HEC **For hire:** **Prices:** 13.70 Mobile home hire 250 **Facilities:** Play Area **Services:** **Off-site:** P R

CRÉVECOEUR-EN-BRIE — SEINE-ET-MARNE

Des 4 Vents

The Camping and Caravanning Club The Friendly Club

rue de Beauregard, 77610
164074111 164074507
e-mail: f.george@free.fr
web: www.caravaning-4vents.fr

Well-kept family-run site in an excellent location.

C&CC Report *With the George family's welcome, the lovingly tended grounds and a peaceful location in easy striking distance of Disneyland® Resort Paris, Parc Astérix and Paris itself, this is an understandably popular site. Nearby medieval Provins is well worth a visit, with fabulous re-enactments of battles of the Middle Ages, while the châteaux at Vaux-le-Vicomte, Fontainebleau and Versailles are some of France's finest. And if all that isn't enough excitement, a superb big cats' safari park is only five minutes drive away.*

dir: *A4 exit 13 in direction Provins D231.*

GPS: 48.7506, 2.8971

Open: 15 Mar-1 Nov **Site:** 10HEC **For hire:** **Prices:** 28 **Facilities:** Wi-fi Play Area **Services:** **Leisure:** P **Off-site:**

FRANCE

CROTOY, LE — SOMME

Camping le Ridin

lieu dit Mayocq, 80550
322270322 322277076
e-mail: leridin@baiedesommepleinair.com
web: www.campingleridin.com

Situated in the heart of the Somme Bay, conveniently located for Paris and Lille. Kids' club available in July and August.

dir: *From Calais take A16 exit 23 towards Le Crotoy. At rdbt straight ahead, then 2nd right.*

GPS: 50.2391, 1.6318

Open: 31 Mar-6 Nov **Site:** 4.5HEC **For hire:** **Prices:** 17.20-22.70 Mobile home hire 260-518 **Facilities:** Wi-fi (charged) Kids' Club Play Area **Services:** **Leisure:** P **Off-site:** S

Flower Camping les Aubépines

800 rue de la Maye, St Firmin, 80550
322270134 322271366
e-mail: lesaubepines@baiedesommepleinair.com
web: www.camping-lesaubepines.com

Peaceful site located in the heart of the Somme Bay. The nearest beach, 1km away, is part of a nature reserve. There are cycle paths to Crotoy. Kids' club available 15 July to 15 August.

dir: *D940 from Abbeville, follow signs for Le Crotoy at 1st rdbt straight over, 2nd rdbt turn right then 1st left.*

GPS: 50.2494, 1.6115

Open: Apr-5 Nov **Site:** 4HEC **For hire:** **Prices:** 16-29.50 Mobile home hire 250-721 **Facilities:** Wi-fi (charged) Kids' Club Play Area **Services:** **Leisure:** P **Off-site:** S

FRANCE

DUNKERQUE (DUNKIRK) — NORD

Licorne

1005 bld de l'Europe, 59240
328692668 328695621
e-mail: contact@campingdelalicorne.com
web: www.campingdelalicorne.com

A quiet site not far from Dunkerque. There is daily entertainment in July and August.

GPS: 51.0519, 2.4204

Open: Apr-Nov **Site:** 10HEC **Prices:** 17.70-21.95 **Facilities:** Wi-fi Play Area **Services:** **Off-site:** P S

ÉPERLECQUES — PAS-DE-CALAIS

Château du Gandspette

62910
321934393 321957498
e-mail: contact@chateau-gandspette.com
web: www.chateau-gandspette.com

A peaceful site, surrounded by woodland.

dir: *11.5km NW on D943 & D207.*

GPS: 50.8189, 2.1775

Open: Apr-Sep **Site:** 11HEC **For hire:** **Prices:** 14-24 Mobile home hire 340-595 **Facilities:** Wi-fi (charged) Play Area **Services:** **Leisure:** P **Off-site:**

EQUIHEN-PLAGE — PAS-DE-CALAIS

CM la Falaise

rue C-Cazin, 62224
321312261 321805401
e-mail: camping.equihen.plage@orange.fr
web: www.camping-equihen-plage.fr

Between Boulogne and Le Touquet.

Open: Apr-Oct **Site:** 8HEC **For hire:** **Facilities:** Play Area **Services:** **Off-site:** S

FELLERIES — NORD

CM La Boissellerie

rue de la Place, 59740
327590650 327590288
e-mail: mairie.felleries@wanadoo.fr

Shaded site.

dir: *Take RN2 southbound.*

GPS: 50.1431, 4.0286

Open: 15 Apr-Sep **Site:** 1HEC **Prices:** 15 **Facilities:** **Off-site:** L P R

FERTÉ-SOUS-JOUARRE, LA — SEINE-ET-MARNE

Bondons

47/49 rue des Bondons, 077260
160220098 160229701
e-mail: castel@chateaudesbondons.com
web: www.caravaningdesbondons.com

Set in a beautiful wooded park. Reserved for caravans.

dir: *2km NE via D402 & D70.*

GPS: 48.9478, 3.1483

Open: All Year. **Site:** 28HEC **Prices:** 27 **Facilities:** Play Area **Services:** **Off-site:** P R

FEUILLÈRES SOMME

Camping du Château et de l'Oseraie

10 rue du Château, 80200

322831759 322830414

e-mail: jsg-bred@wanadoo.fr

web: www.camping-chateau-oseraie.com

Located in the historical surrounding of the Somme region, pitches are shaded. Leisure facilities include a tennis court and games room.

dir: *A1 exit 13.1.*

GPS: 49.9478, 2.8442

Open: Apr-Oct **Site:** 3HEC **For hire:** **Prices:** 14.40-15.10 Mobile home hire 343-470 **Facilities:** Wi-fi (charged) Play Area **Services:** **Leisure:** P **Off-site:**

FORT-MAHON-PLAGE SOMME

Royon

rte de Quend, 80120

322234030 322236515

e-mail: info@campingleroyon.com

web: www.campingleroyon.com

A family site with good facilities and well-marked pitches, 2.5km from the beach.

Open: 10 Mar-1 Nov **Site:** 5.5HEC **For hire:** **Facilities:** **Services:** **Leisure:** P **Off-site:** S

GOUVIEUX OISE

Le Mont César

rte de Toutevoie 10, 60270

344570205

e-mail: lemontcesar@wanadoo.fr

web: www.lemontcesar.com

On a hill overlooking the River Oise.

dir: *A1 to Gouvieux town centre, then towards Creil.*

Open: Apr-Oct **Site:** 6HEC **For hire:** **Prices:** 13.80-15.50 Mobile home hire 250-380 **Facilities:** Wi-fi Play Area **Services:** **Off-site:** P

GRAND-FORT-PHILIPPE NORD

Camping de la Plage

rue Ml-Foch, 59153

328653195 328653599

web: www.camping-de-la-plage.info

On a level meadow separated from the beach (0.5km).

dir: *Leave A16 onto D218 through Gravelines and onto Grand-Fort-Philippe.*

Open: Apr-Oct **Site:** 1.5HEC **For hire:** **Facilities:** **Services:** **Off-site:** R S

GREZ-SUR-LOING SEINE-ET-MARNE

CM Près

chemin des Près, 77880

164457275 164457275

e-mail: camping-grez@wanadoo.fr

web: www.camping-grez-fontainebleau.info

In a natural setting with partly shaded pitches. Hiking and cycling tracks in the surrounding area.

dir: *NE towards Loing.*

Open: end Mar-11 Nov **Site:** 6HEC **Prices:** 10.25-13.90 **Facilities:** Play Area **Services:** **Off-site:** R

GUINES PAS-DE-CALAIS

Bien Assise

The Camping and Caravanning Club The Friendly Club

62340

321352077 321367920

e-mail: castels@bien-assise.com

web: www.bien-assise.com

Rural site near to a forest and next to a charming little town.

C&CC Report *A pretty, well-established and very welcoming site with excellent facilities, close to the beautiful Opal Coast, with its impressive cliffs and golden beaches. Ideal for short breaks, first-time holidays abroad, long stays and overnight stops alike. As well as being very handy for Calais ferry port and the Channel Tunnel, time spent here lazily exploring the Picardy countryside, coast, towns and historic sites reaps many rewards.*

dir: *D231 towards Marquise.*

Open: 30 Mar-21 Sep **Site:** 12HEC **For hire:** **Prices:** 19-28 Mobile home hire 380-800 **Facilities:** Wi-fi Play Area **Services:** **Leisure:** P **Off-site:**

ISQUES — PAS-DE-CALAIS

Cytises

chemin Georges Ducrocq, 62360
☎ 321311110 🖷 321311110
e-mail: campcytises@orange.fr
web: www.lescytises.fr

A pleasant rural setting beside the River Liane.

dir: *A16 exit 28.*

GPS: 50.6777, 1.6427

Open: Apr-15 Oct **Site:** 2.5HEC **For hire:** **Facilities:** Wi-fi Play Area **Services:** **Off-site:** L R S

JABLINES — SEINE-ET-MARNE

International de Jablines

Base de Loisirs, 77450
☎ 160260937 🖷 160264333
e-mail: welcome@camping-jablines.com
web: www.camping-jablines.com

Only 9km from Disneyland® Resort Paris and 30km from Paris.

dir: *A1 or A3 towards Marne-la-Vallée, onto N3.*

GPS: 48.9133, 2.7342

Open: 31 Mar-29 Sep **Site:** 3.5HEC **For hire:** **Prices:** 25-30 Mobile home hire 476-680 **Facilities:** Play Area **Services:** **Off-site:** L

LICQUES — PAS-DE-CALAIS

Canchy

rue de Canchy, 62850
☎ 321826341 🖷 321826341
e-mail: camping.lecanchy@wanadoo.fr
web: www.camping-lecanchy.com

A quiet site on an open, level meadow. Well situated for the ferries and the Channel Tunnel.

Open: 15 Mar-Oct **Site:** 1HEC **For hire:** **Facilities:** **Services:** **Leisure:** R **Off-site:**

Pommiers des Trois Pays

273 rue de Breuil, 62850
☎ 321350202 🖷 321350202
e-mail: contact@pommiers-3pays.com
web: www.pommiers-3pays.com

Small, relaxing site with large pitches separated by hedges.

dir: *D215 Guines-Licques/D224 Ardres-Licques, then follow D191.*

GPS: 50.7797, 1.9476

Open: Apr-Oct **Site:** 2.5HEC **For hire:** **Facilities:** Wi-fi Play Area **Services:** **Leisure:** P **Off-site:** R

MAISONS-LAFFITTE — YVELINES

Camping International de Maisons-Laffitte

1 rue Johnson, 78600
☎ 139122191 🖷 139127050
e-mail: ci.mlaffitte@wanadoo.fr
web: www.campint.com

A well-kept site in a residential area on the banks of the Seine. Modern installations, heated in cold weather. Camping Card International (CCI) is advisable.

dir: *8km N of St-Germain-en-Laye. Or A86 exit Colombes-Ouest.*

GPS: 48.9402, 2.1451

Open: 30 Mar-Oct **Site:** 6.5HEC **For hire:** **Prices:** 29 **Facilities:** Wi-fi (charged) Play Area **Services:** **Leisure:** R **Off-site:** P

MAUBEUGE — NORD

Camping Municipal de Clair de Lune

212 rte de Mons, 59600
☎ 327622548 🖷 327602594
e-mail: camping@ville-maubeuge.fr
web: www.ville-maubeuge.fr/php/decouvrir/camping.php

Peaceful site close to the town centre with pitches divided by hedges. Ideally located for discovering Maubeuge's cultural and historic heritage.

dir: *1.5km N via N2 Bruxelles road.*

Open: Apr-Sep **Site:** 2.13HEC **Prices:** 11-15.35 **Facilities:** Play Area **Services:** **Off-site:**

MELUN — SEINE-ET-MARNE

Belle Étoile

Quai Maréchal Joffre, 77000
☎ 164394812 🖷 164372555
e-mail: info@campinglabelleetoile.com
web: www.campinglabelleetoile.com

Pleasant grassy site with three central blocks, in wooded, peaceful countryside and yet convenient for visiting Paris and Disneyland® Resort Paris.

dir: *At La Rochette on River Seine, 1km from town.*

Open: 31 Mar-14 Oct **Site:** 3.5HEC **For hire:** **Prices:** 17.50-25 Mobile home hire 306-640 **Facilities:** Wi-fi (charged) Kids' Club Play Area **Services:** **Leisure:** P **Off-site:** P R

FRANCE

MERLIMONT — PAS-DE-CALAIS

St-Hubert

RD 940, 62155

321891010 321891012

e-mail: sthubert62@wanadoo.fr

web: www.sthubert62.com

Pleasant wooded surroundings with good recreational facilities.

dir: *3km S via D940, near Parc de Bagatelle.*

Open: Apr-Oct **Site:** 16HEC **Facilities:** **Services:** **Leisure:** P

MIANNAY — SOMME

Clos Cacheleux

rte de Bouillancourt, 80132

322191747 322313533

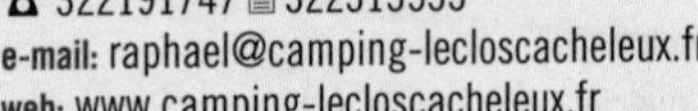

e-mail: raphael@camping-lecloscacheleux.fr

web: www.camping-lecloscacheleux.fr

Situated in the grounds of an 18th-century castle, bordered with woodland and with very large pitches. Organised activities plus a fishing pond and farm animals. Other facilities include use of a swimming pool at a neighbouring site under the same ownership.

C&CC Report *A recently developed site, with huge pitches, ideally situated for exploring the Somme Valley with its historic monuments and the Marquenterre bird sanctuary. Great for short breaks or longer stays, peace and quiet is the order of the day. Campers can use the facilities on the nearby sister site, Le Val de Trie, including covered and outdoor pools, bar, shop and restaurant.*

dir: *From A28 exit 2 at Abbéville take D925 towards Eu & Le Tréport (not towards Moyenville). Left in Miannay on D86 towards Toeufles. Left to Bouillancourt-sous-Miannay after 2km, site signed in village.*

GPS: 50.0864, 1.7156

Open: 15 Mar-15 Oct **Site:** 8HEC **Prices:** 18.90-25.90 **Facilities:** Wi-fi Kids' Club Play Area **Services:** **Off-site:** L P R

MILLY-LA-FORÊT — ESSONNE

Musardière

rte des Grandes Vallées, 91490

164989191 164989191

e-mail: lamusardiere91@orange.fr

Pleasant wooded surroundings.

dir: *4km SE via D948.*

Open: 16 Feb-20 Nov **Site:** 12HEC **For hire:** **Facilities:** Play Area **Services:** **Leisure:** P **Off-site:** R

MONNERVILLE — ESSONNE

Bois de la Justice

91930

164950534 164951731

web: campingboislajustice.pagesperso-orange.fr

Pitches separated by trees and hedges in beautiful natural woodland with good facilities.

dir: *N20 Orléans to Étampes.*

GPS: 48.3325, 2.0470

Open: Feb-Nov **Site:** 5.5HEC **For hire:** **Prices:** 19.50 **Facilities:** Play Area **Services:** **Leisure:** P

MONTREUIL-SUR-MER — PAS-DE-CALAIS

CM Fontaine des Clercs

1, rue de l'Église, 62170

321060728

e-mail: desmarest.mi@wanadoo.fr

web: www.campinglafontainedesclercs.fr

Quiet, shady site, 15 minutes from beaches and 200 metres from the railway station.

dir: *N of town on N1.*

Open: All Year. **Site:** 2HEC **For hire:** **Facilities:** **Services:** **Leisure:** R **Off-site:** P

MOYENNEVILLE — SOMME

Val de Trie

Bouillancourt-sous-Miannay, 80870

322314888 322313533

e-mail: raphael@camping-levaldetrie.fr

web: www.camping-levaldetrie.fr

A small site in a picturesque wooded location with good facilities.

dir: *1km from D925. On A28, exit 3 (Moyennes16), signed.*

GPS: 50.0860, 1.7149

Open: Apr-15 Oct **Site:** 3HEC **For hire:** **Prices:** 16.50-25.80 Mobile home hire 300-700 **Facilities:** Wi-fi Kids' Club Play Area **Services:** **Leisure:** P **Off-site:** L R

FRANCE

NAMPONT SAINT MARTIN — SOMME

Camping La Ferme des Aulnes

Fresne, 80120

☎ 322292269

e-mail: contact@fermedesaulnes.com

web: www.fermedesaulnes.com

Family-friendly site located on an old farm but with modern facilities including a covered swimming pool. Kids' club available in July and August.

Open: Apr-1 Nov **Site:** 4.5HEC **For hire:** **Prices:** 21-23 Mobile home hire 390-790 **Facilities:** Wi-fi Kids' Club Play Area **Services:** **Leisure:** P **Off-site:** R S

NESLES-LA-VALLÉE — VAL-D'OISE

Parc de Séjour de l'Étang

10 chemin des Belles Vues, 95690

☎ 134706289

e-mail: brehinier1@hotmail.fr

web: www.campingparcset.fr

Level site near a small lake.

dir: *A16 exit at L'Isle d'Adam then D64. A15 exit 10 onto D915 then D64.*

GPS: 49.1279, 2.1843

Open: Mar-Oct **Site:** 6HEC **Prices:** 16.50 **Facilities:** **Services:** **Off-site:** P R

OYE-PLAGE — PAS-DE-CALAIS

Oyats

272 Digue Vert, 62215

☎ 321851540 328603833

e-mail: billiet.nicolas@wanadoo.fr

web: www.les-oyats.com

Beside the sea and with direct access to the beach. Leisure facilities include a swimming pool, volleyball and petanque.

dir: *4.5km NW on beach.*

Open: May-Sep **Site:** 5HEC **Facilities:** **Services:** **Leisure:** P S

PARIS

Bois de Boulogne

2 allée du Bord de l'Eau, 75016

☎ 145243000 142244295

e-mail: paris@campingparis.fr

web: www.campingparis.fr

This popular site is close to the city centre and it can be crowded during the summer, as it is the only site in central Paris.

Open: All Year. **Site:** 7HEC **For hire:** **Facilities:** **Services:**

PLESSIS-FEU-AUSSOUX — SEINE-ET-MARNE

Château-de-Chambonnières

77540

☎ 164041585 164041336

e-mail: campingchambonnieres@orange.fr

In wooded area, popular site for visits to Disneyland® Resort Paris.

dir: *On D231 towards Provins.*

Open: Apr-Sep **Site:** 5HEC **Facilities:** **Services:** **Off-site:** P R

POIX-DE-PICARDIE — SOMME

Bois des Pêcheurs

rte de Forges-les-Eaux, 80290

☎ 322901171 322903291

e-mail: camping@ville-poix-de-picardie.fr

web: www.ville-poix-de-picardie.fr

A quiet riverside location with a high standard of sanitary facilities.

dir: *A29 exit 13.*

Open: Apr-Sep **Site:** 2.35HEC **Facilities:** **Services:** **Off-site:** P R

POMMEUSE — SEINE-ET-MARNE

Chêne Gris

24 pl de la gare de Faremoutiers, 77515

☎ 164042180 164200589

e-mail: info@lechenegris.com

web: www.lechenegris.com

Woodland site within easy travelling distance of Disneyland® Resort Paris and the capital itself.

dir: *N34 towards Coulommiers-Crécy, onto D25 to Pommeuse, signed on right after station.*

Open: 31 Mar-3 Nov **Site:** 6HEC **For hire:** **Prices:** 25-44 **Facilities:** Wi-fi (charged) Kids' Club Play Area **Services:** **Leisure:** P **Off-site:** R

PORT-LE-GRAND — SOMME

Château des Tilleuls

rte de la Baie, 80132

☎ 322240775 322242380

web: www.chateaudestilleuls.com

On gently sloping meadow surrounding a farm.

dir: *1km SE on D40A.*

Open: Mar-Oct **Site:** 5HEC **For hire:** **Facilities:** **Services:** **Leisure:** P **Off-site:** R

PROYART SOMME

Loisir la Violette

rte de Mericourt, 80340

322858136 322851737

Close to the N29 and A29, this site overlooks marshes and fishponds.

Open: Apr-Oct **Site:** 1.8HEC **For hire:** **Facilities:** **Off-site:**

QUEND-PLAGE-LES-PINS SOMME

Roses

80120

322277617 322239306

e-mail: info@campingdesroses.com

web: www.campingdesroses.com

Well-kept site with trees and hedges surrounding individual pitches.

dir: *Off D940 at Quend onto D102, site 0.5km on left.*

Open: 15 Mar-23 Oct **Site:** 9HEC **For hire:** **Facilities:** **Services:** **Leisure:** L P **Off-site:** S

Vertes Feuilles

25 rte de la Plage, Monchaux, 80120

322235512 322190752

e-mail: lesvertesfeuilles@baiedesommepleinair.com

web: www.baiedesommepleinair.com

Situated 3km from the sea between the Somme Bay and Authe Bay. Kids' club available in July and August.

dir: *A16 exit 24, follow D32 towards Quend Plage.*

GPS: 50.3198, 1.6063

Open: Apr-Oct **Site:** **For hire:** **Facilities:** Wi-fi Kids' Club Play Area **Services:** **Leisure:** P **Off-site:** L R S

RAMBOUILLET YVELINES

Huttopia Rambouillet

rte du Château d'Eau, 78120

130410734 130410017

e-mail: rambouillet@huttopia.com

web: www.huttopia.com

In the heart of the forest of Rambouillet, beside the Etang d'Or (Golden Pond). Kids' club available in July and August. 1 dog per pitch.

dir: *From Paris take A13, then A12 then N10 cross Trappes then Rambouillet from N10 exit Les Eveuses.*

GPS: 48.6263, 1.8442

Open: 29 Mar-8 Nov **Site:** 8HEC **For hire:** **Prices:** 17.80-27 Mobile home hire 560.70-718.20 **Facilities:** Kids' Club Play Area **Services:** **Leisure:** L P **Off-site:**

ST-AMAND-LES-EAUX NORD

Mont des Bruyères

806 rue Basly, 59230

327485687 327485687

e-mail: lemontdesbruyeres@orange.fr

web: www.campingmontdesbruyeres.com

A quiet site on the edge of a large forest. A discount may be available on presentation of this guide.

dir: *3.5km SE in forest of St-Amand.*

Open: 15 Mar-30 Oct **Site:** 3.5HEC **For hire:** **Prices:** 14.62-17.62 Mobile home hire 225-275 **Facilities:** Wi-fi (charged) Play Area **Services:** **Off-site:** L P R

ST-CHÉRON ESSONNE

Parc des Roches

La Petite Beauce, 91530

164566550 164565450

e-mail: info@camping-parcdesroches.com

web: www.camping-parcdesroches.com

Set in a wooded park.

Open: Mar-15 Dec **Site:** 23HEC **For hire:** **Facilities:** Wi-fi (charged) Play Area **Services:** **Leisure:** P **Off-site:** R

FRANCE

ST-CYR-SUR-MORIN SEINE-ET-MARNE

Choisel

Courcelles la Roue, 77750

160238493 160248174

e-mail: campingduchoisel@wanadoo.fr

web: www.camping-du-choisel.com

A pleasant location. Separate car park for arrivals after 22.00hrs.

dir: *2km W via D31.*

Open: Mar-Nov **Site:** 3.5HEC **For hire:** **Facilities:** **Services:** **Off-site:** L P R

ST-LEU-D'ESSERENT OISE

Campix

60340

344560848 344562875

e-mail: campix@orange.fr

web: www.campingcampix.com

Set in wooded surroundings within easy reach of Chantilly. Facilities include a snack bar and a swimming pool.

C&CC Report *If you like to get back to nature and just relax, this simple green hide-away site, in its lush, irregular and rambling surroundings has a picturesque swimming pool, paddling pool and large sunbathing terrace that together provide its focus. Monsieur Ozon, the friendly, English-speaking owner is always around to help and advise. The château of Chantilly is just a short drive away and nearby Parc Astérix is a great fun day out.*

dir: *3.5km NE via D12.*

Open: 7 Mar-1 Dec **Site:** 6HEC **For hire:** **Prices:** 12.50-20 **Facilities:** Wi-fi (charged) **Services:** **Leisure:** P **Off-site:** L

ST-VALÉRY-SUR-SOMME SOMME

Domaine du Château de Drancourt

80230

322269345 322268587

e-mail: chateau.drancourt@wanadoo.fr

web: www.chateau-drancourt.com

Set within the grounds of a former hunting lodge surrounded by woods, fields and lakes.

dir: *3.5km S via D48.*

GPS: 50.1533, 1.3809

Open: 30 Mar-23 Sep **Site:** 15HEC **For hire:** **Facilities:** Wi-fi Kids' Club **Services:** **Leisure:** P **Off-site:** L S

SALENCY OISE

Étang du Moulin

54 rue du Moulin, 60400

344099981

A small site opposite a trout fishing lake and recreational area under the ownership of the site proprietors.

dir: *3km from Noyon on N32 towards Chauny.*

Open: All Year. **Site:** 0.36HEC **Prices:** 15.10 **Facilities:** **Services:** **Off-site:** P R

SERAUCOURT-LE-GRAND AISNE

Camping du Vivier aux Carpes

10 rue Charles-Voyeux, 02790

323605010

e-mail: contact@camping-picardie.com

web: www.camping-picardie.com

A peaceful site bordered by lakes. Separate car park for arrivals after 22.00hrs.

C&CC Report *This pristine, immaculately kept little site is a paradise for anglers and makes for an ideal break not far from home. In the heart of the Somme region, nearer to Paris than Calais and close to many cathedral cities and Great War sites, it makes a superb base for exploring historic Picardy and further afield. There is plenty of useful advice and information available from the new owners, who have also added on-site food and drink services. Cycle routes lead into this lovely area straight from the site.*

dir: *A26 exit 11, left onto D1, onto D72 Essigny.*

GPS: 49.7817, 3.2117

Open: Mar-Oct **Site:** 3HEC **For hire:** **Prices:** 20 Mobile home hire 385 **Facilities:** Wi-fi Play Area **Services:** **Off-site:** R

STELLA-PLAGE PAS-DE-CALAIS

Camping la Forêt

149 bld de Berck, 62780

321947501

e-mail: info@laforetstella.fr

web: www.laforetstella.fr

1.3km from the sea, family friendly site with facilities including a games room.

GPS: 50.4734, 1.5918

Open: 11 Mar-7 Nov **Site:** 3HEC **For hire:** **Facilities:** Wi-fi (charged) Play Area **Services:** **Off-site:** S

FRANCE

THIEMBRONNE — PAS-DE-CALAIS

Pommiers

rte de Desvres, 62560

321395019

e-mail: campinglespommiers62@orange.fr

web: www.camping-pommiers.com

A family site in pleasant wooded surroundings.

dir: *NW on D132.*

Open: 15 Mar-15 Oct **Site:** 3HEC **For hire:** **Facilities:** **Services:** **Leisure:** P **Off-site:** R

TOLLENT — PAS-DE-CALAIS

Val d'Authie

rte de Berck, 62390

321471427 321471427

e-mail: campingduvaldauthie@orange.fr

web: www.campingduvaldauthie.fr

A pleasant wooded location with wide, well-marked pitches.

dir: *SE via D119.*

Open: Apr-Sep **Site:** 5.7HEC **For hire:** **Prices:** 18 Mobile home hire 470 **Facilities:** Wi-fi Play Area **Services:** **Leisure:** L P **Off-site:** R

TORCY — SEINE-ET-MARNE

Parc de la Colline

rte de Lagny, 77200

160054232 164800517

e-mail: camping.parc.de.la.colline@wanadoo.fr

web: www.camping-de-la-colline.com

An ideal base for visiting Paris (30 minutes from the centre by Metro). Separate car park for arrivals after 22.00hrs.

dir: *A104 exit 10, onto D10E.*

Open: All Year. **Site:** 13HEC **For hire:** **Facilities:** **Services:** **Off-site:** L P

TOUQUIN — SEINE-ET-MARNE

Étangs Fleuris

rte de la Couture, 77131

164041636 164041228

e-mail: contact@etangs-fleuris.com

web: www.etangsfleuris.com

Wooded surroundings with well-defined pitches and modern facilities. Ideally located for visiting Disneyland® Resort Paris.

dir: *A4 exit 13 towards Provins. In Touquin follow signs.*

GPS: 48.7331, 3.0470

Open: 31 Mar-15 Sep **Site:** 5.5HEC **For hire:** **Prices:** 21 Mobile home hire 390-640 **Facilities:** Wi-fi Play Area **Services:** **Leisure:** P **Off-site:**

TOURNEHEM-SUR-LA-HEM — PAS-DE-CALAIS

Hôtel Bal Camping - Caravaning

500 rue du Vieux Château, 62890

321356590 321351857

e-mail: hotelbal@yahoo.fr

A peaceful site in rural surroundings with modern facilities.

C&CC Report *A convenient location for an overnight stop. Set in the grounds of a hotel, 1km from a medieval village and with an on-site bar, restaurant and take-away.*

dir: *D218 from village centre.*

Open: All Year. **Site:** 1.6HEC **For hire:** **Facilities:** **Services:** **Off-site:** R

VAILLY-SUR-AISNE — AISNE

Domaine de la Nature

chemin de Boufaud, Pont de Vailly, 02370

323547455

e-mail: domainedelanature@orange.fr

web: www.domainedelanature.fr

A pleasant rural setting alongside the canal with well-defined pitches and modern sanitary facilities.

dir: *4km W via D144 near canal & lake.*

Open: All Year. **Site:** 3HEC **For hire:** **Facilities:** **Services:** **Off-site:** R

VERSAILLES — YVELINES

Huttopia Versailles

31 rue Berthelot, 78000
139512361 139536829
e-mail: versailles@huttopia.com
web: www.huttopia.com
Site in forest location 2.5km from the palace of Versailles. Very convenient for Paris.
dir: *A13 from Paris, exit Versailles centre, follow signs.*
GPS: 48.7946, 2.1612
Open: 22 Mar-8 Nov **Site:** 4HEC **For hire:** **Prices:** 26.10-33.90 **Facilities:** Wi-fi Play Area **Services:** **Leisure:** P **Off-site:**

VILLENNES-SUR-SEINE — YVELINES

Club des Renardières

rte de Vernouillet, 78670
139758897
Site for caravans only, in beautiful hilly park laid out with hedges, lawns and flower beds. Fully divided into completely separated pitches.
dir: *D113 to Maison Blanche, turn right for 3km.*
Open: All Year. **Site:** 7HEC **Facilities:** **Services:** **Off-site:** L P R

VILLERS-SUR-AUTHIE — SOMME

Val d'Authie

20 rte de Vercourt, 80120
322299247 322299330
e-mail: camping@valdauthie.fr
web: www.valdauthie.fr
A well-designed site between the forest of Crécy and the sea.
dir: *Via N1.*
Open: Apr-8 Oct **Site:** 7HEC **For hire:** **Facilities:** Wi-fi (charged) Kids' Club Play Area **Services:** **Leisure:** P **Off-site:** R

VILLIERS SUR ORGE — ESSONNE

Camping le Beau Village de Paris

1 Voie des Prés, 91700
160161786 160163146
e-mail: le-beau-village@wanadoo.fr
web: www.beau-village.com
20 minutes by train from the centre of Paris and with a range of local amenities close by. Restaurant for guests' use between June and 20 September.
GPS: 48.6551, 2.3042
Open: All Year. **Site:** 2.5HEC **For hire:** **Prices:** 14.50-16.50 Mobile home hire 250-440 **Facilities:** Wi-fi Play Area **Services:** **Leisure:** R **Off-site:** L P

VIRONCHAUX — SOMME

Peupliers

221 rue du Cornet, 80150
322235427
e-mail: les-peupliers3@orange.fr
web: www.campingpeupliers.fr
A peaceful site 3km from the forest of Crécy.
dir: *Via N1 & D938.*
Open: Apr-Oct **Site:** 2.5HEC **For hire:** **Prices:** 18.80-19.80 Mobile home hire 350-441 **Facilities:** Wi-fi **Services:**

WACQUINGHEN — PAS-DE-CALAIS

Éscale

62250
321320069 321320069
e-mail: camp-escale@wanadoo.fr
web: www.escale-camping.com
A landscaped park with modern facilities close to the coast.
dir: *Via A16 & D231.*
Open: 15 Mar-15 Oct **Site:** 11HEC **For hire:** **Prices:** Mobile home hire 290-550 **Facilities:** Wi-fi (charged) Play Area **Services:** **Leisure:** L **Off-site:**

FRANCE

AUVERGNE

ALLANCHE — CANTAL

Camping Les Gentianes

15160
471204587 471204181
e-mail: campingallanche@orange.fr
Family-friendly site, quiet and shaded.
dir: *1km S on D679 towards St-Flour.*
Open: 15 Jun-15 Sep **Site:** 3HEC **For hire:** **Facilities:** **Services:** **Leisure:** R **Off-site:**

ALLEYRAS — HAUTE-LOIRE

CM

43580
471575686 471575686
e-mail: mairie.camping-municipal@akeonet.com
Pleasant surroundings on level ground beside the River Allier.
dir: *2.5km NW.*
Open: 15 Apr-15 Oct **Site:** 1HEC **For hire:** **Facilities:** **Services:** **Off-site:** R

AMBERT — PUY-DE-DÔME

Trois Chênes

rte du Puy, 63600
473823468 473823468
e-mail: tourisme@ville-ambert.fr
web: www.camping-ambert.com
On the outskirts of Ambert the site is well presented with an emphasis on green areas.
Open: May-Sep **Site:** **For hire:** **Facilities:** Play Area **Services:** **Leisure:** P **Off-site:** L

ARNAC — CANTAL

Gineste

15150
471629190 471629272
e-mail: contact@village-vacances-cantal.com
web: www.village-vacances-cantal.com
Situated on a peninsula in Lake Enchanet with modern facilities and access to ski slopes.
dir: *NW of Arnac towards lake.*
Open: All Year. **Site:** 3HEC **For hire:** **Prices:** Mobile home hire 200-430 **Facilities:** Play Area **Services:** **Leisure:** L P **Off-site:** R

ARPAJON-SUR-CÈRE — CANTAL

Cère

rue F-Ramond, 15130
471645507
e-mail: tourisme@caba.fr
web: www.caba.fr/camping
Bordering the Cèze River with leisure facilities including a swimming pool and fishing.
dir: *S towards Rodez on D920, site beside river.*
Open: Jun-Sep **Site:** 2HEC **For hire:** **Facilities:** **Services:** **Leisure:** P R **Off-site:**

AUREC SUR LOIRE — HAUTE-LOIRE

Camping Club A.Tou.Vert - Le Port Buisson

Le Port Buisson, 43110
477352465 477352465
e-mail: atouvert.aurec@wanadoo.fr
web: www.atouvert.com
With direct access to the Loire river and also an on-site pond. Organised activities take place.
dir: *From Puy-en-Velay take N88, exit Monistrol then towards Bas-en-Basset and take D46 to Aurec. From St Étienne take N88 to Firminy then D42 to Aurec.*
Open: 15 Apr-Sep **Site:** 5HEC **For hire:** **Prices:** 9-11.50 Mobile home hire 260-300 **Facilities:** Wi-fi **Services:** **Leisure:** R **Off-site:** P

BELLERIVE-SUR-ALLIER — ALLIER

Acacias

rue Claude-Decloître, 03700
470323622 470598852
e-mail: camping-acacias03@orange.fr
web: www.camping-acacias.com
Well-managed site, sub-divided into numbered pitches by hedges. Clean sanitary installations. Library, billiard room. Water sports are available on nearby lake.
dir: *From Vichy left after bridge beside fuel station & along river for 0.5km.*
Open: Apr-10 Oct **Site:** 3HEC **For hire:** **Prices:** 12.60-16.90 Mobile home hire 259-660 **Facilities:** Wi-fi Kids' Club Play Area **Services:** **Leisure:** L P R **Off-site:**

FRANCE

Beau Rivage

rue Claude Decloître, 03700
☎ 470322685 470320394
e-mail: camping-beaurivage@wanadoo.fr
web: www.camping-beaurivage.com
Neat meadowland with marked out pitches. Well-kept sanitary installations.
dir: *Over bridge onto left bank of River Allier.*
Open: Apr-Oct **Site:** 1.5HEC **For hire:** **Facilities:** **Services:** **Leisure:** P R **Off-site:** L

BOURBON-L'ARCHAMBAULT — ALLIER

CM de Bourbon L'Archambault

Parc Jean Bignon, 03160
☎ 470670883 470673535
Shady site in parkland.
dir: *1km SW on N153, rte de Montluçon, turn right.*
Open: Mar-Oct **Site:** 3HEC **Prices:** 7.09-7.44 **Facilities:** Wi-fi (charged) **Services:** **Off-site:** P

BOURG-ARGENTAL — LOIRE

Camping de l'Astrée

42220
☎ 477397297 477397621
e-mail: prl@bourgargental.fr
web: www.bourg-argental.fr
Pleasant surroundings at the heart of the Pilat Regional Natural Park, with good recreational facilities.
dir: *Via N82.*
Open: All Year. **Site:** 2HEC **For hire:** **Prices:** 12-14.50 **Facilities:** Wi-fi Play Area **Services:** **Leisure:** P R **Off-site:**

BRAIZE — ALLIER

Champ de la Chapelle

03360
☎ 470061545
e-mail: champdelachapelle@wanadoo.fr
web: www.champdelachapelle.com
A family site in the centre of the Tronçais forest with good recreational facilities.
dir: *7km SE via D28 & D978.*
GPS: 46.6431, 2.6544
Open: mid Apr-mid Oct **Site:** 5.6HEC **For hire:** **Prices:** 12.50-15.50 Mobile home hire 320-400 **Facilities:** Wi-fi Play Area **Services:** **Leisure:** P **Off-site:** L R

BRIVES-CHARENSAC — HAUTE-LOIRE

Audinet

av des Sports, 43700
☎ 471091018 471091018
e-mail: camping.audinet@wanadoo.fr
web: www.camping-audinet.fr
A peaceful site in a wooded setting beside the River Loire with good recreational facilities.
dir: *E on N88.*
Open: 30 Apr-22 Sep **Site:** 4.5HEC **For hire:** **Prices:** 11.50-16.90 **Facilities:** Play Area **Services:** **Leisure:** P R **Off-site:**

CANET-DE-SALARS — AVEYRON

Le Caussanel

Lac de Pareloup, 12290
☎ 565468519 565468985
e-mail: info@lecaussanel.com
web: www.lecaussanel.com
Well-equipped site on the shore of Lake Pareloup. Kids' club in high season.
dir: *Via D911.*
GPS: 44.2150, 2.7645
Open: 14 May-8 Sep **Site:** 10HEC **For hire:** **Prices:** 14.50-29.20 Mobile home hire 345-812 **Facilities:** Wi-fi (charged) Kids' Club Play Area **Services:** **Leisure:** L P

Soleil Levant

Lac de Pareloup, 12290
☎ 565460365
e-mail: contact@camping-soleil-levant.com
web: www.camping-soleil-levant.com
A peaceful family site set on terraces on the shores of Lac de Pareloup with good recreational facilities.
dir: *S of Canet-de-Salars on D933 towards Salles-Curan.*
GPS: 44.2149, 2.7779
Open: May-Sep **Site:** 11HEC **For hire:** **Prices:** 14-25 Mobile home hire 180-695 **Facilities:** Wi-fi Kids' Club Play Area **Services:** **Leisure:** L **Off-site:**

FRANCE

CAPDENAC-GARE AVEYRON

CM Rives d'Olt

bld Paul-Ramadier, 12700
565808887
e-mail: camping.capdenac@wanadoo.fr
A quiet site on level ground with pitches divided by hedges on the bank of a river.
dir: *7km from Figeac via N140 towards Rodez, onto D35 to Capendac.*
GPS: 44.5731, 2.0727
Open: Apr-Sep **Site:** 1.3HEC **For hire:** **Prices:** 12.40 **Facilities:** Wi-fi **Services:** **Leisure:** R **Off-site:** P

CEYRAT PUY-DE-DOME

Camping Le Chanset

The Camping and Caravanning Club The Friendly Club

63122
473613073 473613073
e-mail: camping.lechanset@wanadoo.fr
web: www.campingdeceyrat63.com
With a hilltop setting in the town of Ceyrat, the site has pitches for tents and motor homes. Greenery, surrounded by pine trees and chestnut trees in the Natural Regional Park of the Volcanoes of Auvergne. Kids' club available in July and August.
C&CC Report *Six and a half kilometres from Clermont-Ferrand, with views over the village towards the surrounding hills and countryside and 800m to the village centre.*
Site: **For hire:** **Facilities:** Wi-fi Kids' Club Play Area **Services:** **Leisure:** P

CHAMPAGNAC-LE-VIEUX HAUTE-LOIRE

Chanterelle

Le Plan d'Eau, 43440
471763400 471763400
e-mail: camping@champagnac.com
web: www.champagnac.com
Situated in the heart of the Auvergne beside a wooded lake.
dir: *1km N via D5.*
GPS: 45.3656, 3.5062
Open: Apr-Oct **Site:** 4HEC **For hire:** **Prices:** 11.62-15.50 Mobile home hire 276-756 **Facilities:** Wi-fi **Services:** **Leisure:** L **Off-site:** R

CHAMPS-SUR-TARENTAINE CANTAL

Tarentaine

15270
471787125 471787509
e-mail: contact@champs-marchal.org
An attractive location surrounded by lakes and woodland.
dir: *1km SW via D679 & D22 beside River Tarentaine.*
Open: 15 Jun-15 Sep **Site:** 4HEC **For hire:** **Facilities:** **Services:** **Leisure:** R **Off-site:** P

CHÂTEL-DE-NEUVRE ALLIER

Deneuvre

rue Moulins, 03500
470420451
e-mail: campingdeneuvre@wanadoo.fr
web: www.deneuvre.com
Pleasant surroundings within a nature reserve beside the River Allier.
dir: *0.5km N via D9.*
Open: Apr-Sep **Site:** 1HEC **Prices:** 13.50-17.80 **Facilities:** **Services:** **Leisure:** R **Off-site:**

CHÂTEL-GUYON PUY-DE-DÔME

Clos de Balanède

rue de la Piscine, 63140
473860247 473860564
e-mail: clos-balanede.sarl-camping@wanadoo.fr
web: www.balanede.com
A pleasant site set in an orchard.
dir: *Via A71 & D685.*
Open: 15 Apr-Oct **Site:** 4.4HEC **For hire:** **Facilities:** Wi-fi (charged) **Services:** **Leisure:** P **Off-site:** R

FRANCE

CHÂTEL-MONTAGNE ALLIER

Croix Cognat

03250

☎ 470593138

e-mail: campinglacroixcognat@hotmail.fr

web: www.campinglacroixcognat.com

Well-equipped family site at an altitude of 540 metres. Leisure facilities include a trampoline and table tennis.

dir: *0.5km NW on D25 towards Vichy.*

Open: Jul-Aug **Site:** 1HEC **For hire:** **Prices:** 13 Mobile home hire 360 **Facilities:** Wi-fi Kids' Club Play Area **Services:** **Leisure:** P **Off-site:** R

CHAUDES-AIGUES CANTAL

Camping le Couffour

15110

☎ 471235708 471235708

e-mail: blas.berthou@orange.fr

web: www.camping-chaudes-aigues.fr

Tastefully sited around the town football pitch in the local leisure area.

dir: *2km S via D921.*

GPS: 44.8449, 3.0011

Open: Apr-Oct **Site:** 2.5HEC **Prices:** 9.60-12.80 **Facilities:** Wi-fi Play Area **Services:** **Off-site:** L P R

CONDRIEU RHÔNE

Belle Rive

La Plaine, 69420

☎ 474595108

Wooded surroundings bordering the Rhône.

dir: *11km S of Vienne on N86.*

Open: Apr-Sep **Site:** 5HEC **For hire:** **Prices:** 14.20-16.40 Mobile home hire 400-470 **Facilities:** Wi-fi **Services:** **Leisure:** P R

CONQUES AVEYRON

Beau Rivage

12320

☎ 565698223

e-mail: camping.conques@wanadoo.fr

web: www.campingconques.com

Peaceful site beside the river with spacious, well-marked pitches.

dir: *On D901.*

Open: Apr-Sep **Site:** 1HEC **For hire:** **Facilities:** Wi-fi Play Area **Services:** **Leisure:** P R **Off-site:**

COURNON-D'AUVERGNE PUY-DE-DÔME

CM Pré des Laveuses

rue de Laveuses, 63800

☎ 473848130 473846590

web: www.cournon-auvergne.fr/camping

A rural setting beside a 7-hectare lake, close to the River Allier.

dir: *1.5km E towards Billom.*

Open: Apr-Oct **Site:** 5HEC **For hire:** **Facilities:** **Services:** **Leisure:** L R **Off-site:** P

DALLET PUY-DE-DÔME

Ombrages

rte de Pont-du-Château, 63111

☎ 473831097

e-mail: lesombrages@hotmail.com

web: www.lesombrages.nl

Wooded location beside the River Allier. English is spoken at this family campsite with friendly staff and clean modern facilities including swimming pools. A short drive from many of the regions tourist attractions.

Open: 15 May-15 Sep **Site:** 4HEC **For hire:** **Prices:** 14-23 **Facilities:** Wi-fi (charged) Play Area **Services:** **Leisure:** P R **Off-site:**

DARDILLY RHÔNE

Camping Indigo International Lyon

The Camping and Caravanning Club The Friendly Club

Porte de Lyon, 69570

☎ 478356455 472170426

e-mail: lyon@camping-indigo.com

web: www.camping-indigo.com

Located at the gateway to the capital of the Rhône Alpes region, this site is an ideal base for visiting Lyon and the Beaujolais region.

C&CC Report *Ideally situated, just off the A6 motorway north of Lyon, for a stopover on the road to the south. Buses leave from outside the site entrance so visits to Lyon and its UNESCO listed buildings are both easy and interesting. If you're not just stopping over en-route, take time to enjoy the history and gastronomy of one of France's finest cities.*

dir: *A6 exit N of Lyon signed Dardilly, follow signs to Porte de Lyon.*

GPS: 45.8195, 4.7617

Open: All Year. **Site:** 6HEC **For hire:** **Prices:** 16.50-18.90 Mobile home hire 196-565 **Facilities:** Play Area **Services:** **Leisure:** P **Off-site:**

Site 6HEC (site size) grass sand stone little shade partly shaded mainly shaded motorvans accepted bungalows for hire mobile homes for hire tents for hire no dogs site fully accessible for wheelchairs **Prices** amount quoted is per night, for 2 adults and car, plus tent or caravan Mobile home hire is a weekly rate.

EBREUIL — ALLIER

Filature de la Sioule

Ile de Nieres, 03450

470907201

e-mail: camping.filature@gmail.com

web: www.campingfilature.com

A peaceful, well-equipped site in an orchard beside the River Sioule.

dir: *A71 exit 12, site signed.*

GPS: 46.1083, 3.0733

Open: 30 Mar-1 Oct **Site:** 3.6HEC **For hire:** **Prices:** 12-18 Mobile home hire 240-560 **Facilities:** Wi-fi **Services:** **Leisure:** R **Off-site:**

FLAGNAC — AVEYRON

Port de Lacombe

12300

565641008

e-mail: accueil@campingleportdelacombe.fr

web: www.campingleportdelacombe.fr

A shady site in the Lot Valley. Water activities including fishing and canoeing on the river and an aquatic area incorporating a large water chute.

dir: *A75 towards Rodez, turn for Decazeville/Flagnac.*

Open: Apr-Sep **Site:** 4HEC **For hire:** **Prices:** 12.40-23.30 Mobile home hire 196-728 **Facilities:** Wi-fi (charged) Play Area **Services:** **Leisure:** P R **Off-site:**

FLEURIE — RHÔNE

CM la Grappe Fleurie

69820

474698007 474698571

e-mail: camping@fleurie.org

web: www.camping-beaujolais.com

A good quality municipal site in a picturesque setting in the heart of the Beaujolais region.

dir: *0.6km SE on D119 E.*

Open: mid Mar-mid Oct **Site:** 2.46HEC **For hire:** **Facilities:** **Services:** **Leisure:** P **Off-site:**

GOUDET — HAUTE-LOIRE

Au Bord de l'Eau

Plaine du Chambon, 43150

471571682

e-mail: campingauborddeleau@live.fr

web: www.campingauborddeleau.com

Well-equipped site in wooded surroundings below the ruins of the castle. Music classes available for children.

dir: *W via D49, beside River Loire.*

Open: May-Sep **Site:** 4HEC **For hire:** **Prices:** 18 Mobile home hire 225-480 **Facilities:** Wi-fi Play Area **Services:** **Leisure:** P R **Off-site:**

ISLE-ET-BARDAIS — ALLIER

Écossais

03360

470666257 470066399

e-mail: ecossais@campingstroncais.com

web: www.campingstroncais.com

A peaceful location in the heart of the forest of Tronçais, beside the Pirot lake.

dir: *Via A71/E11.*

GPS: 46.6666, 2.7833

Open: Apr-Sep **Site:** 25HEC **For hire:** **Prices:** 7.28-8.68 Mobile home hire 218-450 **Facilities:** Wi-fi **Services:** **Leisure:** L **Off-site:**

JENZAT — ALLIER

Champ de Sioule

rte de Chantelle, 03800

470568635 470568538

e-mail: camping-jenzat@orange.fr

web: www.bassin-gannat.com

Situated close to the River Sioule, in a good location for canoeing and fishing.

dir: *From A71 exit signed Gannat, then onto RD2009. At Saulzet, left onto D42.*

GPS: 46.1660, 3.1897

Open: May-25 Sep **Site:** 1HEC **Facilities:** Play Area **Services:** **Off-site:** R

FRANCE

LACAPELLE-VIESCAMP — CANTAL

Puech des Ouilhes

15150

471464238 471464238

e-mail: truyere@aol.com

web: www.cantal-camping.fr

On a wooded peninsula on Lake St-Étienne-Cantalès.

Open: 15 May-15 Sep **Site:** 2HEC **For hire:** **Facilities:** **Services:** **Leisure:** L P

LANGEAC — HAUTE-LOIRE

Gorges de l'Allier

Domaine du Prad'Eau, 43300

471770501 471772734

e-mail: infos@campinglangeac.com

web: www.campinglangeac.com

Set in wooded surroundings within a nature reserve, 0.8km from the river. Good recreational facilities.

dir: *Off N102.*

Open: Apr-Oct **Site:** 14HEC **For hire:** **Facilities:** Play Area **Services:** **Leisure:** P R **Off-site:**

LAPEYROUSE — PUY-DE-DÔME

CM Les Marins

La Loge, 63700

473523706 473520389

web: 63lapeyrouse.free.fr

A modern, lakeside site with good facilities set among the rolling hills of the Combtaille.

dir: *2km E via D998.*

Open: 15 Jun-1 Sep **Site:** 2HEC **For hire:** **Facilities:** Play Area **Services:** **Leisure:** L **Off-site:** P

LEMPDES — HAUTE-LOIRE

Camping le Pont d'Allagnon

Rue René Filiol, 43410

471765369

e-mail: centre.auvergne.camping@orange.fr

web: www.campingenauvergne.com

Close to the village and on the l'Allagnon river, quiet site ideal for activities such as hiking and canoeing.

GPS: 45.3870, 3.2660

Open: May-Sep **Site:** 2HEC **For hire:** **Prices:** 9-14 Mobile home hire 257-392 **Facilities:** Wi-fi Play Area **Services:** **Leisure:** P R **Off-site:** L

LOUBEYRAT — PUY-DE-DÔME

Colombier

63410

473866694

web: www.campingducolombier.com

A welcoming campsite in parkland.

dir: *1.5km S via D16.*

Open: May-Sep **Site:** 1.3HEC **For hire:** **Facilities:** **Services:** **Leisure:** P

MALZIEU-VILLE, LE — LOZÈRE

Piscine

48140

466314763

Peaceful shaded site on the banks of a river near to the municipal sports complex.

Open: Jun-Aug **Site:** 1HEC **Prices:** 12.90-15.40 **Facilities:** **Services:** **Off-site:** P R

MARTRES-DE-VEYRE, LES — PUY-DE-DÔME

Camping la Font de Bleix

rue des Roches, 63730

473397272

A pleasant site beside the River Allier. A good centre for touring the surrounding area.

dir: *SE via D225 beside River Allier.*

Open: All Year. **Site:** 1.3HEC **For hire:** **Facilities:** **Services:** **Leisure:** R **Off-site:**

MENDE — LOZÈRE

Tivoli

av des Gorges-du-Tarn, 48000

466650038 466650038

e-mail: camping.tivoli0601@orange.fr

web: www.campingtivoli.com

A level site in wooded surroundings beside the river.

dir: *2km from town via A75 or N88.*

Open: All Year. **Site:** 1.8HEC **For hire:** **Prices:** 19.60-22.50 Mobile home hire 255-565 **Facilities:** Wi-fi Play Area **Services:** **Leisure:** P R **Off-site:**

Site 6HEC (site size) 🐛 grass 🌊 sand 🐛 stone ♣ little shade 🌲 partly shaded 🌳 mainly shaded 🚍 motorvans accepted
🏠 bungalows for hire 🚐 mobile homes for hire 🅰 tents for hire ⊗ no dogs & site fully accessible for wheelchairs
Prices amount quoted is per night, for 2 adults and car, plus tent or caravan Mobile home hire is a weekly rate.

FRANCE

MEYRUEIS LOZÈRE

Ayres

rte de la Brêze, 48150
☎ 466456051 🖹 466456051
e-mail: campinglechampdayres@wanadoo.fr
web: www.campinglechampdayres.com

On a wooded meadow with well-defined pitches and modern sanitary installations within easy reach of the picturesque Gorges de la Jonte. Plenty of recreational facilities.

dir: *A75 sortie S44-1.*

GPS: 44.1807, 3.4352

Open: 6 Apr-22 Sep **Site:** 1.5HEC **For hire:** **Prices:** 10-22 Mobile home hire 250-640 **Facilities:** Wi-fi Kids' Club Play Area **Services:** **Leisure:** P **Off-site:** R

Capelan

48150
☎ 466456050 🖹 466450647
e-mail: info@campingcapelan.com
web: www.campingcapelan.com

Set in picturesque surroundings alongside the Gorges de la Jonte with good sports facilities. Dogs not permitted in mobile homes.

dir: *Via A75, exit 44.1 Aguessac towards Meyrueis.*

Open: 5 May-15 Sep **Site:** 4HEC **For hire:** **Prices:** 15-28.50 Mobile home hire 175-755 **Facilities:** Wi-fi Play Area **Services:** **Leisure:** P R **Off-site:**

MILLAU AVEYRON

CM Millau Plage

rte de Millau Plage, 12100
☎ 565601097 🖹 565601688
e-mail: info@campingmillauplage.com
web: www.campingmillauplage.com

Beside the River Tarn, flat shady parkland.

dir: *Via D187.*

Open: 28 Mar-Sep **Site:** 5HEC **For hire:** **Facilities:** **Services:** **Leisure:** P R

Côté Sud

av de L'Aigoual, 12100
☎ 565611883
e-mail: camping-cotesud@orange.fr
web: www.camping-cotesud.fr

A variety of pitches are available, with swimming in the heated outdoor pool or River Dourbie, which runs around the site.

dir: *1km E on D591 next to River Dourbie.*

Open: Apr-Sep **Site:** 3.5HEC **For hire:** **Facilities:** Wi-fi **Services:** **Leisure:** P R

Rivages

860 av de l'Aigoual, 12100
☎ 565610107 🖹 565590356
e-mail: info@campinglesrivages.com
web: www.campinglesrivages.com

A family site with good facilities beside the River Dourbie. Kids' club available in July and August.

dir: *1.7km E via D991.*

GPS: 44.1013, 3.0958

Open: 15 Apr-Sep **Site:** 7HEC **For hire:** **Prices:** 15-34 Mobile home hire 234-742 **Facilities:** Wi-fi Kids' Club Play Area **Services:** **Leisure:** P R **Off-site:**

Viaduc

121 av de Millau Plage, 12100
☎ 565601575 🖹 565613651
e-mail: info@camping-du-viaduc.com
web: www.camping-du-viaduc.com

Located on the banks of the River Tarn, site facilities include swimming pools, waterslides and evening entertainment. Kids' club available in July and August.

dir: *From N, A75 exit 45; from S, A75 exit 47.*

Open: 27 Apr-1 Oct **Site:** 5HEC **For hire:** **Prices:** 15-28 Mobile home hire 224-707 **Facilities:** Wi-fi (charged) Kids' Club Play Area **Services:** **Leisure:** P R

MONTAIGUT-LE-BLANC PUY-DE-DÔME

CM

Le Bourg, 63320
☎ 473967507 🖹 473957005
e-mail: montaigut-le-blanc@wanadoo.fr
web: www.ville-montaigut-le-blanc.fr

A quiet, level municipal site with good recreational facilities.

Open: May-Sep **Site:** 1.5HEC **For hire:** **Facilities:** **Services:** **Leisure:** P R **Off-site:** L

FRANCE

MONT-DORE, LE PUY-DE-DÔME

CM du L'Esquiladou

rte des Cascades, 63240

473652374 473652374

e-mail: camping.esquiladou@orange.fr

web: www.mairie-mont-dore.fr

Mountainous location within a national park.

Open: 20 Apr-30 Oct **Site:** 2HEC **For hire:** **Prices:** 10.50-12 Mobile home hire 260-520 **Facilities:** Wi-fi Play Area **Services:** **Leisure:** P **Off-site:** R

MORNANT RHÔNE

CM de la Trillonière

bld du Général-de-Gaulle, 69440

478441647 478449170

e-mail: accueil@ville-mornant.fr

web: www.ville-mornant.fr

A rural setting on the southern outskirts of the town at an altitude of 333 metres. 25km to Lyon, bus service available.

dir: *Off D30 towards La Condamine.*

GPS: 45.6166, 4.6710

Open: May-Sep **Site:** 1.6HEC **Facilities:** Wi-fi Play Area **Services:** **Leisure:** R **Off-site:** L P

MUROL PUY-DE-DÔME

Europe

63790

473397666 473397661

e-mail: europe.camping@orange.fr

web: www.camping-europ.fr

A family site in rural surroundings on the slopes of a forested valley close to the banks of Lake Chambon.

dir: *Via A71/75 & D996.*

Open: 26 May-2 Sep **Site:** 5.5HEC **For hire:** **Prices:** 11.50-19 Mobile home hire 359-939 **Facilities:** Kids' Club Play Area **Services:** **Leisure:** P **Off-site:** L R

Pré-Bas

Lac Chambon, 63790

473886304 473886593

e-mail: prebas@lac-chambon.com

web: www.campingauvergne.com

On the side of Lake Chambon with direct access to beaches including one where windsurfing is possible.

dir: *SW off D996.*

Open: May-Sep **Site:** 3.5HEC **For hire:** **Prices:** 13.10-24.10 Mobile home hire 276-935 **Facilities:** Wi-fi Play Area **Services:** **Leisure:** L P **Off-site:** R

NANT AVEYRON

Val de Cantobre

12230

565584300 565621036

e-mail: cantobre@rcn.fr

web: www.rcn-valdecantobre.fr

The Camping and Caravanning Club The Friendly Club

Beside the river in the picturesque Gorges de la Dourbie with fine views from the terraced pitches.

C&CC Report *This continues to be an exceptional site, in a stunningly beautiful area, with facilities being of the highest standard. An idyllic setting, any time of the season, with wonderful views from many pitches. You can choose just to relax on site, visit this geologically fascinating area or try one of the many activity sports available locally.*

dir: *4km N of Nant, off D991 towards Millau.*

GPS: 44.0447, 3.3023

Open: 6 Apr-29 Sep **Site:** 6.5HEC **For hire:** **Prices:** 20.70-45.65 Mobile home hire 210.70-1127 **Facilities:** Wi-fi (charged) Kids' Club Play Area **Services:** **Leisure:** P R

NAUSSAC LOZÈRE

Terrasses du Lac

Lac de Naussac, 48300

466692962 466692478

e-mail: info@naussac.com

web: www.naussac.com

Situated beside the lake at an altitude of 1000 metres with fine views.

dir: *Autoroute 75 exit 88 for Langogne.*

Open: 15 Apr-Sep **Site:** 5.8HEC **For hire:** **Facilities:** **Services:** **Leisure:** L P **Off-site:**

FRANCE

NÉBOUZAT PUY-DE-DÔME

Domes

Les Quatre routes de Nébouzat, 63210
☎ 473871406
e-mail: camping.les-domes@wanadoo.fr
web: www.les-domes.com

A comfortable site with hard-standing for caravans.

dir: *Off RN89 Clermont-Bordeaux.*

Open: May-16 Sep **Site:** 1HEC **For hire:** **Facilities:** **Services:** **Leisure:** P **Off-site:** R

NÉRIS-LES-BAINS ALLIER

Camping Municipal du Lac

av Marx-Dormoy, 03310
☎ 470032470 470037999
web: www.ville-neris-les-bains.fr

Situated in a spa town, close to the centre. Some pitches are close to a road, the remainder are in a shaded valley by a stream.

Open: 4 Apr-early Nov **Site:** 7.05HEC **For hire:** **Facilities:** **Services:** **Off-site:** P

NEUVÉGLISE CANTAL

Camping le Belvédère

Lanau, 15260
☎ 471235050
e-mail: belvedere.cantal@wanadoo.fr
web: www.campinglebelvedere.com

Located in the Truyère Valley in a peaceful location with south-facing pitches.

dir: *5km S on D921.*

Open: 31 Mar-29 Sep **Site:** 5HEC **For hire:** **Prices:** 13-28 Mobile home hire 280-745 **Facilities:** Wi-fi (charged) Kids' Club Play Area **Services:** **Leisure:** P **Off-site:** L R

OLLIERGUES PUY-DE-DÔME

Camping les Chelles

63880
☎ 473955434
e-mail: info@camping-les-chelles.com
web: www.camping-les-chelles.com

A family site in wooded surroundings with good leisure facilities.

dir: *5km from town centre.*

GPS: 45.6904, 3.6327

Open: Apr-Oct **Site:** 3.5HEC **For hire:** **Prices:** 13.50 Mobile home hire 200 **Facilities:** Wi-fi Kids' Club Play Area **Services:** **Leisure:** P **Off-site:**

ORCET PUY-DE-DÔME

Le Clos Auroy

The Camping and Caravanning Club The Friendly Club

rue de la Narse, 63670
☎ 473842697 473842697
e-mail: contact@campingclub.info
web: www.camping-le-clos-auroy.com

Terraced site in a green valley next to a small river.

C&CC Report *Le Clos Auroy is great for younger families and anyone seeking tranquil camping in a region of outstanding natural beauty. The owners are eager to share their vast local knowledge, with lots of information on walks and touring. Some of the most unspoilt parts of France are a short drive away, with lakes, volcanoes, mountain rivers and beautiful villages to discover.*

dir: *A75 exit 5 to Orcet, signed.*

GPS: 45.7002, 3.1695

Open: 4 Jan-1 Oct **Site:** 2.5HEC **For hire:** **Prices:** 15-23.80 Mobile home hire 275-650 **Facilities:** Wi-fi Kids' Club Play Area **Services:** **Leisure:** P R **Off-site:** L

POLLIONNAY RHÔNE

Col de la Luère

chemin de Roche Coucou, 69290
☎ 478458111
e-mail: contact@camping-coldelaluere.com
web: camping-coldelaluere.com

Situated in the Monts du Lyonnais, 20 minutes from Lyon.

GPS: 45.7508, 4.6430

Open: All Year. **Site:** 5HEC **For hire:** **Prices:** 12.70-15.10 Mobile home hire 320-380 **Facilities:** Wi-fi Kids' Club Play Area **Services:** **Leisure:** P **Off-site:** R

POMEYS RHÔNE

Camping d'Hurongues

Zone de Loisirs d'Hurongues, 69590
☎ 478484429
e-mail: campinghurongues@orange.fr
web: www.camping-hurongues.com

Site bordered by oak trees, suitable for families, with large pitches. Activities available close by include mountain biking, hiking and canoeing.

dir: *Off road between St Symphorien sur Croise and Chazelles sur Lyon.*

GPS: 45.6345, 4.4280

Open: 17 Apr-17 Oct **Site:** 3.6HEC **For hire:** **Prices:** 10-17 Mobile home hire 238-588 **Facilities:** Wi-fi (charged) Play Area **Services:** **Leisure:** P **Off-site:** R

FRANCE

PONT-DE-SALARS — AVEYRON

Terrasses du Lac

rte du Vibal, 12290

☎ 565468818 🖹 565468538

e-mail: campinglesterrasses@orange.fr

web: www.campinglesterrasses.com

Pleasant lake-side site with terraced pitches overlooking the Pont-de-Salars lake.

dir: *4km N via D523.*

Open: Apr-Sep **Site:** 6HEC **For hire:** **Prices:** 12.50-23.90 Mobile home hire 230-693 **Facilities:** Wi-fi Kids' Club Play Area **Services:** **Leisure:** L P

PONTGIBAUD — PUY-DE-DÔME

CM

rte de la Miouze, 63230

☎ 473889699 🖹 473887777

e-mail: mairie.pontgibaud@wanadoo.fr

web: www.ville-pontgibaud.fr

Set in a wooded area beside the River Sioule.

dir: *0.5km SW on D986 towards Rochefort-Montagne.*

Open: 15 Apr-15 Oct **Site:** 4.5HEC **For hire:** **Facilities:** **Services:** **Leisure:** R **Off-site:** L

PRADEAUX, LES — PUY-DE-DÔME

Châteaux la Grange Fort

63500

☎ 473710593 🖹 473710769

e-mail: chateau@lagrangefort.eu

web: www.lagrangefort.com

Set in a park surrounding a château on the River Allier.

dir: *A75 exit 13 for Parentignat, onto D999 & signed.*

GPS: 45.5088, 3.2849

Open: Etr-15 Oct **Site:** 22HEC **For hire:** **Prices:** 15-26.75 Mobile home hire 250-765 **Facilities:** Wi-fi (charged) Play Area **Services:** **Leisure:** P R **Off-site:**

PUY, LE — HAUTE-LOIRE

Camping du Puy-en-Velay

43000

☎ 471095509 🖹 471095509

web: www.camping-bouthezard-43.com

On a wooded meadow with a section reserved for motor caravans.

dir: *From town centre towards Clermont-Ferrand, right at lights by church of St-Laurent, signed, site 0.5km on left.*

Open: 15 Mar-15 Oct **Site:** 1HEC **Facilities:** **Services:** **Off-site:** P

RIVIÈRE-SUR-TARN — AVEYRON

Peyrelade

rte des Gorges-du-Tarn, 12640

☎ 565626254 🖹 565626561

e-mail: campingpeyrelade@orange.fr

web: www.campingpeyrelade.com

Wooded surroundings close to the Gorges du Tarn.

dir: *2km E via D907, beside River Tarn.*

GPS: 44.1909, 3.1573

Open: 15 May-15 Sep **Site:** 4HEC **For hire:** **Prices:** 15-39 Mobile home hire 266-713 **Facilities:** Wi-fi Kids' Club Play Area **Services:** **Leisure:** P R

RODEZ — AVEYRON

CM Layoule

12000

☎ 565670952 🖹 565671143

Clean, tidy site in valley below town, completely divided into pitches.

dir: *NE of town centre, signed.*

Open: Jun-Sep **Site:** 3HEC **Facilities:** **Services:** **Off-site:**

FRANCE

ROYAT PUY-DE-DÔME

Camping Indigo Royat

rte de Gravenoire, 63130

473359705 473356769

e-mail: royat@camping-indigo.com

web: www.camping-indigo.com

A natural setting at the foot of the Puy de Dôme and overlooking Clermont Ferrand. The pitches are laid out in terraces and are comfortably shaded. Kids' club available in July and August. 1 dog per pitch.

dir: *From A71/A72 exit 15 follow Clermont-Ferrand Nord then Tulle-Bordeaux/Chamalières-Royat.*

GPS: 45.7638, 3.0429

Open: 28 Mar-8 Nov **Site:** 7HEC **For hire:** **Prices:** 14.50-22.50 Mobile home hire 341.25-763 **Facilities:** Kids' Club Play Area **Services:** **Leisure:** P **Off-site:** L R

RUYNES-EN-MARGERIDE CANTAL

Petit Bois

15320

471234226 467363542

web: www.revea-vacances.fr/campings

A pleasant, well-equipped, park-like site on the bank of the River Charente.

dir: *0.5km SW on D13 rte de Garabit, signed.*

Open: 5 May-14 Sep **Site:** 7HEC **For hire:** **Facilities:** **Services:** **Off-site:** P

SAIGNES CANTAL

Bellevue

15240

471406840 471406165

e-mail: saignes.mairie@wanadoo.fr

web: saignes-mairie.fr

A pleasant rural site in the Sumène Valley.

Open: Jul-Aug **Site:** 0.9HEC **For hire:** **Facilities:** **Services:** **Off-site:** P

ST-ALBAN-SUR-LIMAGNOLE LOZÈRE

Galier

48120

466315880 466314183

e-mail: accueil@campinglegalier.fr

web: www.campinglegalier.fr

Well-equipped site beside the river.

dir: *A75 exit 34.*

Open: Mar-Oct **Site:** 4HEC **For hire:** **Facilities:** **Services:** **Leisure:** P R **Off-site:**

ST-AMANS-DES-COTS AVEYRON

Village Center les Tours

12460

499572121 467516389

e-mail: contact@village-center.com

web: www.village-center.com/midi-pyrenees/camping-campagne-les-tours.php

On the shore of Selves Lake with some pitches having direct access to the water. Comprehensive leisure facilities available.

dir: *From N A75 exit St Flour; from S A75 exit Séverac le Château.*

GPS: 44.6676, 2.6812

Open: 27 Apr-9 Sep **Site:** 15HEC **For hire:** **Prices:** 18-35 Mobile home hire 210-909 **Facilities:** Wi-fi (charged) Kids' Club **Services:** **Leisure:** P **Off-site:** L

ST-AMANT-ROCHE-SAVINE PUY-DE-DÔME

CM Saviloisirs

63890

473957360 473957262

e-mail: saviloisirs@wanadoo.fr

web: www.saviloisirs.com

Situated in the Livradois mountains, at an altitude of 905 metres. Quiet site run by the local tourist authority with plenty of sports facilities within easy reach.

dir: *Via Clermont-Ferrand then Billom or St-Etienne then Ambert.*

Open: May-Sep **Site:** 1.5HEC **For hire:** **Prices:** 10.90-12.30 **Facilities:** Wi-fi (charged) Play Area **Services:** **Off-site:** L P R

FRANCE

ST-BONNET-TRONÇAIS — ALLIER

Champ-Fossé

03360

☎ 470061130 🖷 470061501

e-mail: champfosse@campingstroncais.com

web: www.campingstroncais.com

Set in the forest of Tronçais beside a lake with plenty of recreational facilities.

dir: *Via A71-E11.*

GPS: 46.6500, 2.6833

Open: Apr-Oct **Site:** 35HEC **For hire:** **Prices:** 12.22-14.50 Mobile home hire 278-470 **Facilities:** Wi-fi **Services:** **Leisure:** L P **Off-site:**

ST-CLÉMENT-DE-VALORGUE — PUY-DE-DÔME

Narcisses

63660

☎ 473954576 🖷 473954576

e-mail: ptipois2@wanadoo.fr

web: www.campinglesnarcisses.com

A beautiful natural setting within the Livradois-Forez regional park.

Open: May-Sep **Site:** 1.3HEC **For hire:** **Facilities:** **Services:** **Leisure:** P R **Off-site:** L

ST-GAL-SUR-SIOULE — PUY-DE-DÔME

Pont de St-Gal

63440

☎ 473974471

e-mail: campingdesaintgal@orange.fr

A pleasant site with shaded, well-defined pitches, and access to the river for boating and fishing.

dir: *E on D16 towards Ebreuil, beside River Sioule.*

Open: May-Sep **Site:** 1HEC **For hire:** **Facilities:** **Services:** **Leisure:** R

ST-GENIEZ-D'OLT — AVEYRON

Marmotel

12130

☎ 565704651 🖷 565463619

e-mail: info@marmotel.com

web: www.marmotel.com

Grassy family site on River Lot with a variety of recreational facilities.

dir: *A75 exit 41.*

Open: 2 May-22 Sep **Site:** 5HEC **For hire:** **Facilities:** Wi-fi Kids' Club Play Area **Services:** **Leisure:** P R **Off-site:**

ST-GERMAIN-DE-CALBERTE — LOZÈRE

La Garde

48370

☎ 466459482

e-mail: campinglagarde@orange.fr

web: www.causses-cevennes.com/lagarde

A pleasant location on the edge of the Cévennes national park.

dir: *Via A7 or A75.*

Open: Jun-Sep **Site:** 2.4HEC **For hire:** **Facilities:** Wi-fi Play Area **Services:** **Leisure:** P **Off-site:** R

ST-GÉRONS — CANTAL

Domaine du Lac

Espinet, 15150

☎ 471622798

e-mail: prldomainedulac@orange.fr

web: www.prl-domainedulac.fr

A relaxing stay is assured on the shores of Lake St Etienne Cantalès, where fishing is available.

GPS: 44.9351, 2.2301

Open: Apr-Oct **Site:** 4HEC **For hire:** **Prices:** Mobile home hire 350-550 **Facilities:** Wi-fi Play Area **Services:** **Leisure:** L P **Off-site:**

FRANCE

Les Rives du Lac

Espinet, 15150
☎ 625346289
e-mail: info@lesrivesdulac.fr
web: www.lesrivesdulac.fr
Wooded and shady site on the shore of Lake St Etienne Cantalès. Fishing is a popular activity here, with fishing permits available on site.
GPS: 44.9360, 2.2305
Open: 15 Apr-Oct **Site:** 4HEC **For hire:** **Prices:** 13-18 Mobile home hire 250-500 **Facilities:** Wi-fi Play Area **Services:** **Leisure:** L P

ST-GERVAIS-D'AUVERGNE PUY-DE-DÔME

CM de l'Étang Philippe

rte de St-Eloy-les-Mines, 63390
☎ 473857484
e-mail: campingstgervais@wanadoo.fr
web: www.camping-loisir.com
A small municipal site beside a small lake.
dir: *Via N987.*
Open: Apr-Sep **Site:** 5HEC **For hire:** **Facilities:** **Services:** **Leisure:** L **Off-site:**

ST-JACQUES-DES-BLATS CANTAL

CM des Blats

rte de la Gare, 15800
☎ 471470590 471470709
e-mail: i-tourisme-st-jacques@wanadoo.fr
A small site on the banks of the River Cère. A good centre for exploring the surrounding Auvergne Volcanic Park area.
Open: May-Sep **Site:** 1HEC **Facilities:** **Services:** **Leisure:** R **Off-site:**

ST-JUST CANTAL

CM

Le Bourg, 15320
☎ 471737048 471737144
e-mail: commune.stjust@wanadoo.fr
web: www.saintjust.com
Pleasant site on flat ground close to shops. Activities include tennis, climbing, cycling and fishing. Children's activities take place during July and August.
dir: *A75 exit at juncts 31 or 32.*
GPS: 44.8896, 3.209
Open: May-Sep **Site:** 2HEC **For hire:** **Prices:** 8-9.80 Mobile home hire 229-415 **Facilities:** Wi-fi (charged) Play Area **Services:** **Leisure:** P **Off-site:** R

ST-MARTIN-VALMEROUX CANTAL

Moulin du Teinturier

Mont Joly, 15140
☎ 471694312 471692452
e-mail: lemoulinduteinturier@orange.fr
Wooded valley site close to a medieval market town.
dir: *Off D922 Aurillac-Mauriac.*
Open: Jun-Sep **Site:** 2.8HEC **For hire:** **Facilities:** Play Area **Services:** **Leisure:** R **Off-site:** P

ST-NECTAIRE PUY-DE-DÔME

Vallée Verte

rte des Granges, 63710
☎ 473885268
web: www.campinglavalleeverte.com
Wooded surroundings by a river within the Auvergne volcanic park.
dir: *On R146, 400m from R996.*
Open: 15 Apr-Sep **Site:** 2.5HEC **For hire:** **Facilities:** **Services:** **Leisure:** R **Off-site:** P R

ST-OURS PUY-DE-DÔME

Bel-Air

63230
☎ 473887214
e-mail: contact@campingbelair.fr
web: www.campingbelair.fr
In a park setting with spacious pitches. Facilities include an area for games and barbecues.
dir: *1km SW on D943.*
GPS: 45.8444, 2.8767
Open: May-Sep **Site:** 2HEC **For hire:** **Prices:** 14.10 **Facilities:** Wi-fi (charged) Play Area **Services:** **Off-site:** L

ST-PAULIEN HAUTE-LOIRE

Camping de la Rochelambert

Rte de Lanthenas, 43350
☎ 471005402
e-mail: infos@camping-rochelambert.com
web: www.camping-rochelambert.com
Bordered by a river and nature trail, ideal for water sports enthusiasts with activities including fishing.
GPS: 45.1203, 3.7935
Open: Apr-Sep **Site:** 4HEC **For hire:** **Prices:** 12.20-16.60 **Facilities:** Wi-fi Play Area **Services:** **Leisure:** P R **Off-site:**

FRANCE

ST-PIERRE-COLAMINE — PUY-DE-DÔME

Ombrage

63610

473967787

e-mail: campombrage@orange.fr

web: www.campombrage.com

A pleasant site in peaceful wooded surroundings at an altitude of 800 metres on the edge of the Auvergne Volcano Park. All the usual services are provided and there are good recreational facilities.

dir: *300m from D978.*

GPS: 45.5381, 2.9778

Open: All Year. **Site:** 2HEC **For hire:** **Prices:** 11.48-14.25 **Facilities:** Wi-fi Play Area **Services:** **Leisure:** P **Off-site:** R

ST-RÉMY-SUR-DUROLLE — PUY-DE-DÔME

CM Chanterelles

63550

473943171 473943171

e-mail: leschanterelles0549@orange.fr

web: www.revea-vacances.fr

Pleasant wooded surroundings close to the lake.

dir: *3km NE via D201.*

Open: May-Sep **Site:** 6HEC **For hire:** **Facilities:** **Services:** **Off-site:** L P

ST-ROME-DE-TARN — AVEYRON

Cascade

12490

565625659 565625862

e-mail: contact@camping-cascade-aveyron.com

web: www.campingdelacascade.com

Terraced site beside the river Tarn.

dir: *0.3km N via D993.*

Open: All Year. **Site:** 4HEC **For hire:** **Facilities:** **Services:** **Leisure:** L P R **Off-site:**

ST-SALVADOU — AVEYRON

Muret

12200

565818069 565818069

e-mail: info@lemuret.com

web: www.campinglemuret.com

A modern site in peaceful, rural surroundings beside the lake.

dir: *3km SE.*

Open: Apr-Oct **Site:** 3HEC **For hire:** **Facilities:** **Services:** **Leisure:** L **Off-site:**

STE-CATHERINE — RHÔNE

CM du Châtelard

69440

478818060 478818773

e-mail: mairie-ste-catherine@wanadoo.fr

web: www.mairie-saintecatherine.fr

A quiet, well-equipped site providing magnificent views over the surrounding countryside.

dir: *2km S.*

Open: Mar-Nov **Site:** 4HEC **Prices:** 6.10-7.05 **Facilities:** Play Area **Services:** **Off-site:** R

STE-SIGOLÈNE — HAUTE-LOIRE

Kawan Village Camping de Vaubarlet

The Camping and Caravanning Club — The Friendly Club

rte de Grazac, Vaubarlet, 43600

471666495 471661198

e-mail: camping@vaubarlet.com

web: www.vaubarlet.com

Set in a beautiful wooded valley beside the River Dunières with a variety of supervised family activities including a kids' club in summer months.

C&CC Report *For those who love nature and want friendly welcoming site owners and a green-award winning camp site, le Vaubarlet is ideal. The hill walking and mountain bike routes, the on-site first category fishing river, heated pools and the relaxing atmosphere provide the makings of great holidays. Visits to the gorges of the Loire and their châteaux, the spectacular volcanic town of Le Puy-en-Velay, the local towns and markets and the various museums will remain long in the memory.*

dir: *D44 exit to Ste-Sigolène, D43 towards Grazac, signed after 10km.*

GPS: 45.2161, 4.2126

Open: May-Sep **Site:** 3.5HEC **For hire:** **Prices:** 22-25 **Facilities:** Wi-fi Kids' Club Play Area **Services:** **Leisure:** P R

Site 6HEC (site size) grass sand stone little shade partly shaded mainly shaded motorvans accepted bungalows for hire mobile homes for hire tents for hire no dogs site fully accessible for wheelchairs
Prices amount quoted is per night, for 2 adults and car, plus tent or caravan Mobile home hire is a weekly rate.

SALLES-CURAN — AVEYRON

Beau Rivage

rte des Vernhes, Lac de Pareloup, 12410
565463332
e-mail: camping-beau-rivage@orange.fr
web: www.beau-rivage.fr

A small terraced site with a family atmosphere located on the shore of Lac de Pareloup. Kids' club available in July and August. Activities on the lake include sailing, fishing and water sports.

dir: *A75 exit 44.1, follow D991.*

Open: Apr-Oct **Site:** 2HEC **For hire:** **Prices:** 14-29.90 Mobile home hire 182-784 **Facilities:** Wi-fi Kids' Club Play Area **Services:** **Leisure:** L P

Genêts

12410
565463534 565780072
e-mail: contact@camping-les-genets.fr
web: www.camping-les-genets.fr

On the edge of the Pareloup lake.

dir: *7km W via D577.*

Open: Jun-Sep **Site:** 3HEC **For hire:** **Prices:** 18-34 **Facilities:** Wi-fi (charged) Kids' Club **Services:** **Leisure:** L P

SAZERET — ALLIER

Petite Valette

03390
470076457
e-mail: la.petite.valette@wanadoo.fr
web: www.valette.nl

A well-equipped site attached to a farm with well-defined pitches and organised activities for children.

dir: *A71 exit 11 & signed.*

Site: 4HEC **For hire:** **Facilities:** **Services:** **Leisure:** L P

SEMBADEL-GARE — HAUTE-LOIRE

Casses

43160
471009472 471009179

A family site in a rural setting at an altitude of 1000 metres, 2km from a lake.

dir: *1km W via D22.*

Open: Jul-20 Sep **Site:** 2.4HEC **Facilities:** **Services:** **Off-site:** L R

SÉNERGUES — AVEYRON

Étang du Camp

12320
565460195
e-mail: info@etangducamp.fr
web: www.etangducamp.fr

Well-equipped site, with spacious pitches and clean facilities, in a tranquil wooded setting beside the lake.

dir: *6km SW via D242.*

GPS: 44.5581, 2.4627

Open: Apr-Sep **Site:** 3HEC **For hire:** **Prices:** 12-16 **Facilities:** Wi-fi Play Area **Services:** **Off-site:** P

SÉVÉRAC-L'ÉGLISE — AVEYRON

Grange de Monteillac

Monteillac, 12310
565702100 565702101
e-mail: info@la-grange-de-monteillac.com
web: www.la-grange-de-monteillac.com

A family site in a quiet wooded location with good recreational facilities.

dir: *Via A75 & N88.*

Open: 15 May-15 Sep **Site:** 4.5HEC **For hire:** **Prices:** 13.40-34.90 Mobile home hire 255-833 **Facilities:** Wi-fi Kids' Club Play Area **Services:** **Leisure:** P **Off-site:**

SINGLES — PUY-DE-DÔME

Moulin de Serre

Vallee de la Burande, 63690
473211606
e-mail: moulindeserre@orange.fr
web: www.moulindeserre.com

A spacious and well maintained campsite beside the River Burande with pitches raised and separated by hedges. Friendly atmosphere with activities for both adults and children.

dir: *1.7km S of La Guinguette via D73.*

GPS: 45.5431, 2.5428

Open: 7 Apr-17 Sep **Site:** 7HEC **For hire:** **Prices:** 10.05-18.30 Mobile home hire 154-672 **Facilities:** Wi-fi Kids' Club Play Area **Services:** **Leisure:** P R

FRANCE

THÉRONDELS AVEYRON

La Source

Presqu'ile de Laussac, 12600

☎ 565660562 565662100

e-mail: info@camping-la-source.com

web: www.camping-la-source.com

A beautiful location beside Lake Sarrans.

dir: *From Clermont Ferrand A75 exit St Flour, onto D921 then D990 to Pierrefort. After Pierrefort take D34 to Laussac.*

GPS: 44.8536, 2.7716

Open: 17 May-9 Sep **Site:** 4.5HEC **For hire:** **Prices:** 17-29 Mobile home hire 196-833 **Facilities:** Wi-fi (charged) Kids' Club Play Area **Services:** **Leisure:** L P

TRIZAC CANTAL

Pioulat

15400

☎ 471786420 471786540

e-mail: mairie.trizac@wanadoo.fr

In a tranquil village setting with good facilities.

Open: 16 Jun-16 Sep **Site:** 4.71HEC **For hire:** **Facilities:** **Services:** **Leisure:** L R **Off-site:**

VERRIÈRES-EN-FOREZ LOIRE

Ferme Le Soleillant

Le Soleillant, 42600

☎ 477762273

e-mail: camille.rival@wanadoo.fr

web: www.le-soleillant.com

A small terraced site within the grounds of a farm.

dir: *RD496 between Montbrison & St Anthème. Campsite signed.*

GPS: 45.5777, 3.9944

Open: All Year. **Site:** 3.2HEC **For hire:** **Facilities:** **Services:** **Off-site:** R

VIC-SUR-CÈRE CANTAL

Pommeraie

15800

☎ 471475418 471496330

e-mail: pommeraie@wanadoo.fr

web: camping-la-pommeraie.com

A well-equipped family site in a peaceful location with good recreational facilities.

dir: *2km SE.*

Open: May-15 Sep **Site:** 2.5HEC **For hire:** **Facilities:** **Services:** **Leisure:** P **Off-site:** R

VILLEFORT LOZÈRE

Palhère

rte du Mas de la Barque, 48800

☎ 466468063 466468063

e-mail: campinglapalhere@orange.fr

web: www.everyoneweb.fr/campinglapalhere

A well-equipped, peaceful site on the edge of the Parc National des Cévennes.

dir: *4km SW via D66 beside river.*

Open: May-Sep **Site:** 3HEC **For hire:** **Prices:** 14 **Facilities:** Play Area **Services:** **Leisure:** P R **Off-site:** L

VILLEFRANCHE-DE-PANAT AVEYRON

Cantarelles

Alrance, 12430

☎ 565464035 565464035

e-mail: cantarelles@wanadoo.fr

web: www.lescantarelles.com

On level grassland by Lac de Villefranche-de-Panat.

dir: *On D25 3km N.*

Open: May-Sep **Site:** 3.5HEC **For hire:** **Facilities:** **Services:** **Leisure:** L

FRANCE

VILLEFRANCHE-DE-ROUERGUE AVEYRON

Camping du Rouergue

35 bis av de Fondies, 12200
☎ 565451624 🖷 565451624
e-mail: campingrouergue@wanadoo.fr
web: www.campingdurouergue.com

A comfortable site in a pleasant, shady location beside the River Aveyron.

dir: *1.5km SW via D47 rte de Monteils.*

GPS: 44.3406, 2.0264

Open: Apr-Sep **Site:** 2HEC **For hire:** **Facilities:** Wi-fi Play Area **Services:** **Leisure:** P **Off-site:** R

SOUTH COAST/RIVIERA

AGAY VAR

Agay Soleil

1152 bld de la Plage, rte de Cannes D559, 83530
☎ 494820079 🖷 494828870
e-mail: camping-agay-soleil@wanadoo.fr
web: www.agay-soleil.com

A small site in a shady position directly on a sandy beach. The facilities are good and water sports are available nearby.

dir: *Between N98 & sea.*

Open: 25 Mar-5 Nov **Site:** 0.7HEC **For hire:** **Facilities:** **Services:** **Leisure:** S **Off-site:**

Estérel

av des Golfs, 83530
☎ 494820328 🖷 494828737
e-mail: contact@esterel-caravaning.fr

A pleasant family-site with Provençal architecture. There is plenty to entertain all age groups day and evening. Riding and cycling can be enjoyed nearby in the surrounding hills and woods. Just 3km away from the sandy beach of Agay.

dir: *A8 exit 38 Fréjus/St Raphaël in direction of St Raphaël 3km N of Agay-Plage follow signs for Agay par Valescure or Agay par l'interior, near golf course.*

GPS: 43.4534, 6.8326

Open: Apr-Sep **Site:** 15HEC **Prices:** 18-343 **Facilities:** Wi-fi (charged) Kids' Club Play Area **Services:** **Leisure:** P **Off-site:** L R S

AGDE HÉRAULT

Champs Blancs

rte de Rochelongue, Rochelongue-Plage, 34300
☎ 467942342 🖷 467948781
e-mail: champs.blancs@wanadoo.fr
web: www.champs-blancs.fr

Quiet shady site with hedged pitches and surrounded by exotic vegetation. Good sports and entertainment facilities.

Open: 5 Apr-Sep **Site:** 4HEC **For hire:** **Facilities:** Wi-fi (charged) Kids' Club Play Area **Services:** **Leisure:** P **Off-site:** R S

Escale

rte de la Tamarissière, 34300
☎ 467212109 🖷 467211024
e-mail: info@camping-lescale.com
web: www.camping-lescale.com

A riverside site, 0.9km from the sea, with good recreational facilities.

Open: Apr-Sep **Site:** 3HEC **For hire:** **Facilities:** **Services:** **Leisure:** P R **Off-site:** S

Mer et Soleil

88 chemin de Notre Dame, à Saint Martin, 34300
☎ 467942114 🖷 467948194
e-mail: contact@camping-mer-soleil.com
web: www.camping-mer-soleil.com

A modern, well-equipped family site within easy reach of the beach. Spa facilities are available.

GPS: 43.2855, 3.4778

Open: 31 Mar-6 Oct **Site:** 7.9HEC **For hire:** **Prices:** 17-41 Mobile home hire 210-1253 **Facilities:** Wi-fi (charged) Kids' Club Play Area **Services:** **Leisure:** P **Off-site:** R S

Romarins

rte du Grau, 34300
☎ 467941859 🖷 467265880
e-mail: contact@romarins.com
web: www.romarins.com

Located in a busy Mediterranean fishing village south of the city of Agde. On the left bank of the Herault river with fine sandy beaches. Kids' club available in July and August. No dogs in mobile homes.

Open: Apr-Sep **Site:** 2.2HEC **For hire:** **Prices:** 13.70-25 Mobile home hire 230-965 **Facilities:** Wi-fi (charged) Kids' Club Play Area **Services:** **Leisure:** P **Off-site:** R S

FRANCE

Village Center Les 7 Fonts

chemin de Baldy, 34300
☎ 499572121 🖷 467516389
e-mail: contact@village-center.com
web: www.village-center.com/languedoc-roussillon/camping-les-sept-fonts.php
Close to the Canal du Midi, Les 7 Fonts is set in a waterpark.
dir: *A9 exit 34, follow RN312 then RN112 towards Agde/Sète, then Agde, turn right after garden centre.*
GPS: 43.3112, 3.4992
Open: 27 May-18 Sep **Site:** 5.5HEC **For hire:** **Facilities:** Wi-fi (charged) Kids' Club Play Area **Services:** **Leisure:** P

AIGUES MORTES — GARD

Camping Fleur de Camargue

St-Laurent-d'Aigouze, 30220
☎ 466881542
e-mail: contact@fleur-de-camargue.com
web: www.fleur-de-camargue.com
1 dog per pitch, pets not permitted in mobile homes.
C&CC Report *This friendly, family site is a quieter alternative to the sites nearer the coast and there is much to see and do in the area. You can cycle along the canals, go to the beach, spot the flamingoes of the Camargue, visit Montpellier or venture into the beautiful Languedoc interior for a day out.*
GPS: 43.6111, 4.2089
For hire: **Facilities:** Play Area **Leisure:** P

The Camping and Caravanning Club The Friendly Club

Yelloh Village La Petite Camargue

Quartier du Môle, 30220
☎ 466539898 🖷 466539880
e-mail: info@yellohvillage-petite-camargue.com
web: www.yellohvillage-petite-camargue.com
A grassy site among vineyards on the D62, 3.5km from the sea.
dir: *Autoroute exit Gallargues for La Grande Motte. From Aigues Mortes A62 towards La Grande Motte/Montpellier. Site 1km after rdbt with flamingo on.*
GPS: 43.5669, 4.1558
Open: 20 Apr-16 Sep **Site:** 10HEC **For hire:** **Prices:** 17-44 Mobile home hire 273-1533 **Facilities:** Wi-fi Kids' Club Play Area **Services:** **Leisure:** P **Off-site:** S

AIX-EN-PROVENCE — BOUCHES-DU-RHÔNE

Arc en Ciel

Pont de Trois Sautets, 50 av Malacrida, 13100
☎ 442261428
e-mail: camping-arcenciel@neuf.fr
web: www.campingarcenciel.com
A pleasant terraced site on both sides of a stream.
dir: *N7 exit 31 Aix Val Saint André for Toulon, 3km SE near Pont des Trois Sautets.*
Open: Apr-Sep **Site:** 2HEC **Prices:** 19.50-22.90 **Facilities:** Wi-fi Play Area **Services:** **Leisure:** P R **Off-site:**

Chantecler

Val St Andre, 13100
☎ 442261298 🖷 442273353
e-mail: info@campingchantecler.com
web: www.campingchantecler.com
Extensive, uneven site on a hill with terraced pitches. A kids' club is available in July and August.
dir: *A8 exit Aix-Est, 2.5km SE of town.*
Open: All Year. **Site:** 8HEC **For hire:** **Facilities:** Wi-fi (charged) Kids' Club Play Area **Services:** **Leisure:** P **Off-site:** S

ALBARON — BOUCHES-DU-RHÔNE

Domaine du Crin Blanc

CD37 Hameau de Saliers, 13123
☎ 466874878 🖷 466871866
e-mail: camping-crin.blanc@wanadoo.fr
web: www.campingcrinblanc.com
Two swimming pools, plus a paddling pool for campers' use, with many leisure and entertainment activities taking place during July and August.
Open: Apr-Sep **Site:** 5HEC **For hire:** **Facilities:** Wi-fi Kids' Club Play Area **Services:** **Leisure:** P **Off-site:** R

ALET-LES-BAINS — AUDE

Val d'Aleth

chemin de la Paoulette, 11580
468699040
e-mail: camping@valdaleth.com
web: www.valdaleth.com

Picturesque surroundings beneath the historic ramparts, on the banks of the River Aude.

dir: *D118 S from Carcassonne, through Limoux, site 8km S off D118.*

GPS: 42.9951, 2.2561

Open: All Year. **Site:** 0.5HEC **For hire:** **Prices:** 15-16 **Facilities:** Wi-fi (charged) Play Area **Services:** **Leisure:** R **Off-site:** P

ANDUZE — GARD

Arche

30140
466617408 466618894
e-mail: resa@camping-arche.fr
web: www.camping-arche.fr

A beautiful location on the River Gard in the Cévennes region.

dir: *A7 exit Bollène onto D907.*

Open: Apr-Sep **Site:** 10HEC **For hire:** **Prices:** 19.50-39.80 Mobile home hire 370-1080 **Facilities:** Wi-fi Kids' Club Play Area **Services:** **Leisure:** P R

Brise des Pins

rte de St-Félix de Pallières, 30140
466616339

A terraced site offering fine panoramic views over the surrounding countryside.

dir: *3km from Anduze.*

Open: Jun-15 Sep **Site:** **Facilities:** **Services:**

Castel Rose

610 chemin de Recoulin, 30140
466618015
e-mail: castelrose@wanadoo.fr
web: www.castelrose.com

A spacious, wooded and well-equipped site on the banks of the River Gardon.

dir: *1km NW on D907.*

Open: Apr-Sep **Site:** 7HEC **For hire:** **Facilities:** Wi-fi Kids' Club Play Area **Services:** **Leisure:** P R **Off-site:**

Cévennes Provence

30140
466617310 466616074
e-mail: marais@camping-cevennes-provence.com
web: www.camping-cevennes-provence.com

Situated in a valley bordered by two rivers. A quiet site with a choice of pitches in varying levels of shade and terrain.

dir: *From Anduze take D907 towards St Jean du Gard for 3km, turn right to Corbes on D284.*

GPS: 44.0733, 3.9647

Open: 20 Mar-1 Oct **Site:** 30HEC **For hire:** **Prices:** 14.90-23.90 **Facilities:** Wi-fi Play Area **Services:** **Leisure:** R

ANNEYRON — DRÔME

Flower Camping La Châtaigneraie

rte de Mantaille, 26140
475314333 475038467
e-mail: contact@chataigneraie.com
web: www.chataigneraie.com

Family site in peaceful surroundings with fine views of the Rhône Valley and the mountains of the Ardèche. Large grassy pitches, clearly marked with a choice of sunny or shady position and large secure play areas for children. Wi-fi free for 30 minutes.

dir: *A7 exit 12 (Chanas), take N7 towards Valence/St Vallier. Before Le Creux de la Thine left onto D1 for Anneyron, site signed.*

GPS: 45.255, 4.904

Open: Apr-Sep **Site:** 2HEC **For hire:** **Prices:** 15.50-27 Mobile home hire 210-721 **Facilities:** Wi-fi (charged) Kids' Club Play Area **Services:** **Leisure:** P

ANTHÉOR-PLAGE — VAR

Viaduc

bld des Lucioles, 83530
494448231 494448231
e-mail: camping.viaduc@gmail.com

A quiet site 150 metres from a sandy beach, with good facilities.

dir: *Via N98.*

Open: Jun-Sep **Site:** 1.1HEC **Prices:** 26-31 **Facilities:** Wi-fi Play Area **Services:** **Off-site:** S

FRANCE

ANTIBES ALPES-MARITIMES

Logis de la Brague

1221 rte de Nice, La Brague, 06600

☎ 493335472 📠 493746257

e-mail: contact@camping-logisbrague.com

web: www.camping-logisbrague.com

On a level meadow beside a small river, 50 metres from the beach.

dir: *On N7, follow signs to Marineland.*

Open: 2 May-Sep **Site:** 1.7HEC **For hire:** **Facilities:** Play Area **Services:** **Leisure:** R S **Off-site:** P

ARGELÈS-SUR-MER PYRÉNÉES-ORIENTALES

Criques de Porteils

La Corniche de Collioure, 66700

☎ 468811273 📠 468958576

e-mail: contactcdp@lescriques.com

web: www.lescriques.com

The site has good facilities and the restaurant has a terrace with a beautiful view.

dir: *D914, exit 13. Turn right at Hotel du Golfe & follow signs.*

Open: 31 Mar-20 Oct **Site:** 5.5HEC **For hire:** **Prices:** 22.50-42 Mobile home hire 205-1079 **Facilities:** Wi-fi Kids' Club Play Area **Services:** **Leisure:** P S

Dauphin

rte de Taxo à la Mer, 66704

☎ 468811754 📠 468958260

e-mail: info@campingledauphin.com

web: www.campingledauphin.com

On a long stretch of grassland shaded by poplars, 1.5km from the sea. Kids' club for 6 to 12 year olds in July and August.

dir: *3km N of town, turn right at Taxo d'Avall.*

GPS: 42.5724, 3.0217

Open: 12 May-21 Sep **Site:** 8.5HEC **For hire:** **Prices:** 20-55 Mobile home hire 273-1183 **Facilities:** Kids' Club Play Area **Services:** **Leisure:** P **Off-site:** L R S

Galets

rte de Taxo à la Mer, 66700

☎ 468810812 📠 468816876

e-mail: lesgalets@campinglesgalets.fr

web: www.campmed.com

A well-equipped family site with trees, bushes and exotic plants.

dir: *4km N.*

Open: 4 Apr-Sep **Site:** 5HEC **For hire:** **Facilities:** **Services:** **Leisure:** P **Off-site:** R S

Marsouins

chemin de la Retirada, 66702

☎ 468811481 📠 468959358

e-mail: marsouins@campmed.com

web: www.campmed.com

A large family site close to the sea, with good facilities and activities for both adults and children.

dir: *2km NE towards Plage Nord.*

Open: 16 Apr-24 Sep **Site:** 10HEC **For hire:** **Facilities:** Wi-fi Kids' Club Play Area **Services:** **Leisure:** P **Off-site:** S

Massane

66702

☎ 468810685 📠 468815918

e-mail: info@camping-massane.com

web: www.camping-massane.com

Shady, well-planned site, 1km from the sea.

dir: *Beside D618 near municipal sports field.*

Open: 15 Mar-15 Oct **Site:** 3HEC **For hire:** **Facilities:** **Services:** **Leisure:** P **Off-site:** S

Ombrages

av du Général-de-Gaulle, 66702

☎ 468812983 📠 468958187

e-mail: contact@les-ombrages.com

web: www.les-ombrages.com

A picturesque wooded setting 300 metres from the beach. The well-equipped site has good recreational facilities and defined pitches.

Open: Jun-Sep **Site:** 4HEC **For hire:** **Prices:** 10-29 Mobile home hire 240-640 **Facilities:** Wi-fi Play Area **Services:** **Off-site:** L P R S

Pins

av du Tech, 66702
☎ 468811046
e-mail: camping@les-pins.com
web: www.les-pins.com

A peaceful family site on a narrow stretch of grassland with some poplar trees.

Open: May-Sep **Site:** 4HEC **For hire:** **Facilities:** **Services:** **Off-site:** P S

Pujol

rte du Tamariguer, 66700
☎ 468810025 468812121

A lush setting with a variety of recreational facilities.

dir: *0.5km from village, 1km from beach.*

Open: Jun-Sep **Site:** 6.3HEC **For hire:** **Facilities:** **Services:** **Leisure:** P **Off-site:** S

Sirène

rte de Taxo d'Avall, 66702
☎ 468810461 468816974
e-mail: contact@camping-lasirene.fr
web: www.camping-lasirene.fr

A well-appointed family site with good facilities in a delightful wooded setting.

dir: *4km NE.*

Open: 22 Apr-24 Sep **Site:** 17HEC **For hire:** **Facilities:** Kids' Club Play Area **Services:** **Leisure:** P **Off-site:** S

Soleil

rte du Littoral, Plage Nord, 66702
☎ 468811448 468814434
e-mail: camping.soleil@wanadoo.fr
web: campmed.com

Peaceful site in wide meadow surrounded by tall trees. Private beach, natural harbour.

dir: *N from town & 1.5km towards beach.*

GPS: 42.5706, 3.0408

Open: 28 Apr-22 Sep **Site:** 13HEC **For hire:** **Facilities:** Wi-fi Kids' Club Play Area **Services:** **Leisure:** P R S

Village Center le Neptune

av de la Retirada - Plage Nord, 66702
☎ 499572121 467516389
e-mail: contact@village-center.com
web: www.village-center.com/languedoc-roussillon/camping-mer-neptune.php

Located 500 metres from the sea, a site with both sunny and shady pitches.

dir: *N114 exit 11, in Argelès follow signs to Plage Nord.*

GPS: 42.5653, 3.0367

Open: 8 Apr-2 Oct **Site:** 3.4HEC **For hire:** **Facilities:** Wi-fi (charged) Kids' Club Play Area **Services:** **Leisure:** P **Off-site:** S

ARLES — BOUCHES-DU-RHÔNE

Rosiers

145 Draile Marseillaise, Pont de Crau, 13200
☎ 490960212
e-mail: lesrosiers.arles@wanadoo.fr
web: www.arles-camping-club.com

On level ground, shaded by bushes.

dir: *Autoroute exit Arles Sud. Or via N443.*

Open: All Year. **Site:** 3.5HEC **For hire:** **Facilities:** **Services:** **Leisure:** P **Off-site:** L R

ARLES-SUR-TECH — PYRÉNÉES-ORIENTALES

Camping du Riuferrer

66150
☎ 468391106 468391209
e-mail: campingriuferrer@libertysurf.fr
web: www.campingduriuferrer.com

Quiet holiday site on gently sloping ground in pleasant area. Clean sanitary installations. Separate area reserved for overnight stops.

dir: *Signed from N115.*

Open: Mar-Oct **Site:** 4.5HEC **For hire:** **Prices:** 11.50-15 Mobile home hire 200-470 **Facilities:** Wi-fi (charged) Play Area **Services:** **Leisure:** R **Off-site:** P

FRANCE

ARPAILLARGUES — GARD

Mas de Rey

rte d'Anduze, 30700

☎ 466221827 📠 955681833

e-mail: info@campingmasderey.com

web: www.campingmasderey.com

Site run by friendly English speaking owners and staff and set in quiet wooded surroundings with pitches divided by trees and bushes. There are good sports facilities and modern sanitary arrangements.

dir: *3km from Uzès towards Anduze.*

Open: Apr-15 Oct **Site:** 3HEC **For hire:** **Prices:** 17.60-27.10 **Facilities:** Play Area **Services:** **Leisure:** P **Off-site:**

AUBIGNAN — VAUCLUSE

Brégoux

410 chemin du Vas, 84810

☎ 490626250 📠 490626521

e-mail: camping-lebregoux@ventoux-comtat.com

web: www.camping-lebregoux.fr

A level site with good views of Mont Ventoux. Right in the heart of Provence, at Aubignan, in the Ventoux-Comtat Venaissin district.

dir: *On S outskirts of town. D7 onto D55 towards Caromb for 0.5km.*

GPS: 44.0982, 5.0362

Open: Mar-Oct **Site:** 3.5HEC **For hire:** **Facilities:** Wi-fi Play Area **Services:** **Off-site:** R

AUPS — VAR

International

rte de Fox-Amphoux, 83630

☎ 494700680 📠 494701051

e-mail: info@internationalcamping-aups.com

web: www.internationalcamping-aups.com

Wooded surroundings with well-defined pitches and good recreational facilities. A good base for exploring the magnificent Gorges du Verdon.

dir: *0.5km W on D60 towards Fox-Amphoux.*

Open: Apr-Sep **Site:** 4HEC **For hire:** **Facilities:** **Services:** **Leisure:** P **Off-site:**

see advert on this page

AURIBEAU — ALPES-MARITIMES

Parc des Monges

635 chemin du Gabre, 06810

☎ 493609171 📠 493609171

e-mail: contact@parcdesmonges.fr

web: www.parcdesmonges.com

Wooded setting on the banks of a good fishing river, surrounded by mimosa fields.

dir: *A8 exit Mandelieu for Grasse.*

GPS: 43.6061, 6.9025

Open: 21 Apr-29 Sep **Site:** 1.4HEC **For hire:** **Prices:** 17-25 Mobile home hire 300-710 **Facilities:** Wi-fi (charged) Play Area **Services:** **Leisure:** P R **Off-site:**

AVIGNON — VAUCLUSE

Bagatelle

25 allée Antoine Pinay, Ile de la Barthelasse, 84000

☎ 490863039 📠 490271623

e-mail: camping.bagatelle@wanadoo.fr

web: www.campingbagatelle.com

Pleasant site with tall trees on the Ile de la Barthelasse. All pitches are numbered, on hard standing and divided by hedges. Separate section for young people.

dir: *Along town wall & river to Rhône bridge (Nîmes road), signed on right.*

GPS: 43.9522, 4.7992

Open: All Year. **Site:** 4HEC **Prices:** 14.60-24 **Facilities:** Wi-fi (charged) Play Area **Services:** **Off-site:** P

CM Pont St-Bénézet

10 chemin de la Barthelasse, 84000

☎ 490806350 📠 490852212

e-mail: info@camping-avignon.com

web: www.camping-avignon.com

Set on an island near the bridge with fine views of town. Several tiled sanitary blocks with individual wash cabins. Individual pitches with divisions for tents and caravans. Several playing fields for volleyball and basketball.

dir: *NW of town on right bank of Rhône, 370m upstream from bridge on right. (N100 towards Nîmes).*

Open: Mar-Oct **Site:** 7.5HEC **For hire:** **Facilities:** **Services:** **Leisure:** P

AXAT — AUDE

Crémade

11140

☎ 468205064

e-mail: lacremade@hotmail.fr

web: www.lacremade.com

A shady, peaceful site, ideal for water sports.

Open: May-Sep **Site:** 4HEC **For hire:** **Prices:** 12.50-12.90 Mobile home hire 230-370 **Facilities:** Wi-fi **Services:** **Off-site:** P R

Moulin du Pont d'Alies

11140

☎ 468205327 📠 874762003

e-mail: contact@alies.fr

web: www.alies.fr

A picturesque location at the entrance to the Gorges de la Pierre.

dir: *Junct D117 & D118, 0.8km from Axat.*

Open: Apr-Oct **Site:** 2HEC **For hire:** **Facilities:** **Services:** **Leisure:** P R

BALARUC-LES-BAINS — HÉRAULT

Camping le Mas du Padre

4 chemin du Mas du Padre, 34540

☎ 467485341 📠 467480894

e-mail: contact@mas-du-padre.com

web: www.mas-du-padre.com

2km from the centre of the village and Thau lake. Relaxing, family friendly site with facilities including ping-pong, volleyball and weekly discos. Kids' club in July and August. Dogs must be on a lead, no dangerous dogs.

GPS: 43.4522, 3.6924

Open: 31 Mar-21 Oct **Site:** 1.8HEC **For hire:** **Prices:** 16.50-31.20 Mobile home hire 266-714 **Facilities:** Wi-fi Kids' Club Play Area **Services:** **Leisure:** P **Off-site:** L

BANDOL — VAR

Vallongue

83150

☎ 494294955 📠 494294955

e-mail: camping.vallongue@gmail.com

web: www.campingvar.com

Parts of this terraced site have lovely sea views.

Open: Apr-Sep **Site:** 1.5HEC **For hire:** **Facilities:** **Services:** **Leisure:** P **Off-site:**

BARCARÈS, LE — PYRÉNÉES-ORIENTALES

Bousigues

av des Corbières, 66420

☎ 468861619 📠 468862844

e-mail: lasbousigues@wanadoo.fr

web: www.camping-barcares.com

Well-equipped family site 1km from the sea. Bar and café only open July and August.

dir: *D83 exit 10.*

Open: 29 Mar-28 Sep **Site:** 3HEC **For hire:** **Facilities:** **Services:** **Leisure:** P **Off-site:** L R S

California

rte de St-Laurent, 66423

☎ 468861608 📠 468861820

web: www.camping-california.fr

A friendly family site with regular organised entertainment in a pleasant wooded location close to the beach. Kids' club available in July and August.

dir: *1.5km SW via D90.*

Open: 12 Apr-15 Sep **Site:** 5.5HEC **For hire:** **Prices:** 14-36 **Facilities:** Wi-fi (charged) Kids' Club Play Area **Services:** **Leisure:** P **Off-site:** L R S

FRANCE

Europe

The Camping and Caravanning Club The Friendly Club

rte de St-Laurent, 66420
☎ 468861536 📠 468864788
e-mail: reception@europe-camping.com
web: www.europe-camping.com

A holiday village type of site with good recreational facilities, 0.5km from the beach. Kids' club available in July and August.

C&CC Report *Located in a summer resort, this site is a good stopover in winter for travelling into Spain, with an individual sanitation block on each pitch. The local area can be very quiet in winter.*

dir: *Via D90 2km SW, 200m from Agly.*

Open: All Year. **Site:** 6HEC **For hire:**
Prices: 19-49 Mobile home hire 280-1100 **Facilities:** Wi-fi (charged) Kids' Club Play Area
Services: **Leisure:** P **Off-site:** R S

Oasis

rte de St Laurent, 66420
☎ 468861243 📠 468864683
e-mail: camping.loasis@wanadoo.fr
web: www.camping-oasis.com

1km from the sea and close to shops. The aquatic area has three swimming-pools, a 33 metre slide and a large sun terrace. Supervised activities for children.

dir: *A9 exit 41 Perpignan Centre/Nord, take D83 for Le Barcarès, exit 9 & D81 towards Canet. 1st exit passing St Laurent on right, under bridge for Le Bacarès, site on left.*

Facilities: **Services:** **Leisure:** P
Off-site: S

see advert on this page

Presqu'île

66420
☎ 468861280 📠 468862509
e-mail: contact@lapresquile.com
web: www.lapresquile.com

A well-equipped family site on the edge of Lake Leucate and close to the beach.

dir: *2km on rte de Leucate, turn right.*

Open: 9 Apr-1 Nov **Site:** 3.5HEC **For hire:**
Facilities: **Services:**
Leisure: L P **Off-site:** R S

Tamaris

rte de St Laurent, 66420
☎ 468860818 📠 468862309
e-mail: tamaris@altranet.fr
web: www.tamaris.com

Large, secure site with leisure facilities including pool area, karaoke and disco.

dir: *Off A9 motorway.*

Open: All Year. **Site:** 17HEC **For hire:**
Facilities: **Services:**
Leisure: P **Off-site:** L R S

FRANCE

BÉNIVAY-OLLON DRÔME

Domaine de L'Ecluse

Quartier Barastrage, 26170
475280732 475281687
e-mail: camp.ecluse@wanadoo.fr
web: www.campecluse.com

Situated on a farm with fruit trees, olive fields and vineyards. A choice of sunny, shaded or semi-shaded pitches separated by hedges.

dir: *D538 (Nyons-Vaison la Romaine), after 11km take D46 to Buis-les-Baronnies, then left for D147 to Bénivay.*

Open: May-15 Sep **Site:** 3HEC **For hire:** **Facilities:** **Services:** **Leisure:** P

BIOT ALPES-MARITIMES

Antipolis

av du Pylone, La Brague, 06600
493339399 492910200
e-mail: contact@camping-antipolis.com
web: www.camping-antipolis.com

Site close to the sea. Shady pitches separated with hedges.

dir: *A8 exit Antibes-Biot, towards Marineland. Turn right after 800m.*

Open: Apr-Sep **Site:** 4.5HEC **For hire:** **Facilities:** **Services:** **Leisure:** P **Off-site:** S

Eden

chemin du Val-de-Pome, 06410
493656370 493655422
e-mail: campingeden@wanadoo.fr
web: www.camping-eden.fr

Site on level meadowland.

dir: *On D4.*

Open: Apr-30 Oct **Site:** 2.5HEC **For hire:** **Prices:** 20-27 Mobile home hire 250-650 **Facilities:** Wi-fi Play Area **Services:** **Leisure:** P **Off-site:** S

Pylône

BP 39, 06601
493335286 493333054
e-mail: camping.pylone@wanadoo.fr
web: www.campingdupylone.com

Situated between Cannes and Nice, a family site with good facilities.

dir: *N7 onto D4 for Biot, 1st left.*

Open: All Year. **Site:** 16HEC **For hire:** **Facilities:** **Services:** **Leisure:** P R **Off-site:** S

BOISSET-ET-GAUJAC GARD

Domaine de Gaujac

2406 chemin de la Madelaine, 30140
466616757 466605390
e-mail: contact@domaine-de-gaujac.com
web: www.domaine-de-gaujac.com

A family site in wooded surroundings on the banks of a river.

dir: *Via D910.*

Open: Apr-20 Sep **Site:** 10HEC **For hire:** **Facilities:** **Services:** **Leisure:** P R

BOISSON GARD

Château de Boisson

30500
466248561 466248014
e-mail: reception@chateaudeboisson.com
web: www.chateaudeboisson.com

A peaceful, well-equipped site in the beautiful Cévennes region. Painting and bridge courses are available. Kids' club in July and August. Dogs allowed except July and August.

dir: *D7 towards Fumades, Boisson 10km on right, site signed.*

GPS: 44.2093, 4.2568

Open: 9 Apr-24 Sep **Site:** 7.8HEC **For hire:** **Facilities:** Wi-fi (charged) Kids' Club Play Area **Services:** **Leisure:** P

BOLLÈNE VAUCLUSE

Barry

Lieu Dit St-Pierre, 84500
490301320 490404864

Well-kept site near ruins of Barry troglodyte village.

dir: *Signed from Bollène via D26.*

Open: All Year. **Site:** 3HEC **For hire:** **Facilities:** **Services:** **Leisure:** P **Off-site:** L R

Simioune

Quartier Guffiage, 84500
490304462
e-mail: la-simioune@orange.fr
web: www.la-simioune.fr

Pleasant wooded surroundings close to the River Rhône. Pony club and riding school available.

dir: *Off A7, 3rd right for Carpertras, at 3rd x-rds turn left for Lambisque, site is signed.*

Open: All Year. **Site:** 3HEC **For hire:** **Facilities:** Wi-fi **Services:** **Leisure:** P **Off-site:** R

FRANCE

BORMES-LES-MIMOSAS VAR

Camp du Domaine

La Faviere, 83230

494710312 494151867

e-mail: mail@campdudomaine.com

web: www.campdudomaine.com

A very attractive setting with a long sandy beach and numbered pitches. Fine views of sea and sports facilities. Kids' club available in July and August.

dir: *0.5km E of Bormes-Cap Bénat road.*

Open: 30 Mar-Oct **Site:** 45HEC **For hire:** **Prices:** 19.50-43 Mobile home hire 500-970 **Facilities:** Wi-fi (charged) Kids' Club Play Area **Services:** **Leisure:** S

Camping Manjastre

150 chemin des Girolles, 83230

494710328 494716362

e-mail: info@campingmanjastre.com

web: www.campingmanjastre.com

A peaceful site 6km from the Mediterranean beaches. Dogs allowed out of season.

dir: *5km NW via D98 on road to La Môle/Cogolin.*

GPS: 43.1625, 6.3216

Open: All Year. **Site:** 8HEC **For hire:** **Prices:** 15-27.40 **Facilities:** Wi-fi (charged) Play Area **Services:** **Leisure:** P **Off-site:** S

Clau Mar Jo

895 chemin de Benat, 83230

494715339 494243873

e-mail: contact@camping-clau-mar-jo.fr

web: www.camping-clau-mar-jo.fr

A well-shaded site with good facilities two kilometres from the sea between Hyères and Lavandou.

dir: *N98 onto D298.*

Open: 15 Mar-15 Oct **Site:** 1HEC **For hire:** **Facilities:** Wi-fi Play Area **Services:** **Off-site:** S

BOULOU, LE PYRÉNÉES-ORIENTALES

Mas Llinas

66165

468832546

e-mail: info@camping-mas-llinas.com

web: www.camping-mas-llinas.com

A family site in wooded surroundings with a variety of leisure facilities.

dir: *3km N via N9.*

GPS: 42.5431, 2.8319

Open: Feb-Nov **Site:** 15HEC **For hire:** **Prices:** 15.10-20.60 Mobile home hire 260-565 **Facilities:** Wi-fi Play Area **Services:** **Leisure:** P **Off-site:** L R

BOULOURIS-SUR-MER VAR

Ile d'Or

4415 rte de la Corniche, 83700

494945213 494945213

A quiet location with well-equipped pitches, 50 metres from a private beach.

dir: *E off N98.*

GPS: 43.4178, 6.8347

Open: Apr-15 Nov **Site:** 10HEC **For hire:** **Prices:** 28.50 **Facilities:** Wi-fi (charged) **Services:** **Leisure:** S

BOURDEAUX DRÔME

Couspeau

Quartier Bellevue, Le Poët-Célard, 26460

475533014 475533723

e-mail: info@couspeau.com

web: www.couspeau.com

A beautiful natural setting with well-maintained facilities.

dir: *1.3km SE via D328A.*

Open: 15 Apr-Sep **Site:** 8HEC **For hire:** **Facilities:** **Services:** **Leisure:** P

BROUSSES-ET-VILLARET AUDE

Martinet Rouge

11390

☎ 619344160

e-mail: camping.lemartinetrouge@orange.fr

web: www.camping-lemartinetrouge.com

A pleasant, well-equipped site on gently sloping terrain. Terraced, with well-marked pitches.

dir: *NE of Carcassonne, A61 exit22/23.*

Open: Jun-Aug **Site:** 2.8HEC **For hire:** **Prices:** 20-29 Mobile home hire 200-700 **Facilities:** Wi-fi (charged) **Services:** **Leisure:** P **Off-site:** L R

CADENET VAUCLUSE

Le Val de Durance

Les Routes, 84160

☎ 442204725 442950363

e-mail: info@homair.com

web: www.homair.co.uk

A well-equipped family site on the shore of a lake and close to the River Durance.

dir: *Site 20km from A7.*

Open: 6 Apr-Sep **Site:** 11HEC **For hire:** **Prices:** 15-29 Mobile home hire 245-994 **Facilities:** Wi-fi (charged) Kids' Club Play Area **Services:** **Leisure:** L P **Off-site:**

CAGNES-SUR-MER ALPES-MARITIMES

Colombier

35 chemin de Ste-Colombe, 06800

☎ 493731277 493731277

e-mail: campinglecolombier06@wanadoo.fr

web: www.campinglecolombier.com

Well-equipped site in a wooded location, 2km from the sea.

Open: Apr-1 Oct **Site:** 0.6HEC **For hire:** **Prices:** 22 Mobile home hire 590 **Facilities:** Wi-fi (charged) Play Area **Services:** **Leisure:** P **Off-site:** R S

Green Park

159 Vallon-des-Vaux, 06800

☎ 442204725 442950363

e-mail: info@homair.com

web: www.homair.co.uk

Modern sites with well-defined pitches in pleasant wooded surroundings with good recreational facilities.

dir: *8km from A8.*

Open: 6 Apr-Sep **Site:** 1.6HEC **For hire:** **Prices:** 24-44 Mobile home hire 294-1225 **Facilities:** Wi-fi (charged) Kids' Club Play Area **Services:** **Leisure:** P **Off-site:** S

Rivière

168 chemin des Salles, 06800

☎ 493206227 493207253

e-mail: contact@campinglariviere06.fr

web: www.campinglariviere06.fr

Secluded wooded surroundings with modern facilities.

dir: *4km N beside River Cagne.*

Open: 15 Mar-15 Oct **Site:** 1.2HEC **For hire:** **Prices:** 17-19.50 Mobile home hire 240-430 **Facilities:** Play Area **Services:** **Leisure:** P **Off-site:** S

see advert on this page

CAMURAC AUDE

Sapins

11340

☎ 468203811 468314123

e-mail: info@lessapins-camurac.com

web: www.lessapins-camurac.com

A picturesque wooded site on the edge of a forest with views of the surrounding mountains.

dir: *1.5km from village.*

Open: Apr-15 Oct **Site:** 3HEC **For hire:** **Facilities:** **Services:** **Leisure:** P **Off-site:** L

FRANCE

CANET-EN-ROUSILLON PYRÉNÉES-ORIENTALES

Le Brasilia

Voie de la Crouste, Zone Technique du Port, 66140
☎ 468802382 468733297
e-mail: info@lebrasilia.fr
web: www.brasilia.fr

Site near the beach, with pitches divided by bushes and flowerbeds in pine woods. Pitches are well maintained.

dir: *Off main road in village towards beach for 2km.*

GPS: 42.7090, 3.0369

Open: 21 Apr-29 Sep **Site:** 15HEC **For hire:** **Prices:** 20-52 **Facilities:** Wi-fi (charged) Kids' Club Play Area **Services:** **Leisure:** P S **Off-site:**

Ma Prairie

The Camping and Caravanning Club The Friendly Club

av des Coteaux, 66140
☎ 468732617 468732882
e-mail: ma.prairie@wanadoo.fr
web: www.maprairie.com

Peaceful grassland site in a hollow surrounded by vineyards at the entrance to Canet-en-Roussillon. Kids' club in July and August.

C&CC Report *A welcoming, family site with excellent facilities. Subject to demand, coach excursions are run weekly to Andorra, Barcelona and other local places of interest, and a wine tasting visit is organised. The medieval Cathar castles, cave paintings and prehistoric remains are highlights of this captivating region, as is a visit to Collioure - a paradise for lovers of art in all its forms.*

dir: *N617 Perpignan-Canet-Plage onto D11 towards Elne.*

Open: 5 May-25 Sep **Site:** 4.5HEC **For hire:** **Facilities:** Wi-fi (charged) Kids' Club **Services:** **Leisure:** P **Off-site:**

Peupliers

av des Anneaux de Rousillon, 66140
☎ 468803587 468733875
e-mail: contact@camping-les-peupliers.fr

Quiet, level site divided into pitches by hedges with a variety of leisure facilities.

Open: Jun-Sep **Site:** 4HEC **For hire:** **Facilities:** **Services:** **Leisure:** P S

CANET-PLAGE PYRÉNÉES-ORIENTALES

Mar Estang

1 rte de St-Cyprien, 66140
☎ 468803553 468733294
e-mail: contactme@marestang.com
web: www.marestang.com

Close to a sandy beach, the site offers varied activities, includes an art school and has a recently renovated water park with heated pool.

dir: *A9 exit 41 follow signs for Canet then towards St Cyprien.*

GPS: 42.6754, 3.0310

Open: 21 Apr-15 Sep **Site:** 15HEC **For hire:** **Prices:** 17-39 Mobile home hire 169-1069 **Facilities:** Wi-fi Kids' Club Play Area **Services:** **Leisure:** P S **Off-site:**

CANNES ALPES-MARITIMES

Parc Bellevue

67 av M Chevalier, 06150
☎ 493472897 493486625
e-mail: contact@parcbellevue.com
web: www.parcbellevue.com

Shaded park location with entertainment available in season.

dir: *A41 exit Cannes, right at 1st lights.*

Open: Apr-Sep **Site:** 4HEC **For hire:** **Facilities:** **Services:** **Leisure:** P **Off-site:** S

Ranch

chemin St-Joseph, L'Aubarède, 06110
☎ 493460011 493464430
web: www.leranchcamping.fr

On a wooded hillside 2km from the local beaches, with good facilities.

dir: *A8 exit 41 or 42.*

Open: 2 Apr-29 Oct **Site:** 2HEC **For hire:** **Facilities:** **Services:** **Leisure:** P **Off-site:** S

CARCASSONNE AUDE

Cité

rte de St-Hilaire, 11000
☎ 468100100 468473313
web: www.campingcitecarcassonne.com

Wooded surroundings beside the River Aude. A good base for exploring the region.

dir: *Via A61 or A9.*

Open: 15 May-10 Oct **Site:** 7HEC **For hire:** **Facilities:** **Services:** **Leisure:** P **Off-site:** L R

FRANCE

CARPENTRAS VAUCLUSE

Lou Comtadou

rte de St Didier, 881 av P-de-Coubertin, 84200
490670316 490460181
e-mail: info@campingloucomtadou.com
web: www.campingloucomtadou.com

Near the Carpentras swimming pool, in pleasant surroundings, with modern facilities.

dir: *SE of town centre towards St-Didier.*

Open: Apr-Sep **Site:** 2.5HEC **For hire:** **Facilities:** **Services:** **Off-site:** P

CARQUEIRANNE VAR

Beau-Vezé

rte de la Moutonne, 83320
494576530 494576530
e-mail: info@camping-beauveze.com
web: www.camping-beauveze.com

Set in a beautiful wooded park with modern facilities.

dir: *2.5km NW via N559 & D76 between Hyères & Toulon.*

Open: May-Sep **Site:** 7HEC **For hire:** **Facilities:** Wi-fi (charged) Kids' Club **Services:** **Leisure:** P S

CASTEIL PYRÉNÉES-ORIENTALES

Domaine St Martin

6 bld de la Cascade, 66820
468055209
e-mail: info@domainestmartin.com
web: www.domainestmartin.com

Quiet site situated in the attractive landscape of the Confluent Valley at the foot of the Massif Canigou in the Pyrénées.

dir: *D116 towards Vernet-les-Bains. Entering Vernet, turn right crossing main street & follow signs for Casteil.*

Open: Apr-15 Oct **Site:** 6HEC **For hire:** **Prices:** 13-20.40 Mobile home hire 250-600 **Facilities:** Wi-fi Play Area **Services:** **Leisure:** P **Off-site:** R

CASTELLANE ALPES-DE-HAUTE-PROVENCE

Collines de Castellane

rte de Grasse Napoléon, Garde-Castellane, 04120
492836896 492837540
e-mail: info@rcn-lescollinesdecastellane.fr
web: www.rcn-campings.fr

Terraced site on wooded grassland with mountain views and fine recreational facilities.

dir: *On Grasse road beyond La Garde.*

Open: 20 Apr-23 Sep **Site:** 10HEC **For hire:** **Facilities:** **Services:** **Leisure:** P

Domaine du Verdon

The Camping and Caravanning Club The Friendly Club

04120
492836129 492836937
e-mail: contact@camp-du-verdon.com
web: www.camp-du-verdon.com

Flat, well-maintained site in gorge on banks of River Verdon.

C&CC Report *A wide range of facilities in the most spectacular but still easily reachable part of the gorge country, on the famous Route Napoléon and with an off-road path to pretty Castellane. A great site in low season for those wanting a peaceful base with many facilities open, but also at any time for active families, with early booking strongly advised. The very best stretches of the truly jaw-dropping Grand Canyon du Verdon, as well as some of the prettiest countryside, lavender fields and towns in lovely Provence, are all within very easy reach.*

dir: *Below D952 towards Gorges du Verdon.*

GPS: 43.8392, 6.4939

Open: 15 May-15 Sep **Site:** 14HEC **For hire:** **Prices:** 21-52 Mobile home hire 336-1155 **Facilities:** Wi-fi Play Area **Services:** **Leisure:** P R **Off-site:** L

Gorges du Verdon

clos d'Arémus, Chasteuil, 04120
492836364 492837472
e-mail: aremus@camping-gorgesduverdon.com
web: www.camping-gorgesduverdon.com

Situated beside the River Verdon at an altitude of 660 metres, surrounded by mountains. Site divided into pitches and split into two by a road. Bathing in the river is not advised due to strong current.

dir: *9.5km S of village.*

Open: 5 May-15 Sep **Site:** 7HEC **For hire:** **Prices:** 16 Mobile home hire 260-729 **Facilities:** Wi-fi Play Area **Services:** **Leisure:** P

FRANCE

International

rte Napoléon, RD4085, 04120
☎ 492836667 492837767
e-mail: info@camping-international.fr
web: www.camping-international.fr

Family site at the foot of the Col des Lèques and close to the Gorges du Verdon.

dir: *1km from village centre, signed.*

Open: 31 Mar-1 Oct **Site:** 6HEC **For hire:** **Prices:** 16-25 Mobile home hire 275-825 **Facilities:** Wi-fi (charged) Kids' Club Play Area **Services:** **Leisure:** P **Off-site:** L R

Nôtre Dame

rte des Gorges du Verdon, 04120
☎ 492836302
e-mail: camping-notredame@wanadoo.fr
web: www.camping-notredame.com

Meadowland site with deciduous and fruit trees.

dir: *0.5km from village centre on D952.*

GPS: 43.8457, 6.5048

Open: Apr-10 Oct **Site:** 0.6HEC **For hire:** **Prices:** 12-18 Mobile home hire 225-550 **Facilities:** Wi-fi **Services:** **Off-site:** L P R

CASTRIES HÉRAULT

Fondespierre

chemin Rioch Viala, 34160
☎ 467912003
e-mail: accueil@campingfondespierre.com
web: www.campingfondespierre.com

Pitches positioned among olive and oak trees. Bikes can be rented.

dir: *A9, exit 28 and take D610 towards Ales, 1.5km after Castries turn left & follow signs.*

Open: All Year. **Site:** 3HEC **For hire:** **Facilities:** Wi-fi (charged) Play Area **Services:** **Leisure:** P **Off-site:** L

CAVALAIRE-SUR-MER VAR

Cros de Mouton

83240
☎ 494641087 494646312
e-mail: campingcrosdemouton@wanadoo.fr
web: www.crosdemouton.com

Terraced site with individual pitches, separated for caravans and tents. Good view of sea 1.5km away.

dir: *Off N559 in town centre & continue inland for 1.5km.*

Open: 15 Mar-4 Nov **Site:** 5HEC **For hire:** **Facilities:** **Services:** **Leisure:** P **Off-site:** S

Pinède

chemin des Mannes, 83240
☎ 494641114 494641925
web: www.la-pinede-camping.com

A family site with well-defined pitches, 0.5km from the sea.

dir: *300m from village centre.*

Open: 15 Mar-15 Oct **Site:** 2HEC **Facilities:** **Services:** **Off-site:** P S

CENDRAS GARD

Croix Clémentine

rte de Mende, 30480
☎ 466865269 466865484
e-mail: clementine@clementine.fr
web: www.clementine.fr

An extensive, partly terraced site, in wooded surroundings.

dir: *Signed W of town on D160 towards La Baume.*

GPS: 44.1519, 4.0431

Open: 31 Mar-12 Sep **Site:** 12HEC **For hire:** **Facilities:** Wi-fi Kids' Club Play Area **Services:** **Leisure:** P **Off-site:** R

CEYRESTE BOUCHES DU RHÔNE

Camping de Ceyreste

av Eugène Julien, 13600
442830768
e-mail: campingceyreste@yahoo.fr
web: www.campingceyreste.com

3km from beaches at La Ciotat, quiet and shady pitches with leisure activities including miniature golf and a fitness trail course. Shop, bar, café, Camping Gaz and kids' club all available in season.

dir: *N9 exit La Ciotat, then Ceyreste.*

GPS: 43.2168, 5.6302

Open: 30 Mar-11 Nov **Site:** 3HEC **For hire:** **Facilities:** Wi-fi Kids' Club Play Area **Services:** **Leisure:** P **Off-site:** S

CHABEUIL DRÔME

Grand Lierne

Les Garalands, 26120
475598314 475598795
e-mail: grand-lierne@franceloc.fr
web: www.grandlierne.com

On the edge of the Vercors Regional Park.

dir: *A7 exit Valence Sud for Chabeuil, site signed.*

Open: 18 Apr-26 Sep **Site:** 7HEC **For hire:** **Facilities:** **Services:** **Leisure:** P **Off-site:** R

CHÂTEAUNEUF-DE-GALAURE DRÔME

Château de Galaure

D51, 26330
1746785100
web: www.galaure.com

Spacious, restful site beside the River Galaure, which has clear water, ideal for swimming or fishing.

dir: *A7 exit 12 (Chanas), take N7 for St Valier, left for D51 towards Châteauneuf de Galaure.*

Open: 27 Apr-29 Sep **Site:** 14HEC **For hire:** **Prices:** 19-35 Mobile home hire 245-833 **Facilities:** Wi-fi (charged) Kids' Club Play Area **Services:** **Leisure:** P R

CHÂTEAUNEUF-SUR-ISÈRE DRÔME

Soleil Fruité

Les Pêches, 26300
475841970 475780585
e-mail: contact@lesoleilfruite.com
web: www.lesoleilfruite.com

Situated in a 3.6 hectare orchard of peach, apricot and olive trees and surrounded by the mountains of the Ardèche and the massif of the Vercors. Dogs allowed except 7 July to 21 August.

dir: *A7 exit 14 Valence Nord. Follow signs for Pont d'Isère/Tain l'Hermitage.*

Open: 26 Apr-15 Sep **Site:** 4HEC **For hire:** **Prices:** 16.60-24.60 Mobile home hire 284-854 **Facilities:** Wi-fi Kids' Club Play Area **Services:** **Leisure:** P

CHAUZON ARDÈCHE

Digue

07120
475396357 475397517
e-mail: info@camping-la-digue.fr
web: www.camping-la-digue.fr

A beautiful wooded location with good recreational facilities.

dir: *1km E, 100m from River Ardèche.*

Open: 20 Mar-30 Oct **Site:** 2.5HEC **For hire:** **Facilities:** **Services:** **Leisure:** P R

CIOTAT, LA BOUCHES-DU-RHÔNE

Les Oliviers

Chemin des Plaines Baronnes, 13600
442204725 442950363
e-mail: info@homair.com
web: www.homair.co.uk

A terraced family site between the N559 and the railway line from Nice.

dir: *7km from A50.*

Open: 2 Apr-2 Oct **Site:** 10HEC **For hire:** **Prices:** 15-27.50 Mobile home hire 259-903 **Facilities:** Wi-fi (charged) Kids' Club Play Area **Services:** **Leisure:** P **Off-site:** S

FRANCE

St Jean

30 av de St-Jean, 13600
☎ 442831301 🖷 442714641

Site on the right side of the coast road in an excellent position with direct access to the beach.

dir: *Between D559 & sea behind motel in NE part of town.*

Open: 2 Jun-22 Sep **Site:** 9.9HEC **For hire:** **Facilities:** **Services:** **Leisure:** S **Off-site:**

Soleil

751 av Emile Bodin, rte de Cassis, 13600
☎ 442715532
e-mail: contact@camping-dusoleil.com
web: www.camping-dusoleil.com

A small site, divided into pitches, 1.5km from the beach.

dir: *A50 exit 9 La Ciotat.*

Open: Apr-Sep **Site:** 0.5HEC **For hire:** **Facilities:** Wi-fi **Services:** **Off-site:** P S

COGOLIN VAR

Argentière

chemin de l'Argentière, 83310
☎ 494546363 🖷 494540615
e-mail: camping-largentiere@wanadoo.fr
web: www.camping-argentiere.com

Landscaped, partly terraced site with leisure facilities and entertainment.

dir: *1.5km NW along D48 rte de St-Maur.*

GPS: 43.255, 6.5131

Open: Apr-Sep **Site:** 6HEC **For hire:** **Prices:** 16-32 Mobile home hire 245-470 **Facilities:** Wi-fi Kids' Club Play Area **Services:** **Leisure:** P **Off-site:** S

COLLE-SUR-LOUP, LA ALPES-MARITIMES

Castellas

rte de Roquefort, 06480
☎ 493329705 🖷 493329705
e-mail: lecastellas.camping@wanadoo.fr
web: www.camping-le-castellas.com

Wooded location with direct access to the river.

Open: All Year. **Site:** 1.2HEC **For hire:** **Prices:** 20-25 Mobile home hire 260-650 **Facilities:** Wi-fi **Services:** **Leisure:** R S **Off-site:** P

Pinèdes

rte du Pont de Pierre, 06480
☎ 493329894 🖷 493325020
e-mail: info@lespinedes.com
web: www.lespinedes.com

Well-kept terraced site on steep slope with woodland providing shade, interesting walks and beautiful views. Kids' club available in July and August.

dir: *A8 exit Cagnes-sur-Mer, onto D6, right for La Colle-sur-Loup.*

Open: 15 Mar-Sep **Site:** 3.8HEC **For hire:** **Prices:** 16-34 Mobile home hire 310-810 **Facilities:** Wi-fi (charged) Kids' Club Play Area **Services:** **Leisure:** P **Off-site:** R

Vallon Rouge

rte Gréolières, 06480
☎ 493328612 🖷 493328009
e-mail: info@auvallonrouge.com
web: www.auvallonrouge.com

A picturesque forest location close to the river with good facilities. Situated between Nice, Monaco and Cannes, 9km from beaches.

dir: *3km W of town. D6 towards Gréolières, site on right.*

Open: 4 Apr-25 Sep **Site:** 3HEC **For hire:** **Facilities:** Wi-fi Kids' Club Play Area **Services:** **Leisure:** P R **Off-site:**

CRAU, LA VAR

Bois de Mont-Redon

480 chemin du Mont-Redon, 83260
☎ 494667408 🖷 494660966
e-mail: mont.redon@wanadoo.fr
web: www.mont-redon.com

Set among oak and pine trees with well-defined pitches and plenty of recreational facilities including table tennis.

dir: *3km NE via D29.*

GPS: 43.1606, 6.1057

Open: Jun-20 Sep **Site:** 5HEC **For hire:** **Prices:** 29.90 **Facilities:** Wi-fi (charged) **Services:** **Leisure:** P

FRANCE

CRESPIAN GARD

Mas de Reilhe

30260

☎ 466778212 🖷 466802650

e-mail: info@camping-mas-de-reilhe.fr

web: www.camping-mas-de-reilhe.fr

Peaceful family site surrounded by pine trees between the Cévennes and Mediterranean beaches. Nearby are signed walks and medieval villages with traditional markets. Good recreational facilities and activities for children.

dir: *A9 exit 25 onto N106 direction Alès, after 4km left at fork in road signed Le Vigan. Right at x-rds (just before Vic-le-Fesq) onto N110 direction Lédignan, site on right before Crespian.*

Open: 14 Apr-17 Sep **Site:** 3HEC **For hire:** **Prices:** 17-23.20 Mobile home hire 385-770 **Facilities:** Wi-fi Play Area **Services:** **Leisure:** P **Off-site:** R

CROIX-VALMER, LA VAR

Selection

12 bld de la Mer, 83420

☎ 494551030 🖷 494551039

e-mail: camping-selection@wanadoo.fr

web: www.selectioncamping.com

Site in a pine wood, protected from wind. Many terraces and divided into pitches. Kids' club available during July and August. No dogs permitted in July and August.

dir: *Off N559 at rdbt at Km78.5, 300m W.*

GPS: 43.1959, 6.5553

Open: 15 Mar-15 Oct **Site:** 3.8HEC **For hire:** **Facilities:** Wi-fi (charged) Kids' Club Play Area **Services:** **Leisure:** P **Off-site:** S

see advert on this page

DARBRES ARDECHE

Camping les Lavandes

Le Village, 07170

☎ 475942065

e-mail: sarl.leslavandes@free.fr

web: www.les-lavandes-darbres.com

Shaded terraces with large pitches. Leisure facilities include a swimming pool, open-air chess, billiard room plus two children's playgrounds and a small shop in July and August. A restaurant is open from mid June to August.

dir: *RN102 to Darbres.*

GPS: 44.6478, 4.5036

Open: 15 Apr-Sep **Site:** 1.5HEC **For hire:** **Prices:** 12.50-19.90 **Facilities:** Play Area **Services:** **Leisure:** P **Off-site:** L R

DIE DRÔME

Pinède

Quartier du Pont-Neuf, 26150

☎ 475221777 🖷 475222273

e-mail: pinedeclub@infonie.fr

web: www.camping-pinede.com

A picturesque mountain setting beside the River Drôme. Kids' club available in July and August. There is a charge for Wi-fi in July and August.

dir: *W via D93, over railway line & river to site.*

GPS: 44.7570, 5.3530

Open: 8 Apr-15 Sep **Site:** 11HEC **For hire:** **Prices:** 15-34 Mobile home hire 240-700 **Facilities:** Wi-fi (charged) Kids' Club Play Area **Services:** **Leisure:** P R

FRANCE

DIEULEFIT — DRÔME

Huttopia Dieulefit

Quartier d'Espeluche, 26220
☎ 475546394 📠 475904276
e-mail: dieulefit@huttopia.com
web: www.huttopia.com

In a natural setting in an area known for lavender production. Large pitches can be shady or in a forest. Bikes are available to hire and a kids' club is held in July and August. Only 1 dog per pitch.

dir: *From N: A7 exit 18 Montelimar Nord, then towards La Coucouarde and continue to Dieulefit via Sauzet and La Begude de Mazenc.*

GPS: 44.5381, 5.0562

Open: 5 Apr-8 Nov **Site:** 17HEC **For hire:** **Prices:** 18-35 **Facilities:** Kids' Club Play Area **Services:** **Leisure:** P **Off-site:** R

ELNE — PYRÉNÉES-ORIENTALES

Florida

rte de Latour Bas Elne, 66200
☎ 468378088 📠 468378076
web: www.campingleflorida.com

Quiet location between sea and mountains but close to local resorts and amenities.

Open: 5 Apr-8 Nov **Facilities:** **Leisure:** P

ENTRECHAUX — VAUCLUSE

Du Bon Crouzet

rte de St-Marcelin, 84340
☎ 490460162 📠 490460162
e-mail: du.bon.crouzet@free.fr
web: du.bon.crouzet.free.fr

On level ground with modern facilities beside the river.

dir: *D938 exit Vaison-la-Romaine for St-Marcelin-les-Vaison for 6km.*

Open: Apr-15 Oct **Site:** 1.2HEC **Prices:** 12-16 **Facilities:** Wi-fi **Services:** **Leisure:** P R

FONT-ROMEU — PYRÉNÉES-ORIENTALES

Huttopia Font-Romeu

rte de Mont-Louis, 66120
☎ 468300932 📠 468045639
e-mail: font-romeu@huttopia.com
web: www.huttopia.com

Spacious and shaded pitches set in a beautiful site with a backdrop of the Pyrénées. Kids' club in July and August.

dir: *N20-E9 (Ax-les-Thermes to Bourg-Madame), take exit for D618.*

GPS: 42.5117, 2.0497

Open: 21 Jun-10 Sep & 3 Dec-10 Apr **Site:** 7HEC **For hire:** **Prices:** 14.50-24.50 **Facilities:** Kids' Club Play Area **Services:** **Leisure:** P **Off-site:** L R

FONTVIEILLE — BOUCHES-DU-RHÔNE

CM Pins

rue Michelet, 13990
☎ 490547869 📠 490548125
e-mail: campingmunicipal.lespins@wanadoo.fr

Set in a pine wood close to the Moulin d'Alphonse Daudet.

dir: *1km from village via D17.*

Open: Apr-26 Sep **Site:** 4HEC **Prices:** 13.80-16.80 **Facilities:** Wi-fi Play Area **Services:** **Off-site:** P

FORCALQUIER — ALPES-DE-HAUTE-PROVENCE

Camping Indigo Forcalquier

rte de Sigonce, 04300
☎ 492752794 📠 492751810
e-mail: forcalquier@camping-indigo.com
web: www.camping-indigo.com

5 minute walk from village centre, family campsite with high quality facilities.

dir: *A7 exit Avignon Sud onto RN100.*

GPS: 43.9620, 5.7874

Open: 26 Apr-7 Oct **Site:** 4HEC **For hire:** **Prices:** 14.50-21.90 Mobile home hire 299-756 **Facilities:** Kids' Club Play Area **Services:** **Leisure:** P **Off-site:**

FRANCE

FRÉJUS — VAR

Domaine du Colombier

1052 rue des Combattants en Afrique du Nord, 83600

494515601 494515557

e-mail: info@clubcolombier.com

web: www.clubcolombier.com

Extensive site between Cannes and St Tropez, 4.5km from the beach. Good recreational facilities including heated swimming pools, lagoon, waterslides, spa, jacuzzi and fitness area. Plenty of activities and entertainment for adults and children.

dir: *A8 exit 38.*

GPS: 43.4458, 6.7269

Open: 6 Apr-Oct **Site:** 10HEC **For hire:** **Prices:** 20-58 Mobile home hire 273-2205 **Facilities:** Wi-fi (charged) Kids' Club Play Area **Services:** **Leisure:** P **Off-site:** S

Holiday Green

rue des Combattants d'Afrique du Nord, 83600

494198830 494198831

e-mail: info@holiday-green.com

web: www.holidaygreen.com

A family site in a beautiful wooded location, offering fine modern facilities and a variety of recreation and entertainment.

dir: *A8 exit 38 towards Bagnols en Forêt.*

Open: Apr-Sep **Site:** 15HEC **For hire:** **Prices:** 35-52 **Facilities:** Wi-fi (charged) Kids' Club Play Area **Services:** **Leisure:** P **Off-site:** L S

Montourey

Quartier Montourey, 83600

494532641 494532675

e-mail: montourey@wanadoo.fr

A well-equipped site close to the beach.

dir: *2km N.*

Open: Apr-Sep **Site:** 5HEC **For hire:** **Facilities:** **Services:** **Leisure:** P

Pierre Verte

rue des Combattants d'Afrique du Nord, 83600

494408830 494407541

e-mail: info@campinglapierreverte.com

web: www.campinglapierreverte.com

A large family site in a pine forest 8km from the coast.

dir: *Exit 38 (Frejus Centre) of the A8, towards Bagnols en Forêt.*

GPS: 43.4883, 6.7154

Open: 7 Apr-Sep **Site:** 28HEC **For hire:** **Prices:** 22-39 Mobile home hire 300-1100 **Facilities:** Wi-fi (charged) Kids' Club Play Area **Services:** **Leisure:** P

Pins Parasols

3360 rue des Combattants en Afrique du Nord, 83600

494408843 494408199

e-mail: lespinsparasols@wanadoo.fr

web: lespinsparasols.com

A modern family site shaded by oaks and pines with spacious, well-defined pitches and good recreational facilities.

C&CC Report *An ideal family site for discovering the RIVIERAa and Provence. None of the Côte d'Azur resorts are far away, but do take time to discover some of the beautiful Provençal villages that lie only a few kilometres inland – as well as the fantastic Gorges du Verdon. Unlike many coastal sites that are now almost static villages, Les Pins Parasols is still a predominantly traditional touring site.*

dir: *4km N via D4.*

Open: 7 Apr-29 Sep **Site:** 4.5HEC **For hire:** **Prices:** 18.40-28.45 Mobile home hire 212-723 **Facilities:** Wi-fi (charged) Play Area **Services:** **Leisure:** P **Off-site:**

FRONTIGNAN — HÉRAULT

Soleil

60 av d'Ingril, 34110

467430202 467533469

e-mail: campingdusoleil@wanadoo.fr

web: www.campingsoleil.fr

Family site bordering the beach.

dir: *NE via D60.*

Open: Apr-Sep **Site:** 1.2HEC **For hire:** **Facilities:** **Services:** **Leisure:** P S **Off-site:**

Tamaris

140 av d'Ingril, 34110

467434477 467189790

e-mail: les-tamaris@wanadoo.fr

web: www.les-tamaris.fr

A family site on level ground with direct access to the beach. Good recreational facilities.

dir: *N112 onto D129 & D60/D50 for 6km.*

GPS: 43.4494, 3.8056

Open: 3 Apr-28 Sep **Site:** 4.5HEC **For hire:** **Prices:** 25-48 Mobile home hire 210-1090 **Facilities:** Wi-fi Kids' Club Play Area **Services:** **Leisure:** P S

FRANCE

GALLARGUES-LE-MONTUEUX — GARD

Amandiers

30660

466352802

web: www.camping-lesamandiers.com

A family site with good facilities in a beautiful wooded location.

dir: *N113 from Lunel towards Nîmes.*

Open: May-10 Sep **Site:** 3HEC **For hire:** **Facilities:** **Services:** **Leisure:** P **Off-site:** R

GALLICIAN — GARD

Camping le Mas de Mourgues

30600

466733088 466733088

e-mail: info@masdemourgues.com

web: www.masdemourgues.com

Situated in an old vineyard with some vines retained to separate pitches. Views overlooking the Camargue, ideal for touring the surrounding area including the historic town of Nîmes.

dir: *On D6572 between St-Gilles & Vauvert at road junct to Gallician.*

Open: 15 Mar-Oct **Site:** 2HEC **For hire:** **Prices:** 12-20.50 Mobile home hire 260-616 **Facilities:** Wi-fi (charged) Play Area **Services:** **Off-site:** L

GASSIN — VAR

Parc St-James Gassin

rte du Bourrian, 83580

494552020 494563477

Park-like site on slopes of a hill.

dir: *2.5km E of N559, via Km84.5 & Km84.9 on D89.*

Site: 32HEC **Facilities:** **Services:** **Leisure:** P

GIENS — VAR

Mediterranée-Les Cigales

354 bld Alsace Lorraine, 83400

494582106 494589673

e-mail: accueil@campinglemed.fr

web: www.campinglemed.fr

A well-kept site with numbered pitches. Special places for caravans.

dir: *300m E of D97.*

Open: Apr-Oct **Site:** 1.5HEC **For hire:** **Prices:** 14-22 Mobile home hire 265-780 **Facilities:** **Services:** **Off-site:** S

GRASSE — ALPES-MARITIMES

Paoute

160 rte de Cannes, 06130

493091142 493400640

e-mail: camppaoute@hotmail.com

web: www.campinglapaoute.com

A family site in a wooded location close to the town centre.

dir: *S of town centre, E of Cannes road just beyond Centre Commercial.*

GPS: 43.6364, 6.9510

Open: Apr-Sep **Site:** 2.5HEC **For hire:** **Facilities:** Wi-fi (charged) **Services:** **Leisure:** P

GRAU-DU-ROI, LE — GARD

Abri de Camargue

rte du Phare de l'Espiguette, Port Camargue, 30240

466515483 466517642

e-mail: contact@abridecamargue.fr

web: www.abridecamargue.fr

A pleasant site near the beach on the edge of the Camargue with well-marked pitches and modern installations. Activities include petanque and multi-sports.

dir: *A9 exit Gallargues onto N313 then D979 to Grau-du-Roi.*

GPS: 43.5225, 4.1488

Open: Apr-Sep **Site:** 4HEC **For hire:** **Prices:** 28-58 Mobile home hire 413-952 **Facilities:** Wi-fi (charged) Kids' Club Play Area **Services:** **Leisure:** P **Off-site:** S

Eden

Port-Camargue, 30240

466514981 466531320

web: www.campingleden.fr

Quiet site on both sides of the access road, 300 metres from the beach.

dir: *On D626 towards Espiguette.*

Open: 7 Apr-Sep **Site:** 5.25HEC **For hire:** **Prices:** 22-48 Mobile home hire 329-1512 **Facilities:** Wi-fi (charged) Kids' Club Play Area **Services:** **Leisure:** P **Off-site:** L S

Site 6HEC (site size) grass sand stone little shade partly shaded mainly shaded motorvans accepted bungalows for hire mobile homes for hire tents for hire no dogs site fully accessible for wheelchairs
Prices amount quoted is per night, for 2 adults and car, plus tent or caravan Mobile home hire is a weekly rate.

Jardins de Tivoli

rte de l'Éspiquette, 30240

466539700 466510981

e-mail: contact@lesjardinsdetivoli.com

web: www.lesjardinsdetivoli.com

A modern site with well-marked pitches in a wooded setting 0.6km from the beach. There are good recreational facilities including mountain bike hire.

dir: *A9 SE through Le Grau-du-Roi.*

Open: Apr-Sep **Site:** 7HEC **For hire:** **Facilities:** **Services:** **Leisure:** P **Off-site:** S

GRIGNAN DRÔME

Les Truffières

1100 chemin Belle Vue d'Air, 26230

475469362

e-mail: info@lestruffieres.com

web: www.lestruffieres.com

Located opposite the Château Grignan this friendly family site is set amongst oak trees and has good facilities.

dir: *A7 exit Montélimar Sud & N7 E.*

GPS: 44.4111, 4.8916

Open: 20 Apr-Sep **Site:** 3HEC **For hire:** **Prices:** 15-19.20 Mobile home hire 240-550 **Facilities:** Wi-fi **Services:** **Leisure:** P **Off-site:** R

HYÈRES VAR

Ceinturon III

L'Ayguade, 2 rue des Saraniers, 83400

494663265 494664843

e-mail: contact@ceinturon3.fr

web: www.ceinturon3.fr

Well-kept site in wooded surroundings divided into numbered pitches. Individual washing cubicles. Kids' club available in July and August.

dir: *4km SE of Hyères on D42.*

GPS: 43.1005, 6.1693

Open: 31 Mar-Sep **Site:** 3HEC **For hire:** **Prices:** 19.35-24.55 **Facilities:** Wi-fi (charged) Kids' Club Play Area **Services:** **Leisure:** P S **Off-site:** S

International

1737 rte de la Madrague, Presqu'ile de Giens, 83400

494589016 494589050

e-mail: thierry.coulomb@wanadoo.fr

web: www.international-giens.com

Site at the far end of the Almanarre beach, 400 metres from the village of Giens and ideal of windsurfers. A private solarium, sheltered from the wind, has direct access to the sea. Other facilities include children's play areas and a heated swimming pool.

Open: 22 Mar-3 Nov **Site:** 2.5HEC **For hire:** **Facilities:** Wi-fi (charged) Play Area **Services:** **Leisure:** P S

Palmiers

rue du Ceinturon, L'Ayguade, 83400

494663966 494664730

e-mail: camping-palmiers@orange.fr

web: www.camping-les-palmiers.fr

A popular site on level meadowland divided into pitches. 300 metres from the sea. Some individual washing cubicles.

dir: *4km SE of Hyères on D42.*

Open: 15 Mar-15 Oct **Site:** 4.8HEC **For hire:** **Facilities:** **Services:** **Leisure:** P **Off-site:** R S

ISLE-SUR-LA-SORGUE, L' VAUCLUSE

Sorguette

rte d'Apt, 84800

490380571 490208461

e-mail: sorguette@wanadoo.fr

web: www.camping-sorguette.com

Tranquil wooded surroundings beside the River Sorguette with good sports and entertainment facilities. Kids' club available during high season.

dir: *N100 towards Apt.*

GPS: 43.9142, 5.0717

Open: 15 Mar-15 Oct **Site:** 2.5HEC **For hire:** **Prices:** 18.40-23.20 Mobile home hire 392-581 **Facilities:** Wi-fi (charged) Kids' Club Play Area **Services:** **Leisure:** R **Off-site:** P

FRANCE

LANUÉJOLS GARD

Domaine de Pradines

rte de Millau D28, 30750
☎ 467827385
e-mail: contact@domaine-de-pradines.com
web: www.domaine-de-pradines.com

A family-run site, situated at 914 metres in the Parc National des Cévennes, between Millau and the Mont Aigoual. Spacious pitches in natural surroundings with stone buildings. Touring pitches available June to 15 September.

dir: *A75 exit Millau, follow towards Montpellier-le-Vieux then Gorges de la Dourbie. On D41, at Roque St Marguerite take D991, follow towards Lanuéjols via D29/D28.*

GPS: 44.1331, 3.3472

Open: Jan-Oct **Site:** 30HEC **For hire:** **Prices:** 12-16 Mobile home hire 360-540 **Facilities:** Wi-fi Play Area **Services:** **Leisure:** P **Off-site:** L R

LARGENTIÈRE ARDÈCHE

Ranchisses

The Camping and Caravanning Club — The Friendly Club

rte de Rocher, 07110
☎ 475883197 🖷 475883273
e-mail: reception@lesranchisses.fr
web: www.lesranchisses.fr

Located on a river with large, shady pitches and comprehensive leisure facilities.

C&CC Report *Les Ranchisses' tranquil valley setting in this lovely part of the Ardèche complements a friendly, relaxing atmosphere and the excellent site facilities. Younger children and couples of all ages love it and the friendly owners Philippe and Véronique have lots of suggestions for visits and outdoor pursuits. Make sure you try the traditional Ardèche fare at the very picturesque, locally renowned site restaurant, and try out their Wellness Centre.*

dir: *D104 road to Uzer, then follow signs for Largentière (D5). Through village and follow signs for Rocher/Valgorge, 2km to campsite.*

Open: 14 Apr-23 Sep **Site:** 7HEC **For hire:** **Facilities:** Wi-fi (charged) Kids' Club Play Area **Services:** **Leisure:** P R **Off-site:**

LAROQUE-DES-ALBÈRES PYRÉNÉES-ORIENTALES

Camping des Albères

rte Moulin de Cassagnes, 66740
☎ 468692364 🖷 468891430
e-mail: camping-des-alberes@wanadoo.fr
web: www.camping-des-alberes.com

9km from the sea at Argèles-sur-Mer and within the Massif des Albères, an area known for its hiking and mountain bike trails. Leisure facilities include swimming and paddling pools and a games room. Kids' club available in July and August. Charge made for dogs.

Open: Apr-15 Oct **Site:** 7HEC **For hire:** **Facilities:** Wi-fi (charged) Kids' Club Play Area **Services:** **Leisure:** P **Off-site:**

Las Planes

117 av du Vallespir, 66740
☎ 468892136 🖷 468890142
e-mail: info@lasplanes.com
web: www.lasplanes.com

A picturesque setting surrounded by trees, bushes and flowers.

dir: *RD11.*

Open: 15 Jun-Aug **Site:** 2.5HEC **Prices:** 21.50 **Facilities:** Play Area **Services:** **Leisure:** P **Off-site:** R

LÉZIGNAN-CORBIÈRES AUDE

CM Pinède

rue des Rousillous, 11200
☎ 468270508 🖷 468270508
e-mail: reception@campinglapinede.fr
web: www.campinglapinede.fr

Well-kept terraced site with numbered pitches and asphalt drives, decorated with bushes and flower beds. Shop only open July and August.

dir: *Signed from N113.*

Open: Mar-Oct **Site:** 3.5HEC **For hire:** **Prices:** 13.30-18.20 Mobile home hire 250-655 **Facilities:** Wi-fi Play Area **Services:** **Leisure:** P **Off-site:**

LONDE-LES-MAURES, LA — VAR

Moulières

83250
494015321 494015322
e-mail: camping.les.moulieres@wanadoo.fr
web: www.campinglesmoulieres.com
Well-tended level meadowland in quiet location. 1km from the sea.
dir: *On W outskirts towards coast.*
Open: 2 Jun-9 Sep **Site:** 3HEC **Prices:** 21-29 **Facilities:** Wi-fi Play Area **Services:** **Off-site:** S

Pansard

83250
494668322 494665612
e-mail: pansardcamping@aol.com
web: www.provence-campings.com/azur/pansard
Beautiful, wide piece of land in a pine forest beside the beach.
dir: *Off N98.*
Open: Apr-Sep **Site:** 6HEC **For hire:** **Facilities:** **Services:** **Leisure:** S

LUC-EN-DIOIS — DRÔME

Camping les Foulons

chemin de la Piscine, 26310
475213614
e-mail: mcsv@neuf.fr
web: www.camping-luc-en-diois.com
Located in an area known for climbing, a shaded site with facilities including tennis court, swimming pool and beach volleyball field.
Open: Apr-Oct **Site:** 2HEC **For hire:** **Facilities:** Wi-fi Kids' Club Play Area **Services:** **Leisure:** P R **Off-site:** P

LUNEL — HÉRAULT

Pont de Lunel

rte de Nîmes, 34400
467711022
e-mail: nb.pontdelunel@wanadoo.fr
web: www.campingdupontdelunel.com
A small, family site with shaded pitches. A games area for football, volleyball and mini-golf. Events include pétanque and ping-pong competitions.
dir: *A9 or RN113.*
GPS: 43.6854, 4.1519
Open: 15 Mar-15 Oct **Site:** 2.8HEC **For hire:** **Facilities:** Wi-fi (charged) Play Area **Services:** **Off-site:** P R

MALLEMORT — BOUCHES-DU-RHÔNE

Durance Luberon

Domaine du Vergon, 13370
490591336
e-mail: duranceluberon@orange.fr
web: www.campingduranceluberon.com
With views of the surrounding Luberon/Alpilles mountains, leisure facilities include a swimming pool plus children's pool.
dir: *2.5km on D23c, 200m from canal.*
Open: Apr-Sep **Site:** 4.37HEC **For hire:** **Facilities:** **Services:** **Leisure:** P **Off-site:** R

MANDELIEU-LA-NAPOULE — ALPES-MARITIMES

Cigales

505 av de la Mer, 06210
493432353 493433045
e-mail: campingcigales@wanadoo.fr
web: www.lescigales.com
A riverside site with well-defined pitches, 0.8km from the sea.
dir: *S on N7.*
Open: 14 Dec-12 Nov **Site:** 2HEC **For hire:** **Prices:** 31.50-42 Mobile home hire 315-940 **Facilities:** Wi-fi Play Area **Services:** **Leisure:** P **Off-site:** L R S

FRANCE

MARSEILLAN-PLAGE HÉRAULT

Beauregard Plage

250 chemin de l'Airette, 34340

☎ 467771545 🖹 467012178

e-mail: campingbeauregardplage@orange.fr

web: www.camping-beauregard-plage.com

A family camping site bordering a sandy beach sheltered by natural sand dunes. High standard sanitary facilities.

dir: *A9 onto N112 exit Agde/Sète tourist office.*

GPS: 43.315, 3.5489

Open: 31 Mar-15 Oct **Site:** 3.3HEC **Facilities:** Wi-fi Play Area **Services:** **Leisure:** S **Off-site:** L

Créole

74 av des Campings, 34340

☎ 467219269 🖹 467265816

e-mail: campinglacreole@wanadoo.fr

web: www.campinglacreole.com

A quiet family site with direct access to a pleasant sandy beach.

GPS: 43.3128, 3.5464

Open: Apr-Oct **Site:** 1.5HEC **For hire:** **Prices:** 13.70-33.50 **Facilities:** Wi-fi (charged) Play Area **Services:** **Leisure:** S **Off-site:**

Languedoc-Camping

117 chemin du Payrollet, 34340

☎ 467219255 🖹 467016375

A family site in wooded surroundings with direct access to the beach.

dir: *On coast road between Mediterranean & Bassin de Thau.*

Open: 15 Mar-Oct **Site:** 1.5HEC **For hire:** **Facilities:** **Services:** **Leisure:** S **Off-site:** L P R

Plage

69 chemin du Payrollet, 34340

☎ 467219254 🖹 467016357

e-mail: info@laplage-camping.net

web: www.laplage-camping.net

A family site with direct access to a sandy beach.

Open: 15 Mar-Oct **Site:** 1.3HEC **For hire:** **Prices:** 15-34.50 Mobile home hire 270-635 **Facilities:** Wi-fi (charged) Play Area **Services:** **Leisure:** S **Off-site:**

Yelloh Village les Méditerranées

av des Campings, 34340

☎ 467219449 🖹 467218105

e-mail: info@nouvelle-floride.com

web: www.lesmediterranees.com

Quiet wooded surroundings with good sanitary facilities, 200 metres from the beach. The site comprises Charlemagne Zone and Nouvelle Floride, with leisure facilities available. Dogs accepted but restrictions apply.

dir: *Via N112 at Marseillan-Plage.*

Open: 15 Apr-1 Oct **Site:** 7.5HEC **For hire:** **Facilities:** Wi-fi Kids' Club Play Area **Services:** **Leisure:** P S **Off-site:**

MAUREILLAS PYRÉNÉES-ORIENTALES

Val Roma Park

Les Thermas du Boulou, 66480

☎ 468398813 🖹 468398813

e-mail: valromapark@wanadoo.fr

web: valromapark.monsite.wanadoo.fr

A mainly shaded site, 5km from the border with Spain.

dir: *2.5km NE on N9.*

Open: May-Sep **Site:** 3.5HEC **For hire:** **Prices:** 14-18.60 Mobile home hire 250-500 **Facilities:** Wi-fi Play Area **Services:** **Leisure:** P R **Off-site:** L

MÉOLANS-REVEL ALPES-DE-HAUTE-PROVENCE

Domaine de Loisirs de l'Ubaye

04340

☎ 492810196 🖹 492819253

e-mail: info@loisirsubaye.com

web: www.loisirsubaye.com

A large terraced site in a delightful wooded valley. There is a small lake, direct access to the river, and good sports and recreational facilities.

dir: *7km NW of Barcelonnette.*

GPS: 44.3966, 6.5455

Open: 2 May-15 Oct **Site:** 10HEC **For hire:** **Prices:** 13.50-23 Mobile home hire 310-610 **Facilities:** Wi-fi Play Area **Services:** **Leisure:** L P R

MIRABEL-ET-BLACONS — DRÔME

Gervanne Camping

26400

475400020 475400397

e-mail: info@gervanne-camping.com

web: www.gervanne-camping.com

A pleasant family site with scattered shade and plenty of facilities beside the River Drôme. Well located in the heart of the Drôme region, close to the natural park of the Vercors.

dir: *Via D164 Crest-Die.*

GPS: 44.7110, 5.0899

Open: 2 Apr-Sep **Site:** 3.8HEC **For hire:** **Prices:** 14-23 Mobile home hire 294-756 **Facilities:** Wi-fi Kids' Club Play Area **Services:** **Leisure:** P R

MONDRAGON — VAUCLUSE

Pinède en Provence

Les Massanes RD 26, 84430

490408298 959921656

e-mail: contact@camping-pinede-provence.com

web: www.camping-pinede-provence.com

Peaceful terraced site with shady pitches located in a pine forest. Most pitches have electricity and water.

dir: *1km SW via N7.*

GPS: 44.2403, 4.7139

Open: All Year. **Site:** 3.5HEC **For hire:** **Facilities:** Wi-fi Kids' Club Play Area **Services:** **Leisure:** P **Off-site:**

MONTBLANC — HÉRAULT

Le Rebau

34290

467985078 970624298

e-mail: gilbert@camping-lerebau.fr

web: www.camping-lerebau.fr

Divided into pitches and surrounded by vineyards.

dir: *N113 from Pézenas to La Bégude de Jordy, onto D18 towards Montblanc for 2km.*

GPS: 43.3987, 3.3736

Open: Mar-Oct **Site:** 3HEC **For hire:** **Facilities:** Wi-fi **Services:** **Leisure:** P **Off-site:** R

MONTCLAR — AUDE

Domaine d'Arnauteille

11250

468268453 468269110

e-mail: info@arnauteille.com

web: www.camping-arnauteille.com

Not far from Carcassonne, this natural wooded park is surrounded by mountains with panoramic views. Well maintained facilities include Roman Bath style aqua-complex with jacuzzi and solarium.

dir: *2.2km SE via D43.*

Open: 3 Apr-23 Sep **Site:** 12HEC **For hire:** **Prices:** 17-38 Mobile home hire 259-763 **Facilities:** Wi-fi (charged) Kids' Club Play Area **Services:** **Leisure:** P **Off-site:** R

MONTPELLIER — HÉRAULT

Floréal

rte de la 1ère écluse, 34970

467929305 467559244

e-mail: contact@campinglefloreal.com

web: www.campinglefloreal.com

On level ground surrounded by vineyards.

dir: *A9 exit Montpellier-Sud, site 0.5km. From town centre D986 for Palavas.*

Open: Apr-3 Nov **Site:** 1.55HEC **For hire:** **Facilities:** **Services:** **Off-site:** P R

MONTPEZAT — ALPES-DE-HAUTE-PROVENCE

Village Center le Coteau de la Marine

Coteau de la Marine, 04500

492775333 492775934

e-mail: contact@village-center.com

web: www.village-center.com/provence-cote-azur/camping-montagne-coteau-marine.php

A pleasant wooded site set within Verdon regional park, providing easy access to the Verdon Gorges and lavender fields of the Valensole.

dir: *Via D11 & D211.*

GPS: 43.7464, 6.1004

Open: 8 Apr-2 Oct **Site:** 12HEC **For hire:** **Prices:** 16.90-29.90 **Facilities:** Wi-fi (charged) Kids' Club Play Area **Services:** **Leisure:** P

MOURIÈS — BOUCHES-DU-RHÔNE

Devenson

13890
☎ 490475201 📠 490476309
e-mail: camping-devenson@orange.fr
web: www.camping-devenson.com

Terraced site among pine and olive trees in Parc Naturel des Alpilles.

dir: *Off N113 at La Samatane & N towards Mouriès, site N of village.*

GPS: 43.7011, 4.8578

Open: 30 Apr-15 Sep **Site:** 3.5HEC **Prices:** 18.40 **Facilities:** Play Area **Services:** **Leisure:** P **Off-site:**

MOUSTIERS-STE-MARIE — ALPES-DE-HAUTE-PROVENCE

St-Jean

rte de Riez, quartier St Jean, 04360
☎ 492746685 📠 492746685
e-mail: contact@camping-st-jean.fr
web: www.camping-st-jean.fr

Quiet and relaxing site located at the gateway to the Gorges du Verdon, close to Ste-Croix Lake.

dir: *Via D952.*

GPS: 43.8433, 6.2158

Open: Apr-16 Oct **Site:** 1.6HEC **For hire:** **Prices:** 15.80-17.50 Mobile home hire 290-585 **Facilities:** Wi-fi Play Area **Services:** **Leisure:** R **Off-site:** L P

Vieux Colombier

Quartier St-Michel, 04360
☎ 492746189
e-mail: contact@lvcm.fr
web: www.lvcm.fr

A family site near the entrance to the Gorges du Verdon at an altitude of 630 metres.

dir: *0.8km S on D952 towards Castellane.*

Open: Apr-Sep **Site:** 2.73HEC **For hire:** **Prices:** 19.40-21.20 Mobile home hire 252-587 **Facilities:** Wi-fi Play Area **Services:** **Off-site:** L P R

MUY, LE — VAR

Cigales

4 chemin de Jas de la Paro, 83490
☎ 494451208 📠 494459280
e-mail: contact@camping-les-cigales-sud.fr
web: www.camping-les-cigales-sud.fr

A family site set among Mediterranean vegetation with excellent facilities. Organised entertainment in summer. Kids' club available in July and August.

dir: *A8 exit Draguignan, after toll booth, take 1st rdbt to the left & follow road to the entrance of the site - signed.*

Open: 15 Mar-15 Oct **Site:** 13.5HEC **For hire:** **Prices:** 19.25-35 Mobile home hire 266-925 **Facilities:** Wi-fi Kids' Club Play Area **Services:** **Leisure:** P **Off-site:** R

NANS-LES-PINS — VAR

Camping Domaine de la Sainte Baume

Quartier Delvieux Sud, 83860
☎ 494789268 📠 494786737
e-mail: ste-baume@wanadoo.fr
web: www.saintebaume.com

Located among pine and oak trees, pitches are flat and shaded. Ideal for families with facilities including a pool complex. There is a compulsory separate car park at certiain times.

dir: *A8 exit 34 towards St Zacharie, then signs for Nans-les-Pins.*

GPS: 43.3769, 5.7881

Open: Apr-21 Oct **Site:** **For hire:** **Facilities:** Wi-fi (charged) Kids' Club Play Area **Services:** **Leisure:** P **Off-site:**

NARBONNE — AUDE

Camping la Nautique

The Camping and Caravanning Club The Friendly Club

11100

468904819 468907339

e-mail: info@campinglanautique.com

web: www.campinglanautique.com

Situated on the salt-water Étang de Bages et de Sigean, this site is particularly well-appointed, each pitch having its own washing and toilet facilities. There are good recreational facilities.

C&CC Report *The friendly owners of this well maintained lakeside site are keen to welcome you. The individual sanitary blocks on each pitch, which can take the largest of units, are a definite plus. Windsurfers will enjoy the easy access to the lake. Day trips to Cathar country should definitely include a trip to the Corbières and Minervois vineyards. The medieval fortified town of Carcassonne is also worth the trip.*

dir: *A9 exit Narbonne Sud.*

GPS: 43.1472, 3.0039

Open: 15 Feb-15 Nov **Site:** 16HEC **For hire:** **Prices:** 19.50-43 Mobile home hire 189-910 **Facilities:** Wi-fi (charged) Kids' Club Play Area **Services:** **Leisure:** P **Off-site:** L

NARBONNE-PLAGE — AUDE

CM Falaise

av des Vacances, 11100

468498077 468751200

web: www.campinglafalaise.fr

On level ground at the foot of the Massif of the Calpe with modern facilities.

dir: *W of Narbonne Plage, 400m from beach.*

Open: Apr-22 Sep **Site:** 8HEC **Facilities:** **Services:** **Off-site:** S

NÉBIAS — AUDE

Fontaulié-Sud

11500

468201762

e-mail: lefontauliesud@free.fr

web: www.fontauliesud.com

A beautiful setting in the heart of the Cathar region.

dir: *0.6km S via D117.*

Open: May-Sep **Site:** 4HEC **For hire:** **Prices:** 22 Mobile home hire 270-550 **Facilities:** Wi-fi Play Area **Services:** **Leisure:** P **Off-site:** L R

NÎMES — GARD

Domaine de la Bastide

rte de Generac, 30900

466620582 466620583

e-mail: immocamp@wanadoo.fr

web: www.camping-nimes.com

A rural setting with excellent facilities.

dir: *5km S of town centre on D13. A9 exit Nîmes-Ouest.*

Open: All Year. **Site:** 5HEC **For hire:** **Facilities:** **Services:** **Off-site:** L P

OLLIÈRES-SUR-EYRIEUX, LES — ARDÈCHE

Domaine des Plantas

07360

475662153 475662365

e-mail: plantas.ardeche@wanadoo.fr

web: www.camping-franceloc.fr

Games room, disco and other leisure activities.

Open: 5 Apr-4 Oct **Site:** 10HEC **For hire:** **Facilities:** **Services:** **Leisure:** P R

ORAISON — ALPES-DE-HAUTE-PROVENCE

Camping les Oliviers

chemin St Sauveur, 04700

492787000

e-mail: camping-oraison@wanadoo.fr

web: www.camping-oraison.com

Spacious, flat pitches amongst olive trees. Entertainment throughout the day in high season. During July and August, a bar, café, restaurant and kids' club are available.

GPS: 43.9232, 5.9246

Open: Apr-Sep **Site:** 2HEC **For hire:** **Facilities:** Wi-fi Kids' Club Play Area **Services:** **Leisure:** P **Off-site:** L R

ORANGE — VAUCLUSE

Jonquier

1321 rue Alexis-Carrel, 84100

490344948 490511697

e-mail: info@campinglejonquier.com

web: www.campinglejonquier.com

Peaceful site ideally located for exploring Provence.

dir: *On NW outskirts.*

Open: Apr-Sep **Site:** 2HEC **For hire:** **Prices:** 21-27 Mobile home hire 380-670 **Facilities:** Wi-fi (charged) Play Area **Services:** **Leisure:** P **Off-site:** R

FRANCE

PALAU DEL VIDRE — PYRÉNÉES-ORIENTALES

Haras

The Camping and Caravanning Club The Friendly Club

66690

☎ 468221450 468379893

e-mail: haras8@wanadoo.fr

web: www.camping-le-haras.com

Family-friendly site with pitches separated by hedges. In high season, activities include archery, volleyball and petanque.

C&CC Report *A delightful little site in this very popular area, away from the hurly-burly of the coast, run by the welcoming Gil family. Luxuriant plant and tree life abound on site. Nearby, in the small town of Palau you can watch glassmakers at work. Car excursions take you to the beaches of the Roussillon coast, its vineyards, the Albères massif, Andorra, Spain and all that Catalan France has to offer.*

dir: *A9, exit Perpignan Sud, then RN114 towards Argelès-Sur-Mer. Exit 9 for Palau del Vidre, site on left before village.*

Open: 20 Mar-20 Oct **Site:** 4.5HEC **For hire:** **Facilities:** **Services:** **Leisure:** P **Off-site:**

PERNES-LES-FONTAINES — VAUCLUSE

Camping les Fontaines

125 chemin de la Chapelette, rte de Sudre, 84210

☎ 490468255

e-mail: contact@campingfontaines.com

web: www.campingfontaines.com

Located 1km from the village, a peaceful site with views of the surrounding mountains. Leisure facilities include both swimming and paddling pools, table tennis and a kids' club in July and August.

Open: Apr-22 Oct **Site:** 2.5HEC **For hire:** **Prices:** 15-25 Mobile home hire 280-680 **Facilities:** Wi-fi Kids' Club **Services:** **Leisure:** P **Off-site:** L

PEYREMALE-SUR-CÈZE — GARD

Drouilhédes

30160

☎ 466250480 466251095

e-mail: info@campingcevennes.com

web: www.campingcevennes.com

A beautiful location beside the River Cèze surrounded by acacia trees.

dir: *Via A6 & D17.*

Open: Apr-Sep **Site:** 2HEC **For hire:** **Prices:** 16-30.40 **Facilities:** Wi-fi Play Area **Services:** **Leisure:** R **Off-site:**

PONT-D'HÉRAULT — GARD

Magnanarelles

Le Rey, 30570

☎ 467824013 467825061

e-mail: info@maxfrance.com

web: www.maxfrance.com

A pleasant mountain setting with well-defined pitches.

dir: *0.3km W via D999, beside river.*

Open: All Year. **Site:** 2HEC **For hire:** **Facilities:** **Services:** **Leisure:** P R

PORT-GRIMAUD — VAR

Camping de la Plage

83310

☎ 494563115 494564961

e-mail: campingplagegrimaud@wanadoo.fr

web: www.camping-de-la-plage.fr

Wide area of land on both sides of road beside sea. Partly terraced and divided into pitches.

dir: *N on N98.*

GPS: 43.2819, 6.5862

Open: 31 Mar-8 Oct **Site:** 18HEC **Prices:** 26.20-33.20 **Facilities:** Wi-fi (charged) Play Area **Services:** **Leisure:** S **Off-site:** P

Camping des Mûres

RD559, 83310

☎ 494561697 494563791

e-mail: info@camping-des-mures.com

web: www.camping-des-mures.com

Located by the beach, a site offering many leisure activities and entertainment. A kids' club is available in July and August.

Open: 31 Mar-6 Oct **Site:** 11HEC **For hire:** **Prices:** 29-35 Mobile home hire 322-1190 **Facilities:** Wi-fi (charged) Kids' Club Play Area **Services:** **Leisure:** S

Club Holiday Marina

The Camping and Caravanning Club The Friendly Club

Le Ginestrel, 83310

☎ 494560843 🖹 494562388

e-mail: info@holiday-marina.com

web: www.holiday-marina.com

Located close to beaches with diving tuition available. Kids' club in July and August.

C&CC Report *A great location near the Gulf of St Tropez, with trendy, chic coastal resorts and exclusive hilltop villages within easy reach. Relaxing site facilities and the innovative private bathrooms make this a very comfortable and good quality site.*

dir: *On N98.*

Open: Mar-Dec **Site:** 3.5HEC **For hire:** **Facilities:** Wi-fi (charged) Kids' Club Play Area **Services:** **Leisure:** P **Off-site:** S

Domaine des Naiades

St-Pons-les-Mûres, 83310

☎ 494556780 🖹 494556781

e-mail: info@lesnaiades.com

web: www.lesnaiades.com

Site on hilly land with terraces divided into pitches and with many modern facilities. A kids' club is available 15 June to 31 August.

dir: *N98 onto D244, turn right & continue uphill.*

Open: 31 Mar-21 Oct **Site:** 27HEC **For hire:** **Prices:** 26.20-56.20 Mobile home hire 329-1645 **Facilities:** Wi-fi (charged) Kids' Club Play Area **Services:** **Leisure:** P **Off-site:** S

PORTIRAGNES-PLAGE — HÉRAULT

Camping Les Mimosas

34420

☎ 467909292 🖹 467908539

e-mail: les.mimosas.portiragnes@wanadoo.fr

web: www.mimosas.com

A well-equipped family site located in a leisure park on the banks of the Canal du Midi, 1.3km from the sea. Kids' club from 1 July.

dir: *A9 exit Béziers Centre direction of airport Béziers/Cap d'Agde, N112 & D37 towards coast.*

Open: 26 May-5 Sep **Site:** 7HEC **For hire:** **Prices:** 20-40 Mobile home hire 231-1386 **Facilities:** Wi-fi (charged) Kids' Club Play Area **Services:** **Leisure:** P R **Off-site:** S

Sablons

rte de Portiragnes, 34420

☎ 467909055 🖹 467908291

e-mail: contact@les-sablons.com

web: les-sablons.com

Large site subdivided into fields by fences, beside the beach. Night club and disco.

dir: *0.5km N on D37.*

Open: Apr-Sep **Site:** 15HEC **For hire:** **Facilities:** **Services:** **Leisure:** P S

PRADET, LE — VAR

Mauvallon

chemin de la Gavaresse, 83220

☎ 494213173

e-mail: mauvallon@wanadoo.fr

web: www.campingmauvallon.fr

A peaceful, family site close to a pine forest, 500 metres from the sea.

dir: *Off N559 in Le Pradet onto D86 for 2.5km towards sea.*

Open: 15 Jun-15 Sep **Site:** 1.2HEC **Prices:** 14.50 **Facilities:** Wi-fi **Services:** **Off-site:** S

PRAMOUSQUIER — VAR

Pramousquier

83980

☎ 494058395 🖹 494057504

e-mail: camping-lavandou@wanadoo.fr

web: www.campingpramousquier.com

A terraced site set in a wooded park 400 metres from a fine sandy beach. Good recreational facilities.

dir: *2km E via D559.*

Open: May-Sep **Site:** 3HEC **For hire:** **Facilities:** **Services:** **Off-site:** S

PREIXAN — AUDE

Airotel Grand Sud "Le Breil d'Aude"

rte de Limoux, Preixan, 11250

☎ 468268818 🖹 468268507

e-mail: sudfrance@wanadoo.fr

web: www.camping-grandsud.com

Wooded location beside a private lake with free fishing.

dir: *1.5km N via D118.*

Open: Apr-Sep **Site:** 11HEC **For hire:** **Facilities:** Wi-fi Play Area **Services:** **Leisure:** P R **Off-site:**

FRANCE

PRIVAS ARDÈCHE

Ardeche

rte de Montélimar, 07000
475640580 475645968
e-mail: jcray@wanadoo.fr
web: www.ardechecamping.fr
A comfortable site with good facilities in the heart of the Ardèche region.
Open: Apr-Sep **Site:** 5.5HEC **For hire:** **Facilities:** **Services:** **Leisure:** P R **Off-site:** P

PUGET-SUR-ARGENS VAR

Aubrèdes

408 chemin des Aubrèdes, 83480
494455146 494452892
e-mail: campingaubredes@wanadoo.fr
web: campingaubredes.com
Situated on undulating meadowland surrounded by pine trees with modern facilities.
dir: *A8 exit Puget-sur-Argens, site 0.85km.*
Open: 8 May-12 Sep **Site:** 3.8HEC **For hire:** **Facilities:** **Services:** **Leisure:** P

Bastiane

1056, chemin des Suvières, 83480
494555594 494555593
e-mail: info@labastiane.com
web: www.labastiane.com
Hilly site divided into numbered pitches in a pine and oak wood. Individual washing cubicles. Separate car park for arrivals after 23.00hrs. Kids' club in July and August.
dir: *Via A8 exit 37.*
GPS: 43.4685, 6.6765
Open: 5 Apr-21 Oct **Site:** 3.05HEC **For hire:** **Prices:** 16.78-43.78 Mobile home hire 266-861 **Facilities:** Wi-fi (charged) Kids' Club Play Area **Services:** **Leisure:** P **Off-site:** L R

QUINSON ALPES-DE-HAUTE-PROVENCE

Village Center les Prés du Verdon

04500
499572121 467516389
e-mail: contact@village-center.com
web: www.village-center.com/provence-cote-azur/camping-montagne-pres-verdon.php
Ideal for exploring the Verdon gorges, the site has many leisure facilities with a nearby water sports centre offering canoeing and kayaking.
GPS: 43.6969, 6.0415
Open: 8 Apr-2 Oct **Site:** 3.5HEC **For hire:** **Facilities:** Kids' Club Play Area **Services:** **Leisure:** P **Off-site:**

RACOU, LE PYRÉNÉES-ORIENTALES

Bois de Valmarie

66700
468810992 468958058
e-mail: contact@camping-lasirene.fr
web: www.camping-lasirene.fr
A family site with plentiful recreational facilities.
dir: *N114 exit Perpignan Sud.*
Open: 22 Apr-24 Sep **Site:** 7HEC **For hire:** **Facilities:** Wi-fi Play Area **Services:** **Leisure:** P S **Off-site:**

RAMATUELLE VAR

Yelloh Village Tournels

rte de Camarat, 83350
494559090 494559099
e-mail: info@tournels.com
web: www.tournels.com
Lovely views to Pampelonne Bay from part of this site. 1km to beach. Swimming pool area includes lazy river, slides and a children's pool.
dir: *Off D93 Croix-Valmer to St-Tropez, signs to Cap Camarat.*
GPS: 43.2058, 6.6507
Open: 23 Mar-9 Jan **Site:** 20HEC **For hire:** **Prices:** 17-62 Mobile home hire 273-2065 **Facilities:** Wi-fi (charged) Kids' Club Play Area **Services:** **Leisure:** P **Off-site:** S

FRANCE

REMOULINS GARD

Soubeyranne

rte de Beaucaire, 30210

466370321 466371465

e-mail: soubeyranne@franceloc.fr

web: www.soubeyranne.com

A picturesque location close to the River Gard with modern facilities.

dir: *S on D986.*

Open: Apr-23 Sep **Site:** 6HEC **For hire:** **Facilities:** **Services:** **Leisure:** P **Off-site:** R

Sousta

av du Pont-du-Gard, 30210

466371280 466372369

e-mail: info@lasousta.com

web: www.lasousta.com

Picturesque forest site with access to the river, a short distance from the Pont du Gard.

dir: *2km NW. A9 exit for Remoulins, right after bridge towards Pont de Gard.*

Open: Mar-Oct **Site:** 14HEC **For hire:** **Prices:** 13.90-23.90 **Facilities:** Wi-fi Play Area **Services:** **Leisure:** P R

REVENS GARD

Lou Triadou

Le Bourg, 30750

467827358

e-mail: lou.triadou@wanadoo.fr

web: camping_lou_triadou.voila.net

A well-equipped site in the heart of the Causse Noir.

dir: *Via D159/D151.*

Open: 15 Apr-1 Sep **Site:** 0.78HEC **For hire:** **Prices:** 10.50 Mobile home hire 185-300 **Facilities:** **Services:** **Leisure:** P

RIA PYRÉNÉES-ORIENTALES

Bellevue

18 rue Bellevue, 66500

468964896

e-mail: camping.bellevue@free.fr

web: www.camping-bellevue-riasirach.com

Beautifully terraced site beside a former vineyard. Very well-kept.

dir: *2km S on N116, onto road to Sirach, turn right for 0.6km up driveway.*

Open: 9 Apr-15 Oct **Site:** 2.5HEC **For hire:** **Facilities:** Wi-fi Play Area **Services:** **Leisure:** P **Off-site:** L P R

ROQUEBRUNE-SUR-ARGENS VAR

Domaine de la Bergerie

Valleé du Fournel, 83520

498114545 498114546

e-mail: info@domainelabergerie.com

web: www.domainelabergerie.com

A large, well-run family site set in pleasant Provençal countryside with fine recreational facilities.

dir: *A8 exit Le Muy, onto N7 & D7.*

Open: 28 Apr-Sep **Site:** 60HEC **For hire:** **Facilities:** Wi-fi (charged) Kids' Club Play Area **Services:** **Leisure:** L P

Leï Suves

Quartier du Blavet, 83520

494454395 494816313

e-mail: camping.lei.suves@wanadoo.fr

web: www.lei-suves.com

Set in a picturesque forested area with good recreational facilities.

dir: *4km N via N7.*

GPS: 43.4778, 6.6389

Open: 31 Mar-15 Oct **Site:** 7.4HEC **For hire:** **Prices:** 22-42 Mobile home hire 360-970 **Facilities:** Wi-fi (charged) Kids' Club Play Area **Services:** **Leisure:** P **Off-site:** L

see advert on page 284

FRANCE

cilities shower electric points for razors electric points for caravans motorvan service point parking by tents permitted npulsory separate car park shop **Services** café/restaurant bar Camping Gaz International gas other than Camping Gaz first aid facilities laundry **Leisure** swimming L-Lake P-Pool R-River S-Sea **Off-site** All facilities within 5km

Pêcheurs

83520

☎ 494457125 🖷 494816513

e-mail: info@camping-les-pecheurs.com

web: www.camping-les-pecheurs.com

A pleasant site with direct access to the river in a wooded location at the foot of the Roquebrune crag. Kids' club available in July and August.

dir: *0.5km NW via D7, near lake.*

Open: Apr-Sep **Site:** 5HEC **For hire:** **Prices:** 17.50-41 Mobile home hire 350-1095 **Facilities:** Wi-fi (charged) Kids' Club Play Area **Services:** **Leisure:** L P R

ROQUE-D'ANTHÉRON, LA — BOUCHES-DU-RHÔNE

Village Center le Domaine des Iscles

Le Plan d'Eau, 13640

☎ 499572121 🖷 467516389

e-mail: contact@village-center.com

web: www.village-center.com/provence-cote-azur/camping-campagne-les-iscles.php

On the banks of the River Durance.

dir: *A7 exit 26 (Sénas) towards Aix en Provence. At Pont Royal rdbt, exit towards Charleval, then La Roque d'Anthéron on D561.*

GPS: 43.7282, 5.3210

Open: 8 Apr-2 Oct **Site:** 10HEC **For hire:** **Facilities:** Wi-fi (charged) Kids' Club Play Area **Services:** **Leisure:** L P

FRANCE

Site 6HEC (site size) grass sand stone little shade partly shaded mainly shaded motorvans accepted bungalows for hire mobile homes for hire tents for hire no dogs site fully accessible for wheelchairs
Prices amount quoted is per night, for 2 adults and car, plus tent or caravan Mobile home hire is a weekly rate.

ROQUETTE-SUR-SIAGNE, LA ALPES-MARITIMES

Panoramic

1630 av de la République, Quartier St-Jean, 06550

492190777 492190777

e-mail: campingpanoramic@wanadoo.fr

web: www.campingpanoramic.fr

In the centre of a holiday resort, a well-equipped, modern site in a wooded location with shaded terraces, affording magnificent views of the surrounding hills.

dir: *N of village off D9.*

Open: All Year. **Site:** 1HEC **For hire:** **Prices:** 30.50 Mobile home hire 700 **Facilities:** Wi-fi (charged) Play Area **Services:** **Leisure:** P **Off-site:** R S

SAILLAGOUSE PYRÉNÉES-ORIENTALES

Cerdan

11 rte d'Estavar, 66800

468047046

e-mail: lecerdan@lecerdan.com

web: www.lecerdan.com

Picturesque setting in meadow with some terraces. Hot meals served during peak season.

dir: *N116 in the direction of Andorra and Mont-Louis.*

Open: Nov-Sep **Site:** 2.8HEC **For hire:** **Prices:** 12-13 Mobile home hire 300-600 **Facilities:** Wi-fi (charged) Play Area **Services:** **Off-site:** P R

ST-ALBAN-AURIOLLES ARDÈCHE

Camping Ranc Davaine

Rte de Chandolas, 07120

475396055 475393850

e-mail: camping.ranc.davaine@wanadoo.fr

web: www.camping-ranc-davaine.fr

Within easy reach of St-Alban and popular areas of the Ardèche, the site has direct access to a riverside beach. Recreational facilities include a covered pool with slides, jacuzzi and sauna. There is an entertainment programme in high season.

dir: *2.3km SW via D58.*

GPS: 44.4143, 4.2730

Open: 31 Mar-16 Sep **Site:** 12HEC **For hire:** **Prices:** 21-45 Mobile home hire 343-1330 **Facilities:** Wi-fi Kids' Club Play Area **Services:** **Leisure:** P R **Off-site:**

ST-AMBROIX GARD

Beau-Rivage

Le Moulinet, 30500

466241017

e-mail: marc@camping-beau-rivage.fr

web: www.camping-beau-rivage.fr

A good location between the sea and the Cévennes mountains, set beside the River Cèze.

dir: *3.5km SE on D37.*

GPS: 44.2374, 4.2019

Open: Apr-Sep **Site:** 3.5HEC **Facilities:** Wi-fi **Services:** **Leisure:** R **Off-site:**

Clos

30500

466241008 466602562

e-mail: campingleclos@wanadoo.fr

web: www.camping-le-clos.fr

A quiet site in a pleasant setting beside the River Cèze with modern facilities.

dir: *Off Church Square.*

Open: Apr-Oct **Site:** 1.8HEC **For hire:** **Prices:** 9.50-19 Mobile home hire 215-650 **Facilities:** Wi-fi **Services:** **Leisure:** P R **Off-site:** L

ST-AYGULF VAR

L'Étoile d'Argens

chemin des Étangs, 83370

494810141 494812145

e-mail: info@etoiledargens.com

web: www.etoiledargens.com

3km from the beach, on the banks of the River Argens. A water shuttle bus takes campers to the sea. Extensive leisure facilities include three swimming pools and four tennis courts.

dir: *A8 exit Puget sur Argens, then towards Frejus, onto D8 towards Roquebrune sur Argens.*

Open: Apr-Sep **Site:** 11.2HEC **For hire:** **Prices:** 16-56 Mobile home hire 288-1560 **Facilities:** Wi-fi (charged) Kids' Club Play Area **Services:** **Leisure:** P R **Off-site:** L S

Paradis des Campeurs

La Gaillarde Plage, 83380

☎ 494969355 🖹 494496299

web: www.paradis-des-campeurs.com

A quiet family site in a picturesque location with direct access to the beach.

dir: *2.5km towards Gaillarde-Plage between St-Aygulf & Ste-Maxime.*

Open: 31 Mar-2 Oct **Site:** 3.7HEC **For hire:** **Prices:** 17.30-30.30 Mobile home hire 290-730 **Facilities:** Wi-fi (charged) Play Area **Services:** **Leisure:** S

Pont d'Argens

RN98, 83370

☎ 494511497 🖹 494512944

e-mail: campinglepontdargens@yahoo.fr

web: www.camping-caravaning-lepontdargens.com

A pleasant site with good facilities beside the river and sea.

dir: *A8 exit 37 Puget-sur-Argens.*

GPS: 43.4098, 6.7258

Open: Apr-15 Oct **Site:** 7HEC **For hire:** **Prices:** 21-32.50 Mobile home hire 400-1000 **Facilities:** Wi-fi (charged) Kids' Club Play Area **Services:** **Leisure:** P R S

see advert on this page

St-Aygulf Plage

270 av Salvarelli, 83370

☎ 494176249 🖹 494810316

web: www.campingdesaintaygulf.fr

A well-equipped family site in wooded surroundings with direct access to the beach.

dir: *Inland from N98 at Km881.3 N of town.*

Open: Apr-Oct **Site:** 22HEC **For hire:** **Facilities:** **Services:** **Leisure:** S

ST-CHAMAS BOUCHES-DU-RHÔNE

Canet Plage

13250

☎ 490509689 🖹 490508751

e-mail: info@camping-lecanet.fr

web: www.camping-lecanet.fr

A well-equipped site beside the Étang de Berre with a range of recreational facilities.

dir: *On D10, S of Salon-de-Provence towards La Fare les Oliviers.*

Open: All Year. **Site:** 3HEC **For hire:** **Facilities:** **Services:** **Leisure:** L P **Off-site:**

ST-CYPRIEN PYRÉNÉES-ORIENTALES

Cala Gogo

av Armand Lanoux, Les Capellans, 66750

☎ 468210712 🖹 468210219

e-mail: camping.calagogo@wanadoo.fr

web: www.campmed.com

Family site close to the beach and overlooked by the Pyrénées. Special offers for mobile homes are available.

dir: *4km S towards Les Capellans.*

GPS: 42.5994, 3.0373

Open: 28 Apr-22 Sep **Site:** 12HEC **For hire:** **Prices:** 20-42.40 Mobile home hire 259-1330 **Facilities:** Wi-fi Play Area **Services:** **Leisure:** P S

Roussillon

Cami de la Mar, 66750

☎ 468210645 🖹 251339404

e-mail: info@chadotel.com

web: www.chadotel.com

Close to the Spanish border, flanked on one side by the Mediterranean sea and on the other by the Pyrénées. Leisure facilities available along with a programme of entertainment.

GPS: 42.6188, 3.0160

Open: Apr-Sep **Site:** 3.05HEC **For hire:** **Facilities:** Wi-fi (charged) Play Area **Services:** **Leisure:** P **Off-site:** S

ST-CYR-SUR-MER VAR

Clos Ste-Thérèse

rte de Bandol, 83270

☎ 494321221 🖷 494322962

e-mail: camping@clos-therese.com

web: www.clos-therese.com

Located within an area of vineyards overlooking the sea. A well-shaded family site with well-defined pitches on terraces.

dir: *Autoroute A50.*

GPS: 43.1594, 5.7302

Open: Apr-Sep **Site:** 4HEC **For hire:** **Prices:** 15.80-25.20 Mobile home hire 300-870 **Facilities:** Wi-fi (charged) Play Area **Services:** **Leisure:** P **Off-site:** S

ST-JEAN-LE-CENTENIER ARDÈCHE

Camping les Arches

rte de Mirabel, 07580

☎ 475367545 🖷 475367545

e-mail: info@camping-les-arches.com

web: www.camping-les-arches.com

A family site in a wooded location with direct access to the river. Activities for children.

dir: *A7 exit Montélimar Nord, N102 to Mirabel, onto D458 for 0.5km.*

Open: 29 Apr-18 Sep **Site:** 4HEC **For hire:** **Facilities:** Wi-fi Kids' Club Play Area **Services:** **Leisure:** R **Off-site:**

ST-JEAN-PLA-DE-CORTS PYRÉNÉES-ORIENTALES

Casteillets

66490

☎ 468832683 🖷 468833967

e-mail: jc@campinglescasteillets.com

web: www.campinglescasteillets.com

A family site between the sea and the mountains close to the River Tech.

dir: *A9 exit le Boulu.*

GPS: 42.5103, 2.7828

Open: All Year. **Site:** 5HEC **For hire:** **Prices:** 10.90-18.50 Mobile home hire 260-815 **Facilities:** Wi-fi (charged) Kids' Club Play Area **Services:** **Leisure:** P **Off-site:** L R

ST-JULIEN-DE-LA-NEF GARD

Isis en Cévennes

Domaine de St-Julien, 30440

☎ 467738028 🖷 467738848

e-mail: aa@isisencevennes.com

web: www.isisencevennes.fr

Set in wooded surroundings with direct access to the River Hérault. Plenty of sports facilities.

dir: *5km from Ganges towards Le Vigan.*

Open: Mar-Oct **Site:** 14HEC **For hire:** **Facilities:** **Services:** **Leisure:** P R

ST-LAURENT-DU-VAR ALPES-MARITIMES

Magali

1814 rte de la Baronne, 06700

☎ 493315700 🖷 492120133

e-mail: contact@camping-magali.com

web: www.camping-magali.com

A family site on level meadowland, surrounded by trees and bushes at the foot of the southern Alps.

dir: *A8 exit St-Laurent-du-Var, cross industrial zone turn left, after 100m turn right, site in 2km.*

Open: Feb-Oct **Site:** 1.2HEC **For hire:** **Prices:** 17.20-26.90 Mobile home hire 309-599 **Facilities:** Wi-fi Play Area **Services:** **Leisure:** P **Off-site:**

ST-MARTIN-D'ARDÈCHE ARDÈCHE

Camping Indigo le Moulin

07700

☎ 475046620 🖷 475046012

e-mail: moulin@camping-indigo.com

web: www.camping-indigo.com

Site bordering the Ardèche river, with its own beach. Shady, spacious pitches are available. During the summer months, sports tournaments take place. Kids' club takes place in July and August. 1 dog per pitch.

dir: *A7 exit Bollene, then Pont St Esprit. Follow Gorges de l'Ardèche signs.*

GPS: 44.3004, 4.5713

Open: 5 Apr-7 Oct **Site:** 7HEC **For hire:** **Prices:** 15-24 Mobile home hire 284-636 **Facilities:** Kids' Club Play Area **Services:** **Leisure:** P R **Off-site:**

FRANCE

ST-MAXIMIN-LA-STE-BAUME VAR

Provençal

rte de Mazaugues, 83470
☎ 494781697
e-mail: camping.provencal@wanadoo.fr
web: www.camping-le-provencal.com

A family site in wooded surroundings with plenty of recreational facilties. Bar, café and swimming pool only open July and August.

dir: *2.5km S via D64.*

Open: Apr-Sep **Site:** 5HEC **For hire:** **Prices:** 14.50-18.30 Mobile home hire 225-700 **Facilities:** Wi-fi (charged) Play Area **Services:** **Leisure:** P **Off-site:**

ST-PAUL-EN-FORÊT VAR

Parc

83440
☎ 494761535 494847184
e-mail: contact@campingleparc.com
web: www.campingleparc.com

Quiet, fairly isolated site surrounded by woodland.

dir: *3km N on D4.*

GPS: 43.5843, 6.6898

Open: Apr-Sep **Site:** 3.1HEC **For hire:** **Prices:** 29 Mobile home hire 712-914 **Facilities:** Wi-fi (charged) Kids' Club Play Area **Services:** **Leisure:** P **Off-site:** L

ST-RAPHAËL VAR

Dramont

83700
☎ 494820768 494827530

Located in a pine forest with direct access to the beach and modern facilities.

dir: *Via N98 at St-Raphaël, between Boulouris & Agay.*

Open: 15 Mar-15 Oct **Site:** 6.5HEC **For hire:** **Facilities:** **Services:** **Leisure:** S

ST-RÉMY-DE-PROVENCE BOUCHES-DU-RHÔNE

Camping du Mas de Nicolas

av Plaisance du Touch, 13210
☎ 490922705 490923683
e-mail: camping-masdenicolas@nerim.fr

Close to the centre of St-Rémy-de-Provence, this secure site has a swimming pool with spa and fitness room.

Open: Mar-Oct **Site:** 3HEC **For hire:** **Facilities:** Wi-fi Kids' Club Play Area **Services:** **Leisure:** P **Off-site:** L

Monplaisir

chemin Monplaisir, 13210
☎ 490922270 490921857
e-mail: reception@camping-monplaisir.fr
web: www.camping-monplaisir.fr

Located in the middle of Alpilles Natural Regional Park, pitches are shady and screened with hedges. A bar and kids' club are available in July and August.

Open: 6 Mar-Oct **Site:** 2.8HEC **For hire:** **Facilities:** Wi-fi Kids' Club Play Area **Services:** **Leisure:** P

Pégomas

av Jean Moulin, 13210
☎ 490920121 490920121
e-mail: contact@campingpegomas.com
web: www.campingpegomas.com

Well-tended grassland, with trees and bushes, divided into several fields by high cedars providing shade. Recently renovated facilities which are heated in the autumn and spring. Within easy walking distance of the town centre.

dir: *0.5km E of village, signed.*

GPS: 43.7892, 4.8417

Open: 12 Mar-27 Oct **Site:** 2HEC **For hire:** **Prices:** 15-25 Mobile home hire 200-550 **Facilities:** Wi-fi Play Area **Services:** **Leisure:** P **Off-site:** L

ST-ROMAIN-EN-VIENNOIS VAUCLUSE

Soleil de Provence

rte de Nyons, 84110
☎ 490464600 490464037
e-mail: info@camping-soleil-de-provence.fr
web: www.camping-soleil-de-provence.fr

Peaceful site on an uphill meadow 12km from the foot of Mont Ventoux, with superb views of the surrounding mountains. Large swimming pool with an island and palm trees.

dir: *4km from Vaison-la-Romaine.*

Open: 15 Mar-Oct **Site:** 5HEC **For hire:** **Facilities:** **Services:** **Leisure:** P

FRANCE

ST-SAUVEUR-DE-MONTAGUT ARDÈCHE

Ardechois

Le Chambon, Gluiras, 07190

475666187 475666367

e-mail: ardechois.camping@wanadoo.fr

web: www.ardechois-camping.fr

Set in the grounds of a restored 18th-century farm in rolling countryside. Fine views of the surrounding hills.

dir: *8.5km W on D102, beside River Gluèyre.*

Open: 24 Apr-Sep **Site:** 5.5HEC **For hire:** **Facilities:** **Services:** **Leisure:** P R

ST-SORLIN-EN-VALLOIRE DRÔME

Château de la Pérouze

26210

475317021 475317575

A well-appointed family site with a variety of recreational facilities.

dir: *2.5km SE via D1.*

Open: 15 Jun-15 Sep **Site:** 14HEC **For hire:** **Facilities:** **Services:** **Leisure:** L P

ST-THIBÉRY HÉRAULT

Pin Parasol

Le Causse, 34630

467778429 467778429

e-mail: camping-pin-parasol@wanadoo.fr

web: www.campinglepinparasol.com

Pleasant wooded surroundings 1km from the River Hérault.

dir: *A9 exit Agde-Pézenas.*

Open: Jun-Sep **Site:** 2.7HEC **For hire:** **Facilities:** **Services:** **Leisure:** P **Off-site:** R

ST-VALLIER-DE-THIEY ALPES-MARITIMES

Parc des Arboins

06460

493426389

Pleasantly terraced site on a hillside with some oak trees.

dir: *Off N85 at KmV36.*

Open: All Year. **Site:** 4HEC **For hire:** **Facilities:** Play Area **Services:** **Leisure:** P **Off-site:** R

STE-MARIE PYRÉNÉES-ORIENTALES

Camping le Sainte Marie

Rue des Clauses, 66470

468804810 468734222

e-mail: contact@campingsaintemarie66.com

web: www.campingsaintemarie66.com

Close to Mediterranean beaches, pitches are spacious and separated by trees and hedges. Entertainment is available for children including treasure hunts and magic shows.

dir: *A9 exit 41, towards Barcarés/Canet, then Ste-Marie.*

GPS: 42.7138, 3.0313

Open: 7 Apr-10 Nov **Site:** 15HEC **For hire:** **Prices:** 10-25 Mobile home hire 160-550 **Facilities:** Wi-fi Kids' Club Play Area **Services:** **Leisure:** P R **Off-site:** L S

STES-MARIES-DE-LA-MER BOUCHES-DU-RHÔNE

Clos-du-Rhône

BP 74, 13460

490978599 490977885

e-mail: info@camping-leclos.fr

web: www.camping-leclos.fr

A family site with direct access to the sea. Kids' club available in July and August.

dir: *2km W via D38, near beach.*

Open: Apr-5 Nov **Site:** 7HEC **For hire:** **Facilities:** Kids' Club **Services:** **Leisure:** P R S

CM Brise

13460

490978467 490977201

e-mail: info@camping-labrise.fr

web: www.camping-labrise.fr

A well-equipped family site with direct access to the beach, situated in the heart of the Camargue. Modern sanitary blocks and facilities for a variety of sports. Kids' club available in July and August.

dir: *NE on D85A towards beach.*

GPS: 43.4558, 4.4362

Open: 17 Dec-11 Nov **Site:** 19HEC **For hire:** **Prices:** 13-21.50 Mobile home hire 309-780 **Facilities:** Wi-fi Kids' Club Play Area **Services:** **Leisure:** P S **Off-site:** R

FRANCE

SALAVAS — ARDÈCHE

Chauvieux

40 chemin de la Plage, 07150

475880537 475880537

e-mail: camping.chauvieux@wanadoo.fr

web: www.camping-le-chauvieux.com

A popular site in a wooded location close to the River Ardèche with plenty of recreational facilities.

dir: *NE off D579.*

Open: 29 Apr-12 Sep **Site:** 2.3HEC **For hire:** **Facilities:** Wi-fi (charged) Play Area **Services:** **Leisure:** P R

SALERNES — VAR

Arnauds

Quartier des Arnauds, 83690

494675195 494707557

e-mail: lesarnauds@ville-salernes.fr

web: www.village-vacances-lesarnauds.com

Level site alongside a river and a lake.

dir: *Via D560 just beyond village.*

GPS: 43.5661, 6.2252

Open: 2 May-Sep **Site:** 3HEC **For hire:** **Prices:** 20.15-26.77 **Facilities:** Wi-fi (charged) Play Area **Services:** **Leisure:** R **Off-site:**

SALINS-D'HYÈRES, LES — VAR

Port Pothuau

101 chemin les Ourledes, 83400

494664117 494663309

e-mail: pothuau@free.fr

web: www.campingportpothuau.com

A peaceful holiday village ideal for families, completely divided into pitches with good leisure facilities and entertainment. Kids' club in July and August.

dir: *6km E of Hyères on N98 & D12.*

GPS: 43.1208, 6.1846

Open: 2 Apr-16 Oct **Site:** 6HEC **For hire:** **Facilities:** Wi-fi (charged) Kids' Club Play Area **Services:** **Leisure:** P **Off-site:** R S

SALON-DE-PROVENCE — BOUCHES-DU-RHÔNE

Nostradamus

rte d'Eyguières, 13300

490560836 490562341

e-mail: gilles.nostra@gmail.com

web: www.camping-nostradamus.com

Pleasant wooded surroundings with good sports facilities.

dir: *5km W on D17 towards Eyguières & Arles.*

Open: Mar-Oct **Site:** 2.2HEC **For hire:** **Facilities:** Wi-fi (charged) Play Area **Services:** **Leisure:** P R **Off-site:**

SALVETAT, LA — HÉRAULT

Goudal

rte de Lacaune, 34330

467976044 467976268

e-mail: info@goudal.com

web: www.goudal.com

A natural mountain setting within the Haut Languedoc park.

dir: *Via D907.*

Open: May-Sep **Site:** 5HEC **For hire:** **Facilities:** **Services:** **Leisure:** L **Off-site:** R

SAMPZON — ARDÈCHE

Aloha-Plage

07120

608988503 475891026

web: www.campingalohaplage.fr

A fine location beside the River Ardèche, midway between Ruoms and Vallon-Pont-d'Arc. The site has two private swimming pools.

dir: *50m from river.*

Open: Apr-20 Sep **Site:** 3HEC **For hire:** **Facilities:** **Services:** **Leisure:** P R **Off-site:**

Site 6HEC (site size) 🍃 grass ⬤ sand 🍃 stone 🌳 little shade 🍂 partly shaded 🌲 mainly shaded 🚍 motorvans accepted 🏠 bungalows for hire 🚐 mobile homes for hire 🏕 tents for hire ⊗ no dogs 🚻 site fully accessible for wheelchairs **Prices** amount quoted is per night, for 2 adults and car, plus tent or caravan Mobile home hire is a weekly rate.

RCN La Bastide en Ardèche

The Camping and Caravanning Club The Friendly Club

1 rte d'Alès (D111), 07120
☎ 475396472
e-mail: bastide@rcn.fr
web: www.rcn.fr

In a pleasant wooded location next to the Ardèche river, which provides a private sandy beach, for use in July and August.

C&CC Report *A top quality site, with high quality facilities in the heart of one of France's most beautiful and renowned areas, in a great position on the river Ardèche at the foot of Sampzon castle. Good for young families, with a lovely pool, and for walking in stunning countryside or just relaxing amid outstanding scenery.*

dir: *4km SW on the banks of the Ardèche.*

GPS: 44.4229, 4.3217

Open: 31 Mar-6 Oct **Site:** 8HEC **For hire:** **Prices:** 25.50-55 Mobile home hire 295-1030 **Facilities:** Wi-fi (charged) Kids' Club Play Area **Services:** **Leisure:** P R **Off-site:**

Riviera

07120
☎ 475396757 475939557
e-mail: leRIVIERAa@wanadoo.fr
web: www.campingleRIVIERAa.com

Located on the banks of the Ardèche river, just a short distance from the Pont d'Arc.

dir: *From Valence exit autoroute at Montelimar Nord for Le Teil/ Ruoms/Sampzon.*

Open: Apr-Sep **Site:** 6HEC **For hire:** **Prices:** 19.50-41 **Facilities:** Wi-fi Kids' Club Play Area **Services:** **Leisure:** P R **Off-site:**

Soleil Vivarais

07120
☎ 475396756 475396469
e-mail: info@soleil-vivarais.com
web: www.soleil-vivarais.com

An exceptionally well-appointed, terraced site surrounded by the imposing scenery of the Ardèche Gorge. An excellent canoeing centre with opportunities for outdoor and water activities, and regular organised entertainment.

dir: *D579 from Vallon towards Ruoms for 5km & over River Ardèche.*

GPS: 44.4292, 4.3553

Open: 31 Mar-16 Sep **Site:** 12HEC **For hire:** **Prices:** 17-45 **Facilities:** Wi-fi Kids' Club Play Area **Services:** **Leisure:** P R **Off-site:**

SANARY-SUR-MER VAR

Pierredon

652 chemin Raoul Coletta, 83110
☎ 494742502 494746142
e-mail: pierredon@campasun.com
web: www.campasun.com

A well-equipped, wooded site providing a variety of family entertainment, 3km from the sea.

dir: *A50 exit Bandol or Sanary.*

Open: 5 Apr-15 Sep **Site:** 4HEC **For hire:** **Facilities:** **Services:** **Leisure:** P **Off-site:**

SAUVIAN HÉRAULT

Gabinelle

34410
☎ 467395087
e-mail: info@lagabinelle.com
web: www.lagabinelle.com

A modern site in pleasant wooded surroundings with good facilities.

dir: *D19 from Sauvian towards Valras Plage.*

Open: 15 Apr-15 Sep **Site:** 4HEC **For hire:** **Prices:** 20.50 Mobile home hire 560 **Facilities:** Wi-fi Kids' Club Play Area **Services:** **Leisure:** P **Off-site:** R S

SÉRIGNAN-PLAGE HÉRAULT

Camping Village Aloha

Allée des dunes, 34410
☎ 467397130 467325815
e-mail: info@alohacamping.com
web: www.alohacamping.com

Small family site next to the Mediterranean sea, with direct access to the beach. Good facilities including a swimming pool with slides, jacuzzi and children's pool.

dir: *From Lyon/Toulouse A9 exit 35. Left at lights towards Sérignan/Valras-Plage, then onto D37E signed Sérignan/ Sérignan-Plage. From Clermont-Ferrand A75 exit Millau, towards Béziers on N9. Left at rdbt then follow signs to Sérignan/ Sérignan-Plage.*

GPS: 43.2677, 3.3347

Open: 27 Apr-17 Sep **Site:** 10HEC **For hire:** **Prices:** 15-48 Mobile home hire 35-225 **Facilities:** Wi-fi (charged) Kids' Club Play Area **Services:** **Leisure:** P S **Off-site:** R

FRANCE

Clos Virgile

34410

☎ 467322064 467320542

e-mail: contact@leclosvirgile.fr

web: www.leclosvirgile.com

Situated 400 metres from the beach, the site is on level meadowland with large pitches, heated pools and has three well-kept sanitary blocks.

GPS: 43.2699, 3.3312

Open: May-15 Sep **Site:** 5HEC **For hire:** **Facilities:** Wi-fi (charged) Kids' Club Play Area **Services:** **Leisure:** P S

Yelloh Village Le Sérignan-Plage

34410

☎ 467323533 467326839

e-mail: info@leserignanplage.com

web: www.leserignanplage.com

On a fine sandy beach, this is a family site with good recreational facilities including a swimming pool, spa and jacuzzi. There is also evening entertainment, a kids' club and disco for children. Dogs are not permitted in rental accommodation and there is a compulsory separate car park for second vehicles.

dir: *A9 exit 35 Béziers Centre or A75 exit 64 then towards Valras Plage/Sérignan.*

GPS: 43.2631, 3.3198

Open: 26 Apr-2 Oct **Site:** 27HEC **For hire:** **Prices:** 17-54 Mobile home hire 203-2254 **Facilities:** Wi-fi (charged) Kids' Club Play Area **Services:** **Leisure:** P S

SÈTE HÉRAULT

Village Center le Castellas

RN112, 34200

☎ 499572121 467516389

e-mail: contact@village-center.com

web: www.village-center.com/languedoc-roussillon/camping-mer-le-castellas.php

Facing the sea, the site has a wide range of leisure activities and entertainment. Cycles can be hired and a mini-train operates in high season.

GPS: 43.3400, 3.5820

Open: 8 Apr-2 Oct **Site:** 24HEC **For hire:** **Facilities:** Wi-fi (charged) Kids' Club Play Area **Services:** **Leisure:** P S

SEYNE-SUR-MER, LA VAR

Mimosas

av M-Paul, 83500

☎ 494947315 494873613

e-mail: camping-des-mimosas@wanadoo.fr

In an attractive woodland setting, facing the fortress of Six-Fours. 3km from the sea.

dir: *A50 exit 13 for La Seyne centre & towards Sanary-Bandol.*

Open: All Year. **Site:** 1.08HEC **For hire:** **Facilities:** Wi-fi (charged) Play Area **Services:** **Off-site:** P

SIX-FOURS-LES-PLAGES VAR

International St-Jean

av de la Collégiale, 83140

☎ 494875151 494062823

e-mail: campingstjean@gmail.com

web: www.campingstjean.com

Site with pitches, separated by hedges and reeds. Well managed, it lies just below the Fort Six-Fours.

dir: *Via N559 & D63, via chemin de St-Jean.*

Open: All Year. **Site:** 2HEC **For hire:** **Facilities:** **Services:** **Leisure:** P

Playes

419 rue Grand, 83140

☎ 494255757 494071990

e-mail: camplayes@wanadoo.fr

web: www.camplayes.com

Terraced site on north side of town. Trees abound in this excellent location.

dir: *Via N559 & D63, via chemin de St-Jean.*

Open: All Year. **Site:** 1.5HEC **For hire:** **Facilities:** Wi-fi Play Area **Services:** **Leisure:** P **Off-site:** S

FRANCE

Site 6HEC (site size) grass sand stone little shade partly shaded mainly shaded motorvans accepted bungalows for hire mobile homes for hire tents for hire no dogs site fully accessible for wheelchairs
Prices amount quoted is per night, for 2 adults and car, plus tent or caravan Mobile home hire is a weekly rate.

SOMMIÈRES GARD

Camping de Massereau

rte d'Aubais, 30250
☎ 466531120 🖷 411715020
e-mail: info@massereau.fr
web: www.massereau.co.uk

Family owned site located between the Camargue and Mediterranean Sea. There is a swimming pool complex, sauna and jacuzzi. Kids' club available in July and August.

dir: *A9/E15 exit 26 Gallargue or exit 27 Lunel then signed Sommières.*

Open: Apr-Nov **Site:** 10HEC **For hire:** **Prices:** 16.90-56.90 Mobile home hire 209.30-652.40 **Facilities:** Wi-fi (charged) Kids' Club Play Area **Services:** **Leisure:** P **Off-site:** R

see advert on this page

SOSPEL ALPES-MARITIMES

Domaine Ste-Madeleine

rte de Moulinet, 06380
☎ 493041048
e-mail: camp@camping-sainte-madeleine.com
web: camping-sainte-madeleine.com

A peaceful site in beautiful, unspoiled surroundings.

dir: *4.5km NW via D2566.*

Open: 31 Mar-30 Oct **Site:** 3.5HEC **For hire:** **Prices:** 16.40-20 **Facilities:** Wi-fi (charged) **Services:** **Leisure:** P **Off-site:** R

SOUBÈS HÉRAULT

Les Rials

rte de Poujols, 34700
☎ 467441553
e-mail: lesrials@hotmail.fr
web: campinglesrials.free.fr

A terraced site in wooded surroundings on the banks of the River Lergue.

dir: *4km from Lodève. 10km from Lac du Salagou.*

GPS: 43.7725, 3.3275

Open: Jul-Aug **Site:** 3.5HEC **For hire:** **Prices:** 16.50 Mobile home hire 450 **Facilities:** Wi-fi **Services:** **Leisure:** P R **Off-site:**

Sources

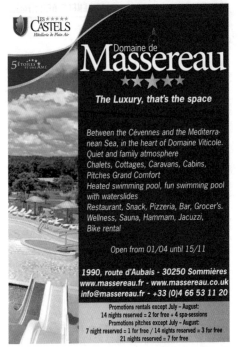

1445 chemin d'Aubaygues, 34700
☎ 467443202 🖷 467884875
e-mail: camping-sources@orange.fr
web: www.camping-sources.com

A small, friendly site in a quiet location beside a river.

dir: *5km NE, signed on N9.*

Open: Apr-15 Oct **Site:** 1.3HEC **For hire:** **Facilities:** **Services:** **Leisure:** P R **Off-site:** L

TAIN-L'HERMITAGE DRÔME

CM Lucs

24 av Prés-Roosevelt, 26600
☎ 475083282 🖷 475083282
e-mail: camping.tainlhermitage@wanadoo.fr
web: www.campinglesIucs.fr

Good overnight stopping place but some traffic noise. Caravan limit 5.5 metres.

dir: *S of town near N7. Turn towards River Rhône at fuel station.*

GPS: 45.0699, 4.8391

Open: 15 Mar-Oct **Site:** 1.5HEC **Prices:** 17.50-17.90 **Facilities:** Play Area **Services:** **Leisure:** P **Off-site:** R

FRANCE

TORREILLES — PYRÉNÉES-ORIENTALES

Dunes

66440

☎ 468283829 🖹 468283257

e-mail: contact@camping-lesdunes.fr

web: www.camping-lesdunes.fr

A well-equipped site in wooded surroundings with direct access to the beach.

dir: *E of village off D81.*

Open: 15 Mar-15 Oct **Site:** 16HEC **For hire:** **Facilities:** **Services:** **Leisure:** P S **Off-site:** R

Spa Marisol

plage de Torreilles, 66440

☎ 468280407 🖹 468281823

e-mail: marisol@camping-marisol.com

web: www.camping-marisol.com

A family site with a variety of sports and entertainment facilities in a pleasant park-like setting, 350 metres from the beach with direct access from the site.

dir: *Off D81 towards sea.*

Open: 28 Apr-29 Sep **Site:** 9HEC **For hire:** **Prices:** 19-56 **Facilities:** Wi-fi Kids' Club Play Area **Services:** **Leisure:** P S **Off-site:** R

Trivoly

bld des Plages, 66440

☎ 468282028 🖹 251339404

e-mail: info@chadotel.com

web: www.chadotel.com

A modern site with excellent facilities and well-defined pitches, 0.8km from the beach.

dir: *Autoroute exit Perpignan Nord for Le Barcarès.*

Open: 7 Apr-22 Sep **Site:** 5HEC **For hire:** **Prices:** 20-32.50 **Facilities:** **Services:** **Leisure:** P **Off-site:** S

TOURNON-SUR-RHÔNE — ARDÈCHE

Camping Manoir

rte de Lamastre, 07300

☎ 475080250

e-mail: info@lemanoir-ardeche.com

web: www.lemanoir-ardeche.com

Picturesque wooded surroundings with modern facilities.

dir: *Off N86 onto Lamastre road for 3km.*

GPS: 45.0648, 4.7898

Open: Apr-Sep **Site:** 2HEC **For hire:** **Prices:** 12-19 Mobile home hire 210-585 **Facilities:** Wi-fi (charged) Play Area **Services:** **Leisure:** P R **Off-site:**

Tournon HPA

1 promenade Roche de France, 07300

☎ 475080528

e-mail: camping@camping-tournon.com

web: www.camping-tournon.com

Well laid-out site in town centre beside River Rhône.

dir: *NW on N86.*

Open: All Year. **Site:** 1.1HEC **For hire:** **Prices:** 15 **Facilities:** Wi-fi Play Area **Services:** **Leisure:** R **Off-site:** P

TOURRETTES-SUR-LOUP — ALPES-MARITIMES

Camassade

523 rte de Pie Lombard, 06140

☎ 493593154 🖹 493593181

e-mail: courrier@camassade.com

web: www.camassade.com

Quiet site under oak trees and pines with several terraces.

dir: *From Vence turn left just after Tourrette.*

GPS: 43.7051, 7.0505

Open: All Year. **Site:** 2HEC **For hire:** **Prices:** 20-25 Mobile home hire 306-600 **Facilities:** Wi-fi Play Area **Services:** **Leisure:** P **Off-site:** R

FRANCE

Rives du Loup

rte de la Colle, 06140
☎ 493241565 📠 493245370
e-mail: info@rivesduloup.com
web: www.rivesduloup.com
Small friendly site in a wooded riverside setting at the heart of the Loup Valley. There are modern facilities and children's activities five days a week. 20 minutes from the coast and ideally located for excursions on the French Riviera.
dir: *Between Vence & Grasse, 3km from Pont-du-Loup on road to La Colle-sur-Loup CD6.*
GPS: 43.6981, 7.0078
Open: Apr-Sep **Site:** 2.2HEC **For hire:** **Facilities:** Wi-fi (charged) Play Area **Services:** **Leisure:** P R **Off-site:**

UCEL ARDÈCHE

Domaine de Gil

rte de Vais les Bains, Quartier Chamboulas, 07200
☎ 475946363 📠 475940195
e-mail: info@domaine-de-gil.com
web: www.domaine-de-gil.com
Pleasant location on the River Ardèche, surrounded by beautiful countryside.
dir: *N of Aubenas off N104.*
Open: 17 Apr-19 Sep **Site:** 4.5HEC **For hire:** **Facilities:** **Services:** **Leisure:** P R

UR PYRÉNÉES-ORIENTALES

Gare

rte d'Espagne, 66760
☎ 468048095
e-mail: info@camping-cerdagne.com
web: www.camping-cerdagne.com/camping.html
A pleasant mountainous setting with well-defined pitches, 0.5km from the village.
Open: Nov-Sep **Site:** 1HEC **For hire:** **Facilities:** **Services:** **Off-site:** R

UZÈS GARD

Moulin Neuf

St Quentin-la-Poterie, 30700
☎ 466221721 📠 466229182
e-mail: lemoulinneuf@yahoo.fr
web: www.le-moulin-neuf.fr
Quiet site on extensive meadowland within an estate.
dir: *4km NE on D982.*
Open: Apr-23 Sep **Site:** 5HEC **For hire:** **Prices:** 19.50-23 **Facilities:** Wi-fi Kids' Club Play Area **Services:** **Leisure:** P

VAISON-LA-ROMAINE VAUCLUSE

Domaine Carpe Diem

rte de St-Marcellin, 84110
☎ 490360202 📠 490363690
e-mail: contact@camping-carpe-diem.com
web: www.camping-carpe-diem.com
Wooded surroundings close to Mont Ventoux with a variety of leisure facilities.
dir: *S of town towards Malaucène.*
Open: 23 Mar-1 Nov **Site:** 10HEC **For hire:** **Facilities:** **Services:** **Leisure:** P **Off-site:** R

Théâtre Romain

Quartier des Arts, chemin du Brusquet, 84110
☎ 490287866 📠 490287876
e-mail: info@camping-theatre.com
web: www.camping-theatre.com
A peaceful site with some leisure facilities.
dir: *0.5km from town centre near Roman theatre.*
GPS: 44.2446, 5.0793
Open: 15 Mar-5 Nov **Site:** 1.5HEC **For hire:** **Prices:** 14-22.50 Mobile home hire 220-650 **Facilities:** Wi-fi Play Area **Services:** **Leisure:** P **Off-site:** L R

FRANCE

VALENCE — DRÔME

Eperviére

chemin de l'Epervière, 26000

☎ 475423200 475562067

e-mail: eperviere26@orange.fr

A well-equipped site bordering the Rhône.

dir: *A7 exit Valence Sud.*

Open: Feb-15 Dec **Site:** 3.5HEC **Facilities:** **Services:** **Leisure:** P **Off-site:**

VALLABRÈGUES — GARD

Lou Vincen

30300

☎ 466592129 466590741

e-mail: campinglouvincen@wanadoo.fr

web: www.campinglouvincen.com

A pleasant shady location in a Provençal village.

GPS: 43.8549, 4.6259

Open: 24 Mar-30 Oct **Site:** 1.4HEC **For hire:** **Prices:** 15.10-19.50 Mobile home hire 313-606 **Facilities:** Wi-fi (charged) Play Area **Services:** **Leisure:** P **Off-site:** L R

VALLERAUGUE — GARD

Camping la Corconne

Pont d'Hérault, 30570

☎ 467824682

e-mail: contact@lacorconne.com

web: www.lacorconne.com

Relaxing and unspoiled site in the Cévennes. Spacious terraced pitches blending into the wooded landscape. The river Hérault is wonderful for swimming. Shop, café and bar open in July and August only.

dir: *3km from Pont d'Hérault on road to Valleraugue.*

Open: Apr-Oct **Site:** 7HEC **For hire:** **Prices:** 16.50-18.50 **Facilities:** Wi-fi Play Area **Services:** **Leisure:** R

VALLON-PONT-D'ARC — ARDÈCHE

Camping Nature Parc L'Ardechois

07150

☎ 475880663 475371497

e-mail: ardecamp@bigfoot.com

web: www.ardechois-camping.com

A pleasant location in the Ardèche gorge. Good access for caravans and plentiful sports facilities.

dir: *D290 from Vallon towards St-Martin, site signed.*

GPS: 44.3980, 4.3990

Open: 31 Mar-Sep **Site:** 6HEC **For hire:** **Prices:** 26-49 Mobile home hire 357-1210 **Facilities:** Wi-fi (charged) Kids' Club Play Area **Services:** **Leisure:** P R **Off-site:**

Camping La Roubine

rte de Ruoms, 07150

☎ 475880456 475880456

e-mail: roubine.ardeche@wanadoo.fr

web: www.camping-roubine.com

Family friendly site with large, separated and shady pitches on the banks of the River Ardèche. Leisure facilities include table tennis, volleyball and basketball. Kids' club in summer. Dogs allowed on leads.

dir: *D579 exit Vallon-Pont-d'Arc, direction Ruoms.*

GPS: 44.4081, 4.3782

Open: 23 Apr-15 Sep **Site:** 7HEC **For hire:** **Facilities:** Wi-fi Kids' Club Play Area **Services:** **Leisure:** R

Mondial

rte des Gorges de l'Ardèche, 07150

☎ 475880044 475371373

e-mail: reserv-info@mondial-camping.com

web: www.mondial-camping.com

Modernised site on the banks of the Ardèche with good sanitary arrangements.

Open: 20 Mar-Sep **Site:** 4.2HEC **For hire:** **Facilities:** **Services:** **Leisure:** P R

Plage Fleurie

Les Mazes, 07150
475880115 475881131
e-mail: info@laplagefleurie.com
web: www.laplagefleurie.com
Holiday site in an unspoiled village beside the river.
dir: *D579 towards Ruoms, 2.5km left towards Les Mazes.*
Open: 29 Apr-15 Sep **Site:** 12HEC **For hire:**
Facilities: **Services:** **Leisure:** P R

VALRAS-PLAGE HÉRAULT

Lou Village

chemin des Montilles, 34350
467373379 467375356
e-mail: info@louvillage.com
web: www.louvillage.com
Situated along a sandy beach, bordered by dunes.
dir: *2km SW, 100m from beach.*
Open: May-14 Sep **Site:** 8HEC **For hire:** **Facilities:** **Services:** **Leisure:** P S
Off-site: R

Sables du Midi

BP29, 34350
467323386 467325820
e-mail: sablesdumidi@siblu.fr
web: www.siblu.fr
Family site on rising ground to the north of town, 1km from the beach.
dir: *A9 exit Béziers-Est for Valras.*
Open: 31 May-8 Aug **Site:** 15HEC **For hire:**
Facilities: **Services:** **Leisure:** P
Off-site: R S

Yole

34350
467373387 467374489
e-mail: infocamping@layolewineresort.com
web: www.campinglayole.com
Very comfortable site divided into pitches. Good sanitary installations with individual washing cubicles. Leisure facilities include several swimming pools with slides and nearby are pedalos for hire and riding stables. Compulsory separate car park for second vehicles.
dir: *SW of D37E towards Vendres.*
Open: 28 Apr-22 Sep **Site:** 23HEC **For hire:**
Prices: 21-51 Mobile home hire 310-1428 **Facilities:** Wi-fi (charged) Kids' Club Play Area **Services:** **Leisure:** P **Off-site:** S

VEDÈNE VAUCLUSE

Flory

385 rte d'Entraigues, 84270
490310051
e-mail: infos@campingflory.com
web: www.campingflory.com
Well-kept site with good facilities on a pine covered hill.
dir: *Off motorway onto D942 for 0.8km.*
GPS: 43.9906, 4.9131
Open: 15 Mar-Sep **Site:** 6.5HEC **For hire:**
Facilities: Play Area **Services:**
Leisure: P

VENCE ALPES-MARITIMES

Domaine de la Bergerie

1330 chemin de la Sine, 06140
493580936 493598044
e-mail: info@camping-domainedelabergerie.com
web: www.camping-domainedelabergerie.com
Peaceful and well-kept site on hilly land near to a wood. Ideally located for exploring the Côte d'Azur. Shop, bar, restaurant and café open from May to the end of September. It is advisable to have a Camping Card International (CCI).
dir: *3km W on D2210.*
GPS: 43.7117, 7.0905
Open: 25 Mar-15 Oct **Site:** 14HEC **For hire:**
Prices: 17-23.50 **Facilities:** Play Area
Services: **Leisure:** P

VERCHENY DRÔME

Acacias

26340
475217251 475217398
e-mail: infos@campinglesacacias.com
web: campinglesacacias.com
Pleasant site beside the River Drôme.
dir: *D93 to Die Gap, 4km from Saillans.*
Open: Apr-Sep **Site:** 3.7HEC **For hire:**
Facilities: Wi-fi Kids' Club Play Area
Services: **Leisure:** R

FRANCE

VÉREILLES HÉRAULT

La Sieste

34260

☎ 467237296 467237538

e-mail: camping.sieste@orange.fr

web: pagesperso-orange.fr/camping.sieste

A rural setting on the River Orb.

dir: *NE of Bédarieux, 10km from Lodève.*

Open: 30 Apr-3 Sep **Site:** 2HEC **For hire:** **Prices:** 16 **Facilities:** **Services:** **Leisure:** P R

VERS-PONT-DU-GARD GARD

Gorges du Gardon

762 chemin Barque Vieille, 30210

☎ 466228181 466229012

e-mail: gorges-gardon@franceloc.fr

web: www.campings-franceloc.fr

A peaceful wooded location beside the River Gardon. 1km from Pont du Gard.

dir: *1km from aqueduct on D981 Uzès road.*

Open: Apr-Sep **Site:** 4.2HEC **For hire:** **Prices:** 16-29 **Facilities:** Wi-fi Kids' Club Play Area **Services:** **Leisure:** P R

VIAS HÉRAULT

Air Marin

34450

☎ 467216490 467217679

e-mail: info@camping-air-marin.fr

web: www.camping-air-marin.fr

A well-equipped family site in wooded surroundings, a 10-minute walk from the beach. Facilities includes tennis and a fitness centre.

dir: *A6 exit Bierre-les-Semur/RN954.*

Open: 15 May-15 Sep **Site:** 7HEC **For hire:** **Prices:** 20-24 Mobile home hire 290-920 **Facilities:** Wi-fi Kids' Club Play Area **Services:** **Leisure:** P **Off-site:** R S

California Plage

Côte Ouest, 34450

☎ 467216469 467215462

e-mail: californie.plage@wanadoo.fr

web: www.californie-plage.fr

Very tidy site completely divided into pitches, beside sea.

dir: *S on D137 past bridge over Canal du Midi turn right & follow signs.*

GPS: 43.2925, 3.4017

Open: Apr-Sep **Site:** 5.5HEC **For hire:** **Prices:** 16-39.50 Mobile home hire 196-1008 **Facilities:** Wi-fi (charged) Kids' Club Play Area **Services:** **Leisure:** P S

Cap Soleil

Côte Ouest, 34450

☎ 467216477 467217066

e-mail: cap.soleil@wanadoo.fr

web: www.capsoleil.fr

On level land near sea. Divided into pitches.

dir: *Cross Canal du Midi, S of town, then turn W.*

Open: All Year. **Site:** 5HEC **For hire:** **Facilities:** **Services:** **Leisure:** P **Off-site:** S

Carabasse

rte de Farinette, 34450

☎ 467216401 467217687

e-mail: lacarabasse@siblu.fr

web: www.siblu.com

A lively camping park with a range of activites, especially for young families and teenagers, centred around a lagoon pool complex and entertainment terrace.

dir: *1.5m NE of Vias.*

Open: 15 Apr-14 Sep **Site:** **For hire:** **Facilities:** **Services:** **Leisure:** P **Off-site:** S

Hélios

Vias-Plage, 34450

☎ 467216366 467216366

e-mail: franceschi.louis@wanadoo.fr

web: www.campinghelios-viasplage.com

On level ground divided into pitches.

dir: *On D137 S of village signed Farinette.*

Open: May-Sep **Site:** 3.5HEC **For hire:** **Facilities:** **Services:** **Off-site:** R S

International le Napoléon

1171 av de la Mediterranée, 34450

☎ 467010780 🖷 467010785

e-mail: reception@camping-napoleon.fr

web: www.camping-napoleon.fr

A well-equipped family site surrounded by tropical vegetation with direct access to the beach. Entertainment shows take place in July and August.

dir: *A9 exit 34, Agde-Vias.*

Open: 6 Apr-Sep **Site:** 3.4HEC **For hire:** **Facilities:** Wi-fi (charged) Kids' Club Play Area **Services:** **Leisure:** P S **Off-site:** R

Meditérranée Plage

34450

☎ 467909907 🖷 467909917

e-mail: contact@mediterranee-plage.com

web: www.meditérranée-plage.com

Direct access to a fine sandy beach. The campsite village has excellent facilities and good service.

dir: *A75/A9 exit Béziers Centre/Cabrials in direction of Portiragnes.*

GPS: 43.2823, 3.3710

Open: 30 Mar-Sep **Site:** 7HEC **For hire:** **Prices:** 16.90-41.80 Mobile home hire 260-1250 **Facilities:** Wi-fi Kids' Club Play Area **Services:** **Leisure:** P S

Sunêlia Domaine de la Dragonnière

RD 612, 34450

☎ 467010310 🖷 467217339

e-mail: contact@dragonniere.com

web: www.dragonniere.com

A busy family site, located between the popular resorts of Vias and Portiragnes with three heated pools, one with slides and games for children. In high season there is a lively entertainment programme and a free shuttle to the beach.

dir: *From the A9, exit 34/36, onto the A75, take exit 64 towards Béziers Centre. Follow signs for Aéroport Béziers Cap d'Agde. At crossroads by airport turn right.*

GPS: 43.3139, 3.3606

Open: 9 Apr-18 Sep **Site:** 30HEC **For hire:** **Facilities:** Kids' Club Play Area **Services:** **Leisure:** P

Yelloh Village Farret

34450

☎ 467216445 🖷 467217049

e-mail: farret@wanadoo.fr

web: www.camping-farret.com

On level meadow beside flat sandy beach, ideal for children. A spa includes sauna, steam room and jacuzzi. Evening entertainment available.

dir: *A9 exit Agde-Vias.*

GPS: 43.2908, 3.4186

Open: 29 Mar-29 Sep **Site:** 14HEC **For hire:** **Prices:** 17-52 Mobile home hire 294-1134 **Facilities:** Wi-fi (charged) Kids' Club Play Area **Services:** **Leisure:** P S **Off-site:** R

VIC-LA-GARDIOLE HÉRAULT

Village Center l'Europe

31 rte de Frontignan, 34110

☎ 499572121 🖷 467516389

e-mail: contact@village-center.com

web: www.village-center.com/languedoc-roussillon/camping-mer-l-europe.php

Close to the town centre, a Mediterranean-village style site with a relaxed atmosphere.

dir: *1.5km W via D114.*

GPS: 43.4916, 3.7792

Open: 24 Jun-4 Sep **Site:** 5HEC **For hire:** **Facilities:** Wi-fi (charged) Kids' Club Play Area **Services:** **Leisure:** P

VILLARS-COLMARS ALPES-DE-HAUTE-PROVENCE

Haut-Verdon

04370

☎ 492834009 🖷 492835661

e-mail: campinglehautverdon@wanadoo.fr

web: www.lehautverdon.com

A comfortable site in a picturesque wooded location beside the River Verdon.

dir: *N on D908.*

Open: May-Sep **Site:** 3.5HEC **For hire:** **Facilities:** Wi-fi Play Area **Services:** **Leisure:** P R **Off-site:**

FRANCE

VILLEMOUSTAUSSOU — AUDE

Pinhiers

chemin du Pont Neuf, 11620
☎ 468478190 🖷 468714349
e-mail: campingdaspinhiers@wanadoo.fr
web: www.camping-carcassonne.net

5km from Carcassonne and 2km from Canal du Midi, leisure facilities include a swimming pool, table tennis and mini-golf.

dir: *A61 towards Mazamet.*

Open: Mar-Nov **Site:** 2HEC **For hire:** **Facilities:** **Services:** **Leisure:** P **Off-site:**

VILLENEUVE-DE-BERG — ARDÉCHE

Domaine le Pommier

07170
☎ 475948281 🖷 475948390
e-mail: info@campinglepommier.com
web: www.campinglepommier.com

Holiday site in beautiful setting with terraces divided into pitches. Kids' club available where Dutch is spoken. Dogs admitted onto pitches.

dir: *On winding private road off N102, 2km from village.*

GPS: 44.5744, 4.5077

Open: 15 Apr-17 Sep **Site:** 20HEC **For hire:** **Facilities:** Wi-fi (charged) Kids' Club Play Area **Services:** **Leisure:** P R

VILLENEUVE-DE-LA-RAHO — PYRÉNÉES-ORIENTALES

Rives-du-Lac

chemin de la Serre, 66180
☎ 468558351 🖷 468558637
e-mail: camping.villeneuveraho@wanadoo.fr

A quiet family site beside the lake.

dir: *Via RN9.*

Open: Apr-Oct **Site:** 2.5HEC **For hire:** **Facilities:** **Services:** **Off-site:** L

VILLENEUVE-LÈS-AVIGNON — GARD

Île des Papes

The Camping and Caravanning Club — The Friendly Club

30400
☎ 490151590 🖷 490151591
e-mail: ile-des-papes@campeole.com
web: www.avignon-camping.com

A well-equipped site on an island between the Rhône Canal and the River Rhône.

C&CC Report *This relaxing, well-maintained, modern Provençal site makes a convenient base for a terrific area rich in scenery and history. There's medieval Villeneuve, beautiful Avignon with its Pope's Palace, the famous vineyards of Châteauneuf-du-Pape, and breathtaking Roman sites such as the amphitheatre at Orange and the Pont du Gard aqueduct. Easy day trips include Van Gogh's Arles, the Camargue, the Ardèche, majestic Mont Ventoux and Provence's lavender-scented hills and gorges. In springtime, don't miss Fontaine de Vaucluse, where a fully formed river rises straight out of the ground.*

dir: *From A9 junct 22, follow Roquemaure, Sauveterre and Villeneuve-lès-Avignon. Before Volleneuve, D780 to site.*

GPS: 43.9936, 4.8177

Open: 27 Mar-6 Nov **Site:** 20HEC **For hire:** **Prices:** 15-24.90 **Facilities:** Kids' Club Play Area **Services:** **Leisure:** P

VILLENEUVE-LOUBET — ALPES-MARITIMES

Panorama

06270
☎ 493209153

Small terraced site, mainly for tents, 0.8km from the sea.

dir: *0.5km from Nice-Cannes autoroute.*

Open: All Year. **Site:** 1HEC **For hire:** **Facilities:** **Services:** **Off-site:** R S

Parc des Maurettes

730 av du Dr-Lefèbvre, 06270
☎ 493209191 🖷 493737720
e-mail: info@parcdesmaurettes.com
web: www.parcdesmaurettes.com

Terraced site in a pine forest with modern facilities, including jacuzzi and sauna.

dir: *A8 exit Villeneuve-Loubet-Plage, RD6007 towards Antibes for 1km.*

GPS: 43.6309, 7.1298

Open: 10 Jan-15 Nov **Site:** 1.8HEC **For hire:** **Prices:** 17.50-32 **Facilities:** Wi-fi (charged) Play Area **Services:** **Off-site:** P S

Parc St-James Sourire

rte de Grasse, 06270

493209611 493220752

e-mail: lesourire@camping-parcsaintjames.com

web: www.camping-parcsaintjames.com

Parkland dominated by an 11th-century monastery. Restaurant open July and August only.

dir: *2km W on D2085.*

GPS: 43.6569, 7.1019

Open: 7 Apr-29 Sep **Site:** 5.5HEC **For hire:** **Facilities:** Wi-fi Play Area **Services:** **Leisure:** P **Off-site:** R

Vieille Ferme

296 bld des Groules, 06270

493334144 493333728

e-mail: info@vieilleferme.com

web: www.vieilleferme.com

A quiet, peaceful family friendly site 1km from the sea. Close to Marineland.

dir: *A8 exit 44 (Antibes) towards Biot/Marineland, then RN7 towards Nice. 100m after La Toscana restaurant.*

GPS: 43.6200, 7.1254

Open: All Year. **Site:** 2.8HEC **For hire:** **Prices:** 19-35 **Facilities:** Wi-fi (charged) Play Area **Services:** **Leisure:** P **Off-site:** S

VILLEROUGE-LA-CRÉMADE AUDE

Pinada

11200

468436788 468436861

e-mail: lepinada@libertysurf.fr

web: camping-le-pinada.com

Pleasant rural surroundings on edge of forest.

dir: *0.6km NW on D106.*

Open: Apr-15 Oct **Site:** 4.5HEC **For hire:** **Facilities:** **Services:** **Leisure:** P **Off-site:**

VILLES-SUR-AUZON VAUCLUSE

Verguettes

rte de Carpentras, 84570

490618818

e-mail: info@provence-camping.com

web: www.provence-camping.com

Small shady site in a fine location with good facilities and views of Mont Ventoux.

dir: *W via D942.*

Open: 7 Apr-Sep **Site:** 2HEC **For hire:** **Prices:** 14-23.50 Mobile home hire 220-700 **Facilities:** Wi-fi (charged) **Services:** **Leisure:** P **Off-site:** L

VITROLLES BOUCHES-DU-RHÔNE

Marina Plage

13127

442893146 442795990

e-mail: information@marina-plage.com

web: www.marina-plage.com

A family site in pleasant wooded surroundings with good recreational facilities.

dir: *A7 exit Vitrolles, RN113 for Roquac, left at 2nd rdbt.*

Open: All Year. **Site:** 11HEC **For hire:** **Facilities:** **Services:** **Leisure:** L

VIVIERS ARDÈCHE

Rochecondrie Loisirs

07220

475527466 475527466

e-mail: campingrochecondrie@wanadoo.fr

web: www.campingrochecondrie.com

A level site with good facilities beside the River l'Escoutay.

dir: *A7 exit Montelimar Sud. N of town on N86.*

GPS: 44.4897, 4.6768

Open: Apr-15 Oct **Site:** 1.8HEC **For hire:** **Prices:** 12-20 Mobile home hire 230-510 **Facilities:** Play Area **Services:** **Leisure:** P R **Off-site:**

FRANCE

VOGÜÉ — ARDÈCHE

Domaine du Cros d'Auzon

Hotellerie de Plein Air, 07200
☎ 475370414 📠 475370102
e-mail: camping.auzon@wanadoo.fr
web: www.domaine-cros-auzon.com

Wooded surroundings close to the Gorges de l'Ardèche with good recreational facilities. Kids' club available in July and August.

dir: *2.5km via D579 bordering river.*

Open: 7 Apr-22 Sep **Site:** 20HEC **For hire:** **Prices:** 18-30.50 Mobile home hire 196-986 **Facilities:** Wi-fi Kids' Club Play Area **Services:** **Leisure:** P R **Off-site:**

VOLONNE — ALPES-DE-HAUTE-PROVENCE

Hippocampe

rte Napoléon, 04290
☎ 492335000 📠 492335049
e-mail: camping@l-hippocampe.com
web: www.l-hippocampe.com

Several strips of land, interspersed with trees, and running down the edge of the lake. Surrounded by fields and gardens.

dir: *On S edge of town, 2km E of N85.*

GPS: 44.1061, 6.0156

Open: 7 Apr-Sep **Site:** 8HEC **For hire:** **Prices:** 16-44 Mobile home hire 294-1064 **Facilities:** Wi-fi (charged) Kids' Club Play Area **Services:** **Leisure:** P

CORSICA

BONIFACIO — CORSE-DU-SUD

Rondinara

Suartone, 20169
☎ 495704315 📠 495705679
e-mail: reception@rondinara.fr
web: www.rondinara.fr

A beautiful location 300 metres from the beach with modern facilities and opportunities for water sports.

dir: *On N198 midway between Porto-Vecchio & Bonifacio.*

GPS: 41.4731, 9.2625

Open: 15 May-Sep **Site:** 6HEC **For hire:** **Prices:** 18-25 Mobile home hire 400-900 **Facilities:** **Services:** **Leisure:** P S

CALVI — HAUTE-CORSE

Dolce Vita

Ponte Bambino, 20260
☎ 495650599 📠 495653125
web: www.dolce-vita.fr

Set in extensive woodland with defined pitches and modern facilities.

Open: May-Sep **Site:** 6HEC **Facilities:** Wi-fi (charged) Play Area **Services:** **Leisure:** R S **Off-site:** L

CARGESE — CORSE-DU-SUD

Torraccia

Bagghiuccia, 20130
☎ 495264239 📠 495264239
e-mail: contact@camping-torraccia.com
web: www.camping-torraccia.com

Terraced site close to the Chiuni and Pero beaches and backed by some fine mountain scenery. There is a swimming pool with slide and a jacuzzi.

dir: *4km N on D81.*

Open: May-Sep **Site:** 3.5HEC **For hire:** **Facilities:** Wi-fi (charged) **Services:** **Off-site:** S

CASTELLARE DI CASINCA — HAUTE-CORSE

Village Center le Domaine d'Anghione

20213
☎ 499572121 📠 467516389
e-mail: contact@village-center.com
web: www.village-center.com/corse/camping-domaine-anghione.php

With direct access to the sea and ideal for families. Leisure facilities include tennis, squash courts and horse riding (at an extra charge).

dir: *N193 then N198.*

GPS: 42.4765, 9.5296

Open: 8 Apr-2 Oct **Site:** 40HEC **For hire:** **Facilities:** Wi-fi (charged) Kids' Club Play Area **Services:** **Leisure:** P S

FRANCE

GALÉRIA HAUTE-CORSE

Deux Torrents

20245
☎ 495620067 🖷 495620332
e-mail: 2torrents@corsica-net.com
A spacious, well-equipped site nestling between two torrents at the foot of the mountains.
dir: *5km E on D51 towards Calenzana.*
Open: Jun-Sep **Site:** 6.3HEC **For hire:** **Prices:** 18-28 Mobile home hire 180-700 **Facilities:** Wi-fi (charged) **Services:** **Off-site:** R

GHISONACCIA HAUTE-CORSE

Arinella-Bianca

20240
☎ 495560478 🖷 495561254
e-mail: arinella@arinellabianca.com
web: www.arinellabianca.com
Wooded surroundings beside the beach with good recreational facilities.
Open: 14 Apr-6 Oct **Site:** 10HEC **For hire:** **Prices:** 23-41 Mobile home hire 240-1350 **Facilities:** Wi-fi (charged) Kids' Club Play Area **Services:** **Leisure:** P R S

LOZARI HAUTE-CORSE

Clos des Chênes

rte de Belgodère, 20226
☎ 495601513 🖷 495602116
e-mail: cdc.lozari@wanadoo.fr
web: www.closdeschenes.fr
A delightful wooded setting 1km from a fine sandy beach. Shop and restaurant open in July and August.
dir: *1.5km S on N197 towards Belgodère.*
GPS: 42.6273, 9.0125
Open: May-Sep **Site:** 5.5HEC **For hire:** **Prices:** 20.90-27.80 Mobile home hire 285-730 **Facilities:** Play Area **Services:** **Leisure:** P **Off-site:** S

LUMIO HAUTE-CORSE

Panoramic

rte de Lavataggio 1, 20260
☎ 495607313 🖷 495607313
e-mail: panoramic@web-office.fr
web: www.le-panoramic.com
Quiet site with friendly atmosphere close to beaches. Very clean and tidy, divided into pitches.
dir: *From Calvi, 12km on N197, 200m from main road.*
Open: May-20 Sep **Site:** 6HEC **For hire:** **Facilities:** **Services:** **Leisure:** P **Off-site:** S

OLMETO-PLAGE CORSE-DU-SUD

Esplanade

20113
☎ 495760503 🖷 495761622
e-mail: campinglesplanade@orange.fr
web: www.camping-esplanade.com
A pleasant natural park, 100 metres from the sea. The campsite is located 5km from Propriano and Olmeto. Weight limit for dogs is 10kg.
Open: Apr-Oct **Site:** 4.75HEC **For hire:** **Facilities:** **Services:** **Leisure:** P S **Off-site:** R

PIANOTTOLI CORSE-DU-SUD

Kevano Plage

plage de Kevano, 20131
☎ 495718322 🖷 495718383
web: www.campingkevano.com
A beautiful setting in the middle of woodland with modern facilities, 400 metres from the beach.
Open: May-Sep **Site:** 6HEC **For hire:** **Facilities:** **Services:** **Off-site:** S

FRANCE

PISCIATELLO — CORSE-DU-SUD

Benista

20166

495251930 495259370

e-mail: camping.benista@orange.fr

web: www.benista.fr

A beautiful wooded setting 5 minutes from the beaches. Pitches are divided by hedges and there are good sports facilities.

GPS: 41.9102, 8.8260

Open: Apr-Oct **Site:** 5HEC **For hire:** **Prices:** 22.50-28.50 Mobile home hire 330-1050 **Facilities:** Wi-fi (charged) Play Area **Services:** **Leisure:** P R **Off-site:** S

PORTO-VECCHIO — CORSE-DU-SUD

Vetta

rte de Bastia, 20137

495700986 483076004

e-mail: info@campinglavetta.com

web: www.campinglavetta.com

Set in natural parkland with modern facilities, 3km from the sea.

dir: *5.5km N on N198.*

GPS: 41.6329, 9.2936

Open: Jun-Oct **Site:** 8HEC **For hire:** **Prices:** 19.64-27.64 **Facilities:** Wi-fi **Services:** **Leisure:** P **Off-site:** S

ST-FLORENT — HAUTE-CORSE

U Pezzo

rte de la Roya, 20217

495370165 495370165

e-mail: contact@upezzo.com

web: www.upezzo.com

Pleasant site, partly level, partly terraced under eucalyptus trees. Private access to large beach.

dir: *S of town on road to beach.*

Open: Apr-15 Oct **Site:** 2HEC **For hire:** **Prices:** 16-19 Mobile home hire 400-1500 **Facilities:** Play Area **Services:** **Leisure:** S **Off-site:** R

SAN NICOLAO — HAUTE-CORSE

Camping Merendella

RN198, Moriani Plage, 20230

495385347 495384401

e-mail: merendella@orange.fr

web: www.merendella.com

Site in a wooded setting overlooking a 300 metre long beach. Leisure facilities include a swimming pool, games room and home theatre. Dogs are only accepted in low season.

dir: *Just off RN198.*

Open: Apr-Oct **Site:** 6.5HEC **For hire:** **Facilities:** Wi-fi (charged) Play Area **Services:** **Leisure:** P S **Off-site:** L R

SOTTA — CORSE-DU-SUD

U Moru

20114

495712340 495712619

e-mail: u-moru@wanadoo.fr

web: www.u-moru.com

A quiet family site 5 minutes from the beach.

dir: *4km SW via D859.*

Open: 15 Jun-15 Sep **Site:** 6HEC **For hire:** **Prices:** 23-26.70 Mobile home hire 670-940 **Facilities:** Wi-fi **Services:** **Leisure:** P

TIUCCIA — CORSE-DU-SUD

Couchants

rte de Casaglione, 20111

495522660 495593177

e-mail: camping.les-couchants@wanadoo.fr

web: camping-lescouchants.fr

A quiet location facing the vast Sagone Bay and close to the Liamone River.

dir: *3km from sea.*

Open: May-Oct **Site:** 5HEC **For hire:** **Facilities:** Wi-fi **Services:** **Off-site:** R S

Drinking and driving

If the level of alcohol in the bloodstream is 0.050% or more, penalties include fines and the licence holder can be banned from driving in Germany. The blood alcohol level is nil percent for drivers aged under 21 or drivers who have held their licence for less than 2 years, should even a small amount of alcohol be detected in the blood the fine is 250.

Driving licence

Minimum age at which a UK licence holder may drive a temporarily imported car and/or motorcycle 18.

Fines

On-the-spot fine or deposit. Should a foreign motorist refuse to pay their vehicle can be confiscated. Motorists can be fined for such things as exceeding speed limits, using abusive language and making derogatory signs.

Wheel clamps are not used in Germany but vehicles causing obstruction can be towed away.

Fuel

Unleaded petrol (95 and 98 octane) and diesel available. LPG is also available from more than 5000 stations.

No leaded petrol (lead substitute additive available). Petrol in cans permitted but forbidden aboard ferries.

Credit cards accepted at most filling stations; check with your card issuer for usage in Germany before travel.

High Ethanol petrol: E10 (petrol containing 10% Ethanol) is now widely available in Germany but is not suitable for use in all vehicles. Pumps are clearly marked 'E10' but this should only be used if you are sure it is suitable – check with the car manufacturer or refer to this list published by the European Car Manufacturers' Association.

Alternatives to E10 – 'Super' (95 octane) and 'Super Plus' (Super unleaded) continue to be widely available.

Lights

It is recommended to use dipped headlights or day time running lights at all times. It is compulsory during daylight hours if fog, snow or rain restrict visibility.

Driving with sidelights (parking lights) alone is not allowed. Vehicles must have their lights on in tunnels.

Motorcycles

Use of dipped headlights at all times is compulsory. The wearing of a crash helmet is compulsory for both driver and passenger of a moped and motorcycle.

Drivers of trikes and quads capable of exceeding 20km/h must wear a helmet unless the vehicle is constructed with seat belts and they are worn.

Motor insurance

Third-party compulsory.

Passengers/children in cars

A child under 12 years of age and measuring less than 1.5m travelling in any type of vehicle, must be seated in a child seat or use a child restraint. It is prohibited to use a child seat in the front seat of a vehicle if the airbag has not been deactivated. All child restraints/seats used, must conform to ECE 44/03 or ECE 44/04.

It is the responsibility of the driver to ensure that all children are safely restrained.

Seat belts

Compulsory for front and rear seat occupants to wear seat belts, if fitted.

Speed limits

Standard legal limits, which may be varied by signs

Private vehicles without trailers	
Built-up areas	50km/h
Outside built-up areas	100km/h
Motorways/dual carriageways	130km/h
Private vehicles with trailer	
Motorways/dual carriageways	100km/h
Other roads	80km/h
Camper van up to 3.5t, with trailer	
Motorways/dual carriageways	80km/h
Other roads	80km/h
Vehicle over 3.5t with a trailer	
Motorways/dual carriageways	80km/h
Other roads	60km/h

The speed limit for caravans on a motorway is 80km/h UK or Irish caravanners wishing to travel at 100km/h on German motorways will first have to pass a TÜV (MOT) test in Germany to confirm that their outfit is suitable for travelling at 100km/h. For full current information please see www.germany-tourism.co.uk/EGB/practical_information/driving_in_germany_10326.htm The use of German motorways is only permitted with vehicles with a designed speed of more than 60km/h.

In bad weather conditions, when visibility is below 50m, the maximum speed limit is 50km/h.

The maximum speed limit for vehicles with snow chains is 50km/h.

Compulsory equipment in Germany

Winter tyres/equipment (See Tyres section).

Other rules/requirements

It is not compulsory for visiting UK motorists to carry a warning triangle, but they are strongly advised to do so, as all drivers must signal their vehicle in case of breakdown, and it is a compulsory requirement for residents.

It is recommended that visitors equip their vehicle with a first-aid kit (its carriage is compulsory for vehicles registered in Germany) and set of replacement bulbs.

Slow-moving vehicles must stop at suitable places and let others pass. It is prohibited to overtake or pass a school bus that is approaching a stopping point, indicated by flashing hazard lights. In all other cases of passing buses it has to be with caution. A fine will be imposed for non-compliance.

Spiked tyres are prohibited.

A GPS based navigation system which has maps indicating the location of fixed speed cameras must have the 'fixed speed camera PoI (Points of Interest)' function deactivated. Should you be unable to deactivate this function the GPS system must not be carried.

The use of radar detectors is prohibited.

All motorists have the obligation to adapt their vehicles to winter weather conditions. This includes but is not limited to winter tyres. Extreme weather may additionally require snow chains.

Tyres

On the 4th December 2010, new regulations regarding winter tyre requirements were introduced in Germany.

This new regulation applies to all motorised vehicles using roads in Germany, including those registered abroad, so vehicles registered in the United Kingdom are affected. It is now prohibited to use summer tyres in Germany during winter weather conditions - summer tyres are predominantly fitted to vehicles in the United Kingdom.

Winter weather conditions include black ice, snow, ice, slush and hoarfrost. Please bear in mind that these conditions may also be present even if the temperature is above 0 degrees.

German law specifies that the tyres must be winter tyres or all season tyres designed for use in wintry conditions. Suitable tyres will normally be marked 'M+S', however these can also be marked with a snowflake or snowy mountains symbol.

Motorists, whose car is equipped with summer tyres may not take the car on the road in winter weather conditions. Motorists in violation face fines of 40. If they actually obstruct traffic, the fine is 80. You may also be prevented from continuing your journey unless the tyres are changed or the weather conditions change.

Emission Zones

Restrictions on the circulation of vehicles are enforced in several German cities, in order to reduce the levels of emission of fine particles in some areas. The areas where restrictions apply will be indicated by signs "Umweltzone" showing coloured vignettes ("Plakette") - green, yellow and red. To enter these areas, drivers will have to stick a vignette on their vehicle windscreen, this can be obtained from technical inspection centres or approved garages, fine for non-compliance 40.

The owner of the vehicle (German or foreign) is required to present the registration certificate of the vehicle and pay a fee of 5 to 10 Euros. The colour of the vignette issued will depend on the type of engine and the Euro classification of the vehicle.

The fee is a 'one-off' charge and remains valid in any German City as long as it remains fixed in the vehicle i.e. not transferred to another vehicle.

Owners of foreign-registered vehicles can obtain a sticker by sending an email to the Berlin vehicle registration authority at kfz-zulassung@labo.verwalt-berlin.de attaching a copy of the vehicle registration certificate specifying the emission code or a manufacturer's certificate (preferably pdf files).

Upon verification of the documents, the registration authority will send a payment request by advance email including the bank details to the applicant. A 6 administration/handling fee will be charged per sticker. The sticker will be sent to the applicant by direct mail. As order processing may take two to three weeks, the sticker should be ordered well in advance.

Alternatively you can now obtain a sticker from the Cologne vehicle registration office by sending an application including a copy of the vehicle documents and 5 (cash or crossed cheque) to Kfz-Zulassungsstelle, Max-Glomsda-Straße 4, D-51105 Köln. For further information, visit www.stadt-koeln.de/3/umwelt/umweltzone/

For maps and detailed information of the environmental zone areas, please see

www.umweltbundesamt.de/umweltzonen

Tolls Currency Euro (€)	Car	Car Towing Caravan/Trailer
Tunnels		
Herren Tunnel (104 nr Lubeck)	€1.30	€1.30
Warnow Tunnel (105 nr Rostock) Summer prices	€2.90	€4.20

SOUTH EAST

AACH BEI OBERSTAUFEN — BAYERN

Aach

87534

☎ 08386 363 · 08386 961721

e-mail: info@camping-aach.de

web: www.camping-aach.de

A terraced site with beautiful views of the mountains. Sauna, solarium, games room.

dir: *B308 from Oberstaufen towards Austrian border for 7km.*

Open: All Year. **Site:** 2.5HEC **For hire:** **Facilities:** **Services:** **Off-site:** R

AITRANG — BAYERN

Elbsee

Am Elbsee 3, 87648

☎ 08343 248 · 08343 1406

e-mail: info@elbsee.de

web: www.elbsee.de

On the eastern shore of the lake with good bathing facilities. Section reserved for campers with dogs.

dir: *NW from Marktoberdorf centre to Ruderatshofen & W towards Aitrang, site signed S of Aitrang (narrow winding road).*

Open: All Year. **Site:** 5HEC **For hire:** **Prices:** 22.40-24.50 **Facilities:** Wi-fi (charged) Play Area **Services:** **Leisure:** L **Off-site:** P

ARLACHING — BAYERN

Kupferschmiede

Trostberger Str 4, 83339

☎ 08667 446 · 08667 16198

e-mail: campingkupfer@aol.com

web: www.campingkupferschmiede.de

On meadowland and close to a forest. Partially gravel.

dir: *On Seebruck-Traunstein road.*

Open: Apr-Oct **Site:** 2.5HEC **Prices:** 17.90-21.30 **Facilities:** Wi-fi (charged) Play Area **Services:** **Leisure:** L **Off-site:** P R

AUGSBURG — BAYERN

Augusta

Mühlhauser Str 54B, 86169

☎ 0821 707575 · 0821 705883

e-mail: info@caravaningpark.com

web: www.caravaningpark.com

Hard standings for caravans. Separate section for residential caravans.

dir: *E11 exit Augsburg-Ost, N towards Neuburg & 400m right.*

Open: All Year. **Site:** 6.6HEC **For hire:** **Facilities:** **Services:** **Leisure:** L **Off-site:**

BAMBERG — BAYERN

Insel

Bug, 96049

☎ 0951 56320 · 0951 56321

e-mail: campinginsel@web.de

web: www.campinginsel.de

The site lies on the bank of the River Regnitz. Park and Ride scheme into Bamberg.

dir: *A73 exit Bamberg S, B505/B4 towards Bamberg, signed on left.*

Open: All Year. **Site:** 5HEC **Prices:** 18.60 **Facilities:** Wi-fi **Services:** **Leisure:** R

BERCHTESGADEN — BAYERN

Allweglehen

Allweggasse 4, 83471

☎ 08652 2396 · 08652 63503

e-mail: urlaub@allweglehen.de

web: www.allweglehen.de

A terraced site at the foot of the Untersalzberg Mountain surrounded by woods. There is also a steep and narrow asphalt access road with passing places. A truck is available for towing caravans.

dir: *B305 towards Schellenberg for 3.5km.*

Open: All Year. **Site:** 4HEC **For hire:** **Prices:** 27.95 **Facilities:** Wi-fi Play Area **Services:** **Leisure:** P **Off-site:** R

BERGEN BAYERN

Wagnerhof

Campingstr 11, 83346

☎ 08662 8557 08662 5924

e-mail: info@camping-bergen.de

web: www.camping-bergen.de

Open all year round, this level site is surrounded by mountains and forest, close to the bottom of Hochfelln, an excellent vantage point. Plenty to do for children, table tennis room and tennis court available.

dir: *München-Salzburg motorway exit Bergen, right at sawmill before town.*

Open: All Year. **Site:** 2.8HEC **For hire:** **Facilities:** **Services:** **Off-site:** L P

BISCHOFSWIESEN BAYERN

Winkl-Landthal

Winkl bei Berchtesgaden, 83483

☎ 08652 8164 08652 979831

e-mail: camping-winkl@t-online.de

web: www.camping-winkl.de

Meadowland site between the B20 and the edge of woodland in the Berchtesgaden National Park.

dir: *From Bad Reichenhall to Berchtesgaden for 8km.*

Open: Dec-Oct **Site:** 2.5HEC **For hire:** **Prices:** 25-29 Mobile home hire 525 **Facilities:** Wi-fi (charged) Play Area **Services:** **Leisure:** R

BRUNNEN FORGGENSEE BAYERN

Brunnen

Seestr 81, 87645

☎ 08362 8273 08362 8630

e-mail: info@camping-brunnen.de

web: www.camping-brunnen.de

Situated on the eastern shore of Lake Forggensee. Kids' club available in high season.

dir: *B17 from Füssen to Schwangau, then N on minor road.*

Open: 15 Dec-5 Nov **Site:** 6HEC **Facilities:** Wi-fi (charged) Kids' Club Play Area **Services:** **Leisure:** L **Off-site:** P

BUXHEIM BAYERN

See International

Am Weiherhaus 7, 87740

☎ 08331 71800 08331 63554

web: www.camping-buxheim.de

Terraced site beyond public bathing area. Recreational facilities include two playgrounds and table tennis.

dir: *Leave Um-Kempten motorway at Memminger Kreuz then right to Buxheim.*

Open: 15 May-Sep **Site:** 42HEC **Facilities:** Wi-fi (charged) Play Area **Services:** **Leisure:** L **Off-site:** P R

DIESSEN BAYERN

St-Alban

86911

☎ 08807 7305 08807 1057

e-mail: ivan.pavic@t-online.de

web: www.camping-ammersee.de

Clean site next to St-Alban, lakeside with private bathing beach and reserved section for residential campers. Good sanitary installations also used by the public.

dir: *B12 from München towards Landsberg/Lech, near Greifenberg turn left, continue via Utting to St-Alban.*

Open: Apr-Oct **Site:** 3.8HEC **Facilities:** **Services:** **Leisure:** L **Off-site:**

DINKELSBÜHL BAYERN

Romantische Strasse

91550

☎ 09851 7817 09851 7848

e-mail: campdinkelsbuehl@aol.com

web: www.campingplatz-dinkelsbuehl.de

Terraced site with some hedges and trees. Separate field for young people. Good sports facilities.

dir: *Signed.*

Open: All Year. **Site:** 9HEC **Facilities:** **Services:** **Leisure:** L **Off-site:**

GERMANY

ENDORF, BAD — BAYERN

Camping Stein

See 10, 83093
☎ 08053 9349 08053 798745
e-mail: info@camping-stein.de
web: www.camping-stein.de

A family site in wooded surroundings on the shore of the Simssee. Dogs not accepted 15 July until 20 August.

dir: *A8.*

GPS: 47.8839, 12.2696

Open: Apr-Oct **Site:** 2.5HEC **Facilities:** Wi-fi (charged) Play Area **Services:** **Leisure:** L **Off-site:**

ERLANGEN — BAYERN

Rangau

Campingstr 44, 91056
☎ 09135 8866 09135 724743
e-mail: info@camping-rangau.de
web: www.camping-rangau.de

On a long stretch of land behind the sports ground, next to the Dechsendorfer Weiher lake, in a nature reserve.

dir: *A3 exit Erlangen W.*

Open: Apr-Sep **Site:** 18HEC **Prices:** 20.50 **Facilities:** **Services:** **Off-site:** L

ESCHERNDORF — BAYERN

Escherndorf-Main

97332
☎ 09381 2889 09381 710945
e-mail: info@campingplatz-mainschleife.de
web: www.campingplatz-escherndorf.de

Site lies on meadowland by the River Main, next to the ferry station (River Ferry Nordheim).

dir: *A7 exit Würzburg/Estenfeld, E for Volkach or A3 exit Kitzingen.*

GPS: 49.8598, 10.1767

Open: Apr-Oct **Site:** 1.5HEC **Prices:** 20 **Facilities:** Wi-fi (charged) **Services:** **Leisure:** R **Off-site:** P

ESTENFELD — BAYERN

Camping Estenfeld

Maidbronner Str 38, 97230
☎ 09305 228 09305 8006
e-mail: cplestenfeld@freenet.de
web: www.camping-estenfeld.de

On meadowland next to sportsground and gardens on the outskirts of Estenfeld.

dir: *A7 exit Würzburg/Estenfeld, B19 S for 1km.*

GPS: 49.8325, 9.9981

Open: 15 May-23 Dec **Site:** 0.5HEC **For hire:** **Prices:** 17-23 Mobile home hire 109-230 **Facilities:** Play Area **Services:** **Off-site:** P

FEILNBACH, BAD — BAYERN

Tenda Camping-Park

Reithof 2, 83075
☎ 08066 884400 08066 8844029
e-mail: info@tenda-camping.de
web: www.tenda-camping.de

Well-organised site on level grassland with pitches laid out in circles and hardstandings for tourers near the entrance.

dir: *A8 exit Bad Aibling, 4km S on minor road.*

GPS: 47.7891, 12.0058

Open: All Year. **Site:** 14HEC **For hire:** **Prices:** 19-27 **Facilities:** Wi-fi (charged) Kids' Club Play Area **Services:** **Leisure:** P **Off-site:** L

FICHTELBERG — BAYERN

Fichtelsee

95686
☎ 09272 801 09272 909045
e-mail: info@camping-fichtelsee.de
web: www.camping-fichtelsee.de

Gently sloping meadow amid pleasant woodland 100 metres from Lake Fichtelsee.

dir: *A9 exit Bad Berneck, B303 to Fichtelsee Leisure Centre turning.*

GPS: 50.0163, 11.8552

Open: 16 Dec-3 Nov **Site:** 2.6HEC **Prices:** 18.50-22.50 **Facilities:** Wi-fi (charged) Kids' Club Play Area **Services:** **Off-site:** L P

GERMANY

FINSTERAU BAYERN

Nationalpark-Ost

94151

☎ 08557 768 🖷 08557 1062

e-mail: berghof-frank@berghof.frank.de

web: www.camping-nationalpark.eu

Terraced site on edge of extensive woodland area at the entrance to a national park.

dir: *N of Freyung towards frontier.*

Open: All Year. **Site:** 3HEC **Prices:** 19.20 **Facilities:** **Services:** **Off-site:**

FRICKENHAUSEN BAYERN

KNAUS Camping Park Frickenhausen

Ochsenfurter Str 49, 97252

☎ 09331 3171 🖷 09331 5784

e-mail: frickenhausen@knauscamp.de

web: www.knauscamp.de

On level meadow in a small poplar wood beside River Main.

dir: *On N bank of River Main 0.5km E of Ochsenfurt.*

Open: 14 Mar-3 Nov **Site:** 3.5HEC **For hire:** **Facilities:** **Services:** **Leisure:** P **Off-site:** P R

FÜRTH IM WALD BAYERN

Einberg

Daberger Str 33, 93437

☎ 09973 1811 🖷 09973 803220

e-mail: camping@stadtwerke-furth.de

web: www.stadtwerke-furth.de

Municipal site in Daberger Str, near swimming pool.

dir: *NE of Cham on B20.*

Open: Mar-Oct **Site:** 2HEC **Facilities:** **Services:** **Leisure:** R **Off-site:** L P

FÜSSEN BAYERN

Hopfensee

Fischerbichl 17, 87629

☎ 08362 917710 🖷 08362 917720

e-mail: info@camping-hopfensee.de

web: www.camping-hopfensee.de

A quiet location beside a lake with a private beach. Ski-safari in winter.

dir: *4km N of Füssen.*

GPS: 47.6013, 10.6833

Open: 17 Dec-4 Nov **Site:** 8HEC **Prices:** 33.85-37.60 **Facilities:** Wi-fi (charged) Kids' Club Play Area **Services:** **Leisure:** L P **Off-site:**

FÜSSING, BAD BAYERN

Kur-Camping Fuchs

94072

☎ 08537 356 🖷 08537 912083

e-mail: info@kurcamping-fuchs.de

web: www.kurcamping-fuchs.de

On meadow divided into pitches and 1km from spa baths at Bad Füssing.

dir: *Turn at Passau end of Tutling on B12 to Kircham & signs to site on Egglfinger Str, 2km from Bad Füssing.*

Open: All Year. **Site:** 1.5HEC **For hire:** **Facilities:** **Services:** **Leisure:** P **Off-site:** R

Max I

Falkenstr 12, Egglfing, 94072

☎ 08537 96170 🖷 08537 961710

e-mail: info@campingmax.de

web: www.campingmax.de

On a level meadow with some trees. Good modern facilities.

dir: *S of Bad Füssing via B12.*

Open: All Year. **Site:** 3.5HEC **For hire:** **Facilities:** Play Area **Services:** **Leisure:** L P

GADEN BAYERN

Schwanenplatz

Am Schwanenplatz 1, 83329

☎ 08681 281 🖷 08681 4276

e-mail: info@schwanenplatz.de

web: www.schwanenplatz.de

Site lies on a meadow, divided into sections beside Waginger See.

dir: *From Traunstein to Waging, right towards Freilassing for 1km, left to lake.*

GPS: 47.9366, 12.7607

Open: 27 Apr-3 Oct **Site:** 4HEC **Prices:** 18.65-22.95 **Facilities:** Wi-fi (charged) Kids' Club Play Area **Services:** **Leisure:** L R **Off-site:**

GARMISCH-PARTENKIRCHEN BAYERN

Zugspitze

Griesener Str 4, 82491

☎ 08821 3180 🖷 08821 947594

A beautiful setting at the foot of the Zugspitze between the road and the Loisach.

dir: *On B24 towards Austrian border.*

Open: All Year. **Site:** 2.9HEC **Facilities:** **Services:** **Leisure:** R **Off-site:** L P

GERMANY

GEMÜNDEN AM MAIN — BAYERN

Saaleinsel

Duivenallee 7, 97737

09351 8574

The municipal site lies a short distance off the main road bordering the River Fränkische Saale. It is in the grounds of a sports field and has a swimming pool.

dir: *Signed off B26.*

Open: Apr-15 Oct **Site:** 7HEC **Facilities:** Play Area **Services:** **Leisure:** P R **Off-site:**

GEMÜNDEN-HOFSTETTEN — BAYERN

Spessart-Camping Schönrain

97737

09351 8645 09351 8721

e-mail: info@spessart-camping.de

web: www.spessart-camping.de

Slightly sloping, partly terraced meadowland east of River Main. Many castles and parks in the surrounding area.

dir: *From Gemünden/Main over the bridge, then right and right again after Hofstetten (site signed).*

Open: Apr-Sep **Site:** 7HEC **For hire:** **Prices:** 18.70 **Facilities:** Play Area **Services:** **Leisure:** P

GRIESBACH, BAD — BAYERN

Kur-Und Feriencamping Dreiquellenbad

94086

08532 96130 08532 961350

e-mail: info@camping-bad-griesbach.de

web: www.camping-bad-griesbach.de

Pleasant wooded surroundings with modern facilities.

dir: *1km S of Griesbach Spa, on the Karpfham-Schwaim road.*

GPS: 48.4208, 13.1919

Open: All Year. **Site:** 4.5HEC **For hire:** **Prices:** 20-25.50 **Facilities:** Wi-fi (charged) Play Area **Services:** **Leisure:** L P **Off-site:** R

HASLACH — BAYERN

Feriencenter Wertacher Hof

87466

08361 770

Well-kept site on Lake Grüntensee.

dir: *Near Wertach-Haslach railway station.*

Open: All Year. **Site:** 3.5HEC **Facilities:** **Services:** **Leisure:** L

HOFHEIM — BAYERN

Brugger am Riegsee

Seestr 2, 82418

08847 728 08847 228

e-mail: office@camping-brugger.de

web: www.camping-brugger.de

A lakeside site in a rural setting with modern facilities and a view to the mountain range Zugspitze and Alpspitze.

Open: May-8 Oct **Site:** 6HEC **Prices:** 19-25 **Facilities:** Wi-fi Kids' Club Play Area **Services:** **Leisure:** L

INGOLSTADT — BAYERN

AZUR Camping Auwaldsee

Am Auwaldsee, 85053

0841 9611616 0841 9611617

e-mail: ingolstadt@azur-camping.de

web: www.azur-camping.de/ingolstadt

Near to Auwaldsee, this site lies in a beautiful setting beside the München-Ingolstadt motorway.

dir: *A9 exit Ingolstadt-Süd.*

Open: All Year. **Site:** 10HEC **Facilities:** Play Area **Services:** **Leisure:** L **Off-site:** P

ISSIGAU — BAYERN

Schloss Issigau

Altes Schloss 3, 95188

09293 7173 09293 933385

e-mail: schloss_issigau@t.online.de

web: www.schloss-issigau.de

Close to Issigau in a central position for a holiday or stopover site.

dir: *A9 exit Berg/Bad Steben, 5km W.*

GPS: 50.3738, 11.7211

Open: 15 Mar-Oct & Xmas-New Year **Site:** 2HEC **For hire:** **Prices:** 16.50-17.50 **Facilities:** Play Area **Services:** **Off-site:**

JODITZ BAYERN

Auensee

95189

☎ 09295 381 🖹 09281 1706666

e-mail: rathaus@gemeinde-koeditz.de

web: www.auensee-camping.de

Municipal site on partly terraced meadowland above lake.

dir: *München-Berlin motorway exit Berg-Bad Steben, site 4km E.*

Open: All Year. **Site:** 9HEC **Prices:** 10.50-13 **Facilities:** Play Area **Services:** **Leisure:** L **Off-site:** P R

KIPFENBERG BAYERN

AZUR-Camping Altmühltal

Campingstr 1, 85110

☎ 08465 905167 🖹 08465 3745

e-mail: kipfenberg@azur-camping.de

web: www.azur-camping.de/kipfenberg

Well-equipped site in an unspoiled wooded location with good canoeing facilities.

Open: Apr-Oct **Site:** 4HEC **Prices:** 18-24 **Facilities:** Wi-fi (charged) **Services:** **Leisure:** R **Off-site:** P

KIRCHZELL BAYERN

AZUR-Camping Odenwald

Am Campingplatz 1, 63931

☎ 09373 566 🖹 09373 7375

e-mail: kirchzell@azur-camping.de

web: www.azur-camping.de/kirchzell

Site on natural terraced meadowland in wooded hilly country.

dir: *From Amorbach towards Eberbach road for 5km, site 1km from town.*

Open: Apr-Oct **Site:** 7HEC **Facilities:** **Services:** **Leisure:** P

KISSINGEN, BAD BAYERN

Bad Kissingen

Euerdorfer Str 1, 97688

☎ 0971 5211 🖹 0971 6990820

e-mail: campingpark-badkissingen@web.de

web: www.campingpark-badkissingen.de

Set in a park beside the River Saale in central location, ideal for touring the area.

Open: Apr-30 Oct **Site:** 1.8HEC **For hire:** **Facilities:** Wi-fi (charged) Play Area **Services:** **Off-site:** P R

KITZINGEN BAYERN

Schiefer Turm

Marktbreiter Str 20, 97318

☎ 09321 33125 🖹 09321 384795

e-mail: info@camping-kitzingen.de

web: www.camping-kitzingen.de

Quiet location but close to the town with cycle paths leading directly from the site, to explore the surrounding countryside.

dir: *A3 exit Biebelried/Kitzingen.*

Open: Apr-15 Oct **Site:** 2.3HEC **For hire:** **Facilities:** **Services:** **Leisure:** R **Off-site:** P

KLINGENBRUNN BAYERN

NationalPark

94518

☎ 08553 727 🖹 08553 6930

web: www.camping-nationalpark.de

Pleasant wooded surroundings set around the restaurant on southern slope between Klingenbrunn and Spiegelau.

dir: *Off B85 12km SE of Regen near Kirchdorf, 6km E towards Klingenbrunn.*

Open: All Year. **Site:** 5HEC **Prices:** 17 **Facilities:** Wi-fi **Services:** **Off-site:** L P

KÖNIGSDORF BAYERN

Königsdorf

Am Bibisee, 82549

☎ 08171 81580 🖹 08171 81165

e-mail: mail@camping-koenigsdorf.de

web: www.camping-koenigsdorf.de

Unspoiled site in natural setting in meadowland. A number of individual pitches for tourers.

dir: *2km N of town off B11, just beyond edge of forest.*

Open: All Year. **Site:** 8.6HEC **Facilities:** **Services:** **Leisure:** L **Off-site:** P R

KÖNIGSSEE BAYERN

Mühlleiten

83477

☎ 08652 4584 🖹 08652 69194

e-mail: info@muehlleiten.eu

web: www.muehlleiten.eu

A pleasant site in wooded surroundings adjacent to a small guesthouse. Beautiful views of the Berchtesgaden mountains.

dir: *N of Königssee towards Berchtesgaden.*

Open: All Year. **Site:** 1.8HEC **Facilities:** Wi-fi **Services:** **Leisure:** R **Off-site:** L P

GERMANY

KRUN — BAYERN

Tennsee

The Camping and Caravanning Club The Friendly Club

82493

08825 170 08825 17236

e-mail: info@camping-tennsee.de

web: www.camping-tennsee.de

A partially terraced site with fine views of the Karwendel and Zugspitze mountains.

C&CC Report *A really friendly site with top-notch facilities, a beautiful Alpine setting and outstanding Bavarian cuisine. There are discounts for local attractions and a wealth of day trips. Fairytale castles including Neuschwanstein, of* Chitty-Chitty-Bang-Bang *fame, grace the lovely Alpine scenery, while Venice, Lake Garda, Innsbruck and the Dolomites can all be reached as day trips by car, or through the site with the local coach tour company.*

dir: *From München-Garmisch-Partenkirchen motorway B2 to Mittenwald & signed.*

Open: 15 Dec-4 Nov **Site:** 5.2HEC **Facilities:** Wi-fi (charged) Play Area **Services:** **Off-site:** L

KÜHNHAUSEN — BAYERN

Stadler

Strandbadstr 11, 83367

08686 8037 08685 1049

web: www.camping-stadler.de

Level meadow on lake with private beach.

dir: *2m E shore of Lake Waginger.*

Open: Apr-Sep **Site:** 0.8HEC **For hire:** **Facilities:** **Services:** **Leisure:** L S **Off-site:**

LACKENHÄUSER — BAYERN

Knaus Campingpark Lackenhäuser

Lackenhäuser 127, 94089

08583 311 08583 91079

e-mail: lackenhaeuser@knauscamp.de

web: www.knauscamp.de

Extensive site with woodland parks, waterfalls. Many health resort facilities.

Open: 16 Dec-3 Nov **Site:** 15HEC **For hire:** **Facilities:** **Services:** **Leisure:** P **Off-site:** L

LANGLAU — BAYERN

SeeCamping Langlau

Seestr 30, 91738

09834 96969 09834 96968

e-mail: mail@seecamping-langlau.de

web: www.seecamping-langlau.de

On the shores of the Kleiner Brombachsee. Kids' club available during summer and Whitsun holidays.

dir: *From Gunzevhausen towards Pleinfield for 10km.*

Open: Mar-15 Nov **Site:** 12.4HEC **For hire:** **Prices:** 20.50 **Facilities:** Wi-fi (charged) Kids' Club Play Area **Services:** **Off-site:** L

LENGFURT — BAYERN

Main-Spessart-Park

Spessartstr 30, 97855

09395 1079 09395 8295

e-mail: info@camping-main-spessart.de

web: www.camping-main-spessart.de

Site lies partly on terraced meadowland and partly on the eastern slopes of the Main Valley. Some water sports and nearby private mooring on the River Main.

dir: *A3 exit Markheidenfeld, N to Altfeld, 6km E to Lengfurt (NW edge of village).*

GPS: 49.8183, 9.5886

Open: All Year. **Site:** 10HEC **Facilities:** Play Area **Services:** **Off-site:** P R

LINDAU — BAYERN

Campingpark Gitzenweiler Hof

The Camping and Caravanning Club The Friendly Club

Gitzenweiler 88, 88131

08382 94940 08382 949415

e-mail: info@gitzenweiler-hof.de

web: www.gitzenweiler-hof.de

Located in hilly meadow ground near Lake Constance surrounded with trees and hedges. Cars may only be parked by tents in certain areas.

C&CC Report *This large, friendly and very well run site has great international appeal, plus a wide range of services and activities available most of the year, making it perfect for active families of all ages. Don't miss the lovely historic island town of Lindau and a boat trip on stunning Lake Constance, or the award-winning Friedrichshafen Zeppelin museum.*

dir: *A96 exit Weissensberg. B31a exit Lindau.*

GPS: 47.5853, 9.7066

Open: All Year. **Site:** 14HEC **For hire:** **Prices:** 22-35 Mobile home hire 300-900 **Facilities:** Wi-fi (charged) Kids' Club Play Area **Services:** **Leisure:** P **Off-site:** L

Lindau am See

Fraunhoferstr 20, Zech, 88131
08382 72236 08382 976106
e-mail: info@park-camping.de
web: www.park-camping.de
Site lies on meadowland with trees, reaching down to the lake. Very large sanitary blocks. Common room, reading room, field for ball games and a separate common room for young people.
dir: *B31 from Lindau towards Bregenz, turn right (signed) before level crossing, site 0.5km.*
Open: 15 Mar-10 Nov **Site:** 5HEC **Prices:** 17-28.50 **Facilities:** Wi-fi (charged) Kids' Club Play Area **Services:** **Leisure:** L **Off-site:** P

MÖRSLINGEN — BAYERN

Mörslingen

89435
09074 4024
e-mail: mail@camping-moerslingen.de
web: www.camping-moerslingen.de
Attractive well equipped site close to LEGOLAND® Günzburg.
dir: *6km N of Dillengen.*
Open: All Year. **Site:** 1HEC **For hire:** **Facilities:** **Services:** **Leisure:** L P **Off-site:**

MÜHLHAUSEN BEI AUGSBURG — BAYERN

Lech Camping

Seeweg 6, 86444
08207 2200 08207 2202
e-mail: info@lech-camping.de
web: www.lech-camping.de
Level grassland with swimming facilities beside lake. Close to LEGOLAND® Munich and Augsburg.
dir: *A8 exit 73. 4km N towards Neuburg.*
GPS: 48.4375, 10.9291
Open: Apr-Oct **Site:** 3HEC **Prices:** 22.90-24.90 **Facilities:** Wi-fi (charged) Play Area **Services:** **Leisure:** L **Off-site:** P

Ludwigshof am See

Augsburger Str 36, 86444
08207 96170 08207 961770
e-mail: info@bauer-caravan.de
web: www.bauer-caravan.de
Clean site with small lake away from motorway, near restaurant of the same name.
dir: *Motorway exit 73 Augsburg Ost, 1.5km N towards Neuburg.*
Open: Apr-Oct **Site:** 12HEC **Facilities:** **Services:** **Leisure:** L **Off-site:** P R

MÜNCHEN (MUNICH) — BAYERN

München-Obermenzing

Lochhausener Str 59, Obermenzing, 81247
089 8112235 089 8144807
e-mail: campingplatz-obermenzing@t-online.de
web: www.campingplatz-muenchen.de
Park-like site near motorway.
dir: *1km from end of Stuttgart-München motorway. A99 exit München-Lochhauser then follow signs for campsite.*
GPS: 48.1747, 11.4469
Open: 15 Mar-Oct **Site:** 5.5HEC **For hire:** **Facilities:** Wi-fi (charged) Play Area **Services:** **Off-site:** L P R

NEUBÄU — BAYERN

Seecamping

Seestr 4, 93426
09469 331 09469 397
e-mail: r.notka@see-campingpark.de
web: www.see-campingpark.de
Meadowland site along lakeshore.
dir: *B85 from Schwandorf towards Cham.*
Open: All Year. **Site:** 5HEC **Facilities:** **Services:** **Leisure:** L

NEUKIRCHEN VORM WALD — BAYERN

Rotbrunn

Pilling 22, 94154
08504 920260 08504 920265
e-mail: camping.rotbrunn@vr-web.de
Terraced and partially shaded site on edge of small town with shops and services.
dir: *A3 exit Aicha W, 6km to Neukirchen.*
Open: All Year. **Site:** **Facilities:** **Services:** **Leisure:** L **Off-site:**

NEUSTADT BAYERN

Main-Spessart-Camping-International

97845

09393 639 09393 1607

e-mail: info@camping-neustadt-main.de

web: www.camping-neustadt-main.de

Beautiful location alongside the River Main. Water sports include water skiing.

dir: *A3 exit Marktheidenfeld towards Lohr.*

GPS: 49.9117, 9.5833

Open: Apr-Sep **Site:** 5.6HEC **Prices:** 19 **Facilities:** Wi-fi (charged) Kids' Club Play Area **Services:** **Leisure:** P R **Off-site:**

NÜRNBERG (NUREMBERG) BAYERN

Knaus Campingpark Nürnberg

Hans-Kalb-Str 56, 90471

0911 9812717 0911 9812718

e-mail: nuernberg@knauscamp.de

web: www.knauscamp.de

Well-kept site in a beautiful forest location between a stadium with a swimming pool and the Trade Fair Centre.

dir: *A9 exit Nürnberg-Fischbach towards stadium.*

Open: All Year. **Site:** 2.7HEC **For hire:** **Facilities:** **Services:** **Off-site:** L P

OBERAMMERGAU BAYERN

Oberammergau

Ettaler Str 56, 82487

08822 94105 08822 94197

e-mail: service@camping-oberammergau.de

web: www.campingpark-oberammergau.de

A year-round site with modern facilities and fine views of the Bavarian Alps.

dir: *Signed from town.*

Open: All Year. **Site:** 2HEC **For hire:** **Facilities:** **Services:** **Leisure:** R **Off-site:** P

OBERSTDORF BAYERN

Oberstdorf

Rubinger Str 16, 87561

08322 6525 08322 809760

e-mail: camping-oberstdorf@t-online.de

web: www.camping-oberstdorf.de

Level grassland site with fine mountain views.

dir: *0.8km N of town centre near railway line.*

Open: All Year. **Site:** 16HEC **Facilities:** **Services:** **Off-site:** L P R

OBERWÖSSEN BAYERN

Litzelau

83246

08640 8704 08640 5265

e-mail: camping-litzelau@t-online.de

web: www.camping-litzelau.de

Almost level meadowland surrounded by forested slopes.

dir: *A8 exit 106 Bernau, B305 S through Marquartstein & Unterwössen.*

Open: All Year. **Site:** 4.5HEC **For hire:** **Facilities:** Wi-fi (charged) Kids' Club Play Area **Services:** **Leisure:** R **Off-site:** L P

PASSAU BAYERN

Dreiflüsse

Am Sonnenhang 8, 94113

08546 633 08546 2686

e-mail: dreifluessecamping@t-online.de

web: www.dreifluessecamping.privat.t-online.de

A well-equipped site in pleasant wooded surroundings. Close to the city of Passau in the upper Danube valley.

dir: *A3 exit Passau-Nord, site signed.*

Open: Apr-Oct **Site:** 5HEC **For hire:** **Facilities:** Wi-fi **Services:** **Leisure:** P

GERMANY

PFRAUNDORF BAYERN

Kratzmühle

85125

☎ 08461 64170 🖷 08461 641717

e-mail: info@kratzmuehle.de

web: www.kratzmuehle.de

Terraced site, divided into pitches, on a wooded hillside overlooking the River Altmühl.

dir: *From village turn to Kratzmühle.*

GPS: 49.0033, 11.4519

Open: All Year. **Site:** 9.6HEC **For hire:** **Facilities:** Wi-fi Play Area **Services:** **Leisure:** L R

PIDING BAYERN

Campingplatz Staufeneck

Strailachweg 1, 83451

☎ 08651 2134 🖷 08651 710450

e-mail: camping-staufeneck@t-online.de

web: www.camping-berchtesgadener-land.de

Beautiful and quiet location beside the River Saalach.

dir: *A8 exit Bad Reichenall for 2.5km & turn right.*

Open: Apr-Oct **Site:** 2.7HEC **Prices:** 20-22.30 **Facilities:** Play Area **Services:** **Leisure:** R **Off-site:** L P

PIELENHOFEN BAYERN

Naabtal-Pielenhofen

The Camping and Caravanning Club The Friendly Club

93188

☎ 09409 373 🖷 09409 723

e-mail: camping.pielenhofen@t-online.de

web: www.camping-pielenhofen.de

The site is well-situated beside the River Naab, and has a special section for overnight visitors.

C&CC Report *This well-established, family-run, friendly and traditional site is constantly improving, with the main washblock in particular recently renovated to a very high standard, and the play area also renewed. The very good touring pitches are mainly on or near the riverside, while the site is bordered by the Bachs' own peaceful farmland. This is a perfect base for visiting enchanting Regensburg, but the area's wooded valleys are great for walking or cycling year round and dotted with lovely castles and other stately buildings. Alternatively, you can always relax with a meal in the site's traditional biergarten.*

dir: *A3 exit Nittendorf, via Etterzhausen.*

Open: All Year. **Site:** 6HEC **For hire:** **Prices:** 18.10 **Facilities:** Wi-fi Play Area **Services:** **Leisure:** R

PRIEN AM CHIEMSEE BAYERN

Hofbauer

Bernauerstr 110, 83209

☎ 08051 4136 🖷 08051 62657

e-mail: ferienhaus-campingpl.hofbauer@t-online.de

web: www.camping-prien-chiemsee.de

A peaceful location among the Bavarian foothills of the Alps with fine views of the mountains. Site divided into separate plots.

dir: *A8 exit 106 for Bernau, right for Prien, site 3km on left.*

Open: Apr-Oct **Site:** 2HEC **For hire:** **Prices:** 22.50 **Facilities:** Wi-fi (charged) Play Area **Services:** **Leisure:** P **Off-site:** L

ROTHENBURG OB DER TAUBER BAYERN

Tauber-Idyll

Detwang 28A, 91541

☎ 09861 3177 🖷 09861 92848

e-mail: camping-tauber-idyll@t-online.de

web: www.rothenburg.de/tauber-idyll

The well-kept site lies on a meadow scattered with trees and bushes, on the outskirts of the northern suburb of Detwang and next to the River Tauber.

dir: *B25 from Nordinger Str W along River Tauber towards Bad Mergentheim. Signed from main roads.*

Open: 1wk before Etr-1 Nov **Site:** 0.5HEC **Prices:** 17 **Facilities:** Wi-fi **Services:** **Off-site:** P R

Tauber-Romantik

Detwang 39, 91541

☎ 09861 6191 🖷 09861 9368889

e-mail: info@camping-tauberromantik.de

web: www.camping-tauberromantik.de

Modern campsite in the pleasant Tauber valley.

GPS: 49.3878, 10.1678

Open: 15 Mar-4 Nov **Site:** 1.2HEC **For hire:** **Prices:** 18.50 **Facilities:** Wi-fi Play Area **Services:** **Off-site:** R

GERMANY

ROTH-WALLESAU BAYERN

Camping Waldsee

Badstr 37, 91154

09171 5570 09171 843245

e-mail: info@camping-waldsee.de

web: www.camping-waldsee.de

On the banks of a lake and surrounded by woods, in an area known for its hiking and cycling trails. Swimming, boating and fishing are all possible on the lake. Kids' club for 4-14 year olds during holiday season.

GPS: 49.1892, 11.1244

Open: All Year. **Site:** 4HEC **For hire:** **Prices:** 17.20-18.20 **Facilities:** Kids' Club Play Area **Services:** **Leisure:** L

ROTTENBUCH BAYERN

Terrassen-Camping am Richterbichl

82401

08867 1500 08867 8300

e-mail: info@camping-rottenbuch.de

web: www.camping-rottenbuch.de

Several pleasant terraces with good views.

dir: *On S outskirts on B23.*

Open: All Year. **Site:** 1.2HEC **For hire:** **Facilities:** Wi-fi (charged) Play Area **Services:** **Leisure:** L **Off-site:** P R

RUHPOLDING BAYERN

Ortnerhof

Ort 5, 83324

08663 1764 08663 5073

e-mail: camping-ortnerhof@t-online.de

web: www.camping-ruhpolding.de

Well-kept site on a meadow at the foot of the Rauschberg Mountain, opposite the cable-car station.

dir: *Off Deutsche Alpenstr (B305).*

Open: All Year. **Site:** 3.6HEC **Prices:** 24.80 **Facilities:** Play Area **Services:** **Off-site:** P

SCHECHEN BAYERN

Campingplatz Erlensee KG

Rosenheimer Str 63, 83135

08039 1695 08039 9416

The site lies on the shores of an artificial lake.

dir: *From Rosenheim, 10km N onto B15 towards Wasserburg, turn right entering Schechen.*

Open: All Year. **Site:** 6HEC **Prices:** 19.40 **Facilities:** **Services:** **Leisure:** L **Off-site:**

SEEFELD BAYERN

Strandbad Pilsensee

Graf Toerringstr 11, 82229

08152 7232 08152 78473

e-mail: campingplatz@toerring-seefeld.de

web: www.schloss-seefeld.de

Within easy reach of the A8 and A96 at the centre of the Bavarian five lake area.

dir: *S towards Pilsensee.*

GPS: 48.0312, 11.1981

Open: All Year. **Site:** 10HEC **For hire:** **Prices:** 19.89 **Facilities:** Wi-fi Play Area **Services:** **Leisure:** L **Off-site:**

SOMMERACH AM MAIN BAYERN

Katzenkopf am See

97334

09381 9215 09381 6028

web: www.camping-katzenkopf.de

On level ground beside the river Main, not far from the village. The site has good recreational facilities, pitches divided by bushes, and clean washrooms.

dir: *A3 exit Kitzingen-Schwarzach-Volkach for Volkach after 4km follow signs to Sommerach, then follow camping signs.*

GPS: 49.8258, 10.2005

Open: Apr-28 Oct **Site:** 7HEC **Prices:** 17.40-18.20 **Facilities:** Play Area **Services:** **Leisure:** L R **Off-site:** P

STADTSTEINACH BAYERN

Stadtsteinach

Badstr 5, 95346

09225 800394

e-mail: info@camping-stadtsteinach.de

web: www.camping-stadtsteinach.de

Terraced site on south-eastern facing slope with a view over the town and surrounding hills.

dir: *Via Badstr.*

Open: All Year. **Site:** 3.8HEC **Facilities:** **Services:** **Off-site:** P

TETTENHAUSEN — BAYERN

Gut Horn

83329

☎ 08681 227 ▤ 08681 4282

e-mail: info@gut-horn.de

web: www.gut-horn.de

Quiet site sheltered by forest in a central location, divided into pitches, on lake shore.

dir: *SE on Wagingersee.*

GPS: 47.9464, 12.7561

Open: Mar-Nov **Site:** 5HEC **For hire:** **Prices:** 20.50-22 **Facilities:** Wi-fi (charged) Play Area **Services:** **Leisure:** L **Off-site:**

TITTMONING — BAYERN

Seebauer

Furth 9, 84529

☎ 08683 1216 ▤ 08683 7175

e-mail: info@camping-seebauer.de

web: www.camping-seebauer.de

On meadow with a few terraces. In a quiet situation near a farm, beside a lake overlooking the Bavarian and Austrian Alps.

dir: *3km NW towards Burghausen.*

GPS: 48.0727, 12.7394

Open: 15 Apr-Sep **Site:** 2.3HEC **Prices:** 19.50 **Facilities:** Wi-fi (charged) Play Area **Services:** **Leisure:** L P **Off-site:** R

TRAUSNITZ — BAYERN

Trausnitz

92555

☎ 09655 1304 ▤ 09655 1304

web: www.camping-trausnitz.de

Wooded surroundings on the shores of a lake with modern facilities.

dir: *A93 exit Pfreimd.*

Open: All Year. **Site:** 3.5HEC **Facilities:** **Services:** **Leisure:** L R

VELBURG — BAYERN

Am Hauenstein

Seestr 9-11, 92355

☎ 09182 454 ▤ 09182 902251

e-mail: campingamhauenstein@t-online.de

web: www.campingamhauenstein.de

A well-appointed site, lies on several terraces with generous spaces enjoying the Jura scenery.

dir: *A3 exit Velburg, S signed Naturbad & Camping.*

GPS: 49.2172, 11.6686

Open: All Year. **Site:** 5HEC **Prices:** 18.40-19.40 **Facilities:** Play Area **Services:** **Off-site:** L P

VIECHTACH — BAYERN

Knaus Campingpark Viechtach

Waldfrieden 22, 94234

☎ 09942 1095 ▤ 09942 902222

e-mail: viechtach@knauscamp.de

web: www.knauscamp.de

Site on slightly undulating meadow, divided by rows of trees. The site has modern installations.

dir: *Off Freibad Viechtach onto B85, signed.*

Open: 16 Dec-3 Nov **Site:** 5.7HEC **For hire:** **Facilities:** **Services:** **Leisure:** P

WAGING — BAYERN

Strandcamping

Am See 1, 83329

☎ 08681 552 ▤ 08681 45010

e-mail: info@strandcamp.de

web: www.strandcamp.de

Extensive, level grassland site divided in two by access road to neighbouring sailing club. The site lies near the Strandbad and Kurhaus bathing area and spa, and the Casino. There is a Kneipp (hydrotherapeutic) pool in the camp.

dir: *Signed to Strandbad bathing area.*

Open: Mar-Oct **Site:** 34HEC **For hire:** **Facilities:** Wi-fi (charged) Kids' Club Play Area **Services:** **Leisure:** L

GERMANY

WALTENHOFEN BAYERN

Insel-Camping am See Allgäu

87448

☎ 08379 881 🖹 08379 7308

e-mail: info@insel-camping.de

web: www.insel-camping.de

A well-equipped site beside the lake with access to ski slopes.

dir: *A7 exit onto 980 towards Waltenhofen. From Waltenhofen take OA22 towards Memhölz, then left to site.*

GPS: 47.6403, 10.2786

Open: All Year. **Site:** 1.6HEC **Prices:** 16-19 **Facilities:** Wi-fi (charged) Play Area **Services:** **Leisure:** L **Off-site:** P R

WEISSACH BAYERN

Wallberg

Rainerweg 10, 83700

☎ 08022 5371 🖹 08022 670274

e-mail: campingplatz-wallberg@web.de

web: www.campingplatz-wallberg.de

This well-kept site lies on a level meadow with a few trees, beside a stream.

dir: *B318 from Gmund to Tegernsee, Bad Wiessee to Weissach, continue 9km.*

Open: All Year. **Site:** 3HEC **For hire:** **Facilities:** **Services:** **Leisure:** R **Off-site:** L P

WEISSENSTADT BAYERN

Weissenstadt

Badstr 91, 95163

☎ 09253 288 🖹 09253 8507

e-mail: whuettel-stadtbad@t-online.de

web: www.campingplatz-weissenstadt.de

This municipal site is in close proximity to a swimming pool and a lake, so offering numerous sports facilities.

dir: *1km NW of town.*

Open: All Year. **Site:** 1.7HEC **Facilities:** **Services:** **Leisure:** L P **Off-site:**

WERTACH BAYERN

Grüntensee-International

Grüntenseestr 41, 87497

☎ 08365 375 🖹 08365 1221

e-mail: info@camping-gruentensee.de

web: www.camping-gruentensee.de

A modern site beside Lake Grünten in the middle of the lovely Allgäuer mountain landscape.

dir: *From Kempten, turn right entering Nesselwang-Werlach & signed.*

Open: All Year. **Site:** 5HEC **Facilities:** Play Area **Services:** **Leisure:** L

ZWIESEL BAYERN

Ferienpark Arber

Waldesruhweg 34, 94227

☎ 09922 802595 🖹 09922 802594

e-mail: info@ferienpark-arber.de

web: www.ferienpark-arber.de

A modern family site, in the middle of a nature reserve in the Bavarian forest.

Open: All Year. **Site:** 16HEC **For hire:** **Prices:** 26-28 **Facilities:** Wi-fi Kids' Club Play Area **Services:** **Off-site:** P

SOUTH WEST

ABTSGMÜND BADEN-WÜRTTEMBERG

Hammerschmiede-See

Hammerschmiede 2, Pommertsweiler, 73453

☎ 07963 369 🖹 07963 840032

e-mail: hug.hammerschmiede@t-online.de

web: www.hug-hammerschmiede.de

A terraced site in a wooded setting beside the lake. Partly divided into pitches with concrete paths.

dir: *From Abtsgmünd for 3km then N to Pommertsweiler, signed.*

Open: May-Sep **Site:** 5HEC **Prices:** 11.10-13.10 **Facilities:** Play Area **Services:** **Leisure:** L **Off-site:**

GERMANY

ACHERN BADEN-WÜRTTEMBERG

Staedtischer Campingplatz am Achernsee

Am Achernsee 8, 77855
07841 25253 07841 508835
e-mail: camping@achern.de
web: www.achern.de
A family site close to attractive lake with bathing.
Open: All Year. **Site:** 6.5HEC **Facilities:** Play Area **Services:** **Leisure:** L
Off-site: P

ALPIRSBACH BADEN-WÜRTTEMBERG

Camping Alpirsbach

Grezenbühler Weg 18, 72275
07444 6313 07444 917815
e-mail: info@camping-alpirsbach.de
web: www.camping-alpirsbach.de
Quiet, family friendly site, ideal for hiking and cycling in the surrounding countryside. Fishing is available, along with table tennis and cycle hire.
Open: All Year. **Site:** 1.2HEC **For hire:** **Facilities:** Wi-fi Play Area **Services:**

ALTNEUDORF BADEN-WÜRTTEMBERG

Steinachperle

69250
06228 467 06228 8568
e-mail: campingplatz-steinachperle@t-online.de
The site lies in the narrow shady valley of the River Steinach.
dir: *Next to Gasthaus zum Pflug on outskirts of Altneudorf.*
Open: Apr-Sep **Site:** 3.5HEC **Facilities:** **Services:** **Leisure:** R

BADENWEILER BADEN-WÜRTTEMBERG

Badenweiler

Weilertalstr 73, 79410
07632 1550 07632 5268
e-mail: info@camping-badenweiler.de
web: www.camping-badenweiler.de
Level meadowland site surrounded by beautiful Black Forest scenery. Good facilities for local walking.
dir: *A5 exit Neuenburg.*
Open: 16 Jan-14 Dec **Site:** 1.6HEC **For hire:**
Prices: 21.43-29.10 Mobile home hire 329.40-354 **Facilities:** Wi-fi (charged) Play Area **Services:** **Leisure:** P

BUCHHORN BEI ÖHRINGEN BADEN-WÜRTTEMBERG

Seewiese

Seestr 11, 74629
07941 61568 07941 38527
e-mail: campingseewiese@t-online.de
web: www.camping-seewiese.de
A well-equipped site on a meadow beside a lake with fine views of the surrounding mountains. Good recreational facilities.
dir: *7km S of Öhringen via Pfedelbach.*
Open: All Year. **Site:** 5.5HEC **Facilities:** Play Area **Services:** **Leisure:** L P

BÜHL BADEN-WÜRTTEMBERG

Adam

Campingstr 1, 77185
07223 23194 07223 8982
e-mail: info@campingplatz-adam.de
web: www.campingplatz-adam.de
On level grassland, by lake.
dir: *A5 exit Bühl, 1km towards Lichtenau.*
Open: All Year. **Site:** 15HEC **For hire:**
Prices: 18.80-26.30 **Facilities:** Wi-fi (charged) Play Area **Services:** **Leisure:** L
Off-site: P

CREGLINGEN BADEN-WÜRTTEMBERG

Camping Romantische Strasse

97993
07933 20289 07933 990019
e-mail: camping.hausotter@web.de
web: www.camping-romantische-strasse.de
The site lies on the southern outskirts of Münster and is divided into pitches. Sanitary facilities include individual washing cubicles.
dir: *From Bad Mergentheim or Rothenburg/Tauber onto Romantic road to Creglingen, turn S for 3km to Münster.*
Open: 15 Mar-15 Nov **Site:** 6HEC **For hire:**
Facilities: Wi-fi (charged) Play Area **Services:** **Leisure:** P R **Off-site:** L

GERMANY

DINGELSDORF BADEN-WÜRTTEMBERG

Fliesshorn

78465

07533 5262

e-mail: info@fliesshorn.de

web: www.fliesshorn.de

At a farm, on meadowland with fine trees.

dir: *In town turn off Stadd-Dettingen road & signed NW for 1.3km.*

Open: Apr-3 Oct **Site:** 5HEC **Facilities:** **Services:** **Off-site:** L S

DONAUESCHINGEN BADEN-WÜRTTEMBERG

Riedsee Camping

78166

0771 5511 0771 15138

e-mail: info@riedsee-camping.de

web: www.riedsee-camping.de

Level meadow on lakeside. Kids' club available in July and August.

dir: *A81 exit Geisingen, B31 towards Pfohren, 13km left, continue 1km.*

Open: All Year. **Site:** 8HEC **Facilities:** Wi-fi (charged) Kids' Club Play Area **Services:** **Leisure:** L

ELLWANGEN-JAGST BADEN-WÜRTTEMBERG

AZUR Ellwangen

Rotenbacherstr 45, 73479

07961 7921 07961 562330

e-mail: ellwangen@azur-camping.de

web: www.azur-camping.de/ellwangen

A modern site with good facilities in a wooded loaction on the banks of the River Jagst.

Open: Apr-Oct **Site:** 3.5HEC **Facilities:** **Services:** **Leisure:** R **Off-site:** L P

ERPFINGEN BADEN-WÜRTTEMBERG

AZUR Rosencamping Schwäbische Alb

72820

07128 466 07128 30137

e-mail: info@azur-camping.de

web: www.azur-camping.de

Extensive family site with an emphasis on child care in a beautiful area.

dir: *From Reutlingen on B312 SE to Grooengstingen, then S on Schwabische Albstr (B313) for 3.5km to Haid, right to Erpfingen, site on W outskirts.*

Open: All Year. **Site:** 9HEC **For hire:** **Prices:** 18-22.50 Mobile home hire 294-616 **Facilities:** Wi-fi (charged) Play Area **Services:** **Leisure:** P **Off-site:** L

ETTENHEIM BADEN-WÜRTTEMBERG

Oase

77955

07822 445918 07822 445919

e-mail: info@campingpark-oase.de

web: www.campingpark-oase.de

Wooded location with modern facilities close to the Black Forest.

dir: *A5 exit Ettenheim.*

Open: Etr-5 Oct **Site:** 5HEC **Prices:** 21-23 **Facilities:** Wi-fi (charged) Play Area **Services:** **Off-site:** P

FREIBURG IM BREISGAU BADEN-WÜRTTEMBERG

Breisgau-Silbersee

Seestr 20, 79108

07665 2346 07665 2346

Extensive level grassland site on outskirts of town. Section reserved for campers with dogs.

dir: *Autobahn exit Freiburg Nord, site 0.5km E.*

Open: All Year. **Site:** 18HEC **Prices:** 19.50 **Facilities:** Play Area **Services:** **Leisure:** L **Off-site:**

Camping am Möslepark

Waldseestr 77, 79117

0761 7679333 0761 7679336

e-mail: information@camping-freiburg.com

web: www.camping-freiburg.com

On outskirts of town near Busse's Waldschänke inn.

dir: *Right after town hall over railway & Waldseestr towards Littenweiler.*

Open: 20 Mar-28 Oct **Site:** 0.7HEC **For hire:** **Prices:** 20-21 **Facilities:** Wi-fi Play Area **Services:** **Off-site:** L P R

GERMANY

FREUDENSTADT BADEN-WÜRTTEMBERG

Langenwald

Strassburgerstr 167, 72250

☎ 07441 2862 📠 07441 2893

e-mail: info@camping-langenwald.de

web: www.camping-langenwald.de

The site consists of several sections and lies next to a former mill beside the River Forbach.

dir: *4km W of Freudenstadt below B28.*

Open: Apr-Nov **Site:** 2HEC **Prices:** 24.50 **Facilities:** Wi-fi Play Area **Services:** **Leisure:** P R

HALLWANGEN BADEN-WÜRTTEMBERG

Königskanzel

72280

☎ 07443 6730 📠 07443 4574

e-mail: info@camping-koenigskanzel.de

web: www.camping-koenigskanzel.de

Set on an elevated position in the centre of the Black Forest.

dir: *B28 from Freudenstadt towards Altensteig, past Hallwangen junct, signed on right.*

GPS: 48.4808, 8.5005

Open: All Year. **Site:** 6HEC **For hire:** **Prices:** 18.50-23.30 **Facilities:** Play Area **Services:** **Leisure:** P **Off-site:**

HAUSEN BADEN-WÜRTTEMBERG

Wagenburg

Kirchstr 24, 88637

☎ 07579 559

e-mail: info@camping-wagenburg.de

web: www.camping-wagenburg.de

On meadowland between the railway bank and the Danube. Site has spectacular view of surrounding landscape. Entrance through subway.

Open: 16 Apr-3 Oct **Site:** 1.2HEC **Prices:** 14.70-16.70 **Facilities:** **Services:** **Leisure:** R

HEIDELBERG BADEN-WÜRTTEMBERG

Heidelberg-Neckartal

Schlierbacher Landstr 151, 69118

☎ 06221 802506

e-mail: mail@camping-heidelberg.de

web: www.camping-heidelberg.de

Located on the river, 5 minutes by bus to the city centre.

Open: Apr-15 Oct **Site:** 3HEC **For hire:** **Prices:** 18.50-24 **Facilities:** **Services:** **Leisure:** R

HERBOLZHEIM BADEN-WÜRTTEMBERG

Herbolzheim

Im Laue 1, 79336

☎ 07643 1460 📠 07643 913382

e-mail: s.hugoschmidt@t-online.de

web: www.laue-camp.de

A pleasant rural setting with good facilities, a short distance from the Europa-Park Rust amusement park.

dir: *On A5 between Freiburg & Offenburg.*

Open: 15 Apr-3 Oct **Site:** 3.8HEC **Prices:** 23 **Facilities:** Wi-fi (charged) Play Area **Services:** **Off-site:** L P

HÖFEN AN DER ENZ BADEN-WÜRTTEMBERG

Quellgrund

75339

☎ 07081 6984 📠 07081 6984

Well-maintained municipal site on grassland between B294 and the River Enz.

dir: *B294 SW from Pforzheim to Quelle inn/fuel station at entrance to Höfen, turn right.*

Open: Nov-Sep **Site:** 3.6HEC **Facilities:** Play Area **Services:** **Leisure:** R **Off-site:** P

HORB BADEN-WÜRTTEMBERG

Schüttehof

72160

☎ 07451 3951 📠 07451 623215

e-mail: camping-schuettehof@t-online.de

web: www.camping-schuettehof.de

Situated on a flat mountain top at the forest edge and 1km from the historic village of Horb on Neckar – the Gate to the Black Forest.

dir: *From Horb towards Freudenstadt, 1.5km after town boundary turn towards stables & site, continue 1km.*

Open: All Year. **Site:** 6HEC **For hire:** **Prices:** 13.60-17 **Facilities:** Play Area **Services:** **Leisure:** P **Off-site:** R

GERMANY

ISNY — BADEN-WÜRTTEMBERG

Waldbad Camping Isny

Lohbauerstr 59-69, 88316

07562 2389 07562 2004

e-mail: info@waldbad-camping-isny.de

web: www.waldbad-camping-isny.de

Attractive wooded surroundings beside a lake.

dir: *Lindau-Kempten B12, exit Isny-Mitte.*

GPS: 47.6792, 10.0294

Open: All Year. **Site:** 4.2HEC **Prices:** 14-24 **Facilities:** Play Area **Services:** **Leisure:** L P **Off-site:**

KEHL — BADEN-WÜRTTEMBERG

Kehl-Strassburg

77694

07851 2603 07851 73076

web: www.campingplatz-kehl.de

Park-like site divided into separate sections for young campers, transit and holiday campers.

dir: *Turn left at Rhine dam on outskirts of town.*

Open: 15 Mar-Oct **Site:** 2.3HEC **Facilities:** **Services:** **Off-site:** P R

KIRCHBERG — BADEN-WÜRTTEMBERG

Christophorus

Werte 61, 88486

07354 663 07354 91314

e-mail: info@camping-christophorus.de

web: www.camping-christophorus.de

Completely enclosed, clean site.

dir: *A7 exit Illereichen Allenstadt to town centre & towards railway station.*

Open: All Year. **Site:** 9.2HEC **Facilities:** **Services:** **Leisure:** L P

KIRCHZARTEN — BADEN-WÜRTTEMBERG

Camping Kirchzarten

Diefenbacher Str 17, 79199

07661 9040910 07661 61624

e-mail: info@camping-kirchzarten.de

web: www.camping-kirchzarten.de

Extensive site with trees providing shade, at the entrance to Freiburg, in the heart of the Southern Black Forest. Kids' club available in summer.

dir: *8km E of Freiburg im Breisgau off B31.*

Open: All Year. **Site:** 5.9HEC **For hire:** **Prices:** 22.60-30.80 **Facilities:** Wi-fi (charged) Kids' Club Play Area **Services:** **Leisure:** P

KRESSBRONN — BADEN-WÜRTTEMBERG

Gohren am See

88079

07543 60590 07543 605929

e-mail: info@campingplatz-gohren.de

web: www.campingplatz-gohren.de

A large site beside the lake. Older parts of the site are divided by hedges and reserved for residential campers. The newer section has fewer bushes.

dir: *3km from Kressbronn, signed from B31.*

Open: 14 Mar-15 Oct **Site:** 38HEC **For hire:** **Facilities:** **Services:** **Leisure:** L **Off-site:** P

LAICHINGEN — BADEN-WÜRTTEMBERG

Heidehof

Heidehofstr 50, 89150

07333 6408 07333 21463

e-mail: info@heidehof.info

web: www.camping-heidehof.de

Well-cared for site on hillside with some tall firs. Divided by asphalt roads with a separate section for overnight campers.

dir: *A8 exit Merkingen, site 2km S via Machtolsheim.*

Open: All Year. **Site:** 25HEC **For hire:** **Prices:** 19-21 **Facilities:** Play Area **Services:** **Leisure:** P

LAUTERBURG — BADEN-WÜRTTEMBERG

Hirtenteich

Hasenweide 2, 73457

07365 296 07365 251

e-mail: camphirtenteich@aol.com

web: www.campingplatz-hirtenteich.de

This site lies on gently sloping terrain, near the Hirtenteich recreation area.

dir: *Off B29 in Essingen, S for 5km.*

Open: All Year. **Site:** 4HEC **For hire:** **Facilities:** Wi-fi (charged) **Services:** **Leisure:** P

GERMANY

LENZKIRCH BADEN-WÜRTTEMBERG

Kreuzhof

Bonndorfer Str 65, 79853

☎ 07653 700 🖹 07653 6623

e-mail: info@brauerei-rogg.de

web: www.brauerei-rogg.de

Grassland near former farm below the Rogg Brewery.

dir: *B317 from Titisee towards Schaffhausen, onto B315 to Lenzkirch, site 2km from centre.*

Open: All Year. **Site:** 2HEC **For hire:** **Facilities:** Wi-fi (charged) Play Area **Services:** **Leisure:** L P

LIEBELSBERG BADEN-WÜRTTEMBERG

Erbenwald

75387

☎ 07053 7382 🖹 07053 3274

e-mail: info@camping-erbenwald.de

web: www.camping-erbenwald.de

Pleasant site on edge of wood.

dir: *B463 S from Calw, 6km turn right just before Neubulach, continue N for 2km.*

GPS: 48.6772, 8.6891

Open: All Year. **Site:** 7.2HEC **For hire:** **Facilities:** Wi-fi (charged) Play Area **Services:** **Leisure:** P

LIEBENZELL, BAD BADEN-WÜRTTEMBERG

Bad-Liebenzell

Pforzheimerstr 34, 75378

☎ 07052 935680 🖹 07052 935681

e-mail: campingpark@abelundneff.de

web: www.campingpark-badliebenzell.de

Municipal site with trees, near tennis courts. Divided by hedges and asphalt roads.

dir: *B463 S from Pforzheim for 19km, left 500m before Bad Liebenzell to site beside River Nagold.*

Open: All Year. **Site:** 3HEC **For hire:** **Facilities:** **Services:** **Leisure:** P R **Off-site:**

MARKDORF BADEN-WÜRTTEMBERG

Wirthshof

88677

☎ 07544 96270 🖹 07544 962727

e-mail: info@wirthshof.de

web: www.wirthshof.de

Family friendly site offering a high standard of comfort and lots of activities.

Open: 15 Mar-3 Nov **Site:** 10HEC **For hire:** **Prices:** 25.20-33.70 **Facilities:** Play Area **Services:** **Leisure:** P **Off-site:** L

MÖRTELSTEIN BADEN-WÜRTTEMBERG

Germania

Mühlwiese 1, 06951

☎ 06262 1795 🖹 06262 1795

The site lies between the River Neckar and a wooded hillside.

dir: *B292 W towards Sinsheim, just after Oberigheim N onto narrow steep road into Neckar Valley.*

Open: 2 Apr-2 Oct **Site:** 0.8HEC **Facilities:** **Services:** **Leisure:** R **Off-site:**

MÜNSTERTAL BADEN-WÜRTTEMBERG

Münstertal

Dietzelbachstr 6, 79244

☎ 07636 7080 🖹 07636 7448

e-mail: info@camping-muenstertal.de

web: www.camping-muenstertal.de

Well equipped level, grassy site in pleasant location with fine views. Activities and film screenings for kids.

dir: *A5 exit Bad Krozingen, SE via Staufen, after 3km left, then right signed Münstertal.*

Open: All Year. **Site:** 7HEC **For hire:** **Prices:** 25.10-28.35 **Facilities:** Play Area **Services:** **Leisure:** P

MURRHARDT BADEN-WÜRTTEMBERG

Waldsee

Fornsbach, 71540

☎ 07192 6436 🖹 07192 935717

e-mail: camping-waldsee@t-online.de

web: www.campingplatz-waldsee-murrhardt.de

The site lies near Lake Waldsee. Asphalt paths and pitches, with gravel surface.

dir: *Murrhardt towards Fornsbach, site on E shore of lake.*

Open: All Year. **Site:** 2HEC **For hire:** **Facilities:** **Services:** **Leisure:** L

NEUENBURG BADEN-WÜRTTEMBERG

Gugel

Oberer Wald, 79395

☎ 07631 7719 🖹 07631 7719

e-mail: info@camping-gugel.de

web: www.camping-gugel.de

An extensive site with many entirely separate pitches. There is a restaurant, as well as an attractive swimming pool and beach bar. Kids' club at Easter and during summer holidays.

dir: *A5 exit Müllheim/Neuenburg, 3km to site.*

GPS: 47.7964, 7.5497

Open: All Year. **Site:** 12.8HEC **Prices:** 21.50-23.50 **Facilities:** Wi-fi Kids' Club Play Area **Services:** **Leisure:** P **Off-site:** L R

NUSSDORF BADEN-WÜRTTEMBERG

Nell

Zur Barbe 5, Bodensee, 88662

☎ 07551 4254 🖹 07551 944458

e-mail: info@campingplatz-nell.de

web: www.camping-nell.de

Located within an orchard between a farm and lakeside promenade. Small private beach.

dir: *Off B31.*

GPS: 47.7516, 9.1905

Open: Apr-20 Oct **Site:** 0.6HEC **Prices:** 19.80-21.60 **Facilities:** **Services:** **Leisure:** L **Off-site:** P

ÖSTRINGEN BADEN-WÜRTTEMBERG

Kraichgau Camping Wackerhof

76684

☎ 07259 361

e-mail: info@wackerhof.de

web: www.wackerhof.de

Between the Black Forest and Odenwald, a peaceful modern terraced site.

dir: *A5 exit Kronau/Bad Schönborn, B292 to Östringen. Campsite in 5km, follow signs.*

GPS: 49.2005, 8.7602

Open: 25 Mar-15 Oct **Site:** 3HEC **Prices:** 10 **Facilities:** **Services:** **Off-site:** P

PFORZHEIM BADEN-WÜRTTEMBERG

International Schwarzwald

Freibadweg 4, 75242

☎ 07234 6517 🖹 07234 5180

e-mail: fam.frech@t-online.de

web: www.camping-schwarzwald.de

Site on edge of wood with southerly aspect. Separate fields for residential, overnight and holiday campers.

dir: *S through Huchenfeld from Pforzheim to Schellbron (15km).*

GPS: 48.8188, 8.7347

Open: All Year. **Site:** 4.5HEC **For hire:** **Facilities:** Play Area **Services:** **Leisure:** P **Off-site:** R

RHEINMÜNSTER BADEN-WÜRTTEMBERG

Freizeitcenter-Oberrhein

Stollhofen, 77836

☎ 07227 2500 🖹 07227 2400

e-mail: info@freizeitcenter-oberrhein.de

web: www.freizeitcenter-oberrhein.de

Modern leisure complex next to the Rhine.

dir: *10km from A5 Baden-Baden/Iffezheim exit from N or Bühl from S.*

GPS: 48.7736, 8.0402

Open: All Year. **Site:** 36HEC **For hire:** **Prices:** 19-29 Mobile home hire 455-623 **Facilities:** Wi-fi (charged) Kids' Club Play Area **Services:** **Leisure:** L

ROSENBERG BADEN-WÜRTTEMBERG

Hüttenhof

Hüttenhof 1, 73494

☎ 07963 203 🖹 07963 8418894

e-mail: rodolayh@t-online.de

web: www.waldcamp.de

Flat meadow on incline in quiet woodland area, next to large farm.

dir: *From Ellwangen N towards Crailsheim for 3km, turn W towards Adelmannsfelden & 8km turn N at Gaishardt.*

Open: 15 Apr-Oct **Site:** 4HEC **For hire:** **Prices:** 15.50 Mobile home hire 350 **Facilities:** Wi-fi (charged) Play Area **Services:** **Leisure:** L

GERMANY

ST PETER BADEN-WÜRTTEMBERG

Steingrübenhof

79271

☎ 07660 210 🖷 07660 1604

e-mail: info@camping-steingrubenhof.de

web: www.camping-steingrubenhof.de

On a level plateau, surrounded by delightful mountain scenery.

dir: *Via A5 & B294.*

Open: All Year. **Site:** 2HEC **For hire:** **Facilities:** Wi-fi (charged) **Services:** **Off-site:** P

SCHAPBACH BADEN-WÜRTTEMBERG

Alisehof

77776

☎ 07839 203 🖷 07839 1263

e-mail: info@camping-online.de

web: www.camping-online.de

The site lies on well-kept ground with several terraces and is separated from the road by the River Wolfach.

dir: *Off B924 in Wolfach at Kinzighbrücke, then 8km N to Schapbach, site 1km N of village.*

GPS: 48.3833, 8.2997

Open: All Year. **Site:** 3HEC **For hire:** **Prices:** 17.20-22.90 Mobile home hire 295 **Facilities:** Wi-fi (charged) Play Area **Services:** **Leisure:** R **Off-site:** L P

SCHILTACH BADEN-WÜRTTEMBERG

Schiltach

77761

☎ 07836 7289 🖷 07836 7466

e-mail: info@campingplatz-schiltach.de

web: www.campingplatz-schiltach.de

The site lies on meadowland on the banks of the River Kinzig and is well-placed for excursions.

Open: 5 Apr-7 Oct **Site:** 3.6HEC **For hire:** **Prices:** 16.60 Mobile home hire 251 **Facilities:** Play Area **Services:** **Leisure:** R **Off-site:** P

SCHÖMBERG BADEN-WÜRTTEMBERG

Höhen-Camping-Langenbrand

Schömberger Str 32, 75328

☎ 07084 6131 🖷 07084 931435

e-mail: info@hoehencamping.de

web: www.hoehencamping.de

Located at the edge of the Black Forest, ideal for exploring the area and surrounding hiking trails.

Open: All Year. **Site:** 1.6HEC **For hire:** **Facilities:** **Services:** **Off-site:**

SCHUSSENRIED, BAD BADEN-WÜRTTEMBERG

Reiterhof von Steinhausen

Reiterhof, 88427

☎ 07583 3060 🖷 07583 1004

e-mail: heikeschmid@web.de

A pleasant rural setting.

dir: *Via B30 Ulm-Bad Waldsee.*

Open: All Year. **Site:** 1HEC **Facilities:** **Services:** **Off-site:** L P R

SCHWÄBISCH GMÜND BADEN-WÜRTTEMBERG

Schurrenhof

Rechberg, 73072

☎ 07165 8190 🖷 07165 1625

e-mail: info@schurrenhof.de

web: www.schurrenhof.de

The site lies in a beautiful setting on the edge of a forest, and has a lovely view of the surrounding countryside.

dir: *B29 S from Schwäbisch Gmünd, through Strassdorf & Rechberg towards Reichenbach on B10, turn towards Schurrenhof.*

Open: All Year. **Site:** 3HEC **For hire:** **Facilities:** **Services:** **Leisure:** P

SCHWÄBISCH HALL BADEN-WÜRTTEMBERG

Steinbacher See

Mühlsteige 26, 74523

☎ 0791 2984 🖷 0791 9462758

e-mail: thomas.seitel@t-online.de

web: www.camping-schwaebisch-hall.de

A modern site in the beautiful Kocher Valley. There are good sports facilities and many places of interest nearby, in the medieval town.

dir: *Via B14/19 to Steinbach.*

GPS: 49.0981, 9.7419

Open: Feb-Nov **Site:** 1.4HEC **Prices:** 18.30-22 **Facilities:** Wi-fi Play Area **Services:** **Off-site:**

GERMANY

STAUFEN — BADEN-WÜRTTEMBERG

Belchenblick

The Camping and Caravanning Club — The Friendly Club

Münstertaler Str 43, 79219

07633 7045 07633 7908

e-mail: info@camping-belchenblick.de

web: www.camping-belchenblick.de

Well-kept site on level ground.

C&CC Report *With a range of excellent facilities for a site of this size, plus the traditional buildings hung with flowers, this is a great base for visiting the Black Forest and for making day trips to Switzerland. Staufen and its castle are very pretty, but picturesque Freiburg is nearby too – if you brave the spiral steps up into the tower of its beautiful minster, the effort is well rewarded.*

dir: *Motorway exit Bad Krozingen/Staufen, site 4km SE.*

GPS: 47.8725, 7.7352

Open: All Year. **Site:** 2.4HEC **Facilities:** Wi-fi (charged) Kids' Club Play Area **Services:** **Leisure:** P R

STEINACH — BADEN-WÜRTTEMBERG

Kinzigtal

77790

07832 8122 07832 6619

e-mail: webmaster@campingplatz-kinzigtal.de

web: www.campingplatz-kinzigtal.de

Site on level meadowland with tall trees, situated next to the municipal heated swimming pool. Kids' club available in July and August.

dir: *Signed from Steinach.*

Open: All Year. **Site:** 2.6HEC **For hire:** **Facilities:** Wi-fi Kids' Club Play Area **Services:** **Off-site:** P R

STUTTGART — BADEN-WÜRTTEMBERG

Cannstatter Wasen

Mercedesstr 40, 70372

0711 556696 0711 557554

e-mail: info@campingplatz-stuttgart.de

web: www.campingplatz-stuttgart.de

Level site with tall poplar trees alongside the River Neckar.

dir: *Via Bad Cannstatt near sports stadium.*

GPS: 48.7938, 9.2186

Open: All Year. **Site:** 1.7HEC **Prices:** 20-23 **Facilities:** Wi-fi (charged) Play Area **Services:** **Off-site:** P R

TENGEN — BADEN-WÜRTTEMBERG

Hegau-Familien-Camping

An der Sonnenhalde 1, 78250

07736 92470 07736 9247124

e-mail: info@hegau-camping.de

web: www.hegau-camping.de

Quiet, peaceful location close to the Swiss border and with panoramic views. Large pitches. Facilities include an indoor swimming pool with steam bath, whirlpool and sauna.

dir: *10km from A81.*

GPS: 47.8236, 8.6536

Open: All Year. **Site:** 8.5HEC **For hire:** **Facilities:** Wi-fi Kids' Club Play Area **Services:** **Leisure:** L P

TITISEE-NEUSTADT — BADEN-WÜRTTEMBERG

Bankenhof

Bruderhalde 31a, 79822

07652 1351

e-mail: info@camping-bankenhof.de

web: www.camping-bankenhof.de

A family site in a wooded location close to the lake. Access road closed 22.00-06.00 hrs.

dir: *From Titisee signed Camping Platz.*

Open: All Year. **Site:** 3.5HEC **For hire:** **Facilities:** **Services:** **Leisure:** R **Off-site:** L

Bühlhof

Bühlhofweg 13, 79822

07652 1606 07652 1827

e-mail: hertha-jaeger@t-online.de

web: www.camping-buehlhof.de

Pleasant location on a hillside above a lake.

dir: *Signed from Titisee.*

Open: 15 Dec-Oct **Site:** 10HEC **Prices:** 17-20 **Facilities:** Wi-fi (charged) Play Area **Services:** **Off-site:** L P

Sandbank

79822

07651 8243 07651 8286

e-mail: info@camping-sandbank.com

web: www.camping-sandbank.com

Lakeside terrain landscaped with trees, upper part terraced.

dir: *From Titisee, N bank of lake, turn onto old Feldbergstr, left at SW end of lake onto private road through Camping Bankenhof (closed 22.00-06.00 hrs) to site, 0.7km on SE bank of lake.*

Open: Apr-20 Oct **Site:** 3HEC **Facilities:** **Services:** **Leisure:** L **Off-site:** P

Weiherhof am Titiseeufer

Bruderhalde 26, 79822

☎ 07652 1468 07652 1478

e-mail: kontakt@camping-titisee.de

web: www.camping-titisee.de

Mainly level site with trees, bordering on lake shore for some 400 metres.

dir: *Signed from Titisee.*

Open: May-Oct **Site:** 2HEC **For hire:** **Prices:** 24 **Facilities:** Wi-fi (charged) Kids' Club Play Area **Services:** **Leisure:** L **Off-site:** P R

TODTNAU **BADEN-WÜRTTEMBERG**

Camping Hochschwarzwald

79674

☎ 07671 1288 07671 9999943

e-mail: camping.hochschwarzwald@web.de

web: www.camping-hochschwarzwald.de

Terraced site, partially grassland, by ski-lift.

dir: *6km NW of Todtnau.*

Open: All Year. **Site:** 2.5HEC **Prices:** 18 **Facilities:** Play Area **Services:** **Leisure:** R

TÜBINGEN **BADEN-WÜRTTEMBERG**

Neckarcamping Tübingen

Rappenberghalde 61, 72070

☎ 07071 43145 07071 793391

e-mail: mail@neckarcamping.de

web: www.neckarcamping.de

A quiet site directly on the banks of the River Neckar and near to the old town. Leisure facilities include fishing, table tennis, punting trips and bike hire.

dir: *From Europastr (Tübingen-Rottenburg) turn off at railway station onto Derendinger Allee (site signed).*

GPS: 48.5100, 9.0352

Open: 31 Mar-Oct **Site:** 1HEC **For hire:** **Prices:** 20-22.90 Mobile home hire 336 **Facilities:** Wi-fi Play Area **Services:** **Leisure:** R **Off-site:** L P

ÜBERLINGEN **BADEN-WÜRTTEMBERG**

Überlingen

Bahnhofstr 57, 88662

☎ 07551 64583 07551 945895

e-mail: info@campingpark-ueberlingen.de

web: www.campingpark-ueberlingen.de

The site lies on the western outskirts of the town, between the railway line and road on one side, and the concrete shore wall on the other. It is divided into several sections by low wooden barriers and has a very small beach.

dir: *Off B31 towards lake.*

Open: Apr-10 Oct **Site:** 3HEC **For hire:** **Facilities:** **Services:** **Leisure:** L **Off-site:** P

UHLDINGEN **BADEN-WÜRTTEMBERG**

Seeperle

Seefelden Hausnr 6, 88690

☎ 07556 5454 07556 966221

e-mail: info@camping-seeperle.de

web: www.camping-seeperle.de

This site has some large trees along the shore of the lake and a landing stage.

dir: *Off B31 at Oberuhldingen towards Seefelden, site 1km.*

Open: 15 Apr-15 Sep **Site:** 0.7HEC **Facilities:** **Services:** **Leisure:** L **Off-site:** P

WALDKIRCH **BADEN-WÜRTTEMBERG**

Elztalblick

79183

☎ 07681 4212 07681 4213

e-mail: eltztalblick@t-online.de

web: www.camping-elztalblick.de

A small site with terraced pitches in the heart of the Black Forest.

dir: *Autobahn exit Waldkirch Ost, signed for 3km.*

Open: 15 Apr-20 Oct **Site:** 2HEC **Prices:** 25.20 **Facilities:** Wi-fi Play Area **Services:** **Off-site:** P

GERMANY

WALDSHUT BADEN-WÜRTTEMBERG

Rhein-Camping

Jahnweg 22, 79761
07751 3152 07751 3252
e-mail: info@rheincamping.de
web: www.rheincamping.de
Wooded surroundings beside the River Rhine.
dir: *1km from Waldshut towards Swiss border.*
GPS: 47.6112, 8.2253
Open: All Year. **Site:** 8HEC **For hire:**
Prices: 17.60-21.60 **Facilities:** **Services:** **Leisure:** R **Off-site:** P

WERTHEIM BADEN-WÜRTTEMBERG

AZUR Wertheim

An den Christwiesen 35, 97877
09342 83111 09342 83171
e-mail: wertheim@azur-camping.de
web: www.azur-camping.de/wertheim
Site lies on a level, long stretch of meadowland on the banks of the River Main next to a swimming pool.
dir: *Towards Miltenberg, 1km right at fuel station towards site.*
Open: Apr-25 Oct **Site:** 7HEC **Facilities:**
Services: **Leisure:** R **Off-site:** P

Wertheim-Bettingen

Geiselbrunnweg 31, Bettingen, 97877
09342 7077 09342 913077
Peaceful wooded area beside a river.
dir: *A3 exit 66 Wertheim/Lengfurt, site 1km.*
Open: Apr-Oct **Site:** 7.5HEC **Facilities:** Wi-fi Play Area **Services:** **Leisure:** R

WILDBAD IM SCHWARZWALD BADEN-WÜRTTEMBERG

Kleinenzhof

75323
07081 3435 07081 3770
e-mail: info@kleinenzhof.de
web: www.kleinenzhof.de
A family site with modern facilities.
dir: *Via B294 3km S of Calmbach.*
GPS: 48.7378, 8.5764
Open: All Year. **Site:** 8HEC **For hire:**
Prices: 26.60-27.90 **Facilities:** Wi-fi (charged) Play Area **Services:** **Leisure:** P R
Off-site:

BERLIN AND EASTERN PROVINCES

ALT SCHWERIN MEKLENBURG-VORPOMMERN

See

An der Schaftannen Nr 1, 17214
039932 42073 039932 42072
e-mail: info@camping-alt-schwerin.de
web: www.camping-alt-schwerin.de
A pleasant lakeside site with modern facilities situated north of the lake.
dir: *Via B192.*
GPS: 53.5229, 12.3184
Open: Apr-Oct **Site:** 3.6HEC **For hire:**
Prices: 22.50-28.50 **Facilities:** Wi-fi Kids' Club Play Area **Services:** **Leisure:** L

BODSTEDT MECKLENBURG-VORPOMMERN

Bodstedt

Damm 43, 18356
038231 4226 038231 4820
A pleasant site on the shore of the Saaler Bodden with good boating facilities.
dir: *B105 exit Fuhlendorf/Barth.*
Site: 3.5HEC **For hire:** **Prices:** 14-17.50
Facilities: Wi-fi Play Area **Off-site:** L R

CAPUTH BRANDENBURG

Himmelreich

Wentorfinsel, Geltow, 14542
033209 70475 033209 20100
e-mail: himmelreich@campingplatz-caputh.de
web: www.campingplatz-caputh.de
An ideal site for enjoying watersports, with boat hire and moorings available. Also sailing, fishing and beach access.
Open: All Year. **Site:** 7.5HEC **Facilities:**
Services: **Leisure:** L R

DRESDEN SACHSEN

Wostra

An der Wostra 7, 01259
0351 2013254 0351 2025448
e-mail: cp-wostra@freenet.de
web: www.dresden.de
Site is close to river and motorway. Good facilities and amenities for all the family.
dir: *B172 towards Heidenau, site signed.*
Open: Apr-Oct **Site:** 1.8HEC **Facilities:**
Services: **Off-site:** L P

GERMANY

FALKENBERG BRANDENBURG

Erholungsgebiet Kiebitz

Hörsteweg 2, 04895

035365 2135 035365 38533

e-mail: info@erholungsgebiet-kiebitz.de

web: www.erholungsgebiet-kiebitz.de

Large leisure complex on Lake Kiebitz with 1.35km of beach. Bikes and boats are available for rental. There is a nature reserve to explore.

dir: *E55 exit Duben, B87/B101 for Herzberg.*

Open: Apr-Oct **Site:** 5.2HEC **For hire:** **Facilities:** **Services:** **Leisure:** L **Off-site:**

GROSS-LEUTHEN BRANDENBURG

EuroCamp Spreewaldtor

Neue Str 1, Märkische Heide, 15913

035471 303 035471 310

e-mail: info@eurocamp-spreewaldtor.de

web: www.eurocamp-spreewaldtor.de

On a level meadow beside the Gross Leuthener See.

dir: *N of town off B179.*

GPS: 52.0481, 14.0392

Open: All Year. **Site:** 9HEC **For hire:** **Facilities:** Wi-fi (charged) Play Area **Services:** **Off-site:** L

GROSS-QUASSOW MECKLENBURG-VORPOMMERN

Camping-und Ferienpark Havelberge

17237

03981 24790 03981 247999

e-mail: info@haveltourist.de

web: www.haveltourist.de

A rural setting on the lake shore with wooded, hilly terraces.

dir: *1.5km S of town, signed.*

Open: All Year. **Site:** 24HEC **For hire:** **Prices:** 12.90-23 **Facilities:** Wi-fi (charged) Kids' Club Play Area **Services:** **Leisure:** L

KELBRA THÜRINGEN

Seecamping Kelbra

Lange Str 150, 06537

034651 45290 034651 45292

e-mail: info@seecampingkelbra.de

web: www.seecampingkelbra.de

On the shore of a 2.5 hectare lake with leisure facilities including sailing/surfing lessons and cycle hire.

Open: All Year. **Site:** 6.5HEC **For hire:** **Prices:** 15.50-18.50 **Facilities:** Wi-fi (charged) Play Area **Services:** **Leisure:** L P **Off-site:**

KLADOW THÜRINGEN

DCC Else-Eckert-Platz

Krampnitzer Weg 111-117, 14089

030 3652797 030 3651245

e-mail: info@dccberlin.de

web: www.dccberlin.de

Large site in woodland close to the lake. Modern facilities.

dir: *B5 & B2 exit Berlin Spandau.*

GPS: 52.455, 13.1133

Open: All Year. **Site:** 7HEC **Facilities:** Play Area **Services:** **Off-site:** L R

KLEINMACHNOW BRANDENBURG

Yacht-Caravan-Club

Bäkehang 9a, 14532

033203 79684 033203 77913

e-mail: spandau@city-camping-berlin.de

web: www.city-camping-berlin.de

A riverside site with an hotel.

dir: *SW of town off A115*

Open: All Year. **Site:** 2.2HEC **For hire:** **Facilities:** Wi-fi (charged) Play Area **Services:** **Leisure:** R

GERMANY

KLEINRÖHRSDORF SACHSEN

LuxOase

Arnsdorfer Str 1, 01900
☎ 035952 56666 🖷 035952 56024
e-mail: info@luxoase.de
web: www.luxoase.de

A beautiful, peaceful location among meadows and woods, bordering a lake. Situated in the centre of the attractions of Dresden, Saxon Switzerland, Meissen and Upper Lusatia. New sanitary building and spa, plus four modern apartments to rent. Dogs must be kept on a lead.

C&CC Report *Few sites are so peaceful, friendly,homely, well-equipped or better at helping you get the most out of your stay. Thomas and Dagmar take you step-by-step through all the details, right down to roads, bus numbers, train stops, and times. The fantastic wellness centre opened in 2011, giving campers a wide choice of ways to unwind and relax. The excursions programme includes coach trips to Prague and Dresden, while Saxony itself offers the fantastic rock formations and forests of the area known as 'Saxon Switzerland', plus beautifully restored Dresden and Colditz Castle's escape museum.*

dir: *A4 exit Pulsnitz for Radeberg, 1km after Leppersdorf turn left.*

GPS: 51.1205, 13.9808

Open: All Year. **Site:** 7.2HEC **For hire:** **Prices:** 17-24 **Facilities:** Wi-fi (charged) Kids' Club Play Area **Services:** **Leisure:** L P

KLEINSAUBERNITZ SACHSEN

Olbasee

Olbaweg 16, 02694
☎ 035932 30232 🖷 035932 30886
e-mail: natur@campingplatz-olbasee.de
web: www.campingplatz-olbasee.de

A rural location on the Olbasee.

dir: *Via S109.*

Open: 16 Apr-17 Oct **Site:** 7HEC **For hire:** **Facilities:** **Services:** **Leisure:** L **Off-site:**

KÖNIGSTEIN SACHSEN

Königstein

Schandauer Str 25e, 01822
☎ 035021 68224
e-mail: camp.koenigstein@t-online.de
web: www.camping-koenigstein.de

On level ground in a wooded location with fine views of the surrounding mountains.

dir: *B172 within Königstein near Dresden.*

Open: Apr-Oct **Site:** 2.4HEC **For hire:** **Prices:** 17-23 **Facilities:** **Services:** **Leisure:** R **Off-site:** P

LASSAN MEKLENBURG-VORPOMMERN

Lassan

Garthof 5-6, 17440
☎ 038374 80373 🖷 038374 80373
e-mail: naturcampingplatzlassan@gmx.de
web: www.campingplatz-lassan.de

A pleasant site on the Achterwasser.

dir: *Via B110.*

Open: Apr-Sep **Site:** 1.8HEC **Facilities:** Play Area **Services:** **Leisure:** L R S **Off-site:** P

MÜHLBERG THÜRINGEN

Drei Gleichen

Am Gut Ringhofen, 99869
☎ 036256 22715 🖷 036256 86801
e-mail: service@campingplatz-muehlberg.de
web: www.campingplatz-muehlberg.de

Pleasant wooded surroundings.

dir: *A4 exit Wandersleben junct 43, Mühlberg signed.*

GPS: 50.8747, 10.8088

Open: Apr-Oct **Site:** 2.8HEC **Prices:** 16-22 **Facilities:** **Services:** **Off-site:** L P

NIESKY SACHSEN

Tonschächt

02902
☎ 03588 205771 🖷 03588 259315
e-mail: info@campingplatz-tonschacht.de
web: www.campingplatz-tonschacht.de

Surrounded by forest the site has a wide range of facilities and amenities for many activities. All pitches have electrical connection. Separate naturist area.

Open: 15 Apr-15 Oct **Site:** 15HEC **Facilities:** **Services:** **Leisure:** L **Off-site:**

GERMANY

NIEWISCH — BRANDENBURG

Schwielochsee-Camping Niewisch

Uferweg Nord 16, 15848

☎ 033676 5186 🖷 033676 5226

e-mail: camping.niewisch@freenet.de

web: www.camping-niewisch.de

A family site in pleasant wooded surroundings on the banks of the Schwielochsee.

Open: All Year. **Site:** 4.2HEC **For hire:** **Facilities:** Play Area **Services:** **Leisure:** L

PLÖTZKY — SACHSEN

Ferienpark Plötzky

Campingplatz Kleiner Waldsee 1, 39245

☎ 039200 50155 🖷 039200 76082

e-mail: info@ferienpark-ploetzky.de

web: www.ferienpark-ploetzky.de

Set in a wooded location beside a small lake with well-defined pitches close to the town of Schönebeck.

dir: *Access via A2 & B246.*

GPS: 52.0628, 11.8003

Open: All Year. **Site:** 12HEC **For hire:** **Facilities:** Wi-fi (charged) **Services:** **Leisure:** L

POTSDAM — BRANDENBURG

Sanssouci zu Potsdam/Berlin

An der Pirscheide 41, Templiner See, 14471

☎ 0331 9510988 🖷 0331 9510988

e-mail: info@camping-potsdam.de

web: www.camping-potsdam.de

Wooded surroundings close to Templiner See.

dir: *Signed from B1.*

GPS: 52.3617, 13.0069

Open: 30 Mar-3 Nov **Site:** 6HEC **For hire:** **Prices:** 33.90 **Facilities:** Wi-fi Play Area **Services:** **Leisure:** L R **Off-site:** P

REICHENBERG — SACHSEN

Bad Sonnenland

Dresdner Str 115, 01468

☎ 0351 8305495 🖷 0351 8305494

e-mail: info@bad-sonnenland.de

web: www.bad-sonnenland.de

A pleasant location beside the lake with modern facilities.

dir: *A4 exit Wilder Mann. 3km S of Moritzburg.*

Open: Apr-Oct **Site:** 18HEC **For hire:** **Prices:** 15.50-24.50 **Facilities:** Play Area **Services:** **Leisure:** L **Off-site:** P

SCHMÖCKWITZ — BERLIN

Campingplatz Krossinsee

Wernsdorfer Str 38, 12527

☎ 030 6758687 🖷 030 70761058

e-mail: info@campingplatz-krossinsee.de

web: www.campingplatz-krossinsee.de

Quiet grassy site on city outskirts.

dir: *27km SE of Berlin centre. From A10 W ring road exit 9 Niederlehme, in direction of Erkner (Wernsdorf), follow camping signs.*

Open: All Year. **Site:** **For hire:** **Facilities:** **Services:** **Leisure:** L **Off-site:**

ZINNOWITZ — MECKLENBURG-VORPOMMERN

Pommernland

Dr Wachsmann-Str 40, 17454

☎ 038377 40348 🖷 038377 40349

e-mail: camping-pommernland@m-vp.de

web: www.camping-pommernland.m-vp.de

Wooded surroundings on the coast.

dir: *Via B111.*

Open: All Year. **Site:** 7.7HEC **For hire:** **Facilities:** **Services:** **Leisure:** S **Off-site:** P

GERMANY

CENTRAL

ASBACHERHÜTTE — RHEINLAND-PFALZ

Harfenmühle

Harfenmühle 2, 55758

06786 7076 06786 7570

e-mail: mail@harfenmuehle.de

web: www.harfenmuehle.net

A quiet site, beautifully situated in the Fischbach Valley. Level grassland, partly terraced. Activities for children include gold digging and looking for gemstones, as well as a sports ground and three playgrounds.

dir: *3km NW of B327 towards Kempfeld.*

GPS: 49.8036, 7.2694

Open: All Year. **Site:** 6.2HEC **For hire:** **Prices:** 19 **Facilities:** Wi-fi (charged) Play Area **Services:** **Leisure:** L

ATTENDORN — NORDRHEIN-WESTFALEN

Biggesee-Waldenburg

57439

02722 95500 02722 955099

e-mail: info@camping-waldenburg.de

web: www.biggesee.com

Generously terraced recreational site on the northern shore of the Bigge reservoir, with adjoining public bathing area. Private sunbathing area.

dir: *A45/A4 exit Olpe then towards Attendorn.*

GPS: 51.1106, 7.9019

Open: Apr-Oct **Site:** 6.5HEC **For hire:** **Prices:** 20.70-23 **Facilities:** Wi-fi (charged) Play Area **Services:** **Leisure:** L **Off-site:** P

Hof Biggen

Finnentroper Str 131, 57439

02722 95530 02722 955366

e-mail: info@biggen.de

web: www.biggen.de

Well-equipped terraced site, surrounded by woodlands. Kids' club during regional holidays.

dir: *Atterdorn road to Ahauser reservoir, entrance near Haus am See inn.*

Open: All Year. **Site:** 18HEC **For hire:** **Prices:** 21 Mobile home hire 200-312 **Facilities:** Kids' Club Play Area **Services:** **Off-site:** L R

BALHORN — HESSEN

Erzeberg

34308

05625 5274 05625 7116

e-mail: info@campingplatz-erzeberg.de

web: www.campingplatz-erzeberg.de

Site lies on meadowland on slightly sloping ground above the village.

dir: *On B450 between Istha & Fritzlar.*

Open: All Year. **Site:** 5HEC **For hire:** **Prices:** 16 **Facilities:** Play Area **Services:** **Leisure:** P **Off-site:**

BARNTRUP — NORDRHEIN-WESTFALEN

Ferienpark Teutoburger Wald

Badeanstaltsweg 4, 32683

05263 2221 05263 956991

e-mail: info@ferienparkteutoburgerwald.de

web: www.ferienparkteutoburgerwald.de

A well-kept site next to an open-air swimming pool and kids' club available in summer months.

dir: *Signed from Barntrup on B66.*

Open: Apr-Oct **Site:** 2.4HEC **For hire:** **Facilities:** Wi-fi Kids' Club Play Area **Services:** **Leisure:** P **Off-site:**

BERNKASTEL-KUES — RHEINLAND-PFALZ

Kueser Werth

Am Hafen 2, 54470

06531 8200 06531 8282

web: www.camping-kueser-werth.de

Grassy site near Mosel and boating marina, with view of Landshut castle.

dir: *On S outskirts of town.*

Open: Apr-Oct **Site:** 2.2HEC **Facilities:** **Services:**

GERMANY

BIRKENFELD RHEINLAND-PFALZ

Campingpark Waldwiesen

55765

06782 5215 06782 5219

e-mail: info@waldwiesen.de

web: www.waldwiesen.de

A quiet, natural campsite in a wooded location, close to the lake.

dir: *Off B41 E of Birkenfeld, signed.*

GPS: 49.655, 7.1819

Open: Etr-15 Oct **Site:** 9.5HEC **For hire:** **Prices:** 16.75-20.25 **Facilities:** Wi-fi (charged) Play Area **Services:** **Leisure:** L **Off-site:** P R

BÖMIGHAUSEN HESSEN

Barenberg

34508

05632 1044 05632 1044

e-mail: berthold.trachte@t-online.de

Beautifully terraced site at Neerdar reservoir.

dir: *Via B251 between Korbach & Brilon.*

Open: All Year. **Site:** 0.5HEC **Facilities:** **Services:** **Leisure:** L R

BRAUNFELS HESSEN

Braunfels

Am Weiherstieg 2, 35619

06442 4366 06442 6895

A terraced site surrounded by a pine forest and deciduous trees. Separate meadow for touring campers.

dir: *A45 exit Limburg, B49 towards town.*

Open: All Year. **Site:** 5.2HEC **For hire:** **Facilities:** **Services:** **Off-site:** P

BREISIG, BAD RHEINLAND-PFALZ

Rheineck

53498

02633 95645 02633 472008

e-mail: info@camping-rheineck.de

web: www.camping-rheineck.de

A quiet, well-kept site on a level meadow in Vinxtbach Valley.

dir: *B9 NW from Koblenz to Bad Breisig, turn left, over railway & continue 400m.*

Open: All Year. **Site:** 6HEC **Facilities:** Play Area **Services:** **Leisure:** R **Off-site:** P

BRUNGERSHAUSEN HESSEN

Auenland

Zum Dammhammer, 35094

06420 7172 06420 822846

e-mail: info@campingplatz-auenland.de

web: www.campingplatz-auenland.de

Attractive location in a protected area at the foot of the Rimberg mountains. Large variety of bird and plant life.

dir: *A2/A3 from N to A45 exit Dillenburg towards Biedenkopf on B62. Exit Brungershausen, site signed.*

Open: All Year. **Site:** 2.4HEC **Facilities:** **Services:** **Leisure:** P R **Off-site:**

BULLAY RHEINLAND-PFALZ

Bären-Camp

Am Moselufer 1/3, 56859

06542 900097 06542 900098

e-mail: info@baeren-camp.de

web: www.baeren-camp.de

On a level meadow beside the Mosel, next to the football ground with good views.

dir: *Via B49 Cochem-Alf, over bridge, through village, signed.*

Open: Etr-1 Nov **Site:** 1.8HEC **Facilities:** **Services:** **Leisure:** R **Off-site:** P

COCHEM RHEINLAND-PFALZ

Altes Forsthaus

Haupstr 2, Landkern, 56814

02671 8701 02671 8722

e-mail: info@landkern.com

web: www.landkern.com

The partly terraced site lies near woodland in the valley below Landkern.

dir: *A48 exit Kaisersesch, S to Landkern, site signed.*

Open: All Year. **Site:** 10HEC **Facilities:** **Services:** **Leisure:** P **Off-site:**

Mosel-Camping-Cochem

Stadionstr, 56812

02671 4409 02671 910719

e-mail: info@campingplatz-cochem.de

web: www.campingplatz-cochem.de

Level meadowland with trees beside the Mosel, downstream from the swimming pool and sports ground.

dir: *From B49 in Cochem follow Freizeitzentrum signs, over downstream bridge, left after swimming pool.*

Open: Etr-Oct **Site:** 2.8HEC **For hire:** **Facilities:** **Services:** **Leisure:** R **Off-site:** P

GERMANY

DAHN — RHEINLAND-PFALZ

Büttelwoog

66994

☎ 06391 5622 06391 5326

e-mail: buettelwoog@t-online.de

web: www.camping-buettelwoog.de

Site lies in a magnificent pine forest, partly surrounded by steep hills and rocks. Section reserved for young people with tents.

dir: *B10 from Pirmasens to Hinterweidenthal then B427 S to Dahn.*

Open: Mar-10 Nov **Site:** 6HEC **Prices:** 20 **Facilities:** Wi-fi Play Area **Services:** **Off-site:** P

DATTELN — NORDRHEIN-WESTFALEN

Erholungspark Wehlingsheide

Schorfheide 3, 45711

☎ 02363 34503 02363 34592

e-mail: info@wehlingsheide.de

web: www.wehlingsheide.de

Pitches are separated by hedges or in a large meadow. Features of the site are a pond, waterfall and swimming area with a sandy beach.

GPS: 51.6822, 7.3058

Open: All Year. **Site:** 60HEC **For hire:** **Prices:** 18 Mobile home hire 320 **Facilities:** Play Area **Services:**

DAUSENAU — RHEINLAND-PFALZ

Lahn-Beach

Hallgarten 16, 56132

☎ 02603 13964 02603 919935

e-mail: info@canutours.de

web: www.campingplatz-dausenau.de

A riverside site in a wooded setting.

GPS: 50.3277, 7.7552

Open: Apr-Oct **Site:** 3HEC **Prices:** 16-20 **Facilities:** Wi-fi (charged) Play Area **Services:** **Leisure:** R **Off-site:**

DIEZ — RHEINLAND-PFALZ

Oranienstein

Strandbadweg 1a, 65582

☎ 06432 2122 06432 924193

e-mail: info@camping-diez.de

web: www.camping-diez.de

On a meadow beside the River Lahn, below Schloss Oranienstein.

dir: *From N A3 exit Diez (from S exit Limburg-Nord), onto B54 for 7km.*

Open: Apr-Oct **Site:** 7HEC **For hire:** **Prices:** 15.90-16.90 **Facilities:** Wi-fi (charged) Play Area **Services:** **Leisure:** R **Off-site:** L

DORSEL AN DER AHR — RHEINLAND-PFALZ

Stahlhütte

53533

☎ 02693 438 02693 511

web: www.campingplatz-stahlhuette.de

Site with individual pitches, on meadowland with trees near River Ahr.

dir: *Off B258 Aachen-Koblenz road.*

Open: All Year. **Site:** 7HEC **Prices:** 19 **Facilities:** Play Area **Services:** **Leisure:** R

DORTMUND — NORDRHEIN-WESTFALEN

Hohensyburg

Syburger Dorfstr 69, 44265

☎ 0231 774374 0231 7749554

e-mail: info@camping-hohensyburg.de

web: www.camping-hohensyburg.de

Terraced site on hilly grassland near Weitkamp inn.

dir: *Via B54.*

Open: All Year. **Site:** 10HEC **Facilities:** **Services:** **Leisure:** L R

DREIEICH-OFFENTHAL — HESSEN

Offenthal

Bahnhofstr 77, 63303

☎ 06074 5629 06074 629133

e-mail: info@campingplatz-dreieich.de

web: www.campingplatz-dreieich.de

A well-equipped site in wooded surroundings.

dir: *Off B486 at Dreieich-Offenthal towards Dietzenbach.*

GPS: 49.9858, 8.7572

Open: All Year. **Site:** 3.2HEC **Prices:** 15-16 **Facilities:** Play Area **Services:** **Leisure:** P **Off-site:**

DROLSHAGEN — NORDRHEIN-WESTFALEN

Gut Kalberschnacke

Kalberschnacke 8, 57489
02763 7501 / 02763 7879
e-mail: camping-kalberschnacke@t-online.de
web: www.camping-kalberschnacke.de

Terraced site above the Bigge-Lister reservoir in wooded area.

dir: *A45 exit Drolshagen-Bergneustadt, site 4km NE.*

Open: All Year. **Site:** 13.5HEC **Facilities:** Play Area **Services:** **Off-site:** L

DÜLMEN — NORDRHEIN-WESTFALEN

Tannenwiese

Borkenbergestr 217, 48249
02594 991759
web: www.camping-tannenwiese.de

The site lies on meadowland in a well-wooded area, near the gliderdrome.

dir: *B51 from Recklinghausen to Hausdülmen, follow sign Segelflügplatz Borkenberge.*

Open: Mar-30 Oct **Site:** 3.7HEC **Prices:** 12.50-14 **Facilities:** Play Area **Services:** **Off-site:**

DÜRKHEIM, BAD — RHEINLAND-PFALZ

Knaus Bad Dürkheim

In den Almen 3, 67098
06322 61356 / 06322 8161
e-mail: badduerkheim@knauscamp.de
web: www.knauscamp.de

Lakeside site on level meadow between vineyards, adjoining a sportsfield.

dir: *Access from E outskirts of town. Turn N at railway viaduct, near fuel station.*

Open: Dec-Oct **Site:** 16.4HEC **For hire:** **Facilities:** **Services:** **Leisure:** L **Off-site:** P

DÜSSELDORF — NORDRHEIN-WESTFALEN

Unterbacher See

Kleiner Torfbruch 31, 40627
0211 8992038 / 0211 8929132
e-mail: service@unterbachersee.de
web: www.unterbachersee.de

Site on sloping grassland.

dir: *From Düsseldorf B326 to Erkrath exit, left by Unterbacher lake.*

Open: Apr-Oct **Site:** 6.5HEC **Facilities:** Play Area **Services:** **Leisure:** L **Off-site:**

EPPSTEIN — HESSEN

TaunusCamp

Bezirksstr 2, 65817
06198 7000 / 06198 7002
e-mail: info@taunuscamp.de
web: www.taunuscamp.de

Relaxing terraced site located in Taunus countryside, ideal for cycling and hiking.

dir: *E35 exit 46 onto B455.*

GPS: 50.1475, 8.3619

Open: All Year. **Site:** 7HEC **For hire:** **Facilities:** Play Area **Services:** **Off-site:** P

ESCHWEGE — HESSEN

Knaus Campingpark Eschwege

Am Werratalsee 2, 37269
05651 338883 / 05651 338884
e-mail: eschwege@knauscamp.de
web: www.knauscamp.de

Site beside the Werratalsee.

dir: *A7 exit Eschwege, signed.*

Open: 26 Mar-2 Nov **Site:** 6.8HEC **For hire:** **Facilities:** **Services:** **Leisure:** L **Off-site:**

ESSEN — NORDRHEIN-WESTFALEN

Essen-Werden

Im Lowental 67, Werden, 45239
0201 492978 / 0201 8496132
e-mail: stadtcamping-essen@t-online.de
web: www.dcc-stadtcamping-essen-werden.de

Several fields divided by bushes and surrounded by thick hedges.

dir: *From Essen centre towards Werden, turn towards railway station, site in 500m (signed).*

Open: All Year. **Site:** 6HEC **Prices:** 18.90 **Facilities:** Wi-fi Play Area **Services:** **Leisure:** R **Off-site:** P

GERMANY

Site 6HEC (site size) grass sand stone little shade partly shaded mainly shaded motorvans accepted bungalows for hire mobile homes for hire tents for hire no dogs site fully accessible for wheelchairs
Prices amount quoted is per night, for 2 adults and car, plus tent or caravan Mobile home hire is a weekly rate.

EXTERTAL — NORDRHEIN-WESTFALEN

Extertal

1 Beurteilung, Eimke 4, 32699
05262 3307 05262 992404
e-mail: info@campingpark-extertal.de
web: www.campingpark-extertal.de

Extensive, partly terraced site on slightly sloping meadowland with two ponds.

dir: *A2 exit 35, B238 past Rinteln, left onto Extertal-Barntrup road for 18km.*

Open: All Year. **Site:** 20HEC **For hire:** **Prices:** 14 **Facilities:** Wi-fi (charged) Play Area **Services:** **Leisure:** L **Off-site:** P

FÜRTH IM ODENWALD — HESSEN

Nibelungen-Camping am Schwimmbad

Tiefertswinkel 20, 64658
06253 5804 06253 3717
e-mail: info@camping-fuerth.de
web: www.camping-fuerth.de

Pleasantly landscaped modern site in beautiful setting next to the municipal open-air swimming pool, with shops and restaurants nearby.

dir: *A5 Darmstadt-Heidelberg exit Heppenheim or Weinheim.*

GPS: 49.6594, 8.7839

Open: 15 Mar-1 Nov **Site:** 4.2HEC **Prices:** 20 **Facilities:** Wi-fi (charged) Play Area **Services:** **Off-site:** P

GAMMELSBACH — HESSEN

Freienstein

Neckartalstr 172, 64743
06068 912122 06068 912121
e-mail: info@camp-freienstein.de
web: www.camp-freienstein.de

The site lies just off the B45 in a landscaped preservation area. It is terraced and divided into pitches.

Open: All Year. **Site:** 5HEC **For hire:** **Facilities:** Play Area **Services:** **Off-site:** L P

GEISENHEIM — HESSEN

Geisenheim

Postfach 1323, 65366
06722 75600 06722 406655
e-mail: info@rheingaucamping.de
web: www.rheingaucamping.de

Pleasant level grassland waterside site.

dir: *Between B42 road & River Rhine.*

Open: Mar-Oct **Site:** 5HEC **Facilities:** **Services:** **Leisure:** R **Off-site:** P

GERBACH — RHEINLAND-PFALZ

AZUR-Camping Pfalz

Kahlenbergweiher 1, 67813
06361 8287 06361 22523
e-mail: gerbach@azur-camping.de
web: www.azur-camping.de/gerbach

A site for nature lovers to enjoy, ideally located for exploring the well known surrounding cities.

dir: *A8 junct Enkenbach-Hochspeyer, N on B48 via Rockenhausen, at Dielkirchen 4.5km E to Gerbach.*

Open: Apr-Oct **Site:** 8.8HEC **Prices:** 17-22.50 **Facilities:** Play Area **Services:** **Leisure:** P

GILLENFELD — RHEINLAND-PFALZ

Feriendorf Pulvermaar

Vulkanstr, 54558
06573 287 06592 982662
e-mail: info@feriendorf-pulvermaar.de
web: www.feriendorf-pulvermaar.de

Partly terraced private site on a slightly sloping meadow above the volcanic lake of Pulvermaar, bordered by woods on one side.

dir: *A48 exit Mehren/Daun, right onto B421 towards Zell, 2nd turning to Gillenfeld, 200m on right.*

GPS: 50.1301, 6.9319

Open: All Year. **Site:** 4HEC **For hire:** **Prices:** 13.50-17 **Facilities:** Wi-fi (charged) Play Area **Services:** **Off-site:** L P

GIROD — RHEINLAND-PFALZ

Eisenbachtal

56412

06485 766 06485 4938

Close to an old volcano situated in the Nassau nature reserve, an ideal area for walking, rare plants and bird watching.

dir: *A3 exit 41, 5km towards Montabaur.*

Open: All Year. **Site:** 3HEC **Prices:** 16 **Facilities:** Play Area **Services:** **Off-site:** P

GLÜDER — NORDRHEIN-WESTFALEN

Waldcamping Glüder

Balkhauser Weg 240, 42659

0212 242120 0212 2421234

e-mail: info@camping-solingen.de

web: www.camping-solingen.de

Site on level terrain surrounded by woodland on banks of the River Wupper.

dir: *B299/B224 from Solingen towards Witzhelden via Burg Hohenscheid.*

Open: All Year. **Site:** 2HEC **Prices:** 14.40-16.40 **Facilities:** Play Area **Services:** **Leisure:** R **Off-site:** P

GRÜNBERG — HESSEN

Spitzer Stein

Alsfelderstr 57, 35305

06401 804117 06401 804103

e-mail: s.moebus@gruenberg.de

web: www.gruenberg.de

Beautiful location in a forest, with a swimming pool.

dir: *A5 exit Grünberg.*

Open: Mar-Oct **Site:** 4HEC **Prices:** 16 **Facilities:** Play Area **Services:** **Leisure:** P **Off-site:**

GRUNDMÜHLE BEI QUENTEL — HESSEN

Grundmühle Quentel

37235

05602 3659 05602 915811

e-mail: info@grundmühle-quentel.de

web: www.grundmühle-quentel.de

Set in a beautiful landscape, this sunny site is in the Meissner Forest.

dir: *B83 from Melsungen to Röhrenfurth, right towards Furstenhagen & via Eiterhagen to Quentel.*

Open: All Year. **Site:** 1.8HEC **For hire:** **Facilities:** **Services:** **Leisure:** P **Off-site:**

GULDENTAL — RHEINLAND-PFALZ

Campingpark Lindelgrund

The Camping and Caravanning Club — The Friendly Club

Im Lindelgrund 1, 55452

06707 633

e-mail: info@lindelgrund.de

web: www.lindelgrund.de

Tranquil site with facilities including volleyball and cycle hire.

C&CC Report *Conveniently situated near the motorway on the way south through the Rhine valley, Guldental is worthy of a longer stay in order to visit the spa towns of Bad Kreuznach, Bad Sobernheim and Bad Münster-am Stein-Ebernburg, in the Rhine and Nahe valleys. The friendly site owners can arrange winetastings at the local vineyards and sometimes they bring the wines to the site for on-site tastings.*

dir: *1m SE off L242.*

Open: All Year. **Facilities:** Play Area **Services:** **Off-site:** P

HALDERN — NORDRHEIN-WESTFALEN

Strandhaus Sonsfeld

46459

02857 2247 02857 7171

On meadowland at the Hagener-Meer next to B8 and railway line.

Open: All Year. **Site:** 15HEC **Facilities:** **Services:** **Leisure:** L

HAUSBAY — RHEINLAND-PFALZ

Schinderhannes

56291

06746 80280 06746 802814

e-mail: info@countrycamping.de

web: www.countrycamping.de

Terraced site on south facing slope, interspersed by trees and shrubs beside a small lake. Separate section for young people. Ideal to use as a stop over point, as caravans can stay hooked up on certain pitches. Restrictions apply to certain dog breeds.

dir: *E of B327. 29km S of Koblenz.*

GPS: 50.1060, 7.5675

Open: All Year. **Site:** 30HEC **Prices:** 16-23 **Facilities:** Wi-fi (charged) Play Area **Services:** **Leisure:** L **Off-site:**

HEIDENBURG — RHEINLAND-PFALZ

Moselhöhe

54426

06509 99016 06509 99017

e-mail: info@cpmh.de

web: www.cpmh.de

A small quiet, well-appointed site on terraces in open meadow.

dir: *A1 exit Mehring towards Thalfang am Erbeskopf.*

Open: Jan-Oct & Dec **Site:** 3HEC **For hire:** **Prices:** 16.50-18 **Facilities:** Wi-fi Play Area **Services:** **Leisure:** P **Off-site:** R

HEIMBACH — NORDRHEIN-WESTFALEN

Rurthal

52396

02446 3377 02446 911126

e-mail: info@campingplatz-rurthal.de

web: www.campingplatz-rurthal.de

Site with individual pitches on meadowland beside the River Ruhr.

dir: *From Düren S via Nideggen & Abenden to Blens, over bridge & left.*

Open: All Year. **Site:** 7HEC **For hire:** **Prices:** 12.80-13.50 **Facilities:** Play Area **Services:** **Leisure:** P **Off-site:** R

HEIMERTSHAUSEN — HESSEN

Heimertshausen

Ehringshauser Str, 36320

06635 206

e-mail: info@campingplatz-heimertshausen.de

web: www.campingplatz-heimertshausen.de

Near swimming pool in extensive, grassy, wooded valley.

dir: *A5 exit Alsfeld W, continue via Romrod & Zell.*

GPS: 50.7362, 9.1526

Open: Apr-Sep **Site:** 3.6HEC **For hire:** **Prices:** 17-18 **Facilities:** Play Area **Services:** **Off-site:** P

HELLENTHAL — NORDRHEIN-WESTFALEN

Hellenthal

Platiss 1, 53940

02482 1500 02482 2171

e-mail: info@camphellenthal.de

web: www.camphellenthal.de

On extensive meadowland, not far from the Belgian border.

dir: *0.5km S of town.*

Open: All Year. **Site:** 6HEC **Facilities:** Play Area **Services:** **Leisure:** P **Off-site:**

HIRSCHHORN AM NECKAR — HESSEN

Odenwald

Langenthalerstr 80, 69430

06272 809 06272 3658

e-mail: odenwald-camping-park@t-online.de

web: www.odenwald-camping-park.de

Extensive site in wooded valley. Divided by River Ülfenbach and hedges.

dir: *Off B37 towards Wald-Michelbach & continue 1.5km.*

Open: Apr-4 Oct **Site:** 8HEC **For hire:** **Facilities:** **Services:** **Leisure:** P R

HONNEF, BAD — NORDRHEIN-WESTFALEN

Camping Jillieshof

Ginsterbergweg 6, 53604

02224 972066 02224 972067

e-mail: information@camping-jillieshof.de

web: www.camping-jillieshof.de

A quiet, family site at the edge of Aegidienberg, conveniently close to the motorway.

dir: *Via A3 2km.*

GPS: 50.6491, 7.3002

Open: All Year. **Site:** 4HEC **For hire:** **Prices:** 17.50-19.50 **Facilities:** Play Area **Services:** **Off-site:**

HORN-BAD MEINBERG — NORDRHEIN-WESTFALEN

Eggewald

Kempener Str 33, 32805

05255 236 05255 1375

e-mail: j.glitz@traktoren-museum.de

web: www.traktoren-museum.de

Site lies in well-wooded countryside. A tractor museum is also on site.

dir: *Off B1 in Horn-Bad Meinberg at Waldschlosschen onto Altenbeken road for 8km to Kempen.*

GPS: 51.8033, 8.9431

Open: All Year. **Site:** 2HEC **Prices:** 14 **Facilities:** **Services:** **Leisure:** P

GERMANY

HÜNFELD HESSEN

Knaus Campingpark Praforst

Dr Detlev-Rudelsdorff-Allee 6, 36088
☎ 06652 749090 🖷 06652 749091
e-mail: huenfeld@knauscamp.de
web: www.knauscamp.de
Site in mixed woodland, with good amenities.
dir: *For access follow B27 from Hünfeld to Shlitz, turn right, 2km to site.*
Open: Jan-Oct **Site:** 3HEC **For hire:** **Facilities:** **Services:**

HUTTEN HESSEN

Camping Hutten Heiligenborn

Am Heiligenborn 6, 36381
☎ 06661 2424 🖷 06661 917581
e-mail: helga.herzog-gericke@online.de
Site lies at Heiligenborn and has a pleasant southerly aspect.
dir: *B40 from Fulda towards Frankfurt to Flieden for 19km, turn left via Rückers to Hutten (8km).*
Open: All Year. **Site:** 3.5HEC **Prices:** 14 **Facilities:** **Services:** **Off-site:** P

INGENHEIM RHEINLAND-PFALZ

SC Klingbachtal

76831
☎ 06349 6278
web: www.klingbachtal.de
Municipal site lies on level meadowland at the edge of the village, next to the sports ground.
dir: *8km S of Landau via B38, signed.*
Open: Apr-Oct **Site:** 1.5HEC **Facilities:** **Services:** **Off-site:** P

IRREL RHEINLAND-PFALZ

Nimseck

54666
☎ 06525 314 🖷 06525 1299
e-mail: info@camping-nimseck.de
web: www.camping-nimseck.de
A family-run site on a long grassy strip in wooded valley on the bank of River Nims. Leisure facilities include a heated outdoor pool along with special events in high season.
dir: *B257 SW from Bitburg, at turning from bypass to Irrel turn left.*
Open: 15 Mar-2 Nov **Site:** 7HEC **For hire:** **Facilities:** Wi-fi (charged) Kids' Club Play Area **Services:** **Leisure:** P R **Off-site:**

KELL RHEINLAND-PFALZ

Freibad Hochwald

54427
☎ 06589 1695
On meadow on slightly sloping wooded hillside, near a public open-air swimming pool.
dir: *2km from B407 towards Trier.*
Open: Jun-Aug **Site:** 2HEC **Facilities:** **Services:** **Leisure:** P

KIRCHHEIM HESSEN

Seepark Kirchheim

36275
☎ 06628 1525 🖷 06628 8664
e-mail: info@campseepark.de
web: www.campseepark.de
This terraced site, with individual pitches, is part of an extensive and well-equipped leisure and recreation centre.
Open: All Year. **Site:** 10HEC **For hire:** **Facilities:** **Services:** **Leisure:** L P

KIRN RHEINLAND-PFALZ

Papiermühle

Krebsweilererstr 8, 55606
☎ 06752 2267
e-mail: infos@papiermuehle-campingplatz.de
web: www.papiermuehle-campingplatz.de
Quiet terraced site in attractive valley.
dir: *B41 exit Kirn W, then Meisenheim.*
Open: 15 Mar-15 Nov **Site:** 6HEC **Prices:** 14 **Facilities:** Play Area **Services:**

KOBLENZ (COBLENCE) RHEINLAND-PFALZ

Ziehfurt

Raiffeisen Str 16, 56333
☎ 02606 1800 & 357 🖷 02606 2566
e-mail: ferieninsel-winningen@t-online.de
web: www.mosel-camping.com
Site lies on level wooded meadowland.
dir: *From Koblenz B416 towards Trier for 11km, access to site at Schwimmbad (swimming pool).*
GPS: 50.3113, 7.4997
Open: Etr-Sep **Site:** 7HEC **Prices:** 20.50-23 **Facilities:** Wi-fi Play Area **Services:** **Leisure:** R **Off-site:** P

GERMANY

KÖLN (COLOGNE) NORDRHEIN-WESTFALEN

Berger

Uferstr 71, Rodenkirchen, 50996
0221 9355240 0221 9355246
e-mail: camping.berger@t-online.de
web: www.camping-berger-koeln.de

Situated on a meadow beside the River Rhine. Beautiful surrounding area and modern facilities.

Open: All Year. **Site:** 6HEC **Prices:** 22.20 **Facilities:** Play Area **Services:** **Leisure:** R

KÖNEN RHEINLAND-PFALZ

Horsch

Könenerstr 36, 54329
06501 17571

Site close to the Saar River.

Open: Apr-14 Oct **Site:** **For hire:** **Prices:** 17-19 **Facilities:** **Services:** **Leisure:** R **Off-site:** P

KREUZBERG RHEINLAND-PFALZ

Viktoria Station

53505
02643 8338 02643 3391
e-mail: mail@viktoria-station.de
web: www.viktoria-station.de

Shady site on meadows by the River Ahr, close to a forest, vineyards and castles.

dir: *A61 exit Meckenheim for Altenahr, site 7km.*

GPS: 50.5075, 6.9794

Open: Apr-Oct **Site:** 5.5HEC **For hire:** **Prices:** 17.60-21.60 **Facilities:** Wi-fi (charged) Play Area **Services:** **Leisure:** R **Off-site:** P

KRÖV RHEINLAND-PFALZ

Kröver-Berg

54536
06541 70040 06541 700444
e-mail: info@erlebnis-laendchen.de
web: www.erlebnis-laendchen.de

In a forest setting, family friendly site with leisure activities.

GPS: 49.9894, 7.0772

Open: All Year. **Site:** 2.6HEC **For hire:** **Prices:** 9.50-14 **Facilities:** Wi-fi Play Area **Services:** **Off-site:** P R

LADBERGEN NORDRHEIN-WESTFALEN

Waldsee

Waldseestr 81, 49549
05485 1816 05485 3560
e-mail: info@waldsee-camping.de
web: www.waldsee-camping.de

Site lies at the inn, near the bathing area of the lake.

dir: *2km N. A1 exit Ladbergen for Saerbeck/Emsdetten, 100m turn right.*

GPS: 52.15, 7.7283

Open: All Year. **Site:** 10.5HEC **For hire:** **Prices:** 17.10 Mobile home hire 210 **Facilities:** Kids' Club Play Area **Services:** **Leisure:** L P **Off-site:** R

LAHNSTEIN RHEINLAND-PFALZ

Burg Lahneck

The Camping and Caravanning Club The Friendly Club

Am Burgweg, 56112
02621 2765 02621 18290
web: www.camping-burg-lahneck.de

Level grassland site with a sunny aspect and terraces that provide shade. Situated next to Lahneck castle with a pleasant view of the Rhine Valley.

C&CC Report *Few sites enjoy a setting as good as this, overlooking the Rhine valley, with a range of public facilities next door at discount prices for campers. Run with friendly efficiency by Frau Mischke, this is an excellent base for visiting the "Romantic Rhine" area, with its ancient ruins, vine-clad valleys and walking and cycling routes – or the owner's castle, next door.*

dir: *B42 from Koblenz to Lahnstein, follow signs Burg Lahneck, 1.5km to site.*

Open: Apr-Oct **Site:** 1.8HEC **Prices:** 19.50-21.50 **Facilities:** **Services:** **Off-site:** P

LEIWEN RHEINLAND-PFALZ

AEGON-Ferienpark Sonnenberg

54340
06507 93690
e-mail: sonnenberg@landal.de
web: www.landal.de

Extensive terraced site in one of the largest wine growing areas of this district. Lies above the River Mosel.

dir: *Off B53 (Mosel Valley road) over River Mosel at Thornich then via Leiwen to site.*

Open: 4 Feb-22 Jan **Site:** 25HEC **For hire:** **Facilities:** **Services:** **Leisure:** P R **Off-site:**

GERMANY

LEMGO NORDRHEIN-WESTFALEN

Campingpark Lemgo

Regenstorstr 10, 32657
05261 14858 0521 459017
e-mail: lemgo@meyer-zu-bentrup.de
web: www.camping-lemgo.de

The site lies by the swimming pool directly on the river, close to the city.

GPS: 52.025, 8.9086

Open: Mar-Nov **Site:** 2.5HEC **For hire:** **Prices:** 17-21 Mobile home hire 242.55-269.50 **Facilities:** Wi-fi Play Area **Services:** **Off-site:** P R

LIBLAR NORDRHEIN-WESTFALEN

Liblarer See

50374
02235 3899
web: camping-liblar.de

This site lies at Lake Liblar, with its own bathing area.

dir: *SW from Köln (Cologne) on B265 for 15km, 1km before Liblar left towards lake.*

Open: All Year. **Site:** 10HEC **Facilities:** Play Area **Services:** **Leisure:** L

LIEBENAU-ZWERGEN HESSEN

Ponyhof Camping Club

Teichweg 1, 34396
05676 1509 05676 8880
e-mail: info@ponyhofcamping.de
web: www.ponyhofcamping.de

A south-facing terraced site among magnificent scenery, 300 metres from a swimming pool.

dir: *Off B83 at Hofgeismar W towards Liebenau. Or off B7 at Obemeiser N towards Liebenau.*

Open: 20 Mar-10 Nov **Site:** 7HEC **For hire:** **Facilities:** **Services:** **Leisure:** R **Off-site:** L P

LINDENFELS HESSEN

Terrassencamping Schlierbach

Am Zentbuckel 11, 64678
06255 630 06255 3526
e-mail: info@terrassencamping-schlierbach.de
web: www.terrassencamping-schlierbach.de

Site is fenced and lies on sloping terrain.

dir: *B47 Bensheim-Michelstadt, turn off in Lindenfels SW to Schlierbach.*

Open: Mar-Oct **Site:** 3.2HEC **Prices:** 15.10-17 **Facilities:** Wi-fi Play Area **Services:** **Off-site:** P

LINGERHAHN RHEINLAND-PFALZ

Mühlenteich

56291
06746 533 06746 1566
e-mail: info@muehlenteich.de
web: www.muehlenteich.de

Site lies on slightly sloping meadowland, divided into sections by trees. Isolated location at the edge of woodland and adjoining the forest swimming pool (free entry for campers). Trout fishing.

dir: *A61 exit Laudert.*

Open: All Year. **Site:** 15HEC **Prices:** 16-24 **Facilities:** Wi-fi (charged) Play Area **Services:** **Leisure:** P **Off-site:** R

LORCH HESSEN

Suleika

Im Bodenthal 2, 65391
06726 9464 06726 9440
e-mail: suleika-camping@t-online.de
web: www.suleika-camping.de

Well laid-out terraced site in an ideal location for exploring the Rhine Valley.

dir: *B42 from Assmannshausen towards Lorch for 3km, turn right to site through railway underpass (2.2m high - large caravans turn right 1km before Lorch).*

Open: 15 Mar-1 Nov **Site:** 4HEC **For hire:** **Prices:** 18-24 Mobile home hire 340 **Facilities:** Play Area **Services:** **Off-site:** L R

GERMANY

LOSHEIM SAARLAND

Camping Girtenmühle

Girtenmühle 1, 66679
☎ 06872 90240 06872 902411
e-mail: info@girtenmuehle.de
web: www.girtenmuehle.de
Quiet forest location, ideal for hikers.
dir: *Via B268 Trier-Losheim.*
Open: Apr-Oct **Site:** 5HEC **For hire:** **Prices:** 16-22.30 **Facilities:** Play Area **Services:** **Off-site:** L P

MARBURG AN DER LAHN HESSEN

GC Lahnaue

Trojedamm 47, 35037
☎ 06421 21331 06421 175882
e-mail: info@lahnaue.de
web: www.lahnaue.de
Situated on the River Lahn, a municipal site on level meadowland next to the Sommerbad (swimming pool).
dir: *W of town.*
Open: Apr-30 Oct **Site:** 1HEC **For hire:** **Facilities:** **Services:** **Leisure:** R **Off-site:** P

MEERBUSCH NORDRHEIN-WESTFALEN

Rheincamping Meerbusch

Zur Rheinfähre 21, 40668
☎ 02150 707571 02150 912289
e-mail: info@rheincamping.com
web: www.rheincamping.com
A peaceful location on the Rhine within easy reach of Düsseldorf.
dir: *Via A57 Neuss-Krefeld.*
Open: Apr-15 Oct **Site:** 3.8HEC **For hire:** **Prices:** 26.50 **Facilities:** Wi-fi (charged) Play Area **Services:** **Leisure:** R **Off-site:** P

MEHLEM NORDRHEIN-WESTFALEN

Genienau

53179
☎ 0228 344949 0228 3294989
The site lies opposite the Drachenfels.
Open: All Year. **Site:** 1.8HEC **Facilities:** **Services:** **Leisure:** R **Off-site:** P

MEINHARD HESSEN

Meinhardsee

37276
☎ 05651 6200 05651 992301
e-mail: info@werra-meissner-camping.de
web: www.werra-meissner-camping.de
A lakeside site with facilities for water sports.
dir: *Via B27 & B249.*
Open: Apr-Oct **Site:** 7HEC **Facilities:** **Services:** **Leisure:** L **Off-site:** P

MESCHEDE NORDRHEIN-WESTFALEN

Knaus Campingpark Hennesee

Mielinghausen 7, 59872
☎ 0291 952720 0291 9527229
e-mail: hennesee@knauscamp.de
web: www.knauscamp.de
Terraced site on the eastern side of a lake in an attractive location of mountains and forests.
Open: 16 Dec-3 Nov **Site:** 17HEC **For hire:** **Facilities:** **Services:** **Leisure:** L P

MESENICH RHEINLAND-PFALZ

Family Camping Club

56820
☎ 02673 4556
e-mail: info@family-camping.de
web: www.family-camping.de
A family site with plenty of recreational facilities beside the River Moselle. Pitches are divided by trees and hedges.
Open: May-Sep **Site:** 3HEC **For hire:** **Facilities:** **Services:** **Leisure:** P R

MITTELHOF RHEINLAND-PFALZ

Camping Im Eichenwald

57537
☎ 02742 910643 02742 910645
e-mail: camping@hatzfeldt.de
web: www.camping-im-eichenwald.de
Set in an oak wood, mainly divided into pitches.
dir: *B62 from Siegen towards Wissen, turn to site 4km NE of Wissen.*
Open: All Year. **Site:** 10HEC **For hire:** **Prices:** 15-16 **Facilities:** Play Area **Services:** **Leisure:** P **Off-site:** R

GERMANY

MONSCHAU NORDRHEIN-WESTFALEN

Perlenau

Eifel, 52156

☎ 02472 4136 📠 02472 4493

e-mail: familie.rasch@monschau-perlenau.de

web: www.monschau-perlenau.de

Family-run, natural site set in woods with an outdoor swimming pool and children's playground.

GPS: 50.5439, 6.2375

Open: Apr-Oct **Site:** 2HEC **For hire:** **Prices:** 19 **Facilities:** Wi-fi Play Area **Services:** **Leisure:** P R **Off-site:**

MÖRFELDEN-WALLDORF HESSEN

Arndt Mörfelden

Am Zeltplatz 5, 64546

☎ 06105 22289 📠 06105 277459

e-mail: campingplatz.moerfelden@t-online.de

web: www.campingplatz-moerfelden.de

Well laid-out site in two sections near the motorway. Surrounded by forest and grassland.

dir: *A5 exit Langen/Mörfelden, site 0.3km, signed.*

Open: All Year. **Site:** 6HEC **Facilities:** **Services:** **Off-site:** L P

MÜLHEIM AN DER RUHR NORDRHEIN-WESTFALEN

Entenfangsee

45481

☎ 0203 760111 📠 0203 765162

Extensive site near a lake. Touring pitches near railway line. Adventure playground.

dir: *Motorway exit Duisburg-Wedau for Bissingheim & lake.*

Open: All Year. **Site:** 12.5HEC **For hire:** **Facilities:** **Services:** **Leisure:** L **Off-site:** P

MÜLLENBACH RHEINLAND-PFALZ

Nürburgring

53520

☎ 02692 224 📠 02692 1020

e-mail: rezeption@camping-am-nuerburgring.de

web: www.camping-am-nuerburgring.de

A large, well-equipped site in a wooded location with direct access to the Nürburgring Grand Prix circuit.

dir: *Via A61/A48 & B412.*

Open: All Year. **Site:** 30HEC **For hire:** **Facilities:** **Services:**

NEHREN RHEINLAND-PFALZ

Nehren

56820

☎ 02673 4612 📠 02671 910754

e-mail: info@campingplatz-nehren.de

web: www.campingplatz-nehren.de

On level terrain beside the River Mosel. Separate section for teenagers. Liable to flood at certain times of the year.

dir: *Off B49 in Nehren.*

Open: Apr-15 Oct **Site:** 5HEC **Facilities:** Wi-fi **Services:** **Leisure:** R

NEUERBURG RHEINLAND-PFALZ

In der Enz

In der Enz 25, 54673

☎ 06564 2660 📠 06564 2979

e-mail: info@camping-inderenz.com

web: www.camping-neuerburg.de

2km outside the historic town of Neuerburg, the site is surrounded by wooded hills and crossed by the River Enz. It offers a peaceful, rural location.

dir: *Access via the B50 (Bitburg-Vianden). At Sinspett turn N, continue to site on N outskirts (7km).*

Open: Mar-Oct & Dec-Jan **Site:** 2HEC **Facilities:** **Services:** **Leisure:** R **Off-site:**

NIEDERKRÜCHTEN NORDRHEIN-WESTFALEN

Lelefeld

Lelefeld 4, 41372

☎ 02163 81203 📠 02163 81203

e-mail: info@camping-lelefeld.com

web: www.camping-lelefeld.com

A quiet wooded location on the outskirts of the village.

dir: *Signed from Elmpt.*

Open: All Year. **Site:** 1.5HEC **Prices:** 12-14.60 **Facilities:** **Services:** **Off-site:** L P R

GERMANY

NIEDERSFELD NORDRHEIN-WESTFALEN

Camping An Der Vossmecke

Am Eschenberg 1a, 59955
02985 8418 02985 553
e-mail: info@camping-vossmecke.de
web: www.camping-vossmecke.de
A pleasant wooded location with facilities for winter camping.
dir: *Off B480 towards Winterberg.*
GPS: 51.1981, 8.5225
Open: All Year. **Site:** 4HEC **Prices:** 14.50-26.40 **Facilities:** Play Area **Services:** **Off-site:** L P

OBERSGEGEN RHEINLAND-PFALZ

Reles-Mühle

Kapellenweg 3, 54675
06566 8741 06566 931064
e-mail: info@eifelcamping.com
web: www.eifelcamping.com
Set in rural surroundings next to a farmhouse, on a level meadow by a brook with trees and bushes.
dir: *B50 from Bitburg towards Vianden, site near Luxembourg frontier.*
Open: All Year. **Site:** 2HEC **For hire:** **Facilities:** **Services:** **Leisure:** R **Off-site:** P

OBERWEIS RHEINLAND-PFALZ

Prümtal-Camping

In der Klaus 17, 54636
06527 92920 06527 929232
e-mail: info@pruemtal.de
web: www.pruemtal.de
A family site in pleasant wooded surroundings with good sports and camping facilities. Kids' club available during July and August.
dir: *B50 from Bitburg towards B51 Vianden, Luxembourg border.*
Open: All Year. **Site:** 3.8HEC **For hire:** **Facilities:** Wi-fi (charged) Kids' Club Play Area **Services:** **Leisure:** P R

ODERSBACH HESSEN

Odersbach

Runkler Str 5A, 35781
06471 7620 06471 379603
e-mail: info@camping-odersbach.de
web: www.camping-odersbach.de
A modern and quiet camp site in an attractive setting beside the River Lahn.
dir: *On S outskirts of town.*
GPS: 50.4758, 8.2411
Open: Apr-Oct **Site:** 6HEC **For hire:** **Prices:** 14.60 Mobile home hire 455 **Facilities:** Wi-fi (charged) Play Area **Services:** **Leisure:** P R **Off-site:**

OLPE-SONDERN NORDRHEIN-WESTFALEN

Biggesee-Vier Jahreszeiten

Sonderner Kopf 3, 57462
02761 944111 02761 944122
e-mail: info@camping-sonderner.de
web: www.biggesee.com
A popular site in wooded surroundings on the shore of the Biggesee.
dir: *A45 exit Olpe for Attendorn, 6km turn for Erholungsanlage Biggesee-Sondern.*
GPS: 51.0736, 7.8564
Open: All Year. **Site:** 6HEC **For hire:** **Prices:** 20.70-24 **Facilities:** Play Area **Services:** **Leisure:** L **Off-site:** P

PORTA WESTFALICA NORDRHEIN-WESTFALEN

Grosser Weserbogen

32457
05731 6188 05731 6601
e-mail: info@grosserweserbogen.de
web: www.grosserweserbogen.de
Lake-side site with extensive leisure facilities and organised entertainment.
dir: *A2 towards Dortmund, exit Porta Westfalica-Minden.*
Open: All Year. **Site:** 9HEC **Facilities:** Play Area **Services:** **Leisure:** L

GERMANY

PRÜM — RHEINLAND-PFALZ

Waldcampingplatz

54591

06551 2481 06551 6555

e-mail: info@waldcamping-pruem.de

web: www.waldcamping-pruem.de

Site lies on both sides of the River Prüm and is surrounded by woods. Divided into three sections of level meadowland.

dir: *On NW edge of Prüm.*

Open: All Year. **Site:** 3.5HEC **Facilities:** **Services:** **Leisure:** R **Off-site:** P

REINSFELD — RHEINLAND-PFALZ

AZUR Camping Hunsrück

Parkstr 1, 54421

06503 95123 06503 95124

e-mail: reinsfeld@azur-camping.de

web: www.azur-camping.de/reinsfeld

A peaceful location close to Trier on the Luxembourg border, surrounded by hills.

dir: *Via B52 or B407.*

Open: All Year. **Site:** 20HEC **For hire:** **Facilities:** **Services:** **Leisure:** P

ROTHEMANN — HESSEN

Rothemann

Maulkuppenstr 17, 36124

06659 2285

A small, well-kept site surrounded by a hedge, next to the main Fulda road.

dir: *A7 onto A66 exit Fulda Süd, 3km S on B27 towards Bad Brükenau.*

Open: Apr-Oct **Site:** 5.4HEC **Facilities:** **Services:** **Off-site:**

RÜDESHEIM — HESSEN

Campingplatz am Rhein

Kastanienallee, 65385

06722 2528 06722 406783

e-mail: mail@campingplatz-ruedesheim.de

web: www.campingplatz-ruedesheim.de

Near the open-air swimming pool, town centre, museums and the River Rhine.

GPS: 49.9777, 7.9408

Open: May-3 Oct **Site:** 3HEC **Prices:** 23 **Facilities:** Play Area **Services:** **Off-site:** P

SAARBURG — RHEINLAND-PFALZ

Landal Greenpark Warsberg

54439

06581 91460 06581 914615

e-mail: warsberg@landal.de

web: www.landal.com

Open site in a quiet hilltop location. A chairlift (700 metres) goes down to the town. Kids' club available in high season.

dir: *Signed at N end of town off B51 Trier road, 3km uphill.*

Open: 31 Mar-Oct **Site:** 12HEC **For hire:** **Prices:** 19-34 **Facilities:** Wi-fi (charged) Kids' Club Play Area **Services:** **Leisure:** P

Leukbachtal

54439

06581 2228 06581 5008

e-mail: service@campingleukbachtal.de

web: www.campingleukbachtal.de

Municipal site on level meadows on both sides of the Leuk-Bach (brook).

dir: *B51 from Saarburg towards Trassen, turn left after x-rds.*

GPS: 49.5991, 6.5413

Open: Mar-1 Nov **Site:** 2.5HEC **For hire:** **Prices:** 18.50 **Facilities:** Play Area **Services:** **Off-site:** P R

Waldfrieden

Im Fichtenhain 4, 54439

06581 2255 06581 5908

e-mail: info@campingwaldfrieden.de

web: www.campingwaldfrieden.de

Site lies next to the Café Waldfrieden on unspoiled, slightly rising meadowland in woods.

dir: *S of town off B51 or B407 towards Nennig (Luxembourg), 200m to site.*

GPS: 49.6008, 6.5283

Open: 8 Feb-15 Nov **Site:** 6.5HEC **Prices:** 18.50 **Facilities:** Wi-fi (charged) Play Area **Services:** **Leisure:** P

SAARLOUIS — SAARLAND

Campingplatz Dr. Ernst Dadder

Marschall-Ney-Weg 2, 66740
☎ 06831 3691 🖷 06831 122970
e-mail: info@campingplatz-saarlouis.de
web: www.campingplatz-saarlouis.de

Centrally located yet peaceful site in the heart of Saarlouis.

dir: *Off B51 in suburb of Roden, over new bridge over River Saar to site beyond sports hall.*

Open: 15 Mar-Oct **Site:** 2HEC **Prices:** 19.50 **Facilities:** **Services:** **Off-site:** P R

ST GOAR — RHEINLAND-PFALZ

Friedenau

Gruendelbach 103, 56329
☎ 06741 368 🖷 06741 368
e-mail: info@camping-friedenau.de
web: www.camping-friedenau.de

On level, narrow stretch of meadowland at Gasthaus Friedenau.

dir: *Off B9 in St-Goar, through railway underpass towards Emmelshausen for 1km.*

Open: Mar-1 Dec **Site:** 2HEC **For hire:** **Prices:** 15.80-17 **Facilities:** Play Area **Services:** **Leisure:** R **Off-site:** P

ST GOARSHAUSEN — RHEINLAND-PFALZ

Camping Loreleystadt

56346
☎ 06771 2592 🖷 06771 802369
e-mail: info@camping-loreleystadt.de
web: www.camping-loreleystadt.de

Set beside the Rhine and opposite Rheinfels castle. Discounts available on boat tours. Dogs must be kept on leads.

dir: *A61/A3.*

GPS: 50.1596, 7.7084

Open: 15 Mar-Oct **Site:** 1.3HEC **For hire:** **Prices:** 22-25 **Facilities:** Wi-fi (charged) **Services:** **Leisure:** R **Off-site:**

SCHACHEN — HESSEN

Hochrhön

36129
☎ 06654 7836 🖷 06654 7836
e-mail: campinghochrhoen@aol.com
web: www.rhoenline.de/camping-hochrhoen

Site lies 1.5km from the Kneipp (hydrotherapeutic) Spa area of Gersfeld.

dir: *2km N of Gersfeld.*

Open: All Year. **Site:** 3HEC **Prices:** 16 **Facilities:** Play Area **Services:** **Off-site:** L P

SCHALKENMEHREN — RHEINLAND-PFALZ

Camp am Maar

Maarstr 22, 54552
☎ 06592 95510 🖷 06592 955140
e-mail: info@hotelschneider.de
web: www.hotelschneider.de

Terraced lakeside site on meadowland at the Schalkenmehrener Maar (water-filled crater). Towing help for caravans.

dir: *A48 exit Mehren/Daun, B42 to Mehren, turn SW.*

GPS: 50.1663, 6.8572

Open: All Year. **Site:** 1HEC **Facilities:** **Services:** **Leisure:** L P **Off-site:**

SCHLEIDEN — NORDRHEIN-WESTFALEN

Schleiden

Im Wiesengrund 39, 53937
☎ 02445 7030 🖷 02445 5980

Site lies on hilly, well-wooded country.

dir: *On B258 to Monschau, 1km to site.*

Open: All Year. **Site:** 5HEC **Facilities:** **Services:** **Off-site:** P

SCHÖNENBERG-KÜBELBERG — RHEINLAND-PFALZ

Campingpark Ohmbachsee

66901
☎ 06373 4001 🖷 06373 4002
e-mail: jungfleisch@campingpark-ohmbachsee.de
web: www.campingpark-ohmbachsee.de

Terraced site on sloping ground above east bank of the Ohmbachsee. Separate field for young people.

dir: *Signed.*

Open: All Year. **Site:** 7.8HEC **For hire:** **Prices:** 21.90 **Facilities:** Wi-fi (charged) **Services:** **Leisure:** P **Off-site:** L

GERMANY

SCHOTTEN HESSEN

Nidda-Stausee

Vogelsbergstr 184, 63679
☎ 06044 1418 🖷 06044 987995
e-mail: campingplatz@schotten.de
web: www.schotten.de

A pleasant family site on the shore of a lake.

dir: *Via B455.*

Open: All Year. **Site:** 3.2HEC **Facilities:** **Services:** **Off-site:** L P

SECK RHEINLAND-PFALZ

Weiherhof

56479
☎ 02664 8555 🖷 02664 6388
e-mail: info@camping-park-weiherhof.de
web: www.camping-park-weiherhof.de

The site lies on level meadowland next to a small lake in a wooded nature reserve and is ideally located for hiking.

dir: *B255 from Rennerod to Hellenbahn-Schellenberg, turn S for 2km.*

Open: All Year. **Site:** 10HEC **For hire:** **Prices:** 18-22 **Facilities:** Play Area **Services:** **Leisure:** L

SENHEIM RHEINLAND-PFALZ

Internationaler Holländischer Hof

56820
☎ 02673 4660 🖷 02673 4100
e-mail: holl.hof@t-online.de
web: www.moselcamping.com

On level meadowland, divided into pitches beside the River Mosel. There are mooring facilities, and a kids' club in July and August.

dir: *B49 from Cochem towards Zell, at Senhals over bridge & left.*

Open: 11 Apr-1 Nov **Site:** 4HEC **For hire:** **Facilities:** Wi-fi Kids' Club Play Area **Services:** **Leisure:** R

SENSWEILER MÜHLE RHEINLAND-PFALZ

Oberes Idartal

55758
☎ 06786 2114 🖷 06786 2222
e-mail: cpoberesidartal@t-online.de
web: www.oberes-idartal.de

Site surrounded by forest lies on a farm by the Idar, set on several small meadows and partly on terraced terrain next to Camping Sensweiler-Mühle.

dir: *B422 from Idar-Oberstein for 10km NW, site between Katzenloch & Allenbach.*

GPS: 49.7691, 7.2073

Open: All Year. **Site:** 2HEC **For hire:** **Prices:** 12.20-14.30 **Facilities:** Play Area **Services:** **Leisure:** R **Off-site:** P

Sensweiler-Mühle

Bundestr 422, 55758
☎ 06786 2395 🖷 06781 35147
e-mail: info@sensweiler-muehle.de
web: www.sensweiler-muehle.de

On extensive grassland beside the Idar, partially terraced, in rural area near a farm. Views of wooded range of hills. Next to Camping Oberes Idartal. Separate section for young groups.

dir: *B422 from Idar-Oberstein for 10km NW, site between Katzenloch & Allenbach.*

Open: Mar-Oct **Site:** 3HEC **Prices:** 16.50 **Facilities:** Play Area **Services:** **Leisure:** R **Off-site:** L

STADTKYLL RHEINLAND-PFALZ

Landal Wirfttal

54589
☎ 06597 92920 🖷 06597 929250
e-mail: wirfttal@landal.de
web: www.landal.com

Extensive, level grassland beside the upper of two small reservoirs, 1km outside the town.

dir: *A1 S from Euskirchen, through Blankenheim towards Stadtkyll.*

Open: All Year. **Site:** 6.4HEC **For hire:** **Facilities:** **Services:** **Leisure:** P

GERMANY

STEINEN RHEINLAND-PFALZ

Hofgut Schönerlen

56244

02666 207 02666 8429

e-mail: camping-kopper@t-online.de

web: www.camping-westerwald.de

Beautiful and quiet site at Lake Hausweiher. Young campers under 18 years old not accepted unless with adults. Dogs are permitted in a separate area.

dir: *B8 to Steinen & left to site.*

GPS: 50.5644, 7.8125

Open: Dec-Oct **Site:** 15HEC **For hire:** **Prices:** 15-17 **Facilities:** Play Area **Services:** **Leisure:** L **Off-site:**

STUKENBROCK NORDRHEIN-WESTFALEN

Campingplatz Am Furlbach

Am Furlbach 33, 33758

05257 3373 05257 940373

e-mail: info@campingplatzamfurlbach.de

web: www.campingplatzamfurlbach.de

Extensive site, partly on level, open meadow and partly in woodland. The shop stocks organic products. Cycling and hiking trails nearby.

dir: *A33 Osnabrück-Paderborn exit 23, Hollywood Safari park.*

Open: 15 Mar-1 Nov **Site:** 9HEC **Prices:** 16-16.50 **Facilities:** Play Area **Services:** **Off-site:**

TANN HESSEN

Ulstertal

Dippach 4, 36142

06682 8292 06682 10086

Terraced site on slightly sloping meadowland.

dir: *Off B278 Bischofsheim-Tann in Wendershausen SE to Dippach.*

Open: All Year. **Site:** 2.4HEC **Facilities:** **Services:**

TREIS-KARDEN RHEINLAND-PFALZ

Mosel-Islands

56253

02672 2613 02672 912102

e-mail: info@mosel-islands.de

web: www.mosel-islands.de

An extensive, level site on a grassy island in the Mosel next to a yacht marina.

dir: *Off B49 in Treis onto S coast road.*

Open: Apr-Oct **Site:** 4.5HEC **Prices:** 18 **Facilities:** Play Area **Services:** **Leisure:** R **Off-site:** P

TRENDELBURG HESSEN

Trendelburg

34388

05675 301 05675 5888

e-mail: conradi-camping@t-online.de

web: www.campingplatz-trendelburg.de

Site located at the foot of the castle, subdivided on the banks of the River Diemel. Covered tennis court. Dogs permitted except in restaurant.

dir: *B83 N from Kessel via Hofgeismar to Trendelburg, over bridge & sharp left to site.*

Open: All Year. **Site:** 2.7HEC **For hire:** **Facilities:** Wi-fi (charged) **Services:** **Leisure:** R **Off-site:** P

TRIER RHEINLAND-PFALZ

Treviris

Luxemburger Str 81, 54294

0651 8200911 0651 8200567

e-mail: info@camping-treviris.de

Level site owned by the Rowing Club Treviris, beside the Mosel 1.6km from the city centre.

dir: *On Luxembourg road between Romer bridge & Adenauer bridge.*

Open: Apr-19 Dec **Site:** 1.5HEC **For hire:** **Facilities:** **Services:** **Leisure:** R **Off-site:** P

GERMANY

TRIPPSTADT RHEINLAND-PFALZ

Sägmühle

Sägmühle 1, 67705

06306 92190 06306 2000

e-mail: info@saegmuehle.de

web: www.saegmuehle.de

The site lies in a wooded valley beside Sägmühle (Saw Mill) lake. It consists of several unconnected sections, some of them terraced. Kids' club in July and August.

dir: *16km S of Kaiserslautern.*

Open: 15 Dec-Oct **Site:** 10HEC **For hire:** **Prices:** 21.40-28 Mobile home hire 330-590 **Facilities:** Wi-fi (charged) Kids' Club Play Area **Services:** **Leisure:** L **Off-site:** P

VINKRATH BEI GREFRATH NORDRHEIN-WESTFALEN

Ferienpark Waldfrieden

An der Paas 13, 47929

02158 3855 02158 3685

e-mail: ferienpark-waldfrieden@t-online.de

web: www.ferienpark-waldfrieden.de

Site within a nature reserve.

dir: *Off B509 at Grefrath N towards Wankum, 3km turn right.*

Open: All Year. **Site:** 4.5HEC **For hire:** **Prices:** 14.50-17.50 **Facilities:** Play Area **Services:** **Leisure:** L **Off-site:** P R

VLOTHO NORDRHEIN-WESTFALEN

Borlefzen

Borlefzen 2, 32602

05733 80008 05733 89728

e-mail: info@borlefzen.de

web: www.borlefzen.de

Family-run site on a lake, ideal for fishing.

Open: Apr-Oct **Site:** 40HEC **For hire:** **Facilities:** **Services:** **Leisure:** L R

WARBURG NORDRHEIN-WESTFALEN

Eversburg

34414

05641 8668

Site lies next to restaurant of the same name on the south-east outskirts of the town.

Open: All Year. **Site:** 4.5HEC **Facilities:** **Services:** **Leisure:** R **Off-site:** P

WASSERFALL NORDRHEIN-WESTFALEN

Aurora

Aurorastr 9, 59909

02905 332

Terraced site surrounded by woodland, next to Fort Fun leisure centre. Little room for touring campers during the winter.

dir: *Turn S off B7 10km E of Meschedes, pass Gevelinghausen to Wasserfall.*

Open: All Year. **Site:** 0.7HEC **For hire:** **Facilities:** **Services:** **Off-site:** P R

WAXWEILER RHEINLAND-PFALZ

Eifel Ferienpark Prümtal

Schwimmbadstr 7, 54649

06554 92000 06554 920029

e-mail: info@ferienpark-waxweiler.de

web: www.ferienpark-waxweiler.de

Site lies on level terrain and is divided into pitches, with a separate field on the opposite side of the River Prüm. There is a kids' club during peak season.

dir: *From N end of Waxweiler turn towards River Prüm.*

Open: Apr-Oct **Site:** 3HEC **For hire:** **Prices:** 8.50-16.50 **Facilities:** Wi-fi (charged) Kids' Club Play Area **Services:** **Leisure:** P R **Off-site:**

WISSEL NORDRHEIN-WESTFALEN

Freizeitpark Wisseler See

Zum Wisseler See 15, 47546

02824 96310 02824 963131

e-mail: info@wisseler-see.de

web: www.wisseler-see.de

Well-kept municipal site with modern equipment beside Lake Wissel. There is a separate car park next to the open-air swimming pool. The pool belongs to the camp. Kids' club during the summer holidays.

dir: *B57 from Kieve towards Xanten, 9km turn left, continue 3km towards Wissel.*

GPS: 51.7611, 6.2847

Open: All Year. **Site:** 35HEC **For hire:** **Prices:** 27-31 **Facilities:** Wi-fi (charged) Kids' Club Play Area **Services:** **Leisure:** L

WITZENHAUSEN HESSEN

Camping Platz Werratal

Am Sande 11, 37213

☎ 05542 1465

e-mail: info@campingplatz-werratal.de

web: www.campingplatz-werratal.de

The site lies on meadow between the outskirts of Witzenhausen and the banks of the Werra.

dir: *Hannover-Kassel motorway exit Werratal, onto B80 to Witzenhausen, signed from market place.*

GPS: 51.3474, 9.8687

Open: All Year. **Site:** 3HEC **For hire:** **Prices:** 15-17.30 Mobile home hire 273 **Facilities:** Play Area **Services:** **Leisure:** R **Off-site:** L P

WOLFSTEIN RHEINLAND-PFALZ

Camping am Königsberg

Am Schwimmbad 1, 67752

☎ 06304 4143 06304 7543

e-mail: info@campingwolfstein.de

web: www.campingwolfstein.de

In the middle of an attractive nature zone at the foot of a mountain. The site has an informal atmosphere and good equipment, beside River Lauter.

dir: *Site at S end of Wolfstein on right of B270 from Kaiserslautern.*

Open: All Year. **Site:** 3.8HEC **For hire:** **Prices:** 15-25 Mobile home hire 500-550 **Facilities:** Wi-fi (charged) Kids' Club Play Area **Services:** **Leisure:** P R **Off-site:** L

ZERF RHEINLAND-PFALZ

Rübezahl

54314

☎ 06587 814 06587 814

e-mail: seyffardt-zerf@t-online.de

Meadowland site in natural grounds on wooded hillside.

dir: *B268 from Zerf S towards Saarbrücken & turn towards Oberzerf, site 2.5km. Or B407 from Saarburg, turn right after Vierherrenhorn onto track for 60m.*

Open: Apr-Oct **Site:** 2.5HEC **Prices:** 13 **Facilities:** Play Area **Services:** **Leisure:** P

ZWESTEN, BAD HESSEN

Waldcamping

34596

☎ 05626 379 06695 1320

e-mail: info@doering-jesberg.de

web: www.waldcamping.de

Site in bend of River Schwalm. For touring campers there is an overflow site.

dir: *Access from Kassel in SW direction via Fritzlar to Zwesten.*

Open: All Year. **Site:** 5HEC **Facilities:** **Services:** **Leisure:** P R **Off-site:**

NORTH

ALTENAU NIEDERSACHSEN

Okertalsperre

Kornhardtweg 2, 38707

☎ 05328 702 05328 911708

e-mail: camping-okertal@t-online.de

web: www.camping-okertalsperre.de

On a long stretch of grassland at the southern end of the Oker reservoir.

dir: *Signed from B498 Oker-Altenau.*

Open: All Year. **Site:** 3.5HEC **Prices:** 18.35-20.10 **Facilities:** Wi-fi Play Area **Services:** **Leisure:** L R

BLECKEDE NIEDERSACHSEN

Alt-Garge (ADAC)

Am Waldbad 23, 21354

☎ 05854 311 05854 1640

e-mail: adac-camping-altgarge@t-online.de

web: www.camping-altgarge.de

A modern site at the south-eastern end of Alt-Garge, next to a heated swimming pool in the woods.

dir: *5km SE of Bleckede.*

GPS: 53.2592, 10.8053

Open: All Year. **Site:** 6.6HEC **For hire:** **Prices:** 20.50-24.50 **Facilities:** Wi-fi (charged) Play Area **Services:** **Leisure:** P **Off-site:** L R

GERMANY

BODENWERDER NIEDERSACHSEN

Himmelspforte

Ziegeleiweg 1, 37619
☎ 05533 4938 05533 4432
e-mail: himmelspforte01@yahoo.de
web: www.camping-weserbergland.de

Site on grassland, with a fruit orchard, next to River Weser. Watersports available. Separate section and common room for young campers.

dir: *Cross River Weser & right towards Rühle, site 2km.*

Open: All Year. **Site:** 11HEC **Facilities:** **Services:** **Leisure:** R **Off-site:** P

Rühler Schweiz

Grosses Tal, 37619
☎ 05533 2486 05533 5882
e-mail: info@brader-ruehler-schweiz.de
web: www.brader-ruehler-schweiz.de

This site lies on well-kept meadowland by the River Weser.

dir: *4km from Weser bridge in Bodenwerder straight ahead towards Rühle.*

GPS: 51.9431, 9.5106

Open: Mar-Oct **Site:** 7HEC **For hire:** **Prices:** 9 **Facilities:** Play Area **Services:** **Leisure:** P R

BOTHEL NIEDERSACHSEN

Hanseat

27384
☎ 04266 355 04266 355
e-mail: info@campingpark-hanseat.de

Small, quality site on the edge of the town.

Open: All Year. **Site:** 4.5HEC **For hire:** **Facilities:** **Services:** **Off-site:** P

BREMEN BREMEN

Stadtwaldsee

Hochschulring 1, 28359
☎ 0421 8410748 0421 8410749
e-mail: contact@camping-stadtwaldsee.de
web: www.camping-stadtwaldsee.de

Situated near a lake in forest close to the city.

dir: *A27 exit 18.*

Open: All Year. **Site:** 5.8HEC **For hire:** **Facilities:** Wi-fi (charged) Play Area **Services:** **Off-site:** L P

BRIETLINGEN-REIHERSEE NIEDERSACHSEN

Reihersee 1

Alte Salzstr 8, 21382
☎ 04133 3671 & 3577 04133 3577

Divided into pitches by hedges and pine trees. Private bathing area.

dir: *Turn E at car park 2km beyond Brietlingen towards Reihersee for 0.8km.*

Open: All Year. **Site:** 6.2HEC **Facilities:** **Services:** **Leisure:** L R **Off-site:**

BÜCHEN SCHLESWIG-HOLSTEIN

Waldschwimmbad

21514
☎ 04155 5360 04155 499140
e-mail: camping-hintz@t-online.de
web: www.camping-buechen.de

On gently sloping grassland.

dir: *From Lauenburg or Mölln to Büchen then signed.*

Open: All Year. **Site:** 1.6HEC **For hire:** **Facilities:** **Services:** **Off-site:** P R

BURGWEDEL NIEDERSACHSEN

Erholungsgebiet Springhorstsee

30938
☎ 05139 3232 05139 27070
e-mail: springhorstsee@aol.com
web: www.springhorstsee.de

On level ground beside a lake with well-defined pitches and modern facilities.

dir: *A7 exit 54, site 2km.*

Open: All Year. **Site:** 29HEC **For hire:** **Facilities:** Play Area **Services:** **Leisure:** L P **Off-site:**

BUTJADINGEN NIEDERSACHSEN

Knaus Campingpark Burhave

Burhave Strand, 26969
☎ 04733 1683 04733 173206
e-mail: burhave@knauscamp.de
web: www.knauscamp.de

Situated next to a national park with access to fine beaches.

Open: 14 Apr-20 Oct **Site:** 10HEC **For hire:** **Facilities:** **Services:** **Leisure:** S

GERMANY

CLAUSTHAL-ZELLERFELD NIEDERSACHSEN

Prahljust

An den langen Bruchen 4, 38678
☎ 05323 1300 🖷 05323 78393
e-mail: camping@prahljust.de
web: www.prahljust.de

The site lies on slightly sloping grassland in an area of woodland and lakes.

dir: *B242 SE from outskirts towards Braunlage, 2km turn right, site 1.5km.*

Open: All Year. **Site:** 13HEC **For hire:** **Facilities:** Play Area **Services:** **Leisure:** L P **Off-site:** R

Waldweben

Spiegelthalerstr 31, 38678
☎ 05323 81712 🖷 05323 962134
e-mail: waldweben@t-online.de
web: www.campingplatz-waldweben.de

Holiday village with individual pitches in open meadow and coniferous woodland by three small lakes.

dir: *Signed from B241 towards Goslar.*

GPS: 51.8231, 10.3166

Open: All Year. **Site:** 4.5HEC **For hire:** **Facilities:** Wi-fi Play Area **Services:** **Off-site:** L P

DAHRENHORST NIEDERSACHSEN

Irenensee

31311
☎ 05173 98120 🖷 05173 981213
e-mail: info@irenensee.de
web: www.irenensee.de

A lakeside site on meadowland, partly surrounded by woods, with separate section for tourers, statics and residentials.

dir: *B188 from Burgdorf towards Uetze for 15km.*

Open: Apr-Oct **Site:** 120HEC **For hire:** **Facilities:** **Services:** **Leisure:** L

DETERN NIEDERSACHSEN

Jümmesee

26847
☎ 04957 1808 🖷 04957 8112
e-mail: info@detern.de
web: www.detern.de

Family site with leisure complex and a central lake.

dir: *Via B72 Aurich-Cloppenburg.*

Open: All Year. **Site:** 11.5HEC **Facilities:** Play Area **Services:** **Leisure:** L R **Off-site:**

DORUM NIEDERSACHSEN

AZUR Nordseecamp Dorumer Tief

Am Kutterhafen, 27632
☎ 04741 5020 🖷 04741 914061
e-mail: dorum@azur-camping.de
web: www.azur-camping.de/dorum

Next to a small harbour. Separated from the beach by a dyke.

dir: *Via A27 Bremerhaven-Cuxhaven.*

Open: Apr-Sep **Site:** 7HEC **Facilities:** **Services:** **Leisure:** P S

ECKWARDERHÖRNE NIEDERSACHSEN

Knaus Camping Park Eckwarderhörne

Butjadinger Str 116, 26969
☎ 04736 1300 🖷 04736 102593
e-mail: eckwarderhoerne@knauscamp.de
web: www.knauscamp.de

Parkland site adjoining the North Sea.

Open: 30 Mar-5 Nov **Site:** 7.7HEC **For hire:** **Facilities:** **Services:** **Leisure:** S

EGESTORF NIEDERSACHSEN

Regenbogen Camp Egestorf

Alte Dorfstr/Hundornweg 1, 21272
☎ 04175 661 🖷 04175 8383
e-mail: egestorf@regenbogen-camp.de
web: www.regengogen-camp.de

Modern site on wooded heathland on the edge of the Lüneburg Heath nature reserve, 2km south of town on slightly sloping terrain with asphalt internal roads.

dir: *A7 exit Evendorf, towards Egestorf.*

Open: Apr-Oct **Site:** 22HEC **For hire:** **Prices:** 12-26.50 **Facilities:** Wi-fi (charged) Play Area **Services:** **Leisure:** P **Off-site:**

ELISABETH SOPHIENKOOG (ISLAND OF NORDSTRAND) SCHLESWIG-HOLSTEIN

Elisabeth-Sophienkoog

Nordstrand, 25845
☎ 04842 8534 🖷 04842 8306
e-mail: camping-nordstrand@t-online.de
web: www.nordstrandcamping.de

On meadowland behind the sea dyke with bathing beach. A quiet site with good facilities for campers.

dir: *Via Husum to Island of Nordstrand.*

Open: Apr-Oct **Site:** 1.7HEC **For hire:** **Prices:** 20-22 Mobile home hire 250-350 **Facilities:** Wi-fi (charged) Play Area **Services:** **Leisure:** L S **Off-site:** P

GERMANY

ESENS-BENSERSIEL — NIEDERSACHSEN

Bensersiel

Am Strand 8, 26427
04971 917121 04971 917190
e-mail: camping@bensersiel.de
web: www.camping-bensersiel.de

Well-managed, extensive leisure centre with harbour, good fish restaurant and reading room. Swimming pools have sea water and artificial waves.

dir: *B210 NE from Aurich to Ogenbargenn then via Esens.*

GPS: 53.6752, 7.5699

Open: Apr-15 Oct **Site:** 10HEC **For hire:** **Facilities:** Wi-fi (charged) Kids' Club Play Area **Services:** **Leisure:** P S **Off-site:** L R

EUTIN-FISSAU — SCHLESWIG-HOLSTEIN

Prinzenholz

Prinzenholzweg 20, 23701
04521 5281 04521 790693
e-mail: info@nc-prinzenholz.de
web: www.nc-prinzenholz.de

Terraced lakeside site divided by trees and bushes.

dir: *N of town onto Malente road, 2km turn right.*

Open: Apr-Oct **Site:** 2HEC **For hire:** **Prices:** 25.50 **Facilities:** Wi-fi Play Area **Services:** **Leisure:** L **Off-site:** P

FALLINGBOSTEL — NIEDERSACHSEN

Böhmeschlucht

Vierde 22, 29683
05162 5604 05162 5160
e-mail: campingplatz-boehmeschlucht@t-online.de
web: www.boehmeschlucht.de

Site located in a nature reserve beside the river Böhme.

dir: *A7 exit 47, site signed 3km N.*

GPS: 52.8792, 9.7217

Open: All Year. **Site:** 4HEC **For hire:** **Prices:** 19.70 **Facilities:** Play Area **Services:** **Leisure:** R **Off-site:** P

FEHMARNSUND (ISLAND OF FEHMARN) — SCHLESWIG-HOLSTEIN

Miramar

Fehmarnsund 70, 23769
04371 3220 04371 868044
e-mail: campingmiramar@t-online.de
web: www.camping-miramar.de

A family site on meadowland at the southern end of the island.

dir: *Off B207 at 1st turn after Sundbrücke (bridge) towards Svendorf.*

GPS: 54.4075, 11.145

Open: All Year. **Site:** 13HEC **For hire:** **Prices:** 19-26 **Facilities:** Kids' Club Play Area **Services:** **Leisure:** L S

GANDERSHEIM, BAD — NIEDERSACHSEN

DCC Kur-Campingpark

Braunschweiger Str 12, 37581
05382 1595 05382 1599
e-mail: info@camping-bad-gandersheim.de
web: www.camping-bad-gandersheim.de

On a level meadow, divided in two by a brook beside a public park. Good sports facilities. Separate section for young people.

dir: *A7 exit 67 Soesen onto B64 W.*

Open: All Year. **Site:** 9HEC **Prices:** 16.90 **Facilities:** **Services:** **Off-site:** P

GARBSEN — NIEDERSACHSEN

Blauer See

30823
05137 89960 05137 899677
e-mail: info@camping-blauer-see.de
web: www.camping-blauer-see.de

On a small lake beside the Garbsen service area on the A2 motorway.

Open: All Year. **Site:** 22HEC **For hire:** **Facilities:** **Services:** **Leisure:** L

GLÜCKSBURG SCHLESWIG-HOLSTEIN

Ostseecamp Glücksburg-Holnis

An der Promenade 1, 24960

04631 622071 04631 622072

e-mail: info@ostseecamp-holnis.de

web: www.ostseecamp-holnis.de

Next to a sandy beach on the Baltic Sea in a quiet, sheltered location. Leisure facilities include fishing, mini-golf and boat hire.

Open: Apr-Oct **Site:** 6HEC **For hire:** **Facilities:** Wi-fi Play Area **Services:** **Off-site:** S

HADDEBY SCHLESWIG-HOLSTEIN

Haithabu

Haddebyer Chaussee 15, 24866

04621 32450 04621 33122

e-mail: info@campingplatz-haithabu.de

web: www.campingplatz-haithabu.de

Clean, tidy site beside the River Schlei.

dir: *B76 from Schleswig towards Eckernförde.*

Open: Apr-Oct **Site:** 5HEC **For hire:** **Facilities:** Play Area **Services:** **Leisure:** R

HAHNENKLEE NIEDERSACHSEN

Kreuzeck

38644

05325 2570 05325 3392

e-mail: kreuzeck@aol.com

web: www.kreuzeck.de

Terraced site in a forest beside a lake. Separate section for dog owners.

dir: *Beside Café am Kreuzeck at junct B241 & road to Hahnenklee.*

Open: All Year. **Site:** 5HEC **For hire:** **Facilities:** **Services:** **Leisure:** L P **Off-site:**

HARDEGSEN NIEDERSACHSEN

Ferienpark Solling

Auf dem Gladeberg 1, 37181

05505 2272 05505 5585

e-mail: ferienparksolling@web.de

Terraced site in forested area. Separate field for touring pitches.

dir: *In town onto Waldgebiet Gladeberg road.*

GPS: 51.6405, 9.831

Open: All Year. **Site:** 2.4HEC **For hire:** **Prices:** 15 **Facilities:** **Services:** **Off-site:** P

HASSENDORF NIEDERSACHSEN

Stürberg

27367

04264 9124 04264 821440

e-mail: campingpark-stuerberg@gmx.de

web: www.stuerberg.de

Pleasant wooded surroundings beside a lake.

dir: *A1 exit 50 Stuckenborstel, B75 for Rotenburg for 5km.*

GPS: 53.1202, 9.2783

Open: Apr-Oct **Site:** 2HEC **Facilities:** Wi-fi Play Area **Services:** **Leisure:** L **Off-site:** P

HATTEN NIEDERSACHSEN

Freizeitzentrum Hatten

Kreyenweg 8, 26209

04482 677 04482 928027

e-mail: info@fzz.hatten.de

web: www.fzz-hatten.de

Well equipped site at the edge of Kirchhatten.

Open: All Year. **Site:** 2HEC **For hire:** **Prices:** 14.50-19.50 **Facilities:** **Services:** **Leisure:** P

HATTORF NIEDERSACHSEN

Oderbrücke

37197

05521 4359 05521 4360

e-mail: info@oderbruecke.info

web: www.oderbruecke.info

A pleasant wooded location with good recreational and sanitary facilities.

dir: *On B27 towards Herzberg.*

GPS: 51.6280, 10.2708

Open: All Year. **Site:** 2.5HEC **Prices:** 12.20 **Facilities:** Play Area **Services:** **Leisure:** R **Off-site:** L P

GERMANY

HEIKENDORF — SCHLESWIG-HOLSTEIN

Möltenort

24226

☎ 0431 241316 🖷 0431 2379920

e-mail: gronau.heikendorf@freenet.de

web: www.camping-ostsee-online.de

Terraced site by the Kieler Förde.

dir: *15km NE of Kiel to W of road B502. Access via narrow, winding road.*

Open: Apr-1 Oct **Site:** 2HEC **Facilities:** **Services:** **Leisure:** S **Off-site:** P

HEMELN — NIEDERSACHSEN

Wesercamping Hemeln

Unterdorf 34, 34346

☎ 05544 1414 🖷 05544 1439

e-mail: info@wesercamping.de

web: www.wesercamping.de

Well-kept site on northern outskirts of village, beside the River Weser and close to Hann Münden Naturpark.

dir: *A7 exit Göttingen, B3 to Dransfeld & signed.*

GPS: 51.5041, 9.6027

Open: All Year. **Site:** 2.4HEC **For hire:** **Prices:** 16-17 **Facilities:** Wi-fi Play Area **Services:** **Leisure:** R **Off-site:** P

HERMANNSBURG — NIEDERSACHSEN

Örtzetal

Dicksbarg 46, 29320

☎ 05052 3072 & 1555

web: www.campingplatz-oldendorf.de

Site lies on meadows on the eastern bank of the River Örtze, set in unspoiled woodlands on Lüneburg Heath. Boat landing stage.

dir: *Off B3 in Bergen NE towards Hermannsburg & Eschwege.*

Open: 15 Mar-Oct **Site:** 6HEC **For hire:** **Facilities:** **Services:** **Leisure:** R **Off-site:** P

HOHEGEISS — NIEDERSACHSEN

Bärenbache

Bärenbachweg 10, 38700

☎ 05583 1306 🖷 05583 1300

e-mail: info@campingplatz-hohegeiss.de

web: www.campingplatz-hohegeiss.de

Terraced site, divided by hedges on south-facing slope. A short walk from the town centre.

Open: All Year. **Site:** 3HEC **For hire:** **Facilities:** **Services:** **Off-site:** P

HOLLE — NIEDERSACHSEN

Seecamp-Derneburg

An der B6, Derneburg, 31188

☎ 05062 565

e-mail: info@seecamp-derneburg.de

web: www.seecamp-derneburg.de

A terraced lakeside site on a hill slope with a southerly aspect. Separate towing field. Useful stopover site near autobahn.

dir: *Motorway exit Derneburg onto B6.*

Open: Apr-15 Sep **Site:** 7.8HEC **For hire:** **Facilities:** **Services:** **Leisure:** L **Off-site:** R

HÖSSERINGEN — NIEDERSACHSEN

Hardausee

29556

☎ 05826 7676 🖷 05826 8303

e-mail: info@camping-hardausee.de

web: www.camping-hardausee.de

Grassland site without firm internal roads. Statics have individual pitches and outbuildings. Separate fields for tourers.

dir: *From Uelzen S on B4, 9km turn right, continue via Suderburg to site on right before Hösseringen.*

Open: Mar-Oct **Site:** 12HEC **For hire:** **Prices:** 16-20 **Facilities:** Play Area **Services:** **Off-site:** L

ISERNHAGEN — NIEDERSACHSEN

Parksee Lohne

Alter Postweg 12, 30916

☎ 05139 88260 🖷 05139 891665

e-mail: parksee-lohne@t-online.de

web: www.parksee-lohne.de

Recreation area by a lake. On the flight approach path for Hannover Langenhagen airport. Separate section for tourers.

dir: *Motorway exit Kirchorst, Altwarmbüchen road to Isernhagen.*

Open: Apr-15 Oct **Site:** 13HEC **Facilities:** **Services:** **Leisure:** L

GERMANY

KLAUSDORF (ISLAND OF FEHMARN) SCHLESWIG-HOLSTEIN

Klausdorfer Strand

23769

04371 2549 04371 2481

e-mail: info@camping-klausdorferstrand.de

web: www.camping-klausdorferstrand.de

A grassy site with sea views, divided into pitches with a sandy beach.

dir: *From Burg turn off main road 2.5km before Klausdorf onto narrow asphalt road.*

GPS: 54.4572, 11.2719

Open: Apr-15 Oct **Site:** 12HEC **For hire:** **Prices:** 14-24 **Facilities:** Wi-fi (charged) Kids' Club Play Area **Services:** **Leisure:** S **Off-site:** L P

KLEINWAABS SCHLESWIG-HOLSTEIN

Ostsee Heide

24369

04352 2530 04352 1398

e-mail: info@waabs.de

web: www.waabs.de

Divided into pitches and pleasantly landscaped. Large games room for teenagers.

Open: Mar-Oct **Site:** 22HEC **For hire:** **Prices:** 17-33 **Facilities:** Wi-fi (charged) Kids' Club Play Area **Services:** **Leisure:** P S

KLINT-BEI-HECHTHAUSEN NIEDERSACHSEN

Geesthof

Am Ferienpark 1, 21755

04774 512 04774 9178

e-mail: info@geesthof.de

web: www.geesthof.de

On dry meadowland next to the River Oste, in quiet setting with trees.

dir: *Off B73 in Hechthausen, W towards Lamstedt for 3km.*

Open: All Year. **Site:** 15HEC **For hire:** **Prices:** 12-19 **Facilities:** Wi-fi (charged) Play Area **Services:** **Leisure:** L P

LOOSE SCHLESWIG-HOLSTEIN

Gut Ludwigsburg

24369

04358 370 04358 460

e-mail: info@ostseecamping-ludwigsburg.de

web: www.ostseecamping-ludwigsburg.de

A well presented site with good amenities and recreational facilities between the old Hanseatic cities of Lübeck and Wismar. Kids' club in July and August.

dir: *From Eckernförde towards Klein-Wabbs, at Gut Ludwigsburg onto track for 2km.*

GPS: 54.5031, 9.9577

Open: Apr-Sep **Site:** 10HEC **For hire:** **Facilities:** Wi-fi Kids' Club Play Area **Services:** **Leisure:** L S

LÜGDE NIEDERSACHSEN

Eichwald

Obere Dorfstr 80, 32676

05283 335 05283 640

e-mail: info@camping-eichwald.de

web: www.camping-eichwald.de

Pleasant grassy site near woodland and a pool.

dir: *S of Lüdge towards Rischenau to Elbrinxen.*

Open: All Year. **Site:** 10HEC **For hire:** **Facilities:** **Services:** **Off-site:** P

MALENTE-GREMSMÜHLEN SCHLESWIG-HOLSTEIN

Schwentine

Wiesenweg 14, 23714

04523 4327 04523 207602

e-mail: info@camping-bad-malente.de

web: www.camping-bad-malente.de

A park-like setting with trees and bushes, at a river within the village of Malente.

dir: *A1 Hamburg/Lübeck/Puttgarden, then Eutin B76 in direction of Süsel and Eutin. A7 Hamburg/Flensburg.*

Open: Apr-Oct **Site:** 2.5HEC **Prices:** 16-20 **Facilities:** Wi-fi Play Area **Services:** **Leisure:** R **Off-site:** L P

NEUSTADT **SCHLESWIG-HOLSTEIN**

Strande

Sandberger Weg 94, 23730
04561 4188 04361 7125
e-mail: info@amstrande.de
web: www.amstrande.de

The site is divided into small sections and slopes down to the sea. Narrow sandy beach.

dir: *From Neustadt towards Schön Klinik, 1st site on right.*

Open: Apr-Sep **Site:** 4.7HEC **For hire:** **Facilities:** Wi-fi (charged) **Services:** **Leisure:** S **Off-site:**

NORTHEIM **NIEDERSACHSEN**

Sultmer Berg

Sultmerberg 3, 37154
05551 51559 05551 5656
e-mail: campingplatzmajora@web.de
web: www.campingplatzsultmerberg.de

Grassland site with views of surrounding hills.

dir: *B3 from town centre.*

Open: 15 Feb-Oct **Site:** 2.7HEC **Prices:** 18.70 **Facilities:** **Services:** **Leisure:** P **Off-site:** L R

ORTSTEIL GÖTTINGERODE **NIEDERSACHSEN**

Harz-Camp Göttingerode

Kreisstr 66, 38667
05322 81215 05322 877533
e-mail: harz-camp@t-online.de
web: www.harz-camp.de

Partly terraced site on the edge of a forest with modern facilities. There is a sauna and jacuzzi. Ideally located for exploring the northern slopes of the Harz mountains.

dir: *On L501 between Bad Harzburg & Goslar.*

Open: All Year. **Site:** 6.5HEC **Prices:** 22.70 **Facilities:** Wi-fi (charged) Play Area **Services:** **Leisure:** P **Off-site:**

OSNABRÜCK **NIEDERSACHSEN**

Niedersachsenhof

Nordstr 109, 49084
0541 77226 0541 70627
e-mail: osnacamp@aol.com
web: www.osnacamp.de

The site lies on a gently sloping meadow bordering a forest, near a converted farmhouse with an inn.

dir: *5km NW from town centre on B51/65 towards Bremen, turn right, site 300m.*

Open: All Year. **Site:** 3HEC **For hire:** **Prices:** 17.50 **Facilities:** Play Area **Services:** **Off-site:** P R

OSTRHAUDERFEHN **NIEDERSACHSEN**

Camping-Und Frieizeitanlage Idasee

Idafehn-Nord 77 B, 26842
04952 994297 04952 808628
e-mail: info@campingidasee.de
web: www.campingidasee.de

A lakeside site between Oldenburg and the Dutch border with good water sports.

dir: *Via B27 Cloppenburg-Aurich.*

GPS: 53.1507, 7.6399

Open: All Year. **Site:** 11HEC **Prices:** 14.30-17.70 **Facilities:** Wi-fi (charged) **Services:** **Leisure:** L **Off-site:** P

OTTERNDORF **NIEDERSACHSEN**

See Achtern Diek

Am Campingplatz 3, 21762
04751 2933 04751 3016
e-mail: campingplatz.otterndorf@ewetel.net
web: www.otterndorf.de

A family site with good facilities close to the coast.

dir: *Via B73 Cuxhaven-Hamburg.*

Open: Apr-Oct **Site:** 15HEC **Prices:** 14.60-20 **Facilities:** Kids' Club Play Area **Services:** **Leisure:** L **Off-site:** P R S

Site 6HEC (site size) grass sand stone little shade partly shaded mainly shaded motorvans accepted bungalows for hire mobile homes for hire tents for hire no dogs site fully accessible for wheelchairs
Prices amount quoted is per night, for 2 adults and car, plus tent or caravan Mobile home hire is a weekly rate.

OYTEN — NIEDERSACHSEN

Knaus Campingplatz Oyten

Erholungsgebiet Oyter See, 28876

☎ 04207 2878 ▤ 04207 909005

e-mail: oyten@knauscamp.de

web: www.knauscamp.de

Parkland site next to a 1.5km long lake on the outskirts of Bremen. Ideal starting point for the Wümme trail

Open: 14 Mar-3 Nov **Site:** 15.6HEC **Facilities:** **Services:** **Leisure:** L

PLÖN — SCHLESWIG-HOLSTEIN

Spitzenort

Ascheberger Str 76, 24306

☎ 04522 2769 ▤ 04522 4574

web: www.spitzenort.de

A pleasant site with hedges surrounded by Plön lake on three sides. Ideal for water sports.

dir: *B430 from Plön towards Neumünster.*

Open: Apr-15 Oct **Site:** 4.5HEC **Facilities:** **Services:** **Leisure:** L **Off-site:** P

RIESTE — NIEDERSACHSEN

Alfsee

Am Campingpark 10, 49597

☎ 05464 92120 ▤ 05464 5837

e-mail: info@alfsee.de

web: www.alfsee.com

Situated around a large lake with a wide range of activities available including a sailing and surfing school, boat and bike rental.

Open: All Year. **Site:** 16HEC **For hire:** **Facilities:** **Services:** **Leisure:** L

RINTELN — NIEDERSACHSEN

Doktor-See

am Doktorsee 8, 31722

☎ 05751 964860 ▤ 05751 964888

e-mail: info@doktorsee.de

web: www.doktorsee.de

A beautiful location beside a recreation area and the Doktor-See bathing beach. Section for touring campers.

dir: *In town turn downstream at River Weser bridge along left bank for 1.5km.*

GPS: 52.1864, 9.0597

Open: All Year. **Site:** 152HEC **For hire:** **Prices:** 15.50-20.80 Mobile home hire 299-352 **Facilities:** Play Area **Services:** **Leisure:** L **Off-site:** P R

ROSENFELDE-GRUBE — SCHLESWIG-HOLSTEIN

Rosenfelder Strand Ostsee Camping

Rosenfelder Strand 1, 23749

☎ 04365 979722 ▤ 04365 979594

e-mail: info@rosenfelder-strand.de

web: www.rosenfelder-strand.de/camping-baltic-sea/index.html

Excellently managed family site beside the sea with a 1km-long beach. Divided into separate fields by rows of bushes. Children's playground in woodland between site and sea.

dir: *E47/A1 Hamburg/Lübeck/Oldenburg-H exit 12 towards Grube then left onto B501 towards Heiligenhafen. After 4km turn right toward Rosenfelde; pass farm then left at sign.*

GPS: 54.2651, 11.0776

Open: 23 Mar-14 Oct **Site:** 24HEC **For hire:** **Prices:** 16.60-26 Mobile home hire 237-580 **Facilities:** Wi-fi (charged) Kids' Club Play Area **Services:** **Leisure:** S

RÖTGESBÜTTEL — NIEDERSACHSEN

Campingplatz Glockenheide

Glockenheide 1, 38531

☎ 05304 1581 ▤ 05304 918076

e-mail: info@glockenheide.de

web: www.glockenheide.de

Tranquil site in heathland. Discounts for Camping Card International (CCI) holders.

dir: *From B4 Rötgesbüttel turn left towards railway station & after level crossing turn left again. After 1km turn left, campsite signed.*

GPS: 52.4064, 10.5115

Open: All Year. **Site:** 5HEC **For hire:** **Prices:** 11.60-12.80 **Facilities:** Play Area **Services:** **Off-site:** L P R

SCHOBÜLL — SCHLESWIG-HOLSTEIN

Seeblick

Nordseestr 39, 25813

☎ 04841 3321 ▤ 04841 5773

e-mail: info@camping-seeblick.de

web: www.camping-seeblick.de

Beautiful location beside the sea. Site divided into two sections.

dir: *Off B5 on N outskirts of Husum towards Insel Nordstrand for 4km to Schobüll.*

Open: 23 Mar-21 Oct **Site:** 3.4HEC **Prices:** 14.50 **Facilities:** Wi-fi Play Area **Services:** **Leisure:** S **Off-site:** P

GERMANY

STRUKKAMPHUK (ISLAND OF FEHMARN) SCHLESWIG-HOLSTEIN

Strukkamphuk

23769

☎ 04371 2194 🖹 04371 87178

e-mail: camping@strukkamphuk.de

web: www.strukkamphuk.de

Site in the south of the Island of Fehmarn, situated behind the dyke, directly on the Baltic Sea.

GPS: 54.4106, 11.1006

Open: All Year. **Site:** 20HEC **Prices:** 13.60-32.50 **Facilities:** Kids' Club Play Area **Services:** **Leisure:** L S

STUHR NIEDERSACHSEN

Steller See

Zum Steller See 15, 28816

☎ 04206 6490 🖹 04206 6668

e-mail: steller.see@t-online.de

web: www.steller-see.de

Located on a nature reserve with good access to the motorway. On-site lake where water sports are available.

dir: *Dreieck Stuhr exit off motorway A1.*

GPS: 53.0075, 8.6925

Open: Apr-Sep **Site:** 16HEC **Prices:** 15.50 **Facilities:** Play Area **Services:** **Leisure:** L

TARMSTEDT NIEDERSACHSEN

Rethbergsee

27412

☎ 04283 422 🖹 04283 980139

e-mail: camping-rethbergsee@t-online.de

web: www.rethbergsee-wochenendpark.de

Level site on a grand scale.

dir: *Halfway between Bremen-Lilienthal & Zeven.*

Open: All Year. **Site:** 10HEC **For hire:** **Prices:** 18 **Facilities:** Play Area **Services:** **Leisure:** L **Off-site:**

TELLINGSTEDT SCHLESWIG-HOLSTEIN

Tellingstedt

Teichstr, 25782

☎ 04838 657 🖹 04836 99060

e-mail: info@amt-eider.de

Divided by a row of high shrubs.

dir: *Off B203 towards swimming pool.*

Open: May-15 Sep **Site:** 1.2HEC **Facilities:** **Services:** **Leisure:** P **Off-site:**

TÖNNING SCHLESWIG-HOLSTEIN

Lilienhof

Katinger Landstr 5, 25832

☎ 04861 439 🖹 04861 610159

e-mail: info@camping-lilienhof.de

web: www.camping-lilienhof.de

Well-maintained site in the woodland grounds of an old manor house next to a quiet country road.

dir: *Off B202 at end of Tönning & 2km W towards Welt.*

GPS: 54.3114, 8.9036

Open: All Year. **Site:** 2HEC **For hire:** **Prices:** 12.50-18.50 Mobile home hire 266-318.50 **Facilities:** Play Area **Services:** **Off-site:** P R S

TOSSENS NIEDERSACHSEN

Knaus Campingpark Tossens

Tossener Deich, 26969

☎ 04736 219 🖹 04736 102168

e-mail: tossens@knauscamp.de

web: www.knauscamp.de

Situated next to the beach facing the North Sea.

Open: 14 Apr-20 Oct **Site:** 8HEC **Facilities:** **Services:** **Leisure:** S **Off-site:** P

WALKENRIED NIEDERSACHSEN

Knaus Campingpark Walkenried

Ellricher Str 7, 37445

☎ 05525 778 🖹 05525 2332

e-mail: walkenried@knauscamp.de

web: www.knauscamp.de

An attractive location in the southern Harz area.

dir: *A7 exit Seesen, B243 via Herzberg & Bad Sachsa.*

Open: 16 Dec-3 Nov **Site:** 5.5HEC **For hire:** **Facilities:** **Services:** **Off-site:**

WALLENSEN NIEDERSACHSEN

Humboldt See

31020

☎ 05186 957140 🖹 05186 957139

web: www.campingpark-humboldtsee.de

Close to Humboldt Lake, the site is ideally located for hiking and walking holidays in mountainous country surrounding the River Weser and the town of Hameln.

Open: All Year. **Site:** 6.5HEC **For hire:** **Facilities:** **Services:** **Off-site:** L

GERMANY

WEISSENHAUS — SCHLESWIG-HOLSTEIN

Triangel

23758

☎ 04361 507890 04361 5078969

e-mail: info@campingplatz-triangel.de

web: www.campingplatz-triangel.de

Eco-friendly campsite set in attractive countryside close to the dunes and a Baltic Sea beach.

dir: *E47/E22 Hamburg-Puttgarden, exit Oldenburg in the centre of Holstein. Direction towards Kiel, exit Weissenhäuser Strand.*

Open: 31 Mar-21 Oct **Site:** 12HEC **For hire:** **Facilities:** Wi-fi (charged) Play Area **Services:** **Leisure:** S

WIETZENDORF — NIEDERSACHSEN

Südsee

Südsee-Camp 1, 29649

☎ 05196 980116 05196 980299

e-mail: info@suedseecamp.de

web: www.5-sterne-camping.de

Beautiful location in a forest beside a lake in the middle of the Lünerburger Heide.

dir: *A7 exit 45 Soltau-Süd, B3 S towards Bergen for 2km, at underpass in Bokel left for Wietzendorf for 4km.*

Open: All Year. **Site:** 80HEC **For hire:** **Facilities:** Wi-fi (charged) Kids' Club Play Area **Services:** **Leisure:** L P

WILSUM — NIEDERSACHSEN

AZUR-Ferienpark Wilsumer Berge

Zum Feriengebiet 1, 49849

☎ 05945 995580 05945 995599

e-mail: info@wilsumerberge.nl

web: www.wilsumerberge.nl

Parts of the site adjoin a large lake. The separate section for touring campers has its own sanitary building.

dir: *B403 from Nordhorn via Uelsen to Wilsum, turn right near Wilsum.*

Open: All Year. **Site:** 88HEC **For hire:** **Facilities:** **Services:** **Leisure:** L

WINGST — NIEDERSACHSEN

Knaus Campingpark Wingst

Schwimmbadallee 13, 21789

☎ 04778 7604 04778 7608

e-mail: wingst@knauscamp.de

web: www.knauscamp.de

This modern comfortable site extends over several terraces, above a small artificial lake on the northern edge of an extensive forested area. Municipal recreation centre across the road.

dir: *Off B73 between Stade & Cuxhaven, 3km S of Cadenberge.*

Open: 14 Mar-3 Nov **Site:** 11.6HEC **For hire:** **Facilities:** Wi-fi (charged) Play Area **Services:** **Off-site:** P R

WINSEN — NIEDERSACHSEN

Hüttensee

29308

☎ 05056 941880 05056 941881

e-mail: info@campingpark-huettensee.de

web: www.campingpark-huettensee.de

Site beside a large stretch of water on Lüneburg Heath, suitable for swimming and water sports. Fine sandy beach. The area is rich in wildlife.

Open: All Year. **Site:** 17HEC **For hire:** **Facilities:** **Services:** **Leisure:** L P

WINSEN-ALLER — NIEDERSACHSEN

Campingplatz Winsen

29308

☎ 05143 93199 05143 93144

web: www.campingplatz-winsen.de

Site lies on meadowland at the River Aller. Water sports available.

dir: *NW from Celle to Winsen.*

Open: All Year. **Site:** 12HEC **Facilities:** **Services:** **Leisure:** R **Off-site:** P

GERMANY

WITTENBORN SCHLESWIG-HOLSTEIN

Weisser Brunnen

23829

☎ 04554 1757 & 1413 04554 4833

e-mail: gert.petzold@t-online.de

web: www.naturcamping-weisser-brunnen.de

A lakeside site consisting of several sections, hilly in parts, next to Lake Mözen. A public road, leading to the lake, passes through part of the site.

dir: *Off B206 at Km23.6 towards lake.*

GPS: 53.9214, 10.2339

Open: Apr-24 Oct **Site:** 7HEC **Prices:** 17-20 **Facilities:** Play Area **Services:** **Leisure:** L

WULFEN (ISLAND OF FEHMARN) SCHLESWIG-HOLSTEIN

Wulfener Hals

23769

☎ 04371 86280 04371 3723

e-mail: camping@wulfenerhals.de

web: www.wulfenerhals.de

A meadowland site beside the Baltic Sea and an inland lake (Burger Binnensee), with a 1.7km long private beach.

dir: *Off B20 (Vogelfluglinie) after Sundbrücke towards Avendorf, then Wulfen & Wulfener Hals.*

Open: All Year. **Site:** 34HEC **For hire:** **Prices:** 11.80-43.60 Mobile home hire 231-903 **Facilities:** Wi-fi (charged) Kids' Club Play Area **Services:** **Leisure:** P S

ZORGE NIEDERSACHSEN

Harz Camping Im Waldwinkel

37449

☎ 05586 1048 05586 8113

e-mail: campingzorge@aol.com

web: www.campingplatz-im-waldwinkel.de

A site on different levels, surrounded by high trees, 200 metres from an open-air woodland pool in Kunzen Valley.

GPS: 51.6416, 10.6502

Open: All Year. **Site:** 1.5HEC **For hire:** **Prices:** 16.70 **Facilities:** Wi-fi (charged) Play Area **Services:** **Off-site:** P

GERMANY

Greece

Drinking and driving

If the level of alcohol in the bloodstream is 0.05% or more it is a criminal offence. 0% of alcohol allowed in drivers' blood applies to drivers who have held a licence for less than two years, and to motorcyclists.

Driving licence

Minimum age at which a UK licence holder may drive temporarily imported car and/or motorcycle (over 50cc) 17.

Fines

Police can impose fines but not collect them on-the-spot. The fine must be paid at a Public Treasury office within 10 days. You can be fined for the unnecessary use of a car horn. Vehicles may be towed away if parked illegally, or if violating traffic regulations.

Fuel

Unleaded petrol (95 and 98 octane) and diesel (petreleo) is available. No leaded petrol (lead replacement petrol available as 'Super 2002' 98 octane). It is forbidden to carry petrol in a can in a vehicle. LPG may not be used in private cars, only in taxis. Credit cards accepted at some filling stations. Check with your card issuer for use in Greece before travel.

Lights

Dipped headlights should be used in poor daytime visibility. The use of full beam headlights in towns is strictly prohibited.

Motorcycles

Use of dipped headlights during the day compulsory. The wearing of crash helmets is compulsory.

Motor insurance

Third-party compulsory.

Passengers/children in cars

Children under 3 years must be placed in a suitable child restraint. Approved child restraints are those conforming with standard ECE R44/03 (or later).

Children between 3 and 11 years, measuring less than 1.35m must be seated in an appropriate child restraint for their size.

From the age of 12, children measuring over 1.35m can wear an adult seat belt.

Placing a rear-facing child restraint in the front passenger seat is allowed only on condition that the passenger airbag is deactivated.

Seat belts

Compulsory for front and rear seat occupants to wear seat belts, if fitted.

Speed limits

Standard legal limits, which may be varied by signs

Private vehicles without trailers	
Built-up areas	50km/h
Outside built-up areas	90km/h or 110km/h
Motorways	130km/h
Cars towing a light trailer	
Motorways	90km/h
Built-up areas	50km/h
Cars towing a trailer	
Motorways	80km/h
Built-up areas	50km/h
Motorhomes	
Motorways	90km/h
Built-up areas	50km/h
Motorhomes towing a trailer	
Motorways	80km/h
Built-up areas	50km/h

The above limits are the maximum unless a lower limit is stated by traffic signs

Pictured: Olive grove, Corfu

Greece

Compulsory equipment in Greece

Fire extinguisher

First-aid kit

Warning triangle (excludes two-wheeled vehicles)

Other rules/requirements

The police are empowered to confiscate the number plates of illegally parked vehicles throughout Greece. Generally this only applies to Greek-registered vehicles, but the drivers of foreign registered vehicles should beware of parking illegally.

Snow chains may be used when roads are covered with snow or ice, usually between November and March. The maximum speed limit for cars with chains is 50km/h.

Tolls Currency Euro (€)	Car
A1/E75 - Afidnes - Athens	€2.05
A1/E75 - Thessaloniki - Katerini	€2.00
A1/E75 - Lamia - Thiva	€2.25
A1/E75 - Thiva - Afidnes	€2.35
A1/E75 - Katerini - Larisa	€5.10
A1/E75 - Larisa - Lamia	€5.20
A2/E90 - Thessaloniki - Grevena	€2.80
A7/E65 - Athens - Tripoli	€3.10
A8/E65-E55 - Korinthos - Patra	€2.90
A8/E94 - Attiki Odos	€2.80
A8/E94 - Athens - Patras	€3.10

Bridges/Tunnels Currency Euro (€)	Car
A7/E65 - Artemission Tunnel	€1.70
A8/E65-E55 - The Rion-Antirio Bridge	€12.90
E55 - Aktion Tunnel	€3.00

AGIÓKAMBOS — THESSALY

Aegeas

40003

☎ 24940 51580 📠 24940 51581

Shady site with marked pitches situated on the coast by a sandy beach.

Open: May-Sep **Site:** 1.2HEC **For hire:** **Facilities:** **Services:** **Off-site:** P S

ALEXANDROÚPOLI — THRACE

Camping Alexandroúpolis

Makris Av, 68100

☎ 25510 28735 📠 25510 28735

e-mail: camping@ditea.gr

web: www.ditea.gr

A large site on a meadow near the waterfront with concrete pitches.

dir: *Between Thessaloniki-Istanbul road & beach to W of town.*

GPS: 40.8467, 25.8563

Open: All Year. **Site:** 7HEC **Prices:** 15.73-17.76 **Facilities:** Wi-fi Play Area **Services:** **Leisure:** S

ATHÍNAI (ATHENS) — ATTICA

Athens

Leoforos Athinon 198, Peristeri, 12136

☎ 210 5814114 📠 210 5820353

e-mail: info@campingathens.com.gr

web: www.campingathens.com.gr

Pitches of a reasonable size and generally well-shaded, although some are near a busy road. Convenient for visiting the city.

dir: *From N E75 signed Athina-Pireas, 2nd exit to Korinthos E94. Site 2km on right. From S NR8 signed Athina-Pireas, site is 4km after Dafni Monastery, keep in right hand land and turn after 1.2km to go back in other direction.*

GPS: 38.0086, 23.6719

Open: All Year. **Site:** 1.4HEC **For hire:** **Prices:** 26-31 **Facilities:** Wi-fi **Services:**

GREECE

Nea Kifissia

60 Potamou & Dimitsanas Adames, Nea Kifissia, 14564

210 8075579 210 8075579

e-mail: camping@hol.gr

A small family-run site with level pitches, some shady. Quiet location but very convenient for visiting the sites of the city.

dir: *16km N of Athens. Signed from Aharnes exit on Athens-Lamia motorway.*

Open: All Year. **Site:** 2.2HEC **For hire:** **Facilities:** **Services:** **Leisure:** P

DELFOÍ (DELPHI) — CENTRAL GREECE

Camping Apollon

Old National Rd, 33054

22650 82762 22650 82888

e-mail: apollon4@otenet.gr

web: www.apolloncamping.gr

Located within easy reach of the ancient site of Delphi, the site offers take-away meals and an internet café.

Open: All Year. **Site:** **For hire:** **Prices:** 23-26 Mobile home hire 350 **Facilities:** Wi-fi (charged) Play Area **Services:** **Leisure:** P **Off-site:**

Chrissa

33054

22650 82050 22650 83148

e-mail: info@chrissacamping.gr

web: www.chrissacamping.gr

Terraced site on a hill overlooking the sea with fine views of Delphi and the Corinth Bay. Leisure facilities include football and basketball court. There is a tavern offering take-away meals.

dir: *6km on Delphi-Itea-Amfissa highway near village of Chrisso.*

GPS: 38.4728, 22.4586

Open: All Year. **Site:** 1.6HEC **For hire:** **Prices:** 18-22 Mobile home hire 280-350 **Facilities:** Wi-fi (charged) Play Area **Services:** **Leisure:** P **Off-site:** S

EPIDAVROS — PELOPONNESE

Camping Bekas

Gialasi Beach, 21059

27530 99930 27530 99931

e-mail: info@bekas.gr

web: www.bekas.gr

Quiet site next to the beach with green surroundings.

Open: Apr-25 Oct **Site:** 2.8HEC **Facilities:** Wi-fi **Services:** **Leisure:** S **Off-site:** P

EVIA, ISLAND OF — CENTRAL GREECE

Milos

Lepira, 34008

22290 60420 22290 60360

e-mail: info@camping-in-evia.gr

web: www.camping-in-evia.gr

A site with modern facilities close to the sea. Set against a background of mountains, and convenient for visiting Athens.

dir: *On island of Evia route 44. Campsite 1.5km before Eretria on right. Signed.*

Open: Apr-Sep **Site:** 1.8HEC **For hire:** **Prices:** 21-23.60 **Facilities:** Wi-fi **Services:** **Leisure:** P S **Off-site:**

FINIKOUNDA — PELOPONNESE

Loutsa

24006

27230 71169 27230 71445

web: www.finikounda.at/camping-loutsa

Picturesque site in shady natural surroundings next to a fine beach.

dir: *National road Methoni-Koroni.*

Open: May-Oct **Site:** 0.8HEC **Facilities:** **Services:** **Leisure:** S **Off-site:** P

GIALOVA — PELOPONNESE

Navarino Beach

24001

27230 22973 27230 23512

e-mail: info@navarino-beach.gr

web: www.navarino-beach.gr

Most pitches face the sea and are shaded by trees. The shallow sandy beach is ideal for children.

Open: All Year. **Site:** 2.4HEC **For hire:** **Prices:** 19-25 **Facilities:** Wi-fi Play Area **Services:** **Leisure:** S **Off-site:**

GREECE

GLIFA — PELOPONNESE

Ionion Beach

27050

26230 96395 26230 96425

e-mail: ioniongr@otenet.gr

web: www.ionion-beach.gr

Family-run site in a shady location by the sea.

dir: *From national road Patras-Pyrgos turn right via Gatsouni & Vartalomia at 67km sign towards Loutra Killini. Left at fork towards Glifa Beach. Follow signs.*

Open: All Year. **Site:** **For hire:** **Facilities:** Wi-fi (charged) Play Area **Services:** **Leisure:** P S

GYTHEIO — PELOPONNESE

Mani Beach

23200

27330 23450 27330 25400

e-mail: info@manibeach.gr

web: www.manibeach.gr

Site with many facilities close to a fine sandy beach with clear water. Several interesting tourist sites nearby.

dir: *4 km S of Gythion on Aeropolis road.*

Open: All Year. **Site:** 3.5HEC **For hire:** **Facilities:** **Services:** **Off-site:** S

ITÉA — CENTRAL GREECE

Ayannis

33200

22650 32555 22650 33870

The site stretches over several terraces and is scattered with small olive trees and strengthened by stone walls. There are fine views over the Gulf of Corinth.

Open: Apr-Oct **Site:** 2HEC **For hire:** **Facilities:** **Services:** **Leisure:** S

KATO ALISSOS — PELOPONNESE

Kato Alissos

25002

26930 71249 26930 71150

e-mail: demiris-cmp@otenet.gr

web: www.camping-kato-alissos.gr

Shady site located in an olive grove.

dir: *Take National Road from Patras to Pyrgos for 21km, turn right following signs for 500m.*

Open: Apr-25 Oct **Site:** 1.2HEC **For hire:** **Facilities:** **Services:** **Leisure:** S **Off-site:** R

KATO GATZEA — THESSALY

Hellas

Volos, 38500

24230 22267 24230 22492

e-mail: info@campinghellas.gr

web: www.campinghellas.gr

The site lies in an olive grove on sloping ground between the road and the beach.

dir: *10km W of Volos, take route Pilio-Argalasti for 18 km, site signposted.*

Open: Apr-Oct **Site:** 2.8HEC **For hire:** **Prices:** 19-27 **Facilities:** Wi-fi **Services:** **Leisure:** S

Sikia

38500

24230 22279 24230 22720

e-mail: info@camping-sikia.gr

web: www.camping-sikia.gr

Family-run terraced site by the seashore, with apartments available to hire.

dir: *From Volos follow coastal road towards Argalasti. Site 18km on right after Kato Gatzea.*

GPS: 39.3088, 23.1098

Open: Apr-Oct **Site:** 3HEC **For hire:** **Facilities:** Wi-fi **Services:** **Leisure:** S **Off-site:**

KAVALA — MACEDONIA

Batis Multiplex

65500

2510 245918 2510 245690

e-mail: info@batis-sa.gr

web: www.batis-sa.gr

Secure site with trees providing natural shade, located next to a beach 4km west of Kavala. Swimming pool and first aid facilities available in high season only.

Open: All Year. **Site:** 3.3HEC **Facilities:** Wi-fi Play Area **Services:** **Leisure:** P S **Off-site:**

GREECE

KÉRKIRA (CORFU)

DASSIA

Karda Beach

49083

26610 93595 26610 93595

e-mail: campco@otenet.gr

web: www.kardacamp.gr

Situated in an olive grove, 100 metres from a good, clean beach.

dir: *12km N of Kérkira, on right of main road from Kérkira-Kassiopi.*

GPS: 39.6861, 19.8383

Open: 9 Apr-30 Oct **Site:** 2.6HEC **For hire:** **Prices:** 23.90-25.20 **Facilities:** Wi-fi Play Area **Services:** **Leisure:** P **Off-site:** S

KRÍTI (CRETE)

RÉTHYMNO

Elizabeth

Ionias 84, Misiria, 74100

28310 28694 28310 28694

e-mail: info@camping-elizabeth.net

web: www.camping-elizabeth.net

A quiet family site, directly on the beach, with spacious pitches under shady trees. Please contact site for winter bookings.

dir: *3km E. From Heraklion, before Réthymno, exit Platanes/Arkadi. Follow road towards Réthymno, site 1km on the right along short, unsurfaced road.*

Open: All Year. **Site:** 25HEC **For hire:** **Prices:** 17.20-23.30 **Facilities:** Wi-fi **Services:** **Leisure:** S **Off-site:** P

LECHEON — PELOPONNESE

Blue Dolphin

20011

27410 25766 27410 85959

e-mail: skouspos@otenet.gr

web: www.camping-blue-dolphin.gr

Situated adjacent to the beach on the Corinthian Gulf. There is an abundance of shade, which is created by the trees and roofing made from bamboo sticks.

dir: *6km W of Corinth off Athens-Patras road.*

Open: Apr-Oct **Site:** 4HEC **For hire:** **Facilities:** Wi-fi Play Area **Services:** **Leisure:** S **Off-site:** P

LITÓCHORO — MACEDONIA

Mytikas

60200

23520 61275 23520 61276

e-mail: camp.mitikas@gmail.com

web: www.campingmitikas.com

A family-run campsite located 100 metres from a fine beach, with a magnificent view of Mount Olympus.

dir: *Approx 15km S of Katerini, turn towards Gritsa Beach. Site on right beyond railway line.*

Open: Apr-15 Oct **Site:** 8.5HEC **For hire:** **Prices:** 17-22 **Facilities:** Wi-fi **Services:** **Leisure:** P S

MARATHONAS — ATTICA

Ramnous

Posidonos 174, 19007

22940 55855 22940 55244

web: www.ramnous.gr

Peaceful site in a beach location with a regular bus to Athens.

dir: *Athens-Marathon road, right at lights about 6km past Nea Makri, right at Kato Souli Schinias sign, then follow signs for 4.5km.*

Open: Apr-Oct **Site:** 20HEC **For hire:** **Facilities:** **Services:** **Leisure:** S **Off-site:** L

PLATARIÁ — MACEDONIA

Camping Elena's Beach

46100

26650 71414 26650 71414

e-mail: info@campingelena.gr

web: www.campingelena.gr

With direct access to its own beach, this site has mainly shaded pitches. Traditional Greek nights are held in the restaurant with singing and dancing.

Open: 4 Apr-Oct **Site:** 1.2HEC **Prices:** 20.50-22.50 **Facilities:** Wi-fi (charged) Play Area **Services:** **Leisure:** S

Kalami Beach

P.O. Box 8, 46100

☎ 26650 71211 📠 26650 71245

e-mail: info@campingkalamibeach.gr

web: www.campingkalamibeach.gr

Site close to Corfu in green surroundings with views of a fine clean beach.

dir: *Igoumenitsa to Platariá road, after 7km 1st campsite on right, signed.*

Open: Apr-Oct **Site:** 1.2HEC **Facilities:** **Services:**

PYLOS — PELOPONNESE

Camping Erodios

Gialova, 24001

☎ 27230 23269 📠 27230 28240

e-mail: erodioss@otenet.gr

web: www.erodioss.gr

Close to Gialova and 15 minutes from Pylos, the site is set in olive trees by the sea.

GPS: 36.9508, 21.7008

Open: 15 Apr-15 Oct **Site:** 4.3HEC **For hire:** **Prices:** 21-32 Mobile home hire 163.80-371.70 **Facilities:** Wi-fi Play Area **Services:** **Leisure:** S

RIO — PELOPONNESE

Rion

26500

☎ 26109 91585 📠 26109 93388

Site beside the sea on level ground with asphalt roads and concrete pitches for caravans. Pines and poplar trees offer shade.

dir: *9km E of Patras on Rion Beach.*

Open: Feb-1 Dec **Site:** 5HEC **Facilities:** **Services:** **Leisure:** S

SARTI — MACEDONIA

Armenistis Camping

63072

☎ 23750 91487 📠 23750 91497

e-mail: info@armenistis.com.gr

web: www.armenistis.com.gr

Located next to a white, sandy beach, shaded by pine trees. Facilities include a crêperie, summer cinema and a kids' club in July and August.

dir: *Via Perimtriki Sithonias.*

Open: 20 May-15 Sep **Site:** 6HEC **For hire:** **Prices:** 19.76-26.70 **Facilities:** Wi-fi Kids' Club Play Area **Services:** **Leisure:** S

SÉRIFOS, ISLAND OF

LIVADAKIA

Coralli Camping Bungalows

84005

☎ 22810 51500 📠 22810 51073

e-mail: info@coralli.gr

web: www.coralli.gr

Located on the Island of Sérifos next to a sandy beach.

Site: **For hire:** **Prices:** 17-20 **Facilities:** Wi-fi **Services:** **Leisure:** P S **Off-site:**

STYLIDA — CENTRAL GREECE

Interstation

230km National Rd, Athens-Thessaloniki, 35300

☎ 22380 23827/8 📠 22380 23828

web: www.campinginterstation.com

Site located among hills and national parks with good facilities.

Open: All Year. **Site:** 8HEC **For hire:** **Facilities:** **Services:** **Leisure:** S

GREECE

Hungary

Drinking and driving

Nil percentage of alcohol allowed in drivers' blood; amounts of less than 0.08% incur a fine, more than 0.08% legal proceedings.

Driving licence

Minimum age at which a UK driving licence holder may drive a temporarily imported car and/or motorcycle 17. All valid UK driving licences should be accepted in Hungary. This includes the older all-green style UK licences (in Northern Ireland older paper style with photographic counterpart) although the EC appreciates that these may be more difficult to understand and that drivers may wish to voluntarily update them before travelling abroad, if time permits. Alternatively, older licences may be accompanied by an International Driving Permit (IDP).

Fines

On-the-spot, the police must hand over the payment order to transfer the amount of the fine within 30 days. The fine is only payable in HUF, credit cards are not accepted. Cash should not be given to a policeman at the roadside. Wheel clamps are in use.

Fuel

Unleaded petrol (95 octane), diesel (Dizel or Gazolaj) and LPG available. No leaded petrol. Petrol in a can permitted, maximum 10 litres. Credit cards accepted at some filling stations, check with your card issuer for usage in Hungary before travel. Cash is the most usual form of payment.

Lights

Use of dipped headlights compulsory at all times outside built-up areas. At night the use of full beam, in built-up areas, is prohibited.

Motorcycles

Use of dipped headlights compulsory at all times. The wearing of crash helmets is compulsory for both driver and passenger.

Motor insurance

Third-party compulsory. Should a visitor cause an accident with a Hungarian citizen they must report it to the Association of Hungarian Insurance Companies.

Passengers/children in cars

A child under 3 years of age may only travel in a vehicle if using a suitable child restraint system appropriate for their weight, they are permitted to travel in the front of the vehicle using this restraint if it is rear facing and there is no airbag or it has been deactivated. Children under 1.5m and over 3 years of age must use a suitable child restraint system and be seated in the rear of the vehicle.

Seat belts

Compulsory for front and rear seat occupants to wear seatbelts, where fitted.

Speed limits

Standard legal limits, which may be varied by signs

Private vehicles without trailers	
In built-up areas	50km/h
Outside built-up areas	90km/h
Semi-motorways	110km/h
Motorways	130km/h

Vehicle towing a caravan or trailer	
Built up areas	50km/h
Motorways	80km/h
Semi-motorway	70km/h

Lower speed limits may apply on the approach to level crossings. Vehicles with snow chains must not exceed 50km/h. In city centres, areas with a 30km/h speed limit are increasingly common.

Compulsory equipment in Hungary

First-aid kit

Warning triangle

Reflective Jacket - All pedestrians walking on a road, or road shoulder outside a built-up area must wear a reflective jacket at night and in case of bad visibility. Any person exiting a vehicle outside a built-up area in a breakdown situation becomes a pedestrian and therefore must wear a reflective jacket.

Snow chains - The use of or their presence in a car can be made compulsory on some roads when weather conditions require.

Other rules/requirements

Recommended that the driver of a conspicuously damaged vehicle entering Hungary obtain a police report confirming the damage at the time of entry, otherwise lengthy delays may be encountered at the frontier when leaving Hungary. This report should be obtained from the police of the country where the car was damaged.

Motorway tax payable for use of:

M1 (Budapest – Hegyeshalom), M3 (Budapest -Gorbehaza – Nyiregyhaza), M5 (Budapest – Kiskunfelegyhaza – Szeged - Roszke/border with Serbia), M6 (M0- Erd - Dunaujvaros), M7 (Budapest - Lake Balaton – Letenye, border with Croatia), M30 (Emod - Miskolc), M35 (Gorbehaza-Debrecen)

Leaflets are distributed at the border to foreign motorists, explaining about the vignette. The electronic vignette and any toll charges must be paid in forints. Credit cards accepted: Visa, Eurocard/Mastercard, DKV and UTA. The vignette can be purchased in person, online, or by telephone (land line or mobile). When a motorist has purchased an e-vignette, a confirmation message will be sent or a coupon issued.

This document must be kept for one year after the expiry of validity. The motorway authorities check all vehicles electronically, and verify the registration number, the category of toll paid and the validity of the e-vignette.

Further information

www.motorway.hu – available for 4 days (vehicles up to 3.5t only), 1 week, 1 month or 13 months. Fines imposed for non-display. The Hungarian Motoring Association, recommend foreign motorists wishing to purchase a vignette at the border have cash in Hungarian Forints. Vignettes should only be purchased from outlets where the prices are clearly displayed at the set rate.

Motorists should be wary of contrived incidents, particularly on the Vienna – Budapest motorway, designed to stop motorists and expose them to robbery.

A new directive by the Hungarian authorities means that traffic will be restricted from entering Budapest when the dust in the air exceeds a fixed level on two consecutive days. The restriction depends upon the number which a registration plate ends, licence plates ending in odd numbers will be permitted to enter Budapest on odd numbered days, even number on even days.

The restriction also applies to UK registered vehicles, however as UK registration plates tend to end in a letter rather than a number we are waiting for confirmation as to how the restriction will apply. The restriction will be applicable from 0600 to 2200 with a fine imposed for non compliance.

Spiked tyres are prohibited. The use of the horn is prohibited in built-up areas, except in the case of danger.

Tolls Currency Forints (HUF)	Car	Car Towing Caravan/Trailer
M1/M3/M5/M7 4 Day Vignette	1650HUF	1650HUF
M1/M3/M5/M7 Weekly Vignette	2750HUF	2750HUF
M1/M3/M5/M7 Monthly Vignette	4500HUF	4500HUF
M1/M3/M5/M7 1 year	40000HUF	40000HUF

ALSÓÖRS **VESZPRÉM**

Balatontourist Camping Európa

Füredi utca 1, 8226

☎ 87 555021 🖹 87 555022

e-mail: europa@balatontourist.hu

web: www.balatontourist.hu

Large site with neat pitches on the lake shore. Entertainment available with a choice of restaurants nearby. Dogs allowed in certain areas of the site only.

GPS: 46.9755, 17.9569

Open: 11 May-9 Sep **Site:** 20HEC **For hire:** **Facilities:** Wi-fi (charged) **Services:** **Leisure:** L P **Off-site:**

BALATONAKALI **VESZPRÉM**

Balatontourist Camping Naturist Levendula

Hókuli utca 25, 8243

☎ 87 544011 🖹 87 544012

e-mail: levendula@balatontourist.hu

web: www.balatontourist.hu

Different-sized pitches divided by hedges are available at this naturist campsite on the shores of Lake Balaton.

dir: *Rte 71.*

GPS: 46.8794, 17.7422

Open: 11 May-9 Sep **Site:** 2.2HEC **For hire:** **Facilities:** Wi-fi (charged) Play Area **Services:** **Leisure:** L **Off-site:**

Balatontourist Camping Strand-Holiday

Strand utca 2, 8243

87 544021 87 544022

e-mail: strand@balatontourist.hu

web: www.balatontourist.hu

On the shores of Lake Balaton with facilities including sunbathing platforms, children's beach and an outdoor theatre. Ideal for families.

dir: *Rte 71.*

GPS: 46.8811, 17.7452

Open: 6 Apr-Sep **Site:** 9HEC **For hire:**
Prices: 3250-4800 **Facilities:** Wi-fi (charged) Play Area **Services:** **Leisure:** L

BALATONALMÁDI — VESZPRÉM

Balatontourist Camping Yacht

Véghely D utca 18, 8220

87 584101 87 584102

e-mail: yacht@balatontourist.hu

web: www.balatontourist.hu

A short walk from the town centre, a well-equipped site with a beach on Lake Balaton. Swimming pool available for children.

GPS: 47.0114, 18.0029

Open: 27 Apr-23 Sep **Site:** 2.7HEC **For hire:**
Prices: 4240-5340 **Facilities:** Wi-fi Kids' Club Play Area **Services:** **Leisure:** L

BALATONBERÉNY — SOMOGY

Balatontourist Camping Naturist Berény

Hétvezér utca 2, 8649

85 377299 85 377715

e-mail: bereny@balatontourist.hu

web: www.balatontourist.hu

Biggest naturist site on the shores of Lake Balaton with a motel and apartments also available. Sporting facilities.

dir: *Rte 7.*

GPS: 46.7131, 17.3106

Open: 13 May-11 Sep **Site:** 5.5HEC **For hire:**
Facilities: Wi-fi (charged) Play Area **Services:** **Leisure:** L

BALATONFÜRED — VESZPRÉM

Balatontourist Camping & Bungalows Füred

Széchenyi utca 24, 8230

87 580241 87 342341

e-mail: fured@balatontourist.hu

web: www.balatontourist.hu

Largest campsite on Lake Balaton with sunny and shaded pitches. Daily programmes (including sports) for both adults and children.

dir: *Rte 71.*

GPS: 46.9457, 17.8771

Open: 27 Apr-Sep **Site:** 21HEC **For hire:**
Facilities: Wi-fi (charged) Play Area
Services: **Leisure:** L P

BALATONSZEMES — SOMOGY

Balatontourist Camping & Bungalows Vadvirág

Lellei utca 1-2, 8636

84 360114 84 360115

e-mail: vadvirag@balatontourist.hu

web: www.balatontourist.hu

Directly on the shore of Lake Balaton, with a good range of sporting facilities including a children's swimming pool. Paddle boats, cycles, scooters etc can be hired.

dir: *Rte 71 & M7.*

GPS: 46.8009, 17.7402

Open: 27 Apr-9 Sep **Site:** 20HEC **For hire:**
Facilities: Wi-fi (charged) Play Area
Services: **Leisure:** L P **Off-site:**

Balatontourist Camping Lidó

Ady Endre utca 8, 8636

84 360112 84 360112

e-mail: lido@balatontourist.hu

web: www.balatontourist.hu

Directly on the shore of Lake Balaton, with shallow water and a beach suitable for families with small children. Leisure facilities include table tennis and tennis court.

dir: *Rte 7 & M7.*

GPS: 46.8133, 17.7739

Open: 4 May-9 Sep **Site:** 1.8HEC **For hire:**
Facilities: Wi-fi (charged) **Services:**
Leisure: L **Off-site:**

HUNGARY

BALATONSZEPEZD VESZPRÉM

Balatontourist Camping Venus

Halász utca 1, 8252

☎ 87 568061 🖹 87 568062

e-mail: venus@balatontourist.hu

web: www.balatontourist.hu

A family friendly site and popular with fishermen, located on the shores of Lake Balaton. Cycles can be rented to explore the surrounding national park.

Open: 11 May-9 Sep **Site:** 2.8HEC **For hire:** **Facilities:** Wi-fi (charged) **Services:** **Leisure:** L **Off-site:**

BUDAPEST BUDAPEST

Arena Camping - Budapest

Pilisi utca 7, 1106

☎ 302969129

e-mail: info@budapestcamping.hu

web: www.budapestcamping.hu

In a green quiet setting in Budapest, 5-10 minutes to the centre of the city by underground train.

dir: *8km from M10.*

GPS: 47.5042, 19.1583

Open: All Year. **Site:** 0.5HEC **For hire:** **Prices:** 4400-5800 **Facilities:** Wi-fi Play Area **Services:** **Off-site:** P

Camping Haller

Haller utca 27, 1096

☎ 1 476 3418

e-mail: info@hallercamping.hu

web: www.hallercamping.hu

Centrally located with 24-hour reception. Discounts are available for stays of four nights.

dir: *M5 highway.*

GPS: 47.4758, 19.0829

Open: 10 May-Sep **Site:** 1.5HEC **For hire:** **Prices:** 5700-6800 **Facilities:** Wi-fi **Services:** **Off-site:** P

BÜKFÜRDŐ VAS

Romantik

Thermal Krt 12, 9740

☎ 94 558050 🖹 94 558051

e-mail: info@romantikcamping.com

web: www.romantikcamping.com

Flat wooded site with unmarked pitches 2km from the spa town of Buk.

Open: All Year. **Site:** 6HEC **For hire:** **Facilities:** Wi-fi Play Area **Services:** **Leisure:** P **Off-site:**

ÉRD PEST

Flamingo

Furdo utca 4, 2030

☎ 23 375328 🖹 23 375328

e-mail: flamingocamp@t-online.hu

Good transport links to the centre of Budapest, sightseeing trips can be arranged.

dir: *On Highway 7.*

Open: Apr-Oct **Site:** 1HEC **For hire:** **Facilities:** Wi-fi Play Area **Services:** **Leisure:** P **Off-site:** R

ESZTERGOM KOMÁRON-ESZTERGOM

Gran Camping, Bungalow & Youth Hostel

Nagy Duna sétány 3, 2500

☎ 33 402513 🖹 33 411953

e-mail: fortanex@t-online.hu

web: www.grancamping-fortanex.hu

Scenic site on the island of Primas by the River Danube. Short walk to the town centre and to the bridge across the Danube to Slovakia.

dir: *From Tat via route 11 to Esztergom. In Esztergom, at rdbt towards Parkany/Sturovo. Campsite over bridge, beyond bend.*

Open: May-Sep **Site:** 4HEC **For hire:** **Prices:** 5240-5640 **Facilities:** Wi-fi **Services:** **Leisure:** P **Off-site:** L

FELSÖPAHOK ZALA

Fortuna Camping

Szent Istvan utca 89, 8395

☎ 83 344630 📠 83 340363

e-mail: fortuna.camping@gmail.com

web: www.fortuna-camping.hu

Quiet site very close to the natural thermal lake of Spa Heviz.

Open: Apr-20 Oct **Site:** 0.8HEC **For hire:** **Facilities:** **Services:** **Off-site:** L

FONYÓD-BÉLATELEP SOMOGY

Balatontourist Camping & Bungalows Napsugár

Wekerle utca 5, 8640

☎ 85 361211 📠 85 361024

e-mail: napsugar@balatontourist.hu

web: www.balatontourist.hu

Located in a shady, wooded area, the grassy beach on Lake Balaton is separated from the pitches by a railway.

GPS: 46.7327, 17.5326

Open: 11 May-2 Sep **Site:** 9.5HEC **For hire:** **Facilities:** Wi-fi (charged) Play Area **Services:** **Leisure:** L **Off-site:**

GYENESDIÁS ZALA

Wellness Park Pension & Camping

Napfény utca 6, 8315

☎ 83 316483 📠 83 316483

e-mail: info@wellness-park.hu

web: www.wellness-park.hu

Close to Lake Balaton, part of a complex that includes a guest house and spa, with tennis and petanque courts. Charge made for dogs. Ideal for cyclists as site is connected to Balaton cycle path. 10km from thermal lake at Hévíz.

dir: *M7 then M71.*

GPS: 46.7642, 17.3025

Open: All Year. **Site:** 2HEC **For hire:** **Facilities:** Wi-fi Play Area **Services:** **Leisure:** P **Off-site:** L

KEMENESKÁPOLNA VAS

Vulkán Resort

Szabadság utca 02, 9553

☎ 95 466060 📠 95 466056

e-mail: info@vulkanresort.com

web: www.vulkanresort.com

A site based on the principles of Feng Shui. A small health spa includes an indoor swimming pool and massage room.

GPS: 47.2147, 17.1004

Open: Apr-Oct **Site:** 5HEC **For hire:** **Facilities:** Wi-fi (charged) Play Area **Services:** **Leisure:** P **Off-site:**

KESZTHELY ZALA

Balatontourist Camping & Bungalows Zala

Entz Géza sétány 1, 8360

☎ 83 312782 📠 83 312782

e-mail: zala@balatontourist.hu

web: www.balatontourist.hu

Quiet site to the south of the town on the shore of Lake Balaton, with its own beach. Cycle route runs adjacent to the site and bikes are available to rent.

dir: *Rte 71.*

GPS: 46.7467, 17.2442

Open: 15 Apr-2 Oct **Site:** 7.2HEC **For hire:** **Facilities:** Wi-fi (charged) Play Area **Services:** **Leisure:** L P **Off-site:**

NESZMÉLY KOMÁROM-ESZTERGOM

Eden

Dunapart, 2544

☎ 33 474183 📠 33 474327

e-mail: eden@mail.holop.hu

web: www.edencamping.com

Site on the banks of the Danube next to a nature conservation area. Activities for children and shop available from 1 July to 20 August. Restaurant open from May to September.

dir: *Main route 10 from Gyor-Budapest, campsite between villages of Neszmély & Sutto.*

Open: Apr-Sep **Site:** 4HEC **For hire:** **Prices:** 3170-4830 **Facilities:** Wi-fi Play Area **Services:** **Leisure:** P R

RÉVFÜLÖP VESZPRÉM

Balatontourist Camping Napfény

Halász utca 5, 8253
☎ 87 563031 🖹 87 464309
e-mail: napfeny@balatontourist.hu
web: www.balatontourist.hu

Site with grassy area on the shores of Lake Balaton, ideal for bathing and windsurfing. Friendly atmosphere with neat pitches. Swimming pool available for children.

dir: *Rte 71.*

GPS: 46.8292, 17.6400

Open: 27 Apr-Sep **Site:** 7.2HEC **For hire:** **Prices:** 3000-4750 **Facilities:** Wi-fi (charged) Play Area **Services:** **Leisure:** L **Off-site:**

SIÓFOK SOMOGY

Balatontourist Camping & Bungalows Aranypart

Szent Lászlo utca 183-185, 8600
☎ 84 353399 🖹 84 352801
e-mail: aranypart@balatontourist.hu
web: www.balatontourist.hu

5km from the centre of town directly on the lake shore. Entertainment for children in high season and water-skiing nearby.

GPS: 46.9281, 18.1032

Open: 20 Apr-9 Sep **Site:** 9.1HEC **For hire:** **Facilities:** Wi-fi (charged) Play Area **Services:** **Leisure:** L **Off-site:** P

Balatontourist Camping Ifjúság

Pusztatorony tér, 8604
☎ 84 352851 🖹 84 352571
e-mail: ifjusag@balatontourist.hu
web: www.balatontourist.hu

Peaceful setting, 9km from city centre and 150 metres from Lake Balaton.

GPS: 46.9375, 18.1290

Open: 25 May-2 Sep **Site:** 8.2HEC **Prices:** 4600-5500 **Facilities:** Wi-fi (charged) Play Area **Services:** **Off-site:** L

SZENTENDRE PEST

Pap-Sziget Camping, Bungalow-Park & Youth Hostel

2000
☎ 26310697 🖹 26310909
e-mail: info@pap-sziget.hu
web: www.pap-sziget.hu

Family-friendly site, north of Budapest, with good transport links to the city. Thermal pool for guests' use. A wooden bridge crosses the River Danube which leads to the site.

dir: *Via rd 11.*

GPS: 47.6817, 19.0829

Open: 4 Apr-15 Oct **Site:** 3.5HEC **For hire:** **Prices:** 4200-5700 **Facilities:** Wi-fi Play Area **Services:** **Off-site:** P R

ÜRÖM PEST

Jumbo Camping

Budakalászi út 23-25, 2096
☎ 26 351251 🖹 26 351251
e-mail: jumbo@campingbudapest.com
web: www.campingbudapest.com

Family-run site on a south-facing hillside with terraced pitches.

GPS: 47.6014, 19.0194

Open: Apr-Oct **Site:** 1HEC **Prices:** 4050-5515 **Facilities:** Wi-fi Play Area **Services:** **Leisure:** P **Off-site:** L

VAJTA FEJÉR

Camping Park Vajta

Termálsor 1, 7041
☎ 25 229700 🖹 25 229700
e-mail: info@camping-park-vajta.nl
web: www.camping-park-vajta.nl

Dutch-owned site, surrounded by forests. A swimming pool plus a thermal pool are available for guests' use. Fishing permits can be purchased for a 700 hectare lake nearby.

GPS: 46.7299, 18.6587

Open: 14 Apr-23 Sep **Site:** 3.5HEC **For hire:** **Facilities:** Play Area **Services:** **Leisure:** P **Off-site:**

VONYARCVASHEGY ZALA

Balatontourist Camping & Bungalows Park

Szent Mihály-domb, 8314

☎ 83 348044 🖹 83 348044

e-mail: park@balatontourist.hu

web: www.balatontourist.hu

In a sheltered and quiet position at the foot of St Michael Hill. Leisure facilities include a beach, volleyball and fishing.

dir: *Rte 71.*

GPS: 46.7511, 17.3333

Open: 15 Apr-2 Oct **Site:** 4.7HEC **For hire:** **Facilities:** Wi-fi (charged) Play Area **Services:** **Leisure:** L

ZALAKAROS ZALA

Balatontourist Camping Termál

Gyógyfürdő tér 6, 8749

☎ 93 340105 🖹 93 340105

e-mail: termal@balatontourist.hu

web: www.balatontourist.hu

Located in a spa town known for its thermal pools, a relaxing site with shop nearby.

GPS: 46.7511, 17.3333

Open: Apr-30 Oct **Site:** 4HEC **For hire:** **Prices:** 3900-4400 **Facilities:** Wi-fi (charged) **Services:** **Off-site:** P

ZAMÁRDI SOMOGY

Balatontourist Camping Autós

Szent István út hrsz 3512, 8621

☎ 84 348931 🖹 84 348931

e-mail: autos@balatontourist.hu

web: www.balatontourist.hu

Picturesque views from this peaceful site, ideal for families with children. Some pitches are located next to Lake Balaton.

GPS: 46.8807, 17.9156

Open: 27 Apr-9 Sep **Site:** 6.7HEC **For hire:** **Prices:** 5550-6300 **Facilities:** Wi-fi (charged) **Services:** **Leisure:** L **Off-site:**

Drinking and driving

If the level of alcohol in the bloodstream is 0.051% or more, severe penalties include fines, confiscation of vehicle and imprisonment. Professional drivers, and drivers with less than three years driving experience, the alcohol limit is zero, it is prohibited.

Driving licence

Minimum age at which a UK licence holder may drive temporarily imported car and/or motorcycle (over 125cc or with passenger) 18. All valid UK driving licences should be accepted in Italy. This includes the older all-green style UK licences (in Northern Ireland older paper style with photographic counterpart) although the EC appreciates that these may be more difficult to understand and that drivers may wish to voluntarily update them before travelling abroad, if time permits. Alternatively, older licences may be accompanied by an International Driving Permit (IDP).

Fines

On-the-spot. Fines are particularly heavy for speeding offences. The police can impose the fine and collect 1 quarter of the maximum fine, and must give a receipt for the amount of the fine paid. Fines for serious offences committed at night between 2200 and 0700 hours are increased by one third, serious offences include speeding, going through a red light etc. Illegally parked vehicles can be clamped or towed away and a fine imposed.

Fuel

Unleaded petrol (95 and 98 octane), diesel (Gasolio) and LPG is available. No leaded petrol (lead substitute additive available). Petrol in a can permitted. Credit cards accepted at most filling stations; check with your card issuer for usage in Italy & San Marino before travel.

Lights

Use of dipped headlights during the day compulsory outside built-up areas and during snow and rain/poor visibility. Rear fog lights may only be used when visibility is less than 50 metres or in case of strong rain or intense snow. Lights must be switched on in tunnels.

Motorcycles

Use of dipped headlights during the day compulsory on all roads. The wearing of crash helmets is compulsory for both driver and passenger. The vehicle can be seized for non-compliance. It is prohibited to carry a child less than 5 years on a moped or motorcycle. The registration certificate must state that the moped/motorcycle is designed to carry a passenger. Motorcycles under 150cc are not allowed on motorways.

Motor insurance

Third-party compulsory.

Passengers/children in cars

Children travelling in foreign registered vehicles i.e. in a UK registered vehicle must be secured according to UK legislation.

Seat belts

Compulsory for front/rear seat occupants to wear seat belts, if fitted.

Speed limits

Standard legal limits, which may be varied by signs

Private vehicles without trailers	
Built-up areas	50km/h
Outside built-up areas	90km/h
Dual carriageways	110km/h
Motorways	130km/h

Private vehicle with caravan or trailer	
Built-up areas	50km/h
Outside built-up areas	70km/h
Motorways	80km/h

Camper Vans up to 3.5t	
Built-up areas	50km/h
Outside built-up areas	90km/h
Dual carriageways	110km/h
Motorways	130km/h

Camper Vans 3.5t to 12t	
Built-up areas	50km/h
Outside built-up areas	80km/h
Motorways	100km/h

Newly qualified drivers must not exceed a speed limit of 90km/h outside built-up areas (100km/h permitted on motorways) for three years after passing their test.

Note: In wet weather lower speed limits of 90km/h apply on dual carriageways and 110km/h on motorways.

Compulsory equipment in Italy and San Marino

Warning triangle - For all vehicles with more than two wheels.

Reflective jacket - The wearing of reflectorised jacket/waistcoat compulsory if driver and/or passenger(s) exits vehicle which is immobilised on the carriageway at night or in poor visibility. Not applicable to two wheeled vehicles.

Snow chains - Between the 15th October and the 15th April, or at other times if conditions dictate. Provinces can introduce their own legislation making the use of winter tyres or snow chains compulsory. Maximum speed limit if using snow chains is 50km/h.

Other rules/requirements

Any vehicle with an overhanging load (e.g. carrying bicycle at rear) must display a fully reflectorised square panel 50cm x 50cm which is red and white diagonally striped, a fine may be imposed if the sign is not displayed. This also applies to vehicles such as cars/caravans carrying bicycles at the rear.

Tolls are levied on the majority of motorways.

In built-up areas the use of the horn is prohibited except in cases of immediate danger .

The transportation or use of radar detectors is prohibited. Violation of this regulation will result in a fine between 708 and 2834 Euros and confiscation of the device.

Eco-pass: An experimental pollution charge is levied in the centre of Milan. Charges apply Mon-Fri and generally from 7.30am until 7.30pm. Drivers must purchase an eco-pass before entering the restricted zone. Tariffs vary according to the emissions of the vehicle. Full information can be found by clicking on the following link (this is only available in Italian) www.comune.milano.it/dseserver/ecopass/richiedere.html

Traffic is restricted in many historical centres/major towns known as 'Zone a Traffico Limitato' or ZTL's, circulation is only permitted for residents.

Entering such areas normally results in a fine by post.

Either winter tyres or snow chains may be used on roads where chains are compulsory.

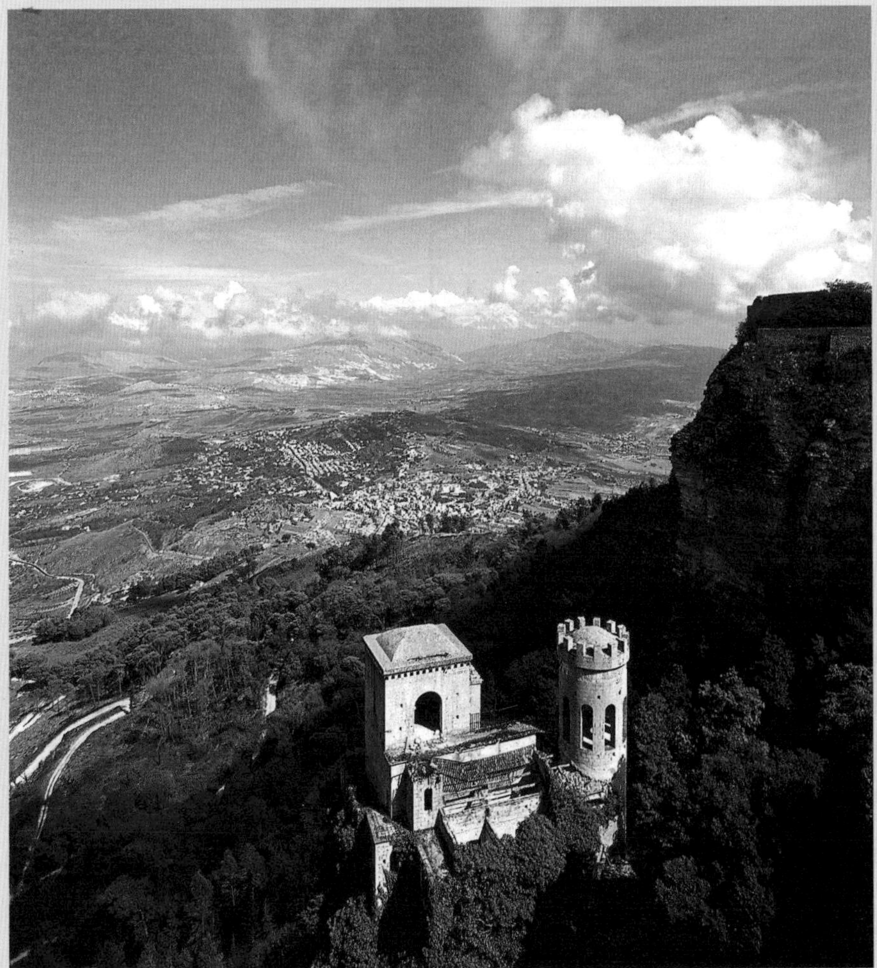

Pictured: Torretta Pepoli, Erice, Sicily

Tolls & Tunnels

Tolls Currency Euro (€)	Car	Car Towing Caravan/Trailer
A1 - Bologna - Firenze	€6.50	€8.30
A1 - Roma - Napoli	€11.60	€15.00
A1 - Milano - Bologna	€12.00	€15.50
A1 - Firenze - Roma	€14.60	€18.80
A1 - Milano - Napoli	€48.70	€58.30
A10 - Genova - Savona	€2.40	€3.00
A10 - Savona - Ventimiglia - (French Border)	€11.50	€21.70
A11 - Firenze - Pisa Nord	€5.90	€7.80
A12 - La Spezia - Livorno	€6.60	€9.30
A12 - Livorno - Roma	€8.30	€11.00
A12 - Genova - La Spezia	€9.20	€12.40
A12 - Genova - Viareggio	€11.40	€15.60
A12 - Genova - Livorno	€14.00	€19.30
A13 - Bologna - Ferrara	€1.90	€2.40
A13 - Ferrara - Pádova	€4.50	€5.80
A13 - Bologna - Pádova	€6.00	€7.20
A14 - Bari - Taranto	€3.80	€5.00
A14 - Ancona - Pescara	€8.70	€11.20
A14 - Bologna - Ancona	€11.40	€14.70
A14 - Pescara - Bari	€17.80	€23.00
A14 - Pescara - Taranto	€21.60	€23.20
A14 - Bologna - Taranto	€42.50	€54.90
A15 - Parma - La Spezia	€11.90	€15.20
A16 - Napoli - Bari	€15.70	€20.20
A18 - Messina - Catania	€3.60	€14.80
A20 - Messina - Caccamo	€10.40	€30.60
A21 - Piacenza - Brescia	€3.80	€5.00
A21 - Alessandria - Piacenza	€4.90	€6.40
A21 - Torino - Alessandria	€5.90	€7.70
A21 - Torino - Piacenza	€11.30	€14.80
A22 - Verona - Modena	€5.30	€6.90
A22 - Trento - Verona	€5.50	€7.10
A22 - Brenner Pass - Trento	€8.00	€10.30
A22 - Brenner Pass (Austrian Border) - Modena	€18.80	€24.20
A23 - Udine - Tarvisio (Austria)	€6.50	€7.70
A24 - Roma - Teramo	€15.70	€14.80
A25 - Roma - Pescara	€13.60	€17.60
A26 - Genova - Alessandria	€4.30	€5.50
A26 - Genova - Iselle (Swiss Frontier)	€12.50	€16.00
A27 - Venezia - Belluno	€6.60	€8.40
A3 - Napoli - Salerno	€2.00	€3.50
A30 - Caserta - Salerno	€5.00	€4.30
A31 - Vicenza - Trento	€1.70	€2.00
A32 - Torino - Tunnel du Frejus (France)	€10.70	€17.60
A33 - Asti - Cuneo	€9.90	0.00
A4 - Padova - Venezia	€2.70	€3.60
A4 - Brescia - Verona	€2.90	€3.80
A4 - Verona - Padova	€3.70	€4.90
A4 - Milano - Brescia	€5.60	€7.10
A4 - Venezia - Trieste	€7.00	€9.20
A4 - Torino - Milano	€9.60	€12.10
A4 - Milano - Venezia	€15.70	€20.40
A5 - Santhia - Aosta	€11.30	€17.00
A5 - Torino - Aosta	€12.90	€19.30
A6 - Torino - Savona	€11.10	€14.70
A7 - Milano - Tortona	€3.60	€4.70
A7 - Milano - Génova	€9.10	€9.80
A8 - Milano - Varese	€3.50	€3.40
A8/A9 - Milano - Chiasso (Swiss Frontier)	€4.10	€4.10

Tunnels Currency Euro (€)	Car	Car Towing Caravan/Trailer
On A32 (E70) -Tunnel del Frejus	€36.80	€48.70
T2 - Grand St Bernard Tunnel	€22.80	€36.30
On A5 (E25) -Mont Blanc Tunnel	€36.80	€48.70
Munt La Schera Tunnel - Livigno	€10.00	€20.00

NORTH WEST/ALPS & LAKES

ANFO BRESCIA

Pilù

via Venturi 4, 25070
☎ 0365 809037 0365 809207
e-mail: info@pilu.it
web: www.pilu.it

A well-maintained, slightly sloping site subdivided by trees and rows of shrubs. Separated from the pebble beach by a public footpath.

dir: *On the banks of Lake Idro approached via SS237 and SS669, signed on S outskirts.*

Open: Apr-Sep **Site:** 2HEC **For hire:** **Prices:** 16-31.50 **Facilities:** Wi-fi (charged) Play Area **Services:** **Leisure:** L P R **Off-site:**

ANGERA VARESE

Città di Angera

via Bruschera 99, 21021
☎ 0331 930736 0331 960367
e-mail: info@campingcittadiangera.it
web: www.campingcittadiangera.it

Large family site with plenty of recreational facilities.

dir: *A8/A26 exit Vergiate onto SS33 to Sesto Calende then SS69 to Angera, signed.*

Open: 15 Feb-14 Nov **Site:** 10HEC **Facilities:** Kids' Club Play Area **Services:** **Leisure:** L P **Off-site:**

ARVIER AOSTA

Arvier

via Chaussa 17, 11011
☎ 0165 069006 0165 99045
e-mail: campingarvier@yahoo.it
web: www.campingarvier.com

Quiet wooded site close to mountains and a peaceful village.

Open: Jun-Aug **Site:** 1HEC **For hire:** **Prices:** 26.40-27.90 **Facilities:** Wi-fi Play Area **Services:** **Leisure:** P **Off-site:** R

BASTIA MONDOVI CUNEO

Cascina

Loc Pieve 23, 12060
☎ 0174 60181 0174 60181
e-mail: info@campinglacascina.it
web: www.campinglacascina.it

A peaceful site on level land surrounded by mountains.

dir: *A6/SP12 to Bastia Mondovi.*

Open: Jan-30 Aug & Oct-Dec **Site:** 4HEC **For hire:** **Facilities:** **Services:** **Leisure:** P R

BAVENO NOVARA

Tranquilla

via Cave-Oltrefiume 02, 28831
☎ 0323 923452 0323 923452
e-mail: info@tranquilla.com
web: www.tranquilla.com

A peaceful location with panoramic views of the surrounding mountains and Lake Maggiore (800 metres away). Modern facilities with trekking opportunities nearby.

dir: *4km from Stresa. 1km from Baveno.*

GPS: 45.9124, 8.4886

Open: 15 Mar-15 Oct **Site:** 1.8HEC **For hire:** **Prices:** 17.60-26.50 **Facilities:** Wi-fi Play Area **Services:** **Leisure:** P **Off-site:** L R

BELLAGIO COMO

Azienda Agricola Clarke

via Valassina 170/c, 22021
☎ 031 951325
e-mail: elizabethclarke@tin.it
web: www.bellagio-camping.com

A small, secluded site on a horsebreeding farm close to Lake Bellagio, up towards the mountains with fine views. No dogs allowed.

Open: Jun-Sep **Site:** 0.5HEC **Prices:** 30 **Facilities:** Wi-fi (charged) **Off-site:** L P

BOLZANO-BOZEN BOLZANO

Moosbauer

Moritzingerweg 83, 39100
☎ 0471 918492 0471 204894
e-mail: info@moosbauer.com
web: www.moosbauer.com

Small site in attractive valley at the Gateway to the Dolomites.

Open: All Year. **Site:** 1.2HEC **Facilities:** **Services:** **Leisure:** P **Off-site:**

ITALY

BRÉCCIA COMO

International

via Cecilio, 22100
031 521435 031 521435
e-mail: campingint@hotmail.com
web: www.camping-internazionale.it
On a level meadow near the motorway.
dir: *Off A9 Como-Milan.*
Open: 28 Mar-30 Oct **Site:** 1.3HEC **For hire:** **Facilities:** Play Area **Services:** **Leisure:** P

BRESSANONE-BRIXEN BOLZANO

Löwenhof-Leone

via Brennero 60 - quartiere Leone, 39040
0472 836216 0472 801337
e-mail: info@loewenhof.it
web: www.loewenhof.it
Site offers rafting and canoeing school as well as a sauna and pool, which are avaliable in the Dolomiti resort 8km away.
dir: *Bolzano-Brenner motorway exit Varna, site just before Brixen.*
GPS: 46.7344, 11.6472
Open: Mar-26 Oct **Site:** 0.5HEC **Prices:** 24-35 **Facilities:** Wi-fi (charged) Play Area **Services:** **Leisure:** P R **Off-site:** L

CALCERANICA TRENTO

Al Pescatore

via dei Pescatori 1, 38050
0461 723062 0461 724212
e-mail: trentino@campingpescatore.it
web: www.campingpescatore.it
The site consists of several sections of meadowland, inland from the lake shore road to Lago di Caldonazzo. Well maintained with private beach.
Open: 22 May-15 Sep **Site:** 3.8HEC **Facilities:** **Services:** **Leisure:** L P **Off-site:**

Fleiola

via Trento 42, 38050
0461 723153 0461 724386
e-mail: info@campingfleiola.it
web: www.campingfleiola.it
Site is divided into sectors beside lake.
dir: *Verona-Brenner motorway exit Trento, signs for Pergine & Caldonazzo.*
Open: Apr-5 Oct **Site:** 1.2HEC **For hire:** **Facilities:** Wi-fi Kids' Club Play Area **Services:** **Leisure:** L **Off-site:**

Riviera

viale Venezia 10, 38050
0461 724464 0461 718689
e-mail: riviera@dnet.it
web: www.camping-riviera.net
10 metres from the southern shore and beach of Lake Caldonazzo. Pitches are grassy and well-shaded.
Open: Etr-15 Sep **Site:** 1.5HEC **Prices:** 20-33 **Facilities:** Wi-fi (charged) Play Area **Services:** **Leisure:** L **Off-site:**

CAMPITELLO DI FASSA TRENTO

Miravalle

vicolo camping 15, streda de Greva 39, 38031
0462 750502 0462 751563
e-mail: info@campingmiravalle.it
web: www.campingmiravalle.it
Wooded mountain setting beside the River Avisio and close to the town centre.
dir: *A22 exit Egna/Ora then follow SS48 for approx 55km to village, signed.*
Open: Jun-Sep & Dec-30 Mar **Site:** 3HEC **For hire:** **Prices:** 25-35 **Facilities:** Wi-fi (charged) Play Area **Services:** **Off-site:** P

CANAZEI TRENTO

Marmolada

via Pareda 60, 38032
0462 601660 0462 601722
e-mail: campingmarmolada@virgilio.it
Grassland site extending to the river, part of it in spruce woodland.
dir: *On S outskirts on right of road to Alba Penia.*
Open: All Year. **Site:** 3HEC **Facilities:** **Services:** **Leisure:** R **Off-site:** P

CANNOBIO NOVARA

International Paradis

via Casali Darbedo 12, 28822
0323 71227 0323 72591
e-mail: info@campinglagomaggiore.it
web: www.campinglagomaggiore.it
A level site on the bank of a lake.
dir: *Off SS34 at Km35/V.*
Open: 20 Mar-15 Oct **Site:** 1.2HEC **For hire:** **Prices:** 28-36 **Facilities:** Wi-fi (charged) **Services:** **Leisure:** L **Off-site:** R

Residence Campagna

via Casali Darbedo 20/22, 28822
☎ 0323 70100 🖷 0323 71190
e-mail: info@campingcampagna.it
web: www.campingcampagna.it
A well-equipped site in a pleasant lakeside location.
dir: *Off SS34 to Locarno at Km35/V on N outskirts of village. W of lake on road 21.*
GPS: 46.0711, 8.6936
Open: 20 Mar-23 Oct **Site:** 1.2HEC **For hire:** **Facilities:** Wi-fi (charged) Play Area **Services:** **Leisure:** L **Off-site:** R

Valle Romantica

via Valle Cannobina, 28822
☎ 0323 71249 🖷 0323 71249
e-mail: valleromantica@riviera-valleromantica.com
web: www.riviera-valleromantica.com
A pleasant site with trees, shrubs and flowers. Internal roads are asphalted and a mountain stream provides bathing facilities as well as a swimming pool.
dir: *1.5km W off road to Malesco.*
Open: 25 Mar-16 Sep **Site:** 50HEC **For hire:** **Prices:** 25-33 **Facilities:** Wi-fi (charged) Play Area **Services:** **Leisure:** P R **Off-site:** L

CASTELLETTO TICINO — NOVARA

Italia Lido

via Cicognola 104, 28053
☎ 0331 923032 🖷 0331 923032
e-mail: info@campingitalialido.it
web: www.campingitalialido.it
A large family site with its own private beach on Lake Maggiore. The site is popular with families and there are good recreational facilities.
dir: *A8 onto A26 & signed.*
Open: Mar-30 Oct **Site:** 3HEC **For hire:** **Facilities:** Play Area **Services:** **Leisure:** L **Off-site:**

CASTIGLIONE INTELVI — COMO

Campeggio ai Colli Fioriti

via Case Sparse 10, 22023
☎ 0318 30564 🖷 0318 30564
e-mail: colli.fioriti@tiscali.it
web: www.campeggioaicollifioriti.it
In a valley setting surrounded by meadows with leisure facilities that include tennis, table tennis and volleyball.
GPS: 45.9589, 9.0731
Open: All Year. **Site:** 2.7HEC **For hire:** **Prices:** 17.20-21.50 Mobile home hire 290-370 **Facilities:** Wi-fi (charged) Play Area **Services:** **Off-site:** P R

CHIUSA-KLAUSEN — BOLZANO

Gamp

Griesbruck 10, 39043
☎ 0472 847425 🖷 0472 845067
e-mail: info@camping-gamp.com
web: www.camping-gamp.com
The site lies next to the Gasthof Gamp, between the Brenner railway line and the motorway bridge, which passes high above the site.
dir: *Motorway exit onto SS12, signed.*
Open: All Year. **Site:** 0.6HEC **Facilities:** **Services:** **Leisure:** P **Off-site:** P

CHIUSI DELLA VERNA — TRENTO

La Verna

Vezzano, 52010
☎ 0575 532121 🖷 0575 532041
e-mail: info@campinglaverna.it
web: www.campinglaverna.it
On the borders of the Casentino Forest Park in attractive Tuscan scenery. Pitches are of varying sizes and levels of shade.
Open: 11 Apr-4 Oct **Site:** 2.2HEC **For hire:** **Facilities:** **Services:** **Leisure:** P **Off-site:** R

ITALY

COLFOSCO — BOLZANO

Colfosco

via Sorega 15, 39030
☎ 0471 836515 🖹 0471 830801
e-mail: info@campingcolfosco.org
web: www.campingcolfosco.org

A beautiful setting at the foot of the Sella mountains.

Open: Dec-10 Apr & Jun-Sep **Site:** 2.5HEC **For hire:** **Facilities:** Wi-fi (charged) Play Area **Services:** **Leisure:** R **Off-site:** L

COLOMBARE — BRESCIA

Sirmione

via Sirmioncino 9, 25019
☎ 030 919045 🖹 030 919045
e-mail: info@camping-sirmione.it
web: www.camping-sirmione.it

A well-equipped site in a beautiful location on the Sirmione peninsula, with direct access to Lake Garda.

dir: *SS11 towards Sirmione, 0.4km turn right.*

Open: 25 Mar-5 Oct **Site:** 3.5HEC **For hire:** **Facilities:** Play Area **Services:** **Leisure:** L P **Off-site:**

DESENZANO DEL GARDA — BRESCIA

Villaggio Turistico Vò

via Vò 9, 25015
☎ 030 9121325 🖹 030 9120773
e-mail: vo@voit.it
web: www.voit.it

Situated on Lake Garda, 1.5km from Desenzano, surrounded by meadows and woods.

dir: *Between Padenghe & Sirmione on Lake Garda, 2km from Desenzano.*

Open: Apr-Sep **Site:** 5HEC **For hire:** **Prices:** 26-38 **Facilities:** Wi-fi (charged) Play Area **Services:** **Leisure:** L P **Off-site:**

DIMARO — TRENTO

Dolomiti Camping Village

via Gole 105, 38025
☎ 0463 974332 🖹 0463 973200
e-mail: info@campingdolomiti.com
web: www.campingdolomiti.com

The site has large flat plots surrounded by tall pines. Good sports facilities and tuition for canoeing and white-water rafting. There is a spa available and a kids' club in July and August. Dogs not permitted between 10 July and 20 August.

dir: *Off SS42 at Km173.5.*

GPS: 46.3253, 10.8631

Open: 19 May-29 Sep & 3 Dec-15 Apr **Site:** 4HEC **For hire:** **Prices:** 25.50-36 **Facilities:** Wi-fi (charged) Kids' Club Play Area **Services:** **Leisure:** P **Off-site:** R

DOMASO — COMO

Gardenia

via Case Sparse 164, 22013
☎ 0344 96262 🖹 0344 83381
e-mail: info@domaso.biz
web: www.domaso.biz

A family-run site on the west bank of Lake Como, ideally located for sports and relaxation.

dir: *N at Case Sparse.*

GPS: 46.1528, 9.3344

Open: Apr-Sep **Site:** 8.5HEC **For hire:** **Prices:** 21-23.30 **Facilities:** Wi-fi (charged) Play Area **Services:** **Leisure:** L **Off-site:** P R

DORMELLETTO — NOVARA

Lago Azzurro

via E-Fermi 2, 28040
☎ 0322 497197 🖹 0322 497197
e-mail: info@campinglagoazzurro.it
web: www.campinglagoazzurro.it

A lakeside site in beautiful surroundings with fine sports facilities.

dir: *S of Arona off SS Sempione 33.*

GPS: 45.7374, 8.5765

Open: All Year. **Site:** 2.5HEC **For hire:** **Prices:** 21.50-33 **Facilities:** Wi-fi (charged) **Services:** **Leisure:** L P

Lago Maggiore

via L-da-Vinci 7, 28040
0322 497193 0322 498600
e-mail: info@lagomag.com
web: www.lagomag.com
Well-maintained site divided into plots, pleasantly landscaped by the lakeside.
dir: *Off SS33, signed.*
GPS: 45.735, 8.5752
Open: Apr-Sep **Site:** 7HEC **For hire:** **Prices:** 18-38 Mobile home hire 354-1290 **Facilities:** Wi-fi (charged) Kids' Club Play Area **Services:** **Leisure:** L P **Off-site:**

Lido Holiday Inn

via M-Polo 1, 28040
0322 497047 0322 497047
e-mail: info@campingholidayinn.com
web: www.campingholidayinn.com
Site on bank of the lake, with some trees.
dir: *A8/A26, exit for Castelletto Ticino, site 2km.*
Open: All Year. **Site:** 3.5HEC **For hire:** **Facilities:** **Services:** **Leisure:** L P **Off-site:**

Smeraldo

via Cavour 131, 28040
0322 497031 0322 498789
e-mail: info@camping-smeraldo.com
web: www.camping-smeraldo.com
Well-landscaped site in woodland beside a lake. Divided into plots.
dir: *Off SS33.*
Open: Mar-Oct **Site:** 24HEC **For hire:** **Facilities:** **Services:** **Leisure:** L P **Off-site:**

EDOLO BRESCIA

Adamello

via Campeggio 10, 25048
0364 71694 0364 71694
e-mail: info@campingadamello.it
web: www.campingadamello.it
A terraced site in wooded surroundings, 1km from the lake.
dir: *1.5km W of SS39.*
Open: All Year. **Site:** 1.2HEC **For hire:** **Prices:** 22-27 **Facilities:** Play Area **Services:** **Off-site:** L P R

FERIOLO NOVARA

Orchidea

via 42 Martiri 20, 28831
0323 28257 0323 28573
e-mail: info@campingorchidea.it
web: www.campingorchidea.it
A modern family site on Lake Maggiore with good sports and entertainment facilities.
dir: *Via SS33.*
Open: 21 Mar-10 Oct **Site:** 4HEC **For hire:** **Facilities:** Wi-fi (charged) Kids' Club Play Area **Services:** **Leisure:** L **Off-site:** P R

FONDOTOCE NOVARA

Camping Village Continental

via 42 Martiri 156, 28924
0323 496300 0323 496218
e-mail: info@campingcontinental.com
web: www.campingcontinental.com
By Lake Mergozzo and 1km from Lake Maggiore. Dogs not permitted in accommodation.
dir: *On right of road Verbania Fondotoce-Gravellona.*
Open: 30 Mar-24 Sep **Site:** 10HEC **For hire:** **Prices:** 20.30-52.40 Mobile home hire 305.82-1155.00 **Facilities:** Wi-fi (charged) Kids' Club Play Area **Services:** **Leisure:** L P **Off-site:** R

Lido Toce Camping

via per Feriolo 41, 28924
0323 496298 0323 496220
e-mail: info@campinglidotoce.eu
web: www.campinglidotoce.eu
A beautiful location with spectacular views on the eastern shore of the lake. Good recreational facilities.
GPS: 45.9373, 8.4879
Open: Apr-Oct **Site:** 2HEC **Prices:** 19.90-27.90 **Facilities:** Wi-fi (charged) Play Area **Services:** **Leisure:** L R **Off-site:** P

ITALY

ITALY

Village Isolino

via Per Feriolo 25, 28924
☎ 0323 496080 🖷 0323 496414
e-mail: info@isolino.com
web: www.isolino.it

Peaceful site with panoramic views and large pitches. Swimming pool complex 28 April to 16 September. Kids' club available 28 April to 9 September. Dogs accepted but restrictions apply.

GPS: 45.9427, 8.4869

Open: 30 Mar-24 Sep **Site:** 12HEC **For hire:** **Prices:** 19.30-49.30 Mobile home hire 299.80-1295 **Facilities:** Wi-fi (charged) Kids' Club Play Area **Services:** **Leisure:** L P **Off-site:** R

FUCINE DI OSSANA — TRENTO

Camping Cevedale

via di Sotto Pila 4, 38026
☎ 0463 751630 🖷 0463 751630
e-mail: info@campingcevedale.it
web: www.campingcevedale.it

A well-equipped site in a peaceful location at an altitude of 900 metres, close to the local ski resorts. Kids' club available in June and July.

dir: *A22 exit San Michele direction Tonale.*

GPS: 46.3083, 10.7336

Open: All Year. **Site:** 3.8HEC **For hire:** **Prices:** 25-32 **Facilities:** Wi-fi Kids' Club Play Area **Services:** **Leisure:** R **Off-site:** L P

GHIRLA — VARESE

Trelago

via Trelago 20, 21030
☎ 0332 716583 🖷 0332 719650
e-mail: info@3lagocamping.com
web: www.3lagocamping.com

Lakeside site with grassy pitches shaded by tall trees.

dir: *Signs from Milan to Varese & Ghirla, site 15km from Varese.*

Open: Apr-Sep **Site:** 3.3HEC **For hire:** **Prices:** 20.50 **Facilities:** Wi-fi Play Area **Services:** **Leisure:** L P **Off-site:** R

IDRO — BRESCIA

AZUR Rio Vantone

25074
☎ 0365 83125 🖷 0365 823663
e-mail: idro@azur-camping.de
web: www.riovantone.it

The site lies at the mouth of the river of same name beside Lake Idro. Subdivided into pitches (separate pitches for youths) on grass and woodland at the foot of distinctive rock formations.

dir: *Approach from Idro towards Vantone & signed.*

Open: Apr-Oct **Site:** 4.5HEC **For hire:** **Prices:** 19-32.50 Mobile home hire 385-686 **Facilities:** Wi-fi (charged) Kids' Club Play Area **Services:** **Leisure:** L P R

Vantone Pineta

via Vantone 39, 25074
☎ 0365 823385
e-mail: info@vantonepineta.it
web: www.vantonepineta.it

On eastern shore of lake. Grassland enclosed by rush and willow fencing. Part of the site is in a small wood on the bank of a stream.

dir: *Approach from Idro & signs for Camping Idro Rio Vantone.*

Open: 31 Mar-Sep **Site:** 2HEC **For hire:** **Prices:** 23.50-31.50 **Facilities:** Wi-fi (charged) Play Area **Services:** **Leisure:** L P **Off-site:**

ISEO — BRESCIA

Camping del Sole

via Per Rovato, 25049
☎ 030 980288 🖷 030 9821724
e-mail: info@campingdelsole.it
web: www.campingdelsole.it

Family-friendly holiday park on the banks of Lake Iseo, with direct access to a sandy beach. Leisure facilities include a wide range of sports plus evening entertainment. Dogs are only permitted in a small area of the site.

dir: *Milan-Venice motorway exit Ospitaletto or Rovato.*

Open: 2 Apr-23 Sep **Site:** 4HEC **For hire:** **Prices:** 23-41.60 **Facilities:** Wi-fi Kids' Club Play Area **Services:** **Leisure:** L P **Off-site:**

Punta d'Oro

via Antonioli 51/53, 25049
030 980084 030 980084
e-mail: info@camping-puntadoro.com
web: www.camping-puntadoro.com

A well-set out site, directly on the lake shore, with roads and paths to every pitch.

dir: *A4 exit Rovato, signs for Iseo.*

Open: Apr-Oct **Site:** 0.6HEC **For hire:** **Prices:** 17-32.50 Mobile home hire 259-588 **Facilities:** Wi-fi Play Area **Services:** **Leisure:** L **Off-site:** P

Quai

via Antonioli 73, 25049
0309 821610 0309 981161
e-mail: info@campingquai.it
web: www.campingquai.it

Shady site close to the edge of Lake Iseo.

dir: *W of town, signed.*

GPS: 45.6661, 10.0628

Open: 8 Apr-26 Sep **Site:** 1.3HEC **For hire:** **Facilities:** Wi-fi (charged) **Services:** **Leisure:** L **Off-site:** P

Sassabanek

via Colombera 2, 25049
030 980300 030 9821360
e-mail: sassabanek@sassabanek.it
web: www.sassabanek.it

A pleasant wooded location on the shore of Lake Iseo with good recreational facilities.

Open: Apr-Sep **Site:** 3.5HEC **Facilities:** **Services:** **Leisure:** L P **Off-site:**

LAIVES-LEIFERS BOLZANO

Steiner

Kennedystr 34, 39055
0471 950105 0471 593141
e-mail: info@campingsteiner.com
web: www.campingsteiner.com

The site lies in the Etsch valley, only 8km from Bolzano. There are 140 pitches set amongst apple and elm trees. Facilities include swimming pools, a TV room and a shop.

dir: *Off SS12 on N outskirts of village.*

Open: 24 Mar-4 Nov **Site:** 2.5HEC **For hire:** **Prices:** 26-33 **Facilities:** Wi-fi (charged) Play Area **Services:** **Leisure:** P **Off-site:**

LATSCH BOLZANO

Latsch an der Etsch

Reichstr 4, 39021
0473 623217 0473 622333
e-mail: info@camping-latsch.com
web: www.camping-latsch.com

A terraced site beside the river.

dir: *Signed on SS38.*

GPS: 46.7102, 11.0791

Open: 11 Dec-10 Dec **Site:** 2.2HEC **For hire:** **Prices:** 28.40-33.20 Mobile home hire 520.80-632.80 **Facilities:** Wi-fi (charged) Play Area **Services:** **Leisure:** P R **Off-site:** L

LECCO COMO

Rivabella

via Alla Spiaggia 35, 23900
0341 421143 0341 421143
e-mail: rivabellalecco@libero.it
web: www.rivabellalecco.it

On a private, guarded beach on the shore of Lake Como.

dir: *3km S towards Bergamo.*

Open: 25 Apr-Sep **Site:** 2HEC **Prices:** 25 **Facilities:** Wi-fi Play Area **Services:** **Leisure:** L **Off-site:** P

LEVICO TERME TRENTO

Due Laghi

Loc Costa 3, 38056
0461 706290 0461 707381
e-mail: info@campingclub.it
web: www.campingclub.it

Mainly family site with 400 large, flat, grass pitches.

dir: *From Trento signs for Pergine & Lake Caldonazza.*

Open: 18 May-12 Sep **Site:** 12HEC **For hire:** **Prices:** 16-40 **Facilities:** Wi-fi (charged) Kids' Club Play Area **Services:** **Leisure:** L P

ITALY

ITALY

Jolly

Loc Pleina, 38056

☎ 0461 706934 🖷 0461 700227

e-mail: info@lagolevico.com

web: www.lagolevico.com

The site is divided into plots and lies 200 metres from the lake. Three indoor swimming pools.

dir: *SS47 exit Levico/Caldonazzo & follow signs for site.*

GPS: 46.0077, 11.2838

Open: Apr-14 Oct **Site:** 3.5HEC **For hire:** **Facilities:** Wi-fi Kids' Club Play Area **Services:** **Leisure:** L P **Off-site:** R

Levico

38056

☎ 0461 706491 🖷 0461 707735

e-mail: info@lagolevico.com

web: www.lagolevico.com

Site is by Lake Levico with a private beach.

dir: *SS47 exit Levico/Caldonazzo, site signed.*

GPS: 46.0077, 11.2838

Open: Apr-14 Oct **Site:** 5HEC **For hire:** **Facilities:** Wi-fi Kids' Club Play Area **Services:** **Leisure:** L P R

LIMONE PIEMONTE — CUNEO

Luis Matlas

12015

☎ 0171 927565 🖷 0171 927565

This tidy site offers winter facilities, and skiing lessons are provided by the owner. Fishing is also available.

dir: *N of town off Limone-Nice road.*

Open: Jan-7 May & 18 May-Sep & Nov-Dec **Site:** 1.5HEC **Prices:** 21.50-24.50 **Facilities:** Play Area **Services:** **Leisure:** R **Off-site:**

LIMONE SUL GARDA — BRESCIA

Nanzel

via 4 Novembre 3, 25010

☎ 0365 954155 🖷 0365 954468

e-mail: campingnanzel@libero.it

web: www.campingnanzel.it

Well-managed site, with low terraces in olive grove.

dir: *Access from Km101.2 (Hotel Giorgiol).*

Open: 30 Mar-21 Oct **Site:** 0.7HEC **For hire:** **Prices:** 24-32.50 **Facilities:** **Services:** **Leisure:** L **Off-site:**

MACCAGNO — VARESE

Lagocamp-Parkcamping Maccagno

via Corsini 3, 21010

☎ 0332 560203 🖷 0332 561263

e-mail: maccagno@lagocamp.com

web: www.lagocamp.com

A popular site on the shore of the lake.

dir: *Off SS394 in village at Km43/III towards lake, 0.5km turn right.*

Open: 17 Mar-3 Nov **Site:** 1.2HEC **For hire:** **Prices:** 20-36 **Facilities:** Wi-fi (charged) Kids' Club Play Area **Services:** **Leisure:** L R **Off-site:**

Lido

via Pietraperzia 13, 21010

☎ 0332 560250 🖷 0332 560250

e-mail: lido@boschettoholiday.it

web: www.boschettoholiday.it/lido

Lakeside site with good facilities, 200 metres from the river.

Open: Apr-Sep **Site:** 0.8HEC **For hire:** **Facilities:** **Services:** **Leisure:** L **Off-site:** R

MANERBA DEL GARDA — BRESCIA

Belvedere

via Cavalle 5, 25080

☎ 0365 551175 🖷 0365 552350

e-mail: info@camping-belvedere.it

web: www.camping-belvedere.it

Terraced site by Lake Garda.

dir: *Signed from SS572.*

Open: 15 Mar-5 Oct **Site:** 2.1HEC **For hire:** **Facilities:** **Services:** **Leisure:** L P **Off-site:**

Rio Ferienglück

via del Rio 37, 25080

☎ 0365 551075 🖷 0365 551044

A quiet site on the banks of Lake Garda.

dir: *Off SS572 Desenzano-Salò between Km8 & Km9, site 4km N.*

Open: Apr-Sep **Site:** 5HEC **For hire:** **Facilities:** Wi-fi (charged) Play Area **Services:** **Leisure:** L P R

Rocca

via Cavalle 22, 25080
0365 551738 0365 551755
e-mail: info@laroccacamp.it
web: www.laroccacamp.it
A picturesque location with fine views over the gulf of Manerba.
Open: 31 Mar-Sep **Site:** 5HEC **For hire:** **Prices:** 19-42 Mobile home hire 275-975 **Facilities:** Wi-fi (charged) Play Area **Services:** **Leisure:** L P

Zocco

via del Zocco 43, 25080
0365 551605 0365 552053
e-mail: info@campingzocco.it
web: www.campingzocco.it
On the banks of Lake Garda with direct access to a beach and private landing stage. Leisure facilities include tennis courts and a football pitch.
dir: *0.5km S of Gardonicino di Manerba.*
GPS: 45.5397, 10.5560
Open: 4 Apr-23 Sep **Site:** 5HEC **For hire:** **Prices:** 16-32.30 Mobile home hire 300-826 **Facilities:** Wi-fi **Services:** **Leisure:** L P

MARONE **BRESCIA**

Riva di San Pietro

via Cristini 9, 25054
030 9827129 030 9827129
e-mail: info@rivasanpietro.it
web: www.rivasanpietro.it
A modern site on the eastern side of Lake Iseo. Plenty of recreational facilities.
dir: *Milano-Venezia road exit Rovato or Palazzolo for Iseo, Marone 10km N.*
Open: May-Sep **Site:** 2HEC **For hire:** **Facilities:** Wi-fi (charged) Play Area **Services:** **Leisure:** L P **Off-site:**

MOLVENO **TRENTO**

Camping Spiaggia-Lago di Molveno

via Lungolago 27, 38018
0461 586978 0461 586330
e-mail: camping@molveno.it
web: www.campingmolveno.it
A picturesque setting by the lake, at the foot of the Brenta Dolomites.
dir: *Signed from SS421.*
Open: All Year. **Site:** 4HEC **For hire:** **Prices:** 20-46 **Facilities:** Wi-fi Play Area **Services:** **Off-site:** L P

MONIGA DEL GARDA **BRESCIA**

Camping Piantelle

via San Cassiano 1/A, 25080
0365 502013 0365 502637
e-mail: info@piantelle.com
web: www.piantelle.com
Quiet, family site on the shores of Lake Garda. Pitches are shaded by oak and poplar trees. Two swimming pools are available, plus a kids' club in July and August.
dir: *From A4 Milano-Venezia motorway take Desenzano exit. Follow signs for Salò, then Moniga del Garda.*
GPS: 45.5201, 10.5295
Open: 6 Apr-7 Oct **Site:** 8.5HEC **For hire:** **Prices:** 23-50 **Facilities:** Wi-fi Kids' Club Play Area **Services:** **Leisure:** L P **Off-site:**

Fontanelle

via Magone 13, 25080
0365 502079 0365 503324
e-mail: info@campingfontanelle.it
web: www.campingfontanelle.it
Peaceful site on the shores of Lake Garda shaded by olive trees. A kids' club is available in high season.
Open: 24 Apr-16 Sep **Site:** 45HEC **For hire:** **Prices:** 23-46 **Facilities:** Wi-fi (charged) Kids' Club Play Area **Services:** **Leisure:** L P **Off-site:**

ITALY

San Michele

via San Michele 8, 25080
0365 502026 0365 503443
e-mail: info@campingsanmichele.it
web: www.campingsanmichele.it
A family site with good facilities and direct access to the lake via a private beach.
dir: *A4 exit Desenzano, site 8km towards Salò.*
Open: 10 Mar-2 Nov **Site:** 3HEC **For hire:** **Facilities:** **Services:** **Leisure:** L P **Off-site:**

Villa Garuti

via del Porto 5, 25080
030 9907134 030 9907817
e-mail: info@villagaruti.it
web: www.villagaruti.it
A campsite and holiday village in the garden of the old Villa Garuti, beside the lake with its own beach.
dir: *A4 exit Desenzano, SS572 to Padenghe.*
Open: Apr-10 Oct **Site:** 1.5HEC **For hire:** **Prices:** 25-42 **Facilities:** Wi-fi Kids' Club Play Area **Services:** **Leisure:** L P **Off-site:**

NOVATE MEZZOLA — SONDRIO

El Ranchero

via Nazionale 3, 23025
0343 44169 0343 44169
e-mail: info@elranchero.it
web: www.elranchero.it
Located on the edge of the Mezzola Lake in front of a spectacular view of the mountains.
Open: May-15 Oct **Site:** 1HEC **For hire:** **Facilities:** Wi-fi (charged) Play Area **Services:** **Leisure:** L **Off-site:** P R

ORTA SAN GIULIO — NOVARA

Camping Cusio

Lago d'Orta, via Don Boslo, 5, 28016
0322 90290 0322 90290
e-mail: cusio@tin.it
web: www.campingcusio.it
Site surrounded by woodland on Lake Orta in a picturesque alpine valley. Good facilities.
dir: *S of Omegna towards Borgomanero.*
Open: Apr-Nov **Site:** 2HEC **For hire:** **Prices:** 17.80-31.50 **Facilities:** Wi-fi (charged) Play Area **Services:** **Leisure:** P **Off-site:** L

PADENGHE — BRESCIA

La Cá

via della Colombaia 6, 25080
030 9907006 030 9907693
e-mail: info@campinglaca.it
web: www.campinglaca.it
A park-like setting on terraced ground.
dir: *Off road along Lake Garda, 1.5km N turn for Padenghe & down steep road towards lake.*
Open: Mar-30 Oct **Site:** 2HEC **For hire:** **Prices:** 13.20-32.90 Mobile home hire 154-329 **Facilities:** Wi-fi (charged) **Services:** **Leisure:** L P

PEIO — TRENTO

Val di Sole

Loc Dossi di Cavia, 38024
0463 753177 0463 753176
e-mail: valdisole@camping.it
web: www.valdisolecamping.it
The site lies on terraced slopes at the foot of the Ortier mountain range.
dir: *400m off SP87.*
Open: Jun-5 Nov & Dec-5 May **Site:** 2.3HEC **For hire:** **Facilities:** **Services:** **Off-site:** P

PERA DI FASSA — TRENTO

Soal

Strada Dolomites 190, 38036
0462 764519 0462 764519
e-mail: info@campingsoal.com
web: www.campingsoal.com
Breath-taking location among the Dolomites, ideal for skiing and walking.
Open: All Year. **Site:** 30HEC **For hire:** **Facilities:** Play Area **Services:** **Leisure:** R

PÉRGINE — TRENTO

Punta Indiani

Lago di Caldonazzo, 38057
0461 548062 0461 548607
e-mail: info@campingpuntaindiani.it
web: www.campingpuntaindiani.it
On level ground surrounded by trees with direct access to 400 metres of private beach on the banks of the lake.
dir: *A22 exit Trento, signs for Pergine, S Cristoforo & Caldonazzo.*
GPS: 46.0267, 11.2303
Open: 27 Apr-Sep **Site:** 1.5HEC **Prices:** 20-36 **Facilities:** Wi-fi (charged) **Services:** **Leisure:** L **Off-site:**

San Cristoforo

via dei Pescatori, 38057
0461 512707 0461 707381
e-mail: info@campingclub.it
web: www.campingclub.it
A family-run site in a prime position on the sunniest side of lake.
dir: *SS47 from Trento towards Venice for 14km, site in centre of San Cristoforo.*
Open: 20 May-12 Sep **Site:** 2.5HEC **For hire:**
Facilities: **Services:** **Leisure:** L P
Off-site:

PIEVE DI MANERBA BRESCIA

Faro

via Repubblica 52, 25080
0365 651704 0365 651704
e-mail: campeggioilfaro@virgilio.it
web: www.campingilfaro.it
Set in a peaceful rural area close to the sea.
dir: *Off A4 at Desenzano onto N572 to Manerba del Garda.*
Open: 15 Apr-15 Sep **Site:** 1HEC **For hire:**
Prices: 16-30 **Facilities:** **Services:**
Leisure: P **Off-site:** L

PISOGNE BRESCIA

Eden

via Piangrande 3, 25055
0364 880500 0364 880500
e-mail: info@campeggioeden.com
web: www.campeggioeden.com
The site lies on the eastern shore of the lake with tall trees and a level beach.
dir: *Off SS510 at Km37/VII, over railway towards lake.*
Open: May-15 Sep **Site:** 2.5HEC **For hire:**
Prices: 21.50-26.50 **Facilities:** **Services:**
Leisure: L **Off-site:** P R

PORLEZZA COMO

OK La Rivetta

via Calbiga,30, 22018
0344 70393 0344 70715
e-mail: info@campingoklarivetta.com
web: www.campingoklarivetta.com
The site lies in meadowland on the north eastern shore of the lake.
dir: *S from SS340.*
Open: 15 Mar-15 Nov **Site:** 5HEC **For hire:**
Facilities: **Services:** **Leisure:** L P
Off-site: R

POZZA DI FASSA TRENTO

Rosengarten

Strada de Pucia, 4, Loc Puccia, 38036
0462 763305 0462 762247
e-mail: info@catinacciorosengarten.com
web: www.catinacciorosengarten.com
A well-tended site in the heart of the Dolomites, only 200 metres from the town of Pozza Di Fassa. A good base for a skiing or walking holiday, there is a free bus to the ski slopes. A new addition for 2012 is a sauna with Turkish bath and private bathrooms.
dir: *Signed from SS48.*
Open: 10 Jun-20 Oct & 5 Dec-25 Apr **Site:** 3HEC **For hire:** **Prices:** 21-31.40 **Facilities:** Wi-fi Kids' Club Play Area **Services:** **Leisure:** R
Off-site: P

Vidor Family & Wellness Resort

Strada de Ruf de Ruacia 15, 38036
0462 760022 0462 762007
e-mail: info@campingvidor.it
web: www.campingvidor.it
A traditional family-run site in a pine forest. Ideal for skiers, nature lovers and families. Health and beauty spa on site.
dir: *Signed from SS48.*
GPS: 46.4205, 11.7076
Open: Jan-Oct & Dec **Site:** 2.8HEC **For hire:**
Prices: 14.50-36 **Facilities:** Wi-fi (charged) Kids' Club Play Area **Services:** **Leisure:** P
Off-site: R

RASUN BOLZANO

Corones

39030
0474 496490 0474 498250
e-mail: info@corones.com
web: www.corones.com
A modern site in an ideal mountain location with good sports facilities.
dir: *Milan-Brenner motorway exit Val Pusteria, through Brunico & Valdaora to Rasun.*
Open: May-Oct & Dec-Mar **Site:** 2.7HEC **For hire:**
Facilities: Wi-fi (charged) Kids' Club Play Area
Services: **Leisure:** P

RIVA DEL GARDA — TRENTO

Brione

via Brione 32, 38066
☎ 0464 520885 0464 520890
e-mail: info@campingbrione.com
web: www.campingbrione.com

This quiet site is at the foot of a hill covered with olive trees, ideally located near Lake Garda.

GPS: 45.8803, 10.8591

Open: Apr-Oct **Site:** 3.3HEC **For hire:**
Prices: 26-30.50 **Facilities:** Wi-fi (charged) Play Area **Services:** **Leisure:** P **Off-site:** L

Camping Bavaria

viale Rovereto 100, 38066
☎ 0464 552524 0464 559126
e-mail: info@bavarianet.it
web: www.bavarianet.it

Site faces directly onto a lake, ideal for watersports enthusiasts.

dir: *On SS240 towards Rovereto.*

GPS: 45.8797, 10.8561

Open: Apr-Oct **Site:** 0.6HEC **Prices:** 25-31
Facilities: Wi-fi Play Area **Services:**
Leisure: L **Off-site:**

RIVOLTELLA — BRESCIA

San Francesco

Strada Vicinale San Francesco, 25010
☎ 030 9110245 030 9119464
e-mail: moreinfo@campingsanfrancesco.com
web: www.campingsanfrancesco.com

This well-kept site is divided into many sections by drives, vineyards and orchards and has a private gravel beach.

dir: *At Km268 on SSN11.*

Open: Apr-28 Sep **Site:** 10.4HEC **For hire:**
Prices: 25-56 Mobile home hire 455-1260 **Facilities:** Wi-fi (charged) Play Area **Services:**
Leisure: L P

ST-VINCENT — AOSTA

Paradise Village Camping

via Trieste 19, 11027
☎ 0166 513669 0166 546309
e-mail: info@villageparadise.com
web: www.villageparadise.com

Peaceful site with large pitches, divided into terraces and pleasantly shaded by trees. Close to a spa town and ski-runs.

Open: All Year. **Site:** 7.5HEC **For hire:**
Prices: 29.50-31.50 **Facilities:** Wi-fi
Services: **Off-site:** R

SAN ANTONIO DI MAVIGNOLA — TRENTO

Fae

38086
☎ 0465 507178 0465 507178
e-mail: info@campingfae.it
web: www.campingfae.it

Situated in the winter skiing region of Madonna di Campiglio. Good base for climbing in the Brenta range. Set on on four gravel terraces, and an alpine meadow in a hollow.

dir: *Off SS239.*

Open: Jun-Sep & Dec-Apr **Site:** 2.1HEC **For hire:**
Prices: 27-34 **Facilities:** Play Area
Services: **Off-site:** L P R

SAN FELICE DEL BENACO — BRESCIA

Camping Europa-Silvella

via Silvella 10, 25010
☎ 0365 651095 0365 654395
e-mail: info@europasilvella.it
web: www.europasilvella.it

Site separated in two by the approach road. The beach is 80 metres below.

dir: *A4 exit Desenzano del Garda and follow signs to Salò and Riva continue for 10km, signed.*

Open: 25 Apr-20 Sep **Site:** 7.5HEC **For hire:**
Facilities: **Services:** **Leisure:** L P

Fornella

via Fornella 1, 25010
☎ 0365 62294 0365 559418
e-mail: fornella@fornella.it
web: www.fornella.it

A quiet site in an ideal location on the shore of Lake Garda. Kids' club in high season.

dir: *Signed from SS572 Salò-Desenzano.*

Open: 18 Apr-23 Sep **Site:** 9.2HEC **For hire:**
Prices: 24-44.10 **Facilities:** Wi-fi (charged) Kids' Club Play Area **Services:** **Leisure:** L P

Gardiola

via Gardiola 36, 25010
0365 559240 0365 690724
e-mail: info@lagardiola.com
web: www.baiaholiday.com

A terraced site with a variety of good facilities on the shore of Lake Garda.

dir: *S of San Felice del Benaco off SS572.*

Open: Apr-22 Oct **Site:** 0.37HEC **For hire:** **Facilities:** Wi-fi (charged) **Services:** **Leisure:** L **Off-site:** P R

Ideal Molino

25010
0365 62023 0365 559395
e-mail: info@campingmolino.it
web: www.campingmolino.it

Charming and quiet site beside Lake Garda, set among beautiful scenery 1km from San Felice. On the beach there is a pier and boat moorings. Pedal boats can be hired for lake trips.

GPS: 45.5786, 10.5547

Open: 24 Mar-7 Oct **Site:** 2HEC **For hire:** **Prices:** 22.30-47.50 Mobile home hire 399-1134 **Facilities:** Kids' Club Play Area **Services:** **Leisure:** L P **Off-site:**

Weekend

The Camping and Caravanning Club — The Friendly Club

via Vallone della Selva 2, 25010
0365 43712 0365 42196
e-mail: info@weekend.it
web: www.weekend.it

A quiet family site with modern facilities, situated in an olive grove overlooking Lake Garda.

C&CC Report *A lovely site in a really spectacular setting. The views from the pool and from the bar's garden terrace are truly exceptional. Boat trips run from nearby Portese, and a visit to any of the towns around the lake, from Riva del Garda in the north to the beautiful fortified lake town of Sirmione in the south, is really rewarding. Just a short walk away you can go wine-tasting at Portese, while back on site, the weekly Italian buffet is very popular with the visiting campers from all over Europe and one of the highlights of the site's popular activities programme.*

dir: *A4 exit Desenzano, to Cisano, signed San Felice D-B.*

Open: 20 Apr-20 Sep **Site:** 9HEC **For hire:** **Facilities:** Wi-fi (charged) Kids' Club Play Area **Services:** **Leisure:** P **Off-site:** L

SAN MARTINO DI CASTROZZA TRENTO

Sass Maor

via Laghetto 48, 38058
0439 68347 0439 68347
e-mail: info@campingsassmaor.it
web: www.campingsassmaor.it

A winter sports site in a beautiful mountain setting.

dir: *From Trento to Ora, Cavalese & S Martino di Castrozza.*

Open: All Year. **Site:** 0.19HEC **Facilities:** Wi-fi **Services:** **Off-site:**

SAN PIETRO DI CORTENO GOLGI BRESCIA

Camping Villaggio Aprica

via Nazionale 507, 25040
0342 710001
e-mail: info@campingaprica.it
web: www.campingaprica.it

A small natural park ideal for winter skiing and summer walking or cycling.

dir: *On SS39 Aprica-Edolo.*

Open: All Year. **Site:** 2.1HEC **For hire:** **Facilities:** Wi-fi Play Area **Services:** **Leisure:** R **Off-site:** L P

SAN VIGILIO DI MAREBBE BOLZANO

Al Plan

39030
0474 501694 0474 506550
e-mail: camping.alplan@rolmail.net
web: www.campingalplan.com

Surrounded by the Dolomites, at an altitude of 1200 metres, this quiet site offers plenty of summer and winter activities.

dir: *Off A22.*

Open: 3 Dec-15 Apr & Jun-14 Oct **Site:** 1.2HEC **For hire:** **Prices:** 24-31 **Facilities:** Play Area **Services:** **Off-site:** R

ITALY

ITALY

SARRE AOSTA

Monte Bianco

Fraz St Maurice 15, 11010
☎ 0165 257523 🖷 0165 257275
e-mail: info@campingmontebianco.it
web: www.campingmontebianco.it
Wooded surroundings close to the town centre.
dir: *SS26 towards Aosta & Courmayer.*
GPS: 45.7171, 7.2612
Open: 15 May-20 Sep **Site:** 7.5HEC **Prices:** 21.90-23.50 **Facilities:** Wi-fi Play Area **Services:** **Leisure:** R **Off-site:** P

SEXTEN BOLZANO

Sexten

St-Josefstr 54, 39030
☎ 0474 710444 🖷 0474 710053
e-mail: info@patzenfeld.com
web: www.patzenfeld.com
This family-run site, located in the Dolomite mountain region, has modern facilities. The site offers swimming pools, a spa and plenty of activities, including skiing in winter. A kids' club is available in high season.
GPS: 46.6678, 13.3991
Open: All Year. **Site:** 6.5HEC **For hire:** **Facilities:** Wi-fi (charged) Kids' Club Play Area **Services:** **Leisure:** P R

SORICO COMO

La Riva

via Pomciome 3, 22010
☎ 0344 94571 🖷 0344 94571
e-mail: info@campinglariva.com
web: www.campinglariva.com
Set in stunning countryside in the Italian Lakes area.
Open: Apr-3 Nov **Site:** 1.4HEC **Facilities:** Wi-fi Play Area **Services:** **Leisure:** L P **Off-site:**

TORBOLE TRENTO

Camping Al Porto

via al Cor 3, 38069
☎ 0464 505891 🖷 0464 505891
e-mail: info@campingalporto.it
web: www.campingalporto.it
A site with modern facilities, situated in a quiet position near the lake, ideal for families. Good sports facilities and apartments for hire.
dir: *From Torbole onto SS240, signed.*
Open: 25 Mar-3 Nov **Site:** 1.1HEC **Prices:** 19.60-29 **Facilities:** Wi-fi (charged) Play Area **Services:** **Off-site:** L P R

TORRE DANIELE TORINO

Mombarone

via Nazionale 54, 10010
☎ 0125 757907 🖷 0125 757396
e-mail: info@campingmombarone.it
web: www.campingmombarone.it
With views of the surrounding mountains, a mainly grassy site with local amenities nearby.
dir: *13km N of Ivrea on SS26. Close to river.*
GPS: 45.5650, 7.8161
Open: All Year. **Site:** 2HEC **For hire:** **Prices:** 20.50-23 **Facilities:** Wi-fi **Services:** **Leisure:** R **Off-site:**

VALNONTEY AOSTA

Lo Stambecco

11012
☎ 0165 74152
e-mail: infotiscali@campeggiolostambecco.it
web: www.campeggiolostambecco.it
Site with terraced pitches, ideal for hiking in surrounding mountains.
Open: 15 May-25 Sep **Site:** 1.6HEC **For hire:** **Facilities:** **Services:** **Leisure:** R **Off-site:**

VENICE/NORTH

ARSIE — BELLUNO

Gajole

Loc Soravigo, 32030
0439 58505 0439 58505
e-mail: info@campinggajole.it
web: www.campinggajole.it

A delightful, peaceful setting on the shore of Lake Corlo. Suitable for families with children.

dir: *Off SS50.*

Open: Apr-Sep **Site:** 1.8HEC **Prices:** 20-24 **Facilities:** Wi-fi (charged) Play Area **Services:** **Leisure:** L **Off-site:**

ASIAGO — VICENZA

Ekar

Loc Ekar, 36012
0424 455157 0424 455161
e-mail: info@campingasiagoekar.com
web: www.campingasiagoekar.com

On a level meadow in a striking setting among wooded hills in a popular skiing region.

Open: 5 May-Sep & 15 Nov-6 Apr **Site:** 3.5HEC **Facilities:** **Services:**

AURISINA — TRIESTE

Agrituristico Imperial

Aurisina Cave 55, 34011
040 200459 040 200459
e-mail: campimperial@libero.it
web: www.campingimperialcarso.it

A well-maintained site in a secluded, wooded location.

dir: *Via SS14 Sistiana-Aurisina.*

GPS: 45.7574, 13.6590

Open: 20 May-20 Sep **Site:** 1.2HEC **Prices:** 17.50-26.50 **Facilities:** **Services:** **Leisure:** P **Off-site:** S

BARDOLINO — VERONA

Continental

Loc Reboin, 37011
045 7210192 045 7211756
e-mail: camping.continental@campingarda.it

A pleasant site directly on the lake with modern facilities.

Open: Etr-10 Oct **Site:** 3.5HEC **For hire:** **Facilities:** Wi-fi (charged) Play Area **Services:** **Leisure:** L **Off-site:**

Rocca

Loc S Pietro, 37011
045 7211111 045 7211300
e-mail: info@campinglarocca.com
web: www.campinglarocca.com

Slightly sloping grassland broken by rows of trees, separated from the lake by a public path (no cars). Part of site is on the other side of the main road, terraced among vines and olives with a lovely view of the lake.

dir: *Below SS249 at Km40/IV.*

Open: 26 Mar-4 Oct **Site:** 8HEC **For hire:** **Facilities:** **Services:** **Leisure:** L P **Off-site:**

BIBIONE — VENEZIA

Villaggio Turistico Internazionale

via Colonie 2, 30020
0431 442611 0431 442699
e-mail: info@vti.it
web: www.vti.it

Mostly sandy terrain under pine trees. Some meadowland with a few deciduous trees. Wide sandy beach. Leisure facilities include tennis court, swimming pool complex and direct access to a private beach.

dir: *A4 E of Venice take Latisana exit then 354 towards Lignano after 12km turn right to Bevazzana & left to Bibione. Signed along approach road.*

GPS: 45.635, 13.0375

Open: 2 Apr-Sep **Site:** 15HEC **For hire:** **Prices:** 20.50-61 Mobile home hire 252-1064 **Facilities:** Wi-fi (charged) Kids' Club Play Area **Services:** **Leisure:** P S

CA'NOGHERA — VENEZIA

Alba d'Oro

via Triestina 214G, 30030
041 5415102 041 5415971
e-mail: albadoro@ecvacanze.it
web: www.ecvacanze.it

On level ground directly on the lagoon with modern facilities including moorings for small boats. Regular bus service to Venice.

dir: *Off SS14.*

Open: 15 Apr-14 Nov **Site:** 7HEC **For hire:** **Facilities:** **Services:** **Leisure:** P R **Off-site:** L S

CAORLE — VENEZIA

Camping Laguna Village

via del Cacciatori 5, 30021
0421 210165 0421 217085
e-mail: info@campinglagunavillage.com
web: www.campinglagunavillage.com

Close to the Caorle lagoon, family-friendly site with three styles of pitch. There is an outdoor swimming pool complex and activities throughout the summer.

GPS: 45.6165, 12.9062

Open: 12 May-16 Sep **Site:** 10.7HEC **For hire:** **Prices:** 17-37 **Facilities:** Wi-fi (charged) Kids' Club Play Area **Services:** **Leisure:** P S **Off-site:**

Pra'delle Torri

viale Altanea 201, 30021
0421 299063 0421 299035
e-mail: info@pradelletorri.it
web: www.pradelletorri.it

Extensive site on flat ground.

dir: *3km W by beach.*

GPS: 45.5728, 12.8135

Open: 21 Apr-Sep **Site:** 120HEC **For hire:** **Prices:** 17.30-46.30 **Facilities:** Wi-fi (charged) Kids' Club Play Area **Services:** **Leisure:** P S

CA'SAVIO — VENEZIA

Ca'Savio

The Camping and Caravanning Club The Friendly Club

via di Ca'Savio 77, 30013
041 966017 041 5300707
e-mail: fuin@casavio.it
web: www.casavio.it

Flat site among trees next to beach.

C&CC Report *A large, well-equipped and very well run site, great for combining a lively beach holiday in a popular tourist area with visits to the marvel that is Venice, the famous glass-making island of Murano, or beyond. From here you arrive in Venice in best Marco Polo fashion – by sea, taking a ferry across the lagoon to St. Mark's Square.*

dir: *Jesolo-Punta Sabbione road, on left.*

Open: May-Sep **Site:** 26.8HEC **For hire:** **Facilities:** Wi-fi Kids' Club Play Area **Services:** **Leisure:** P S **Off-site:**

CASSONE — VERONA

Bellavista

via Gardesana, 37018
045 7420244 045 7420244
e-mail: info@campingbellavistamalcesine.com
web: www.campingbellavistamalcesine.com

A fine position in an olive grove overlooking Lake Garda with modern sanitary installations. Access to the lake is by an underpass and water sports are available.

Open: All Year. **Site:** 27HEC **For hire:** **Facilities:** **Services:** **Leisure:** L **Off-site:** P R

CASTELLETTO DI BRENZONE — VERONA

Le Maior

via Croce N.10, 37010
045 7430333 045 7430333
e-mail: campinglemaior@brenzone.com
web: www.campinglemaior.it

A comfortable, modern site in a pleasant, quiet location.

Open: Etr-29 Sep **Site:** 8HEC **For hire:** **Facilities:** Wi-fi **Services:** **Off-site:** L

San Zeno

via A Vespucci 97, 37010
045 7430231 045 4430171
e-mail: info@campingsanzeno.it
web: www.campingsanzeno.it

Situated close to the lake and surrounded by hundred-year old olive groves.

dir: *Motorway exit Rovereto/Trento, continue S, site 10km S of Malcesine.*

Open: May-Sep **Site:** 1.4HEC **For hire:** **Prices:** 25-30 **Facilities:** **Services:** **Off-site:** L

CAVALLINO VENEZIA

Cavallino

via delle Batterie 164, 30013
041 966133 041 5300827
e-mail: info@campingcavallino.com
web: www.baiaholiday.com
Located on the seafront with a long, wide sandy beach. Pitches are mainly shaded by pine trees and are separated by hedges. Ideal for families with facilities including a swimming pool and mini-golf.
GPS: 45.4567, 12.5006
Open: 24 Mar-Oct **Site:** 10.7HEC **For hire:** **Facilities:** Wi-fi (charged) Kids' Club Play Area **Services:** **Leisure:** P S **Off-site:**

Europa Camping Village

via Fausta 332, 30013
041 968069 041 5370150
e-mail: info@campingeuropa.com
web: www.campingeuropa.com
Located on the Cavallino coast, this family site has modern facilities. A kids' club is available from mid May to mid September.
dir: *Signed on Punta Sabbioni road.*
Open: 2 Apr-Sep **Site:** 11HEC **For hire:** **Facilities:** Wi-fi (charged) Kids' Club Play Area **Services:** **Leisure:** P S **Off-site:**

Italy Camping Village

via Fausta 272, 30013
041 968090 041 5370076
e-mail: info@campingitaly.it
web: www.campingitaly.it
Small family site on a peninsula 6km from Lido di Jesolo. Venice can be reached by public ferry.
dir: *Brenner-Venezia motorway exit signs for Jesolo-Cavallino.*
Open: 20 Apr-16 Sep **Site:** 3.9HEC **For hire:** **Prices:** 18.10-41 Mobile home hire 350-693 **Facilities:** Wi-fi (charged) Kids' Club Play Area **Services:** **Leisure:** P S **Off-site:**

Residence Village

via F-Baracca 47, 30013
041 968027 041 5370340
e-mail: info@residencevillage.com
web: www.residencevillage.com
Well-laid out family site on level, wooded grassland. Located by a sandy beach between Jesolo and Cavallino.
dir: *Leave A4 and follow signs to Jesolo and Cavallino, signed.*
GPS: 45.4805, 12.5744
Open: 6 May-16 Sep **Site:** 8.5HEC **For hire:** **Prices:** 10.60-42.70 **Facilities:** Wi-fi (charged) Kids' Club Play Area **Services:** **Leisure:** P S **Off-site:** R

Sant' Angelo

via F-Baracca 63, 30013
041 968882 041 5370242
e-mail: info@santangelo.it
web: www.santangelo.it
A large beach site decorated by trees and flower beds. Good entertainment, sports and eating facilities.
dir: *Outside Venice signs for Caposile & Jesolo, cross bridge just after Lido di Jesolo & right to coast.*
Open: 6 May-24 Sep **Site:** 20HEC **For hire:** **Facilities:** **Services:** **Leisure:** P S

Scarpiland

via A-Poerio 14, 30013
041 966488 041 966488
e-mail: info@scarpiland.com
web: www.scarpiland.com
A beautiful location surrounded by a pine wood with sea views and direct access to the beach.
GPS: 45.455, 12.4886
Open: 24 Apr-18 Sep **Site:** 4.5HEC **For hire:** **Prices:** 15.70-34.30 Mobile home hire 175-595 **Facilities:** Wi-fi (charged) Kids' Club Play Area **Services:** **Leisure:** S

Silva

via F-Baracca 53, 30013

☎ 041 968087 🖷 041 968087

e-mail: info@campingsilva.it

web: www.campingsilva.it

The site lies on sand and grassland and is located between road and beach, divided by a vineyard. The section of site near the beach is quiet.

dir: *From Jesolo in the direction of Punta Sabbioni.*

Open: 4 May-16 Sep **Site:** 3.3HEC **For hire:** **Prices:** 17-35 Mobile home hire 175-455 **Facilities:** Play Area **Services:** **Leisure:** S **Off-site:** R

Union-Lido

via Fausta 258, 30013

☎ 041 2575111 🖷 041 5370355

e-mail: info@unionlido.com

web: www.unionlido.com

This large site lies on a long stretch of land next to a 1km-long beach. Separate section for tents and caravans. Ideal for families.

dir: *Motorway from Tarvisio via Udine, San Dona di Piave then signed to Jesolo & Cavallino.*

GPS: 45.4675, 12.5314

Open: 21 Apr-23 Sep **Site:** 60HEC **For hire:** **Prices:** 48.60-65.60 Mobile home hire 121-166 **Facilities:** Wi-fi (charged) Kids' Club Play Area **Services:** **Leisure:** P S

Vela Blu Camping Village

via Radaelli 10, 30013

☎ 041 968068 🖷 041 5371003

e-mail: info@velablu.it

web: www.velablu.it

Set in a pinewood, directly next to the sea and with a private beach. There is a traditional swimming pool plus a children's pool with three slides. Activities take place throughout the day.

GPS: 45.4578, 12.5064

Open: 2 Apr-29 Sep **Site:** 10HEC **For hire:** **Prices:** 17.20-42.60 **Facilities:** Wi-fi (charged) Kids' Club Play Area **Services:** **Leisure:** P S **Off-site:**

Villa al Mare

via del Faro 12, 30013

☎ 041 968066 🖷 041 5370576

e-mail: info@villaalmare.com

web: www.villaalmare.com

Level site divided into plots on a peninsula behind the lighthouse. Direct access to a long, sandy beach.

Open: Apr-Sep **Site:** 2HEC **For hire:** **Facilities:** **Services:** **Leisure:** P R S

CHIOGGIA VENEZIA

Miramare

via A-Barbarigo 103, 30015

☎ 041 490610 🖷 041 490610

e-mail: campmir@tin.it

web: www.miramarecamping.com

A peaceful site, divided into two parts, with a private beach. Sports facilities and entertainment for children in high season.

dir: *SS309 Strada Romeo towards Chioggia Sottomarina, turn right at beach, site 0.5km.*

GPS: 45.1903, 12.3033

Open: 20 Apr-19 Sep **Site:** 6HEC **For hire:** **Facilities:** Wi-fi (charged) Kids' Club Play Area **Services:** **Leisure:** P S **Off-site:**

Villaggio Turistico Isamar

via Isamar 9, Isolaverde, 30015

☎ 041 5535811 🖷 041 490440

e-mail: info@villaggioisamar.com

web: www.villaggioisamar.com

The site lies on level grassland at the mouth of the River Etsch. Shade is provided by high poplars. Good beach.

dir: *Off SS309. NB Caravans are advised to approach via Km84/VII near Brenta.*

Open: 15 May-10 Sep **Site:** 33HEC **For hire:** **Facilities:** Wi-fi (charged) Kids' Club Play Area **Services:** **Leisure:** P R S

CHIOGGIA SOTTOMARINA — VENEZIA

Oasi

via A-Barbarigo 147, 30019
041 5541145 041 490801
e-mail: info@campingoasi.com
web: www.campingoasi.com

A well-equipped site on a wooded peninsula near the mouth of the Brenta River with a wide private beach.

dir: *W of town centre towards river & beach.*

GPS: 45.1814, 12.3075

Open: 30 Mar-Sep **Site:** 3HEC **For hire:** **Prices:** 20.50-35.90 **Facilities:** Wi-fi (charged) Kids' Club Play Area **Services:** **Leisure:** P R S **Off-site:**

CISANO — VERONA

Camping Cisano

via Peschiera 52 CP 126, 37011
045 6229098 045 6229059
e-mail: cisano@camping-cisano.it
web: www.camping-cisano.it

Quiet, partly terraced site beside Lake Garda with good water sports and entertainment.

dir: *Brenner-Verona motorway exit AFFI, site 8km.*

Open: 24 Mar-8 Oct **Site:** 14HEC **For hire:** **Prices:** 18.50-43 **Facilities:** Wi-fi Kids' Club Play Area **Services:** **Leisure:** L P

San Vito

via Pralesi 3, CP 126, 37011
045 6229026 045 6229059
e-mail: cisano@camping-cisano.it
web: www.camping-cisano.it

A tranquil and shady site with many modern facilities.

dir: *8km from Brenner motorway, exit signed AFFI.*

Open: 24 Mar-8 Oct **Site:** 5HEC **For hire:** **Prices:** 18.50-43 **Facilities:** Wi-fi Kids' Club Play Area **Services:** **Leisure:** L P

CORTINA D'AMPEZZO — BELLUNO

Cortina

via Campo 2, 32043
0436 867575 0436 867917
e-mail: campcortina@tin.it
web: www.campingcortina.it

This site lies among pine trees several hundred metres from the edge of town.

dir: *Off Dolomite road towards Belluno, site 1km by small river.*

Open: All Year. **Site:** 4.6HEC **Prices:** 20-26 **Facilities:** Wi-fi (charged) Play Area **Services:** **Leisure:** P R **Off-site:**

Dolomiti

via Campo di Sotto, 32043
0436 2485 0436 5403
e-mail: campeggiodolomiti@tin.it
web: www.campeggiodolomiti.it

The site is beautifully situated on grassland with pine trees in a hollow, not far from the Olympic ski jump.

dir: *2.7km S of Cortina. Off Dolomite road towards Belluno, site 1.5km.*

Open: Jun-19 Sep **Site:** 5.4HEC **Prices:** 20-26 **Facilities:** Play Area **Services:** **Leisure:** R **Off-site:** L

Olympia

Fiames 1, 32043
0436 5057 0436 5057
e-mail: info@campingolympiacortina.it
web: www.campingolympiacortina.it

A very beautiful site set in the centre of the magnificent Dolomite landscape.

dir: *N of town off SS51.*

Open: 5 Dec-5 Nov **Site:** 4HEC **Prices:** 17-26 **Facilities:** Wi-fi (charged) Play Area **Services:** **Leisure:** R **Off-site:** L P

Rocchetta

via Campo 1, 32043
0436 5063 0436 5063
e-mail: camping@sunrise.it
web: www.campingrocchetta.it

Set in beautiful wooded surroundings.

dir: *S from Cortina via SS51.*

GPS: 46.5225, 12.1342

Open: Jun-20 Sep & Dec-10 Apr **Site:** 2.5HEC **Facilities:** Wi-fi (charged) Play Area **Services:** **Leisure:** R **Off-site:** L

ITALY

ERACLEA MARE — VENEZIA

Portofelice

viale dei Fiori 15, 30020
0421 66411 0421 66021
e-mail: info@portofelice.it
web: www.portofelice.it

A well-equipped family village site separated from the beach by a pine wood. A variety of recreational facilities is available.

dir: *From A4 Venice/Trieste exit San Donà/Noventa di Piave & travel S through San Donà di Piave & Eraclea and Ercalea Mare, then follow signs for site.*

GPS: 45.5536, 12.7664

Open: 12 May-15 Sep **Site:** 17.5HEC **For hire:** **Prices:** 16.20-45.60 Mobile home hire 273-045 **Facilities:** Wi-fi (charged) Kids' Club Play Area **Services:** **Leisure:** P S **Off-site:** R

FUSINA VENEZIA — VENEZIA

Fusina

via Moranzani 79, 30030
041 5470055 041 5470050
e-mail: info@campingfusina.com
web: www.campingfusina.com

This well-equipped site is ideal for those visiting Venice and the Lagoon. There is a regular water bus service to Venice.

GPS: 45.4194, 12.2558

Open: All Year. **Site:** 5.5HEC **For hire:** **Prices:** 33-35 **Facilities:** Wi-fi (charged) Play Area **Services:** **Leisure:** S

GEMONA DEL FRIÚLI — UDINE

Ai Pioppi

via del Bersaglio 118, 33013
0432 980358
e-mail: bar-camping-taxi@aipioppi.it
web: www.aipioppi.it

Quiet, well-equipped site in a pleasant mountain setting.

dir: *1km from town centre via N13.*

Open: 15 Mar-30 Oct **Site:** 11HEC **For hire:** **Facilities:** Wi-fi (charged) **Services:** **Off-site:** P R

GRADO — GORIZIA

Tenuta Primero

via Monfalcone 14, 34073
0431 896900 0431 896901
e-mail: info@tenuta-primero.com
web: www.tenuta-primero.com

The site lies on extensive level grassland between the road and the dam, which is 2 metres high along the narrow and level beach.

dir: *Signed off Monfalcone road.*

Open: Apr-Sep **Site:** 20HEC **For hire:** **Prices:** 19-49 **Facilities:** Wi-fi (charged) Kids' Club Play Area **Services:** **Leisure:** P S **Off-site:** R

Villaggio Europa

34073
0431 80877 0431 82284
e-mail: info@villaggioeuropa.com
web: www.villaggioeuropa.com

Level terrain under half-grown poplars, and partly in pine forest.

dir: *On road to Monfalcone, 20km from Palmanova via Aquileia.*

GPS: 45.6967, 13.4550

Open: 21 Apr-23 Sep **Site:** 22HEC **For hire:** **Prices:** 23-42 **Facilities:** Kids' Club Play Area **Services:** **Leisure:** P S

JÉSOLO, LIDO DI — VENEZIA

Malibu Beach

viale Oriente 78, 30017
0421 362212 0421 961338
e-mail: info@campingmalibubeach.com
web: www.campingmalibubeach.com

Set in a pine wood facing the sea and a fine sandy beach.

dir: *From Venezia via Cavallino on coast road to Cortellazzo.*

Open: 12 May-16 Sep **Site:** 10HEC **For hire:** **Prices:** 23-44.50 **Facilities:** Wi-fi Kids' Club Play Area **Services:** **Leisure:** P S

Waikiki

viale Oriente 144, 30016
0421 980186 0421 378040
e-mail: info@campingwaikiki.com
web: www.campingwaikiki.com

A family site in a pine wood with direct access to the beach. Regular bus service to Venice passes the site.

Open: 12 May-16 Sep **Site:** 5.2HEC **For hire:** **Prices:** 18.25-36 **Facilities:** Wi-fi (charged) Kids' Club Play Area **Services:** **Leisure:** P S **Off-site:** R

ilities shower electric points for razors electric points for caravans motorvan service point parking by tents permitted
npulsory separate car park shop **Services** café/restaurant bar Camping Gaz International gas other than Camping Gaz
first aid facilities laundry **Leisure** swimming L-Lake P-Pool R-River S-Sea **Off-site** All facilities within 5km

LAZISE VERONA

Camping La Quercia

37017
045 6470577 045 6470243
e-mail: laquercia@laquercia.it
web: www.laquercia.it

The site is divided into many large sections by tarmacked drives and lies on terraced ground, sloping gently down to a lake. There is a large private beach.

dir: *Off SS49 at Km31/8 & site 400m.*

Open: Apr-Sep **Site:** 20HEC **For hire:** **Facilities:** Wi-fi (charged) Kids' Club Play Area **Services:** **Leisure:** L P **Off-site:**

see advert on page 399

Parc

via Gardesana 110, 37017
045 7580127 045 6470150
e-mail: duparc@campingduparc.com
web: www.campingduparc.com

Well-kept, lakeside site off main road.

dir: *From Garda, site on S side of Lazise just after turning for Verona.*

Open: 15 Mar-30 Oct **Site:** 6HEC **For hire:** **Facilities:** Wi-fi Kids' Club Play Area **Services:** **Leisure:** L P **Off-site:**

LIGNANO SABBIADORO UDINE

Camping Sabbiadoro

via Sabbiadoro 8, 33054
0431 71455 0431 721355
e-mail: campsab@lignano.it
web: www.campingsabbiadoro.it

A tranquil site in the shelter of a pine grove near the beach and the centre of Lignano.

dir: *Via A4 Venice-Trieste (exit Latisana) onto S354.*

Open: 31 Mar-7 Oct **Site:** 13HEC **For hire:** **Prices:** 22.10-40 Mobile home hire 252-1095.50 **Facilities:** Wi-fi (charged) Kids' Club Play Area **Services:** **Leisure:** P **Off-site:** S

MALCESINE VERONA

Claudia

Gardesana 394, 37018
045 7400786 045 7400786
e-mail: info@campingclaudia.it
web: www.campingclaudia.it

Flat, grassy site only 30 metres from the lake. Excellent facilities, especially for water sports.

dir: *From Rome/Brenner motorway, continue via Trento, Arco & Torbole, site on outskirts of Malcesine.*

Open: Apr-20 Oct **Site:** 1HEC **Facilities:** **Services:** **Off-site:** L

MALGA CIAPELA BELLUNO

Malga Ciapela Marmolada

32020
0437 722064 0437 722064
e-mail: camping.mc.marmolada@dolomiti.com

A terraced site in tranquil wooded surroundings at the foot of Monte Marmolada.

dir: *Brenner-Verona motorway exit Bozen, signs for Canazei, Malga Ciapela & site at Marmolada.*

Open: Dec-25 Apr & Jun-20 Sep **Site:** 3HEC **Facilities:** **Services:** **Leisure:** R **Off-site:**

MASARÈ BELLUNO

Alleghe

32022
0437 723737 0437 723874
e-mail: alleghecamp@dolomites.com
web: www.camping.dolomiti.com/alleghe

Several terraces on a wooded incline below a road.

Open: 6 Dec-Apr & 14 Jun-29 Sep **Site:** 2HEC **Facilities:** **Services:** **Off-site:** L P

MONTEGROTTO TERME PADOVA

Sporting Center

35036
049 793400 049 8911551
e-mail: sporting@sportingcenter.it
web: www.sportingcenter.it

A peaceful site in a pleasant setting in the Euganean hills with good facilities including a thermal treatment centre.

Open: Mar-12 Nov **Site:** 6.5HEC **For hire:** **Facilities:** **Services:** **Leisure:** P **Off-site:**

Site 6HEC (site size) grass sand stone little shade partly shaded mainly shaded motorvans accepted bungalows for hire mobile homes for hire tents for hire no dogs site fully accessible for wheelchairs
Prices amount quoted is per night, for 2 adults and car, plus tent or caravan Mobile home hire is a weekly rate.

ITALY

ORIAGO VENEZIA

Serenissima

via Padana 334, 30034

☎ 041 921850 🖹 041 920286

e-mail: info@campingserenissima.it

web: www.campingserenissima.it

A well-looked after site with shade provided by the local woodland. Local bus service every 20 minutes to Venice.

dir: *A4 to Venice, SS11 at Oriago.*

Open: Etr-10 Nov **Site:** 2HEC **For hire:** **Facilities:** Play Area **Services:** **Leisure:** R

PACENGO VERONA

Camping Lido

via Peschiera 2, 37017

☎ 045 7590030 🖹 045 7590611

e-mail: info@campinglido.it

web: www.campinglido.it

On the lake shore with a pebble beach and boat moorings for rent, pitches are bordered by hedges. Other leisure facilities include two swimming pools and a fitness centre.

Open: Apr-Oct **Site:** 10HEC **For hire:** **Facilities:** Wi-fi (charged) Kids' Club Play Area **Services:** **Leisure:** L P

PALAFAVERA BELLUNO

Palafavera

32010

☎ 0437 788506 🖹 0437 788857

e-mail: palafavera@sunrise.it

web: www.camping.dolomiti.com/palafavera

A beautiful location in the heart of the Dolomites at an altitude of 1514 metres. Modern sanitary installations and plenty of recreational facilities.

Open: Dec-Apr & Jun-Sep **Site:** 5HEC **Prices:** 19.60-24 **Facilities:** Play Area **Services:** **Leisure:** L P R

PESCHIERA DEL GARDA VERONA

Bella Italia

via Bella Italia 2, 37019

☎ 045 6400688 🖹 045 6401410

e-mail: info@camping-bellaitalia.it

web: www.camping-bellaitalia.it

Extensive lakeside site. No animals or motorcycles allowed. No credit cards accepted. Kids' club available for 4-10 year olds.

dir: *Off Brescia road between Km276.2 & Km275.8 towards lake.*

Open: 24 Mar-28 Oct **Site:** 30HEC **For hire:** **Prices:** 26.30-53.50 **Facilities:** Wi-fi (charged) Kids' Club Play Area **Services:** **Leisure:** P **Off-site:** L R

Bergamini

Strada Bergamini 51, Porto Bergamini, 37019

☎ 045 7550283 🖹 045 7550283

e-mail: info@campingbergamini.it

web: www.campingbergamini.it

Ideal for young families as site has two children's pools and extensive play areas.

dir: *Signs for Porto Bergamini.*

GPS: 45.4503, 10.6706

Open: May-20 Sep **Site:** 1.4HEC **For hire:** **Prices:** 27-44 **Facilities:** Wi-fi Kids' Club Play Area **Services:** **Leisure:** L P **Off-site:** R

San Benedetto

Strada Bergamini 14, 37019

☎ 045 7550544 🖹 045 7551512

e-mail: info@campingsanbenedetto.it

web: www.campingsanbenedetto.it

A family site in a fine position overlooking the lake.

Open: 15 Mar-Sep **Site:** 22HEC **For hire:** **Facilities:** **Services:** **Leisure:** L P **Off-site:** R

PUNTA SABBIONI VENEZIA

Marina di Venezia

via Montello 6, 30013
041 5302511 041 966036
e-mail: camping@marinadivenezia.it
web: www.marinadivenezia.it

Extensive, well-organised and well-maintained holiday centre, amply shaded by trees. A section of the site is designated for dog owners, caravans and tents.

dir: *Along coast road, 0.5km before end turn onto narrow asphalt road towards sea, signed.*

GPS: 45.4375, 12.4381

Open: 21 Apr-Sep **Site:** 70HEC **For hire:** **Prices:** 19.80-45.10 **Facilities:** Wi-fi (charged) Kids' Club Play Area **Services:** **Leisure:** P S

Miramare

Lungomare D-Alighieri 29, 30013
041 966150 041 5301150
e-mail: info@camping-miramare.it
web: www.camping-miramare.it

A magnificent location overlooking the lagoon.

Open: Apr-Nov **Site:** 1.8HEC **For hire:** **Facilities:** **Services:** **Off-site:** S

ROSOLINA MARE ROVIGO

Campeggio Vittoria

Strada Sud 340, 45010
0426 68128 0426 68148
e-mail: info@campingvittoria.it
web: www.campingvittoria.it

Situated between a pine wood and private sandy beach, pitches vary from beach front with artificial shades, or in among the pine trees. Leisure facilities include evening entertainment for all the family.

GPS: 45.1167, 12.3253

Open: 24 Apr-9 Sep **Site:** 17HEC **For hire:** **Prices:** 22-30 **Facilities:** Kids' Club Play Area **Services:** **Leisure:** P R S **Off-site:**

Rosapineta

Strada Nord 24, 45010
0426 68033 0426 68105
e-mail: info@rosapineta.it
web: www.rosapineta.com

The site lies in the grounds of an extensive holiday camp. Pitches for caravans and tents are separate. Dogs are accepted but restrictions apply.

dir: *Strada Romea towards Ravenna & over River Adige, 0.8km turn off, over bridge towards Rosolina Mare & Rosapineta (8km).*

GPS: 45.1388, 12.3236

Open: 11 May-15 Sep **Site:** 47HEC **For hire:** **Prices:** 23.60-35.70 Mobile home hire 161-469 **Facilities:** Wi-fi (charged) Kids' Club Play Area **Services:** **Leisure:** P S **Off-site:** R

SISTIANA TRIESTE

Marepinetá

34019
040 299264 040 299265
e-mail: info@marepineta.com
web: www.baiaholiday.com

A modern site in a pleasant wooded location near the harbour and beach with a range of recreational facilities. Free bus service to the beach.

dir: *A4 exit Duino, 1km on SS14.*

Open: Apr-18 Oct **Site:** 10.8HEC **For hire:** **Facilities:** **Services:** **Leisure:** P **Off-site:** S

TREPORTI VENEZIA

Camping Village Mediterráneo

via delle Batterie 38, Ca'Vio, 30013
041 966721 041 966944
e-mail: mediterraneo@vacanze-natura.it
web: www.campingmediterraneo.it

A family site with pitches near the beach or surrounded by pine trees.

dir: *Signed from Jesolo continue towards Punta Sabbione until Ca'Vio.*

GPS: 45.4542, 12.4814

Open: 18 Apr-28 Sep **Site:** 17HEC **For hire:** **Facilities:** Wi-fi (charged) Kids' Club Play Area **Services:** **Leisure:** P S **Off-site:** R

Ca' Pasquali Village

via Poerio 33, 30013
041 966110 041 5300797
e-mail: info@capasquali.it
web: www.capasquali.it
Sandy, meadowland site with poplar and pine trees.
dir: *Off Cavallino-Punta Sabbioni coast road onto asphalt road for 400m.*
GPS: 45.4525, 12.4901
Open: 21 Apr-22 Sep **Site:** 9.8HEC **For hire:** **Prices:** 19.60-50.70 Mobile home hire 127.50-940.80 **Facilities:** Wi-fi (charged) Kids' Club Play Area **Services:** **Leisure:** P S **Off-site:**

Fiori

via Vettor Pisani 52, 30013
041 966448 041 966724
e-mail: fiori@vacanze-natura.it
web: www.deifiori.it
The site stretches over a wide area of dunes and pine trees with separate sections for caravans and tents.
dir: *A4 from Venice onto coast road via Jesolo to Lido del Cavallino.*
GPS: 45.4494, 14.4494
Open: 20 Apr-Sep **Site:** 11HEC **For hire:** **Prices:** 17.90-45.20 **Facilities:** Wi-fi (charged) Kids' Club Play Area **Services:** **Leisure:** P S

VICENZA VICENZA

Vicenza

via U Scarpelli 35, 36100
0444 582311 0444 582434
e-mail: info@campingvicenza.it
web: www.ascom.vi.it/camping
A modern, well-equipped site.
dir: *A4 exit Vicenza-Est.*
Open: Apr-Sep **Site:** 3HEC **For hire:** **Facilities:** Play Area **Services:** **Off-site:** R

ZOLDO ALTO BELLUNO

Pala Favera

32010
0437 788506 0437 788857
e-mail: palafavera@sunrise.it
web: www.campingpalafavera.com
Site with some woodland, at the foot of Monte Pelmo.
Open: Dec-Apr & Jun-Sep **Site:** 5HEC **For hire:** **Facilities:** Play Area **Services:** **Leisure:** R **Off-site:** P

NORTH WEST/MED COAST

ALBENGA SAVONA

Bella Vista

Campochiesa, Reg Campore 23, 17031
0182 540213 0182 554925
e-mail: info@campingbellavista.it
web: www.campingbellavista.it
A friendly, family orientated site with good facilities. Pitches are divided by bushes and flowerbeds.
dir: *1km from Km613.5 on SS1.*
Open: 15 Mar-15 Nov **Site:** 1.4HEC **For hire:** **Prices:** 15-40 **Facilities:** Wi-fi (charged) **Services:** **Leisure:** P **Off-site:** S

Roma

Regione Foce, 17031
0182 52317 0182 555075
e-mail: info@campingroma.com
web: www.campingroma.com
The site is divided into pitches and laid out with many flower beds.
dir: *N of bridge over Centa, turn left.*
GPS: 44.0422, 8.2225
Open: Apr-29 Sep **Site:** 1HEC **For hire:** **Prices:** 22-35 **Facilities:** Play Area **Services:** **Leisure:** R S **Off-site:** P

ALBINIA GROSSETO

Acapulco

via Aurelia Km155, 58010
0564 870165 0564 870165
e-mail: info@campeggioacapulco.com
web: www.campeggioacapulco.com
Set on hilly terrain in pine woodland.
dir: *Off via Aurelia at Km155 onto coast road.*
Open: May-14 Sep **Site:** 2HEC **For hire:** **Prices:** 18.50-34.50 Mobile home hire 315-980 **Facilities:** Wi-fi Play Area **Services:** **Leisure:** S

Hawaii

58010

☎ 0564 870164

e-mail: info@campinghawaii.it

web: www.campinghawaii.it

The site lies in a pine forest on rather hilly ground.

dir: *Off via Aurelia at Km154/V towards sea.*

Open: 16 Apr-27 Sep **Site:** 4HEC **For hire:** **Facilities:** **Services:** **Leisure:** S

BIBBONA, MARINA DI LIVORNO

Camping Casa di Caccia

via del Mare 40, 57020

☎ 0586 600000 0586 600000

e-mail: info@campingcasadicaccia.com

web: www.campingcasadicaccia.com

A tranquil site by the sea, with direct access to a private beach and pitches nestled amongst pine trees. A kids' club is available in high season.

dir: *A12 exit Rosignano, SS1 direction Grosseto, exit La California, site 4km; From Rome SS1 direction Livorno, exit Donoratico, site 8km.*

Open: 24 Mar-28 Oct **Site:** 3.5HEC **For hire:** **Prices:** 19.50-43.50 Mobile home hire 210-600 **Facilities:** Wi-fi (charged) Kids' Club Play Area **Services:** **Leisure:** S

Capanne

via Aurelia Km273, 57020

☎ 0586 600064 0586 600198

e-mail: info@campinglecapanne.it

web: www.campinglecapanne.it

A pleasant family site set in a spacious wooded park in magnificent Tuscan scenery. Defined pitches and a variety of recreational facilities.

dir: *Access from Km273 via Aurelia travelling inland.*

Open: 21 Apr-23 Sep **Site:** 9HEC **For hire:** **Prices:** 21.60-43 **Facilities:** Wi-fi (charged) Kids' Club Play Area **Services:** **Leisure:** P **Off-site:** L S

Capannino

via Cavalleggeri Sud 26, 57020

☎ 0586 600252 0586 600720

e-mail: capannino@capannino.it

web: www.capannino.it

Well-tended park site in pine woodland with private beach.

dir: *Off via Aurelia at Km272/VII towards sea.*

Open: 6 Apr-16 Sep **Site:** 3HEC **For hire:** **Prices:** 30-53 **Facilities:** Wi-fi (charged) Play Area **Services:** **Leisure:** S **Off-site:** P

Forte

via dei Platani 58, 57020

☎ 0586 600155 0586 600123

e-mail: campeggiodelforte@campeggiodelforte.it

web: www.campeggiodelforte.it

Level site, grassy, sandy terrain.

dir: *SS1 direction Grosseto, exit La California, take SS Aurelia direction San Vicenzo, after 2km right to Marina di Bibbona.*

GPS: 43.2344, 10.5349

Open: 23 Apr-18 Sep **Site:** 8HEC **For hire:** **Facilities:** Kids' Club Play Area **Services:** **Leisure:** P **Off-site:** S

Free Beach

via Cavalleggeri Nord 88, 57020

☎ 0586 600388 0586 602984

e-mail: info@campingfreebeach.it

web: www.campingfreebeach.it

Situated 300 metres from the sea through pine woods.

dir: *From SS206 at Cecina signs to San Guido.*

Open: 22 Apr-19 Sep **Site:** 9HEC **For hire:** **Facilities:** Wi-fi Play Area **Services:** **Leisure:** P **Off-site:** S

Il Gineprino

via dei Platani, 56a, 57020

☎ 0586 600550 0586 636866

e-mail: info@ilgineprino.it

web: www.ilgineprino.it

A modern site situated on the Tuscany coast and shaded by a pine wood. There are good recreational facilities and the beach is within 700 metres. Cars parked by tents in low season. A kids' club is available during high season.

dir: *Motorway exit La California for Marina di Bibbona.*

Open: Apr-Sep **Site:** 1.5HEC **For hire:** **Prices:** 22-34.50 Mobile home hire 170-650 **Facilities:** Kids' Club Play Area **Services:** **Leisure:** P **Off-site:** S

BOGLIASCO — GENOVA

Genova Est

via Marconi, Cassa, 16031
010 3472053 010 3472053
e-mail: info@camping-genova-est.it
web: www.camping-genova-est.it
Quiet and shady site 1km from the sea. A free bus service operates from the site to the railway station for links to Genoa and Portofino.
dir: *A12 exit Nervi, 8km E.*
GPS: 44.3807, 9.0723
Open: 31 Mar-15 Oct **Site:** 1.2HEC **For hire:** **Prices:** 21-23.20 **Facilities:** Wi-fi **Services:** **Off-site:** P S

BOTTAI — FIRENZE

Internazionale Firenze

via S Cristoforo 2, 50029
055 2374704 055 2373412
e-mail: internazionale@florencecamping.it
web: www.campingflorence.com
Situated on the Florentine hills, the site offers a relaxing atmosphere close to many historic sites.
Open: Apr-29 Oct **Site:** 6HEC **For hire:** **Facilities:** Wi-fi (charged) **Services:** **Leisure:** P **Off-site:** L R

CAPANNOLE — AREZZO

Chiocciola

via G-Cesare 14, 52020
055 995776 055 995776
web: www.campinglachiocciola.com
A modern site in a rural setting among chestnut trees at an altitude of 250 metres.
Open: Mar-1 Nov **Site:** 3HEC **For hire:** **Facilities:** **Services:** **Leisure:** P **Off-site:** L R

CAPRAIA E LIMITE — FIRENZE

San Giusto

via Castra 71, 50050
055 8712304 055 8711856
e-mail: info@campingsangiusto.it
web: www.campingsangiusto.it
A useful site on slightly sloping ground within easy reach of Florence, Pisa, Siena and Lucca by car or public transport.
Open: Etr-Oct **Site:** 7.3HEC **For hire:** **Prices:** 22.50-28 Mobile home hire 280-400 **Facilities:** Wi-fi Play Area **Services:** **Leisure:** P **Off-site:** L R

CASALE MARITTIMO — PISA

Valle Gaia

via Cecinese 87, 56040
0586 681236 0586 683551
e-mail: info@vallegaia.it
web: www.vallegaia.it
Site among pines and olive trees in a quiet rural location.
dir: *Autostrada/superstrada exit Casale Marittimo for Cecina, site signed.*
Open: 31 Mar-6 Oct **Site:** 4HEC **For hire:** **Prices:** 16.40-33.30 **Facilities:** Wi-fi Play Area **Services:** **Leisure:** P **Off-site:**

CASTAGNETO CARDUCCI — LIVORNO

Climatico Le Pianacce

via Bolgherese, 57022
0565 763667 0565 766085
e-mail: info@campinglepianacce.it
web: www.campinglepianacce.it
Terraced site on slopes of mountain in typical Tuscany countryside, enhanced by site landscaping. Pleasant climate due to altitude.
dir: *Off via Aurelia at Km344/VIII towards Castagneto Carducci/ Sassetta, 3.2km left for Bolgheri, 0.5km right towards mountains.*
Open: 21 Apr-23 Sep **Site:** 9HEC **For hire:** **Prices:** 20-47 **Facilities:** Wi-fi (charged) Kids' Club Play Area **Services:** **Leisure:** P

ITALY

CASTEL DEL PIANO — GROSSETO

Amiata

via Roma 15, 58033
☎ 0564 955107 📠 0564 955107
e-mail: info@amiata.org
web: www.amiata.org

A grassland site with a separate section for dog owners.

GPS: 42.8841, 11.5366

Open: All Year. **Site:** 4.2HEC **For hire:** **Prices:** 16.50-22.80 **Facilities:** Play Area **Services:** **Off-site:** P

CASTIGLIONE DELLA PESCAIA — GROSSETO

Santa Pomata

Strada della Rocchette, 58043
☎ 0564 941037 📠 0564 941221
e-mail: info@campingsantapomata.it
web: www.campingsantapomata.it

Site in hilly woodland terrain with some pitches among bushes. Flat clean sandy beach.

dir: *Off SS322 at Km20 towards Le Rocchette 4.5km NW, continue to sea, site 1km on left.*

Open: 20 Apr-20 Oct **Site:** 6HEC **For hire:** **Prices:** 25-39 Mobile home hire 315-455 **Facilities:** **Services:** **Leisure:** S

CERIALE — SAVONA

Baciccia

via Torino 19, 17023
☎ 0182 990743 📠 0182 993839
e-mail: info@campingbaciccia.it
web: www.campingbaciccia.it

An orderly site, lying inland off the via Aurelia, 0.5km from the sea.

dir: *Entrance 100m W of Km612/V.*

GPS: 44.0817, 8.2175

Open: 20 Mar-5 Nov & Dec-10 Jan **Site:** 1.5HEC **For hire:** **Prices:** 20-38 Mobile home hire 350-731.50 **Facilities:** Wi-fi (charged) Play Area **Services:** **Leisure:** P **Off-site:** S

CERVO — IMPERIA

Lino

via N Sauro 4, 18010
☎ 0183 400087 📠 0183 400089
e-mail: info@campinglino.it
web: www.campinglino.com

A clean, well-managed seaside site shaded by grape vines. There is a knee-deep lagoon suitable for children.

dir: *Off via Aurelia at Km637/V near railway underpass onto via Nazionale Sauro towards sea.*

GPS: 43.9239, 8.1081

Open: 31 Mar-20 Oct **Site:** 1.1HEC **For hire:** **Prices:** 22-44 **Facilities:** Wi-fi (charged) Play Area **Services:** **Leisure:** P S **Off-site:**

CUTIGLIANO — PISTOIA

Betulle

via Cantamaggio 6, 51024
☎ 0573 68004 📠 0573 68004
web: www.campeggiolebetulle.it

A pleasant year-round site with good facilities in a central location with access to three popular ski stations.

Open: All Year. **Site:** 4HEC **For hire:** **Facilities:** **Services:** **Leisure:** L R **Off-site:** P

DEIVA MARINA — LA SPEZIA

La Sfinge

Gea 5, 19013
☎ 0187 825464 📠 0187 825464
e-mail: lasfinge@camping.it
web: www.campinglasfinge.com

Partly terraced site in pleasant wooded surroundings. Ideal for both nature lovers and families. Compulsory separate car park for tent campers.

dir: *Via A12 Genova-La Spezia.*

Open: All Year. **Site:** 1.8HEC **For hire:** **Facilities:** **Services:** **Leisure:** R S

Villaggio Turistico Arenella

Arenella, 19013

0187 825259 0187 826884

e-mail: info@campingarenella.it

web: www.campingarenella.it

Set in a beautiful quiet valley 1.5km from the sea with good facilities.

dir: *Via A12 Genoa-La Spezia.*

Open: Dec-Oct **Site:** 16.2HEC **For hire:** **Facilities:** Wi-fi (charged) **Services:** **Off-site:** S

DONORATICO LIVORNO

Continental

via I Maggio, Marina di Castagneto, 57024

0565 744014 0565 744168

e-mail: info@campingcontinental.it

web: www.campingcontinental.it

Situated directly on a blue flag beach within an ancient pine forest.

Open: Apr-Sep **Site:** 6.5HEC **Facilities:** **Services:** **Leisure:** S

LACONA, ISLE OF ELBA

Lacona Pineta

Lacona CP 186, 57037

0565 964322 0565 964087

e-mail: info@campinglaconapineta.com

web: www.campinglaconapineta.com

A picturesque location on a thickly wooded hillside sloping gently towards a sandy beach, with plenty of recreational facilities.

Open: Apr-Oct **Site:** 4HEC **For hire:** **Facilities:** **Services:** **Leisure:** P S

NISPORTO, ISLE OF ELBA

Sole e Mare

57039

0565 934907 0565 961180

e-mail: info@soleemare.it

web: www.soleemare.it

A well-equipped, modern site in pleasant wooded surroundings close to the beach. A variety of recreational facilities is available.

dir: *Ferry from Piombino to Rio Marina then road to Rio nell' Elba towards Nisporto.*

GPS: 42.8253, 10.3806

Open: Apr-15 Oct **Site:** 2HEC **For hire:** **Facilities:** Wi-fi (charged) Kids' Club Play Area **Services:** **Leisure:** S

OTTONE, ISLE OF ELBA

Rosselba le Palme

57037

0565 933101 0565 933041

e-mail: info@rosselbalepalme.it

web: www.rosselbalepalme.it

Pitches are on varying heights up from the beach. Shade is provided by large palm trees.

dir: *8km from Portoferraio around bay via Bivo Bagnaia.*

Open: 24 Apr-12 Oct **Site:** 30HEC **For hire:** **Facilities:** Wi-fi (charged) **Services:** **Leisure:** P S

PORTO AZZURRO, ISLE OF ELBA

Reale

57036

0565 95678 0565 920127

e-mail: campingreale@tin.it

web: www.isolaelbacampingreale.com

A well-equipped site in a wooded location with direct access to the beach.

dir: *From Portoferraio towards Porto Azzurro for 2.5km, towards Rio Marina for 12km & signed.*

Open: Apr-Oct **Site:** 2HEC **For hire:** **Prices:** 25-43 Mobile home hire 470-945 **Facilities:** Wi-fi Play Area **Services:** **Leisure:** S **Off-site:** P

PORTOFERRAIO, ISLE OF ELBA

Acquaviva Village Camping

57037

0565 919103 0565 915592

e-mail: campingacquaviva@elbalink.it

web: www.campingacquaviva.it

This seafront site is surrounded by trees and has excellent facilities for scuba diving and water sports. Cars may be parked by tents in low season only.

dir: *3km W of town.*

Open: Etr-Oct **Site:** 2HEC **For hire:** **Prices:** 24.90-48.50 Mobile home hire 210-805 **Facilities:** Wi-fi (charged) Kids' Club Play Area **Services:** **Leisure:** S **Off-site:**

ITALY

ITALY

Enfola

Enfola, Casella Postale 147, 57037
☎ 0565 939001 🖷 0565 918613
e-mail: info@campingenfola.it
web: www.campingenfola.it

Located on the Isle of Elba, ideal for scuba-diving and sailing.

Open: Etr-Oct **Site:** 0.8HEC **For hire:** **Facilities:** **Services:** **Off-site:** S

Scaglieri

via Biodola 1, 57037
☎ 0565 969940 🖷 0565 969834
e-mail: info@campingscaglieri.it
web: www.campingscaglieri.it

Sloping terraces 10 metres from the sea make up this site. Facilities such as tennis and golf are avaliable at the nearby Hotel Hermitage.

dir: *Island accessable by plane & ferry. Site on N coast 7km from Portoferraio.*

Open: 10 Apr-20 Oct **Site:** 1.7HEC **For hire:** **Facilities:** Wi-fi (charged) Kids' Club Play Area **Services:** **Leisure:** P **Off-site:** S

FIÉSOLE — FIRENZE

Panoramico

via Peramonda 1, 50014
☎ 055 599069 🖷 055 59186
e-mail: panoramico@florencecamping.com
web: www.florencecamping.com

Site stretches over wide terraces on the Fiésole hillside surrounded by tall evergreens. There is a free shuttle bus to Fiésole.

dir: *A1 exit Firenze Sud, signs through city to Fiésole, site on SS Bolognese.*

Open: All Year. **Site:** 5HEC **For hire:** **Prices:** 30-35 **Facilities:** Wi-fi (charged) Play Area **Services:** **Leisure:** P **Off-site:**

FIGLINE VALDARNO — FIRENZE

Norcenni Girasole Club

The Camping and Caravanning Club The Friendly Club

via Norcenni 7, 50063
☎ 055 915141 🖷 055 9151402
e-mail: girasole@ecvacanze.it
web: www.ecvacanze.it

Terraced site on partial slope. Kids' club available in high season.

C&CC Report *Large, lively, popular site with superb facilities, excursions and activities, yet a family atmosphere and traditional style still permeate this beautiful Tuscan hillside location. You can count on terrific holidays for families of all ages, but this is also a wonderful low season base for discovering the real Tuscany.*

dir: *A1 exit onto road 69 for Figline, right for Greve & signed.*

GPS: 43.6133, 11.4494

Open: 31 Apr-13 Oct **Site:** 15HEC **For hire:** **Prices:** 25-58 **Facilities:** Wi-fi (charged) Kids' Club Play Area **Services:** **Leisure:** P **Off-site:**

FIRENZE (FLORENCE)

See Troghi

GROSSETO, MARINA DI — GROSSETO

Le Marze

Strada Provinciale 158, 58046
☎ 0564 35501 🖷 0564 744503
e-mail: lemarze@boschettoholiday.it
web: www.boschettoholiday.it/lemarze

Located in a pine wood, ideal for touring the local area.

dir: *Via SS322.*

GPS: 42.7444, 10.945

Open: 30 Mar-7 Oct **Site:** 20HEC **For hire:** **Prices:** 18.60-45.30 **Facilities:** Wi-fi (charged) Kids' Club Play Area **Services:** **Leisure:** P R S

Rosmarina

via delle Colonie 37, 58046
☎ 0564 36319 🖷 0564 34758
e-mail: info@campingrosmarina.it
web: www.campingrosmarina.it

A modern site in a pine wood close to the sea. Beautiful views, and various sports and entertainment for everyone.

Open: Apr-Sep **Site:** 1.4HEC **For hire:** **Prices:** 17-42 **Facilities:** Wi-fi **Services:** **Leisure:** S

LERICI — LA SPEZIA

Maralunga

via Carpanini 61, Maralunga, 19032

0187 966589 0187 966589

e-mail: info@campeggiomaralunga.it

This terraced site is directly on the seafront and surrounded by olive groves.

dir: *Access from Sarzana-La Spezia motorway.*

Open: Jun-Sep **Site:** 1HEC **Prices:** 40-55.50 **Facilities:** **Services:** **Leisure:** S **Off-site:** P

MARCIALLA — FIRENZE

Panorama del Chianti

via Marcialla 349, Certaldo, 50020

0571 669334 0571 669334

e-mail: info@campingchianti.it

web: www.campingchianti.it

A sloping, terraced site with good facilities, surrounded by vineyards and olive groves. There is a charge for Wi-fi from 10 July to 20 August.

dir: *Autostrada del Sole exit Firenze-Certosa. Or Autostrada del Palio exit Tavarnelle Valpesa.*

Open: 15 Mar-15 Oct **Site:** 2.17HEC **For hire:** **Facilities:** Wi-fi Play Area **Services:** **Leisure:** P **Off-site:** L

MASSA, MARINA DI — MASSA CARRARA

Giardino

viale delle Pinete 382, 54100

0585 869291 0585 240781

web: www.campinggiardino.com

Site in pine woodland and on two meadows, shade provided by roof matting.

dir: *On island side of SS328 to Pisa.*

Open: Apr-Sep **Site:** 3.2HEC **For hire:** **Facilities:** **Services:** **Leisure:** P **Off-site:** S

MONÉGLIA — GENOVA

Villaggio Smeraldo

Preata, 16030

0185 49375 0185 490484

e-mail: info@villaggiosmeraldo.it

web: www.villaggiosmeraldo.it

A pleasant site in a pine wood overlooking the sea with modern facilities and direct access to the beach.

dir: *Via A12/SS1.*

Open: All Year. **Site:** 1.5HEC **For hire:** **Prices:** 26-52 **Facilities:** Wi-fi **Services:** **Leisure:** S

MONTECATINI TERME — PISTOIA

Belsito

via delle Vigne 1/A, Vico, 51016

0572 67373 0572 67373

e-mail: info@campingbelsito.it

web: www.campingbelsito.it

A quiet site at an altitude of 250 metres, with good sized pitches.

Open: Apr-Sep **Site:** 6HEC **For hire:** **Prices:** 22.50-37 **Facilities:** Wi-fi (charged) Play Area **Services:** **Leisure:** P

MONTERIGGIONI — SIENA

Luxor Quies

Loc Trasqua, 53032

0577 743047 0577 743131

e-mail: info@luxorcamping.com

web: www.luxorcamping.com

Lies on a flat-topped hill, partly in an oak wood, partly in meadowland.

dir: *Off SS2 at Km239/II or Km238/IX, site 2.5km over railway line. Very steep & winding road to site.*

GPS: 43.3997, 11.2484

Open: 19 May-9 Sep **Site:** 1.5HEC **Prices:** 29.80 **Facilities:** Play Area **Services:** **Leisure:** P

ITALY

MONTESCUDÁIO LIVORNO

Montescudáio

via del Poggetto, 56040
☎ 0586 683477 📠 0586 630932
e-mail: info@camping-montescudaio.it
web: www.camping-montescudaio.it

This modern site on a hill is divided into individual pitches, some of which are naturally screened.

dir: *From SS1 via Aurelia at Cecinia towards Guardistallo for 2.5km.*

Open: 13 May-15 Sep **Site:** 25HEC **For hire:** **Facilities:** Wi-fi **Services:** **Leisure:** P S **Off-site:**

MONTICELLO AMIATA GROSSETO

Lucherino

Lucherino, 58044
☎ 0564 992975 📠 0564 992975
e-mail: info@campinglucherino.net
web: www.campinglucherino.net

A peaceful site 735 metres above sea level on the slopes of Monte Amiata. The shady but sloping site is ideal for walkers and historians.

dir: *SS223 to Paganico then signs to Monte Amiata.*

GPS: 42.8824, 11.4766

Open: May-Sep **Site:** 2HEC **For hire:** **Prices:** 23-33 Mobile home hire 294-420 **Facilities:** Wi-fi Play Area **Services:** **Leisure:** P **Off-site:** R

PEGLI GENOVA

Villa Doria

via al Campeggio 15n, 16156
☎ 010 6969600 📠 010 6969600
e-mail: villadoria@camping.it
web: www.camping.it/liguria/villadoria

Quiet site in pleasant wooded surroundings.

dir: *Signed via SS1.*

Open: 7 Feb-7 Jan **Site:** 0.45HEC **For hire:** **Facilities:** Wi-fi (charged) **Services:** **Off-site:** S

PISA PISA

Camping Village Torre Pendente

viale della Cascine 86, 56122
☎ 050 561704 📠 050 561734
e-mail: info@campingtorrependente.com
web: www.campingtorrependente.com

Pleasant, modern site with spacious pitches on level ground in a rural setting. 1km walk to the Leaning Tower and ideal for visiting the ancient city centre. Kids' club in high season.

dir: *SS12 from Lucca to Pisa, continue N with town on left for 1km, site on right.*

GPS: 43.7242, 10.3831

Open: Apr-15 Oct **Site:** 2.5HEC **For hire:** **Prices:** 29-33.50 **Facilities:** Wi-fi (charged) Kids' Club Play Area **Services:** **Leisure:** P **Off-site:** R

SAN BARONTO FIRENZE

Barco Reale

via Nardini 11, 51035
☎ 0573 88332 📠 0573 856003
e-mail: info@barcoreale.com
web: www.barcoreale.com

A well-equipped site in a hilly, wooded location.

dir: *S of A11 & E of SS436. Signed from Lamporecchio.*

Open: 3 Apr-29 Sep **Site:** 10HEC **For hire:** **Prices:** 24.90-40.90 **Facilities:** Wi-fi (charged) Kids' Club Play Area **Services:** **Leisure:** P

SAN GIMIGNANO SIENA

Boschetto di Piemma

Santa Lucia, 38/c, 53037
☎ 0577 907134 📠 0577 907453
e-mail: info@boschettodipiemma.it
web: www.boschettodipiemma.it

This small grassy site is well-equipped and has many facilities for both families and individuals. Kids' club available in July and August.

GPS: 43.4535, 11.0550

Open: Mar-Oct **Site:** 6HEC **For hire:** **Prices:** 24-36 **Facilities:** Wi-fi (charged) Kids' Club Play Area **Services:** **Leisure:** P **Off-site:**

SAN PIERO A SIEVE — FIRENZE

Village Mugello Verde

via Massorondinaio 39, 50037
055 848511 055 8486910
e-mail: mugelloverde@florencecamping.com
web: www.florencecamping.com

Terraced site in wooded surroundings.

dir: *A1 exit 18 & signed.*

GPS: 43.9610, 11.3101

Open: All Year. **Site:** 12HEC **For hire:** **Prices:** 21-27 **Facilities:** Wi-fi (charged) Play Area **Services:** **Leisure:** P **Off-site:** L R

SAN VINCENZO — LIVORNO

Park Albatros

The Camping and Caravanning Club The Friendly Club

Pineta di Torre Nuova, 57027
0565 701018 0565 701400
e-mail: parkalbatros@ecvacanze.it
web: www.ecvacanze.it

The site lies among beautiful tall pine trees, 1km from the sea. Kids' club available for 4-11 year olds.

C&CC Report *An ideal site for those who like to combine lazy days on the beach with visits to the fascinating towns and cities of Tuscany. The great range of facilities, including the extensive pool complex, makes it difficult to leave the site. For the more adventurous why not try a day trip to the beautiful island of Elba, last home of the exiled Napoleon Bonaparte.*

dir: *Off SP23 beyond San Vincenzo at Km7/III & continue 0.6km inland.*

GPS: 43.0274, 10.5341

Open: 27 Apr-16 Sep **Site:** 30HEC **For hire:** **Prices:** 26.50-54 **Facilities:** Wi-fi (charged) Kids' Club Play Area **Services:** **Leisure:** P **Off-site:** S

SARTEANO — SIENA

Parco delle Piscine

via del Bagno Santo 29, 53047
0578 26971 0578 265889
e-mail: info@parcodellepiscine.it
web: www.parcodellepiscine.it

A well shaded location on a plateau surrounded by hills. The three pools on the site are fed by mineral rich spring water. A kids' club is available in July and August.

dir: *A1 exit 29 Chiusi-Chianciano terme. Follow signs to Sarteano for 5km. Cross main square, follow main road, site on left.*

GPS: 42.9875, 11.8647

Open: Apr-Sep **Site:** 15HEC **For hire:** **Prices:** 34-55 Mobile home hire 385-840 **Facilities:** Wi-fi (charged) Kids' Club Play Area **Services:** **Leisure:** P

SARZANA — LA SPEZIA

Iron Gate

via XXV Aprile 54, 19038
0187 676370 0187 675014
e-mail: info@marina3b.it

A modern site with good facilities attached to the Iron Gate Marina.

Open: All Year. **Site:** 2HEC **For hire:** **Prices:** 20.70-32.80 **Facilities:** Wi-fi Play Area **Services:** **Leisure:** P R **Off-site:**

SIENA — SIENA

Camping Siena Colleverde

Strada di Scacciapensieri 47, 53100
0577 334080 0577 334005
e-mail: info@sienacamping.com
web: www.sienacamping.com

The site offers both large areas for caravans and mobile homes and a large grassy area for tents. There is a local bus service, 100 metres from the site, to the centre of Siena.

GPS: 43.3375, 11.3306

Open: Mar-Dec **Site:** 5HEC **For hire:** **Prices:** 30.20-34.80 **Facilities:** Wi-fi (charged) Play Area **Services:** **Leisure:** P **Off-site:**

ITALY

Montagnola

Sovicille, 53018

☎ 0577 314473 🖹 0577 314473

e-mail: montagnolacamping@libero.it

Quiet site in an oak wood with individual plots separated by hedges. Facilities are modern and extensive.

dir: *A1 W exit Siena, site signed towards Sovicille.*

Open: Etr-29 Sep **Site:** 2.5HEC **For hire:** **Facilities:** **Services:** **Off-site:**

Le Soline

Casciano di Murlo, 53016

☎ 0577 817410 🖹 0577 817415

e-mail: camping@lesoline.it

web: www.camping.it/toscana/lesoline

Terraced hilly site surrounded by woodland with a variety of sports facilities and family entertainment.

dir: *Via SS223.*

GPS: 43.1552, 11.3323

Open: All Year. **Site:** 6HEC **For hire:** **Prices:** 15-23.50 **Facilities:** Wi-fi Play Area **Services:** **Leisure:** P **Off-site:** R

STELLA SAN GIOVANNI — SAVONA

Dolce Vita

via Rio Basco 62, 17044

☎ 019 703269 🖹 019 703269

e-mail: campingdolcevita@libero.it

web: www.campingdolcevita.it

Wooded surroundings with well-defined pitches, 5.5km from the coast.

dir: *Via SS334.*

GPS: 44.3856, 8.5022

Open: All Year. **Site:** 10HEC **For hire:** **Prices:** 21-31 **Facilities:** Wi-fi Play Area **Services:** **Leisure:** P **Off-site:** S

TORRE DEL LAGO PUCCINI — LUCCA

Burlamacco

viale G-Marconi Int, 55049

☎ 0584 359544 🖹 0584 359387

e-mail: info@campingburlamacco.com

web: www.campingburlamacco.com

A beautiful wooded location 1km from the sea on the Versilia Riviera, close to the former home of Puccini. A variety of facilities are available.

Open: Apr-Sep **Site:** 4.5HEC **For hire:** **Prices:** 19.30-30.30 Mobile home hire 210-280 **Facilities:** Play Area **Services:** **Leisure:** P **Off-site:** L S

Camping Italia

52 viale dei Tigli, 55049

☎ 0584 359828 🖹 0584 341504

e-mail: info@campingitalia.net

web: www.campingitalia.net

This site is divided into pitches and lies in meadowland planted with poplar trees. A kids' club is available during July and August. Separate car park for mobile homes.

dir: *Inland off Viareggio road (viale dei Tigli).*

GPS: 43.8291, 10.2725

Open: 18 Apr-22 Sep **Site:** 9HEC **For hire:** **Facilities:** Wi-fi (charged) Kids' Club Play Area **Services:** **Leisure:** P **Off-site:** L S

Europa

viale dei Tigli, 55049

☎ 0584 350707 🖹 0584 342592

e-mail: info@europacamp.it

web: www.europacamp.it

Site in pine and poplar woodland. A kids' club is available in June, July and August. Dogs permitted in low season only.

dir: *From Viareggio, on land side of viale dei Tigli.*

GPS: 43.8311, 10.2706

Open: Apr-13 Oct **Site:** 60HEC **For hire:** **Prices:** 18-41 **Facilities:** Wi-fi (charged) Kids' Club Play Area **Services:** **Leisure:** P **Off-site:** R S

Tigli

viale dei Tigli, 54, 55049

☎ 0584 341278 🖹 0584 341278

e-mail: info@campingdeitigli.com

web: www.campingdeitigli.com

Shady site close to a Regional Park, Lake Massaciuccoli, and the villa where Puccini wrote much of his music.

Open: Apr-Sep **Site:** 9HEC **For hire:** **Prices:** 20-35 **Facilities:** Kids' Club Play Area **Services:** **Leisure:** P **Off-site:** L S

Site 6HEC (site size) grass sand stone little shade partly shaded mainly shaded motorvans accepted bungalows for hire mobile homes for hire tents for hire no dogs site fully accessible for wheelchairs
Prices amount quoted is per night, for 2 adults and car, plus tent or caravan Mobile home hire is a weekly rate.

TROGHI FIRENZE

Camping Village Il Poggetto

Strada Provinciale 1, Aretina KM 14, 50067
☎ 055 8307323 🖷 055 8307323
e-mail: info@campingilpoggetto.com
web: www.campingilpoggetto.com

A modern site with good facilities. Large, level, grassy pitches. Good bus connections to Florence.

dir: *A1 exit Incisa-Reggello, site 5km.*

GPS: 43.7014, 11.4053

Open: 31 Mar-15 Oct **Site:** 4.5HEC **For hire:** **Prices:** 29.50-35 **Facilities:** Wi-fi (charged) Kids' Club Play Area **Services:** **Leisure:** P **Off-site:** L R

VADA LIVORNO

Camping Molino a Fuoco

via Cavalleggeri no 32, 57018
☎ 0586 770150 🖷 0586 770031
e-mail: info@campingmolinoafuoco.com
web: www.campingmolinoafuoco.com

Family-friendly site, 100 metres from the beach and with direct access. Grassy pitches are shaded by a variety of trees and divided by hedges. Cycles, canoes and pedaloes are all available for rent. Kids' club available June to August. Dogs are not accepted in high season.

dir: *A12 exit Rosignano/SS1 exit Vada. Follow signs to Vada.*

GPS: 43.3319, 10.4597

Open: 30 Mar-13 Oct **Site:** 5HEC **For hire:** **Prices:** 21-37 Mobile home hire 287-539 **Facilities:** Wi-fi (charged) Kids' Club Play Area **Services:** **Leisure:** P S **Off-site:**

Fiori

Loc Campo di Fiori 4, 57018
☎ 0586 770096 🖷 0586 770323
e-mail: campofiori@multinet.it
web: www.campingcampodeifiori.it

Level grassland surrounded by fields, with trees providing a good deal of shade.

dir: *A12 to Rosignano.*

Open: 23 Apr-25 Sep **Site:** 15HEC **For hire:** **Facilities:** Play Area **Services:** **Leisure:** P **Off-site:** S

VIAREGGIO LUCCA

Camping Pineta SRL

via dei Lecci 107, 55049
☎ 0584 383397
e-mail: campinglapineta@interfree.it
web: www.campinglapineta.com

A well-organised site in a wooded location, 1km from a private beach. Dogs not permitted in July and August.

dir: *Via SSN1 between Km354 & Km355.*

Open: 5 Apr-23 Sep **Site:** 3.2HEC **For hire:** **Prices:** 16.50-34.50 **Facilities:** Kids' Club Play Area **Services:** **Leisure:** P **Off-site:** S

Viareggio

via Comparini 1, 55049
☎ 0584 391012 🖷 0584 391012
e-mail: info@campingviareggio.it
web: www.campingviareggio.it

The site lies in a poplar wood 0.7km from the beach.

dir: *1.5km S of town. From Km354/V towards coast.*

Open: Apr-Sep **Site:** 3HEC **For hire:** **Prices:** 20-33 **Facilities:** Wi-fi (charged) Play Area **Services:** **Leisure:** P **Off-site:** L S

ZINOLA SAVONA

Buggi International

via N S del Monte 15, 17049
☎ 019 860120 🖷 019 804573

A well-equipped site with plenty of space for tents, 0.9km from the sea.

dir: *4km W of Savona.*

Open: All Year. **Site:** 2HEC **For hire:** **Prices:** 26 Mobile home hire 350-560 **Facilities:** **Services:** **Off-site:** S

ITALY

NORTH EAST/ADRIATIC

ASSISI PERUGIA

Village Assisi

Campiglione No 110, 06081

075 813710 075 812335

e-mail: info@campingassisi.it

web: www.campingassisi.it

Set at the foot of the hill on which Assisi stands, this modern, well-equipped site is a good touring base.

dir: *W via SS147.*

GPS: 43.5744, 12.0755

Open: Apr-Oct **Site:** 3HEC **For hire:** **Prices:** 26-34 Mobile home hire 350-560 **Facilities:** Wi-fi (charged) Play Area **Services:** **Leisure:** P **Off-site:** R

BARREA L'AQUILA

Genziana

Parco Nazionale d'Abruzzo, Tre Croci, 67030

0864 88101 0864 88101

e-mail: pasettanet@tiscali.it

web: www.campinglagenzianapasetta.it

Located in the Parco Nazionale d'Abruzzo with views over Barrea lakes. The owner is an expert in alpine walking and can provide information about local walks.

GPS: 41.755, 14.001

Open: All Year. **Site:** 2HEC **For hire:** **Prices:** 27.50-31.50 **Facilities:** Play Area **Services:** **Off-site:** L

BASCHI TERNI

Camping Gole del Forello

SS448, 05023

0335 8171500 0763 300182

e-mail: info@goledelforello.it

web: www.goledelforello.it

In a quiet countryside location and close to Orvieto and Todi, the site has two swimming pools, football and tennis courts.

Open: 5 Apr-Sep **Site:** 4.5HEC **Facilities:** Wi-fi **Services:** **Leisure:** L P **Off-site:** R

BELLARIA FORLI

Happy Camping Village

via Panzini 228, 47814

0541 346102 0541 346408

e-mail: info@happycamping.it

web: www.happycamping.it

The site is in a quiet position on the sea shore close to the centre of town.

dir: *A14/SS16 exit Bellaria Cagnona S Mauro Mare, signs for Acquabell, over level crossing, site on right.*

GPS: 44.1603, 12.4483

Open: All Year. **Site:** 4HEC **For hire:** **Prices:** 26.50-44 **Facilities:** Wi-fi (charged) Kids' Club Play Area **Services:** **Leisure:** P S **Off-site:** R

BEVAGNA PERUGIA

Camping Pian di Boccio

Via Pian di Boccio 10, 06031

0742 360164 0742 360391

e-mail: info@piandiboccio.com

web: www.piandiboccio.com

In wooded surroundings in the centre of the Umbria region. Leisure facilities include a swimming pool, children's pool, archery, tennis and a fishing lake. Kids' club in July and August.

GPS: 44.9119, 12.5867

Open: Apr-Sep **Site:** 8HEC **For hire:** **Facilities:** Wi-fi (charged) Kids' Club Play Area **Services:** **Leisure:** P **Off-site:**

BOLOGNA BOLOGNA

Citta di Bologna

via Romita 12/IVA, 40127

051 325016 051 325318

e-mail: info@hotelcamping.com

web: www.hotelcamping.com

Situated close to the centre of Bologna with good transport links to the city. Facilities include a fitness gym.

GPS: 44.5239, 11.3739

Open: 10 Jan-20 Dec **Site:** 6.3HEC **For hire:** **Prices:** 24-32 **Facilities:** Wi-fi (charged) Play Area **Services:** **Leisure:** P **Off-site:**

BORGHETTO PERUGIA

Badiaccia

via Pratovecchio 1, 06061
075 9659097 075 9659019
e-mail: info@badiaccia.com
web: www.badiaccia.com

A well-equipped site with large grassy pitches and direct access to the lake.

dir: *A1 exit Valdichiana for Perugia & signs for Lake Trasimeno.*

GPS: 43.1803, 12.0161

Open: Apr-Sep **Site:** 5.5HEC **For hire:** **Facilities:** Wi-fi (charged) Kids' Club Play Area **Services:** **Leisure:** L P **Off-site:**

CASAL BORSETTI RAVENNA

Reno

via Spallazzi 11, 48123
0544 445020 0544 442056
e-mail: info@campingreno.it
web: www.campingreno.it

In a natural pinewood with direct access to the sea. Pitches are of various dimensions.

dir: *Off SS309 at Km8 or Km14.*

GPS: 44.5347, 12.2772

Open: Apr-Oct **Site:** 3.3HEC **For hire:** **Prices:** 18.80-28.60 Mobile home hire 238-482.50 **Facilities:** Play Area **Services:** **Off-site:** S

CASTIGLIONE DEL LAGO PERUGIA

Listro

via Lungolago 9, 06061
075 951193 075 951193
e-mail: listro@listro.it
web: www.listro.it

Attractive site on a peninsula in Lake Trasimeno.

GPS: 43.1340, 12.0446

Open: Apr-Sep **Site:** 1HEC **Prices:** 15.20-18.70 **Facilities:** Wi-fi (charged) **Services:** **Leisure:** L **Off-site:** P

CERVIA RAVENNA

Adriatico

via Pinarella 90, 48015
0544 71537 0544 72346
e-mail: info@campingadriatico.net
web: www.campingadriatico.net

Level meadowland site with plenty of shade, pleasantly landscaped with olive trees, willows, elms and maples.

dir: *Site before Pinarella di Cervia off SS16 Cadulti per le Liberta, 0.6km from sea.*

Open: 22 Apr-12 Sep **Site:** 3.4HEC **For hire:** **Facilities:** **Services:** **Leisure:** P S **Off-site:** L

CESENATICO FORLI

Cesenatico

via Mazzini 182, 47042
0547 81344 0547 672452
e-mail: info@campingcesenatico.it
web: www.campingcesenatico.com

200 metres from the beach and close to the city centre. Facilities include two swimming pools and a jacuzzi.

dir: *1.5km N, off the SS16 at Km178 towards sea.*

Open: All Year. **Site:** 18HEC **For hire:** **Facilities:** **Services:** **Leisure:** P S **Off-site:**

Zadina

via Mazzini 184, 47042
0547 82310 0547 702381
e-mail: info@campingzadina.it

Very pleasant terrain in dunes on two sides of a canal.

Open: 23 Apr-16 Sep **Site:** 6HEC **For hire:** **Facilities:** **Services:** **Leisure:** S

CITTA DI CASTELLO PERUGIA

La Montesca

06012
075 8558566 075 852018
e-mail: info@lamontesca.it
web: www.lamontesca.it

Set in a large wooded park with excellent facilities. A good base for exploring the area.

dir: *3km from town beside River Tiber.*

Open: 15 May-15 Sep **Site:** 5HEC **For hire:** **Facilities:** **Services:** **Leisure:** P **Off-site:** R

ITALY

ITALY

COLOGNA SPIAGGIA — TERAMO

Stork Camping Village

via del Mare 11, 64026
085 8937076 085 8937542
e-mail: info@storkcampingvillage.com
web: www.storkcampingvillage.com

Situated next to a sand/shingle beach, wide camping pitches are available. Leisure facilities include two tennis courts, volleyball and a games room. Cars may be parked next to tents in low season.

dir: *A14 (Bologna-Taranto) exit Teramo-Guilianova, continue on SS80 towards Guilianova.*

Open: 15 May-15 Sep **Site:** 7HEC **For hire:** **Prices:** 16-38.50 **Facilities:** Wi-fi (charged) Kids' Club Play Area **Services:** **Leisure:** P S

COSTACCIARO — PERUGIA

Villaggio Rio Verde

Loc Fornace 1, 06021
075 9170138 075 9170181
e-mail: info@campingrioverde.it
web: www.campingrioverde.it

Located in a pine wood in the grounds of a country house, with an abundance of wildlife.

GPS: 43.3508, 12.6845

Open: 20 Apr-Sep **Site:** 5HEC **For hire:** **Facilities:** Wi-fi Play Area **Services:** **Leisure:** P R **Off-site:**

CUPRA MARITTIMA — ASCOLI PICENO

Calypso

via Boccabianca 8, 63012
0735 778686 0735 778106
e-mail: calypso@camping.it
web: www.campingcalypso.it

On the Adriatic coast with shady pitches close to the beach. Leisure and entertainment facilities are available.

Open: Apr-29 Sep **Site:** 26HEC **For hire:** **Facilities:** **Services:** **Leisure:** P S

DANTE, LIDO DI — RAVENNA

Classe

viale Catone, 48100
0544 492005 0544 492058
e-mail: info@campingclasse.it
web: www.campingclasse.it

Level meadowland in grounds of former farm.

dir: *Off SS16 at Km154/V towards sea, 9km to site.*

Open: 28 Mar-10 Oct **Site:** 7HEC **For hire:** **Facilities:** **Services:** **Leisure:** P S **Off-site:** L R

FANO — PESARO & URBINO

Mare Blu

61032
0721 884201 0721 884389
e-mail: info@campingmareblu.net
web: www.campingmareblu.net

The site is surrounded by tall poplars with direct access to a sandy beach. Facilities for most water sports, and entertainment for children and families.

dir: *A14 exit Fano, site 3km S.*

Open: Apr-Sep **Site:** 3HEC **For hire:** **Prices:** 20-36 **Facilities:** Wi-fi Play Area **Services:** **Leisure:** P S **Off-site:** R

FERRARA — FERRARA

Estense

via Gramicia 76, 44100
0532 752396 0532 752396
e-mail: camping.estense@libero.it
web: www.campeggioestense.it

A good overnight stop on the way south. A charge may be made for Wi-fi.

dir: *NE outskirts of Ferrara.*

Open: 27 Feb-9 Jan **Site:** 3.3HEC **Prices:** 18.50-21 **Facilities:** Wi-fi **Off-site:** P R

FIORENZUOLA DI FOCARA — PESARO & URBINO

Panorama

Strada Panoramica, 61121

0721 208145 0721 209799

e-mail: info@campingpanorama.it

web: www.campingpanorama.it

Located in a park 100 metres above sea level this site welcomes families, animals, cyclists and those wishing to relax.

dir: *Signed off SS16. 10km from Gabicce, 7km from Pesaro.*

Open: 15 Apr-Sep **Site:** 2.2HEC **For hire:** **Prices:** 26-36 **Facilities:** Wi-fi (charged) Play Area **Services:** **Leisure:** P S

GATTEO MARE — FORLI

Delle Rose

via Adriatica 29, 47043

0547 86213 0547 87583

e-mail: info@villaggiorose.com

web: www.villaggiorose.com

A peaceful setting close to the sea and the town centre, within a natural pine forest.

dir: *Off SS16 at Km186.*

Open: 19 May-18 Sep **Site:** 4HEC **For hire:** **Prices:** 23-41 Mobile home hire 175-600 **Facilities:** Kids' Club Play Area **Services:** **Leisure:** P S **Off-site:** R

GIULIANOVA LIDO — TERAMO

Don Antonio Camping Residence Village

via Padova, 64021

085 8008928 085 8006172

e-mail: info@campingdonantonio.it

web: www.campingdonantonio.it

A family site in a wooded location with direct access to a private beach, which is free for campers. A variety of sports and entertainment facilities are available, particularly in July and August, when all cars must use the designated car park. Dogs allowed during low season.

dir: *Access via A14 & SS80.*

GPS: 42.7781, 13.9556

Open: 16 May-16 Sep **Site:** 5HEC **For hire:** **Prices:** 20-44 **Facilities:** Wi-fi (charged) Kids' Club Play Area **Services:** **Leisure:** P S **Off-site:** R

GUBBIO — PERUGIA

Villa Ortoguidone

Fraz. Cipolleto 49, Ortoguidone, 06024

075 9272037

e-mail: info@gubbiocamping.com

web: www.gubbiocamping.com

One of two well-equipped sites in the same location. Plenty of space for tents. Dogs accepted, restrictions apply.

dir: *Via SS298 Gubbio-Perugia.*

GPS: 43.3217, 12.5687

Open: 4 Apr-16 Sep **Site:** 0.5HEC **For hire:** **Prices:** 24-31 Mobile home hire 252-770 **Facilities:** Play Area **Services:** **Leisure:** P **Off-site:**

MARCELLI DI NUMANA — ANCONA

Conero Azzurro

via Litoranea, 60026

071 7390507 071 7390986

e-mail: info@coneroazzurro.it

Well-equipped site between the Adriatic and Monte Conero.

Open: Jun-15 Sep **Site:** 5HEC **For hire:** **Facilities:** **Services:** **Leisure:** P S **Off-site:**

MAROTTA — PESARO & URBINO

Gabbiano

via Faa' di Bruno 95, 61035

0721 96691 0721 96691

e-mail: info@campingdelgabbiano.it

web: www.campingdelgabbiano.it

Quiet location surrounded by trees overlooking the sea.

dir: *A14 exit Marotta, SS16 for Fano for 2.5km.*

Open: May-Sep **Site:** 1.9HEC **For hire:** **Facilities:** **Services:** **Leisure:** P S

ITALY

ITALY

MARTINSICURO — TERAMO

Duca Amedeo

Lungomare Europa 158, 64014
☎ 0861 797376 🖷 0861 797264
e-mail: ducaamedeo@camping.it
web: www.ducaamedeo.it

A pleasant location close to the sea, surrounded by trees and lush vegetation.

dir: *A14 exit Martinsicuro.*

GPS: 42.8811, 13.9206

Open: 30 Apr-27 Sep **Site:** 3.7HEC **For hire:** **Prices:** 15-45 Mobile home hire 160-432 **Facilities:** Wi-fi Kids' Club Play Area **Services:** **Leisure:** P S **Off-site:**

MARZABOTTO — BOLOGNA

Piccolo Paradiso

via Ca' Bianca, 40043
☎ 051 842680 🖷 051 6756581
e-mail: piccoloparadiso@aruba.it
web: www.campingpiccoloparadiso.eu

Pleasant site with plenty of trees. A sports centre less than 100 metres from the site provides excellent facilities for sports and recreation.

dir: *A1 exit for town, towards Vado for 2km, signed.*

Open: 15 Mar-15 Oct **Site:** 6.5HEC **For hire:** **Facilities:** **Services:** **Leisure:** L P **Off-site:** R

MILANO MARITTIMA — RAVENNA

Romagna

viale Matteotti 190, 48016
☎ 0544 949326 🖷 0544 949345
e-mail: info@campeggioromagna.it
web: www.campeggioromagna.it

This site lies beside a pine forest on the Adriatic coast and has direct access to the beach.

dir: *SS16 Strada Adriatica, turn off after Milano Marittima & signed.*

Open: 12 Apr-10 Sep **Site:** 40HEC **For hire:** **Prices:** 18-36.50 **Facilities:** Play Area **Services:** **Leisure:** P S **Off-site:**

MODENA — MODENA

International Camping

Strada Cave di Ramo 111, 41123
☎ 059 332252 🖷 059 823235
e-mail: internationalcamping.int@tin.it
web: www.internationalcamping.org

5km from Modena and close to the motorway. Pitches vary in terrain and are shaded.

GPS: 44.6544, 10.8675

Open: All Year. **Site:** 2.3HEC **Prices:** 29-32.50 **Facilities:** Wi-fi Play Area **Services:** **Leisure:** P **Off-site:**

MONTECRETO — MODENA

Parcodei Castagni SRL

via del Parco 5, 41025
☎ 0536 63595 🖷 0536 63630
e-mail: camping@parcodeicastagni.it
web: www.parcodeicastagni.it

Site set among mature chestnut trees in an environmentally friendly location, with pitches separated by small trees. A chair lift provides access to the surrounding high mountains.

GPS: 44.2467, 10.7119

Open: All Year. **Site:** 0.9HEC **For hire:** **Prices:** 24-27 **Facilities:** Play Area **Services:** **Leisure:** P **Off-site:** R

MONTENERO, MARINA DI — CAMPOBASSO

Costa Verde

86036
☎ 0873 803144 🖷 0873 9931179
e-mail: info@costaverde.it
web: www.costaverde.it

A level site with good facilities and direct access to the beach east of San Salvo Marino.

dir: *Off SS16 coast road at Km525/VII onto farm road for 300m.*

Open: 15 May-15 Sep **Site:** 1HEC **For hire:** **Prices:** 17.80-33 **Facilities:** Wi-fi Kids' Club Play Area **Services:** **Leisure:** P R S **Off-site:**

NARNI — TERNI

Monti del Sole

Strada di Borgaria 22, 05035
0744 796336 0744 796336
e-mail: info@campingmontidelsole.it
web: www.campingmontidelsole.it
A spacious wooded site, shaded and flat. All plots are grassed and easily reached by firm lanes.
dir: *A1 exit Magliano Sabina for Terni, signs for Narni.*
Open: Apr-Sep **Site:** 8HEC **For hire:** **Prices:** 23.50-26.50 **Facilities:** Wi-fi Play Area **Services:** **Leisure:** P

NAZIONI, LIDO DELLE — FERRARA

Tahiti Camping

viale Libia 133, 44020
0533 379500 0533 379700
e-mail: info@campingtahiti.com
web: www.campingtahiti.com
Attractively planned site, 0.65km from the sea. The site's private beach is accessible via a miniature railway.
dir: *Off SS309 near Km32.5 & 2km to site, signed.*
GPS: 44.7347, 12.2316
Open: 24 Apr-23 Sep **Site:** 12HEC **For hire:** **Prices:** 24.80-37.90 **Facilities:** Wi-fi (charged) Kids' Club Play Area **Services:** **Leisure:** P **Off-site:** L S

PASSIGNANO — PERUGIA

Kursaal

viale Europa 24, 06065
075 828085 075 827182
e-mail: info@campingkursaal.it
web: www.campingkursaal.it
The site lies on the banks of Lake Trasimeno, between Umbria and Tuscany.
dir: *Off SS75 at Km35.2.*
GPS: 43.1826, 12.1508
Open: Apr-Oct **Site:** 1.5HEC **Prices:** 24-30 **Facilities:** Wi-fi **Services:** **Leisure:** L P **Off-site:**

La Spiaggia

viale Europa 22, 06065
075 827246 075 827276
e-mail: info@campinglaspiaggia.it
web: www.campinglaspiaggia.it
On the northern shore of Lake Trasimeno in a tranquil wooded location. Large grassy pitches.
GPS: 43.1839, 12.1486
Open: 31 Mar-7 Oct **Site:** 1.8HEC **Prices:** 24-28 **Facilities:** Wi-fi Play Area **Services:** **Leisure:** L P **Off-site:**

PERUGIA — PERUGIA

Rocolo

Strada Fontana la Trinita 1/N, 06132
075 5181635 075 5181635
e-mail: giaco86@hotmail.it
web: www.ilrocolo.it
A quiet site with good facilities and pitches surrounded by oak and cypress trees.
GPS: 43.1100, 12.3272
Open: 15 Apr-Oct **Site:** 2.4HEC **For hire:** **Facilities:** Wi-fi Play Area **Services:** **Off-site:** P

PIEVEPELAGO — MODENA

Rio Verde

via M di Canossa 34, 41027
0536 72204 0536 72204
e-mail: campingrioverde@alice.it
web: www.camping-rioverde.it
Wooded mountain setting close to the river with modern facilities.
dir: *SS12 from Modena.*
Open: All Year. **Site:** 1.8HEC **For hire:** **Facilities:** Play Area **Services:** **Leisure:** R **Off-site:** L P

PINARELLA — RAVENNA

Safari

viale Titano 130, 48015
0544 987356 0544 987356
e-mail: csafari@cervia.com
web: www.campingsafari.it
The site is divided into several sections. Only families are accepted.
Open: 19 Apr-10 Sep **Site:** 3.1HEC **Prices:** 25-34 **Facilities:** **Services:** **Off-site:** S

ITALY

ITALY

PINETO TERAMO

International Torre Cerrano

Loc Torre Cerrano, 64025
☎ 085 930639 🖷 085 930639
e-mail: info@internationalcamping.it
web: www.internationalcamping.it

Site on level terrain with young poplars. Sunshade roofing on the beach.

dir: *Off SS16 at Km431.2 & under railway underpass, site next to railway line.*

GPS: 42.5814, 14.0929

Open: May-Sep **Site:** 1.5HEC **For hire:** **Prices:** 17.50-42 **Facilities:** Wi-fi Play Area **Services:** **Leisure:** S

POMPOSA FERRARA

International I Tre Moschettieri

via Capanno Garibaldi 22, 44020
☎ 0533 380376 🖷 0533 380377
e-mail: info@tremoschettieri.com
web: www.tremoschettieri.com

In a quiet peaceful area the site is set beneath pine trees next to sea. Extensive choice of good quality services.

dir: *Signed from SS309.*

GPS: 44.7267, 12.2361

Open: 20 Apr-16 Sep **Site:** 11HEC **For hire:** **Prices:** 21-37 **Facilities:** Wi-fi (charged) Play Area **Services:** **Leisure:** P S **Off-site:** L

PORTO SANT'ELPÍDIO FERMO

La Risacca

via Europa 100, 63821
☎ 0734 991423 🖷 0734 997276
e-mail: info@larisacca.it
web: www.larisacca.it

Clean, well-kept site on level meadowland, with some trees surrounded by fields. Dogs not permitted 3-25 August.

dir: *Off SS16 N of village, towards sea under railway (narrow underpass maximum height 3m) & 1.2km along field paths to site. Caravan access 400m further S along SS16, under railway & along field paths to site.*

Open: 21 Apr-1 May & 19 May-14 Sep **Site:** 8HEC **For hire:** **Prices:** 16-38 Mobile home hire 182-441 **Facilities:** Wi-fi (charged) Kids' Club Play Area **Services:** **Leisure:** P S **Off-site:** R

PRECI PERUGIA

Il Collaccio

Castelvecchio di Preci, 06047
☎ 0743 939005 🖷 0743 939094
e-mail: info@ilcollaccio.com
web: www.ilcollaccio.com

Beautiful natural surroundings with plenty of roomy pitches and good recreational facilities. Dogs permitted in certain areas only.

dir: *Via SS209.*

Open: Apr-Sep **Site:** 10HEC **For hire:** **Prices:** 21-33.50 **Facilities:** Wi-fi (charged) **Services:** **Leisure:** P **Off-site:** R

PUNTA MARINA TERME RAVENNA

Adriano Camping Village

via dei Campeggi 7, 48100
☎ 0544 437230 🖷 0544 438510
e-mail: info@adrianocampingvillage.com
web: www.adrianocampingvillage.com

A landscaped site among the dunes of the Punta Marina, 300 metres from the sea.

dir: *On SS309 via Lido Adriano to Punta Marina.*

Open: 21 Apr-18 Sep **Site:** 14HEC **For hire:** **Facilities:** Wi-fi (charged) Kids' Club Play Area **Services:** **Leisure:** P S **Off-site:**

RAVENNA, MARINA DI RAVENNA

Piomboni Camping Village

viale Della Pace 421, 48122
☎ 0544 530230 🖷 0544 538618
e-mail: info@campingpiomboni.it
web: www.campingpiomboni.it

Site on slightly undulating mainly grassy terrain with pines and poplars. Separate section for tents and a kids' club from mid June to August. Some dog breeds may not be accepted.

dir: *Access from SS309 or A14.*

GPS: 44.4664, 12.2853

Open: 20 Apr-16 Sep **Site:** 5HEC **For hire:** **Facilities:** Wi-fi Kids' Club Play Area **Services:** **Leisure:** S **Off-site:** P

RICCIONE FORLI

Alberello

via Torino 80, 47838
0541 615402 0541 615248
e-mail: direzione@alberello.it
web: www.alberello.it

On the seafront connected to the beach by a private subway. Popular with families, with a range of recreational facilities.

dir: *Via A14 & SS16.*

GPS: 43.9872, 12.6883

Open: 5 Apr-24 Sep **Site:** 4HEC **For hire:** **Prices:** 18.90-38 **Facilities:** Wi-fi (charged) Kids' Club Play Area **Services:** **Off-site:** L P R S

Fontanelle

via Torino 56, 47838
0541 615449 0541 610193
e-mail: info@campingfontanelle.net
web: www.campingfontanelle.net

On southern outskirts, separated from the beach by the coast road. The public beach is reached by an underpass.

dir: *Off SS16 between Km216 & Km217.*

Open: 5 Apr-Sep **Site:** 6HEC **Prices:** 18.90-38 **Facilities:** Wi-fi (charged) Kids' Club Play Area **Services:** **Leisure:** S **Off-site:** P R

Riccione

via Marsala N10, 47838
0541 690160 0541 690044
e-mail: info@campingriccione.it
web: www.campingriccione.it

Extensive flat meadowland with poplars, 400 metres from the sea. Dogs permitted on site in low season only.

dir: *Off SS16 on S outskirts of town towards sea for 200m.*

GPS: 43.9853, 12.6786

Open: 5 Apr-23 Sep **Site:** 6.5HEC **For hire:** **Prices:** 23.40-42.30 **Facilities:** Wi-fi (charged) Kids' Club Play Area **Services:** **Leisure:** P S

ROSETO DEGLI ABRUZZI TERAMO

Eurcamping

Lungomare Trieste 90, 64026
085 8993179 085 8930552
e-mail: eurcamping@camping.it
web: www.eurcamping.it

A quiet site, near to the beach, offering pitches shaded by trees.

dir: *Off SS16 in town, site 0.5km.*

GPS: 42.6577, 14.0353

Open: May-Oct **Site:** 5HEC **For hire:** **Prices:** 15-42.50 **Facilities:** Wi-fi (charged) Kids' Club Play Area **Services:** **Leisure:** P S **Off-site:** R

SALSOMAGGIORE TERME PARMA

Arizona

via Tabiano 42 A, 43039
0524 565648 0524 567589
e-mail: info@camping-arizona.it
web: www.camping-arizona.it

Family site with plenty of activities, and close to two thermal therapeutic establishments.

dir: *Off A1 to Tabiano.*

Open: Apr-15 Oct **Site:** 13HEC **For hire:** **Prices:** 20-32 Mobile home hire 329-756 **Facilities:** Wi-fi (charged) Play Area **Services:** **Leisure:** P **Off-site:**

S ARCANGELO SUL TRASIMENO PERUGIA

Camping Polvese

via Montivalle, 06063
075 848078 075 848050
e-mail: polvese@polvese.com
web: www.polvese.com

A peaceful location beside Lake Trasimeno with plenty of recreational facilities.

GPS: 43.0819, 12.1422

Open: Apr-Sep **Site:** 5HEC **For hire:** **Prices:** 18-22 **Facilities:** Wi-fi (charged) Kids' Club Play Area **Services:** **Leisure:** L P

Camping Villaggio Italgest

via Martiri di Cefalonia, 06063

☎ 075 848238 🖷 075 848085

e-mail: camping@italgest.com

web: www.italgest.com

On the border between Umbria and Tuscany, the site is situated on the banks of a lake and surrounded by woodland. There are modern facilities, and various activities are available. Kids' club available in July and August.

GPS: 43.0881, 12.1564

Open: Apr-Sep **Site:** 5.5HEC **For hire:** **Prices:** 21-28.50 **Facilities:** Wi-fi (charged) Kids' Club Play Area **Services:** **Leisure:** L P

SAN MARINO

Centro Vacanze San Marino

Strada San Michele 50, 47893

☎ 0549 903964 🖷 0549 907120

e-mail: info@centrovacanzesanmarino.com

web: www.centrovacanzesanmarino.com

A quiet wooded location close to the centre of the Republic of San Marino.

dir: *A14 exit Rimini Sud.*

Open: All Year. **Site:** 10HEC **For hire:** **Facilities:** Wi-fi Kids' Club Play Area **Services:** **Leisure:** P **Off-site:**

SAVIGNANO MARE — FORLI

Camping Village Rubicone

via Matrice Destra 1, 47039

☎ 0541 346377 🖷 0541 346999

e-mail: info@campingrubicone.com

web: www.campingrubicone.com

Located on the sea front, this large family site has direct access to a private, sandy beach.

dir: *A14 from Bologna, exit Rimini Nord, then SS16 direction Ravenna, exit Savignano Mare.*

GPS: 44.1648, 12.4416

Open: 23 May-16 Sep **Site:** 13HEC **For hire:** **Prices:** 22-38.90 Mobile home hire 476-945 **Facilities:** Wi-fi (charged) Kids' Club Play Area **Services:** **Leisure:** P R S **Off-site:**

SCACCHI, LIDO DEGLI — FERRARA

Florenz

via Alpi Centrali 199, 44020

☎ 0533 380193 🖷 0533 381456

e-mail: info@campingflorenz.com

web: www.campingflorenz.com

Site with dunes extending to the sea.

dir: *Off Strada Romea for Lido Degli Scacchi, continue on asphalt road to beach.*

Open: 15 Mar-28 Sep **Site:** 8HEC **For hire:** **Facilities:** **Services:** **Leisure:** P S

SENIGALLIA — ANCONA

Summerland

via Podesti 236, 60019

☎ 071 7926816 🖷 071 7927758

e-mail: info@campingsummerland.it

web: www.campingsummerland.it

A pleasant site with good facilities, 150 metres from the sea.

dir: *SS16 exit Senigallia, site 3km.*

Open: Jun-15 Sep **Site:** 4.5HEC **For hire:** **Prices:** 25-40 **Facilities:** Wi-fi Kids' Club Play Area **Services:** **Off-site:** P S

SILVI — TERAMO

Centro Vacanze Europe Garden

Contrada Vallescura 10, 64028

☎ 085 930137 🖷 085 932846

e-mail: info@europegarden.it

web: www.europegarden.it

Set in the shade of olive trees with panoramic views over the Adriatic. Extensive leisure facilities include access to a large private beach with a shuttle bus service, two swimming pools, volleyball, archery and 5-a-side football.

GPS: 42.5678, 14.0925

Open: 23 Apr-17 Sep **Site:** 5HEC **For hire:** **Facilities:** Wi-fi Kids' Club Play Area **Services:** **Leisure:** P S **Off-site:**

SPINA, LIDO DI — FERRARA

International Camping Mare e Pineta

via delle Acacie 67, 44029
0533 330110 0533 330052
e-mail: info@campingmarepineta.com
web: www.campingmarepineta.com

Located in the middle of a pinewood, with direct access to a sandy beach, this site has touring pitches, mobile homes and bungalows. Leisure facilities include four swimming pools. Small dogs only are accepted.

dir: *2km SE of Port Garibaldi.*

GPS: 44.6558, 12.2453

Open: 19 Apr-17 Sep **Site:** 16HEC **For hire:** **Prices:** 18.80-36.85 Mobile home hire 329-966 **Facilities:** Wi-fi (charged) Kids' Club **Services:** **Leisure:** P S **Off-site:**

Spina Camping Village

via del Campeggio 99, 44029
0533 330179 0533 333566
e-mail: info@spinacampingvillage.com
web: www.spinacampingvillage.com

Extensive site on level meadowland and slightly hilly dune terrain. Separate section for dog owners.

dir: *Signed off SS309.*

Open: Apr-Sep **Site:** 24HEC **For hire:** **Facilities:** **Services:** **Leisure:** P S **Off-site:**

TORINO DI SANGRO MARINA — CHIETI

Belvedere

66020
0873 911381 0873 911122
e-mail: campingbelvedere@hotmail.it

Well equipped coastal campsite close to sandy beaches.

Open: Jun-6 Sep **Site:** 1.5HEC **For hire:** **Facilities:** Play Area **Services:** **Leisure:** S **Off-site:** P

TUORO SUL TRASIMENO — PERUGIA

Camping Village Punta Navaccia

via Navaccia 4, 06069
075 826357 075 8258147
e-mail: navaccia@camping.it
web: www.puntanavaccia.it

On the shores of Lake Trasimeno with piers and floating platforms. Two heated swimming pools plus a covered amphitheatre where films are shown. Extensive sports facilities plus evening entertainment.

Open: 13 Mar-Oct **Site:** 7HEC **For hire:** **Prices:** 19-28.50 **Facilities:** Wi-fi (charged) Kids' Club Play Area **Services:** **Leisure:** L P **Off-site:**

VALLICELLA DI MONZUNO — BOLOGNA

Le Querce

Strada Prov 61, 40036
051 6770394 051 6770394
e-mail: contatti@campinglequerce.com
web: www.campinglequerce.com

A well-equipped site in a wooded mountain setting.

dir: *Access via Autostrada del Sole.*

Open: Apr-Sep **Site:** 12HEC **For hire:** **Prices:** 20-30 **Facilities:** Kids' Club Play Area **Services:** **Leisure:** L P R

VASTO — CHIETI

Grotta del Saraceno

via Osca 6, 66054
0873 310213 0873 310295
e-mail: info@grottadelsaraceno.it
web: www.grottadelsaraceno.it

Site in olive grove on steep coastal cliffs with lovely views. Steep path to beach.

dir: *Off SS16 at Km512.2.*

Open: 15 Jun-12 Sep **Site:** 14HEC **For hire:** **Facilities:** Kids' Club Play Area **Services:** **Leisure:** S **Off-site:**

Pioppeto

66055
0873 801466 0873 801466
e-mail: infocampeggio@ilpioppeto.it
web: www.ilpioppeto.it

Next to a sandy beach, site shaded by poplars and eucalyptus trees. Activities take place in season.

Open: 15 May-14 Sep **Site:** 1HEC **For hire:** **Prices:** 26-36.90 **Facilities:** Wi-fi (charged) Kids' Club Play Area **Services:** **Leisure:** S **Off-site:** P R

ITALY

ZOCCA — MODENA

Montequestiolo

via Montequestiolo 184, 41059

059 986800 059 986800

e-mail: biocampus@campeggiomontequestiolo.it

web: www.campeggiomontequestiolo.it

Located within a mountainous landscape, ideal for cyclists and hikers.

Open: Mar-Oct **Site:** 1.8HEC **For hire:** **Prices:** 16-22 **Facilities:** Play Area **Services:** **Off-site:** P

ROME

BOLSENA — VITERBO

Blu International

via Cassia km 111.650, 01023

0761 798855 0761 798855

e-mail: info@blucamping.it

web: www.blucamping.it

A modern site with good facilities in a wooded location on the shore of Lake Bolsena.

dir: *A1 exit Orvieto onto SS71.*

GPS: 42.6312, 11.9945

Open: 14 Apr-Sep **Site:** 3HEC **For hire:** **Prices:** 19-25 **Facilities:** Wi-fi (charged) Play Area **Services:** **Leisure:** L P **Off-site:**

Lido

via Cassia km111, 01023

0761 799258 0761 796105

e-mail: info@lidocampingvillage.it

web: www.lidocampingvillage.it

A lakeside family site with modern facilities including supermarket and restaurant/pizzeria. Kids' club available in July and August.

dir: *A1 exit Orvieto & continue for 18km to Bolsena.*

GPS: 42.6272, 11.9941

Open: 21 Apr-Sep **Site:** 10HEC **For hire:** **Prices:** 23.50-30 **Facilities:** Kids' Club Play Area **Services:** **Leisure:** L P

BRACCIANO — ROMA

Porticciolo

via Porticciolo, 00062

06 99803060 06 99803030

e-mail: info@porticciolo.it

web: www.porticciolo.it

A family site in a pleasant location on the shore of a lake.

dir: *SS493 to Bracciano.*

Open: Apr-Sep **Site:** 3.2HEC **For hire:** **Facilities:** **Services:** **Leisure:** L **Off-site:**

FIANO ROMANO — ROMA

Family Park I Pini

The Camping and Caravanning Club — The Friendly Club

via delle Sassete 1A, 00065

0765 453349 0765 1890941

e-mail: ipini@camping.it

web: www.ecvacanze.it

A modern, well-equipped site within easy reach of the centre of Rome. A good base for excursions. Kids' club in high season.

C&CC Report *A lovely campsite set in woodland with plenty of activities on site. Children are catered for with the animation programme and great swimming pools, and the surrounding woodland area is ready to be explored. The shuttle service to Rome from the site makes it easy to explore the history and culture of this famous city.*

dir: *A1 exit Roma Nord-Fiano Romano, follow signs for Fiano Romano. At 1st rdbt after Palace Inn, turn right. After 2km, at 2nd rdbt straight on to lights. Take left, follow signs for Park I Pini.*

Open: 28 Apr-25 Sep **Site:** 5HEC **For hire:** **Prices:** 25-36 **Facilities:** Wi-fi Kids' Club Play Area **Services:** **Leisure:** P

FORMIA — LATINA

Gianola

via delle Vigne, 04023

0771 720223 0771 720223

e-mail: gianolacamping@tiscali.it

web: www.gianolacamping.it

A narrow grassland area near a stream and trees amid agricultural land. Pleasant sandy beach edged by rocks.

dir: *Off Roma-Napoli road, 0.8km from S Croce.*

Open: Apr-Sep **Site:** 4HEC **For hire:** **Facilities:** Play Area **Services:** **Leisure:** R S **Off-site:** L P

MINTURNO, MARINA DI — LATINA

Golden Garden

via Pantano Arenile 74, 04026
0771 681425 0771 614059
e-mail: servizio.clienti@goldengarden.it
web: www.goldengarden.it

Secluded quiet site within agricultural area by the sea.

dir: *A1 Milano-Napoli exit Cassino in direction fo Formia then SS7 over river bridge (Garigliano), continue 4.6km (last 1km sandy track).*

Open: May-5 Sep **Site:** 2.3HEC **For hire:** **Facilities:** Kids' Club Play Area **Services:** **Leisure:** S **Off-site:** P R

MONTALTO DI CASTRO, MARINA DI — VITERBO

California Camping Village

01014
0766 802848 0766 801210
e-mail: info@californiacampingvillage.com
web: www.californiacampingvillage.com

Situated on the coast below an ancient pine grove with good facilities for sports and leisure. Kids' club available in July and August.

Open: May-14 Sep **Site:** 14HEC **For hire:** **Facilities:** Kids' Club Play Area **Services:** **Leisure:** P S

Internazionale Pionier Etrusco

via Vulsinia, 01014
0766 802199 0766 801214
e-mail: info@campingpionieretrusco.it
web: www.campingpionieretrusco.eu

Situated in a pine forest close to the beach. Various leisure and sports activities, and a relaxing atmosphere.

Open: Mar-15 Oct **Site:** 8HEC **For hire:** **Facilities:** **Services:** **Off-site:** R S

ROMA (ROME) — ROMA

Flaminio Village

via Flaminia Nuova 821, 00189
06 3332604 06 3330653
e-mail: info@villageflaminio.com
web: www.villageflaminio.com

An extensive site with good facilities, set on narrow hill terraces in a quiet valley.

dir: *Off ring road onto SS3 (via Flaminia) for 2.5km towards city centre.*

GPS: 41.9562, 12.4824

Open: All Year. **Site:** 10HEC **For hire:** **Prices:** 29.50-34.70 **Facilities:** Wi-fi (charged) Play Area **Services:** **Leisure:** P **Off-site:** R

Happy

via del Prato della Corte 1915, 00123
06 33626401 06 33613800
e-mail: info@happycamping.net
web: www.happycamping.net

Convenient location in the north of the town. Modern installations.

dir: *Grande Raccordo Anulare (ring road) exit Cassia Veientama-Viterbo.*

GPS: 42.0033, 12.4527

Open: Mar-8 Jan **Site:** 3.6HEC **For hire:** **Prices:** 23.80-34.50 **Facilities:** Wi-fi (charged) **Services:** **Leisure:** P **Off-site:**

Roma

via Aurelia 831, 00165
06 6623018 06 66418147
e-mail: campingroma@ecvacanze.it
web: www.ecvacanze.it

The site lies on terraces on a hill near the AGIP Motel. Various excursions can be arranged.

dir: *From ring road onto SS1 (via Aurelia) for 1.5km towards town centre, turn to site at Km8/11.*

GPS: 41.8875, 12.4044

Open: All Year. **Site:** 7HEC **For hire:** **Prices:** 28.40-38.10 **Facilities:** Wi-fi Play Area **Services:** **Leisure:** P **Off-site:**

ITALY

Seven Hills

via Cassia 1216, 00189

06 30310826 06 30310039

e-mail: info@sevenhills.it

web: www.sevenhills.it

A fine, partly terraced site in beautiful rural surroundings. Well placed for access to the city by bus or underground.

dir: *Outer ring road exit 3, site 2.5km NE.*

Open: Mar-1 Nov **Site:** 5HEC **For hire:** **Facilities:** **Services:** **Leisure:** P

Tiber

via Tiberina Km1400, 00188

06 33610733 06 33612314

e-mail: info@campingtiber.com

web: www.campingtiber.com

On level grassland, shaded by poplars beside the Tiber.

dir: *Ring road exit 3, site signed N of city. From S signs for Prima Porta.*

Open: 15 Mar-Oct **Site:** 5HEC **For hire:** **Facilities:** **Services:** **Leisure:** P R

SALTO DI FONDI — LATINA

Holiday Village

via Flacca Km 6800, 04020

0771 555009 0771 556282

e-mail: info@holidayvillage.it

web: www.holidayvillage.it

A well-shaded and well-equipped site beside the Mediterranean.

Open: Jan-Sep **Site:** 4HEC **For hire:** **Prices:** 22-58 **Facilities:** Kids' Club Play Area **Services:** **Leisure:** P S

TERRACINA — LATINA

Badino

Porto Badino, 04019

0773 764430 0773 764430

Wooded surroundings with direct access to the beach.

dir: *Off Roma-Napoli road towards canal (Porto Canale Badi-no) & sea.*

Open: Apr-15 Oct **Site:** 1.8HEC **For hire:** **Facilities:** Play Area **Services:** **Leisure:** S **Off-site:**

SOUTH

BAIA DOMIZIA — CASERTA

Baia Domizia Villaggio Camping

81030

0823 930164 0823 930375

e-mail: info@baiadomizia.it

web: www.baiadomizia.it

Part of this extensive seaside site is laid out with flower beds. Good sports and leisure facilities. Ideal for families.

dir: *Off SS7 at Km6/V & 3km towards sea.*

GPS: 41.2075, 13.7908

Open: 6 May-17 Sep **Site:** 30HEC **For hire:** **Prices:** 24.90-47.80 **Facilities:** Wi-fi (charged) Kids' Club Play Area **Services:** **Leisure:** P S

BRIATICO — CATANZARO

Dolomiti

89817

0963 391355 0963 393009

e-mail: info@dolomitisulmare.com

web: www.dolomitisulmare.com

The site is in a delightful setting on two terraces planted with olive trees. It lies by the road and 150 metres from the railway.

dir: *Off road SS522 between Km17 & Km18 towards sea.*

Open: 24 Jun-10 Sep **Site:** 5HEC **For hire:** **Facilities:** **Services:** **Leisure:** P S **Off-site:**

CAPO VATICANO — CATANZARO

Il Gabbiano

San Nicolo di Ricadi, 89865

0963 663384 0963 665442

e-mail: info@villaggioilgabbiano.com

web: www.villaggioilgabbiano.com

High quality facilities in holiday village by the sea.

Open: Apr-Oct **Site:** **For hire:** **Facilities:** Wi-fi Kids' Club Play Area **Services:** **Leisure:** P S

CIRÒ MARINA — CATANZARO

Punta Alice

88811

0962 31160 0962 373823

e-mail: info@puntalice.it

web: www.puntalice.it

Meadowland among lush Mediterranean vegetation, bordering a fine gravel beach 50 metres wide.

dir: *2km from town. Off SS106 Strada Ionica at Km290 to Cirò Marina, through village & beach road towards lighthouse.*

Open: Apr-Sep **Site:** 5.5HEC **For hire:** **Facilities:** **Services:** **Leisure:** P S

CORIGLIANO CÁLABRO — COSENZA

Thurium

Contrada Ricota Grande, 87064

0983 851101 0983 851955

e-mail: info@campingthurium.com

web: www.campingthurium.com

Situated close to the beach, the site has leisure facilities including football, evening entertainment and guided tours. Dogs accepted but restrictions apply.

GPS: 39.6911, 16.5222

Open: 3 Apr-26 Nov **Site:** 16HEC **For hire:** **Prices:** 13.40-47.90 Mobile home hire 170-950 **Facilities:** Wi-fi (charged) **Services:** **Leisure:** P S

EBOLI — SALERNO

Paestum

Litoranea Loc Foce Sele, 84025

0828 691003 0828 691204

e-mail: info@campingpaestum.it

web: www.campingpaestum.it

Sandy, meadowland site in tall poplar wood by the mouth of a river. Steps and bus service to private beach, 0.6km from site.

dir: *Off Litoranea at Km20 at fork to Santa Cecilia, continue 300m, signed.*

GPS: 40.4924, 14.9418

Open: 15 May-15 Sep **Site:** 8HEC **For hire:** **Prices:** 22-36 Mobile home hire 280-1155 **Facilities:** Wi-fi (charged) Kids' Club Play Area **Services:** **Leisure:** P **Off-site:** R S

GALLIPOLI — LECCE

Baia di Gallipoli

73014

0833 273210

e-mail: info@baiadigallipoli.com

web: www.baiadigallipoli.com

A holiday village set amid pine woods close to the sea with good facilities.

dir: *5km SE of Gallipoli.*

Open: Etr-Sep **Site:** 14HEC **For hire:** **Facilities:** **Services:** **Leisure:** P **Off-site:** S

LEPORANO, MARINA DI — TARANTO

Porto Pirrone

Litoranea Salentina, 74020

099 5315184 099 5315184

e-mail: info@portopirronecamping.it

web: www.portopirronecamping.it

Set in a pine wood offering flat large plots for both tents and caravans. Good sports and entertainment.

dir: *A14 from Massafra towards Taranto & Leporano, site near marina.*

Open: Mar-Oct **Site:** 3.2HEC **For hire:** **Facilities:** Kids' Club **Services:** **Leisure:** S **Off-site:**

MÁCCHIA — FOGGIA

Monaco

71030

0884 530280 0884 565737

e-mail: info@baiadelmonaco.it

web: www.baiadelmonaco.it

A pleasant location with good facilities and direct access to the beach.

Open: Jun-15 Sep **Site:** 5.3HEC **For hire:** **Facilities:** **Services:** **Leisure:** P S

MANFREDONIA — FOGGIA

Ippocampo

SS159, 71043

0884 571121

e-mail: campingippocampo@email.it

web: www.campingippocampo.it

Set in the grounds of a holiday village.

Open: May-Sep **Site:** 8HEC **For hire:** **Facilities:** **Services:** **Leisure:** S **Off-site:** P

OTRANTO — LECCE

Mulino d'Acqua

via S Stefano, 73028
☎ 0836 802191 🖹 0836 802196
e-mail: mulino.camping@anet.it
web: www.mulinodacqua.it

Shaded by olive trees, close to the beach, and with plenty of organised activities. Only small dogs allowed.

Open: end May-mid Sep **Site:** 10HEC **For hire:** **Facilities:** Wi-fi (charged) Play Area **Services:** **Leisure:** P S **Off-site:**

PESCHICI — FOGGIA

Centro Turistico San Nicola

Loc San Nicola, 71010
☎ 0884 964024

Terraced site in lovely location by the sea, in a bay enclosed by rocks.

dir: *Off Peschici-Vieste coast road, signed along winding road to site in 1km.*

Open: Apr-15 Oct **Site:** 14HEC **For hire:** **Facilities:** **Services:** **Leisure:** S

Internazionale Manacore

71010
☎ 0884 911020 🖹 0884 911049
e-mail: manacore@grupposaccia.it
web: www.grupposaccia.it

Meadowland with a few terraces in attractive bay, surrounded by wooded hills.

dir: *Off Peschici-Vieste coast road towards sea on wide U bend.*

Open: Apr-9 Oct **Site:** 22HEC **For hire:**
Prices: 22.50-54 **Facilities:** Kids' Club Play Area
Services: **Leisure:** S

PIZZO — CATANZARO

Villaggio Camping Pinetamare

88812
☎ 0963 534871 🖹 0963 534871
e-mail: info@villaggiopinetamare.com
web: www.villaggiopinetamare.it

A sandy site surrounded by tall pine trees. Most water sports are available along the private beach, and families are welcome.

dir: *Salerno-Reggio motorway exit Pizzo, site N of town.*

Open: Jun-15 Sep **Site:** 10HEC **For hire:**
Facilities: **Services:**
Leisure: P S **Off-site:** L

POMPEI — NAPOLI

Spartacus

via Plinio 127, 80045
☎ 081 8624078 🖹 081 8624078
e-mail: staff@campingspartacus.it
web: www.campingspartacus.it

Site on a level meadow with orange trees. Close to the main entrance for the Pompeii ruins and a good location for visiting nearby resorts.

dir: *Motorway exit Pompei West, off Napoli road, opposite Scavi di Pompei, near fuel station.*

GPS: 40.7456, 14.4839

Open: All Year. **Site:** 9HEC **For hire:**
Prices: 13-21 **Facilities:** Wi-fi Play Area
Services: **Leisure:** P

POZZUOLI — NAPOLI

Vulcano Solfatara

via Solfatara 161, 80078
☎ 081 5267413 🖹 081 5263482
e-mail: info@solfatara.it
web: www.solfatara.it

Clean and orderly site in a forest near the crater of the extinct Solfatara Volcano.

dir: *From Nuova via Domiziana (SS7) at Km60/1 (6km before Napoli) turn inland through stone gate.*

GPS: 46.8292, 14.1382

Open: All Year. **Site:** 3HEC **For hire:** **Prices:** 29-34.50
Facilities: Wi-fi (charged) Play Area
Services: **Leisure:** P **Off-site:** L S

PRÁIA A MARE — COSENZA

International Camping Village

Lungomare Sirimarco, 87028
☎ 0985 72211 🖹 0985 72211
e-mail: reception@campinginternational.it
web: www.campinginternational.it

A beautiful location on the gulf of Policastro with fine recreational facilities.

dir: *A3 to Falerna, onto SS18 (south); A3 Logonegro (north).*

Open: May-Sep **Site:** 5.5HEC **For hire:** **Facilities:** Play Area **Services:**
Leisure: S

RODI GARGANICO FOGGIA

Ripa

Contrada Ripa, 71012
0884 965367 0884 965695
e-mail: info@villaggioripa.it
web: www.villaggioripa.it
Well-equipped and attractive site close to the beach.
Open: 15 Jun-15 Sep **Site:** 6HEC **For hire:**
Facilities: Wi-fi Play Area **Services:**
Leisure: P S **Off-site:** L

ROSSANO SCALO COSENZA

Marina di Rossano

Contrada Leuca, 87068
0983 516054 0983 514106
e-mail: marina.club@tiscalinet.it
web: www.marinadirossano.it
Wooded surroundings close to the beach with modern facilities.
dir: *A3 exit Rossano via N106.*
Open: 15 May-29 Sep **Site:** 7HEC **For hire:**
Facilities: Wi-fi Kids' Club Play Area
Services: **Leisure:** P S **Off-site:**

SAN MENÁIO FOGGIA

Valle d'Oro

Loc Aia del Cervone, 71010
0884 991580 0884 991580
e-mail: info@campingvalledoro.it
web: www.campingvalledoro.it
Site in an olive grove with some terraces and surrounded by wooded hills, 2km from the sea.
dir: *Off SS89 onto SS528 to site at Km1.800.*
Open: 15 Jun-15 Sep **Site:** 3HEC **For hire:**
Facilities: **Services:** **Off-site:** P S

SANTA CESÁREA TERME LECCE

Scogliera

via Litoranea per Castro, 73020
0836 949802 0836 949802
Attractive site close to the sea.
dir: *1km S on SS173.*
Open: All Year. **Site:** 8HEC **For hire:** **Facilities:**
Services: **Leisure:** P **Off-site:** S

SANTA MARIA DI CASTELLABATE SALERNO

Trezene

84072
0974 965027 0974 965013
e-mail: info@trezene.com
web: www.trezene.com
The site is partly divided into pitches and consists of two sections lying either side of the access road. Pitches between road and fine sandy beach are reserved for touring campers.
Open: Apr-Oct **Site:** 2.5HEC **For hire:** **Facilities:**
Services: **Leisure:** S **Off-site:**

SORRENTO NAPOLI

International Camping Nube d'Argento

via Capo 21, 80067
081 8781344 081 8073450
e-mail: info@nubedargento.com
web: www.nubedargento.com
The site lies on narrow terraces just off a steep concrete road between the beach and the outskirts of the town. Access difficult for caravans.
Open: 20 Mar-14 Jan **Site:** 1.5HEC **For hire:**
Prices: 25-42 **Facilities:** Wi-fi Play Area
Services: **Leisure:** P S **Off-site:**

Santa Fortunata Campogaio

via Capo 39, 80067
081 8073579 081 8073590
e-mail: info@santafortunata.eu
web: www.santafortunata.eu
A well-appointed, terraced site shaded by olive trees and with direct access to the sea (50 metres).
dir: *2km from town centre. 400m after exit from SS145 on road towards Massa Lubrense.*
GPS: 40.6274, 14.3374
Open: 7 Apr-17 Oct **Site:** 20HEC **For hire:**
Prices: 20-36 **Facilities:** Wi-fi (charged) Kids' Club Play Area **Services:** **Leisure:** P S

SPECCHIOLLA, LIDO DI — BRINDISI

Pineta al Mare

72012
0831 987024 0831 994057
e-mail: info@campingpinetamare.com
web: www.campingpinetamare.com

Site in pine woodland with sandy beach and some rocks.

dir: *E of Bari-Brindisi road at Km21.5.*

Open: Apr-20 Sep **Site:** 5.5HEC **For hire:** **Prices:** 23-42 **Facilities:** Wi-fi (charged) Kids' Club Play Area **Services:** **Leisure:** P S **Off-site:**

TORRE RINALDA — LECCE

Torre Rinalda Camping Village

Litoranea Salentina CP152, 73100
0832 382161 0832 382565
e-mail: info@torrerinalda.it
web: www.torrerinalda.it

An extensive level meadow separated from the sea by dunes. There is a disco and a kids' club in high season.

dir: *SS613 Brindisi-Lecce exit Trepuzzi, coast road for 1.5km.*

Open: 5 May-16 Sep **Site:** 15HEC **For hire:** **Prices:** 19.50-56.30 **Facilities:** Wi-fi (charged) Kids' Club Play Area **Services:** **Leisure:** P S

UGENTO — LECCE

Riva di Ugento

Litoranea Gallipoli-SM di Leuca, 73059
0833 933600 0833 933601
web: www.rivadiugento.it

A well-equipped site in wooded surroundings close to the beach.

Open: 14 May-Sep **Site:** 32HEC **For hire:** **Facilities:** Wi-fi Play Area **Services:** **Leisure:** P S

VARCATURO, MARINA DI — NAPOLI

Partenope

80014
081 5091076 081 5096767
e-mail: info@campingpartenope.it
web: www.campingpartenope.it

Partially undulating terrain in woodland with access to a private beach. Leisure facilities include tennis, football and evening entertainment.

dir: *Off SS7 (via Domiziana) at Km45/II towards sea for 300m.*

Open: Jun-8 Sep **Site:** 6HEC **For hire:** **Facilities:** **Services:** **Leisure:** R S

VICO EQUENSE — NAPOLI

Sant' Antonio

Marina Aequa, 80069
081 8028570 081 8028570
e-mail: info@campingsantantonio.it
web: www.campingsantantonio.it

A modern site set among fruit trees, close to the beach with fine views over the Bay of Naples.

GPS: 40.6588, 14.4186

Open: 15 Mar-Oct **Site:** 1HEC **For hire:** **Prices:** 26-30 **Facilities:** Wi-fi (charged) **Services:** **Leisure:** S **Off-site:** P

Seiano Spiaggia

Marina Aequa, via Murrano 15, 80069
081 8028560 081 8028560
e-mail: info@campingseiano.it
web: www.campingseiano.it

Set in a plantation of evergreen and orange trees close to the sea. There are good facilities and the site is well situated for Pompeii, Naples and Vesuvius.

dir: *A3 exit Castellammare di Stabia, highway 145, after Seiano tunnel & bridge right to Marina Aequa. By train Naples-Sorrento line to Seiano. Daily steamer from nearby beach to Capri.*

GPS: 40.6602, 14.4203

Open: Apr-Sep **Site:** 1HEC **For hire:** **Prices:** 22.50-26 **Facilities:** **Services:** **Off-site:** P S

Villaggio Turistico Azzurro

via Marina Aequa 9, 80066
081 8029984 081 8029176
e-mail: info@villaggioazzurro.net
web: www.villaggioazzurro.net
Shaded site among ancient olive groves, by the sea and in close proximity to the Isle of Capri.
dir: *A3 exit Castellammare, signs for Vico Equense, after 3rd tunnel & bridge right to Marina Aequa.*
Open: Mar-1 Dec **Site:** 11HEC **For hire:** **Facilities:** Play Area **Services:** **Leisure:** S **Off-site:**

VIESTE FOGGIA

Capo Vieste

71019
0884 706326 0884 705993
e-mail: info@capovieste.it
web: www.capovieste.it
The site lies on a large area of unspoiled land, planted with a few rows of poplar and pine trees. It is by the sea and has a large bathing area.
dir: *Off coast road to Peschici, 7km beyond Vieste.*
Open: 20 Apr-15 Oct **Site:** 6HEC **For hire:** **Facilities:** **Services:** **Leisure:** P S

Umbramare

Casella Postale 313, Santa Maria di Merino, 71019
0884 706174 0884 706174
e-mail: umbramarevieste@tiscali.it
web: www.umbramarevieste.it
Site with access to a private beach and a small children's play park. Separate car park for bungalows.
dir: *Off A14 at Poggio Imperiale onto route via Rodi Gargánico & Peschici.*
Open: Apr-Oct **Site:** 10.5HEC **For hire:** **Prices:** 15-36 **Facilities:** Play Area **Services:** **Leisure:** S **Off-site:**

Vieste Marina

Litoranea Vieste-Peschici Km 5, 71019
0884 706471 0884 706471
e-mail: viestemarina@tiscali.it
web: www.garganovacanze.it
Tree-lined level site adjacent to the coast road in a quiet location with good facilities.
dir: *5km N of Vieste, signed.*
Open: May-Sep **Site:** 5HEC **For hire:** **Facilities:** **Services:** **Leisure:** P S **Off-site:**

Village Punta Lunga

Defensola, CP 339, 71019
0884 706031 0884 706910
e-mail: info@puntalunga.it
web: www.puntalunga.it
A terraced site in wooded surroundings encompassing two sandy bathing bays and a rocky peninsula.
dir: *2km N of Vieste, signed from coast road.*
Open: 28 Apr-1 Oct **Site:** 6HEC **For hire:** **Facilities:** **Services:** **Leisure:** S

THE ISLANDS

SARDEGNA (SARDINIA)

AGLIENTU SASSARI

Baia Blu la Tortuga

Pineta di Vignola Mare, 07020
079 602200 079 602040
e-mail: info@baiablu.com
web: www.baiaholiday.com
Site in pine forest by the sea. A beautiful setting with wide choice of facilities and leisure activities.
GPS: 41.1261, 9.0672
Open: Apr-20 Oct **Site:** 17HEC **For hire:** **Prices:** 16-55 **Facilities:** Wi-fi (charged) Kids' Club Play Area **Services:** **Leisure:** S

ARBATAX NUORO

Telis

Porto Frailis, 08041
0782 667261 0782 667140
e-mail: telisca@tiscali.it
web: www.campingtelis.com
Located in the bay of Porto Frailis, this terraced site is surrounded by beautiful scenery. There are good facilities and pitches surrounded by eucalyptus and mimosa trees.
dir: *SS125 between Cagliari & Olbia.*
Open: All Year. **Site:** 3HEC **For hire:** **Prices:** 22-40 **Facilities:** Wi-fi Kids' Club Play Area **Services:** **Leisure:** P S **Off-site:**

CALASETTA — CAGLIARI

Le Saline

09011

☎ 0781 88615 📠 0781 435510

e-mail: info@campinglesaline.com

web: www.campinglesaline.com

Wooded surroundings close to the beach, 0.5km from the village with good recreational facilities.

Open: May-Oct **Site:** 7HEC **For hire:** **Facilities:** Play Area **Services:** **Leisure:** S **Off-site:**

CANNIGIONE-ARZACHENA — SASSARI

Centro Vacanze Isuledda

07021

☎ 0789 86003 📠 0789 86089

e-mail: info@isuledda.it

web: www.isuledda.it

Near the beautiful Costa Smeralda with modern sanitary installations and plentiful sports and entertainment facilities.

GPS: 41.4408, 9.4408

Open: Apr-Oct **Site:** 15HEC **For hire:** **Prices:** 20.50-54 Mobile home hire 280-1057 **Facilities:** Wi-fi (charged) Kids' Club Play Area **Services:** **Leisure:** S

LOTZORAI — NUORO

Cernie

via Case Sparse 17, 08040

☎ 0782 669472 📠 06 91659297

e-mail: info@campinglecernie.com

web: www.campinglecernie.com

Close to the beach with beautiful views on all sides. Varied sports and leisure activities.

Open: May-Oct **Site:** 1.5HEC **For hire:** **Facilities:** Play Area **Services:** **Leisure:** S **Off-site:**

OROSEI — NUORO

Campeggio Il Golfo

via Marzellinu 1, 08028

☎ 0784 91036 📠 0784 187 0144

e-mail: info@campeggioilgolfo.com

web: www.campeggioilgolfo.com

On the east of the island, 400 metres from a white sandy beach.

Open: Jun-Sep **Site:** 7HEC **For hire:** **Prices:** 20-38 **Facilities:** Wi-fi Play Area **Off-site:** S

PORTO ROTONDO — SASSARI

Cugnana

Loc Cugnana, 07026

☎ 0789 33184 📠 0789 33398

e-mail: info@campingcugnana.it

web: www.campingcugnana.it

A well-appointed family site with good recreational facilities and free transport to the local beaches.

Open: Apr-10 Oct **Site:** 5HEC **For hire:** **Facilities:** **Services:** **Leisure:** P **Off-site:** S

PORTO TRAMATZU — CAGLIARI

Porto Tramatzu

09019

☎ 070 9283027 📠 070 9283028

e-mail: coop.proturismo@libero.it

web: www.camping.it

With extensive facilities and large individual plots. The site is less than 100 metres from the beautiful Porto Tramatzu.

dir: *SS195 from Cagliari.*

Open: Etr-Oct **Site:** 3.5HEC **For hire:** **Facilities:** **Services:** **Leisure:** S

SANTA LUCIA — NUORO

Calapineta

SS Orientale Sarda 125, 08029

☎ 0784 819184 📠 0784 818128

e-mail: info@calapineta.it

web: www.calapineta.it

Well-equipped site 1.5km from a white sand beach.

Open: Jun-15 Sep **Site:** 10HEC **For hire:** **Facilities:** Play Area **Services:** **Leisure:** S

Selema

08029

☎ 0784 37349

e-mail: info@selemacamping.com

web: www.selemacamping.com

A beach site in the shadow of a pine grove. Large plots with good facilities and amenities close to a small ancient fishing village.

Open: Apr-15 Oct **Site:** 7.5HEC **For hire:** **Prices:** 21-45 Mobile home hire 490-1000 **Facilities:** Wi-fi Play Area **Services:** **Leisure:** P S **Off-site:**

SANT'ANTIOCO — CAGLIARI

Tonnara

Loc Calasapone, 09017
☎ 0781 809058 🖷 0781 809036
e-mail: mail@camping-tonnara.it
web: www.campingtonnara.it

Situated in the centre of Cala Sapone Bay with enclosed plots, good sports facilities and access to a sandy beach.

dir: *S of Carbonia, road to island of Sant' Antioco.*

Open: Apr-Oct **Site:** 7HEC **For hire:** **Facilities:** **Services:** **Leisure:** P S

TORRE SALINAS — CAGLIARI

Torre Salinas

09043
☎ 070 999032 🖷 070 999001
e-mail: information@camping-torre-salinas.de
web: www.camping-torre-salinas.de

On south-eastern coast of Sardinia, close to a lagoon.

Open: Apr-14 Oct **Site:** 1.5HEC **For hire:** **Prices:** 19-40 **Facilities:** **Services:** **Leisure:** S

VALLEDORIA — SASSARI

La Foce

via Ampurias 110, 07039
☎ 079 582109 🖷 079 582191
e-mail: info@lafoce.eu
web: www.lafoce.eu

A delightful wooded setting separated from the beach by the River Coghinas, which can be crossed by ferry. Modern sanitary installations and plenty of recreational facilities, including a kids' club in July and August.

GPS: 40.9336, 8.8172

Open: 21 Apr-Sep **Site:** 20HEC **For hire:** **Prices:** 18-50 **Facilities:** Wi-fi Kids' Club Play Area **Services:** **Leisure:** P R S **Off-site:** L

Valledoria International Camping

07039
☎ 079 584070 🖷 079 584058
e-mail: info@campingvalledoria.com
web: www.campingvalledoria.com

Located in a pine wood, this site has both white sand beaches and rocky cliffs.

Open: 15 May-29 Sep **Site:** 10HEC **For hire:** **Prices:** 17.50-31.50 Mobile home hire 240-360 **Facilities:** Wi-fi (charged) Play Area **Services:** **Leisure:** S **Off-site:**

SICILIA (SICILY)

AVOLA — SIRACUSA

Sabbiadoro

via Chiusa di Carlo, 96012
☎ 0931 822415 🖷 0931 822415 & 560000
e-mail: info@campeggiosabbiadoro.com
web: www.campeggiosabbiadoro.com

Site with magnificent views located in a picturesque area directly on the beach and surrounded by trees and tropical plants.

GPS: 36.9361, 15.1753

Open: All Year. **Site:** 2.2HEC **For hire:** **Prices:** 28-32 **Facilities:** Wi-fi (charged) **Services:** **Leisure:** S **Off-site:** P R

CASTEL DI TUSA — MESSINA

Scoglio

98079
☎ 0921 334345 🖷 0921 334345
e-mail: loscoglio@loscoglio.net
web: www.loscoglio.net

A terraced site. No shade on the gravel beach.

dir: *A20 from Uscita, off SS113 Km 164.*

GPS: 38.0100, 14.2307

Open: Apr-Sep **Site:** 1.5HEC **For hire:** **Prices:** 16-42.50 Mobile home hire 290-840 **Facilities:** Wi-fi (charged) Play Area **Services:** **Leisure:** P S

CASTELVETRANO — TRAPANI

Camping Helios

via 1 n 271, Triscina di Selinunte, 91022
☎ 0924 84301 🖷 0924 84301
e-mail: info@campinghelios.it
web: www.campinghelios.it

Family-run campsite next to the beach and with direct access. Facilities include cycle rental and the site is ideally located for visiting local historical sites. There is a compulsory separate car park in high season.

GPS: 37.5826, 12.7697

Open: Apr-Oct **Site:** 12HEC **For hire:** **Prices:** 21-31 **Facilities:** Play Area **Services:** **Leisure:** S **Off-site:**

ITALY

CATÁNIA — CATANIA

Jonio

via Villini a Mare 2, 95126
☎ 095 491139 095 492277
e-mail: info@campingjonio.com
web: www.jonioeventi.it
On a clifftop plateau. Access to beach via steps.
dir: *Off SS14 N of town towards sea.*
Open: All Year. **Site:** 1.2HEC **For hire:** **Facilities:** **Services:** **Leisure:** S

FINALE DI POLLINA — PALERMO

Rais Gerbi

90010
☎ 0921 426570 0921 426577
e-mail: camping@raisgerbi.it
web: www.raisgerbi.it
A well-equipped, modern site with its own private beach in picturesque wooded surroundings. Kids' club summer only.
dir: *Off SS113 at Km172.9.*
Open: All Year. **Site:** 5HEC **For hire:** **Prices:** 19-40 Mobile home hire 250-600 **Facilities:** Wi-fi (charged) Kids' Club Play Area **Services:** **Leisure:** P S **Off-site:**

FÚRNARI MARINA — MESSINA

Village Bazia

Contrada Bazia, 98054
☎ 0941 800130 0941 81006
e-mail: info@bazia.it
web: www.bazia.it
A pleasant seaside site with plenty of recreational facilities.
Open: Jun-10 Sep **Site:** 4HEC **For hire:** **Facilities:** **Services:** **Leisure:** P S **Off-site:**

ÍSOLA DELLE FÉMMINE — PALERMO

La Playa

viale Marino 55, 90040
☎ 091 8677001 091 8677001
e-mail: campinglaplaya@virglio.it
web: www.laplayacamping.it
A ideal site for a relaxing holiday with beautiful views and quiet woodland walks. Beach lies in front of the campsite.
dir: *A29 Palermo to Trapani & SS113.*
Open: 21 Mar-15 Oct **Site:** 2.2HEC **For hire:** **Prices:** 20.50-31 Mobile home hire 315-700 **Facilities:** Wi-fi (charged) Play Area **Services:** **Leisure:** S **Off-site:**

MENFI — AGRIGENTO

Palma

via delle Palme n 29, 92013
☎ 0925 78392 0925 78392
e-mail: campinglapalma@libero.it
web: www.campinglapalma.com
On the Mediterranean coast, shaded site with a pizzeria and bar.
dir: *6km S A29, exit Castelvetrano towards Menfi.*
Open: All Year. **Site:** 1HEC **For hire:** **Facilities:** **Services:** **Leisure:** S

OLIVERI — MESSINA

Marinello

Contrada Marinello, 98060
☎ 0941 313000 0941 313702
e-mail: marinello@camping.it
web: www.villaggiomarinello.it
Site consists of small pitches set in a woodland area 100 metres from the sea. Dogs not permitted in July and August.
dir: *A20 exit Falcone.*
Open: All Year. **Site:** 3.2HEC **For hire:** **Facilities:** **Services:** **Leisure:** S **Off-site:**

PUNTA BRACCETTO — RAGUSA

Camping Luminoso

viale dei Canalotti sn, 97017
☎ 0932 918401 0932 918455
e-mail: info@campingluminoso.com
web: www.campingluminoso.com
Relaxing site, ideal for families, with direct access to a sandy beach. Kids' club in July and August. Cars can be parked by tents except July and August.
GPS: 36.8172, 14.4658
Open: All Year. **Site:** 15HEC **For hire:** **Facilities:** Wi-fi (charged) Kids' Club Play Area **Services:** **Leisure:** S **Off-site:**

Rocca dei Tramonti

97017
☎ 0932 863208 0932 918054
web: www.roccadeitramonti.it
The site lies in a quiet setting on rather barren land near a beautiful sandy bay surrounded by cliffs.
dir: *From Marina di Ragusa 10km W on coast road to Punta Braccetto.*
Open: May-Sep **Site:** 3HEC **For hire:** **Prices:** 23-27 Mobile home hire 350 **Facilities:** Play Area **Leisure:** S **Off-site:**

SANT' ALESSIO SICULO — MESSINA

Focetta Sicula

Contrada Siena 40, 98030

☎ 0942 751657 🖷 0942 756708

e-mail: lafocetta@camping.it

web: www.lafocetta.it

A well-equipped site with a private beach in a quiet beautiful location.

GPS: 37.9314, 15.3556

Open: All Year. **Site:** 1.2HEC **For hire:** **Facilities:** Wi-fi (charged) Play Area **Services:** **Leisure:** S **Off-site:**

SECCAGRANDE — AGRIGENTO

Kamemi Camping Village

92016

☎ 0925 69212 🖷 0925 69212

e-mail: info@kamemivillage.com

web: www.kamemivillage.com

Wooded surroundings close to the beach with good recreational facilities.

Open: All Year. **Site:** 5HEC **For hire:** **Prices:** 13-50 Mobile home hire 250-1000 **Facilities:** Kids' Club **Services:** **Leisure:** P S **Off-site:**

TORRE FARO — MESSINA

Nuovo Camping dello Stretto

via Circuito, 98164

☎ 090 3223051 🖷 090 3223051

e-mail: info@campingdellostretto.it

web: www.campingdellostretto.it

11km north of Messina, large pitches are available and a shuttle service takes campers to nearby beaches.

GPS: 38.2617, 15.6333

Open: 25 Apr-Sep **Site:** **For hire:** **Prices:** 21.50-27.50 **Facilities:** Wi-fi (charged) Kids' Club Play Area **Services:** **Leisure:** P **Off-site:** S

Above: Julius Ceasar with Foro Romano behind, Fori Imperiali

Luxembourg

Drinking and driving
If the level of alcohol in the bloodstream is 0.05 per cent or more severe penalties include fines and/or prison. Young driver's blood alcohol level and novice driver's blood alcohol level is 0.019 per cent.

Driving licence
Minimum age at which a UK licence holder may drive a temporarily imported car and/or motorcycle 18.

Fines
On-the-spot, they can be settled by cash or by bank card. Unauthorised and dangerous parking can result in the car being impounded or removed.

Fuel
Unleaded petrol (95 and 98 octane) and diesel available. LPG is available in a few petrol stations (approximately 12). It is forbidden to carry petrol in a can. Credit cards accepted at filling stations, check with your card issuer for usage in Luxembourg before travel.

Lights
The use of dipped headlights during the day recommended. Sidelights required when parking where there isn't any public lighting. When visibility is reduced to fewer than 100 metres due to fog, snow, heavy rain etc, dipped headlights must be used. It is compulsory to flash headlights at night when overtaking outside built-up areas. In tunnels indicated by a sign, drivers must use their passing lights.

Motorcycles
Use of dipped headlights during the day compulsory. The wearing of crash helmets is compulsory for both driver and passenger. Children under 12 are not permitted as a passenger.

Motor insurance
Third-party compulsory.

Passengers/children in cars
Children under 3 years of age must be seated in an approved restraint system. Children aged 3 to 17 years and/or under 1.5m must be seated in an appropriate restraint system. If their weight is over 36kg a seatbelt can be used but only on the rear seat of the vehicle. Rearward facing child restraint systems are prohibited on seats with frontal airbags unless the airbag is deactivated.

Seat belts
Compulsory for front/rear seat occupants to wear seat belts, if fitted.

Speed limits
Standard legal limits, which may be varied by signs

Private vehicles without trailers	
Built-up areas	50km/h
Outside built-up areas	90km/h
Motorways	130km/h
In case of rain or snow	110km/h
Vehicles with spiked tyres	70km/h
Private vehicle with trailer	
Built-up areas	50km/h
Outside built-up areas	75km/h
Motorways	90km/h

Compulsory equipment in Luxembourg
Reflective jacket - It is compulsory for the driver and passengers to wear a reflective waistcoat when exiting a vehicle in a breakdown situation on a motorway or outside built-up areas, at night and in bad visibility.

Warning triangle - compulsory for all vehicles with 4 or more wheels.

Tyres – All tyres on a car must be of the same type, either winter tyres marked M&S on the sidewall or summer tyres.

Other rules/requirements
The use of spiked tyres is permitted from the 1st December until the 31st March. Use of snow chains permitted, in case of snow or ice.

Any vehicle immobilised on the motorway must use warning signals, a warning triangle and a flashing light at the rear.

In built-up areas the use of the horn is prohibited except in case of immediate danger .

'Zone de rencontre' – This new road sign which can be seen in residential and commercial areas indicates a maximum speed of 20 km/h. Within this zone pedestrians have priority and may cross the road whenever they choose to, if they do not unnecessarily impede the traffic.

CLERVAUX

Official de Clervaux

33 rue Klatzewee, 9714

920042 929728

e-mail: info@camping-clervaux.lu

web: www.camping-clervaux.lu

Situated next to the sports stadium, between the La Clerve stream and the railway, in a forested area. Trains only run during the day and there is little noise. Separate field for tents.

dir: *0.5km SW from village.*

Open: 15 Mar-30 Oct **Site:** 3HEC **For hire:** **Facilities:** **Services:** **Leisure:** P R **Off-site:**

DIEKIRCH

Bleesbruck

9359

803134 802718

e-mail: info@camping-bleesbruck.lu

web: www.camping-bleesbruck.lu

A modern site in tranquil wooded surroundings, with a separate naturist area.

Open: Apr-Oct **Site:** 4HEC **For hire:** **Facilities:** Play Area **Services:** **Leisure:** R **Off-site:** P

Op der Sauer

rte de Gilsdorf, 9201

808590 809470

web: www.campsauer.lu

This site provides spacious pitches and many facilities around the park. Younger guests are well provided for, as there is a children's pool and a kids' club in July and August.

dir: *0.5km from town centre on road to Gilsdorf, near stadium.*

Open: All Year. **Site:** 5HEC **For hire:** **Facilities:** Wi-fi (charged) Kids' Club Play Area **Services:** **Leisure:** R **Off-site:**

DILLINGEN

Wies-Neu

12 rue de la Sûre, 6350

836110 26876438

web: www.camping-wies-neu.lu

A comfortable family site on the bank of the River Sûre.

dir: *Between Diekirch & Echternacht.*

Open: Apr-30 Oct **Site:** 45HEC **For hire:** **Facilities:** **Services:** **Leisure:** R **Off-site:**

ECHTERNACH

Official

17 rte de Diekirch, 6430

720272 26720847

e-mail: info@camping-echternach.lu

web: www.camping-echternach.lu

Just 10 minutes from the centre of Echternach, this terraced site is divided into three areas. A kids' club is available from mid July to mid August.

dir: *E42 to Echternach.*

Open: 15 Mar-1 Nov **Site:** 7HEC **For hire:** **Prices:** 17.10-19.60 Mobile home hire 250-350 **Facilities:** Wi-fi Kids' Club Play Area **Services:** **Leisure:** P **Off-site:** L R

ENSCHERANGE

Val d'Or

9747

920691 929725

e-mail: valdor@pt.lu

web: www.valdor.lu

Quiet family site in a beautiful natural setting beside the River Clerve. Wi-fi available free of charge for one hour daily.

dir: *8km S of Clervaux between Drauffelt & Wilwerwiltz.*

GPS: 50.0001, 5.9910

Open: Apr-1 Nov **Site:** 4HEC **For hire:** **Prices:** 16-20 Mobile home hire 210-650 **Facilities:** Wi-fi Kids' Club Play Area **Services:** **Leisure:** R **Off-site:**

ESCH-SUR-ALZETTE

Gaalgebierg

4001

541069 549630

web: www.gaalgebierg.lu

A level park-like site with lovely trees on a hillock.

dir: *N6 SE from town centre towards Dudelange, right at motorway underpass, steep climb uphill.*

Open: All Year. **Site:** 2.5HEC **For hire:** **Facilities:** **Services:** **Off-site:** P

HEIDERSCHEID

Fuussekaul

4 Fuussekaul, 9156

2688881 26888828

e-mail: info@fuussekaul.lu

web: www.fuussekaul.lu

A level grassland family site adjoining a woodland area. Good recreational facilities.

dir: *Off N15 Bastogne-Diekirch.*

Open: All Year. **Site:** 18HEC **For hire:** **Prices:** 18.50-35 Mobile home hire 288-875 **Facilities:** Wi-fi (charged) Kids' Club Play Area **Services:** **Leisure:** P **Off-site:** L R

INGLEDORF

Gritt

rue du Pont, 9161

802018 802019

web: www.campinggritt.lu

Set on the southern bank of the Sûre between Ettelbruck and Diekirch. A beautiful country setting ideal for fishing.

Open: Apr-Oct **Site:** 5HEC **For hire:** **Prices:** 16.60-22.10 **Facilities:** Wi-fi **Services:** **Leisure:** R **Off-site:** L

KOCKELSCHEUER

Kockelscheuer

22 rte de Bettembourg, 1899

471815 401243

e-mail: caravani@pt.lu

web: www.camp-kockelscheuer.lu

A modern site on the edge of a forest.

dir: *4km from Luxembourg off N31.*

GPS: 49.5722, 6.1083

Open: Etr-Oct **Site:** 3.8HEC **Prices:** 13 **Facilities:** **Services:** **Off-site:**

LAROCHETTE

Kengert

7633

837186 878323

e-mail: info@kengert.lu

web: www.kengert.lu

On gently sloping meadow in a pleasant rural location.

C&CC Report *The Ardennes is a gorgeous region in which to unwind, with its beautiful, unspoiled, uncrowded countryside of high, forested, rolling hills and deep, lush valleys peppered with striking rock formations. Popular for short and long stays alike, Auf Kengert is a particularly welcoming and homely site, while the free local transport and entry to attractions throughout the Grand Duchy, with the special Luxembourg Card, are a major bonus.*

dir: *N8 towards Mersch, CR119 towards Nommern, 2km turn right.*

GPS: 49.8003, 6.1985

Open: Mar-7 Nov **Site:** 4HEC **For hire:** **Prices:** 20-30 **Facilities:** Wi-fi Play Area **Services:** **Leisure:** P

MAULUSMÜHLE

Woltzdal

Maison 12, 9974

998938 979739

e-mail: info@woltzdal-camping.lu

web: www.campingwoltzdal.com

Quiet family site in the deep Woltz Valley.

dir: *N30 from Liège to Bastogne, N874 to Clervaux & onto N12.*

GPS: 50.0921, 6.0278

Open: Apr-Oct **Site:** 1.5HEC **For hire:** **Prices:** 17-21 Mobile home hire 475-670 **Facilities:** Wi-fi (charged) Play Area **Services:** **Leisure:** R

MERSCH

Krounebierg

rue du Camping, 7572

329756 327987

e-mail: contact@campingkrounebierg.lu

web: www.campingkrounebierg.lu

A clean, well-kept site on five terraces, split into sections by hedges.

dir: *0.5km W of village church.*

Open: Apr-Oct **Site:** 5.5HEC **For hire:** **Prices:** 19.80-31.90 **Facilities:** Wi-fi Kids' Club Play Area **Services:** **Leisure:** P

NOMMERN

Europacamping Nommerlayen

rue Nommerlayen, 7465
878078 879678
e-mail: nommerlayen@vo.lu
web: www.nommerlayen-ec.lu

A terraced site in wooded surroundings with plenty of recreational facilities. A kids' club is available during the school holidays.

Open: 18 Feb-Oct **Site:** 15HEC **For hire:**
Prices: 22.50-40 Mobile home hire 365-880 **Facilities:** Wi-fi (charged) Kids' Club Play Area **Services:** **Leisure:** P

OBEREISENBACH

Kohnenhof

1 Kounenhaff, 9838
929464 929690
e-mail: kohnenhof@pt.lu
web: www.campingkohnenhof.lu

Quiet site in a rural setting in the River Our valley. The site has an excellent restaurant in an old farmhouse.

Open: Apr-Oct **Site:** 6HEC **For hire:**
Prices: 16-29 Mobile home hire 350-800 **Facilities:** Wi-fi (charged) Kids' Club Play Area **Services:** **Leisure:** R

ROSPORT

Barrage

rte d'Echternach, 6580
730160 735155
e-mail: campingrosport@pt.lu
web: www.campingrosport.com

Situated by Lake Sûre on the German border at the entrance to Luxembourg's Little Switzerland.

dir: *Main road from Echternach to Wasserbillig.*

Open: 15 Mar-Oct **Site:** 3.2HEC **Facilities:** Wi-fi (charged) Play Area **Services:** **Leisure:** L P R
Off-site:

STEINFORT

Steinfort

72 rte de Luxembourg, 8440
398827 397410
e-mail: campstei@pt.lu
web: www.camping-steinfort.lu

A small family site with good recreational and entertainment facilities, well situated for exploring the Seven Castles area.

dir: *E25 exit Steinfort.*

GPS: 49.6593, 5.9274

Open: All Year. **Site:** 3.5HEC **For hire:**
Prices: 15-23 **Facilities:** Wi-fi Kids' Club Play Area **Services:** **Leisure:** P **Off-site:**

LUXEMBOURG

Netherlands

Drinking and driving
If the level of alcohol in the bloodstream is over 0.05 per cent, severe penalties include fine, withdrawal of driving licence and imprisonment. The lower limit of 0.02 per cent applies to new drivers for the first five years and moped riders up to the age of 24. In some cases a blood test will be necessary after a breath test.

Driving licence
Minimum age at which a UK licence holder may drive a temporarily imported car and/or motorcycle 18.

Fines
On-the-spot. In the case of illegal parking, the police can impose and collect on-the-spot fines or tow the vehicle away. Vehicles can be confiscated in cases of heavy excess of speed and drink driving.

Fuel
Unleaded petrol (95 and 98 octane), diesel and LPG (Autogas) are available. No leaded petrol (lead substitute petrol available as 'super' 98 octane). Petrol in a can permitted but it is forbidden aboard ferries. Credit cards accepted at most filling stations; check with your card issuer for use in the Netherlands before travel.

Lights
The use of dipped headlights during the day is recommended. At night it is prohibited to drive with only sidelights.

Motorcycles
The use of dipped headlights during the day is recommended. The wearing of crash helmets is compulsory for all motorcycles which are capable of exceeding 25 km/h this is also applicable to drivers and passengers of open micro cars without seatbelts.

Motor insurance
Third-party compulsory.

Passengers/children in cars
Children up to the age of 18 and less than 1.35m in height cannot travel as a front or rear seat passenger unless using a suitable restraint system adapted to their size. Suitable child restraint systems must meet the safety approval of ECE 44/03 or 44/04. If the vehicle is not fitted with rear seat belts children under 3 are not permitted to travel in the vehicle. Children under 3 are permitted to travel in the front seats if using a rear facing child seat with the airbag deactivated (if fitted). If the vehicle's front seats are not fitted with seat belts, only passengers measuring 1.35m or more may travel in the front seat.

Seat belts
Compulsory for front and rear seat occupants to wear seat belts, if fitted.

Speed limits
Standard legal limits, which may be varied by signs

Private vehicles without trailers	
Built-up areas	50km/h
Outside built-up areas	80km/h or 100 km/h
Motorways	120km/h
Private vehicles with trailer or camper van under 3.5t	
Built-up areas	50km/h
Motorways	90km/h
Main roads	90km/h
Other roads	80km/h
Private vehicles with trailer or camper van over 3.5t	
Built-up areas	50km/h
Motorways	80km/h
Main roads	80km/h
Other roads	80km/h

No minimum speed on motorways.

Other rules/requirements in the Netherlands
Warning triangle or hazard warning lights must be used in case of accident or breakdown (recommended that warning triangle always be carried).

Buses have right of way when leaving bus stops in built-up areas.

Trams have right of way except when crossing a priority road. Beware of large numbers of cyclists and skaters.

Spiked tyres are prohibited.

The use of a radar detector is prohibited, if a person is caught using such a device by the police the radar detector will be confiscated and you will be fined 250.

Horns should not be used at night and only used in moderation during the day. Parking discs can be obtained from local stores.

Tolls Vignette Currency Euro (€)	Car	Car Towing Caravan/Trailer
Bridges and Tunnels		
Kil Tunnel	€5.00	€5.00
Westerschelde Tunnel	€4.80	€7.15

NORTH

AMEN DRENTHE

Vakantiepark Diana Heide

53 Amen, 9446

0592 389297 0592 389432

e-mail: info@dianaheide.nl

web: www.dianaheide.nl

An ideal site for relaxation, set away from traffic among forest and heathland.

dir: *E35 from Assen, through Amen towards Hooghalen.*

Open: Apr-Oct **Site:** 30HEC **For hire:** **Facilities:** Wi-fi (charged) Kids' Club Play Area **Services:** **Leisure:** L P **Off-site:** R

ANNEN DRENTHE

Hondsrug

Annerweg 3, 9463

0592 271292 0592 271440

e-mail: info@hondsrug.nl

web: www.hondsrug.nl

A family site in a pleasant rural setting with good recreational facilities.

dir: *On N34 SE of Annen.*

GPS: 53.0361, 6.7392

Open: Apr-1 Oct **Site:** 18HEC **For hire:** **Facilities:** Wi-fi (charged) Kids' Club **Services:** **Leisure:** P

ASSEN DRENTHE

Vakantiepark Witterzomer

Witterzomer 7, 9405

0592 393535 0592 393530

e-mail: info@witterzomer.nl

web: www.witterzomer.nl

A large site with internal asphalt roads, lying in mixed woodland near a nature reserve. Separate sections for dog owners. Individual washing facilities for disabled people.

dir: *Off A28.*

Open: All Year. **Site:** 75HEC **For hire:** **Prices:** 18-26 Mobile home hire 225-725 **Facilities:** Wi-fi (charged) **Services:** **Leisure:** L P

BERGUM FRIESLAND

Bergumermeer

Solcamastr 30, 9262

0511 461385 0511 463955

e-mail: info@bergumermeer.nl

web: www.bergumermeer.nl

Pleasant wooded surroundings with good recreational facilities, close to the marina on Bergumermeer. Kids' club available in July to August.

dir: *N355 onto N356 S, exit E to Sumar towards Oostermeer.*

Open: 27 Mar-Oct **Site:** 29HEC **For hire:** **Facilities:** Wi-fi (charged) Kids' Club **Services:** **Leisure:** L P

BORGER DRENTHE

Vakantiepark Hunzedal

De Drift 3, 9531

0599 234698 0599 235183

e-mail: info@hunzedal.nl

web: www.vakantiegevoel.nl

The site is clean, well-kept and lies north east of the village.

dir: *Off road towards Buinen, over Buinen-Schoondoord canal, 200m E turn S for 1km.*

Open: 29 Mar-1 Nov **Site:** 30HEC **For hire:** **Facilities:** **Services:** **Leisure:** L P

DIEVER DRENTHE

Hoeve aan den Weg

Bosweg 12, 8439

0521 387269 0521 387413

e-mail: camping@hoeveaandenweg.nl

web: www.hoeveaandenweg.nl

Pleasant wooded surroundings with good recreational facilities.

dir: *Off A32, E of Steenwijk.*

Open: Apr-Oct **Site:** 9HEC **For hire:** **Facilities:** **Services:** **Leisure:** P

DWINGELOO DRENTHE

Noordster

Noordster 105, 7991

0521 597238 0521 597589

e-mail: noordster@rcn.nl

web: www.rcn.nl

A large family site with static and touring pitches, surrounded by woodland.

dir: *3km S on E35.*

Open: All Year. **Site:** 42HEC **For hire:** **Prices:** 20.80-28.30 Mobile home hire 240-640 **Facilities:** **Services:** **Leisure:** P

NETHERLANDS

EERNEWOUDE — FRIESLAND

It Wiid

Kooidijk 10, 9264
0511 539223 0511 539335
e-mail: info@wiid.nl
web: www.wiid.nl

In the centre of a national park, with many islands and waterways. Pitches are available by the water or more sheltered. Kids' club in high season. Certain breeds of dog may be restricted. Boats can be hired.

Open: Apr-Sep **Site:** 28HEC **For hire:** **Prices:** 28.45-36.10 Mobile home hire 250-500 **Facilities:** Wi-fi (charged) Kids' Club Play Area **Services:** **Leisure:** L P

FRANEKER — FRIESLAND

Bloemketerp

Burg J Dykstraweg 3, 8801
0517 395099 0517 395150
e-mail: info@bloemketerp.nl
web: www.bloemketerp.nl

Set in a well-equipped leisure centre near the historic city centre of Franeker.

Open: All Year. **Site:** 5HEC **For hire:** **Facilities:** **Services:** **Off-site:** L P R S

GRONINGEN — GRONINGEN

Stadspark

Campinglaan 6, 9727
050 5251624 050 5250099
e-mail: info@campingstadspark.nl
web: www.campingstadspark.nl

A well-kept site on patches of grass between rows of bushes and groups of pine and deciduous trees. Some of its pitches are naturally screened.

dir: *From SW outskirts of town towards Peize & Roden.*

Open: 15 Mar-15 Oct **Site:** 6HEC **For hire:** **Facilities:** **Services:** **Off-site:** L P

HARLINGEN — FRIESLAND

Camping De Zeehoeve

8862
0517 413465 0517 416971
e-mail: info@zeehoeve.nl
web: www.zeehoeve.nl

A well-kept meadowland site divided into large sections by rows of bushes.

dir: *1km S of Harlingen near a dyke.*

Open: Apr-Sep **Site:** 10HEC **For hire:** **Prices:** 21.50 **Facilities:** Wi-fi (charged) Kids' Club **Services:** **Leisure:** S **Off-site:**

HEE (ISLAND OF TERSCHELLING) — FRIESLAND

Camping de Kooi

Heester Kooiweg 20, 8882
0562 442743 0562 442835
e-mail: info@campingdekooi.nl
web: www.campingdekooi.nl

Quiet and spacious site by a lake and surrounded by woodland.

dir: *5km from harbour.*

GPS: 53.3814, 5.2563

Open: 15 Apr-21 Sep **Site:** 8.5HEC **For hire:** **Prices:** 20.60-23.60 **Facilities:** **Services:** **Leisure:** L **Off-site:** P S

HINDELOOPEN — FRIESLAND

Hindeloopen

Westerdijk 9, 8713
0514 521452 0514 523221
e-mail: info@campinghindeloopen.nl
web: www.campinghindeloopen.nl

A peaceful site on the Ijsselmeer with fishing and water sports.

dir: *Via N359.*

Open: Apr-Oct **Site:** 16HEC **Prices:** 16.50-23.50 **Facilities:** Wi-fi Kids' Club Play Area **Services:** **Leisure:** L

KOUDUM — FRIESLAND

De Kuilart

Kuilart 1, 8723
0514 522221 0514 523010
e-mail: info@kuilart.nl
web: www.kuilart.nl

A camping and water-sports centre on the shores of De Fluessen lake.

dir: *Via N359.*

Open: All Year. **Site:** 37HEC **For hire:** **Facilities:** **Services:** **Leisure:** L P **Off-site:** S

LAUWERSOOG — GRONINGEN

Lauwersoog

Strandweg 5, 9976
0519 349133 0519 349195
e-mail: info@lauwersoog.nl
web: www.lauwersoog.nl

A pleasant location on the shores of Lauwersmeer. A good excursion centre with water sports.

Open: All Year. **Site:** 35HEC **For hire:** **Facilities:** **Services:** **Leisure:** L S

MAKKUM — FRIESLAND

Holle Poarte

Holle Poarte 2, 8754
0515 231344 0515 231339
e-mail: info@hollepoarte.nl
web: www.hollepoarte.nl

A modern site with water sports on the Ijsselmeer.

Open: All Year. **Site:** 32HEC **For hire:** **Facilities:** **Services:** **Leisure:** L

OPENDE — FRIESLAND

Strandheem

Parkweg 2, 9865
0594 659555 0594 658592
e-mail: info@strandheem.nl
web: www.strandheem.nl

A family site next to a large lake with sandy beach. Modern sanitary blocks and a variety of recreational facilities.

dir: *A7/E22 exit 31.*

Open: Apr-1 Oct **Site:** 15HEC **For hire:** **Prices:** 17.50-25.50 Mobile home hire 175-700 **Facilities:** Wi-fi Kids' Club Play Area **Services:** **Leisure:** L P

RUINEN — DRENTHE

Wiltzangh

Witteveen 2, 7963
0522 471227 0522 472178
e-mail: info@dewiltzangh-ruinen.nl
web: www.dewiltzangh.com

Set in the middle of a coniferous and deciduous forest, and within the grounds of a big holiday village.

dir: *From Ruinen towards Ansen, 3km turn N.*

Open: Apr-Oct **Site:** 13HEC **For hire:** **Facilities:** **Services:** **Leisure:** P

TERMUNTERZIJL — GRONINGEN

Zeestrand Eems-Dollard

Schepperbuurt 4a, 9948
0596 601443 0596 601209
e-mail: campingzeestrand@online.nl
web: www.campingzeestrand.nl

Overlooking Wadden See with views of Germany, and close to a beach. Family site with children's activities.

dir: *A7 exit 45 for Delfzijl, site signed.*

Open: Apr-1 Nov **Site:** 6.5HEC **For hire:** **Prices:** 17.80 Mobile home hire 200-500 **Facilities:** Wi-fi (charged) Kids' Club Play Area **Services:** **Leisure:** L P R S **Off-site:**

WEDDE — GRONINGEN

Wedderbergen

Molenweg 2, 9698
0597 561673
e-mail: info@wedderbergen.nl
web: www.wedderbergen.nl

Meadowland site divided by deciduous trees and hedges.

dir: *From E outskirts of village onto narrow asphalt road N, 3.2km onto Spanjaardsweg & Molenweg to site.*

GPS: 53.0861, 7.0819

Open: Apr-Sep **Site:** 40HEC **For hire:** **Prices:** 22-29.50 Mobile home hire 250-545 **Facilities:** Wi-fi (charged) Kids' Club Play Area **Services:** **Leisure:** L R **Off-site:** P

NETHERLANDS

CENTRAL

ALKMAAR NOORD-HOLLAND

Alkmaar

Bergerweg 201, 1817
☎ 072 5116924
e-mail: info@campingalkmaar.nl
web: www.campingalkmaar.nl

The site is well-kept and divided into many sections by rows of trees and bushes.

dir: *On NW outskirts of town, off Bergen road.*

Open: Mar-Oct **Site:** 3HEC **For hire:** **Facilities:** **Services:** **Off-site:** P

ALMERE FLEVOLAND

Camping Waterhout

Archerpad 6, 1234
☎ 036 5470632
e-mail: info@waterhout.nl
web: www.waterhout.nl

On the southern banks of Weerwater, spacious site laid out in a circular style. Numerous activities take place including sailing and a diving school.

dir: *A6 exit 4.*

GPS: 52.3569, 5.2250

Open: 31 Mar-14 Oct **Site:** 4.4HEC **For hire:** **Prices:** 20-24.50 **Facilities:** Wi-fi Kids' Club Play Area **Services:** **Leisure:** L **Off-site:** P

AMSTELVEEN NOORD-HOLLAND

Het Amsterdam Bos

Kleine Noorddijk 1, 1432
☎ 020 6416868 020 6402378
e-mail: info@campingamsterdam.com
web: www.campingamsterdam.com

The site is in a park-like setting in the Amsterdam wood. The camp is near the airport flight path and is subject to noise depending on the wind direction.

dir: *From The Hague along motorway, turn at N edge of airport towards Amstelveen, signs for Aalsmeer. From Utrecht, motorway exit Amstelveen for Aalsmeer, through Bovenkerk.*

GPS: 52.2942, 4.8231

Open: Apr-Oct **Site:** 6.8HEC **For hire:** **Prices:** 15-24.50 **Facilities:** Wi-fi **Services:** **Off-site:** L P R

AMSTERDAM NOORD-HOLLAND

Camping Zeeburg

Zuider Ijdijk 20, 1095
☎ 020 6944430 020 6946238
e-mail: info@campingzeeburg.nl
web: www.campingzeeburg.nl

On an island in the Ijmeer, 15 minutes from the city centre, with good facilities. Popular with backpackers and holidaymakers.

dir: *A10 exit S114 for Zeeburg.*

GPS: 52.3653, 4.9594

Open: All Year. **Site:** 4HEC **For hire:** **Prices:** 17-28 **Facilities:** Wi-fi **Services:** **Leisure:** L **Off-site:** P

Gaasper Camping Amsterdam

Loosdrechtdreef 7, 1108
☎ 020 6967326 020 6969369
web: www.gaaspercamping.nl

Situated on the edge of the beautiful Gaasperpark within easy reach, by metro, to the centre of Amsterdam.

dir: *A9 exit Weesp (S113), campsite signed.*

GPS: 52.3128, 4.9906

Open: 15 Mar-1 Nov **Site:** 5.5HEC **Prices:** 19.75-23.50 **Facilities:** Wi-fi Play Area **Services:** **Off-site:** L

ANDIJK NOORD-HOLLAND

Vakantiedorp Het Grootslag

Proefpolder 4, 1619
☎ 0228 592944 0228 592457
e-mail: info@andijkvakanties.nl
web: www.andijkvakanties.nl

A well-equipped site situated on the banks of lake Ijsselmeer. Individual bathrooms are allocated to some of the pitches and a range of recreational facilities are available, including pony rides for children.

dir: *A7 exit Hoorn-Noord/Enkhuizen/Lelystad, left for Andijk, signs for Het Grootslag & Dijkweg.*

GPS: 52.1925, 5.1925

Open: Apr-30 Oct **Site:** 40HEC **For hire:** **Prices:** 19-31 **Facilities:** Play Area **Services:** **Leisure:** L P

NETHERLANDS

APPELTERN — GELDERLAND

Het Groene Eiland

Lutenkampstr 2, 6629
0487 562130 0487 561540
e-mail: info@hetgroeneeiland.nl
web: www.hetgroeneeiland.nl

Recently refurbished and set in a water recreation park with plenty of sports facilities and sauna.

dir: *A15 exit Leeuwen & signed.*

Open: 20 Feb-9 Jan **Site:** 16HEC **For hire:** **Prices:** 15.28-19.10 Mobile home hire 321-610 **Facilities:** Wi-fi (charged) Kids' Club Play Area **Services:** **Leisure:** L R **Off-site:**

ARNHEM — GELDERLAND

Arnhem

Kemperbergerweg 771, 6816
026 4431600 026 4457705
e-mail: info@recreatieparkarnhem.nl
web: www.recreatieparkarnhem.nl

The site lies on grassland and is surrounded by trees.

dir: *NW of town & S of E36.*

Open: Apr-Oct **Site:** 36HEC **For hire:** **Facilities:** **Services:** **Leisure:** P

Droompark Hooge Veluwe

Koningsweg 14, 6816
026 4432272 026 4436809
e-mail: info@hoogeveluwe.nl
web: www.hoogeveluwe.nl

Situated in a pleasant natural park with good facilities.

dir: *E36 exit Apeldoorn, NW towards Hooge Veluwe.*

Open: 31 Mar-28 Oct **Site:** 18HEC **For hire:** **Prices:** 19-31 Mobile home hire 195-710 **Facilities:** Wi-fi (charged) Kids' Club Play Area **Services:** **Leisure:** P **Off-site:**

Warnsborn

Bakenbergseweg 257, 6816
026 4423469 026 4421095
e-mail: info@campingwarnsborn.nl
web: www.campingwarnsborn.nl

The site is surrounded by woodland and lies on slightly sloping meadowland. Near a zoo and open-air museum.

dir: *Near E36 NW of town towards Utrecht. 200m S of fuel station, continue W for 0.7km.*

Open: Apr-Oct **Site:** 3.5HEC **For hire:** **Prices:** 17.70-19.80 Mobile home hire 280-450 **Facilities:** Wi-fi (charged) **Services:** **Off-site:** P

BABBERICH — GELDERLAND

Rivo Torto

Beekseweg 8, 6909
0316 247332 0316 246628
e-mail: info@rivotorto.nl
web: www.rivotorto.nl

A riverside site with good recreational facilities.

dir: *3km W on E36.*

Open: 15 Mar-Oct **Site:** 8.5HEC **Facilities:** **Services:** **Off-site:**

BEERZE-OMMEN — OVERIJSSEL

Camping De Roos

Beerzerweg 10, 7736
0523 251234 0523 250958
e-mail: info@campingderoos.nl
web: www.campingderoos.nl

A small river tributary runs through the site with a sandy beach, and pitches are in natural surroundings. Cycle hire is available and many walking/cycle routes start from the campsite. There is a compulsory separate car park in July and August.

dir: *From Zwolle take A28 to Meppel exit Ommen then onto N340. In Ommen right over Vechterbridge towards Beerze, then left onto R103 for 7km, site on left 200m after sign for Beerze.*

GPS: 52.5107, 6.5151

Open: 6 Apr-1 Oct **Site:** 25HEC **For hire:** **Prices:** 16.70-19.70 **Facilities:** Wi-fi (charged) Play Area **Services:** **Leisure:** R

BERKHOUT — NOORD-HOLLAND

Westerkogge

Lysbeth Tysweg 7, 1647
0229 551208 0229 551390
e-mail: info@westerkogge.nl
web: www.westerkogge.nl

A fine location with sheltered pitches and a good range of recreational facilities.

dir: *A7 exit Hoorn-Berkhout or Berkhout-Avenhorn.*

Open: Apr-Oct **Site:** 11HEC **For hire:** **Prices:** 15-25 Mobile home hire 250-400 **Facilities:** Wi-fi (charged) **Services:** **Leisure:** P **Off-site:** L S

NETHERLANDS

BIDDINGHUIZEN FLEVOLAND

Riviera Park

Spijkweg 15, 8256
☎ 0321 331344 🖷 0321 331402
e-mail: info@riviera.nl
web: www.riviera.nl

Grassland site surrounded by shrubs near a deciduous forest.

dir: *On Polder beside Veluwemeer, 5km S of Biddinghuizen turn left.*

Open: Apr-30 Oct **Site:** 60HEC **For hire:** **Facilities:** **Services:** **Leisure:** L P

BILTHOVEN UTRECHT

Bospark Bilthoven

Burg v.d Borchlaan 7, 3722
☎ 030 2286777 🖷 030 2293888
e-mail: info@bosparkbilthoven.nl
web: www.bosparkbilthoven.nl

Family site in wooded surroundings with asphalt drives.

dir: *Signed from town centre.*

Open: Apr-Oct **Site:** 20HEC **For hire:** **Facilities:** **Services:** **Leisure:** P **Off-site:**

BLOKZIJL OVERIJSSEL

Tussen de Diepen

Duinigermeerweg 1A, 8356
☎ 0527 291565 🖷 0527 292203
e-mail: camping@tussendediepen.nl
web: www.tussendediepen.nl

Secluded site surrounded by water. Fishing, water sports and sailing.

Open: Apr-Oct **Site:** 5.2HEC **For hire:** **Facilities:** **Services:** **Leisure:** L R **Off-site:** P

BUURSE OVERIJSSEL

't Hazenbos

Oude Buurserdijk 1, 7481
☎ 053 5696338
e-mail: info@hazenbos.nl
web: www.hazenbos.nl

On several meadows, partially surrounded by trees.

dir: *7km from German border.*

Open: 15 Mar-Oct **Site:** 6HEC **Prices:** 13.45-15.60 **Facilities:** Play Area **Services:** **Off-site:** L

CALLANTSOOG NOORD-HOLLAND

Recreatiecentrum de Nollen

Westerweg 8, 1759
☎ 0224 581281 🖷 0224 582098
e-mail: info@denollen.nl
web: www.denollen.nl

A modern family site with plenty of facilities, less than 1.9km from the beach.

dir: *E of town towards N9.*

Open: 31 Mar-28 Oct **Site:** 9HEC **For hire:** **Prices:** 16.36-32.86 Mobile home hire 300-650 **Facilities:** Wi-fi (charged) Kids' Club Play Area **Services:** **Off-site:** P S

Tempelhof

Westerweg 2, 1759
☎ 0224 581522 🖷 0224 582133
e-mail: info@tempelhof.nl
web: www.tempelhof.nl

Well-equipped site on level meadowland.

dir: *N9 5km W.*

GPS: 52.8472, 4.7153

Open: All Year. **Site:** 12.7HEC **For hire:** **Prices:** 17-37 Mobile home hire 385-609 **Facilities:** Wi-fi (charged) Kids' Club Play Area **Services:** **Leisure:** P **Off-site:** S

COCKSDORP, DE (ISLAND OF TEXEL) NOORD-HOLLAND

Vakantiepark De Krim

Roggeslootweg 6, 1795
☎ 0222 390112 🖷 0222 390123
e-mail: info@krim.nl
web: www.krim.nl

Large site close to the beach and sand dunes. Pitches vary in size and amenities, in large and small fields. Extensive leisure facilities include outdoor and indoor swimming pools, mini-golf and cycle hire. Kids' club available in holiday season.

dir: *Den Helder ferry, situated in the north of the island.*

Open: All Year. **Site:** 32HEC **For hire:** **Prices:** 26-46 Mobile home hire 260-1230 **Facilities:** Wi-fi (charged) Kids' Club Play Area **Services:** **Leisure:** P **Off-site:** S

DENEKAMP — OVERIJSSEL

Papillon

Kanaalweg 30, 7591
05413 51670 05413 55217
e-mail: info@depapillon.nl
web: www.depapillon.nl

Mostly a chalet site on meadowland in a coniferous and deciduous forest, 2km north of Denekamp. There are a few naturally screened pitches.

dir: *Off E72 towards Nordhorn (Germany) 300m N of sign for Almelo-Nordhorn canal, continue NE 1.5km.*

Open: Apr-1 Oct **Site:** 16.5HEC **For hire:** **Facilities:** Wi-fi Kids' Club Play Area **Services:** **Leisure:** L P

DIEPENHEIM — OVERIJSSEL

Molnhofte

Nyhofweg 5, 7478
0547 351514 0547 351641
e-mail: info@molnhofte.nl
web: www.molnhofte.nl

A family site in a rural setting with modern bungalows for hire.

dir: *E of town off N824.*

Open: All Year. **Site:** 6HEC **For hire:** **Prices:** 15.50-20.50 **Facilities:** Wi-fi (charged) **Services:** **Leisure:** P

DOETINCHEM — GELDERLAND

Wrange

Rekhemseweg 144, 7004
0314 324852 0314 378470
e-mail: info@dewrange.nl
web: www.dewrange.nl

On the eastern outskirts of the town, set in meadowland and surrounded by bushes and deciduous trees.

dir: *200m E of link road between roads to Varsseveld & Terborg.*

Open: All Year. **Site:** 12HEC **For hire:** **Facilities:** **Services:** **Leisure:** P

DOORN — UTRECHT

Het Grote Bos

Hydeparklaan 24, 3941
0343 513644 0343 512324
e-mail: het-grote-bos@rcn.nl
web: www.rcn.nl

Well laid-out site on wooded grassland. Varied leisure activities for children and adults.

dir: *1km NW of Doorn.*

Open: All Year. **Site:** 80HEC **For hire:** **Facilities:** **Services:** **Leisure:** P

EDAM — NOORD-HOLLAND

Strandbad-Edam

Zeevangszeedijk 7a, 1135
0299 371994 0299 371510
e-mail: info@campingstrandbad.nl
web: www.campingstrandbad.nl

A friendly family site on Ijssel Lake with plenty of facilities and close to the historical town of Edam.

dir: *20km from Amsterdam. N247 exit signed Edam North.*

Open: Apr-Sep **Site:** 5HEC **For hire:** **Prices:** 17.70-19.95 **Facilities:** Wi-fi (charged) Play Area **Services:** **Leisure:** L **Off-site:** P

EERBEEK — GELDERLAND

Landal Greenparks Coldenhove

Boshoffweg 6, 6961
0313 659101 0313 654776
e-mail: coldenhove@landal.nl
web: www.landal.com

Set in woodland.

dir: *From Apeldoorn-Dieren road 2km SW, then NW for 1km.*

Open: 23 Mar-5 Nov **Site:** 74HEC **For hire:** **Facilities:** Kids' Club Play Area **Services:** **Leisure:** P

Robertsoord

Doonweg 4, 6961
0313 651346 0313 655751
e-mail: info@robertsoord.nl
web: www.robertsoord.nl

Wooded location with good recreational facilities.

dir: *1km SE A50 exit Loenen/Eerbeek.*

Open: Apr-Oct **Site:** 2.5HEC **For hire:** **Facilities:** Wi-fi **Services:** **Off-site:** P

ENSCHEDE OVERIJSSEL

De Twentse Es

Keppelerdijk 200, 7534
☎ 053 4611372 053 4618558
e-mail: info@twentse-es.nl
web: www.twentse-es.nl

Wooded location with good recreational facilities.

dir: *Signed on A35.*

Open: All Year. **Site:** 10HEC **For hire:** **Prices:** 26.50 **Facilities:** Wi-fi Kids' Club Play Area **Services:** **Leisure:** P

ERMELO GELDERLAND

Haeghehorst

Fazantlaan 4, 3852
☎ 0341 553185 0341 562751
e-mail: info@haeghehorst.nl
web: www.haeghehorst.nl

Well-equipped site in pleasant wooded surroundings.

dir: *A28 towards Amersfoort, onto N303.*

Open: All Year. **Site:** 10HEC **For hire:** **Facilities:** **Services:** **Leisure:** P

GROOTE KEETEN NOORD-HOLLAND

Callassande

Voorweg 5A, 1759
☎ 0224 581663 0224 582588
e-mail: info@callassande.nl
web: www.callassande.nl

A large site with fine facilities close to the sea.

Open: Apr-Oct **Site:** 12HEC **For hire:** **Facilities:** Wi-fi (charged) **Services:** **Leisure:** P **Off-site:** S

HAAKSBERGEN OVERIJSSEL

't Stien'n Boer

Scholtenhagenweg 42, 7481
☎ 053 5722610 053 5729394
e-mail: info@stien-nboer.nl
web: www.stien-nboer.nl

A family site with good recreational facilities, including indoor swimming pool with separate pool for children, near the town. Ideal for cycling and walking.

Open: Apr-Oct **Site:** 10.5HEC **For hire:** **Prices:** 13-21.50 Mobile home hire 229-483 **Facilities:** Wi-fi (charged) Kids' Club Play Area **Services:** **Leisure:** P **Off-site:** L

HALFWEG NOORD-HOLLAND

Droompark Spaarnwoude

Zuiderweg 2, 1165
☎ 020 4972796 020 4975887
e-mail: info@droomparkspaarnwoude.nl
web: www.droomparkspaarnwoude.nl

Grassy site on several levels subdivided by trees, hedges and shrubs. Separate section for young campers and hiker cabins are rentable. Kids' club available in school holidays.

dir: *A5 exit Spaarnwoude, site signed.*

Open: Apr-Oct **Site:** 13HEC **For hire:** **Facilities:** Wi-fi (charged) Kids' Club Play Area **Services:** **Leisure:** L **Off-site:** P

HATTEM GELDERLAND

Molecaten Park de Leemkule

Leemkuilen 6, 8051
☎ 038 4441945 038 4446280
e-mail: info@leemkule.nl
web: www.leemkule.nl

The holiday centre is in one of the largest nature reserves in the country. Kids' club available during Dutch school holidays.

dir: *2.5km SW.*

Open: Apr-Oct **Site:** 16HEC **For hire:** **Prices:** 18-22.50 Mobile home hire 398-708 **Facilities:** Wi-fi (charged) Kids' Club **Services:** **Leisure:** P **Off-site:**

HEILOO NOORD-HOLLAND

Heiloo

De Omloop 24, 1852
☎ 072 5355555 072 5355551
e-mail: info@campingheiloo.nl
web: www.campingheiloo.nl

One of the best sites in the area. It is divided into many large squares by hedges.

Open: Apr-Oct **Site:** 4HEC **For hire:** **Facilities:** Wi-fi **Services:** **Off-site:** L P

HELDER, DEN — NOORD-HOLLAND

Donkere Duinen

Jan Verfailleweg 616, 1783
0223 614731
e-mail: info@donkereduinen.nl
web: www.donkereduinen.nl
A quiet, pleasant site with good facilities.
dir: *Signs for Nieuw-Den Helder Strand, 0.8km towards beach.*
Open: 23 Apr-30 Aug **Site:** 7HEC **Facilities:** **Services:** **Leisure:** S **Off-site:** P

't Noorder Sandt

Noorder Sandt 2, Julianadorp aan Zee, 1787
0223 641266 0223 645600
e-mail: noordersandt@ardoer.com
web: www.ardoer.com/noordersandt
A flat, well-maintained site on meadowland, with good sanitary blocks. Kids' club during July and August.
dir: *Access from Den Helder to Callantsoog coast road.*
Open: 26 Mar-26 Oct **Site:** 11HEC **For hire:** **Prices:** 12.50-39 **Facilities:** Wi-fi Kids' Club Play Area **Services:** **Leisure:** P **Off-site:** S

HENGELO — OVERIJSSEL

Zwaaikom

Kettingbrugweg 60, 7552
074 2916560 074 2916785
e-mail: smink_zwaaikom@planet.nl
web: www.dezwaaikom.tk
A family site on the Twente canal, with good facilities.
dir: *SE towards Enschede between canal & road.*
Open: 15 Apr-15 Sep **Site:** 4HEC **Prices:** 14.80 **Facilities:** Wi-fi (charged) **Services:** **Leisure:** P

HEUMEN — GELDERLAND

Camping Heumens Bos

Vosseneindseweg 46, 6582
024 3581481 024 3583862
e-mail: info@heumensbos.nl
web: www.heumensbos.nl
One of the best sites in the area with modern facilities and spacious pitches.
dir: *A73 exit 3 & follow signs.*
Open: All Year. **Site:** 16HEC **For hire:** **Prices:** 17-32 Mobile home hire 280-460 **Facilities:** Wi-fi (charged) Kids' Club Play Area **Services:** **Leisure:** P **Off-site:** R

HOENDERLOO — GELDERLAND

Pampel

Woeste Hoefweg 35, 7351
055 3781760 055 3781992
e-mail: info@pampel.nl
web: www.pampel.nl
A most attractive site in pleasant wooded surroundings with good facilities for families, including a heated indoor pool, indoor play area and kids' club in high season.
Open: All Year. **Site:** 14.5HEC **For hire:** **Prices:** 19-27.50 **Facilities:** Wi-fi (charged) Kids' Club Play Area **Services:** **Leisure:** P **Off-site:**

HOORN, DEN (ISLAND OF TEXEL) — NOORD-HOLLAND

Texelcamping Loodsmansduin

Rommelpot 19, 1797
0222 317208 0222 317018
e-mail: info@texelcampings.nl
web: www.texelcampings.nl
Close to Den Hoorn in the middle of the National Park of the Dunes of Texel. A section of the site is reserved for naturists and there is a naturist beach 1.5km away.
dir: *N501 follow signs for Den Hoorn, then small green signs.*
Open: All Year. **Site:** 38HEC **For hire:** **Prices:** 14.50-28.20 **Facilities:** Wi-fi (charged) Kids' Club Play Area **Services:** **Leisure:** P **Off-site:** S

KESTEREN — GELDERLAND

Camping Betuwe

Hogedijkseweg 40, 4041
0488 481477 0488 482599
e-mail: info@campingbetuwe.nl
web: www.campingbetuwe.nl
On level meadowland surrounded by bushy hedges and divided into individual pitches. 100 metres from private beach and pool.
dir: *2km N of village, turn W off main Rhenen-Kesteren road, continue 2.7km.*
Open: All Year. **Site:** 30HEC **Facilities:** **Services:** **Leisure:** L

KOOG, DE (ISLAND OF TEXEL) **NOORD-HOLLAND**

Kogerstrand

Badweg 33, 1796
☎ 0222 327806 🖹 0222 317018
e-mail: info@texelcampings.nl
web: www.texelcampings.nl

Located in the National Park of the Dunes of Texel, next to the sea. There is a separate area for young people aged 15-25 and dogs are only allowed on the southside. There is a restricted traffic policy and cars are parked in a central car park.

dir: *From ferry proceed to De Koog, continue along road (Nikadel). Pass Catholic church, continue along Badweg to end of road. Located behind the big hill/dune.*

Open: Apr-Oct **Site:** 52HEC **For hire:** **Prices:** 17-26.20 **Facilities:** Wi-fi (charged) Kids' Club Play Area **Services:** **Leisure:** S **Off-site:** P

Om de Noord

Boodtlaan 80, 1796
☎ 0222 317208 🖹 0222 317018
e-mail: info@texelcampings.nl
web: www.texelcampings.nl

Site with spacious pitches located close to woodlands, dunes and the beach.

dir: *From ferry to De Koog, continue along road (Nikadel), pass Catholic church on right, turn right at junct with Boodtlaan, continue to football pitch, driveway on left.*

Open: Apr-Oct **Site:** 3.3HEC **Prices:** 20.70-39.50 **Facilities:** Wi-fi (charged) Kids' Club Play Area **Services:** **Off-site:** P S

Shelter

Boodtlaan 43, 1796
☎ 0222 317208 🖹 0222 317018
e-mail: info@texelcampings.nl
web: www.texelcampings.nl

Small family camping site close to a forest, the beach and national parks.

dir: *N501 to De Koog. Follow road to Motel Texel, turn left, 500m on left.*

Open: All Year. **Site:** 1.1HEC **For hire:** **Prices:** 20.70-39.50 **Facilities:** Wi-fi (charged) Kids' Club Play Area **Services:** **Off-site:** P S

LATHUM **GELDERLAND**

De Mars

Marsweg 6, 6988
☎ 0313 631131
e-mail: info@campingdemars.nl
web: www.campingdemars.nl

Divided into pitches on level meadowland beside a dammed tributary of River Ijssel.

dir: *Off Arnhem-Doesburg road N of village & W for 1.7km.*

Open: Apr-Oct **Site:** 10HEC **Prices:** 16.60-18.60 **Facilities:** **Services:** **Leisure:** L

LUTTENBERG **OVERIJSSEL**

Luttenberg

Heuvelweg 9, 8105
☎ 0572 301405 🖹 0572 301757
e-mail: info@luttenberg.nl
web: www.luttenberg.nl

A large holiday park with spacious, well-defined pitches separated by bushes. Variety of recreational facilities.

Open: Apr-Sep **Site:** 9HEC **For hire:** **Prices:** 19.50 **Facilities:** Wi-fi (charged) Kids' Club Play Area **Services:** **Leisure:** P

MAARN **UTRECHT**

Laag-Kanje

Laan van Laag-Kanje 1, 3951
☎ 0343 441348 🖹 0343 443295
e-mail: allurepark@laagkanje.nl
web: www.laagkanje.nl

Pleasant site with good facilities situated 0.5km from the lake.

dir: *N of A12 & S of N224, 2km NE.*

Open: Apr-Sep **Site:** 28HEC **Facilities:** Wi-fi (charged) Kids' Club **Services:** **Off-site:** L

MIJNDEN **UTRECHT**

Recreatiecentrum Mijnden

Bloklaan 22a, 1231
☎ 0294 233165 🖹 0294 233402
e-mail: info@mijnden.nl
web: www.mijnden.nl

Situated on Loosdrechtse Plassen lake with good sports facilities. Kids' club available during high season.

dir: *A2 exit Hilversum, after bridge turn right, through Loenen & left.*

Open: 15 Apr-25 Sep **Site:** 25HEC **Prices:** 21-26 **Facilities:** Wi-fi (charged) Kids' Club **Services:** **Leisure:** L **Off-site:** P

NETHERLANDS

NOORD SCHARWOUDE NOORD-HOLLAND

Molengroet Droompark

Molengroet 1, 1723

☎ 0226 393444 📠 0226 391426

e-mail: info@molengroet.nl

web: www.molengroet.nl

Site with modern facilities within easy reach of the beach and the Geestmerambacht water park. Kids' club available in high season.

dir: *Signed on N245.*

Open: Apr-Oct **Site:** 11HEC **For hire:** **Prices:** 9.50-30 **Facilities:** Wi-fi (charged) Kids' Club **Services:** **Leisure:** L P **Off-site:** S

NUNSPEET GELDERLAND

Vossenberg

Groenlaantje 25, 8071

☎ 0341 252458 📠 0341 279500

e-mail: info@vrijetijdspark.nl

web: www.campingdevossenberg.nl

Natural site within Veluwe forest and close to Nunspeet. Entertainment programmes for children are organised, in season.

Open: Apr-1 Nov **Site:** 3.6HEC **For hire:** **Facilities:** **Services:** **Off-site:** L P

OTTERLO GELDERLAND

Camping de Zanding

The Camping and Caravanning Club — The Friendly Club

6731

☎ 0318 596111

e-mail: info@droomparkdezanding.nl

web: www.droomparkdezanding.nl

Spacious pitches in a lake side setting. Water sports and activities are available.

C&CC Report *This very well equipped campsite is ideally situated for exploring this fascinating region of the Netherlands – for history buffs the sites of the battle of Arnhem, the subject of the film* A Bridge Too Far, *are a must, whilst nature lovers can visit Arnhem's extensive Zoo or the Hoge Veluwe National Park, adjacent to the campsite. Children will love the wide range of activities on site during the day, and the whole family can choose between the restaurant/pizzeria or the Dutch Pancake House for a bite to eat.*

GPS: 52.0929, 5.7776

Open: 31 Mar-28 Oct **Facilities:** Wi-fi Play Area **Services:** **Leisure:** L

PUTTEN GELDERLAND

Strandpark Putten

Strandboulevard 27, 3882

☎ 0341 361304 📠 0341 361210

Campsite is by a lake and has a private beach. Excellent facilities for windsurfing and yachting.

dir: *Off A28.*

Open: Apr-Oct **Site:** 8HEC **For hire:** **Facilities:** **Services:** **Leisure:** L **Off-site:** P

REUTUM OVERIJSSEL

De Molenhof

Kleijsenweg 7, 7667

☎ 0541 661165 📠 0541 662032

e-mail: info@demolenhof.nl

web: www.demolenhof.nl

A large family site in wooded surroundings with plenty of modern facilities.

dir: *Via A1 6km SW of Ootmarsum.*

Open: 4 Apr-27 Sep **Site:** 16HEC **For hire:** **Facilities:** **Services:** **Leisure:** P

RHENEN UTRECHT

Thymse Berg

Nieuwe Veenendaalseweg 229, 3911

☎ 0317 612384 📠 0317 618119

e-mail: allurepark@thijmseberg.nl

web: www.thijmseberg.nl

Family site with spacious pitches. Leisure facilities include a swimming and paddling pool and children's entertainment.

dir: *N of town.*

Open: Apr-Oct **Site:** 10HEC **For hire:** **Facilities:** Wi-fi Kids' Club Play Area **Services:** **Leisure:** P **Off-site:** L R

NETHERLANDS

ST MAARTENSZEE — NOORD-HOLLAND

St Maartenszee

Westerduinweg 30, 1753
0224 561401
e-mail: info@campingsintmaartenszee.nl
web: www.campingsintmaartenszee.nl

Completely surrounded and divided into pitches by hedges, lying on meadowland beside a wide belt of dunes.

dir: *Via N9 towards Den Helder, signed in village St Maartensvlotbrug.*

Open: 30 Mar-Sep **Site:** 5HEC **For hire:** **Prices:** 23-37 **Facilities:** Wi-fi (charged) Kids' Club **Services:** **Off-site:** L P S

STEENWIJK — OVERIJSSEL

Kom

Bultweg 25, 8346
0521 513736 0521 518736
e-mail: info@campingdekom.nl
web: www.campingdekom.nl

Split into two sections, lying near a country house, and surrounded by a beautiful oak forest.

dir: *Off Steenwijk-Frederiksoord road (NB easy to miss).*

Open: All Year. **Site:** 12.5HEC **For hire:** **Facilities:** **Services:** **Leisure:** P

UITDAM — NOORD-HOLLAND

Uitdam

Zeedijk 2, 1154
020 4031433 020 4033692
e-mail: info@campinguitdam.nl
web: www.campinguitdam.nl

A well-maintained site on the Markermeer adjoining the marina.

dir: *Via N247 Amsterdam-Monnickendam.*

Open: Mar-Oct **Site:** 21HEC **For hire:** **Facilities:** **Services:** **Leisure:** L

VOGELENZANG — NOORD-HOLLAND

Vogelenzang

Doodweg Tweede 17, 2114
023 5847014 023 5849249
e-mail: camping@vogelenzang.nl
web: www.vogelenzang.nl

Quiet, family site.

dir: *1km W.*

Open: Etr-15 Sep **Site:** 16HEC **Facilities:** Kids' Club Play Area **Services:** **Leisure:** P **Off-site:** S

WIJDENES — NOORD-HOLLAND

Het Hof

Zuideruitweg 64, 1608
0229 501435 0229 503244
e-mail: info@campinghethof.nl
web: www.campinghethof.nl

A series of fields in a sheltered position on the shore of the Ijsselmeer.

dir: *A7 exit 8 Hoorn, onto N506 for Enkhuizen, right to Wijdenes & signed.*

Open: 30 Mar-Sep **Site:** 3.9HEC **Facilities:** **Services:** **Leisure:** L P

WINTERSWIJK — GELDERLAND

Twee Bruggen

Meenkmolenweg 11, 7109
0543 565366 0543 565222
e-mail: info@detweebruggen.nl
web: www.detweebruggen.nl

A family site in pleasant wooded surroundings with modern facilities.

Open: All Year. **Site:** 34HEC **For hire:** **Prices:** 21-45.50 Mobile home hire 279-599 **Facilities:** Wi-fi (charged) Kids' Club Play Area **Services:** **Leisure:** L P

ZEIST — UTRECHT

Allurepark de Krakeling

Woudenbergseweg 17, 3707
030 6915374
e-mail: info@dekrakeling.nl
web: www.dekrakeling.nl

Relaxing, family site with varied pitches. An à la carte restaurant is available for meals or drinks.

dir: *Signed from A12 (Utrecht-Arnhem) exit Driebergen-Zeist.*

Open: Apr-Sep **Site:** **Prices:** 23.50 **Facilities:** Wi-fi Kids' Club Play Area **Services:** **Off-site:** L P

SOUTH

AFFERDEN — LIMBURG

Klein Canada

Dorpsstr 1, 5851
☎ 0485 531223 🖷 0485 532218
e-mail: info@kleincanada.nl
web: www.kleincanada.nl
Situated among heath and woodland close to the River Meuse.

Open: All Year. **Site:** 12.5HEC **For hire:** **Prices:** 19-33.50 Mobile home hire 210-560 **Facilities:** Wi-fi (charged) **Services:** **Leisure:** P

BAARLAND — ZEELAND

Comfort Camping Scheldeoord

Landingsweg 1, 4435
☎ 0113 639900 🖷 0113 639500
e-mail: info@scheldeoord.nl
web: www.scheldeoord.nl
A popular family site in a beautiful location by the River Westerschelde.

dir: *S of town on coast.*

Open: Apr-Oct **Site:** 16HEC **For hire:** **Facilities:** Wi-fi (charged) Kids' Club **Services:** **Leisure:** P S

BERG EN TERBLIJT — LIMBURG

Oriëntal

Rijksweg 6, 6325
☎ 043 6040075 🖷 043 6042912
e-mail: info@campingoriental.nl
web: www.campingoriental.nl
Quietly situated in an outstanding spot on the Mergelland, close to the city of Maastricht. The site sits concealed among the greenery of a former orchard.

dir: *On Maastricht-Valkenburg road, 3km from Maastricht.*

Open: Apr-Oct **Site:** 5.5HEC **For hire:** **Facilities:** **Services:** **Leisure:** P

BERGEYK — NOORD-BRABANT

Paal

De Paaldreef 14, 5571
☎ 0497 571977 🖷 0497 577164
e-mail: info@depaal.nl
web: www.depaal.nl
Site catering especially for families with young children.

dir: *A67 in direction of Antwerp exit 30 toward Bergeyk - signed.*

Open: Apr-Oct **Site:** 41HEC **For hire:** **Prices:** 31-49 **Facilities:** Wi-fi (charged) Kids' Club Play Area **Services:** **Leisure:** P **Off-site:** L

BOSSCHENHOOFD — NOORD-BRABANT

Langoed de Wildert

Pagnevaartdreef 3, 4744
☎ 0165 312582 🖷 0165 310941
web: www.landgoeddewildert.nl
Peaceful location in woodland.

dir: *A58 exit 21 to Bosschenhoofd, pass church on right, site 0.5km on left.*

Open: Apr-Sep **Site:** 15HEC **Prices:** 23 **Facilities:** **Services:** **Off-site:** P

BRESKENS — ZEELAND

Napoleon Hoeve

Zandertje 30, 4511
☎ 0117 383838 🖷 0117 383550
e-mail: info@napoleonhoeve.nl
web: www.napoleonhoeve.nl
A family site with access to the beach.

Open: All Year. **Site:** 13HEC **For hire:** **Facilities:** Wi-fi (charged) Play Area **Services:** **Leisure:** P S

Schoneveld

Schoneveld 1, 4511
☎ 0117 383220 🖷 0117 383650
e-mail: info@droomparkschoneveld.nl
web: www.beachparcschoneveld.nl
Large, sheltered pitches close to a wide, sandy beach. Leisure facilities include a heated indoor swimming pool, children's play area and bowling alley.

dir: *3km S at beach.*

Open: All Year. **Site:** 14HEC **For hire:** **Facilities:** **Services:** **Leisure:** P S

NETHERLANDS

BRIELLE ZUID-HOLLAND

Krabbeplaat

Oude Veerdam 4, 3231
☎ 0181 412363 🖷 0181 412093
e-mail: info@krabbeplaat.nl
web: www.krabbeplaat.com

On level ground scattered with trees and groups of bushes. Nearest site to the coast and ferries.

dir: *S of N15 on Braise Meer, signed.*

Open: Apr-Oct **Site:** 18HEC **For hire:** **Facilities:** **Services:** **Leisure:** L

BROEKHUIZENVORST LIMBURG

Kasteel Ooijen

Blitterswijkseweg 2, 5871
☎ 077 4631307 🖷 077 4632765
e-mail: info@kasteelooijen.nl
web: www.kasteelooijen.nl

Site with swimming pool complex and waterslides. Other leisure facilities include tennis courts.

dir: *Off A73.*

Open: Apr-Oct **Site:** 16HEC **For hire:** **Facilities:** **Services:** **Leisure:** P **Off-site:**

BROUWERSHAVEN ZEELAND

Osse

Blankersweg 4, 4318
☎ 0111 691513 🖷 0111 691058
e-mail: denosse@zeelandnet.nl
web: www.campingdenosse.nl

An attractive site with good water sports.

Open: Apr-6 Nov **Site:** 8.3HEC **For hire:** **Facilities:** Wi-fi (charged) Kids' Club Play Area **Services:** **Leisure:** P S **Off-site:** L

BURGH-HAAMSTEDE ZEELAND

Camping Ginsterveld

Maireweg 10, 4328
☎ 0111 651590 🖷 0111 653040
e-mail: info@ginsterveld.nl
web: www.ginsterveld.nl

A family holiday centre with well-defined pitches on level ground and plenty of recreational facilities.

dir: *NW of town, signed from R107.*

Open: Apr-Oct **Site:** 14HEC **Prices:** 19-36 **Facilities:** Wi-fi Kids' Club Play Area **Services:** **Leisure:** P **Off-site:** S

DELFT ZUID-HOLLAND

Delftse Hout

The Camping and Caravanning Club The Friendly Club

Korftlaan 5, 2616
☎ 015 2130040 🖷 015 2131293
e-mail: info@delftsehout.nl
web: www.delftsehout.nl

On a level meadow surrounded by woodland close to the lake. Kids' club available during school holidays.

C&CC Report *A great site for all ages wanting a well-placed, comfortable base to explore picturesque Delft, The Hague, Rotterdam, Amsterdam and the coastal resorts and other attractions of central Holland. Many destinations are accessible by public transport, including Delft city centre itself, but it's also a great area for the classic Dutch mode of transport – the bike.*

dir: *1.6km E of A13, signed.*

Open: Apr-1 Nov **Site:** 5.5HEC **For hire:** **Prices:** 24-30 Mobile home hire 295-895 **Facilities:** Wi-fi Kids' Club Play Area **Services:** **Leisure:** P **Off-site:** L

ECHT LIMBURG

Marisheem

Brugweg 89, 6102
☎ 0475 481458 🖷 0475 488018
e-mail: info@marisheem.nl
web: www.marisheem.nl

The site is well-kept and lies east of the village. There is a snack bar and a kids' club is available in high season.

dir: *From town towards Echterbosch & border, 2.2km turn left.*

GPS: 51.0921, 5.9112

Open: Mar-Oct **Site:** 12HEC **Prices:** 20.90-32.90 **Facilities:** Wi-fi (charged) Kids' Club **Services:** **Leisure:** P **Off-site:**

EERSEL NOORD-BRABANT

Ter Spegelt

Postelseweg 88, 5521
☎ 0497 512016 🖷 0497 514162
e-mail: info@terspegelt.nl
web: www.terspegelt.nl

A large family-orientated site with good recreational facilities.

dir: *A67 Venlo-Antwerp, follow signs for Eersel then Ter Spegelt.*

Open: Apr-30 Oct **Site:** 63HEC **For hire:** **Prices:** 21.50-65 **Facilities:** Wi-fi (charged) Kids' Club Play Area **Services:** **Leisure:** L P

GROEDE — ZEELAND

Groede

Zeeweg 1, 4503
0117 371384 0117 372277
e-mail: info@strandcampinggroede.nl
web: www.strandcampinggroede.nl
A large family site with a variety of leisure facilities and close to the beach.
Open: Apr-Oct **Site:** 20HEC **For hire:** **Prices:** 17.20-45.50 **Facilities:** Wi-fi (charged) Kids' Club Play Area **Services:** **Leisure:** S

HELLEVOETSLUIS — ZUID-HOLLAND

't Weergors

Zuiddyk 2, 3221
0181 312430 0181 311010
e-mail: weergors@pn.nl
web: www.weergors.nl
A pleasant, peaceful site on a level meadow close to the beach. A good overnight stopping place or holiday site. Kids' club available during summer holiday.
Open: Apr-Oct **Site:** 9.7HEC **For hire:** **Prices:** 23.20 Mobile home hire 350-550 **Facilities:** Wi-fi (charged) Kids' Club Play Area **Services:** **Leisure:** S **Off-site:** L P R

HERPEN — NOORD-BRABANT

Herperduin

Schaijkseweg 12, 5373
0486 411383 0486 416171
e-mail: info@herperduin.nl
web: www.herperduin.nl
Situated in extensive woodland.
Open: Apr-20 Oct **Site:** 7HEC **For hire:** **Facilities:** **Services:** **Leisure:** P

HOEK — ZEELAND

Braakman Holiday Park

Middenweg 1, 4542
0115 481730 0115 482077
e-mail: info@braakman.co.uk
web: www.braakman.co.uk
A large family site on the edge of extensive nature reserves. The pitches are shaded by woodland and there is direct access to Braakman lake. Plenty of recreational facilities.
dir: *4km W of town, signed from N61.*
Open: All Year. **Site:** 80HEC **For hire:** **Facilities:** **Services:** **Leisure:** L P

HOEK VAN HOLLAND — ZUID-HOLLAND

Hoek van Holland

Wierstr 100, 3151
0174 382550 0174 310210
e-mail: camping.hvh@hetnet.nl
web: www.campinghoekvanholland.nl
On grass, surrounded by bushes and paved drives.
dir: *From N, off E36 to beach.*
Open: 14 Mar-24 Oct **Site:** 5.5HEC **Facilities:** **Services:** **Off-site:** S

HOEVEN — NOORD-BRABANT

Molecaten Park Bosbad Hoeven

Oude Antwerpse Postbaan 81b, 4741
0165 502570 0165 504254
e-mail: info@bosbadhoeven.nl
web: www.bosbadhoeven.nl
Extensive site with modern facilities including a waterpark, indoor playground and pool.
dir: *A58 exit 20 St Willebrord, follow signs for Hoeven.*
Open: Apr-Oct **Site:** 35HEC **For hire:** **Prices:** 18-30 Mobile home hire 195-690 **Facilities:** Wi-fi (charged) Kids' Club Play Area **Services:** **Leisure:** P

KAMPERLAND — ZEELAND

Roompot

Mariapolderseweg 1, 4493
0113 374000 0113 374170
e-mail: info@roompot.nl
web: www.roompot.nl
A level, well-maintained site with a private beach.
dir: *Off Kamperland-Wissenkerke road & N for 0.5km.*
Open: All Year. **Site:** 33HEC **For hire:** **Facilities:** Wi-fi (charged) Kids' Club Play Area **Services:** **Leisure:** P S

KATWIJK AAN ZEE — ZUID-HOLLAND

Recreatiecentrum De Noordduinen

Campingweg 1, 2221
071 4025295 071 4033977
e-mail: info@noordduinen.nl
web: www.noordduinen.nl
Family site among dunes close to the sea.
dir: *W of A44 via Hoorneslaan.*
Open: All Year. **Site:** 11HEC **For hire:** **Facilities:** Wi-fi Kids' Club Play Area **Services:** **Leisure:** P S

NETHERLANDS

KORTGENE — ZEELAND

De Paardekreek

Havenweg 1, 4484
☎ 0113 302051 🖷 0113 302280
e-mail: paardekreek@ardoer.com
web: www.ardoer.com/paardekreek
A municipal site next to the Veerse Meer canal.
dir: *Off Zierikzee-Goes road at fuel station towards Kortgene, through village & continue SW.*
Open: Apr-Oct **Site:** 10HEC **For hire:** **Facilities:** **Services:** **Leisure:** L P

KOUDEKERKE — ZEELAND

Dishoek

Dishoek 2, 4371
☎ 0118 551348 🖷 0118 552990
e-mail: info@campingdishoek.nl
web: www.roompot.nl
Situated next to the beach, with organised activities for children and evening entertainment.
dir: *W on Vlissingen-Dishoek road.*
Open: 18 Mar-23 Oct **Site:** 6HEC **Facilities:** **Services:** **Off-site:** S

Duinzicht

Strandweg 7, 4371
☎ 0118 551397 🖷 0118 553222
e-mail: info@campingduinzicht.nl
web: www.campingduinzicht.nl
A small family site with good facilities.
dir: *1.5km SW of Koudekerke.*
Open: Apr-Oct **Site:** 6.5HEC **For hire:** **Facilities:** **Services:** **Off-site:** S

LAGE MIERDE — NOORD-BRABANT

Vakantiecentrum de Hertenwei

Wellenseind 7-9, 5094
☎ 013 5091295
e-mail: receptie@hertenwei.nl
web: www.hertenwei.nl
Pleasant wooded site with modern facilities. A kids' club is available during school holidays.
dir: *2km N on N269 (Tilburg-Reusel).*
GPS: 51.4203, 5.1422
Open: All Year. **Site:** 20HEC **For hire:** **Prices:** 16.40-27.50 Mobile home hire 275-540 **Facilities:** Wi-fi Kids' Club Play Area **Services:** **Leisure:** P

LUYKSGESTEL — NOORD-BRABANT

Zwarte Bergen

Zwarte Bergen Dreef 1, 5575
☎ 0497 541373 🖷 0497 542673
e-mail: info@zwartebergen.nl
web: www.zwartebergen.nl
Isolated and very quiet site in a pine forest.
dir: *From Eindhoven through Valkenswaard & Bergiejkl, signed.*
Open: 2 Apr-2 Oct **Site:** 25.5HEC **For hire:** **Facilities:** **Services:** **Leisure:** P

MAASBREE — LIMBURG

BreeBronne

Lange Heide 9, 5993
☎ 077 4652360 🖷 077 4652095
e-mail: info@breebronne.nl
web: www.breebronne.nl
A family site in quiet surroundings with good facilities.
dir: *On E3 just before Venlo, on German border.*
Open: Mar-Oct **Site:** 23HEC **For hire:** **Facilities:** Wi-fi Kids' Club Play Area **Services:** **Leisure:** L P **Off-site:** R

MIERLO — NOORD-BRABANT

Wolfsven

Patrijslaan 4, 5731
☎ 0492 661661 🖷 0492 663895
e-mail: info.wolfsven@rpholidays.nl
web: www.roompot.nl
Large site with wooded areas and several lakes. Asphalt drives.
Open: 3 Apr-1 Nov **Site:** 67HEC **For hire:** **Facilities:** **Services:** **Leisure:** L P **Off-site:**

NIEUWVLIET — ZEELAND

Pannenschuur

Zeedijk 19, 4504
☎ 0117 372300 🖷 0117 371415
e-mail: info@pannenschuur.nl
web: www.pannenschuur.nl
A modern site with good facilities. Close to the beach.
dir: *NW of town, signed.*
Open: All Year. **Site:** 14HEC **For hire:** **Facilities:** **Services:** **Leisure:** P S

NETHERLANDS

NOORDWELLE ZEELAND

Camping Agri-Nova

Kooijmansweg 8, 4326

☎ 0111 461304 0111 462726

e-mail: info@agricamping.nl

web: www.agricamping.nl

Situated close to the beach and dunes, spacious pitches in natural surroundings. Ideal for relaxing and cycling holidays.

dir: *N652.*

GPS: 51.7170, 3.7735

Open: 17 Mar-28 Oct **Site:** 5HEC **Prices:** 15-28 **Facilities:** Wi-fi (charged) **Services:** **Off-site:** L P S

NOORDWIJK ZUID-HOLLAND

Parc du Soleil

Kraaierslaan 7, 2204

☎ 0252 374225 0252 376450

e-mail: info@parcdusoleil.nl

web: www.parcdusoleil.nl

A pleasant location near the bulb fields and the sea.

dir: *Signed.*

Open: Apr-Nov **Site:** 5.5HEC **For hire:** **Facilities:** Play Area **Services:** **Leisure:** P **Off-site:** L S

Recreatiepark Noordwijkse Duinen

Kapelleboslaan 41, 2204

☎ 0252 372485 0252 340140

e-mail: info@noordwijkseduinen.nl

web: www.noordwijkseduinen.nl

A well-equipped family site in a wooded location 2km from the beach.

dir: *A44 - N206.*

Open: All Year. **Site:** 6HEC **For hire:** **Prices:** 15-30 Mobile home hire 275-695 **Facilities:** Wi-fi (charged) Kids' Club Play Area **Services:** **Leisure:** P **Off-site:** L S

OISTERWIJK NOORD-BRABANT

Reebok

Duinenweg 4, 5062

☎ 013 5282309 013 5217592

e-mail: info@dereebok.nl

web: www.dereebok.nl

Situated in a large pine forest within attractive surroundings with numerous small lakes. There is a kids' club available in high season.

dir: *SE of town.*

GPS: 51.5733, 5.2322

Open: All Year. **Site:** 8HEC **For hire:** **Facilities:** Wi-fi (charged) Kids' Club Play Area **Services:** **Off-site:** L P

OOSTERHOUT NOORD-BRABANT

Katjeskelder

Katjeskelder 1, 4904

☎ 0162 453539 0162 454090

e-mail: kkinfo@katjeskelder.nl

web: www.katjeskelder.nl

A large, modern family site with good sanitary and recreational facilities.

dir: *A27 exit 17 & signed.*

Open: All Year. **Site:** 25HEC **For hire:** **Facilities:** **Services:** **Leisure:** P **Off-site:**

OOSTKAPELLE ZEELAND

Dennenbos

Duinweg 64, 4356

☎ 0118 581310 0118 583773

e-mail: dennenbos@zeelandnet.nl

web: www.dennenbos.nl

A well-maintained family site in a wooded location, 0.5km from the beach.

Open: Mar-Nov **Site:** 3HEC **For hire:** **Facilities:** Kids' Club Play Area **Services:** **Leisure:** P S

NETHERLANDS

In de Bongerd

Brouwerijstr 13, 4356

0118 581510 0118 581510

e-mail: info@campingindebongerd.nl

web: www.campingindebongerd.nl

A well-kept family site, set in a meadow with hedges and apple trees. There are fine recreational facilities and the beach is within easy reach.

dir: *0.5km N.*

Open: 30 Mar-28 Oct **Site:** 7.4HEC **For hire:** **Facilities:** **Services:** **Leisure:** P S

Ons Buiten

Aagtekerkseweg 2a, 4356

0118 581813 0118 583771

e-mail: onsbuiten@ardoer.com

web: www.ardoer.com/onsbuiten

A beautiful location with a choice of recreational activities.

dir: *From church S towards Grijpskerke, turn W for 400m.*

Open: 31 Mar-Oct **Site:** 11.5HEC **Facilities:** **Services:** **Leisure:** P S

Pekelinge

Landmetersweg 1, 4356

0118 582820 0118 583782

e-mail: pekelinge@ardoer.com

web: www.ardoer.com/pekelinge

A spacious site for families, with pitches also available for the less able-bodied. Kids' club and indoor swimming pool available during weekends and holidays.

Open: Apr-Oct **Site:** 18HEC **For hire:** **Prices:** 19-55 Mobile home hire 315-875 **Facilities:** Wi-fi Kids' Club Play Area **Services:** **Leisure:** P **Off-site:** S

OOSTVOORNE ZUID-HOLLAND

Kruininger Gors

Gorspl 2, 3233

0181 482711 0181 485957

e-mail: info@kruiningergors.nl

web: www.kruiningergors.nl

Located on the shores of Lake Brielle, a lively site with private sandy beaches and moorings for boats.

dir: *Via A15/N218.*

Open: Apr-Sep **Site:** 108HEC **Prices:** 17-20 **Facilities:** Wi-fi (charged) Kids' Club Play Area **Services:** **Leisure:** L **Off-site:** S

OUDDORP ZUID-HOLLAND

Klepperstee

Vrijheidsweg 1, 3253

0187 681511 0187 683060

e-mail: info@klepperstee.com

web: www.klepperstee.com

On level meadow divided by hedges and trees.

dir: *N57 exit Ouddorp.*

Open: Apr-Oct **Site:** 40HEC **Facilities:** **Services:** **Leisure:** P **Off-site:** L S

PLASMOLEN LIMBURG

Eldorado

Witteweg 18, 6586

024 6961914 024 6963017

e-mail: info@eldorado-mook.nl

web: www.eldorado-mook.nl

Well-equipped site in wooded surroundings on the Mooker See.

dir: *S of N271.*

Open: Apr-1 Oct **Site:** 6HEC **Facilities:** **Services:** **Leisure:** L

RENESSE ZEELAND

International

Scharendijkseweg 8, 4325

0111 461391 0111 462571

e-mail: info@camping-international.net

web: www.camping-international.net

On grassland, between rows of tall shrubs and trees. Between dyke road and main road to Scharendijk on eastern outskirts of village.

Open: Mar-Nov **Site:** 3HEC **For hire:** **Prices:** 27.45-31.95 **Facilities:** Wi-fi (charged) Play Area **Services:** **Leisure:** S **Off-site:** P

Wijde Blick

Lagezoom 23, 4325

0111 468888 0111 468889

e-mail: wijdeblick@ardoer.com

web: www.ardoer.com

A family site with good facilities.

dir: *W of N651, signed.*

Open: All Year. **Site:** 10HEC **For hire:** **Facilities:** **Services:** **Leisure:** P **Off-site:** S

RETRANCHEMENT ZEELAND

De Zwinhoeve

Duinweg 1, 4525
0117 392120 0117 392248
e-mail: info@zwinhoeve.nl
web: www.zwinhoeve.nl
A beautiful position backed by dunes with easy access to the fine beaches of the Zeeuws-Vlaanderen coast.
Open: 19 Mar-26 Oct **Site:** 9HEC **For hire:** **Facilities:** **Services:** **Leisure:** S **Off-site:** P

RIJNSBURG ZUID-HOLLAND

Koningshof

The Camping and Caravanning Club The Friendly Club

Elsgeesterweg 8, 2231
071 4026051 071 4021336
e-mail: info@koningshofholland.nl
web: www.koningshofholland.nl
Modern site on level meadow near the flower fields. Maximum of one dog per pitch.
C&CC Report *A friendly site with very good facilities, close to many attractions. A great site for younger children. Beaches, cities and countryside are all in easy driving distance. Keukenhof gardens and the bulb fields are a particular delight in spring. Cycling on the excellent cycle path network is highly recommended for getting around, too.*
dir: *A44 exit 7 to Rijnsburg, site 1km N, signed.*
Open: Apr-Nov **Site:** 7.5HEC **For hire:** **Prices:** 24.50-29.50 Mobile home hire 355-639 **Facilities:** Wi-fi Kids' Club Play Area **Services:** **Leisure:** P **Off-site:** S

ROCKANJE ZUID-HOLLAND

Waterboscamping

Duinrand 11, 3235
0181 401900 0181 404233
e-mail: info@waterboscamping.nl
web: www.waterboscamping.nl
A small, pleasant site near the beach, with large trees, a pond and a playground.
dir: *Via N15.*
Open: Apr-Sep **Site:** 7HEC **For hire:** **Facilities:** Wi-fi (charged) Kids' Club Play Area **Services:** **Off-site:** S

ROERMOND LIMBURG

Resort Marina Oolderhuuske

Oolderhuuske 1, 6041
0475 588686 0475 582652
e-mail: info@oolderhuuske.nl
web: www.oolderhuuske.nl
A well-equipped site within the marina area on the Maasplassen. A kids' club is available during the holidays.
Open: Apr-Oct **Site:** 22HEC **For hire:** **Facilities:** Wi-fi Kids' Club **Services:** **Leisure:** L P R

ROOSENDAAL NOORD-BRABANT

Zonneland

Turfvaartsestr 6, 4709
0165 365429
e-mail: info@zonneland.nl
web: www.zonneland.nl
Site in woodland convenient to the motorway.
dir: *S of town towards Belgian border.*
GPS: 51.4944, 4.485
Open: Mar-1 Oct **Site:** 14HEC **Prices:** 27 **Facilities:** Wi-fi **Services:** **Leisure:** P

SCHIN OP GEUL LIMBURG

Vinkenhof

The Camping and Caravanning Club The Friendly Club

Engwegen 2a, 6305
043 4591389 043 4591780
e-mail: info@campingvinkenhof.nl
web: www.campingvinkenhof.nl
Small, friendly site on flat ground at foot of hill and on edge of village. There are modern facilities and a new swimming pool. Kids' club available in July and August.
C&CC Report *Woods, farms and rolling hills, full of wildlife, provide the backdrop for this lovely, village site, that continues to improve each year. The Weijts family continue to offer a warm welcome at Vinkenhof, with the attractive bar terrace and cosy restaurant adding to the homely feel. Pretty Valkenburg with its Roman catacombs is a must to visit, while Belgium, Germany and Maastricht, are all within easy reach, as are the Dutch hills fringing the atmospheric Ardennes.*
dir: *A76, exit at Nuth for Schin op Geul.*
GPS: 50.8500, 5.8730
Open: Mar-2 Jan **Site:** 2.2HEC **For hire:** **Prices:** 13-27.25 Mobile home hire 225-350 **Facilities:** Wi-fi (charged) Kids' Club Play Area **Services:** **Leisure:** P **Off-site:**

Facilities 🛪 shower ⊙ electric points for razors 🔌 electric points for caravans ⛴ motorvan service point ℗ parking by tents permitted
compulsory separate car park 🏪 shop **Services** 🍽 café/restaurant 🍺 bar ⌀ Camping Gaz International 🚿 gas other than Camping Gaz

NETHERLANDS

SEVENUM — LIMBURG

Schatberg

Midden Peelweg 5, 5975
☎ 077 4677777 🖹 077 4677799
e-mail: receptie@schatberg.nl
web: www.schatberg.nl

A well-appointed family site in wooded surroundings with plenty of leisure facilities.

dir: *A67 exit 38 for Schatberg & SW towards Eindhoven.*

Open: All Year. **Site:** 86HEC **For hire:** **Facilities:** Play Area **Services:** **Leisure:** L P

'S-GRAVENZANDE — ZUID-HOLLAND

Jagtveld

Nieuwlandsedijk 41, 2691
☎ 0174 413479 🖹 0174 422127
e-mail: info@jagtveld.nl
web: www.jagtveld.nl

A quiet family site on level meadowland with good facilities.

dir: *Via N220.*

Open: Apr-Sep **Site:** 3.3HEC **Facilities:** **Services:** **Off-site:** S

SLUIS — ZEELAND

Meidoorn

Hoogstr 68, 4524
☎ 0117 461662 🖹 0117 461662
e-mail: meidoorn@zeelandnet.nl
web: www.campingdemeidoorn.nl

A meadowland site surrounded by rows of deciduous trees.

dir: *N on road to Zuidzande.*

Open: Apr-22 Oct **Site:** 6.5HEC **For hire:** **Facilities:** **Services:** **Off-site:**

VENRAY — LIMBURG

de Oude Barrier

Maasheseweg 93, 5817
☎ 0478 582305
e-mail: info@deoudebarrier.nl
web: www.deoudebarrier.nl

A quiet site recommended for young children and older campers.

dir: *Via A73. NE of town.*

Open: Apr-Sep **Site:** 14HEC **For hire:** **Prices:** 12.70-13.50 Mobile home hire 165-450 **Facilities:** Wi-fi Play Area **Services:** **Leisure:** P **Off-site:** R

VROUWENPOLDER — ZEELAND

Oranjezon

Koningin Emmaweg 16a, 4354
☎ 0118 591549 🖹 0118 591920
e-mail: oranjezon@oranjezon.nl
web: www.oranjezon.nl

Situated to the west of the village, a well-kept site with pitches between tall, thick hedges and bushes. Kids' club available in high season.

dir: *Towards Oostkapelle, 2.5km turn N for 300m.*

Open: Apr-Oct **Site:** 9.75HEC **For hire:** **Facilities:** Wi-fi (charged) Kids' Club **Services:** **Leisure:** P S

Zandput

Vroondijk 9, 4354
☎ 0118 597210 🖹 0118 591954
web: www.roompot.nl

On level ground behind dunes and close to the beach.

dir: *2km N.*

Open: 3 Apr-1 Nov **Site:** 12HEC **For hire:** **Facilities:** **Services:** **Off-site:** L S

WASSENAAR — ZUID-HOLLAND

Duinhorst

Buurtweg 135, 2244
☎ 070 3242270 🖹 070 3246053
e-mail: info@duinhorst.nl
web: www.duinhorst.nl

A peaceful site in wooded surroundings with modern facilities and opportunities for sports and entertainment.

Open: Apr-Sep **Site:** 11HEC **Prices:** 20-24 **Facilities:** Kids' Club **Services:** **Leisure:** P

Holidaypark Duinrell

The Camping and Caravanning Club — The Friendly Club

Duinrell 1, 2242
☎ 070 5155255 🖷 070 5155371
e-mail: info@duinrell.nl
web: www.duinrell.nl

A very well-maintained site with a recreation centre adjacent, which is free for campers. Some aircraft noise. Toilets have facilities for the disabled. Restricted area for cars in some parts of site.

C&CC Report *Duinrell is much, much more than just a campsite – with its own amusement park (free to campers), fantastic Tiki Pool complex (payable on site), and themed restaurants, children of all ages will find plenty to do. The site's location in the beautiful woodland and dune area on the coast of South Holland, next to the beach and within walking distance of the attractive village of Wassenaar, makes Duinrell the perfect place to visit, all year round.*

dir: *Off A44 at lights in Wassenaar, signed.*

GPS: 52.1458, 4.3869

Open: All Year. **Site:** 110HEC **For hire:** **Prices:** 40.26-50.26 Mobile home hire 275-1095 **Facilities:** Wi-fi (charged) Kids' Club **Services:** **Leisure:** P **Off-site:** L S

WEERT — LIMBURG

De Yzeren Man

Herenvennenweg 60, 6006
☎ 0495 533202 🖷 0495 546812
web: www.resortdeijzerenman.nl

Well-kept site with asphalt drives, set in a big nature reserve with zoo, heath and forest.

dir: *A2 Eindhoven-Maastricht.*

Open: Apr-1 Nov **Site:** 8.5HEC **Facilities:** **Services:** **Leisure:** P **Off-site:**

WELL — LIMBURG

Vakantiepark Leukermeer

De Kamp 5, 5855
☎ 0478 502444 🖷 0478 501260
e-mail: vakantie@leukermeer.nl
web: www.leukermeer.nl

Beautiful surroundings on Leukermeer with modern facilities and plenty of leisure activities.

dir: *Signed from N271.*

GPS: 51.5669, 6.0594

Open: Apr-1 Nov **Site:** 14HEC **For hire:** **Prices:** 22.90-41.40 Mobile home hire 199-669 **Facilities:** Wi-fi (charged) Kids' Club Play Area **Services:** **Leisure:** L P **Off-site:**

WEMELDINGE — ZEELAND

Linda

Oostkanaalweg 4, 4424
☎ 0113 621259 🖷 0113 622638
e-mail: info@campinglinda.nl
web: www.campinglinda.nl

On meadowland surrounded by rows of tall shrubs. At the Eastern National Park and a short walk from the historic village Wemeldinge.

dir: *Turn opposite bridge in town for 100m, over bridge to site.*

Open: Apr-Nov **Site:** 8HEC **For hire:** **Facilities:** Wi-fi Kids' Club Play Area **Services:** **Leisure:** S

WESTKAPELLE — ZEELAND

Boomgaard

Domineeshofweg 1, 4361
☎ 0118 571377 🖷 0118 572383
e-mail: info@deboomgaard.info
web: www.deboomgaard.info

A flat grassy site.

dir: *Signed off Middleburg road on S outskirts of town.*

Open: 27 Mar-24 Oct **Site:** 8HEC **For hire:** **Facilities:** **Services:** **Leisure:** P **Off-site:** S

NETHERLANDS

Facilities shower electric points for razors electric points for caravans motorvan service point parking by tents permitted compulsory separate car park shop **Services** café/restaurant bar Camping Gaz International gas other than Camping Gaz first aid facilities laundry **Leisure** swimming L-Lake P-Pool R-River S-Sea **Off-site** All facilities within 5km

Drinking and driving

The maximum level of alcohol in the bloodstream is 0.02%. Between 0.021% and 0.05% per cent a heavy fine imposed and suspension of licence. Over 0.05% the fine is determined by a tribunal along with the prison sentence and suspension of licence.

Driving licence

Minimum age at which a UK licence holder may drive a temporarily imported car and/or motorcycle (over 125cc) 18. All valid UK driving licences should be accepted in Poland.

Fines

On-the-spot. An official receipt should be obtained. The Police are authorised to request foreign motorists to pay their fines in cash. Wheel clamps are in use. Illegally parked cars causing an obstruction may be towed away and impounded.

Fuel

Unleaded petrol (95 and 98 octane), diesel and LPG available. No leaded petrol (95 octane petrol with lead replacement additive available). Up to 10 litres of petrol in a can is permitted but forbidden aboard ferries. Credit cards accepted at most filling stations; check with your card issuer for usage in Poland before travel.

Lights

Dipped headlights or daytime running lights are compulsory for all vehicles at all times. Fine imposed for non-compliance.

Motorcycles

Dipped headlights or daytime running lights are compulsory for all vehicles at all times. The wearing of crash helmets is compulsory for both driver and passenger.

Motor insurance

Third-party compulsory.

Passengers/children in cars

Children under 12 and 1.5m in height cannot travel as front or a rear seat passenger unless using a suitable restraint system adapted to their size. If a car is equipped with front seat airbags it is prohibited to place a child in a rear facing seat.

Seat belts

Compulsory for front/rear seat occupants to wear seat belts, if fitted.

Speed limits

Standard legal limits, which may be varied by signs

Private vehicles without trailers

Built-up areas (2300hrs to 0500hrs)	60km/h
Built-up areas (0500hrs to 2300hrs)	50km/h
Outside built-up areas	90km/h
Express roads (2x1 lanes)	100km/h
Express roads (2x2 lanes)	110km/h
Motorways	130km/h

Private vehicle towing a trailer or caravan

Built-up areas	30km/h
Motorways	80km/h
Express roads (2x2 lanes and 2x1 lane) and dual carriageways	80km/h
Other roads	70km/h.
Minimum speed on motorways	40km/h
Some residential zones	20km/h

Compulsory equipment in Poland

Warning triangle - compulsory for all vehicles with more than two wheels

Other rules/requirements

It is recommended that visitors equip their vehicle with a first aid kit and a set of replacement bulbs.

It is also recommended that a fire extinguisher be carried as its carriage is compulsory for Polish registered vehicles.

The use of spiked tyres is prohibited. Snow chains may be used only on roads covered with snow. It is prohibited to carry or/and use a radar detector. The use of the horn is prohibited in built-up areas except to avoid an accident.

Tolls Currency Zlotys (PLN)	Car	Car Towing Caravan/Trailer
A1 Rusocin - Nowe Marzy	17.60PLN	41.80PLN
A2 Komoraiki - Now/Tomysl	13PLN	27PLN
A2 Krzesiny - Wrzesia	13PLN	27PLN
A2 Wrzesnia - Konin	13.50PLN	24.50PLN
A4 Katowice - Krakow	16PLN	27PLN

CHMIELNO — ZACHODNIOPOMORSKIE

Tamowa

Zawory 47, 83-333
058 6842535 058 6842535
e-mail: camping@tamowa.pl
web: www.tamowa.pl
Site on the shore of Lake Klodno with private beach. Recreational facilities include boating, water sports and fishing. Walking and cycle routes nearby.
dir: *Route 211 Stupsk-Gdansk.*
Open: All Year. **Site:** 2HEC **For hire:** **Prices:** 34-50 **Facilities:** Wi-fi (charged) Play Area **Services:** **Leisure:** L **Off-site:**

DZIWNÓWEK — ZACHODNIOPOMORSKIE

Bialy Dom

ulica Kamienska 11-12, 72-420
091 3811171 091 3811446
web: www.campingbialydom.com
Site located 50 metres from the beach.
GPS: 54.0352, 14.8036
Open: Mar-Oct **Site:** 2.5HEC **For hire:** **Prices:** 51-88 **Facilities:** Wi-fi (charged) Play Area **Services:** **Off-site:** L P S

GIZYCKO — WARMIŃSKO-MAZURSKIE

Elixir Hotelik Caravan Camping

Guty 9, 11-500
087 4282826
e-mail: office@elixirhotel.com
web: www.elixirhotel.com
With lake shoreline and jetties for fishing, this site offers peace and quiet to visitors. Children are well catered for with scooters, bicycles and go-karts available. Other recreational facilities include table tennis and pedaloes.
dir: *Route 59 then 592.*
Open: May-Oct **Site:** 3.5HEC **For hire:** **Facilities:** Wi-fi Kids' Club Play Area **Services:** **Leisure:** L **Off-site:**

JELENIA GÓRA — DOLNOSLASKIE

Camping Sloneczna Polana

ulica M Rataja 9, 58-560
075 7552566
e-mail: info@campingpolen.com
web: www.campingpolen.com
A quiet, family site with spacious plots. Facilities include satellite TV, safe rental and sports.
dir: *On route from Jelenia Góra to the Czech Republic border (E3).*
Open: May-Sep **Site:** 2.5HEC **For hire:** **Facilities:** Wi-fi Play Area **Services:** **Leisure:** P R **Off-site:**

KRAKÓW — MALOPOLSKIE

Krakowianka

ulica Zywiecka Boczna 2, 30-427
012 2681135 012 2681417
e-mail: noclegi@krakowianka.info
web: www.krakowianka.info
Located on the outskirts of Kraków in a park complex with good recreational facilities.
GPS: 50.0147, 19.9247
Open: All Year. **Site:** 3.8HEC **For hire:** **Prices:** 50-90 **Facilities:** Wi-fi **Services:** **Off-site:** L

MIELNO — ZACHODNIOPOMORSKE

Rodzinny

ulica Chrobrego 51, 76-032
094 3189385 094 3475008
e-mail: recepcja@campingrodzinny.pl
web: www.campingrodzinny.pl
Family run campsite close to the sea and a marina.
dir: *Route 11 onto 165.*
GPS: 54.2628, 16.0722
Open: 15 Apr-15 Nov **Site:** 0.5HEC **Prices:** 45-55 **Facilities:** Wi-fi (charged) Play Area **Services:** **Off-site:** L P S

POLAND

MIKOLAJKI WARMIŃSKO-MAZURSKIE

Camping Kama

Talty 36, 11-730
087 4216575 087 4216575
e-mail: camping@kama.mazury.pl
web: kama.mazury.pl
Situated on the bank of Lake Talty. Excellent for fishing and water sports.
dir: *Route 16.*
Open: May-15 Oct **Site:** 2HEC **For hire:** **Prices:** 56-72 **Facilities:** Wi-fi (charged) Play Area **Services:** **Leisure:** L **Off-site:** P R

PRZEWORSK PODKARPACKIE

Pastewnik

ulica Lancucka 2, 37-200
016 6492300 016 6492301
e-mail: zajazdpastewnik@hot.pl
web: www.pastewnik.pl
A unique place which functions as an inn, camping site, and open-air museum.
dir: *From Przeworsk on A4 (E40) towards Rzeszow, campsite on right after bridge.*
Open: May-Sep **Site:** 2HEC **For hire:** **Facilities:** Wi-fi Play Area **Services:** **Off-site:** P

PRZYWIDZ POMORSKIE

Camping nr 20

ulica Gdańska 19, 83-047
0602 623091 058 6825265
e-mail: biuro@camping.vti.pl
web: www.camping.vti.pl
On a lake side, a site in a quiet setting with watersports equipment for guests' use.
GPS: 54.1947, 18.3239
Open: All Year. **Site:** 2HEC **For hire:** **Prices:** 55-80 **Facilities:** Wi-fi Kids' Club Play Area **Services:** **Leisure:** L **Off-site:** P

SOPOT POMORSKIE

Przy Plazy

Bitwy pod Plowcami 73, 81-831
058 5516523
e-mail: camping67@sopot.pl
web: www.camping67.sopot.pl
Next to a beach in a shaded woody location.
Open: 15 Jun-Aug **Site:** 3HEC **Facilities:** **Services:** **Off-site:**

WOLIBÓRZ DOLNOSLASKIE

Lesny Dwor-Waldgut

Woliborz 12b, 57-431
074 8724590
e-mail: waldgut@waldgut.de
web: www.waldgut.de
Campsite in grounds of a manor house in attractive mountainous location.
dir: *On Wat Brzych-Ktodzko route 381: near Nowa Rudna follow signs towards Wolibórz. Campsite signed.*
Open: All Year. **Site:** 2HEC **For hire:** **Facilities:** **Services:** **Leisure:** P **Off-site:**

WROCLAW DOLNOSLASKIE

Stadion Olimpijski

ulica Paderewskieg 35, 51-612
071 3484651 071 3483928
Site close to the Stadium. Convenient for short breaks to the city.
Open: May-15 Oct **Site:** 2HEC **For hire:** **Facilities:** **Services:** **Off-site:** L

ZAKOPANE MALOPOLSKIE

Pod Krokwia

ulica Zeromskiego, 34-500
018 2012256 018 2012256
e-mail: camp@podkrokwia.pl
web: www.podkrokwia.pl
Close to a national park area with mountain views.
dir: *In Zakopane turn left at 1st rdbt, straight over next rdbt, right at 3rd rdbt, campsite 150mtrs on right.*
Open: All Year. **Site:** 4HEC **For hire:** **Facilities:** **Services:** **Off-site:** P R

Ustup

Ustup 5B, 34-500
060 5950007
e-mail: camping.ustup@gmail.com
web: www.camping-ustup.pl
On the rivers Zakopianka and Olczyski Potok with fine views of Tatry Mountains.
dir: *Route DK7-DK47 Kraków - Zakopane.*
GPS: 49.3220, 19.9856
Open: May-Sep **Site:** 0.8HEC **For hire:** **Prices:** 48-53 **Facilities:** Wi-fi **Services:** **Off-site:** L P R

POLAND

Drinking and driving

If the level of alcohol in the bloodstream is 0.05% to 0.08%, fine and withdrawal of the driving licence for a minimum of one month to a maximum of one year; more than 0.08%, fine and withdrawal of driving licence for a minimum of two months up to a maximum of two years. The police are also empowered to carry out testing on drivers for narcotics.

Driving licence

Minimum age at which a UK licence holder may drive a temporarily imported car and/or motorcycle (over 50cc) 17; however visitors under the age of 18 years may encounter problems even though they hold a valid UK licence. All valid UK driving licences should be accepted in Portugal. This includes the older all-green style UK licences (in Northern Ireland older paper style with photographic counterpart) although the EC appreciates that these may be more difficult to understand and that drivers may wish to voluntarily update them before travelling abroad if time permits. Alternatively, older licences may be accompanied by an International Driving Permit (IDP).

Fines

On-the-spot and must be paid in Euros. Most traffic police vehicles are equipped with portable ATM machines for immediate payment of the fines. An official receipt showing the maximum amount of the fine should be obtained.

Note: foreign motorists refusing to pay an on-the-spot fine will be asked for a deposit to cover the maximum fine for the offence committed. If a motorist refuses to do this, the police can take the driving licence, registration document or failing that they can confiscate the vehicle.

Wheel-clamping and towing are in operation for illegally parked vehicles.

Fuel

Unleaded petrol (95 and 98 octane), diesel and LPG available. No leaded petrol (lead replacement petrol available as 98 octane). Petrol in a can permitted.

Credit cards accepted at most filling stations; check with your card issuer for use in Portugal before travel. Note: A tax of 0.50 is added to credit card transactions.

Lights

Dipped headlights compulsory in poor daytime visibility and in tunnels.

Motorcycles

Use of dipped headlights during the day compulsory. The wearing of crash helmets is compulsory. Child under seven not permitted as passenger.

Motor insurance

Third-party compulsory.

Passengers/children in cars

Children under 12 and less than 1.50m in height cannot travel as front seat passengers. They must travel in the rear in a special restraint system adapted to their size, unless the vehicle has only two seats, or is not fitted with seat belts. Children under 3 can be seated in the front passenger seat if using a suitable child restraint however, the airbag must be switched off if using a rear-facing child restraint system.

Seat belts

Compulsory for front/rear seat occupants to wear seat belts, if fitted.

Speed limits

Standard legal limits, which may be varied by signs

Private vehicles without trailers	
Built-up areas	50km/h
Outside built-up areas	90km/h or 100km/h
Motorways	120km/h
Private vehicle towing a trailer or caravan	
Built-up areas	50km/h
Outside built-up areas	70km/h or 80km/h
Motorways	100km/h
Minimum speed on motorways	50km/h

Motorists who have held a driving licence for less than one year must not exceed 90km/h or any lower speed limit.

Compulsory equipment in Portugal

Photographic proof of identity - It is a legal requirement in Portugal that everyone carries photographic proof of identity at all times

Reflective jacket – compulsory for residents, recommended for visitors*

Temporary Electronic Toll Device (DEM) – Since the 15th October 2010

you are required to have a temporary automatic toll device for using certain motorways. We have been advised that these are the A4, A17, A25, A28, A29, A41 and A42 – this may be extended. The device must be pre-loaded with a minimum of 10. The device can be obtained from some motorway service stations, CTT which is the post company in Portugal and Via Verde shops, with a 27 deposit. When leaving Portugal the device must be returned to one of the selected outlets. The deposit paid for the device and any unused monies should be credited to you.

Other rules/requirements

Carrying a warning triangle recommended as the use of hazard warning lights or a warning triangle is compulsory in an accident/breakdown situation.

It is prohibited to carry and/or use a radar detector. Spiked tyres and winter tyres are prohibited. Snow chains may be used, where the weather conditions require. It is illegal to carry bicycles on the back of a passenger car.

In built-up areas the use of the horn is prohibited during the hours of darkness except in the case of immediate danger.

*The wearing of reflectorised jacket/waistcoat is recommended if the driver and/or passenger(s) exits a vehicle which is immobilised on the carriageway of all motorways and main or busy roads. We recommend the jacket be carried in the passenger compartment of the vehicle (not the boot). This is a compulsory requirement for residents.

Pictured: Alfama, Lisbon

Tolls & Bridges

Tolls Currency Euro (€)	Car with or without Caravan/Trailer
A1 Lisboa - Porto	€19.55
A10 A9 - Arruda dos Vinhos - A13	€2.10
A11 A28/Braga (A3) - Guimaraes (A7) - A4	€0.80
A12 Setubal - Pte Vasco de Gama	€1.95
A13 Santo Estevao - Marateca (A2/A6)	€8.90
A14 Figueira da Foz - Coimbra Nord	€2.20
A15 Caldas da Rainha - Santarem	€3.55
A2 Lisboa - VLA (Algarve)	€18.40
A21 Malveria (A8) - Ericeira	€1.80
A3 Porto - Valença do Minho (Spain/Vigo)	€7.85

Tolls Currency Euro (€)	Car Towing Caravan/Trailer
A4 Porto - Amarante	€3.65
A5 Lisboa - Cascais	€1.25
A6/A2 A2/Marateca - Elvas (Spanish border)	€11.90
A7 Vila Nova de Famalicao - Guimaraes	€1.55
A8 Lisboa - Leiria	€10.20
A9 Alverca - Oeiras	€2.95
Bridges and Tunnels	
25 de Abril Bridge (Ponte 25 de Abril) On A2 (payable in one direction - north into Lisboa - only. No toll in August)	€1.45
Vasco da Gama Bridge On A12 (North only) (Ponte Vasco da Gama)	€2.40

SOUTH

ALBUFEIRA — ALGARVE

Albufeira

The Camping and Caravanning Club The Friendly Club

8200-555

289587629 289587633

e-mail: campingalbufeira@mail.telepac.pt

web: www.campingalbufeira.net

A modern, purpose-built site with excellent sanitary blocks and a variety of sports and entertainment facilities.

C&CC Report *Albufeira is in an area renowned among golfers and sunseekers throughout Europe and is a firm perennial favourite. A new walkway and cycle path from the site means the town centre, 3km away, is within easy reach, giving you great access to many good quality restaurants, beaches and other local towns and attractions. For trips further afield, you are only 5km from the motorway, which travels the length of the Algarve, giving you the opportunity to visit many of the towns and attractions that the area has to offer. With site improvements already underway, including pitch drainage, we are sure that Albufeira will continue to be a popular destination.*

dir: *1.5km from Albufeira, signed from N125.*

Open: All Year. **Site:** 19HEC **For hire:** **Facilities:** **Services:** **Leisure:** P **Off-site:** S

ALVITO — BAIXO ALENTEJO

Markádia

Barragem de Odivelas, Apartado 17, 7920-999

284763141 284763102

e-mail: markadia@hotmail.com

web: www.markadia.net

Partly wooded site beside a lake with modern facilities. Dogs not accepted in July and August.

dir: *2 km S of N257.*

GPS: 38.1838, -8.1036

Open: All Year. **Site:** 10HEC **For hire:** **Prices:** 11.60-23.20 **Facilities:** Play Area **Services:** **Leisure:** L **Off-site:** P

BEJA — BAIXO ALENTEJO

Parque de Campismo Municipal de Beja

av Vasco da Gama, 7800-397

284311911 284311911

e-mail: campismo@cm-beja.pt

web: www.cm-beja.pt

Shaded site laid out around a central street, enhanced by flower beds and trees.

dir: *A2 onto IP2.*

Open: All Year. **Site:** 1HEC **Prices:** 4.30-10.95 **Facilities:** **Services:** **Off-site:** P

LAGOS — ALGARVE

Turiscampo

The Camping and Caravanning Club The Friendly Club

E N125, 8600-109

282789265 282788578

e-mail: info@turiscampo.com

web: www.turiscampo.com

Site with large shaded pitches offering entertainment and extensive leisure facilities, including swimming pool and jacuzzi. Shower blocks have been recently renovated.

C&CC Report *This high quality modern campsite, in the western Algarve, continues to receive rave reviews from campers for its friendly welcome and for the quality of its facilities. The Coll family are carefully redeveloping the site with priority being given to good-sized pitches and quality facilities for campers. The local area is ideal for both those who like to relax and for those who want to be more active. Within easy reach are white sandy beaches and a picturesque rocky coastline, with the most south-westerly point of Europe, Cape St Vincent, with its famous lighthouse just 19km away. The nearby town of Lagos is steeped in history, from Roman times through to the occupation by the Moors, then to more recent Portuguese explorers. A great site where you can enjoy the Mediterranean climate and easily explore the surrounding area.*

dir: *From A22/IC4 exit 1, Lagos-Vila do Bispo, towards Lagos, then N125 towards Sagres until approaching Espiche.*

Open: All Year. **Site:** 7.5HEC **For hire:** **Prices:** 18-40 Mobile home hire 315-868 **Facilities:** Wi-fi (charged) Kids' Club Play Area **Services:** **Leisure:** P **Off-site:** S

PORTUGAL

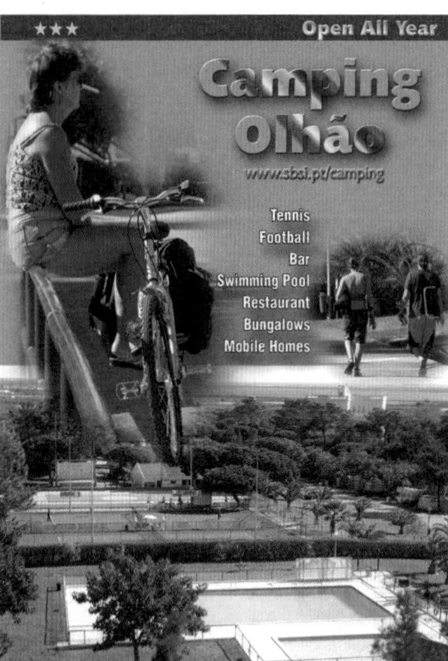

MEXILHOERIA GRANDE — ALGARVE

Camping Chickenrun

Varzea do Farello, 8500-160
☎ 968451636
e-mail: chickenrun4077@aol.com
web: www.chickenrun.vpweb.co.uk

Rural, rustic site with large pitches set among olive and citrus trees. Horse riding, golf and cycle routes available locally. The local shop can deliver and gas can be collected for campers.

dir: *EN125.*

GPS: 37.1729, -8.6127

Open: All Year. **Site:** 6HEC **For hire:** **Prices:** 3-7 **Facilities:** Wi-fi (charged) **Services:** **Leisure:** P R S

ODEMIRA — BAIXO ALENTEJO

Zmar

7630-011
☎ 707200626
e-mail: info@zmar.eu
web: www.zmar.eu

Dogs allowed at an extra charge, no dangerous dogs.

C&CC Report *Zmar is the first Eco Camping Resort in Portugal and you will be amazed at the quality of the main facilities. These facilities are shared with the permanent accommodation, with wash blocks adjacent to the camping areas. The permanent accommodation does not impact on the camping areas, as these wooden chalets (approximately 200) are spread out in separate areas around this very spacious site and make a minimal impact on the environment. This is a campsite where you can either pamper yourself in the spa (extra charge) or simply enjoy all the inclusive facilities. The south west corner of the Alentejo district of Portugal is completely unspoilt by tourist development. In an easily accessible area there are gently rolling hills and a national park. Beautiful beaches can be found at nearby Almograve and Zambujeira do Mar. If all you know of Portugal is the Algarve then you are in for a great surprise in discovering this area.*

dir: *From the N393 take N393/1 heading for Cabo Sardao/ Zambujeira.*

Site: **For hire:** **Facilities:** Play Area **Services:** **Leisure:** P

OLHÃO — ALGARVE

Olhão

Pinheiros de Marim, 8700-914
☎ 289700300 289700390
e-mail: parque.campismo@sbsi.pt

Near Ria Formosa Natural Park, large site with facilities for live entertainment.

C&CC Report *Olhão is an excellent location for exploring the less developed eastern Algarve, and Camping Olhão offers an easy-going environment with good on-site facilities. The town of Olhão itself has a working fishing port, renowned for its shellfish and little touched by tourism. You'll still see traditional buildings and traditionally dressed locals. Nearby Tavira is known as the 'Aristocrat of the Algarve' for its beautiful churches, elegant houses and flower-filled squares. Boat trips to the sandbanks off Tavira and Olhão reveal fabulous beaches, bars and restaurants. Spain is close and a day trip to historic Seville is highly recommended.*

GPS: 37.0352, -7.8225

Open: All Year. **Site:** 10HEC **For hire:** **Prices:** 8.40-19.50 **Facilities:** Wi-fi (charged) **Services:** **Leisure:** P **Off-site:** S

see advert on this page

PORTUGAL

PORTIMÃO — ALGARVE

Da Dourada

Alvor, 8500-053

282459178 282459178

e-mail: campingdourada@hotmail.com

Set in a park-like area close to the beach with good facilities.

dir: *N off Portimão-Lagos road.*

Open: All Year. **Site:** 4HEC **For hire:** **Facilities:** **Services:** **Leisure:** P R S

PRAIA DA LUZ — ALGARVE

Orbitur

Estrada da Praia da Luz, Valverde, 8600-148

282789211 282789213

e-mail: valverde@orbitur.pt

web: www.orbitur.pt

Well-equipped site with children's playground and tennis courts.

dir: *Off N125 Lagos-Cape St Vincent road. 4km from Lagos.*

Open: All Year. **Site:** 9.1HEC **For hire:** **Facilities:** **Services:** **Leisure:** P **Off-site:** S

PRAIA DE SALEMA — ALGARVE

Quinta dos Carriços

Praia da Salema, 8650-196

282695201 28265122

e-mail: quintacarrico@oninet.pt

web: www.quintadoscarricos.com

A well-equipped site with good facilities. There is a naturist section in a separate valley with its own facilities.

Open: All Year. **Site:** 20HEC **For hire:** **Prices:** 23.40-29.95 **Facilities:** **Services:** **Off-site:** S

QUARTEIRA — ALGARVE

Orbitur

Estrada da Forte Santa, av Sá Carneiro, 8125-618

The Camping and Caravanning Club — The Friendly Club

289302826 289302822

e-mail: quarteira@orbitur.pt

web: www.orbitur.pt

A terraced site at the top of a hill.

C&CC Report *Orbitur Quarteira is particularly well-suited to campers who like local facilities such as shops, restaurants and buses to be within reasonable walking distance. This site is great for, and much appreciated by, those who prefer quieter sites. Quarteira is one of the smaller modern resorts of this much-loved coastal region and is well placed for day trips to many of the Algarve's places of interest. Vilamoura and Val de Lobo are both easily reached and well worth visiting for golfers and non-golfers alike.*

dir: *Off M125 in Almoncil, signs to Quarteira, left 0.5km before sea.*

Open: All Year. **Site:** 9.7HEC **For hire:** **Facilities:** **Services:** **Leisure:** P **Off-site:** S

see advert on this page

SAGRES — ALGARVE

Orbitur

Cerro das Moitas, 8650-998

282624371 282624445

e-mail: sagres@orbitur.pt

web: www.orbitur.pt

Situated in a dune and forest area.

dir: *1.5km W of N268.*

Open: All Year. **Site:** 6.7HEC **For hire:** **Facilities:** **Services:** **Off-site:** S

SÃO MARCOS DA SERRA — ALGARVE

Quinta de Odelouca

Vale Grande CxP 644-5, 8375
☎ 282361718
e-mail: info@quintaodelouca.com
web: www.quintaodelouca.com

Built in 2010 and located in the Ribeira de Odelouca river basin, quiet site with a swimming pool.

dir: *Via IC1. Site 5km from blue railway bridge, signed.*

Open: All Year. **Site:** 2HEC **For hire:** **Prices:** 16.50 **Facilities:** Wi-fi (charged) **Services:** **Leisure:** P **Off-site:** R

VILA NOVA DE MILFONTES — BAIXO ALENTEJO

Milfontes

7645-300
☎ 283996104 283996104
e-mail: geral@campingmilfontes.com
web: www.campingmilfontes.com

Close to the beach and located in a pine forest, with pitches of varied shade and privacy.

Open: All Year. **Site:** 6.5HEC **For hire:** **Facilities:** **Services:** **Off-site:** R S

NORTH

ANGEIRAS — DOURO LITORAL

Orbitur

4455-039
☎ 229270571 229271178
e-mail: angeiras@orbitur.pt
web: www.orbitur.pt

A modern, well-kept site in a pine wood on a hill overlooking the sea.

dir: *W of N13 x-rds at Km12.1. E of Vila do Pinheiro towards sea for 5km.*

Open: All Year. **Site:** 7HEC **For hire:** **Facilities:** **Services:** **Leisure:** P **Off-site:** S

CAMINHA — MINHO

Orbitur

Mata do Camarido, E N13, Km 90, 4910-180
☎ 258921295 258921473
e-mail: caminha@orbitur.pt
web: www.orbitur.pt

On undulating sandy ground with trees.

dir: *Off N13 at Km89.7, W along Rio Minho for 0.8km & left.*

Open: Jan-Nov **Site:** 2.1HEC **For hire:** **Facilities:** **Services:** **Off-site:** S

CAMPO DO GERES — MINHO

Cerdeira

4840-030
☎ 253351005 253353315
e-mail: info@parquecerdeira.com
web: www.parquecerdeira.com

A picturesque wooded location with mature oak trees surrounding the pitches.

Open: All Year. **Site:** 7HEC **For hire:** **Prices:** 12.20-26.40 **Facilities:** Wi-fi **Services:** **Leisure:** P **Off-site:** L R

CANDEMIL — MINHO

Camping Convivio

Rua de Badão, 4920-020
☎ 251794404
e-mail: campingconvivio@sapo.net
web: www.campingconvivio.net

Small relaxing site with terraced pitches among a wide variety of fruit trees. Facilities include a salt-water swimming pool, table tennis and bike rental. Cars may only be parked by tents at certain times.

dir: *A3 (Valença-Porto).*

GPS: 41.9436, 8.6936

Open: 15 Mar-15 Oct **Site:** 0.5HEC **For hire:** **Prices:** 14.80-17.80 **Facilities:** Wi-fi (charged) Play Area **Services:** **Leisure:** P **Off-site:** R

CANEDO DE BASTO — DOURO LITORAL

Quinta do Rio

Celorico de Basto, 4890-140
962462131
e-mail: quintadorio@kanguru.pt
web: www.quintadorio.nl

On the Tamega River, spacious site with terraced pitches between vines or shaded spots under a variety of trees. Kayak trips can be organised.

dir: *S of A7.*

GPS: 41.4491, 7.9606

Open: All Year. **Site:** 3HEC **For hire:** **Prices:** 15.50-19.50 **Facilities:** Play Area **Services:** **Leisure:** P R **Off-site:** L

FAFE — MINHO

Parque de Campismo da Barragem de Queimadela

Rua da Barragem, Revelhe, 4820-560
253504084 253504085
e-mail: naturfafe@naturfafe.pt
web: www.naturfafe.pt

Close to the city of Fafe, ideal for exploring the surrounding walking trails and fishing in the Queimadela Dam.

dir: *A11.*

GPS: 41.5033, -8.1619

Open: Mar-5 Jan **Site:** 0.7HEC **Prices:** 9-11.50 **Facilities:** Play Area **Services:** **Leisure:** L R **Off-site:**

PÓVOA DE VARZIM — DOURO LITORAL

Rio Alto

E N13 - Km 13, Estela-Rio Alto, 4570-275
252615699 252615599
e-mail: rioalto@orbitur.pt
web: www.orbitur.pt

Situated near dunes, 150 metres from the sea.

dir: *Off N13 towards Viana.*

Open: All Year. **Site:** 7.9HEC **For hire:** **Facilities:** **Services:** **Leisure:** P S

RIBAS — MINHO

Quinta Valbom

Quintã, 4890-505
253653048
e-mail: info@quintavalbom.nl
web: www.quintavalbom.nl

Pitches laid out over three terraces, with views of the Ribas valley. Ideal for hiking in the surrounding countryside.

dir: *S of A7 & N206.*

GPS: 41.4619, -8.0111

Open: Apr-Oct **Site:** 5HEC **For hire:** **Prices:** 17.95-21.90 **Facilities:** Wi-fi Play Area **Services:** **Leisure:** P **Off-site:** R

VIANA DO CASTELO — MINHO

Orbitur

Rua Diogo Álvares, Cabedelo, 4900-161
258322167 258321946
e-mail: viana@orbitur.pt
web: www.orbitur.pt

A well-equipped site with direct access to a sandy beach.

dir: *Approach via N13 Porto-Viana do Castelo.*

Open: All Year. **Site:** 3HEC **For hire:** **Facilities:** **Services:** **Leisure:** P S

VIEIRA DO MINHO — MINHO

Parque de Campismo da Cabreira

Lugar de Entre os Rios, Cantelães, 4850
253648665 253646889
e-mail: geral@epmar.pt
web: www.epmar.pt

Situated between two rivers, the site has natural shade. Leisure facilities include a swimming pool and tennis court. Bikes can be hired to explore the surrounding countryside.

dir: *A3 then N103.*

Open: Mar-Oct **Site:** **Prices:** 10-15 **Facilities:** Play Area **Services:** **Leisure:** L P R **Off-site:**

PORTUGAL

VILA NOVA DE GAIA — DOURO LITORAL

Orbitur

Rua do Cerro, 608, Praia da Madalena, 4405-736
227122520 227122534
e-mail: madalena@orbitur.pt
web: www.orbitur.pt
Well-equipped site in a pine wood 0.5km from Madalena beach.
Open: All Year. **Site:** 2.4HEC **For hire:** **Facilities:** **Services:** **Leisure:** P **Off-site:** R S

VILA REAL — TRÁS-OS-MONTES

Parque Campismo de Vila Real

Rua Dr-Manuel Cardona, 5000-558
259324724
Quiet terraced site in woodland close to lake.
dir: *In E part of town off N2 by fuel station.*
Open: Mar-Nov **Site:** 4HEC **For hire:** **Facilities:** **Services:** **Off-site:** P R

CENTRAL

ALENQUER — ESTREMADURA

Alenquer Camping & Bungalows

Estrada National no 9 - km 94, 2580-330
263710375 263710375
e-mail: camping@dosdin.pt
web: www.dosdin.pt/camping
Located 30km north of Lisbon this modern well-equipped terraced site is surrounded by walnut trees.
dir: *Via A1 & N9.*
GPS: 39.0589, -9.0281
Open: All Year. **Site:** 1HEC **For hire:** **Prices:** 10-15 Mobile home hire 350-455 **Facilities:** Wi-fi Play Area **Services:** **Leisure:** P **Off-site:** R

ARGANIL — BEIRA LITORAL

Arganil

Sarzedo, 3300-432
235200133 235200134
e-mail: camping@mail.telepac.pt
web: www.cm-arganil.pt
A pleasant location among pine trees, close to the River Alva.
dir: *On N342-4.*
Open: All Year. **Site:** 3HEC **For hire:** **Facilities:** **Services:** **Leisure:** R **Off-site:**

BEIRÃ-MARVÃO — ALTO ALENTEJO

Camping Beirã-Marvão Alentejo

Monte de Bica, Painel de Bica Cx 60, 7330-013
245992360 245992360
e-mail: info@camping-beira-marvao.com
web: www.camping-beira-marvao.com
Set in a protected natural park, a small site with a wide variety of fruit and olive trees. Dogs are permitted on leads. Bike hire is on a first-come first-served basis.
GPS: 39.4278, -7.3856
Open: All Year. **Site:** 3HEC **Prices:** 8 **Facilities:** Wi-fi **Services:** **Leisure:** P **Off-site:** L R

BREJO — BEIRA LITORAL

Parque de Campismo Quinta do Porto

Rua Quinta do Porto, 3420-252
936183194
e-mail: info@quintadoporto.com
web: www.quintadoporto.com
Natural, quiet site set in an olive grove, with spacious pitches. Walks can be accessed directly from the site. One dog allowed per pitch.
dir: *IC6 exit 7, follow signs to Campismo.*
GPS: 40.3332, -8.0603
Open: All Year. **Site:** 1.8HEC **For hire:** **Prices:** 12-14 Mobile home hire 200 **Facilities:** Wi-fi (charged) **Services:** **Leisure:** P **Off-site:** L R

CALDAS DA RAINHA — ESTREMADURA

Orbitur Foz do Arelho

Rua Maldonado Freitas, Foz do Arelho, 2500-516
262978683 262978685
e-mail: fozarelho@orbitur.pt
web: www.orbitur.pt
Situated in a fine lagoon on the Arelho estuary.
dir: *3km SE of Foz do Arelho.*
Open: All Year. **Site:** 6HEC **For hire:** **Facilities:** **Services:** **Leisure:** P **Off-site:** L S

Site 6HEC (site size) grass sand stone little shade partly shaded mainly shaded motorvans accepted bungalows for hire mobile homes for hire tents for hire no dogs site fully accessible for wheelchairs
Prices amount quoted is per night, for 2 adults and car, plus tent or caravan Mobile home hire is a weekly rate.

CASFREIRES BEIRA ALTA

Quinta Chave Grande

Rua do Barreiro 462, Ferreira d'Aves, 3560-043
☎ 232665552 🖹 232665552
e-mail: chave-grande@sapo.pt
web: www.chavegrande.com

A terraced site overlooking a beautiful valley. There are modern installations and leisure facilities.

Open: Apr-15 Oct **Site:** 10HEC **For hire:** **Prices:** 18-22.50 Mobile home hire 300-400 **Facilities:** Wi-fi (charged) Kids' Club Play Area **Services:** **Leisure:** P **Off-site:** L R

COSTA DA CAPARICA ESTREMADURA

Orbitur

Av Afonso de Albuquerque, Quinta de St António, 2825-450
☎ 212901366 🖹 212900661
e-mail: caparica@orbitur.pt
web: www.orbitur.pt

This site has a small touring section and is 200 metres from a fine sandy beach.

dir: *After crossing Ponte Sul on road to Caparica, turn right at lights, site 1km on left.*

Open: All Year. **Site:** 5.7HEC **For hire:** **Facilities:** **Services:** **Off-site:** S

ÉVORA ALTO ALENTEJO

Orbitur

The Camping and Caravanning Club The Friendly Club

Estrada de Alcacovas, Herdade Esparragosa, 7005-206
☎ 266705190 🖹 266709830
e-mail: evora@orbitur.pt
web: www.orbitur.pt

Site in wooded surroundings with modern facilities.

C&CC Report *Located about a 1.5km from the Lisbon to Beja road in the southern suburbs of Évora, just over 1km from the city walls of this UNESCO World Heritage city.*

dir: *2km S near Km94.5.*

Open: All Year. **Site:** 3.3HEC **For hire:** **Facilities:** **Services:** **Leisure:** P

ÉVORA DE ALCOBAÇA ESTREMADURA

Rural de Silveira

Capuchos, 2460-479
☎ 262509573
e-mail: silveira.capuchos@gmail.com
web: www.campingsilveira.com

Set in a rural wooded location, between the sea and the mountains.

dir: *3km from Alcobaça on N86.*

GPS: 39.5261, -8.9658

Open: 15 May-15 Sep **Site:** 0.5HEC **Prices:** 12-14 **Facilities:** Play Area **Services:** **Off-site:** R

FERNÃO FERRO ESTREMADURA

Parque Verde

Avenida Casal do Sapo - Fontainhas, 2865-060
☎ 212108999 🖹 212103263
e-mail: info@parqueverde.pt
web: www.parqueverde.pt

30km from Lisbon, a family site with health club and other leisure activities throughout the year. Kids' club available in summer.

GPS: 38.5508, -9.0667

Open: All Year. **Site:** 17.5HEC **For hire:** **Prices:** 22-27 **Facilities:** Kids' Club Play Area **Services:** **Leisure:** P

FERREIRA DO ZÊZERE BEIRA LITORAL

Quinta da Cerejeira

2240-333
☎ 249361756
e-mail: info@cerejeira.com
web: www.cerejeira.com

Originally a wine farm, the site has wide, partially shaded pitches among fruit and olive trees. Live musical entertainment takes place during the summer.

dir: *A1 (Lisboa-Porto) exit Torres Novas, onto A23 towards Tomar then IC3 to Ferreira do Zêzere.*

GPS: 39.7007, -8.2781

Open: Feb-Sep **Site:** 1HEC **For hire:** **Prices:** 10-18.25 **Facilities:** Wi-fi Play Area **Services:** **Leisure:** P **Off-site:** L R

PORTUGAL

FIGUEIRA DA FOZ — BEIRA LITORAL

Orbitur

E N109 - Km 4, Gala, 3080-458
☎ 233431492 🖹 233431231
e-mail: info@orbitur.pt
web: www.orbitur.pt

An enclosed area set within a municipal park on top of Guarda hill.

dir: *On NW outskirts of town. Turn left off N16 Porto road at Km177, uphill for 0.5km.*

Open: All Year. **Site:** 6HEC **For hire:** **Facilities:** **Services:** **Leisure:** P **Off-site:** S

FIGUEIRÓ DOS VINHOS — BEIRA LITORAL

Quinta da Fonte

Fontainhas, 3260-328
☎ 933011017
e-mail: l.schieving@kanguru.pt
web: www.quintadafonte.nl

Small, rural campsite with pitches available among olive trees or in a field bordering a stream. Meals are freshly prepared daily, and served on the terrace, weather permitting. Only one pitch suitable for caravans and motorvans.

dir: *IC8 until Figueiró dos Vinhos (N237).*

Open: All Year. **Site:** 1HEC **For hire:** **Prices:** 16-18 Mobile home hire 210 **Facilities:** Play Area **Services:** **Off-site:** L P R

GOUVEIA — BEIRA LITORAL

Curral do Negro

6290-528
☎ 961350810 🖹 238458041
e-mail: info@curraldonegro.com
web: www.curraldonegro.com

A mountain setting surrounded by woodland.

dir: *Signed.*

Open: 18 Jan-30 Oct **Site:** 2HEC **Facilities:** **Services:** **Leisure:** P

Quinta das Cegonhas

Nabainhos, 6290-122
☎ 23874886 🖹 238748094
e-mail: cegonhas@cegonhas.com
web: www.cegonhas.com

At the northern end of Serra da Estrela Natur Park, pitches are arranged on wide terraces. Facilities include table tennis and swimming/children's pool. Wi-fi free for first hour.

GPS: 40.5208, -7.5417

Open: All Year. **Site:** 2HEC **Prices:** 14.55-20.90 **Facilities:** Wi-fi (charged) Play Area **Services:** **Leisure:** P

GUINCHO — ESTREMADURA

Orbitur

The Camping and Caravanning Club — The Friendly Club

E N247-6, Lugar de Areia, 2750-053
☎ 214870450 🖹 214857413
e-mail: guincho@orbitur.pt
web: www.orbitur.pt

On hilly ground in a pine wood in the Parque du Guincho, near the Boca do Inferno.

C&CC Report *Very convenient for Lisbon, with regular bus services from the site to Cascais and a good train connection from there to the capital.*

dir: *5km NW of Cascais, off road 247-7.*

Open: All Year. **Site:** 7.7HEC **For hire:** **Facilities:** **Services:** **Off-site:** S

IDANHA-A-NOVA — BEIRA BAIXA

Orbitur Idanha-a-Nova

E N354 - Km 8, Barragem de Idanha-a-Nova, 6060-166
☎ 277202793 🖹 277202945
e-mail: info@orbitur.pt
web: www.orbitur.pt

The campsite is near the Marechal Carmona Dam and near the Monfortinho hot springs in an area rich in history and architectural heritage. Individual marked pitches. Good for families and outdoor sports.

dir: *Off E N353, S from Fundão.*

Open: All Year. **Site:** 8HEC **For hire:** **Facilities:** **Services:** **Leisure:** P **Off-site:** L R

LUSO BEIRA LITORAL

Luso

E N336, Pampilhosa, Quinta Do Vale Do Jorge, 3050-246
☎ 231107551
e-mail: parquecampismoluso@gmail.com
On Portugal's Silver Coast, the wooded site has good facilities and is close to the motorway junction.
Open: All Year. **Site:** 3HEC **For hire:** **Facilities:** **Services:** **Off-site:** L P

MIRA BEIRA LITORAL

Vila Caia Camping

Travessa da Carreira do Tiro, 3070-176
☎ 231451524 231451861
e-mail: geral@vilacaia.com
web: www.vilacaia.com
2.5km from the beach, a quiet site shaded by trees close to a natural lake. Dogs are permitted, on leads. Many facilities only available in high season.
dir: *A17.*
GPS: 40.4472, -8.7569
Open: Jan-Nov **Site:** 6.5HEC **For hire:** **Prices:** 11.55-20.10 **Facilities:** Play Area **Services:** **Leisure:** P R **Off-site:** L S

MONTARGIL ALTO ALENTEJO

Orbitur

E N2, 7425-017
☎ 242901207 242901220
e-mail: montargil@orbitur.pt
web: www.orbitur.pt
A beautiful wooded location with good recreational facilities close to the River Alva.
dir: *N off N2.*
Open: All Year. **Site:** 6HEC **For hire:** **Facilities:** **Services:** **Off-site:** L

NAZARÉ ESTREMADURA

Orbitur Valado

Rua dos Combatentes do Ultramar 2, 2450-148
☎ 262561111 262561137
e-mail: valado@orbitur.pt
web: www.orbitur.pt
Set in a pine wood 2km from the village with good facilities.
dir: *300m E of village, S of road E N8-5 Nazaré-Alcobaça.*
Open: Feb-Oct **Site:** 6.3HEC **For hire:** **Facilities:** **Services:** **Off-site:** S

Vale Paraiso

E N242, 2450-138
☎ 262561800 262561900
e-mail: info@valeparaiso.com
web: www.valeparaiso.com
Situated in a beautiful natural park among tall pines. The site is well appointed with high standards of hygiene and varied recreational facilities. Massages and gym available.
GPS: 39.6203, -9.0564
Open: Jan-16 Dec, 27-31 Dec **Site:** 8.3HEC **For hire:** **Prices:** 13-23.70 **Facilities:** Wi-fi Play Area **Services:** **Leisure:** P **Off-site:** S

OUTEIRO DE LOURIÇAL BEIRA LITORAL

Tamanco

Rua do Louriçal 11, Casas Brancas, 3105-158
☎ 236952551 236952551
e-mail: tamanco@me.com
web: www.campismo-o-tamanco.com
Small site with a pleasant atmosphere and a good restaurant. Nearby are places of interest and beaches.
dir: *Via N109 or A1.*
GPS: 39.9917, -8.7889
Open: All Year. **Site:** 1.5HEC **For hire:** **Prices:** 10.50-18.90 **Facilities:** **Services:** **Leisure:** P **Off-site:**

PENICHE ESTREMADURA

CM

av Monsenhor Bastos, 2520-206
☎ 262789529 262789529
e-mail: campismo-peniche@sapo.pt
web: www.cm-peniche.pt
On a sandy hillock, partly wooded, 0.5km from sea.
dir: *2km E.*
Open: All Year. **Site:** 12.6HEC **Prices:** 4.50-7.55 **Facilities:** Play Area **Services:** **Off-site:** P S

Peniche Praia

Estrada Marginal Norte, 2520-605
☎ 262783460 262785334
e-mail: geral@penichepraia.pt
web: www.penichepraia.pt
On level ground 0.5km from the sea.
dir: *N towards Cabo Carudeiro.*
Open: All Year. **Site:** 1.5HEC **For hire:** **Facilities:** **Services:** **Off-site:** P S

PORTUGAL

PRAIA DE MIRA — BEIRA LITORAL

Orbitur

Estrada Florestal 1 - km 2, Dunas de Mira, 3070-792
231471234 231472047
e-mail: mira@orbitur.pt
web: www.orbitur.pt
Site lies in a dense forest.
dir: *N off N334 at Km2 towards Videira, opposite road fork.*
Open: Jan-Nov **Site:** 3HEC **For hire:** **Facilities:** **Services:** **Leisure:** S **Off-site:** L

QUIAIOS — BEIRA LITORAL

Orbitur Quiaios

Praia de Quiaios, 3080-515
233919995 233919996
e-mail: info@orbitur.pt
web: www.orbitur.pt
Situated adjacent to the beach in an area abounding in architectural heritage. The surrounding pine wood adds to the peaceful and relaxing environment.
dir: *8km from Figueira da Foz.*
Open: All Year. **Site:** **For hire:** **Facilities:** **Services:** **Leisure:** S **Off-site:** L

SANTO ANTÓNIO DAS AREIAS — ALTO ALENTEJO

Camping Asseiceira

Caixa Postal 2, Asseiceira, 7330-204
245992940
e-mail: gary-campingasseiceira@hotmail.com
web: www.campingasseiceira.com
British-owned site, situated in an olive grove, with views of the local village and castle. Walking maps to explore the surrounding countryside are provided.
Open: Dec-Oct **Site:** 1HEC **For hire:** **Prices:** 14-16 **Facilities:** Wi-fi **Services:** **Leisure:** P **Off-site:**

SÃO JACINTO — BEIRA LITORAL

Orbitur

E N327 - Km 20, 3800-901
234838284 234838122
e-mail: sjacinto@orbitur.pt
web: www.orbitur.pt
Set in a dense pine wood, towards the sea from the uneven paved Ovar road that runs alongside the lagoon.
dir: *1.5km from sea, W of N237.*
Open: Feb-Oct **Site:** 2.25HEC **For hire:** **Facilities:** **Services:** **Leisure:** R **Off-site:** S

SÃO PEDRO DE MOEL — ESTREMADURA

Orbitur

Rua Volta do Sete, 2430-440
244599168 244599148
e-mail: spedro@orbitur.pt
web: www.orbitur.pt
On a hill among pine trees.
dir: *Off road 242-2 from Marinha Grande at rdbt near fuel station on E outskirts of village, N for 100m.*
Open: All Year. **Site:** 7HEC **For hire:** **Facilities:** **Services:** **Leisure:** P **Off-site:** S

SOURE — BEIRA LITORAL

Termas da Azenha

Rua João Henriques Foja Oliveira, Vinha da Rainha, 3130-433
916508145 239508493
e-mail: info@termas-da-azenha.com
web: www.termas-da-azenha.com
Natural site with no marked pitches, popular with families as there are activities for children. Dogs are permitted on leads. Cars may be parked by tents except in high season.
Open: All Year. **Site:** **For hire:** **Prices:** 15-18 **Facilities:** Wi-fi Play Area **Services:** **Leisure:** P **Off-site:**

Drinking and driving
Strictly forbidden. Nil percentage of alcohol allowed in drivers' blood. Driving Licence can be suspended for a maximum of 90 days or prison sentence for offenders.

Driving licence
Minimum age at which a UK licence holder may drive a temporarily imported car and/or motorcycle (for up to 90 days) 18. Driving licences issued in the UK that do not incorporate a photograph must be accompanied by an International Driving Permit (IDP).

Fines
Police can impose fines and collect them on-the-spot, a receipt must be obtained. A vehicle which is illegally parked may be clamped and removed. If a fine is paid within 48 hours, the fine amount is halved.

Fuel
Lead replacement petrol (95 and 98 octane), unleaded petrol, diesel and LPG available. Petrol in a can permitted (must be empty when leaving Romania). Tax is payable on petrol and diesel in the vehicle tank when leaving Romania.

Credit cards are accepted at many stations; check with your card issuer for usage in Romania before travel. Payment is usually made in local currency.

Lights
Forbidden to drive at night if vehicle lighting faulty. Additional headlamps prohibited. Dipped headlights must be used outside built-up areas during the day.

Motorcycles
Use of dipped headlights during the day compulsory. Wearing of crash helmets is compulsory for driver and passenger of machines 50cc and over.

Motor insurance
Green Card/third party insurance compulsory. Drivers of vehicles registered abroad who are not in possession of a valid green card must take out short term insurance at the frontier.

Passengers/children in cars
Child under 12 cannot travel as a front seat passenger .

Seat belts
Compulsory for front/rear seat occupants to wear seat belts, if fitted.

Speed limits
Standard legal limits, which may be varied by signs

Private vehicles without trailers	
Built-up areas	50km/h
Outside built-up areas	90km/h
Dual carriageways	100km/h
Motorways	130km/h

Private vehicles with caravans or trailers & motorhomes or camper vans	
Built-up areas	50km/h
Motorways	110km/h
Main roads	90km/h
Other roads	80km/h

No minimum speed on motorways.

A 10km/h reduction of the standard speed limit applies if towing. A driver who has held a licence for less than 1 year is restricted to a speed limit of 20 km/h below the indicated speed. The speed limit for mopeds is 45 km/h inside and outside built-up areas.

Compulsory equipment in Romania
First aid kit

Fire extinguisher

Red warning triangle - not required for two wheeled vehicles.

Reflective jacket – All persons exiting a vehicle to walk on the road when in a breakdown or emergency situation must wear a reflective jacket.

Other rules/requirements
It is against the law to drive a dirty car.

If a temporarily imported vehicle is damaged before arrival in Romania, the importer must ask a Romanian Customs or Police Officer to write a report on the damage so that they can export the vehicle without problems. If any damage occurs inside the country a report must be obtained at the scene of the accident. Damaged vehicles may only be taken out of the country on production of this evidence. "Claxonarea interzisa" – use of horn prohibited. The use of the horn is prohibited between 2200hrs and 0600hrs in built-up areas.

Spiked tyres are prohibited.

The use of snow chains recommended for winter journeys to mountains and may be compulsory in case of heavy snow.

Since 1st October 2010, the road tax 'stickers' known as "rovinieta" have been replaced by a system of electronic tax. The tax is payable at the National Road Administration offices at border crossing points, from post office branches in Romania or some petrol stations.

The driver must give details of the vehicle, his identity and place of residence. You must advise of the number of days in Romania and pay the tax accordingly. This information is then entered into a database of the Road Information Centre. Cameras are situated along roads. This enables the traffic police to check your vehicle number plate against the database. The cost depends on the vehicle emissions category and period of use in Romania. Fine for non-compliance or expired road tax is between 50 and 900.

Bulgaria

Drinking and driving

If the level of alcohol in the bloodstream is 0.05 per cent or more the driver will be prosecuted and receive a fine and driving suspension. The police carry out random breath tests. If the test is positive, the driver will be required to undergo a blood test carried out by a hospital doctor. The police can test drivers for the use of drugs at the roadside.

Driving licence

Minimum age at which a UK driving licence holder may drive a temporarily imported car and/or motorcycle 18. It is recommended that an International Driving Permit (IDP) accompanies older licences that are not a EC model.

Fines

On-the-spot. An official receipt should be obtained. Wheel clamps are in use for illegally parked cars. Vehicles causing an obstruction will be towed away.

Fuel

Leaded petrol is no longer available. Unleaded petrol (95 and 98 octane), diesel and LPG are available. Credit cards accepted at most filling stations but not all local stations in small towns accept international cards; check with your card issuer for usage in Bulgaria before travel. Importation of fuel in a spare can prohibited.

Lights

The use of dipped headlights during daylight hours throughout the year is recommended, however their use is compulsory from the 1st November to the 1st March.

Motorcycles

Wearing of crash helmets compulsory for both driver and passenger. Motorcyclists must have their lights on at all times.

Motor insurance

Third party insurance compulsory. Green Cards are recognised.

Passengers/children in cars

Children under the age of 3 may not be transported in vehicles not fitted with child restraints. Children aged 3 or over, measuring less than 1.5m may travel in a vehicle without restraints but they must occupy a rear seat.

Seat belts

Compulsory for front/rear seat occupants to wear seat belts.

Speed limits

Standard legal limits, which may be varied by signs

Private vehicles without trailers	
Built-up areas	50km/h
Outside built-up areas	90km/h
Motorways	130km/h
Private vehicles with caravan or trailer	
Built-up areas	50km/h
Outside built-up areas	70km/h
Motorways	100 km/h

Compulsory equipment in Bulgaria

Fire extinguisher – Not required for two wheeled vehicles.

First-aid kit

Warning triangle - not required for two wheeled vehicles.

Reflective jackets - Wearing a reflective jacket is compulsory for any person who has to step out of a vehicle, day or night in case of breakdown or emergency on a motorway. This regulation also applies to motorcyclists.

Other rules/requirements

In built-up areas it is prohibited to use the horn between 2200hrs and 0600hrs (0900hrs on public holidays), and between 1200hrs and 1600hrs.

Visiting motorists are required to drive through a liquid disinfectant on entry for which the charge is (approx) 4, and also purchase a 'vignette' (road tax). The vignette is available at the border, UAB offices, most petrol stations and offices of the CI and DZI Bank, weekly, monthly or annually. Heavy fines are imposed for non-compliance.

Winter tyres are recommended in winter. Snow chains are permitted. Their use can become compulsory according to road conditions, in which case this is indicated by the international road sign. Maximum speed limit with snow chains is 50km/h. Spiked tyres are forbidden.

Drivers of luxury or 4 x 4 vehicles are advised to use guarded car parks.

A GPS based navigation system which has maps indicating the location of fixed speed cameras must have the 'fixed speed camera PoI (Points of Interest)' function deactivated. The use of radar detectors is prohibited.

In one way streets parking is on the left only.

Tolls Bulgarian Lev (BGN)	Car
7 day vignette	BGN60.63
1 month vignette	BGN72.12
E85 across River Danube - Ruse - Giurgiu (Romania)	BGN4.00

Please note: Although the official currency of Romania is the Romanian leu, the campsites featured in this guide have quoted their prices in Euros.

ROMANIA

AUREL VLAICU — ARAD

Aurel Vlaicu

Stradă Principale 155, 335401
☎ 0254 245541
e-mail: zeerom@zeelandnet.nl
web: www.campingaurelvlaicu.ro
Situated in a quiet village with fine views of the mountains.

Open: 15 Apr-Sep **Site:** 0.7HEC **For hire:** **Facilities:** **Services:** **Leisure:** P **Off-site:** R

BLAJEL — SIBIU

Doua Lumi

Stradă Tudor Vladimirescu 87-89, 557050
☎ 0269 851079
e-mail: info@doualumi.com
web: www.doualumi.com
Small, well-kept family site, with a friendly atmosphere and clean facilities. Located in the heart of Transylvania, information can be provided about the area and tours. Leisure facilities include a swimming pool and bike hire.

dir: *Off DN14a in centre of village.*

GPS: 46.2114, 24.3242

Open: Apr-Oct **Site:** 0.5HEC **For hire:** **Prices:** 13-16.50 **Facilities:** Wi-fi Play Area **Services:** **Leisure:** P **Off-site:**

BRAN — BRASOV

Vampire Camping

Stradă Principala 77C, 507025
☎ 0316 2583909
e-mail: info@vampirecamping.com
web: www.vampirecamping.com
Peaceful location bordered by hills and mountains. Ideally located for visiting Bran Castle, most commonly known as Dracula's Castle, home of the famous fictional vampire.

Open: Apr-1 Nov **Site:** 3.5HEC **For hire:** **Facilities:** **Services:** **Off-site:** P

CÂRTA — SIBIU

De Oude Wilg

Stradă Prundului 311, 557070
☎ 0269 521347
e-mail: de_oude_wilg@yahoo.com
web: www.campingdeoudewilg.nl
Centrally located, north of the Fagaras mountains in a broad valley. Small site with level pitches in the heart of the village.

Open: All Year. **Site:** 1HEC **Prices:** 11-15 **Facilities:** Wi-fi **Services:** **Leisure:** R **Off-site:**

CISNADIOARA — SIBIU

Ananas Camping

Stradă Cimitirului 32, 555301
☎ 0269 566066
e-mail: info@ananas7b.de
web: www.ananas7b.de
Situated in the heart of Transylvania with a mountain landscape, forests and meadows.

Open: 15 Apr-15 Oct **Site:** **For hire:** **Prices:** 8-12 **Facilities:** Wi-fi Play Area **Services:** **Leisure:** P **Off-site:**

DARMANESTI — SUCEAVA

Camperland Camping Trotus Valley

Calea Trotusului 272, 605300
☎ 0744 665567 0234 374705
e-mail: info@camperland.ro
web: www.camperland.ro
Site located in mountainous region in east of country between the Black Sea and the monasteries in Northern Moldova. Trips can be arranged for small groups.

dir: *Off DN12A (Adjud-Mercuiri).*

Open: 15 Apr-15 Oct **Site:** 1.5HEC **For hire:** **Facilities:** **Services:** **Off-site:** R

EFORIE — CONSTANTA

Meduza

Stradă Sportului, 905350
☎ 0767 707122
e-mail: n_t_sco@yahoo.com
Site located near 4km of beaches and Lake Techirghiol with its spa properties.

Open: Jun-15 Sep **Site:** 2.2HEC **Facilities:** **Services:** **Off-site:** S

GILAU — CLUJ

Eldorado

DN1-E60, 407310

☎ 0264 371688 🖷 0264 371688

e-mail: info@campingeldorado.com

web: www.campingeldorado.com

Situated in the tourist area of Transylvania at the foot of the Apuseni Mountains. Tents are available for hire for groups.

dir: *Off E60.*

GPS: 46.7669, 23.3530

Open: 15 Apr-15 Oct **Site:** 3.8HEC **For hire:** **Prices:** 10-13.50 **Facilities:** Wi-fi Play Area **Services:** **Leisure:** L P **Off-site:**

MINIŞ — ARAD

Camping Route Roemenië

317137

☎ 0742 678111

e-mail: camping.route.roemenie@gmail.com

web: www.routeroemenie.nl

Small, relaxing site surrounded by mountains, 3km from a lake where fishing and swimming are available. Compulsory separate car park in high season. There is a shopping service available and organised excursions.

dir: *From centre of Arad follow signs to Deva on E68, then in Paulis follow signs to site.*

GPS: 46.1336, 21.5983

Open: 15 Apr-15 Sep **Site:** 0.5HEC **Prices:** 11-16 **Facilities:** Wi-fi Play Area **Services:** **Leisure:** P **Off-site:** L R

MURIGHIOL — TULCEA

Camping Lac Murighiol

827150

☎ 0740 501297

e-mail: contact@campinglacmurighiol.ro

web: www.campinglacmurighiol.ro

Peaceful site situated near the Danube Delta. Organised trips are available for campers to experience the wildlife and ecology of the area. Charge made for dogs.

dir: *On Main St.*

GPS: 45.0464, 29.1606

Open: All Year. **Site:** 0.25HEC **Prices:** 8.50-13.50 **Facilities:** Wi-fi Play Area **Services:** **Off-site:** L R

RUCAR — ARGES

Panorama

Stradă Brasovului 219, 117630

☎ 0740 666279

e-mail: campingpanorama@hotmail.com

Situated in the spectacular Carpathian mountain area.

dir: *Route E574 Brasov-Pitesti.*

Open: May-Sep **Site:** 1.1HEC **For hire:** **Facilities:** **Services:** **Off-site:**

SÓVATA — MURES

Vasskert

Stradă Prinzipala 129/A, 545500

☎ 0265 570902 🖷 0265 570902

e-mail: vasskert@szovata.hu

web: www.szovata.hu

Unspoilt location with mountain streams and forests, close to the famous Bear Lake with its spa properties.

Open: May-Sep **Site:** 0.8HEC **For hire:** **Prices:** 11-14.50 **Facilities:** Wi-fi Play Area **Services:** **Leisure:** R **Off-site:** L P

ROMANIA

Please note: Although the official currency of Bulgaria is the Bulgarian lev, the campsites featured in this guide have quoted their prices in Euros.

BULGARIA

DRYANOVO — GABROVO

Strinava

Dryanovo Monastery, 5370
☎ 0676 72332
e-mail: bacho_kiro2@abv.bg
web: www.dryanovo.com

Site situated near the outskirts of Dryanovo Monastery, by the banks of the river Dryanovska in an attractive location with much natural wildlife. Booking required in April and September.

dir: *1km from the main road Veliko Tarnovo - Gabrovo.*

Open: Apr-Sep **Site:** **For hire:** **Facilities:** **Leisure:** R **Off-site:** P

HARMANLI — HASKOVO

Sakar Hills Camping

2 Georgi Rakovski St, Biser, 6470
☎ 0885 504338
e-mail: mail@sakar-hills.com
web: www.sakar-hills.com

Located close to the Greek and Turkish borders, large pitches and a covered outdoor seating area for campers use.

dir: *1km from E85 Sofia-Istanbul road.*

GPS: 41.8703, 25.9913

Open: Apr-Oct **Site:** 0.5HEC **Facilities:** Wi-fi **Services:** **Off-site:** L P R

LYASKOVETS — VELIKO TARNOVO

Camping Veliko Tarnovo

70 Vail Levski St, Dragizhevo Village, 5145
☎ 0619 42777
e-mail: office@campingvelikotarnovo.com
web: www.campingvelikotarnovo.com

Set in a rural, picturesque valley and close to tourist attractions. Fully serviced pitches and family bathroom available.

dir: *A4/E772 Veliko Tarnovo - Varna.*

GPS: 43.0669, 25.7531

Open: Mar-Oct **Site:** 1.5HEC **For hire:** **Prices:** 12-30 **Facilities:** Wi-fi Play Area **Services:** **Leisure:** P **Off-site:** L R

Please note: Although the official currency of Romania is the Romanian leu, the campsites featured in this guide have quoted their prices in Euros.

Drinking and driving

If the level of alcohol in the bloodstream is 0.05% or more, severe penalties include fine or suspension of driving licence. 0% of alcohol is permitted in the drivers' blood if the licence has been held for less than two years, the person is under 21 or employed as a professional driver. The driver can still be fined for levels under 0.05% if the driver is unable to drive safely. These rules also apply to narcotics.

Driving licence

Minimum age at which a UK licence holder may drive a temporarily imported car and/or motorcycle (exceeding 125cc) 18. An IDP (International Driving Permit) is compulsory for holders of driving licences not incorporating a photograph.

Fines

On-the-spot, they must be paid in local currency. Refusal to pay could result in your passport being held. Illegally parked vehicles will be towed away or clamped.

Fuel

Unleaded petrol (95 and 98 octane), diesel and LPG available. No leaded petrol (lead substitute additive available). Petrol in a can permitted. Credit cards accepted at filling stations, check with your card issuer for usage before travel.

Lights

Use of dipped headlights during the day compulsory.

Motorcycles

Use of dipped headlights during the day compulsory. Wearing of crash helmets is compulsory for both driver and passenger. Children under 12 not permitted as a passenger.

Motor insurance

Third-party compulsory.

Passengers/children in cars

Child under 12 and smaller than 1.5m must use suitable restraint system for their age and size. Children over 12 may wear normal seat belts.

Seat belts

Compulsory for front/rear seat occupants to wear seat belts, if fitted.

Speed limits

Standard legal limits, which may be varied by signs

Private vehicles without trailers

Built-up areas	50km/h
Outside built-up areas	90km/h
Dual carriageways ("fast roads")	100km/h
Motorways	130km/h

Some areas have a restricted speed limit of 30km/h.

Minimum speed on motorways	60km/h

Private vehicle towing a trailer or caravan

Built-up areas	50km/h
Motorways	80km/h
Dual carriageways ("fast roads")	80km/h
Other roads	80km/h
Vehicles equipped with snow chains	50km/h

In bad weather and when visibility is reduced to less than 50m due to bad weather, maximum speed limit 50km/h

Compulsory equipment in Slovenia

Reflective jacket – (not motorcycles) The reflective waistcoat/s should be kept in the vehicle and not in the boot as any person exiting the vehicle must wear a reflective safety jacket as soon as they leave their vehicle in an accident/breakdown situation, fine for non-compliance.

Warning triangle – two if towing a trailer. Not required for two wheeled vehicles.

Snow chains – must be carried between 15 November and 15 March (and at other times under winter weather conditions) by private cars and vehicles up to 3.5tonnes unless the vehicle is fitted with four winter tyres marked M&S. Minimum tyre tread depth for use in winter weather conditions is 3mm.

Other rules/requirements

Warning triangle and/or hazard warning lights must be used in an accident/ breakdown situation.

At night if hazard lights fail, in addition to a warning triangle a yellow flashing light or position lights must mark the vehicle.

Fire extinguisher, first-aid kit and set of replacement bulbs recommended, replacements bulbs are compulsory for residents.

Foreign drivers involved in an accident are advised to call the police and obtain a written report.

It is prohibited to overtake a bus transporting children when passengers are getting on/off.

Drivers must not indicate when entering a roundabout, they must use indicators when leaving the roundabout.

Use of the horn is prohibited in built-up areas or at night, except in cases of danger/injury/illness. The use of the horn is generally prohibited in the vicinity of hospitals.

A vignette system has been introduced which replaces tolls. The vignette will have to be displayed when travelling on motorways and expressways and will be available to purchase from filling stations in Slovenia and in neighbouring countries. The vignettes are available with validities of 1 year (vehicle up to 3.5t 95), per month (vehicle up to 3.5t 30) and for 7 days (vehicle up to 3.5t 15), with the yearly one being valid from 1st December to the 31st January the following year, fine for non-display 300 minimum. Further information can be found on www.dars.si

The use of spiked tyres is prohibited. Hazard warning lights must be used when reversing.

Vignettes Currency Euro (€)	Car	Car Towing Caravan/Trailer
weekly vignette	€15.00	€15.00
monthly vignette	€30.00	€30.00
annual vignette	€95.00	€95.00
Jesenice - St Jakob (Austrian Border)	€6.50	€6.50

ANKARAN — PRIMORSKA

Camp Adria Ankaran

Jadranska cesta 25, 6280
05 663 7350 05 663 7360
e-mail: camp@adria-ankaran.si
web: www.adria-ankaran.si

Quiet, family site on the coast, with leisure facilities including an Olympic-size swimming pool, spa and bowling.

dir: *Via A1 & H5.*

Open: 14 Apr-15 Oct **Site:** 7HEC **For hire:** **Prices:** 22-27 **Facilities:** Wi-fi (charged) Kids' Club Play Area **Services:** **Leisure:** P S **Off-site:**

BANOVCI — POMURJE

Banovci

Banovci 1a, 9241
02 513 1400 02 587 1703
e-mail: terme@terme-banovci.si
web: www.terme-banovci.si

Site in a thermal spa location with pool complex featuring whirlpools, fountains and waterslides. Separate naturist section.

dir: *On Ormoz-Radenci road, past Ljutomer & right after level crossing, campsite signed.*

Open: All Year. **Site:** 8HEC **For hire:** **Facilities:** **Services:** **Leisure:** P **Off-site:** R

BLED — GORENJSKA

Bled

Kidriceva 10c, 4260
04 575 2000 04 575 2002
e-mail: info@camping-bled.com
web: camping-bled.com

Well-run site in stunning location with many activities.

C&CC Report *The Julian Alps are an especially beautiful part of Europe's greatest mountain range, with vast limestone crags topping steep and densely wooded slopes. Friendly, well run and with very good facilities, Camping Bled is in a stunning location by the unspoilt lake. Gems to visit include Slovenia's only island, on Lake Bled; lovely Lake Bohinj; Europe's largest show caves at Postojna; Pokljuka plateau, with its soaring pine forests, wild flowers and tiny farming villages; and General Tito's former residence. The Bled Days festival is held on the fourth weekend in July each year and includes Bled Night, with thousands of candles adrift on the lake.*

dir: *Drive from Bled along the lake in direction of Bohinjska Bistrica. Turn right after 1.5 km, campsite 1km.*

Open: 20 Mar-15 Oct **Site:** 6.5HEC **For hire:** **Facilities:** **Services:** **Leisure:** L **Off-site:** P

BOHINJSKA BISTRICA — GORISKA

Danica

Triglavska 60, 4264
04 572 1702 04 572 3330
e-mail: info@camp-danica.si
web: www.camp-danica.si

Site ringed by the Julian Alps and in a pleasant location by the River Sava and Lake Bohinj.

Open: May-Oct **Site:** 4.5HEC **Facilities:** **Services:** **Leisure:** R **Off-site:** L P

SLOVENIA

BOVEC GORISKA

Polovnik

Ledina 8, 5230

☎ 05 389 6007 🖷 05 389 6006

e-mail: kamp.polovnik@siol.net

web: www.kamp-polovnik.com

Located in a beautiful park in the Soea Valley and a short walk from the centre of Bovec. The layout of the campsite enables guests to reach all the local attractions by foot.

dir: *N side of Bovec, follow camping signs. Approach via Passo de Predil not recommended for large caravans.*

Open: Apr-15 Oct **Site:** 1.2HEC **Prices:** 16.02-19.02 **Facilities:** Wi-fi **Services:** **Off-site:** P R

IZOLA PRIMORSKA

Belvedere

Dobrava 1a, 6310

☎ 05 660 5100 🖷 05 660 5182

e-mail: belvedere@belvedere.si

web: www.belvedere.si

On a hill, near the coast overlooking the Bay of Trieste. On-site shop open in July and August.

dir: *From Koper, campsite 1km after Izola. NB Do not take Izola exit but drive towards Portoroz & follow campsite signs.*

Open: Apr-Sep **Site:** 3HEC **Prices:** 22-28 **Facilities:** **Services:** **Leisure:** P S **Off-site:**

KOBARID GORISKA

Kamp Nadiža Podbela

Stresova ulica 18, 5222

☎ 04 144 3535

e-mail: info@kamp-nadiza.com

web: www.kamp-nadiza.com

Suitable for families with small children and on the banks of Nadiža river.

Open: 15 Mar-Oct **Site:** 3HEC **For hire:** **Facilities:** Wi-fi Kids' Club Play Area **Services:** **Leisure:** R **Off-site:** R

Koren

Ladra 1B, 5222

☎ 05 389 1311 🖷 05 389 1310

e-mail: info@kamp-koren.si

web: www.kamp-koren.si

In a picturesque location by the Soca river and under Mount Krn. Good facilities for water sports, hiking and mountaineering.

dir: *At Drežnica, 5km E of Kobarid (Bovec-Tolmin road).*

GPS: 46.2508, 13.5867

Open: All Year. **Site:** 2HEC **For hire:** **Prices:** 21-24 **Facilities:** Wi-fi (charged) Play Area **Services:** **Leisure:** R **Off-site:**

LESCE GORENJSKA

Camping Šobec

Šobčeva resta 25, 4248

☎ 04 535 3700 🖷 04 535 3701

e-mail: sobec@siol.net

web: www.sobec.si

In a wooded area on lake shore.

dir: *Via A2/E61.*

GPS: 46.3561, 14.1499

Open: 16 Apr-2 Oct **Site:** 16HEC **For hire:** **Prices:** 21.40-25.60 **Facilities:** Wi-fi Kids' Club Play Area **Services:** **Leisure:** L R **Off-site:** P

LJUBLJANA GORENJSKA

Ljubljana Resort

Dunadska cesta 270, 1000

☎ 01 568 3913 🖷 01 568 3912

e-mail: ljubljana.resort@gpl.si

web: www.ljubljanaresort.si

A shaded site by the Sava river, part of larger complex which includes a hotel.

GPS: 46.0978, 14.5189

Open: 14 Mar-Dec **Site:** 3HEC **For hire:** **Facilities:** Wi-fi (charged) Kids' Club Play Area **Services:** **Leisure:** P R **Off-site:**

MOJSTRANA — GORENJSKA

Camping Kamne

Dovje 9, 4281

☎ 04 589 1105 🖷 04 589 1105

e-mail: campingkamne@telemach.net

web: www.campingkamne.com

In the immediate vicinity of Triglav National park, an area of mountains and scenic valleys.

dir: *E of Dovje, off Kranjska Gora-Jesenice road.*

GPS: 46.4645, 13.9579

Open: All Year. **Site:** 1.5HEC **For hire:** **Prices:** 13.40-17.60 **Facilities:** Play Area **Services:** **Leisure:** P **Off-site:**

MORAVSKE TOPLICE — POMURJE

Camping Terme 3000

Kranjčeva 12, 9226

☎ 02 512 1200 🖷 02 512 1148

e-mail: recepcija.camp2@terme3000.si

web: www.sava-hotels-resorts.com

Shaded by trees, this site has modern facilities and access is available to the Terme 3000 waterpark.

GPS: 46.6801, 16.2206

Open: All Year. **Site:** 7HEC **For hire:** **Facilities:** Wi-fi (charged) Kids' Club Play Area **Services:** **Off-site:** P

PODČETRTEK — SAVINJSKO

Terme Olimia - Camp Natura

Zdravliška Cesta 24, 3524

☎ 03 829 7000 🖷 03 582 9009

e-mail: alenka.brglez@terme-olimia.com

web: www.terme-olimia.com

Well-presented site, close to a swimming pool/spa complex.

Open: Apr-Oct **Site:** **For hire:** **Prices:** 29.80-33.80 **Facilities:** Wi-fi Kids' Club Play Area **Services:** **Leisure:** P **Off-site:**

PORTOROZ — PRIMORSKA

Lucija

Seca 204, 6320

☎ 05 690 6000 🖷 05 690 6900

e-mail: camp@metropolgroup.si

web: www.metropol-hotels.com

Close to the Adriatic seaside resort of Portoroz with its many attractions. Dance and music evenings organised on the site.

Open: 10 Apr-4 Oct **Site:** 5.5HEC **Facilities:** **Services:** **Leisure:** S **Off-site:** P

RECICA OB SAVINJI — SAVINJSKO

Menina

Varpolje 105, 3332

☎ 04 052 5266

e-mail: info@campingmenina.com

web: www.campingmenina.com

Peaceful site set in a scenic location by the Savinja River and the Kamnik-Savinja Alps.

dir: *800m off main Mozirje - Ljubno road.*

Open: All Year. **Site:** 8.5HEC **For hire:** **Prices:** 15-24 Mobile home hire 400-585 **Facilities:** Wi-fi Kids' Club Play Area **Services:** **Leisure:** L R **Off-site:**

Drinking and driving
If the level of alcohol in the bloodstream is 0.05% or more, severe penalties include fines and withdrawal of visitor's driving licence. Drivers with less than 2 years experience, 0.03%. Severe penalties include imprisonment for non compliance

Driving licence
Minimum age at which a UK licence holder may drive a temporarily imported car 18. Motorcycles up to 125cc 16, over 125cc 18. All valid UK driving licences should be accepted in Spain. This includes the older all-green style UK licences (in Northern Ireland older paper style with photographic counterpart) although the EC appreciates that these may be more difficult to understand and that drivers may wish to voluntarily update them before travelling abroad, if time permits. Alternatively, older licences may be accompanied by an International Driving Permit (IDP).

Fines
On-the-spot. An official receipt should be obtained. Illegally parked vehicles can be towed away. Wheel clamps are also in use.

Fuel
Unleaded petrol (95 and 98 octane) available. No leaded petrol. Petrol in a can permitted. Diesel (Gasoleo 'A' or Gas-oil) available Note: Gasoleo 'B' is heating oil only.

LPG is available under the name of "Autogas", but there are only a few sales outlets at present. For locations please see map on website at www.repsolypf.com or www.spainautogas.com. Credit cards accepted at most filling stations; check with your card issuer for usage in Spain before travel.

Lights
The use of full headlights in built-up areas is prohibited; use sidelights or dipped headlights depending on how well lit the roads are. Dipped headlights must be used in tunnels.

Motorcycles
Use of dipped headlights during the day compulsory. Wearing of crash helmets compulsory, this includes trikes and quads unless they are equipped with seat belts. A child between 7 and 11 years old may be transported as a passenger on a motorcycle driven by his mother, father or authorised person. He/she must wear a helmet suitable for his/her size. Moped drivers under the age of 18 can not transport passengers. A child under the age of 7 can not be transported at all.

Motor insurance
Third-party compulsory.

Passengers/children in cars
Children up to the age of 12, measuring less than 135 cm must be seated in a child restraint system adapted to their size and weight, except when travelling in a taxi in an urban area. Children measuring more than 135 cm may use an adult seatbelt.

Seat belts
Compulsory for front/rear seat occupants to wear seat belts, if fitted.

Speed limits
Standard legal limits, which may be varied by signs

Private vehicles without trailers	
Built-up areas	50km/h
2nd category roads	90km/h
1st category roads	100 km/h
Motorways	120km/h
On motorways/dual carriageways in built-up areas	80km/h
Minimum speed on motorways/dual carriageways	60km/h
Some residential zones are 20km/h	
Camping car (motorhome) & Car towing a trailer up to 750kg	
Motorways and dual carriageways	90km/h
2nd category roads	70km/h
1st category roads	80km/h
Vehicle towing a trailer over 750kg	
Motorways and dual carriageways	80km/h
2nd category roads	70km/h
1st category roads	80km/h

Compulsory equipment in Spain
Spare tyre – or tyre repair kit and the equipment to change the tyre.

Warning triangle - one warning triangle compulsory for foreign registered vehicles but carrying two is recommended as, in an accident/breakdown situation; local officials may impose a fine if only one is produced. Not required for two wheeled vehicles.

Reflective jacket - The wearing of reflectorised jacket/waistcoat compulsory if driver and/or passenger(s) exits vehicle which is immobilised on the carriageway of all motorways and main or busy roads. However, it is not mandatory to carry a reflectorised jacket in the vehicle and Spanish police cannot fine a foreign motorist who does not carry one. Be aware as car hire companies are not under legal obligation to supply them to persons hiring vehicles, so often don't.

Other rules/requirements
It is recommended that a driver who wears glasses should carry a spare pair with them if this is noted on your driving licence.

Apparatus with a screen which can distract a driver (such as television, video, DVD equipment) should be positioned in places where the driver is unable to see them. This excludes GPS systems. It is prohibited to touch or program the device unless parked in a safe place.

The use of radar detectors is prohibited, severe penalty for non compliance.

In urban areas it is prohibited to sound the horn at any time, except in an emergency. Lights may be flashed in place of using the horn.

The use of snow chains is recommended in snowy weather conditions, police can stop vehicles not fitted with snow chains. Maximum speed when using snow chains is 50 km/h. The winter period is usually from November to March.

The use of spiked tyres is prohibited.

In case of a car towing a caravan/trailer exceeding 12m, there must be two yellow reflectors at the rear of the towed caravan or trailer.

A load may exceed the length of a private vehicle at the rear by up to 10% of its length. The load must be indicated by a panel with diagonal red and white stripes. If you wish to carry bicycles on the rear of your vehicle, you will need a 50 x 50 cm reflectorised panel, which can be brought from most caravan/motor home accessory shops or from www.fiamma.com – they are available in plastic or aluminium.

In some cities in one way streets, vehicles must be parked on the side of the road where houses bear uneven numbers on uneven days of the month, and on the side of even numbers on even days.

Only fully hands-free phone systems are permitted. The use of earpieces or headphones while driving is banned. Failure to comply carries a fine of 200.

Motorists should be aware of contrived incidents. Foreign registered vehicles, especially those towing caravans, and hire cars are often targeted in service areas or tricked in to stopping on the hard shoulder by the occupant of a passing vehicle. They will gesture that something is wrong with the vehicle. Lock all doors and keep bags out of sight. The number of thefts by bogus policemen has increased in Madrid and Catalonia.

Tolls (Private car, with or without trailer)	
A1 Burgos - A68 (near Miranda de Ebro)	€8.75
A12 Leon - Astorga	€3.85
A15/A68 Pamplona (Irunea) - Tudela	€12.05
A19 Barcelona - Blanes	€3.97
A2 Zaragoza - Tarragona	€16.25
A3 Madrid - Casa de la Moraleja	€3.40
A4 Cadiz - Dos Hermanas (Sevilla)	€5.90
A41 Madrid - Toledo	€2.20
A51 Madrid - Avila	€8.10
A55 La Coruna - Carballo	€2.30
A57 Vigo - Baiona	€1.45
A6 Villalba - Adanero	€9.35
A61 Madrid - Segovia	€7.35
A66 Leon - Oviado	€10.60
A68 Miranda de Ebro - Bilbao (Bilbo)	€8.80
A68 Zaragoza - Miranda de Ebro	€17.65
A7 Alicante (Alacant) - Cartagena	€3.15
A7 Barcelona - Tarragona	€11.26
A7 La Jonquera (French Frontier) - Barcelona	€12.56
A7 Malaga - Gibraltar	€13.15
A7 Valencia - Alicante (Alacant)	€13.90
A7 Tarragona - Valencia	€22.00
A8 Bilbao (Bilbo) - Irun (French Frontier)	€8.59
A9 Ferrol - La Coruna	€3.60
A9 La Coruna - Santiago de Compostela	€5.15
A9 Santiago de Compostela - Vigo	€7.35
AP53 Santiago de Compostela - Ourense	€5.15
C16 Barcelona - Puigcerda (Tunel del Cadi)	€20.83
C32 Barcelona - Tarragona	€11.26
E9 Barcelona - Tunel de Vallviderol	€3.52
M12 Madrid (Barajas) Airport - Alcobendas (E5/A1)	€1.75
R2 Madrid - Guadalajara	€6.85
R5 Madrid - Navadcarnero	€3.50
Tunnels	
Tunel del Cadi (Spanish/French border)	€11.00
Tunels de Vallvidrera - Barcelona	€3.52

Andorra

Drinking and driving

The permitted level of alcohol in the bloodstream is 0.05 per cent.

Driving licence

Minimum age at which a UK licence holder may drive temporarily imported car and/or motorcycle 18.

Fines

On-the-spot.

Fuel

Leaded (98 octane), unleaded petrol (95 and 98 octane) and Diesel (Gasoil) is available but not LPG available. It is forbidden to carry petrol in a can. Credit cards are accepted at most filling stations, check with your card issuer for usage in Andorra before travel.

Lights

Dipped headlights should be used in poor daytime visibility. Motorcycles: Use of dipped headlights during the day compulsory. The wearing of a crash helmet is compulsory.

Motor insurance

Third party insurance is compulsory.

Passengers/children in cars

Children under 10 years and measuring less than 1.5m must be placed in a restraint system adapted to their size, of an EU approved design. If they are travelling in the front of the car, the airbag must be deactivated.

Seat belts

Compulsory for front seat occupants to wear seat belts, if fitted.

Speed limits

Standard legal limits, which may be varied by signs

Private vehicles with or without trailers	
Built-up areas	50km/h
Outside built-up areas	between 60km/h and 90km/h

Compulsory equipment in Andorra

Spare bulbs
Warning triangle
Reflective yellow waistcoat

Other rules/requirements

Winter tyres are recommended. Snow chains must be used when road conditions or signs indicate.

NORTH EAST COAST

ALBANYÀ — GIRONA

Bassegoda Park

ctra de Bassegoda, 17733
972 542020 972 542021
e-mail: info@bassegodapark.com
web: www.bassegodapark.com

Set within a National Park in a peaceful, natural setting. Ideal for hiking in the surrounding countryside. On-site facilities include an outdoor swimming pool, games room and sports area.

Open: 3 Mar-9 Dec **Site:** 4.5HEC **For hire:** **Prices:** 23.85-29.50 **Facilities:** Wi-fi Play Area **Services:** **Leisure:** L P R

BEGUR — GIRONA

Begur

ctra D'Esclanya km2, 17255
972 623201 972 624566
e-mail: info@campingbegur.com
web: www.campingbegur.com

A terraced site in a wooded valley.

dir: *1.4km SE of town. Right of road to Palafrugell, 400m after turning for Fornells & Aiguablava.*

Open: Apr-Sep **Site:** 8HEC **For hire:** **Prices:** 25-44.10 **Facilities:** Wi-fi Kids' Club Play Area **Services:** **Leisure:** P **Off-site:** S

Maset

Playa de sa Riera, 17255
972 623023 972 623901
e-mail: info@campingelmaset.com
web: www.campingelmaset.com

A well-kept terraced site, divided into pitches in a beautiful valley, 300 metres from the sea.

dir: *2km N of Begur. If entering from W, turn left just before town.*

Open: 13 May-13 Oct **Site:** 1.2HEC **For hire:** **Prices:** 23.20-33.80 Mobile home hire 385-735 **Facilities:** Wi-fi Play Area **Services:** **Leisure:** P **Off-site:** S

Site 6HEC (site size) grass sand stone little shade partly shaded mainly shaded motorvans accepted bungalows for hire mobile homes for hire tents for hire no dogs site fully accessible for wheelchairs
Prices amount quoted is per night, for 2 adults and car, plus tent or caravan Mobile home hire is a weekly rate.

BLANES GIRONA

Bella Terra

av Vila de Madrid 35-40, 17300

972 348017 972 348275

e-mail: info@campingbellaterra.com

web: www.campingbellaterra.com

A large family site in a lovely pine wood beside the beach with modern facilities. Dogs are not permitted in rentals.

dir: *Via N11.*

GPS: 41.6581, 2.7792

Open: Apr-Sep **Site:** 10.5HEC **For hire:** **Prices:** 44.10-54.60 **Facilities:** Wi-fi (charged) Kids' Club Play Area **Services:** **Leisure:** P S

Blanes

av Villa de Madrid 33, 17300

972 331591 972 337063

e-mail: info@campingblanes.com

web: www.campingblanes.com

Set in a pine forest with direct path to the beach, 1km from the town centre reached along a sea promenade.

dir: *On left of Paseo Villa de Madrid coast road towards town.*

GPS: 41.6591, 2.7795

Open: All Year. **Site:** 2HEC **Prices:** 25.50-36.95 **Facilities:** Wi-fi (charged) Play Area **Services:** **Leisure:** P S **Off-site:** R

Masia

calle Colon 44, Los Pinos, 17300

972 331013 972 333128

e-mail: info@campinglamasia.com

web: www.campinglamasia.com

A pleasant family site on level ground with shady pitches, 150 metres from the sea.

dir: *50m inland from Paseo Villa de Madrid coast road.*

Open: May-Sep **Site:** 9HEC **For hire:** **Facilities:** Wi-fi (charged) Kids' Club Play Area **Services:** **Leisure:** P R S

Pinar

av Villa de Madrid, 17300

972 331083 972 331100

e-mail: camping@elpinarbeach.com

web: www.elpinarbeach.com

Divided into two by the coastal road. Partially meadow under poplars.

dir: *1km on Paseo Villa de Madrid coast road.*

Open: Apr-Sep **Site:** 5HEC **For hire:** **Facilities:** **Services:** **Leisure:** P S

S'Abanell

av Villa de Madrid 7-9, 17300

972 331809 972 350506

e-mail: info@sabanell.com

web: www.sabanell.com

Set within a pine wood, part of which is inland and open to the public.

dir: *On either side of Avenida Villa de Madrid road. Off coast road S of Blanes.*

Open: 8 Jan-23 Dec **Site:** 3.3HEC **For hire:** **Facilities:** Wi-fi (charged) **Services:** **Leisure:** S

SPAIN

CALELLA DE LA COSTA BARCELONA

Botanic Bona Vista

08370

93 7692488 93 7695804

e-mail: info@botanic-bonavista.net

web: www.botanic-bonavista.net

Subdivided and well-tended terraced site on a hillside, beautifully landscaped. Steep internal roads. Access to the beach via a pedestrian underpass.

dir: *Off NII at Km665, site round blind corner.*

Open: All Year. **Site:** 2.85HEC **Facilities:** **Services:** **Leisure:** P S

Far

08370

93 7690967 93 7693197

e-mail: info@campingelfar.com

web: www.campingelfar.com

Terraced site on a hillock under deciduous trees with lovely view of Calella and out to sea. Steep internal roads.

dir: *S on NII, site before left bend at Km 666.*

Open: Apr-Sep **Site:** 2.5HEC **For hire:** **Facilities:** **Services:** **Leisure:** P **Off-site:** S

CASTELL D'ARO GIRONA

Castell d'Aro

crta S'Agaro, 17249

972 819699 972 829005

e-mail: campingcastelldaro@gmail.com

web: www.campingcastelldaro.com

A quiet family site, 2km from the beach, with good recreational facilities.

Open: Apr-Sep **Site:** 8HEC **For hire:** **Prices:** 25-37.50 **Facilities:** Wi-fi (charged) Play Area **Services:** **Leisure:** P **Off-site:** S

CASTELLÓ D'EMPURIES — GIRONA

Castell-Mar

Platja de la Rubina, 17486

972 450822 972 452330

e-mail: cmar@campingparks.com

web: www.campingparks.com

A modern family site close to the beach on the edge of a national park. Entertainment nightly during July and August.

dir: *AP 7 exit 3 (Figueras-Roses) onto C260 in direction of Roses at km40 exit La Rubina. Pass the restaurant, site at end of the road.*

GPS: 42.2552, 3.14

Open: 19 May-23 Sep **Site:** 5HEC **For hire:** **Prices:** 19-50 **Facilities:** Wi-fi (charged) Kids' Club Play Area **Services:** **Leisure:** P **Off-site:** S

see advert on opposite page

Mas-Nou

carrer/ Mas Nou No 7, 17486

972 454175 972 454358

e-mail: info@campingmasnou.com

web: www.campingmasnou.com

A family site with good recreational facilities, 2.5km from the coast. Kids' club available in July and August. Dogs are not permitted in chalets or mobile homes.

dir: *Off A7 onto Figueres-Roses road.*

Open: 31 Mar-Sep **Site:** 7.8HEC **For hire:** **Prices:** 20.70-38.70 Mobile home hire 311.70-799.40 **Facilities:** Wi-fi Kids' Club Play Area **Services:** **Leisure:** P **Off-site:** R S

Nautic Almata

17486

972 454477 972 454686

e-mail: info@almata.com

web: www.almata.com

A level meadowland site reaching as far as the sea and bordering the River Fluvia, which has been made into a canal. Shade, good facilities. Boating is possible in the canal, which flows into the sea.

Open: 19 May-23 Sep **Site:** 22HEC **For hire:** **Prices:** 25-59 **Facilities:** Wi-fi (charged) Kids' Club Play Area **Services:** **Leisure:** P R S

CUBELLES — BARCELONA

La Rueda

08880

938 950207 938 950347

e-mail: larueda@la-rueda.com

web: www.la-rueda.com

Level terrain between road and railway. Access to beach by means of an underpass.

dir: *1km N of Cunit near C31 Km146.2.*

GPS: 41.1998, 1.6433

Open: 31 Mar-11 Sep **Site:** 6HEC **For hire:** **Prices:** 18-41 **Facilities:** Wi-fi (charged) Play Area **Services:** **Leisure:** P **Off-site:** S

ESCALA, L' — GIRONA

Maite

Playa Riells, 17130

972 770544 972 770599

e-mail: maite@campings.net

web: www.campings.net/maite

An extensive site, lying inland, but near the sea, at a small lake. Partly on a hillock under pine trees.

Open: Jun-15 Sep **Site:** 6HEC **Facilities:** **Services:** **Leisure:** L S

Neus

Cala Montgó, 17130

972 770403 972 222409

e-mail: info@campingneus.cat

web: www.campingneus.cat

Peaceful location among pine trees. A small family site 0.8km from the beach.

dir: *A7 exit 5 onto GI 623 to L'Escala, then follow directions to Cala Montgó. 1km before the beach turn right for 500m & follow signs to campsite.*

GPS: 42.1050, 3.1583

Open: 25 May-16 Sep **Site:** 5HEC **For hire:** **Prices:** 21.70-45.20 **Facilities:** Wi-fi Kids' Club Play Area **Services:** **Leisure:** P **Off-site:** S

Site 6HEC (site size) grass sand stone little shade partly shaded mainly shaded motorvans accepted bungalows for hire mobile homes for hire tents for hire no dogs site fully accessible for wheelchairs
Prices amount quoted is per night, for 2 adults and car, plus tent or caravan Mobile home hire is a weekly rate.

ESTARTIT, L' GIRONA

Castell Montgri

17258

972 751630 972 750906

e-mail: cmontgri@campingparks.com

web: www.campingparks.com

On a large terraced meadow in pine woodlands. The site is at the foot of the Rocamaura mountain, set in a large plot of land, at the entrance to the coastal village of l'Estartit. Integrated into the natural surroundings and not far from the village.

Open: 14 May-25 Sep **Site:** 25HEC **For hire:** **Facilities:** Wi-fi (charged) Play Area **Services:** **Leisure:** P **Off-site:** S

see advert on this page

Estartit

Cap Villa Primavera 12, 17258

972 751909 972 750991

e-mail: campingestartit@hotmail.com

web: www.campingestartit.com

Set in a valley on sloping ground, which can be steep in places. Close to town and beach. Some terraces are shaded by pines. Dogs are not permitted during July and August.

dir: *200m from church & road from Torroella de Montgri.*

GPS: 42.0568, 3.1974

Open: Apr-Sep **Site:** 2.5HEC **For hire:** **Prices:** 11.66-25.93 Mobile home hire 175-434 **Facilities:** Wi-fi (charged) **Services:** **Leisure:** L P R S **Off-site:**

Medes

17258

972 751805 972 750413

e-mail: info@campinglesmedes.com

web: www.campinglesmedes.com

Quiet holiday site in rural surroundings with clearly marked pitches and modern facilities.

Open: Dec-Oct **Site:** 2.6HEC **For hire:** **Prices:** 18.70-37.05 **Facilities:** Wi-fi (charged) Kids' Club Play Area **Services:** **Leisure:** P **Off-site:** S

GUARDIOLA DE BERGUEDA BARCELONA

El Bergueda

08694

93 8227432 93 8227432

e-mail: info@campingbergueda.com

web: www.campingbergueda.com

Located next to the Cadí-Moixeró natural park this peaceful site is in the middle of a forest at an altitude of 900 metres. There is a variety of sports facilities and tourist attractions nearby.

dir: *On B400.*

GPS: 42.2166, 1.8375

Open: 24 Jun-1 Sep **Site:** 3HEC **For hire:** **Prices:** 20.52-22.80 **Facilities:** Wi-fi Play Area **Services:** **Leisure:** P **Off-site:** R

GUILS DE CERDANYA GIRONA

Pirineus

17528

☎ 972 881062 🖷 972 882471

e-mail: guils@stel.es

web: www.stel.es

A fine level location at an altitude of 1200 metres with views over the Cerdanya Valley.

dir: *On Puigcerdà-Guils de Cerdanya road.*

Open: 22 Jun-11 Sep **Site:** 5HEC **For hire:** **Prices:** 30.60-42.80 **Facilities:** Wi-fi Play Area **Services:** **Leisure:** P

LLORET DE MAR GIRONA

Tucan

ctra de Lloret a Blanes, 17310

☎ 972 369965 🖷 972 360079

e-mail: info@campingtucan.com

web: www.campingtucan.com

A modern family site, close to the sea, with plenty of recreational facilities.

dir: *A7 exit 9 to Lloret de Mar.*

Open: Apr-25 Sep **Site:** 4HEC **For hire:** **Facilities:** Wi-fi (charged) Kids' Club Play Area **Services:** **Leisure:** P **Off-site:** S

PALAFRUGELL GIRONA

Kim's Camping SL

Font d'En Xeco 1, 17211

☎ 972 301156 🖷 972 610894

e-mail: info@campingkims.com

web: www.campingkims.com

Terraced site with large flat areas, lying on the wooded slopes of a beautiful valley leading to the sea.

dir: *Turn right off Palafrugell-Tamariu road for 1km, pass Club Tennis Llafranc, 400m from sea.*

GPS: 41.8989, 3.1864

Open: 30 Mar-Sep **Site:** 5.8HEC **For hire:** **Prices:** 16-43.85 **Facilities:** Wi-fi (charged) Kids' Club Play Area **Services:** **Leisure:** P **Off-site:** S

Relax-Ge

ctra Girona-Palamós, C-31 km 329, 17253

☎ 972 301549 🖷 972 601100

e-mail: info@campingrelaxge.com

web: www.campingrelaxge.com

Level meadow under poplars and olive trees.

dir: *Off C255 at Km38.7 & 4km towards sea.*

Open: Apr-Sep **Site:** 3HEC **For hire:** **Facilities:** **Services:** **Leisure:** P **Off-site:** S

PALAMÓS GIRONA

Cala Gogo

Calonge, 17251

☎ 972 651564 🖷 972 650553

e-mail: calagogo@calagogo.es

web: www.calagogo.es

Terraced site in tall pine woodland and poplars with some good views of the sea. Underpass across to section of site with private beach. Some internal dusty roads.

dir: *From Palamós 4km S on C253 coast road, site on right after Km47.*

GPS: 41.8312, 3.0837

Open: 28 Apr-16 Sep **Site:** 20HEC **For hire:** **Prices:** 20.30-52 Mobile home hire 288-1218 **Facilities:** Wi-fi Kids' Club Play Area **Services:** **Leisure:** P S

Castell Park

17253

☎ 972 315263 🖷 972 315263

e-mail: info@campingcastellpark.com

web: www.campingcastellpark.com

Level and gently sloping meadow with poplars and pine woodland on a hill. Quiet, family campsite.

dir: *At Km328 to right of C31 to Palamós, 3km S of Montras.*

GPS: 41.8819, 3.1408

Open: 31 Mar-16 Sep **Site:** 4.5HEC **For hire:** **Prices:** 16.70-36.40 Mobile home hire 270-665 **Facilities:** Play Area **Services:** **Leisure:** P **Off-site:** S

Internacional de Calonge

Calonge, 17251

☎ 972 651233 🖷 972 652507

e-mail: info@intercalonge.com

web: www.intercalonge.com

Set on a pine covered hill overlooking the sea within easy reach of a sandy beach.

Open: All Year. **Site:** 13HEC **For hire:** **Facilities:** Wi-fi **Services:** **Leisure:** P S

Internacional Palamós

Cami Cap de Planes s/n, 17230

972 317436 972 317626

e-mail: info@internacionalpalamos.com

web: www.internacionalpalamos.com

A family site in a picturesque wooded location close to the beach and the town centre. Well equipped with good facilities and larger pitches for families.

GPS: 41.8572, 3.1381

Open: 31 Mar-Sep **Site:** 5.2HEC **For hire:** **Prices:** 34.45-55.35 **Facilities:** Wi-fi (charged) Play Area **Services:** **Leisure:** P S **Off-site:**

Palamós

ctra la Fosca 12, 17230

972 314296 972 601100

e-mail: campingpal@grn.es

web: www.campingpalamos.com

A picturesque location on a wooded headland overlooking the sea.

Open: 2 Apr-25 Sep **Site:** 5.5HEC **For hire:** **Facilities:** Wi-fi Play Area **Services:** **Leisure:** P S **Off-site:**

PALS GIRONA

Cypsela

carrer/Rodors, 7, 17256

972 667696 972 667300

e-mail: info@cypsela.com

web: www.cypsela.com

Well-kept grassy site in a pine wood.

dir: *Turn towards sea N of Pals towards Playa de Pals, turn left after Km3.*

GPS: 41.9861, 3.1809

Open: 18 May-16 Sep **Site:** 20HEC **For hire:** **Prices:** 36.78-82.10 **Facilities:** Wi-fi (charged) Kids' Club Play Area **Services:** **Leisure:** P **Off-site:** R S

Mas Patoxas

ctra C31, Palafrugell-Pals Km 339, 17256

972 636928 972 667349

e-mail: info@campingmaspatoxas.com

web: www.campingmaspatoxas.com

A family site in a quiet location close to the sea. Modern sanitary blocks and plenty of recreational facilities.

dir: *At Km5 on Palafrugell to Torroella.*

Open: 13 Jan-16 Dec **Site:** 5.5HEC **For hire:** **Prices:** 18.50-52 Mobile home hire 257.25-805 **Facilities:** Wi-fi (charged) Kids' Club Play Area **Services:** **Leisure:** P **Off-site:** S

Playa Brava

av del Grau, 1, 17256

972 636894 972 636952

e-mail: info@playabrava.com

web: www.playabrava.com

On level terrain adjoining pine woodlands, golf course, lake and sea. Direct access to the beach of Pals. Kids' club July to August.

dir: *From AP7/E15 Girona, exit 6 towards Palamós on C-66, 7.5km past La Bisbal, exit to Pals on GIV-6502 & follow signs for Platja de Pals. Site on left just before road ends at beach car park.*

GPS: 42.0011, 3.1938

Open: 12 May-12 Sep **Site:** 11HEC **Prices:** 32.60-55.80 **Facilities:** Wi-fi (charged) Kids' Club Play Area **Services:** **Leisure:** L P R S

PINEDA DE MAR BARCELONA

Camell

av Tarrongers 12, 08397

93 7671520 93 7629181

e-mail: campingcamell@yahoo.es

Surrounded by deciduous trees next to a small wood owned by the Taurus Hotel.

dir: *Off NII at Km670 onto av de los Naranjos towards sea.*

Open: May-Sep **Site:** 2.2HEC **Facilities:** **Services:** **Leisure:** P S **Off-site:**

PLATJA D'ARO, LA GIRONA

Valldaro

Cami Vell 63, 17250

972 817515 972 816662

e-mail: info@valldaro.com

web: www.valldaro.com

Extensive level meadowland under poplars, pines and eucalyptus trees. Kids' club in July and August.

GPS: 41.8238, 3.0522

Open: Apr-25 Sep **Site:** 18HEC **For hire:** **Facilities:** Wi-fi (charged) Kids' Club Play Area **Services:** **Leisure:** P **Off-site:** S

PUIGCERDÀ — GIRONA

Stel

ctra Llivia, 17520
972 882361 972 140419
e-mail: puigcerda@stel.es
web: www.stel.es

Modern site in the Pyrénées on level land. Has wonderful views of the mountains and surrounding area. Good sanitary installations.

dir: *N154 between Comarruga & Tarragona.*

Open: Jun-11 Sep **Site:** 7HEC **For hire:**
Prices: 30.60-38.10 **Facilities:** Wi-fi Play Area
Services: **Leisure:** P

SALDES — BARCELONA

Repos del Pedraforca

08697
93 8258044
e-mail: pedra@campingpedraforca.com
web: www.campingpedraforca.com

A well-equipped site situated in an area of natural beauty. Activities for children in summer.

dir: *C-17/E9 exit Guardiola de Berguedà, then B-400 direction Saldes.*

GPS: 42.2275, 1.7597

Open: All Year. **Site:** 4HEC **For hire:**
Prices: 22.55-27.85 **Facilities:** Wi-fi Play Area
Services: **Leisure:** P **Off-site:** R

SANTA CRISTINA D'ARO — GIRONA

Mas St Josep

ctra Sta Cristina, 17246
972 835108 972 837018
e-mail: info@campingmassantjosep.com
web: www.campingmassantjosep.com

A family site with plenty of recreational facilities.

GPS: 41.8116, 3.0182

Open: 6 Apr-11 Sep **Site:** 35HEC **For hire:**
Prices: 17-49 **Facilities:** Wi-fi (charged) Kids' Club Play Area **Services:** **Leisure:** P
Off-site: S

SANT ANTONI DE CALONGE — GIRONA

Eurocamping

av Catalunya 15, 17252
972 650879 972 661987
e-mail: info@euro-camping.com
web: www.euro-camping.com

A family site in a peaceful location close to the sea with fine recreational facilities.

dir: *E of A7 exit 6.*

Open: 21 Apr-23 Sep **Site:** 13HEC **For hire:**
Prices: 27-50.25 **Facilities:** Kids' Club Play Area
Services: **Leisure:** P **Off-site:** S

Treumal

San Feliu Guixols a Palamós, Km 47.5, 17250
972 651095 972 651671
e-mail: info@campingtreumal.com
web: www.campingtreumal.com

A peaceful family site in a beautiful location between a pine wood and the beach.

dir: *AP7 exit 7 or 9 km47.5 onto C-253 for Playa de Aro and San Feliu de Guixols.*

GPS: 41.8364, 3.0872

Open: 31 Mar-Sep **Site:** 8HEC **For hire:**
Prices: 23.70-49.30 **Facilities:** Wi-fi (charged) Play Area **Services:** **Leisure:** P S

see advert on opposite page

SANT CEBRIÁ DE VALLALTA — BARCELONA

La Verneda

av Maresme 35, 08396
93 7631185 93 7631185
e-mail: verneda50@hotmail.com
web: www.campinglaverneda.com

A level family site with 150 shady pitches. Located 3km from the fishing village of Sant Pol de Mar, 40km from Girona and 50km from Barcelona, the site is an ideal base.

dir: *Off NII Girona-Barcelona at end of Sant Pol de Mar, turn inland at Km670, 2km to edge of village & right before bridge over river.*

Open: Apr-Sep **Site:** 1.6HEC **For hire:** **Prices:** 25
Mobile home hire 350 **Facilities:** Wi-fi (charged)
Kids' Club **Services:** **Leisure:** P
Off-site: S

Site 6HEC (site size) grass sand stone little shade partly shaded mainly shaded motorvans accepted bungalows for hire mobile homes for hire tents for hire no dogs site fully accessible for wheelchairs
Prices amount quoted is per night, for 2 adults and car, plus tent or caravan Mobile home hire is a weekly rate.

SANT FELIU DE GUIXOLS GIRONA

Sant Pol

Doctor Fleming 1, 17220
☎ 972 327269 🖷 972 222409
e-mail: info@campingsantpol.cat
web: www.campingsantpol.cat

Wooded surroundings near the beach with good facilities. The site is within walking distance of the town and is ideal for families as well as couples seeking relaxation.

dir: *0.8km from town centre towards Palamós.*

Open: 30 Mar-4 Nov **Site:** 1.17HEC **For hire:** **Prices:** 22-55 **Facilities:** Wi-fi (charged) Kids' Club Play Area **Services:** **Leisure:** P **Off-site:** S

SANT PERE PESCADOR GIRONA

Amfora

av J-Terradellas 2, 17470
☎ 972 520540 🖷 972 520539
e-mail: info@campingamfora.com
web: www.campingamfora.com

A pleasant site, directly on the beach, with modern sanitary facilities. There are plentiful leisure facilities. Bungalows and mobile homes to hire.

Open: 15 Apr-Sep **Site:** 12HEC **For hire:** **Facilities:** Wi-fi (charged) Kids' Club Play Area **Services:** **Leisure:** P R S **Off-site:** L

Aquarius

The Camping and Caravanning Club The Friendly Club

17470
☎ 972 520003 🖷 972 550216
e-mail: camping@aquarius.es
web: www.aquarius.es

Level site between fields and meadows. Partially in shade, quiet well-organised site by the lovely sandy beach of Bahia de Rosas.

C&CC Report *Popular with campers from all over Europe, the relaxed atmosphere of this friendly and attractive site adds to its appeal for families who love the beach. Musical events, set around a beautiful flower-filled courtyard on site, are complemented by local beauty spots, such as the traditional fishing village of Cadaqués, where you can also visit the house of Salvador Dalí. Meanwhile in Figueres, the surrealist master's museum features some of his more bizarre works and offers an interesting day out.*

dir: *Towards l'Escala & signed towards beach.*

GPS: 42.178, 3.108

Open: 15 Mar-Oct **Site:** 8HEC **For hire:** **Prices:** 20.80-47.10 Mobile home hire 483.70-1098.30 **Facilities:** Wi-fi (charged) Kids' Club Play Area **Services:** **Leisure:** S

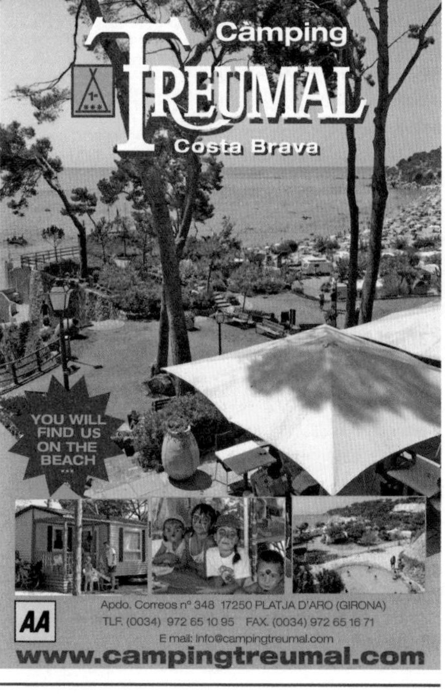

Camping
TREUMAL
Costa Brava
YOU WILL FIND US ON THE BEACH
AA
Apdo. Correos nº 348 17250 PLATJA D'ARO (GIRONA)
TLF. (0034) 972 65 10 95 FAX. (0034) 972 65 16 71
E mail: info@campingtreumal.com
www.campingtreumal.com

Ballena Alegre

17470
☎ 902 510520 🖷 902 510521
web: www.ballena-alegre.com

Extensive site near wide sandy beach with dunes. Large shopping complex. Modern washing and sanitary facilities.

dir: *Travelling with caravan or camper exit 5 AP-7 (E-15) L'Escala/Empuries. Then GI-623, after 18.5 km at rdbt turn left to San Martí D'Empuries, 1 km to site.*

GPS: 42.1522, 3.1117

Open: 14 May-26 Sep **Site:** 24HEC **For hire:** **Facilities:** Wi-fi (charged) Kids' Club Play Area **Services:** **Leisure:** P S **Off-site:** L R

SPAIN

Dunas

17470

☎ 972 521717 972 550046

e-mail: info@campinglasdunas.com

web: www.campinglasdunas.com

Level extensive grassland site with young poplars, some of medium height, on the beach, totally subdivided.

Open: May-Sep **Site:** 30HEC **For hire:**
Facilities: **Services:**
Leisure: P S

see advert on this page

Palmeras

ctra de la Platja, 17470

☎ 972 520506 972 550285

e-mail: info@campinglaspalmeras.com

web: www.campinglaspalmeras.com

On level grassland with plenty of shade. Family friendly facilities close to the beach.

dir: *From Sant Pere Pescador to beach, 200m from sea.*

Open: 31 Mar-20 Oct **Site:** 5HEC **For hire:**
Prices: 20.50-48.90 **Facilities:** Wi-fi (charged) Kids' Club **Services:** **Leisure:** P S
Off-site: R

SITGES BARCELONA

El Garrofer

ctra C 246A Km 39, 08870

☎ 93 8941780 93 8110623

e-mail: info@garroferpark.com

web: www.garroferpark.com

An area close to the beach with many pine trees, surrounded by a golf course and the Garraf nature reserve.

GPS: 41.2336, 1.7808

Open: 28 Jan-18 Dec **Site:** 8HEC **For hire:**
Prices: 18.80-36.30 **Facilities:** Wi-fi (charged) Kids' Club Play Area **Services:** **Leisure:** P
Off-site: S

TAMARIU GIRONA

Tamariu

17212

☎ 972 620422

e-mail: info@campingtamariu.com

web: www.campingtamariu.com

Terraced site with mixture of high young pines. Direct access to the beach.

dir: *Turning to site at beach parking area, continue 300m.*

Open: May-Sep **Site:** 2HEC **For hire:** **Prices:** 19-24.30 Mobile home hire 300-450 **Facilities:** Wi-fi (charged) Play Area **Services:** **Leisure:** P **Off-site:** S

TARADELL BARCELONA

La Vall

Cami de la Vallmitjana, 08552

☎ 93 8126336 93 8126027

e-mail: lavallpark@campinglavallpark.cat

web: www.campinglavall.com

Set in the mountains on the outskirts of Taradell near the Guilleries-Montseny, with good recreational facilities.

dir: *C-17 (Barcelona-Puigcerdà) exit 54 Taradell.*

GPS: 41.865, 2.295

Open: 7 Jan-13 Dec **Site:** 8HEC **For hire:** **Prices:** 21.60-26.95 **Facilities:** Wi-fi Play Area **Services:** **Leisure:** P

TORROELLA DE MONTGRI GIRONA

Delfin Verde

17257

☎ 972 758450 972 760070

e-mail: info@eldelfinverde.com

web: www.eldelfinverde.com

On undulating ground with some pine trees, and an open meadow beside the long sandy beach.

dir: *2km S of Torroella de Montgri towards Begur, left towards Maspinell & sea for 4.8km.*

Open: Apr-Sep **Site:** 35HEC **For hire:** **Facilities:** **Services:** **Leisure:** P R S

TOSSA DE MAR GIRONA

Cala Llevadó

17320

☎ 972 340314 972 341187

e-mail: info@calallevado.com

web: www.calallevado.com

Magnificent terraced site with hairpin roads overlooking three bays, all suitable for bathing. The narrow, winding drives are quite steep in parts. Separate section for caravans.

dir: *Coast road towards Lloret de Mar, 4km turn towards sea.*

Open: May-Sep **Site:** 17HEC **For hire:** **Prices:** 31.40-49.90 **Facilities:** Wi-fi Kids' Club Play Area **Services:** **Leisure:** P S

Camping Can Martí

17320

☎ 972 340851 972 342461

e-mail: info@campingcanmarti.com

web: www.campingcanmarti.com

Pleasant, unspoiled site in a partly wooded location. Good modern facilities.

dir: *1km from sea.*

Open: Apr-Sep **Site:** 10HEC **Prices:** 12-32 **Facilities:** Play Area **Services:** **Leisure:** P **Off-site:** L R S

VALLROMANES BARCELONA

El Vedado

08188

☎ 93 5729026 93 5729621

e-mail: info@campingelvedado.com

web: www.campingelvedado.com

A valley site surrounded by wooded mountains with the beach only a short drive away. Ideal for visiting Barcelona, as there is a bus from the site.

dir: *AP7 exit 13 for Masnou, C32 exit 86 for Granollers.*

GPS: 41.5236, 2.2936

Open: Mar-6 Nov **Site:** 100HEC **For hire:** **Prices:** 22-32 **Facilities:** **Services:** **Leisure:** P **Off-site:** S

Facilities: ☊ shower ⊙ electric points for razors ⊕ electric points for caravans ⅄ motorvan service point ⓟ parking by tents permitted
compulsory separate car park ⓢ shop **Services** ⦿ café/restaurant ⛙ bar ⊘ Camping Gaz International ⛏ gas other than Camping Gaz

SPAIN

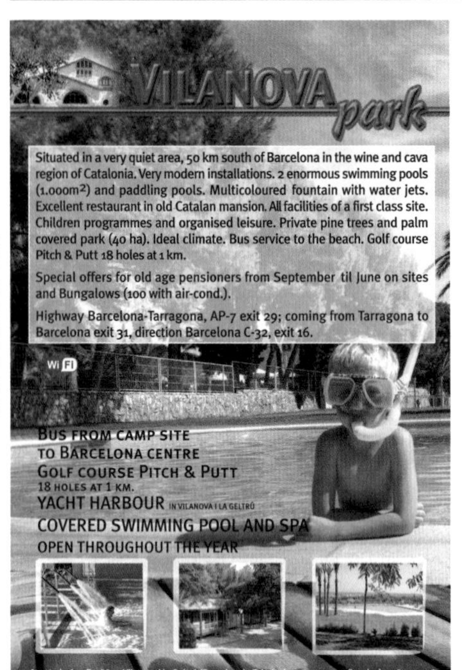

VILALLONGA DE TER — GIRONA

Conca de Ter

ctra Camprodon-Setcases s/n, 17869
☎ 972 740629 🖷 972 130171
e-mail: concater@concater.com
web: www.concater.com

A pleasant family site in wooded surroundings with a variety of recreational facilities.

dir: *Between Camprodón & Setcases, 20km from French border.*

Open: All Year. **Site:** 3.2HEC **For hire:** **Facilities:** **Services:** **Leisure:** P R **Off-site:** R

VILANOVA I LA GELTRÚ — BARCELONA

Vilanova Park

The Camping and Caravanning Club — The Friendly Club

BV-2115 ctra Arboç km2.5, 08800
☎ 93 8933402 🖷 93 8935528
e-mail: info@vilanovapark.com
web: www.vilanovapark.com

A well-equipped family site on the edge of a densely wooded area close to the coast in the Catalonian wine-producing area. Modern sanitary blocks. Kids' club mid April to mid September and weekends.

C&CC Report *Whatever the time of year you go, Vilanova Park takes some beating, with its pleasant climate and its high quality facilities open all year. Within easy reach are Barcelona, (direct buses from the site entrance to the city centre), some of Europe's best beaches, Sitges' old-world charm, Vilafranca's wine cellars to which the site runs excursions, and Montserrat's mountain monastery.*

dir: *A7 exit 29.*

GPS: 41.2319, 1.6905

Open: All Year. **Site:** 45HEC **For hire:** **Prices:** 31.35-51.70 Mobile home hire 510-945 **Facilities:** Wi-fi (charged) Kids' Club Play Area **Services:** **Leisure:** P **Off-site:** L S

see advert on this page

CENTRAL

ALBARRACIN — TERUEL

Ciudad de Albarracin

Cami de Gea, Arrabal, 44100
☎ 978 710197 🖷 978 710197
e-mail: campingalbarracin5@hotmail.com
web: www.campingalbarracin.com

A modern site on mainly level ground with good facilities.

dir: *Signed from A1512.*

GPS: 40.4116, -1.4272

Open: Mar-7 Nov **Site:** 2.5HEC **For hire:** **Prices:** 16.15 **Facilities:** Wi-fi Play Area **Services:** **Off-site:** L P R

Site 6HEC (site size) grass sand stone little shade partly shaded mainly shaded motorvans accepted bungalows for hire mobile homes for hire tents for hire no dogs site fully accessible for wheelchairs
Prices amount quoted is per night, for 2 adults and car, plus tent or caravan Mobile home hire is a weekly rate.

ARANJUEZ MADRID

Internacional de Aranjuez

Soto Del Rebollo S/N, 28300
91 8911395 91 8920406
e-mail: info@campingaranjuez.com
web: www.campingaranjuez.com

Site divided in two parts with trees and lawns in a castle's large park.

C&CC Report *Located in the town of Aranjuez in the former grounds of the castle, convenient for visiting Madrid by train.*

dir: *Off NIV at Km46 into village, 200m beyond fuel station turn sharp NE for 1km.*

GPS: 40.0421, -3.5993

Open: All Year. **Site:** 3.3HEC **For hire:**
Prices: 8.09-31.10 **Facilities:** Wi-fi (charged) **Services:** **Leisure:** P R

see advert on this page

CABRERA, LA MADRID

Pico de la Miel

ctra A-1, Salida 57, 28751
91 8688082 91 8688541
e-mail: info@picodelamiel.com
web: www.picodelamiel.com

Good quality camping just forty minutes from Madrid with regular bus service available. Attractive location with access to arts and culture.

C&CC Report *Just off the A1 Madrid to Burgos motorway, at the foot of the Sierra de Guadarrama and the honey-coloured peak from which the site takes its name. Shops and local village services 500m.*

dir: *A1 exit Km57 or Km60.*

Open: All Year. **Site:** 10.5HEC **For hire:**
Prices: 18-24 **Facilities:** Wi-fi (charged) Kids' Club Play Area **Services:** **Leisure:** P **Off-site:** L R

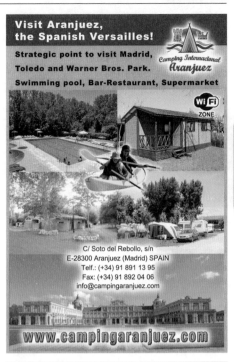

CÁCERES CÁCERES

Camping Cuidad de Cáceres

ctra N630, km 549.5, 10005
927 233100 927 235896
e-mail: info@campingcaceres.com
web: www.campingcaceres.com

Located 2km from the city centre. Leisure facilities include a swimming pool and a children's pool. Dogs must be kept on leads.

C&CC Report *Not far from Cáceres and the A66 motorway, with bus services into town. Cáceres is a UNESCO World Heritage site because of its wide range or architecture, cobbled streets and medieval, fortified homes. Each pitch has its own sanitation block which is popular with campers.*

dir: *N630 km 549.5 or A66 exit 545.*

GPS: 39.4886, -6.4128

Open: All Year. **Site:** 5HEC **For hire:**
Prices: 20-22 **Facilities:** Wi-fi Kids' Club Play Area **Services:** **Leisure:** P **Off-site:**

cilities shower electric points for razors electric points for caravans motorvan service point parking by tents permitted
mpulsory separate car park shop **Services** café/restaurant bar Camping Gaz International gas other than Camping Gaz
first aid facilities laundry **Leisure** swimming L-Lake P-Pool R-River S-Sea **Off-site** All facilities within 5km

CUENCA — CUENCA

Cuenca

ctra Cuenca-Tragacete KM7, 16147
969 231656 969 231656
e-mail: info@campingcuenca.com
web: www.campingcuenca.com
A modern site in a peaceful wooded location.

dir: *N on CM-2106 towards Mariana.*

Open: 15 Apr-16 Oct **Site:** 23HEC **For hire:** **Facilities:** **Services:** **Leisure:** P **Off-site:** L R

ESCORIAL, EL — MADRID

El Escorial

ctra Guadarrama, km 3500, 28280
918 902412 918 961062
e-mail: info@campingelescorial.com
web: www.campingelescorial.com
Pleasant wooded surroundings with good recreational facilities.

GPS: 40.6269, -4.1

Open: All Year. **Site:** 40HEC **For hire:** **Prices:** 29.80-36.20 **Facilities:** Kids' Club Play Area **Services:** **Leisure:** P

FUENTE DE SAN ESTEBAN, LA — SALAMANCA

Cruce

37200
923 440130
e-mail: campingelcruce@yahoo.es
web: www.campingelcruce.com
Useful stopover site in a quiet location in the Castillian countryside.

dir: *50m from N620 at Km291. 400m A-62 exit 293.*

Open: May-Sep **Site:** 0.5HEC **For hire:** **Prices:** 13.50-16 **Facilities:** Wi-fi **Services:** **Off-site:** P R

GARGANTILLA DE LOZOYA — MADRID

Monte Holiday

28739
91 8695278 91 8695278
web: www.monteholiday.com
A terraced site with modern facilities in a beautiful mountain setting and near a large nature reserve. The area is ideal for anglers and walkers and many outdoor sports enthusiasts. Mainly flat pitches with grass or gravel surfaces and shade from mature trees. Children's activities in high season.

dir: *Off N1 at Km69 towards Cobos for 10km.*

Open: All Year. **Site:** 30HEC **For hire:** **Facilities:** Wi-fi (charged) **Services:** **Leisure:** P **Off-site:** L R

GETAFE — MADRID

Alpha

calle de la Calidad 1, 28906
91 6958069 91 6831659
e-mail: info@campingalpha.com
web: www.campingalpha.com
Surrounded by pine woods at roughly the geographical centre of Spain with well-defined pitches and modern facilities. Direct bus service to Madrid.

dir: *A4 km14,400.*

GPS: 40.3172, -3.6889

Open: All Year. **Site:** 4.8HEC **For hire:** **Facilities:** Wi-fi (charged) **Services:** **Leisure:** P

MADRID — MADRID

Arco Iris

28670
91 6160387 91 6160059
e-mail: madrid@bungalowsarcoiris.com
web: www.bungalowsarcoiris.com
A family site in a peaceful location, yet with easy access to Madrid. Dogs not permitted in bungalows.

dir: *M40 ring road exit 36, then M501, continue up to KM7100.*

GPS: 40.3818, -3.9080

Open: All Year. **Site:** 4HEC **For hire:** **Prices:** 16-28 **Facilities:** Wi-fi **Services:** **Leisure:** P **Off-site:** R

Camping Osuna

Calle de los Jardines de Aranjuez, 28042

☎ 91 7410510

e-mail: osunacamping@gmail.com

web: www.campingosuna.com

On long stretch of land, shade being provided by pines, acacias and maple. Some noise from airfield, road and railway. Close to two parks, Juan Carlos I and El Capricho.

dir: *M11 from town centre towards Barajas, 7.5km turn right at Km1 after railway underpass.*

GPS: 40.4538, -3.6033

Open: All Year. **Site:** 2.3HEC **Prices:** 23.50-27 **Facilities:** Wi-fi Play Area **Services:** **Off-site:** L P R

MALPARTIDA DE PLASENCIA — CÁCERES

Parque Natural de Monfrague

ctra Plasencia-Trujillo km-10, 10680

☎ 927 459220 927 459233

e-mail: contacto@campingmonfrague.com

web: www.campingmonfrague.com

A modern site with well-defined pitches and good facilities.

dir: *9km from EX208.*

Open: All Year. **Site:** 7HEC **For hire:** **Prices:** 16.40 **Facilities:** Wi-fi Kids' Club Play Area **Services:** **Leisure:** P **Off-site:**

MÉRIDA — BADAJOZ

Mérida

Apto. 465, 06800

☎ 924 303453

e-mail: info@campingmerida.com

web: www.campingmerida.com

Ideal for outdoor activities holidays including cycling and climbing.

dir: *3km off A5.*

Open: All Year. **Site:** **Facilities:** **Services:**

MIRANDA DEL CASTAÑAR — SALAMANCA

El Burro Blanco

37660

☎ 923 161100

e-mail: camping.elburroblanco@gmail.com

web: www.elburroblanco.net

A well-equipped site in an area of woodland overlooking the village.

dir: *1km from village centre.*

GPS: 40.4749, -5.9985

Open: Apr-Sep **Site:** 3.5HEC **Prices:** 19 **Facilities:** **Services:** **Off-site:** P R

NAVALAFUENTE — MADRID

Camping Piscis

ctra Guadalix a Navalafuente, km3, 28729

☎ 91 8432253 91 8432253

e-mail: campiscis@campiscis.com

web: www.campiscis.com

Spacious pitches surrounded by oak trees.

dir: *N1 exit 50 towards Guadalix de la Sierra.*

Open: All Year. **Site:** 23HEC **For hire:** **Facilities:** Wi-fi (charged) **Services:** **Leisure:** P

RIAZA — SEGOVIA

Riaza

ctra de la Estacion s/n, 40500

☎ 921 550580 921 550580

e-mail: info@camping-riaza.com

web: www.camping-riaza.com

Located on the outskirts of a medieval town, a site with individual pitches divided by laurel hedges. Leisure facilities include swimming pools and tennis.

dir: *From Burgos A1 exit 104. From Madrid A1 exit 103 direction Riaza and Soria (N110). Right at rdbt after 12km. Campsite on left.*

GPS: 41.2830, -3.4666

Open: All Year. **Site:** 12HEC **For hire:** **Prices:** 16-24 **Facilities:** Wi-fi (charged) Kids' Club Play Area **Services:** **Leisure:** P **Off-site:** L R

SPAIN

SALAMANCA — SALAMANCA

Camping Olimpia

Pedrosillo el Ralo, 37427
923 080854
e-mail: info@campingolimpia.com
web: www.campingolimpia.com

Large pitches bordered by trees and shrubs.

C&CC Report *An ideal en route stop just off the A62 motorway, where you can have an evening meal in the site restaurant and be assured of clean, modern facilities in this small, friendly and well kept site.*

dir: *12km NE of city on A62 junct 225.*

Open: All Year. **Site:** 0.7HEC **Facilities:** Wi-fi **Services:**

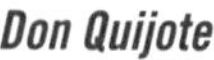

Don Quijote

ctra Aldealengua km 4, Cabrerizos, 37193
923 209052 923 209052
e-mail: info@campingdonquijote.com
web: www.campingdonquijote.com

Near to the town centre, quiet, family campsite.

dir: *NE of town towards Aldealengua.*

GPS: 40.975, -5.6030

Open: Mar-Oct **Site:** 6.5HEC **For hire:** **Facilities:** Wi-fi (charged) Play Area **Services:** **Leisure:** P R

SANTA MARTA DE TORMES — SALAMANCA

Regio

ctra Salamanca/Madrid Km4, 37900
923 138888 923 138044
e-mail: recepcion@campingregio.com
web: www.campingregio.com

A pleasant site, divided into several fields.

C&CC Report *An ideal base for visiting historic Salamanca. Located about 500m from the N501 Salamanca to Ávila road, in the southern suburbs of Salamanca, about 1.5km from city centre – hourly bus from site.*

dir: *100m from N501 Salamanca-Ávila, behind Hotel Jardin-Regio.*

Open: All Year. **Site:** 3HEC **For hire:** **Facilities:** **Services:** **Leisure:** P R

SEGOVIA — SEGOVIA

Acueducto

ctra de la Granja, 40004
921 425000 921 425000
e-mail: informacion@campingacueducto.com
web: www.campingacueducto.com

Located 3km from Segovia city, in a characteristic Castilian landscape with magnificent views to the mountain range. A well equipped site offering many facilities.

dir: *SE next to N601 at Km112.*

Open: Apr-Sep **Site:** 3HEC **For hire:** **Prices:** 23-24.60 **Facilities:** **Services:** **Leisure:** P **Off-site:** L

TOLEDO — TOLEDO

Greco

45004
925 220090 925 220090
e-mail: campingelgreco@telefonica.net
web: www.campingelgreco.es

Few shady terraces on slope leading down to the River Tajo. On south-western outskirts of town.

dir: *From town centre C401 Carretera Comarcal SW for 2km, right at Km28, 300m towards Puebla de Montalban.*

Open: All Year. **Site:** 2.5HEC **For hire:** **Prices:** 26.20 **Facilities:** Wi-fi Play Area **Services:** **Leisure:** P R **Off-site:**

VALDEMAQUEDA — MADRID

El Canto la Gallina

28295
091 8984820 091 8984823
e-mail: camping@elcantolagallina.com
web: www.elcantolagallina.com

Wooded location at the foot of a mountain.

Open: All Year. **Site:** 12.5HEC **For hire:** **Facilities:** **Services:** **Leisure:** P **Off-site:** R

Site 6HEC (site size) grass sand stone little shade partly shaded mainly shaded motorvans accepted bungalows for hire mobile homes for hire tents for hire no dogs site fully accessible for wheelchairs
Prices amount quoted is per night, for 2 adults and car, plus tent or caravan Mobile home hire is a weekly rate.

SOUTH EAST COAST

ALCOSSEBRE CASTELLÓN

Playa Tropicana

The Camping and Caravanning Club The Friendly Club

12579

964 412463 964 412805

e-mail: info@playatropicana.com

web: www.playatropicana.com

On a 0.5km long sandy beach, 3km from the village.

C&CC Report *Playa Tropicana is a top quality site opposite a long sandy beach on this tranquil part of the coastline, with high quality facilities in lovely surroundings. The site lives up to its name with exotic plants, palm trees and classical statues lining the roads. The site owners are adding to Playa Tropicana's already excellent facilities with a new heated covered pool and jacuzzi planned to be open for winter 2011-12. The reception staff will be able to help you with ideas for local visits, walking and cycling routes and local festivals. Local fishing clubs welcome visitors and if you are interested in diving then speak with the site owner, Vera, about visiting the protected Columbretes isles - "one of the best diving spots in the Mediterranean", she proudly tells us.*

dir: *Motorway exit 44, onto N340 N for 3km, turn towards sea at Km1018.*

GPS: 40.22, 0.2681

Open: All Year. **Site:** 3HEC **For hire:** **Prices:** 16-52 **Facilities:** Wi-fi (charged) Kids' Club Play Area **Services:** **Leisure:** P S

Ribamar

Partida Ribamar s/n, 12579

964 761163 964 994082

e-mail: info@campingribamar.com

web: www.campingribamar.com

Quiet wooded site with individual pitches, set between the sea and mountains.

dir: *AP7 exit 44 (Torreblanca-Alcossebre) onto N340.*

Open: All Year. **Site:** 2.2HEC **For hire:** **Prices:** 17.40-41.50 **Facilities:** Wi-fi (charged) Play Area **Services:** **Leisure:** P **Off-site:** S

ALTEA ALICANTE

Cap Blanch

Playa del Cap-Blanch, 03590

96 5845946 96 5844556

e-mail: capblanch@ctv.es

web: www.camping-capblanch.com

A well-equipped site on Albir beach backed by imposing mountains. Good sports and recreational facilities.

dir: *A7 exit 65.*

GPS: 38.5774, -0.0645

Open: All Year. **Site:** 4HEC **For hire:** **Prices:** 21-25 **Facilities:** Wi-fi Play Area **Services:** **Leisure:** S **Off-site:**

AMETLLA DE MAR, L' TARRAGONA

Camping Ametlla

Paratge Santes Creus, 43860

977 267784 977 267868

e-mail: info@campingametlla.com

web: www.campingametlla.com

A modern site with good facilities and direct access to two beaches. Kids' club in July and August. Dogs are not permitted in bungalows.

dir: *2km W, S of A7.*

GPS: 40.8650, 0.7789

Open: All Year. **Site:** 8HEC **For hire:** **Prices:** 14-37.20 **Facilities:** Wi-fi (charged) Kids' Club Play Area **Services:** **Leisure:** P S

BENICARLÓ CASTELLÓN

Alegria del Mar

Playa Norte, 12580

964 470871 964 470871

e-mail: info@campingalegria.com

web: www.campingalegria.com

Small site which is British owned and managed. Suitable for long and short term camping close to the beach and Benicarlo.

dir: *Via N340, 1046km.*

GPS: 40.4263, 0.4374

Open: All Year. **Site:** 10HEC **For hire:** **Prices:** 14-23 **Facilities:** Wi-fi (charged) Play Area **Services:** **Leisure:** P S

SPAIN

BENICASIM — CASTELLÓN

Bonterra Park

av Barcelona 47, 12560
☎ 964 300007 🖷 964 100669
e-mail: info@bonterrapark.com
web: www.bonterrapark.com

Well situated site with large, shady pitches, 300 metres from the beach and 300 metres from the town centre. Dogs not accepted in July and August.

C&CC Report *Bonterra Park is a high quality site with its covered heated pool, bar, restaurant facilities and proximity to local services. There is a lot to do in the area, both on the coast and inland, from fascinating València and the vineyards and bodegas of Requena-Utiel, to the numerous natural parks. This is an ideal site for motorhome owners and cyclists alike, being within walking distance of a town with a lovely beach, and with convenient public transport near the site entrance.*

dir: *300m N towards Las Villas de Benicasim.*

Open: All Year. **Site:** 5HEC **For hire:**
Prices: 24.26-56.26 **Facilities:** Wi-fi (charged) Kids' Club Play Area **Services:** **Leisure:** P **Off-site:** S

BENIDORM — ALICANTE

Arena Blanca

av Dr Severo Ochoa 44, 03503
☎ 96 5861889 🖷 96 5861107
e-mail: info@camping-arenablanca.es
web: www.camping-arenablanca.es

A modern family site not far from a sandy beach. Kids' club available in July and August.

dir: *Via N332 Benidorm-Altea.*

GPS: 38.5511, -0.0965

Open: All Year. **Site:** 2.2HEC **For hire:**
Prices: 11.34-32.40 **Facilities:** Wi-fi Kids' Club **Services:** **Leisure:** P S

Armanello

av Comunidad Valenciana S/N, 03503
☎ 96 5853190 🖷 96 5853100
e-mail: info@campingarmanello.com
web: www.campingarmanello.com

Divided by bushes with large pitches on terraces under olive and palm trees next to a small orange grove.

dir: *N of town off N332 at Km123.1.*

Open: All Year. **Site:** 1.6HEC **For hire:**
Facilities: Wi-fi **Services:** **Leisure:** P **Off-site:** S

CAMPELLO — ALICANTE

Costa Blanca

calle Convento 143, 03560
☎ 965 630670 🖷 965 630670
e-mail: info@campingcostablanca.com
web: www.campingcostablanca.com

On mostly level ground scattered with old olive and eucalyptus trees. The Alicante-Denia railway line runs behind the camp.

dir: *Off N332 at Km94.2 & fuel station onto narrow gravel track towards sea for 0.5km.*

GPS: 38.4364, -0.3872

Open: All Year. **Site:** 1.1HEC **For hire:**
Prices: 17.11-29.82 **Facilities:** Wi-fi (charged) Play Area **Services:** **Leisure:** P
Off-site: S

CUNIT — TARRAGONA

Mar de Cunit

Playa Cunit, 43881
☎ 977 674058 🖷 977 675006
e-mail: mardecunit@seker.es
web: www.mardecunit.com

A friendly site on level ground overlooking the beach.

Open: 15 May-15 Sep **Site:** 1.2HEC **For hire:**
Facilities: **Services:** **Leisure:** L S **Off-site:**

GUARDAMAR DEL SEGURA — ALICANTE

Marjal Camping & Bungalows Resort

Cartagena-Alicante Rd (N 332), 03140
☎ 966 727070 🖷 966 726695
e-mail: camping@marjal.com
web: www.campingmarjal.com

Located in Dunas de Guardamar Natural Park next to the Segura estuary, alongside pine and eucalyptus forests with access to fine sandy beaches.

C&CC Report *Popular Marjal is one of the most modern sites on the Mediterranean. In an excellent location on the Costa Blanca, with its normally mild climate, offering both a relaxing environment and opportunities to avail yourselves of the site's very high quality facilities, including the free and very well-equipped sports complex where you can keep fit or simply unwind. The site's restaurant offers ample opportunity for any cook in your party to take a break, with reasonably priced menus catering for all tastes.*

dir: *A7 exit 72, then N332 towards Cartagena, at km73.4.*

GPS: 38.1092, -0.6547

Open: All Year. **Site:** 3.5HEC **For hire:**
Prices: 33-65 **Facilities:** Wi-fi Kids' Club Play Area **Services:** **Leisure:** P
Off-site: S

see advert on opposite page

Site 6HEC (site size) grass sand stone little shade partly shaded mainly shaded motorvans accepted bungalows for hire mobile homes for hire tents for hire no dogs site fully accessible for wheelchairs
Prices amount quoted is per night, for 2 adults and car, plus tent or caravan Mobile home hire is a weekly rate.

Palm Mar

03140

☎ 96 5728856 🖷 96 5728856

e-mail: campingpalmmar@hotmail.com

web: www.campingpalmmar.es

On the seafront and with direct access to the beach.

Open: Jun-Sep **Site:** 2HEC **Facilities:** **Services:** **Leisure:** S **Off-site:** P

HOSPITALET DE L'INFANT, L' TARRAGONA

El Templo del Sol

Platja del Torn, 43890

☎ 977 823434 🖷 977 823464

e-mail: info@eltemplodelsol.com

web: www.eltemplodelsol.com

Site with modern sanitary installations and good recreational facilities on a 1.5km-long beach. This is a naturist site. Only families or holders of an International Naturism Carnet are allowed.

dir: *A3 exit 38, 4km towards sea.*

Open: 29 Mar-22 Oct **Site:** 14HEC **For hire:** **Facilities:** Wi-fi (charged) **Services:** **Leisure:** P S

MARINA, LA ALICANTE

Internacional la Marina

03194

☎ 96 5419200 🖷 96 5419110

e-mail: info@campinglamarina.com

web: www.campinglamarina.com

A large modern site in a wooded setting, 0.5km from a sandy beach.

dir: *A7 exit 72 junct with N332 in direction of Cartagena. Continue until the village of La Marina & 2km S on the old highway. Site entrance at KM76.*

GPS: 38.1297, -0.6497

Open: All Year. **Site:** 6.3HEC **For hire:** **Prices:** 11.98-59.40 **Facilities:** Wi-fi (charged) Kids' Club Play Area **Services:** **Leisure:** P **Off-site:** S

see advert on page 506

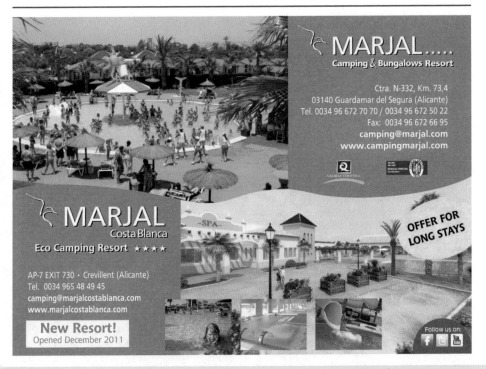

MIRAMAR PLAYA VALENCIA

Coelius

av del Mar, 46711
☎ 96 2819574 96 2818897
e-mail: camping@coelius.com
web: www.coelius.com

A site with modern facilities, 0.5km from Miramar beach.

dir: *A7 exit 61 then N332 in direction of Gandia and then Bellereguard-Miramar.*

Open: All Year. **Site:** 2HEC **For hire:** **Facilities:** Wi-fi Play Area **Services:** **Leisure:** P **Off-site:** S

MONCOFA CASTELLÓN

Monmar

carrer/ Serratelles, s/n, 12593
☎ 964 588592 964 588592
e-mail: campingmonmar@terra.es
web: www.campingmonmar.blogspot.com

The Camping and Caravanning Club The Friendly Club

Close to road network, beach and town.

C&CC Report *A site with high quality facilities, situated in an expanding town, with owners and staff who look after campers exceptionally well. The surrounding region is fascinating and has not yet been spoilt by the tourist invasion. Nearby Vall d'Uixo has a street market and the longest underground river in Europe, while the area is also well-known for its ceramics. València with its historic centre, the jaw-dropping architecture of the modern City of Arts and Sciences and the world-famous Lladró porcelain is a short drive away. A great site in particular for motorhomes with the site's cost-effective minibus available and shops in close proximity to the site. With the minibus stopping at Nules station you can also benefit from train travel.*

dir: *23km S of Castellon city.*

GPS: 39.8083, -0.1272

Open: All Year. **Site:** 3HEC **For hire:** **Prices:** 11-26.50 **Facilities:** Wi-fi Play Area **Services:** **Leisure:** L P S

SPAIN

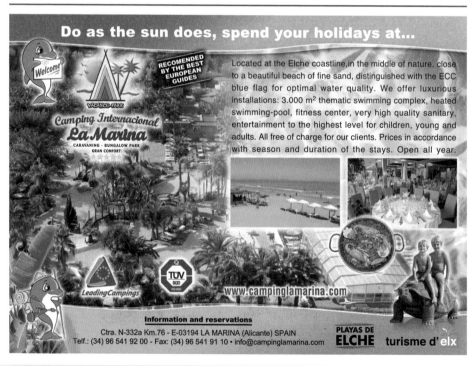

MONT-ROIG DEL CAMP TARRAGONA

Camping Els Prats Village

ctra N-340 km 1137, 43892

☎ 977 810027 🖹 977 170901

e-mail: info@campingelsprats.com

web: www.campingelsprats.com

Pleasant site near to the beach, ideal for relaxing and water sports. Dogs are permitted in one area only. 5 hours Wi-fi available free.

dir: *AP-7 exit 37-38 or A7 exit 1138, then onto N-340.*

GPS: 41.0407, 0.9821

Open: 16 Mar-4 Nov **Site:** **For hire:** **Prices:** 24.50-60 Mobile home hire 360-1190 **Facilities:** Wi-fi Kids' Club Play Area **Services:** **Leisure:** P S

Playa Montroig

43300

☎ 977 810637 🖹 977 811411

e-mail: info@playamontroig.com

web: www.playamontroig.com

An ideal holiday centre for the whole family with sanitary installations of the highest quality. Situated on a fine sandy beach and surrounded by tropical gardens, this site offers a range of sports and recreational facilities and is noted for its helpful and friendly staff.

dir: *AP7 exit 37 or 38, onto N340, left at Km1136.*

Open: 23 Mar-4 Nov **Site:** 35HEC **For hire:** **Facilities:** Wi-fi Play Area **Services:** **Leisure:** P S

Torre Del Sol

43300

☎ 977 810486 🖹 977 811306

e-mail: info@latorredelsol.com

web: www.latorredelsol.com

A level tidy grassland site on two levels, with young poplars and some of medium height, between a long stretch of beach and the railway.

dir: *Off N340 at Km224.1 towards sea.*

Open: 15 Mar-Oct **Site:** 24HEC **For hire:** **Facilities:** Wi-fi Kids' Club Play Area **Services:** **Leisure:** P S

see advert below

SPAIN

NAVAJAS CASTELLÓN

Altomira

The Camping and Caravanning Club The Friendly Club

12470
☎ 964 713211 🖷 964 713512
e-mail: reservas@campingaltomira.com
web: www.campingaltomira.com

Terraced site in the Pàlancia Valley, with touring pitches on the higher levels. Ideal place for walkers and cyclists as the site is close to one of the longest walking and cycling routes in Spain. Kids' club in high season.

C&CC Report *Conveniently located just outside the town of Navajas, with easy access to the A23 motorway. Very convenient for visiting València by train with the train station within 500 metres.*

dir: *A23 Sagunto to Teruel exit 33 Navajas.*

Open: All Year. **Site:** 2.5HEC **For hire:** **Prices:** 16.52-22.10 **Facilities:** Wi-fi (charged) Kids' Club Play Area **Services:** **Leisure:** P **Off-site:** L R

OLIVA VALENCIA

Azul

Apartado de Correos 96, 46780
☎ 96 2854106 🖷 96 2854096
e-mail: campingazul@ctv.es
web: www.campingazul.com

A well-equipped site with spacious individual plots and direct access to the beach. Kids' club July to 1 September.

GPS: 38.9069, -0.0686

Open: Mar-Oct **Site:** 2.5HEC **For hire:** **Prices:** 10.62-25.60 Mobile home hire 190-755 **Facilities:** Wi-fi (charged) Kids' Club Play Area **Services:** **Leisure:** S **Off-site:** R

Euro Camping

46780
☎ 96 2854098 🖷 96 2851753
e-mail: info@eurocamping-es.com
web: www.eurocamping-es.com

On a wide sandy beach between orange groves. Well-shaded with poplar and eucalyptus trees.

dir: *Off N332 at Km184.9, 0.6km from Oliva, towards sea for 3.3km, site signed. Narrow access road & blind corners.*

GPS: 38.9053, -0.0665

Open: All Year. **Site:** 4.5HEC **For hire:** **Prices:** 14.90-44.39 **Facilities:** Wi-fi (charged) Play Area **Services:** **Leisure:** S **Off-site:** L R

Ferienplatz Olé

46780
☎ 96 2857517 🖷 96 2857517
e-mail: camping-ole@hotmail.com
web: www.camping-ole.com

An extensive site with some pitches among dunes.

dir: *Off N332 at Km209.9 5km S of Oliva, 3km onto part asphalt road through orchard.*

Open: All Year. **Site:** 46HEC **For hire:** **Facilities:** **Services:** **Leisure:** P S

Kiko Park

The Camping and Caravanning Club The Friendly Club

Playa de Oliva, 46780
☎ 96 2850905 🖷 96 2854320
e-mail: kikopark@kikopark.com
web: www.kikopark.com

Family holiday camp, divided into paddocks, lying between marshland and vineyards. The sea can be reached by crossing a dyke and there are sunshade roofs.

C&CC Report *Camping Kiko Park is in an excellent location, offering a relaxing environment, very good on-site facilities and the opportunity to explore the coastal region as well as the inland Valèncian region. The outdoor pool and indoor spa (charged) have been welcome additions to the site's facilities. The popular campsite bar/restaurant offers high-quality regional and international dishes, with a renowned special festival of Valèncian rice dishes each February. Light meals are also available, or you can just enjoy a drink at the bar. The site overlooks the fine, sandy Blue Flag beach across the renaturalised dunes and the small yachting harbour.*

dir: *A7 exit 61, onto N332 towards Oliva.*

Open: All Year. **Site:** 4HEC **For hire:** **Facilities:** Wi-fi (charged) **Services:** **Leisure:** P S

OROPESA DEL MAR CASTELLÓN

Didota

av de la Didota, 12594
☎ 964 319551 🖷 964 319568

Family campsite with good facilities and close to the sea.

Open: All Year. **Site:** 1.7HEC **For hire:** **Facilities:** **Services:** **Leisure:** P **Off-site:** S

PEÑISCOLA CASTELLÓN

Eden

av Papa Luna, Km6, 12598
☎ 964 480562 🖷 964 489828
e-mail: camping@camping-eden.com
web: www.camping-eden.com

A modern, well-appointed site on level ground close to the seafront.

dir: *Off A7 for Peñiscola, turn towards Peñiscola.*

GPS: 40.3715, 0.4027

Open: All Year. **Site:** 4HEC **For hire:** **Prices:** 10-62 **Facilities:** Wi-fi (charged) Kids' Club Play Area **Services:** **Leisure:** P **Off-site:** S

Spa Natura Resort

Partida Villarroyos s/n, 12598
☎ 964 475480 🖷 964 785051
e-mail: info@spanaturaresort.com
web: www.spanaturaresort.com

Family friendly site, close to sandy beaches with extensive leisure facilities including a spa and mini-golf. Ideal for hiking and horse riding in the surrounding countryside.

dir: *A7 exit 43.*

GPS: 40.4016, 0.3813

Open: All Year. **Site:** 3HEC **For hire:** **Prices:** 15-45 **Facilities:** Wi-fi (charged) Play Area **Services:** **Leisure:** P **Off-site:** S

PILAR DE LA HORADADA ALICANTE

Camping Lo Monte

av Comunidada Valenciana No 157, 03190
☎ 96 6766782 🖷 96 6746536
e-mail: info@campinglomonte-alicante.es
web: www.campinglomonte-alicante.es

A slightly sloping site just 1km from sandy beaches. Extensive leisure facilities including three swimming pools, gym, spa and bike hire. Nearby are golf courses, hiking trails and water sports.

GPS: 37.8792, -0.7656

Open: All Year. **Site:** 7.2HEC **For hire:** **Prices:** 28.08-47.84 **Facilities:** Wi-fi Play Area **Services:** **Leisure:** P **Off-site:** S

SALOU TARRAGONA

Sanguli-Salou

43840
☎ 977 381641 🖷 977 384616
e-mail: mail@sanguli.es
web: www.sanguli.es

A large, family site in pleasant wooded surroundings, 50 metres from the beach, with extensive sports and entertainment facilities.

dir: *3km SW from Port Aventura, 50m inland from coast road to Cambrils.*

Open: 14 Mar-2 Nov **Site:** 24HEC **For hire:** **Facilities:** **Services:** **Leisure:** P S

see advert on page 510

TAMARIT TARRAGONA

Caledonia

43008
☎ 977 650098 🖷 977 652867
e-mail: caledonia@campingcaledonia.com
web: www.campingcaledonia.com

A well-appointed site in wooded surroundings, 0.8km from the sea. Kids' club open from July to August.

dir: *On N340 at Km1172.*

GPS: 41.1388, 1.3541

Open: 15 May-20 Sep **Site:** 3.5HEC **For hire:** **Prices:** 14.80-30 **Facilities:** Wi-fi (charged) Kids' Club **Services:** **Leisure:** P **Off-site:** S

Trillas Platja Tamarit

43008
☎ 977 650249 🖷 977 650926
e-mail: info@campingtrillas.com
web: www.campingtrillas.com

On several terraces planted with olive trees next to a farm, 50 metres from the sea.

dir: *Off N340 at Km1.172 8km N of Tarragona, over narrow railway bridge (beware oncoming traffic).*

Open: Apr-2 Oct **Site:** 4HEC **For hire:** **Facilities:** **Services:** **Leisure:** P R S

SPAIN

Site 6HEC (site size) grass sand stone little shade partly shaded mainly shaded motorvans accepted bungalows for hire mobile homes for hire tents for hire no dogs site fully accessible for wheelchairs
Prices amount quoted is per night, for 2 adults and car, plus tent or caravan Mobile home hire is a weekly rate.

TARRAGONA — TARRAGONA

Tamarit-Park

Platja Tamarit, 43008

977 650128 977 650451

e-mail: resort@tamarit.com

web: www.tamarit.com

Well-kept site at the sea beneath Tamarit castle. One section lies under tall shady trees, and another lies in a meadow with some trees.

dir: *Off N340 at Km1171.5 towards beach, left at end of road.*

Open: 7 Apr-Oct **Site:** 17HEC **For hire:** **Facilities:** **Services:** **Leisure:** P R S

VILANOVA DE PRADES — TARRAGONA

Serra de Prades

Sant Antoni, 43439

977 869050 977 869050

e-mail: info@serradeprades.com

web: www.serradeprades.com

A fine quiet site close to the mountains and within easy reach of Barcelona and the Port Aventura theme park. Kids' club summer only.

dir: *Via N240.*

GPS: 41.3486, 0.9588

Open: All Year. **Site:** 5HEC **For hire:** **Prices:** 15-33 **Facilities:** Wi-fi (charged) Kids' Club Play Area **Services:** **Leisure:** P **Off-site:** R

VILLARGORDO DEL CABRIEL — VALENCIA

Kiko Park Rural

ctra Embalse Contreras km3, 46317

96 2139082 96 2139337

e-mail: kikoparkrural@kikopark.com

web: www.kikopark.com/rural

Campsite built on site of a small village and farm with former buildings used for amenities and many young trees planted for shade. Pitches divided by hedges and all have fine views.

dir: *A3 (Madrid-Valencia), exit 255 towards Villargordo Cabriel. Signed.*

Open: All Year. **Site:** 2.2HEC **For hire:** **Facilities:** **Services:** **Leisure:** P **Off-site:** L R

NORTH COAST

AJO-BAREYO — CANTABRIA

Cabo de Ajo

Av al Faro 2024, 39170

942 907500 942 621400

e-mail: info@campingcabodeajo.com

web: www.campingcabodeajo.com

Well-equipped site located 26km from Santander and not far from the coast. Transfers to the beach are available in summer. Leisure facilities include a swimming pool and table tennis. Dogs are accepted, except dangerous breeds.

dir: *A8 exit Beranga Km185.*

Open: 15 Jan-15 Dec **Site:** 1.6HEC **For hire:** **Prices:** 20.63-28.08 **Facilities:** Play Area **Services:** **Leisure:** P **Off-site:** R S

BAREYO — CANTABRIA

Los Molinos de Bareyo

ctra Bareyo-Güemes, 39190

942 670569 942 670569

e-mail: losmolinosdebareyo@ceoecant.es

web: www.campinglosmolinos.com

A quiet location with fine views.

dir: *A8 exit km 185, then towards Ajo.*

Open: Jun-Sep & Etr **Site:** 12HEC **For hire:** **Prices:** 15-22 **Facilities:** Wi-fi **Services:** **Leisure:** P **Off-site:** R S

BARREIROS — LUGO

Camping Poblado Gaivota

Playa de Barreiros, 27790

982 124451

web: www.campingpobladogaivota.com

Site leads down to a sandy beach with windsurfing. The main buildings have been designed and built by the owner, who is a painter.

GPS: 43.5622, -7.2075

Open: Apr-15 Oct **Site:** 1HEC **For hire:** **Prices:** 18.36-21.82 **Facilities:** Wi-fi Play Area **Services:** **Leisure:** S **Off-site:** P R

SPAIN

CADAVEDO ASTURIAS

Camping La Regalina

ctra de la Playa SN, 33788
98 5645056 98 4980167
e-mail: info@laregalina.com
web: www.camping-asturias.com

Small, well-equipped site, with a swimming pool available 15 June to 15 October.

dir: *A3/N632 Cadavedo, continue following signs for site.*

GPS: 43.5497, -6.3846

Open: All Year. **Site:** 1HEC **For hire:** **Prices:** 20-24 **Facilities:** Wi-fi Play Area **Services:** **Leisure:** P **Off-site:** R S

COMILLAS CANTABRIA

Comillas

ctra M-Noriga, 39520
942 720074 942 215206
e-mail: info@campingcomillas.com
web: www.campingcomillas.com

Level grassland site to the right of the road to the beach.

dir: *E on C6316 at Km23.*

Open: Jun-Sep **Site:** 3HEC **Prices:** 25.50 **Facilities:** **Services:** **Leisure:** S **Off-site:** P

FRANCA, LA ASTURIAS

Las Hortensias

Playa de la Franca, 33590
985 412442 985 5412153
e-mail: lashortensias@campinglashortensias.com
web: www.campinglashortensias.com

A well-maintained site with good facilities beside the La Franca beach.

Open: Jun-Sep **Site:** 2.8HEC **Facilities:** Wi-fi Play Area **Services:** **Leisure:** R S **Off-site:**

ISLARES CANTABRIA

Playa Arenillas

39798
942 863152 942 863152
e-mail: cueva@mundivia.es
web: www.campingplayaarenillas.com

Well-equipped site in meadowland with some pine trees, 100 metres from the beach.

dir: *N off N634 at Km155.8 for 100m. Steep entrance.*

Open: Apr-Sep **Site:** 2HEC **For hire:** **Prices:** 24.21 **Facilities:** Wi-fi (charged) Play Area **Services:** **Leisure:** S

LLANES ASTURIAS

Palacio de Garaña

33591
98 5410075 98 5410298
e-mail: info@palaciodegarana.com
web: www.palaciodegarana.com

Situated in the grounds of the former Palace of the Marquis of Argüelles, the site is enclosed by stone walls and has good facilities.

Open: 22 Jun-15 Sep **Site:** 2.8HEC **For hire:** **Prices:** 21.49-26.03 **Facilities:** Wi-fi Play Area **Services:** **Leisure:** P **Off-site:** R S

La Paz

The Camping and Caravanning Club The Friendly Club

Playa de Vidiago, 33597
98 5411012 98 5411235
e-mail: delfin@campinglapaz.com
web: www.campinglapaz.com

On the seafront, and with views of the sea and mountains. Pitches are arranged in terraces.

C&CC Report *It's hard to overstate just how special La Paz's location is. Many pitches have breathtaking views – with the Picos de Europa behind and a superb beach below. This is Green Spain at its absolute best. An ideal site for active and adventurous couples and families. There is even help siting units on the terraces for those who want it.*

dir: *Access to site at km292 from town centre on N634.*

Open: Apr-Sep **Site:** **Facilities:** **Services:** **Leisure:** S

LUARCA ASTURIAS

Cantiles

33700
98 5640938 98 4111458
e-mail: cantiles@campingloscantiles.com
web: www.campingloscantiles.com

Meadowland site beautifully situated high above the cliffs. Limited shade from bushes. Footpath to the bay 70 metres below.

dir: *A8 exit 467 from Oviedo, turn at Km308.5 towards Faro de Luarca after fuel station, in Villar de Luarca turn right & 1km to site.*

GPS: 43.5488, -6.5241

Open: All Year. **Site:** 2.3HEC **For hire:** **Facilities:** Wi-fi (charged) **Services:** **Off-site:** P R S

MOTRICO (MUTRIKU) GUIPÚZCOA

Aitzeta

20830

☎ 943 603356 ▤ 943 603106

On two sloping meadows, partially terraced. Lovely view of the sea 1km away.

dir: *0.5km NE on C6212 turn at KmSS56.1.*

GPS: 43.3055, -2.3780

Open: May-Sep **Site:** 1.5HEC **Facilities:** Play Area **Services:** **Leisure:** S **Off-site:**

NOJA CANTABRIA

Los Molinos

av Ris s/n, 39180

☎ 942 630426 ▤ 942 630725

e-mail: losmolinos@ceoecant.es

web: www.campinglosmolinos.com

Pleasant surroundings close to the Emerald coast and fine beaches. Various leisure and sports activities.

dir: *A8 exit km185 in direction of Noja.*

Open: Etr & Jun-Sep **Site:** 18HEC **For hire:** **Prices:** 19-28 **Facilities:** Wi-fi (charged) **Services:** **Leisure:** P **Off-site:** S

Playa Joyel

The Camping and Caravanning Club The Friendly Club

Playa de Ris, 39180

☎ 942 630081 ▤ 942 631294

e-mail: playajoyel@telefonica.net

web: www.playajoyel.com

Set in a level meadow on a peninsula with direct access to the beach.

C&CC Report *A wide range of high quality facilities, set among mature trees and next to the beach, make this an outstanding high or low season site. Ideal for those who like lots going on. Close by is the excellent municipal sports centre. The Guggenheim museum in Bilbao, and the Costa Verde's stunning mountains, are among other attractions close to hand.*

dir: *Between Laredo & Solares via A8, exit 185.*

Open: 15 Apr-2 Oct **Site:** 24HEC **For hire:** **Facilities:** Wi-fi (charged) **Services:** **Leisure:** P S

ORIO GUIPÚZCOA

CM Playa de Orio

20810

☎ 943 834801 ▤ 943 133433

e-mail: kanpina@terra.es

web: www.oriora.com

On two flat terraces along cliffs and surrounded by hedges. Wheelchair accessible everywhere except swimming pool.

dir: *Off N634 near Km12.5 in Orio, before bridge over River Orio turn towards sea for 1.5km.*

Open: Mar-1 Nov **Site:** 3HEC **Prices:** 18.65-30.10 **Facilities:** Wi-fi **Services:** **Leisure:** P **Off-site:** R S

PECHÓN CANTABRIA

Arenas

39594

☎ 942 717188 ▤ 942 717188

e-mail: info@campinglasarenas.com

web: www.campinglasarenas.com

On terraces between rocks, reaching down to the sea.

dir: *Off N634 E of Unquera at Km74 towards sea & onto road S.*

Open: 2 Jun-29 Sep **Site:** 12HEC **Facilities:** Wi-fi Play Area **Services:** **Leisure:** P R S

PERLORA-CANDAS ASTURIAS

Perlora

33491

☎ 98 5870048 ▤ 98 5870048

e-mail: recepcion@campingperlora.com

web: www.campingperlora.com

On top of a large hill on a peninsula with a few terraced pitches.

dir: *7km W of Gijon. Off N632 towards Luanco for 5km.*

GPS: 43.5838, -5.7560

Open: All Year. **Site:** 1.4HEC **Facilities:** **Services:** **Leisure:** S **Off-site:**

REINANTE LUGO

Reinante

27279

☎ 982 134005 ▤ 982 134005

Longish site beyond a range of dunes on a lovely sandy beach.

dir: *On N634 at Km391.7.*

Open: All Year. **Site:** 32HEC **For hire:** **Facilities:** **Services:** **Leisure:** L R S

SPAIN

SAN SEBASTIÁN (DONOSTIA) GUIPÚZCOA

Camping Bungalows Igueldo

Aita Orkolaga Pasealekua 69, Igueldo, 20008
☎ 943 214502 ▤ 943 280411
e-mail: info@campingigueldo.com
web: www.campingigueldo.com

5km from San Sebastián, terraced site on Monte Igueldo divided by hedges. Good public transport links.

dir: *From town signs for Monte Igueldo & beach road for 4.5km.*

GPS: 43.3046, -2.0459

Open: All Year. **Site:** 5HEC **For hire:** **Facilities:** Wi-fi Play Area **Services:** **Off-site:** P R S

SANTIAGO DE COMPOSTELA LA CORUÑA

As Cancelas

rue do 25 de Xullo 35, 15704
☎ 981 580266 ▤ 981 575553
web: www.campingascancelas.com

Quiet site located 2km from the city centre.

Open: All Year. **Site:** 1.8HEC **For hire:** **Facilities:** **Services:** **Leisure:** P

VALDOVIÑO LA CORUÑA

Valdoviño

ctra de la Playa, 15552
☎ 981 487076 ▤ 981 486131
e-mail: campingvaldovino@yahoo.com
web: www.turvaldovino.com

Six gently sloping fields partly in shade. Located behind Cafeteria Andy and block of flats with several villas beyond.

dir: *Off C646 towards Cedeira & sea, 0.7km to site.*

Open: Etr wk & Jun-Sep **Site:** 2HEC **For hire:** **Prices:** 26.20-27.80 **Facilities:** Wi-fi **Services:** **Off-site:** L P R S

VIVEIRO LUGO

Vivero

27850
☎ 982 560004
e-mail: campingvivero@gmail.com

Set in tall woodland near the beach road and sea.

dir: *Off C642 Barreois-Ortueire at Km443.1 & signed.*

Open: Jun-Sep **Site:** 1.2HEC **Facilities:** **Services:** **Off-site:** R S

ZARAUZ (ZARAUTZ) GUIPÚZCOA

Talai Mendi

20800
☎ 943 830042 ▤ 943 830042

A meadowland site on a hillside with shade, 0.5km from the sea. Divided by internal roads.

dir: *On outskirts of town, off N634 at Km17.5 by fuel station towards sea for 350m (narrow asphalt road).*

Open: Jul-Aug **Site:** 3.8HEC **Prices:** 30-33 **Facilities:** Wi-fi **Services:** **Leisure:** S **Off-site:** R

Zarautz

Monte Talai-Mendi, 20800
☎ 943 831238 ▤ 943 132486
e-mail: info@grancampingzarautz.com
web: www.grancampingzarautz.com

Site with terraces separated by hedges. At the foot of Monte Talai-Mendi, the eastern end of Zarautz, from here admire the impressive panorama of the beach and surrounding areas. A fully equipped site with modern facilities.

dir: *1.8km from N634 San Sebastian-Bilbao road. Asphalt access road from Km15.5.*

GPS: 43.2894, -2.1466

Open: All Year. **Site:** 5HEC **Facilities:** **Services:** **Off-site:** P R S

NORTH EAST

ARANDA DE DUERO — BURGOS

Costajàn

09400

947 502070 947 511354

e-mail: campingcostajan@camping-costajan.com

Wooded setting with good facilities.

dir: *Off N1 Burgos-Madrid at Km162.1 N of town.*

Open: All Year. **Site:** 1.8HEC **For hire:** **Facilities:** **Services:** **Leisure:** P **Off-site:** L R

BELLVER DE CERDANYA — LLEIDA

Solana del Segre

25720

973 510310

e-mail: info@solanadelsegre.com

web: www.solanadelsegre.com

A well-equipped site on the River Segre, known for its trout fishing.

dir: *Off N260 km198.*

Open: Jul-Aug **Site:** 6.5HEC **For hire:** **Facilities:** Wi-fi Play Area **Services:** **Leisure:** P R **Off-site:** L

BONANSA — HUESCA

Baliera

22486

974 554016 974 554099

e-mail: info@baliera.com

web: www.baliera.com

A well-equipped site in a beautiful Pyrenean location on the bank of a river and near Aigüestortes National Park. Kids' club available in July and August.

dir: *At Km 355.5 on N260.*

GPS: 42.4392, 0.6989

Open: 26 Dec-Oct & 1-16 Dec **Site:** 5HEC **For hire:** **Prices:** 25.28-31.60 **Facilities:** Wi-fi Kids' Club Play Area **Services:** **Leisure:** L P R **Off-site:**

BORDETA, LA — LLEIDA

Prado Verde

25551

973 647172 973 647172

web: www.campingpradoverde.es

Level meadowland on River Garona with sparse trees and sheltered by high hedges from traffic noise.

dir: *On N230 at Km199 behind fuel station.*

Open: All Year. **Site:** 1.7HEC **For hire:** **Facilities:** **Services:** **Leisure:** L P R

BOSSOST — LLEIDA

Bedurá-Park

ctra N230 km. 174.4, Era Bordeta, 25551

973 648293 973 647038

e-mail: info@bedurapark.com

web: www.bedurapark.com

A terraced site in the Aran Valley offering spectacular views over the surrounding mountains. The site, in wooded surroundings, offers all modern facilities and a variety of sports opportunities.

dir: *Via N230 Km174.4.*

Open: Apr-15 Sep **Site:** 5HEC **For hire:** **Prices:** 23.92-27.10 **Facilities:** Wi-fi Play Area **Services:** **Leisure:** P R **Off-site:** L

ESPOT — LLEIDA

Sol I Neu

ctra d'Espot, 25597

973 624001 973 624107

e-mail: camping@solineu.com

web: www.solineu.com

A peaceful site in a beautiful mountain setting with modern facilities. Organised excursions available.

dir: *From C13 take Espot road.*

GPS: 42.5719, 1.0975

Open: Jul-Aug **Site:** 1.5HEC **Prices:** 25.10 **Facilities:** Wi-fi Play Area **Services:** **Leisure:** P R **Off-site:** L

ESTELLA — NAVARRA

Lizarra

Paraje de Ordoiz, 31200

948 551733 948 554755

e-mail: info@campinglizarra.com

web: www.campinglizarra.com

Site offering two swimming pools, football and mini-golf. Entertainment takes place during the summer.

Open: All Year. **Site:** 4HEC **For hire:** **Facilities:** **Services:** **Leisure:** P

GAVIN HUESCA

Gavin

ctras N260 km 503, 22639
974 485090 974 485017
e-mail: info@campinggavin.com
web: www.campinggavin.com

Located at the mouth of the Tena Valley, a campsite with modern, comfortable installations and a comprehensive range of facilities and services.

C&CC Report *Expect a friendly welcome from the helpful staff at Camping Gavin. The high-quality facilities are in traditional-style buildings and the site enjoys a south-facing location, as well as easy access via French motorways. Camping Gavin offers snow-covered mountains, lakes and rivers, as well as the culture and restaurants of the local towns and villages. The Aragon region is different to any other. Once you have discovered it, you will want to return again.*

GPS: 42.6203, -0.3110

Open: All Year. **Site:** 7.2HEC **For hire:** **Facilities:** Wi-fi Play Area **Services:** **Leisure:** P **Off-site:** L R

HARO LA RIOJA

Haro

av Miranda 1, 26200
941 312737 941 312068
e-mail: campingdeharo@fer.es
web: www.campingdeharo.com

On the outskirts of the city on the banks of the river Tirón. Kids' club during high season.

C&CC Report *Well situated in the Rioja wine region, near to major route, suitable for overnight stops and for short breaks.*

dir: *AP68 exit 9.*

GPS: 42.5783, -2.8543

Open: 20 Jan-9 Dec **Site:** 5HEC **For hire:** **Prices:** 21.35-26.95 **Facilities:** Wi-fi (charged) Kids' Club Play Area **Services:** **Leisure:** P **Off-site:** R

HUESCA HUESCA

San Jorge

Ricardo del Arco, 22004
974 227416 974 227416
e-mail: contacto@campingsanjorge.com
web: campingsanjorge.com

Site with sports field surrounded by high walls. Subdivided by hedges, sparse woodland.

dir: *M123 from town centre towards Zaragoza for 1.5km & signed.*

Open: 15 Mar-15 Oct **Site:** 0.7HEC **Facilities:** Wi-fi **Services:** **Leisure:** P **Off-site:**

LABUERDA HUESCA

Peña Montañesa

ctra Aínsa-Francia, Km2, 22360
974 500032 974 500991
e-mail: info@penamontanesa.com
web: www.penamontanesa.com

A well-equipped family site in a wooded location near the entrance to the Ordesa and Monte Perdido national park.

Open: All Year. **Site:** 10HEC **For hire:** **Prices:** 25.25-30.30 **Facilities:** Wi-fi Play Area **Services:** **Leisure:** P **Off-site:** L R

MENDIGORRÍA NAVARRA

Errota - El Molino

31150
948 340604 948 340082
e-mail: info@campingelmolino.com
web: www.campingelmolino.com

Site includes both individual plots separated by hedges, and a free area with no division. River on site and canoes and pedal boats for hire.

dir: *Access from the N111 (Pamplona - Logroño). At Puente la Reina, take N6030 to Mendigorría, after 6km, take turn for Larraga by Arga River.*

Open: All Year. **Site:** 15HEC **For hire:** **Facilities:** **Services:** **Leisure:** P R **Off-site:**

NÁJERA LA RIOJA

Ruedo

ctra C-31, 26300
941 360102

Set among poplars but with very little shade.

dir: *Off N120 Logroño-Burgos in Nájera, along river just before stone bridge across River Majerilla & left.*

Open: Etr-10 Sep **Site:** 0.5HEC **Facilities:** **Services:** **Off-site:** P R

NUEVALOS ZARAGOZA

Lago Park

ctra Alhama de Aragón-Nuevalos, 50210
976 849038 976 849038
e-mail: reservas@campinglagopark.com
web: www.campinglagopark.com

A pleasant location 100 metres from Laguna de la Tranquera.

dir: *NE towards Alhama de Aragón.*

Open: Apr-Oct **Site:** 3HEC **For hire:** **Facilities:** Wi-fi **Services:** **Leisure:** L P R

ORICAIN NAVARRA

Ezcaba

ctra Francia-Irun km7, 31194
948 330315 948 331316
e-mail: info@campingezcaba.com
web: www.campingezcaba.com
Gently sloping meadowland and a few terraces on a flat topped hill.
dir: *N of Pamplona. Off N121 at Km7.3 towards Berriosuso, after River Ulzama turn right & uphill.*
GPS: 42.8571, -1.6235
Open: All Year. **Site:** 2HEC **For hire:** **Prices:** 17.70-27.40 **Facilities:** Wi-fi (charged) Play Area **Services:** **Leisure:** P **Off-site:** R

PANCORBO BURGOS

Desfiladero

09280
947 354027
e-mail: campingeldesfiladero@hotmail.com
web: www.eldesfiladero.com
A well-appointed site close to the river.
C&CC Report *With impressive views over the canyon in which the site is situated, El Desfiladero is only a few kilometres to the south-west of Miranda de Ebro and just off the AP1 motorway. This makes it a convenient stop-over for routes from Santander to most Spanish destinations and from Bilbao to winter destinations in Spain and Portugal.*
dir: *Off N1 at Km305.2.*
Open: All Year. **Site:** 13HEC **For hire:** **Prices:** 15.12-16.47 **Facilities:** **Services:** **Leisure:** L **Off-site:** P R

PUEBLA DE CASTRO, LA HUESCA

Lago Barasona

crta Nacional 123 A km25, 22435
974 545148 974 545148
e-mail: info@lagobarasona.com
web: www.lagobarasona.com
A well-equipped, terraced site in a beautiful setting beside the lake and backed by mountains.
Open: Mar-12 Dec **Site:** 5HEC **For hire:** **Facilities:** Wi-fi Kids' Club **Services:** **Leisure:** P **Off-site:** L R

RIBERA DE CARDÓS LLEIDA

Cardós

25570
973 623112 973 623183
web: www.campingdelcardos.com
Long stretch of meadowland divided by four rows of poplars.
dir: *Near electricity plant in Llavorsi turn NE onto Ribera road for 9km, site near hostel Soly Neu.*
Open: Apr-29 Sep **Site:** 3HEC **For hire:** **Facilities:** **Services:** **Leisure:** P R

SANTO DOMINGO DE LA CALZADA LA RIOJA

Bañares

26250
941 342804 941 340131
web: www.campingbanares.es
Situated in a valley surrounded by the Cantabria mountains, a swimming pool is available for campers' use.
Open: All Year. **Site:** 12HEC **For hire:** **Facilities:** **Services:** **Leisure:** P

SOLSONA LLEIDA

Solsonès

25280
973 482861 973 481300
e-mail: info@campingsolsones.com
web: www.campingsolsones.com
A well-equipped site in a picturesque mountain setting with facilities for both summer and winter holidays.
Open: 8 Jan-8 Dec **Site:** 6.3HEC **For hire:** **Prices:** 22.50-25 Mobile home hire 445.55-644 **Facilities:** Wi-fi Kids' Club Play Area **Services:** **Leisure:** P

TORLA HUESCA

Camping Ordesa

ctra de Ordesa s/n, 22376
974 117721 974 486347
e-mail: infocamping@campingordesa.es
web: www.campingordesa.es
On three terraces between well-kept hedges.
dir: *2km N of village at Km96 & N of C138.*
Open: Apr-15 Oct **Site:** 4HEC **For hire:** **Prices:** 19.50 **Facilities:** Wi-fi Play Area **Services:** **Leisure:** P **Off-site:** R

SPAIN

SPAIN

VILLOSLADA DE CAMEROS — LA RIOJA

Los Cameros

ctra La Virgen, 26125

☎ 941 747021 🖷 941 742091

e-mail: info@camping-loscameros.com

web: www.camping-loscameros.com

Situated in the Sierra Cebollera national park in the Iberian mountain range.

dir: *Off N111 towards Soria & onto Villoslada.*

Open: All Year. **Site:** 4HEC **For hire:** **Facilities:** **Services:** **Leisure:** R

ZARAGOZA — ZARAGOZA

Ciudad de Zaragoza

San Juan Bautista de la Salle, 50012

☎ 876 241495

e-mail: info@campingzaragoza.com

web: www.campingzaragoza.com

Surburban campsite, around 3km from the centre of Zaragoza.

C&CC Report *Located in a suburb of Zaragoza, with local shops within 500m and with easy access from the motorway. Being 3km from Zaragoza centre by bus, the campsite is convenient for visiting this capital of Aragon with its 2,000 years of history.*

dir: *Z40 (Zaragova ring road), exit 33a then NII. Situated off Maurice Ravel Street.*

GPS: 41.6379, -0.9431

Open: All Year. **For hire:** **Facilities:** Wi-fi Play Area **Services:** **Leisure:** P

NORTH WEST

BAYONA — PONTEVEDRA

Bayona Playa

ctra Vigo-Bayona km 19.4, 36393

☎ 986 350035 🖷 986 352952

e-mail: campingbayona@campingbayona.com

web: www.campingbayona.com

On a long sandy peninsula on the Galicia coast with direct access to the beach. The site has modern facilities and a variety of water sports are available.

dir: *Autopista AP9 Salida No 5 (Baiona Norte).*

Open: All Year. **Site:** 4HEC **For hire:** **Facilities:** **Services:** **Leisure:** P R S

CARRIÓN DE LOS CONDES — LÉON

Camping El Edén

14620

☎ 979 880200

e-mail: administracion@campingeleden.es

web: www.campingeleden.es

Modern facilities with large pitches.

C&CC Report *On the banks of a river, just a few minutes' walk from the centre of the small town of Carrión de los Condes. Close to the main route from the northern Spanish ferry ports to western Spain and to Portugal.*

GPS: 42.3357, -4.6044

Open: All Year. **Site:** **Facilities:** Wi-fi **Services:**

CUBILLAS DE SANTA MARTA — VALLADOLID

Cubillas

47290

☎ 983 585002 🖷 983 585016

e-mail: info@campingcubillas.com

web: www.campingcubillas.com

Meadowland with young trees, subdivided by hedges. Steep ascent to the site.

dir: *On right of N620 from Burgos between km100 & km101.*

GPS: 41.8051, -4.5871

Open: 9 Jan-16 Dec **Site:** 4HEC **For hire:** **Prices:** 18.75-25.40 **Facilities:** Wi-fi (charged) Play Area **Services:** **Leisure:** P **Off-site:** R

PORTONOVO — PONTEVEDRA

Paxariñas

36970

☎ 986 723055 🖷 986 721356

e-mail: info@campingpaxarinas.com

web: www.campingpaxarinas.com

Slightly sloping site towards a bay, among dunes and tall pines and young deciduous trees. The site and surrounding area has many leisure activities and lovely beaches.

GPS: 42.3926, -8.8448

Open: Etr-15 Oct **Site:** 2HEC **For hire:** **Prices:** 15-30 Mobile home hire 300-595 **Facilities:** Wi-fi Play Area **Services:** **Leisure:** S **Off-site:** P

SANTA MARINA DE VALDEON — LÉON

El Cares

24915

☎ 987 742676 🖷 987 742676

Wooded mountain setting with good facilities.

dir: *N off N621 from Portilla de la Reina.*

Open: Jun-Sep **Site:** 15HEC **For hire:** **Facilities:** **Services:** **Leisure:** R **Off-site:** L

SAN VICENTE DO MAR — PONTEVEDRA

Siglo XXI

36988

☎ 986 738100 🖷 986 738113

e-mail: info@campingsiglo21.com

web: www.campingsiglo21.com

A popular modern site with individual sanitary facilities attached to each pitch.

Open: Jun-Sep **Site:** 1.5HEC **Prices:** 24 **Facilities:** Wi-fi Play Area **Services:** **Leisure:** P **Off-site:** S

TORDESILLAS — VALLADOLID

Astral

Cami de Pollos 8, 47100

☎ 983 770953 🖷 983 770953

e-mail: info@campingelastral.es

web: www.campingelastral.es

A well-equipped site in a pleasant rural location close to the River Duero.

dir: *Motorway exit Tordesillas & signed.*

GPS: 41.4953, -5.0052

Open: Apr-Sep **Site:** 3HEC **For hire:** **Prices:** 17.80- 26.40 **Facilities:** Wi-fi (charged) Kids' Club Play Area **Services:** **Leisure:** P **Off-site:** R

VALENCIA DE DON JUAN — LÉON

Pico Verde

ctra C621 Mayorga-Astorga, 24200

☎ 987 750525 🖷 987 750525

e-mail: campingpicoverd@terra.es

web: www.verial.es/campingpicoverde

A green and quiet site, just off A66.

dir: *6km off A66.*

Open: 15 Jun-4 Sep **Site:** 2.7HEC **Facilities:** Play Area **Services:** **Leisure:** P **Off-site:** R

SOUTH

BAÑOS DE FORTUNA — MURCIA

Fuente

30620

☎ 968 685017 🖷 968 685125

e-mail: info@campingfuente.com

web: www.campingfuente.com

A camping ground within a hotel complex with individual bathroom facilities attached to each pitch and good recreational facilities.

dir: *C3223 from Fortuna à Pinoso to Balneario de Fortuna, signed.*

GPS: 38.2064, -1.1072

Open: All Year. **Site:** 1.9HEC **For hire:** **Prices:** 16.74-18.90 **Facilities:** Wi-fi (charged) **Services:** **Leisure:** P **Off-site:**

CABO DE GATA — ALMERIA

Cabo de Gata

The Camping and Caravanning Club The Friendly Club

04150

☎ 950 160443 🖷 950 916821

e-mail: info@campingcabodegata.com

web: www.campingcabodegata.com

Natural parkland site with separate pitches, 1km from the beach. Kids' club available in summer.

C&CC Report *Many choose Cabo de Gata for its very peaceful surroundings in the semi-arid Cabo de Gatar-Nijar natural park, on the Gulf of Almería, one of the most southerly and reputedly driest points in Europe. With good modern facilities, the site makes a good base for visiting the natural park with its salinas (salt pans) and their abundant birdlife. You can walk out of the campsite entrance straight into the park's famous flat sand dunes. The park is also known for the richness of its diverse flora growing in the volcanic soil, and for its beaches, rocky cliffs and salt flats.*

dir: *E15 or N340 exit 460 or 467.*

GPS: 36.8008, -2.2461

Open: All Year. **Site:** 3.6HEC **For hire:** **Prices:** 10.74-24.85 **Facilities:** Wi-fi (charged) Kids' Club Play Area **Services:** **Leisure:** P S

see advert on page 520

CARCHUNA — GRANADA

Don Cactus

Carchuna-Motril, 18730
☎ 958 623109 958 624294
e-mail: camping@doncactus.com
web: www.doncactus.com

A well established modern site adjoining the beach.

dir: *On N340 Carchuna-Motril at Km343.*

GPS: 36.6958, -3.4433

Open: All Year. **Site:** 4HEC **For hire:**
Prices: 9.23-30.75 **Facilities:** Wi-fi (charged) Kids' Club Play Area **Services:**
Leisure: P S

CARLOTA, LA — CORDOBA

Carlos III

ctra N4 km 430, 14100
☎ 957 300697 957 3000697
e-mail: camping@campingcarlosIII.com
web: www.campingcarlosIII.com

Wooded surroundings with modern facilities. Wooden bungalows to rent with breakfast included.

dir: *A4 exit 432/NIV exit La Carlota.*

GPS: 37.6825, -4.9180

Open: All Year. **Site:** 7HEC **For hire:**
Prices: 17.85-20.50 **Facilities:** Wi-fi (charged) Kids' Club Play Area **Services:**
Leisure: P **Off-site:**

CASTILLO DE BAÑOS — GRANADA

Castillo de Baños

The Camping and Caravanning Club – The Friendly Club

La Mamola, 18750
☎ 958 829528 958 829768
e-mail: info@campingcastillo.com
web: www.campingcastillo.com

Well-equipped site next to the beach. Kids' club in July and August.

C&CC Report *This is a small simple site with a relaxing atmosphere, for those who want something a bit different. As well as for longer stays, the site's location also makes it a convenient place to break the journey when travelling between the Mediterranean and Atlantic campsites. To make the most out of this area you will need to use your own vehicle to get out and about. Many of the best parts of beautiful Andalucía are within easy day-trip reach. Granada with its historic jewel - the Alhambra Palace - is just one recommendation, but there are many others too.*

dir: *At Km360 on N340 Castillo de Baños-La Mamola.*

GPS: 36.7408, -3.3011

Open: All Year. **Site:** 3HEC **For hire:**
Prices: 7.70-25.65 **Facilities:** Wi-fi (charged) Kids' Club Play Area **Services:**
Leisure: P S

CONIL DE LA FRONTERA CÁDIZ

Camping La Rosaleda

ctra del Pradillo km1.3, 11140
956 443327 956 443385
e-mail: info@campinglarosaleda.com
web: www.campinglarosaleda.com

Situated on the Costa de la Luz, the site has good sporting facilities and entertainment programme. Dogs are accepted, except in July and August.

C&CC Report *Camping La Rosaleda is a gem of a site. Family owned and run, the campsite is very well kept and the owners and staff are always on hand to provide local information. Activities, entertainment and excursions are organised regularly, even a trip to Tangiers in Morocco, subject to minimum numbers. This green and verdant region offers several interesting itineraries to follow. The campsite is central to several natural parks and the coast is very good for exploring by bike.*

GPS: 39.2928, -6.0958

Open: All Year. **Site:** 5HEC **For hire:**
Prices: 18-38.50 **Facilities:** Wi-fi Kids' Club Play Area **Services:** **Leisure:** P
Off-site: S

Fuente del Gallo

Fuente del Gallo, 11140
956 440137 956 442036
e-mail: camping@campingfuentedelgallo.com
web: www.campingfuentedelgallo.com

A well-equipped site in a wooded location 300 metres from the beach.

dir: *Signed from N340, Km23 or A48 exit 15 onto main road to Km23.*

Open: Apr-Sep **Site:** 2.5HEC **For hire:**
Prices: 20-32.50 **Facilities:** Wi-fi (charged) Play Area **Services:** **Leisure:** P **Off-site:** S

Roche

Carril de Pilahito, s/n, 11149
956 442216 956 443002
e-mail: info@campingroche.com
web: www.campingroche.com

Spread among pine groves with well-defined pitches close to the beach. Ideal for walking and cycling.

dir: *Via N340 from Cádiz to Algeciras, 19.5km.*

Open: All Year. **Site:** 5HEC **For hire:**
Prices: 15.96-28 **Facilities:** Wi-fi Play Area
Services: **Leisure:** P **Off-site:** R S

see advert below

This is a wonderful place to experience the sunshine and culture of Spain.

Camping Roche is situated in a pine forest near white sandy beaches. Ideal place for enjoying the landscape and nature. The campsite is next to Conil, a lovely town in the south of Spain. A recently built extension provides further pitches: spacious and luxury pitches equipped with electricity (10 A), water and water waste.

Carril de Pilahito, E-11149
Conil de la Fra., Cádiz
Tlf. 956 44 22 16 / 956 44 26 24
Fax: 956 44 30 02
info@campingroche.com
www.campingroche.com

A **40%** *discount in low season. We have off-season deals for longer stays:*
1 month for 2 persons + tent/caravan + electricity and car for € 285.

acilities shower electric points for razors electric points for caravans motorvan service point parking by tents permitted compulsory separate car park shop **Services** café/restaurant bar Camping Gaz International gas other than Camping Gaz first aid facilities laundry **Leisure** swimming L-Lake P-Pool R-River S-Sea **Off-site** All facilities within 5km

EL ROCÍO — HUELVA

Aldea

ctra del Rocío km 25, 21750
959 442677 959 442582
e-mail: info@campinglaaldea.com
web: www.campinglaaldea.com

Situated in the village of El Rocío, at the entrance of Doñana, a national and natural park.

C&CC Report *El Rocío is a fantastic location for nature lovers and those wanting to get immersed in traditional Spain. With its sand streets and hitch rails for horses it is a popular place of pilgrimage, especially on Sundays. La Aldea is a modern campsite offering a wide range of high quality facilities and services. Visitors will not fail to be impressed by the area and the friendliness of campsite staff and locals. Located on the edge of the most important protected nature area in Europe, the unique Doñana natural park – an area with more than 300 bird species, including one of the world's largest colonies of Spanish imperial eagles. The natural areas are accessible through a number of visitor centres, nature trails with guided half-day safari trips in four-wheel drive vehicles, horse-guided routes, waymarked walks and boardwalks, visitor centres and observatories.*

dir: *A49/H612, follow directions for Matalascanas.*

Open: All Year. **Site:** 5.8HEC **For hire:** **Facilities:** Wi-fi (charged) Play Area **Services:** **Leisure:** P

ESTEPONA — MÁLAGA

Parque Tropical

ctra A7, 29680
952 793618 952 793618
e-mail: parquetropicalcamping@hotmail.com
web: www.parquetropicalcamping.com

A modern site at the foot of the Sierra Bermeja mountains, a short walk from the sea.

dir: *Via N340 at Km162.*

Open: All Year. **Site:** 12.4HEC **For hire:** **Prices:** 10-25 **Facilities:** Wi-fi (charged) **Services:** **Leisure:** P **Off-site:** S

FUENTE DE PIEDRA — MÁLAGA

Espacios Rurales

Cami de la Rábita s/n, 29520
952 735294 952 735461
e-mail: info@camping-rural.com
web: www.camping-rural.com

Situated within a wildlife reserve on the shores of a lagoon. Leisure facilities include a swimming pool available in summer and mini-golf.

Open: All Year. **Site:** 2HEC **For hire:** **Prices:** 14.40-20 **Facilities:** Wi-fi Kids' Club Play Area **Services:** **Leisure:** L P **Off-site:**

GALLARDOS, LOS — ALMERIA

Gallardos

04280
950 528324 950 469596
e-mail: campinglosgallardos@hotmail.com
web: www.campinglosgallardos.com

Level site with individual pitches, 11km from the sea and 10km from the old Moorish village of Mojácar.

dir: *0.5km from Km525 on N340.*

Open: All Year. **Site:** 3.5HEC **Facilities:** **Services:** **Leisure:** P

GRANADA — GRANADA

Sierra Nevada

av Juan Pablo II, 23, 18014
958 150062 958 150954
e-mail: campingmotel@terra.es
web: www.campingsierranevada.com

Almost level grassy and shady site, in numerous sections, within a motel complex. Good transport links to the city centre.

dir: *A44 exit 123 signed bus station.*

GPS: 37.1981, -3.6175

Open: Mar-Oct **Site:** 3HEC **For hire:** **Prices:** 25.80 **Facilities:** Wi-fi Play Area **Services:** **Leisure:** P **Off-site:** L R

GÜÉJAR-SIERRA GRANADA

Las Lomas

ctra Güéjar-Sierra Km 6.5, 18160
958 484742 958 484000
e-mail: info@campinglaslomas.com
web: www.campinglaslomas.com

With views of the surrounding countryside, pitches are divided by hedges. Kids' club available in July and August. Dogs permitted except in bungalows.

C&CC Report *Peaceful hillside setting above reservoir with spectacular Sierra Nevada views, with modern wash blocks and private bathrooms for hire. Convenient for visiting Granada, the Alhambra palace and the scenery and traditional villages of the Sierra Nevada mountains.*

dir: *E902 (Motril-Jaén), exit 132 to Ronda Sur. Follow Sierra Nevada. Take right hand lane 3km past the tunnel then turn left. Follow signs 'Güéjar Sierra' and 'Las Lomas'.*

GPS: 37.1594, -3.4544

Open: All Year. **Site:** 2HEC **For hire:** **Prices:** 20-27 **Facilities:** Wi-fi (charged) Kids' Club Play Area **Services:** **Leisure:** P **Off-site:** L R

GUIJARROSA, LA CORDOBA

Campiña

14547
957 315303 957 315303
e-mail: info@campinglacampina.com
web: www.campinglacampina.com

A quiet rural setting surrounded by olive trees and elms with modern facilities, and a bus from the gate to Cordoba. Breakfast is included in pitch prices. Between November and February booking is necessary.

dir: *Off N4/E5 at Km424 (Aldea Quintana La Victoria) or Km441 (La Rambla Montilla).*

GPS: 37.6228, -4.8594

Open: Mar-Oct **Site:** 0.7HEC **For hire:** **Prices:** 14-22 **Facilities:** Wi-fi **Services:** **Leisure:** P

HUMILLADERO MÁLAGA

Sierrecilla

The Camping and Caravanning Club
The Friendly Club

29531
951 199090
e-mail: info@lasierrecilla.com
web: www.lasierrecilla.com

Modern and luxurious facilities with plots of different sizes. 40 minutes from the beaches of Málaga and 1 hour from Granada, Seville and Cordoba, an ideal place to discover Andalucia. Eagles, vultures and falcons can be seen locally.

C&CC Report *Conveniently located, just over 1.5km from the A92 Granada-Seville motorway, this recently redeveloped site is on the outskirts of the village of Humilladero, with local shops, bars and restaurants within 900m.*

dir: *A 92 exit 138 at 1st rdbt to Humilladero at town entrance rdbt take 2nd exit, follow to bottom turn right & next corner to left.*

GPS: 37.1081, -4.6871

Site: **For hire:** **Facilities:** Wi-fi **Services:** **Leisure:** P

ISLA CRISTINA HUELVA

Giralda

21410
959 343318 959 343318
e-mail: recepcion@campinggiralda.com
web: www.campinggiralda.com

On level ground dotted with trees within easy reach of the beach. Modern facilities and plenty of entertainment.

dir: *On Isla Cristina-La Antilla road.*

Open: All Year. **Site:** 15HEC **For hire:** **Facilities:** **Services:** **Leisure:** P R **Off-site:** S

ISLA PLANA MURCIA

Madriles

ctra de la Azohia Km45, 30868
968 152151 968 152092
e-mail: camplosmadriles@terra.es
web: www.campinglosmadriles.com

A large family site with a variety of recreational facilities including tennis, table tennis and a swimming pool. Pitches on stepped terraces overlook the sea.

dir: *Via Mazarron-Cartagena road.*

GPS: 37.5780, -1.1963

Open: All Year. **Site:** 7.2HEC **For hire:** **Prices:** 16-30.78 **Facilities:** Wi-fi (charged) Play Area **Services:** **Leisure:** P S **Off-site:**

SPAIN

cilities shower electric points for razors electric points for caravans motorvan service point parking by tents permitted mpulsory separate car park shop **Services** café/restaurant bar Camping Gaz International gas other than Camping Gaz first aid facilities laundry **Leisure** swimming L-Lake P-Pool R-River S-Sea **Off-site** All facilities within 5km

MANGA DEL MAR MENOR, LA — MURCIA

La Manga

Autovia de la Manga, Salida 11, 30386
968 563014 968 563426
e-mail: lamanga@caravaning.es
web: www.caravaning.es

A large family site on the Mar Menor lagoon. Pitches separated by hedges or trees. Good recreational facilities. Kids' club in high season.

C&CC Report *A great location and a high quality site. La Manga resort, the beautiful coastal area of Calblanque and fishing villages such as Cabo de Palos are all nearby. Several golf courses are close by, too. The area can be bustling with visitors from across Europe and space is usually at a premium. During Semana Santa (Holy Week) leading up to Easter Monday, the campsite and the local area are likely to be very busy as the Spanish come to celebrate. During this week local celebrations are liable to last well into the night and provide an insight into how the Spanish love to fiesta.*

dir: *Off Cartagena motorway via MU-312.*

Open: All Year. **Site:** 32HEC **For hire:** **Prices:** 20-29.50 **Facilities:** Wi-fi (charged) Kids' Club Play Area **Services:** **Leisure:** P S

MARBELLA — MÁLAGA

Buganvilla

29600
952 831973 952 831974
e-mail: info@campingbuganvilla.com
web: www.campingbuganvilla.com

A well-equipped site in a pine forest close to the beach.

dir: *E of Marbella off N340 coast road towards Mijas.*

Open: All Year. **Site:** 4HEC **For hire:** **Facilities:** **Services:** **Leisure:** P S **Off-site:**

Cabopino

29600
952 834373 952 850106
e-mail: info@campingcabopino.com
web: www.campingcabopino.com

A well run site in a pleasant location 175 metres from the beach. There is an indoor and outdoor swimming pool and an entertainment programme all year round. High quality restaurant available.

C&CC Report *A well-located site in the heart of the Costa del Sol. Like the surrounding area, the site is busy all year round and space is at a premium. Across the road is Puerto Cabopino, a tiny port where convertibles sit beside powerboats and cruisers. Among the places to visit are Marbella with its jet-set port at Puerto Banús joined by a 7km long promenade. Also visit old Marbella with its small shops, art galleries, bars and bistros, plus its Alcazaba Moorish fortification dating back to the 9th century. Gibraltar is about 80km away and a favourite to visit. Inland from Marbella, the stunning, gorge-spanning town of Ronda is a beautiful drive away, while numerous nature reserves and small sierras offer a very peaceful contrast to the non-stop hustle and bustle of the coast.*

dir: *Off N340 (A7) km194.7.*

GPS: 36.4886, -4.7427

Open: All Year. **Site:** 11HEC **For hire:** **Facilities:** Wi-fi (charged) Kids' Club Play Area **Services:** **Leisure:** P **Off-site:** S

MAZAGÓN — HUELVA

Mazagón

cuesta de la Barca s/n, 21130
959 376208 959 536256
e-mail: info@campingplayamazagon.com
web: www.campingplayamazagon.com

Undulating terrain among dunes in a sparse pine forest. Long sandy beach. Small dogs only accepted.

dir: *Off N431 Sevilla-Huelva before San Juan del Puerto towards Moguer, continue S via Palso de la Frontera.*

Open: All Year. **Site:** 8HEC **Prices:** 30 **Facilities:** Wi-fi (charged) Play Area **Services:** **Leisure:** P **Off-site:** S

Site 6HEC (site size) grass sand stone little shade partly shaded mainly shaded motorvans accepted bungalows for hire mobile homes for hire tents for hire no dogs site fully accessible for wheelchairs
Prices amount quoted is per night, for 2 adults and car, plus tent or caravan Mobile home hire is a weekly rate.

MOJÁCAR ALMERIA

Sopalmo

Sopalmo, 04637
950 473002
e-mail: info@campingsopalmoelcortijillo.com
web: www.campingsopalmoelcortijillo.com

Site with panoramic views of the surrounding countryside and at the foot of the Sierra Cabrera mountains.

GPS: 37.0653, -1.8688

Open: All Year. **Site:** 9HEC **For hire:** **Prices:** 6.50-18 **Facilities:** Wi-fi Play Area **Services:** **Off-site:** S

MORATALLA MURCIA

La Puerta

ctra del Canal, Paraje La Puerta Km8, 30440
968 730008 968 706365
e-mail: info@campinglapuerta.com
web: www.campinglapuerta.com

Wooded site alongside the river Alhárabe with big pitches and pleasant views.

dir: *A30 Albacete to Murcia, onto C415 to Moratalla.*

Open: All Year. **Site:** 10HEC **For hire:** **Facilities:** **Services:** **Leisure:** P R **Off-site:**

MOTRIL GRANADA

Playa de Poniente

Playa de Poniente s/n, 18613
958 820303 958 604191
e-mail: info@campingplayadeponiente.com
web: www.campingplayadeponiente.com

Situated on a beach and within an area that has a sub-tropical climate. Leisure activities include tennis and paddle tennis.

GPS: 36.7180, -3.5463

Open: All Year. **Site:** 2.4HEC **For hire:** **Prices:** 11-24.75 **Facilities:** Wi-fi (charged) Play Area **Services:** **Leisure:** P S

OTURA GRANADA

Suspiro del Moro

18630
958 555411 958 555411
e-mail: campingsuspirodelmoro@yahoo.es
web: www.campingsuspirodelmoro.com

A modern, quiet, pleasant site with good facilities close to the town centre.

dir: *10km S of Granada via N323 follow signs for Padul, site at km145 on x-rds to Alm necar.*

Open: All Year. **Site:** 1HEC **For hire:** **Prices:** 19-22.10 **Facilities:** Wi-fi (charged) Play Area **Services:** **Leisure:** P **Off-site:** R

PELIGROS GRANADA

Granada

Autovía Granada - Jaén (A44), Salida 121, 18210
958 340548 958 340548
e-mail: pruizlopez1953@yahoo.es
web: www.campinggranada.es

Wooded location with panoramic views.

dir: *A44 (Autovia Serra Nevada), exit 121.*

Open: 15 Mar-Sep **Site:** 2.2HEC **Prices:** 23.76 **Facilities:** **Services:** **Leisure:** P

PUERTO DE SANTA MARÍA, EL CÁDIZ

Playa Las Dunas

Paseo Maritimo de la Puntilla S/N, 11500
956 872210 956 860117
e-mail: info@lasdunascamping.com
web: www.lasdunascamping.com

Large site with good recreational facilities close to the beach.

GPS: 36.5875, -6.2408

Open: All Year. **Site:** 13.2HEC **For hire:** **Prices:** 18.50-24.40 **Facilities:** Wi-fi (charged) **Services:** **Leisure:** P **Off-site:** R S

SPAIN

RONDA MÁLAGA

El Sur

ctra de Algeciras A369 2.8km, 29400
952 875939 952 877054
e-mail: info@campingelsur.com
web: www.elsur.com
A beautiful location in the heart of the Serrania of Ronda.
GPS: 36.7211, -5.1717
Open: Feb-1 Nov **Site:** 4HEC **For hire:** **Prices:** 19.40-23.90 **Facilities:** Wi-fi (charged) Play Area **Services:** **Leisure:** P

ROQUETAS-DE-MAR ALMERIA

Roquetas

Los Parrales, 04740
950 343809 950 342525
e-mail: info@campingroquetas.com
web: www.campingsroquetas.com
A family site on the coast with good facilities. Discounts available in low season.
dir: *Access by road 340. 1.7km from Km428.6.*
Open: All Year. **Site:** 8HEC **For hire:** **Prices:** 8.08-20.22 **Facilities:** Wi-fi (charged) Play Area **Services:** **Leisure:** L P S

SANTA ELENA JAÉN

Despeñaperros

The Camping and Caravanning Club The Friendly Club

23213
953 664192 953 664192
e-mail: info@campingdespenaperros.com
web: www.campingdespenaperros.com
A clean, restful site in a nature reserve with views of the surrounding mountains.
C&CC Report *Very convenient for routes south and south-west, and for the Despeñaperros Natural Park, with villages services within 500m.*
dir: *On A4-E5 at Km257 (Madrid-Sevilla) or km259 (Sevilla-Madrid).*
Open: All Year. **Site:** 5HEC **For hire:** **Prices:** 13.45-14.50 **Facilities:** Wi-fi **Services:** **Leisure:** P

TARIFA CÁDIZ

Paloma

11380
956 684203 956 684233
e-mail: campingpaloma@yahoo.es
web: www.campingpaloma.com
A modern site in a secluded location next to the prehistoric Necropolis de los Algarbes, 400 metres from the beach and. Fine views of the African coast across the Straits of Gibraltar.
dir: *Via N340 Cádiz-Málaga at Km74.*
Open: All Year. **Site:** 4.9HEC **For hire:** **Facilities:** **Services:** **Leisure:** P **Off-site:** R S

Rió Jara

11380
956 680570 956 680570
e-mail: campingriojara@terra.es
web: www.campingriojara.com
Extensive site on meadowland with good tree cover. Long sandy beach.
dir: *Off N340 at Km81 towards sea.*
Open: All Year. **Site:** 3HEC **Facilities:** Wi-fi **Services:** **Leisure:** R S

Tarifa

11380
956 684778 956 684778
e-mail: info@campingtarifa.es
web: www.campingtarifa.es
A terraced site in wooded surroundings, 100 metres from the sea.
dir: *N340 at Km78 on Málaga-Cádiz road.*
GPS: 36.0548, -5.6494
Open: Mar-Oct **Site:** 3.2HEC **For hire:** **Prices:** 22-35.50 **Facilities:** Wi-fi Play Area **Services:** **Leisure:** P **Off-site:** R S

TORROX-COSTA — MÁLAGA

El Pino

Torrox-Park s/n, 29793

☎ 952 530006 🖷 952 532578

e-mail: info@campingelpino.com

web: www.campingelpino.com

Quiet site with a family atmosphere, surrounded by avocado and tropical trees, offering shade in summer.

dir: *Autovia del Mediterraneo km 285, 500m from rdbt & bridge access to Torrox Park.*

GPS: 36.7392, -3.9497

Open: All Year. **Site:** 50HEC **For hire:** **Prices:** 13-18 **Facilities:** Wi-fi Play Area **Services:** **Leisure:** P **Off-site:** S

see advert on this page

VILLAFRANCA DE CÓRDOBA — CÓRDOBA

Albolafia

Cami de la Vega s/n, 14420

☎ 957 190835 🖷 957 190835

e-mail: informacion@campingalbolafia.com

web: www.campingalbolafia.com

A site with modern, well designed facilities. The entrance buildings are in a semicircular way, with a central fountain built on an ancient well. Córdoba is within easy reach and there are good transport links.

dir: *Autovia A4 at km 377, site in 1.8km.*

GPS: 38.5933, -4.9283

Open: All Year. **Site:** 3HEC **For hire:** **Facilities:** Wi-fi Play Area **Services:** **Leisure:** P R

ANDORRA

SANT JULIÀ DE LÒRIA

Huguet

ctra de Fontaneda, 600

☎ 376843718 🖷 376843803

On level strip of meadowland with rows of fruit and deciduous trees.

Open: All Year. **Site:** 1.5HEC **Facilities:** **Services:** **Leisure:** R **Off-site:** L P

Drinking and driving

If the level of alcohol in the bloodstream is 0.05 per cent or more, severe penalties include fine or prison. The police may request any driver to undergo a breath test or drugs test. Visiting motorists may be forbidden from driving in Switzerland for a minimum of one month.

Driving licence

Minimum age at which a UK licence holder may drive temporarily imported car 18, motorcycle (up to 50cc) 16, motorcycle (50cc or over) 18.

Fines

On-the-spot fines imposed in certain cases. Vehicle clamps are not used in Switzerland but vehicles causing an obstruction can be removed. Speeding fines are severe.

Fuel

Unleaded petrol (95 and 98 octane) and Diesel (Gasoil) is available. No leaded petrol (lead substitute additive available). There is limited LPG availability (only eight outlets). Petrol in a can permitted.

Credit card acceptance variable, especially at night due to automatic pumps not recognising UK card PIN; check with your card issuer for usage in Switzerland before travel. Some automatic pumps accept bank notes.

Lights

Use of dipped headlights during the day recommended for all vehicles. Compulsory when passing through tunnels even if they are well lit, a fine will be imposed for non-compliance.

Motorcycles

Wearing of crash helmets compulsory. Use of dipped headlights during the day recommended.

Motor insurance

Third-party compulsory.

Passengers/children in cars

Vehicles registered outside Switzerland, i.e. visiting Switzerland must comply with the requirements of their country of registration with regard to child restraint regulations. Children up to 12 years of age have to be placed in a child restraint type approved complying with UN ECE regulation 44.03. Children measuring more than 150 cm will not be included.

Seat belts

Compulsory for front and rear seat occupants to wear seat belts, if fitted.

Speed limits

Standard legal limits, which may be varied by signs

Private vehicles without trailers	
Built-up areas	50km/h
Outside built-up areas	80km/h
Semi-motorways	100km/h)
Motorways	120km/h

Private vehicles (up to 3.5t) with trailer	
Semi-motorways and motorways	80km/h
Built-up areas	50km/h
Open road	80km/h

Minimum speed on motorways: 80km/h

NOTE Towing of cars on a motorway only permitted up to the next exit, at a maximum speed of 40km/h.

Compulsory equipment in Switzerland

Snow chains – compulsory in areas indicated by appropriate sign and must be fitted on at least two drive wheels.

Warning triangle – Each motor vehicle must be equipped with a warning triangle which must be kept within easy reach (not in the boot). This must be used in any breakdown/emergency situation. Excludes motorcycles.

Other rules/requirements

Hitchhiking prohibited on motorways and semi-motorways.

The Swiss authorities levy an annual motorway tax and a vehicle sticker (costing CHF40 (or 29 EUR) for vehicles up to 3.5 tonnes maximum total weight and known locally as a 'vignette') must be displayed in the prescribed manner by each vehicle (including motorcycles, trailers and caravans) using Swiss motorways and semi- motorways. The fine for non-display of the vignette is the cost of vignette(s) plus CHF100. Motorists may purchase the stickers in the UK (telephone the Swiss Centre on free-phone 0800 100 20030 for information) or in Switzerland from customs offices at the frontier or service stations and garages throughout the country.

Vehicles over 3.5 tonnes maximum total weight are taxed on all roads; i.e. caravans pay a fixed tax for periods of one day, 10 days, one month or one year.

A GPS based navigation system which has maps indicating the location of fixed speed cameras must have the 'fixed speed camera PoI (Points of Interest)' function deactivated.

Radar detectors are prohibited even if not switched on.

All vehicles with spiked tyres are prohibited on motorways

and semi-motorways except for certain parts of the A13 and A2.

Snow tyres are not compulsory, however vehicles which are not equipped to travel through snow and which impede traffic are liable to a fine.

Drivers who are involved in an accident who decide not to call the police must complete a European Accident Claim Form.

During daylight hours outside built-up areas drivers must sound their horns before sharp bends where visibility is limited, after dark this warning must be given by flashing headlights.

In Switzerland, pedestrians generally have right of way and expect vehicles to stop. Some pedestrians may just step in to the road when on crosswalks and will expect your vehicle to stop.

Blue zone parking discs are available from many petrol stations, garages, kiosks, restaurants and police stations.

Tolls Currency Swiss Franc (CHF)	Car	Car Towing Caravan/Trailer
Annual vignette (includes use of Gotthard Tunnel and San Bernardino Tunnel)	40CHF	40CHF
Bridges and Tunnels		
Munt La Schera Tunnel	15CHF	20CHF
Grand St Bernard Tunnel	30CHF	46.70CHF
Lotschberg Tunnel (Kandersteg - Goppenstern) (Fri-Sun & BH 27CHF)	22CHF	22CHF

NORTH

KÜNTEN — AARGAU

Sulz

5444

☎ 056 4964879 & 079 6607426 (mob)

056 4964847

e-mail: info@camping-sulz.ch

web: www.camping-sulz.ch

Situated by a river, with good sized pitches.

dir: *A1 exit Baden towards Bremgarten.*

Open: 15 Mar-Oct **Site:** 3HEC **For hire:** **Prices:** 20-30 **Facilities:** Wi-fi (charged) Play Area **Services:** **Leisure:** P R

MÖHLIN — AARGAU

Bachtalen

4313

☎ 061 8515095 & 079 4079971 (mob)

e-mail: info@camping-moehlin.ch

web: www.camping-moehlin.ch

A pleasant site in a wooded rural setting.

dir: *2km N towards the Rhine.*

Open: Apr-Oct **Site:** 1HEC **For hire:** **Facilities:** **Services:** **Off-site:** P R

REINACH — BASEL

Waldhort

Heideweg 16, 4153

☎ 061 7116429 061 7139835

e-mail: info@camping-waldhort.ch

web: www.camping-waldhort.ch

Pleasant wooded surroundings close to the Basle-Delémont road.

GPS: 47.5102, 7.6047

Open: Mar-Oct **Site:** 3.3HEC **Prices:** 38 **Facilities:** Wi-fi Play Area **Services:** **Leisure:** P **Off-site:**

SOLOTHURN — SOLOTHURN

Camping TCS Lido Solothurn

Glutzenhofstr, 4500

☎ 032 6218935 032 6218939

e-mail: camping.solothurn@tcs.ch

web: www.campingtcs.ch/solothurn

On the River Aare, close to the city, with a grassy beach and a paddling pool. Boating is a feature with rentals and trips available.

dir: *A5 exit Solothurn-West, then towards Weststadt.*

GPS: 47.1983, 7.5236

Open: 3 Mar-2 Dec **Site:** 2.5HEC **For hire:** **Prices:** 40.90-50.90 **Facilities:** Wi-fi (charged) Play Area **Services:** **Leisure:** R

cilities shower electric points for razors electric points for caravans motorvan service point parking by tents permitted mpulsory separate car park shop **Services** café/restaurant bar Camping Gaz International gas other than Camping Gaz first aid facilities laundry **Leisure** swimming L-Lake P-Pool R-River S-Sea **Off-site** All facilities within 5km

ZURZACH AARGAU

Oberfeld

5330

☎ 056 2492575 🖹 056 2492579

e-mail: presi@camping-zurzach.ch

web: www.camping-zurzach.ch

Close to the spa town of Zurzach, the site offers modern facilities, with cycling and hiking trails in the surrounding countryside.

Open: 24 Mar-27 Oct **Site:** 2HEC **For hire:** **Facilities:** **Services:** **Leisure:** P R

NORTH EAST

ALTNAU THURGAU

Ruderbaum

Ruderbaum 3, 8595

☎ 071 6952965 🖹 071 6900631

e-mail: camping@ruderbaum.ch

web: www.ruderbaum.ch

A small site with ample facilities.

dir: *Close to railway station by Lake Bodensee between Constance & Romanshorn.*

Open: Apr-Oct **Site:** 7.5HEC **Prices:** 24.50-29.50 **Facilities:** Play Area **Services:** **Leisure:** L **Off-site:** P

APPENZELL APPENZELL

Eischen

Kaustr 123, 9050

☎ 071 7875030 🖹 071 7875660

e-mail: info@eischen.ch

web: www.eischen.ch

A woodland site with modern installations.

dir: *S of Appenzell towards Wattwil.*

Open: All Year. **Site:** 2HEC **Facilities:** **Services:**

ESCHENZ THURGAU

Hüttenberg

Hüttenberg, 8264

☎ 052 7412337 🖹 052 7415671

e-mail: info@huettenberg.ch

web: www.huettenberg.ch

Terraced site with good facilities lying above village.

dir: *1km SW.*

GPS: 47.6447, 8.8597

Open: Apr-Oct **Site:** 6HEC **For hire:** **Prices:** 27.50-36.50 **Facilities:** Wi-fi Play Area **Services:** **Leisure:** P **Off-site:** L R

FLAACH ZÜRICH

Camping TCS Flaach am Rhein

Steubisallmend 761, 8416

☎ 052 3181413 🖹 052 3182683

e-mail: camping.flaach@tcs.ch

web: www.campingtcs.ch/flaach

Family-friendly site on the banks of the River Rhine. Leisure facilities include a swimming pool with waterslide, badminton and table tennis.

dir: *Via Winterthur then Flaach. Take turning next to Ziegelhütte restaurant and continue for 500m.*

GPS: 47.5786, 8.5825

Open: 4 Apr-7 Oct **Site:** 2HEC **Prices:** 42-50 **Facilities:** Wi-fi (charged) Play Area **Services:** **Leisure:** P R

GOLDINGEN ST-GALLEN

Atzmännig

8638

☎ 055 2846434 🖹 055 2846435

e-mail: info@atzmaennig.ch

web: www.atzmaennig.ch

Suitable for summer and winter holidays, the site is close to the main cable car and ski-lift stations and giant mountainside slide.

Open: All Year. **Site:** 1.5HEC **Facilities:** **Services:** **Off-site:**

KRUMMENAU ST-GALLEN

Adler

9643

☎ 071 9941030

The site is in an ideal location for winter sports and the hiking trails of this beautiful area.

dir: *On edge of village.*

Open: All Year. **Site:** 0.8HEC **Prices:** 22-28 **Facilities:** **Services:**

LANGWIESEN ZÜRICH

Camping TCS Rheinwiese

Hauptstr, 8246

052 6593300 052 6593355

e-mail: camping.schaffhausen@tcs.ch

web: www.campingtcs.ch/schaffhausen

On the grassy shores of the River Rhine, site activities are based around the water. There is also a snack bar for guests. 2.5km to the city of Schaffhausen.

dir: *A4 exit Schaffhausen, then towards Kreuzlingen.*

GPS: 47.6869, 8.6558

Open: 20 Apr-7 Oct **Site:** 1.25HEC **Prices:** 33.60-41.10 **Facilities:** Wi-fi (charged) Play Area **Services:** **Leisure:** R **Off-site:** P

MAMMERN THURGAU

Guldifuss

Guldifusstr 1, 8265

052 7411320 052 7411342

web: www.guldifuss.ch

A terraced site directly on the Untersee.

Open: Apr-Oct **Site:** 1.6HEC **Prices:** 30 **Facilities:** **Services:** **Leisure:** L **Off-site:**

OTTENBACH ZÜRICH

Reussbrücke

Muristr 24, 8913

044 7612022 044 7612042

e-mail: reussbruecke8913@bluewin.ch

web: www.campingzurich.ch

By river of same name.

Open: Apr-Oct **Site:** 1.8HEC **For hire:** **Facilities:** Wi-fi (charged) Play Area **Services:** **Leisure:** P R **Off-site:**

SCHÖNENGRUND APPENZELL

Camping Kronenfeld

Hauptstr 43, 9105

071 3611268 071 3611166

e-mail: camp.schoenengrund@bluewin.ch

web: www.schoenengrund.ch

A comfortable, partly residential site with well-defined touring pitches.

Open: All Year. **Site:** 1HEC **Facilities:** Play Area **Services:** **Off-site:** P

WAGENHAUSEN SCHAFFHAUSEN

Wagenhausen

Hauptstr 82, 8259

052 7414271 052 7414157

e-mail: campingwagenhausen@bluewin.ch

web: www.campingwagenhausen.ch

A delightful wooded location beside the River Rhine, close to the historic city Stein am Rhein. Between Bodensee and Rhine Falls.

Open: Apr-Oct **Site:** 4.5HEC **For hire:** **Prices:** 30-36 **Facilities:** Wi-fi Play Area **Services:** **Leisure:** P R

WALENSTADT ST-GALLEN

See-Camping

8880

081 7351896 081 7351841

e-mail: kontakt@see-camping.ch

web: www.see-camping.ch

A well-equipped family site with direct access to the Walensee.

dir: *Motorway Zürich-Chur exit.*

Open: May-Sep **Site:** 1.2HEC **Facilities:** Play Area **Services:** **Leisure:** L **Off-site:** P

WILDBERG ZÜRICH

Weid

8489

052 3853388 052 3853477

e-mail: campingweid@bluewin.ch

web: www.campingwildberg.ch

On a terraced meadow in a very peaceful location surrounded by woods.

dir: *From Winterthur signs for Tösstal, right after spinning-mill in Turbenthal.*

Open: All Year. **Site:** 6.1HEC **For hire:** **Prices:** 24 Mobile home hire 490 **Facilities:** Play Area **Services:** **Off-site:** P R

SWITZERLAND

WINTERTHUR — ZÜRICH

Schützenweiher

Eichliwaldstr 4, 8400
☎ 052 2125260 🖷 052 2125260
e-mail: campingplatz@win.ch
web: www.campingwinterthur.ch

Site set amongst trees and shrubs and located on a lake.

dir: *To the left of the Schaffhausen road, near Schützenhaus restaurant.*

GPS: 47.5194, 8.7163

Open: All Year. **Site:** 0.8HEC **Prices:** 28-38 **Facilities:** Wi-fi Play Area **Services:** **Off-site:** P

NORTH WEST/CENTRAL

AESCHI — BERN

Panorama

3703
☎ 033 2233656
e-mail: postmaster@camping-aeschi.ch
web: www.camping-aeschi.ch

A well kept campsite surrounded by trees and mountains, close to Lake Thun.

dir: *400m SE of Camping Club Bern.*

Open: 15 May-15 Oct **Site:** 1HEC **For hire:** **Facilities:** **Services:** **Off-site:** P

BÖNIGEN — BERN

Camping TCS Seeblick

Campingstr 14, 3806
☎ 033 8221143 🖷 033 8221162
e-mail: camping.boenigen@tcs.ch
web: www.campingtcs.ch/boenigen

On Lake Brienz in a holiday resort area with paddling pools and playground suitable for families with children, plus a snack bar.

dir: *From Lucenne A8 exit 27 Bönigen. From Berne A8 exit 26 Interlaken-Ost, then towards Bönigen.*

GPS: 46.6911, 7.8936

Open: 4 Apr-7 Oct **Site:** 1.5HEC **Prices:** 39.60-49.90 **Facilities:** Wi-fi (charged) Play Area **Services:** **Leisure:** L P

BRENZIKOFEN — BERN

Wydeli

Wydeli 60, 3671
☎ 031 7711141
e-mail: info@camping-brenzikofen.ch
web: www.camping-brenzikofen.ch

Small site in pleasant countryside.

dir: *8km N of Thun.*

Open: May-Sep **Site:** 1.3HEC **For hire:** **Facilities:** Play Area **Services:** **Leisure:** P **Off-site:**

BRUNNEN — SCHWYZ

Hopfreben

6440
☎ 041 8201873 🖷 041 8201873
web: www.camping-brunnen.ch

On the right bank of the Muotta stream, 100 metres before it flows into the lake.

dir: *1km W.*

GPS: 46.9968, 8.5934

Open: 6 Apr-22 Sep **Site:** 1.5HEC **Prices:** 37-45 **Facilities:** Wi-fi Play Area **Services:** **Leisure:** L P R

BUOCHS — NIDWALDEN

Camping TCS Sportzentrum

6374
☎ 041 6203474 🖷 041 6206484
e-mail: camping.buochs@tcs.ch
web: www.campingtcs.ch/buochs

On Lake Vierwaldstätten between a sports ground and a beach. Ideal for touring the surrounding mountains and lakes. On-site facilities include a games room and cycle rental.

dir: *A2 exit 34.*

GPS: 46.9794, 8.4181

Open: 4 Apr-7 Oct **Site:** 2.2HEC **Prices:** 42.80-53.20 **Facilities:** Wi-fi (charged) Play Area **Services:** **Leisure:** L

COLOMBIER — NEUCHÂTEL

Paradis-Plage

allée du Port 8, 2013
032 8412446 032 8414305
e-mail: info@paradisplage.ch
web: www.paradisplage.ch
A delightful setting beside Lake Neuchâtel with modern facilities.
dir: *Leave A5 exit 9*
GPS: 46.9672, 6.8702
Open: Mar-Oct **Site:** 4HEC **For hire:** **Prices:** 35-43 Mobile home hire 630-840 **Facilities:** Wi-fi Play Area **Services:** **Leisure:** L

ERLACH — BERN

Mon Plaisir

3235
032 3381358 032 3381305
e-mail: info@camping24.ch
web: www.camping24.ch
Well-equipped site beside the lake.
Open: All Year. **Site:** 0.6HEC **For hire:** **Facilities:** **Services:** **Leisure:** L **Off-site:** P R

EUTHAL — SCHWYZ

Hotel Post Garni and Camping

Euthalerstr 10, 8844
079 5017673 055 4127673
e-mail: info@hotelposteuthal.ch
web: www.hotelposteuthal.ch
On the shore of the Sihlsee in a beautiful mountain setting.
GPS: 47.0997, 8.8072
Open: May-Oct **Site:** 1HEC **Prices:** 30-38 **Facilities:** Wi-fi Play Area **Services:** **Leisure:** L **Off-site:** P R

FLÜELEN — URI

Urnersee

6454
041 8709222 041 8709216
e-mail: info@windsurfing-urnersee.ch
web: www.windsurfing-urnersee.ch
On level ground on the shore of the Vierwaldstättersee with plenty of sports facilities.
Open: 15 Apr-Oct **Site:** 4.5HEC **Facilities:** **Services:** **Leisure:** L R **Off-site:** P

FRUTIGEN — BERN

Grassi

3714
033 6711149 033 6711380
e-mail: campinggrassi@bluewin.ch
web: www.camping-grassi.ch
Site scattered with fruit trees beside a farm on the River Engstilgern. Shop open July and August.
dir: *From the Haupstr, turn right at Simplon Hotel.*
Open: All Year. **Site:** 1.5HEC **For hire:** **Prices:** 27.40-33.40 **Facilities:** Wi-fi Play Area **Services:** **Off-site:** P

GAMPELEN — BERN

Fanel

Seestr 50, 3236
032 3132333 032 3131407
e-mail: camping.gampelen@tcs.ch
web: www.campingtcs.ch/gampelen
A level site on the shore of Lake Neuchâtel protected by trees and bushes. 2 dogs per pitch.
dir: *On A5 towards Gampelen.*
Open: 4 Apr-7 Oct **Site:** 11.3HEC **For hire:** **Prices:** 38.60-47.70 Mobile home hire 490-840 **Facilities:** Wi-fi (charged) Play Area **Services:** **Leisure:** L **Off-site:** R

GISWIL — OBWALDEN

Giswil

Campingstr 11, 6074
041 6752355 041 6752351
e-mail: giswil@camping-international.ch
web: www.camping-international.ch
On the shores of Lake Sarnen, pitches are separated by trees and hedges. Lake swimming is possible with a grass/sand beach area.
GPS: 46.8530, 8.1874
Open: Apr-14 Oct **Site:** 1.9HEC **Prices:** 37.50-42.40 **Facilities:** Wi-fi Play Area **Services:** **Leisure:** L

SWITZERLAND

GOLDAU SCHWYZ

Bernerhöhe-Ranch

Gotthardstr 107, 6410
☎ 041 8554161 041 8555970
e-mail: camping.bernerhoehe@gmail.com
On the edge of a forest with a beautiful view of Lake Lauerz. Separate field for tents. Bar, café and restaurant open during summer.
dir: *1.5km SE & turn left.*
Open: All Year. **Site:** 2.5HEC **Facilities:** Play Area **Services:**

GRINDELWALD BERN

Aspen

3818
☎ 033 8544000 033 8544004
e-mail: aspen@grindelwald.ch
web: www.hotel-aspen.ch
Sunny hill terraces.
Open: Jun-15 Oct **Site:** 2.5HEC **Facilities:** **Services:** **Off-site:** P R

GSTAAD BERN

Bellerive

3780
☎ 033 7446330 033 7446345
e-mail: bellerive.camping@bluewin.ch
web: www.bellerivecamping.ch
Surrounded by mountains, ideal for outdoor pursuits holidays.
Open: All Year. **Site:** 0.8HEC **For hire:** **Facilities:** **Services:** **Leisure:** R **Off-site:** P

GWATT BERN

Camping TCS Thunersee

Gwattstr 103, 3645
☎ 033 3364067 033 3364017
e-mail: camping.gwatt@tcs.ch
web: www.campingtcs.ch/gwatt
With direct access to a beach on Lake Thun, the site provides a large lawned area for recreation or relaxing. Fishing is available on the lake.
dir: *A6 (Bern-Thun-Interlaken) exit 17 Thun-Sud, then towards Gwatt.*
GPS: 46.7278, 7.6275
Open: 4 Apr-7 Oct **Site:** 1.5HEC **Prices:** 42.10-53.50 **Facilities:** Wi-fi (charged) **Services:** **Leisure:** L

HINTERKAPPELEN BERN

Camping TCS Bern-Eymatt

Wohlenstr 62c, 3032
☎ 031 9011007 031 9012591
e-mail: camping.bern@tcs.ch
web: www.campingtcs.ch/bern
In a meadow setting on a bow of the River Aare, with good public transport links to Bern. Leisure facilities include table tennis and badminton.
dir: *From Bern A1/A12 (direction Morat-Neuchâtel) exit Bern-Bethlehem, then towards Wohlen/Aarbers.*
GPS: 46.9639, 7.3839
Open: All Year. **Site:** 3.5HEC **For hire:** **Prices:** 38.50-46.10 **Facilities:** Wi-fi (charged) Play Area **Services:** **Leisure:** P **Off-site:** R

INNERTKIRCHEN BERN

Aareschlucht

Hauptstr 34, 3862
☎ 033 9715532 033 9715344
e-mail: campaareschlucht@bluewin.ch
web: www.camping-aareschlucht.ch
A beautiful Alpine location with superb mountain views.
Open: May-Oct **Site:** 0.5HEC **For hire:** **Facilities:** **Services:** **Off-site:** R

Grund

3862
☎ 033 9714409 033 9714767
e-mail: info@camping-grund.ch
web: www.camping-grund.ch
Next to farm on southern outskirts of village.
dir: *Turn S off main road in village centre at Hotel Urweider, 0.3km turn right.*
Open: All Year. **Site:** 120HEC **For hire:** **Facilities:** **Services:** **Off-site:** R

INTERLAKEN BERN

Camping TCS Interlaken

Brienzstr 24, 3800
☎ 033 8224434 🖷 033 8224456
e-mail: camping.interlaken@tcs.ch
web: www.campingtcs.ch/interlaken

In a picturesque setting on the banks of the Aare river and 300 metres from Lake Brienz. Cycle and kayak rental available on site.

dir: *A8 (Interlaken-Ost) exit 26 Ringenberg.*

GPS: 46.6925, 7.8686

Open: 4 Apr-7 Oct **Site:** 1.2HEC **Prices:** 38.40-46.60
Facilities: Wi-fi (charged) Play Area
Services: **Off-site:** L

Hobby 3

Lehnweg 16, 3800
☎ 033 8229652 🖷 033 8229657
e-mail: info@campinghobby.ch
web: www.campinghobby.ch

Family site in a quiet location with fine views of the surrounding mountains and within easy walking distance of Interlaken. Free travel on the local public transport system.

dir: *N8 exit 24 for Unterseen, follow camping sign No 3. Or N8 exit 24 (right lane in tunnel), turn right & follow camping sign No 3.*

GPS: 46.6855, 7.8311

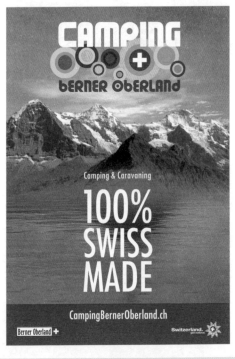

Open: Apr-Sep **Site:** 1.5HEC **Prices:** 34-50.60
Facilities: Wi-fi Play Area **Services:**
Off-site: L P R

Jungfraublick

Gsteigstr 80, 3800
☎ 033 8224414 🖷 033 8221619
e-mail: info@jungfraublick.ch
web: www.jungfraublick.ch

A family site with clean, modern facilities in a fine central location.

dir: *A8 exit 25, site 300m on left towards Matteu-Interlaken.*

GPS: 46.673, 7.866

Open: May-20 Sep **Site:** 1.3HEC **Prices:** 32-42
Facilities: Wi-fi **Services:**
Leisure: P **Off-site:** L R

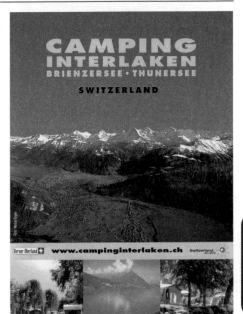

SWITZERLAND

Jungfraucamp

Steindlerstr 60, 3800
☎ 033 8227107 🖷 033 8225730
e-mail: info@jungfraucamp.ch
web: www.jungfraucamp.ch

Beautiful views of the Eiger, the Mönch and the Jungfrau.

dir: *Turn right at Unterseen, through Schulhaus & Steindlerstr to site.*

Open: 15 May-20 Sep **Site:** 2.5HEC **Facilities:** **Services:** **Leisure:** P **Off-site:** L R

Lazy Rancho 4

Lehnweg 6, 3800
☎ 033 8228716 🖷 033 8231920
e-mail: info@lazyrancho.ch
web: www.lazyrancho.ch

The Camping and Caravanning Club The Friendly Club

A family site in a magnificent position with views of the Eiger, Mönch and Jungfrau with good facilities.

C&CC Report *Dump the car! The great Swiss integrated boat, rail and bus transport system starts five minutes' walk from this quiet family site, with free bus and train transport throughout the Interlaken area. Cycling on Interlaken's speed-restricted roads is a dream. To many of us this region is classic Switzerland, and the camp site owners are a mine of local information, so take your pick of Alpine activities on land or water or in the air – or just look at it all.*

dir: *A8 exit Unterseen for Gunten, 2km turn right, left at Landhotel Golf.*

GPS: 46.6855, 7.8308

Open: 6 Apr-20 Oct **Site:** 16HEC **For hire:** **Facilities:** Wi-fi Play Area **Services:** **Leisure:** P **Off-site:** L R

Manor Farm 1

3800
☎ 033 8222264 🖷 033 8222279
e-mail: manorfarm@swisscamps.ch
web: www.manorfarm.ch

A well-equipped site in a beautiful mountain setting.

dir: *A8 exit Gunten/Beatenberg, signed.*

Open: All Year. **Site:** 7.5HEC **For hire:** **Facilities:** **Services:** **Leisure:** L R **Off-site:** P

KANDERSTEG — BERN

Rendez-Vous

Hubleweg, 3718
☎ 033 6751534 🖷 033 6751737
e-mail: rendez-vous.camping@bluewin.ch
web: www.camping-kandersteg.ch

A delightful mountain setting with modern facilities.

dir: *0.75km E of town.*

GPS: 46.4967, 7.6836

Open: All Year. **Site:** 1HEC **Prices:** 27.80-39.30 **Facilities:** Wi-fi (charged) **Services:** **Off-site:** L P

KRATTIGEN — BERN

Stuhlegg

3704
☎ 033 6542723 🖷 033 6546703
e-mail: campstuhlegg@bluewin.ch
web: www.camping-stuhlegg.ch

On a quiet and sunny terrace in Krattigen, above Lake Thun, 5km from the motorway at Spiez. Its central position allows day excursions over the Bernese Oberland.

Open: Jan-Oct & Dec **Site:** 2.4HEC **Prices:** 30-38 **Facilities:** Wi-fi Play Area **Services:** **Leisure:** P **Off-site:** L

LANDERON, LE — NEUCHÂTEL

Peches

2525
☎ 032 7512900 🖷 032 7516354
e-mail: info@camping-lelanderon.ch
web: www.camping-lelanderon.ch

A small site at the meeting point of the River Thielle and the Lac de Bienne.

Open: 15 Apr-15 Oct **Site:** 2.1HEC **For hire:** **Prices:** 41 Mobile home hire 765-905 **Facilities:** Wi-fi Play Area **Services:** **Off-site:** L P R

LAUTERBRUNNEN — BERN

Jungfrau

3822
☎ 033 8562010 🖷 033 8562020
e-mail: info@camping-jungfrau.ch
web: www.camping-jungfrau.ch

Widespread site in meadowland crossed by a stream. Partly divided into pitches.

dir: *Turn right 100m before church, campsite in 400m.*

Open: All Year. **Site:** 5HEC **For hire:** **Facilities:** **Off-site:** P

Schützenbach

3822

033 8551268 033 8551275

e-mail: info@schuetzenbach.ch

web: www.schuetzenbach.ch

A fine Alpine location close to the main skiing areas, with a free ski bus in the winter, and 300 metres from the lake.

dir: *0.8km S of village on left of road to Stechelberg opp B50.*

Open: All Year. **Site:** 3HEC **For hire:** **Facilities:** Wi-fi (charged) Play Area **Services:** **Off-site:** P R

LIGNIÈRES NEUCHÂTEL

Fraso-Ranch

2523

032 7514616 032 7514614

e-mail: camping.fraso-ranch@bluewin.ch

A modern family site with good recreational facilities and a separate section for tourers.

dir: *NE of Lignières on Nods road, signed.*

Open: 24 Dec-Oct **Site:** 8.7HEC **Facilities:** **Services:** **Leisure:** P

LUNGERN OBWALDEN

Obsee

6078

041 6781463 041 6782163

e-mail: camping@obsee.ch

web: www.obsee.ch

A beautiful setting between the lake and the mountains with facilities for water sports.

dir: *A2/A8 - 1km W of Lungern.*

Open: All Year. **Site:** 1.5HEC **For hire:** **Prices:** 38.40 **Facilities:** Play Area **Services:** **Leisure:** L R **Off-site:** P

LUZERN (LUCERNE) LUZERN

Steinibachried (TCS)

Horw, 6048

041 3403558 041 3403556

e-mail: camping.horw@tcs.ch

web: www.campingtcs.ch/horw

A gently sloping meadow next to the football ground and the beach, separated from the lake by a wide belt of reeds.

dir: *3.2km S of Luzern.*

Open: 4 Apr-7 Oct **Site:** 2HEC **For hire:** **Prices:** 21.40 **Facilities:** Wi-fi (charged) Play Area **Services:** **Off-site:** L P

MOSEN LUZERN

Camping-Seeblick

6295

041 9171666 041 9171666

e-mail: infos@camping-seeblick.ch

web: www.camping-seeblick.ch

Set on two strips of land on edge of lake, divided by paths into several squares.

dir: *N on A26.*

GPS: 47.2447, 8.2244

Open: Mar-Oct **Site:** 2.5HEC **Prices:** 26-35 **Facilities:** Wi-fi (charged) Play Area **Services:** **Leisure:** L **Off-site:**

NOTTWIL LUZERN

St Margrethen

6207

041 9371404

e-mail: st-margrethen@swisscamps.ch

web: www.camping-nottwil.ch

Natural meadowland with fruit trees, with own access to lake.

dir: *Off road to Sursee 400m NW of Nottwil, towards lake for 100m.*

GPS: 47.1429, 8.1239

Open: Apr-Oct **Site:** 1.4HEC **Prices:** 29.80-31.80 **Facilities:** Wi-fi (charged) Play Area **Services:** **Leisure:** L **Off-site:** P

PRÊLES BERN

Prêles

2515

032 3151716 032 3155160

e-mail: info@camping-jura.ch

web: www.camping-jura.ch

On a wooded plateau overlooking Lake Biel.

dir: *Off Biel-Neuchâtel road at Twann & signs for Prêles, through village, site on left.*

Open: Apr-Oct **Site:** 6HEC **For hire:** **Facilities:** **Services:** **Leisure:** P

SWITZERLAND

SAANEN — BERN

Saanen beim Kappeli

Campingstr 15, 3792

☎ 033 7446191 📠 033 7446184

e-mail: info@camping-saanen.ch

web: www.camping-saanen.ch

Set in a long meadow between the railway and the River Saane.

dir: *1km SE of town.*

Open: Jan-Oct & Dec **Site:** 0.8HEC **For hire:** **Facilities:** Wi-fi Play Area **Services:** **Leisure:** R **Off-site:** P

SACHSELN — OBWALDEN

Ewil

Brünigstr 258, 6072

☎ 041 6663270

e-mail: info@camping-ewil.ch

web: www.camping-ewil.ch

On a level meadow on the south-western shore of the Sarnensee.

dir: *W of Sachseln-Ewil road towards lake.*

Open: Apr-Sep **Site:** 1.5HEC **For hire:** **Prices:** 25.40-32.90 **Facilities:** Wi-fi **Services:** **Leisure:** L **Off-site:** P R

SEMPACH — LUZERN

Seeland

6204

☎ 041 4601466 📠 041 4604766

e-mail: camping.sempach@tcs.ch

web: www.campingtcs.ch/sempach

Rectangular, level site on south-western shore of lake. Kids' club available during high season only.

dir: *0.7km S on Luzern road by lake.*

Open: 4 Apr-7 Oct **Site:** 5.2HEC **For hire:** **Prices:** 34.60-58.20 **Facilities:** Wi-fi (charged) Kids' Club Play Area **Services:** **Leisure:** L

STECHELBERG — BERN

Breithorn

3824

☎ 033 8551225 📠 033 8553561

e-mail: breithorn@stechelberg.ch

A beautiful location in the Lauterbrunnen Valley.

dir: *3km S of Lauterbrunnen.*

Open: All Year. **Site:** 1HEC **Prices:** 27.40-31.40 **Facilities:** **Services:**

SURSEE — LUZERN

Camping Sursee

Baselstr, Waldheim, 6210

☎ 041 9211161

e-mail: info@camping-sursee.ch

web: www.camping-sursee.ch

Natural and quiet site, 1.2km from shopping centre and railway station.

dir: *A2 Basel-Gotthard exit 20 Sursee, direction Sursee, Basel 2 (blue signs at 4 rdbts).*

GPS: 47.175, 8.0869

Open: Apr-Sep **Site:** 1.7HEC **For hire:** **Prices:** 22.60-28.60 Mobile home hire 300-500 **Facilities:** Wi-fi (charged) Play Area **Services:** **Off-site:** L P

VITZNAU — LUZERN

Vitznau

The Camping and Caravanning Club — The Friendly Club

6354

☎ 041 3971280 📠 041 3972457

e-mail: info@camping.vitznau.ch

web: www.camping-vitznau.ch

Well-tended terraced site, on edge of village with fine views of lake.

C&CC Report *The wonderful combination of a spectacular setting, a very friendly welcome, superb travel deals and a short hop to Lucerne, constitutes the recipe for a relaxing and invigorating holiday. Miles of walking are possible on Mount Rigi, after the ride up Europe's first rack railway, while the world's steepest cog railway runs up Mount Pilatus.*

dir: *From N turn towards mountain at church & signed.*

Open: Apr-Oct **Site:** 1.8HEC **For hire:** **Prices:** 40.70-53.70 **Facilities:** **Services:** **Leisure:** P **Off-site:** L

WABERN — BERN

SC Eichholz

Strandweg 49, 3084

☎ 031 9612602 📠 031 9613526

e-mail: info@campingeichholz.ch

web: www.campingeichholz.ch

Set in municipal parkland with a separate section for caravans.

dir: *Approach via Gossetstr & track beside river.*

GPS: 46.9330, 7.4558

Open: 20 Apr-Sep **Site:** 2HEC **For hire:** **Prices:** 36-39 **Facilities:** Wi-fi (charged) Play Area **Services:** **Leisure:** R **Off-site:** P

SWITZERLAND

WILDERSWIL — BERN

Oberei

Obereigasse 9, 3812
033 8221335 033 8221335
e-mail: oberei8@swisscamps.ch
web: www.campingwilderswil.ch

A peaceful site in a picturesque village with fine views of the Jungfrau and surrounding mountains. There are good facilities. Well situated for walks and excursions to the mountains by train, 6 minutes away.

GPS: 46.6686, 7.8744

Open: May-15 Oct **Site:** 0.55HEC **For hire:** **Prices:** 32.60-36.60 **Facilities:** Play Area **Services:** **Off-site:** L P R

ZUG — ZUG

Zugersee

Chamer Fussweg 36, 6300
041 7418422 041 7418430
e-mail: camping.zug@tcs.ch
web: www.campingtcs.ch

Pleasant location with beautiful view of Lake Zug and the surrounding mountains. The nearby railway can get very busy.

dir: *A4 exit Zug-Ouest in direction of Zug, 1km NW by lake.*

GPS: 47.1774, 8.4936

Open: 4 Apr-7 Oct **Site:** 1.1HEC **Prices:** 37.90-46 **Facilities:** Wi-fi (charged) Play Area **Services:** **Leisure:** L

EAST

ANDEER — GRAUBÜNDEN

Sut Baselgia

7440
081 6611453 081 6307077
e-mail: camping.andeer@bluewin.ch
web: www.campingandeer.ch

A pleasant, peaceful setting north towards Chur.

GPS: 46.6065, 9.4263

Open: All Year. **Site:** 1.2HEC **Prices:** 28.70-40.70 **Facilities:** Wi-fi **Services:** **Off-site:** P

AROSA — GRAUBÜNDEN

Arosa Tourismus

7050
081 3787034 081 3773005
e-mail: sportanlagen@arosa.ch
web: www.arosa.ch

Gently sloping site in a park-like setting, at an altitude of 1800 metres. Dogs must be on a lead.

Open: All Year. **Site:** 0.6HEC **Facilities:** **Services:** **Off-site:** L P

DISENTIS — GRAUBÜNDEN

Camping TCS Fontanivas

via Fontanivas 9, 7180
081 9474422 081 9474431
e-mail: camping.disentis@tcs.ch
web: www.campingtcs.ch/disentis

In a meadow setting, surrounded by mountains. The on-site lake provides opportunities for swimming, boating and other activities.

dir: *A2 exit Göschenen, then rte Cantonale Andermatt-Oberalp.*

GPS: 46.6967, 8.8531

Open: 20 Apr-23 Sep **Site:** 2.5HEC **For hire:** **Prices:** 41.70-49.70 **Facilities:** Wi-fi (charged) Play Area **Services:** **Leisure:** L **Off-site:** R

LANDQUART — GRAUBÜNDEN

Camping TCS Neue Ganda

Ganda 21, 7302
081 3223955 081 3226864
e-mail: camping.landquart@tcs.ch
web: www.campingtcs.ch/landquart

Surrounded by mountains, site has facilities both in summer and winter. A bus service runs to the nearby ski areas in season.

dir: *A13 exit Landquart, then towards Davos.*

GPS: 46.9706, 9.5936

Open: 16 Mar-14 Oct & 7 Dec-26 Feb **Site:** 4.5HEC **Prices:** 36.80-42.90 **Facilities:** Wi-fi (charged) Play Area **Services:** **Off-site:** P

SWITZERLAND

LENZ — GRAUBÜNDEN

St Cassian

7083

☎ 081 3842472 📠 081 3842489

e-mail: info@st-cassian.ch

web: www.st-cassian.ch

A level, shady site in a beautiful location at an altitude of 1415 metres above sea level. There are good facilities and the site is 1km from the town.

dir: *Motorway exit Chur-Süd, signs for Lenzerheide/St Moritz, up good mountain road.*

Open: All Year. **Site:** 25HEC **Prices:** 31-36.60 **Facilities:** ® **Services:** **Off-site:**

LENZERHEIDE — GRAUBÜNDEN

Camping TCS Gravas

7078

☎ 081 3842335 📠 081 3563206

e-mail: camping.lenzerheide@tcs.ch

web: www.campingtcs.ch/lenzerheide

Direct access to ski lifts and cross-country trails from the site. Ideal for cycling and walking.

dir: *A13 exit Coire-Sud, then towards Lenzerheide.*

GPS: 46.7225, 9.5550

Open: 25 May-30 Mar **Site:** 1HEC **Prices:** 38.90-45.80 **Facilities:** Wi-fi (charged) Play Area **Services:** **Off-site:** L P

POSCHIAVO — GRAUBÜNDEN

Boomerang

7745

☎ 081 8440713 📠 081 8441575

e-mail: info@camping-boomerang.ch

web: www.camping-boomerang.ch

A quiet setting in the heart of green countryside of the Rhaetian Alps. The site is equipped with all modern comforts.

dir: *2km SE.*

GPS: 46.3099, 10.0747

Open: All Year. **Site:** 1.5HEC **For hire:** **Facilities:** Wi-fi Play Area ® **Services:** **Off-site:** L P R

ST MORITZ — GRAUBÜNDEN

Camping TCS Olympiaschanze

7500

☎ 081 8334090 📠 081 8344096

e-mail: camping.stmoritz@tcs.ch

web: www.campingtcs.ch/stmoritz

Set on two meadows and a small forest, the site has a snack bar and is an ideal base for walking or mountain biking.

dir: *1km from St Moritz towards Maloja and Julierpass.*

GPS: 46.4783, 9.8250

Open: 25 May-Sep **Site:** 1.5HEC **Prices:** 38.80-47.20 **Facilities:** Wi-fi (charged) ® **Services:**

SAMEDAN — GRAUBÜNDEN

Punt Muragl

via da Puntraschigna 56, 7503

☎ 081 8428197 📠 081 8428197

e-mail: camping.samedan@tcs.ch

web: www.campingtcs.ch/samedan

A summer and winter site in a pleasant alpine setting.

dir: *Near Bernina railway halt, to right of fork of roads Samedan & Celerina/Schlarigna to Pontresina.*

GPS: 46.51, 9.8794

Open: 25 May-7 Oct, 25 Nov-15 Apr **Site:** 2HEC **For hire:** **Prices:** 43.30-48.80 **Facilities:** Wi-fi (charged) Play Area ® **Services:** **Off-site:** L P

SCUOL — GRAUBÜNDEN

Camping TCS Gurlaina

7550

☎ 081 8641501 📠 081 8640760

e-mail: camping.scuol@tcs.ch

web: www.campingtcs.ch/scuol

Surrounded by forest, pitches are on meadowland and there is a snack bar. Nearby are health resorts and ski runs.

GPS: 46.7912, 10.2982

Open: 7 Dec-15 Apr & 17 May-21 Oct **Site:** 3HEC **Prices:** 42-50.40 **Facilities:** Wi-fi (charged) Play Area **Services:** **Off-site:** P

SWITZERLAND

SPLÜGEN GRAUBÜNDEN

Camping Auf dem Sand

7435
081 6641476 081 6641460
e-mail: camping@splugen.ch
web: www.campingsplugen.ch

On the River Hinterrhein. Ideal starting point for skiing, cross country skiing or, throughout the year, hiking. Parking restrictions apply at certain times of the year.

dir: *Off main road in village & signed.*

GPS: 46.5491, 9.3141

Open: All Year. **Site:** 0.8HEC **Prices:** 43-48 **Facilities:** Wi-fi Play Area **Services:** **Leisure:** R

THUSIS GRAUBÜNDEN

Viamala

7430
081 6512472 081 6512472
e-mail: info@camping-thusis.ch
web: www.camping-thusis.ch

Pleasant wooded surroundings near the River Hinterrhein and close to the beautiful Viamala gorge.

dir: *NE towards Chur.*

Open: May-Sep **Site:** 4.5HEC **For hire:** **Facilities:** **Services:** **Off-site:** P R

TSCHIERV GRAUBÜNDEN

Staila

Chasa Maruya, 7532
081 8585628
e-mail: maruya@gmx.net
web: www.muenstertal.ch

Site in the village behind the Sternen Hotel.

dir: *Between Ofen Pass & Santa Maria.*

Open: Jul-Aug **Site:** 1HEC **Prices:** 30 **Facilities:** Play Area **Services:** **Leisure:** P R

SOUTH

AGNO TICINO

Eurocampo

via Molinazzo 9, 6982
091 6052114 091 6053187
e-mail: eurocampo@ticino.com
web: www.eurocampo.ch

Part of site is near its own sandy beach and is divided by groups of trees.

dir: *0.6km E on Lugano-Ponte Tresa road, opp Aeroport sign & MIGROS building.*

Open: Apr-Oct **Site:** 6.5HEC **Prices:** 38-45 **Facilities:** **Services:** **Leisure:** L R

BELLINZONA TICINO

Camping TCS Bosco di Molinazzo

6500
091 8291118 091 8292355
e-mail: camping.bellinzona@tcs.ch
web: www.campingtcs.ch/bellinzona

Close to the A2 highway, shaded site on a river bank with a snack bar. Ideal for a stop-over or longer stay.

dir: *A2 exit Bellinzona-Nord, towards Bellinzona, site signed.*

GPS: 46.2122, 9.0386

Open: 4 Apr-14 Oct **Site:** 1HEC **Prices:** 40.90-49.90 **Facilities:** Wi-fi (charged) Play Area **Services:** **Leisure:** P **Off-site:** R

CUGNASCO TICINO

Park-Camping Riarena

6516
091 8591688 091 8592885
e-mail: camping.riarena@bluewin.ch
web: www.camping-riarena.ch

Beautiful park-like family site in level, natural woodland. All facilities are well-maintained and Lake Maggiore is within easy reach.

dir: *1.5km NW. Off road 13 at fuel station 9km NE of Locarno & continue 0.5km.*

Open: Mar-20 Oct **Site:** 3.2HEC **For hire:** **Facilities:** **Services:** **Leisure:** P **Off-site:** R

GORDEVIO TICINO

Bellariva

6672

☎ 091 7531444 🖷 091 7531764
e-mail: camping.gordevio@tcs.ch
web: www.campingtcs.ch/gordevio

A quiet location between the road and the River Maggia.

Open: 4 Apr-14 Oct **Site:** 2.5HEC **For hire:** **Prices:** 44.20-57.40 Mobile home hire 595-980 **Facilities:** Wi-fi (charged) Play Area **Services:** **Leisure:** P R

LOCARNO TICINO

Delta

via Respini 7, 6600

☎ 091 7516081 🖷 091 7512243
e-mail: info@campingdelta.com
web: www.campingdelta.com

A beautiful, well-equipped and well-organised site at Lake Maggiore.

dir: *2km from city.*

Open: Mar-Oct **Site:** 5.4HEC **For hire:** **Prices:** 21-106 **Facilities:** Wi-fi (charged) Kids' Club Play Area **Services:** **Leisure:** L R **Off-site:** P

MERIDE TICINO

Camping TCS Parco al Sole

6866

☎ 091 6464330 🖷 091 6460992
e-mail: camping.meride@tcs.ch
web: www.campingtcs.ch/meride

Shady, relaxing site in a countryside setting. In high season, entertainment and activities take place.

dir: *A2 to Lugano Mendrisio exit Stabio-Varese onto motorway, then exit Rancate and follow signs to Arzo then Serpiano.*

GPS: 45.8892, 8.9483

Open: 20 Apr-23 Sep **Site:** 1.2HEC **Prices:** 42-51.40 **Facilities:** Wi-fi (charged) Play Area **Services:** **Leisure:** P

MOLINAZZO DI MONTEGGIO TICINO

Tresiana

6995

☎ 091 6083342 🖷 091 6083142
e-mail: info@camping-tresiana
web: www.camping-tresiana.ch

A family site on meadowland with trees on riverbank.

dir: *Right after bridge in Ponte Tresa, site 5km.*

Open: 31 Mar-21 Oct **Site:** 1.5HEC **For hire:** **Facilities:** Wi-fi (charged) **Services:** **Leisure:** P R **Off-site:** L

MUZZANO TICINO

Camping TCS La Piodella

via alla Foce 14, 6933

☎ 091 9947788 🖷 091 9946708
e-mail: camping.muzzano@tcs.ch
web: www.campingtcs.ch/muzzano

Directly on Lake Lugano and with a grassy beach. Wide range of leisure activities, for children train rides are available and there is a kids' club in high season.

dir: *A2 exit Lugano-Nord, then towards Aérodrome.*

GPS: 45.9953, 8.9086

Open: All Year. **Site:** 4.7HEC **Prices:** 54.60-67.20 **Facilities:** Wi-fi (charged) Kids' Club Play Area **Services:** **Leisure:** L P

TENERO TICINO

Campofelice

via alle Brere 7, 6598

☎ 091 7451417 🖷 091 7451888
e-mail: camping@campofelice.ch
web: www.campofelice.ch

A beautifully situated and extensive site on the shores of Lake Maggiore, divided into pitches and crossed by asphalt drives.

dir: *1.9km S, signed.*

GPS: 46.1688, 8.8558

Open: 22 Mar-Oct **Site:** 15HEC **For hire:** **Prices:** 39-90 **Facilities:** Wi-fi (charged) Play Area **Services:** **Leisure:** L R **Off-site:** P

Lido Mappo

via Mappo, 6598
☎ 091 7451437 🖷 091 7454808
e-mail: camping@lidomappo.ch
web: www.lidomappo.ch

A well-appointed site, beautifully situated by a lake. Teenagers not accepted unaccompanied. Minimum stay, one week in July and August.

dir: *A2 exit for Bellinzona Sud, towards Locarno & exit for Tenero, site signed.*

GPS: 46.1769, 8.8419

Open: 23 Mar-28 Oct **Site:** 6.5HEC **Prices:** 36-93 **Facilities:** Wi-fi Play Area **Services:** **Leisure:** L **Off-site:** P R

Tamaro

via Mappo 32, 6598
☎ 091 7452161 🖷 091 7456636
e-mail: info@campingtamaro.ch
web: www.campingtamaro.ch

Well-equipped site with direct access to the lake. Groups of young persons must be accompanied by adults.

dir: *4km from Locarno, signed from motorway.*

GPS: 46.1755, 8.8444

Open: 10 Mar-28 Oct **Site:** 5HEC **For hire:** **Prices:** 37-66 Mobile home hire 540-1470 **Facilities:** Wi-fi (charged) Play Area **Services:** **Leisure:** L P **Off-site:** R

SOUTH WEST

AGARN — VALAIS

Gemmi

Briannenstr 4, 3952
☎ 027 4731154 🖷 027 4734295
e-mail: info@campinggemmi.ch
web: www.campinggemmi.ch

A very pleasant location on the outskirts of the town, with outstanding views of the surrounding mountains. There are clean, modern facilities and individual bathrooms are available for weekly hire.

dir: *A9 exit Agarn, signed.*

Open: 17 Apr-16 Oct **Site:** 0.9HEC **Facilities:** **Services:** **Off-site:** P R

AROLLA — VALAIS

Petit Praz

1986
☎ 027 2832295
e-mail: camping@arolla.com
web: www.camping-arolla.com

An imposing mountain setting.

GPS: 46.0266, 7.4852

Open: Jun-20 Sep **Site:** 1HEC **Prices:** 25-28 **Facilities:** Wi-fi **Services:** **Off-site:**

BALLENS — VAUD

Bois Gentil

1144
☎ 021 8095120 🖷 021 8095120
e-mail: py30@bluewin.ch

Level grassy site.

dir: *200m S of station.*

Open: Apr-Oct **Site:** 2.5HEC **Facilities:** **Services:** **Leisure:** P

BOUVERET, LE — VALAIS

Camping Rive-bleue

130 rte de la Plage, 1897
☎ 024 4812161 🖷 024 4812108
e-mail: info@camping-rive-bleue.ch
web: www.camping-rive-bleue.ch

Set beside a lake with a natural sandy beach and modern facilities.

dir: *Off A37 to Monthey in SW outskirts of Bouveret & continue NE for 0.8km.*

Open: Apr-17 Oct **Site:** 3HEC **For hire:** **Facilities:** **Services:** **Leisure:** L P **Off-site:** R

BULLET — VAUD

Cluds

1453
☎ 024 4541440 🖷 024 4541440
e-mail: vd28@campings-ccyverdon.ch
web: www.campings-ccyverdon.ch

A beautiful mountain setting among pine trees.

dir: *1.5km NE.*

Open: All Year. **Site:** 1.2HEC **For hire:** **Facilities:** Wi-fi (charged) Play Area **Services:** **Off-site:**

SWITZERLAND

CHÂTEAU-D'OEX VAUD

Berceau

1837

☎ 026 9246234 026 9242526

web: www.chateau-doex.ch

On level strip of grass between the mountain and the river bank.

dir: *1km SE at junct roads 77 & 76.*

Open: All Year. **Site:** 1HEC **Facilities:** **Services:** **Leisure:** P R **Off-site:**

CHÂTEL-ST-DENIS FRIBOURG

Bivouac

rte des Paccots, 1618

☎ 021 9487849 021 9487849

e-mail: info@le-bivouac.ch

web: www.le-bivouac.ch

Beautiful views of the rolling Swiss countryside. Various sports and leisure activities.

dir: *Turn E in Châtel-St Denis & continue 2km.*

Open: Apr-Sep **Site:** 2HEC **Facilities:** **Services:** **Leisure:** P R

CHESSEL VAUD

Grand Bois

1846

☎ 024 4814225 024 4815113

e-mail: au.grand-bois@bluewin.ch

web: www.augrandbois.ch

On a level meadow close to a canal, only a few kilometres from Lake Geneva.

dir: *N of town towards lake.*

GPS: 46.3561, 6.8991

Open: All Year. **Site:** 4HEC **For hire:** **Prices:** 20-28 Mobile home hire 450-600 **Facilities:** Wi-fi Play Area **Services:** **Leisure:** P R **Off-site:** L

CUDREFIN VAUD

Camping Communal de Cudrefin

Grand rue 2, 1588

☎ 026 6773277 026 6770767

e-mail: camping@cudrefin.ch

web: www.camping-cudrefin.ch

Surrounded by nature overlooking the Jura mountains. The site is by the lake, 0.5km from the town centre.

dir: *Leave A1 at Avenches/Cudrefin exit.*

GPS: 49.9602, 7.0280

Open: 15 Mar-Oct **Site:** 6HEC **For hire:** **Prices:** 30 Mobile home hire 624-1144 **Facilities:** Wi-fi (charged) Play Area **Services:** **Leisure:** L **Off-site:** R

DÜDINGEN FRIBOURG

Schiffenensee

3186

☎ 026 4931917

e-mail: info@camping-schiffenen.ch

web: www.camping-schiffenen.ch

On the shore of Lake Schiffenen and with access to the lake and boat/pedalo rentals. Other leisure facilities include tennis and mini-golf.

dir: *A12 exit Düdingen & N towards Murten.*

Open: Apr-Oct **Site:** 9HEC **Facilities:** **Services:** **Leisure:** L P **Off-site:**

EVOLÈNE VALAIS

Evolène

1983

☎ 027 2831144 027 2833255

e-mail: info@camping-evolene.ch

web: www.camping-evolene.ch

On a level meadow with fine views of the surrounding mountains.

dir: *200m from town.*

Open: All Year. **Site:** 10HEC **For hire:** **Prices:** 25-28 Mobile home hire 300-480 **Facilities:** Wi-fi Play Area **Services:** **Leisure:** P **Off-site:** R

FOULY, LA VALAIS

Glaciers

1944

☎ 027 7831826 027 7833605

e-mail: info@camping-glaciers.ch

web: www.camping-glaciers.ch

At end of village in a beautiful Alpine location with fine views of the surrounding mountains.

Open: 15 May-Sep **Site:** 7HEC **For hire:** **Facilities:** **Services:** **Off-site:**

GRANDSON VAUD

Pécos

VD24, 1422
☎ 024 4454969 🖷 024 4462904
e-mail: vd24@campings-ccyverdon.ch
web: www.campings-ccyverdon.ch
Shaded by trees and with access to a lake, where water sports are available.
dir: *400m SW of railway station between railway & lake.*
Open: Apr-Sep **Site:** 2HEC **For hire:** **Facilities:** **Services:** **Leisure:** L

GUMEFENS FRIBOURG

Camping du Lac

1643
☎ 026 9152162 🖷 026 9152168
e-mail: info@campingdulac-gruyere.ch
web: www.campingdulac-gruyere.ch
On the borders of the lake.
GPS: 46.6756, 7.085
Open: Jul-Aug & wknds May-Jun & Sep **Site:** 1.5HEC **Facilities:** Wi-fi **Services:** **Leisure:** L

LAUSANNE VAUD

Vidy

chemin du Camping 3, 1007
☎ 021 6225000 🖷 021 6225001
e-mail: info@clv.ch
web: www.clv.ch
A delightful location among trees and flowerbeds overlooking Lac Léman.
GPS: 46.5176, 6.5976
Open: All Year. **Site:** 4.5HEC **For hire:** **Facilities:** Wi-fi (charged) Play Area **Services:** **Leisure:** L P

LEYSIN VAUD

Soleil

1854
☎ 024 4943939
e-mail: info@camping-leysin.ch
web: www.camping-leysin.ch
A picturesque Alpine setting.
dir: *Enter village & left at fuel station, site 400m.*
Open: Dec-Oct **Site:** 1.1HEC **For hire:** **Facilities:** Wi-fi **Services:** **Off-site:** P

MARTIGNY VALAIS

Camping TCS Les Neuvilles

rue du Levant, 1920
☎ 027 7224544 🖷 027 7223544
e-mail: camping.martigny@tcs.ch
web: www.campingtcs.ch/martigny
Flat, grassy site with good transport links to the city of Martigny. Mini-golf and paddling pool for children, also table tennis and bowls available.
dir: *A9 towards Grand-St-Bernard exit Martigny Expo, site signed.*
GPS: 46.0969, 7.0786
Open: 4 Apr-28 Oct **Site:** 2.5HEC **Prices:** 37.70-45.50 **Facilities:** Wi-fi (charged) Play Area **Services:** **Leisure:** P **Off-site:**

MORGES VAUD

Camping TCS Le Petit Bois

Promenade du Petit Bois 15, 1110
☎ 021 8011270 🖷 021 8033869
e-mail: camping.morges@tcs.ch
web: www.campingtcs.ch/morges
Close to the town centre and the shore of Lake Genève. On site facilities are table tennis and a children's train.
dir: *A1 exit 15 Morges-Bière, then towards the lake.*
GPS: 46.5044, 6.4889
Open: 4 Apr-14 Oct **Site:** 3.2HEC **For hire:** **Prices:** 42.30-56 **Facilities:** Wi-fi (charged) Play Area **Services:** **Leisure:** L **Off-site:** P

MORGINS VALAIS

La Mare au Diable Morgins

Case postale 61, 1875
☎ 024 4772361 🖷 024 4773708
e-mail: serge.monay@bluewin.ch
web: www.morgins.ch
Terraced site below a pine forest.
dir: *Left at end of village towards Pas de Morgins near Swiss customs.*
GPS: 46.2402, 6.8497
Open: All Year. **Site:** 1.3HEC **Prices:** 23.40-29.40 **Facilities:** Wi-fi **Services:** **Off-site:** P R

ORBE — VAUD

Camping TCS Le Signal

rte du Signal 9, 1350

Peaceful, relaxing site in the Swiss countryside. Mini-golf is available along with free access to the swimming pool situated next door.

dir: *A9 exit N3, follow signs to Cossonay then Lausanne.*

GPS: 46.7361, 6.5322

Open: 4 Apr-7 Oct **Site:** 2.1HEC **For hire:** **Prices:** 34.20-42.80 **Facilities:** Wi-fi (charged) Play Area **Services:** **Off-site:** P

RARON — VALAIS

Santa Monica

Kantonsstr 56, 3942

027 9342424 027 9342450

e-mail: info@santa-monica.ch

web: www.santa-monica.ch

Ideal for visiting the surrounding Valais mountains. Facilities include a heated swimming pool.

Open: Apr-Oct **Site:** 4HEC **For hire:** **Facilities:** **Services:** **Leisure:** P **Off-site:** L R

RECKINGEN — VALAIS

Residence Camping Augenstern

3998

027 9731395 027 9732677

e-mail: info@campingaugenstern.ch

web: www.campingaugenstern.ch

On an alpine meadow close to the River Rhône.

dir: *400m S on bank of Rhône.*

GPS: 46.465, 8.245

Open: Jan-20 Mar, 12 May-19 Oct & 16-31 Dec **Site:** 3HEC **For hire:** **Prices:** 32.70-36.70 **Facilities:** Wi-fi (charged) Play Area **Services:** **Leisure:** R **Off-site:** P R

RIED-BRIG — VALAIS

Tropic

3911

027 9232537

In the sunny Valais, Brig and surrounding area offers a wide variety of sporting and cultural events, activities and recreational opportunities.

dir: *On left of Simplon road near entrance to village. 3km above Brig.*

Open: Jun-Aug **Site:** 1.5HEC **For hire:** **Facilities:** **Services:** **Off-site:**

SAAS-GRUND — VALAIS

Kapellenweg

3910

027 9574997 027 9573316

e-mail: camping@kapellenweg.ch

web: www.kapellenweg.ch

On a level meadow in a picturesque mountain setting in the Saas Valley. Modern facilities.

dir: *Over bridge & right towards Saas-Almagell.*

Open: 15 May-15 Oct **Site:** 1.46HEC **For hire:** **Prices:** 25 Mobile home hire 252.50 **Facilities:** Wi-fi (charged) **Services:** **Leisure:** R **Off-site:** P

SALAVAUX — VAUD

Camping TCS Salavaux Plage

chemin de la Plage 10, 1585

026 6771476 026 6773744

e-mail: camping.salavaux@tcs.ch

web: www.campingtcs.ch/salavaux

100 metres from the shore of Lake Murten, large site with partly shaded pitches. Cycles can be hired and entertainment for all the family is available.

dir: *A1 exit Murten, then follow signs to Salavaux.*

GPS: 46.9136, 7.0339

Open: 4 Apr-7 Oct **Site:** 6HEC **Prices:** 39-60.20 **Facilities:** Wi-fi (charged) Play Area **Services:** **Leisure:** L

SALGESCH — VALAIS

Swiss Plage

3970

027 4816023 027 4813215

e-mail: info@swissplage.ch

web: swissplage.ch

Situated beside a small lake and surrounded by vineyards. Good recreational facilities.

Open: Etr-1 Nov **Site:** 10HEC **For hire:** **Facilities:** **Services:** **Leisure:** L R **Off-site:** P

SATIGNY GENÈVE

Bois-de-Bay

1242

022 3410505 022 3410606

e-mail: boisdebay@sccv.ch

web: www.sccv.ch

On the banks of the Rhône, pitches are flat with hedges and trees.

dir: *Off A1 at Bernex & signed.*

Open: 17 Jan-10 Dec **Site:** 2.8HEC **For hire:** **Facilities:** Wi-fi (charged) Play Area **Services:**

SIERRE VALAIS

Bois de Finges

3960

027 4550284 027 4553351

web: www.campingtcs.ch

Situated in a pine forest with well-defined pitches set on terraces.

dir: *Motorway exit Sierre-Ouest for Sierre.*

Open: 24 Apr-27 Sep **Site:** 5HEC **For hire:** **Facilities:** **Services:** **Leisure:** P **Off-site:** L R

SION VALAIS

Camping TCS les Iles

chemin du Camping 6, 1951

027 3464347 027 3466847

e-mail: camping.sion@tcs.ch

web: www.campingtcs.ch/sion

Large site, close to the city, with a wide range of leisure activities. A bus service to the ski runs is available in winter.

dir: *A9 exit 25 Vétroz-Conthey, site signed.*

GPS: 46.2117, 7.3139

Open: 21 Dec-28 Oct **Site:** 8HEC **For hire:** **Prices:** 39.20-48.80 **Facilities:** Wi-fi (charged) Play Area **Services:** **Leisure:** L P

SORENS FRIBOURG

Forêt

rte Principale 271, 1642

026 9151882 026 9150363

e-mail: info@camping-la-foret.ch

web: www.camping-la-foret.ch

A pleasant site on a level meadow surrounded by woodland.

dir: *Off A12 to village.*

Open: All Year. **Site:** 4HEC **Prices:** 25.70 **Facilities:** Wi-fi (charged) Play Area **Services:** **Leisure:** P **Off-site:** L

SUSTEN VALAIS

Bella-Tola

Waldstr 57, 3952

027 4731491 027 4733641

e-mail: info@bella-tola.ch

web: www.bella-tola.ch

A peaceful, terraced site at an altitude of 750 metres, shielded by a belt of woodland. Good, clean modern facilities.

dir: *Off A9, 2km from village.*

Open: 26 Apr-26 Oct **Site:** 3.6HEC **Prices:** 20.15-28.25 **Facilities:** **Services:** **Leisure:** P

ULRICHEN VALAIS

Camping Nufenen

3988

027 9731437

e-mail: info@camping-nufenen.ch

web: www.camping-nufenen.ch

Family friendly, secluded campsite, 1km south-east of Ulrichen.

dir: *1km SE to right of road to Nufenen Pass.*

Open: 16 May-14 Oct **Site:** 8HEC **For hire:** **Facilities:** Wi-fi **Services:** **Leisure:** R **Off-site:** L P

VALLORBE VAUD

Pré sous Ville

1337

021 8432309

e-mail: christophe.wirz@aapv.ch

web: www.aapv.ch

A wooded riverside location. The neighbouring swimming pool is available free to campers.

dir: *On left bank of River Orbe.*

Open: mid Apr-mid Oct **Site:** 1HEC **For hire:** **Prices:** 30.50 **Facilities:** Wi-fi Play Area **Services:** **Leisure:** P R **Off-site:** L

VERS-L'ÉGLISE VAUD

Murée

1864

079 4019915

e-mail: dagonch@bluewinch.ch

web: www.camping-caravaningvd.com

Partially terraced site by a stream.

dir: *N9 exit Aigle-Aprés, take direction Aigle-Le Supey. 8km in direction of Les Diablerets/Col du Pillon at entrance to village, site signed on right.*

GPS: 46.3550, 7.1266

Open: All Year. **Site:** 1.1HEC **For hire:** **Prices:** 27.40-28.40 **Facilities:** **Services:** **Leisure:** R **Off-site:**

VÉSENAZ GENÈVE

Pointe à la Bise

Chemin de la Bise, 1222

022 7521296 022 7523767

e-mail: camping.geneve@tcs.ch

web: www.campingtcs.ch

A pleasant wooded setting on the shore of Lake Léman.

dir: *NE between Vésenaz & Collonge-Bellerive, on route du Lac in direction of Evian.*

GPS: 46.245, 6.1933

Open: 4 Apr-7 Oct **Site:** 3.2HEC **Prices:** 45.50-56 **Facilities:** Wi-fi (charged) Play Area **Services:** **Leisure:** L P

VÉTROZ VALAIS

Botza

rte du Camping 1, 1963

027 3461940 027 3462535

e-mail: info@botza.ch

web: www.botza.ch

On a level meadow with pitches divided by hedges. Fine panoramic views and good leisure facilities.

GPS: 46.2058, 7.2786

Open: All Year. **Site:** 3HEC **For hire:** **Prices:** 21.80-42.80 **Facilities:** Wi-fi Kids' Club Play Area **Services:** **Leisure:** P **Off-site:** L

YVONAND VAUD

VD 8 Pointe D'Yvonand

1462

024 4301655 024 4302463

e-mail: vd8@campings-ccyverdon.ch

web: www.campings-ccyverdon.ch

Site borders Lake Neuchâtel with a private beach 1km away. Boat moorings, private jetty and boat hire.

dir: *3km W, signed.*

Open: Apr-Sep **Site:** 5HEC **For hire:** **Facilities:** **Services:** **Leisure:** L

SWITZERLAND

Turkey

Accident & emergency numbers

Turkey only uses the European emergency number for medical emergencies. These are the current numbers for emergency services:

Police 155 Medical 112 110 Fire

Drinking and driving

If the level of alcohol in the bloodstream is 0.05% or more, penalties are severe. For drivers of cars with caravans or trailers the alcohol level in the bloodstream is 0%.

Driving licence

Minimum age at which a UK licence holder may drive a temporarily imported car and/or motorcycle 18. UK driving licence valid for 90 days; licences that do not have a photo must be accompanied by an International Driving Permit (IDP).

Fines

On-the-spot. Vehicles may be towed away if causing an obstruction.

Fuel

Leaded (95 octane), unleaded petrol (95 and 98 octane) and diesel are available. LPG is available in large centres. Petrol in a can permitted (fireproof container). Credit cards accepted at many filling stations, check with your card issuer for usage in Turkey before travel.

Lights

Dipped headlights should be used in poor daytime visibility, and after sunset in built-up areas.

Motorcycles

Wearing of crash helmets compulsory.

Motor Insurance

Third party insurance compulsory. Foreign insurance e.g. UK insurance is recognised in the European part of Turkey, check to ensure your policy covers Turkey.

Visiting motorists driving vehicles registered in the UK may use a valid Green Card when driving in Turkey. The Green Card must cover the whole of Turkey, i.e. both the European Part and the Asian part (Anatolia). Visiting motorists who are not in possession of a valid Green Card or who are not in possession of a valid UK insurance policy (validated for the whole of Turkey) must take out short term insurance at the border or TTOK offices.

Passengers/children in cars

Child under 12 cannot travel as front seat passenger.

Seat belts

Compulsory for front and rear seat occupants to wear seat belts, where fitted.

Speed limits

Standard legal limits, which may be varied by signs

Private vehicles without trailers

Built-up areas	50km/h
Outside built-up areas (cars)	90km/h
Outside built-up areas (motorcycles)	70km/h
Motorways (cars)	120km/h
Motorways (motorcycles)	80km/h
Minimum speed on motorways	40km/h

Vehicle with trailer

Built-up areas	40km/h
Outside built-up areas	80km/h
Motorways	110km/h

Motorhome with trailer

Built-up areas	40km/h
Outside built-up areas	70km/h
Motorways	80km/h

Compulsory equipment in Turkey

First aid kit – Not required for two wheeled vehicles

Fire extinguisher – Not required for two wheeled vehicles

Warning triangle – two required

Other rules/requirements

The use of the horn is generally prohibited in towns between 2200 hours until sunrise.

The use of spiked tyres, snow chains and studded tyres are permitted but only where their use does not damage the road surface. It is recommended that winter tyres are used in snowy areas and snow chains are carried.

In the event of an accident it is compulsory for the police to be called and a report obtained.

Tolls Currency Turkish Lire (TRY)	Car	Car Towing Caravan/Trailer
O21 (E90) Pozanti - Tarus	2.00TRY	6.50TRY
O3 (E80) Edirne - Istanbul	6.50TRY	15.25TRY
O31 (E87) Izmir - Aydin	2.75TRY	6.50TRY
O32 (E881) Izmir - Cesme	2.00TRY	5.00TRY
O4 (E80/E89) Istanbul - Ankara	13.50TRY	30.50TRY
O52 (E51) Adana - Mersin	2.75TRY	7.75TRY
O53 (E91) Ceyhan - Iskenderun	2.75TRY	7.00TRY
Bridges and Tunnels		
Bosphorus and Fatih Sultan Mehmet Bridge Istanbul on E80 (Eastbound only)	3.75TRY	23.50TRY

Please note: Although the official currency of Turkey is the Turkish lira, the campsites featured in this guide have quoted their prices in Euros.

BERGAMA **AEGEAN**

Bergama Caravan Camping

Atatürk Bulvari No 148, 35700
0232 6333902 0232 6331792
e-mail: info@caravancamping.net
web: www.caravancamping.net

A small site that welcomes campers including motorcyclists. There is a large restaurant on-site.

Open: All Year. **Site:** 0.5HEC **Prices:** 15-17 **Facilities:** Wi-fi Play Area **Services:** **Leisure:** P **Off-site:**

BODRUM **AEGEAN**

Zetas Camping Gumbet

Mahallesi Etem Kaptan 10, 48400
0252 3192231 0252 3195741

Located in one of the most picturesque areas of Turkey with a scenic coastline and a picturesque harbour. The campsite is located directly on Gumbet Beach.

dir: *3km from centre of Bodrum.*

Open: All Year. **Site:** 1.2HEC **Facilities:** Wi-fi Play Area **Services:** **Leisure:** S

BOGAZKALE **CENTRAL ANATOLIA**

Asikoglu Tourist Camp

Ankara Sungurlu Asfaiti, 19310
0364 4522004 0364 4522171
e-mail: info@hattusas.com
web: www.hattusas.com

Site in an historic location dating back to the Bronze Age. Nearby are the ruins of Hattusas and the Bogazkale Hittite Museum.

dir: *From Corum towards Bogazkale, campsite on right at 1st crossing in Bogazkale.*

Open: 15 Mar-15 Nov **Site:** 1HEC **Prices:** 8-10 **Facilities:** Wi-fi **Services:** **Leisure:** L **Off-site:**

GÖREME **CENTRAL ANATOLIA**

Goreme Panorama Teras

50180
0384 2712352 0384 2712632
e-mail: panoramacamping@hotmail.com
web: www.goremepanoramacamping.com

A family-owned site with 24hr access in the centre of Cappadocia. All local amenities and sightseeing options may be arranged at preferential rates. Medical assistance on call.

dir: *250km from Ankaran. Nevcehir-Göreme road, campsite on left entering Göreme.*

Open: All Year. **Site:** 1HEC **For hire:** **Prices:** 15 **Facilities:** Wi-fi **Services:** **Leisure:** P **Off-site:**

KAŞ **ANTALYA**

Olympos Mocamp

07580
0242 8362252 0242 8362252
e-mail: cerci_82@hotmail.com
web: www.kasolympos.com

2km from the town centre, mainly shaded site. Access to the beach is across a road.

Open: Apr-29 Sep **Site:** **For hire:** **Facilities:** Wi-fi Play Area **Services:** **Leisure:** S **Off-site:**

KEMER **ANTALYA**

Sundance Camp

Faselis cad. 1015 sokok no 62, 07995
0242 8214165 0242 8215527
e-mail: sundance@sundancecamp.com
web: www.sundancecamp.com

Located next to the beach, with a small area for tents. Activities include horse riding, kayaking and table tennis.

dir: *SE of E90.*

Open: All Year. **Site:** 15HEC **For hire:** **Prices:** 22-30 **Facilities:** Wi-fi **Services:** **Leisure:** S **Off-site:**

TURKEY

KUŞADASI AEGEAN

Önder Camping

Ataturk bul. no 72, 09400

0256 6181590 0256 6181517

e-mail: info@onderotel.com

web: www.ondercamping.com

Large site with grassy pitches. Facilities include an outdoor swimming pool.

Open: Mar-Nov **Site:** 12HEC **For hire:** **Prices:** 9-15 **Facilities:** Wi-fi **Services:** **Leisure:** P **Off-site:** S

SELCUK AEGEAN

Dereli

Pamucak, 35920

0232 8931205 0232 8931203

web: www.dereli-ephesus.com

A short distance from Ephesus overlooking a sandy beach and shaded by eucalyptus trees.

dir: *In Selcuk towards Kuşadasi, at junct straight ahead to Pamucak, campsite signed before left turn.*

Open: Mar-Oct **Site:** 3HEC **For hire:** **Facilities:** **Services:** **Leisure:** S

SULTANHANI CENTRAL ANATOLIA

Kervan

Sultanhani Kasabi, 68190

0382 2422325 0382 2422411

e-mail: kervancamping@mynet.com

web: www.kervancamping.com

Family campsite situated in the middle of the flat plain between Konya and Aksaray at a former oasis on the ancient Silk Road.

dir: *Route 300 from Aksaray to Konya. 39km after Aksaray left at exit Sultanhani, follow signs to campsite on right.*

Open: Mar-Nov **Site:** 4.1HEC **Prices:** 12-15 **Facilities:** Wi-fi **Services:** **Off-site:**

TURKEY

Country Map Section

1 Austria
2 Belgium & Luxembourg
3 France North
4 France South
5 Germany
6 Germany - detail
7 Netherlands
8 Spain & Portugal
9 Italy
10 Switzerland
11 Croatia & Slovenia
12 Czech Republic & Hungary
13 Greece
14 Poland
15 Romania, Bulgaria & Western Turkey

AUSTRIA

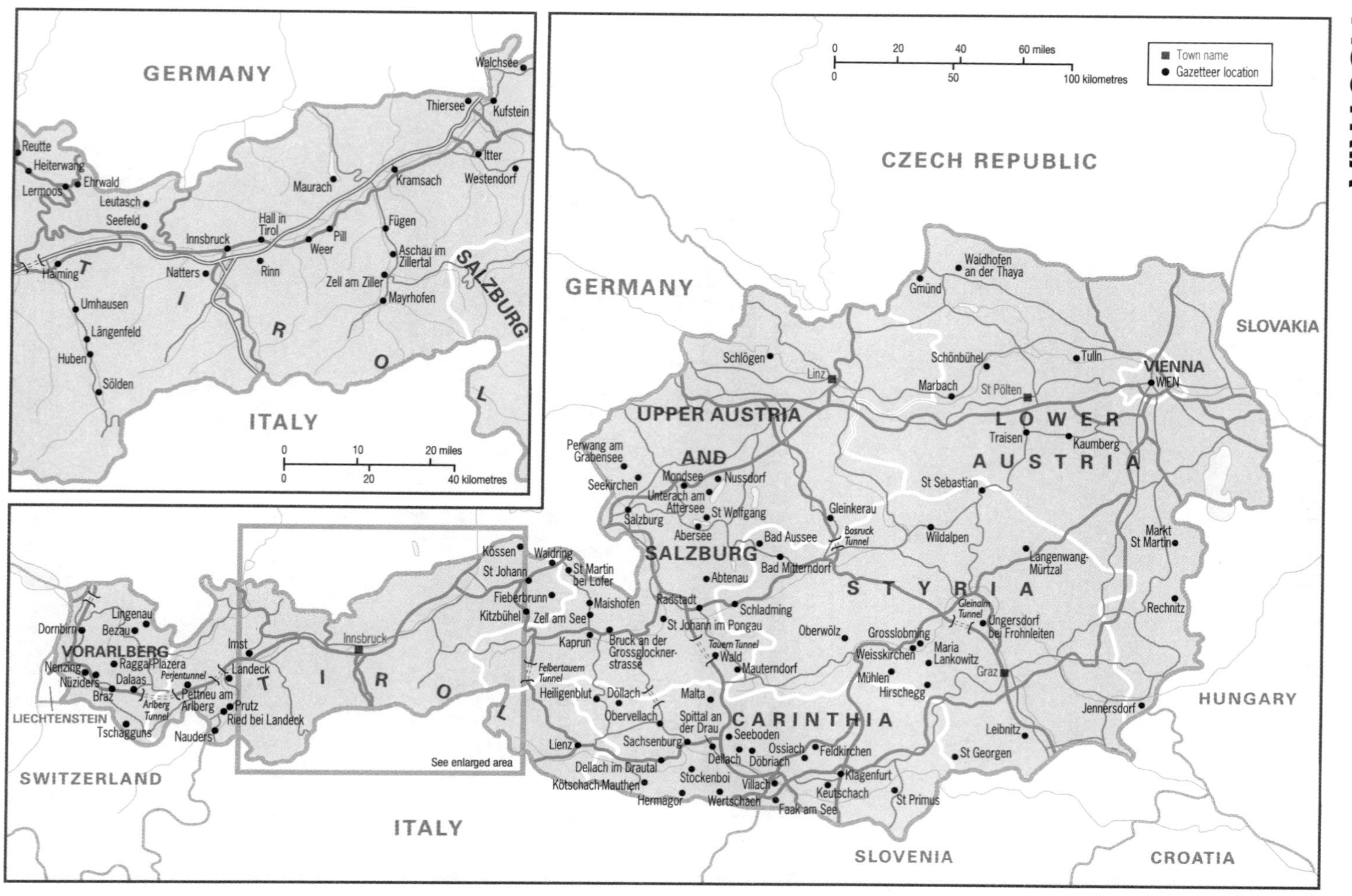

Town name
Gazetteer location
0 20 40 60 miles
0 50 100 kilometres
CZECH REPUBLIC
GERMANY
SLOVAKIA
HUNGARY
CROATIA
SLOVENIA
ITALY
SWITZERLAND
LIECHTENSTEIN
VIENNA
WIEN
LOWER AUSTRIA
UPPER AUSTRIA AND SALZBURG
STYRIA
CARINTHIA
TIROL
VORARLBERG
Waidhofen an der Thaya
Gmünd
Schlögen
Linz
Schönbühel
Tulln
Marbach
St Pölten
Traisen
Kaumberg
St Sebastian
Wildalpen
Markt St Martin
Langenwang-Mürztal
Rechnitz
Gleinalm Tunnel
Ungersdorf bei Frohnleiten
Graz
Jennersdorf
Leibnitz
St Georgen
Grosslobming
Maria Lankowitz
Weisskirchen
Mühlen
Hirschegg
Oberwölz
Perwang am Grabensee
Seekirchen
Mondsee
Nussdorf
Unterach am Attersee
St Wolfgang
Salzburg
Abersee
Gleinkerau
Bosruck Tunnel
Bad Aussee
Bad Mitterndorf
Abtenau
Radstadt
Schladming
St Johann im Pongau
Tauern Tunnel
Wald
Mauterndorf
Malta
Spittal an der Drau
Seeboden
Ossiach
Feldkirchen
Dellach
Döbriach
Klagenfurt
Keutschach
St Primus
Villach
Faak am See
Wertschach
Stockenboi
Hermagor
Sachsenburg
Dellach im Drautal
Kötschach-Mauthen
Lienz
Obervellach
Döllach
Heiligenblut
Felbertauern Tunnel
Kaprun
Bruck an der Grossglockner-strasse
Zell am See
Maishofen
Kitzbühel
Fieberbrunn
St Johann
St Martin bei Lofer
Waidring
Kössen
Innsbruck
See enlarged area
Imst
Landeck
Pettneu am Arlberg
Prutz
Ried bei Landeck
Nauders
Perjentunnel
Arlberg Tunnel
Raggal-Plazera
Dalaas
Braz
Tschagguns
Nenzing
Nüziders
Dornbirn
Bezau
Lingenau
Walchsee
Thiersee
Kufstein
Itter
Westendorf
Kramsach
Maurach
Reutte
Heiterwang
Ehrwald
Lermoos
Leutasch
Seefeld
Innsbruck
Hall in Tirol
Pill
Weer
Fügen
Aschau im Zillertal
Zell am Ziller
Mayrhofen
Rinn
Natters
Haiming
Umhausen
Längenfeld
Huben
Sölden
0 10 20 miles
0 20 40 kilometres

BELGIUM & LUXEMBOURG

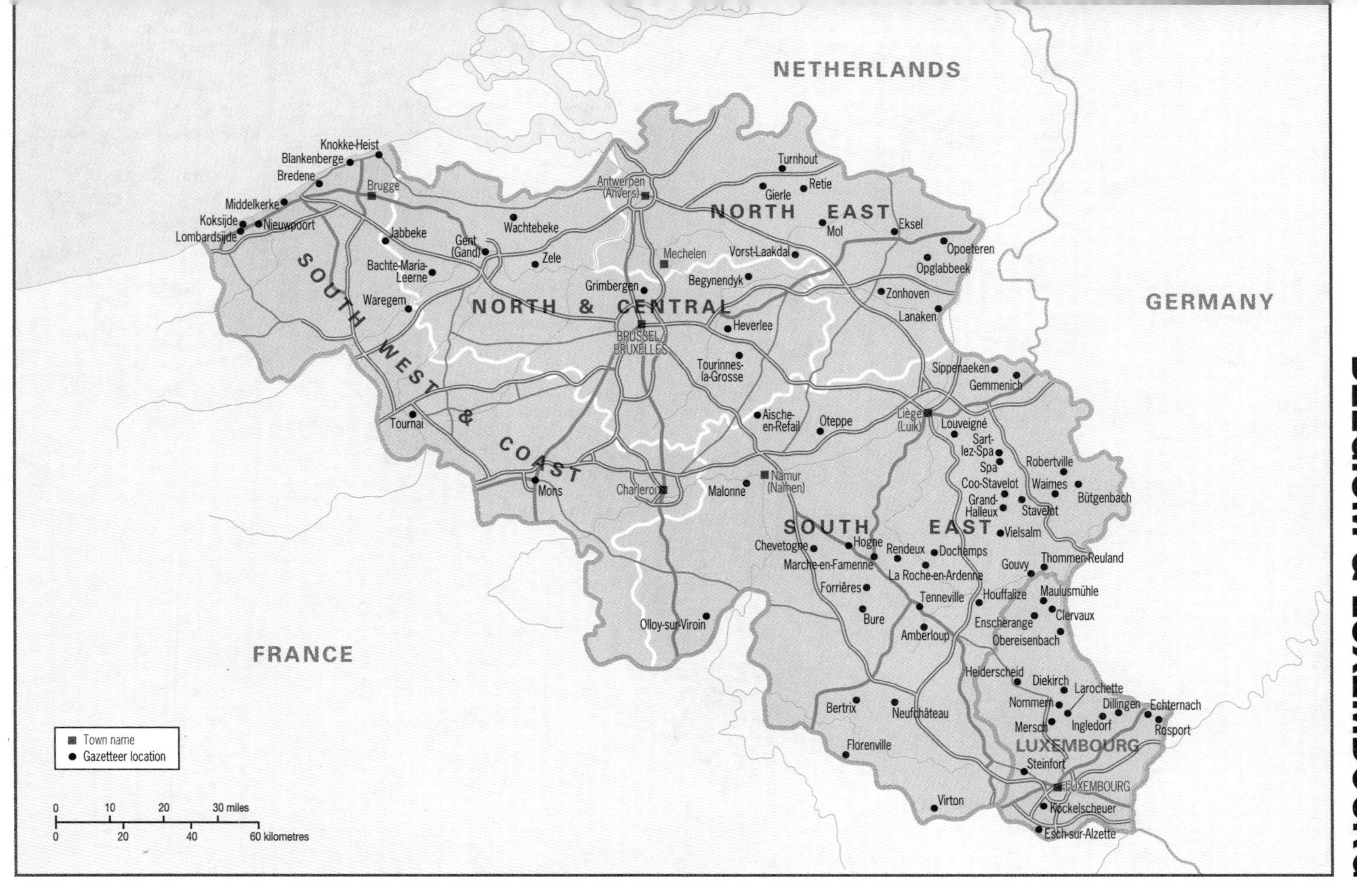

FRANCE

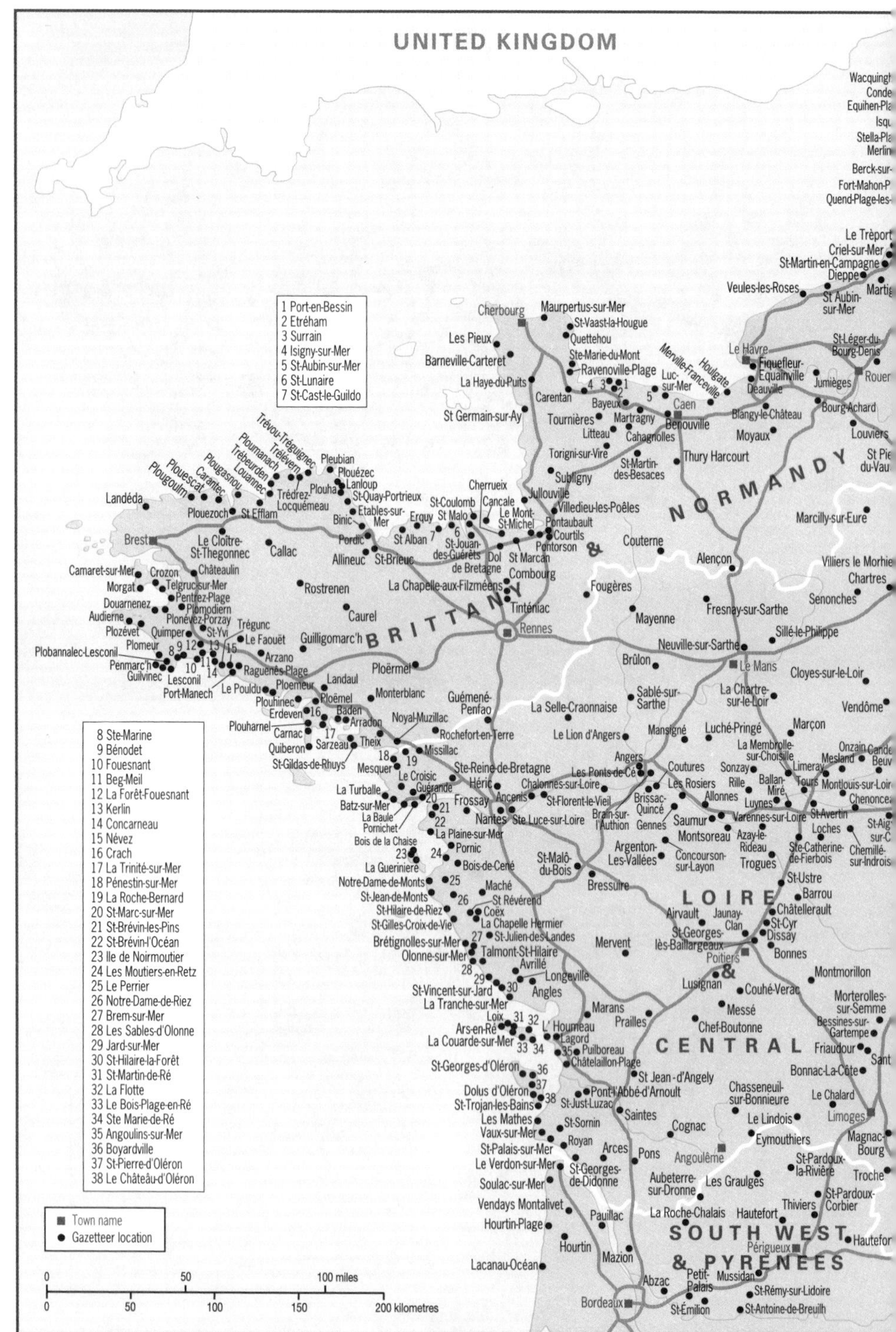

UNITED KINGDOM
NORMANDY
BRITTANY
LOIRE & CENTRAL
SOUTH WEST & PYRENEES
1 Port-en-Bessin
2 Etréham
3 Surrain
4 Isigny-sur-Mer
5 St-Aubin-sur-Mer
6 St-Lunaire
7 St-Cast-le-Guildo
8 Ste-Marine
9 Bénodet
10 Fouesnant
11 Beg-Meil
12 La Forêt-Fouesnant
13 Kerlin
14 Concarneau
15 Névez
16 Crach
17 La Trinité-sur-Mer
18 Pénestin-sur-Mer
19 La Roche-Bernard
20 St-Marc-sur-Mer
21 St-Brévin-les-Pins
22 St-Brévin-l'Océan
23 Ile de Noirmoutier
24 Les Moutiers-en-Retz
25 Le Perrier
26 Notre-Dame-de-Riez
27 Brem-sur-Mer
28 Les Sables-d'Olonne
29 Jard-sur-Mer
30 St-Hilaire-la-Forêt
31 St-Martin-de-Ré
32 La Flotte
33 Le Bois-Plage-en-Ré
34 Ste Marie-de-Ré
35 Angoulins-sur-Mer
36 Boyardville
37 St-Pierre-d'Oléron
38 Le Château-d'Oléron
Town name
Gazetteer location
0 50 100 miles
0 50 100 150 200 kilometres
Cherbourg
Maurpertus-sur-Mer
St-Vaast-la-Hougue
Quettehou
Les Pieux
Barneville-Carteret
Ste-Marie-du-Mont
Ravenoville-Plage
La Haye-du-Puits
Carentan
Bayeux
Caen
Le Havre
Rennes
Brest
Nantes
Le Mans
Poitiers
Limoges
Angoulême
Périgueux
Bordeaux
Rouen

Dunkerque
Bray-Dunes
Oye Plage
Coudekerque
NETHERLANDS
Guînes
Ardres
Éperlecques
Licques
Tournehem-sur-la-Hem
Thiembronne
Lille
BELGIUM
39 Port-le-Grand
40 St Valéry-sur-Somme
41 Villers-sur-Authie
GERMANY
Montreuil-sur-Mer
Nampont
St Martin
Tollent
St-Amand-les-Eaux
Boubers-sur-Canche
Maubeuge
Vironchaux
Le Crotoy
Boiry-Notre-Dame
Felleries
Miannay
Feuillères
Moyenneville
Bertangles
Signy-le-Petit
Blangy-sur-Bresle
Amiens
Proyart
Bourg-Fidèle
Monthermé
Poix-de-Picardie
LUXEMBOURG
Seraucourt-le-Grand
Sedan
PARIS & NORTH
Salency
Vailly-sur-Aisne
Berny-Rivière
Buzancy
Reims
Grandpré
Sivry-sur-Meuse
St-Leu-d'Esserent
Verdun
Ste-Menehould
Metz
Nesles-la-Vallée
Gouvieux
Villennes-sur-Seine
Acy-en-Multien
Maisons-Laffitte
Charly-sur-Marne
Baerenthal
Lauterbourg
Jablines
La Ferte-sous-Jouarre
Châlons-en-Champagne
ALSACE & LORRAINE
Torcy
Oberbronn
St-Cyr-sur-Morin
Versailles
PARIS
Pommeuse
Sézanne
Dabo
Wasselonne
Nancy
Éclaron-Braucourt
Strasbourg
Rambouillet
Villiers sur Orge
Touquin
Plessis-Feu-Aussoux
Villers-lès-Nancy
Obernai
St-Pierre
St Hilaire-sous-Romilly
Giffaumont
St-Chéron
Melun
Le Hohwald
Dambach-la-Ville
Thonnance-les-Moulins
Lièpvre
Sélestat
Crèvecoeur-en-Brie
Pont-Sainte-Marie
Vittel
Gemaingoutte
Ribeauvillé
Milly-la-Forêt
Radonvilliers
Corcieux
Anould
Kaysersberg
Troyes
Grez-sur-Loing
Granges-sur-Vologne
Riquewihr
Soulaines-Dhuys
Rehaupal
Turckheim
Colmar
Boulancourt
Mesnil-St-Père
Froncles
Fontenoy-le-Château
Le Tholy
Munster
Biesheim
Vagney
Ste-Croix-en-Plaine
BURGUNDY & CHAMPAGNE
Montigny-le-Roi
La Bresse
Riel-les-Eaux
Bourbonne-les-Bains
Mittlach
Wattwiller
Nibelle
Moosch
Geishouse
Orleans
Châtillon-sur-Seine
Bannes
St-Maurice-sur-Moselle
Cernay
Olivet
Sully-sur-Loire
Marcenay
Peigney
Bourg
Masevaux
Mulhouse
Auxerre
Port-sur-Saône
Belfort
Heimsbrunn
Muides-sur-Loire
Gien
Villeneuve-les-Genêts
Vincelles
Ancy-le-Franc
ALPS & EAST
Rougemont
Seppois-le-Bas
Bracieux
Pierrefitte-sur-Sauldre
Bonny-sur-Loire
Accolay
Vermenton
Venarey-les-Laumes
Huanne-Montmartin
L'Isle-sur-le-Doubs
42 Luttenbach
43 Wihr-au-Val
44 Xonrupt/Longemer
45 Gérardmer
46 Kruth
47 Bussang
48 Eguisheim
49 Issenheim
Clamecy
Avallon
Dijon
Andryes
Chalezeule
St-Satur
Vandenesse-en-Auxois
Saulieu
Besançon
Auxonne
Chevigny
Arnay-le-Duc
Vignoles
Ornans
Pougues-les-Eaux
Montsauche
Dole
Beaune
Bourges
Montapas
Ounans
Nevers
Epinac
Seurre
Parcey
Arbois
Meursault
Malbuisson
St-Amand-Montrond
Chagny
St-Péreuse
St-Honoré
St Marcel
SWITZERLAND
Champagnole
Châtillon
Decize
Tazilly
Toulon-sur-Arroux
Vellès
Néret
St-Bonnet-Tronçais
Laives
Lons-le-Saunier
Marigny
Bourbon-Lancy
Issy-l'Evêque
Tournus
Doucier
Montgivray
Braize
Isle-et-Bardais
Bourbon-l'Archambault
Gigny-sur-Saône
Mesnois
Patornay
Digoin
Uchizy
Boussac-Bourg
Lugrin
Charolles
St-Claude
Lapeyrouse
Paray-le-Monial
Pont-de-Vaux
Clairvaux-les-Lacs
Sciez
Sazeret
Dompierre-les-Ormes
Montrevel-en-Bresse
Messery
Châtel-de-Neuvre
Matour
Mâcon
Divonne-les-Bains
Gibles
Néris-les-Bains
La Clayette
Crêches-sur-Saône
50
Jenzat
Thoissey
Neydens
Argentière
Ebreuil
Châtel Montagne
Fleurie
Bourg-en-Bresse
Matafelon Granges
Bellerive-sur-Allier
La Clusaz
Passy
St Gal-sur-Sioule
Choisy
Chamonix-Mont-Blanc
St-Gervais-d'Auvergne
Ars-sur-Formans
Villars-les-Dombes
Sevrier
Rumilly
Tunnel du Mont
Miremont
Loubeyrat
AUVERGNE
ALPS & EAST
Talloires
Châtel Guyon
St Jorioz
St-Gervais-les-Bains
St-Léonard-de-Noblat
St-Ours
Doussard
Pontgibaud
Royat
Albens
Dardilly
St-Rémy-sur-Durolle
Bout-du-lac
Séez
Landry
Pollionnay
Ceyrat
Murs-et-Gélignieux
Dallet
Pomeys
Verrières-en-Forez
Trept
Bourg-St-Maurice
Lyon
Le Bourget-du-Lac
La Rosière-de-Montvalezan
Nébouzat
52
51
Cournon-d'Auvergne
St-Jean-de-Couz
St-Germain-les-Belles
Olliergues
Ambert
Mornant
St Clément-de-Valorgue
Ste-Catherine
Les Abrets
La Rochette
Plagne-Montchavin
Murol
Orcet
Les Martres-de-Veyre
Meyrieu-les-Etangs
Entre-deux-Guiers
Le Mont-Dore
Tignes-les-Brevières
St Amant-Roche-Savine
Condrieu
Vernioz
ITALY
Jassat
St-Pierre-Colamine
Les Pradeaux
Allevard
Champs-sur-Tarentaine
St-Martin-sur-la-Chambre
Champagnac-le-Vieux
Miribel-les-Échelles
Saignes
Singles
Bourg-Argental
St-Clair-du-Rhône
Condat sur Ganaveix
Aurec sur Loire
Lempdes
Sembadel-Gare
St-Sorlin-en-Valloire
St-Pierre-de-Chartreuse
Tunnel du Fréjus
50 Cormoranche-sur-Saône
51 Montaigut-le-Blanc
52 St Nectaire
Trizac
Allanche
Ste-Sigolêne
Grenoble
Langeac
St-Paulien
Le Bourg-d'Oisans
Autrans
St Martin-Valmeroux
St-Jacques-des-Blats
Ruynes-en-Margeride
Brives-Charensac
Tain-l'Hermitage
Méaudre
Villard-de-Lans
St-Laurent-en-Beaumont
Tournon-sur-Rhône
Choranche
Val-des-Prés
St-Gérons
Vic-sur-Cère
St Just
Alleyras
Le Puy
Goudet
La Salle-en-Beaumont
Arpajon-sur-Cère
Neuvéglise
Le Malzieu-Ville
Valence
Chabeuil
Gresse-en-Vercors
Arnac
Thérondels
St-Alban-sur-Limagnole
SOUTH COAST & RIVIERA
Chaudes-Aigues

4

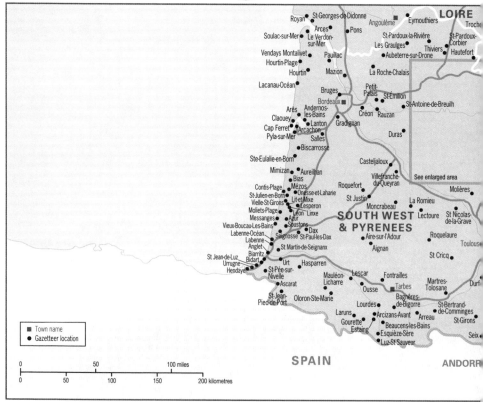

Royan
St-Georges-de-Didonne
Arces
Pons
Soulac-sur-Mer
Le Verdon-sur-Mer
Vendays Montalivet
Pauillac
Hourtin-Plage
Hourtin
Mazion
Lacanau-Océan
Bruges
Bordeaux
Arès
Andernos-les-Bains
Claouey
Lanton
Cap Ferret
Arcachon
Pyla-sur-Mer
Gradignan
Salles
Biscarrosse
Ste-Eulalie-en-Born
Mimizan
Aureilhan
Bias
Contis-Plage
Mézos
St-Julien-en-Born
Onesse-et-Laharie
Vielle-St-Girons
Lit-et-Mixe
Lesperon
Moliets-Plage
Léon
Linxe
Messanges
Azur
Vieux-Boucau-Les-Bains
Soustons
Labenne-Océan
Dax
Labenne
Seignosse
St-Paul-les-Dax
Anglet
St Martin-de-Seignanx
Biarritz
St Jean-de-Luz
Bidart
Urrugne
Urt
Hendaye
Hasparren
St-Pée-sur-Nivelle
Ascarat
St-Jean-Pied-de-Port
Mauléon-Licharre
Oloron-Ste-Marie
Lescar
Ousse
Laruns
Gourette
Estaing
Lourdes
Arcizans-Avant
Beaucens-les-Bains
Esquièze-Sère
Luz-St-Sauveur
Fontrailles
Tarbes
Bagnères-de-Bigorre
Arreau
Martres-Tolosane
St-Bertrand-de-Comminges
St-Girons
Seix
Angoulême
Eymouthiers
LOIRE
Troche
St-Pardoux-la-Rivière
St-Pardoux-Corbier
Les Graulges
Thiviers
Hautefort
Aubeterre-sur-Drone
La Roche-Chalais
Petit-Palais
St-Émilion
St-Antoine-de-Breuilh
Créon
Rauzan
Duras
Casteljaloux
Villefranche-du-Queyran
See enlarged area
Roquefort
St Justin
Molières
Moncrabeau
La Romieu
Lectoure
St Nicolas-de-la-Grave
SOUTH WEST & PYRENEES
Aire-sur-l'Adour
Aignan
Roquelaure
Toulous
St Cricq
Durf
SPAIN
ANDORR

■ Town name
● Gazetteer location

0 50 100 miles
0 50 100 150 200 kilometres

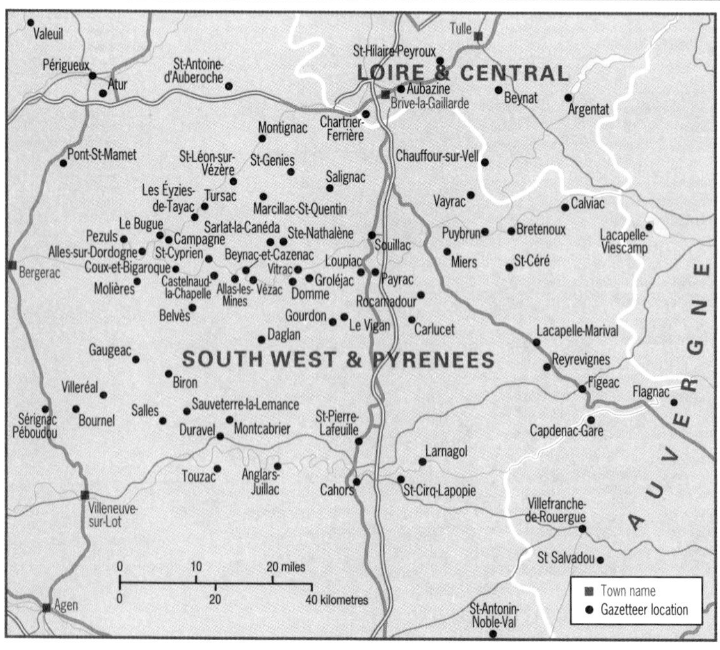

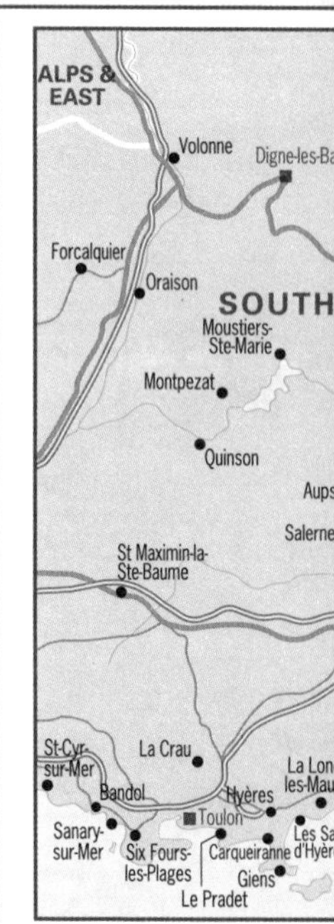

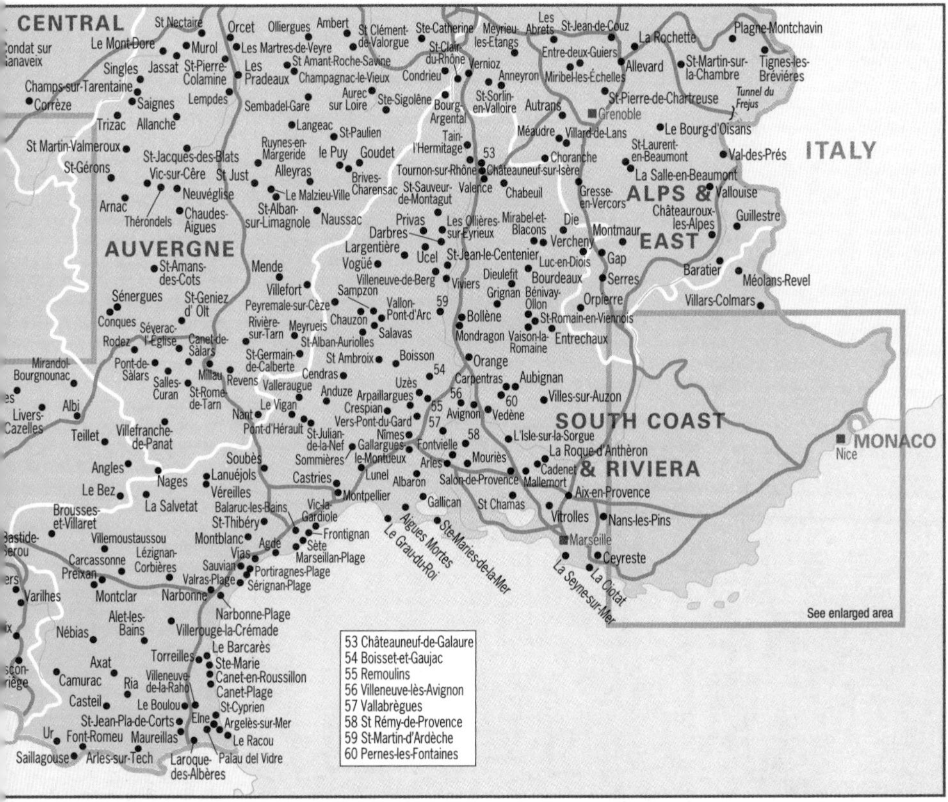

CENTRAL

Condat sur Ganaveix, Le Mont-Dore, St Nectaire, Murol, Orcet, Olliergues, Ambert, St Clément-de-Valorgue, Ste-Catherine, Meyrieu-les-Etangs, Les Abrets, St-Jean-de-Couz, La Rochette, Plagne-Montchavin, Singles, Jassat, St-Pierre-Colamine, Les Martres-de-Veyre, Les Pradeaux, St Amant-Roche-Savine, Champagnac-le-Vieux, St-Clair-du-Rhône, Condrieu, Vernioz, Entre-deux-Guiers, Miribel-les-Échelles, Allevard, St-Martin-sur-la-Chambre, Tignes-les-Bréviéres, Champs-sur-Tarentaine, Corrèze, Saignes, Lempdes, Sembadel-Gare, Aurec-sur Loire, Ste-Sigolène, Bourg-Argental, Anneyron, St-Sorlin-en-Valloire, Autrans, Grenoble, St-Pierre-de-Chartreuse, Tunnel du Frejus, Trizac, Allanche, Langeac, St-Paulien, Méaudre, Villard-de-Lans, Le Bourg-d'Oisans, St Martin-Valmeroux, Ruynes-en-Margeride, Le Puy, Goudet, Tain-l'Hermitage, 53, St-Laurent-en-Beaumont, Val-des-Prés, ITALY, St-Jacques-des-Blats, Choranche, St-Gérons, Vic-sur-Cère, St Just, Alleyras, Brives-Charensac, Tournon-sur-Rhône, Châteauneuf-sur-Isère, La Salle-en-Beaumont, Neuvéglise, Le Malzieu-Ville, St-Sauveur-de-Montagut, Valence, Chabeuil, Gresse-en-Vercors, ALPS & EAST, Vallouise, Arnac, Thérondels, Chaudes-Aigues, St-Alban-sur-Limagnole, Naussac, Privas, Les Ollières-sur-Eyrieux, Mirabel-et-Blacons, Die, Châteauroux-les-Alpes, Guillestre, Darbres, Montmaur, AUVERGNE, Largentière, Ucel, St-Jean-le-Centenier, Vercheny, Luc-en-Diois, Gap, St-Amans-des-Cots, Mende, Vogüé, Villeneuve-de-Berg, Dieulefit, Bourdeaux, Serres, Baratier, Méolans-Revel, Villefort, Sampzon, Viviers, Grignan, Bénivay-Ollon, Orpierre, Sénergues, St-Geniez-d' Olt, Peyremale-sur-Cèze, Vallon-Pont-d'Arc, 59, Villars-Colmars, Conques, Séverac-l'Eglise, Rivière-sur-Tarn, Meyrueis, Chauzon, Bollène, St-Romain-en-Viennois, Rodez, Canet-de-Salars, St-Alban-Auriolles, Salavas, Mondragon, Vaison-la-Romaine, Entrechaux, Mirandol-Bourgnounac, Pont-de-Salars, St-Germain-de-Calberte, St Ambroix, Boisson, Orange, Millau, Cendras, 54, Salles-Curan, Revens, Valleraugue, Uzès, Carpentras, Aubignan, Livers-Cazelles, Albi, St-Rome-de-Tarn, Anduze, Arpaillargues, 56, 60, Villes-sur-Auzon, Le Vigan, Crespian, 55, Avignon, Vedène, Nant, Pont-d'Hérault, Vers-Pont-du-Gard, 57, SOUTH COAST & RIVIERA, Teillet, Villefranche-de-Panat, St-Julian-de-la-Nef, Nîmes, 58, L'Isle-sur-la-Sorgue, MONACO, Nice, Gallargues-le-Montueux, Fontvielle, La Roque-d'Anthèron, Soubès, Sommières, Arles, Mouriès, Cadenet, Angles, Lanuéjols, Castries, Lunel, Albaron, Salon-de-Provence, Mallemort, Le Bez, Nages, Véreilles, Montpellier, Gallican, St Chamas, Aix-en-Provence, La Salvetat, Balaruc-les-Bains, Vic-la-Gardiole, Vitrolles, Nans-les-Pins, Brousses-et-Villaret, St-Thibéry, Frontignan, Aigues Mortes, Ste-Maries-de-la-Mer, Le Grau-du-Roi, Bastide-Serou, Villemoustaussou, Montblanc, Agde, Sète, Marseille, Carcassonne, Lézignan-Corbières, Vias, Marseillan-Plage, Ceyreste, Preixan, Sauvian, Portiragnes-Plage, Valras-Plage, Sérignan-Plage, La Seyne-sur-Mer, La Ciotat, Varilhes, Montclar, Narbonne, Narbonne-Plage, See enlarged area, Alet-les-Bains, Nébias, Villerouge-la-Crémade, Torreilles, Le Barcarès, Axat, Ste-Marie, Camurac, Ria, Villeneuve-de-la-Raho, Canet-en-Roussillon, Canet-Plage, Casteil, Le Boulou, St-Cyprien, St-Jean-Pla-de-Corts, Elne, Argelès-sur-Mer, Ur, Font-Romeu, Maureillas, Le Racou, Saillagouse, Arles-sur-Tech, Laroque-des-Albères, Palau del Vidre

53 Châteauneuf-de-Galaure
54 Boisset-et-Gaujac
55 Remoulins
56 Villeneuve-lès-Avignon
57 Vallabrègues
58 St Rémy-de-Provence
59 St-Martin-d'Ardèche
60 Pernes-les-Fontaines

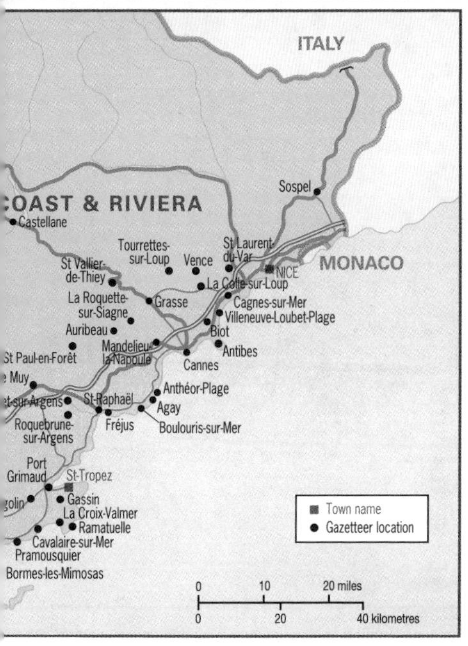

GERMANY

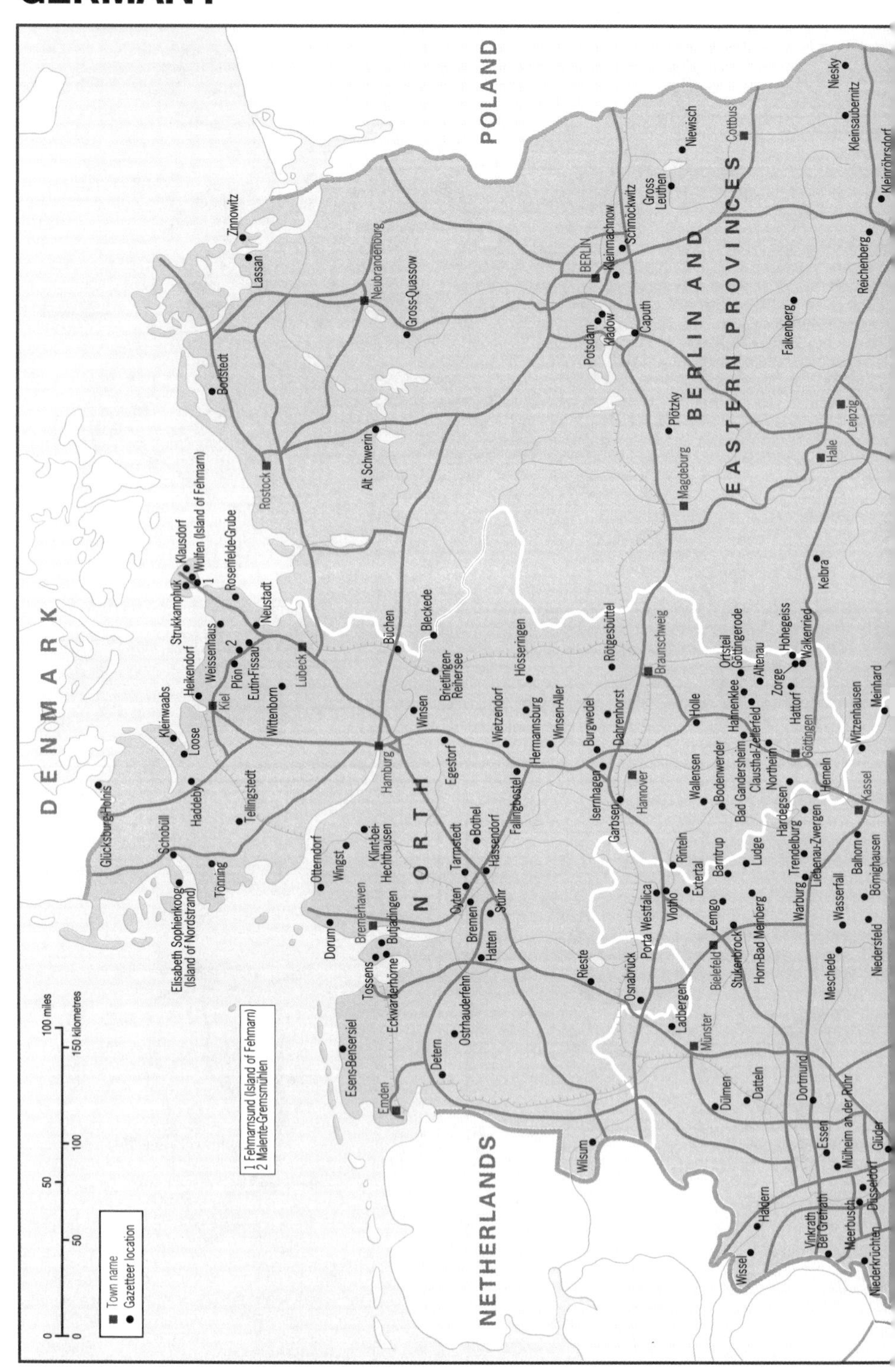

DENMARK
POLAND
NETHERLANDS
NORTH
BERLIN AND EASTERN PROVINCES
Town name
Gazetteer location
0
50
100 miles
0
50
100
150 kilometres
1 Fehmarnsund (Island of Fehmarn)
2 Malente-Gremsmühlen
Glücksburg-Holnis
Schobüll
Elisabeth Sophienkoog (Island of Nordstrand)
Tönning
Haddeby
Tellingstedt
Loose
Kleinwaabs
Heikendorf
Kiel
Weissenhaus
Strukkamphuk
Klausdorf
Wulfen (Island of Fehmarn)
Rosenfelde-Grube
Neustadt
Plön
Eutin-Fissau
Wittenborn
Lubeck
Rostock
Bodstedt
Lassan
Zinnowitz
Neubrandenburg
Gross-Quassow
Alt Schwerin
Büchen
Bleckede
Hamburg
Winsen
Brietlingen-Reihersee
Egestorf
Otterndorf
Wingst
Klint-bei-Hechthausen
Bremerhaven
Dorum
Butjadingen
Tossens
Eckwarderhörne
Esens-Bensersiel
Emden
Detern
Ostrhauderfehn
Hatten
Bremen
Oyten
Stuhr
Tarmstedt
Bothel
Hassendorf
Fallingbostel
Wietzendorf
Hermannsburg
Hösseringen
Winsen-Aller
Burgwedel
Dahrenhorst
Rötgesbüttel
Braunschweig
Isernhagen
Hannover
Garbsen
Wilsum
Rieste
Osnabrück
Porta Westfalica
Vlotho
Rinteln
Extertal
Barntrup
Lemgo
Bielefeld
Stukenbrock
Horn-Bad Meinberg
Ladbergen
Münster
Dülmen
Datteln
Dortmund
Essen
Mülheim an der Ruhr
Glüder
Düsseldorf
Haldern
Wissel
Vinkrath Bei Grefrath
Meerbusch
Niederkrüchten
Wallensen
Bodenwerder
Bad Gandersheim
Clausthal-Zellerfeld
Northeim
Holle
Hahnenklee
Ortsteil Göttingerode
Altenau
Zorge
Hattorf
Hohegeiss
Walkenried
Göttingen
Hemeln
Hardegsen
Lüdge
Trendelburg
Liebenau-Zwergen
Warburg
Kassel
Balhorn
Bömighausen
Wasserfall
Meschede
Niedersfeld
Witzenhausen
Meinhard
Kelbra
Magdeburg
Plötzky
Halle
Leipzig
Potsdam
Kladow
Caputh
BERLIN
Kleinmachnow
Schmöckwitz
Gross Leuthen
Niewisch
Cottbus
Niesky
Kleinsaubernitz
Kleinröhrsdorf
Reichenberg
Falkenberg

5

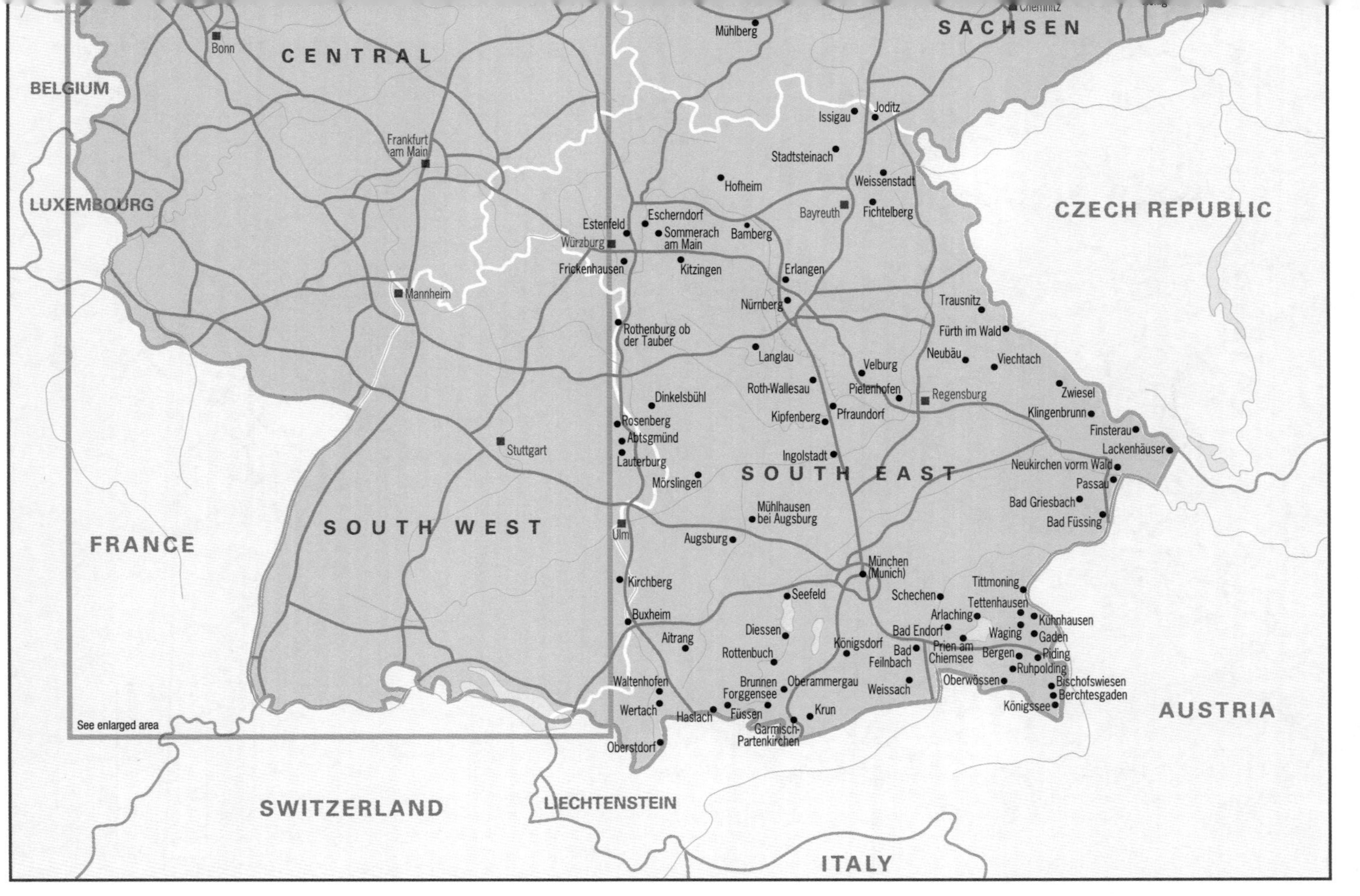

SACHSEN
CZECH REPUBLIC
AUSTRIA
ITALY
LIECHTENSTEIN
SWITZERLAND
FRANCE
LUXEMBOURG
BELGIUM
CENTRAL
SOUTH EAST
SOUTH WEST
See enlarged area
Bonn
Frankfurt am Main
Mannheim
Stuttgart
Würzburg
Estenfeld
Frickenhausen
Escherndorf
Sommerach am Main
Kitzingen
Mühlberg
Hofheim
Bamberg
Stadtsteinach
Issigau
Joditz
Weissenstadt
Fichtelberg
Bayreuth
Erlangen
Nürnberg
Rothenburg ob der Tauber
Langlau
Dinkelsbühl
Rosenberg
Abtsgmünd
Lauterburg
Mörslingen
Ulm
Roth-Wallesau
Kipfenberg
Pfraundorf
Velburg
Pielenhofen
Regensburg
Neubäu
Trausnitz
Fürth im Wald
Viechtach
Zwiesel
Klingenbrunn
Finsterau
Lackenhäuser
Neukirchen vorm Wald
Passau
Bad Griesbach
Bad Füssing
Ingolstadt
Mühlhausen bei Augsburg
Augsburg
Kirchberg
Buxheim
Aitrang
Waltenhofen
Wertach
Oberstdorf
Haslach
Füssen
Brunnen Forggensee
Rottenbuch
Diessen
Seefeld
Oberammergau
Garmisch-Partenkirchen
Krun
Königsdorf
München (Munich)
Schechen
Bad Feilnbach
Weissach
Bad Endorf
Arlaching
Prien am Chiemsee
Tettenhausen
Tittmoning
Kühnhausen
Waging
Gaden
Bergen
Piding
Ruhpolding
Oberwössen
Bischofswiesen
Berchtesgaden
Königssee

GERMANY

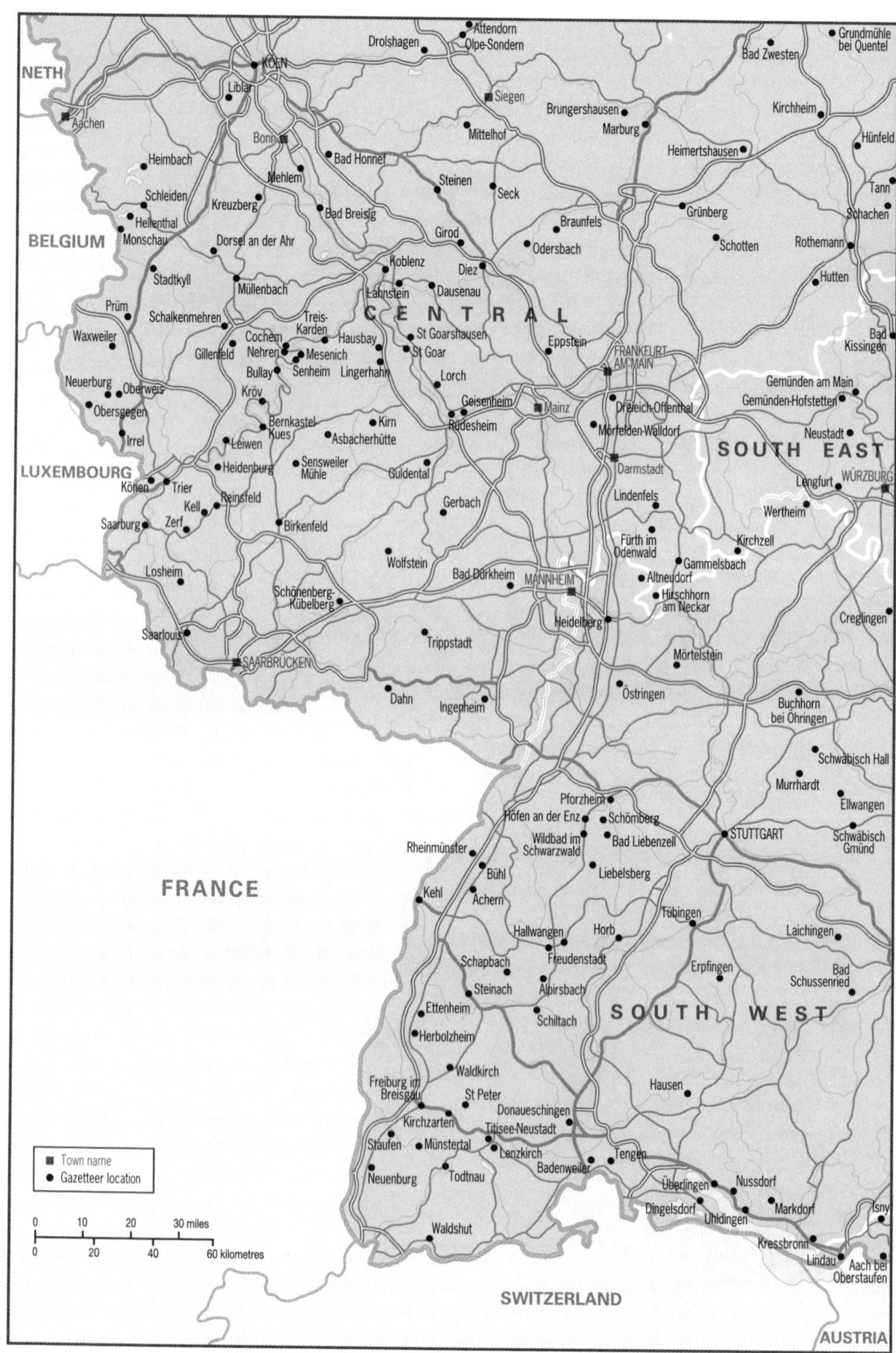
NETH
BELGIUM
LUXEMBOURG
FRANCE
SWITZERLAND
AUSTRIA
CENTRAL
SOUTH EAST
SOUTH WEST
Attendorn
Olpe-Sondern
Drolshagen
KÖLN
Liblar
Aachen
Siegen
Bad Zwesten
Grundmühle bei Quentel
Brungershausen
Marburg
Kirchheim
Hünfeld
Mittelhof
Bonn
Heimbach
Bad Honnef
Heimertshausen
Mehlem
Steinen
Seck
Tann
Schleiden
Kreuzberg
Hellenthal
Bad Breisig
Grünberg
Schachen
Monschau
Braunfels
Girod
Schotten
Rothemann
Dorsel an der Ahr
Odersbach
Koblenz
Diez
Stadtkyll
Hutten
Müllenbach
Lahnstein
Dausenau
Prüm
Schalkenmehren
Treis-Karden
Bad Kissingen
Waxweiler
Cochem
Hausbay
St Goarshausen
Eppstein
Gillenfeld
Nehren
Mesenich
St Goar
FRANKFURT AM MAIN
Neuerburg
Bullay
Senheim
Lingerhahn
Lorch
Gemünden am Main
Oberweis
Gemünden-Hofstetten
Obersgegen
Kröv
Geisenheim
Mainz
Dreieich-Offenthal
Bernkastel-Kues
Kirn
Rüdesheim
Mörfelden-Walldorf
Neustadt
Irrel
Leiwen
Asbacherhütte
Darmstadt
Sensweiler Mühle
Heidenburg
Guldental
Lengfurt
WÜRZBURG
Könen
Trier
Reinsfeld
Lindenfels
Kell
Gerbach
Wertheim
Saarburg
Zerf
Birkenfeld
Fürth im Odenwald
Kirchzell
Wolfstein
Gammelsbach
Losheim
Bad Dürkheim
MANNHEIM
Altneudorf
Schönenberg-Kübelberg
Hirschhorn am Neckar
Creglingen
Heidelberg
Saarlouis
Trippstadt
SAARBRÜCKEN
Mörtelstein
Östringen
Dahn
Ingenheim
Buchhorn bei Öhringen
Schwäbisch Hall
Murrhardt
Pforzheim
Ellwangen
Höfen an der Enz
Schömberg
STUTTGART
Wildbad im Schwarzwald
Bad Liebenzell
Schwäbisch Gmünd
Rheinmünster
Bühl
Liebelsberg
Kehl
Achern
Tübingen
Hallwangen
Horb
Laichingen
Freudenstadt
Schapbach
Erpfingen
Bad Schussenried
Steinach
Alpirsbach
Ettenheim
Schiltach
Herbolzheim
Waldkirch
Freiburg im Breisgau
Hausen
St Peter
Donaueschingen
Kirchzarten
Titisee-Neustadt
Staufen
Münstertal
Lenzkirch
Badenweiler
Tengen
Neuenburg
Todtnau
Überlingen
Nussdorf
Dingelsdorf
Uhldingen
Markdorf
Isny
Waldshut
Kressbronn
Lindau
Aach bei Oberstaufen
Town name
Gazetteer location
0
10
20
30 miles
0
20
40
60 kilometres

NETHERLANDS

Town name
Gazetteer location
0
20
40
60 miles
0
50
100 kilometres
NORTH
CENTRAL
SOUTH
GERMANY
BELGIUM
FRANCE
LUX
Hee
Lauwersoog
Termunterzijl
Groningen
Harlingen
Leeuwarden
Bergum
Franeker
Opende
De Cocksdorp
Eernewoude
De Koog
Annen
Wedde
Makkum
Den Hoorn
Hindeloopen
Assen
Den Helder
Koudum
Amen
Borger
Groote Keeten
Diever
Callantsoog
Dwingeloo
St Maartenszee
Steenwijk
Ruinen
Andijk
Noord Scharwoude
Blokzijl
Berkhout
Heiloo
Alkmaar
Wijdenes
Edam
Zwolle
Beerze-Ommen
Uitdam
Biddinghuizen
Hattem
Reutum
Haarlem
AMSTERDAM
Almere
Nunspeet
Luttenberg
Denekamp
Vogelenzang
Halfweg
Noordwijk
Amstelveen
Ermelo
Hengelo
Rijnsburg
Putten
Apeldoorn
Enschede
Mijnden
Diepenheim
Katwijk aan Zee
Buurse
Haaksbergen
Leiden
Bilthoven
Otterlo
Wassenaar
Eerbeek
Zeist
Maarn
Hoenderloo
DEN HAAG
Hengelo
Lathum
's-Gravenzande
Delft
Doorn
Arnhem
Winterswijk
Hoek Van Holland
Doetinchem
Rhenen
Oostvoorne
Brielle
Rotterdam
Babberich
Kesteren
Rockanje
Nijmegen
Ouddorp
Hellevoetsluis
Appeltern
Renesse
Herpen
Heumen
Brouwershaven
Burgh-Haamstede
Noordwelle
's-Hertogenbosch
Oosterhout
Plasmolen
Afferden
Vrouwenpolder
Kamperland
Breda
Hoeven
Tilburg
Oostkapelle
Oisterwijk
Kortgene
Roosendaal
Bosschenhoofd
Well
Westkapelle
Eindhoven
Venray
Wemeldinge
Broekhuizenvorst
Koudekerke
Mierlo
Lage Mierde
Sevenum
Nieuwvliet
Breskens
Eersel
Maasbree
Baarland
Retranchement
Groede
Bergeyk
Hoek
Luyksgestel
Sluis
Weert
Roermond
Echt
Berg en Terblijt
Schin Op Geul
Maastricht

SPAIN & PORTUGAL

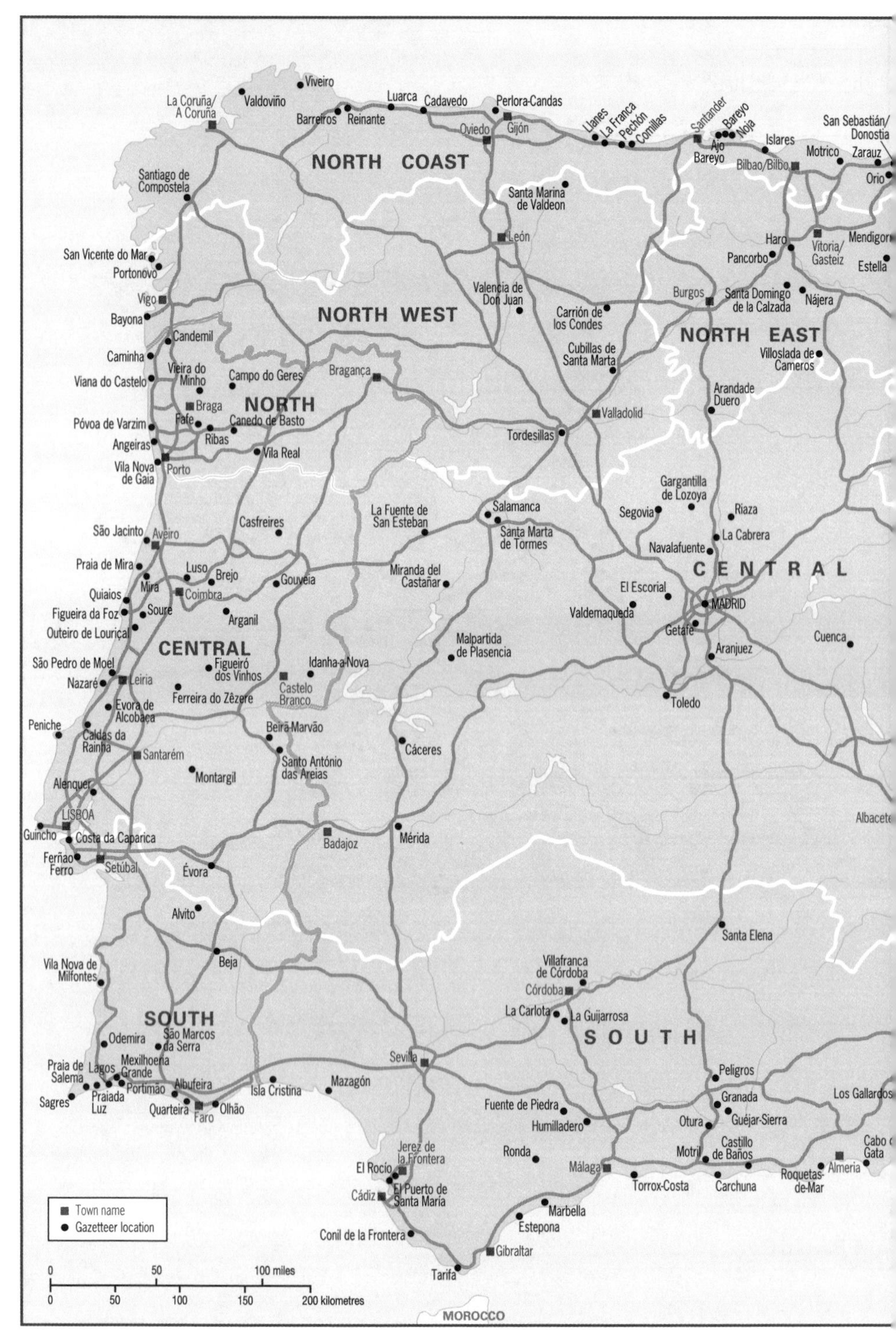

FRANCE
Oricain
Pamplona/
Iruñea
Tunnel de
Somport
Torla
Gavin
Labuerda
Huesca
Bossost
La Bordeta
Espot
Ribera de Cardós
Bonansa
La Puebla
de Castro
ANDORRA
NORTH EAST
COAST
NORTH EAST
Zaragoza
Vilanova
de Prades
BARCELONA
See enlarged area
Nuevalos
Mont-Roig del Camp
Salou
L'Hospitalet de l'infant
L'Ametlla de Mar
SOUTH EAST COAST
Peñiscola
Benicarló
Alcossebre
Albarracin
Oropesa del Mar
Navajas
Benicasim
Moncofa
Villargordo
del Cabriel
Valencia
Palma de
Mallorca
Islas
Baleares
Miramar Playa
Oliva
Altea
Benidorm
Campello
Alicante/Alacant
Baños de
Fortuna
Moratalla
La Marina
Guardamar del Segura
Murcia
Pilar de la Horadada
La Manga del Mar Menor
Cartagena
Isla Plana
Mojácar
FRANCE
ANDORRA
Guils de Cerdanya
Santa Julià
de Lòria
Bellver de
Cerdanya
Puigcerdà
Vilallonga de Ter
Albanyà
Túnel
del Cadí
Guardiola de
Bergueda
Castelló d'Empuries
Sant Pere Pescador
NORTH
EAST
l'Escala
l'Estartit
NORTH EAST
COAST
Torroella de Montgri
Saldes
Gerona/
Girona
Pals
Begur
Solsona
Sant Antoni de Calonge
Tamariu
Taradell
Palafrugell
Palamós
Castell d'Aro
La Platja d'Aro
Santa Cristina d'Aro
Tossa de Mar
Sant Feliu de Guixols
Sant Cebriá
de Vallalta
Lloret de Mar
Blanes
Pineda de Mar
Sabadell
Vallromanes
Calella de
la Costa
SOUTH
EAST
COAST
Badalona
BARCELONA
Cubelles
Sitges
Cunit
Vilanova
i la Geltrú
Tamarit
Tarragona
0
20
40 miles
0
20
40
60 kilometres

ITALY

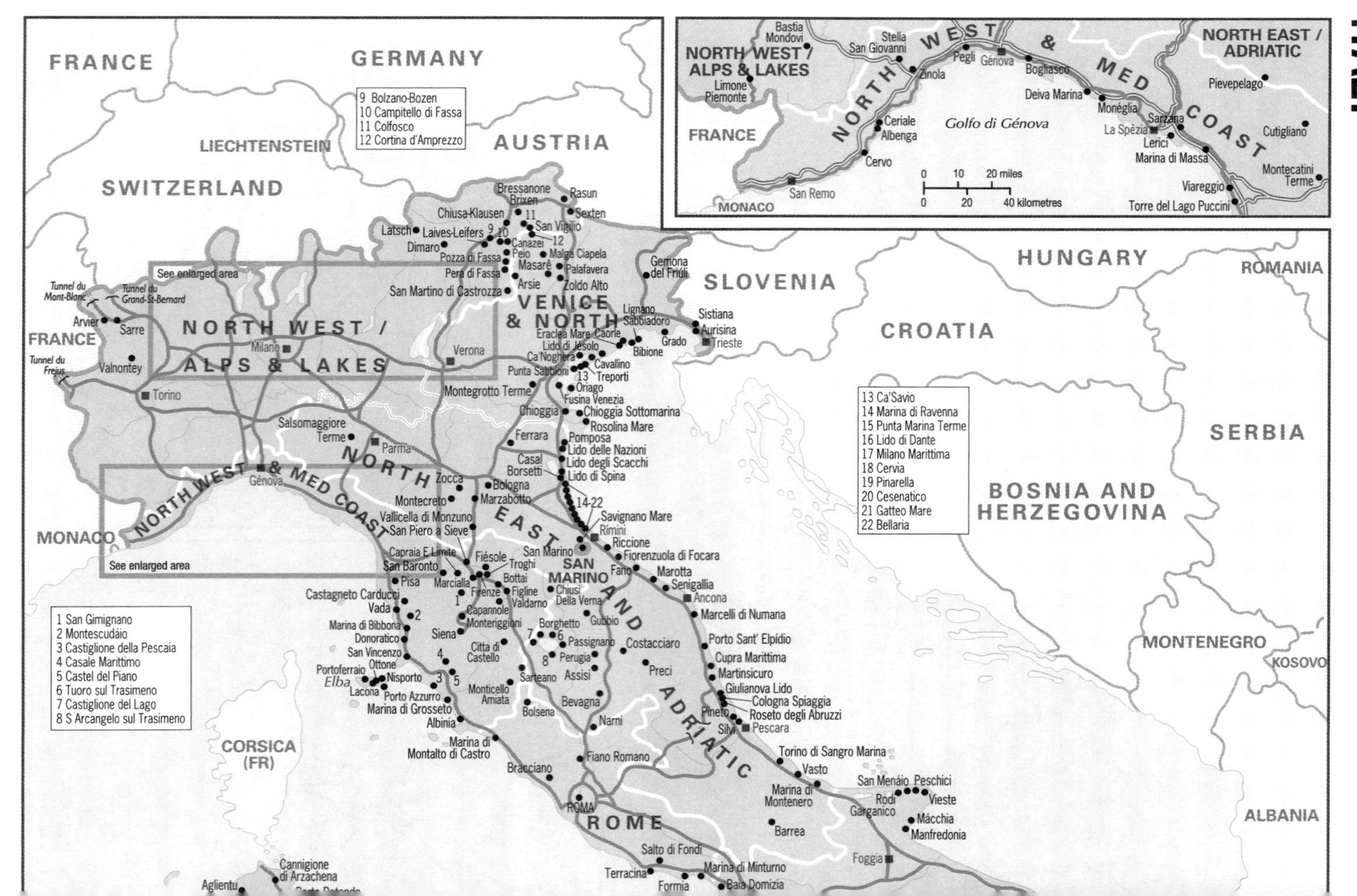

NORTH EAST / ADRIATIC
NORTH WEST & MED COAST
NORTH WEST / ALPS & LAKES
FRANCE
MONACO
Golfo di Génova
0 10 20 miles
0 20 40 kilometres
Bastia Mondovì
Limone Piemonte
Stella San Giovanni
Zinola
Pegli
Génova
Bogliasco
Deiva Marina
Monéglia
Sarzana
La Spèzia
Lerici
Marina di Massa
Pievepelago
Cutigliano
Montecatini Terme
Viareggio
Torre del Lago Puccini
Ceriale
Albenga
Cervo
San Remo
GERMANY
AUSTRIA
SWITZERLAND
LIECHTENSTEIN
HUNGARY
ROMANIA
SLOVENIA
CROATIA
SERBIA
BOSNIA AND HERZEGOVINA
MONTENEGRO
KOSOVO
ALBANIA
CORSICA (FR)
9 Bolzano-Bozen
10 Campitello di Fassa
11 Colfosco
12 Cortina d'Ampezzo
13 Ca'Savio
14 Marina di Ravenna
15 Punta Marina Terme
16 Lido di Dante
17 Milano Marittima
18 Cervia
19 Pinarella
20 Cesenatico
21 Gatteo Mare
22 Bellaria
1 San Gimignano
2 Montescudàio
3 Castiglione della Pescaia
4 Casale Marittimo
5 Castel del Piano
6 Tuoro sul Trasimeno
7 Castiglione del Lago
8 S Arcangelo sul Trasimeno
NORTH WEST / ALPS & LAKES
VENICE & NORTH EAST
NORTH EAST
SAN MARINO AND ADRIATIC
ROME
See enlarged area
Tunnel du Mont-Blanc
Tunnel du Grand-St-Bernard
Tunnel du Fréjus
Arvier
Sarre
Valnontey
Torino
Milano
Verona
Parma
Génova
Salsomaggiore Terme
San Martino di Castrozza
Montegrotto Terme
Latsch
Dimaro
Laives-Leifers
Chiusa-Klausen
Bressanone Brixen
Rasun
Sexten
San Vigilio
Canazei
Peio
Pozza di Fassa
Pera di Fassa
Malga Ciapela
Masarè
Palafavera
Zoldo Alto
Arsie
Gemona del Friuli
Sistiana
Aurisina
Trieste
Grado
Lignano Sabbiadoro
Bibione
Eraclea Mare
Caorle
Lido di Jesolo
Cavallino
Ca'Noghera
Punta Sabbioni
Treporti
Oriago
Fusina Venezia
Chioggia
Chioggia Sottomarina
Rosolina Mare
Pomposa
Lido delle Nazioni
Lido degli Scacchi
Lido di Spina
Ferrara
Casal Borsetti
Bologna
Marzabotto
Zocca
Montecreto
Vallicella di Monzuno
San Piero a Sieve
Capraia E Limite
San Baronto
Pisa
Savignano Mare
Rimini
Riccione
Fiorenzuola di Focara
Marotta
Senigallia
Ancona
Fano
San Marino
Fiésole
Firenze
Troghi
Bottai
Figline Valdarno
Marcialla
Capannole
Monteriggioni
Siena
Chiusi della Verna
Gubbio
Borghetto
Passignano
Perugia
Assisi
Bevagna
Costacciaro
Preci
Narni
Città di Castello
Monticello Amiata
Sarteano
Bolsena
Castagneto Carducci
Vada
Marina di Bibbona
Donoratico
San Vincenzo
Portoferraio
Elba
Ottone
Nisporto
Lacona
Porto Azzurro
Marina di Grosseto
Albinia
Marina di Montalto di Castro
Bracciano
Fiano Romano
ROMA
Marcelli di Numana
Porto Sant' Elpìdio
Cupra Marittima
Martinsicuro
Giulianova Lido
Cologna Spiaggia
Roseto degli Abruzzi
Pineto
Silvi
Pescara
Torino di Sangro Marina
Vasto
Marina di Montenero
Barrea
San Menàio
Peschici
Vieste
Rodi Garganico
Màcchia
Manfredonia
Foggia
Marina di Minturno
Baia Domizia
Formia
Salto di Fondi
Terracina
Cannigione di Arzachena
Aglientu

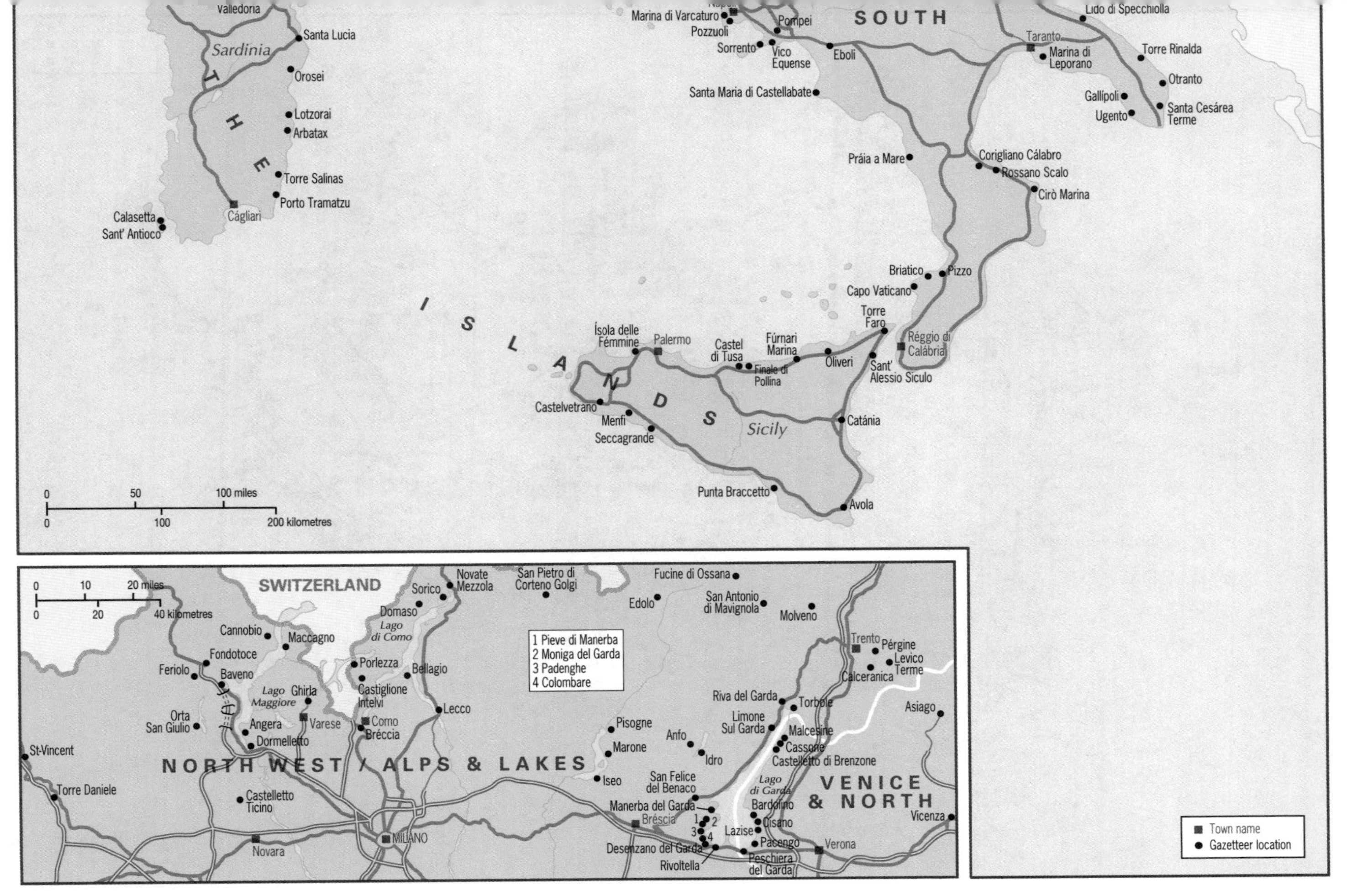

THE ISLANDS
SOUTH
Sardinia
Sicily
Valledoria
Santa Lucia
Orosei
Lotzorai
Arbatax
Torre Salinas
Porto Tramatzu
Cágliari
Calasetta
Sant' Antioco
Marina di Varcaturo
Pozzuoli
Pompei
Sorrento
Vico Equense
Eboli
Santa Maria di Castellabate
Taranto
Marina di Leporano
Lido di Specchiolla
Torre Rinalda
Otranto
Gallipoli
Ugento
Santa Cesárea Terme
Práia a Mare
Corigliano Cálabro
Rossano Scalo
Cirò Marina
Briatico
Pizzo
Capo Vaticano
Torre Faro
Réggio di Calábria
Sant' Alessio Siculo
Ísola delle Fémmine
Palermo
Castel di Tusa
Fúrnari Marina
Finale di Pollina
Oliveri
Castelvetrano
Menfi
Seccagrande
Catánia
Punta Braccetto
Avola
0
50
100 miles
0
100
200 kilometres
SWITZERLAND
NORTH WEST / ALPS & LAKES
VENICE & NORTH
0
10
20 miles
0
20
40 kilometres
Cannobio
Maccagno
Fondotoce
Feriolo
Baveno
Lago Maggiore
Ghirla
Varese
Orta San Giulio
Angera
Dormelletto
St-Vincent
Torre Daniele
Castelletto Ticino
Novara
MILANO
Sorico
Novate Mezzola
Domaso
Lago di Como
Porlezza
Bellagio
Castiglione Intelvi
Como
Bréccia
Lecco
San Pietro di Corteno Golgi
Fucine di Ossana
Edolo
San Antonio di Mavignola
Molveno
1 Pieve di Manerba
2 Moniga del Garda
3 Padenghe
4 Colombare
Pisogne
Marone
Iseo
Anfo
Idro
San Felice del Benaco
Manerba del Garda
Bréscia
Desenzano del Garda
Rivoltella
Riva del Garda
Torbole
Limone Sul Garda
Malcesine
Cassone
Castelletto di Brenzone
Lago di Garda
Bardolino
Cisano
Lazise
Pacengo
Peschiera del Garda
Verona
Trento
Pérgine
Levico Terme
Calceranica
Asiago
Vicenza
Town name
Gazetteer location

SWITZERLAND

CROATIA & SLOVENIA

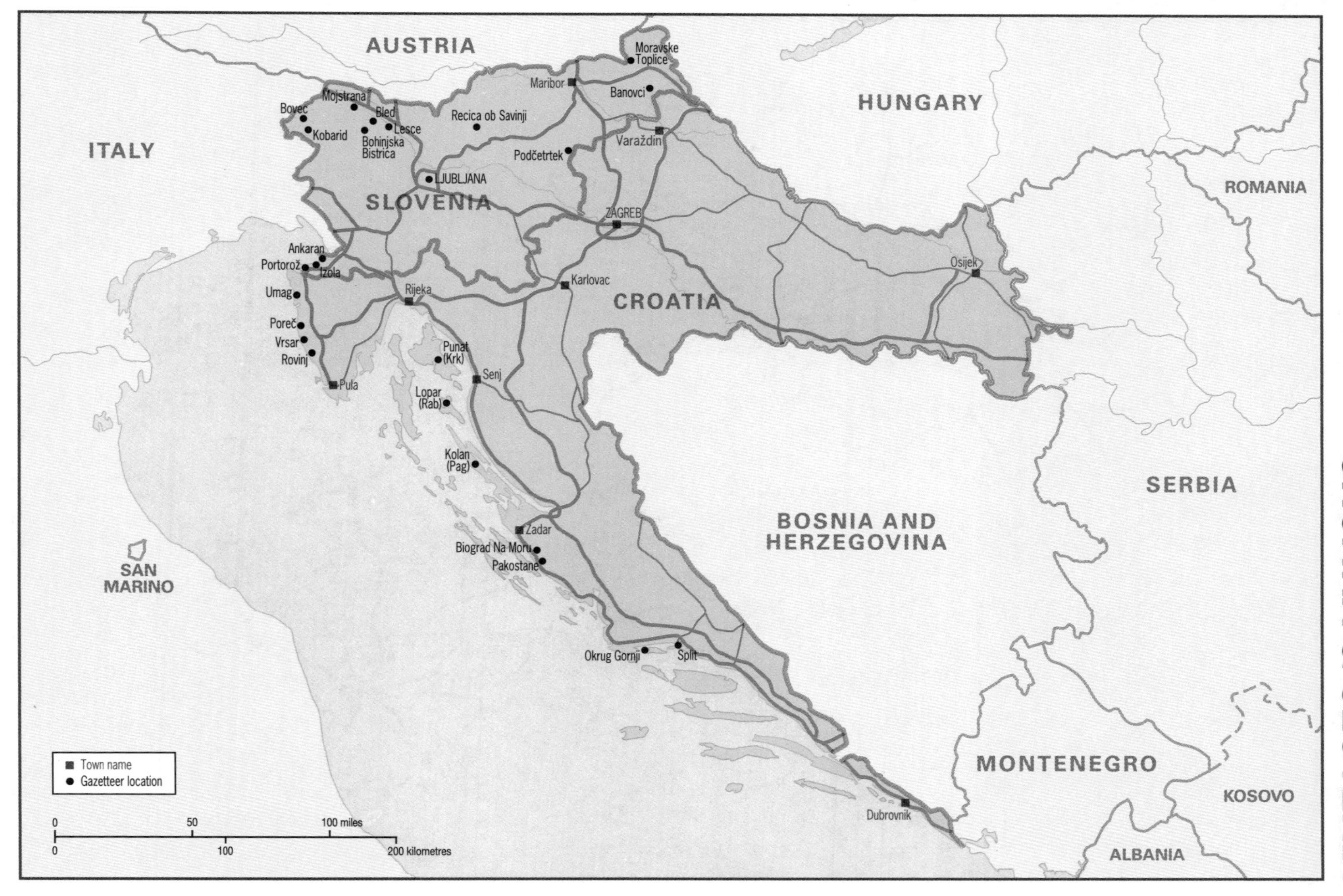

CZECH REPUBLIC & HUNGARY

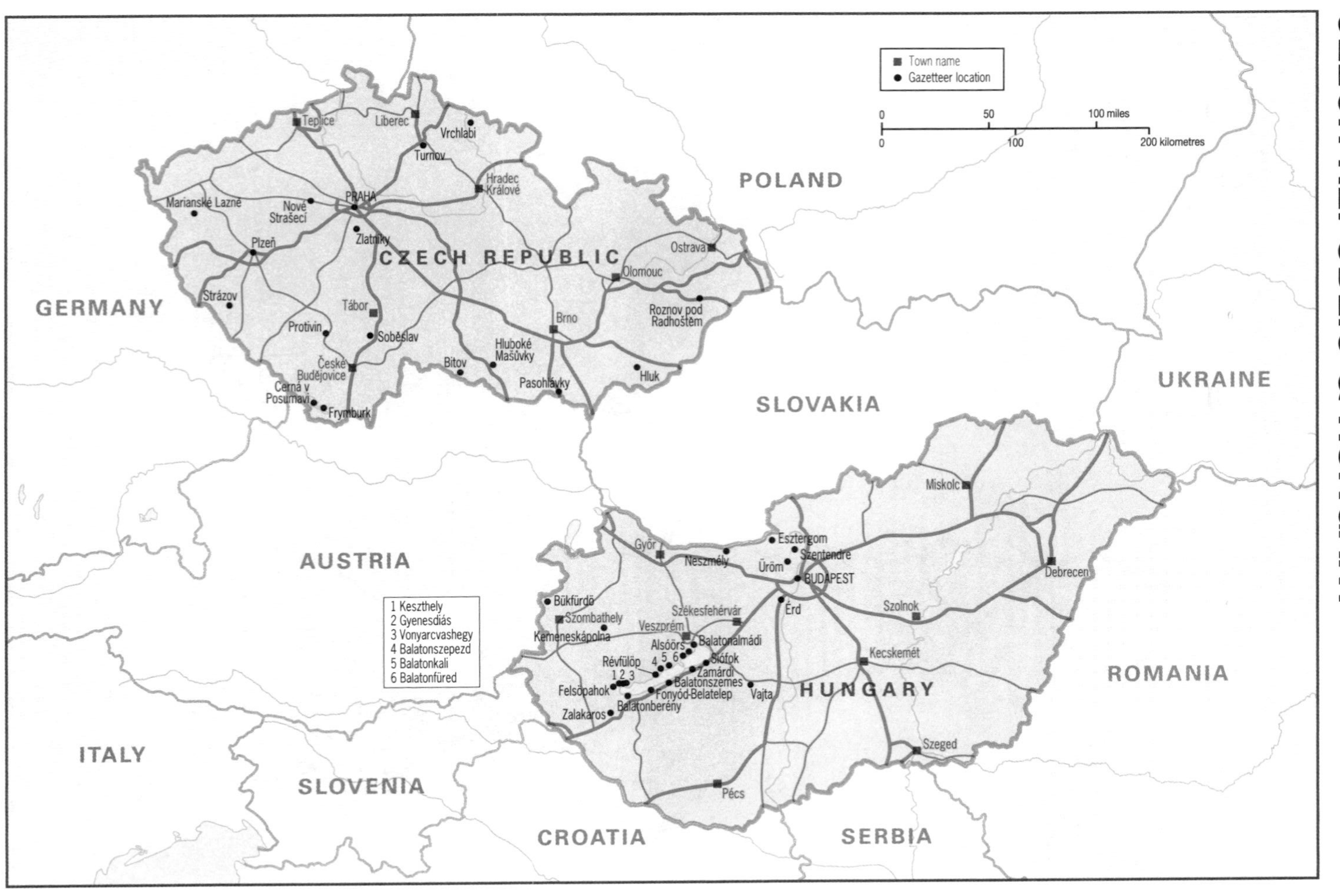

GREECE

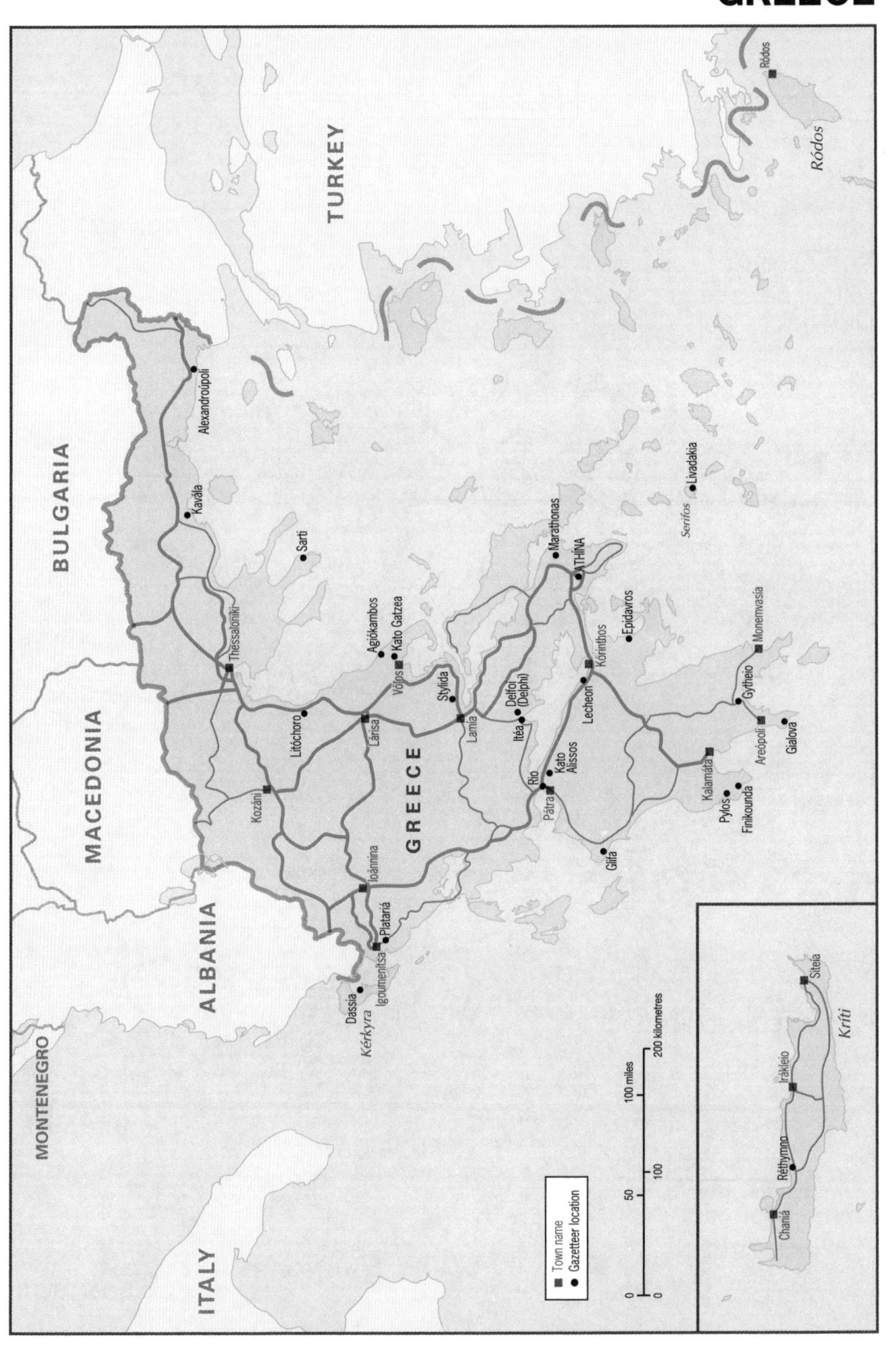

BULGARIA
MACEDONIA
ALBANIA
MONTENEGRO
ITALY
TURKEY
G R E E C E
Alexandroúpoli
Kavála
Sarti
Thessaloníki
Agiókambos
Káto Gatzea
Vólos
Stylída
Litóchoro
Lárisa
Lamía
Delfoi
(Delphi)
Itéa
Kozáni
Ioánnina
Plataria
Igoumenitsa
Dassia
Kérkyra
Rio
Kato
Alissos
Pátra
Lecheon
Kórinthos
Marathonas
ATHÍNA
Epidavros
Glifa
Kalamáta
Pylos
Finikounda
Areópoli
Gialova
Gytheio
Monemvasia
Livadakia
Serífos
Ródos
Ródos
Chaniá
Réthymno
Irákleio
Siteia
Kríti
Town name
Gazetteer location
0 50 100 miles
0 100 200 kilometres

POLAND

Town name
Gazetteer location
0 50 100 miles
0 50 100 150 kilometres
SWEDEN
LATVIA
LITHUANIA
DENMARK
RUSSIA
BELARUS
GERMANY
POLAND
CZECH REPUBLIC
UKRAINE
SLOVAKIA
AUSTRIA
HUNGARY
ROMANIA
Słupsk
Sopot
Gdańsk
Elblag
Mielno
Koszalin
Przywidz
Świnoujście
Dziwnówek
Olsztyn
Gizycko
Mikolajki
Augustów
Szczecin
Bydgoszcz
Toruń
Białystok
Płock
Poznań
WARSZAWA
Kalisz
Łódź
Radom
Lublin
Chmielno
Wrocław
Jelenia Góra
Wolibórz
Częstochowa
Kielce
Katowice
Kraków
Przeworsk
Rzeszów
Zakopane

ROMANIA, BULGARIA & WESTERN TURKEY

Index

A

C

D

E

F

G

H

L

M

N

O

P

Q

R

S

The Automobile Association would like to thank the following photographers, companies and picture libraries for their assistance in the preparation of this book.
Abbreviations for the picture credits are as follows – (t) top; (b) bottom; (c) centre; (l) left; (r) right; (AA) AA World Travel Library

Cover
Front cover: (t) AA/C Sawyer ; (bl) AA/J A Tims; (br) AA/C Sawyer. Back cover: (r) AA/A Mockford & N Bonetti; (c) AA/J A Tims; (r) AA/C Sawyer.

Interior
p1 AA/Clive Sawyer; p2 AA/Mockford & Bonetti; p3 bl AA/Yadid Levy; p3 br AA/Peter Wilson; p4/5 AA/Pete Bennett; p8 AA/Ken Paterson; p9 tl AA/Yadid Levy; p9 br AA/James Tims; p11 AA/Laurie Noble; p12 AA/James Tims; p14 AA/Terence Carter; p17 AA/Alex Kouprianoff; p18 AA/Wyn Voysey; p20 The Camping and Caravanning Club; p21 The Camping and Caravanning Club; p23 The Camping and Caravanning Club; p24 The Camping and Caravanning Club; p25 AA/James Tims; p27 AA/A Baker; p28 AA/Peter Baker; p29 AA/David Noble; p51 AA/Alex Kouprianoff; p67 AA/Pete Bennett; p73 AA/Jonathan Smith; p73 AA/Jon Wyand; p75 AA/Karl Blackwell; p77 AA/Michael Short; p363 AA/Clive Sawyer; p377 AA/Clive Sawyer; p435 AA/Mockford & Bonetti; p465 AA/Monica Wells; p552 AA/Doug Traverso

Every effort has been made to trace the copyright holders, and we apologise in advance for any unintentional omissions or errors. We would be pleased to apply any corrections in a following edition of this publication.